TARGETED EDUCATIONAL SOLUTIONS.

ACT • PLAN • EXPLORE Victory

Classroom Text

ACT • PLAN • EXPLORE • SAT • PSAT • SAT II • GRE • GMAT • LSAT • MCAT • TOEFL • GED • PRAXIS • PSAE • ITBS • CollegePrep™

About Cambridge Educational Services:
Cambridge Educational Services was founded in order to help all students, regardless of income, meet standards and perform to the best of their abilities on standardized tests and in the classroom. Our mission is to provide assessment services and program materials that make quality school improvement programs possible for a wide range of student ability levels. Our goal is to help students achieve test scores that reflect their true potential and ability. Our programs help thousands of students each year reach their goals, such as: becoming National Merit Scholars, gaining admission to the colleges of their choice, and earning valuable scholarships. Cambridge publishes a variety of school improvement and preparation titles and products including textbooks, teacher's guides, skills review manuals, software, and assessment services.

Cambridge Publishing, Inc., Chicago Global Headquarters, Des Plaines 60018

 First edition 1994
Eighth edition 2005

Printed in the United States of America
10 09 08 07 06 2 3 4 5

ISBN-10: 1-58894-036-5
ISBN-13: 978-1-58894-036-0

TARGETED EDUCATIONAL SOLUTIONS.

Dear Student,

The fact that you are reading this book means just one thing: you have a big, important test ahead of you. You want to do well, and we can help you. This course will assist in your success on the ACT, PLAN, and EXPLORE and improve your all-around academic performance.

Since you began going to school, you have been taught thousands of things. No one expects you to remember all of them. However, the ACT, PLAN, and EXPLORE are cumulative tests, which means that you might be tested on concepts that you have forgotten or that you have never learned. Not only that—the ACT, PLAN, and EXPLORE test you in an unfamiliar format. Full preparation requires a targeted review.

Your Cambridge ACT Classroom Text contains all of the materials that you need in order to: (1) refresh or build your understanding of important skills; (2) apply those skills in the particular context of the ACT, PLAN, and EXPLORE; and (3) reduce test anxiety through practice.

You have the tools to succeed. Attend class, participate in learning, do all of your homework, and maintain a positive attitude. You can do it; we have confidence in you.

Good Luck!

The Cambridge Curriculum Committee

TABLE OF CONTENTS

HOW TO USE THIS BOOK

This book is organized into six parts:

1) information to help you make sense of your pre-assessment results (Step One);
2) six skills review chapters (Step Two);
3) items resembling the real ACT, PLAN, and EXPLORE that your instructor will use to teach tested concepts and applicable strategies (Step Three);
4) four full-length ACT practice tests (Step Four);
5) information to help you make sense of your post-assessment results (Step Five);
6) recommendations for continuing your study after the course is done (Step Six).

The following introduction will briefly explain how to use each part of this textbook.

MAKING SENSE OF YOUR OFFICIAL PRE-TEST RESULTS

In order to know where to begin preparing for the ACT, PLAN, or EXPLORE, you have to find out what you already do well and what you could learn to do better. The pre-assessment serves this purpose. First, you will take an official, retired ACT, PLAN, or EXPLORE under actual testing conditions. Then, with the help of your instructor, you will use the results of those tests to determine exactly which topics to review, for how long, and in what order.

Three Winning Strategies sections found in this step will help get you started with Applying to College, Overcoming Test Anxiety, and Time Management.

TARGETED SKILLS REVIEW

The Skills Review section of this book contains items that will enable you to do three things: (1) review material that you may have forgotten; (2) learn material that you may never have learned; and (3) master the skills required to answer the more difficult multiple-choice items on the ACT, PLAN, and EXPLORE.

The Skills Review is divided into six areas:

- Grammar and Mechanics
- Math
- Math Express
- Reading
- Science
- Writing

Each chapter contains concept lessons and corresponding review exercises. For example, the lessons in the Math Skills Review cover the following topics: whole numbers; fractions; signed numbers; decimals; percents; mean, median, and mode; ratios and proportions; exponents and radicals; algebraic operations; algebraic equations and inequalities; geometry; functions, graphs, and coordinate geometry; and story problems. The other Skills Review chapters cover a similar range of topics that are appropriate to each subject.

These exercises do not necessarily contain items that mimic ACT, PLAN, or EXPLORE items. The items are designed to help you learn a concept—not necessarily to help you learn about how the concepts appear on the actual exam. After you have mastered the skills, you will be able to take full advantage of the test-taking strategies that are developed in the Problem-Solving, Concepts, and Strategies section of the book. Your instructor may either review the Skills Review material in class or have you complete the exercises as homework.

SOLVING PROBLEMS THAT LOOK LIKE THOSE FOUND ON THE TEST

Problem-Solving, Concepts, and Strategies make up the heart of this course and, in particular, this textbook. This part of the book contains items that look like those found on the real ACT, PLAN, and EXPLORE. When compared with items on the real tests, the items in this part of the book have similar content, represent the same difficulty levels, and can be solved by using the same problem-solving skills and alternative test-taking strategies.

There are five chapters in the Problem-Solving, Concepts, and Strategies section, each representing a major component of the ACT, PLAN, and EXPLORE:

- English
- Mathematics
- Reading
- Science Reasoning
- Writing

At the beginning of each of the above chapters, there is a Cambridge Course Concept Outline. These outlines act as course syllabi and list the concepts that are tested for each item-type over a two-year testing cycle. The items in each chapter are organized to correspond with the respective course concept outline. For each concept in the outline, there are various clusters of items. A cluster contains a greater number of items if the item-type appears with great frequency on the real test, and it contains a lesser number of items if the item-type appears with less frequency. Although the concepts are not arranged in clusters on the real ACT, PLAN, or EXPLORE, we organize the problems in clusters so that the concepts are emphasized and reinforced. After you learn the concepts, you will be able to practice applying this conceptual knowledge on the practice tests.

TAKING PRACTICE TESTS

In the practice test section of the book, there are four full-length ACT practice tests. In these tests, the items not only mimic the real test in content and difficulty level, but they are also arranged in an order and with a frequency that simulates the real ACT, PLAN, and EXPLORE.

Your instructor will ask you to either complete some or all of these items in class, or he or she will assign them as homework. If you are taking these four tests at home, you should take two with time restrictions and two without time restrictions. Taking the test without time restrictions will help you get a sense of how long it would take for you to comfortably and accurately solve an item. Applying the time pressure then forces you to pace yourself as you would on the real test. If you complete all four of the practice tests, any test anxiety you may have will be greatly reduced.

MAKING SENSE OF YOUR OFFICIAL POST-TEST RESULTS

In order to know how far you've come since the pre-test, you have to take another official retired ACT, PLAN, or EXPLORE. You will take a second official, retired ACT, PLAN, or EXPLORE under actual testing conditions. You will use the results to evaluate your progress and to determine exactly what topics would be the most beneficial for you to review.

FIGURING OUT WHAT TO DO NEXT

Step Six contains a short guide to help you devise a personal study plan for the days or weeks between the end of the course and the official test. You will practice what you learned in the Winning Strategies sections (Step One) to make the most of your remaining study time.

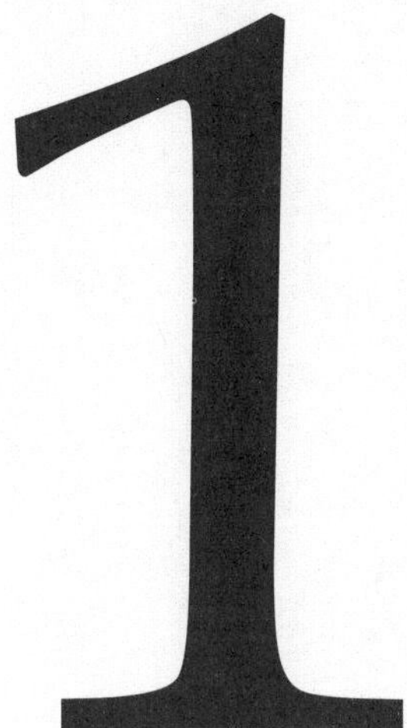

Step One: Pre-Assessment and Course Planning

Step One Highlights:

Take an official test under real testing conditions to gain predictive data on which to base instruction.

Measure your baseline abilities so you can see how far you've come by the course's conclusion.

Learn the top areas where you should focus your efforts so that you will see the greatest improvement.

See first-hand the types of items and pacing you will encounter on your actual test.

Step One Overview:

You start your course with an official test so that you know where you stand on the ACT, PLAN, or EXPLORE. This diagnostic test tells you and your instructor where you need to focus to see the greatest improvement. You should complete this test under real testing conditions so you know what to expect on the day of the actual test. Course instruction hinges on your pre-test performance, so try hard, but it's just a pre-test so don't be too discouraged if you don't perform as well as you hoped. You'll soon be learning tips and core curricular skills to boost your score.

Winning Strategies

TARGETED EDUCATIONAL SOLUTIONS.

Cambridge Course Concept Outline
WINNING STRATEGIES

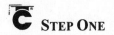

Following the Winning Strategies chapters is the Bubble Sheet for use when taking the ACT, PLAN, or EXPLORE Pre-Test.

APPLYING TO COLLEGE
–Winning Strategies–

Helping you get into the college of your choice is the goal of this six-part section. We have advised tens of thousands of students, interviewed college admissions officers across the country, and attended annual advisors' conferences. Thus, the descriptions, conclusions, and suggestions contained herein have been distilled from a variety of sources.

This section is intended for a range of readers—for those who are already actively working on their applications as well as for those who are only thinking of applying to college. Therefore, some of the points we make are very general and others are very specific. Some of the information may already be familiar, while other points and tips may surprise you. No matter what your status, you will find the following six-part section immediately useful for applying to college and getting into the college of your choice.

A. INTRODUCTION

In order to create the most effective application you can, you must understand and appreciate the function of the admissions process as a social and economic process. Many prospective applicants view the filing of a college application only from their own individual perspective and consider themselves outside spectators who merely benefit from (or are victims of) a bureaucratic juggernaut. For those who share this point of view, we offer the following comments:

Colleges only care about your ACT score.
You cannot get into a really good school unless you know someone.
They really do not read your personal statement.

Such comments reflect an attitude that is based on a misinterpretation of the admissions process—not taking into consideration the social and economic factors. Let us examine this process from two perspectives: yours, and that of a college.

First, from your perspective, you must keep in mind that the college admissions process is much more than merely answering a few questions about your educational background and employment history. Rather, the application process is just the first step on a career path that will last for most of the rest of your life. Decisions you make at this stage may have implications for your life 30 or 40 years from now. An easy way of realizing this is to imagine the different courses your life might follow if you do or do not get into college, or to compare your career prospects if you are or are not accepted by your first choice school.

Now, this is not to say that not getting into a certain school spells disaster. Obviously, becoming a psychologist, engineer, biochemist, computer scientist, economist, chemist, teacher, historian, musician, physicist, geologist, political scientist, or sociologist is not for everyone. Rather, we are simply trying to stress the importance of the admissions process to you as an individual. Indeed, you do not have to look far into the future to appreciate the effect that the admissions process will have on you. Your decisions at this point will determine where you are likely to live for the next four years.

Additionally, you must appreciate the financial commitment that you are making. In the first instance, the cost of the application process alone could easily exceed $1,000. The fees that you pay to take the ACT Assessment with score reports could be as much as $100. Furthermore, the application fees charged by schools run between $25 and $40. If you apply to ten schools, you could easily spend $450 on application fees. In addition, you will probably spend at least $100 on administrative details such as document preparation, copying, postage, and long distance telephone calls. Add another $300 or so for test preparation for the ACT, and you are already committed to $1,000 or more.

On top of application expenses, most schools require that you respond to an acceptance offer by a certain deadline with a non-refundable deposit. You may find yourself in the uncomfortable position of paying such a deposit to ensure that you have a college seat even though you have not yet heard from some other schools. However, these sums pale in comparison to the cost of tuition—as much as $35,000. With the expense of room and board for four years taken into account, the entire expense to obtain your college degree could easily exceed $100,000.

Do not let those numbers frighten you. We are not trying to dissuade you from pursuing a college degree. We are trying to dramatize a point: the decision to apply to college has significant social and economic implications for you as an individual.

On the other side of the coin, from the perspective of the college, there are also social and economic implications. A college, like any educational institution, is a corporate entity, and its admissions decisions reflect social and economic policies adopted by the corporation. Consider first some of the economic implications for a college to accept or reject an applicant.

The college has to be run as any other business entity. It has employees; it owns or rents property; it operates a library; it buys furniture and office equipment; it pays utility bills; and so on. A large part of those expenses is paid using student tuition. A college, therefore, is dependent on a steady flow of tuition income. So, admissions decisions must be made in the context of budgetary constraints. A college simply cannot afford to have large numbers of students dropping out of school. Therefore, one concern of a college admissions officer is to ensure that those applicants who are accepted are committed to completing the course of study. Additionally—though this may not be an explicit concern—colleges rely heavily on alumni donations. Therefore, it would not be surprising to learn that an applicant who shows considerable professional promise would be considered favorably. Moreover, a school that graduates successful B.A. and B.S. students gets a reputation for being a good school and such a reputation in turn tends to attract highly qualified applicants.

We do not mean to give you the impression that an admissions decision is made solely on economic considerations. That is far from the truth. Colleges also have a sense of the social responsibility they bear as educators of B.A. and B.S. students—one of the most influential groups of people in our society. They meet this responsibility in some obvious ways such as actively seeking applicants from groups who are under-represented in the professional community and by establishing programs to train professionals for positions of special need.

The admissions process, then, is the interface between these two perspectives. The process is designed to match individuals and institutions that can mutually satisfy each other's needs. This matching function, however, is somewhat skewed. For decades, there have been more people interested in pursuing professional careers than there are seats available at accredited colleges. In recent times, there have been over two applicants for each available seat. Consequently, applicants are competing for college entrance.

Given the mismatch between the number of available slots and the number of applicants, the application process is turned into a competition. You will have to compete against others for a college seat (or at least for a spot at the college of your choice). To do this, you must make yourself attractive to a college. You must persuade the admissions committee that you will help them satisfy their economic and social needs. That thought must guide you as you create your application.

Using the information in this section, you will create an application that will position you for acceptance—that is, an application that will give a college an affirmative reason for accepting you. In addition to this section, you may also want to consider some other sources. For general information about the accredited colleges in this country, you should buy, or check out from your school's library, the *College Handbook*. The College Entrance Examination Board publishes this book and it contains summaries of approximately 3,200 two- and four-year colleges. Use the *College Handbook* for general guidance. For each school in which you have even a passing interest, request that school's information bulletin. Read those bulletins carefully. They provide listings of faculty members and their qualifications, descriptions of any special programs, information about student activities and campus life, catalogues of financial aid, and much more.

B. HOW THE ADMISSIONS PROCESS WORKS

If we read the title of this section literally, then anything we say about it must be false. This is because there is no "the" admissions process. Rather, each college has its own individual admissions process, and each process differs in ways more or less important from that of every other college in the country.

On the other hand, we cannot talk about the details of the admissions process at each of the approximately 3,200 U.S. Colleges and Universities offering hundreds of degree program areas. Indeed, almost all schools regard the mechanics of the decision-making process as a highly sensitive matter, and they do not share the details of that process with outsiders. In any event, you cannot exercise any control over the way a college makes its decision. As you will see, you do not need "inside" information to create an effective application.

As noted above, the admissions process varies from school to school. Faculty committees may be required to make the decisions by majority vote or unanimous agreement before an applicant is accepted. A professional admissions officer, officers who may not themselves have B.A.s, B.S.s, or Ph.D.s, or a Dean of Admissions (who has a graduate degree but is not a faculty member) may make the decisions. A committee of members drawn from both administration and faculty may make the decisions. Finally, students themselves may have some input into the decisions.

We will not dwell on these different possibilities for two reasons. One, they are outside of your control. Two, regardless of the formal structure of the admissions process, it is designed to satisfy the institution's social and economic goals—as we noted above.

Despite the variety of formal structures, one generalization is possible:

> *Every college relies to some extent on the applicant's Grade Point Average (GPA) and ACT score, but there are few (if any) colleges that rely only on these quantitative factors.*

This statement contains two ideas. Let us look at each.

First, most colleges use the GPA and the ACT score. Again, the exact reliance on these numbers varies from school to school, but many use a formula that combines the two together into an index. The formula is designed to weight the two numbers approximately equal to give admissions officers some idea of how the applicant stacks up against other applicants.

Second, there are schools that claim to minimize the importance of the ACT and the GPA. They claim that the ACT is the very last factor at which they look. Such schools have a very flexible admissions process.

Many schools use the test scores and grades as a screening device to determine how much attention will be given to an application. Applications with very low test scores and grades will receive little attention. The schools reason that unless there is something obvious and compelling in the application to offset the low numbers, then the applicant should be rejected. Applications with very high test scores and grades will receive little attention. The reasoning is that unless there is something obvious and compelling in the application to reject it, it should be accepted. On this theory, the applications with test scores and grades in the middle receive the greatest attention. These are applications from candidates who are at least competitive for the school but who do not command an automatic acceptance. It is in this pool that competition is the most severe.

Here is a table that illustrates what happens at most colleges:

GPA	ACT SCORE (Percentile) 61–70%	71–80%	81–90%	91–100%
3.75+	$\frac{2}{19}$	$\frac{49}{101}$	$\frac{102}{116}$	$\frac{72}{79}$
3.50–3.74	$\frac{6}{112}$	$\frac{75}{275}$	$\frac{301}{361}$	$\frac{120}{129}$
0–3.49	$\frac{10}{160}$	$\frac{90}{601}$	$\frac{375}{666}$	$\frac{201}{250}$

The fractions represent the total number of accepted applicants divided by the total number of applicants.

The categories in the table show what this college did with applications with certain ACT scores (shown in percentile terms) and grade point averages. In the category in the upper right hand corner are candidates with scores above the 90th percentile and GPAs above 3.75. The table shows that 72 of the 79 were accepted and seven rejected.

What is obvious from the table is that some candidates with higher indices were rejected in favor of candidates with lower numbers. For example, of those candidates with scores between the 81st and 90th percentiles, 74 more candidates were accepted with a GPA below 3.50 than were students with a higher GPA between 3.50 and 3.74.

Why would a college reject an applicant with higher numbers for one with lower numbers? The answer lies in our analysis of the admissions process. Apparently, there were factors in the applications of those who were accepted that suggested to the admissions committee that those applicants would better meet the social and economic goals of the institution. Those factors are unquantifiable ones such as motivation, commitment, leadership, experience, and so on.

As you prepare your college applications, you are, of course, saddled with your GPA and your ACT score. You cannot change those factors. (The question of retaking the ACT is discussed below.) This means that the only real control you will have over your application will be those unquantifiable factors. We will show you how to maximize their impact.

There is one final point about the mechanics of the application process is rolling admissions. Rolling admissions is a device used by many colleges that regulates the release of acceptances. A typical college application season opens in October and closes in May or June. Applications are received throughout the application season, and decisions are made on an ongoing basis; this is achieved by targeting an entering class. Based on its admissions history, a college will estimate the expected range of ACT scores and GPAs of the students it will accept in the upcoming year. Then, as it receives applications (say, month by month), it will act on them. Students with very strong applications compared with the target group will receive acceptances; students with weak ones will receive rejections. Applications in the middle are carried over, and the applicants receive either no notification or notification that the application is still pending.

The rolling admissions process has advantages for both the college and the applicant. From the applicant's point of view, the earlier the notification of the disposition of an application the better. That is, you know whether you were accepted or rejected and you can go on from there. From the college's viewpoint, the entering class and therefore the stability of the budget begin to take shape as early as possible.

The rolling admissions process is also a tool you can use to your advantage: apply early. Obviously, schools have greater flexibility and there are more seats available earlier in the admissions season than later. We do not mean to imply that if you apply late in the season you will be rejected. In fact, it is impossible to quantify exactly the advantage that applications received earlier, rather than later, enjoy. Still, if you want to maximize your chances of acceptance, apply early!

C. WHERE TO APPLY

Given the economic commitment that you will be making, one of the obvious questions on your mind will be, "Where should I apply?" You should apply to a group of schools such that, given your economic resources, you maximize your chances of gaining admission to the colleges of your choice.

To apply to a college, you must remit a non-refundable application fee. This means that you are, to speak crudely, gambling with your money. You pay the fee, but you do not know in advance whether you will win or lose. So, hedge your bets. In a gambling situation, a bettor will have several choices. Some will be long shots, others will be almost sure things, and others will lie somewhere in between. The long shots will pay handsome dividends and the sure things a reasonable return. The others will pay in between.

Given these considerations, you should select two or perhaps three "long shot" schools. As the term "long shot" implies, the odds of your being accepted to these schools are not very good, but the potential payoff justifies the gamble. On the other hand, you should also select one or two "sure thing" schools. To do this, you may have to apply to a school in your geographical area that does not enjoy a particularly good reputation or to a school that is located in another part of the country. The rest of your applications should go to your "good bet" schools—schools for which the chances for acceptance are 40% to 75%.

Assume that you have the resources to apply to ten schools and that you have an above average GPA and ACT score. Depending on the exact numbers, you may very well have a chance at one of the top colleges. However, those are your "long shot" schools. You are almost a sure thing at many schools, your "sure thing" schools. Finally, there is a long list of "good bet" schools in the middle. At each of these schools, your application will likely receive serious consideration, but it is not guaranteed for acceptance.

This strategy of "stacking" your applications will maximize your chances of acceptance at a school you want, while minimizing the chance that you will not get into any school. Of course, the way the strategy is implemented will vary from person to person. For people who are lucky enough to have a high GPA and a top ACT score, the middle and bottom tier schools collapse into a single tier. At the other extreme, those who are unlucky enough to have a GPA and ACT score that are below what most schools accept will have to work with the second and third tiers.

As you prepare to implement this strategy, make a realistic assessment of your chances. Candidates unfortunately tend to overestimate the importance of what they believe to be their own interesting or unique factors. For example, we often hear candidates make statements such as, "Well sure my GPA is a little low, but I had to work part-time while I was in school"; and "I know my ACT score is not that good, but I was a member of the high school Student Council." These are valid points and are usually taken into consideration by admissions officers. However, the question is how much weight they will be given, for they (or some similar point) are true of most people applying to college. For example, if you are thinking of applying to a program requiring an average GPA of 3.8 and an average ACT score in the 90th percentile and you do not meet these requirements, then there had better be something really special in your background such as an Olympic medal.

A question related to the "Where should I apply?" question is "What are the top undergraduate schools in the country?" Since there is no single criterion for "best school" that would be accepted by everyone, it is arguable that this question simply cannot be given a meaningful answer. Nevertheless, even though an unequivocal answer cannot be given, it is possible to get an approximate answer. The "U.S. News & World Report" Year 2005 survey of college school deans lists the top twenty-five national universities and top 25 national colleges. (Entries on the list may change each year, as may the rankings.)

TOP 25 NATIONAL UNIVERSITIES

1. Harvard University
   Princeton University (NJ)
3. Yale University (CT)
4. University of Pennsylvania
5. Duke University (NC)
   Massachusetts Inst. of Technology
   Stanford University (CA)
8. California Institute of Technology
9. Columbia University (NY)
   Dartmouth College (NH)
11. Northwestern University (IL)
   Washington Univ. in St. Louis
13. Brown University (RI)
14. Cornell University (NY)
   Johns Hopkins University (MD)
   University of Chicago
17. Rice University (TX)
18. University of Notre Dame (IN)
   Vanderbilt University (TN)
20. Emory University (GA)
21. University of California – Berkeley
22. Carnegie Mellon University (PA)
   Univ. of Michigan – Ann Arbor
   University of Virginia
25. Georgetown University (DC)
   Univ. of California – Los Angeles

TOP 25 NATIONAL LIBERAL ARTS COLLEGES

1. Williams College (MA)
2. Amherst College (MA)
   Swarthmore College (PA)
4. Wellesley College (MA)
5. Carleton College (MN)
   Pomona College (CA)
7. Bowdoin College (ME)
   Davidson College (NC)
9. Haverford College (PA)
   Wesleyan University (CT)
11. Middlebury College (VT)
12. Vassar College (NY)
13. Claremont McKenna College (CA)
   Smith College (MA)
   Washington and Lee Univ. (VA)
16. Colgate University (NY)
   Grinnell College (IA)
   Harvey Mudd College (CA)
19. Colby College (ME)
   Hamilton College (NY)
21. Bryn Mawr College (PA)
22. Bates College (ME)
23. Oberlin College (OH)
24. Mount Holyoke College (MA)
   Trinity College (CT)

D. CREATING YOUR APPLICATION

The title of this section echoes our analysis of the admissions process given above. To maximize your chances of success, you must create an application that satisfies the needs of the school to which you are applying. This does not mean that you create an application out of whole cloth, but it does mean that you organize and present your experiences in a way that depicts you in the most favorable light.

Most of the questions you will be asked need only short answers. Did you work while you were in school? What clubs did you join? What honors or awards did you receive? You do not have much room to maneuver here. However, you should try to communicate as much information as possible in your short answers. Compare the following pairs of descriptions:

Member of Orchestra
Second Violinist of the Orchestra

Played Intra-Mural Volleyball
Co-captain of the Volleyball Team

Member of the AD's CSL
One of three members on the Associate Dean's Committee on Student Life

Worked at Billy's Burger Barn
Assistant Manager at Billy's Burger Barn (25 hours/week)

In addition to the short answer questions, most applications invite you to make a personal statement. Some applications ask for very little additional information. For example: "In a paragraph explain to us why you want to go to college." Other applications are open-ended: "On a separate sheet of paper, tell us anything else you think we ought to know about you." The point of the question is for you to give the admissions committee any information that might not be available from test scores, GPA, and short-answer questions.

You should consider the personal statement to be the most important part of your application for two reasons. First, the personal statement should be your argument to the admissions committee for your acceptance. It should give them reasons to accept you. Second, the personal statement is the one aspect of the application over which you can exercise any real control. Your GPA is already settled; your work experience was accumulated over the years; your ACT has been scored. These aspects of the application cannot easily be manipulated. The personal statement, however, is under your control.

What should go into a personal statement? You should include arguments that interpret your academic, employment, and personal history in such a way as to indicate that you have the ability complete college and that you are committed to studying and later to pursuing a career in your chosen area of study. Importantly, the personal statement must not be a simple restatement of facts already in the application. Imagine, for example, a personal statement that reads as follows:

> *I went to high school where I got a 3.5 GPA. I was a member of the Associate Dean's Committee on Student Life, and I worked as the assistant manager on the night shift at Billy's Burger Barn. Then I took the ACT and got a 24. I know I will be a good B.A. candidate and will enjoy my job.*

This is not very interesting. Furthermore, all of that information is already included in your answers to the standard questions on the application. There is no point in simply repeating it.

Instead, you *interpret* the facts of your life to make them *reasons* for accepting you. You should start with your GPA. Try to bring out facts that suggest that the GPA is really better than it looks. Did you have one particularly bad semester, during which you took physics, calculus, and Latin, which pulled your average down? Was there a death in the family or some other difficult time that interfered with your studies? How many hours did you work in an average week? What extracurricular or family commitments took time away from your studies? Did you follow an unusual course of study such as an honors program? Were your classes particularly challenging, such as Advance Placement classes? Did you participate in any unusual courses such as field research?

These are the points that the admissions committee wants to hear. For example:

> *The committee will see that my final GPA is 3.5. I should point out that the average would have been higher had I not needed to work 20 hours each week to save for my college education. Additionally, my grades in the first semester of my junior year were disappointing because my grandmother, who lived with my family and with whom I was very close, died. Finally, in order to fulfill the requirements for the honors program, I wrote a 20-page honors thesis on the Dutch fishing industry of the 18th century. I have included a copy of the introduction to my thesis with this application.*

You should take the same approach to your work experience. For example:

> *During my junior and senior years in high school, I worked an average of 20 hours per week at Billy's Burger Barn as the manager on the night shift. I would report to work at midnight and get off at four a.m. As night manager, I supervised eight other employees and was responsible for making emergency repairs on kitchen equipment. For example, once I was able to keep the deep fryer in operation by using a length of telephone cable to repair a faulty thermostat. The night manager was also responsible for maintaining order. It is not an easy job to convince intoxicated students who become too rowdy to leave without calling the police. Moreover, we were robbed at gunpoint not once but twice.*

Of course, if you have considerable work experience, *e.g.*, if you graduated from high school several years ago, you will want to go into that experience in more detail than if you had only student work experience.

Can you say anything about the ACT score? Probably not much—the ACT score is straightforward and not usually open to interpretation. However, there are some exceptions. One such exception is a history of poor scores on standardized exams. Consider the following:

> *I believe that my ACT score of 24 understates my real ability, for I have never had much success on aptitude tests. Yet, I finished high school with a 3.6 GPA.*

> *The committee will see that I have two ACT scores: 18 and 24. During the first test, I had the flu and a fever and simply could not concentrate.*

These are the two most common excuses for a disappointing ACT score.

Finally, you must also persuade the admissions committee that you are serious about obtaining your college degree. You must be able to show the committee something in your background that explains why you want to go to college. In addition, it will help your case if you can suggest what you might do with a college degree. For example:

> *As a prospective science major, I interned with the Student Environmental Association. Working with private company executives, whom had themselves satisfied E.P.A. emissions standards, we convinced the University to stop polluting the Ten-Mile Run Creek. From this experience, I learned how business helps to protect our environment. I plan to make environmental resources my area of study, and I hope to work for the government or a private agency to protect the environment.*

A word of warning is in order here. Your career objectives have to be believable. It is not sufficient to write, "I plan to solve the environmental problems of American industry." That is much too abstract. Nor are college admissions officers interested in a general discourse on the advantages of democracy or the hardship of poverty. If you write, "I want to eliminate damage to the planet and to help private industries help themselves environmentally" then there had better be something in your experience that makes this believable.

Finally, with regard to motivation, do not imagine that there is a preferred political position that you should adopt. College admissions officers span the political spectrum. To be sure, some are political liberals, but there are also conservatives. You do not have to make up a "tear-jerker" essay in order to be accepted.

Thus far, we have discussed the issues of ability and motivation. You may also wish to include in your personal statement information that shows that you have something that will help the school create a diverse student body. This additional information can be something dramatic:

> *One morning, a patron choked on a burger and lost consciousness. I used the Heimlich maneuver to dislodge the food and performed CPR until a team of paramedics arrived. The patron recovered fully, in large part, according to her doctors, because of my first aid.*

Conversely, the information may not be dramatic:

> *My parents are Armenian immigrants, so I am fluent in Armenian as well as English. I would enjoy meeting others who share an interest in the politics, legal developments, and culture of that part of the world.*

However, do not overestimate the value of this kind of information. It is, so to speak, the icing on the cake. It makes you a more interesting individual and might tip the scale in your favor when all other things are equal. It will not, however, get you an acceptance at a school for which you are not otherwise competitive in terms of ACT and GPA.

Now we turn our attention to matters of style. When you marshal your arguments for acceptance, you need to present them in an organized fashion. There is no single preferred format, but you might start with the following outline:

I. I have the ability
   A. My high school studies are good
      1. I had one bad semester
      2. I was in the accelerated program
      3. I wrote a thesis
   B. My work experience is good
      1. I worked while in high school
      2. I was promoted to shift leader at my job
II. I want to earn my college degree
   A. I worked with Ph.D.s on the pollution problem during my internship
   B. I would become a specialist in environmental chemistry
III. There is something interesting about me

The prose you use should be your own natural style of writing. Do not try something cute. Admissions officers detest essays that try to look like manuscripts and footnote "documentary evidence." You should create your outline, using all the arguments of which you can think. Then you must begin to edit. For most people, the final document should not be more than a page to a page and a half—typed of course! During the editing process, you will strive for an economy of language, so that you can convey as much information as possible. Additionally, you will be forced to make considered judgments about the relative importance of various points. You will be forced to delete those ideas that are not that compelling. To obtain a superior personal statement, it may be necessary to reduce five or six pages to a single page, and the process may require more than 20 drafts.

E. LETTERS OF RECOMMENDATION

Perhaps the best advice that we can give you about so-called letters of recommendation is to think of them as evaluations rather than recommendations. Indeed, many admissions officers refer to letter-writers as evaluators. These letters can be very important factors in an application, so who should write them?

First, some schools require a letter from the dean of students (or some similar functionary) at your high school. This is not optional on your part. Even if you have never met the dean, you must get this letter. However, colleges do not really expect the dean to have much to say. The requirement is in essence an inquiry to the school about your behavior. It is intended to evoke any information about disciplinary problems that might not otherwise surface. So the best letter from a dean, and the one most people get, is just a statement to the effect that there is nothing to say about you. In addition to the dean's letter, most schools require or at least permit you to submit two or three letters of evaluation from other sources. Who should write these? First, let us dispose of a common misunderstanding. A letter of evaluation does not have to come from a famous person. How effective is the following letter?

Francis Scott
Chairperson of the Board

To the Admissions Committee:

I am recommending Susan Roberts for college. Her mother is a member of our board of directors. Susan's mother earned her doctorate at the University of Chicago and she regularly makes significant contributions to our corporate meetings. Susan, following her mother's example, will make a fine college candidate.

Sincerely,
Francis Scott

The letterhead holds great promise, but then the letter itself is worthless. It is obvious that the letter-writer does not really have any basis for his conclusion that the candidate will make a good college candidate.

The best letters of evaluation will come from people who know you very well: a teacher with whom you took several courses, your intern supervisor, or an associate with whom you have worked closely. A good evaluation will incorporate personal knowledge into the letter and reference specific events and activities. For example:

Mary P. Weiss
White, Weiss, and Blanche

To the Admissions Committee:

White, Weiss, and Blanche is a consulting firm that advises corporations on environmental concerns. Susan Roberts has worked for us as an intern for the past two summers. Her work is outstanding, and she is an intelligent and genial person.

Last summer, as my assistant, Susan wrote a five-page report that outlined a way of altering a client's exhaust stack to reduce sulfur emissions. The report was organized so that it was easy to follow and written in a style that was clear and easy to understand. Additionally, Susan assisted with a live presentation during a meeting with the client's board of directors and engineers. She was confident and handled some very difficult questions in an easy manner.

Finally, Susan made an important contribution to our company softball team. The team finished in last place, but Susan played in every game. Her batting average was not anything to brag about, but her enthusiasm more than made up for it.

Sincerely,
Mary Weiss

To get a letter such as this, you will have to ask someone who knows you well.

F. TAKING THE ACT

We have already emphasized the important role that the ACT plays in the admissions process. It is only common sense that you do everything you can to maximize your score. You should not take the ACT until you are certain that you are ready to do your best. Colleges receive all of your ACT test scores—not just your best one. In addition, many colleges average multiple scores. You are already heading in the right direction by taking the Cambridge ACT Review Course—we will provide you with everything you need to succeed on the ACT. The rest is up to you. Good luck!

OVERCOMING TEST ANXIETY
–Winning Strategies–

Test anxiety can manifest itself in various forms—from the common occurrences of "butterflies" in the stomach, mild sweating, or nervous laughter, to the more extreme occurrences of overwhelming fear, anxiety attacks, and unmanageable worry. It is quite normal for students to experience some mild anxiety before or during testing without being greatly affected. On the other hand, more intense worry, fear, or tension can prevent students from performing successfully on standardized tests. Some experts who study human performance propose that light stress may actually help to focus a person's concentration on the task at hand. However, stress that reaches beyond minimum levels and remains for a long period of time can block a student's ability to quickly recall facts, remember strategies, analyze complex problems, and creatively approach difficult items. When taking a test, being calm and collected promotes clear and logical thinking. Therefore, a relaxed state of mind is not only important to you as a test-taker, but it is also essential. The following strategies provide practical hints and methods to help alleviate debilitating test anxiety.

A. PLAN—HAVE A STUDY PLAN AND STICK TO IT

Putting off important test review assignments until the last minute naturally causes high stress for anyone who is seriously anxious about test day. Even the brightest student experiences nervousness when he or she walks into a test site without being fully prepared. Therefore, stress reduction methods should begin weeks or even months in advance. Prepared test-takers are more relaxed, confident, and focused, so you should begin to review materials earlier rather than later in order to reduce anxiety.

Be warned that it is almost impossible to successfully cram for standardized tests, such as the SAT, ACT, GRE, GMAT, or LSAT. Waiting until the day or week before the test to begin studying will only serve to elevate your anxiety level. Cramming at the last minute, which may have worked for you in the past with quizzes or less comprehensive tests, will not work to prepare you for long, comprehensive, standardized tests. Such comprehensive tests require extended and intensive study methods. Trying to cram will leave you feeling frustrated, unprepared, overwhelmed, and nervous about the pending test day.

So, the key to combating test anxiety is to plan ahead so that you are not unprepared. Do not procrastinate—develop a study plan, start early, and stick to it. A study plan is a written set of daily goals that will help you track the content and the sequence of your test review. This plan will help you tell yourself what, when, where, and how much you will study. (See the Time Management section on page 25 for a further description on how to organize your time effectively.)

By planning your work and working your plan, you can alleviate any unnecessary anxiety. Here are some tips on how to produce your study plan.

➢ *Record a Plan on Paper*

A written study plan is more concrete and dependable than one that simply rattles around in your head. So, you should use a piece of paper and a pencil to write out a plan for reviewing all of the materials that are necessary to succeed on the test. Record important items and dates on your calendar (Time Management), and post the study plan in a place where you will see it often (*e.g.*, your bedroom door or your refrigerator). When you accomplish one of the goals on your plan (*e.g.*, taking a timed practice exam or reviewing a certain number of items), designate its completion with a checkmark. This system of recording your goals will give you a sense of achievement.

➢ *Break the Test into Pieces*

Standardized tests are segmented into multiple sections according to subject area. However, you should not try to learn all of the material related to a particular subject area in one sitting. The subject matter that is covered is far too broad to learn in a few short minutes, so you should not try to learn every test strategy at once or review the whole test in one day. Instead, you should break the test into smaller portions and then study a portion until you are confident that you can move on to another. You should also vary the sections that you study in order to ward off boredom. For example, on Monday, study a Math section, and on Tuesday, study a Reading section.

In addition to breaking the test into smaller portions, you should always remember to review sections that you have already studied. This review will keep all of the sections fresh in your mind for test day. No two students are capable of learning at an identical rate. Some students can learn huge chunks of information at once, while other students need to review smaller amounts of information over a greater period of time. Determine the amount of material that you can comfortably and adequately cover in one day; then, attack that amount of material on each day.

For most students, the study plan is determined by the Cambridge Review Course schedule. The class schedule and sequence have been developed to help you improve your test score. So, follow the guidance of your class instructor and mold your personal study plan around the schedule.

➢ ***Do Some Studying or Preparation Every Day***

Yes. It is very important that you study something every single day. Once you get the "study snowball" rolling, the momentum will help you overcome the temptation to quit. Be consistent. It is far better to study sixty minutes per day for seven straight days than to study seven straight hours only once per week.

➢ ***Study at the Same Time and Place***

Find somewhere quiet to study, where there are few distractions, the lighting is good, and you feel comfortable. Since most tests are given either at desks, tables, or computer terminals, avoid studying in bed or in a lounge chair. Simulate the test conditions by studying at a desk or table. Turn off the television or the radio. Shut down the computer, unless of course you are using it as a study tool. Give yourself uninterrupted quality time to study. Find a consistent time when you can study and lock it into your schedule. Do not let yourself off the hook. Study each day at the same time and place so that you can become accustomed to your work environment.

➢ ***Set Goals and Reward Yourself***

Set a weekly goal for the amount of time that you will study and the amount of material that you will review. When you meet these weekly goals, reward yourself. Offer yourself special incentives that will motivate you to reach your next goal.

➢ ***Find a Study Partner or Someone to Hold You Accountable for Your Progress***

There really is strength in numbers. Find at least one person who will help you stay on course with your goals. Have this person ask you, every few days, whether or not you are sticking to your plan. Consider finding a "study buddy." Push each other to set and reach high test preparation goals.

Early and consistent test preparation means that you will walk calmly and confidently into the testing center on test day, knowing that you have done your very best to prepare for the test.

B. PREPARE POSITIVELY—REPLACE ANXIETY WITH POSITIVITY

Positive thinking helps overcome test anxiety. For years, psychologists have studied how attitudes affect and alter achievement. These studies suggest that students with positive attitudes consistently score higher than students with negative attitudes.

Here are some practical ways to create a positive mindset:

➢ ***Talk Positively to Yourself***

Success comes in a "can," not a "cannot." So, learn to think positively by mentally replacing "cannot" with "can." Negative statements such as, "I will never pass this test," "I know I can't get this," or "I'm not smart enough to get a good score," are counterproductive, and they hinder both studying and the test-taking process. In order to eliminate negative thoughts, you must first take note of them when they occur and then take steps to remove them from your mind. As soon as you recognize a negative thought, immediately replace it with a positive thought. It is quite easy. Whenever you hear phrases such as "I can't do this," or "I'm not smart enough," think to yourself, "I can do this," "I will understand this," or "I am smart enough." Furthermore, as you walk into the classroom on the day of the test, repeatedly say to yourself, "I have studied, I will do my best, and I will succeed."

➢ ***Think Positively About Yourself***

Think positively with the help of visualization. Try this: While in a relaxed mood, close your eyes and envision yourself walking into the test room, perfectly calm and confident. Now, imagine yourself taking each section of the test without any difficulty and with great calmness. See yourself answering the items quickly and correctly. Watch yourself exiting the test area with confidence because you know that you performed extremely well. With these visualization techniques, you can mentally and emotionally practice taking the test in a confident and calm manner. You can practice visualizing yourself at any time and for any given situation. Many students find that it works well close to bedtime. Coaches encourage their peak performing athletes to use daily visualization exercises in order to increase their abilities in running, jumping, shooting, *etc.* Every single day, from now until the test day, practice visualization and picture yourself taking the test quickly, easily, confidently, and calmly. Visualization can help you exude a positive attitude and overcome test anxiety. Get the picture?

➢ ***Act Positively Toward Yourself***

On the day of the test, act positively. Even if you do not "feel" completely confident, you should stride into the test site with your head held high and a bounce in your step. Show both yourself and your peers that you are at ease and in complete control of the situation. Present yourself as someone who knows that he or she will be successful. Acting confidently will actually help you feel confident.

Practice these strategies in order to instill a positive mental attitude. Positive thinking means believing in yourself. Believe that you can achieve your highest goal under any circumstances. Know that you can do it. Dare to try.

C. PUT AWAY NEGATIVE THOUGHTS—THEY FUEL TEST ANXIETY

Since you will be practicing positive thinking, you should also learn to recognize and eliminate distorted, or twisted, thinking. Avoid thinking any of the following distorted things about yourself:

"I must always be perfect." The reality is that everyone makes mistakes. In testing situations, perfectionists mentally fuss and fume about a single mistake instead of celebrating all of the items that they answered correctly. Dwelling on mistakes wastes time and creates more tension. Push mistakes behind you and move forward to the next set of items. Remember that we all reserve the right to learn and grow.

"I failed the last time, so I'll fail this time." Past failure does not lead to future failure. People do get better the more that they practice. Because you did poorly on something in the past does not guarantee a poor performance either this time or in the future. Use this test as an opportunity for a fresh start. Forget yesterday's failures and realize that today is a brand new beginning.

"People won't like me if I do poorly." It is preferable to have good relations with people and to have them approve of you or even to love you—but it is not necessary. You will not be unhappy unless you make yourself unhappy. Rely on self-approval, not on the approval of others. Do your best because you want to and you can, not because you want to please someone else.

"I have been anxious when taking tests before; therefore, I'll always be anxious." This twisted logic implies that you have no control over your behavior; however, that is not the case. You can change and learn to control your anxiety. It might take time and hard work to build calmness and confidence, but it is certainly within your reach.

D. POWER UP PHYSICALLY—RELEASE STRESS WITH PHYSICAL EXERCISE

Physical exercise is an excellent way to both reduce anxiety levels and cope with the effects of stress. Start a regular program of physical fitness that includes stretching and cardiovascular activities. If necessary, check with a doctor or a health professional in order to develop a customized fitness program.

E. PRACTICE BEING CALM—LEARN TO MENTALLY AND PHYSICALLY RELAX

You may not realize that mental and physical relaxation play significant parts in the studying process. By setting aside time for clearing your mind and body of stress and anxiety, you will refresh your mental and physical energy reserves. Spend quality time studying and reviewing for the test. Then, spend time relaxing your mind and body so that you are re-energized for your next study session.

Practice the following relaxation exercises to calm the body and mind.

➢ *Physical Relaxation Exercise*

Pick a quiet room where there are few distractions. Shut off all intrusive lights. Sit in a chair or lie down in a bed. If you wear glasses, take them off. Get comfortable, loosening any tight or binding clothing. Close your eyes, and take a deep breath. Blow out all of the air in your lungs, and then breathe in deeply. Now, focus on your tense muscles and consciously relax them. Start by focusing on your toes, your feet, and your calves. Tense and release your muscles to fully relax them. Move upward through each muscle group in your body, up to and including your facial muscles. Continue to breathe slowly, steadily, and fully during this exercise. Repeat this process, while consciously relaxing tense muscles, until you relax your entire body. Rest in this state for a few minutes. When you are finished, open your eyes, and remain still for another minute or two before rising.

➢ *Breathing Exercise*

Deep and relaxed breathing will calm your nerves and reduce stress. Whenever you start feeling anxious, take time out to perform this simple breathing exercise. Place you hands upon your stomach and breathe in slowly and deeply through your nose, feeling your rib cage rise. Pause and hold your breath for a second, thinking to yourself, "I am calm." Release your breath slowly and fully, blowing it out through your mouth. Repeat this exercise eight to ten times. Perform this exercise whenever you feel nervous or anxious.

➢ ***Mental Relaxation Exercise***

Meditation, in various forms, has been practiced to allow the mind to release stressful thoughts. Many types of meditation can be learned and then practiced on a regular basis. A popular type of meditation is the passive form. Begin meditating after your body is in a relaxed state. Concentrate on something monotonous until your mind becomes quiet. You may choose to concentrate on a sound, a word, or an object. Observe your thoughts without controlling them. Gently refocus on the sound, word, or object. Passively observe your thoughts when they come, then gently refocus back upon the sound, word, or object.

F. PREPARE—DO NOT LEAVE IMPORTANT ITEMS UNTIL THE LAST MINUTE

You are going to want to remain as relaxed as possible on the day of the test. In order to eliminate the last-minute, frantic rush to find that "one thing" that you cannot locate, make a list of the items that you need for the day of the test. Set out those important items the night before in order to efficiently and effectively speed you on your way toward the testing center.

➢ ***Determine the Items that You Are Expected to Bring***

Carefully read the test packet materials so that you know exactly what you should and should not bring to the test center. You may need to bring an eraser, personal I.D., calculator, or pencils. However, some test centers do not allow food, scratch paper, or alarms. Therefore, determine what things to bring and what things to leave at home.

➢ ***Check the Working Condition of Your Calculator, Watch, etc.***

Okay, this might sound silly, but make sure that your watch and calculator (if allowed) are in good working condition. Replace old calculator batteries with new batteries. Sharpen pencils before arriving at the test center.

➢ ***Gather the Items that You Need***

On the night before the test, gather all of the necessary items so that you can avoid the anxiety of trying to find them at the last minute.

➢ ***Know the Directions to the Test Center***

If you have not been to the test center before, make sure that you are provided with clear and specific directions as soon as possible. If you are at all confused about how to get to the test center, call the center immediately and clarify the directions.

➢ ***Decide Whether to Study the Night Before the Test***

Should you study the night before the test? Well, as mentioned earlier, you certainly should not attempt to cram for the test. You may want to review a few strategies, but you do not want to attempt to learn large amounts of new material. Instead, take some time to review, and then find some entertaining activity to occupy your time. Go to the gym or see a movie with friends. Laughing is always a great way to reduce stress, so you may want to find something humorous to do or watch.

➢ ***Sleep Well***

A good night of sleep will help reduce stress on the test day. Do not stay out late on the night before the test.

➢ ***Get to the Test Site Early***

Your anxiety level will increase if you arrive at the test center late, stand in line to register, run to a seat, and then immediately begin to take the test. So, arrive at the test center early enough to find the room, register, find your seat, set out necessary items (pencil, calculator, *etc.*), and still have a few minutes to relax and compose yourself. You may also need time to locate the restrooms and drinking fountains. However, do not arrive at the test center too early. Students typically get nervous and anxious when they have to wait for a long period of time with nothing to do except think about the upcoming test. So, find the balance between "too early" and "too late" that works best for you.

➢ ***Watch Your Diet***

What you choose to eat can be a physical cause of stress. Therefore, control your eating habits in order to maintain lower stress levels. Eat a healthy breakfast on the day of the test. Restrict your intake of sugar, salt, and caffeine. Remember that sugar and caffeine are found in coffee, cola, cocoa, and tea. These substances trigger a stress response in your body. High levels of sugar and caffeine are associated with nervousness, dizziness, irritability, headaches, and insomnia. Additionally, smoking has been found to decrease a person's ability to handle stress. Cigarettes act as a stimulant because of their nicotine content and will serve to increase stress levels.

➢ ***Dress Comfortably***

The good news is that you are going to a test, not a fashion show. So, wear comfortable clothes to the testing center; choose clothes that are not overly binding or tight. Dressing in layers is always a good idea since testing rooms are notoriously either too hot or too cold.

G. PAUSE—RELEASE PHYSICAL AND MENTAL ANXIETY BEFORE THE TEST

As already stated, relaxation allows you to focus your full attention and energy on the task at hand, rather than be distracted by tension and stress. Release as much tension and anxiety as possible right before taking the test.

➢ ***Release and Relax***

Having arrived early at the test site, take the last few minutes to relax. Do not attempt to study or review at this point. Instead, use a simple relaxation technique. Close your eyes, and breathe in deeply through your nose. Hold that breath for a few seconds. Next, release that breath through your mouth. Repeat this "in-and-out" breathing cycle. Try to gradually slow the pace of the "in-and-out" motion of your breathing. Visualize yourself at a place that you find peaceful and relaxing, such as the beach, the woods, or some other favorite spot. Continue this technique for a few minutes until you feel yourself becoming relaxed and calm.

➢ ***Do Some Low-Level Physical Exercise***

Take a brisk walk. For many people, walking helps lower high stress levels, while positively easing the mind from worrying about the upcoming test. Others find that stretching exercises help loosen tense muscles. Just be sure to return to the site with plenty of time to register and sit down for the test.

➢ ***Massage Tension Away***

While waiting for the test, sit comfortably in your chair. Notice places in your body that feel tense—generally the shoulders, neck, or back. Gently massage tense areas for a few minutes.

H. PRESS ON—CONCENTRATE ON THE CURRENT ITEM, NOT THE LAST OR NEXT

Dwelling on answers to previous items will only elevate test anxiety, so do not worry about those sections or items that you have finished.

➢ ***Focus on One Item at a Time***

Your task on any test is to correctly answer each item, one item at a time. Good test-takers focus only on the item to which they are currently working. Poor test-takers worry about items that they just completed or about items in the upcoming section. Try to stay "in the moment" by concentrating on one item at a time.

I. PROUDLY DEPART—WALK OUT WITH YOUR HEAD HELD HIGH

➢ ***Know that You Have Done Your Best***

If you have followed the strategies listed in this section, attended test preparation classes, and spent time reviewing and studying on your own, you have most likely done your very best to prepare for the test. As you walk out of the test site, remind yourself that you have indeed put forth your best effort.

➢ ***Watch the Labels***

After the test, never label yourself as a "failure," "loser," or "under-achiever." Instead, if you do not feel that you did as well as you expected, use the experience to learn about the test and about yourself. Students are able to re-take standardized tests, so reflect upon what you can do better next time, not upon how poorly you think you did this time.

J. PERSPECTIVE—KEEP LIFE IN PERSPECTIVE

Yes, the test you will take is important, but other things in life are important too. Remember that this test is a means to an end—getting into college, graduate school, or a profession—and not the end itself.

NOTE: Some test-takers, even after applying all of the above strategies, still experience debilitating stress. Intense anxiety or stress that causes nausea, headaches, overwhelming emotional fears, or other severe symptoms may need special attention and care that goes beyond the strategies in these pages. If you suffer from these debilitating stress symptoms, ask your high school or university counseling office what resources are available to help overcome severe test anxiety.

TIME MANAGEMENT
–Winning Strategies–

A. INTRODUCTION

High school students live hectic and exciting lives. In order to succeed in high school, you must learn how to manage your time, which really means that you must learn how to manage yourself by becoming a proactive student. To be proactive means to act assertively and decisively in order to prepare for upcoming events or situations. To be proactive also means to make wise decisions about how to plan the use of your time. Therefore, a proactive student is a well-prepared student.

School classes and homework take up a great deal of the day, but there are also opportunities for recreation, extracurricular activity, and personal development. While jobs, athletics, friends, clubs, concerts, *etc.* may take time away from your academic life, learning to manage your time and juggle multiple responsibilities is essential for succeeding in high school. This section focuses on how to better manage your time by using such powerful tools as the PLAN method and pyramid scheduling.

B. SCHEDULING FOR SUCCESS—HAVE A PLAN

The PLAN method presents four elements for maximizing your time:

PRIORITIZE tasks according to their long-term benefit.
LIST those tasks according to their priority.
ARRANGE those tasks on a schedule.
NEGOTIATE your schedule if those tasks become overwhelming.

1. P...PRIORITIZE

Though many high school activities are important, it is necessary to determine which of these activities are the most important. Students who ***prioritize*** their tasks arrange them in an optimum order that is based on level of importance: More important tasks take precedence over less important tasks. So, in order to prioritize, you need to identify activities that will benefit you most in the long-run.

Different students have different priorities. While most students do not study during all of their free time, successful students generally prioritize academics over other activities. These students devote a majority of their free time to studying so that they can reinforce what they have already learned in class. In order to effectively prioritize your tasks, you must first identify your own long-term goals. With a better understanding of your goals for the future, you can more effectively prioritize your activities in the present.

Here are some questions that you should ask yourself in order to better determine your long-term goals:

- What clubs would I like to join?
- What sports would I like to play?
- What social service groups would I like to join?
- With whom do I want to be friends?
- What type of impact would I like to have on my community?
- What special accomplishments do I want to achieve?
- What types of positive things do I want people to say about me?
- Who do I want to impress? How will I impress them?
- What will make me a happy and fulfilled person?
- Do I want to go to college? If so, which college and what major might I choose?
- What career would I like to pursue?

2. L...LIST

Every week, make a ***list*** of the tasks that you want to accomplish, placing the most important tasks at the top of your list.

3. A...ARRANGE

Each day, ***arrange*** all of your tasks on a daily schedule, prioritizing the most important tasks over tasks that are less important. The key to prioritization is to maintain a clear understanding of what is most important so that you can remain focused on the most significant tasks at hand.

4. N...NEGOTIATE

In any given high school quarter, there are weeks that are especially busy and may prove to be overwhelming. Typically, chapter tests and final exams require considerable amounts of study time. The following are seven tips on how to better ***negotiate*** the details of your schedule in accordance with the potential added pressures of exam time.

1. Anticipate weeks with heavy workloads and note them on your schedule.
2. Meet with your teachers to discuss any problems that you might have with completing class work.
3. Form a study group to help prepare for tests.
4. Get plenty of rest; you will need rest and energy during stressful times.
5. Do not wait until the last week of the quarter to complete major projects; procrastination is unproductive.
6. Attempt to get time off from your job during the most hectic times.
7. Say no to distractions such as watching television and reading books or magazines.

C. MANAGE YOUR TIME BY USING PYRAMID SCHEDULING

A pyramid consists of a large base, or foundation, which transitions into progressively narrower levels until finally reaching a small point at the top. In a similar fashion, pyramid scheduling begins with organizing your long-term projects and then moves on to your more immediate tasks until finally reaching your daily schedule. Purchase an annual calendar or planner so that you can schedule months, weeks, and days, approaching your scheduling process in the following manner:

1. SCHEDULE THE ENTIRE QUARTER

During the first week of each quarter (typically running nine weeks in length), organize all of your major assignments and responsibilities on the calendar. After you have received a syllabus for each of your classes, reference all important dates that coincide with any of the following:

- Class assignments, such as reading selections and projects
- Tests and exams
- Quizzes
- Holidays and vacations
- Personal obligations, such as birthdays and family gatherings
- Job commitments
- Extracurricular activities, such as athletic events and student government meetings

2. SCHEDULE EACH MONTH

Two days before the beginning of each month, review your monthly schedule for all assignments, tests, and quizzes. Then, reference any important dates for monthly activities that do not already appear on your calendar, such as:

- Additional assignments
- Sporting events or concerts that you plan to attend
- Personal commitments, such as work schedule and social engagements
- Study blocks for major projects, exams, tests, or quizzes

3. SCHEDULE EACH WEEK

On Sunday night of each week, review your weekly schedule for all assignments, tests, and quizzes. Look for any personal appointments or special commitments that may be scheduled for the upcoming week. Then, on a weekly calendar, outline a schedule for that upcoming week so that you will have sufficient time for studying and completing assignments. Each day of the weekly schedule should be divided up into mornings, afternoons, and evenings so that you can reference the most important times for certain daily activities, such as:

- Classes
- Class assignments, such as reading selections and projects
- Tests and exams
- Quizzes
- Holidays and vacation days
- Personal commitments, such as work schedule and social engagements
- Employment commitments
- Extracurricular activities, such as athletic events and student government meetings
- Study sessions

4. SCHEDULE EACH DAY

On the night before each school day, create a schedule that outlines important times for the following daily activities:

- Class schedule
- Study times
- Job schedule
- Free time
- Additional appointments, tasks, or responsibilities

5. FINALLY, REMEMBER TO STICK TO YOUR SCHEDULE

Unless emergencies arise, stick to your schedule. Do not change your schedule unless it is absolutely necessary to accommodate and prioritize new activities. Remember that time management is really about self-management. So, remain disciplined so that you can follow your schedule without falling prey to distractions.

D. CONCLUSION

Successful students are able to self-manage themselves by learning and using valuable time management tools. If you start to use these tools now, you can be successful in high school and beyond. Always remember to schedule your work and work your schedule!

PRE-TEST BUBBLE SHEET

Start with number 1 for each new section. If a section has fewer items than answer spaces, leave the extra answer spaces blank. Be sure to erase any errors or stray marks completely.

Name ______________________ Student ID Number ______________________

Date ______________ Instructor ______________________ Course/Session Number ______________

TEST 1—ENGLISH

1 A B C D	16 F G H J	31 A B C D	46 F G H J	61 A B C D
2 F G H J	17 A B C D	32 F G H J	47 A B C D	62 F G H J
3 A B C D	18 F G H J	33 A B C D	48 F G H J	63 A B C D
4 F G H J	19 A B C D	34 F G H J	49 A B C D	64 F G H J
5 A B C D	20 F G H J	35 A B C D	50 F G H J	65 A B C D
6 F G H J	21 A B C D	36 F G H J	51 A B C D	66 F G H J
7 A B C D	22 F G H J	37 A B C D	52 F G H J	67 A B C D
8 F G H J	23 A B C D	38 F G H J	53 A B C D	68 F G H J
9 A B C D	24 F G H J	39 A B C D	54 F G H J	69 A B C D
10 F G H J	25 A B C D	40 F G H J	55 A B C D	70 F G H J
11 A B C D	26 F G H J	41 A B C D	56 F G H J	71 A B C D
12 F G H J	27 A B C D	42 F G H J	57 A B C D	72 F G H J
13 A B C D	28 F G H J	43 A B C D	58 F G H J	73 A B C D
14 F G H J	29 A B C D	44 F G H J	59 A B C D	74 F G H J
15 A B C D	30 F G H J	45 A B C D	60 F G H J	75 A B C D

TEST 2—MATHEMATICS

1 A B C D E	13 A B C D E	25 A B C D E	37 A B C D E	49 A B C D E
2 F G H J K	14 F G H J K	26 F G H J K	38 F G H J K	50 F G H J K
3 A B C D E	15 A B C D E	27 A B C D E	39 A B C D E	51 A B C D E
4 F G H J K	16 F G H J K	28 F G H J K	40 F G H J K	52 F G H J K
5 A B C D E	17 A B C D E	29 A B C D E	41 A B C D E	53 A B C D E
6 F G H J K	18 F G H J K	30 F G H J K	42 F G H J K	54 F G H J K
7 A B C D E	19 A B C D E	31 A B C D E	43 A B C D E	55 A B C D E
8 F G H J K	20 F G H J K	32 F G H J K	44 F G H J K	56 F G H J K
9 A B C D E	21 A B C D E	33 A B C D E	45 A B C D E	57 A B C D E
10 F G H J K	22 F G H J K	34 F G H J K	46 F G H J K	58 F G H J K
11 A B C D E	23 A B C D E	35 A B C D E	47 A B C D E	59 A B C D E
12 F G H J K	24 F G H J K	36 F G H J K	48 F G H J K	60 F G H J K

TEST 3—READING

1 A B C D	9 A B C D	17 A B C D	25 A B C D	33 A B C D
2 F G H J	10 F G H J	18 F G H J	26 F G H J	34 F G H J
3 A B C D	11 A B C D	19 A B C D	27 A B C D	35 A B C D
4 F G H J	12 F G H J	20 F G H J	28 F G H J	36 F G H J
5 A B C D	13 A B C D	21 A B C D	29 A B C D	37 A B C D
6 F G H J	14 F G H J	22 F G H J	30 F G H J	38 F G H J
7 A B C D	15 A B C D	23 A B C D	31 A B C D	39 A B C D
8 F G H J	16 F G H J	24 F G H J	32 F G H J	40 F G H J

TEST 4—SCIENCE REASONING

1 A B C D	9 A B C D	17 A B C D	25 A B C D	33 A B C D
2 F G H J	10 F G H J	18 F G H J	26 F G H J	34 F G H J
3 A B C D	11 A B C D	19 A B C D	27 A B C D	35 A B C D
4 F G H J	12 F G H J	20 F G H J	28 F G H J	36 F G H J
5 A B C D	13 A B C D	21 A B C D	29 A B C D	37 A B C D
6 F G H J	14 F G H J	22 F G H J	30 F G H J	38 F G H J
7 A B C D	15 A B C D	23 A B C D	31 A B C D	39 A B C D
8 F G H J	16 F G H J	24 F G H J	32 F G H J	40 F G H J

Step Two: Targeted Skills Review

Step Two Highlights:

Build a strong foundation of verbal basics in the Grammar and Mechanics Skills Review.

Review the most commonly tested math concepts in the Math Skills Review.

Use the Math Express Skills Review for quick reference.

Discover careful reading techniques applicable to each section of the test in the Reading Skills Review.

Practice the components of solid essay writing in the Writing Skills Review.

Refresh yourself on key science concepts in the Science Skills Review.

Step Two Overview:

Before learning specific test-taking strategies in Step Three, you may first be asked to complete part or all of the items in this step. The lessons and corresponding items in this section of the textbook are designed to reinforce the standards-based skills that you have already learned in school. Mastery of these skills will boost your performance on the ACT, PLAN, and EXPLORE and in the classroom. Focus your efforts on the Skills Review chapters that you find the most challenging.

Grammar and Mechanics Skills Review

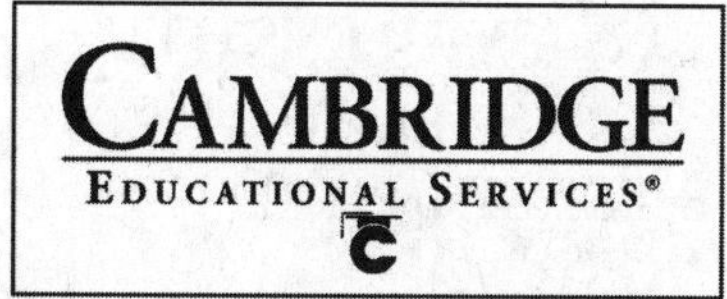

TARGETED EDUCATIONAL SOLUTIONS.

Cambridge Course Concept Outline
GRAMMAR AND MECHANICS SKILLS REVIEW

Parts of Speech

Nouns

A ***noun*** is a word that refers to any one of the following items: persons, animals, plants, objects, times, places, and ideas.

Examples:

Persons:	Bob, woman, niece, student, doctor, men, brothers, teachers
Animals:	dog, mouse, cow, cats, elephants, birds
Plants:	grass, tree, bushes, oaks
Objects:	glove, car, building, sidewalk, desks, buses
Times:	hour, 8 o'clock, Thanksgiving, Mondays, weekends
Places:	home, office, city, Puerto Rico, Poland, Africa
Ideas:	democracy, love, youth, sisterhood, dreams

Pronouns

A ***pronoun*** is a word that can substitute for a noun.

Examples:

Hernandez hit a home run. <u>He</u> waved to the crowd.
The woman went into the store. <u>She</u> bought a book.
My sisters live in St. Louis. <u>They</u> are coming to visit.
The bull escaped from the pasture. The farmer caught <u>him</u>.
The plant seems dry. Julie should water <u>it</u>.

Verbs

A ***verb*** is a word that expresses activity, change, feeling, or existence.

Examples:

The dog <u>is running</u> down the street.
Mary <u>wrote</u> a letter.
Kevin <u>sewed</u> a button on the shirt.
The weather <u>became</u> cold.
The sky <u>darkened</u>.
John <u>likes</u> Mary.
Carl <u>worries</u> that he might not pass the test.
The house <u>is</u> green.
The letter <u>was</u> several days late.

Modifiers

A ***modifier*** gives further detail to nouns and verbs.

Examples:

The blue car ran into the red car.
The tall woman was carrying an expensive umbrella.
The farmer patiently waited for the cows.
Margaret walked quickly into the kitchen.

Conjunctions

A ***conjunction*** joins together nouns or ideas.

Examples:

Paul and Mary ate dinner.
I like coffee, but George likes tea.
You can take the subway or the bus.
Harry played while Sam sang.
Although Ed had not arrived, we ate anyway.

Prepositions

A ***preposition*** shows the relationship between an idea and a noun in the sentence.

Examples:

Patty sat on the chair.
Cliff gave the apples to Tom.
Geneva is the owner of the diner.
The mop is in the closet beside the broom.

EXERCISE 1

Parts of Speech

DIRECTIONS: In Items #1-20, identify each underlined word's part of speech. Use the following key:

N = Noun	V = Verb
Pro = Pronoun	M = Modifier
C = Conjunction	Prep = Preposition

Answers are on page 907.

1. The ambulance weaved in and out of traffic as it hurried to the hospital.

   ambulance ____ traffic ____ it ____
   hurried ____ hospital ____

2. The movers unloaded the sofa and put it in the living room.

   movers ____ unloaded ____ and ____
   it ____ in ____

3. The dark clouds completely blocked our view of the mountains and the lake.

   dark ____ clouds ____ blocked ____
   our ____ and ____

4. After dinner, we cleared the dishes from the table, put them in the kitchen sink, and sat down to watch the game.

   dinner ____ cleared ____ table ____
   and ____ sat ____

5. One room in the library was filled with books written by authors of Polish ancestry.

   room ____ was filled ____ with ____
   authors ____ Polish ____

6. Some of the first television shows were adaptations of earlier radio versions of the same programs.

   first ____ shows ____ were ____
   earlier ____ programs ____

7. When the waiter arrived, Victor ordered pie with ice cream, chocolate syrup, and a cherry.

   waiter ____ arrived ____ Victor ____
   ordered ____ and ____

8. The building inspector finally approved the plans and allowed the construction to continue.

   inspector ____ finally ____ approved ____
   and ____ allowed ____

9. The superintendent notified the tenants in the building that the water would be off for two hours.

   notified ____ in ____ water ____
   would be ____ hours ____

10. Just as the band finished the number, the crowd burst into loud applause.

    band ____ finished ____ crowd ____
    burst ____ loud ____

11. Carlos telephoned Iris to tell her that he would be late for their date.

    telephoned ____ her ____ would be ____
    their ____ date ____

12. The cat was sleeping on the windowsill in the warmth of the afternoon sun.

    cat ____ was sleeping ____ warmth ____
    of ____ sun ____

13. As the train pulled into each station, the conductor called out the name of that station and the name of the next station.

    train ____ pulled ____ called ____
    name ____ and ____

14. By the time we got to Woodstock, the children were sound asleep in the rear of the car.

    we ____ children ____ were ____
    in ____ rear ____

15. Before they leave the camp, the guides teach the hikers how to identify poison ivy and warn them to avoid it.

    they ____ leave ____ teach ____
    hikers ____ and ____

16. Chuck covered the steaming hot pancakes with plenty of melted butter and sweet, sticky syrup.

    covered ____ steaming ____ melted ____
    sticky ____ syrup ____

17. Last weekend, we made a special trip to the mountains to see the brilliant colors of the beautiful fall leaves.

    weekend ____ made ____ special ____
    brilliant ____ beautiful ____

18. After that eventful afternoon, Art wrote to Cathy several times, but his letters all came back unopened.

    eventful ____ wrote ____ but ____
    his ____ unopened ____

19. Through the morning mist, we could just barely make out the headlights of the bus as it turned off the highway.

barely ____ make out ____ bus ____
as ____ it ____

20. Our host offered us a choice of coffee or tea and served some little cakes, which were delicious.

offered ____ us ____ or ____
were ____ delicious ____

DIRECTIONS: In Items #21-36, correct the underlined preposition if necessary. If the original sentence is correct, choose (A); if the sentence requires no preposition, choose (D). Answers are on page 907.

21. This class is different than the other.
A. NO CHANGE
B. of
C. from
D. OMIT the underlined portion.

22. Where are you going to?
A. NO CHANGE
B. from
C. in
D. OMIT the underlined portion.

23. He has not yet taken advantage off the sale.
A. NO CHANGE
B. of
C. from
D. OMIT the underlined portion.

24. The teacher broke the news to the student.
A. NO CHANGE
B. too
C. two
D. OMIT the underlined portion.

25. Due to decreased sales, the workers were laid off by the company.
A. NO CHANGE
B. of
C. down
D. OMIT the underlined portion.

26. The manager promised to look in to the customer's complaint.
A. NO CHANGE
B. into
C. unto
D. OMIT the underlined portion.

27. He took it up on himself to schedule the meeting.
A. NO CHANGE
B. on
C. upon
D. OMIT the underlined portion.

28. She found it below her to clean her own house.
A. NO CHANGE
B. beneath
C. be neat
D. OMIT the underlined portion.

29. The office will open sometime in a half hour.
A. NO CHANGE
B. within
C. inside
D. OMIT the underlined portion.

30. Are you under the weather?
A. NO CHANGE
B. below
C. beneath
D. OMIT the underlined portion.

31. There are many students waiting on the instructor during her offPice hours.
A. NO CHANGE
B. for
C. to
D. OMIT the underlined portion.

32. Please save energy by turning of the lights before you leave the house.
A. NO CHANGE
B. off
C. in
D. OMIT the underlined portion.

33. The dancers swung in motion when the music started.
A. NO CHANGE
B. in to
C. into
D. OMIT the underlined portion.

34. I work at the bank in the corner of Main and Packard.
A. NO CHANGE
B. on
C. around
D. OMIT the underlined portion.

35. The lawyer voiced his objection on the recount of the votes.
A. NO CHANGE
B. to
C. about
D. OMIT the underlined portion.

36. Ralph had difficulty getting to sleep till very late.
A. NO CHANGE
B. up to
C. until
D. OMIT the underlined portion.

Common Grammatical Errors

Subject-Verb Agreement

One common grammatical error is lack of agreement between subject and verb. The simplest subject-verb disagreements are usually obvious, as in the following examples. Note: ✓ = correct, ✗ = wrong.

Examples:

The books <u>is</u> on the shelf. ✗

The books <u>are</u> on the shelf. ✓

The teacher <u>admonish</u> the class to calm down. ✗

The teacher <u>admonishes</u> the class to calm down. ✓

In order to test your ability to spot such errors, test-writers may use one of the three following tricks:

WHAT OBSCURES SUBJECT-VERB AGREEMENT

1. Material Inserted Between Subject and Verb
2.  Inverted Sentence Structure
3. Use of Compound Subjects

1. Material Inserted Between Subject and Verb

The test-writers insert material between the subject and verb to obscure their connection. If you are not careful, by the time you reach the verb, you will have forgotten the subject; as a result, it will not be easy to determine whether the verb agrees with the subject. Consider the following examples:

Examples:

Star <u>performers</u> in the movies or on television usually <u>earns</u> substantial income from royalties. ✗

One school of thought maintains that the federal <u>deficit</u>, not exorbitant corporate profits or excessively high wages, <u>cause</u> most of the inflation we are now experiencing. ✗

A recent survey shows that a <u>household</u> in which both the wife and the husband are pursuing careers <u>stand</u> a better chance of surviving intact than one in which only the husband works. ✗

In each of these three sentences, the subject and verb do not agree: "performers…earns," "deficit…cause," and "household…stand." However, the errors may not be immediately evident because of the intervening material. In the first sentence, the subject is separated from the verb by prepositional phrases. In the second sentence, the subject and the verb are separated by a parenthetical expression. In the third sentence, a clause intervenes between the subject and the verb.

The plausibility of the incorrect verb choice, and therefore the chance that the error will go unnoticed, is strengthened when test-writers place a word or phrase near the verb that might be mistaken for the subject: "television…earns," "profits and wages…cause," and "careers…stand." If the first word of each of these pairs had been the subject, then there would have been no failure of agreement.

2. *Inverted Sentence Structure*

A second common problem of subject-verb agreement is ***inverted sentence structure***. In an inverted sentence, the verb precedes the subject. You should pay careful attention to the agreement between subject and verb, no matter how those elements are ordered.

Examples:

> Although the first amendment to the Constitution does guarantee freedom of speech, the Supreme Court has long recognized that there has to be some restrictions on the exercise of this right. ✘
>
> Jennifer must have been doubly pleased that day, for seated in the gallery to watch her receive the award was her brother, her parents, and her husband. ✘

In both of these sentences, the subjects and verbs do not agree. The relationships are obscured by the order in which the elements appear in the sentence—the verbs come before the subjects. These sentences should read:

> Although the first amendment to the Constitution does guarantee freedom of speech, the Supreme Court [illegible] long recognized that there <u>have</u> to be some restrictions on the exercise of this right. ✓
>
> Jennifer must have been doubly pleased that day, for seated in the gallery to watch her receive the award <u>were</u> her brother, her parents, and her husband. ✓

WATCH FOR INVERTED SENTENCE STRUCTURES

Regardless of the order of the sentence—subject-verb or verb-subject—the verb must always agree with its subject. If a sentence has a complex structure, it often helps to look at each element in isolation.

3. *Use of Compound Subjects*

Finally, be alert for ***compound subjects***. Usually, when the subject of a [illegible]nce consists of two or more elements joined by the conjunction "and," the [illegible] is consi[illegible]red plural and requires a plural ver[illegible] [illegible]onsider the following example:

Example:

> Of the seven candidates, [illegible]hn, Bill, and Jim <u>was</u> past office holders. ✘

The subject, "John, Bill, and Jim," [illegible] compound (joined by "and") and requires the plural verb "were"—even though the individual nouns are singular.

WATCH FOR COMPOUND SUBJECTS

Compound subjects, typically two or more subjects joined by "and," are plural and need a plural verb.

Be careful not to confuse the compound subject with the disjunctive subject. When elements of the subject are joined by "or," the verb must agree with the element nearest to it. Replacing "and" with "or" changes our previous example:

Example:

> Of the seven candidates, John, Bill, or Jim <u>is</u> likely to win. ✓

The elements are joined by "or," so the verb must agree with "John" or "Bill" or "Jim." The verb "is" correctly agrees with the disjunctive subject.

Additionally, watch out for subjects that are designed to look like compound subjects but which are actually singular. Typically, these subjects are disguised using pronouns.

Example:

> Neither one of those fools even know how to change a light bulb. ✗

The subject is not "those fools"; instead, it is the singular subject "Neither one." Thus, the singular verb "knows" is required.

WATCH FOR DISJUNCTIVE AND SINGULAR SUBJECTS

1. If the elements of the subject are joined by "or," the subject is disjunctive. The verb must agree with the closest element of the subject.
2. Be alert for singular subjects that appear to be plural (typically pronouns).

Pronoun Usage

The rules for ***pronoun usage*** are summarized below. Note: ✓ = correct, ✗ = wrong.

PRONOUN USAGE RULES

1. A pronoun must have an antecedent (referent) to which it refers.
2. The pronoun must refer clearly to the antecedent.
3. The pronoun and antecedent must agree.
4. The pronoun must have the proper case.

1. Pronouns Must Have Antecedents

A ***pronoun*** is used as a substitute for a noun. The noun that it replaces is called the ***antecedent*** (referent). With the exception of certain idioms such as "It is raining," a pronoun that does not have an antecedent is used incorrectly.

Examples:

> Although Glen is president of the student body, he has not yet passed his English exam, and because of it, he will not graduate with the rest of his class. ✗
>
> The damage done by Senator Smith's opposition to the policy of equal employment is undeniable, but that is exactly what he attempted to do in his speech on Thursday. ✗

In the first example, what is the antecedent of "it"? It is not "he has not yet passed his English exam," because that is a complete thought, or clause, not just a noun. "It" is not a pronoun substitute for that entire thought. Rather, "it" refers to Glen's "failure" to pass the exam, thereby providing "it" with the required antecedent. However, "failure" does not appear in noun form in the sentence. In other words, "it" wants to refer to a noun, but there is no noun to function as its point of reference. The sentence must be rewritten: "because of that fact, he will not graduate…."

In the second example, "that" functions as a relative pronoun—it relates something in the first clause to the second clause. However, to what does "that" refer? Test possibilities by substituting them for "that" in the second clause. The sentence should make sense when you replace the pronoun with its antecedent. Is the antecedent "damage"?

but damage is exactly what he attempted to do.... ✗

Perhaps, then, the antecedent is opposition or undeniable:

but opposition is exactly what he attempted to do.... ✗

but undeniable is exactly what he attempted to do.... ✗

There are no other candidates for the antecedent, so we must conclude that the use of "that" is incorrect. Most likely, what the writer intended to say was that the Senator attempted to deny the damage:

The damage done by Senator Smith's opposition to the policy of equal employment is undeniable, but he attempted to deny that damage in his speech on Thursday. ✓

PRONOUNS MUST HAVE ANTECEDENTS

Except for a few idiomatic expressions ("It" is getting late, "It" will be sunny today), every pronoun must have an antecedent. An antecedent must be a noun, not a thought or phrase. Identify a pronoun's antecedent and then check that it is correct by substituting it for the pronoun in the sentence.

2. ***Antecedents Must Be Clear***

The antecedent of a pronoun must be made clear from the structure of the sentence. Consider these examples:

Examples:

Edward's father died before he reached his 20th birthday, so he never finished his education. ✗

In 1980, the University Council voted to rescind Provision 3, which made it easier for some students to graduate. ✗

In the first example, it is not clear whether the father died before he reached the age of 20 or before Edward reached the age of 20. Furthermore, it is not clear whose education remained unfinished. Similarly, in the second example, the antecedent of "which" is not clear. "Which" may refer to Provision 3 or it may refer to the University Council's vote to rescind Provision 3.

WATCH FOR UNCLEAR ANTECEDENTS

The antecedent of a pronoun must be clearly identified by the structure of the sentence.

Example:

The letter is on the desk that we received yesterday. ✗

The letter that we received yesterday is on the desk. ✓

Finally, the impersonal use of "it," "they," and "you" tends to produce vague, wordy sentences.

Examples:

In the manual it says to make three copies. ✗

The manual says to make three copies. ✓

They predict we are in for a cold, wet winter. ✗

The almanac predicts a cold, wet winter. ✓

3. *Pronoun-Antecedent Agreement*

The pronoun must agree with its antecedent. Consider the following example:

Example:

Historically, the college dean was also a professor, but today they are usually administrators. ✗

In the example, "they" must refer to "dean," but "dean" is singular and "they" is plural. The sentence can be corrected in one of two ways: by changing the first clause to the plural or by changing the second clause to the singular.

Historically, college deans were also professors, but today they are usually administrators. ✓

Historically, the college dean was also a professor, but today the dean is usually an administrator. ✓

WATCH FOR PRONOUN-ANTECEDENT AGREEMENT

If the antecedent is singular, the pronoun must be singular; if the antecedent is plural, the pronoun must be plural.

Finally, it is incorrect to use different forms of the same pronoun to refer to an antecedent. This error results in the sentence having different antecedents and therefore a *shifting subject.*

WATCH FOR SHIFTING SUBJECTS

Watch for shifting subject errors. These errors occur if different forms of the same pronoun are used to refer to the antecedent.

Example:

The teacher told John that he thought his work was improving. ✗

Does the teacher think that his own work is improving or that John's work is improving? The correct sentence reads: "The teacher told John that John's work was improving."

4. *Pronouns Must Have Proper Case*

A pronoun must agree with its antecedent in case, number, and person. The pronoun's function in a sentence determines which case should be used. You should be familiar with the following three categories of pronoun case: nominative (or subjective), objective, and possessive.

TYPES OF PRONOUN CASE

- *Nominative* (*subjective*) case pronouns are used as subjects of sentences.
- *Objective* case pronouns are used as objects: direct objects, indirect objects, and objects of prepositions. If a prepositional phrase ends with a pronoun, it must be an objective pronoun.
- *Possessive* case pronouns are used to show possession. Use a possessive pronoun preceding a gerund. A gerund is the "-ing" form of a verb that is used as a noun.
- *Interrogative* pronouns stand in for the answer to a question.

The following examples illustrate correct usage of pronoun case.

Examples:

Nominative: I thought he would like the gift we bought. ✓

Objective: The choice for the part is between Bob and me. ✓ (The object pronoun me follows the preposition between.)

Possessive: Do you mind my using your computer? ✓ (The possessive pronoun my precedes the gerund using.)

Interrogative: Who is the starting pitcher for the Orioles today? ✓

EXAMPLES OF PRONOUN CASE

	Nominative Case		*Objective Case*		*Possessive Case*	
	Singular	*Plural*	*Singular*	*Plural*	*Singular*	*Plural*
1st Person:	I	we	me	us	my	our
2nd Person:	you	you	you	you	your	your
3rd Person:	he, she, it	they	him, her, it	them	his, her, its	their
Interrogative:	who	who	whom	whom	whose	whose

The following are additional examples of the *nominative*, or subjective, pronoun case.

Examples:

John and him were chosen. ✗

John and he were chosen. ✓ (He is the subject of the verb; we certainly would not say that him was chosen.)

It was her who was chosen. ✗

She was chosen. ✓

Us student-workers decided to organize into a union. ✗

We student-workers decided to organize into a union. ✓

He is as witty as her. ✗

He is as witty as she is. ✓

Whom do you suppose will win the election? ✗

Who do you suppose will win the election? ✓

The following are additional examples of the *objective* pronoun case.

Examples:

They accused Tom and he of stealing. ✘

They accused Tom and him of stealing. ✓ (*Him* is the object of the verb accused; they accused him, not he.)

The tickets were given to Bill and I. ✘

The tickets were given to Bill and me. ✓ (Me is the object of to; the tickets were given to me, not to I.)

Who did you see? ✘

Whom did you see? ✓ (Hint: Make this a declarative sentence: "You saw him." You would not say, "You saw he.")

An easy way to remember when to use "who" versus "whom" is that in those situations that "him" (or "her") would be appropriate, "whom" should be used; in those situations that "he" (or "she") would be appropriate, "who" should be used.

Finally, personal pronouns that express ownership never require an apostrophe. Also, a pronoun that precedes a gerund ("-ing" verb form used as a noun) is usually the possessive case.

Examples:

This book is your's, not her's. ✘

This book is yours, not hers. ✓

He rejoiced at him going to the party. ✘

He rejoiced at his going to the party. ✓

Some pronouns are either singular or plural, while others can be both. The structure and intended meaning of the sentence indicate whether the pronoun is singular or plural.

 **SINGULAR AND/OR PLURAL PRONOUNS** 

Singular:	anybody, another, everybody, everything, somebody, something, nobody, one, anyone, everyone, someone, no one, each, every, neither, either, much
Plural:	both, few, many, most, several
Singular & Plural:	all, any, half, more, none, some

Technically, pronouns are divided into eight formal categories:

FORMAL CATEGORIES OF PRONOUNS

Personal:	I, we, my, mine, our, ours, me, us, you, your, yours, he, she, it, they, his, hers, its, their, theirs, him, her, them
Demonstrative:	this, these, that, those
Indefinite:	all, any, anything, both, each, either, one, everyone, everybody, everything, few, many, more, neither, none, somebody, someone, something
Relative:	who, whose, whom, which, of which, that, of that, what, of what
Interrogative:	who, whose, whom, which, of which, what, of what
Numerical:	one, two, three, first, second, third
Reflexive/Intensive:	myself, ourselves, yourself, yourselves, himself, herself, itself, themselves
Reciprocal:	each other, one another

For the test, it is not necessary to know the names of the individual categories and which pronouns belong in which categories. However, through your experience in conversation and writing, you should be able to correctly use each type of pronoun, and you should have the ability to spot when each type of pronoun is used incorrectly.

Example:

Many of the students <u>which</u> were participating in the spelling bee had been finalists last year. ✘

In the above example, the pronoun "which" refers to "Many of the students" and it is the incorrect pronoun choice. Instead, the sentence should read: "Many…who were participating…."

Adjectives vs. Adverbs

Note: ✓ = correct, ✘ = wrong.

1. ***Adjectives Modify Nouns, Adverbs Modify Verbs***

   Adjectives are used to modify nouns, while ***adverbs*** are used to modify verbs, adjectives, or other adverbs.

   Example:

   No matter how <u>quick</u> he played, Rich never beat Julie when playing the card game "speed." ✘

   In the above example, "quick" is intended to modify the speed with which Rich played cards. However, "quick" is an adjective and therefore cannot be used to modify a verb. By adding "-ly" to the end of "quick," we can transform it into an adverb and the sentence reads: "No matter how quickly he played…."

The following examples further illustrate the proper use of adjectives and adverbs.

Examples:

Adjectives: Mr. Jackson is a good teacher. ✓
He is a bad driver. ✓
There has been a considerable change in the weather. ✓
My sister is a superb dancer. ✓
The teacher gave a quick explanation of the problem. ✓
This is a slow exercise. ✓

Adverbs: Mr. Jackson teaches well. ✓
He drives badly. ✓
The weather has changed considerably. ✓
My sister dances superbly. ✓
The teacher explained the problem quickly. ✓
This exercise must be done slowly. ✓

The first three of the following examples underscore that adjectives, not adverbs, must be used to modify nouns. The remaining examples show that adverbs, not adjectives, must be used to modify verbs and adjectives.

Examples:

He said that the medicine tasted terribly. ✗
He said that the medicine tasted terrible. ✓

The dog remained faithfully to its master until the end. ✗
The dog remained faithful to its master until the end. ✓

I felt badly about forgetting the appointment. ✗
I felt bad about forgetting the appointment. ✓

He can do the job easier than you can. ✗
He can do the job more easily than you can. ✓

The problem seemed exceeding complex to me. ✗
The problem seemed exceedingly complex to me. ✓

It rained steady all day yesterday. ✗
It rained steadily all day yesterday. ✓

The professor presented an obvious important point in class. ✗
The professor presented an obviously important point in class. ✓

We all agreed that the new film was real funny. ✗
We all agreed that the new film was really funny. ✓

The students found the physics examination extreme difficult. ✗
The students found the physics examination extremely difficult. ✓

If you speak firm, he will listen to you. ✗
If you speak firmly, he will listen to you. ✓

He made considerable more progress than I did. ✗
He made considerably more progress than I did. ✓

2. *Linking Verbs*

Linking verbs are followed by adjectives, not adverbs. The following is a list of common linking verbs.

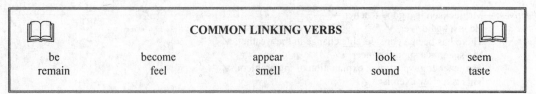

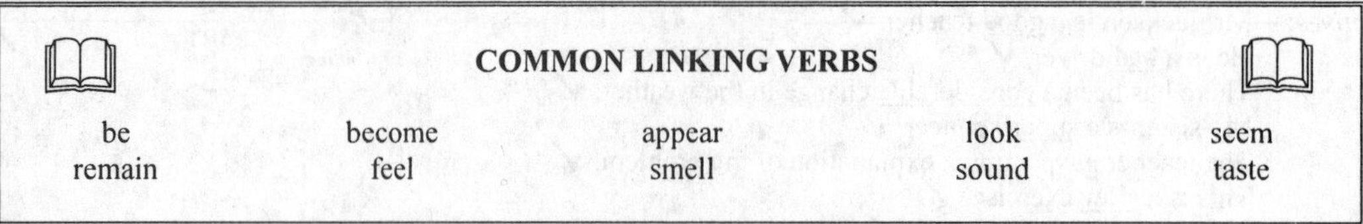

COMMON LINKING VERBS

be	become	appear	look	seem
remain	feel	smell	sound	taste

Note that some of the verbs listed as linking verbs may sometimes function as verbs of action. The following examples illustrate this point.

Examples:

Adjectives: I feel tired. ✓
He looked angry. ✓
The pie tastes delicious. ✓

Adverbs: I felt my way slowly in the darkness. ✓
He looked about the room angrily. ✓
She tasted the pie cautiously. ✓

3. *Watch for Adjectives Posing as Adverbs*

WATCH FOR ADJECTIVE-ADVERB SWITCHING

Be alert for adjectives posing in place of adverbs and vice versa. Adjectives can usually be transformed into adverbs by adding "-ly." However, verbs must be modified by adverbs, not simply an adjective posing as an adverb.

Examples:

The girl looks intelligently. ✗
The girl looks intelligent. ✓

That perfume smells sweetly, doesn't it? ✗
That perfume smells sweet, doesn't it? ✓

The physician appeared nervously when he talked to the patient. ✗
The physician appeared nervous when he talked to the patient. ✓

This bed seems very comfortably. ✗
This bed seems very comfortable. ✓

Several people arrived too lately to be admitted to the performance. ✗ ("Lately" is not an adverb for "late." Instead, "lately" means "as of late.")
Several people arrived too late to be admitted to the performance. ✓

The horse ran fastly enough to win the race. ✗ ("Fastly" is not a word!)
The horse ran fast enough to win the race. ✓

The architect worked hardly to finish his drawings by the next day. ✗ ("Hardly" is not an adverb for "hard." Instead, "hardly" means "barely.")
The architect worked hard to finish his drawings by the next day. ✓

Double Negatives

It is true that we all hear and sometimes say ***double negatives*** in daily conversation. However, double negatives are NOT acceptable in standard written English.

Note: ✗ = wrong.

Example:

I hadn't hardly begun to understand Spanish when I had to move again. ✗

The phrase "hadn't hardly" is a double negative. The sentence should read: "I had hardly begun to understand…."

WATCH FOR DOUBLE NEGATIVES

 Watch for double negatives ("not barely," "hardly nothing")—they are always incorrect.

Nouns and Noun Clauses

Nouns are names of people, places, things, or ideas; they are used to indicate the subject of a sentence. Like pronouns, nouns have a case. Note: ✓ = correct, ✗ = wrong.

TYPES OF NOUN CASE

 *Nominative (Subjective)* case is used when the noun is the subject of the sentence.

 *Objective* case is used when the noun is an indirect or direct object or is the object of a preposition.

 *Possessive* case is used when nouns are intended to show possession.

Sometimes the place of the noun in a sentence is filled by a ***noun clause*** instead of a single noun. A noun clause is a dependent clause.

Example:

That Judy was chosen for the promotion is not surprising. ✓

The failure to properly introduce a noun clause is an error of sentence structure. "That" by itself is not the noun, nor is "Judy was chosen for the promotion" a noun. However, the two combined create a noun clause and function as the noun.

RULE FOR INTRODUCING NOUN CLAUSES

 A noun clause is a group of words that functions as the subject (or another noun usage) of a sentence. "That" is often the best word to use to introduce noun clauses.

Examples:

The reason the saxophone is a popular jazz instrument is <u>because</u> its timbre can approximate that of the human voice. ✗
The reason the saxophone is a popular jazz instrument is <u>that</u> its timbre can approximate that of the human voice. ✓

<u>Why</u> American car manufacturers did not reduce car sizes earlier than they did is a mystery to most market experts. ✗
<u>That</u> American car manufacturers did not reduce car sizes earlier than they did is a mystery to most market experts. ✓

The above examples make the error of introducing noun clauses with <u>because</u> and <u>why</u>. In both sentences, a noun clause is required; <u>that</u> should be used in both cases.

WATCH FOR "BECAUSE" AND "WHY" AS NOUN CLAUSE INTRODUCTIONS

Noun clauses must be introduced by "that," not "because" or "why."

Additionally, do NOT use "where" for "that" in object clauses.

Example:

I saw in the bulletin <u>where</u> Mrs. Wagner's retirement was announced. ✗
I saw in the bulletin <u>that</u> Mrs. Wagner's retirement was announced. ✓

However, if the subject of the sentence actually is about where something is, then use "where."

Examples:

<u>Where</u> the wedding had initially been scheduled is not where it ended up being held. ✓
All I want to know is <u>where</u> we are supposed to go for homeroom attendance. ✓

EXERCISE 2

Common Grammatical Errors

DIRECTIONS: For Items #1-25, circle the letter of the underlined part of the sentence containing the grammatical error. Answers are on page 907.

1. The professor deals harsh (A) with students who are not prepared (B), and he is (C) even more severe (D) with those who plagiarize.

2. A recent study indicates (A) that the average person ignores (B) most commercial advertising and does not buy (C) products because of them (D).

3. Despite the fact (A) that New York City is one of the most (B) densely populated areas in the world, there are (C) many parks where one can sit on a bench under the trees and you can (D) read a book.

4. Charles Dickens wrote (A) about the horrifying (B) conditions in the English boarding schools that (C) he learned about on one of his (D) trips to Yorkshire.

5. André Breton initiated (A) the Surrealist movement with the publication (B) of a manifesto, and it (C) incorporated the theories of Freud as well as (D) his own.

6. The review of the concert published (A) in the morning's paper mentioned that the soloist is (B) a very promising talent and that (C) the orchestra played capable (D).

7. During the war (A), there were many people in the Polish countryside that (B) sheltered those (C) who had escaped (D) from concentration camps.

8. The dean lectured (A) to we students (B) on the privilege and responsibility (C) of attending (D) the university.

9. You taking the initiative (A) in the negotiations (B) will profit (C) the company to a great degree (D).

10. The members of the club insisted that (A) I be (B) the representative of the organization at the conference which (C) was something I had hoped (D) to avoid.

11. No one (A) knows for sure whether there was (B) a real person (C) about which (C) Shakespeare wrote (D) his sonnets.

12. Although (A) the director of the zoo takes (B) great pains to recreate (C) the natural habitats of the animals, few of the exhibits is completely (D) accurate in every detail.

13. Climatic differences between the north and south of some (A) countries helps to (B) account for the differences (C) in temperament of the inhabitants of the two (D) regions.

14. The month of August was particularly cold (A); hardly no daily temperatures (B) were recorded (C) above 80 degrees, and only one was (D) recorded above 90 degrees.

15. The diaries of Stendhal, which make entertaining reading (A), also provides (B) a great wealth of information about musical taste (C) and performance practice in the last century (D).

16. Given the evidence [A] of the existence of a complicated system of communication used by whales, [B] it is necessary to [C] acknowledge its [D] intelligence.

17. Him being at the rally [A] does not necessarily mean [B] that [C] the congressman agrees [D] with the president's entire platform.

18. Although there is no perfect form of government, representative democracy, as it is practiced in America, [A] is a system [B] that is working well [C] and more than satisfactory. [D]

19. George hired [A] a caterer, who [B] he [C] later recommended, [D] after tasting her specialty—spring rolls.

20. After driving past Trinity Church, [A] the bus stopped at [B] the recent constructed [B] Exposition Tower, the tallest [C] building in the city, to allow the passengers to take [D] the special elevators to the observation tower.

21. The student senate passed [A] the resolution banning [B] smoking in the cafeteria [B] with scarcely any [C] dissenting votes which angered [D] many members of the faculty.

22. Most employers assume [A] that one's professional personality and work habits are formed [B] as a result of [C] your [D] early work experience.

23. Only a small number [A] of taxi drivers fail to insure [B] their vehicles, but usually these are the ones [C] who need it [D] most.

24. Angered [A] by the double standard society imposed on [B] women, Edna St. Vincent Millay wrote candid about [C] her [D] opinions and her personal life.

25. Unless they hire players [A] who [B] are [C] better hitters, the fans will gradually lose [D] interest in the team despite the fine efforts of the pitching staff.

DIRECTIONS: For Items #26-41, after identifying each answer choice as an adjective or adverb, determine whether the blank should be filled in with the adjective choice or the adverb choice. Answers are on page 907.

26. Kathy does her homework ________.
slow ________ slowly ________

27. We understand each other ________.
really well ________ real good ________

28. Students should be ________ to their professors at all times.
polite ________ politely ________

29. Paula has adjusted to her new school. She is doing ________.
good ________ well ________

30. I think the cake is done. It smells ________.
good ________ well ________

31. Your room is a ________ mess. Clean it up at once!
terrible ________ terribly ________

32. When I found out that the accident was my fault, I felt __________.

awfully __________ awful __________

33. The movie we saw last night wasn't __________ exciting.

terrible __________ terribly __________

34. Doing a job __________ right away saves time in the long run.

well __________ good __________

35. Cats have a developed sense of smell. They can smell __________.

well __________ good __________

36. "Mrs. Chang, your son works __________ in class. You can be proud of him."

hard __________ hardly __________

37. In order to deliver the package on time, the messenger biked __________.

fast __________ quick __________

38. The college I will be attending in September is __________.

nearly __________ near __________

39. After contracting the disease, Marc's symptoms appeared __________.

slow __________ slowly __________

40. Doctors need to remain __________ even during an epidemic.

healthy __________ healthily __________

41. Leo's stomach felt __________ after the terrific Thanksgiving feast.

heavy __________ heavily __________

Analyzing Sentence Structure

When analyzing the structure of a sentence, ask yourself the following four questions.

CHECKLIST FOR ANALYZING SENTENCE STRUCTURE

1. Is the sentence a run-on sentence?
2. Are the elements of the sentence parallel?
3. Are there any incomplete split constructions?
4. Do the verb tenses correctly reflect the sequence of events?

Run-on Sentences

Be aware of sentences that carelessly run main clauses together without appropriate punctuation or connectors. ***Run-on sentences*** can be corrected in one of three ways: "end-stop" punctuation, a semicolon, or a connector. Note: ✓ = correct, ✗ = wrong.

The most common way to correct a run-on sentence is to divide the sentence using "end-stop" punctuation.

Examples:

The lecture was dull you almost fell asleep. ✗
The lecture was dull. You almost fell asleep. ✓

Was the lecture dull you almost fell asleep. ✗
Was the lecture dull? You almost fell asleep. ✓

The lecture was incredibly dull you almost fell asleep. ✗
The lecture was incredibly dull! You almost fell asleep. ✓

The comma is not an end-mark. DO NOT use a comma by itself to separate two sentences.

Example:

Close the window, there is a draft in the room. ✗
Close the window. There is a draft in the room. ✓

Sometimes, two sentences are very closely related in meaning, and full "end-stop" punctuation may seem too strong. A semicolon can then be used to divide the two sentences.

Example:

It was a beautiful day there was not a cloud in the sky. ✗
It was a beautiful day; there was not a cloud in the sky. ✓

A third way to correct the run-on is to use a connector (conjunction) such as "and," "but," "for," "or," and "nor" if the two sentences are equally important. It is usually advisable to place a comma before these connectors.

Example:

I like to ski, my friend prefers to sit by the fire. ✗
I like to ski, but my friend prefers to sit by the fire. ✓

Particular problem words that may cause run-ons are "however," "therefore," "consequently," and "moreover." These words are not sentence connectors, and when they follow a complete thought, either a period or a semicolon should precede them.

Faulty Parallelism

Faulty parallelism is a common grammatical error for writers. Whenever elements of a sentence perform similar or equal functions, they should have the same form. Consider the following faulty sentences; they are missing necessary words. Note: ✓ = correct, ✗ = wrong.

Examples:

At most colleges, the dominant attitude among students is that gaining admission to professional graduate school is more important than to obtain a well-rounded education. ✗
To demand that additional seasonings be placed on the table is insulting the chef's judgment on the proper balance of ingredients. ✗
The review was very critical of the film, citing the poor photography, the weak plot, and the dialogue was stilted. ✗

In the first example, "gaining admission" and "to obtain" must both have the same form. Either both must be in the gerund form or both must be in the infinitive form. For example: "gaining admission…is more important than obtaining…."

In the second example, the subject ("to demand") and the predicated complement ("insulting") must both have the same form: "To demand…is to insult…."

In the last example, the last element of the list of film criticisms is not of the same form as the other two elements. The sentence should read: "…citing the poor photography, the weak plot, and the stilted dialogue."

CHECK THAT ALL ELEMENTS OF A SENTENCE ARE PARALLEL

 Check that all elements of a sentence are parallel—including verb forms, noun forms, and word pairs such as "this…that," "either…or," and "neither…nor."

Examples:

He spends his time playing cards, swimming, going to the theater, and at school. ✗
He spends his time playing cards, swimming, going to the theater, and going to school. ✓

He manages his business affairs with knowledge, ease, and confidently. ✗
He manages his business affairs with knowledge, ease, and confidence. ✓

He was required by the instructor to go to the library, to take out several books on the Vietnam War, and that he should report to the class on what he had learned. ✗
He was required by the instructor to go to the library, to take out several books on the Vietnam War, and to report to the class on what he had learned. ✓

I am studying the sources of educational theory and how educational theory has evolved. ✗
I am studying the sources and the evolution of educational theory. ✓

He was not only sympathetic but also knew when to be considerate. ✗
He was not only sympathetic but also considerate. ✓

Not only did he enjoy the movie but also the play. ✗
He enjoyed not only the movie but also the play. ✓

I was concerned about the price of the car and if it was comfortable. ✗
I was concerned about the price and the comfort of the car. ✓

Neither does he speak Spanish nor Helen. ✗
Neither he nor Helen speaks Spanish. ✓

Incomplete Split Constructions

Split constructions refer to phrases in which a thought, interrupted by intervening material, is completed later in the sentence. Note: ✓ = correct, ✗ = wrong.

Example:

The officials were not only aware of, but actually encouraged, the misreporting of scores. ✓

This sentence contains a perfectly acceptable split construction. Ordinarily, the object of a preposition closely follows the preposition: "aware of the misreporting." Here, the object of the preposition is separated from the preposition by the phrase "but actually encouraged." This is unobjectionable as long as the thought is properly completed. There is a danger, however, that the intervening material will throw something off in the sentence.

CHECK THAT SPLIT CONSTRUCTIONS ARE COMPLETED

A split construction is a sentence structure in which two otherwise separate ideas are joined together by a later element. Be alert for split constructions and check that any interrupted thought is correctly completed.

Consider the following faulty sentences; they are incomplete split constructions.

Examples:

Her colleagues always speak of Professor Collins as a person who has and will always be sensitive to the needs of younger students. ✗
Judging from the pricing policies of many large corporations, maintaining a stable share of the market is as important, if not more important than, making a large profit. ✗

In the first sentence, the error is in the verb. The auxiliary verb "has" needs the verb "been," but "been" does not appear in the sentence. The sentence could be corrected by completing the construction: "…has been and will always be…."
In the second sentence, the error is an incomplete comparison. The sentence should read: "…as important as, if not more important than,…."

RULE FOR CHECKING FOR SPLIT CONSTRUCTIONS

The intervening material makes it difficult to spot errors of split construction. Therefore, when checking for split constructions, read the sentence without the intervening material—it should make sense, be grammatically correct, and be a complete sentence.

Verb Tense

The same ***verb tense*** should be used whenever possible within a sentence or paragraph. Avoid shifts in verb tense unless there is a valid reason. Note: ✓ = correct, ✗ = wrong.

Example:

Joan came home last week and goes to her home in the country where she spends the last weekend of her vacation. ✗
Joan came home last week and went to her home in the country where she spent the last weekend of her vacation. ✓

1. Principal Parts of Verbs

Verb tense is indicated by changing the verb or by combining certain verb forms with auxiliary verbs. The ***principal parts*** are the verb tenses from which all verb forms are derived: present, past, present perfect, future perfect, and past perfect.

VERB PRINCIPAL PARTS

1. *Present Tense:* talk, write
2. *Past Tense:* talked, wrote

3. *Present Perfect Tense:* have talked, has written
4. *Future Perfect Tense:* will have talked, will have written
5. *Past Perfect Tense:* had talked, had written

Verbs are classified as regular (or weak) and irregular (or strong), according to the way in which their principal parts are formed. Regular verbs form their past, present perfect, future perfect, and past perfect tenses by the addition of "-ed" to the infinitive.

Examples:

Present Tense	*Past Tense*	*Present Perfect Tense*	*Future Perfect Tense*	*Past Perfect Tense*
talk	talked	has (have) talked	will have talked	had talked
help	helped	has (have) helped	will have helped	had helped
walk	walked	has (have) walked	will have walked	had walked

The principal parts of irregular verbs are formed by changes in the verb itself:

Examples:

Present Tense	*Past Tense*	*Present Perfect Tense*	*Future Perfect Tense*	*Past Perfect Tense*
see	saw	has (have) seen	will have seen	had seen
say	said	has (have) said	will have said	had said
go	went	has (have) gone	will have gone	had gone

Examples:

Present Tense

We were taught that vitamins were important for our well-being. ✗
We were taught that vitamins are important for our well-being. ✓

Past Tense

When he spoke, all the people cheer him. ✗
When he spoke, all the people cheered him. ✓

Since he is late, he did not receive a gift. ✗
Since he was late, he did not receive a gift. ✓

Present Perfect Tense

I am told that you had completed the job. ✗
I am told that you have completed the job. ✓

Future Perfect Tense

I have earned enough money for the car by the end of the month. ✗
I will have earned enough money for the car by the end of the month. ✓

Past Perfect Tense

I was told that you have completed the job before you left. ✗
I was told that you had completed the job before you left. ✓

In the first example, the verb tense "are" is used because when expressing a permanent fact, the present tense is used.

The following page contains a summary of the present tense, past tense, and past participles of many common irregular verbs. The past participle is a word that typically expresses completed action, that is traditionally one of the principal parts of the verb, and that is traditionally used in the formation of the perfect tenses in the active voice and of all tenses in the passive voice.

PRINCIPAL PARTS OF COMMON IRREGULAR VERBS

Present	Past	Past Participle
arise	arose	arisen
be	was, were	been
bear	bore	borne
become	became	become
begin	began	begun
bid	bade	bid, bidden
blow	blew	blown
break	broke	broken
bring	brought	brought
build	built	built
buy	bought	bought
catch	caught	caught
choose	chose	chosen
cling	clung	clung
come	came	come
cut	cut	cut
do	did	done
draw	drew	drawn
drink	drank	drunk
drive	drove	driven
eat	ate	eaten
fall	fell	fallen
feed	fed	fed
feel	felt	felt
fight	fought	fought
find	found	found
flee	fled	fled
fling	flung	flung
fly	flew	flown
forget	forgot	forgotten
forgive	forgave	forgiven
freeze	froze	frozen
get	got	gotten
give	gave	given
go	went	gone
grow	grew	grown
hang (a person)	hanged	hanged
hang (an object)	hung	hung
hear	heard	heard
hide	hid	hidden
hold	held	held
hurt	hurt	hurt
keep	kept	kept
know	knew	known
lay	laid	laid

Present	Past	Past Participle
lead	led	led
leave	left	left
lend	lent	lent
lie	lay	lain
light	lit, lighted	lit, lighted
lose	lost	lost
make	made	made
meet	met	met
read	read	read
ride	rode	ridden
ring	rang	rung
rise	rose	risen
run	ran	run
see	saw	seen
send	sent	sent
sew	sewed	sewn
shake	shook	shaken
sit	sat	sat
shoot	shot	shot
shrink	shrank, shrunk	shrunk, shrunken
slay	slew	slain
sleep	slept	slept
slide	slid	slid
speak	spoke	spoken
spend	spent	spent
spin	spun	spun
spring	sprang, sprung	sprung
stand	stood	stood
steal	stole	stolen
sting	stung	stung
swear	swore	sworn
swing	swung	swung
swim	swam	swum
take	took	taken
teach	taught	taught
tear	tore	torn
tell	told	told
think	thought	thought
throw	threw	thrown
wake	waked, woke	waked, woken
wear	wore	worn
weave	wove	woven
win	won	won
wring	wrung	wrung
write	wrote	written

2. ***When to Use the Perfect Tenses***

Use the ***present perfect*** for an action begun in the past and extended to the present.

Example:

I cannot have any more turkey or stuffing; already I have eaten too much food. ✓

In this case, ate would be incorrect. The action have eaten (present perfect) began in the past and extended to the present.

Use the ***past perfect*** for an action begun and completed in the past before some other past action.

Example:

The foreman asked what had happened to my eye. ✓

In this case, "happened" would be incorrect. The action "asked" and the action "had happened" (past perfect) are used because one action (regarding the speaker's eye) is "more past" than the other action (the foreman's asking).

Use the ***future perfect*** for an action begun at any time and completed in the future. When there are two future actions, the action completed first is expressed in the future perfect tense.

Example:

When I reach Chicago tonight, my uncle will have left for Los Angeles. ✓

The action "will have left" is going to take place before the action "reach," although both actions will occur in the future.

3. ***The Subjunctive Mood***

The ***subjunctive*** expresses a condition contrary to a fact, a wish, a supposition, or an indirect command.

WHEN TO USE THE SUBJUNCTIVE MOOD

☺

1. To express a wish not likely to be fulfilled or impossible to realize
2. In a subordinate clause after a verb that expresses a command, a request, or a suggestion
3. To express a condition known or supposed to be contrary to fact
4. After "as if" or "as though"

The most common subjunctives are "were" and "be." "Were" is used instead of the indicative form "was," and "be" is used instead of the indicative form "am."

Examples:

I wish it were possible for us to approve his transfer at this time. ✓
If I were in St. Louis, I should be glad to attend. ✓
If this were a simple case, we would easily agree on a solution. ✓
If I were you, I should not mind the assignment. ✓
He asked that the report be submitted in duplicate. ✓
It is recommended that this office be responsible for preparing the statements. ✓
We suggest that he be relieved of the assignment. ✓

In formal writing and speech, "as if" and "as though" are followed by the subjunctive since they introduce as supposition something not factual. In informal writing and speaking, the indicative is sometimes used.

Examples:

He talked as if he were an expert on taxation. (He is not.) ✓
This report looks as though it were the work of a college freshman. ✓

Avoid shifts in mood. Once you have decided on the mood that properly expresses your message, use that mood throughout the sentence or the paragraph. A shift in mood is confusing to the listener or reader; it indicates that the speaker or writer himself has changed his way of looking at the conditions.

Example:

It is requested that a report of the proceedings be prepared and copies should be distributed to all members. ("Be" is subjunctive; "should be" is indicative.) ✗
It is requested that a report of the proceedings be prepared and that copies be distributed to all members. ✓

EXERCISE 3

Analyzing Sentence Structure

DIRECTIONS: In Sentences #1-30, circle the correct verb choice. Answers are on page 908.

1. Each year, many people who did not graduate from high school (receive, receives) GED diplomas.
2. The books on the top shelf (was, were) all written by Emily Brontë.
3. The stores in the downtown sector's newly renovated mall (offer, offers) brand name fashions at reduced prices.
4. Only a few dust-covered bottles of the vintage wine (remain, remains) in the cellar.
5. Each tourist who visits the caverns (is, are) given a guidebook.
6. Underneath the leaf covering (was, were) several different species of insects.
7. The young boys, who had never before been in trouble with the law, (was, were) worried about what their parents would say.
8. Several barrels containing a highly toxic liquid (has, have) been discovered at the abandoned factory.
9. The sponsors of the arts and crafts fair (hope, hopes) that it will attract several thousand visitors.
10. Dawn, Harriet, and Gloria, who have formed their own singing group, (is, are) auditioning for jobs.
11. According to insiders, the mayor, whose administration has been rocked by several crises, (worry, worries) that more layoffs are inevitable.
12. There (has, have) been several acts of vandalism in the cemetery in recent months.
13. Rock musicians who perform in front of large speakers often (loses, lose) part of their hearing.
14. The leaves from the branches of the tree that hang over the fence (falls, fall) into the neighbor's yard.
15. The computer and the printer, which are sitting on James' desk, (has, have) never been used.
16. Theresa, wearing her hip-length waders, (was, were) fishing in the middle of the stream.
17. The film critic for the *New York Times* (write, writes) that the film is very funny and entertaining.
18. Several of the ingredients that are used in the dish (has, have) to be prepared in advance.
19. The computer that controls the temperature of the living quarters of the ship (was, were) malfunctioning.
20. There (has, have) been some support for a proposal to build a new courthouse in the center of town.
21. Bill and Jean (is, are) going to the game tomorrow.
22. There (was, were) several students absent last week.
23. I hope that no one has left (his or her, their) homework at home.
24. Each of the sisters celebrated (her, their) birthday at the Plaza.
25. The music of Verdi's operas (is, are) filled with dramatic sweep.
26. All the musicians tuned (his, their) instruments.
27. Either Mrs. Martinez or Carlos (go, goes) to church each week.
28. I told you to (have, have had) the dog walked and fed by the time I got home from work.
29. Last month, the storekeeper, having lost most of his business to a conglomerate retail store, (can, could) not pay the monthly rent bill.
30. Once the weather (became, becomes) cold, Jim could no longer ride his bicycle to work.

DIRECTIONS: For Items #31-58, choose the verb form that completes the sentence correctly. Answers are on page 909.

31. A gentleman is __________ to see you.
    A. comes
    B. came
    C. come
    D. coming
    E. will come

32. Bill was __________ to telephone you last night.
    A. to suppose
    B. supposed
    C. suppose
    D. supposing
    E. will suppose

33. My friend has __________ to get impatient.
    A. to begin
    B. began
    C. begin
    D. beginning
    E. begun

34. He has __________ a serious cold.
    A. catched
    B. caught
    C. catch
    D. catching
    E. will catch

35. He could __________ before large groups if he were asked.
    A. sing
    B. sang
    C. sung
    D. singed
    E. singing

36. She has __________ before large groups several times.
    A. sing
    B. sang
    C. sung
    D. singed
    E. singing

37. They have already __________ to the theater.
    A. go
    B. goes
    C. going
    D. gone
    E. will go

38. He has __________ me excellent advice.
    A. give
    B. gave
    C. gived
    D. giving
    E. given

39. He is __________ to his parents.
    A. to devote
    B. devote
    C. devoted
    D. devoting
    E. will devote

40. The engineer has designed and __________ his own home.
    A. to build
    B. builds
    C. building
    D. built
    E. had built

41. He __________ as he ran onto the stage following the clown and the magician.
    A. to laugh
    B. laughing
    C. laughed
    D. laughs
    E. had laughed

42. She __________ the high-jump so well at trials that she is going to the Olympics this summer.
    A. had jumped
    B. to jump
    C. jumping
    D. jumps
    E. jumped

43. It __________ that she continued to blame me even after she knew it wasn't my fault.
    A. hurt
    B. hurts
    C. has hurt
    D. hurting
    E. will hurt

44. The man __________ the murder occur if he had really been on that street corner when he said he was.
    A. see
    B. sees
    C. would have saw
    D. seen
    E. would have seen

45. The child __________ everywhere now that she is able to stand up by herself.
A. to walk
B. walks
C. walked
D. walking
E. had walked

46. Tomorrow morning, Sam __________ his sister.
A. was calling
B. called
C. calling
D. has called
E. will call

47. After she had completed her investigation, the state trooper __________ her report.
A. was writing
B. wrote
C. has written
D. writes
E. will write

48. When I was growing up, we __________ every summer at my grandmother's home in the country.
A. spend
B. will spend
C. have spent
D. were spending
E. spent

49. Whenever we get a craving for a late night snack, we __________ a pizza.
A. order
B. ordered
C. had ordered
D. have ordered
E. were ordering

50. For years now, John __________ his milk at the corner grocery.
A. buys
B. will buy
C. has bought
D. is buying
E. bought

51. We were just leaving when the telephone __________.
A. rang
B. will ring
C. was ringing
D. has rung
E. had rung

52. We arrived at the house by noon, but the wedding __________ over.
A. is
B. will be
C. had been
D. has been
E. was

53. We __________ to drive to the game, but the car stalled.
A. plan
B. will plan
C. had planned
D. are planning
E. have planned

54. The roofers were putting the last shingles on the house while the plumber __________ the water lines.
A. is testing
B. was testing
C. tests
D. will test
E. had tested

55. A large flock of Canadian Geese __________ over the meadow and landed in the pond.
A. will fly
B. were flying
C. fly
D. flew
E. are flying

56. Hui worked very hard to complete her coursework before the baby __________ due.
A. is
B. are
C. was
D. will be
E. were

57. We __________ to drive from Wisconsin to Washington in two days, but we were late.
A. want
B. are wanting
C. were wanted
D. wants
E. had wanted

58. Earl and I __________ to eat lunch together outside if it doesn't rain.
A. will hope
B. had hoped
C. hope
D. did hope
E. hoped

DIRECTIONS: For Items #59-81, circle the letter of the underlined part of the sentence containing the error. Answers are on page 909.

59. The owner of the collection requested that (A) the museum require (B) all people with a camera (C) to leave (D) them at the door.

60. The young comic found (A) that capturing the audience's attention was easy, but to maintain (B) their (C) interest was (D) difficult.

61. The whale had been laying (A) on the beach for over two hours before the rescue teams were able to begin (B) moving (C) it back into (D) the water.

62. The praying mantis is welcomed by (A) homeowners for its (B) ability to control (C) destructive garden pests, unlike the cockroach, which serves no useful function (D).

63. The newly (A) purchased (B) picture was hanged (C) on the back wall nearest (D) the bay window.

64. The opening scene (A) of the film was a grainy, black-and-white (B) shot of an empty town square in which (C) an outlaw was hung (D).

65. We spent (A) an exhausting day shopping we (B) could hardly (C) wait to get (D) home.

66. The fact that she is bright, articulate, and has charisma (A) will serve (B) her well in her campaign for governor, particularly (C) since her opponent has none (D) of those qualities.

67. Puritans such as William Bradford displaying (A) the courage and piety needed to survive (B) in the New World, a world both (C) promising and threatening, which (D) offered unique challenges to their faith.

68. The woman to whom (A) I take my clothes for tailoring (B) has sewed (C) the hem on this skirt perfectly (D).

69. Unfortunately, before (A) cures are found for diseases such as cancer, many lives would have been (B) lost and million of dollars in medical services spent to (C) treat symptoms rather than to (D) provide a cure.

70. The house on (A) the corner was completely (B) empty, no (C) one came (D) to the door.

71. For many people, it is difficult to accept (A) compliments graciously and even more difficult (B) taking (C) criticism graciously (D).

72. Due (A) to the extremely warm (B) weather this winter, the water has not froze (C) on the pond sufficiently (D).

73. The French poet Artaud believed (A) that, (B) following (C) the climax of a drama, the audience experienced (D) a violent catharsis and is thereby "reborn."

74. Where (A) had everyone (B) gone all (C) the lights were off (D).

75. Rather (A) than declaring (B) bankruptcy, he applied (C) for a loan and the bank loaned (D) him the money.

76. Wagering (A) on the Kentucky Derby favorite is (B) a bad betting (C) proposition, for in the last fifteen years, the horse that has been the crowd favorite at post time of the Kentucky Derby loses (D) the race.

77. We entered the cave __very__ (A) __slowly almost__ (B) afraid of what we __might find__ (C) __there__ (D).

78. After he __had learned__ (A) __of__ (B) her suicide, he __drunk__ (C) all of the poison __from the vial__ (D).

79. __During the years__ (A) she spent __searching for a cure__ (B) for the disease, Dr. Thompson interviewed hundreds of patients, ran thousands of tests, and __cross-checking__ (C) __millions of bits of data__ (D).

80. __After struggling with the problem__ (A) for most of the afternoon, he finally __flinged__ (B) the papers __on__ (C) the desk and __ran out of the room__ (D).

81. __Suddenly__ (A), I felt that something __was going to__ (B) __happen__ (C) __my__ (C) heart began to __beat furiously__ (D).

DIRECTIONS: For Sentences #82-96, correct the faulty parallelism if one exists. Answers are on page 909.

82. When at school, he studies, goes to the library, and he works on the computer.

83. In order to get eight hours of sleep, the student prefers sleeping in late in the morning to go to bed early in the evening.

84. I still need to pass Math 252, English 301, and return two overdue books before I am allowed to graduate.

85. You need to talk to either the teacher or the counselor.

86. Dr. Smydra is not only a captivating lecturer, but also an engaging conversationalist.

87. I will either graduate this fall or lose out on a great opportunity with IBM.

88. Our instructor suggested that we study the assignment carefully, go to the library to research the topic extensively, and we should conduct a survey among 20 subjects.

89. The increase of attrition among community college students is caused by a lack of family support and students have a limited income while attending school.

90. Many non-smokers complained about the health risks associated with second-hand smoke; as a result, smoking is banned in the library, in the cafeteria, and smokers have to leave the building to light a cigarette.

91. After talking to financial aid and see your advisor, return to the registrar's office.

92. Professor Walker not only helped me, but many of my classmates as well.

93. In his communications class, he can either work in groups or in pairs.

94. I prefer that other geography textbook because of the clear explanations, numerous exercises, and Mrs. Patrick's vivid teaching style.

95. The question is whether to study tonight or should I get up earlier tomorrow morning?

96. Reasons for the latest tuition increase are the upgraded computers, new library and, last but not least, inflation has increased to 6.5%.

Problems of Logical Expression

Ask yourself the following five questions when checking the logical expression of a sentence.

CHECKLIST FOR LOGICAL EXPRESSION ERRORS

1. Does the sentence contain a faulty or illogical comparison?
2. Does the sentence maintain consistent verb tenses?
3. Does the sentence actually convey the intended meaning?
4. Is the sentence clear and concise?
5. Does the sentence contain any misplaced modifiers?

Faulty or Illogical Comparisons

One problem of logical expression is faulty or illogical comparisons. A faulty comparison is the attempt to compare two things that cannot logically be compared. Consider the following faulty examples. Note: ✓ = correct, ✗ = wrong.

Examples:

Today, life expectancies of both men and women are much higher compared to the turn of the century when living conditions were much harsher. ✗
The average salary of a professional basketball player is higher than the top-level management of most corporations. ✗

A comparison can only be made between like items. Yet, in the first sentence we see an attempt to compare "life expectancies" with "the turn of the century"—two dissimilar concepts. The sentence is corrected by simply adding the phrase "those of" before "the turn of the century." Now we have life expectancies compared to life expectancies, and that is a logical comparison.

The same error occurs in the second sentence. An attempt is made to compare "average salary" to "management." The error can be corrected in the same way as in the first example: "…is higher than those of the top-level management…."

WATCH FOR ILLOGICAL COMPARISONS

Be alert for sentences that attempt to make an illogical comparison between two dissimilar concepts.

When two things are being compared, the comparative form of the adjective is used. The comparative is formed in one of the two following ways.

RULES FOR COMPARISONS BETWEEN TWO OBJECTS

1. Two objects can be compared by adding "-er" to the adjective.
2. Two objects can be compared by placing "more" before the adjective.

Examples:

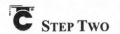

She is more prettier than her sister. ✗
She is more pretty than her sister. ✓
She is prettier than her sister. ✓

Jeremy is more wiser than we know. ✗
Jeremy is wiser than we know. ✓
Jeremy is more wise than we know. ✓

If three or more things are being compared, then the superlative form of the adjective is used. The superlative is formed in one of the two following ways.

RULES FOR COMPARISONS AMONG THREE OR MORE OBJECTS

1. Three or more objects can be compared by adding "-est" to the adjective.
2. Three or more objects can be compared by placing "most" before the adjective.

Examples:

Mary is the shorter of all of her friends. ✗
Mary is the shortest of all of her friends. ✓

This is the most sharpest knife I have. ✗
This is the sharpest knife I have. ✓

Calculus is the most difficult class that I have this year. ✓

Some comparative and superlative modifiers require changing the words themselves. A few of these irregular comparisons are given below; consult your dictionary whenever you are in doubt about the comparisons of any adjective or adverb.

MODIFIERS THAT DO CHANGE

Positive	*Comparative*	*Superlative*
good	better	best
well	better	best
bad (evil, ill)	worse	worst
badly	worse	worst
far	farther, further	farthest, furthest
late	later, latter	latest, last
little	less, lesser	least
many, much	more	most

Some adjectives and adverbs express qualities that go beyond comparison. They represent the highest degree of a given quality and, as a result, they cannot be improved. Some of these words are listed below.

MODIFIERS THAT DO NOT CHANGE

complete	preferable	horizontally	supreme	totally
correct	round	secondly	immortally	unique
dead	deadly	square	infinitely	uniquely
perfectly	exact	squarely	perfect	universally
perpendicularly				

The use of the comparative in such an expression as "This thing is better than any other" implies that "this thing" is separate from the group or class to which it is being compared. In these expressions, a word such as "other" or "else" is required to separate the thing being compared from the rest of the group of which it is a part.

Example:

Our house is cooler than any house on the block. ✗
Since "our house" is one of the houses on the block, it should not be included in the comparison. The sentence should read:
Our house is cooler than any other house on the block. ✓

Example:

He has a better record than any salesman in our group. ✗

Since "he" is himself one of the salesmen in the group, the comparison must separate him from the group. The sentence should read:

He has a better record than any <u>other</u> salesman in our group. ✓

Finally, be aware of incomplete comparisons. The result is illogical and confusing.

Examples:

The plays of Shakespeare are as good as Marlowe. ✗
The plays of Shakespeare are as good as <u>those</u> of Marlowe. ✓

His skill in tennis is far better than other athletes his age. ✗
His skill in tennis is far better than <u>that</u> of other athletes his age. ✓

His poetry is as exciting, if not more exciting than, the poetry of his instructor. ✗
His poetry is as exciting <u>as</u>, if not more exciting than, the poetry of his instructor. ✓

Sequence and Verb Tense

A second common problem of logical expression is poor choice of verb tense. The choice of ***verb tense*** in a correctly written sentence reflects the ***sequence*** of events described. The following examples contain verb tense errors. Note: ✓ = correct, ✗ = wrong.

Examples:

As soon as Linda finished writing her dissertation, she <u>will take</u> a well-earned vacation in Paris. ✗
A recent study shows that many mothers re-enter the labor force after their children <u>left</u> home. ✗

In the first example, both "writing" and "vacation" must be placed in the same time frame. As written, the sentence places the two actions in different, unconnected time frames. Depending on whether Linda has already completed the dissertation, the sentence could be corrected in either of two ways:

As soon as Linda <u>finishes</u> writing her dissertation, she will take a well-earned vacation in Paris. ✓
As soon as Linda finished writing her dissertation, she <u>took</u> a well-earned vacation in Paris. ✓

The first corrected version of the first example states that neither event has yet occurred and that the writing will precede the vacation. The second corrected version of the first example states that the events are completed and that the writing preceded the vacation.

In the second example, the verb "left" is incorrect because the verb "re-enter" is describing a present, ongoing action. The sentence can be corrected by making it clear that "children leaving home" is also a present phenomenon:

A recent study shows that many mothers re-enter the labor force after their children <u>leave</u> home. ✓
A recent study shows that many mothers re-enter the labor force after their children <u>have left</u> home. ✓

Either sentence is acceptable since both make it clear that leaving home is not a completed past action but an ongoing phenomenon.

WATCH FOR SHIFTING VERB TENSES

 Make sure that verb tenses properly reflect the sequence, as well as the duration, of any action described in the sentence.

Examples:

Charles came to town last week and goes to a resort where he rests for three days. ✗
Charles came to town last week and went to a resort where he rested for three days. ✓

Joan came home last week and goes to her home in the country where she spends the last weekend of her vacation. ✗
Joan came home last week and went to her home in the country where she spent the last weekend of her vacation. ✓

Unintended Meanings

Another problem in the category of logical expression relates to whether the sentence actually says what it intends to say. Often, sentences will intend to say one thing but actually say another. Note: ✗ = wrong.

Examples:

A childless charwoman's daughter, Dr. Roberts was a self-made woman. ✗
If the present interest rates fall, the dollar will lose some of its value on the foreign exchange. ✗

At first, both of these sentences may seem plausible, but a closer reading will show that each contains an error of logical expression. The first example is actually self-contradictory. As written, it asserts that Dr. Roberts was the daughter of a childless charwoman. In that case, Dr. Roberts would indeed have been a self-made woman! The sentence intends to say that Dr. Roberts was both childless and the daughter of a charwoman: "A charwoman's daughter and childless, Dr. Roberts was a self-made woman."

The second example is a bit subtler. It suggests that present interest rates can change, but that is internally inconsistent, since if the interest rate changes, the result is a new interest rate, not a changed "present" rate. The sentence is corrected by deleting the word "present."

In this category, there are as many possible examples as there are possible errors in human reasoning. Therefore, when checking for intended meaning, just ask yourself what the logic of the sentence implies.

CHECK THAT THE SENTENCE STRUCTURE HAS INTENDED MEANING

 Determine if the sentence says what it intends to say from the sentence's logical structure.

Conciseness

There are endless possibilities for conciseness errors. Several examples are illustrated below. Note: ✓ = correct, ✗ = wrong.

1. Avoid Awkward Sentences and Passive Verbs

A sentence may be grammatically and logically correct yet be in need of correction because it is awkward.

Examples:

The giant condor is able to spread its wings up to 25 feet. ✗
The giant condor has a wingspan of up to 25 feet. ✓

Although most students would benefit from further study of the sciences, doing so is frightening to most of them in that science courses are more difficult than liberal arts courses. ✗
Although most students would benefit from further study of the sciences, most of them are afraid to take science courses because they are more difficult than liberal arts courses. ✓

Given that the Incas lacked the wheel, the buildings at Machu Picchu are more astonishing than any Greek temples that are comparable as an achievement. ✗
Given that the Incas lacked the wheel, the buildings at Machu Picchu are more astonishing than any comparable Greek temple. ✓

In each case, the second sentence is less awkward and more clearly renders the intended thought by being more direct and concise.

A common error among writers is the use of the passive verb. Each of the following examples illustrates that by replacing weak passive verbs, sentences are rendered both clear and concise.

Examples:

One-fourth of the market was captured by the new computer firm. ✗
The new computer firm captured one-fourth of the market. ✓
The lottery prize being $110 million, there are almost as many tickets sold as there are prize dollars. ✗
When the lottery prize is $110 million, there are almost as many tickets sold as there are prize dollars. ✓
The teacher, having finished the day's lesson, let us leave class early. ✗
Because the teacher finished the day's lesson, she let us leave class early. ✓

AVOID PASSIVE VERBS

Any verb construction using a form of the verb "be" or "have" in addition to the active verb is called a passive verb. Passive verbs are not often used and should be avoided. The active voice is stronger and more direct.

2. ***Avoid Needlessly Wordy Sentences***

Occasionally, an original sentence will be incorrect simply because it is needlessly wordy.

Examples:

The protracted discussion over what route to take continued for a long time. ✗
The discussion over what route to take continued for a long time. ✓

An aim of the proposal is chiefly to ensure and guarantee the academic freedom of students. ✗
An aim of the proposal is to guarantee the academic freedom of students. ✓

To be protracted is to be continued for a long time; an aim is a chief concern, and to ensure is to guarantee. Therefore, each original is needlessly wordy.

Misplaced Modifiers

Another error of logical expression is the infamous misplaced modifier. Generally, a modifier should be placed as close to what it modifies as possible. A modifier that is too far from that which it intends to modify, or too close to some other important element, will seem to modify the wrong part of the sentence. Consider the following faulty sentences. Note: ✓ = correct, ✗ = wrong.

Examples:

Stuffed with herb dressing, trussed neatly, and baked to a golden hue, Aunt Fannie served her famous holiday turkey. ✘

The doctor said gently to the patient that there was nothing wrong with a smile. ✘

At the party, Fred served cold lemonade to his thirsty guests in paper cups. ✘

Consider the first example—poor Aunt Fannie! The proximity of the introductory modifier to Aunt Fannie suggests that she was stuffed, trussed, and baked. The sentence can be corrected by relocating the modifying phrase: "Aunt Fannie served her famous holiday turkey, stuffed with herb dressing, trussed neatly, and baked to a golden hue."

The second example is ambiguous and it could mean either that there is nothing wrong with smiling or that the doctor said, with a smile, that nothing was wrong with the patient. The corrected sentence reads: "With a smile, the doctor said gently to the patient that there was nothing wrong."

Finally, in the third example, the location of the prepositional phrase "in paper cups" implies that the guests are actually inside the paper cups! The sentence is corrected by moving the modifying phrase so that it is closer to what it is intended to modify: "At the party, Fred served cold lemonade in paper cups to his thirsty guests."

WATCH FOR MISPLACED MODIFIERS

 Be alert for sentences with ambiguous or incorrect modification. Correct misplaced modifiers by placing them as close as possible to what they modify.

Examples:

I bought a piano from an old lady with intricate carvings. ✘

I bought a piano with intricate carvings from an old lady. ✓

I read about the destruction of Rome in my history class. ✘

In my history class, I read about the destruction of Rome. ✓

The word "only" often c Examine the following confusing sentences.

Examples:

<u>Only</u> he kissed her. ✓

He <u>only</u> kissed her. ✓

He kissed <u>only</u> her. ✓

All three sentences are possible, but a different meaning is conveyed in each, depending on the positioning of "only."

Finally, problems may be created by the placement of a participle phrase.

Example:

Answering the doorbell, the cake remained in the oven. ✘

It sounds as though the cake answered the doorbell! Correct this sentence by adding a subject to which the phrase can refer:

Answering the doorbell, we forgot to take the cake from the oven. ✓

Example:

Falling on the roof, we heard the sound of the rain. ✗

We heard the sound of the rain falling on the roof. ✓

EXERCISE 4

Problems of Logical Expression

DIRECTIONS: Read the following passage. In Items #1-14, choose the best answer that corrects the sentence without changing its meaning or intent. When correcting the sentences, look at the sentence in the context of the passage in order to check for consistency and logical expression. If the sentence is correct as written, choose (A). Answers are on page 910.

(1) When I was a child, my grandmother's kitchen was the scene of feverish activity during the early fall. (2) Each morning, she would go to the farmers' market and returns with baskets of fruits and vegetables. (3) Then, she would spend the rest of the day preparing the food for the wide-mouthed canning jars that would preserve them through the winter. (4) By late fall, the pantry shelves are lined with rows of jars containing pickled peaches, creamed corn, and many varieties of jams and jellies.

(5) Today, we are able to buy fresh fruits and vegetables at the local grocery store even during the winter. (6) Indeed, years ago, home-canning was a practical solution to one of nature's dilemmas. (7) On the one hand, the harvest produced more fruits and vegetables than could be consumed immediately, so without some way to preserve the produce, they would spoil. (8) On the other hand, during the winter months, fresh produce was not available, so it was important to have preserved foods available.

(9) There are nothing mysterious about home-canning. (10) Fruits or vegetables are packed into special canning jars, fitted with self-sealing lids, and you submerge them in boiling water. (11) The sustained high heat kills dangerous organisms causing the food to spoil. (12) As it gradually cools, a vacuum pulls the lid down against the mouth of the jar to make an airtight seal. (13) Unless the seal is broken, no organisms can enter the jar to cause spoilage.

(14) Although we no longer depend on home-canning, home-canning can be fun. (15) Jams and jellies spread over hot toast on a cold winter morning seems to taste better when you have made them yourself. (16) You also enjoy giving homemade preserves to friends and relatives as gifts. (17) All one needs to do to get started is to find a book about home-canning at the local library or bookstore and follow the directions.

1. Sentence (2): Each morning, she would go to the farmers' market and returns with baskets of fruits and vegetables.
   A. NO CHANGE
   B. is returning
   C. would return
   D. was returning
   E. have returned

2. Sentence (3): Then, she would spend the rest of the day preparing the food for the wide-mouthed canning jars that would preserve them through the winter.
   A. NO CHANGE
   B. would preserve it
   C. preserved them
   D. was preserving them
   E. preserves it

3. Sentence (4): By late fall, the pantry shelves are lined with rows of jars containing pickled peaches, creamed corn, and many varieties of jams and jellies.
   A. NO CHANGE
   B. is lined
   C. were lined
   D. was lined
   E. might be lined

4. Sentence (6): Indeed, years ago, home-canning was a practical solution to one of nature's dilemmas.
   A. NO CHANGE
   B. Indeed
   C. Furthermore,
   D. Moreover,
   E. However,

5. Sentence (7): On the one hand, the harvest produced more fruits and vegetables than could be consumed immediately, so without some way to preserve the produce, they would spoil.
   A. NO CHANGE
   B. it would spoil
   C. they spoil
   D. it spoils
   E. it spoiled

6. Sentence (8): On the other hand, during the winter months, fresh produce was not available, so it was important to have preserved foods available.
   A. NO CHANGE
   B. is
   C. has been
   D. could be
   E. can be

7. Sentence (9): There are nothing mysterious about home-canning.
   A. NO CHANGE
   B. is
   C. was
   D. were
   E. has been

8. Sentence (10): Fruits or vegetables are packed into special canning jars, fitted with self-sealing lids, and you submerge them in boiling water.
   A. NO CHANGE
   B. you submerge it
   C. you submerged them
   D. you submerged it
   E. submerged

9. Sentence (11): The sustained high heat kills dangerous organisms causing the food to spoil.
   A. NO CHANGE
   B. that caused
   C. that could cause
   D. to cause
   E. which caused

10. Sentence (12): As it gradually cools, a vacuum pulls the lid down against the mouth of the jar to make an airtight seal.
    A. NO CHANGE
    B. As they gradually cool,
    C. Gradually cooling,
    D. Gradually cooled,
    E. As the jars gradually cool,

11. Sentence (13): Unless the seal is broken, no organisms can enter the jar to cause spoilage.
    A. NO CHANGE
    B. are entering
    C. entered
    D. have entered
    E. had entered

12. Sentence (15): Jams and jellies spread over hot toast on a cold winter morning seems to taste better when you have made them yourself.
    A. NO CHANGE
    B. seem to taste
    C. seems tasting
    D. will seem to taste
    E. seemed to taste

13. Sentence (16): You also enjoy giving homemade preserves to friends and relatives as gifts.
    A. NO CHANGE
    B. will enjoy giving
    C. enjoyed giving
    D. enjoy to give
    E. enjoys giving

14. Sentence (17): All one needs to do to get started is to find a book about home-canning at the local library or bookstore and follow the directions.
    A. NO CHANGE
    B. your needs
    C. you need
    D. people need
    E. the reader needs

DIRECTIONS: In Items #15-29, circle the letter of the underlined part of the sentence containing the error. Answers are on page 910.

15. Written in almost total isolation from the world, (A) Emily Dickinson spoke of (B) love and (C) death in her (D) poems.

16. Early in his career, (A) the pianist entertained thoughts of becoming (B) a composer; but after receiving bad reviews for his own work, he (C) had given up. (D)

17. The (A) baseball game was halted due to rain and rescheduled (B) for the following day, even though (C) the fans would not leave (D) the stadium.

18. Being highly qualified for the position (A), the bank president will conduct (B) a final interview of the new candidate tomorrow, after which (C) he will make (D) her a job offer.

19. The literature of Native Americans (A) has been overlooked (B) by most scholars, and the reason is because (C) most university courses in literature are taught (D) in departments that also teach a language, such as French.

20. In broken English (A), the police officer patiently listened to the tourist ask for directions to Radio City Music Hall, after which (B) she motioned (C) the tourist and his family into the squad car and drove them (D) to their destination.

21. Bullfighting remains a controversial (A) sport and many (B) are repulsed by it, since (C) Hemingway was an aficionado of the sport and glorified it (D) in his writing.

22. Following the recent crash of the stock market (A), Peter bought (B) a book on portfolio management in order to learn (C) methods to protect his investments from a well-known investment banker (D).

23. Since (A) we have a broader (B) technological base, American scientists believe that our space program will ultimately prove (C) superior to the Soviet Union (D).

24. Although a person may always represent himself (A) in a judicial proceeding, licensed lawyers only (B) may represent others (C) in such (D) proceedings for a fee.

25. Unlike the pale and delicately built ballerinas of (A) romantic ballet (B), Judith Jamison's movement seems more African than (C) European-American, and her physical appearance reinforces (D) the contrast.

26. Market experts predict (A) that in ten years, when the harmful effects of caffeine become more generally known (B), the number of tons of decaffeinated coffee consumed by (C) Americans each year will exceed coffee containing caffeine (D).

27. Illiteracy, a widespread problem in the United States (A), undermines (B) productivity because many mistakes are (C) made by workers who do not know how to read on the job (D).

28. As sailors are often assigned (A) to ships that remain (B) at sea for months at a time, men in the Navy spend (C) more time away from home than any branch of the service (D).

29. Like A. J. Ayer (A), much of Gilbert Ryle's philosophical argumentation relies (B) on analysis of the way people (C) ordinarily (D) use language.

DIRECTIONS: For Sentences #30-44, correct the faulty comparison if one exists. Answers are on page 910.

30. The life of my generation is easier than my parents.

31. My two daughters enjoy different TV shows; the oldest watches game shows, while the youngest prefers talk shows.

32. Her present instructor is better of all the ones she has had so far.

33. In the technology lab, I choose the computer with the more greater memory.

34. According to the counselor, taking these classes in this order is much beneficial than the other way around.

35. Our school is very unique in many aspects.

36. The fraternity he joined is better than all fraternities.

37. Professor Baker's explanations are not as clear as Professor Thomas' explanations.

38. You can learn just as much, if not more, online as in a regular classroom.

39. Which of these three sections is better?

40. I am spending more time on the assignments in my management class than all my other classes combined.

41. You will receive your grades no latest than tomorrow at 2 p.m.

42. There is no need for farther negotiation.

43. She is doing so badly in her art class that she could not do any worst.

44. This exercise seems more difficult than all of them.

DIRECTIONS: Rewrite Sentences #45-54 so that the modified word in each is clear. Answers are on page 910.

45. He tripped on a crack in the pavement going to school.

46. Mary only failed the test; everyone else in her class passed.

47. Did you see the film about the five people on the boat on television?

48. The police officer ordered the man to stop in his patrol car.

49. Upon picking up the phone, the noise became muted.

50. While swimming, a fish nibbled on my toe.

51. He went to the old church to pray for the people on Cemetery Hill.

52. Of all his admirers, his wife only loved him.

53. Upon entering the class, the blackboard came into view.

54. The baby was pushed by his mother in a stroller.

DIRECTIONS: Some of Sentences #55-64 are correct, but most are incorrect. Rewrite each incorrect sentence correctly. Answers are on page 910.

55. She likes tennis, golf, and to go swimming.

56. He could not deliver the supplies. Because the roads had not yet been plowed.

57. If you want to succeed, one must be willing to work hard.

58. Jeff is taller than any boy in his class.

59. To get to school, we nearly walked two miles.

60. The heroine was unbelievable naive.

61. Drive carefully. There may be ice on the roads.

62. Leaning out the window, the garden could be seen below.

63. The hotel room was clean and comfortable that we had reserved.

64. This book is heavier in weight than that one.

Idioms and Clarity of Expression

Standard English contains numerous idioms and two-word verbs that are perfectly acceptable to use. The following is a list of commonly accepted idioms and two-word verbs.

IDIOMS AND TWO-WORD VERBS

about time, about to
above all
act up
add up (*make sense*)
a good deal of
an arm and a leg
at the drop of a hat
back out (of)
bank on
be about to
be an old hand (at)
be a question of
beat around the bush
be bound to
be broke
be fed up (with)
be off
be out of something
be out of the question
be over
be short for, be short of
be the picture of
be up to someone
be warm
bite off more than one can chew
break down, break the ice
break the news (to)
bring about
broken English
brush up on
by and large
by heart, by no means
call off
call on
care for
catch on, catch up (with)
come across, come down with
come out smelling like a rose
cost an arm and a leg
count on, count out
cut down on, cut it close
cut out, cut out for
day in and day out
die down
do over, do with, do without
dream up
drop in (on), drop off
size up
sleep on it
snap out of
speak up (*say something, speak more loudly*)
spell out (for)
stand a chance
stand for
stand out
start up
stay out, stay up
a stone's throw (from)
straighten up
take a chance, take advantage (of)
take after, take in, take into account
every other
fall behind, fall through
a far cry from
feel free
feel like a million bucks
feel up to
few and far between
fill in (for)
fly off the handle
follow in someone's footsteps
for good
get the hang of
get in one's blood
get in the way
get off, get on, get over, get to
get rid of
get the better of
get under way
give a hand (to, with)
go on (with)
go without saying
hand in, hand out
hang up
have a heart
have in mind
have over
hear first hand (from)
hear from, hear of
hit it off
hold on (to), hold still, hold up
how come?
in the dark, in hot water
in the long run, in no time
jump to conclusions
keep an eye on, keep an eye out (for)
keep from, keep on one's toes
keep on (with), keep up (with)
knock it off
lay off
learn the ropes
leave out
let (somebody) alone, let (somebody) know
let go of
look after, look for, look forward to
look into, look out (for)
look up (to)
make a difference, make a point of
make ends meet, make out
take it easy, take off (*leave*)
take one's mind off, take one's time
take over, take pains, take turns
talk over
tangle with
tell apart
think much of
think over
throw cold water on
tie up, tie into
trade in
turn down, turn up, turn into
turn off, turn on, turn out, turn in
under the weather
make sense of, make way for
make up, make up one's mind
mark up, mark down
may as well, might as well
mean to
move on, move up
next to nothing
nose something out
now and then
odds and ends
on a shoestring, on its last leg
on the go
on one's last leg, on one's toes
on pins and needles
on second thought
on the mend, on the road, on the run
on the tip of one's tongue
on the whole
open up
out of order, out of sorts
out of this world, out to win
over and over
part with
pass up
pat oneself on the back
pay off, pay someone a visit
pick out, pick up (learn)
pick up the tab (for)
a piece of cake
play by ear
point out
pull one's leg
put aside, put off
put one's best foot forward
put together, put up (with)
rave about
rough it
rule out
run into, run out of, run short (of)
save one's breath
search me
see off, see to
serve one right
set out
settle down, settle on
sing another tune
show around, show up
shut down
up against
ups and downs
up-to-date
use up
wait for, wait on
warm up (to)
watch out (for)
wear out
a whole new ballgame
with flying colors
without a hitch
work out (*exercise, solve*)
write out
zero in (on)

An expression that is not idiomatic is one that is not acceptable standard written English for any of the following reasons.

CHECKLIST FOR IDIOMATIC EXPRESSION ERRORS

1. Wrong Prepositions

2. Diction
3. Gerunds vs. Infinitives
4. Ambiguity in Scope
5. Low-Level Usage

Wrong Prepositions

In standard written English, only certain prepositions can be used with certain verbs. You should know which prepositions to use with which verbs as a result of daily conversation and writing in standard written English. Note: ✗ = wrong.

Example:

I asked him repeatedly if he was from <u>about</u> here, but he never answered me. ✗

The phrase "was from about here" is not correct. You should recognize the correct phrase from daily conversation: "he was from around here."

Diction

The second category of idiomatic expression errors involves diction, i.e., word choice. Sometimes, a word is used incorrectly, which leads to a construction that is simply not idiomatic or not acceptable according to standard usage. Note: ✓ = correct, ✗ = wrong.

Example:

The techniques of empirical observation in the social sciences are different <u>than</u> those in the physical sciences. ✗

This example is improved by replacing "than" with "from." Rewritten, the sentence reads: "The techniques of empirical observation in the social sciences are different "from" those in the physical sciences."

A variation on this theme uses pairs of words that are often incorrectly used, as the following examples illustrate.

Examples:

John expressed his intention to make the trip, but if he will actually go is doubtful. ✗

John expressed his intention to make the trip, but whether he will actually go is doubtful. ✓

Herbert divided the cake among Mary and Sally. ✗

Herbert divided the cake between Mary and Sally. ✓

Herbert divided the cake between Mary, Sally, and himself. ✗

Herbert divided the cake among Mary, Sally, and himself. ✓

The amount of students in the class declined as the semester progressed. ✗

The number of students in the class declined as the semester progressed. ✓

There are less students in Professor Smith's class than there are in Professor Jones' class. ✗

There are fewer students in Professor Smith's class than there are in Professor Jones' class. ✓

Some sentences are incorrect because they use a word that does not convey the intended meaning. The confusion is understandable because of the similarity between the correct word and the chosen word.

WATCH FOR INAPPROPRIATE DICTION

Be alert for non-idiomatic usage and commonly misused words.

The following list is an extended summary of commonly confused word groups.

CONFUSING WORD GROUPS

accede—*to agree with*	They will *accede* to your request for more information.
exceed—*to be more than*	Unfortunately, her expenditures now *exceed* her income.
concede—*to yield* (not necessarily in agreement)	They *concede* that more information is necessary.
accept—*to receive*, or	I'll *accept* the gift from you.
to agree to something	I will lend you the money if you *accept* my conditions.
except—*to exclude* or *excluding*	Everyone *except* my uncle went home.
access—*availability*, or	The lawyer was given *access* to the grand jury records.
to get at	I could not *access* the files without the proper password.
excess—*state of surpassing specified limits* (noun), or	Expenditures this month are far in *excess* of income.
more than usual (adjective)	The airline charged him fifty dollars for *excess* baggage.
adapt—*to adjust or change*	Children can *adapt* to changing conditions very easily.
adept—*skillful*	Proper instruction makes children *adept* in various games.
adopt—*to take as one's own*	The war orphan was *adopted* by the general and his wife.
adapted to—*original or natural suitability*	The gills of the fish are *adapted to* underwater breathing.
adapted for—*created suitability*	Atomic energy is constantly being *adapted for* new uses.
adapted from—*changed to be made suitable*	Many of Wagner's librettos were *adapted from* Norse sagas.
addition—*the act or process of adding*	In *addition* to a dictionary, he always used a thesaurus.
edition—*a printing of a publication*	The first *edition* of Shakespeare's plays appeared in 1623.
advantage—*a superior position*	He had an *advantage* in experience over his opponent.
benefit—*a favor conferred or earned*	The rules were changed for his *benefit*.
adverse—*unfavorable*	He was very upset by the *adverse* decision.
averse—*having a feeling of repugnance or dislike*	Many writers are *averse* to criticism of their work.
advice—*counsel, opinion* (noun)	Let me give you some free *advice*.
advise—*to offer advice* (verb)	I'd *advise* you to see your doctor.
affect—*to influence* (verb)	The pollution *affected* our health.
effect—*to cause or bring about* (verb), or	Our lawsuit *effected* a change in the law.
a result (noun)	The *effect* of the storm could not be measured.
all ready—*everybody or everything ready*	They were *all ready* to write when the test began.
already—*previously*	They had *already* written the letter.
all together—*everybody or everything together*	The boys and girls stood *all together* in line.
altogether—*completely*	His action was *altogether* strange for a person of his type.
allude—*to make a reference to*	In his essay, he *alludes* to Shakespeare's puns.
elude—*to escape from*	The burglar *eluded* the police.
allusion—*an indirect reference*	The poem is an *allusion* to one of Shakespeare's sonnets.
illusion—*an erroneous concept or perception*	My mirror created the *illusion* of space in the narrow hall.
alongside of—*side by side with*	Bill stood *alongside of* Henry.
alongside—*parallel to the side*	Park the car *alongside* the curb.
among—*a term used with more than two persons or things*	The inheritance was equally divided *among* the four kids.
between—*a term used with two persons or things*	The inheritance was divided *between* the two kids.
angel—*a heavenly creature*	She has been an *angel* in these difficult times.
angle—*a point at which two lines meet*, or	A line perpendicular to another line forms a right *angle*.
an aspect seen from a particular point of view	From that *angle*, the picture looks completely different.
ante—a prefix meaning *before*	The *ante*chamber is the small room before the main room.
anti—a prefix meaning *against*	He is known to be *anti*-American.
assistance—*the act of assisting, aid*	I needed his *assistance* when I repaired the roof.
assistants—*helpers, aides*	The chief surgeon has four *assistants*.
breadth—*width*	The canvas was twice greater in length than in *breadth*.
breath—*an intake of air*	Before you dive in, take a very deep *breath*.
breathe—*to draw air in and give it out*	It is difficult to *breathe* when you have a bad cold.

CONFUSING WORD GROUPS

build—*to erect, construct* (verb), or	I want to *build* a sandcastle.
the physical makeup of a person (noun)	She has a very athletic *build.*
built—the past tense of *build*	We *built* a moat around the sandcastle.
buy—*to purchase*	I want to *buy* a new tie.
by—*near,*	My bloodhound likes to sleep *by* the door at night.
by means of, or	He comes to school *by* public transportation.
not later than	Mary said that she would be back at work *by* noon.
bye—*free pass to next round*	She had a *bye* in the tournament.
canvas—*a heavy, coarse material*	The *canvas* sails were very heavy.
canvass—*to solicit, conduct a survey*	The politicians are going to *canvass* our neighborhood.
capital—*place of government,* or	Paris is the *capital* of France.
wealth	It takes substantial *capital* to open a restaurant.
capitol—*building that houses legislatures*	Congress convenes in the *Capitol* in Washington, D.C.
carat—*a unit of weight*	The movie star wears a ten-*carat* diamond ring.
caret—*a proofreading symbol, indicating where something is to be inserted*	He added a phrase in the space above the *caret.*
carrot—*a vegetable*	Does he feed his pet rabbit a *carrot* every other day?
click—*a brief, sharp sound*	The detective drew his gun when he heard the lock *click.*
clique—*an exclusive group of people or set*	In high school, I was not part of any *clique.*
cease—*to end*	Please *cease* making those sounds.
seize—*to take hold of*	*Seize* him by the collar as he comes around the corner.
choice—*a selection*	My *choice* for a career is teaching.
choose—*to select*	We may *choose* our own advisors.
chose—the past tense of *choose*	I finally *chose* my wedding dress.
cite—*to quote*	He enjoys *citing* Shakespeare to illustrate his views.
sight—*seeing, what is seen*	The *sight* of the accident was appalling.
site—*a place where something is located or occurs*	We are seeking a new *site* for the baseball field.
cloth—*fabric or material*	The seats were covered with *cloth,* not vinyl.
clothe—*to put on clothes, to dress*	Her job is to *clothe* the actors for each scene.
coarse—*vulgar,* or	He was shunned because of his *coarse* behavior.
harsh	The sandpaper was very *coarse.*
course—*a path,* or	The ship took its usual *course.*
a plan of study	How many *courses* are you taking this term?
complement—*a completing part*	His wit was a *complement* to her beauty.
compliment—*an expression of praise or admiration*	He received many *compliments* for his fine work.
confidant—*one to whom private matters are confided* (noun)	His priest was his only *confidant.*
confidence—*a feeling of assurance or certainty* (noun)	The ballplayer is developing *confidence* in his ability.
confident—*having confidence in oneself* (adjective)	Her success in business has given her a *confident* manner.
conscience—*the ability to recognize the difference between right and wrong*	The attorney said the criminal lacked a *conscience.*
conscious—*aware*	He was *conscious* that his actions had consequences.
consul—*a government representative*	Americans abroad should keep in touch with the *consuls.*
council—*an assembly that meets for deliberation*	The student *council* met to discuss a campus dress code.
counsel—*advice* (counselor)	The defendant heeded the *counsel* of his friends.
decent—*suitable*	The *decent* thing to do is to admit your error.
descent—*going down*	The *descent* into the cave was dangerous.
dissent—*disagreement*	Two of the justices filed a *dissenting* opinion.
desert (DEZZ-ert)—*an arid area*	I have seen several movies set in the Sahara *desert.*
desert (di-ZERT)—*abandon,* or	The soldier was warned not to *desert* his company.
a reward or punishment	We're certain that execution is a just *desert* for his crime.
dessert (di-ZERT)—*the final course of a meal*	We had strawberry shortcake for *dessert.*
disburse—*to pay out*	This week the bank has *disbursed* a million dollars.
disperse—*to scatter, distribute widely*	The defeated army began to *disperse.*
discomfit—*to upset*	The general's plan was designed to *discomfit* the enemy.
discomfort—*lack of ease*	This starched collar causes *discomfort.*
dual—*double*	Dr. Jekyll had a *dual* personality.
duel—*a contest between two persons or groups*	Aaron Burr and Alexander Hamilton engaged in a *duel.*
elicit—*to draw forth, evoke*	Her performance *elicited* tears from the audience.
illicit—*illegal, unlawful*	He was arrested because of his *illicit* business dealings.
emigrate—*to leave a country*	They *emigrated* from Norway in the nineteenth century.
immigrate—*to enter a country*	Many Irish *immigrated* to the United States.

CONFUSING WORD GROUPS

eminent—*of high rank, prominent, outstanding* .... He was the most *eminent* physician of his time.
imminent—*about to occur, impending* .... His nomination to the board of directors is *imminent.*

epitaph—*an inscription on a tombstone or monument* .... His *epitaph* was taken from a section of the Bible.
epithet—*a term used to describe or characterize the nature of a person or thing* .... The drunk was shouting *epithets* at the passersby.

expand—*to spread out* .... As the staff increases, we can *expand* our office space.
expend—*to use up* .... Don't *expend* all your energy on one project.

fair—*light in color,* .... I have a very *fair* complexion.
reasonable, or .... Your attitude is not a *fair* one.
beauty .... The *fair* princess rode her horse off into the sunset.
fare—*a set price* .... The *fare* is reduced for senior citizens.

farther—used to express *distance* .... John ran *farther* than Bill walked.
further—used to express *time or degree* .... Please go no *further* in your argument.

faze—*to worry or disturb* .... I tried not to let his mean look *faze* me.
phase—*an aspect* .... A crescent is a *phase* of the moon.

find—*to locate* .... Can you *find* the keys?
fine—*good,* .... He is a *fine* cook.
well, ... After being very sick for two weeks, now I feel absolutely *fine.*
precise, or .... The calibration of the scale requires very *fine* measurements.
a penalty .... I received a parking *fine* for an expired meter.
fined—*penalized* .... The judge *fined* him twenty dollars.

formally—*in a formal way* .... He was dressed *formally* for the dinner party.
formerly—*at an earlier time* .... He was *formerly* a delegate to the convention.

fort (fort)—*a fortified place* .... A small garrison was able to hold the *fort.*
forte (FOR-tay)—*a strong point* .... Conducting Wagner's music was Toscanini's *forte.*
forte (FOR-tay)—*a musical term that means loudly* .... The musical composition was meant to be played *forte.*

idle—*unemployed or unoccupied* .... He didn't enjoy remaining *idle* while he recuperated.
idol—*image or object of worship* .... Rock musicians are the *idols* of many teenagers.

in—indicates *inclusion or location*, or .... The spoons are *in* the drawer.
motion within limits .... We were walking *in* the room.
into—*motion toward one place from another* .... I put the spoons *into* the drawer.

incidence—*to the extent or frequency of an occurrence* .... The *incidence* of rabies has decreased since last year.
incidents—*occurrences, events* .... Luckily, the accidents were just minor *incidents.*

it's—the contraction of *it is*, or .... *It's* a very difficult assignment.
the contraction of *it has* .... *It's* been a very long day.
its—possessive pronoun meaning *belonging to it* .... We tried to analyze *its* meaning.

knew—the past tense of *know* .... I *knew* her many years ago.
new—*of recent origin* .... I received a *new* bicycle for my birthday.

know—*to have knowledge or understanding* .... I *know* your brother.
no—a negative used to express *denial or refusal* .... There are *no* more books available.

later—*after a certain time* .... I'll see you *later.*
latter—*the second of two* .... Of the two speakers, the *latter* was more interesting.

lay—*to put* .... I (*lay, laid, have laid*) the gift on the table.
lie—*to recline* .... I (*lie, lay, have lain*) on my blanket on the beach.

lets—the third person singular present of *let* .... He *lets* me park my car in his garage.
let's—contraction for *let us* .... *Let's* go home early today.

lightening—*making less heavy* .... Removing the books will succeed in *lightening* your bag.
lightning—*electric discharge in the atmosphere*, or .... Thunderstorms often produce startling *lightning* bolts.
moving with great speed .... The horse raced *lightning* fast.

loose—*not fastened or restrained*, or .... The dog got *loose* from the leash.
not tight-fitting .... After my diet, the new pants were too *loose* on me.
lose—*to mislay,* .... Try not to *lose* your umbrella.
to be unable to keep, or .... She *lost* her mind.
to be defeated .... They can't *lose* with their new strategy.

mind—*human consciousness* (noun), ... Make up your *mind* which record you want.
to object (verb), or .... We don't *mind* if you bring a friend.
to watch out for .... I cannot go to the movies because I have to *mind* the children.
mine—*a possessive, showing ownership* .... Use your own sled; that one is *mine.*

moral—*good or ethical* (adjective), or .... The trust administrator had a *moral* obligation to the heirs.
a lesson to be drawn (noun) .... The *moral* of the story is that it pays to be honest.
morale—*spirit* .... The team's *morale* improved after the coach's speech.

passed—the past tense of *to pass* .... The week *passed* very quickly.
past—*just preceding or an earlier time*, or .... The *past* week was a very exciting one.
in a direction going close to and then beyond .... We walked down the block and *past* the old mansion.

CONFUSING WORD GROUPS

patience—*enduring calmly with tolerant understanding* .... He has very little *patience* with fools.
patients—*people under medical treatment* .... There are twenty *patients* waiting to see the doctor.

personal—used to describe *an individual's character, conduct, or private affairs* .... He took a *personal* interest in each of the students.
personnel—*an organized body of individuals* .... The store's *personnel* department is on the third floor.

precede—*to come before* .... What events *preceded* the fight?
proceed—*to go ahead* .... We can *proceed* with our next plan.

principal—*chief or main* (adjective), ... His *principal* support comes from the real estate industry.
a leader, or .... The school *principal* called a meeting of the faculty.
a sum of money (noun) .... He earned 10% interest on the *principal* he invested.
principle—*a fundamental truth or belief* .... As a matter of *principle*, he didn't register for the draft.

prophecy—*prediction* (noun, rhymes with *sea)* .... What is the fortune-teller's *prophecy?*
prophesy—*to predict* (verb, rhymes with *sigh)* .... What did the witches *prophesy?*

quiet—*silent, still* .... My brother is very shy and *quiet.*
quit—*to give up or discontinue* .... I *quit* the team last week.
quite—*very, exactly, or to the greatest extent* .... His analysis is *quite* correct.

raise—*to lift, to erect* .... The neighbors helped him *raise* a new barn.
raze—*to tear down* .... The demolition crew *razed* the old building.
rise—*to increase in value*, or .... The price of silver will *rise* again this month.
to get up or move from a lower to a higher position .... If a judge enters a room, everyone must *rise* from their seats.

seem—*to appear* .... He *seems* to be sleeping.
seen—the past participle of *see* .... Have you *seen* your sister lately?

set—*to place something down* (mainly) .... He (*sets, set, has set*) the lamp on the table.
sit—*to seat oneself* (mainly) .... He (*sits, sat, has sat*) on the chair.

stationary—*standing still* .... Long ago, people thought that the earth was *stationary.*
stationery—*writing material* .... We bought our school supplies at the *stationery* store.

suppose—*to assume or guess* .... I *suppose* you will be home early.
supposed—past tense and past participle of *suppose* .... I (*supposed, had supposed*) you would be home early.
supposed—*ought to or should* (followed by *to*) .... I am *supposed to* be in school tomorrow.

than—used to express *comparison* .... Jim ate more *than* we could put on the large plate.
then—used to express *time*, or .... I knocked on the door, and *then* I entered.
a result or consequence .... If you go, *then* I will go too.

their—*belonging to them* .... We took *their* books home with us.
there—*in that place* .... Your books are over *there* on the desk.
they're—the contraction of *they are* .... *They're* coming over for dinner.

though—*although* or .... *Though* he's my friend, I can't recommend him.
as if (preceded by *as*) .... He acted *as though* nothing had happened.
thought—past tense of *to think* (verb), or .... I *thought* you were serious!
an idea (noun) .... It is the *thought* that counts.
through—*in one side and out another*, ... We enjoyed running *through* the snow.
by way of, or .... They met each other *through* a mutual friend.
finished .... My boyfriend and I are completely *through* with one another.

to—*in the direction of* (preposition), or .... We shall go *to* school.
used before a verb to indicate the *infinitive* .... I like *to* swim.
too—*very, also* .... It is *too* hot today.
two—*the numeral 2* .... I ate *two* sandwiches for lunch.

use—*to employ or put into service* .... I want to *use* your chair.
used—past tense and the past participle of *to use* .... I *used* your chair.
used—*in the habit of or accustomed to*, (followed by *to*) .... I am *used to* your comments.
used— an adjective meaning *not new* .... I bought a *used* car.

weather—*atmospheric conditions* .... I don't like the *weather* in San Francisco.
whether—*introduces a choice* .... He inquired *whether* we were going to the dance.
(*whether* should not be preceded by *of* or *as to*)

were—a past tense of *to be* .... They *were* there yesterday.
we're—the contraction of *we are* .... *We're* in charge of the decorations.
where—*place or location* .... *Where* are we meeting your brother?

who's—the contraction of *who is*, or .... *Who's* the next batter?
the contraction of *who has* .... *Who's* already gone to this movie?
whose—*of whom, implying ownership* .... *Whose* notebook is on the desk?

your—a possessive showing *ownership* .... Please give him *your* notebook.
you're—the contraction of *you are* .... *You're* very sweet.

Gerunds vs. Infinitives

The ***infinitive*** is the "to" form of a verb and the ***gerund*** is the "-ing" form of a verb. Both the infinitive and the gerund forms of a verb may be used as nouns. In some circumstances, use of either verb form is correct.

Examples:

Adding an extra room to the house is the next project.
To add an extra room to the house is the next project.

In this example, each sentence is correct. However, in some circumstances, gerunds and infinitives are NOT interchangeable.

WATCH FOR GERUND-INFINITIVE SWITCHING

 Watch for situations in which the infinitive form of the verb has been switched with the gerund form, or vice versa, when it is not appropriate usage in standard written English.

The following list is a summary of common verbs that are often followed by infinitives.

VERBS OFTEN FOLLOWED BY "*TO*" VERB FORMS

advise**	care	encourage**	implore**	prefer*	teach**
afford	cause**	endeavor	instruct**	prepare	teach…how**
agree	caution**	expect*	intend*	pretend	tell**
allow**	challenge**	fail	invite**	proceed	tend
appear	claim	forbid**	learn	promise*	threaten
appoint**	come	force**	manage	prove	urge**
arrange	command**	forget	mean	refuse	use**
ask*	compel**	get (manage,	motivate**	remind**	volunteer
attempt	consent	have the opportunity)	need*	request**	wait
be	convince**	get** (persuade)	oblige**	require**	want*
be supposed	dare*	happen	offer	seem	warn**
beg*	decide	help*	order**	serve	wish*
begin	demand	hesitate	pay*	show…how**	would like*
believe**	deserve	hire**	permit**	struggle	would love*
can't afford	direct**	hope	persuade**	swear	would prefer*
can't wait	enable**	hurry	plan		

* verb + infinitive, or verb + (noun *or* pronoun) + infinitive ** verb + (noun *or* pronoun) + infinitive

Examples:

Our new physics professor prefers to teach by example; that is, by laboratory experience, rather than by theory.
Our dinner reservations were at such an exclusive restaurant, the host required my date to wear a coat and tie.

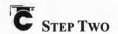

The following list is a summary of common verbs that are often followed by gerunds.

VERBS OFTEN FOLLOWED BY "-*ING*" VERB FORMS

acknowledge	defer	escape	keep (continue)	recommend
admit	delay	excuse	mention	regret
anticipate	deny	explain	mind (object to)	report
appreciate	detest	feel like	miss	resent
avoid	discontinue	finish	postpone	risk
be worth	discuss	forgive	practice	spend time
cannot help	dislike	give up (stop)	prevent	suggest
cannot stand	dispute	go	prohibit	tolerate
celebrate	dread	imagine	quit	understand
complete	endure	involve	recall	
consider	enjoy	justify		

Examples:

My brother recommended bicycling to relieve the knee pain normally caused by running.
In the final written settlement, the company agreed to discontinue testing on animals.

Either infinitives or gerunds may follow certain verbs without changing the original meaning of the verb.

VERBS FOLLOWED BY EITHER INFINITIVES OR GERUNDS WITHOUT CHANGE IN MEANING

attempt	cannot stand	intend	neglect
begin	continue	like	prefer
cannot bear	hate	love	start

Examples:

Following the divorce, she attempted to bring her ex-husband to court on charges of failure to pay alimony.
I had to admit, I preferred eating at a restaurant rather than eating at home when he was cooking!

However, the meanings of certain other verbs do change when followed by infinitives or gerunds.

VERBS FOLLOWED BY EITHER INFINITIVES OR GERUNDS WITH CHANGE IN MEANING

forget	propose	regret	stop
mean	quit	remember	try

Examples:

You can forget having the party here.
I forgot to have the electricity connected by the time we moved into the new house.

Ambiguity in Scope

Watch for ***ambiguity in scope***. This occurs when there is no clear division between two ideas, so that the ideas seem to merge. Note: ✘ = wrong.

Examples:

After the arrest, the accused was charged with resisting arrest and criminal fraud. ✘

The recent changes in the tax law will primarily affect workers who wait tables in restaurants, operate concessions in public places, and drive taxis. ✘

In the first example, the scope of "resisting" is not clear. The sentence can be interpreted to mean that the accused was charged with resisting criminal fraud. The intended scope is made clear by inserting "with": "...charged with resisting arrest and with criminal fraud." The corrected sentence indicates that there are two separate ideas, not one.

In the second example, the use of "and" seems to tie three separate ideas together; that is, it is those workers who do all three jobs who will be affected—clearly not the intent of the sentence. These are three separate ideas that can be clarified by changing "and" to "or," or by making a series of parallel ideas: "...workers who wait tables in restaurants, workers who operate concessions in public places, and workers who drive taxis."

WATCH FOR AMBIGUITY IN SCOPE

Be alert for sentences that run two or more ideas together. Usually the error can be corrected by adding words to clarify the two ideas as distinct and to separate them from one another.

Low-Level Usage

There are a few expressions heard frequently in conversation that are regarded as ***low-level usage*** and are unacceptable in standard written English. The exam measures the ability to recognize the difference between standard and non-standard writing. Note: ✓ = correct, ✘ = wrong.

Example:

She sure is pretty! ✘

She certainly is pretty! ✓

AVOID LOW-LEVEL USAGE

Instead of:	*Say:*	*Instead of:*	*Say:*
ain't	am not; are not; is not	would of	would have
aren't I	am I not	may of	may have
around (2 p.m.)	about (2 p.m.)	might of	might have
being that	since	must of	must have
between you and I	between you and me	off of	off
bunch (of people)	group (of people)	on account of	because
but that	that	plan on	plan to
cannot seem	seems unable	put in	spend, make, or devote
different than	different from	quite a few	many
else than	other than	same as	in the same way as; just as
equally as good	equally good; just as good	sort of	somewhat; rather
have got	have	theirselves	themselves
having took	having taken	try and	try to
in back of	behind	unbeknownst to	without the knowledge of
kind of	somewhat; rather	upwards of	more than
worst kind	very badly	should of	should have

EXERCISE 5

Idioms and Clarity of Expression

DIRECTIONS: In Sentences #1-99, circle the correct word choice. Answers are on page 911.

1. He is the (principal, principle) backer of the play.
2. I hope your company will (accept, except) our offer.
3. We hope to have good (weather, whether) when we are on vacation.
4. Put the rabbit back (in, into) the hat.
5. The attorney will (advice, advise) you of your rights.
6. She is far taller (than, then) I imagined.
7. Are they (all ready, already) to go?
8. She answered the letter on shocking pink (stationary, stationery).
9. What is the (affect, effect) you are trying to achieve?
10. I want to (set, sit) next to my grandfather.
11. He's going to (lay, lie) down for a nap.
12. I'm (all together, altogether) tired of his excuses.
13. He saluted when the flag (passed, past) by.
14. I'd like another portion of (desert, dessert).
15. Try not to (loose, lose) your good reputation.
16. How much will the final examination (effect, affect) my grade?
17. What is it (you're, your) trying to suggest?
18. She's not (use, used) to such cold weather.
19. The cost of the coat will (raise, rise) again.
20. You are (suppose, supposed) to be home at six o'clock.
21. Her cat ran straight for (its, it's) bowl of food.
22. Are you (conscience, conscious) of what you are doing?
23. It will (seen, seem) that we are afraid.
24. His essays are filled with literary (allusions, illusions).
25. This wine will be a good (complement, compliment) to the meal.
26. It's (later, latter) than you think!
27. My cousin has a swimmer's (build, built).
28. I never (knew, new) him before today.
29. She asked her a (personal, personnel) question.
30. The golf (coarse, course) was very crowded.
31. The costume was made from old (cloth, clothe) napkins.
32. The ball carrier was trying to (allude, elude) the tacklers.
33. There are (know, no) more exhibitions planned.
34. I will wait for you in the (ante, anti) room.
35. Her (moral, morale) is very low.
36. Begin the sentence with a (capital, capitol) letter.
37. The fact that he nearly had an accident did not even (faze, phase) him.
38. He earns royalties in (access, excess) of a million dollars a year.
39. Now, may we (precede, proceed) with the debate?
40. Her (fort, forte) is writing lyrics for musical comedy.
41. They wondered how they were going to (disburse, disperse) the huge crowd.
42. Everyone was dressed (formally, formerly) for the dinner party.
43. I am not (adverse, averse) to continuing the discussion at another time.
44. Can something be done to retard the (incidence, incidents) of influenza in that area?
45. "Seeing the film in class will serve a (dual, duel) purpose," he explained.

46. I'm not sure I want to (expand, expend) so much energy on that project.

47. Imagine my (discomfit, discomfort) when she showed up at the party too!

48. He was a famous matinee (idle, idol) many years ago.

49. When did they (emigrate, immigrate) from New York to Paris?

50. I think she is part of a (click, clique) of snobs and creeps.

51. She paid little attention to the fortune-teller's (prophecy, prophesy).

52. The lights went out when the (lightning, lightening) hit the house.

53. I'll provide you (what ever, whatever) assistance you require.

54. We are in (eminent, imminent) danger of losing our reservations.

55. Will she be able to (adapt, adopt) to our way of performing the operation?

56. As we went through the old cemetery, we were fascinated by some of the (epitaphs, epithets).

57. He shared the riches (between, among) Laura, Millie, and Ernestine.

58. The housing law was rewritten for his (advantage, benefit).

59. (Alot, A lot) of the time, he falls asleep at nine o'clock.

60. It was difficult to keep track of the (amount, number) of people who visited him last week.

61. I see him in the park (almost, most) every day.

62. Are you certain that he is (alright, all right) now?

63. She is just beginning to (aggravate, annoy) her mother.

64. He is the school's oldest living (alumni, alumnus).

65. He spotted the riverbank and then guided the canoe up (alongside, alongside of).

66. (Being as, Since) it is Wednesday, we are going to a Broadway matinee.

67. He is (anxious, eager) to be finished with the dental treatment.

68. Where do you want to (meet, meet at)?

69. My aunt just went inside to rest (awhile, a while).

70. It was (about, around) noon when we met for lunch.

71. I brought a (couple, couple of) books for you; both are historical novels.

72. Between (you and I, you and me), I think that her hat is very unbecoming.

73. The (continual, continuous) ticking of the clock was very disconcerting.

74. She (cannot seem, seems unable) to get up early enough to eat breakfast with him.

75. I (assume, expect) that you really earned your salary today.

76. I'm (disinterested, uninterested) in seeing that movie.

77. You must be (every bit as, just as) sleepy as I am.

78. I doubt (that, whether) it will snow today.

79. Sam, Joe, Lou, and Artie have worked with (each other, one another) before.

80. She asked him (if, whether) he wanted to have lunch with her or with her sister.

81. All (humans, human beings) need to take a certain amount of water into their bodies every week.

82. We hope to (conclude, finalize) the deal this month.

83. We were upset when she (flaunted, flouted) her mother's orders.

84. His girlfriend only eats (healthful, healthy) foods.

85. He said such terrible things about her that she is suing him for (libel, slander).

86. I would like to see you in (regard, regards) to the apartment you plan to rent.

87. She is always late for work, (irregardless, regardless) of how early she wakes up in the morning.

88. He'll (loan, lend) you a hand carrying the groceries.

89. The media (are, is) doing the job poorly.

90. The art director was taken (off, off of) the most profitable gallery show.

91. I hope that she will (quit, stop) sending us the job applications.

92. The reason the baby is crying is (because, that) she is hungry.

93. Does he (manage, run) the department efficiently?

94. Anyone who wants to have (his or her, their) conference with me today is invited to meet in my office at ten o'clock.

95. She scored more points than (any, any other) player on the team.

96. His room is very neat (but, while) hers is very messy.

97. He will (try and, try to) be more pleasant to his sister.

98. I shall give it to (whoever, whomever) arrives first.

99. This time, we will not wait (for, on) you for more than ten minutes.

DIRECTIONS: In Sentences #100-114, determine whether the gerund choice (A), the infinitive choice (B), or BOTH the gerund and the infinitive (C), is the correct answer to fill in the blank. Answers are on page 914.

100. After the break, the teacher continued __________.
    A. lecturing
    B. to lecture
    C. BOTH

101. He forgot __________ me at the party last year, so he introduced himself again.
    A. meeting
    B. to meet
    C. BOTH

102. Please remember __________ five minutes early on the day of the test.
    A. arriving
    B. to arrive
    C. BOTH

103. He hesitated __________ for the assignment.
    A. volunteering
    B. to volunteer
    C. BOTH

104. After her speech, the lecturer proceeded __________ questions.
    A. taking
    B. to take
    C. BOTH

105. The politician continued __________ soft money contributions during his campaign.
    A. accepting
    B. to accept
    C. BOTH

106. "I will not tolerate __________," the professor said.
    A. talking
    B. to talk
    C. BOTH

107. Taking sixteen credit hours, the student has neglected __________ some of her essays.
    A. writing
    B. to write
    C. BOTH

108. She has not even begun __________ for the exam even though it is tomorrow.
    A. preparing
    B. to prepare
    C. BOTH

109. The applicant tried __________ for an extension of the deadline, but his request was turned down.
    A. asking
    B. to ask
    C. BOTH

110. The class has been warned not __________.
    A. cheating
    B. to cheat
    C. BOTH

111. The senior anticipates __________ next month.
    A. graduating
    B. to graduate
    C. BOTH

112. Knowing that the deadline is tomorrow has forced me __________ on the project.
    A. concentrating
    B. to concentrate
    C. BOTH

113. Cats cannot stand __________ the sound of a vacuum cleaner.
    A. hearing
    B. to hear
    C. BOTH

114. I do not want to spend any more time __________ these equations.
    A. solving
    B. to solve
    C. BOTH

DIRECTIONS: For Items #115-129, circle the letter of the underlined part of the sentence containing the error and write the correct word or phrase. Answers are on page 914.

115. Economists have established (A) that there i[illegible] [illegible]elation (B)—albeit an indirect one—between the amount (C) of oil imported into this country and the number (D) of traffic accidents.

Correct Word/Phrase: ____________________

116. Ironically, today Elizabeth I and her (A) rival for the English throne, Mary Stuart, whom (B) Elizabeth had (C) executed, lay (D) side by side in Westminster Abbey.

Correct Word/Phrase: ____________________

117. Although the script is interesting and well-written, it is not clear whether (A) it can be adopted (B) for television since the original story contains scenes that could not be broadcast (C) over (D) the public airwaves.

Correct Word/Phrase: ____________________

118. If he had known (A) how difficult law school would be, he would of chosen (B) a different profession or perhaps even have followed (C) the tradition (D) of going into the family business.

Correct Word/Phrase: ____________________

119. When shopping malls and business complexes get built (A), quite often the needs of the handicapped are (B) not considered; as a result, it later becomes necessary to make costly (C) modifications to structures to make them accessible (D) to persons of impaired mobility.

Correct Word/Phrase: ____________________

120. Researchers have found (A) that children experience (B) twice as much deep sleep than (C) adults, a fact which may (D) teach us something about the connection between age and learning ability.

Correct Word/Phrase: ____________________

121. Despite (A) the ample evidence that smoking is hazardous (B) to one's health, many (C) people seem to find the warnings neither frightening or (D) convincing.

Correct Word/Phrase: ____________________

122. No matter how many (A) encores the audience demands, Helen Walker is always willing (B) to sing yet (C) another song which pleases (D) the audience.

Correct Word/Phrase: ____________________

123. In light of recent (A) translations of stone carvings depicting (B) scenes of carnage, scholars are now questioning as to whether (C) the Incas were really (D) a peace-loving civilization.

Correct Word/Phrase: ____________________

124. In galleries containing works of both Gauguin and Cézanne, you will find an equal number (A) of admirers in front of (B) the works of each (C), but most art critics agree that Gauguin is not of the same artistic stature with (D) Cézanne.

Correct Word/Phrase: ____________________

125. The Board of Education will never be (A) fully (B) responsive (C) to the needs of Hispanic children in the school system so long that (D) the mayor refuses to appoint a Hispanic educator to the Board.

Correct Word/Phrase: ____________________

126. The judge sentenced (A) the president of the corporation to ten years in prison for embezzling (B) corporate funds but gave (C) his partner in crime less of a sentence (D).

Correct Word/Phrase: ________________________

127. Scientists have recently discovered (A) that mussels secrete (B) a powerful adhesive that allows them attaching (C) themselves to rocks, concrete pilings, and other (D) stone or masonry structures.

Correct Word/Phrase: ________________________

128. Wall paintings found recently in the caves of Brazil are convincing (A) evidence that cave art developed (B) in the Americas at an earlier time as (C) it (D) did on other continents.

Correct Word/Phrase: ________________________

129. The drop (A) in oil prices and the slump in the computer industry account for (B) the recent raise (C) in unemployment in Texas and the associated (D) decline in the value of real estate in the region.

Correct Word/Phrase: ________________________

Punctuation

Although ***punctuation*** is stressed less than other aspects of standard written English on the exam, it is important to be aware of the principal rules governing punctuation. This section is not intended to give the definitive set of punctuation rules, but rather to provide a basic framework for correct usage.

Commas

USE A COMMA BEFORE COORDINATING CONJUNCTIONS

Coordinating conjunctions ("and," "but," "nor," "or," "for," "yet," "so") join two independent clauses. Use a comma before coordinating conjunctions unless the two clauses are very short.

Note: ✓ = correct, ✗ = wrong.

Examples:

The boy wanted to borrow a book from the library, <u>but</u> the librarian would not allow him to take it until he had paid his fines. ✓

Joe has been very diligent about completing his work, <u>but</u> he has had many problems concerning his punctuality. ✓

I sincerely hope that these exercises prove to be of assistance to you, <u>and</u> I believe that they will help you to make a better showing on your examinations. ✓

Generally, a comma is not used before a subordinate clause that ends a sentence. However, in long, unwieldy sentences, it is acceptable.

If there is no subject following the conjunction, then a comma cannot be used, as this would create a sentence fragment. If there is a subject following the conjunction, but the two clauses are very short, the separating comma may be omitted.

Examples:

She went to the cafe <u>and</u> bought a cup of coffee. ✓

Roy washed the dishes <u>and</u> Helen dried them. ✓

I saw him <u>and</u> I spoke to him. ✓

A restrictive phrase or clause is vital to the meaning of a sentence and cannot be omitted. Do NOT set apart restrictive phrases or clauses with commas.

Example:

A sailboat, without sails, is useless. ✗

A sailboat without sails is useless. ✓

USE COMMAS FOR CLARITY

1. Use a comma if the sentence might be subject to different interpretations without it.
2. Use a comma if a pause would make the sentence clearer and easier to read.

The following examples show how commas change the interpretation of the sentences.

Examples:

The banks that closed yesterday are in serious financial trouble. (Some banks closed yesterday, and those banks are in trouble.)
The banks, which closed yesterday, are in serious financial trouble. (All banks closed yesterday, and all banks are in trouble.)

My cat Leo fell down the laundry chute. (The implication is that I have more than one cat.)
My cat, Leo, fell down the laundry chute. (Here, Leo is an appositive. Presumably, he is the only cat.)

Inside the people were dancing. ✗
Inside, the people were dancing. ✓

After all crime must be punished. ✗
After all, crime must be punished. ✓

Pausing is not infallible, but it is the best resort when all other rules governing use of the comma seem to fail.

USE COMMAS TO SEPARATE COORDINATE ADJECTIVES, WORDS IN A SERIES, AND NOUNS IN DIRECT ADDRESS

1. Coordinate adjectives are adjectives of equal importance that precede the noun that they describe. If the word "and" can be added between the adjectives without changing the sense of the sentence, then use commas.

2. Use a comma between words in a series when three or more elements are present. In such a series, use a comma before "and" or "or." If the series ends in *etc.*, use a comma before *etc.* Do not use a comma after *etc.* in a series, even if the sentence continues.
3. Use commas to set off nouns in direct address. The name of the person addressed is separated from the rest of the sentence by commas.

Examples:

The jolly, fat man stood at the top of the stairs. ✓

He is a wise, charming man. ✓

She is a slow, careful reader. ✓

Coats, umbrellas, and boots should be placed in the closet at the end of the hall. ✓

Pencils, scissors, paper clips, *etc.* belong in your top desk drawer. ✓

Bob, please close the door. ✓

I think, José, you are the one who was chosen. ✓

USE A COMMA TO SEPARATE QUOTATIONS AND INTRODUCTORY PHRASES

1. Use a comma to separate a short, direct quotation from the speaker.
2. Use a comma after an introductory phrase of two or more words.

3. Use a comma after an introductory phrase whenever the comma would aid clarity.
4. Use a comma after introductory gerunds, participles, and infinitives, regardless of their length.

On the other hand, if the subordinate clause follows the main clause, it is not necessary to set it off with a comma.

Examples:

She said, "I must leave work on time today." ✓

"Tomorrow I begin my summer job," he told us. ✓

As a child, she was a tomboy. ✓

She was a tomboy as a child. ✓

To Dan, Phil was a friend as well as a brother. ✓

Phil was a friend as well as a brother to Dan. ✓

In 1998, 300 people lost their lives in an earthquake. ✓

300 people lost their lives in an earthquake in 1998. ✓

When you come home, please ring the bell before opening the door. ✓

Please ring the bell before opening the door when you come home. ✓

Because the prisoner had a history of attempted jailbreaks, he was put under heavy guard. ✓

The prisoner was put under heavy guard because he had a history of attempted jailbreaks. ✓

Finally, commas must be used to set off a phrase or to interrupt the flow of the sentence.

USE PAIRS OF COMMAS TO SET OFF APPOSITIVE, PARENTHETICAL, AND NON-RESTRICTIVE ELEMENTS

1. An appositive phrase follows a noun or pronoun and has the same meaning as that noun or pronoun.

2. Parenthetical expressions are words that interrupt the flow of the sentence ("however," "though," "for instance," "by the way," "to tell the truth," "believe me," "it appears to me," "I am sure," "as a matter of fact") without changing the meaning of the sentence.
3. A non-restrictive element introduces material that is not essential to the sentence and, if removed, will not change the meaning of the original sentence.

Examples:

Mr. Dias, our lawyer, gave us some great advice. ✓

Bob, an industrious and hard-working student, will run for class treasurer. ✓

This book, I believe, is the best of its kind. ✓

Julie and her three dogs, I am sure, will not easily find an apartment to rent. ✓

Sam, who is a very well behaved dog, never strays from the front yard. ✓

Millie, who is a fine student, has a perfect attendance record. ✓

Test for placement of commas in a parenthetical expression by reading the sentence aloud. If you would pause before and after such an expression, then commas should set it off. In general, if you can omit the material without changing the meaning of the main clause, then the material is non-restrictive and it should be set off by commas.

USE COMMAS TO SEPARATE DATES, ADDRESSES, AND SPECIFIC LOCATIONS

Commas, including a comma after the last item, separate the different parts of a date and address.

Examples:

The train will arrive on Friday, February 13, 2003, if it is on schedule. ✓

My new address is: 2040 Winnebago Ave., Apt. #2, Madison, WI. ✓

My daughter traveled from Cambridge, Massachusetts, to Albany, New York, in three hours. ✓

The above rules summarize the most important uses of commas. If you use them in just these situations, then you will not make a serious comma usage mistake.

SITUATIONS IN WHICH NOT TO USE COMMAS

1. Do not use a comma to separate a subject from its verb.
2. Do not use commas to set off restrictive or necessary clauses or phrases.
3. Do not use a comma in place of a conjunction.

Semicolons

Note: ✓ = correct, ✗ = wrong.

USE A SEMICOLON TO SEPARATE TWO COMPLETE IDEAS

A semicolon may be used to separate two complete ideas (independent clauses) in a sentence when the two ideas have a close relationship, and they are NOT connected with a coordinating conjunction.

Example:

The setting sun caused the fields to take on a special glow; all was bathed in a pale light. ✓

The **semicolon** is often used between two or more independent clauses connected by conjunctive adverbs such as "consequently," "therefore," "also," "furthermore," "for example," "however," "nevertheless," "still," "yet," "moreover," and "otherwise." (Note: A comma must follow the adverb.)

USE SEMICOLONS ONLY FOR INDEPENDENT CLAUSES

Unless each clause can function as an independent sentence, it is probably wrong to use a semicolon.

Examples:

He waited at the station for well over an hour; however, no one appeared. ✓

He waited at the station for well over an hour. However, no one appeared. ✓

Anne is working at the front desk on Monday; Ernie will take over on Tuesday. ✓

Anne is working at the front desk on Monday. Ernie will take over on Tuesday. ✓

She waited for her check to arrive in the mail for two weeks; however, the check never appeared. ✓

She waited for her check to arrive in the mail for two weeks. However, the check never appeared. ✓

However, DO NOT use a semicolon between an independent clause and a phrase or subordinate clause.

Example:

She worked extra hours every night; yet, was not able to finish the project on time. ✗

She worked extra hours every night yet was not able to finish the project on time. ✓

To summarize, two main clauses should be separated by a conjunction, by a semicolon, or by a period (two sentences). The same two clauses may be written in any one of three ways, as the following example shows.

Example:

Autumn had come and the trees were almost bare. ✓

Autumn had come; the trees were almost bare. ✓

Autumn had come. The trees were almost bare. ✓

If you are uncertain about how to use a semicolon to connect independent clauses, write two sentences instead.

USE A SEMICOLON TO SEPARATE A SERIES OF PHRASES CONTAINING COMMAS OR A SERIES OF NUMBERS

1. Use a semicolon to separate a series of phrases or clauses, each of which contains commas.
2. Use a semicolon to avoid confusion with numbers.

Examples:

The old gentleman's heirs were Margaret Whitlock, his half-sister; James Bagley, the butler; William Frame, companion to his late cousin, Robert Bone; and his favorite charity, the Salvation Army. ✓

Add the following prices: $.25; $7.50; and $12.89. ✓

Colons

The ***colon*** is always used in the following situations. Note: ✓ = correct, ✗ = wrong.

RULES FOR SITUATIONS REQUIRING A COLON

1. A colon should be placed after the salutation in a business letter.
2. Use a colon to separate hours from minutes.
3. The colon is used to precede a list of three or more items or a long quotation.
4. A colon should be used to introduce a question.
5. A colon is generally used in places where a full stop would leave the beginning of the sentence unchanged in meaning.

Examples:

Dear Board Member: ✓

The eclipse occurred at 10:36 A.M. ✓

Many people refer to four, rather than three, branches of government: executive, judicial, legislative, and media. ✓

My question is this: are you willing to punch a time clock? ✓

Avoid using the colon directly after a verb or when it interrupts the natural flow of language.

Examples:

We played: volleyball, badminton, football, and tag. ✗

We played volleyball, badminton, football, and tag. ✓

We purchased: apples, pears, bananas, and grapes. ✗

We purchased apples, pears, bananas, and grapes. ✓

DO NOT USE COLONS TO CALL ATTENTION IF ALREADY SIGNALED

A colon may be used to introduce or to call attention to elaboration or explanation. However, do not use colons after expressions such as "like," "for example," "such as," and "that is." In fact, colons are intended to replace these terms.

Be careful not to use a colon to introduce or call attention to material that is already signaled by some other element of the sentence.

Example:

We did many different things on our vacation, such as: hiking, camping, biking, canoeing, and kayaking. ✗

We did many different things on our vacation, such as hiking, camping, biking, canoeing, and kayaking. ✓

We did many different things on our vacation: hiking, camping, biking, canoeing, and kayaking. ✓

Periods

RULES FOR SITUATIONS REQUIRING A PERIOD

1. Use a period at the end of a sentence that makes a statement, gives a command, or makes a "polite request" in the form of a question that does not require an answer.
2. Use a period after an abbreviation and after the initial in a person's name.

Examples:

He is my best friend.
There are thirty days in September.
Would you please hold the script so that I may see if I have memorized my lines.
Gen. Robert E. Lee led the Confederate forces.

Note: DO NOT use a period in postal service name abbreviations such as AZ (Arizona) or MI (Michigan).

Exclamation and Question Marks

RULES FOR SITUATIONS REQUIRING EXCLAMATION MARKS

Use exclamation marks after expressions showing strong emotion or issuing a command. Use an exclamation mark only to express strong feeling or emotion or to imply urgency.

Examples:

Wonderful! You won the lottery!
Oh no! I won't go!

RULES FOR SITUATIONS REQUIRING QUESTION MARKS

Use a question mark after a request for information. A question mark is used only after a direct question. A period is used after an indirect question.

Note: A question must end with a ***question mark*** even if the question does not encompass the entire sentence.

Examples:

At what time does the last bus leave?
"Daddy, are we there yet?" the child asked.
Did you take the examination on Friday?
The instructor wanted to know if you took the examination on Friday.

Dashes

The material following the ***dash*** usually directs the reader's attention to the content that precedes it. Unless this material ends a sentence, dashes, like parentheses, must be used in pairs.

RULES FOR SITUATIONS REQUIRING A DASH

1. Use a dash for emphasis or to set off an explanatory group of words.

2. Use a dash before a word or group of words that indicates a summation or reversal of what preceded it.
3. Use a dash to mark a sudden break in thought that leaves a sentence unfinished.

Examples:

The tools of his trade—probe, mirror, and cotton swabs—were neatly arranged on the dentist's tray.
Patience, sensitivity, understanding, and empathy—these are the marks of a friend.
He was not pleased with—in fact, he was completely hostile toward—the takeover.

Dashes in sentences have a function that is similar to commas when they are used to set off parenthetical remarks. The difference between the two is a matter of emphasis. The dashes mark a more dramatic shift or interruption of thought. Do not mix dashes and commas.

Hyphens

RULES FOR SITUATIONS REQUIRING A HYPHEN

1. Use a hyphen with a compound modifier that precedes the noun.
2. Use a hyphen with fractions that serve as adjectives or adverbs.

The following examples demonstrate situations in which it is correct to use a ***hyphen*** and situations in which it is NOT correct to use a hyphen.

Examples:

There was a <u>sit-in</u> demonstration at the office.
We will <u>sit in</u> the auditorium.
I purchased a <u>four-cylinder</u> car.
I purchased a car with <u>four cylinders</u>.

Quotation Marks

Note: ✓ = correct, ✗ = wrong.

WHEN TO USE QUOTATION MARKS

1. Use quotation marks to enclose the actual words of the speaker or writer.

2. Use quotation marks to emphasize words used in a special or unusual sense.
3. Use quotation marks to set off titles of short themes or parts of a larger work.

Examples:

Jane said, "There will be many people at the party." ✓

He kept using the phrase "you know" throughout his conversation. ✓

"Within You, Without You" is my favorite song on the *Sgt. Pepper's Lonely Hearts Club Band* album by The Beatles. ✓

WHEN NOT TO USE QUOTATION MARKS

1. Do not use quotation marks for indirect quotations.
2. Do not use quotation marks to justify a poor choice of words.

Examples:

He said that "he would be happy to attend the meeting." ✗

He said that he would be happy to attend the meeting. ✓

I gave her research summary article a low score because I didn't think she "got it right." ✗

I gave her research summary article a low score because I didn't think she understood the methods or results. ✓

PUNCTUATION RULES FOR SITUATIONS WITH QUOTATIONS

1. Always place periods and commas inside quotation marks.
2. Place question marks inside quotation marks if it is part of a quotation. If the entire sentence, including the quotation, is a question, place the question mark outside the quotation marks.
3. Place exclamation marks inside quotation marks if it is part of a quotation. If the entire sentence, including the quotation, is an exclamation, place the exclamation mark outside the quotation marks.
4. Always place colons and semicolons outside quotation marks.

Examples:

The principal said, "Cars parked in the fire lane will be ticketed." ✓

The first chapter of *The Andromeda Strain* is entitled "The Country of Lost Borders." ✓

My favorite poem is "My Last Duchess," a dramatic monologue written by Robert Browning. ✓

Three stories in Kurt Vonnegut's *Welcome to the Monkey House* are "Harrison Bergeron," "Next Door," and "Epicac." ✓

Mother asked earlier tonight, "Did you take out the garbage?" ✓

Do you want to go to the movies and see "Jurassic Park"? ✓

The sentry shouted, "Drop your gun!" ✓

Save us from our "friends"! ✓

My favorite poem is "My Last Duchess"; this poem is a dramatic monologue written by Robert Browning. ✓

He was quoted as supporting the investigation in the "Washington Post": "I don't know of any proof of misappropriation of funds; however, I support a full investigation into any possible wrongdoing by government officials." ✓

Apostrophes

Errors of ***apostrophe*** usage usually occur when a paper isn't proofread or when a writer isn't sure how to use an apostrophe correctly. The apostrophe is used for possession and contraction. Note: ✓ = correct, ✗ = wrong.

USE APOSTROPHES FOR POSSESSION

 Use apostrophes to indicate the possessive case of nouns. DO NOT use apostrophes with possessive pronouns (*e.g.*, "yours," "hers," "ours," "theirs," and "whose").

Examples:

lady's = belonging to the lady ✓

ladies' = belonging to the ladies ✓

To test for correct placement of the apostrophe, read the apostrophe as "of the."

Examples:

childrens' = of the childrens ✗

children's = of the children ✓

The placement rule applies at all times, even with regard to compound nouns separated by hyphens and with regard to entities made up of two or more names.

Examples:

Lansdale, Jackson, and Smith's law firm = the law firm belonging to Lansdale, Jackson, and Smith ✓

Brown and Sons' delivery truck = the delivery truck of Brown and Sons ✓

If the noun does not end in "s"—whether singular or plural—add "'s"; if the noun ends in "s," simply add the apostrophe.

Examples:

Socrates's philosophy ✗

Socrates' philosophy ✓

Johnsons's house ✗

Johnsons' house ✓

USE APOSTROPHES FOR CONTRACTIONS

 Use an apostrophe to indicate a contraction; insert the apostrophe in place of the omitted letter(s). It is NOT acceptable in standard written English to begin a paragraph with a contraction.

Examples:

haven't = have not ✓

o'clock = of the clock ✓

class of '85 = class of 1985 ✓

Be careful with "its" and "it's." "It's" is the contraction of "it is." "Its" is the third person possessive pronoun. Also, do NOT confuse "they're" ("they are"), "their" (possessive), and "there" (preposition).

Example:

The cat knows when <u>it's</u> time for <u>its</u> bath. ✓

They're happy to be done with <u>their</u> work. ✓

EXERCISE 6

Punctuation

DIRECTIONS: Punctuate Sentences #1-55 with additional commas, semicolons, periods, exclamation marks, question marks, quotation marks, dashes, hyphens, and apostrophes *if necessary.* Answers are on page 914.

1. He was not aware that you had lost your passport
2. Did you report the loss to the proper authorities
3. I suppose you had to fill out many forms
4. What a nuisance
5. I hate doing so much paper work
6. Did you ever discover where the wallet was
7. I imagine you wondered how it was misplaced
8. Good for you
9. At least you now have your passport
10. What will you do if it happens again
11. I dont know if they are coming though I sent them an invitation weeks ago
12. Neurology is the science that deals with the anatomy physiology and pathology of the nervous system
13. Nursery lore like everything human has been subject to many changes over long periods of time
14. Bob read Joyces Ulysses to the class everyone seemed to enjoy the reading
15. In order to provide more living space we converted an attached garage into a den
16. Because he is such an industrious student he has many friends
17. I dont recall who wrote A Midsummer Nights Dream
18. In the writing class students learned about coordinating conjunctions and but so or yet for and nor
19. Those who do not complain are never pitied is a familiar quotation by Jane Austen
20. Howard and his ex wife are on amicable terms
21. Her last words were call me on Sunday and she jumped on the train
22. He is an out of work carpenter
23. This is what is called a pregnant chad
24. Come early on Monday the teacher said to take the exit exam
25. The dog mans best friend is a companion to many
26. The winner of the horse race is to the best of my knowledge Silver
27. Every time I see him the dentist asks me how often I floss
28. The officer was off duty when he witnessed the crime
29. Anna Karenina is my favorite movie
30. Red white and blue are the colors of the American flag
31. Stop using stuff in your essays its too informal
32. She was a self made millionaire
33. The Smiths who are the best neighbors anyone could ask for have moved out
34. My eighteen year old daughter will graduate this spring
35. Dracula lived in Transylvania
36. The students were told to put away their books
37. Begun while Dickens was still at work on Pickwick Papers Oliver Twist was published in 1837 and is now one of the authors most widely read works
38. Given the great difficulties of making soundings in very deep water it is not surprising that few such soundings were made until the middle of this century
39. Did you finishing writing your thesis prospectus on time
40. The root of modern Dutch was once supposed to be Old Frisian but the general view now is that the characteristic forms of Dutch are at least as old as those of Old Frisian

41. Moose once scarce because of indiscriminate hunting are protected by law and the number of moose is once again increasing

42. He ordered a set of books several records and a film almost a month ago

43. Perhaps the most interesting section of New Orleans is the French Quarter which extends from North Rampart Street to the Mississippi River

44. Writing for a skeptical and rationalizing age Shaftesbury was primarily concerned with showing that goodness and beauty are not determined by revelation authority opinion or fashion

45. We tried our best to purchase the books but we were completely unsuccessful even though we went to every bookstore in town

46. A great deal of information regarding the nutritional requirements of farm animals has been accumulated over countless generations by trial and error however most recent advances have come as the result of systematic studies at schools of animal husbandry

47. Omoo Melvilles sequel to Typee appeared in 1847 and went through five printings in that year alone

48. Go to Florence for the best gelato in all of Italy said the old man to the young tourist

49. Although the first school for African Americans was a public school established in Virginia in 1620 most educational opportunities for African Americans before the Civil War were provided by private agencies

50. As the climate of Europe changed the population became too dense for the supply of food obtained by hunting and other means of securing food such as the domestication of animals were necessary

51. In Faulkners poetic realism the grotesque is somber violent and often inexplicable in Caldwells writing it is lightened by a ballad like humorous sophisticated detachment

52. The valley of the Loire a northern tributary of the Loire at Angers abounds in rock villages they occur in many other places in France Spain and northern Italy

53. The telephone rang several times as a result his sleep was interrupted

54. He has forty three thousand dollars to spend however once that is gone he will be penniless

55. Before an examination do the following review your work get a good nights sleep eat a balanced breakfast and arrive on time to take the test

Capitalization and Spelling

Capitalization

CAPITALIZE FIRST WORD OF SENTENCES, PROPER NAMES, DAYS, MONTHS, AND HOLIDAYS

 Capitalize the first word of a sentence, all proper names, the days of the week, the months of the year, and holidays.

Note that the seasons are NOT capitalized.

Examples:

With cooperation, a depression can be avoided.
America, General Motors, Abraham Lincoln, First Congregational Church
The check was mailed on Thursday, the day before Christmas.
In Florida, winter is mild.

CAPITALIZE FIRST WORD AND NOUNS IN SALUTATIONS

 Capitalize the first word and all nouns in the salutation of a letter and the first word of the complimentary close of a letter.

Examples:

Dear Mr. Jones,
My dear Mr. Jones,
Truly yours,
Very truly yours,

CAPITALIZE FIRST AND IMPORTANT WORDS IN TITLES

 Capitalize the first and all other important words in a title.

Example:

The Art of Salesmanship

CAPITALIZE WORDS WHEN PART OF A PROPER NAME

 Capitalize a word used as part of a proper name.

Examples:

William Street
That street is narrow.
Morningside Terrace
We have a terrace apartment.

CAPITALIZE TITLES WHEN REFERRING TO A PARTICULAR PERSON

 Capitalize titles when they refer to a particular official or family member.

Examples:

The report was read by Secretary Marshall.
Our secretary, Miss Shaw, is ill.
Let's visit Uncle Harry.
I have three uncles.

CAPITALIZE "NORTH," "SOUTH," "WEST," AND "EAST"
WHEN REFERRING TO A PARTICULAR REGION

 Capitalize points of a compass when they refer to particular regions of a country but not when they refer to direction in general

Examples:

We're going to the South next week.
New York is south of Albany.
They honeymooned in the Far East.
She transferred here from a university in the Middle East.

CAPITALIZE FIRST WORD IN QUOTATIONS

 Capitalize the first word of a direct quotation.

Example:

Alexander Pope wrote, "A little learning is a dangerous thing."

When a direct quotation sentence is broken, the first word of the second half of the sentence is not capitalized.

Example:

"Don't phone," Lilly told me, "because it will be too late."

CAPITALIZE LANGUAGES

 Capitalize languages, but DO NOT capitalize the names of other school subjects.

Example:

I am enrolled in English, math, history, and French.

Class titles, however, are still titles, so capitalize the first and important words.

Example:

I need four math credits, so I will take Euclidian Geometry.

Spelling

1. "I" Before "E" Rule

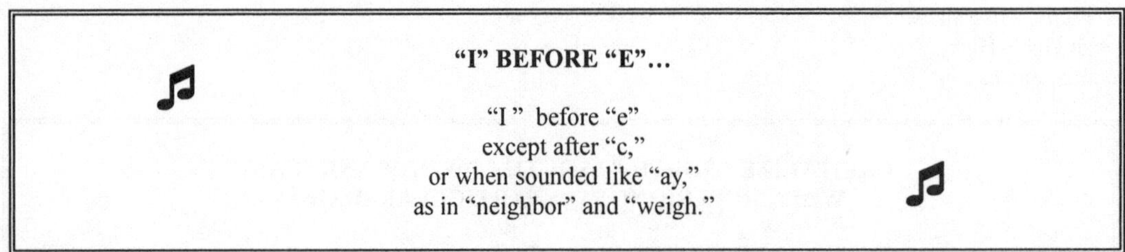

"I" BEFORE "E"...

"I " before "e"
except after "c,"
or when sounded like "ay,"
as in "neighbor" and "weigh."

Examples:

grieve, relief, believe, chief, piece, briefcase
receive, deceive, receipt
neighbor, weight, reign, freight

The "i" before "e" rule has the following three exceptions.

WATCH FOR EXCEPTIONS TO THE "I" BEFORE "E" RULE

1. Words in which both vowels are pronounced use "ie" after "c," as in "society."
2. Words with a "shen" sound use "ie" after "c," as in "sufficient."
3. Other exceptions are: "either" or "neither," "foreign," "height," "seize," "their," and "weird."

2. Adding Suffixes

It is important to know when to double consonants when adding suffixes such as "-ing" and "-ed."

RULES FOR DOUBLING CONSONANTS WHEN ADDING SUFFIXES

1. Double the final consonant of a one-syllable word when the final consonant is preceded by a single vowel.
2. For words with more than one syllable, follow the first rule only when the accent is on the last syllable.
3. DO NOT double the final consonant when the word already ends in two consonants.
4. DO NOT double the final consonant if the consonant is preceded by two vowels.
5. For words ending with "c," add a "k" before adding a suffix.

These rules apply only when the added suffix begins with a vowel. If the suffix begins with a consonant, do NOT double the last letter of the word. Note: If the suffix begins with a vowel and the word ends with a vowel, the last letter of the word should be dropped when the suffix is added.

Examples:

stop ⇒ stopped; pin ⇒ pinned; fit ⇒ fitter; sit ⇒ sitting; nag ⇒ nagging; fat ⇒ fatten
infer ⇒ inferred; permit ⇒ permitted; bellow ⇒ bellowed; frighten ⇒ frightened; commit ⇒ committing
bark ⇒ barked; wink ⇒ winked; work ⇒ worked
soil ⇒ soiled; fail ⇒ failed; heat ⇒ heated
picnic ⇒ picnicking

3. Forming Plurals

RULES FOR FORMING PLURALS OF WORDS

1. Add "-s."
2. Change "y" to "i" and add "-es" for words in which "y" is preceded by a consonant.
3. Add "-s" for words ending in "y" when "y" is preceded by a vowel.
4. For nouns ending in "-ess," add "-es."

Examples:

walnut ⇒ walnuts; salad ⇒ salads
lady ⇒ ladies; enemy ⇒ enemies; policy ⇒ policies; city ⇒ cities
valley ⇒ valleys; play ⇒ plays
princess ⇒ princesses; hostess ⇒ hostesses

EXERCISE 7

Capitalization and Spelling

DIRECTIONS: Indicate whether Words #1-25 should be capitalized. Answers are on page 917.

1. thanksgiving ☐ Yes ☐ No
2. flower ☐ Yes ☐ No
3. airplane ☐ Yes ☐ No
4. ohio ☐ Yes ☐ No
5. france ☐ Yes ☐ No
6. muhammad ali ☐ Yes ☐ No
7. magician ☐ Yes ☐ No
8. tin can ☐ Yes ☐ No
9. rocky mountains ☐ Yes ☐ No
10. governor davis ☐ Yes ☐ No
11. pine tree ☐ Yes ☐ No
12. overcoat ☐ Yes ☐ No
13. television ☐ Yes ☐ No
14. michael jordan ☐ Yes ☐ No
15. arsonist ☐ Yes ☐ No
16. uncle ☐ Yes ☐ No
17. token ☐ Yes ☐ No
18. hamburger ☐ Yes ☐ No
19. halloween ☐ Yes ☐ No
20. morning ☐ Yes ☐ No
21. central park ☐ Yes ☐ No
22. ten o'clock ☐ Yes ☐ No
23. january ☐ Yes ☐ No
24. afternoon ☐ Yes ☐ No
25. monday ☐ Yes ☐ No

DIRECTIONS: For Words #26-35, fill in the missing letters, "*i*" and "*e*," in the appropriate order. Answers are on page 917.

26. f_______ld
27. conc_____t
28. sl_______gh
29. v________n
30. c______ling
31. n_______ce
32. sc_____ntific
33. s______zure
34. consc___ntious
35. anc_______nt

DIRECTIONS: For Words #36-55, add the appropriate suffix. Answers are on page 918.

36. fib + ing = ____________________
37. beg + ing = ____________________
38. control + able = ____________________
39. commit + ment = ____________________
40. color + ful = ____________________
41. stop + ing = ____________________
42. big + est = ____________________
43. quit + ing = ____________________
44. rob + ing = ____________________
45. glad + ly = ____________________
46. bride + al = ____________________
47. force + ible = ____________________
48. force + ful = ____________________
49. imagine + ary = ____________________
50. hope + less = ____________________
51. true + ly = ____________________

52. remove + ing = ____________________

53. life + like = ____________________

54. like + ly = ____________________

55. service + able = ____________________

DIRECTIONS: For each group of Words #56-85, there is one misspelling. Find the misspelled word and spell it correctly on the line provided. Answers are on page 918.

56. carriage, conseeince, association ____________________

57. achievement, chief, aviater ____________________

58. alltogether, almost, already ____________________

59. annual, desireable, despair ____________________

60. independance, ninety, nevertheless ____________________

61. billian, weather, rhyme ____________________

62. quiet, lying, naturaly ____________________

63. speach, straight, valleys ____________________

64. transfered, tragedy, reference ____________________

65. received, reciept, reception ____________________

66. calender, appropriately, casualties ____________________

67. affidavid, colossal, development ____________________

68. diptheria, competent, bigoted ____________________

69. prevelent, precipice, nauseous ____________________

70. fundamentally, obedience, bookeeper ____________________

71. tenant, repetetious, serviceable ____________________

72. cloudiness, donkies, babyish ____________________

73. wholly, wirey, strenuous ____________________

74. successfully, renowned, propagander ____________________

75. recuperate, vacuum, specificaly ____________________

76. innoculate, aeronautics, saboteur ____________________

77. prejudice, panacea, amethist ____________________

78. laringytis, recipe, psychological ____________________

79. scissors, supremacy, cinamon ____________________

80. rarify, resind, thousandth ____________________

81. superstitious, surgeon, irresistably ____________________

82. sophomore, brocoli, synonym ____________________

83. questionnaire, mayonaise, prophecy ____________________

84. jeopardy, narrative, monotonous ____________________

85. primitive, obedience, mocassin ____________________

Math Skills Review

TARGETED EDUCATIONAL SOLUTIONS.

Cambridge Course Concept Outline
MATH SKILLS REVIEW

Whole Numbers

Real Number System

The following diagram outlines the subsets of the ***real number system***. You should be familiar with the terminology and numbers contained in several of these subsets. Each set is a subset of the one above it; for example, the set of natural numbers is a subset of the set of whole numbers, integers, rational numbers, and real numbers. Natural numbers are whole numbers, integers, rational numbers, and real numbers. Refer back to this diagram as often as necessary.

Real Numbers

Real numbers are all the numbers on the number line including fractions, integers, radicals, negatives, and zero.

Rational Numbers

Rational numbers can be expressed as a ratio of two integers $\left(e.g., \frac{2}{7}, -\frac{8}{2}, \frac{9}{10}\right)$. A rational number can be expressed as a number that terminates (*e.g.*, −1, 0, 35, −5.25, 8.0262) or as a non-terminating decimal with a pattern (*e.g.*, 4.333..., 3.2525..., −0.19621962...). Also, $\sqrt{4}$ is a rational number since it can be expressed as $\frac{2}{1}$, or 2.

Irrational Numbers

Irrational numbers cannot be expressed as a ratio of two integers. No pattern exists when irrational numbers are expressed as decimals and they do not terminate (*e.g.*, $\sqrt{2}$, $-\sqrt{3}$, π).

Integers

Integers are signed (positive and negative) whole numbers and the number zero: {..., −2, −1, 0, 1, ...}.

Whole Numbers

Whole numbers are the numbers used for counting and the number zero: {0, 1, 2, 3, ...}.

Natural or Counting Numbers

Natural numbers are the numbers used for counting: {1, 2, 3, ...}.

Terms and Operations

For simplicity, we will introduce the terms and operational concepts associated with all numbers using ***whole numbers***. ***Whole numbers*** are the numbers used for counting, plus the number zero: {0, 1, 2, 3, 4, ...}. Later we will return to the other numbers of the real number system, including fractions, signed numbers, and irrational numbers.

1. Basic Terms

sum (total): The result of adding numbers together. The ***sum***, or total, of 2 and 3 is 5: $2 + 3 = 5$.
difference: The result of subtracting one number from another. The ***difference*** between 5 and 2 is 3: $5 - 2 = 3$.
product: The result of multiplying numbers together. The ***product*** of 2 and 3 is 6: $2 \cdot 3 = 6$.
quotient: The result of dividing one number by another. The ***quotient*** when 6 is divided by 2 is 3: $6 \div 2 = 3$.
remainder: In division, if the quotient is not itself a whole number, the result can be written as a whole number quotient plus a whole number remainder. For example, $7 \div 3 = 2$, plus a ***remainder*** of 1.

2. Symbols of Inclusion

Sets of ***parentheses***, ***brackets***, and ***braces*** indicate the order in which operations are to be performed. The innermost symbol of inclusion indicates which operation should be executed first. Generally, operations in parentheses are done first, operations in brackets are done second, and operations in braces are done third. Parentheses, brackets, and braces have the same meaning—three different symbols are used for clarity.

Examples:

1. $(2+3) \cdot 4 = 20$
2. $2 + (3 \cdot 4) = 14$
3. $\frac{(2 \cdot 3) \cdot (2+1)}{3 \cdot (5-4)} = \frac{(6) \cdot (3)}{3 \cdot (1)} = \frac{18}{3} = 6$

A particularly complex statement might use parentheses, brackets, and even braces if necessary. With problems such as these, work from the inside out. Start with the operations within parentheses; then do the operations within the brackets; and finally complete the indicated operations.

Example:

$$\{[(2 \cdot 3) - 5] \cdot 1\} + [2 \cdot (4-1)] = (6-5) + (2 \cdot 3) = 1 + 6 = 7$$

3. Order of Operations

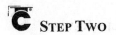

Parentheses, brackets, and braces eliminate ambiguity, but they do not always dictate the order in which operations must be done. Use this mnemonic to remember the order of operations for simplifying expressions: *Please Excuse My Dear Aunt Sally.*

Please: Parentheses, brackets, braces
Excuse: Exponents, radicals
My: Multiplication*
Dear: Division*
Aunt: Addition*
Sally: Subtraction*

*Remember: add/subtract and multiply/divide in expressions as the operations occur from left to right.

Examples:

1. $6 + 4 \cdot 3 - 5 = 6 + 12 - 5 = 18 - 5 = 13$
2. $[2(3+4)](3 \cdot 2) = [2(7)](6) = (14)(6) = 84$
3. $\{(2+7) - [(8 \cdot 6) \div 2] + 25\}\{[2 + 3(2-1)] \div 5\} = [(2+7) - (48 \div 2) + 25]\{[2 + 3(1)] \div 5\} = [(2+7) - 24 + 25]$
$(5 \div 5) = (9 + 25 - 24)(1) = (9 + 1) = 10$

4. Factoring and Canceling

An important point to make is that even when multiplication and addition are combined, you have a choice about order of operations. In the following example, most people would probably do the addition first and then the multiplication. It is also permissible, however, to do the multiplication first.

Example:

$5(2 + 3 + 4) = 5(9) = 45$
$5(2 + 3 + 4) = 5(2) + 5(3) + 5(4) = 10 + 15 + 20 = 45$

Thus, $10 + 15 + 20$ is equal to $5(2) + 5(3) + 5(4)$, which in turn equals $5(2 + 3 + 4)$. This reverse multiplication process is called ***factoring***. Factoring can be a tremendous labor-saving device. While you may be tempted to carry out the operations as indicated using a calculator, it is almost always more efficient to first simplify expressions by factoring.

Example:

$(723)(34) - (723)(33) = 24{,}582 - 23{,}859 = 723$
$(723)(34) - (723)(33) = 723(34 - 33) = 723(1) = 723$

Factoring can be combined with division for even greater simplifying power. Division of factors common to both the numerator and the denominator is called ***canceling***.

Example:

$$\frac{24 + 36}{12} = \frac{12(2 + 3)}{12} = (1)(2 + 3) = 5$$

In this case, 12 can be factored from both 24 and 36. It is then possible to divide 12 by 12, which is 1.

Factors, Multiples, and Primes

Numbers that evenly divide another number are called the ***factors*** of that number. If a number is evenly divisible by another number, it is considered a ***multiple*** of that number. 1, 2, 3, 4, 6, and 12 are all factors of 12: 12 is a multiple of 2, a multiple of 3, and so on. Some numbers are not evenly divisible except by 1 and themselves. A number such as this is called a ***prime*** number. For example, 13 is evenly divisible by 1 and 13 but not by 2 through 12. Note: 1 is NOT considered a prime number even though it is not evenly divisible by any other number. The following are examples of prime numbers: 2, 3, 5, 7, 11, 13, 17, 19, and 23.

Example:

Let $D = 120$. How many positive factors, including 1 and 120, does D have?
➢ Express 120 using prime factors: $120 = 2(2)(2)(3)(5) = 2^3(3)(5)$. The exponents of the prime factors 2, 3, and 5, are 3, 1, and 1, respectively. Add 1 to each exponent and multiple the results together: $(3 + 1)(1 + 1)(1 + 1) = (4)(2)(2) = 16$.

Odd and Even Numbers

An ***odd number*** is not evenly divisible by 2; an ***even number*** is a number that is divisible by 2. Any number with a last digit that is 0, 2, 4, 6, or 8 is divisible by 2 and is even. Any number with a last digit that is 1, 3, 5, 7, or 9 is not evenly divisible by 2 and is odd. Zero is considered an even number. The following are important principles that govern the behavior of odd and even numbers.

PRINCIPLES OF ODD AND EVEN NUMBERS

1. EVEN ± EVEN = EVEN
2. EVEN ± ODD = ODD
3. ODD ± EVEN = ODD
4. ODD ± ODD = EVEN
5. EVEN • EVEN = EVEN
6. EVEN • ODD = EVEN
7. ODD • EVEN = EVEN
8. ODD • ODD = ODD

Examples:

1. $2 + 4 = 6; 2 - 4 = -2$
2. $4 + 3 = 7; 4 - 3 = 1$
3. $3 + 4 = 7; 3 - 4 = -1$
4. $3 + 5 = 8; 3 - 5 = -2$
5. $2 \cdot 4 = 8$
6. $2 \cdot 3 = 6$
7. $3 \cdot 2 = 6$
8. $3 \cdot 5 = 15$

The rules for multiplication do NOT apply to division. For example, if you divide the even number 4 by the even number 8, the result is $\frac{1}{2}$. Odd and even are characteristics of whole numbers and negative integers, but not fractions. A fraction is neither odd nor even.

Consecutive Integers

Consecutive integers immediately follow one another. For example, 3, 4, 5, and 6 are consecutive integers, but 3, 7, 21, and 45 are not. In a string of consecutive integers, the next number is always one more than the preceding number. Thus, if n is the first number in a string of consecutive integers, the second number is $n + 1$, the fourth number is $n + 3$, and so on.

1st	2nd	3rd	4th
n	$n+1$	$n+2$	$n+3$
3	4	5	6

We can also speak of ***consecutive even integers*** and ***consecutive odd integers***. 2, 4, 6, and 8 are consecutive even integers; 3, 5, 7, and 9 are consecutive odd integers. If n is the first number in a string of consecutive even or odd integers, the second number is $n + 2$, the third number is $n + 4$, the fourth number is $n + 6$, and so on.

1st	2nd	3rd	4th
n	$n+2$	$n+4$	$n+6$
3	5	7	9
4	6	8	10

Do not be confused by the fact that the sequence for consecutive odd integers proceeds as n, $n + 2$, $n + 4$, *etc.* Even though 2, 4, *etc.* are even numbers, $n + 2$, $n + 4$, *etc.* will be odd numbers when the starting point, n, is odd.

NOTE: The ACT, PLAN, and EXPLORE allow calculators. Therefore, it is important that you learn how to use a calculator and bring the same calculator with you to the exam. Using a calculator provides greater accuracy and often saves valuable test time.

EXERCISE 1

Whole Numbers

DIRECTIONS: Choose the correct answer to each of the following items. Answers are on page 920.

1. Subtracting 1 from which digit in the number 12,345 will decrease the value of the number by 1,000?

   A. 1 C. 3 E. 5
   B. 2 D. 4

2. Adding 3 to which digit in the number 736,124 will increase the value of the number by 30,000?

   A. 7 C. 6 E. 4
   B. 3 D. 2

3. Adding 1 to each digit of the number 222,222 will increase the value of the number by how much?

   A. 333,333 C. 100,000 E. 1
   B. 111,111 D. 10

4. $(1 \cdot 10{,}000) + (2 \cdot 1{,}000) + (3 \cdot 100) + (4 \cdot 10) + (5 \cdot 1) = ?$

   A. 5,000 C. 12,345 E. 543,210
   B. 15,000 D. 54,321

5. $(1 \cdot 1) + (1 \cdot 10) + (1 \cdot 100) + (1 \cdot 1{,}000) + (1 \cdot 10{,}000) = ?$

   A. 5 C. 11,111 E. 1,111,100
   B. 5,000 D. 111,110

6. $(1 \cdot 100{,}000) + (2 \cdot 10{,}000) + (3 \cdot 1{,}000) = ?$

   A. 123 C. 12,300 E. 1,230,000
   B. 1,230 D. 123,000

7. $(2 \cdot 1{,}000) + (3 \cdot 100) + (1 \cdot 10{,}000) + (2 \cdot 10) + 1 = ?$

   A. 11,223 C. 12,321 E. 32,121
   B. 12,132 D. 23,121

8. $(9 \cdot 10{,}000) + (9 \cdot 100) = ?$

   A. 99 C. 90,009 E. 90,900
   B. 9,090 D. 90,090

9. $(2 \cdot 10{,}000) + (8 \cdot 1{,}000) + (4 \cdot 10) = ?$

   A. 284 C. 2,084 E. 28,040
   B. 482 D. 2,840

10. What is the sum of 2 and 3?

    A. 1 C. 6 E. 10
    B. 5 D. 8

11. What is the sum of 5, 7, and 8?

    A. 12 C. 20 E. 28
    B. 15 D. 25

12. What is the sum of 20, 30, and 40?

    A. 60 C. 80 E. 100
    B. 70 D. 90

13. What is the difference between 8 and 3?

    A. 24 C. 8 E. 3
    B. 11 D. 5

14. What is the difference between 28 and 14?

    A. 2 C. 14 E. 392
    B. 7 D. 42

15. What is the product of 2 and 8?

    A. 4 C. 10 E. 24
    B. 6 D. 16

16. What is the product of 20 and 50?

    A. 70 C. 1,000 E. 100,000
    B. 100 D. 10,000

17. What is the product of 12 and 10?

    A. 2 C. 120 E. 300
    B. 22 D. 240

18. What is the sum of $(5 + 1)$ and $(2 + 3)$?

    A. 4 C. 24 E. 40
    B. 11 D. 33

19. What is the difference between $(5 + 2)$ and $(3 \cdot 2)$?

    A. 0 C. 3 E. 14
    B. 1 D. 10

20. What is the product of the sum of 2 and 3 and the sum of 3 and 4?

    A. 6 C. 35 E. 72
    B. 12 D. 48

21. What is the sum of the product of 2 and 3 and the product of 3 and 4?

    A. 6 C. 18 E. 72
    B. 12 D. 35

22. What is the difference between the product of 3 and 4 and the product of 2 and 3?

    A. 2 C. 6 E. 36
    B. 3 D. 12

23. What is the remainder when 12 is divided by 7?

A. 1
B. 2
C. 3
D. 4
E. 5

24. What is the remainder when 18 is divided by 2?

A. 0
B. 1
C. 3
D. 6
E. 9

25. What is the remainder when 50 is divided by 2?

A. 0
B. 1
C. 3
D. 25
E. 50

26. What is the remainder when 15 is divided by 8?

A. 0
B. 1
C. 4
D. 7
E. 89

27. What is the remainder when 15 is divided by 2?

A. 0
B. 1
C. 7
D. 8
E. 14

28. When both 8 and 13 are divided by a certain number, the remainder is 3. What is the number?

A. 4
B. 5
C. 6
D. 7
E. 8

29. When both 33 and 37 are divided by a certain number, the remainder is 1. What is the number?

A. 4
B. 9
C. 10
D. 16
E. 18

30. When both 12 and 19 are divided by a certain number, the remainder is 5. What is the number?

A. 3
B. 4
C. 5
D. 7
E. 9

31. $(4 \cdot 3) + 2 = ?$

A. 6
B. 9
C. 12
D. 14
E. 26

32. $(2 \cdot 3) \div (2 + 1) = ?$

A. 0
B. 1
C. 2
D. 3
E. 6

33. $[2 \cdot (12 \div 4)] + [6 \div (1 + 2)] = ?$

A. 4
B. 6
C. 8
D. 18
E. 24

34. $[(36 \div 12) \cdot (24 \div 3)] \div [(1 \cdot 3) - (18 \div 9)] = ?$

A. 3
B. 8
C. 16
D. 20
E. 24

35. $[(12 \cdot 3) - (3 \cdot 12)] + [(8 \div 2) \div 4] = ?$

A. 0
B. 1
C. 4
D. 8
E. 16

36. $(1 \cdot 2 \cdot 3 \cdot 4) - [(2 \cdot 3) + (3 \cdot 6)] = ?$

A. 0
B. 1
C. 6
D. 16
E. 24

37. Which of the following statements is (are) true?

I. $(4 + 3) - 6 = 4 + (6 - 2)$
II. $3(4 + 5) = (3 \cdot 4) + (3 \cdot 5)$
III. $(3 + 5) \cdot 4 = 4 \cdot (5 + 3)$

A. I only
B. II only
C. III only
D. II and III only
E. I, II, and III

38. $12 + 24 + 36 = ?$

A. $3 \cdot 12$
B. $12(1 + 2 + 3)$
C. $12(3 + 4 + 5)$
D. $6(2) + 6(3) + 6(4)$
E. $12 \cdot 24 \cdot 36$

39. $25 + 50 + 100 = ?$

A. $5(1 + 2 + 3)$
B. $5(1 + 2 + 4)$
C. $25(1 + 2 + 3)$
D. $25(1 + 2 + 4)$
E. $25(1 + 5 + 10)$

40. $\frac{99(121) - 99(120)}{33} = ?$

A. 1
B. 3
C. 33
D. 99
E. 120

41. $1{,}234(96) - 1{,}234(48) = ?$

A. $1{,}234 \cdot 48$
B. $1{,}234 \cdot 96$
C. $1{,}234(48 + 96)$
D. $(1{,}234 \cdot 1{,}234)$
E. $2 \cdot 1{,}234$

42. How many prime numbers are greater than 20 but less than 30?

A. 0
B. 1
C. 2
D. 3
E. 4

43. How many prime numbers are greater that 50 but less than 60?

A. 0
B. 1
C. 2
D. 3
E. 4

44. Which of the following numbers is (are) prime?

I. 11
II. 111
III. 1,111

A. I only
B. II only
C. I and II only
D. I and III only
E. I, II, and III

45. Which of the following numbers is (are) prime?

I. 12,345
II. 999,999,999
III. 1,000,000,002

A. I only
B. III only
C. I and II only
D. I, II, and III
E. Neither I, II, nor III

46. What is the largest factor of both 25 and 40?

A. 5 C. 10 E. 25
B. 8 D. 15

47. What is the largest factor of both 6 and 9?

A. 1 C. 6 E. 12
B. 3 D. 9

48. What is the largest factor of both 12 and 18?

A. 6 C. 36 E. 216
B. 24 D. 48

49. What is the largest factor of 18, 24, and 36?

A. 6 C. 12 E. 18
B. 9 D. 15

50. What is the largest factor of 7, 14, and 21?

A. 1 C. 14 E. 35
B. 7 D. 21

51. What is the smallest multiple of both 5 and 2?

A. 7 C. 20 E. 40
B. 10 D. 30

52. What is the smallest multiple of both 12 and 18?

A. 36 C. 72 E. 216
B. 48 D. 128

53. Which of the following is (are) even?

I. 12
II. 36
III. 101

A. I only
B. II only
C. I and II only
D. I and III only
E. I, II, and III

54. Which of the following is (are) odd?

I. 24 • 31
II. 22 • 49
III. 33 • 101

A. I only
B. II only
C. III only
D. I and III only
E. I, II, and III

55. Which of the following is (are) even?

I. 333,332 • 333,333
II. 999,999 + 101,101
III. 22,221 • 44,441

A. I only
B. II only
C. I and II only
D. I and III only
E. I, II, and III

56. If n is an even number, then which of the following MAY NOT be even?

A. $(n \cdot n) + n$ C. $n + 2$ E. $\frac{n}{2}$
B. $n \cdot n - n$ D. $3(n + 2)$

57. For any whole number n, which of the following MUST be odd?

I. $3(n + 1)$
II. $3n + 2n$
III. $2n - 1$

A. I only
B. II only
C. III only
D. I and II only
E. I, II, and III

58. If 8 is the third number in a series of three consecutive whole numbers, what is the first number in the series?

A. 0 C. 6 E. 11
B. 1 D. 7

59. If 15 is the fifth number in a series of five consecutive odd numbers, what is the third number in the series?

A. 5 C. 9 E. 13
B. 7 D. 11

60. If m, n, and o are consecutive whole numbers that total 15, what is the largest of the three numbers?

A. 4 C. 6 E. 17
B. 5 D. 14

61. If $A = 2^2(3)(7) = 84$, how many positive factors, including 1 and 84, does A have?

A. 12 C. 36 E. 84
B. 24 D. 42

62. If $B = 5(8)(11) = 440$, how many positive factors, including 1 and 440, does B have?

A. 8 C. 12 E. 24
B. 10 D. 16

63. If $ab(c - d + 2e) = -6$, which of the numbers a, b, c, d, and e CANNOT be 0?

A. a and b only
B. b only
C. c only
D. d only
E. c and d only

64. If $[a - 2(b + c - 3d)]e = 3$, which of the numbers a, b, c, d, and e CANNOT be 0?

A. a C. c E. e
B. b D. d

Fractions

When one whole number is divided by another whole number and the result is not a third whole number, the result is a ***fraction***. For example, when 2 is divided by 3, the result is not a whole number, but rather it is the fraction $\frac{2}{3}$. Note that any whole number can also be expressed as a fraction; *e.g.*, $\frac{12}{3} = 4$, $7 = \frac{7}{1}$.

The number above the division line in the fraction is called the ***numerator***; the number below the line is called the ***denominator***. In a ***proper fraction***, the numerator is less than the denominator, so the fraction has a value of less than 1, *e.g.*, $\frac{1}{2}$ and $\frac{3}{4}$, which are both less than 1. In an ***improper fraction***, the numerator is greater than the denominator, so the fraction has a value greater than 1, *e.g.*, $\frac{3}{2}$ and $\frac{4}{3}$, which are both greater than 1. A ***mixed number*** consists of both a whole number and a fraction written together. For example, $2\frac{1}{2}$ is equivalent to $2 + \frac{1}{2}$, and $3\frac{4}{5}$ is equivalent to $3 + \frac{4}{5}$.

Converting Mixed Numbers to Improper Fractions

Before you add, subtract, multiply, or divide, convert ***mixed numbers*** to ***improper fractions***. To convert a mixed number to an improper fraction, use the following procedure.

Step 1: Use the denominator of the old fractional part of the mixed number as the new denominator.

Step 2: Multiply the whole number part of the mixed number by the denominator of the old fractional part and add to that product the numerator of the old fractional part. This is the new numerator.

Examples:

1. Rewrite $2\frac{3}{7}$ as an improper fraction.

   ➤ The denominator of the improper fraction is 7. The numerator is determined by multiplying 7 by 2 and adding 3 to the result. To summarize: $2\frac{3}{7} \Rightarrow \frac{(2 \cdot 7) + 3}{7} = \frac{14 + 3}{7} = \frac{17}{7}$.

2. $3\frac{1}{4} = \frac{(3 \cdot 4) + 1}{4} = \frac{13}{4}$

3. $6\frac{2}{5} = \frac{(6 \cdot 5) + 2}{5} = \frac{32}{5}$

4. $2\frac{12}{13} = \frac{(2 \cdot 13) + 12}{13} = \frac{38}{13}$

Converting Improper Fractions to Mixed Numbers

To convert an improper fraction to a mixed number, reverse the process described above.

Step 1: Divide the denominator into the numerator. The quotient becomes the whole number part of the mixed number.

Step 2: Use the same denominator for the fraction; the numerator is the remainder of the division process in Step 1.

Examples:

1. Convert $\frac{30}{7}$ into a mixed number.

   ➤ Divide 7 into 30; the result is 4 with a remainder of 2. The 4 is the whole number part of the mixed number. Next, the numerator of the fraction is the remainder 2, and the denominator is 7. Therefore, $\frac{30}{7} = 4\frac{2}{7}$.

2. $\frac{29}{5} = 29 \div 5 = 5$ with a remainder of $4 = 5\frac{4}{5}$
3. $\frac{31}{6} = 31 \div 6 = 5$ with a remainder of $1 = 5\frac{1}{6}$
4. $\frac{43}{13} = 43 \div 13 = 3$ with a remainder of $4 = 3\frac{4}{13}$

Reducing Fractions to Lowest Terms

For reasons of convenience, it is customary to reduce all fractions to their lowest terms. When you reduce a fraction to lowest terms, you really are doing nothing but rewriting it in an equivalent form. This is accomplished by eliminating common factors in both the numerator and the denominator of the fraction.

Example:

$$\frac{8}{16} = \frac{1(8)}{2(8)} = \frac{1}{2}$$

➤ There are various ways of describing what goes on when you reduce a fraction. You might think of taking out a common factor, such as 8 in this example, and then dividing 8 into 8 (canceling). It is also possible to think of the process as dividing both the numerator and the denominator by the same number: $\frac{8}{16} = \frac{8 \div 8}{16 \div 8} = \frac{1}{2}$.

It does not matter how you describe the process, so long as you know how to reduce a fraction to its lowest terms. A fraction is expressed in lowest terms when there is no number (other than 1) that can be evenly divided into both the numerator and the denominator. For example, the fraction $\frac{8}{15}$ is in lowest terms, since there is no number (other than 1) that evenly goes into 8 that also evenly goes into 15. On the other hand, the fraction $\frac{8}{12}$ is not in lowest terms, since both 8 and 12 can be evenly divided by 4. Reducing $\frac{8}{12}$ by a factor of 4 gives $\frac{2}{3}$, which is in lowest terms since nothing (other than 1) evenly divides into both 2 and 3.

Examples:

1. $\frac{12}{36} = \frac{1 \cdot 12}{3 \cdot 12} = \frac{1}{3}$
2. $\frac{42}{48} = \frac{7 \cdot 6}{8 \cdot 6} = \frac{7}{8}$
3. $\frac{50}{125} = \frac{2 \cdot 25}{5 \cdot 25} = \frac{2}{5}$

If a fraction is particularly large, you may need to reduce it in steps. The process is largely a matter of trial and error, but there are a couple of rules that can guide you. Remember that if both the numerator and the denominator are even numbers, you can reduce the fraction by a factor of 2. Finally, if both the numerator and the denominator end in either 0 or 5, they are both divisible by 5.

Examples:

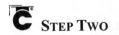

1. $\frac{32}{64}=\frac{16(2)}{32(2)}=\frac{8(2)}{16(2)}=\frac{4(2)}{8(2)}=\frac{2(2)}{4(2)}=\frac{1(2)}{2(2)}=\frac{1}{2}$
2. $\frac{55}{100}=\frac{11(5)}{20(5)}=\frac{11}{20}$

Common Denominators

A ***common denominator*** is a number that is a multiple of the denominators of two or more fractions. For example, 12 is a multiple of both 3 and 4 (both 3 and 4 divide evenly into 12), so it is a suitable common denominator for $\frac{1}{3}$ and $\frac{1}{4}$. Converting a fraction to one with another denominator is the reverse of reducing it to lowest terms. When you multiply both the numerator and the denominator by the same number, you are really just multiplying the fraction by 1, so its value is not changed; *e.g.*, $\frac{3}{3}=1$.

In grade school, you were taught to find the lowest common denominator for fractions. In truth, any common denominator will work. The easiest way to find a common denominator is to multiply the different denominators together. For example, a common denominator for 2 and 3 is 2 • 3, or 6; a common denominator for 3 and 4 is 3 • 4, or 12; a common denominator for 2 and 5 is 2 • 5, or 10.

What was the big deal about lowest common denominators? It is the same as reducing fractions to lowest terms: It is easier to work with smaller numbers. A common denominator for 2 and 8 is 16, but 8 is also a possibility. It is easier to deal with a fraction of denominator 8 than 16. In the final analysis, you can use any common denominator, because you can always reduce a fraction to its lowest terms.

Operations of Fractions

1. *Adding Fractions*

The procedure for adding fractions depends on whether or not the fractions share the same denominator. To add fractions with the same denominator, create a new fraction using that denominator. The new numerator is the sum of the old numerators.

Examples:

1. $\frac{3}{7}+\frac{2}{7}=\frac{5}{7}$
2. $\frac{2}{5}+\frac{2}{5}=\frac{4}{5}$
3. $\frac{1}{7}+\frac{2}{7}+\frac{3}{7}=\frac{6}{7}$

To add fractions with different denominators, you must first find a common denominator and co[illegible] the fractions in the manner described above. For example, $\frac{1}{3}$ and $\frac{1}{5}$. Since these fractions have unlike denominators, yo[illegible]ust find a common denominator such as 15. Next, you convert each fraction to a fraction with a denominator of 15.

Examples:

1. $\frac{1}{3}+\frac{1}{5}=\frac{1(5)}{3(5)}+\frac{1(3)}{5(3)}=\frac{5}{15}+\frac{3}{15}=\frac{8}{15}$
2. $\frac{1}{3}+\frac{2}{7}=\frac{1(7)}{3(7)}+\frac{2(3)}{7(3)}=\frac{7}{21}+\frac{6}{21}=\frac{13}{21}$
3. $\frac{2}{9}+\frac{4}{5}=\frac{2(5)}{9(5)}+\frac{4(9)}{5(9)}=\frac{10}{45}+\frac{36}{45}=\frac{46}{45}$

To add a fraction and a whole number, you can treat the whole number as a fraction with [illegible]enominator of 1.

Example:

$$2+\frac{1}{5}+\frac{1}{2}=\frac{2}{1}+\frac{1}{5}+\frac{1}{2}=\frac{2(10)}{1(10)}+\frac{1(2)}{5(2)}+\frac{1(5)}{2(5)}=\frac{20}{10}+\frac{2}{10}+\frac{5}{10}=\frac{27}{10}$$

To add a fraction and a mixed number, change the mixed number to an improper fraction and add together the two fractions.

Example:

$$2\frac{1}{3}+\frac{1}{3}=\frac{7}{3}+\frac{1}{3}=\frac{8}{3}=2\frac{2}{3}$$

2. ***Subtracting Fractions***

Follow the same procedures for subtraction of fractions as for addition, except subtract rather than add. When the fractions have the same denominators, simply subtract one numerator from the other.

Examples:

1. $\frac{5}{7}-\frac{2}{7}=\frac{3}{7}$
2. $\frac{4}{5}-\frac{3}{5}=\frac{1}{5}$

When fractions have different denominators, it is first necessary to find a common denominator.

Examples:

1. $\frac{7}{8}-\frac{3}{5}=\frac{7(5)}{8(5)}-\frac{3(8)}{5(8)}=\frac{35}{40}-\frac{24}{40}=\frac{11}{40}$
2. $\frac{5}{6}-\frac{1}{5}=\frac{5(5)}{6(5)}-\frac{1(6)}{5(6)}=\frac{25}{30}-\frac{6}{30}=\frac{19}{30}$
3. $2-\frac{7}{6}=\frac{2}{1}-\frac{7}{6}=\frac{2(6)}{1(6)}-\frac{7(1)}{6(1)}=\frac{12}{6}-\frac{7}{6}=\frac{5}{6}$

3. ***"Flying-X" Shortcut***

You do not need to worry about finding a lowest common denominator as long as you remember to reduce the result of an operation to lowest terms. This sets up a little trick for adding and subtracting fractions that makes the process a purely mechanical one—one you do not even have to think about. The trick is called the ***flying-x***.

To add (or subtract) any two fractions with unlike denominators use the following procedure.

Step 1: Multiply the denominators to get a new denominator.
Step 2: Multiply the numerator of the first fraction by the denominator of the second.
Step 3: Multiply the denominator of the first fraction by the numerator of the second.
Step 4: The new numerator is the sum (or difference) of the results of Steps 2 and 3.

Once again, it is more difficult to describe the process than it is to do it. Perhaps the easiest way to learn it is to see it done. To add two fractions: $\frac{a}{b}+\frac{c}{d}=\frac{a}{b}\!\!>\!+\!<\!\!\frac{c}{d}=\frac{ad+bc}{bd}$.

Example:

$$\frac{2}{7}+\frac{1}{5}=\frac{2}{7}\!\!>\!+\!<\!\!\frac{1}{5}=\frac{10+7}{35}=\frac{17}{35}$$

As you can see, the connecting arrows make a figure that looks like an x floating above the ground, or a "flying-x."

The flying-x method also works for subtracting fractions.

Examples:

1. $\frac{3}{5}-\frac{1}{3}=\frac{3}{5}>-<\frac{1}{3}=\frac{9-5}{15}=\frac{4}{15}$
2. $\frac{6}{7}-\frac{5}{6}=\frac{6}{7}>-<\frac{5}{6}=\frac{36-35}{42}=\frac{1}{42}$

Of course, this may not give you the lowest terms of the fractions, so it may be necessary to reduce.

Examples:

1. $\frac{3}{4}-\frac{1}{8}=\frac{3}{4}>-<\frac{1}{8}=\frac{24-4}{32}=\frac{20}{32}=\frac{5}{8}$
2. $\frac{2}{3}-\frac{1}{6}=\frac{2}{3}>-<\frac{1}{6}=\frac{12-3}{18}=\frac{9}{18}=\frac{1}{2}$

4. *Multiplying Fractions*

Multiplication of fractions does not require a common denominator. To multiply fractions, just multiply numerators to create a new numerator, and multiply denominators to create a new denominator.

Examples:

1. $\frac{3}{4}\bullet\frac{1}{5}=\frac{3\bullet 1}{4\bullet 5}=\frac{3}{20}$
2. $\frac{2}{3}\bullet\frac{2}{5}=\frac{2\bullet 2}{3\bullet 5}=\frac{4}{15}$

5. *Dividing Fractions*

Division of fractions is the opposite of multiplication. To divide by a fraction, you invert the divisor (the fraction by which you are dividing) and then multiply the two together.

Examples:

1. $2\div\frac{1}{4}=\frac{2}{1}\bullet\frac{4}{1}=\frac{8}{1}=8$
2. $\dfrac{\frac{2}{3}}{\frac{5}{6}}=\frac{2}{3}\bullet\frac{6}{5}=\frac{12}{15}=\frac{4}{5}$
3. $\frac{1}{3}\div\frac{5}{6}=\frac{1}{3}\bullet\frac{6}{5}=\frac{6}{15}=\frac{2}{5}$
4. $\frac{2}{7}\div 2=\frac{2}{7}\div\frac{2}{1}=\frac{2}{7}\bullet\frac{1}{2}=\frac{2}{14}=\frac{1}{7}$
5. $\frac{1}{5}\div\frac{1}{2}=\frac{1}{5}\bullet\frac{2}{1}=\frac{2}{5}$
6. $3\div\frac{1}{5}=\frac{3}{1}\bullet\frac{5}{1}=\frac{15}{1}=15$

Comparing Fractions

1. *Comparing Decimal Equivalents*

We can compare the values of fractions in several different ways. The first method is the one most commonly used but which often takes up valuable time. Convert the fractions to decimal equivalents and compare these values.

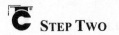

Example:

Find the largest value of the following fractions: $\frac{1}{2}, \frac{2}{3}, \frac{1}{8}$, and $\frac{2}{11}$.

➤ Convert the fractions to decimal equivalents: 0.5, $0.6\overline{6}$, 0.125, and $0.18\overline{18}$. Compare the values: $0.6\overline{6}$ is the largest.

2. ***Upward Cross-Multiplication***

The second method of comparing fractions is often faster. We use ***upward cross-multiplication***—multiply the denominator of the one fraction with the numerator of the other fraction in an upward direction. The fraction with the greatest product above it has the greatest value.

Example:

Find the largest value of the following fractions: $\frac{1}{2}, \frac{2}{3}, \frac{1}{8}$, and $\frac{2}{11}$.

➤ Compare $\frac{1}{2}$ with $\frac{2}{3}$ by multiplying (3)(1) and (2)(2) and place the value above each fraction: $\overset{③}{\frac{1}{2}} \times \overset{④}{\frac{2}{3}}$ ⇒ 4 is larger than 3, so $\frac{2}{3}$ is larger than $\frac{1}{2}$. Now, compare $\frac{2}{3}$ with the other two remaining fractions: $\overset{⑯}{\frac{2}{3}} \times \overset{③}{\frac{1}{8}}$ ⇒ $\frac{2}{3}$ is larger. $\overset{㉒}{\frac{2}{3}} \times \overset{⑥}{\frac{2}{11}}$ ⇒ $\frac{2}{3}$ is larger. Therefore, $\frac{2}{3}$ is the largest value.

Alternatively, you can directly compare fractions by converting all of the fractions to fractions with the same denominator. The fraction with the largest numerator is then the largest value.

Example:

Find the smallest value of the following fractions: $\frac{1}{4}, \frac{5}{14}, \frac{3}{7}$, and $\frac{1}{2}$.

➤ Convert the fractions to fractions with the same denominator: $\frac{1}{4} \cdot \frac{7}{7} = \frac{7}{28}$; $\frac{5}{14} \cdot \frac{2}{2} = \frac{10}{28}$; $\frac{3}{7} \cdot \frac{4}{4} = \frac{12}{28}$; $\frac{1}{2} \cdot \frac{14}{14} = \frac{14}{28}$. Since $\frac{7}{28}$ is the rewritten fraction with the smallest numerator, the fraction equivalent $\frac{1}{4}$ is the smallest value of the given fractions.

NOTE: The ACT, PLAN, and EXPLORE allow calculators. Therefore, it is important that you learn how to use a calculator and bring the same calculator with you to the exam. Using a calculator provides greater accuracy and often saves valuable test time.

EXERCISE 2

Fractions

DIRECTIONS: Choose the correct answer to each of the following items. Use a calculator when necessary. Answers are on page 920.

1. $5\frac{3}{8} = ?$

   A. 1 B. $\frac{15}{8}$ C. $\frac{23}{8}$ D. $\frac{35}{8}$ E. $\frac{43}{8}$

2. $2\frac{3}{4} = ?$

   A. $\frac{1}{4}$ B. $\frac{3}{4}$ C. $\frac{9}{4}$ D. $\frac{11}{4}$ E. $\frac{15}{4}$

3. $3\frac{1}{12} = ?$

   A. $\frac{13}{12}$ B. $\frac{37}{12}$ C. $\frac{41}{12}$ D. $\frac{53}{12}$ E. $\frac{71}{12}$

4. $1\frac{1}{65} = ?$

   A. $\frac{64}{65}$ B. $\frac{65}{66}$ C. $\frac{66}{65}$ D. 66 [illegible] E. $\frac{67}{66}$

5. $5\frac{2}{7} = ?$

   A. $\frac{5}{14}$ B. $\frac{35}{7}$ C. $\frac{37}{7}$ D. $\frac{70}{7}$ E. $\frac{110}{7}$

6. $\frac{12}{8} = ?$

   A. 4 B. 3 C. $2\frac{1}{2}$ D. $1\frac{1}{2}$ E. $1\frac{1}{4}$

7. $\frac{20}{6} = ?$

   A. $3\frac{1}{3}$ B. $3\frac{2}{3}$ C. $4\frac{1}{6}$ D. $4\frac{1}{3}$ E. 6

8. $\frac{23}{13} = ?$

   A. 10 B. $7\frac{7}{13}$ C. $1\frac{10}{13}$ D. $\frac{13}{23}$ E. $\frac{7}{13}$

9. $\frac{25}{4} = ?$

   A. $\frac{4}{25}$ B. $\frac{4}{12}$ C. $1\frac{1}{8}$ D. $1\frac{1}{4}$ E. $6\frac{1}{4}$

10. $\frac{201}{100} = ?$

    A. $1\frac{1}{100}$ B. $1\frac{1}{50}$ C. $2\frac{1}{100}$ D. $2\frac{1}{50}$ E. 101

11. $\frac{3}{12} = ?$

    A. $\frac{1}{6}$ B. $\frac{1}{4}$ C. $\frac{1}{3}$ D. $\frac{1}{2}$ E. $\frac{3}{4}$

12. [illegible]/81 = [illegible]

    A. $\frac{1}{9}$ B. $\frac{2}{9}$ C. $\frac{1}{3}$ D. $\frac{4}{9}$ E. $\frac{2}{3}$

13. $\frac{125}{625} = ?$

    A. $\frac{1}{10}$ B. $\frac{1}{5}$ C. $\frac{2}{5}$ D. $\frac{7}{10}$ E. $\frac{4}{5}$

14. $\frac{39}{52} = ?$

    A. $\frac{1}{5}$ B. $\frac{1}{4}$ C. $\frac{1}{3}$ D. $\frac{1}{2}$ E. $\frac{3}{4}$

15. $\frac{121}{132} = ?$

    A. $\frac{1}{11}$ B. $\frac{1}{10}$ C. $\frac{9}{10}$ D. $\frac{10}{11}$ E. $\frac{11}{12}$

16. Which of the following is equal to $\frac{4}{25}$?

A. $\frac{8}{50}$ B. $\frac{8}{100}$ C. $\frac{12}{150}$ D. $\frac{160}{200}$ E. $\frac{200}{250}$

17. Which of the following is NOT equal to $\frac{3}{8}$?

A. $\frac{6}{16}$ B. $\frac{15}{40}$ C. $\frac{31}{81}$ D. $\frac{33}{88}$ E. $\frac{120}{320}$

18. Which of the following is NOT equal to $\frac{3}{4}$?

A. $\frac{6}{8}$ B. $\frac{12}{16}$ C. $\frac{20}{24}$ D. $\frac{36}{48}$ E. $\frac{300}{400}$

19. Which of the following is NOT equal to $\frac{5}{6}$?

A. $\frac{25}{30}$ B. $\frac{45}{50}$ C. $\frac{50}{60}$ D. $\frac{55}{66}$ E. $\frac{100}{120}$

20. Which of the following is NOT equal to $\frac{1}{6}$?

A. $\frac{2}{12}$ B. $\frac{3}{18}$ C. $\frac{4}{24}$ D. $\frac{5}{30}$ E. $\frac{6}{40}$

21. $\frac{1}{7}+\frac{2}{7}=?$

A. $\frac{2}{7}$ B. $\frac{3}{7}$ C. $\frac{6}{7}$ D. $\frac{8}{7}$ E. $\frac{12}{7}$

22. $\frac{5}{8}+\frac{1}{8}=?$

A. $\frac{1}{2}$ B. $\frac{3}{4}$ C. $\frac{7}{8}$ D. $\frac{8}{5}$ E. $\frac{4}{3}$

23. $\frac{12}{13}+\frac{12}{13}=?$

A. 0 B. 1 C. $\frac{12}{26}$ D. $\frac{24}{13}$ E. $\frac{26}{13}$

24. $\frac{3}{8}+\frac{5}{8}=?$

A. $\frac{2}{8}$ B. 1 C. $\frac{5}{4}$ D. $\frac{8}{5}$ E. $\frac{12}{5}$

25. $\frac{1}{11}+\frac{2}{11}+\frac{7}{11}=?$

A. $\frac{4}{11}$ B. $\frac{7}{11}$ C. $\frac{10}{11}$ D. $\frac{11}{10}$ E. $\frac{11}{7}$

26. $\frac{3}{8}+\frac{5}{6}=?$

A. $\frac{8}{48}$ B. $\frac{8}{14}$ C. $\frac{29}{24}$ D. $\frac{3}{2}$ E. $\frac{14}{8}$

27. $\frac{1}{8}+\frac{1}{7}=?$

A. $\frac{1}{56}$ B. $\frac{1}{27}$ C. $\frac{1}{15}$ D. $\frac{1}{5}$ E. $\frac{15}{56}$

28. $\frac{1}{12}+\frac{1}{7}=?$

A. $\frac{19}{84}$ B. $\frac{19}{42}$ C. $\frac{10}{19}$ D. $\frac{20}{19}$ E. $\frac{5}{4}$

29. $\frac{3}{5}+\frac{2}{11}=?$

A. $\frac{43}{110}$ B. $\frac{43}{55}$ C. $\frac{54}{55}$ D. $\frac{55}{54}$ E. $\frac{100}{43}$

30. $\frac{1}{2}+\frac{1}{3}+\frac{1}{6}=?$

A. $\frac{1}{36}$ B. $\frac{1}{12}$ C. 1 D. $\frac{7}{6}$ E. $\frac{7}{3}$

31. $\frac{2}{3}+\frac{3}{6}+\frac{4}{6}=?$

A. $\frac{9}{20}$ B. $\frac{6}{7}$ C. $\frac{7}{6}$ D. $\frac{11}{6}$ E. $\frac{16}{3}$

32. $\frac{2}{3}-\frac{1}{3}=?$

A. $\frac{1}{6}$ B. $\frac{1}{3}$ C. $\frac{2}{3}$ D. $\frac{4}{3}$ E. $\frac{6}{3}$

33. $\frac{5}{7}-\frac{4}{7}=?$

A. $\frac{9}{7}$ B. 1 C. $\frac{5}{7}$ D. $\frac{1}{7}$ E. $\frac{1}{49}$

34. $\frac{9}{10}-\frac{1}{5}=?$

A. $\frac{7}{10}$ B. $\frac{7}{5}$ C. $\frac{10}{7}$ D. $\frac{18}{7}$ E. $\frac{20}{7}$

35. $\frac{3}{2}-\frac{1}{4}=?$

A. $\frac{5}{4}$ B. $\frac{4}{5}$ C. $\frac{3}{4}$ D. $\frac{2}{3}$ E. $\frac{1}{3}$

36. $2\frac{1}{2}-\frac{7}{8}=?$

A. $\frac{9}{2}$
B. $\frac{5}{2}$
C. $\frac{13}{8}$
D. $\frac{5}{4}$
E. $\frac{4}{5}$

37. $2\frac{2}{3}-1\frac{1}{6}=?$

A. $1\frac{1}{6}$
B. $1\frac{1}{3}$
C. $1\frac{1}{2}$
D. $1\frac{2}{3}$
E. 2

38. $\frac{1}{2}\bullet\frac{2}{3}=?$

A. $\frac{1}{6}$
B. $\frac{1}{3}$
C. $\frac{1}{2}$
D. $\frac{2}{3}$
E. $\frac{3}{4}$

39. $\frac{2}{7}\bullet\frac{1}{4}=?$

A. $\frac{1}{63}$
B. $\frac{1}{14}$
C. $\frac{1}{4}$
D. $\frac{3}{8}$
E. $\frac{5}{9}$

40. $\frac{1}{3}\bullet\frac{1}{3}=?$

A. $\frac{1}{9}$
B. $\frac{1}{6}$
C. $\frac{1}{3}$
D. $\frac{2}{3}$
E. $\frac{3}{2}$

41. $\frac{1}{2}\bullet\frac{1}{2}\bullet\frac{1}{2}=?$

A. $\frac{1}{16}$
B. $\frac{1}{8}$
C. $\frac{3}{16}$
D. $\frac{3}{8}$
E. $\frac{2}{3}$

42. $\frac{2}{3}\bullet\frac{3}{4}\bullet\frac{4}{5}=?$

A. $\frac{2}{5}$
B. $\frac{3}{5}$
C. $\frac{2}{3}$
D. $\frac{3}{4}$
E. $\frac{4}{5}$

43. $\frac{1}{4}\bullet\frac{1}{8}\bullet 3=?$

A. $\frac{3}{32}$
B. $\frac{1}{8}$
C. $\frac{1}{4}$
D. $\frac{1}{2}$
E. $\frac{3}{4}$

44. $\frac{1}{3}\bullet\frac{1}{6}\bullet 12=?$

A. $\frac{1}{3}$
B. $\frac{2}{3}$
C. 1
D. $\frac{3}{2}$
E. 2

45. $\frac{7}{8}\div\frac{3}{4}=?$

A. $\frac{7}{6}$
B. 1
C. $\frac{3}{4}$
D. $\frac{1}{3}$
E. $\frac{1}{8}$

46. $\frac{5}{7}\div\frac{1}{7}=?$

A. $\frac{1}{7}$
B. $\frac{1}{5}$
C. 5
D. 7
E. 12

47. $\frac{1}{12}\div\frac{1}{12}=?$

A. $\frac{1}{144}$
B. 1
C. 12
D. 18
E. 144

48. $2\div\frac{1}{11}=?$

A. 22
B. 11
C. $\frac{11}{2}$
D. $\frac{11}{22}$
E. $\frac{1}{22}$

49. $\frac{8}{9}\div\frac{7}{8}=?$

A. $\frac{64}{63}$
B. $\frac{9}{7}$
C. $\frac{7}{9}$
D. $\frac{1}{2}$
E. $\frac{1}{3}$

50. $\frac{1}{10}\div\frac{3}{5}=?$

A. $\frac{1}{6}$
B. $\frac{1}{5}$
C. $\frac{3}{10}$
D. $\frac{3}{5}$
E. $\frac{5}{3}$

51. $\left(\frac{1}{4}+\frac{2}{3}\right)\bullet\left(\frac{3}{2}+\frac{1}{4}\right)=?$

A. $\frac{21}{47}$
B. $\frac{33}{49}$
C. $\frac{51}{48}$
D. $\frac{77}{48}$
E. $\frac{105}{51}$

52. $\left(\frac{2}{3}\bullet\frac{1}{6}\right)\div\left(\frac{1}{2}\bullet\frac{1}{4}\right)=?$

A. $\frac{1}{18}$
B. $\frac{2}{9}$
C. $\frac{8}{9}$
D. $\frac{11}{8}$
E. $\frac{15}{75}$

53. $\left[\left(\frac{1}{3}+\frac{1}{2}\right)\bullet\left(\frac{2}{3}-\frac{1}{3}\right)\right]\bullet 18=?$

A. 5
B. $\frac{7}{8}$
C. $\frac{5}{6}$
D. $\frac{4}{5}$
E. $\frac{2}{3}$

54. $\left[\left(\frac{1}{3}\div\frac{1}{6}\right)\bullet\left(\frac{2}{3}\div\frac{1}{3}\right)\right]\bullet\left(\frac{1}{2}+\frac{3}{4}\right)=?$

A. 5
B. 4
C. 3
D. 2
E. 1

55. Simplify: $8\left(\frac{1}{3}+\frac{3}{4}\right)$.

A. $\frac{1}{3}$
B. $\frac{4}{3}$
C. $\frac{16}{3}$
D. $\frac{19}{3}$
E. $\frac{26}{3}$

56. Simplify: $\frac{1}{4}-\frac{1}{5}$.

A. $\frac{1}{5}$ C. $\frac{1}{20}$ E. $\frac{4}{5}$
B. $\frac{1}{3}$ D. $\frac{3}{4}$

57. Simplify: $\frac{\frac{4}{9}}{\frac{2}{5}}$.

A. $\frac{1}{2}$ C. $\frac{8}{45}$ E. $1\frac{1}{9}$
B. $\frac{3}{4}$ D. $\frac{11}{9}$

58. Simplify: $\left(-\frac{1}{2}\right)^2+\left(\frac{1}{4}\right)^2+(-2)\left(\frac{1}{2}\right)^2$.

A. $-\frac{3}{16}$ C. $\frac{1}{3}$ E. $\frac{4}{5}$
B. $-\frac{1}{5}$ D. $\frac{3}{4}$

59. Which fraction is the largest?

A. $\frac{9}{16}$ C. $\frac{5}{8}$ E. $\frac{1}{2}$
B. $\frac{7}{10}$ D. $\frac{4}{5}$

60. Jughead eats $\frac{2}{5}$ of a pound of cake each day. How many pounds of cake does Jughead eat in 3 weeks?

A. $4\frac{1}{2}$ C. $5\frac{1}{5}$ E. 10
B. $5\frac{3}{4}$ D. $8\frac{2}{5}$

61. Chompa eats $\frac{3}{8}$ of a bag of candy per day. How many weeks will 42 bags of candy last Chompa?

A. 4 C. 9 E. 16
B. 5 D. 12

62. If Bruce can eat $2\frac{1}{2}$ bananas per day, how many bananas can Bruce eat in 4 weeks?

A. 70 C. 80 E. 90
B. 75 D. 85

63. One brass rod measures $3\frac{5}{16}$ inches long and another brass rod measures $2\frac{3}{4}$ inches long. What is the total length, in inches, of the two rods combined?

A. $6\frac{9}{16}$ C. $5\frac{1}{2}$ E. $5\frac{1}{32}$
B. $6\frac{1}{16}$ D. $5\frac{1}{16}$

64. Which of the following equals the number of half-pound packages of tea that can be taken out of a box that holds $10\frac{1}{2}$ pounds of tea?

A. 5 C. 11 E. 21
B. $10\frac{1}{2}$ D. $20\frac{1}{122}$

65. If each bag of tokens weighs $5\frac{3}{4}$ pounds, how many pounds do 3 bags weigh?

A. $7\frac{1}{4}$ C. $16\frac{1}{2}$ E. $17\frac{1}{2}$
B. $15\frac{3}{4}$ D. $17\frac{1}{4}$

66. During one week, a man traveled $3\frac{1}{2}$, $1\frac{1}{4}$, $1\frac{1}{6}$, and $2\frac{3}{8}$ miles. The next week, he traveled $\frac{1}{4}$, $\frac{3}{8}$, $\frac{9}{16}$, $3\frac{1}{16}$, $2\frac{5}{8}$, and $3\frac{3}{16}$ miles. How many more miles did he travel the second week than the first week?

A. $1\frac{37}{48}$ C. $1\frac{3}{4}$ E. $\frac{47}{48}$
B. $1\frac{1}{2}$ D. 1

67. A certain type of board is sold only in lengths of multiples of 2 feet. The shortest board sold is 6 feet and the longest is 24 feet. A builder needs a large quantity of this type of board in $5\frac{1}{2}$-foot lengths. To minimize waste, which of the following board lengths should be ordered?

A. 6-ft. C. 22-ft. E. 26-ft.
B. 12-ft. D. 24-ft.

68. A man spent $\frac{15}{16}$ of his entire fortune in buying a car for \$7,500. How much money did he possess?

A. \$6,000 C. \$7,000 E. \$8,500
B. \$6,500 D. \$8,000

69. The population of a town was 54,000 in the last census. Since then it has increased $\frac{2}{3}$. Which of the following equals its present population?

A. 18,000 C. 72,000 E. 108,000
B. 36,000 D. 90,000

70. $\frac{1}{3}$ of the liquid contents of a can evaporates on the first day and $\frac{3}{4}$ of the remainder evaporates on the second day. Which of the following equals the fractional part of the original contents remaining at the close of the second day?

A. $\frac{5}{12}$ C. $\frac{1}{6}$ E. $\frac{4}{7}$
B. $\frac{7}{12}$ D. $\frac{1}{2}$

71. A car is run until the gas tank is $\frac{1}{8}$ full. The tank is then filled to capacity by putting in 14 gallons. What is the the gas tank's capacity, in gallons?

A. 14 C. 16 E. 18
B. 15 D. 17

Signed Numbers

Numbers are just positions in a linear system. Each number is one greater than the number to its left and one less than the number to its right. The following number line represents the ***integer number system***, which consists of the signed (positive and negative) whole numbers and zero:

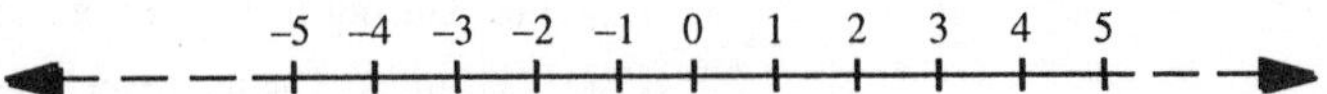

With both positive and negative integers, each position is one more than the position before it and one less than the position after it: −1 is one less than zero and one more than −2; −2 is one less than −1 and one more than −3. The minus sign indicates the direction in which the number system is moving with reference to zero. If you move to the right, you are going in the positive direction; to the left, in the negative direction.

It is natural to use negative numbers in everyday situations, such as games and banking: An overdrawn checking account results in a minus balance. You can manipulate negative numbers using the basic operations (addition, subtraction, multiplication, and division). To help explain these operations, we introduce the concept of absolute value.

Absolute Value

The ***absolute value*** of a number is its value without any sign and so it is always a positive numerical value: $|x| \geq 0$. Therefore, $|x| = x$ **if** $x \geq 0$ and $|x| = -x$ **if** $x < 0$. A number's absolute value is its distance on the number line from the origin, without regard to direction: $|x| = |-x|$.

Examples:

1. $|4| = 4$
2. $|-10| = 10$
3. $|5| - |3| = 5 - 3 = 2$
4. $|-2| + |-3| = 2 + 3 = 5$

This idea of value, without regard to direction, helps to clarify negative number operations.

Adding Negative Numbers

To add negative numbers to other numbers, subtract the absolute value of the negative numbers.

Example:

$10 + (-4) = 10 - |-4| = 10 - 4 = 6$

➢ The number line illustrates the logic: Start at 10 and move the counter four units in the negative direction. The result is 6:

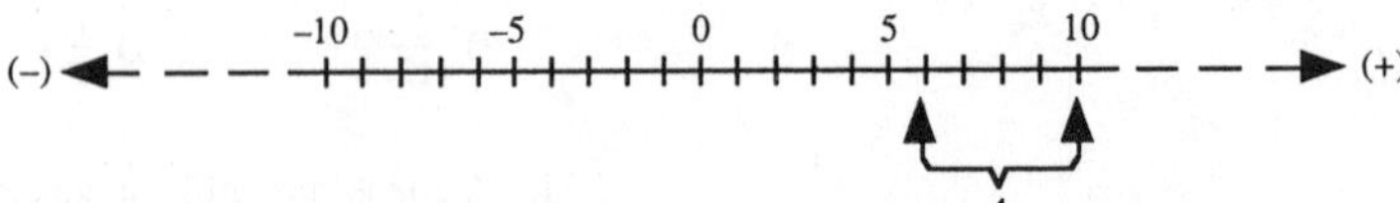

Follow this procedure even if you wind up with a negative result, as illustrated in the following example.

Example:

$10 + (-12) = 10 - |-12| = 10 - 12 = -2$

➢ Start at 10 and move the counter 12 units in a negative direction. The result is two units to the left of zero, or −2:

Similarly, the procedure works when you add a negative number to another negative number.

Example:

$-3 + -2 = -3 - |-2| = -3 - 2 = -5$

➢ Begin at −3, and move the counter two units in the negative direction. The result is −5:

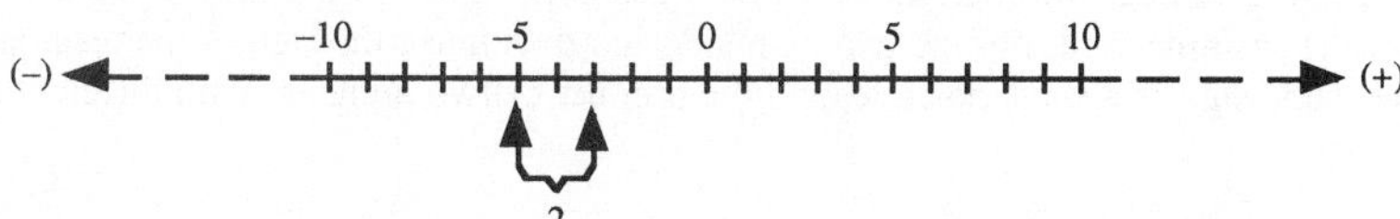

Any addition of a negative number is equivalent to subtraction of a positive number.

Examples:

1. $5 + (-2) = 5 - 2 = 3$
2. $7 + (-7) = 7 - 7 = 0$

Subtracting Negative Numbers

Subtracting negative numbers is a little different. When you subtract a negative number, you are really adding, since the number itself has a negative value. It is like a double negative: "It is not true that Bob's not here" means that Bob is here. To subtract a negative number from another quantity, add the absolute value of the negative number to the other quantity.

Example:

$10 - (-5) = 10 + |-5| = 10 + 5 = 15$

➢ Start at 10: Since the minus signs cancel each other out, move the counter in the positive direction. The result is 15:

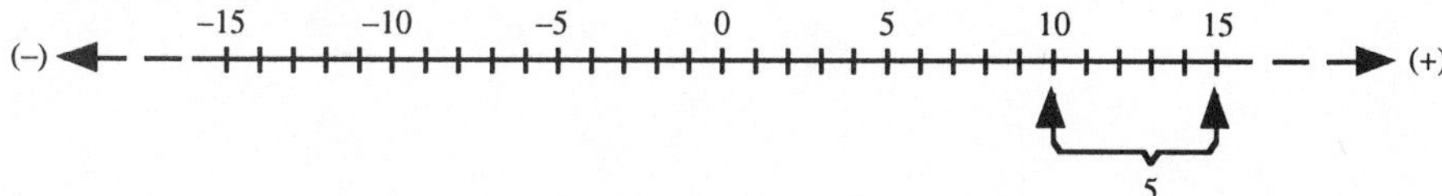

Follow this procedure no matter where you start, even if you are subtracting a negative number from zero or from another negative number.

Example:

$-5 - (-10) = -5 + |-10| = -5 + 10 = 5$

➢ Start at −5: Since the minus signs cancel each other out, move the counter in the positive direction. The result is 5:

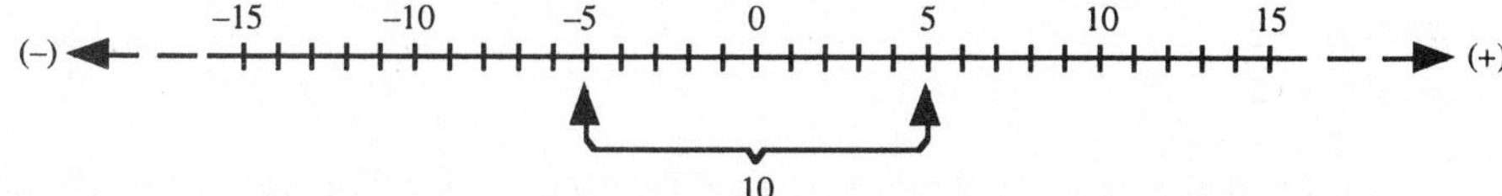

Any subtraction of a negative number is equivalent to addition of a positive number.

Examples:

1. $4-(-4)=4+4=8$
2. $0-(-7)=0+7=7$
3. $-8-(-4)=-8+4=-4$

Multiplying Negative Numbers

We can also explain the rules for multiplying negative numbers through the concept of absolute value. To multiply a positive number by a negative number, simply multiply together the absolute values of the two numbers, and then make the sign of the resultant value negative. The product of two numbers with the same sign is always positive, and the product of two numbers with different signs is always negative.

Examples:

1. $3 \cdot -6 = -(|3| \cdot |-6|) = -(3 \cdot 6) = -18$
2. $-2 \cdot 4 = -(|-2| \cdot |4|) = -(2 \cdot 4) = -8$

A way of remembering this is to think that the minus sign has "tainted" the problem, so the result must be negative.

To multiply a negative number by a negative number, multiply together the absolute values of the two numbers, and then make the sign of this value positive. The product of two negative numbers is always positive.

Example:

$-3 \cdot -6 = |-3| \cdot |-6| = 3 \cdot 6 = 18$

This is like saying that two wrongs DO make a right—a negative times a negative produces a positive.

Any product involving an odd number of negatives will always be negative. Any product involving an even number of negatives will always be positive.

Examples:

1. $-1 \cdot -2 = 2$
2. $-1 \cdot -2 \cdot -3 = -6$
3. $-1 \cdot -2 \cdot -3 \cdot -4 \cdot = 24$
4. $-1 \cdot -2 \cdot -3 \cdot -4 \cdot -5 = -120$

Dividing Negative Numbers

When dividing negative numbers, the same rules apply as with multiplication. If the division involves a positive number and a negative number, divide using the absolute values of the numbers, and then make the sign of the resultant value negative.

Examples:

1. $6 \div -3 = -(|6| \div |-3|) = -(6 \div 3) = -2$
2. $-8 \div 2 = -(|-8| \div |2|) = -(8 \div 2) = -4$

For division involving two negative numbers, divide using the absolute values of the numbers, and then make the sign of this value positive.

Example:

$-8 \div -4 = |-8| \div |-4| = 8 \div 4 = 2$

Any quotient involving an odd number of negatives will always be negative. Any quotient involving an even number of negatives will always be positive.

Examples:

1. $\frac{4}{-2} = -2$
2. $\frac{(-2)(6)}{-4} = \frac{-12}{-4} = 3$
3. $\frac{(3)(-2)(-4)}{(-1)(2)} = -(3 \cdot 4) = -12$

Summary of Signed Numbers

PRINCIPLES FOR WORKING WITH NEGATIVE NUMBERS

1. *Subtraction* of a *negative* number is equivalent to *addition* of a *positive* number.
2. *Addition* of a *negative* number is equivalent to *subtraction* of a *positive* number.
3. *Multiplication* or *division* involving an *odd* number of *negative* numbers always results in a *negative* number.
4. *Multiplication* or *division* involving an *even* number of *negative* numbers always results in a *positive* number.

These rules govern operations with all signed numbers. Be careful how you apply the rules to complicated expressions; just take each item step by step.

Example:

$$\frac{(2 \cdot -3) - (-2 + -12)}{(-8 \div 2) \cdot (2 + -4)} = \frac{(-6) - (-14)}{(-4) \cdot (-2)} = \frac{-6 + 14}{4 \cdot 2} = \frac{14 - 6}{8} = \frac{8}{8} = 1$$

NOTE: The ACT, PLAN, and EXPLORE allow calculators. Therefore, it is important that you learn how to use a calculator and bring the same calculator with you to the exam. Using a calculator provides greater accuracy and often saves valuable test time.

EXERCISE 3

Signed Numbers

DIRECTIONS: Choose the correct answer to each of the following items. Use a calculator when necessary. Answers are on page 920.

Items #1-15: Each of the following items includes a number line and a counter. Select the letter of the correct position for the counter after the indicated operations.

Example:

2 + 3 = ?

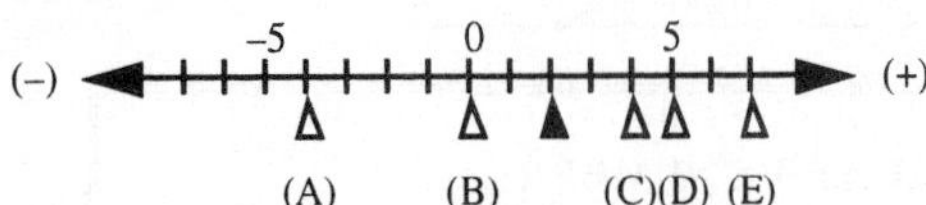

The original position of the counter is 2. If you move it three units in the positive direction, the result is 5, (D).

1. 3 + 1 = ?

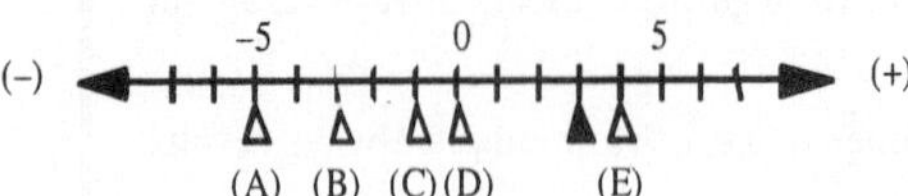

2. 5 − 2 = ?

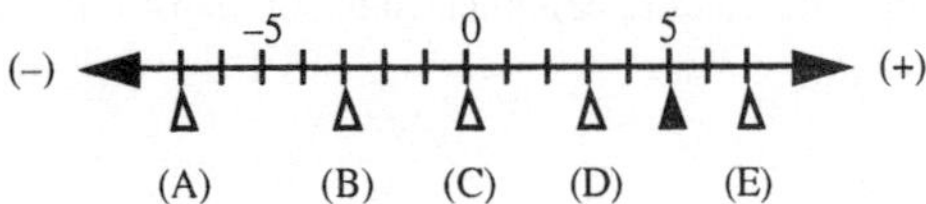

3. 5 + (−2) = ?

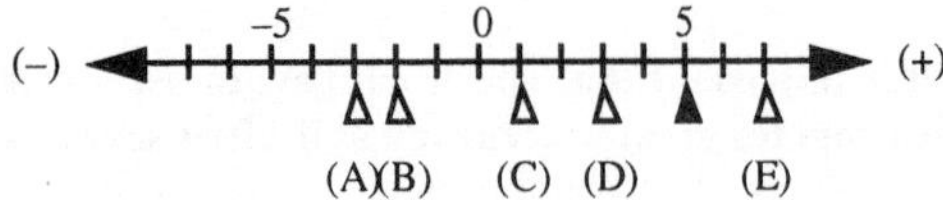

4. 3 + 2 + (−7) = ?

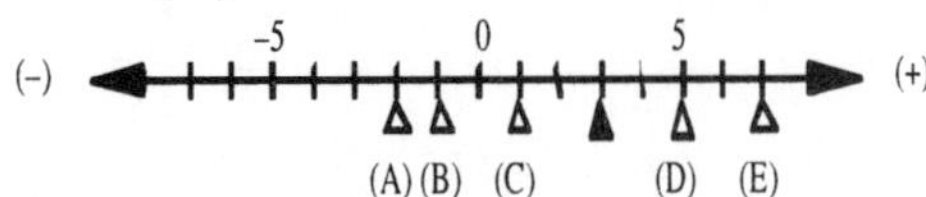

5. 2 + (−4) = ?

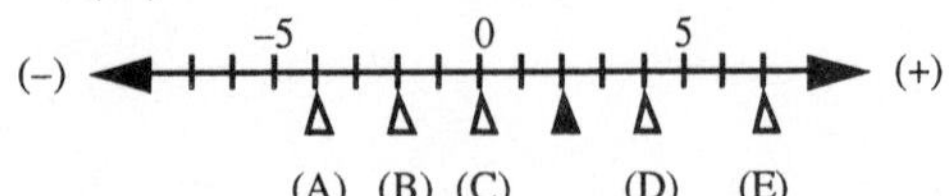

6. −2 + (−2) = ?

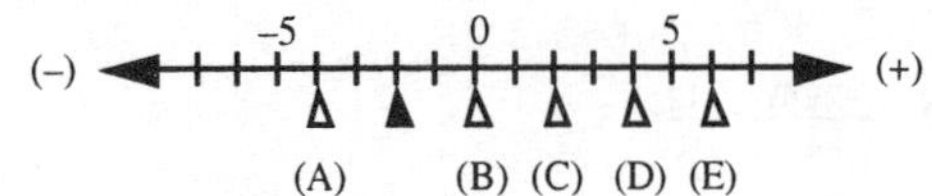

7. 4 + (−2) + (−2) = ?

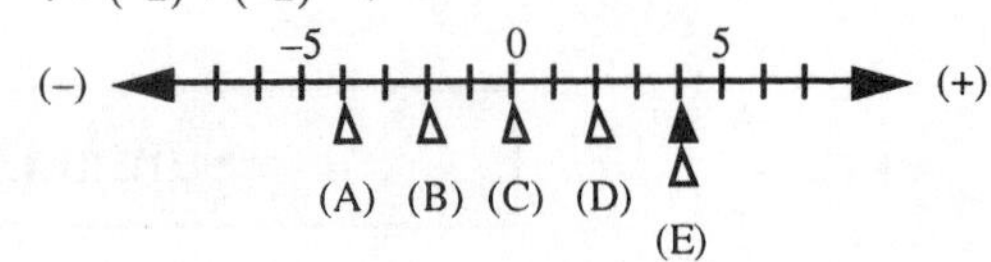

8. −4 + (−1) + (−1) = ?

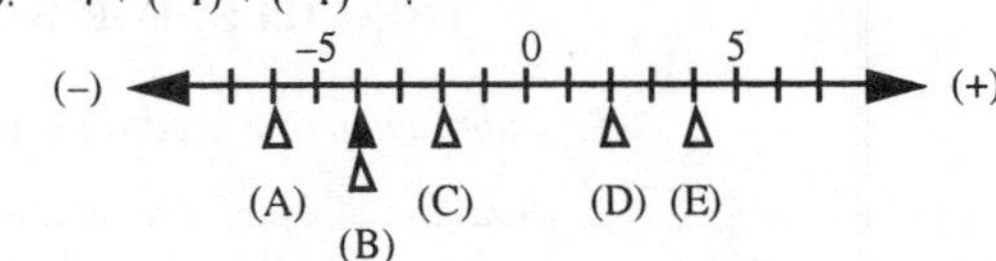

9. −4 + 8 = ?

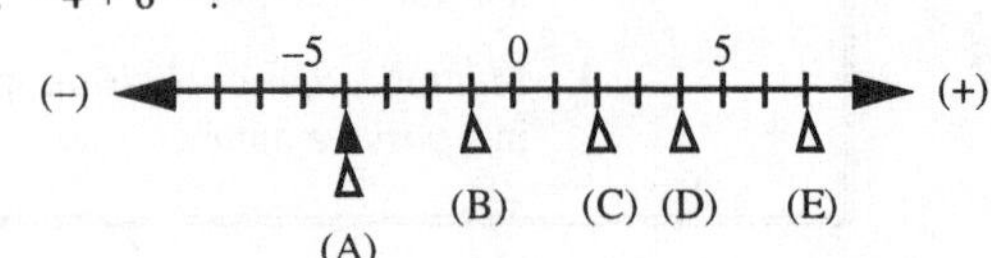

10. −2 + 2 + (−1) = ?

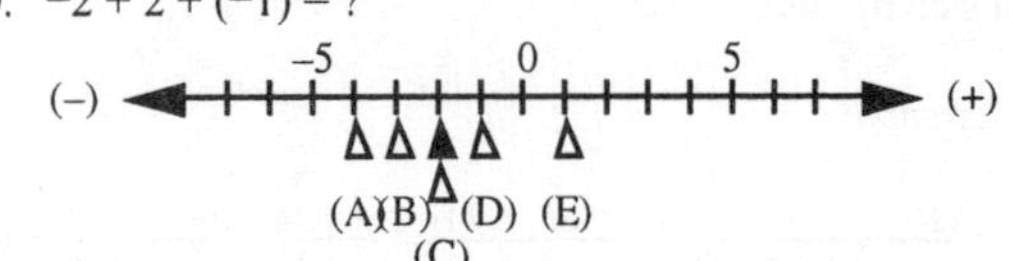

11. 2 − (−1) = ?

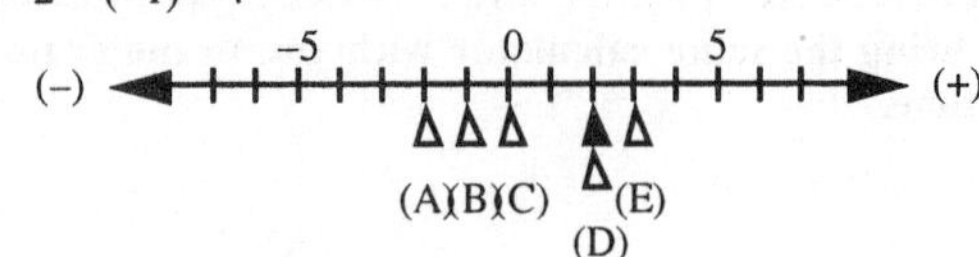

12. 5 − (−2) = ?

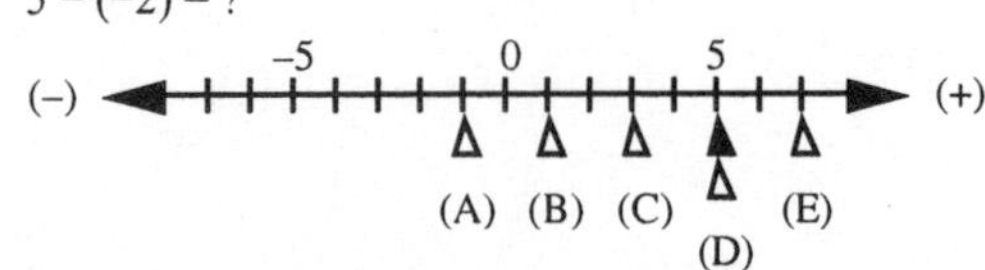

13. 0 − (−4) = ?

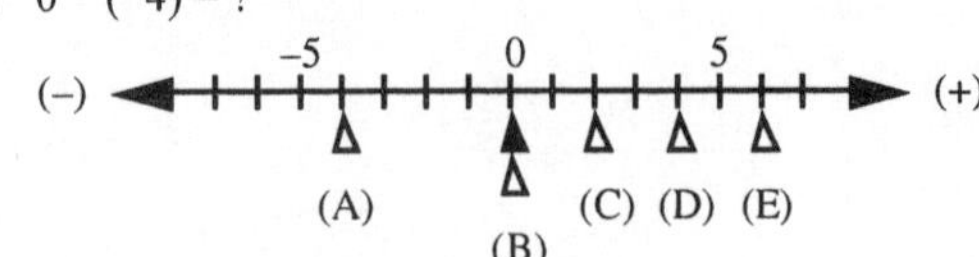

14. $-2-(-1)=?$

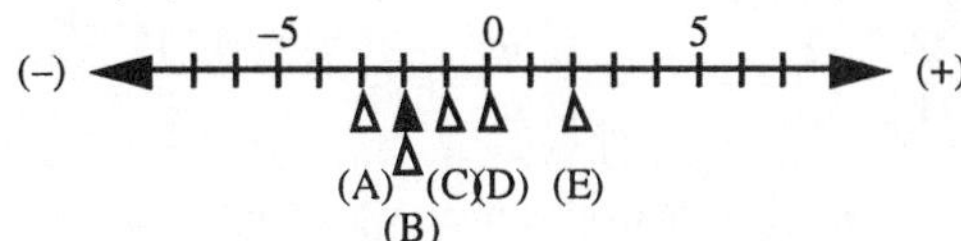

15. $-3-(-1)-(-2)=?$

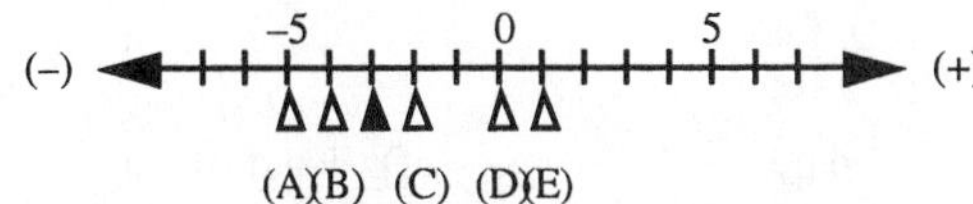

Items #16-60: Determine the correct answer for each of these problems without the aid of a number line.

16. $5+8+(-2)+(-1)=?$
A. 3 B. 7 C. 10 D. 13 E. 23

17. $12-7+6+(-1)=?$
A. 2 B. 6 C. 10 D. 14 E. 18

18. $3+(-3)=?$
A. –6 B. –3 C. 0 D. 3 E. 6

19. $0+(-12)=?$
A. –12 B. –6 C. –1 D. 0 E. 12

20. $-3+1=?$
A. –4 B. –2 C. 2 D. 4 E. 8

21. $-2+(-6)=?$
A. –8 B. –4 C. –2 D. 2 E. 4

22. $-2+(-3)+(-4)=?$
A. –24 B. –9 C. –6 D. 0 E. 6

23. $100+(-99)=?$
A. –199 B. –99 C. –1 D. 1 E. 99

24. $14-(-2)=?$
A. 16 B. 12 C. 4 D. –2 E. –14

25. $2-(-5)=?$
A. 7 B. 3 C. –2 D. –3 E. –7

26. $0-(-4)=?$
A. –8 B. –4 C. 0 D. 4 E. 8

27. $-2-(-3)=?$
A. –6 B. –5 C. –1 D. 1 E. 3

28. $-5-(-1)-1=?$
A. –7 B. –5 C. –3 D. –1 E. 2

29. $(5-1)+(1-5)=?$
A. –5 B. –3 C. 0 D. 3 E. 5

30. $[2-(-6)]-[-2+(-1)]=?$
A. –2 B. –1 C. 1 D. 5 E. 11

31. $1 \bullet -2=?$
A. –2 B. –1 C. $-\frac{1}{2}$ D. 1 E. 2

32. $-8 \bullet 6=?$
A. –48 B. –2 C. 2 D. 14 E. 48

33. $-10 \bullet -10=?$
A. –100 B. –20 C. 0 D. 20 E. 100

34. $-2 \bullet -1 \bullet 1=?$
A. –3 B. –2 C. 1 D. 2 E. 4

35. $-10 \bullet -10 \bullet -10=?$
A. –1,000 B. –30 C. –1 D. 1 E. 1,000

36. $-2 \bullet -2 \bullet -2 \bullet -2=?$
A. –32 B. –8 C. 4 D. 16 E. 32

37. $-1 \bullet -1 \bullet -1 \bullet -1 \bullet -1 \bullet -1 \bullet -1 \bullet -1 \bullet -1 \bullet -1=?$
A. –10 B. –1 C. 0 D. 1 E. 10

38. $4 \div -2=?$
A. –8 B. –2 C. $-\frac{1}{2}$ D. 2 E. 8

39. $-12 \div 4 = ?$

A. –4
B. –3
C. –2
D. 3
E. 4

40. $-12 \div -12 = ?$

A. –144
B. –1
C. 1
D. 24
E. 144

41. $[7 - (-6)] + [3 \cdot (2 - 4)] = ?$

A. –2
B. 0
C. 7
D. 12
E. 23

42. $[2 \cdot (-3)][1 \cdot (-4)][2 \cdot (-1)] = ?$

A. –48
B. –16
C. 2
D. 28
E. 56

43. $(6 \cdot -2) \div (3 \cdot -4) = ?$

A. –12
B. –1
C. 1
D. 3
E. 24

44. $\{[4 - (-3)] + [7 - (-1)]\}[-3 - (-2)] = ?$

A. –25
B. –15
C. –7
D. –1
E. 8

45. $[(2 \cdot -1) + (4 \div -2)][(-6 + 6) - (2 - 3)] = ?$

A. 5
B. 2
C. –2
D. –4
E. –23

46. $(2 - 3)(3 - 2)(4 - 3)(3 - 4)(5 - 4)(4 - 5) = ?$

A. –625
B. –1
C. 1
D. 50
E. 625

47. $[2(3 - 4)] + [(125 \div -25)(1 \cdot -2)] = ?$

A. –12
B. –8
C. 2
D. 8
E. 125

48. $-\frac{1}{2} \cdot 2 \cdot -\frac{1}{2} \cdot 2 \cdot -\frac{1}{2} \cdot 2 = ?$

A. –16
B. –8
C. –1
D. 1
E. 2

49. $[(2 \cdot 3) \div (-6 \cdot 1)][(21 \div 7) \cdot \frac{1}{3}] = ?$

A. –5
B. –1
C. 1
D. 12
E. 36

50. $(-5 \cdot -2) - (-2 \cdot -5) = ?$

A. 0
B. 2
C. 10
D. 12
E. 18

51. $6 \div -\frac{1}{3} = ?$

A. –18
B. $-\frac{1}{2}$
C. 2
D. 3
E. 18

52. $[-3 - (-3)] - [-2 - (-2)] - [-1 - (-1)] = ?$

A. –12
B. –6
C. 0
D. 6
E. 12

53. If n is any negative number, which of the following must also be negative?

I. $n + n$
II. $n \cdot n$
III. $n - n$

A. I only
B. II only
C. I and III only
D. II and III only
E. I, II, and III

54. If n is any negative number, which of the following must also be negative?

I. $n \cdot -n$
II. $-n \cdot -n$
III. $-n + n$

A. I only
B. II only
C. III only
D. II and III only
E. I, II, and III

55. If n is any positive number, which of the following must be negative?

I. $n \cdot -n$
II. $-n + -n$
III. $n - (-n)$

A. I only
B. II only
C. I and II only
D. I and III only
E. I, II, and III

56. If n is any positive number, which of the following must be positive?

I. $-n - (-n)$
II. $-n \cdot -n$
III. $n \div (-n \cdot -n)$

A. I only
B. II only
C. III only
D. I and III only
E. II and III only

57. Given any number such that $n \neq 0$, which of the following must be equal to 0?

I. $-n \cdot -n \cdot -n \cdot -n \cdot -n \cdot -n$
II. $[(n - n) - n] - [(n - n) - n]$
III. $n \div [(n \div n) \div n]$

A. I only
B. II only
C. I and II only
D. I and III only
E. I, II, and III

58. In the figure below, what point between A and B is two times as far from A as from B?

A. 7
B. 10
C. 17
D. 24
E. 31

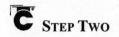

59. In the figure below, what point between A and B is three times as far from A as from B?

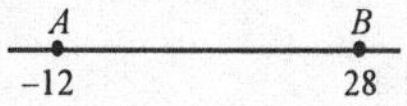

A. 12 C. 20 E. 24
B. 18 D. 21

60. $|1| + |-2| + |3| + |-4| + |5| + |-6| + |7| + |-8| + |9| + |-10| + |11| + |-12| = ?$

A. −12 C. 6 E. 78
B. −6 D. 12

Decimals

A ***decimal*** is nothing more than a special way of writing fractions using a denominator of ten, or one hundred, or one thousand, and so on. Decimals are written with a decimal point to the left of the decimal digits in order to distinguish them from whole numbers.

Examples:

1. The fraction $\frac{3}{10}$ written as a decimal is 0.3.
2. The fraction $\frac{72}{100}$ written as a decimal is 0.72.

The positions to the right of the decimal point are called decimal places. Decimal places are analogous to the positions of the digits in whole numbers (units column, tens column, *etc.*). The number of decimal places indicates the denominator of the fraction. One decimal place indicates a denominator of 10; two places indicate a denominator of 100; three indicate a denominator of 1,000; and so on. 0.335 is read as three hundred thirty-five thousandths and 0.12345 as twelve thousand three hundred forty-five hundred thousandths.

0	.	1	2	3	4	5
		TENTHS	HUNDREDTHS	THOUSANDTHS	TEN THOUSANDTHS	HUNDRED THOUSANDTHS

When a decimal does not include a positive or negative whole number, a zero is placed to the left of the decimal point. This has no mathematical significance; it is there just to make the decimals more readable. Without the zero, someone might fail to see the decimal and read .335 as 335. On the exam, all decimals that do not include a positive or negative whole number are written with a zero to the left of the decimal point.

Converting Fractions to Decimals

If the fraction already has a denominator that is ten, one hundred, one thousand, *etc.*, the conversion is very easy. The numerator of the fraction becomes the decimal. The number of zeros in the denominator governs the placement of the decimal point. Starting just to the right of the last digit of the numerator, you count over one digit to the left for each zero in the denominator. For example, to express $\frac{127}{1,000}$ in decimal form, take the numerator, 127, as the decimal. Then, starting just to the right of the 7, count over three places to the left (one for each zero in 1,000). The decimal equivalent is 0.127.

Examples:

1. $\frac{3}{10} = 0.3$ (One zero in the denominator indicates one decimal place.)
2. $\frac{13}{100} = 0.13$ (Two zeros in the denominator indicate two decimal places.)
3. $\frac{522}{1,000} = 0.522$ (Three zeros in the denominator indicate three decimal places.)

If there are fewer digits in the numerator than zeros in the denominator, add zeros to the left of the number until you have enough decimal places. For example, consider $\frac{53}{1,000}$: the denominator contains three zeros, but 53 is only a two-digit number. Therefore, add one zero to the left of the 5: $\frac{53}{1,000} = 0.053$.

Examples:

1. $\frac{3}{100} = 0.03$ (Two zeros mean two decimal places.)
2. $\frac{71}{10,000} = 0.0071$ (Four zeros mean four decimal places.)
3. $\frac{9}{100,000} = 0.00009$ (Five zeros mean five decimal places.)

To convert a proper fraction with a denominator other than 10, 100, *etc.*, convert the fraction to an equivalent form using a denominator such as ten, one hundred, *etc.* For example, to convert $\frac{3}{4}$ to a decimal, change it into a fraction with a denominator of 100: $\frac{3}{4} = \frac{3 \cdot 25}{4 \cdot 25} = \frac{75}{100}$. Then, $\frac{75}{100}$ is written as 0.75, as described in the previous section.

Examples:

1. $\frac{2}{5} = \frac{2 \cdot 2}{5 \cdot 2} = \frac{4}{10} = 0.4$
2. $\frac{1}{4} = \frac{1 \cdot 25}{4 \cdot 25} = \frac{25}{100} = 0.25$
3. $\frac{3}{8} = \frac{3 \cdot 125}{8 \cdot 125} = \frac{375}{1,000} = 0.375$
4. $\frac{1}{50} = \frac{1 \cdot 2}{50 \cdot 2} = \frac{2}{100} = 0.02$

To determine which denominator you should use, divide the denominator of the fraction into 10, then into 100, then into 1,000, until you find the first denominator that is evenly divisible by the denominator of the fraction. For example, $\frac{3}{8}$ does not have an equivalent form with a denominator of 10, but it does have an equivalent form with a denominator of 1,000. This is the same process used above to find common denominators for fractions. (Note: You can also convert a fraction into a decimal by dividing the numerator of the fraction by its denominator. However, this method obviously presupposes that you know how to divide decimals. We will come back to the topic of converting to decimals when we discuss how to divide decimals.)

Converting Mixed Numbers to Decimals

To change a mixed number to a decimal, convert the fractional part of the mixed number to a decimal as discussed above, and then place the whole number part of the mixed number to the left of the decimal point.

Examples:

1. Convert the mixed number $2\frac{3}{4}$ to a decimal.
   - ➤ First, convert $\frac{3}{4}$ to a decimal: $\frac{3}{4} = 0.75$. Then, place the whole-number part to the left of the decimal point: 2.75. Notice that the extra zero is dropped—there is no reason to write 02.75.
2. $6\frac{1}{10} = 6.1$
3. $12\frac{1}{2} = 12.5$
4. $3\frac{7}{8} = 3.875$

Converting Improper Fractions to Decimals

To convert an improper fraction to a decimal, just treat the improper fraction as a mixed number and follow the procedure just outlined.

Examples:

1. $\frac{9}{4} = 2\frac{1}{4} = 2.25$
2. $\frac{7}{2} = 3\frac{1}{2} = 3.5$
3. $\frac{8}{5} = 1\frac{3}{5} = 1.6$

It is also possible, and often easier, to convert fractions to decimals by dividing the numerator by the denominator. Again, we will postpone this part of the discussion until we have studied division of decimals.

Converting Decimals to Fractions and Mixed Numbers

To convert a decimal back to a fraction, it is necessary only to create a fraction using the digits of the decimal number as a numerator and a denominator of 1 followed by a number of zeros equal to the number of decimal places.

Examples:

1. Convert 0.125 to a fraction.
   ➤ Use 125 as the numerator and 1,000 as the denominator: $\frac{125}{1{,}000}$. Reduce the fraction to lowest terms: $\frac{125}{1{,}000} = \frac{1}{8}$.
2. $0.04 = \frac{4}{100} = \frac{1}{25}$
3. $0.25 = \frac{25}{100} = \frac{1}{4}$
4. $0.005 = \frac{5}{1{,}000} = \frac{1}{200}$

Finally, if the decimal consists of both a whole part and a fraction, the conversion will result in a mixed number. The whole part of the mixed number will be the whole part of the decimal. Then, convert the fractional part of the decimal as just shown.

Examples:

1. Convert 2.05 to a mixed number.
   ➤ Write 0.05 as a fraction: $0.05 = \frac{5}{100} = \frac{1}{20}$. The whole number part is 2, so $2.05 = 2\frac{1}{20}$.
2. $1.75 = 1 + \frac{75}{100} = 1 + \frac{3}{4} = 1\frac{3}{4}$
3. $32.6 = 32 + \frac{6}{10} = 32 + \frac{3}{5} = 32\frac{3}{5}$
4. $2.05 = 2 + \frac{5}{100} = 2 + \frac{1}{20} = 2\frac{1}{20}$
5. $357.125 = 357 + \frac{125}{1{,}000} = 357 + \frac{1}{8} = 357\frac{1}{8}$

Operations of Decimals

1. *Adding and Subtracting Decimals*

Decimals can be manipulated in very much the same way as whole numbers. You can add and subtract decimals.

Examples:

1. $0.2 + 0.3 + 0.1 = 0.6$
2. $0.7 - 0.2 = 0.5$

Adding zeros to the end of a decimal number does not change the value of that number. If the decimals do not have the same number of decimal places, add zeros to the right of those that do not until every number has the same number of decimal places. Then, line up the decimal points and combine the decimals as indicated. Follow the same process for subtracting decimals.

Examples:

1. $0.75 - 0.1125 = \begin{array}{r} 0.7500 \\ \underline{-0.1125} \\ 0.6375 \end{array}$

2. $0.125 + 0.6 + 0.115 = \begin{array}{r} 0.125 \\ 0.600 \\ \underline{+0.115} \\ 0.840 \end{array}$

3. $0.999 - 0.000001 = \begin{array}{r} 0.999000 \\ \underline{-0.000001} \\ 0.998999 \end{array}$

4. $2.14 + 0.125 + 0.0005 = \begin{array}{r} 2.1400 \\ 0.1250 \\ \underline{+0.0005} \\ 2.2655 \end{array}$

5. $0.8 - 0.1111 = \begin{array}{r} 0.8000 \\ \underline{-0.1111} \\ 0.6889 \end{array}$

6. $0.11 + 0.9 + 0.033 = \begin{array}{r} 0.110 \\ 0.900 \\ \underline{+0.033} \\ 1.043 \end{array}$

2. *Multiplying Decimals*

As with fractions, there is no need to find a common denominator when multiplying decimals: The multiplication process generates its own. Simply multiply as with whole numbers and then adjust the decimal point. To find the correct position for the decimal point first, count the total number of decimal places in the numbers that are being multiplied. Then, in the final product, place the decimal point that many places to the left, counting from the right side of the last digit.

Examples:

1. $0.25 \cdot 0.2 = ?$

   ➢ Ignore the decimals and multiply: $25 \cdot 2 = 50$. Now, adjust the decimal point. Since 0.25 has two decimal places, and 0.2 has one decimal place, count three places to the left, starting at the right side of the 0 in 50; the final product is $0.050 = 0.05$.
2. $0.1 \cdot 0.2 \cdot 0.3 = 0.006$ ($1 \cdot 2 \cdot 3 = 6$, and there are three decimal places in the multiplication.)
3. $0.02 \cdot 0.008 = 0.00016$ ($2 \cdot 8 = 16$, and there are five decimal places in the multiplication.)
4. $2 \cdot 0.5 = 1$ ($2 \cdot 5 = 10$, and there is one decimal place in the multiplication.)
5. $2.5 \cdot 2.5 = 6.25$ ($25 \cdot 25 = 625$, and there are two decimal places in the multiplication.)
6. $0.10 \cdot 0.10 \cdot 0.10 = 0.001000 = 0.001$ ($10 \cdot 10 \cdot 10 = 1{,}000$, and there are six decimal places in the multiplication.)

To simplify the process of multiplying decimals, drop any final zeros before multiplying. Thus, in the case of the last example, $0.10 \cdot 0.10 \cdot 0.10 = 0.1 \cdot 0.1 \cdot 0.1 = 0.001$ since there are three decimal places in the multiplication.

3. *Dividing Decimals*

Like multiplication, division generates a common denominator by a suitable adjustment of zeros. However, there are two situations in which division of decimals is a little tricky. Let's review them one at a time.

First, when the divisor (the number doing the dividing) is a whole number, place the decimal point in the quotient (result of division) immediately above the decimal point in the dividend (the number being divided). Then, keep dividing until there is no remainder, adding zeros as needed to the right of the dividend. This is the procedure whenever the divisor is a whole number—even if the dividend is also a whole number.

Examples:

1. $$\begin{array}{r} 0.05 \\ 0.25 \div 5 = 5\overline{)0.25} \\ \underline{-25} \\ 0 \end{array}$$

2. $$\begin{array}{r} 1.25 \\ 2.5 \div 2 = 2\overline{)2.50} \\ \underline{-2} \\ 05 \\ \underline{-4} \\ 10 \\ \underline{-10} \\ 0 \end{array}$$

3. $$\begin{array}{r} 0.07 \\ 1.75 \div 25 = 25\overline{)1.75} \\ \underline{-175} \\ 0 \end{array}$$

4. $$\begin{array}{r} 0.12 \\ 1.44 \div 12 = 12\overline{)1.44} \\ \underline{-144} \\ 0 \end{array}$$

5. $$\begin{array}{r} 0.0004 \\ 0.1 \div 250 = 250\overline{)0.1000} \\ \underline{-1000} \\ 0 \end{array}$$

6. $$\begin{array}{r} 4.5 \\ 9 \div 2 = 2\overline{)9.0} \\ \underline{-8} \\ 10 \\ \underline{-10} \\ 0 \end{array}$$

The second tricky situation occurs when the divisor is a decimal. In these cases, "clear" the fractional part of the decimal by moving the decimal point to the right. For example, if dividing by 0.1, change 0.1 to 1; if dividing by 2.11, convert that to 211 by moving the decimal point two places to the right. However, you must also move the decimal point of the dividend by the same number of places to ensure that their relative values are not changed. Notice that in the following examples both decimal points are moved the same number of places to the right.

Examples:

1. $$\begin{array}{r} 2. \\ 5 \div 2.5 = 2.5.\overline{)5.0.} \\ \underline{-50} \\ 0 \end{array}$$

2. $$\begin{array}{r} 8. \\ 10 \div 1.25 = 1.25.\overline{)10.00.} \\ \underline{-1000} \\ 0 \end{array}$$

3. $$\begin{array}{r} 1000. \\ 50 \div 0.05 = 0.05.\overline{)50.00.} \\ \underline{-5000} \\ 0 \end{array}$$

There are two final things to say about dividing decimals. First, as mentioned previously, you can use division of decimals to convert fractions to decimals. For example, to convert $\frac{9}{2}$ to a decimal number, simply divide 9 by 2.

Examples:

1. $$\begin{array}{r} 4.5 \\ \frac{9}{2} = 2\overline{)9} = 2\overline{)9.0} \\ \underline{-8} \\ 10 \\ \underline{-10} \\ 0 \end{array}$$

2. $$\begin{array}{r} 0.75 \\ \frac{3}{4} = 4\overline{)3} = 4\overline{)3.00} \\ \underline{-28} \\ 20 \\ \underline{-20} \\ 0 \end{array}$$

Second, some fractions do not have exact decimal equivalents. Try converting $\frac{1}{3}$ to a decimal using the division route. You will be at it forever, because you get an endless succession of "3"s. Try converting $\frac{1}{9}$ to a decimal using the division method. Again, you will get an endless succession, this time of repeating "1"s. By convention, repeating decimals are indicated using an overbar: $0.1\overline{1}$.

NOTE: The ACT, PLAN, and EXPLORE allow calculators. Therefore, it is important that you learn how to use a calculator and bring the same calculator with you to the exam. Using a calculator provides greater accuracy and often saves valuable test time.

EXERCISE 4

Decimals

DIRECTIONS: Choose the correct answer to each of the following items. Use a calculator when necessary. Answers are on page 920.

1. What is $\frac{7}{10}$ expressed as a decimal?

A. 70 B. 7 C. 0.7 D. 0.007 E. 0.0007

2. What is $\frac{73}{100}$ expressed as a decimal?

A. 73 B. 7.3 C. 0.73 D. 0.073 E. 0.0073

3. What is $\frac{21}{1,000}$ expressed as a decimal?

A. 0.21 B. 0.021 C. 0.0021 D. 0.00021 E. 0.000021

4. What is $\frac{557}{1,000}$ expressed as a decimal?

A. 5.57 B. 0.557 C. 0.0557 D. 0.0057 E. 0.00057

5. What is $\frac{34}{10,000}$ expressed as a decimal?

A. 0.00034 B. 0.0034 C. 0.034 D. 0.34 E. 3.4

6. What is $\frac{1}{1,000,000}$ expressed as a decimal?

A. 0.01 B. 0.001 C. 0.0001 D. 0.00001 E. 0.000001

7. What is $\frac{30}{100}$ expressed as a decimal?

A. 3 B. 0.3 C. 0.03 D. 0.003 E. 0.0003

8. What is $\frac{1,000}{4,000}$ expressed as a decimal?

A. 0.25 B. 0.025 C. 0.0025 D. 0.00025 E. 0.000025

9. Which of the following is (are) equal to $\frac{1}{10}$?

I. 1.0
II. 0.1
III. 0.1000

A. I only B. II only C. III only D. I and III only E. II and III only

10. Which of the following is (are) equal to $\frac{25}{100}$?

I. 0.25
II. 0.025
III. 0.0025

A. I only B. I and II only C. I and III only D. II and III only E. I, II, and III

11. What is $\frac{257}{100}$ expressed as a decimal?

A. 25.7 B. 2.57 C. 0.257 D. 0.0257 E. 0.00257

12. What is $\frac{57}{10}$ expressed as a decimal?

A. 57 B. 5.7 C. 0.57 D. 0.057 E. 0.0057

13. What is $\frac{5}{8}$ expressed as a decimal?

A. 0.125 B. 0.625 C. 0.850 D. 1.25 E. 5.80

14. What is $\frac{4}{5}$ expressed as a decimal?

A. 0.4 B. 0.6 C. 0.8 D. 1.2 E. 2.4

15. What is $\frac{1}{20}$ expressed as a decimal?

A. 0.05 B. 0.005 C. 0.0005 D. 0.00005 E. 0.000005

16. What is $\frac{1}{50}$ expressed as a decimal?

A. 0.2 B. 0.02 C. 0.002 D. 0.0002 E. 0.00002

17. What is $\frac{3}{200}$ expressed as a decimal?

A. 0.15 B. 0.015 C. 0.0015 D. 0.00015 E. 0.000015

18. What is $\frac{9}{500}$ expressed as a decimal?

A. 0.000018 B. 0.00018 C. 0.0018 D. 0.018 E. 0.18

19. What is $\frac{17}{500}$ expressed as a decimal?

A. 0.175 B. 0.034 C. 0.0175 D. 0.0034 E. 0.00034

20. What is $\frac{123}{200}$ expressed as a decimal?

A. 0.615 B. 0.256 C. 0.0615 D. 0.0256 E. 0.00615

21. $0.1 + 0.1 = ?$

A. 0.002 B. 0.02 C. 0.2 D. 2 E. 20

22. $0.27 + 0.13 + 0.55 = ?$

A. 0.21 B. 0.36 C. 0.47 D. 0.85 E. 0.95

23. $0.528 + 0.116 + 0.227 = ?$

A. 0.871 B. 0.583 C. 0.243 D. 0.112 E. 0.0012

24. $0.7 + 0.013 + 0.028 = ?$

A. 0.741 B. 0.988 C. 1.02 D. 1.224 E. 2.553

25. $1.23 + 0.00001 = ?$

A. 1.24 B. 1.2301 C. 1.23001 D. 1.2300001 E. 1.230000001

26. $57.1 + 23.3 + 35.012 = ?$

A. 412.115 B. 115.412 C. 115.0412 D. 11.5412 E. 1.15412

27. $0.01 + 0.001 + 0.0001 + 0.00001 = ?$

A. 1 B. 0.10 C. 0.1111 D. 0.01111 E. 0.001111

28. $0.9 + 0.09 + 0.009 + 0.0009 = ?$

A. 0.9999 B. 0.09999 C. 0.009999 D. 0.0009999 E. 0.0000999

29. $0.27 + 0.36 + 2.1117 + 3.77777 + 1.42 = ?$

A. 5.44 B. 7.93947 C. 8.11143 D. 12.223479 E. 14.002785

30. $12{,}279.1 + 3{,}428.01 + 3{,}444.99 = ?$

A. 19,151.99 B. 19,152 C. 19,152.09 D. 19,152.1 E. 19,152.11

31. $0.7 - 0.3 = ?$

A. 0.004 B. 0.021 C. 0.04 D. 0.21 E. 0.4

32. $0.75 - 0.25 = ?$

A. 5 B. 1 C. 0.5 D. 0.25 E. 0.005

33. $1.35 - 0.35 = ?$

A. 1 B. 0.35 C. 0.1 D. 0.0035 E. 0.00001

34. $25.125 - 5.357 = ?$

A. 19.768 B. 15.432 C. 12.115 D. 4.108 E. 2.288

35. $1 - 0.00001 = ?$

A. 0.9 B. 0.99 C. 0.999 D. 0.9999 E. 0.99999

36. $0.2 \cdot 0.1 = ?$

A. 0.3 B. 0.2 C. 0.1 D. 0.02 E. 0.006

37. $0.1 \cdot 0.1 \cdot 0.1 = ?$

A. 0.3 B. 0.1 C. 0.01 D. 0.001 E. 0.0001

38. $1.1 \cdot 1.1 \cdot 1.1 = ?$

A. 1.331 B. 1.111 C. 0.111 D. 0.0111 E. 0.00111

39. $0.11 \cdot 0.33 = ?$

A. 0.363 B. 0.0363 C. 0.00363 D. 0.000363 E. 0.0000363

40. $0.2 \cdot 0.5 \cdot 0.2 \cdot 0.5 = ?$

A. 0.1 B. 0.01 C. 0.001 D. 0.0001 E. 0.00001

41. $5 \cdot 0.25 = ?$

A. 1.25 B. 0.125 C. 0.0125 D. 0.00125 E. 0.000125

42. $10 \cdot 0.000001 = ?$

A. 0.00001 B. 0.0001 C. 0.001 D. 0.01 E. 0.1

43. $100 \cdot 0.00052 = ?$

A. 0.0052 B. 0.052 C. 5.2 D. 52 E. 520

44. $1.2 \cdot 1.2 = ?$

A. 0.144 B. 1.44 C. 14.4 D. 144 E. 1,444

45. $1.000 \cdot 1.000 \cdot 1.000 \cdot 1.000 = ?$

A. 1 B. 0.1 C. 0.01 D. 0.001 E. 0.0001

46. $6 \div 0.2 = ?$

A. 0.03 B. 0.3 C. 3 D. 30 E. 300

47. $0.2 \div 5 = ?$

A. 0.4 B. 0.04 C. 0.004 D. 0.0004 E. 0.00004

48. $1 \div 0.001 = ?$

A. 10,000 C. 100 E. 0.0001
B. 1,000 D. 0.001

49. $25.1 \div 2.51 = ?$

A. 100 C. 0.1 E. 0.001
B. 10 D. 0.01

50. $0.25 \div 8 = ?$

A. 4 C. 0.03125 E. 0.003125
B. 0.4 D. 0.004

51. $0.005 \div 0.005 = ?$

A. 1 C. 0.005 E. 0.00005
B. 0.5 D. 0.0005

52. $2 \div 2.5 = ?$

A. 8 C. 0.8 E. 0.008
B. 5 D. 0.5

53. $111 \div 0.111 = ?$

A. 1 C. 11 E. 1,000
B. 10 D. 110

54. $0.12345 \div 0.012345 = ?$

A. 100 C. 1 E. 0.01
B. 10 D. 0.1

55. $0.002 \div 0.00002 = ?$

A. 100 C. 0.1 E. 0.001
B. 10 D. 0.01

56. Express as a decimal: $\frac{3}{5} + \frac{5}{8}$.

A. 1.00 C. 1.225 E. 1.75
B. 1.115 D. 1.50

57. Find the average of $\frac{2}{3}$ and 0.75.

A. $\frac{9}{24}$ C. $\frac{17}{24}$ E. $\frac{23}{24}$
B. $\frac{14}{24}$ D. $\frac{21}{24}$

58. Find the average of 0.1, 0.01, and $\frac{1}{4}$.

A. 0.10 C. 0.50 E. 1.0
B. 0.12 D. 0.75

59. Simplify: $\frac{12\frac{1}{3}}{0.2}$.

A. $\frac{1}{50}$ C. $\frac{85}{2}$ E. $\frac{225}{4}$
B. $\frac{3}{40}$ D. $\frac{185}{3}$

60. Simplify: $0.1\left[\frac{1}{3} - 2\left(\frac{1}{2} - \frac{1}{4}\right)\right]$.

A. $-\frac{2}{15}$ C. $-\frac{1}{90}$ E. $\frac{3}{4}$
B. $-\frac{1}{60}$ D. $\frac{1}{2}$

61. For three months, Pete saved part of his monthly allowance. He saved \$4.56 the first month, \$3.82 the second month, and \$5.06 the third month. How much did Pete save altogether?

A. \$12.04 C. \$13.04 E. \$14.44
B. \$12.44 D. \$13.44

62. The diameter of a rod is required to be 1.51 ± 0.015 inches. Which of the following represents the possible range of measurements for the rod's diameter?

A. 1.490 inches to 1.520 inches
B. 1.495 inches to 1.520 inches
C. 1.495 inches to 1.525 inches
D. 1.495 inches to 1.530 inches
E. 1.500 inches to 1.530 inches

63. From an employee's salary of \$190.57, an employer deducts \$3.05 for social security and \$5.68 for pension. What is the final amount of the check?

A. \$180.84 C. \$181.84 E. \$182.84
B. \$181.04 D. \$182.04

64. If the outer radius of a metal pipe is 2.84 inches and the inner radius is 1.94 inches, what is the thickness of the metal?

A. 0.85 in. C. 1.00 in. E. 1.25 in.
B. 0.90 in. D. 1.18 in.

65. Pete earns \$20.56 on Monday, \$32.90 on Tuesday, and \$20.78 on Wednesday. He spends half of all that he earned during the 3 days. How much does he have left?

A. \$36.12 C. \$37.12 E. \$38.12
B. \$36.72 D. \$37.72

66. What is the total cost of $3\frac{1}{2}$ pounds of meat at \$1.69/lb. and 20 lemons at \$0.60/dozen?

A. \$5.92 C. \$6.92 E. \$7.92
B. \$6.42 D. \$7.42

67. A reel of cable weighs 1,279 pounds. If the empty reel weighs 285 pounds and the cable weighs 7.1 pounds per foot, how many feet of cable are on the reel?

A. 140 C. 160 E. 180
B. 150 D. 170

68. How much will 345 fasteners at \$4.15 per hundred cost?

A. \$13.12 C. \$14.12 E. \$14.82
B. \$13.82 D. \$14.32

Percents

A ***percent*** is a special type of fraction that always has a denominator equal to 100. The percent sign, "%," is shorthand for "$\frac{x}{100}$." For example, $67\% = \frac{67}{100}$.

Converting to and from Percents

Since percents are simply a special type of fraction, both fractions and decimals can be converted to percents, and vice versa. The easiest conversion is to change a decimal to a percent: Move the decimal point two places to the right and add the percent sign.

Examples:

1. $0.27 = 27\%$
2. $0.50 = 50\%$
3. $0.275 = 27.5\%$

This substitutes "%" for two decimal places—simply a matter of changing things from one form into an equivalent form, which is a process we have already used in several ways. To change a percent back to a decimal, move the decimal point two places to the left and drop the percent sign.

Examples:

1. $27\% = 0.27$
2. $50\% = 0.50$
3. $27.5\% = 0.275$

You already know the rules for converting fractions to decimals, and vice versa. To convert a fraction to a percent, just convert the fraction to a decimal and follow the rule above.

Examples:

1. $\frac{3}{4} = 0.75 = 75\%$
2. $\frac{5}{8} = 0.625 = 62.5\%$
3. $\frac{1}{10} = 0.10 = 10\%$

To reverse the process, follow the rule given above for turning percentages back into decimals, and then use the procedure outlined in the previous section for converting decimals to fractions.

Examples:

1. $75\% = 0.75 = \frac{75}{100} = \frac{3}{4}$
2. $62.5\% = 0.625 = \frac{625}{1,000} = \frac{5}{8}$
3. $10\% = 0.1 = \frac{1}{10}$

There are two tricky types of percents: those greater than 100% and those less than 1%. First, it is possible to have a percent that is larger than 100. This would be the result of converting a mixed number, such as $2\frac{3}{4}$, to a percent: $2\frac{3}{4} = 2.75 = 275\%$. Second, percents can also be less than 1, in which case they are written with decimals; for example, 0.5%. However, these numbers follow the general rules outlined above. To convert 0.5% to a fraction: $0.5\% = 0.005 = \frac{5}{1,000} = \frac{1}{200}$. Similarly, fractions smaller than $\frac{1}{100}$ will yield a percent less than 1: $\frac{1}{2,500} = 0.0004 = 0.04\%$.

Operations of Percents

1. Adding and Subtracting Percents

Percents are fractions, so they can be manipulated like other fractions. All percents have 100 as the denominator. It is easy to add and subtract percents because you already have a common denominator.

Examples:

1. Paul originally owned 25 percent of the stock of a certain company. He purchased another 15 percent of the stock privately, and he received a gift of another 10 percent of the stock. What percent of the stock of the company does Paul now own?
   ➤ 25% + 15% + 10% = 50%
2. In a certain election, Peter and Mary received 50 percent of all the votes that were cast. If Peter received 20 percent of the votes cast in the election, what percent of the votes did Mary receive?
   ➤ 50% − 20% = 30%

2. Multiplying Percents

To multiply percents, first convert them to decimals and then multiply. For example, 60% • 80% = 0.60 • 0.80 = 0.48.

Example:

In a certain group, 80 percent of the people are wearing hats. If 60 percent of those wearing hats are also wearing gloves, what percent of the entire group is wearing both a hat and gloves?
➤ 60% of 80% = 60% • 80% = 0.60 • 0.80 = 0.48 = 48%

3. Dividing Percents

To divide percents, first convert them to decimals and then divide. For example, 100% ÷ 12.5% = 1 ÷ 0.125 = 8.

Example:

Peter is purchasing an item on a lay-away plan. If he pays weekly installments of 8% of the purchase price, how many weeks will it take for Peter to payoff the entire purchase price?
➤ 100% ÷ 8% = 1 ÷ 0.08 = 12.5 weeks

Percent Story Problems

Four basic variations of percent problems appear on the exam as story problems:

- What is x percent of something?
- This is what percent of that?
- This is a given percent of what?
- What is the percent change from this quantity to that quantity?

1. "What Is X Percent of Some Quantity?"

Percents are fractions, so in the question, "What is x percent of some quantity?", the *of* indicates multiplication.

Examples:

1. A certain class is made up of 125 students. If 60 percent of the students are men, how many men are in the class?
   ➤ 60% of $125 = 60\% \cdot 125 = 0.60 \cdot 125 = 75$
2. If Sam originally had \$25 and gave 25 percent of that amount to his friend Samantha, how much money did Sam give to Samantha?
   ➤ 25% of $\$25 = 25\% \cdot 25 = 0.25 \cdot 25 = \$6.25$
3. If Paula had 50 marbles and gave 20 percent of them to her friend Paul, how many marbles did Paula give to Paul?
   ➤ 20% of $50 = 20\% \cdot 50 = 0.20 \cdot 50 = 10$

2. *"What Percent Is This of That?"*

A second common item involving percents has the form, "What percent is this of that?"

Example:

What percent is 3 of 12?
➤ Convert $\frac{3}{12}$ to a decimal by dividing 3 by 12 and then change that decimal number to a percent: $\frac{3}{12} = \frac{1}{4} = 0.25 = 25\%$.

There are other ways of phrasing the same question:

- 3 is what percent of 12?
- Of 12, what percent is 3?

Note that all three of the above questions are equivalent and represent the three following general forms:

- What percent is this of that?
- This is what percent of that?
- Of that, what percent is this?

Although the order of words is different, these three questions ask the same thing: to express a fraction as a percent. Here is a little trick to help you avoid confusion. Notice that in each question form, there is the phrase "*of* that" and the phrase "*is* this" ("this *is*"). When you set up a fraction for the percent, always place the "*is* this" value over the "*of* that" value. We call this the "*is* over *of*" method for percents: $\frac{is}{of} = \frac{\%}{100}$.

Example:

5 is what percent of 25? Of 25, what percent is 5? What percent is 5 of 25?
➤ Notice that these questions are equivalent. $\frac{is}{of} = \frac{\%}{100} \Rightarrow \frac{5}{25} = \frac{1}{5} = 0.2 = \frac{\%}{100} \Rightarrow \% = (0.2)(100) = 20\%$.

As long as you place the "*is* this" value in the numerator and the "*of* that" value in the denominator, you cannot make a mistake.

Examples:

1. What percent is 20 of 50?
   ➤ $\frac{20}{50} = \frac{2}{5} = 0.40 = 40\%$
2. Of 125, what percent is 25?
   ➤ $\frac{25}{125} = \frac{1}{5} = 0.20 = 20\%$
3. 12 is what percent of 6?
   ➤ $\frac{12}{6} = 2 = 200\%$

The "*is* over *of*" method can be used to attack any item that presents a variation on this theme. For example, what number is 20% of 25? This is similar to the previous examples, except in this case, the percent is given and one of the two numbers is missing. Still, the "*is* over *of*" method works; "*is* this" is represented by "what number"—simply a slight variation in wording.

Examples:

1. What number is 20% of 25?
   ➤ $\frac{is}{of}=\frac{\%}{100} \Rightarrow \frac{is}{25}=\frac{20}{100} \Rightarrow is=\frac{500}{100}=5$
2. 5 is 20% of what number?
   ➤ $\frac{is}{of}=\frac{\%}{100} \Rightarrow \frac{5}{of}=\frac{20}{100} \Rightarrow of=\frac{500}{20}=25$

Notice that in the second example, the method still applies. No matter how wordy or otherwise difficult such items get, they are all answerable using this method.

Example:

John received a paycheck for $200. Of that amount, he paid Ed $25. What percent of the paycheck did John give Ed?
➤ $200 is the *of* value; $25 is the *is* value: $\frac{is}{of}=\frac{\%}{100} \Rightarrow \frac{25}{200}=\frac{\%}{100} \Rightarrow \%=\frac{25 \cdot 100}{200}=\frac{25}{2}=12.5\%$.

3. *"This Is X Percent of What?"*

In the third type of percent problem, the task is to manipulate a given value and percent to determine the unknown total value. The "*is* over *of*" equation, $\frac{is}{of}=\frac{\%}{100}$, can also be used for this variation.

Examples:

1. Seven students attended a field trip. If these 7 students were $6\frac{1}{4}\%$ of all the 9th-graders, find the total number of 9th-graders.
   ➤ $\frac{is}{of}=\frac{\%}{100} \Rightarrow \frac{7}{x}=\frac{6.25\%}{100} \Rightarrow 7 \cdot 100 = 6.25 \cdot x \Rightarrow x=\frac{7 \cdot 100}{6.25}=112.$
2. A television set discounted by 18% was sold for $459.20. What was the price of the set before the discount?
   ➤ Simplified: "$459.20 is 100% − 18%, or 82%, of what?" $\frac{\$459.20}{x}=\frac{82}{100} \Rightarrow \$459.20 \cdot 100 = x \cdot 82 \Rightarrow x=\frac{\$459.20 \cdot 100}{82}=$ $560.

4. *Percent Change*

The fourth percent item involves a quantity change over time. This type of item asks you to express the relationship between the change and the original amount in percent terms. To solve, create a fraction that is then expressed as a percent. Think of this as the "*change* over *original*" trick, because the fraction places the change over the original amount.

Examples:

1. The price of an item increased from $20 to $25. What was the percent increase in the price?
   ➤ $\frac{Change}{Original\ Amount}=\frac{25-20}{20}=\frac{5}{20}=\frac{1}{4}=0.25=25\%$
2. Mary was earning $16 per hour when she received a raise of $4 per hour. Her hourly wage increased by what percent?
   ➤ $\frac{Change}{Original\ Amount}=\frac{4}{16}=0.25=25\%$

The "*change* over *original*" trick works for decreases as well.

Examples:

1. A stock's value declined from \$50 per share to \$45 per share. What was the percent decline in the value of a share?
   ➤ $\frac{Change}{Original\ Amount} = \frac{5}{50} = \frac{1}{10} = 0.10 = 10\%$
2. Student enrollment at City University dropped from 5,000 students in 1990 to 4,000 students in 2000. What was the percent drop in the number of students enrolled at City University?
   ➤ $\frac{Change}{Original\ Amount} = \frac{1{,}000}{5{,}000} = \frac{1}{5} = 0.20 = 20\%$

NOTE: The ACT, PLAN, and EXPLORE allow calculators. Therefore, it is important that you learn how to use a calculator and bring the same calculator with you to the exam. Using a calculator provides greater accuracy and often saves valuable test time.

EXERCISE 5

Percents

DIRECTIONS: Choose the correct answer to each of the following items. Use a calculator when necessary. Answers are on page 921.

1. What is 0.79 expressed as a percent?
   A. 0.0079% B. 0.079% C. 0.79% D. 7.9% E. 79%

2. What is 0.55 expressed as a percent?
   A. 55% B. 5.5% C. 0.55% D. 0.055% E. 0.0055%

3. What is 0.111 expressed as a percent?
   A. 111% B. 11.1% C. 1.11% D. 0.111% E. 0.0111%

4. What is 0.125 expressed as a percent?
   A. 125% B. 12.5% C. 1.25% D. 0.125% E. 0.0125%

5. What is 0.5555 expressed as a percent?
   A. 5,555% B. 555.5% C. 55.55% D. 5.555% E. 0.555%

6. What is 0.3 expressed as a percent?
   A. 30% B. 3% C. 0.30% D. 0.03% E. 0.003%

7. What is 0.7500 expressed as a percent?
   A. 7,500% B. 750% C. 75% D. 7.5% E. 0.75%

8. What is 2.45 expressed as a percent?
   A. 2,450% B. 245% C. 24.5% D. 2.45% E. 0.245%

9. What is 1.25 expressed as a percent?
   A. 125% B. 12.5% C. 1.25% D. 0.125% E. 0.0125%

10. What is 10 expressed as a percent?
    A. 1,000% B. 100% C. 10% D. 1% E. 0.1%

11. What is 0.015 expressed as a percent?
    A. 15% B. 1.5% C. 0.15% D. 0.015% E. 0.0015%

12. What is 0.099 expressed as a percent?
    A. 99% B. 9.9% C. 0.99% D. 0.099% E. 0.0099%

13. What is 0.0333 expressed as a percent?
    A. 3.33% B. 0.333% C. 0.0333% D. 0.00333% E. 0.000333%

14. What is 0.001 expressed as a percent?
    A. 0.1% B. 0.01% C. 0.001% D. 0.0001% E. 0.00001%

15. What is 0.0100 expressed as a percent?
    A. 1% B. 0.01% C. 0.001% D. 0.0001% E. 0.1%

16. What is 25% expressed as a decimal?
    A. 25.0 B. 2.5 C. 0.25 D. 0.025 E. 0.0025

17. What is 56% expressed as a decimal?
    A. 5.6 B. 0.56 C. 0.056 D. 0.0056 E. 0.00056

18. What is 10% expressed as a decimal?
    A. 100.0 B. 10.0 C. 1.0 D. 0.1 E. 0.001

19. What is 100% expressed as a decimal?
    A. 100.0 B. 10.0 C. 1.0 D. 0.1 E. 0.001

20. What is 250% expressed as a decimal?
    A. 250.0 B. 25.0 C. 2.5 D. 0.25 E. 0.025

21. What is 1,000% expressed as a decimal?
    A. 1,000.0 B. 100.0 C. 10.0 D. 1.0 E. 0.01

22. What is 0.25% expressed as a decimal?
    A. 25.0 B. 0.25 C. 0.025 D. 0.0025 E. 0.00025

23. What is 0.099% expressed as a decimal?
    A. 99 B. 0.99 C. 0.099 D. 0.0099 E. 0.00099

24. What is 0.0988% expressed as a decimal?
A. 0.988 C. 0.00988 E. 9.8
B. 0.0988 D. 0.000988

25. What is 0.00100% expressed as a decimal?
A. 0.01 C. 0.0001 E. 0.000001
B. 0.001 D. 0.00001

26. What is $\frac{1}{10}$ expressed as a percent?
A. 100% C. 1% E. 0.01%
B. 10% D. 0.1%

27. What is $\frac{3}{100}$ expressed as a percent?
A. 300% C. 3% E. 0.03%
B. 30% D. 0.3%

28. What is $\frac{99}{100}$ expressed as a percent?
A. 99% C. 0.99% E. 0.0099%
B. 9.9% D. 0.099%

29. What is $\frac{100}{1,000}$ expressed as a percent?
A. 0.1% C. 10% E. 1,000%
B. 1.0% D. 100%

30. What is $\frac{333}{100}$ expressed as a percent?
A. 333% C. 3.33% E. 0.0333%
B. 33.3% D. 0.333%

31. What is $\frac{9}{1,000}$ expressed as a percent?
A. 9% C. 0.09% E. 0.0009%
B. 0.9% D. 0.009%

32. What is $\frac{3}{4}$ expressed as a percent?
A. 0.0075% C. 0.75% E. 75%
B. 0.075% D. 7.5%

33. What is $\frac{4}{5}$ expressed as a percent?
A. 4.5% C. 45% E. 450%
B. 8% D. 80%

34. What is $\frac{3}{50}$ expressed as a percent?
A. 60% C. 0.6% E. 0.0006%
B. 6% D. 0.006%

35. What is $\frac{3}{75}$ expressed as a percent?
A. 0.004% C. 0.4% E. 40%
B. 0.04% D. 4%

36. What is $\frac{6}{500}$ expressed as a percent?
A. 0.012% C. 1.2% E. 120%
B. 0.12% D. 12%

37. What is $\frac{111}{555}$ expressed as a percent?
A. 222% C. 22% E. 2%
B. 200% D. 20%

38. What is $\frac{8}{5,000}$ expressed as a percent?
A. 16% C. 0.016% E. 0.00016%
B. 0.16% D. 0.0016%

39. What is $1\frac{1}{10}$ expressed as a percent?
A. 110% C. 1.1% E. 0.011%
B. 11% D. 0.11%

40. What is $9\frac{99}{100}$ expressed as a percent?
A. 999% C. 9.99% E. 0.0999%
B. 99.9% D. 0.999%

41. What is $3\frac{1}{2}$ expressed as a percent?
A. 0.35% C. 35% E. 3,500%
B. 3.5% D. 350%

42. What is $1\frac{3}{4}$ expressed as a percent?
A. 175% C. 17.5% E. 1.75%
B. 134% D. 13.4%

43. What is $10\frac{1}{5}$ expressed as a percent?
A. 10.02% C. 100.2% E. 1,020%
B. 10.2% D. 102%

44. What is $3\frac{1}{50}$ expressed as a percent?
A. 302% C. 3.02% E. 0.00302%
B. 30.2% D. 0.0302%

45. What is $\frac{111}{100}$ expressed as a percent?
A. 1,110% C. 11.1% E. 0.0111%
B. 111% D. 1.11%

46. What is $\frac{7}{2}$ expressed as a percent?
A. 0.35% C. 35% E. 3,500%
B. 3.5% D. 350%

47. What is $\frac{13}{5}$ expressed as a percent?
A. 260% C. 2.6% E. 0.026%
B. 26% D. 0.26%

48. What is $\frac{9}{8}$ expressed as a percent?
A. 1,125% C. 11.25% E. 0.1125%
B. 112.5% D. 1.125%

49. What is $\frac{22}{5}$ expressed as a percent?
A. 440% C. 4.4% E. 0.044
B. 44% D. 0.44%

50. What is $\frac{33}{6}$ expressed as a percent?
A. 550% C. 5.5% E. 0.55%
B. 53% D. 5.3%

51. Which of the following is equal to 18%?
A. $\frac{18}{1}$ C. $\frac{18}{100}$ E. $\frac{18}{10,000}$
B. $\frac{18}{10}$ D. $\frac{18}{1,000}$

52. Which of the following is equal to 80%?
A. 80 C. 0.8 E. 0.008
B. 8 D. 0.08

53. Which of the following is equal to 45%?
A. $\frac{1}{9}$ C. $\frac{11}{19}$ E. $\frac{9}{10}$
B. $\frac{9}{20}$ D. $\frac{3}{4}$

54. Which of the following is equal to 7%?
A. 0.007 C. 0.7 E. 70
B. 0.07 D. 7

55. Which of the following is equal to 13.2%?
A. 0.0132 C. 1.32 E. 132
B. 0.132 D. 13.2

56. Which of the following is equal to 1.111%?
A. 0.001111 C. 0.11111 E. 11.11
B. 0.01111 D. 1.111

57. Which of the following is equal to 10.101%?
A. 0.0010101 C. 0.10101 E. 10.101
B. 0.010101 D. 1.0101

58. Which of the following is equal to 33%?
A. $\frac{1}{3}$ C. $\frac{33}{111}$ E. $\frac{333}{10,000}$
B. $\frac{33}{100}$ D. $\frac{333}{1,000}$

59. Which of the following is equal to 80.1%?
A. $80\frac{1}{10}$ C. $\frac{801}{1,000}$ E. 0.00801
B. 8.01 D. 0.0801

60. Which of the following is equal to 0.02%?
A. $\frac{1}{5}$ C. $\frac{1}{500}$ E. $\frac{1}{50,000}$
B. $\frac{1}{50}$ D. $\frac{1}{5,000}$

61. Which of the following is equal to 250%?
A. $\frac{25}{1,000}$ C. $\frac{1}{4}$ E. 25
B. $\frac{25}{100}$ D. 2.5

62. Which of the following is equal to 1,000%?
A. $\frac{1}{10}$ C. 10 E. 1,000
B. 1 D. 100

63. 37% + 42% = ?
A. 6% C. 106% E. 154%
B. 79% D. 110%

64. 210% + 21% = ?
A. 21,021% C. 23.1% E. 0.231%
B. 231% D. 2.31%

65. 8% + 9% + 10% + 110% = ?
A. 17% C. 180% E. 18,000%
B. 137% D. 1,800%

66. 254% + 166% + 342% = ?
A. 900% C. 432% E. 92%
B. 762% D. 111%

67. 0.02% + 0.005% = ?
A. 7% C. 1% E. 0.025%
B. 2.5% D. 0.07%

68. 33% − 25% = ?
A. 0.08% C. 8% E. 800%
B. 0.8% D. 80%

69. 100% − 0.99% = ?
A. 1% C. 11% E. 99.99%
B. 9.9% D. 99.01%

70. 222% − 22.2% = ?
A. 221.88% C. 22.188% E. 1.998%
B. 199.8% D. 19.98%

71. If John read 15 percent of the pages in a book on Monday and another 25 percent on Tuesday, what percent of the book did he read on Monday and Tuesday combined?
A. 7.5% C. 55% E. 80%
B. 40% D. 75%

72. If from 9:00 a.m. to noon Mary mowed 35 percent of a lawn, and from noon to 3:00 p.m. she mowed another 50 percent of the lawn, what percent of the lawn did she mow between 9:00 a.m. and 3:00 p.m.?

A. 17.5% C. 74.3% E. 98%
B. 60% D. 85%

Items #73-75 refer to the following table.

Schedule for Completing Project X	Mon.	Tues.	Wed.	Thurs.	Fri.
% of work to be completed each day	8%	17%	25%	33%	17%

73. By the end of which day is one-half of the work scheduled to be completed?

A. Monday C. Wednesday E. Friday
B. Tuesday D. Thursday

74. By the end of Tuesday, what percent of the work is scheduled to be completed?

A. 8% C. 25% E. 88%
B. 17% D. 50%

75. If production is on schedule, during which day will $\frac{2}{3}$ of the project have been completed?

A. Monday C. Wednesday E. Friday
B. Tuesday D. Thursday

76. A bucket filled to 33% of its capacity has an amount of water equal to $\frac{1}{4}$ of the bucket's capacity added to it. The bucket is filled to what percent of its capacity?

A. 8% C. 33% E. 75%
B. 25% D. 58%

77. If Edward spends 15% of his allowance on a book and another 25% on food, what percent of his allowance remains?

A. 10% C. 45% E. 80%
B. 40% D. 60%

78. 50% of 50% = ?

A. 1% C. 25% E. 250%
B. 2.5% D. 100%

79. 1% of 100% = ?

A. 0.01% C. 1% E. 100%
B. 0.1% D. 10%

80. If a jar contains 100 marbles and 66% of those marbles are red, how many marbles in the jar are red?

A. 6 C. 66 E. 6,660
B. 34 D. 660

81. If 75% of 240 cars in a certain parking lot are sedans, how many of the cars in the parking lot are sedans?

A. 18 C. 60 E. 210
B. 24 D. 180

82. If 0.1% of the 189,000 names on a certain mailing list have the initials *B.D.*, how many names on the list have the initials *B.D.*?

A. 1.89 C. 189 E. 189,000
B. 18.9 D. 18,900

83. What percent of 10 is 1?

A. 0.1% C. 10% E. 1,000%
B. 1% D. 100%

84. What percent of 12 is 3?

A. 2.5% C. 25% E. 400%
B. 3.6% D. 36%

85. 50 is what percent of 40?

A. 125% C. 80% E. 8%
B. 90% D. 12.5%

86. What number is 10% of 100?

A. 0.01 C. 1 E. 1,000
B. 0.1 D. 10

87. What number is 250% of 12?

A. 3 C. 24 E. 36
B. 15 D. 30

88. If Patty's age is 48 and Al's age is 36, then Al's age is what percent of Patty's age?

A. 7.5% C. 75% E. 175%
B. 25% D. $133\frac{1}{3}$%

89. If 25 of the employees at a bank are women and 15 are men, then what percent of the bank's employees are women?

A. 37.5% C. 60% E. 90%
B. 40% D. 62.5%

90. If the price of an item increases from $5.00 to $8.00, the new price is what percent of the old price?

A. 20% C. 62.5% E. 160%
B. 60% D. 92.5%

91. If the price of an item increases from $5.00 to $8.00, the old price is what percent of the new price?

A. 20% C. 62.5% E. 160%
B. 60% D. 92.5%

92. If the price of a share of stock drops from $200 to $160, the new price is what percent of the old price?

A. 20% C. 50% E. 125%
B. 25% D. 80%

93. If the price of a share of stock drops from $200 to $160, the old price is what percent of the new price?

A. 20% C. 50% E. 125%
B. 25% D. 80%

94. If the price of a share of stock drops from $200 to $160, what was the percent decline in the price?

A. 20% C. 50% E. 125%
B. 25% D. 80%

Items #95-99 refer to the following table.

Enrollments for a One-Week Seminar	
Week Number	Number of Enrollees
1	10
2	25
3	20
4	15
5	30

95. The number of people who enrolled for the seminar in Week 1 was what percent of the number of people who enrolled in Week 2?

A. 5% C. 50% E. 250%
B. 40% D. 80%

96. The number of people who enrolled for the seminar in Week 4 was what percent of the number of people who enrolled in Week 5?

A. 15% C. 50% E. 200%
B. 25% D. 100%

97. The number of people who enrolled for the seminar in Week 5 was what percent of the number of people who enrolled in Week 4?

A. 15% C. 50% E. 200%
B. 25% D. 100%

98. What was the percent increase in the number of people enrolled for the seminar from Week 1 to Week 2?

A. 40% C. 100% E. 250%
B. 80% D. 150%

99. What was the percent decrease in the number of people enrolled for the seminar from Week 3 to Week 4?

A. 25% C. 75% E. $133\frac{1}{3}$%

B. $33\frac{1}{3}$% D. 125%

100. If a textbook costs $35, what is 8% sales tax on the textbook?

A. $1.20 C. $2.00 E. $3.20
B. $1.80 D. $2.80

101. If a textbook costs $30 plus 8.5% sales tax, what is the total cost of one textbook?

A. $3.55 C. $23.55 E. $33.55
B. $12.55 D. $32.55

102. How much is 25% of 80?

A. 2 C. 20 E. 45
B. 8 D. 40

103. How much is 2.3% of 90?

A. 1.07 C. 2.17 E. 2.3
B. 2.07 D. 2.7

104. On a test that had 50 items, Gertrude got 34 out of the first 40 correct. If she received a grade of 80% on the test, how many of the last 10 items did Gertrude have correct?

A. 6 C. 10 E. 34
B. 8 D. 12

105. The number of the question you are now reading is what percent of 1,000?

A. 0.1% C. 10.5% E. 1,050%
B. 10% D. 100%

106. 40 is what percent of 50?

A. 5% C. 80% E. 95%
B. 25% D. 90%

107. 80 is what percent of 20?

A. 4% C. 40% E. 400%
B. 8% D. 200%

108. In the junior class, 300 enrolled in a test preparation course, while 500 did not. What percent of the junior class did not enroll in a test preparation course?

A. 7% C. 62.5% E. 90%
B. 35% D. 75%

109. Mary's factory produces pencils at a cost to her company of $0.02 per pencil. If she sells them to a wholesaler at $0.05 each, what is her percent of profit based on her cost of $0.02 per pencil?

A. 25% C. 75% E. 150%
B. 50% D. 100%

110. In a certain class of 30 students, 6 received A's. What percent of the class did not receive an A?

A. 8% C. 60% E. 90%
B. 40% D. 80%

111. If the Wildcats won 10 out of 12 games, to the nearest whole percent, what percentage of their games did the Wildcats win?

A. 3 C. 38 E. 94
B. 8 D. 83

112. On Thursday, Hui made 86 out of 100 free throws. On Friday, she made 46 out of 50 free throws. What was Hui's free throw percentage for the two days?

A. 8.8% C. 28% E. 88%
B. 12.8% D. 82%

113. A stereo was discounted by 20% and sold at the discount price of \$256. Which of the following equals the price of the stereo before the discount?

A. less than \$300
B. between \$300 and \$308
C. between \$308 and \$316
D. between \$316 and \$324
E. more than \$324

114. In a bag of red and black jellybeans, 136 are red jellybeans and the remainder are black jellybeans. If 15% of the jellybeans in the bag are black, what is the total number of jellybeans in the bag?

A. 151 C. 175 E. 906
B. 160 D. 200

115. The regular price of a TV set is \$118.80. Which of the following equals the price of the TV set after a sale reduction of 20%?

A. \$158.60 C. \$138.84 E. \$29.70
B. \$148.50 D. \$95.04

116. A circle graph of a budget shows the expenditure of 26.2% for housing, 28.4% for food, 12% for clothing, 12.7% for taxes, and the balance for miscellaneous items. Which of the following equals the percent for miscellaneous items?

A. 79.3 C. 68.5 E. 20.7
B. 70.3 D. 29.7

117. Two dozen shuttlecocks and four badminton rackets are to be purchased for a playground. The shuttlecocks are priced at \$.35 each and the rackets at \$2.75 each. The playground receives a discount of 30% from these prices. Which of the following equals the total cost of this equipment?

A. \$7.29 C. \$13.58 E. \$19.40
B. \$11.43 D. \$18.60

118. A piece of wood weighing 10 ounces is found to have a weight of 8 ounces after drying. Which of the following equals the moisture content?

A. 80% C. $33\frac{1}{3}$% E. 20%
B. 40% D. 25%

119. A bag contains 800 coins. Of these, 10 percent are dimes, 30 percent are nickels, and the rest are quarters. Which of the following equals the amount of money in the bag?

A. less than \$150
B. between \$150 and \$300
C. between \$301 and \$450
D. between \$450 and \$800
E. more than \$800

120. Six quarts of a 20% solution of alcohol in water are mixed with 4 quarts of a 60% solution of alcohol in water. Which of the following equals the alcoholic strength of the mixture?

A. 80% C. 36% E. 10%
B. 40% D. 25%

121. A man insures 80% of his property and pays a $2\frac{1}{2}$% premium amounting to \$348. What is the total value of his property?

A. \$19,000 C. \$18,000 E. \$13,920
B. \$18,400 D. \$17,400

122. A clerk spent his 35-hour work week as follows: $\frac{1}{5}$ of his time he sorted mail, $\frac{1}{2}$ of his time he filed letters, and $\frac{1}{7}$ of the time he did reception work. The rest of his time was devoted to messenger work. Which of the following approximately equals the percent of time spent on messenger work by the clerk during the week?

A. 6% C. 14% E. 20%
B. 10% D. 16%

123. In a school in which 40% of the enrolled students are boys, 80% of the boys are present on a certain day. If 1,152 boys are present, which of the following equals the total school enrollment?

A. 1,440 C. 3,600 E. 5,760
B. 2,880 D. 5,400

124. Mrs. Morris receives a salary raise from \$25,000 to \$27,500. Find the percent of increase.

A. 19% C. 90% E. $12\frac{1}{2}$%
B. 10% D. 151%

125. The population of Stormville has increased from 80,000 to 100,000 in the last 20 years. Find the percent of increase.

A. 20% C. 80% E. 10%
B. 25% D. 60%

126. The value of Super Company Stock dropped from \$25 a share to \$21 a share. Find the percent of decrease.

A. 4% C. 12% E. 20%
B. 8% D. 16%

127. The Rubins bought their home for \$30,000 and sold it for \$60,000. Find the percent of increase.

A. 100% C. 200% E. 150%
B 50% D. 300%

128. During the pre-holiday rush, Martin's Department Store increased its sales staff from 150 to 200 persons. By what percent must it now decrease its sales staff to return to the usual number of salespersons?

A. 25% C. 20% E. 75%

B. $33\frac{1}{3}$% D. 40%

Mean, Median, and Mode

Mean (or average), ***median***, and ***mode*** are three types of statistics that can be determined for a given set of numbers. These statistics provide particular information about a particular set of data.

Mean

1. *Calculating a Mean (Average)*

To calculate an ***average (arithmetic mean)***, just add the quantities contributing to the average and then divide that sum by the number of quantities involved. For example, the average of 3, 7, and 8 is 6: $3 + 7 + 8 = 18$, and $18 \div 3 = 6$. Typically, on the exam, the term "average" is used instead of "mean" or "arithmetic mean."

Example:

A student's final grade is the average of her scores on five exams. If she receives scores of 78, 83, 82, 88, and 94, what is her final grade?

➢ To find the average, add the five grades and divide that sum by 5: $\frac{78 + 83 + 82 + 88 + 94}{5} = \frac{425}{5} = 85$.

It is possible that an easy item might ask that you find the average of a few numbers, as above; however, items about averages can take several other forms. The generalized formula for an average (arithmetic mean) is given by the following equation.

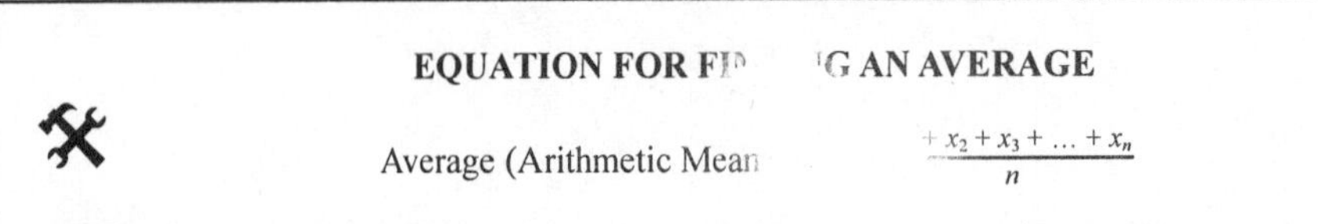

EQUATION FOR FI… G AN AVERAGE

Average (Arithmetic Mean … $+ x_2 + x_3 + \ldots + x_n$ / n

2. *Determining Missing Elem…nts*

Some items provi… a group of numbers and some—but not all—o… …e quantities involved. You are then asked to find the ***missing*** …emen… …xample, if the average of 3, 8, and x is 6, what is the value of x? Since the average of the three numbers is 6, the sum … f the three numbers is $3 \cdot 6 = 18$. The two given numbers are equal to $3 + 8 = 11$, so the third number must be $18 - 11$ … …k the solution by averaging 3, 8, and 7: $3 + 8 + 7 = 18$, and $18 \div 3 = 6$.

Examples:

1. For a certain five-day period, the average high temperature (in degrees Fahrenheit) for Chicago was 30°. If the high temperatures recorded for the first four of those days were 26°, 32°, 24°, and 35°, what was the high temperature recorded on the fifth day?
   ➢ The sum of the five numbers is $5 \cdot 30 = 150$. The sum for the four days we know about is: $26 + 32 + 24 + 35 = 117$. Thus, the fifth day must have had a high temperature of $150 - 117 = 33$.
2. The average of Jose's scores on four tests is 90. If three of those scores are 89, 92, and 94, what is his fourth score?
   ➢ The sum of all four scores must be $4 \cdot 90 = 360$. The three known scores sum to: $89 + 92 + 94 = 275$. Thus, the remaining score must be $360 - 275 = 85$.
3. The average of a group of eight numbers is 9. If one of these numbers is removed from the group, the average of the remaining numbers is 7. What is the value of the number removed?
   ➢ The sum of the original numbers is $8 \cdot 9 = 72$. The sum of the remaining numbers is $7 \cdot 7 = 49$, so the value of the number that was removed must be $72 - 49 = 23$.

A variation on this type of an item might ask about more than one missing element.

Example:

In a group of children, three of the children are ages 7, 8, and 10, and the other two are the same age. If the average of the ages of all five children is 7, what is the age of the other two children?
➤ The total sum of the five ages must be $5 \cdot 7 = 35$. The known ages total only $7 + 8 + 10 = 25$, so the ages of the two other children must total 10. Since there are two of them, each one must be 5 years old.

3. *Calculating Weighted Averages*

In the average problems discussed thus far, each element in the average has been given equal weight. Sometimes, averages are created that give greater weight to one element than to another.

Example:

Cody bought 4 books that cost \$6.00 each and 2 books that cost \$3.00 each. What is the average cost of the 6 books?
➤ The average cost of the 6 books is not just the average of \$6.00 and \$3.00, which is \$4.50. He bought more of the higher priced books, so the average must reflect that fact. One method is to treat each book as a separate expense: $\frac{6+6+6+6+3+3}{6} = \frac{30}{6} = 5$. Another method is to "weigh" the two different costs: $6(4) + 3(2) = 30$ and $\frac{30}{6} = 5$.

Median

The ***median*** of an odd number of data values is the middle value of the data set when it is arranged in ascending or descending order. The median of an even number of data values is the average of the two middle values of the data set when it is arranged in ascending or descending order.

Examples:

1. What is the median of {1, 1, 2, 3, 4, 5, 6, 7, 7, 7, 8, 8, 9}?
   ➤ The set contains an odd number of data values, so the median is the middle value: 6.
2. What is the median of {7, 9, 10, 16}?
   ➤ The set contains an even number of data values, so the median is the average of the two middle values: $\frac{9+10}{2} = 9.5$.

Mode

The ***mode*** is the value that appears most frequently in a set of data. Some data sets have multiple modes, while other data sets have no modes.

Examples:

1. The mode of {2, 4, 5, 5, 5, 6, 6, 19.2} is 5.
2. The group of numbers {–3, 5, 6, –3, –2, 7, 5, –3, 6, 5, 5, –3} is bimodal since –3 and 5 each occur four times.

NOTE: The ACT, PLAN, and EXPLORE allow calculators. Therefore, it is important that you learn how to use a calculator and bring the same calculator with you to the exam. Using a calculator provides greater accuracy and often saves valuable test time.

EXERCISE 6

Mean, Median, and Mode

DIRECTIONS: Choose the correct answer to each of the following items. Use a calculator when necessary. Answers are on page 921.

1. What is the average of 8, 6, and 16?

   A. 10 B. 12 C. 13 D. 15 E. 18

2. What is the average of 0 and 50?

   A. 0 B. 5 C. 10 D. 25 E. 50

3. What is the average of 5, 11, 12, and 8?

   A. 6 B. 8 C. 9 D. 10 E. 12

4. What is the average of 25, 28, 21, 30, and 36?

   A. 25 B. 28 C. 29 D. 34 E. 44

5. What is the average of $\frac{1}{4}$, $\frac{3}{4}$, $\frac{5}{8}$, $\frac{1}{2}$, and $\frac{3}{8}$?

   A. $\frac{3}{32}$ B. $\frac{5}{16}$ C. $\frac{1}{2}$ D. $\frac{5}{8}$ E. $\frac{27}{32}$

6. What is the average of $0.78, $0.45, $0.36, $0.98, $0.55, and $0.54?

   A. $0.49 B. $0.54 C. $0.56 D. $0.60 E. $0.61

7. What is the average of 0.03, 0.11, 0.08, and 0.5?

   A. 0.18 B. 0.25 C. 0.28 D. 0.50 E. 1.0

8. What is the average of 1,001, 1,002, 1,003, 1,004, and 1,005?

   A. 250 B. 1,000 C. 1,003 D. 2,500 E. 5,000

9. What is the average of −8, −6, and −13?

   A. −18 B. −15 C. −13 D. −12 E. −9

10. Jordan receives test scores of 79, 85, 90, 76, and 80. What is the average of these test scores?

    A. 82 B. 83 C. 84 D. 85 E. 86

11. Mr. Whipple bought five different items costing $4.51, $6.25, $3.32, $4.48, and $2.19. What is the average cost of the five items?

    A. $3.40 B. $3.80 C. $3.90 D. $4.00 E. $4.15

12. Nadia received scores of 8.5, 9.3, 8.2, and 9.0 in four different gymnastics events. What is the average of her scores?

    A. 8.5 B. 8.75 C. 8.9 D. 9 E. 9.1

13. Five people have ages of 44, 33, 45, 44, and 29 years. What is the average of their ages in years?

    A. 36 B. 39 C. 40 D. 41 E. 43

14. In a certain government office, if 360 staff hours are needed to process 120 building permit applications, on the average how long (in hours) does it take to process one application?

    A. 3 B. 6 C. 12 D. 24 E. 36

15. In a chemical test for Substance *X*, a sample is divided into five equal parts. If the purity of the five parts is 84 percent, 89 percent, 87 percent, 90 percent, and 80 percent, then what is the overall purity of the sample (expressed as a percent of Substance *X*)?

    A. 83 B. 84 C. 86 D. 87 E. 88

16. The average of three numbers is 24. If two of the numbers are 21 and 23, what is the third number?

    A. 20 B. 24 C. 26 D. 28 E. 30

17. The average of three numbers is 5. If two of the numbers are zero, what is the third number?

    A. 1 B. 3 C. 5 D. 10 E. 15

18. The average of the weight of four people is 166 pounds. If three of the people weigh 150 pounds, 200 pounds, and 180 pounds, what is the weight of the fourth person?

    A. 134 B. 140 C. 155 D. 161 E. 165

19. For a certain student, the average of five test scores is 83. If four of the scores are 81, 79, 85, and 90, what is the fifth test score?

A. 83 B. 82 C. 81 D. 80 E. 79

20. Sue bought ten items at an average price of \$3.60. The cost of eight of the items totaled \$30. If the other two items were the same price, what was the price she paid for each?

A. \$15.00 B. \$7.50 C. \$6.00 D. \$3.00 E. \$1.50

21. In a certain shipment, the weights of twelve books average 2.75 pounds. If one of the books is removed, the weights of the remaining books average 2.70 pounds. What was the weight, in pounds, of the book that was removed?

A. 1.7 B. 2.3 C. 3.0 D. 3.3 E. 4.5

22. The average of a group of seven test scores is 80. If the lowest and the highest scores are thrown out, the average of the remaining scores is 78. What is the average of the lowest and highest scores?

A. 100 B. 95 C. 90 D. 88 E. 85

23. In a certain group, twelve of the children are age 10, and eight are age 15. What is the average of the ages of all the children in the group?

A. 9.5 B. 10.5 C. 11 D. 11.5 E. 12

24. Robert made the following deposits in a savings account:

Amount	*Frequency*
\$15	4 times
\$20	2 times
\$25	4 times

What was the average of all the deposits Robert made?

A. \$18.50 B. \$20.00 C. \$21.50 D. \$22.00 E. \$22.50

25. The average of the weights of six people sitting in a boat is 145 pounds. After a seventh person gets into the boat, the average of the weights of all seven people in the boat is 147 pounds. What is the weight, in pounds, of the seventh person?

A. 160 B. 159 C. 155 D. 149 E. 147

26. Find the mean of the following 5 numbers: 2, 3, 13, 15, and 1.

A. 4.6 B. 6.2 C. 6.8 D. 8.6 E. 16.8

27. Find the mean of the following 6 numbers: −3, 2, 6, 5, 2, and 0.

A. 1 B. 2 C. 5 D. 6 E. 8

28. If the mean of 6 numbers is 10, what is the sixth number if the five given numbers are −3, 5, 6, 13, and 17?

A. 12 B. 16 C. 18 D. 20 E. 22

29. The average of 5 numbers is 56. If two new numbers are added to the list, the average of the 7 numbers is 58. Which of the following equals the average of the two new numbers?

A. 64 B. 63 C. 62 D. 61 E. 60

30. Arranged in some order, $3x + 1$, $2x + 4$, and $x + 10$ represent 3 consecutive whole numbers. If x represents a whole number and the average of the 3 numbers is 13, then solve for x.

A. 2 B. 4 C. 6 D. 8 E. 10

31. Arthur interviewed 100 female corporate officers and found that 34 of them were 55 years old, 28 were 45 years old, 26 were 35 years old, and 12 of them were 25 years old. What was the average of the women's ages?

A. 16 B. 43 C. 43.4 D. 44.3 E. 45

Items #32-34 refer to the following information.

During the last 14 games, a basketball player scored the following points per game: 42, 35, 29, 42, 33, 37, 26, 38, 42, 47, 51, 33, 30, and 40.

32. What is the median score?

A. 35.4 B. 35.7 C. 36 D. 37.5 E. 38

33. What is the mode?

A. 35.4 B. 37.5 C. 38 D. 42 E. 44

34. If after one more game, the player's average for points per game is exactly 37, how many points did the player score in the fifteenth game?

A. 30 B. 37 C. 37.5 D. 42 E. 44

35. Find the median of the following 5 numbers: 1, 3, 7, 2, and 8.

A. 1 B. 2 C. 3 D. 4.2 E. 7

36. Find the median for the following data set: {2, −3, 8, 4, 9, −16, 12, 0, 4, 2, 1}.

A. 4
B. 2.1
C. 2
D. 1
E. 0

37. Find the median for the following data set: {2, −3, 8, 4, 9, −16, 12, 8, 4, 2}.

A. 2
B. 3
C. 3.5
D. 4
E. 4.2

38. Find the mode of the following 5 numbers: 4, 8, 10, 8, and 15.

A. 4
B. 8
C. 9
D. 10
E. 15

39. Find the mode of the following data set: {6, 8, 10, 2, −2, 2, 8, 4, 2}.

A. 6
B. 4.4
C. 4
D. 2
E. 1

40. A set of seven numbers contains the numbers: 1, 4, 5, and 6. The other three numbers are represented by $2x + 8$, $x - 4$, and $7x - 4$. If the mode of these seven numbers is a negative even integer, then what is a possible value for x?

A. 0
B. 1
C. 2
D. 4
E. 5

41. The grades received on a test by twenty students were 100, 55, 75, 80, 65, 65, 95, 90, 80, 45, 40, 50, 85, 85, 85, 80, 80, 70, 65, and 60. What is the average of these grades?

A. 70.5
B. 72.5
C. 77
D. 80.3
E. 100

42. Arthur purchased 75 six-inch rulers costing 15¢ each, 100 one-foot rulers costing 30¢ each, and 50 one-yard rulers costing 72¢ each. What was the average price per ruler?

A. $26\frac{1}{8}$¢
B. $34\frac{1}{3}$¢
C. 39¢
D. 42¢
E. $77\frac{1}{4}$¢

43. What is the average grade for a student who received 90 in English, 84 in algebra, 75 in French, and 76 in music, if the subjects have the following weights: English 4, algebra 3, French 3, and music 1?

A. 81
B. $81\frac{1}{2}$
C. 82
D. $82\frac{1}{2}$
E. 83

Items #44-46 refer to the following information.

A census shows that on a certain neighborhood block the number of children in each family is 3, 4, 4, 0, 1, 2, 0, 2, and 2, respectively.

44. Find the average number of children per family.

A. 4
B. 3
C. $3\frac{1}{2}$
D. 2
E. $1\frac{1}{2}$

45. Find the median number of children.

A. 1
B. 2
C. 3
D. 4
E. 5

46. Find the mode of the number of children.

A. 0
B. 1
C. 2
D. 3
E. 4

Ratios and Proportions

Working with Ratios

1. *Two-Part Ratios*

A ***ratio*** is a statement about the relationship between any two quantities, or we might say a ratio is a statement that compares any two quantities. Suppose that in an English class there are five girls and eight boys. We can compare those quantities by saying that the ratio of girls to boys is 5 to 8. Conversely, the ratio of boys to girls is 8 to 5. Notice that order is very important in stating a ratio. The order of the numbers in the ratio must reflect the order of the categories being compared. In our example, it would be incorrect to say that the ratio of girls to boys is 8 to 5.

A phrase such as "5 to 8" is one way of stating a ratio, but there are several other ways. A ratio can also be described using a colon: "the ratio of girls to boys is 5:8" or "the ratio of boys to girls is 8:5." Alternatively, the ratio can be written in fraction form: "the ratio $\frac{\text{girls}}{\text{boys}}$ is $\frac{5}{8}$," and "the ratio $\frac{\text{boys}}{\text{girls}}$ is $\frac{8}{5}$."

Ratios of the form a:b or a/b can also refer to numbers instead of a number of objects. We can speak abstractly of the ratio 5:8, which is the ratio of any set of five things to any set of eight things. Consequently, ratios can be manipulated in the same way as fractions. Just as you could rewrite a fraction to get a form with a different denominator, you can convert a ratio to an equivalent form by multiplying both terms of the ratio by the same number. For example, $\frac{5}{8} = \frac{5 \cdot 2}{8 \cdot 2} = \frac{10}{16}$ and $\frac{8}{5} = \frac{8 \cdot 3}{5 \cdot 3} = \frac{24}{15}$.

It is customary to reduce a ratio to its lowest terms just as you would reduce fractions to their lowest terms. For example, in a certain classroom, there are ten girls and sixteen boys; the ratio of girls to boys is $\frac{10}{16}$, which is $\frac{5}{8}$. Although you may not be aware of it, you probably also use ratios informally in ordinary conversation. A common phrase that signifies a ratio is "for every (number)...there are (number)...." For example, in the classroom just described, for every 10 girls there are 16 boys, or in lowest terms, for every 5 girls there are 8 boys, and for every 8 boys there are 5 girls.

Finally, a ratio can also be stated as a rate using the word "per." If a car travels 200 miles and uses 10 gallons of fuel, the car gets 200 miles per 10 gallons, or 20 miles per gallon. Cost, too, is often described as a ratio. If it is possible to purchase a dozen greeting cards for \$2.40, the cost of the cards is \$2.40 per dozen, or 20 cents per card.

2. *Three-Part Ratios*

When three quantities are to be compared, they can be stated using ordinary ratios. For example, if a bowl of fruit contains two apples, three pears, and five oranges, the ratio of apples to pears is 2:3; the ratio of apples to oranges is 2:5; and the ratio of pears to oranges is 3:5. This same information can also be conveyed in a single statement. The ratio of apples to pears to oranges is 2:3:5.

A ***three-part ratio*** depends on the middle term to join the two outside terms. Above, the ratio of apples to pears is 2:3, and the ratio of pears to oranges is 3:5. Since 3 is common to both ratios, it can be the middle term. Sometimes it will be necessary to find a common middle term.

Example:

On a certain day, a bank has the following rates of exchange: $\frac{\text{dollar}}{\text{mark}} = \frac{1}{3}$ and $\frac{\text{mark}}{\text{pound}} = \frac{6}{1}$. What is the ratio of dollars to pounds?

➢ To find the ratio dollars:pounds, we will use marks as the middle term. However, the ratio of dollars to marks is 1:3, and the ratio of marks to pounds is 6:1. We must change the first ratio to express it in terms of six marks rather than three marks. This is like finding a common denominator before adding fractions: $\frac{1}{3} = \frac{1 \cdot 2}{3 \cdot 2} = \frac{2}{6}$, so the ratio of dollars to marks is 2:6, and the ratio of dollars to marks to pounds is 2:6:1. Thus, the ratio of dollars to pounds is 2:1.

3. *Using Ratios to Divide Quantities*

An item may require that you divide a quantity according to a certain ratio.

Examples:

1. A \$100 prize is divided between two contestants according to the ratio 2:3. How much does each contestant receive?
   ➤ Add the terms of the ratio to determine by how many parts the prize is to be divided. Divide the prize by that many parts, and multiply the result by the number of parts to be given to each contestant. 2 + 3 = 5, so the prize is to be divided into five parts. Each part is \$100 ÷ 5 = \$20. One contestant gets 2 • \$20 = \$40, and the other contestant receives 3 • \$20 = \$60.

2. Bronze is 16 parts tin and 9 parts copper. If a bronze ingot weighs 100 pounds, how much does the tin weigh (in pounds)?
   ➤ First, the number of parts in the ratio is 16 + 9 = 25. Second, 100 ÷ 25 = 4, so each part is worth 4 pounds. Since there are 16 parts of tin, the tin must weigh 16 • 4 = 64 pounds.

Working with Proportions

A ***proportion*** is the mathematical equivalent of a verbal analogy. For example, 2:3::8:12 is equivalent to "two is to three as eight is to twelve." The main difference between an analogy and a proportion is the precision. A verbal analogy depends upon words that do not have unique and precise meanings, while mathematical proportions are made up of numbers, which are very exact.

In a mathematical proportion, the first and last terms are called the "extremes" of the proportion because they are on the extreme outside, and the two middle terms are called the "means" (mean can mean "middle"). In a mathematical proportion, the product of the extremes is always equal to the product of the means. For example, 2:3::8:12 and 2 • 12 = 3 • 8.

1. Determining the Missing Elements in Proportions

Since any ratio can be written as a fraction, a proportion, which states that two ratios are equivalent, can also be written in fractional forms as an equation. This is the foundation for the process called cross-multiplication, a process that is useful in solving for an unknown element in a proportion.

Examples:

1. $\frac{2}{3}=\frac{8}{12} \Rightarrow \frac{2}{3}\times\frac{8}{12} \Rightarrow 2 \cdot 12 = 3 \cdot 8$
2. $\frac{6}{9}=\frac{12}{x} \Rightarrow \frac{6}{9}\times\frac{12}{x} \Rightarrow 6x = 108 \Rightarrow x = \frac{108}{6} = 18.$
   ➤ After cross-multiplying, divide both sides of the equality by the numerical coefficient of the unknown. Then, check the correctness of this solution by substituting 18 back in to the original proportion: $\frac{6}{9}=\frac{12}{18} \Rightarrow \frac{6}{9}\times\frac{12}{18} \Rightarrow 6 \cdot 18 = 9 \cdot 12.$
3. $\frac{3}{15}=\frac{x}{45} \Rightarrow \frac{3}{15}\times\frac{x}{45} \Rightarrow 3 \cdot 45 = 15x \Rightarrow x = \frac{135}{15} = 9$
   ➤ Check the solution by substitution: $\frac{3}{15}=\frac{9}{45} \Rightarrow \frac{3}{15}\times\frac{9}{45} \Rightarrow 3 \cdot 45 = 15 \cdot 9 \Rightarrow 135 = 135.$

2. Direct Proportions

The use of proportions can be a powerful problem-solving tool. ***Direct proportions*** equate ratios of two quantities having a direct relationship. The more there is of one quantity, the more there is of the other quantity, and vice versa.

Example:

If the cost of a dozen donuts is \$3.60, what is the cost of 4 donuts? Assume there is no discount for buying in bulk.

➤ One method for solving this item is to calculate the cost of one donut (\$3.60/12 = \$0.30), and then multiply that cost by four (\$0.30 • 4 = \$1.20). While this approach is not incorrect, the same result can be reached in a conceptually simpler way. The more donuts being purchased, the greater the total cost, and vice versa. Relate the quantities using a direct proportion: $\frac{\text{Total Cost } X}{\text{Total Cost } Y}=\frac{\text{Number } X}{\text{Number } Y} \Rightarrow \frac{\$3.60}{x}=\frac{12}{4} \Rightarrow 12x = \$3.60 \cdot 4 \Rightarrow x = \frac{\$14.40}{12} = \$1.20.$

In the previous example, we set up the proportion by grouping like terms: "cost" is on one side of the proportion and "number" is on the other side. It is equally correct to set up the proportion as $\frac{\text{Total Cost } X}{\text{Number } X}=\frac{\text{Total Cost } Y}{\text{Number } Y}$. Additionally, it does not matter which quantity is on top or bottom: $\frac{\text{Number } X}{\text{Total Cost } X} = \frac{\text{Number } Y}{\text{Total Cost } Y}$ is equally correct. However, it is generally a good idea to group like terms to avoid confusion.

The LONGER the travel time, the GREATER the distance traveled (assuming a CONSTANT speed).

Example:

If a plane moving at a constant speed flies 300 miles in 6 hours, how far will the plane fly in 8 hours?

➢ Group like terms: $\frac{\text{Time } X}{\text{Time } Y} = \frac{\text{Distance } X}{\text{Distance } Y} \Rightarrow \frac{6}{8} = \frac{300}{x} \Rightarrow \frac{6}{8} >\!=\!< \frac{300}{x} \Rightarrow 6x = 8 \cdot 300 \Rightarrow x = \frac{2{,}400}{6} = 400.$

The LONGER the time of operation, the GREATER the output.

Example:

If an uninterrupted stamping machine operating at a constant rate postmarks 320 envelopes in 5 minutes, how long will it take the machine to postmark 480 envelopes?

➢ Group like terms: $\frac{\text{Time } X}{\text{Time } Y} = \frac{\text{Output } X}{\text{Output } Y} \Rightarrow \frac{5}{x} = \frac{320}{480} \Rightarrow \frac{5}{x} >\!=\!< \frac{320}{480} \Rightarrow 5(480) = x(320) \Rightarrow x = \frac{5(480)}{320} = 7.5$ minutes.

The GREATER the number of items, the GREATER the weight.

Example:

If 20 jars of preserves weigh 25 pounds, how much do 15 jars of preserves weigh?

➢ Group like terms: $\frac{\text{Weight of Jars } X}{\text{Weight of Jars } Y} = \frac{\text{Jars } X}{\text{Jars } Y} \Rightarrow \frac{25}{x} = \frac{20}{15} \Rightarrow \frac{25}{x} >\!=\!< \frac{20}{15} \Rightarrow 25(15) = x(20) \Rightarrow x = \frac{25(15)}{20} = 18.75$ pounds.

3. ***Inverse Proportions***

In some situations, quantities are related inversely; that is, an increase in one results in a decrease in the other. For example, the more workers, or machines, doing a job, the less time it takes to finish. In this case, quantities are related inversely to each other. To solve problems involving inverse relationships, use the following procedure to set up an inverse proportion.

1. Set up an ordinary proportion—make sure to group like quantities.
2. Invert the right side of the proportion.
3. Cross-multiply and solve for the unknown.

Example:

Traveling at a constant rate of 150 miles per hour, a plane makes the trip from Phoenix to Grand Junction in 4 hours. How long will the trip take if the plane flies at a constant rate of 200 miles per hour?

➢ First, set up a proportion, grouping like terms: $\frac{\text{Speed } X}{\text{Speed } Y} = \frac{\text{Time } X}{\text{Time } Y} \Rightarrow \frac{150}{200} = \frac{4}{x}$. Then, invert the right side of the proportion: $\frac{150}{200} = \frac{x}{4} \Rightarrow \frac{150}{200} >\!=\!< \frac{x}{4} \Rightarrow 150(4) = 200x \Rightarrow x = \frac{150(4)}{200} = 3$ hours.

While it is possible, though not advised, to set up a direct proportion without grouping like terms, with an inverse proportion, it is essential to group like terms. This is sufficient reasoning to always group like terms: You will not make a mistake if the item involves an inverse proportion.

NOTE: The ACT, PLAN, and EXPLORE allow calculators. Therefore, it is important that you learn how to use a calculator and bring the same calculator with you to the exam. Using a calculator provides greater accuracy and often saves valuable test time.

EXERCISE 7

Ratios and Proportions

DIRECTIONS: Choose the correct answer to each of the following items. Use a calculator when necessary. Answers are on page 921.

1. If a jar contains 3 blue marbles and 8 red marbles, what is the ratio of blue marbles to red marbles?

   A. 3:11　C. 8:3　E. 4:1
   B. 3:8　D. 11:3

2. If a school has 24 teachers and 480 students, what is the ratio of teachers to students?

   A. $\frac{1}{20}$　C. $\frac{1}{48}$　E. $\frac{1}{200}$
   B. $\frac{1}{24}$　D. $\frac{1}{56}$

3. If a library contains 12,000 works of fiction and 3,000 works of nonfiction, what is the ratio of works of fiction to works of nonfiction?

   A. $\frac{1}{9}$　C. $\frac{1}{4}$　E. $\frac{5}{1}$
   B. $\frac{1}{5}$　D. $\frac{4}{1}$

4. Which of the following is (are) equivalent to $\frac{1}{3}$?

   I. $\frac{40}{120}$
   II. $\frac{75}{100}$
   III. $\frac{120}{360}$

   A. I only　D. II and III only
   B. III only　E. I, II, and III
   C. I and III only

Items #5-6 refer to the following table.

Students at Tyler Junior High School	7th Grade	8th Grade
Girls	90	80
Boys	85	75

5. What is the ratio of seventh-grade girls to the total number of girls at Tyler Junior High School?

   A. $\frac{9}{17}$　C. $\frac{18}{17}$　E. $\frac{17}{9}$
   B. $\frac{8}{9}$　D. $\frac{9}{8}$

6. What is the ratio of eighth-grade girls to the total number of students at Tyler Junior High School?

   A. $\frac{8}{33}$　C. $\frac{8}{15}$　E. $\frac{17}{30}$
   B. $\frac{9}{33}$　D. $\frac{8}{17}$

7. If an airplane flies 275 miles on 25 gallons of fuel, then what is the average fuel consumption for the entire trip expressed in miles per gallon?

   A. 25　C. 15　E. 7
   B. 18　D. 11

8. An assortment of candy includes 12 chocolates, 6 caramels, and 9 mints. What is the ratio of chocolates:caramels:mints?

   A. 4:3:2　C. 3:4:2　E. 2:4:3
   B. 4:2:3　D. 3:2:4

9. If Lucy has twice the amount of money that Ricky has, and Ricky has three times the amount of money that Ethel has, then what is the ratio of the amount of money Ethel has to the amount of money Lucy has?

   A. $\frac{1}{8}$　C. $\frac{1}{4}$　E. $\frac{2}{1}$
   B. $\frac{1}{6}$　D. $\frac{1}{2}$

10. If three farkels buy two kirns, and three kirns buy five pucks, then nine farkels buy how many pucks?

    A. 2　C. 8　E. 17
    B. 5　D. 10

11. If Machine X operates at twice the rate of Machine Y, and Machine Y operates at $\frac{2}{3}$ the rate of Machine Z, then what is the ratio of the rate of operation of Machine X to the rate of operation of Machine Z?

    A. $\frac{4}{1}$　C. $\frac{4}{3}$　E. $\frac{1}{3}$
    B. $\frac{3}{1}$　D. $\frac{3}{4}$

12. If 48 marbles are to be divided between Bill and Carl in the ratio of 3:5, how many marbles should Bill get?

    A. 6　C. 18　E. 30
    B. 8　D. 24

13. If \$10 is to be divided between Janeway and Nelix so that Nelix receives $\frac{1}{4}$ of what Janeway receives, then how much should Janeway receive?

A. \$10.00 C. \$7.50 E. \$2.00
B. \$8.00 D. \$6.00

14. If a \$1,000 reward is to be divided among three people in the ratio of 2:3:5, what is the largest amount that will be given to any one of the three recipients?

A. \$200 C. \$500 E. \$900
B. \$300 D. \$750

15. If $\frac{6}{8}=\frac{x}{4}$, then $x = ?$

A. 12 C. 4 E. 2
B. 6 D. 3

16. If $\frac{14}{x}=\frac{2}{7}$, then $x = ?$

A. 7 C. 28 E. 343
B. 14 D. 49

17. If $\frac{3}{4}=\frac{4}{x}$, then $x = ?$

A. $\frac{3}{16}$ C. $\frac{4}{3}$ E. $\frac{16}{3}$
B. $\frac{3}{4}$ D. $\frac{7}{3}$

18. If 240 widgets cost \$36, what is the cost of 180 widgets?

A. \$8 C. \$24 E. \$32
B. \$16 D. \$27

19. If a kilogram of a certain cheese costs \$9.60, what is the cost of 450 grams of the cheese? (1 kilogram = 1,000 grams)

A. \$2.78 C. \$3.88 E. \$5.12
B. \$3.14 D. \$4.32

20. If 50 feet of electrical wire cost \$4.80, then \$10.80 will buy how many feet of the wire?

A. 60 C. 67.25 E. 112.5
B. 62.5 D. 75

21. In a certain group of people, 100 people have red hair. If only 25 percent of the people have red hair, then how many people do not have red hair?

A. 75 C. 300 E. 500
B. 125 D. 400

22. If a certain fundraising project has raised \$12,000, which is 20 percent of its goal, how much money will have been raised when 50 percent of the goal has been reached?

A. \$60,000 C. \$18,000 E. \$4,800
B. \$30,000 D. \$15,000

23. If 48 liters of a certain liquid weigh 50 kilograms, then how much (in kilograms) will 72 liters of the liquid weigh?

A. 25 C. 75 E. 120
B. 60 D. 90

24. If the trip from Soldier Field to Wrigley Field takes two hours walking at a constant rate of four miles per hour, how long (in hours) will the same trip take walking at a constant rate of five miles per hour?

A. 2.5 C. 1.6 E. 1.25
B. 1.75 D. 1.5

25. A swimming pool is filled by either of two pipes. Pipe *A* supplies water at the rate of 200 gallons per hour and takes eight hours to fill the pool. If Pipe *B* can fill the pool in five hours, what is the rate (in gallons per hour) at which Pipe *B* supplies water?

A. 125 C. 360 E. 575
B. 320 D. 480

26. What is the ratio of 3 to 8 expressed as a decimal?

A. 0.125 C. 0.375 E. 1
B. 0.25 D. 0.50

27. If the ratio of 3 to 4 is the same as the ratio of 15 to x, find x.

A. 5 C. 15 E. 25
B. 10 D. 20

28. Annika can solve 10 math problems in 30 minutes. At this rate, how many math problems can she solve in 48 minutes?

A. 8 C. 32 E. 56
B. 16 D. 46

29. Seung can walk up 6 flights of stairs in 4 minutes. At this rate, how many flights of stairs could he walk up in 18 minutes?

A. 4 C. 14 E. 27
B. 10 D. 20

30. If 4 candy bars cost \$1.04, how much should 6 candy bars cost?

A. \$0.96 C. \$1.56 E. \$2.06
B. \$1.25 D. \$1.85

31. If Baby Andrew takes 8 steps to walk 2 yards, how many steps will he take to walk 5 yards?

A. 5 C. 15 E. 25
B. 10 D. 20

32. If a 40-inch stick is divided in a 3:5 ratio, how long (in inches) is the shorter piece?

A. 5 C. 15 E. 25
B. 10 D. 20

33. Orville claims that 3 bags of his popcorn will yield 28 ounces when popped. If this is the case, how many ounces will 5 bags of his popcorn yield when popped?

A. 23
C. $54\frac{1}{2}$
E. $64\frac{2}{3}$
B. $46\frac{2}{3}$
D. 64

34. In a poll of 1,000 people, 420 said they would vote for Mason. Based on this poll, how many people would be expected to vote for Mason if 60,000,000 people actually vote?

A. 25,200,000
C. 26,000,000
E. 26,500,000
B. 25,500,000
D. 26,200,000

35. In 4 days, a worm grew from 5 cm. to 12 cm. At this rate, how long will the worm be in another 6 days?

A. 21 cm.
C. 22.25 cm.
E. 23 cm.
B. 22 cm.
D. 22.5 cm.

36. Elan can mow 3 lawns in 85 minutes. At this rate, how long would he need to mow 5 lawns?

A. 140 minutes, 20 seconds
B. 141 minutes
C. 141 minutes, 40 seconds
D. 142 minutes
E. 142 minutes, 50 seconds

37. Sarah does $\frac{1}{5}$ of a job in 6 minutes. At this rate, what fraction of the job will she do in 10 minutes?

A. $\frac{1}{4}$
C. $\frac{1}{2}$
E. $\frac{3}{2}$
B. $\frac{1}{3}$
D. $\frac{3}{4}$

38. A snapshot measures $2\frac{1}{2}$ inches by $1\frac{7}{8}$ inches. If it is enlarged so that the longer dimension is 4 inches, what is the length of the enlarged shorter dimension?

A. $2\frac{1}{2}$ in.
C. $3\frac{3}{8}$ in.
E. 5 in.
B. 3 in.
D. 4 in.

39. Three of the men's white handkerchiefs cost \$2.29. How much will a dozen of those handkerchiefs cost?

A. \$27.48
C. \$9.16
E. \$4.58
B. \$13.74
D. \$6.87

40. A certain pole casts a 24 foot long shadow. At the same time another pole that is 3 feet high casts a 4 foot long shadow. How high is the first pole, given that the heights and shadows are in proportion?

A. 18 ft.
C. 20 ft.
E. 24 ft.
B. 19 ft.
D. 21 ft.

41. If a drawing is scaled $\frac{1}{8}$ inch to the foot, what is the actual length represented by $3\frac{1}{2}$ inches on the drawing?

A. 3.5 ft.
C. 21 ft.
E. 120 ft.
B. 7 ft.
D. 28 ft.

42. Aluminum bronze consists of copper and aluminum, usually in the ratio of 10:1 by weight. If an object made of this alloy weighs 77 pounds, how many pounds of aluminum does it contain?

A. 0.7
C. 7.7
E. 77.0
B. 7.0
D. 70.7

43. It costs 31 cents/ft.^{2} to lay vinyl flooring. How much will it cost to lay 180 ft.^{2} of flooring?

A. \$16.20
C. \$55.80
E. \$180.00
B. \$18.60
D. \$62.00

44. If Tuvak earns \$352 in 16 days, how much will he earn in 117 days?

A. \$3,050
C. \$2,285
E. \$1,170
B. \$2,574
D. \$2,080

45. Assuming that on a blueprint $\frac{1}{8}$ inch equals 12 inches of actual length, what is the actual length, in inches, of a steel bar represented on the blueprint by a line $3\frac{3}{4}$ inches long?

A. $3\frac{3}{4}$
C. 36
E. 450
B. 30
D. 360

46. Blake, James, and Staunton invested \$9,000, \$7,000, and \$6,000, respectively. Their profits were to be divided according to the ratio of their investments. If James uses his share of the firm's profit of \$825 to pay a personal debt of \$230, how much will he have left?

A. \$30.50
C. \$34.50
E. \$37.50
B. \$32.50
D. \$36.50

47. If on a road map $1\frac{5}{8}$ inches represents 10 miles, how many miles does 2.25 inches represent?

A. $\frac{180}{13}$ miles
C. $\frac{57}{4}$ miles
E. 3 miles
B. $\frac{53}{4}$ miles
D. $\frac{27}{2}$ miles

48. Jake and Jessie are standing next to each other in the sun. If Jake's shadow is 48 inches long, and he is 72 inches tall, how long is Jessie's shadow, in inches, if she is 66 inches tall?

A. 42
C. 44
E. 46
B. 43
D. 45

49. A blueprint allows 1 inch for every 12 feet. At that rate, 7 inches represents how many yards?

A. $\frac{28}{3}$
C. 84
E. 336
B. 28
D. 252

50. A bug crawls clockwise around the outside rim of a clock from the 12 to the 4 and travels 7 inches. If a second bug crawls around the outside rim from the 6 to the 11, in the same direction, how many inches did the bug travel?

A. 7.75
B. 8
C. 8.25
D. 8.5
E. 8.75

Exponents and Radicals

Powers and Exponents

1. Powers of Numbers

A ***power*** of a number indicates repeated multiplication. For example, "3 to the fifth power" means $3 \cdot 3 \cdot 3 \cdot 3 \cdot 3$, which equals 243. Therefore, 3 raised to the fifth power is 243.

Examples:

1. 2 to the second power $= 2 \cdot 2 = 4$.
2. 2 to the third power $= 2 \cdot 2 \cdot 2 = 8$.
3. 2 to the fourth power $= 2 \cdot 2 \cdot 2 \cdot 2 = 16$.
4. 3 to the second power $= 3 \cdot 3 = 9$.
5. 3 to the third power $= 3 \cdot 3 \cdot 3 = 27$.

The second power of a number is also called the square of the number. This refers to a square with sides equal in length to the number; the square of the number is equal to the area of the aforementioned square.

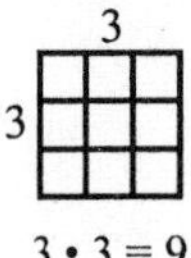

$3 \cdot 3 = 9$

The third power of a number is also called the cube of the number, which refers to a cube with sides equal in length to the number; the cube of the number is equal to the volume of the cube with sides equal in length to that number.

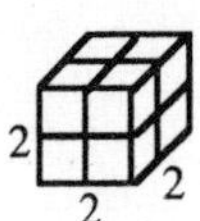

$2 \cdot 2 \cdot 2 = 8$

Beyond the square and the cube, powers are referred to by their numerical names, *e.g.*, fourth, fifth, sixth, and so on.

2. Exponential Notation

The notation system for designating the power of a number is a superscript following the number. The number being multiplied is the ***base,*** and the superscript is the ***exponent.*** The exponent indicates the operation of repeated multiplication.

Examples:

1. The third power of 2 is written as 2^3: base $\rightarrow 2^{3 \leftarrow \text{exponent}} = 2 \cdot 2 \cdot 2$.
2. The fifth power of 2 is written as 3^5: base $\rightarrow 3^{5 \leftarrow \text{exponent}} = 3 \cdot 3 \cdot 3 \cdot 3 \cdot 3$.

A base without an exponent is unchanged and represents the ***first power*** of the number. Since $x^1 = x$, the exponent 1 is not explicitly noted.

Examples:

1. $2^1 = 2$
2. $1{,}000^1 = 1{,}000$

Operations Involving Exponents

There are special rules that apply to operations involving exponents. When you begin working with radicals (fractional exponents) and algebraic expressions, these same rules will apply.

1. *Multiplication Involving Exponents*

The ***product rule*** is used to multiply two identical bases with similar or different exponents. To multiply powers of the same base, add the exponents: $x^m \cdot x^n = x^{m+n}$. To better understand this rule, explicitly write out the multiplication indicated by the exponents.

Example:

$2^2 \cdot 2^3 = 2^{2+3} = 2^5 = (2 \cdot 2)(2 \cdot 2 \cdot 2)$

➤ Writing out the expression and using the product rule give you the same result, but it is much faster to apply the latter.

Therefore, the product rule provides an easy shortcut for multiplying identical bases with exponents.

Examples:

1. $3^2 \cdot 3^5 = 3^{(2+5)} = 3^7$
2. $5^2 \cdot 5^3 \cdot 5^5 = 5^{(2+3+5)} = 5^{10}$
3. $x^3 \cdot x^4 = x^{(3+4)} = x^7$
4. $y^7 \cdot y^2 \cdot y^4 = y^{(7+2+4)} = y^{13}$

Notice that each of these examples has only one base. The product rule does NOT apply to terms with different bases.

Example:

$2^4 \cdot 3^4 = ?$

➤ The product rule cannot be used since 2 and 3 are not equal bases. You must explicitly multiply all of the numbers: $2^4 \cdot 3^4 = (2 \cdot 2 \cdot 2 \cdot 2)(3 \cdot 3 \cdot 3 \cdot 3) = 16 \cdot 81 = 1{,}296$.

Finally, the product rule does NOT apply to addition or subtraction of bases with exponents, even if the bases are identical.

Example:

$2^2 + 2^3 \neq 2^5$, since $2^2 + 2^3 = (2 \cdot 2) + (2 \cdot 2 \cdot 2) = 4 + 8 = 12$ and $2^5 = 2 \cdot 2 \cdot 2 \cdot 2 \cdot 2 = 32$.

2. *Division Involving Exponents*

The ***quotient rule*** is used for division involving identical bases with exponents. When dividing similar bases, subtract the exponent in the denominator from the exponent in the numerator: $\frac{x^m}{x^n} = x^{m-n}$. As with the product rule, the quotient rule can be verified by explicitly carrying out the indicated operations, as illustrated in the first of the following examples.

Examples:

1. $\frac{2^5}{2^3} = 2^{(5-3)} = 2^2$

   ➤ Writing out the expression and using the quotient rule give you the same result: $\frac{2^5}{2^3} = \frac{2 \cdot 2 \cdot 2 \cdot 2 \cdot 2}{2 \cdot 2 \cdot 2} = \frac{32}{8} = 4 = 2^2$.
2. $\frac{5^{10}}{5^9} = 5^{(10-9)} = 5^1 = 5$
3. $\frac{x^8}{x^6} = x^{(8-6)} = x^2$
4. $\frac{y^3}{y^2} = y^{(3-2)} = y^1 = y$

An ***exponent of zero*** results whenever a quantity is divided into itself. Since a quantity divided into itself is equal to 1, any base (except zero) with an exponent of zero is also equal to 1: $\mathbf{x^0 = 1}$ if $x \neq 0$. 0^0 is an undefined operation in math.

Examples:

1. $\frac{5^3}{5^3} = 5^{(3-3)} = 5^0 = 1$
2. $\frac{x^{12}}{x^{12}} = x^{(12-12)} = x^0 = 1$

3. *Raising a Power to a Power*

The ***power rule*** is used when a power of a number is raised to another power. This is done by multiplying the exponents together: $\mathbf{(x^m)^n = x^{mn}}$. Again, we can prove the validity of this shortcut by explicitly carrying out the indicated multiplications.

Examples:

1. $(2^2)^3 = 2^{(2 \cdot 3)} = 2^6$

   ➢ Writing out the expression and using the power rule give you the same result: $(2^2)^3 = (2 \cdot 2)^3 = 4^3 = 4 \cdot 4 \cdot 4 = 64 = 2^6$.

2. $(x^3)^4 = x^{(3 \cdot 4)} = x^{12}$

4. *Raising a Product to a Power*

The ***product power rule*** is used when a product with exponents is raised to a power. The exponent outside the parentheses governs all the factors inside the parentheses. When raising a product to a power, first multiply the exponent on the outside by each exponent on the inside: $\mathbf{(x^m \cdot y^p)^n = x^{mn} \cdot y^{pn}}$.

Examples:

1. $(2 \cdot 3)^2 = 2^2 \cdot 3^2 = 4 \cdot 9 = 36$

   ➢ Writing out the expression and using the product power rule give you the same result: $(2 \cdot 3)^2 = (6)^2 = 36$.

2. $(2^2 \cdot 3^3)^2 = 2^{(2 \cdot 2)} \cdot 3^{(3 \cdot 2)} = (2^4)(3^6) = (16)(729) = 11{,}664$
3. $(x^2 \cdot y^3)^4 = x^{(2 \cdot 4)} \cdot y^{(3 \cdot 4)} = x^8y^{12}$

5. *Raising a Quotient to a Power*

The ***quotient power rule*** is used when a quotient with exponents is raised to a power. It is essentially the same as the previous rule for determining the power of a product. The exponent outside the parentheses governs all the factors inside the parentheses. Determine the power of a quotient by multiplying the exponent on the outside by each exponent on the inside:

$\left(\frac{x^m}{y^p}\right)^n = \frac{x^{mn}}{y^{pn}}$.

Examples:

1. $\left(\frac{2}{3}\right)^3 = \frac{2^3}{3^3} = \frac{8}{27}$

   ➢ Writing out the expression and using the quotient power rule give you the same result: $\left(\frac{2}{3}\right)^3 = \frac{2}{3} \cdot \frac{2}{3} \cdot \frac{2}{3} = \frac{2 \cdot 2 \cdot 2}{3 \cdot 3 \cdot 3} = \frac{8}{27}$.

2. $\left(\frac{1^2}{3^3}\right)^2 = \frac{1^{(2 \cdot 2)}}{3^{(3 \cdot 2)}} = \frac{1^4}{3^6} = \frac{1}{729}$
3. $\left(\frac{x^2}{y^3}\right)^2 = \frac{x^{(2 \cdot 2)}}{y^{(3 \cdot 2)}} = \frac{x^4}{y^6}$

6. *Negative Exponents*

Negative exponents do not signify negative numbers. Instead, they signify fractions. Specifically, a negative exponent indicates the power of the ***reciprocal*** of the base: $x^{-n} = \frac{1}{x^n}$.

Examples:

1. $\frac{2^2}{2^3} = 2^{(2-3)} = 2^{-1} = \frac{1}{2^1} = \frac{1}{2}$ or $\frac{2^2}{2^3} = \frac{2 \cdot 2}{2 \cdot 2 \cdot 2} = \frac{4}{8} = \frac{1}{2}$
2. $3^{-2} = \left(\frac{1}{3}\right)^2 = \frac{1}{9}$
3. $x^{-3} = \left(\frac{1}{x}\right)^3 = \frac{1}{x^3}$

7. *Rational (Fractional) Exponents*

Exponents are not restricted to integer values. ***Rational (fractional) exponents*** are also possible. Later in this chapter, we will use rational exponents when working with radicals. Rational exponents also appear in algebraic expressions, functions, and equations. The rules for working with rational exponents are the same as those for integer exponents.

Examples:

1. $2^{1/2} \cdot 2^{1/2} = 2^1 = 2$
2. $(x^2y^4)^{1/4} = x^{1/2}y$

8. *Working with Exponents*

Complex expressions may require the application of two or more operations involving exponents. No matter how complex an item gets, it can be solved by a series of simple steps following the five rules that are explained above for working with exponents. Remember to follow the rules for order of operations. Also, be careful when negative signs are involved.

Examples:

1. $(2^3 \cdot 3^2)^2 = 2^{3 \cdot 2} \cdot 3^{2 \cdot 2} = 2^6 \cdot 3^4$
2. $\left(\frac{3^3 \cdot 5^5}{3^2 \cdot 5^2}\right)^2 = (3^{3-2} \cdot 5^{5-2})^2 = (3^1 \cdot 5^3)^2 = 3^2 \cdot 5^6$
3. $\left(\frac{x^2 \cdot y^3}{x \cdot y^2}\right)^2 = (x^{2-1} \cdot y^{3-2})^2 = (x \cdot y)^2 = x^2y^2$
4. $(-3)^3(-2)^6 = (-27)(64) = -1{,}728$
5. $-2^4(-3)^2 = -(2^4)(-3)^2 = -(16)(9) = -144$

These rules for working with exponents provide simple shortcuts, as verified by explicitly executing all indicated operations. When you begin to manipulate algebraic expressions, not only will these same shortcuts apply, but they will become indispensable.

SUMMARY OF OPERATIONS INVOLVING EXPONENTS

$x^1 = x; x^0 = 1$

Product Rule: $x^m \cdot x^n = x^{m+n}$

Quotient Rule: $\frac{x^m}{x^n} = x^{m-n}$

Power Rule: $(x^m)^n = x^{mn}$

Product Power Rule: $(x^m \cdot y^p)^n = x^{mn} \cdot y^{pn}$

Quotient Power Rule: $\left(\frac{x^m}{y^p}\right)^n = \frac{x^{mn}}{y^{pn}}$

Negative Exponents: $x^{-n} = \left(\frac{1}{x}\right)^n = \frac{1}{x^n}$

Roots and Radicals

1. *Roots of Numbers*

A ***square root*** of a number x is a solution to the equation $\sqrt{x} = b$, in which $x = b^2$. When you perform the multiplication indicated by an exponent, you are in effect answering the question, "What do I get when I multiply this number by itself so many times?" Now ask the opposite question, "What number, when multiplied by itself so many times, will give me a certain value?" For example, when you raise 2 to the third power, you find out that $2^3 = 8$. Now, ask the question in the other direction. What number, when raised to the third, is equal to 8?

This reverse process is called "finding the root of a number." Why roots? Look at the following diagram; since $2^6 = 64$, the sixth root of 64 is 2. The picture resembles plant roots.

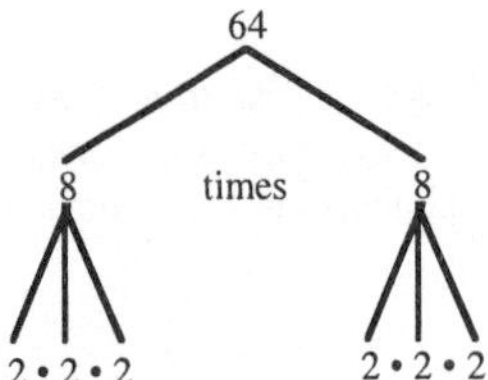

Of course, we rarely deal with sixth roots. Mostly, we deal with two roots: $2 \cdot 2 = 4$, so the second or ***square root*** of 4 is 2; and occasionally with numbers having three roots: $2 \cdot 2 \cdot 2 = 8$, so the third or ***cube root*** of 8 is 2.

The operation of taking a square root of a number is signaled by the ***radical*** sign, $\sqrt{\ }$. ***Radical*** comes from the Latin word "rad," which means "root."

Examples:

1. $\sqrt{1} = 1$ 3. $\sqrt{9} = 3$ 5. $\sqrt{25} = 5$ 7. $\sqrt{49} = 7$ 9. $\sqrt{81} = 9$ 11. $\sqrt{121} = 11$
2. $\sqrt{4} = 2$ 4. $\sqrt{16} = 4$ 6. $\sqrt{36} = 6$ 8. $\sqrt{64} = 8$ 10. $\sqrt{100} = 10$ 12. $\sqrt{144} = 12$

The symbol $\sqrt{\ }$ always denotes a positive number. Later, when we get to the topic of quadratic equations in algebra, we will run across a "±" sign preceding the radical; this signifies both the positive and negative values of the root.

If a radical sign is preceded by a superscript number, then the number, or ***index***, indicates a root other than the square root. In the notation $\sqrt[n]{a}$, n is the root or index, $\sqrt{\ }$ is the radical, and a is the radicand.

Examples:

1. $\sqrt[3]{8} = 2 \Rightarrow$ The cube root of 8 is 2.
2. $\sqrt[4]{81} = 3 \Rightarrow$ The fourth root of 81 is 3.
3. $\sqrt[6]{64} = 2 \Rightarrow$ The sixth root of 64 is 2.

2. *Determining Square Roots*

If a number is a perfect square (*e.g.*, 4, 9, 16, *etc.*), then extracting its square root is easy. Simply use the values given in the examples of square roots above. Not every number, however, has an exact square root. In such cases, you can do one of two things. First, you may be able to find in the number a factor that does have an exact square root and extract that factor from under the radical sign.

Examples:

1. $\sqrt{125} = ?$

   ➢ 125 does not have a perfect square root. However, 25 has a perfect square and is a factor of 125, so factor 125 into 25 and 5: $\sqrt{125} = \sqrt{25 \bullet 5}$. Then, take the square root of 25, which is 5; $\sqrt{25} \bullet \sqrt{5} = 5 \bullet \sqrt{5}$. The final expression is $5\sqrt{5}$, which means 5 multiplied by the square root of 5: $\sqrt{125} = 5\sqrt{5}$.
2. $\sqrt{27} = \sqrt{9 \bullet 3} = \sqrt{9} \bullet \sqrt{3} = 3 \bullet \sqrt{3} = 3\sqrt{3}$
3. $\sqrt{32} = \sqrt{16 \bullet 2} = \sqrt{16} \bullet \sqrt{2} = 4 \bullet \sqrt{2} = 4\sqrt{2}$
4. $\sqrt{52} = \sqrt{4 \bullet 13} = \sqrt{4} \bullet \sqrt{13} = 2 \bullet \sqrt{13} = 2\sqrt{13}$

For the purposes of the exam, knowledge of the approximate values for common square roots may save valuable test time. For example, it is useful to know that $\sqrt{2}$ is approximately 1.4 and that $\sqrt{3}$ is approximately 1.7. Other values can be approximated by using ranges; *e.g.*, $\sqrt{7}$ must be between 2 and 3 ($\sqrt{4} < \sqrt{7} < \sqrt{9}$). Since 7 is closer to 9 than to 4, a good approximation of $\sqrt{7}$ is 2.6 to 2.7. Note that the knowledgeable use of a calculator when applicable can be quite helpful.

Operations Involving Radicals (Rational Exponents)

Radicals can be rewritten using ***rational (fractional) exponents***. This simplifies the process of working with radicals, since all of the rules for exponents apply to fractional exponents and thus to radicals. The relationship between a rational exponent and the radical representing a given root is: $\sqrt[n]{x^m} = x^{m/n}$, where m and n are integers, and $n \neq 0$.

Examples:

1. $\sqrt{4} = 4^{1/2} = 2$
2. $\sqrt[3]{8} = 8^{1/3} = 2$

When you multiply a square root by itself, the result is the radicand: $(\sqrt{x})(\sqrt{x}) = x$. This can be explained using the product rule for exponents as illustrated in the following example.

Example:

$$(\sqrt{2})(\sqrt{2}) = 2^{1/2} \bullet 2^{1/2} = 2^1 = 2$$

The power rules for working with exponents are the ones you are most likely to use when working with radicals. The following example illustrates how the product power rule applies to radicals.

Example:

$$\sqrt{125} = 125^{1/2} = (25 \bullet 5)^{1/2} = 25^{1/2} \bullet 5^{1/2} = (\sqrt{25})(\sqrt{5}) = 5\sqrt{5}$$

Notice that this is just the process of extracting a square root by finding a factor, but what makes this process work is the product power rule of exponents. The quotient power rule is used in the following example.

Example:

$$\sqrt{\frac{4}{9}} = \left(\frac{4}{9}\right)^{1/2} = \frac{4^{1/2}}{9^{1/2}} = \frac{\sqrt{4}}{\sqrt{9}} = \frac{2}{3}$$

Importantly, since radicals are fractional exponents and obey the rules for exponents, you cannot simply add radicals. $\sqrt{4} + \sqrt{9}$ is not equal to $\sqrt{13}$, and you can prove this by taking the square root of 4, which is 2, and the square root of 9, which is 3. 2 + 3 is 5, which does not equal $\sqrt{13}$.

OPERATIONS INVOLVING RADICALS (RATIONAL EXPONENTS)

Product Rule: $\sqrt{x} \cdot \sqrt{x} = x^{1/2}x^{1/2} = x^1 = x$

Quotient Rule: $\dfrac{\sqrt[m]{x}}{\sqrt[n]{x}} = \dfrac{x^{1/m}}{x^{1/n}} = x^{(1/m - 1/n)}$

Power Rule: $(\sqrt[m]{x})^n = (x^{1/m})^n = x^{n/m}$

Product Power Rule: $\sqrt[m]{x^n y^p} = (x^n y^p)^{1/m} = x^{n/m} y^{p/m} = \sqrt[m]{x^n} \cdot \sqrt[m]{y^p}$

Quotient Power Rule: $\sqrt[m]{\dfrac{x^n}{y^p}} = \left(\dfrac{x^n}{y^p}\right)^{1/m} = \dfrac{x^{n/m}}{y^{p/m}} = \dfrac{\sqrt[m]{x^n}}{\sqrt[m]{y^p}}$

NOTE: The ACT, PLAN, and EXPLORE allow calculators. Therefore, it is important that you learn how to use a calculator and bring the same calculator with you to the exam. Using a calculator provides greater accuracy and often saves valuable test time.

EXERCISE 8

Exponents and Radicals

DIRECTIONS: Choose the correct answer to each of the following items. Use a calculator when necessary. Answers are on page 921.

1. What is the third power of 3?

   A. 1 B. 3 C. 9 D. 15 E. 27

2. What is the fourth power of 2?

   A. 2 B. 4 C. 8 D. 16 E. 32

3. What is the first power of 1,000,000?

   A. 0 B. $\frac{1}{1{,}000{,}000}$ C. 1 D. 10 E. 1,000,000

4. $100^0 = ?$

   A. 0 B. 1 C. 10 D. 100 E. 100,000

5. $2^3 \cdot 2^2 = ?$

   A. 6 B. 8 C. 2^5 D. 2^6 E. 4^6

6. $3^{10} \cdot 10^3 = ?$

   I. 30^{30}
   II. $300 \cdot 1{,}000$
   III. $30 + 30$

   A. I only
   B. II only
   C. I and III only
   D. II and III only
   E. Neither I, II, nor III

7. $5^4 \cdot 5^9 = ?$

   A. 25^{36} B. 5^{36} C. 5^{13} D. 5^5 E. 5

8. $2^3 \cdot 2^4 \cdot 2^5 = ?$

   A. 2^{12} B. 2^{60} C. 8^{12} D. 4^{60} E. 8^{60}

9. $(2 + 3)^{20} = ?$

   A. 5^{20} B. $2^{20} + 3^{20}$ C. 6^{20} D. 20^5 E. 20^6

10. $\frac{2^5}{2^3} = ?$

    A. 2^2 B. 4^4 C. 2^8 D. 4^8 E. 2^{15}

11. $\frac{3^{10}}{3^8} = ?$

    A. 3 B. 3^2 C. 9^2 D. 3^{18} E. 3^{80}

12. $\frac{5^2}{5^2} = ?$

    I. 0
    II. 1
    III. 5^0

    A. I and II only
    B. I and III only
    C. II and III only
    D. III only
    E. Neither I, II, nor III

13. $\frac{3^2}{3^3} = ?$

    I. 3^{-1}
    II. $\frac{1}{3}$
    III. -1

    A. I only
    B. II only
    C. I and II only
    D. I and III only
    E. I, II, and III

14. $(2^2)^3 = ?$

    A. 2^5 B. 2^6 C. 4^5 D. 4^6 E. 6^5

15. $(5^2)^6 = ?$

    A. 5^8 B. 5^{12} C. 10^4 D. 10^8 E. 10^{12}

16. $(7^7)^7 = ?$

    A. 21 B. 7^{14} C. 7^{49} D. 21^7 E. 49^{49}

17. $(3 \cdot 2)^2 = ?$

    I. 36
    II. $3 \cdot 3 \cdot 2 \cdot 2$
    III. $3^2 \cdot 2^2$

    A. I only
    B. II only
    C. III only
    D. I and III only
    E. I, II, and III

18. $(5 \cdot 3)^2 = ?$

I. 15^2
II. $5^2 \cdot 3^2$
III. 8^2

A. I only
B. II only
C. III only
D. I and II only
E. I, II, and III

19. $\left(\frac{8}{3}\right)^2 = ?$

I. $\frac{64}{9}$
II. $\frac{8^2}{3^2}$
III. 11^2

A. I only
B. II only
C. I and II only
D. I and III only
E. I, II, and III

20. $\left(\frac{4}{9}\right)^2 = ?$

A. $\frac{2}{3}$
B. $\frac{4}{9}$
C. $\frac{16}{81}$
D. $\frac{4^2}{9}$
E. $\frac{4}{9^2}$

21. $(2 \cdot 2^2 \cdot 2^3)^2 = ?$

A. 2^8
B. 2^{10}
C. 2^{12}
D. 2^{16}
E. 2^{18}

22. $\left(\frac{2^4 \cdot 5^4}{2^2 \cdot 5^2}\right)^2 = ?$

A. $2^4 \cdot 5^4$
B. $2^6 \cdot 2^6$
C. 4^6
D. 4^8
E. 24

23. $\frac{3^6 \cdot 5^3 \cdot 7^9}{3^4 \cdot 5^3 \cdot 7^8} = ?$

A. $3^2 \cdot 5 \cdot 7$
B. $3^2 \cdot 5 \cdot 7^2$
C. $3 \cdot 5 \cdot 7$
D. $3^2 \cdot 5$
E. $3^2 \cdot 7$

24. $\left(\frac{5^{12} \cdot 7^5}{5^{11} \cdot 7^5}\right)^2 = ?$

A. 25
B. 49
C. 5^7
D. 5^{11}
E. 7^5

25. $\left(\frac{12^{12} \cdot 11^{11} \cdot 10^{10}}{12^{12} \cdot 11^{11} \cdot 10^9}\right)^2 = ?$

A. 0
B. 1
C. 10
D. 100
E. 1,000

26. $\sqrt{36} = ?$

I. 6
II. −6
III. $3\sqrt{3}$

A. I only
B. I and II only
C. I and III only
D. II and III only
E. I, II, and III

27. $\sqrt{81} + \sqrt{4} = ?$

I. $\sqrt{85}$
II. $\sqrt{9} + \sqrt{2}$
III. 11

A. I only
B. II only
C. III only
D. I and II only
E. II and III only

28. $\sqrt{27} = ?$

A. 3
B. $3\sqrt{3}$
C. $3\sqrt{9}$
D. 27
E. 81

29. $\sqrt{52} = ?$

A. $\sqrt{5} + \sqrt{2}$
B. 7
C. $2\sqrt{13}$
D. $13\sqrt{4}$
E. 13^2

30. $\sqrt{\frac{9}{4}} = ?$

A. $\frac{\sqrt{3}}{2}$
B. $\frac{3}{\sqrt{2}}$
C. $\frac{3}{2}$
D. 5
E. $\sqrt{5}$

31. $\frac{\sqrt{81}}{\sqrt{27}} = ?$

A. $\sqrt{3}$
B. 3
C. $3\sqrt{3}$
D. 9
E. $9\sqrt{3}$

32. $2\sqrt{2}$ is most nearly equal to which of the following?

A. 2.8
B. 3.4
C. 4
D. 7
E. 12

33. $\sqrt{27}$ is approximately equal to which of the following?

A. 3
B. 4
C. 4.5
D. 5.1
E. 9

34. $\sqrt{12}$ is approximately equal to which of the following?

A. 2
B. 3.4
C. 4
D. 6
E. 8

35. $\sqrt{23}$ is approximately equal to which of the following?

A. 4
B. 4.8
C. 6
D. 7
E. 8

36. $\sqrt{45}$ is approximately equal to which of the following?

A. 5
B. 5.5
C. 6.6
D. 7
E. 7.5

37. Simplify: $(7 + \sqrt{5})(3 - \sqrt{5})$.

A. $4 + 4\sqrt{5}$
B. $4 - \sqrt{5}$
C. $16 + 4\sqrt{5}$
D. $16 - 4\sqrt{5}$
E. 16

38. Simplify: $(5-\sqrt{2})(3-\sqrt{2})$.

A. $17+\sqrt{2}$ C. $17+\sqrt{8}$ E. 25
B. $17-8\sqrt{2}$ D. $17+8\sqrt{2}$

39. Simplify: $(\sqrt{3}+1)(2-\sqrt{3})$.

A. -1 C. $-1+\sqrt{3}$ E. $1+\sqrt{3}$
B. $-1-\sqrt{3}$ D. 1

40. Simplify: $\sqrt{2}\cdot 2\sqrt{3}$.

A. $-2\sqrt{6}$ C. 2 E. $2\sqrt{6}$
B. $-\sqrt{6}$ D. $\sqrt{6}$

41. Simplify: $\sqrt{8}+\sqrt{50}$.

A. $-7\sqrt{2}$ C. $\sqrt{2}$ E. 7
B. $-\sqrt{2}$ D. $7\sqrt{2}$

42. Simplify: $\sqrt{3^2+5^2}$.

A. 6 C. 7 E. 8
B. $\sqrt{34}$ D. $\sqrt{51}$

43. Simplify: $\sqrt{(2\sqrt{3})^2+2^2}$.

A. 1 C. 3 E. 5
B. 2 D. 4

44. Is $(5+\sqrt{2})(5-\sqrt{2})$ rational?

A. Yes
B. No
C. Cannot be determined from the given information

45. Is $\frac{(5+\sqrt{2})}{(5-\sqrt{2})}$ rational?

A. Yes
B. No
C. Cannot be determined from the given information

46. Multiply and simplify: $\frac{\sqrt{2}}{2}\left(\sqrt{6}+\frac{\sqrt{2}}{2}\right)$.

A. $\sqrt{3}+\frac{1}{2}$ C. $\sqrt{6}+1$ E. $\sqrt{6}+2$
B. $\frac{\sqrt{3}}{2}$ D. $\sqrt{6}+1$

47. Divide and simplify: $\frac{15\sqrt{96}}{5\sqrt{2}}$.

A. $7\sqrt{3}$ C. $11\sqrt{3}$ E. $40\sqrt{3}$
B. $7\sqrt{12}$ D. $12\sqrt{3}$

48. Which of the following radicals is a perfect square?

A. $\sqrt{0.4}$ C. $\sqrt{0.09}$ E. $\sqrt{0.025}$
B. $\sqrt{0.9}$ D. $\sqrt{0.02}$

49. $\left(-\frac{1}{3}\right)^4=?$

A. $-\frac{1}{81}$ C. $-\frac{1}{12}$ E. $-\frac{1}{64}$
B. $\frac{1}{81}$ D. $\frac{1}{12}$

50. $-4^4=?$

A. -256 C. -16 E. -8
B. 256 D. 16

51. $\sqrt[12]{x^6}=?$

A. x^6 C. x^2 E. x^{-2}
B. x^{-6} D. $x^{1/2}$

52. $\sqrt[k]{6^{2km}}$ MUST be a positive integer if:

A. k is a positive integer
B. k is a multiple of 3
C. $k<0$
D. m is a non-negative common fraction
E. m is a non-negative integer

Algebraic Operations

Algebra is the branch of mathematics that uses letter symbols to represent numbers. The letter symbols are, in essence, placeholders. They function somewhat like "someone" or "somewhere." For example, in the sentence "Someone took the book and put it somewhere," neither the identity of the person in question nor the new location of the book is known. We can rewrite this sentence in algebraic terms: "x put the book in y place." The identity of x is unknown, and the new location of the book is unknown. It is for this reason that letter symbols in algebra are often referred to as "unknowns."

Algebra, like English, is a language, and for making certain statements, algebra is much better than English. For example, the English statement "There is a number such that, when you add 3 to it, the result is 8" can be rendered more easily in algebraic notation: $x + 3 = 8$. In fact, learning the rules of algebra is really very much like learning the grammar of any language. Keeping this analogy between algebra and English in mind, let's begin by studying the components of the algebraic language.

Elements of Algebra

1. *Algebraic Terms*

The basic unit of the English language is the word. The basic unit of algebra is the ***term***. In English, a word consists of one or more letters. In algebra, a term consists of one or more letters or numbers. For example, x, $2z$, xy, N, 2, $\sqrt{7}$, and π are all algebraic terms. A term can be a product, quotient, or single symbol.

In English, a word may have a root, a prefix, a suffix, an ending, and so on. In algebra, a term may have a coefficient, an exponent, and a sign, etc. Of course, algebraic terms also include a variable, also referred to as the base.

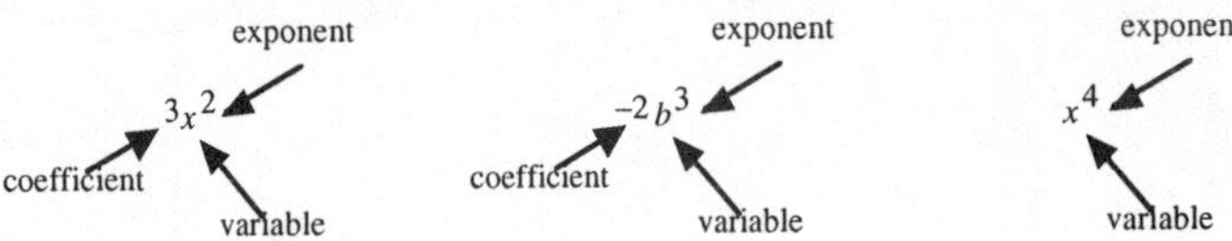

Just as with numbers, when the sign of an algebraic term is positive, the "+" is not written; *e.g.*, $3x$ is equivalent to $+3x$. Additionally, when the coefficient is 1, it is understood to be included and is not written out; *e.g.*, x rather than $1x$.

The elements in an algebraic term are all joined by the operation of multiplication. The coefficient and its sign are multiplied by the variable. For example: $-3x = (-3)(x)$; $5a = (+5)(a)$; and $\frac{1}{2}N = \left(+\frac{1}{2}\right)(N)$.

The exponent, as you have already learned, also indicates multiplication. Thus, x^2 means x times x; a^3 means a times a times a; and N^5 means N times N times N times N times N. Be careful not to confuse the coefficient with the exponent. $3x$ means "+3 times x," while x^3 means "x times x times x." Of course, many terms have both a coefficient and an exponent. Thus, $3x^2$ means "+3 times x times x," and $-5a^3$ means "-5 times a times a times a."

2. *Algebraic Expressions*

In English, words are organized into phrases. In algebra, terms are grouped together in ***expressions***. An expression is a collection of algebraic terms that are joined by addition, subtraction, or both.

Examples:

1. $x + y$
2. $-2x + 3y + z$
3. $3x^2 - 2y^2$
4. $x^2 + y^{20}$

A ***rational expression*** is a fraction containing algebraic terms. In other words, rational expressions are algebraic fractions.

Examples:

1. $\frac{1}{x}$
2. $\frac{x^2}{xy - y^2}$
3. $\frac{3+\frac{1}{x}}{9-\frac{1}{x^2}}$

Algebraic expressions are classified according to the number of terms the expression contains. A ***monomial*** is an algebraic expression with exactly one term. A ***polynomial*** is an algebraic expression with more than one term. A ***binomial*** is a polynomial with exactly two terms. A ***trinomial*** is a polynomial with exactly three terms.

3. *Algebraic Equations*

In algebra, a complete sentence is called an equation. An equation asserts that two algebraic expressions are equal. Equations involving rational expressions are called ***rational equations.***

Examples:

1. $2x + 4 = 3x - 2$
2. $\frac{y^2 - 5y}{y^2 - 4y - 5} = \frac{y}{y+1}$

Operations of Algebraic Terms

1. *Adding and Subtracting Algebraic Terms*

Addition and subtraction are indicated in algebra, as they are in arithmetic, with the signs "+" and "−." In arithmetic, these operations combine the numbers into a third number. For example, the addition of 2 and 3 is equivalent to combining 2 and 3 to form the number 5: $2 + 3 = 5$.

In algebra, however, only ***similar (like) terms*** may be combined. Similar terms are terms with the same variables having the same exponent values. Coefficients do not factor into whether or not terms are similar.

Examples:

1. $3x^2$, $40x^2$, $-2x^2$, and $\sqrt{2}x^2$ are similar terms.
2. xy, $5xy$, $-23xy$, and πxy are similar terms.
3. $10xyz$, $-xyz$, and xyz are similar terms.
4. $3x$ and $3x^2$ are NOT similar terms.
5. xy and x^2y are NOT similar terms.
6. xy, yz, and xz are NOT similar terms.

To simplify an algebraic expression, group similar terms and add/subtract the numerical coefficients of each group. Variables and exponents of combined similar terms remain unchanged.

Examples:

1. $x^2 + 2x^2 + 3x^2 = ?$

   ➢ All three terms are similar since each includes x^2. Combine the terms by adding the coefficients: $1 + 2 + 3 = 6$. Thus, the result is $6x^2$.

2. $y + 2x + 3y - x = ?$

   ➤ With two different types of terms, group the similar terms together: $(2x - x) + (y + 3y)$. Add the coefficients for each type of term. For the x terms, the combined coefficient is $2 - 1 = 1$; for the y terms, $1 + 3 = 4$. The result is $x + 4y$.

3. $x - 3x + 5x - 2x = (1 - 3 + 5 - 2)x = x$
4. $2x - y - 3x + 4y + 5x = (2x - 3x + 5x) + (4y - y) = 4x + 3y$
5. $5x^2 + 3x^3 - 2x^2 + 4x^3 = (5x^2 - 2x^2) + (3x^3 + 4x^3) = 3x^2 + 7x^3$

Notice that when you have combined all similar terms, it is not possible to carry the addition or subtraction any further.

2. *Multiplying and Dividing Algebraic Terms*

Use the arithmetic ***rules of exponents*** to multiply or divide algebraic terms. Remember that $x^0 = 1$ when $x \neq 0$, and $x^1 = x$.

OPERATIONS OF ALGEBRAIC TERMS

Product Rule: $x^m \cdot x^n = x^{m+n}$
$ax^m \cdot bx^n = abx^{m+n}$

Quotient Rule: $\frac{x^m}{x^n} = x^{m-n}$

Power Rule: $(x^m)^n = x^{mn}$

Product Power Rule: $(x^m \cdot y^p)^n = x^{mn} \cdot y^{pn}$

Quotient Power Rule: $\left(\frac{x^m}{y^p}\right)^n = \frac{x^{mn}}{y^{pn}}$

Negative Exponents: $x^{-n} = \frac{1}{x^n}$.

Examples:

Product Rule:
$(x^2)(x^3) = x^{(2+3)} = x^5$
$(3x^2)(xy) = (3 \cdot 1)(x^2 \cdot xy) = 3 \cdot x^{(2+1)} \cdot y = 3x^3y$
$(2xyz)(3xy)(4yz) = (2 \cdot 3 \cdot 4)(xyz \cdot xy \cdot yz) = 24 \cdot x^{(1+1)} \cdot y^{(1+1+1)} \cdot z^{(1+1)} = 24x^2y^3z^2$

Quotient Rule:
$\frac{x^3}{x^2} = x^{(3-2)} = x^1 = x$
$\frac{2x^4y^3}{x^2z} = \frac{2}{1} \cdot \frac{x^4y^3}{x^2z} = 2 \cdot \frac{x^{(4-2)}y^3}{z} = \frac{2x^2y^3}{z}$

Power Rule: $(x^2)^3 = x^{(2)(3)} = x^6$

Product Power Rule: $(x^2y^3)^2 = x^{(2)(2)}y^{(3)(2)} = x^4y^6$

Quotient Power Rule: $\left(\frac{x^2}{y^3}\right)^2 = \frac{x^{(2)(2)}}{y^{(3)(2)}} = \frac{x^4}{y^6}$

Operations of Algebraic Fractions

1. *Adding and Subtracting Algebraic Fractions*

Adding and subtracting algebraic fractions, like adding and subtracting numerical fractions, require common denominators. If the denominators are the same, simply add/subtract the numerators: $\frac{a}{x} \pm \frac{b}{x} = \frac{a \pm b}{x}$.

Examples:

1. $\frac{5}{x}+\frac{3}{x}=\frac{5+3}{x}=\frac{8}{x}$
2. $\frac{2x}{y}-\frac{x}{y}=\frac{2x-x}{y}=\frac{x}{y}$
3. $\frac{a}{cd}+\frac{x}{cd}=\frac{a+x}{cd}$

To add or subtract algebraic fractions with unlike denominators, you must first find a common denominator. Usually, this can be accomplished by using the same "flying *x*" method as with numerical fractions: $\frac{a}{x}\pm\frac{b}{y}=\frac{ay}{xy}\pm\frac{bx}{yx}=\frac{ay\pm bx}{xy}$.

Example:

$$\frac{2x}{y}+\frac{3y}{x}=\frac{2x}{y}+\frac{3y}{x}=\frac{2x^2+3y^2}{xy}$$

2. ***Multiplying and Dividing Algebraic Fractions***

To multiply algebraic fractions, follow the rule for multiplying numeric fractions. Multiply terms in the numerators to create a new numerator, and multiply terms in the denominator to create a new denominator: $\frac{a}{c}\bullet\frac{b}{d}=\frac{ab}{cd}$.

Examples:

1. $\frac{2}{x}\bullet\frac{3}{y}=\frac{6}{xy}$
2. $\frac{x^2y^3}{z}\bullet\frac{x^3y^2}{wz}=\frac{x^5y^5}{wz^2}$

To divide algebraic fractions, follow the rule for dividing numeric fractions. Invert the divisor, or second fraction, and multiply: $\frac{a}{c}\div\frac{b}{d}=\frac{a}{c}\bullet\frac{d}{b}=\frac{ad}{cb}$.

Examples:

1. $\frac{2}{y}\div\frac{3}{x}=\frac{2}{y}\bullet\frac{x}{3}=\frac{2x}{3y}$
2. $\frac{2x^2}{y}\div\frac{y}{x}=\frac{2x^2}{y}\bullet\frac{x}{y}=\frac{2x^3}{y^2}$

Multiplying Algebraic Expressions

A ***polynomial*** is an algebraic expression with one or more terms involving only the operations of addition, subtraction, and multiplication of variables. Polynomial means "many terms," although it is possible to get a monomial by adding two polynomials. A multiplication item such as $(x+y)(x+y)$ requires a special procedure. The fundamental rule for multiplying is that every term of one expression must be multiplied by every term of the other expression.

1. ***Distributive Property***

First, let's look at the case in which a polynomial is to be multiplied by a single term. One way of solving the item is to first add and then multiply. Alternatively, we can use the ***distributive property*** to multiply every term inside the parentheses by the term outside the parentheses, and then we can add the terms: $x(y+z)=xy+xz$. The result is the same regardless of the method used. The following example illustrates these two methods using real numbers.

Example:

$2(3+4+5) = 2(12) = 24$

➢ The distributive property returns the same result: $2(3+4+5) = (2 \cdot 3) + (2 \cdot 4) + (2 \cdot 5) = 6 + 8 + 10 = 24$.

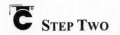

When working with algebraic expressions, use the distributive property, since you cannot add unlike terms. The following examples apply the distributive property to algebraic expressions.

Examples:

1. $x(y+z) = xy + xz$
2. $a(b+c+d) = ab + ac + ad$

To multiply two polynomials, either add the polynomials before multiplying them, or reverse the order of operations using the distributive property.

Example:

$(2+3)(1+3+4) = (5)(8) = 40$

➢ The distributive property returns the same result: $(2+3)(1+3+4) = (2 \cdot 1) + (2 \cdot 3) + (2 \cdot 4) + (3 \cdot 1) + (3 \cdot 3) + (3 \cdot 4) = 2 + 6 + 8 + 3 + 9 + 12 = 40$.

2. ***FOIL Method***

To multiply two binomials using the ***FOIL method***, follow these steps for combining the binomial terms: (1) multiply the first terms, (2) multiply the outer terms, (3) multiply the inner terms, (4) multiply the last terms, and (5) combine like terms. The FOIL method is simply a mnemonic shortcut derived from the distributive property. The following diagram illustrates application of the FOIL method.

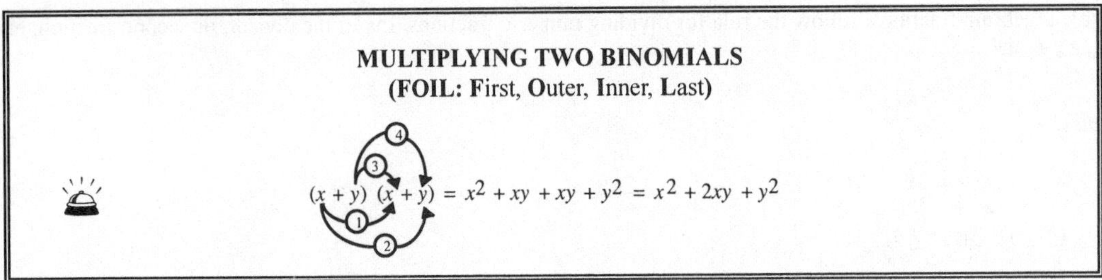

MULTIPLYING TWO BINOMIALS
(FOIL: First, Outer, Inner, Last)
(x + y) (x + y) = x2 + xy + xy + y2 = x2 + 2xy + y2

Examples:

1. $(x+y)(x+y) = ?$

   ➢ First: $(x)(x) = x^2$; Outer: $(x)(y) = xy$; Inner: $(y)(x) = xy$; Last: $(y)(y) = y^2$. Add: $x^2 + xy + xy + y^2 = x^2 + 2xy + y^2$.
2. $(x-y)(x-y) = ?$

   ➢ First: $(x)(x) = x^2$; Outer: $(x)(-y) = -xy$; Inner: $(-y)(x) = -xy$; Last: $(-y)(-y) = y^2$. Add: $x^2 - xy - xy + y^2 = x^2 - 2xy + y^2$.

Three situations, one in addition to the two illustrated in the previous examples, arise with such frequency that you should memorize the results to simplify the calculation.

THREE COMMON MULTIPLICATIONS INVOLVING POLYNOMIALS

1. $(x+y)^2 = (x+y)(x+y) = x^2 + 2xy + y^2$
2. $(x-y)^2 = (x-y)(x-y) = x^2 - 2xy + y^2$
3. $(x+y)(x-y) = x^2 - y^2$

You might be asked to multiply something more complex than two binomials. The process is tedious and time-consuming, but ultimately it is executed the same way.

Example:

$(x + y)^3 = ?$

➢ Apply the FOIL method to the first two binomials, then multiply the last binomial to the resultant trinomial of the first two binomials: $(x + y)^3 = (x + y)(x + y)(x + y) = (x^2 + 2xy + y^2)(x + y) =$
$x(x^2) + x(2xy) + x(y^2) + y(x^2) + y(2xy) + y(y^2) = x^3 + 2x^2y + xy^2 + x^2y + 2xy^2 + y^3 = x^3 + 3x^2y + 3xy^2 + y^3$.

Factoring Algebraic Expressions

Although the term ***factoring*** intimidates many students, factoring is really nothing more than reverse multiplication. For example, if $(x + y)(x + y) = x^2 + 2xy + y^2$, then $x^2 + 2xy + y^2$ can be factored into $(x + y)(x + y)$. Fortunately, for the purposes of taking the test, any factoring you might need to do will fall into one of three categories.

1. Finding a Common Factor

If all the terms of an algebraic expression contain a common factor, then that term can be factored out of the expression.

Examples:

1. $ab + ac + ad = a(b + c + d)$
2. $abx + aby + abz = ab(x + y + z)$
3. $x^2 + x^3 + x^4 = x^2(1 + x + x^2)$
4. $3a + 6a^2 + 9a^3 = 3a(1 + 2a + 3a^2)$

2. Reversing a Known Polynomial Multiplication Process

Three patterns recur with such frequency on the exam that you should memorize them. These patterns are the same as the ones you were encouraged to memorize in the discussion of the FOIL method.

THREE COMMON POLYNOMIAL MULTIPLICATION REVERSALS

1. Perfect square trinomial: $x^2 + 2xy + y^2 = (x + y)(x + y)$
2. Perfect square trinomial: $x^2 - 2xy + y^2 = (x - y)(x - y)$
3. Difference of two squares: $x^2 - y^2 = (x + y)(x - y)$

3. Reversing an Unknown Polynomial Multiplication Process

Occasionally, you may find it necessary to factor an expression that does not fall into one of the three categories presented above. The expression will most likely have the form $ax^2 + bx + c$; *e.g.*, $x^2 + 2x + 1$. To factor such expressions, set up a blank diagram: (   )(   ). Then, fill in the diagram by answering the following series of questions.

1. What factors will produce the first term, ax^2?
2. What possible factors will produce the last term, c?
3. Which of the possible factors from step 2, when added together, will produce the middle term, bx?

Examples:

1. Factor $x^2 + 3x + 2$.

   ➢ • What factors will produce the first term, ax^2? x times x yields x^2, so the factors, in part, are $(x \quad)(x \quad)$.
   • What possible factors will produce the last term? The possibilities are $\{2, 1\}$ and $\{-2, -1\}$.
   • Which of the two sets of factors just mentioned, when added together, will produce a result of $+3x$?
   The answer is $\{2, 1\}$: $2 + 1 = 3$, as the FOIL method confirms: $(x + 2)(x + 1) = x^2 + x + 2x + 2 = x^2 + 3x + 2$.

2. Factor $x^2 + 4x - 12$.

   ➢ • What factors will generate ax^2? $(x \quad)(x \quad)$.
   • What factors will generate -12? $\{1, -12\}$, $\{12, -1\}$, $\{2, -6\}$ $\{6, -2\}$, $\{3, -4\}$, and $\{4, -3\}$.
   • Which factors, when added together, will produce the middle term of $+ 4x$? The answer is $\{6, -2\}$: $6 + (-2) = 4$.
   Thus, the factors are $(x + 6)$ and $(x - 2)$, as the FOIL method confirms: $(x + 6)(x - 2) = x^2 - 2x + 6x - 12 = x^2 + 4x - 12$.

Absolute Value in Algebraic Expressions

Algebraic terms involving absolute values are treated the same way as numeric absolute values. Remember that the absolute value of any term is always a positive numerical value.

PRINCIPLES OF ABSOLUTE VALUE

1. $|x| = x$ if $x \geq 0$; $|x| = -x$ if $x < 0$
2. $|x| = |-x|$
3. $|x| \geq 0$
4. $|x - y| = |y - x|$

Examples:

1. If $w = -3$, $|w| = ?$

   ➢ Since the value of w is less than zero, $|w| = -w = -(-3) = 3$.

2. Let x be a member of the following set: $\{-11, -10, -9, -8, -7, -6, -5, -4, -3, -2, -1, 0, 1, 2, 3, 4\}$. $\frac{|2x - |x||}{3}$ is a positive integer for how many different numbers in the set?

   ➢ If $x < 0$, then $|x| = -x$: $\frac{|2x - |x||}{3} = \frac{|2x - (-x)|}{3} = \frac{|2x + x|}{3} = \frac{|3x|}{3} = |x|$, which is always a positive. Therefore, $\frac{|2x - |x||}{3}$ is a positive integer for all numbers in the set less than zero. If $x \geq 0$, then $|x| = x$: $\frac{|2x - |x||}{3} = \frac{|2x - x|}{3} = \frac{|x|}{3} = \frac{x}{3}$. Thus, the only other number in the set that returns a positive integer is 3. The total number of values in the set that satisfy the condition is: $11 + 1 = 12$.

Radicals in Algebraic Expressions

Radicals in algebraic expressions are manipulated in the same way as numeric radicals using the rules of exponents.

Example:

Does $\frac{3\sqrt{x} + \sqrt{x^3}}{x} = \frac{3}{\sqrt{x}} + \sqrt{x}$?

➢ $\frac{3\sqrt{x} + \sqrt{x^3}}{x} = \frac{3\sqrt{x}}{x} + \frac{\sqrt{x^3}}{x} = \frac{3x^{1/2}}{x} + \frac{x^{3/2}}{x} = 3x^{(1/2 - 1)} + x^{(3/2 - 1)} = 3x^{-1/2} + x^{1/2} = \frac{3}{\sqrt{x}} + \sqrt{x}$.

When simplifying expressions containing roots and radicals that are inverse operations of one another, it is important to note that the sign of the variable impacts the sign of the result. Consider $\sqrt{x^2}$. If $x \geq 0$, then $\sqrt{x^2} = x$; if $x < 0$, then $\sqrt{x^2} = -x$.

Examples:

1. $\sqrt{2^2} = 2$
2. $\sqrt{(-2)^2} = -(-2) = 2$

NOTE: The ACT, PLAN, and EXPLORE allow calculators. Therefore, it is important that you learn how to use a calculator and bring the same calculator with you to the exam. Using a calculator provides greater accuracy and often saves valuable test time.

EXERCISE 9

Algebraic Operations

DIRECTIONS: Choose the correct answer to each of the following items. Use a calculator when necessary. Answers are on page 922.

1. Which of the following is (are) like terms?

   I. $34x$ and $-18x$
   II. $2x$ and $2xy$
   III. x^3 and $3x$

   A. I only
   B. II only
   C. I and III only
   D. II and III only
   E. I, II, and III

2. Which of the following is (are) like terms?

   I. $\sqrt{2}x$ and $\sqrt{3}x$
   II. π and 10
   III. x^2 and $2x^2$

   A. I only
   B. II only
   C. I and II only
   D. I and III only
   E. I, II, and III

3. $x + 2x + 3x = ?$

   A. $6x^6$
   B. x^6
   C. $6x$
   D. $x + 6$
   E. $x - 6$

4. $2x + 3x - x + 4x = ?$

   A. $8x^8$
   B. x^8
   C. $8x$
   D. $x + 8$
   E. $x - 8$

5. $a^3 + a^2 + a = ?$

   A. $3a^3$
   B. a^3
   C. $2a^2$
   D. a^2
   E. $a^3 + a^2 + a$

6. $z^2 + 2z^2 - 5z^2 = ?$

   A. $-9z^2$
   B. $-2z^2$
   C. 0
   D. $2z^2$
   E. $5z^2$

7. $a^3 - 12a^3 + 15a^3 + 2a^3 = ?$

   A. $6a^3$
   B. $2a^2$
   C. $6a$
   D. $3a$
   E. a

8. $3c + 2a - 1 + 4c - 2a + 1 = ?$

   A. $2a + 4c + 1$
   B. $4a + 3c - 2$
   C. $a + c - 1$
   D. $2a + 1$
   E. $7c$

9. $-7nx + 2nx + 2n + 7x = ?$

   A. 0
   B. $-5nx + 2n + 7x$
   C. $18nx$
   D. $9nx + 9xn$
   E. $4nx$

10. $c^2 + 2c^2d^2 - c^2 = ?$

    A. $4c^2d^2$
    B. $2c^2d^2$
    C. c^2d^2
    D. $2cd$
    E. cd

11. $2x^2 + 2x^2 + 2x^2 = ?$

    A. $6x^6$
    B. $2x^6$
    C. $6x^2$
    D. $6x$
    E. 6

12. $3xy + 3x^2y - 2xy + y = ?$

    A. $6xy - y$
    B. $x + xy + y$
    C. $3x^2y + xy + y$
    D. $x^2y^2 + xy$
    E. $3xy + x$

13. $x^2 + 2xy - 3x + 4xy - 6y + 2y^2 + 3x - 2xy + 6y = ?$

    A. $x^2 - 2xy + y^2$
    B. $x^2 + y^2 + 3x + 2y$
    C. $x^2 + 2y^2 + 4xy + 6x + 6y$
    D. $x^2 + 2y^2 + 4xy + 6x$
    E. $x^2 + 2y^2 + 4xy$

14. $8p + 2p^2 + pq - 4p^2 - 14p - pq = ?$

    A. $-2p^2 - 6p$
    B. $-p^2 + 6p$
    C. $2p^2 + 6p$
    D. $p^2 + 3p$
    E. $3p^2 - pq$

15. $pqr + qrs + rst + stu = ?$

    A. $pqrst$
    B. $pq + qr + rs + st + tu$
    C. $pqr + rst$
    D. $4pqrst$
    E. $pqr + qrs + rst + stu$

16. $(x^2)(x^3) = ?$

    A. $x^{2/3}$
    B. x
    C. $x^{3/2}$
    D. x^5
    E. x^6

17. $(a)(a^2)(a^3)(a^4) = ?$

    A. $10a$
    B. $24a$
    C. a^5
    D. a^{10}
    E. a^{24}

18. $y^5 \div y^2 = ?$

    A. $3y$
    B. $7y$
    C. $y^{5/2}$
    D. y^3
    E. y^7

19. $(x^2y)(xy^2) = ?$

    A. $4xy$
    B. x^3y^3
    C. xy^4
    D. x^4y^4
    E. xy^{16}

20. $(abc)(a^2bc^2) = ?$

A. $4abc$
B. a^2bc^2
C. $a^3b^2c^3$
D. $a^3b^3c^3$
E. abc^6

21. $(xy^2)(x^2z)(y^2z) = ?$

A. $8xyz$
B. x^2y^4z
C. $x^3y^4z^2$
D. $x^3y^3z^2$
E. $x^3y^3z^3$

22. $\frac{x^2y^4}{xy} = ?$

A. y^3
B. xy^3
C. x^2y^3
D. x^3y^5
E. xy^8

23. $\frac{a^3b^4c^5}{abc} = ?$

A. $a^2b^3c^4$
B. $a^3b^4c^5$
C. $(abc)^3$
D. $(abc)^{12}$
E. $(abc)^{60}$

24. $(x^2y^3)^4 = ?$

A. $(xy)^9$
B. x^6y^7
C. x^8y^{12}
D. xy^{20}
E. xy^{24}

25. $\left(\frac{a^2}{b^3}\right)^3 = ?$

A. $\frac{a^5}{b}$
B. $\frac{a^6}{b^9}$
C. a^5b
D. a^6b
E. a^6b^9

26. $\frac{x^3y^4z^5}{x^4y^2z} = ?$

A. y^2z^4
B. xy^2z^4
C. $\frac{y^2z^4}{x}$
D. $\frac{y^2z^5}{x}$
E. $\frac{y^6z^6}{x}$

27. $\left(\frac{c^4d^2}{c^2d}\right)^3 = ?$

A. c^5d^3
B. c^5d^5
C. c^6d^3
D. c^6d^4
E. c^6d^6

28. $\left(\frac{x^2y^3}{xy}\right)\left(\frac{x^3y^4}{xy}\right) = ?$

A. x^2y^3
B. x^3y^4
C. x^3y^5
D. x^5y^6
E. x^6y^7

29. $\left(\frac{abc^2}{abc^3}\right)\left(\frac{a^2b^2c}{ab}\right) = ?$

A. $\frac{ab}{c}$
B. $\frac{bc}{a}$
C. ab
D. c
E. 1

30. $\left(\frac{x^5y^3z^2}{x^4y^2z}\right)^2\left(\frac{x^2y^3z^5}{xy^2z^4}\right)^3 = ?$

A. xyz
B. $x^2y^2z^2$
C. $x^5y^5z^5$
D. $x^6y^6z^6$
E. xyz^{12}

31. $\frac{a}{c} + \frac{b}{c} = ?$

A. $\frac{ab}{c}$
B. $\frac{a+b}{c}$
C. $\frac{a+b}{2c}$
D. $\frac{a+b}{c^2}$
E. $\frac{a+b}{abc}$

32. $\frac{x}{2} + \frac{y}{2} + \frac{z}{2} = ?$

A. $\frac{x+y+z}{2}$
B. $\frac{x+y+z}{6}$
C. $\frac{x+y+z}{8}$
D $\frac{xyz}{2}$
E. $\frac{xyz}{8}$

33. $\frac{ab}{x} + \frac{bc}{x} + \frac{cd}{x} = ?$

A. $\frac{abcd}{x}$
B. $\frac{a+b+c+d}{3x}$
C. $\frac{ab+bc+cd}{x}$
D. $\frac{ab+bc+cd}{3x}$
E. $\frac{ab+bc+cd}{x^3}$

34. $\frac{x^2}{k} + \frac{x^3}{k} + \frac{x^4}{k} = ?$

A. $\frac{x^9}{k}$
B. $\frac{x^9}{3k}$
C. $\frac{x^{24}}{k}$
D. $\frac{x^2+x^3+x^4}{k}$
E. $\frac{x^2+x^3+x^4}{3k}$

35. $\frac{2x}{z} - \frac{y}{z} = ?$

A. $\frac{2x-y}{z}$
B. $\frac{2x-y}{2z}$
C. $\frac{2x-y}{z^2}$
D. $\frac{2xy}{z}$
E. $\frac{2xy}{2z}$

36. $\frac{x}{y} + \frac{y}{x} = ?$

A. $\frac{xy}{x+y}$
B. $\frac{x+y}{y+x}$
C. $\frac{x+y}{xy}$
D. $\frac{xy+yx}{xy}$
E. $\frac{x^2+y^2}{xy}$

37. $\frac{a}{b} - \frac{b}{a} = ?$

A. $\frac{ab}{a-b}$
B. $\frac{a-b}{b-a}$
C. $\frac{a-b}{ab}$
D. $\frac{ab-ba}{ab}$
E. $\frac{a^2-b^2}{ab}$

38. $\frac{x^2}{y} + \frac{x^3}{z} = ?$

A. $\frac{x^2+x^3}{yz}$
B. $\frac{x^5}{yz}$
C. $\frac{x^6}{yz}$
D. $\frac{x^2+x^3}{yz}$
E. $\frac{x^2z+x^3y}{yz}$

39. $\frac{x}{a} + \frac{y}{b} + \frac{z}{c} = ?$

A. $\frac{xyz}{abc}$
B. $\frac{x+y+z}{a+b+c}$
C. $\frac{xbc+yac+zab}{abc}$
D. $\frac{xbc+yac+zab}{a+b+c}$
E. $\frac{xa+yb+zc}{abc}$

40. $\frac{x^2}{y^2} - \frac{y^3}{x^3} = ?$

A. $\frac{x^2 - x^3}{y^5}$
B. $\frac{x^3 - x^2}{y^6}$
C. $\frac{x^2 - y^3}{x^2 - y^2}$
D. $\frac{x^5 - y^5}{x^3 y^2}$
E. $\frac{x^6 - y^6}{x^3 y^2}$

41. $2(x + y) = ?$

A. $2xy$
B. $2x + 2y$
C. $2 + x + 2y$
D. $4x$
E. $2x^2 + 2y^2$

42. $a(b + c) = ?$

A. $ab + bc$
B. $ab + ac$
C. $2abc$
D. $ab^2 + b^2c$
E. $ab + ac + bc$

43. $3(a + b + c + d) = ?$

A. $3abcd$
B. $3a + b + c + d$
C. $3a + 3b + 3c + 3d$
D. $3ab + 3bc + 3cd$
E. $12a + 12b + 12c + 12d$

44. $2x(3x + 4x^2) = ?$

A. x^{10}
B. $6x + 8x^2$
C. $5x^2 + 6x^3$
D. $6x^2 + 8x^3$
E. $6(x^2 + x^3)$

45. $3a^2(ab + ac + bc) = ?$

A. $3a^3 b^2 c$
B. $3a^3 + 3b^2 + 3c$
C. $3a^2b + 3a^2c + 3a^2bc$
D. $3a^3b + 3a^3c + 3a^2bc$
E. $3a^5b + 3a^5c$

46. $(x + y)\,(x + y) = ?$

A. $x^2 + y^2$
B. $x^2 - y^2$
C. $x^2 + 2xy - y^2$
D. $x^2 - 2xy + y^2$
E. $x^2 + 2xy$ [illegible] y^2

47. $(a + b)^2 = ?$

A. $a^2 + b^2$
B. $a^2 - b^2$
C. $a^2 + 2ab - b^2$
D. [illegible] $b + b^2$
[illegible] $2ab + b^2$

48. $(x - y)^2 = ?$

A. $x^2 + 2xy - y^2$
B. $x^2 + 2xy + y^2$
C. $x^2 - 2xy + y^2$
D. $x^2 - 2xy - y^2$
E. $x^2 + y^2$

49. $(a + b)(a - b) = ?$

A. $a^2 - b^2$
B. $a^2 + b^2$
C. $a^2 + 2ab + b^2$
D. $a^2 - 2ab + b^2$
E. $a^2 + 2ab - b^2$

50. $(x - 2)^2 = ?$

A. $2x$
B. $4x$
C. $x^2 - 4$
D. $x^2 - 4x + 4$
E. $x^2 - 4x - 4$

51. $(2 - x)^2 = ?$

A. $4 - x^2$
B. $x^2 + 4$
C. $x^2 + 4x + 4$
D. $x^2 - 4x + 4$
E. $x^2 - 4x - 4$

52. $(ab + bc)(a + b) = ?$

A. $a^2b + ab^2 + b^2c + abc$
B. $a^2b + ab^2 + abc$
C. $a^2b + ab^2 + a^2bc$
D. $a^2b + ab + bc + abc$
E. $a^2 + b^2 + c^2 + abc$

53. $(x - y)(x + 2) = ?$

A. $x^2 + 2xy + 2y$
B. $x^2 + 2xy + x + y$
C. $x^2 + 2xy + x - 2y$
D. $x^2 - xy + 2x - 2y$
E. $x^2 + 2x + 2y - 2$

54. $(a + b)(c + d) = ?$

A. $ab + bc + cd$
B. $ab + bc + cd + ad$
C. $ac + bd$
D. $ac + ad + bc + bd$
E. $ab + ac + ad$

55. $(w + x)(y - z) = ?$

A. $wxy - z$
B. $wy + xy - yz$
C. $wy - wz + xy + xz$
D. $wy + wz + xy - xz$
E. $wy - wz + xy - xz$

56. $(x + y)(w + x + y) = ?$

A. $x^2 + wx + wy + xy$
B. $x^2 + y^2 + wx + wy + 2xy$
C. $x^2 + y^2 + wxy$
D. $x^2 + y^2 + wx^2y^2$
[illegible] $x^2y^2 + wxy$

57. $(2$ [illegible] $(3 + x + y) = ?$

A. $x^2 +$ [illegible] $+ 6$
B. $x^2 + 6xy$ [illegible] $3x + 2y + 6$
C. $x^2 + 2xy + 6x + 6y + 6$
D. $x^2 + xy + 5x + 2y + 6$
E. $x^2 + 3xy + 2x + y + 6$

58. $(x + y)^3 = ?$

A. $x^3 + 5x^2y + y^2z + xyz$
B. $x^3 + 3x^3y + 3xy^3 + y^3$
C. $x^3 + 3x^2y + 3xy^2 + y^3$
D. $x^3 + 6x^2y^2 + y^3$
E. $x^3 + 12x^2y^2 + y^3$

59. $(x - y)^3 = ?$

A. $x^3 - 3x^2y + 3xy^2 - y^3$
B. $x^3 + 3x^2y + 3xy^2 + y^3$
C. $x^3 + 3x^2y - 3xy^2 - y^3$
D. $x^3 + 6x^2y^2 + y^3$
E. $x^3 + 6x^2y^2 - y^3$

60. $(a + b)(a - b)(a + b)(a - b) = ?$

A. 1
B. $a^2 - b^2$
C. $a^2 + b^2$
D. $a^4 - 2a^2b^2 + b^4$
E. $a^4 + 2a^2b^2 + b^4$

61. $2a + 2b + 2c = ?$

A. $2(a + b + c)$
B. $2(abc)$
C. $2(ab + bc + ca)$
D. $6(a + b + c)$
E. $8(a + b + c)$

62. $x + x^2 + x^3 = ?$

A. $x(x + 2x + 3x)$
B. $x(1 + 2x + 3x)$
C. $x(1 + 2 + 3)$
D. $x(1 + x + x^2)$
E. $x(1 + 3x)$

63. $2x^2 + 4x^3 + 8x^4 = ?$

A. $2x^2(1 + 2x + 4x^2)$
B. $2x^2(1 + 2x + 4x^3)$
C. $2x^2(x + 2x + 4x^2)$
D. $2x^2(x + 2x^2 + 4x^3)$
E. $2x^2(x^2 + 2x^3 + 4x^4)$

64. $abc + bcd + cde = ?$

A. $ab(c + d + e)$
B. $ac(b + e)$
C. $b(a + c + de)$
D. $c(ab + bd + de)$
E. $d(a + b + c + e)$

65. $x^2y^2 + x^2y + xy^2 = ?$

A. $(x + y)^2$
B. $x^2 + y^2$
C. $x^2y^2(x + y)$
D. $xy(xy + x + y)$
E. $xy(x + y + 1)$

66. $p^2 + 2pq + q^2 = ?$

A. $(p + q)(p - q)$
B. $(p + q)(p + q)$
C. $p^2 - q^2$
D. $p^2 + q^2$
E. $(p - q)^2$

67. $144^2 - 121^2 = ?$

A. 23
B. $(144 + 121)(144 - 121)$
C. $(144 + 121)(144 + 121)$
D. $(23)^2$
E. $(144 + 121)^2$

68. $x^2 - y^2 = ?$

A. $(x + y)(x - y)$
B. $(x + y)(x + y)$
C. $(x - y)(x - y)$
D. $x^2 + y^2$
E. $2xy$

69. $x^2 + 2x + 1 = ?$

A. $(x + 1)(x - 1)$
B. $(x + 1)(x + 1)$
C. $(x - 1)(x - 1)$
D. $x^2 - 1$
E. $x^2 + 1$

70. $x^2 - 1 = ?$

A. $(x + 1)(x + 1)$
B. $(x - 1)(x - 1)$
C. $(x + 1)(x - 1)$
D. $(x - 1)^2$
E. $(x + 1)^2$

71. $x^2 + 3x + 2 = ?$

A. $(x + 1)(x - 2)$
B. $(x + 2)(x + 1)$
C. $(x + 2)(x - 1)$
D. $(x - 2)(x - 1)$
E. $(x + 3)(x - 1)$

72. $a^2 - a - 2 = ?$

A. $(a + 2)(a - 1)$
B. $(a - 2)(a + 1)$
C. $(a + 1)(a + 2)$
D. $(a + 2)(a - 2)$
E. $(a + 1)(a - 1)$

73. $p^2 + 4p + 3 = ?$

A. $(p + 3)(p + 1)$
B. $(p + 3)(p - 1)$
C. $(p - 3)(p - 1)$
D. $(p + 3)(p + 4)$
E. $(p + 3)(p - 4)$

74. $c^2 + 6c + 8 = ?$

A. $(c + 2)(c + 4)$
B. $(c + 2)(c - 4)$
C. $(c + 4)(c - 2)$
D. $(c + 3)(c + 5)$
E. $(c + 8)(c - 1)$

75. $x^2 + x - 20 = ?$

A. $(x + 5)(x - 4)$
B. $(x + 4)(x - 5)$
C. $(x + 2)(x - 10)$
D. $(x + 10)(x - 2)$
E. $(x + 20)(x - 1)$

76. $p^2 + 5p + 6 = ?$

A. $(p + 1)(p + 6)$
B. $(p + 6)(p - 1)$
C. $(p + 2)(p + 3)$
D. $(p - 3)(p - 2)$
E. $(p + 5)(p + 1)$

77. $x^2 + 8x + 16 = ?$

A. $(x + 2)(x + 8)$
B. $(x + 2)(x - 8)$
C. $(x - 4)(x - 4)$
D. $(x + 4)(x - 4)$
E. $(x + 4)(x + 4)$

78. $x^2 - 5x - 6 = ?$

A. $(x + 1)(x + 6)$
B. $(x + 6)(x - 1)$
C. $(x + 2)(x + 3)$
D. $(x - 6)(x + 1)$
E. $(x - 2)(x - 3)$

79. $a^2 - 3a + 2 = ?$

A. $(a - 2)(a - 1)$
B. $(a - 2)(a + 1)$
C. $(a + 1)(a - 2)$
D. $(a - 3)(a + 1)$
E. $(a + 3)(a + 1)$

80. $x^2 + x - 12 = ?$

A. $(x + 6)(x + 2)$
B. $(x + 6)(x - 2)$
C. $(x + 4)(x - 3)$
D. $(x - 4)(x - 3)$
E. $(x + 12)(x + 1)$

81. $x^2 - 8x + 16 = ?$

A. $x + 2$
B. $x + 4$
C. $(x + 2)^2$
D. $(x - 4)^2$
E. $(x + 4)^3$

82. What number must be added to $12x + x^2$ to make the resulting trinomial expression a perfect square?

A. 4
B. 16
C. 25
D. 36
E. 49

83. What number must be added to $4x^2 - 12x$ to make the resulting trinomial expression a perfect square?

A. 2
B. 4
C. 9
D. 12
E. 16

84. $x^2 - 8x + 15 = ?$

A. $(x + 5)(x + 3)$
B. $(x - 5)(x + 3)$
C. $(x + 5)(x - 3)$
D. $(x - 5)(x - 3)$
E. $(x - 15)(x - 1)$

85. $2x^2 + 5x - 3 = ?$

A. $(x - 1)(x + 3)$
B. $(2x - 1)(x + 3)$
C. $(2x + 1)(x - 3)$
D. $(3x + 1)(x + 3)$
E. $(3x - 1)(2x + 3)$

86. $21x + 10x^2 - 10 = ?$

A. $(5x - 2)(2x + 5)$
B. $(5x + 2)(2x + 5)$
C. $(5x + 2)(2x - 5)$
D. $(8x + 2)(4x + 5)$
E. $(10x - 4)(2x - 5)$

87. $ax^2 + 3ax = ?$

A. $3ax$
B. $ax(x - 3)$
C. $ax(x + 3)$
D. $ax^2(x - 3)$
E. $ax^2(x + 3)$

88. $2x^2 - 8x + 3 - (x^2 - 3x + 9) = ?$

A. $(x - 6)(x - 1)$
B. $(x - 6)(x + 1)$
C. $(x + 6)(x + 1)$
D. $(2x - 6)(x - 1)$
E. $(2x + 6)(x + 1)$

89. If $15x^2 + ax - 28 = (5x - 4)(3x + 7)$, then $a = ?$

A. 7
B. 14
C. 23
D. 28
E. 33

90. $x^2 - 9 = ?$

A. $x^2 - 3$
B. $(x - 3)(x - 3)$
C. $(x + 3)(x + 3)$
D. $(x + 3)(x - 3)$
E. $x - 3$

91. $x^2 - 9y^4 = ?$

A. $(x + 3y^2)(x - 3y^2)$
B. $(x - 3y^2)(x - 3y^2)$
C. $(x + 3y^2)(x + 3y^2)$
D. $(2x + 3y^2)(2x + 3y^2)$
E. $(2x - 3y^2)(2x - 3y^2)$

92. $x^2 + 6x - 27 = ?$

A. $(x - 9)(x - 9)$
B. $(x - 9)(x - 3)$
C. $(x - 3)(x - 3)$
D. $(x + 9)(x + 3)$
E. $(x + 9)(x - 3)$

93. Simplify: $\frac{8x^{-4}}{2x}$.

A. $\frac{2}{x^5}$
B. $\frac{4}{x^4}$
C. $\frac{3}{x^5}$
D. $\frac{4}{x^5}$
E. $\frac{8}{x^5}$

94. Simplify: $\frac{3^{-1}x^5y^2}{2xy}$.

A. $\frac{x^2y}{6}$
B. $\frac{x^4y}{6}$
C. $\frac{x^6y^2}{8}$
D. $\frac{x^6y^4}{6}$
E. $\frac{x^6y^2}{10}$

95. Simplify: $\frac{6x^{-5}y^2}{3^{-1}x^{-4}y}$.

A. $\frac{12y^4}{x^4}$
B. $\frac{16y^4}{x^5}$
C. $\frac{16y^5}{x^4}$
D. $\frac{18y}{x}$
E. $\frac{18y^5}{x^6}$

96. Simplify: $\frac{9^2x^3y}{3^{-1}x^{-4}y}$.

A. $243x^7$
B. $244x^3$
C. $248x^7$
D. $252x^2$
E. $256x$

97. If $x = -2$, $x^2 = ?$

A. -4
B. 4
C. 6
D. 8
E. 10

98. If $x = -3$ and $y = 5$, then $x^2y = ?$

A. -50
B. -45
C. 45
D. 50
E. 55

99. If $x = -2$ and $y = -3$, then $x^2 - 4xy - x = ?$

A. -24
B. -20
C. -18
D. -16
E. -14

100. Expand and simplify: $(x - y)(x^2 - 2x + 5)$.

A. $x^3 - 2x^2 + 5x - x^2y + 2xy - 5y$
B. $x^3 + 2x^2 + 5x - x^2y + 2xy - 5y$
C. $x^3 - 2x^2 - 5x - x^2y + 2xy - 5y$
D. $x^3 - 2x^2 + 5x + x^2y + 2xy - 5y$
E. $x^3 - 2x^2 + 5x - x^2y - 2xy - 5y$

101. Expand and simplify: $(2x + \sqrt{3})^2$.

A. $3x^2 + 3x\sqrt{3} + 3$
B. $4x^2 - 4x\sqrt{3} + 3$
C. $4x^2 - 4x\sqrt{3} - 3$
D. $-4x^2 + 4x\sqrt{3} + 3$
E. $4x^2 + 4x\sqrt{3} + 3$

102. If $x = -2$ and $y = 3$, then $2x^2 - xy = ?$

A. 10
B. 12
C. 14
D. 16
E. 18

103. Simplify: $\left(\frac{x^2y^3x^5}{2^{-1}}\right)^2$.

A. $4x^{12}y^4$
B. $4x^{12}y^{66}$
C. $4x^{14}y^4$
D. $4x^{12}y^6$
E. $4x^{14}y^6$

104. Does $\sqrt{x^2 + y^2} = x + y$?

A. Yes
B. No
C. Cannot be determined from the given information

105. Does $\sqrt{(x+y)^2} = \sqrt{x^2 + 2xy + y^2}$?
A. Yes
B. No
C. Cannot be determined from the given information

106. Does $\frac{x}{\sqrt{2x-y}} = x\sqrt{2x+y}$?
A. Yes
B. No
C. Cannot be determined from the given information

107. Does $\frac{6}{\sqrt{2a-3c}} = \frac{6\sqrt{2a-3c}}{(2a-3c)}$?
A. Yes
B. No
C. Cannot be determined from the given information

108. Find the sum of $\frac{n}{6} + \frac{2n}{5}$.
A. $\frac{13n}{30}$
B. $17n$
C. $\frac{3n}{30}$
D. $\frac{17n}{30}$
E. $\frac{3n}{11}$

109. Combine into a single fraction: $1 - \frac{x}{y}$.
A. $\frac{1-x}{y}$
B. $\frac{y-x}{y}$
C. $\frac{x-y}{y}$
D. $\frac{1-x}{1-y}$
E. $\frac{y-x}{xy}$

110. Divide $\frac{x-y}{x+y}$ by $\frac{y-x}{y+x}$.
A. 1
B. −1
C. $\frac{(x-y)^2}{(x+y)^2}$
D. $-\frac{(x-y)^2}{(x+y)^2}$
E. 0

111. Simplify: $\frac{1+\frac{1}{x}}{\frac{y}{x}}$.
A. $\frac{x+1}{y}$
B. $\frac{x+1}{x}$
C. $\frac{x+1}{xy}$
D. $\frac{x^2+1}{xy}$
E. $\frac{y+1}{y}$

112. Find an expression equivalent to $\left(\frac{2x^2}{y}\right)^3$.
A. $\frac{8x^5}{3y}$
B. $\frac{6x^6}{y^3}$
C. $\frac{6x^5}{y^3}$
D. $\frac{8x^5}{y^3}$
E. $\frac{8x^6}{y^3}$

113. Simplify: $\frac{\frac{1}{x}+\frac{1}{y}}{3}$.
A. $\frac{3x+3y}{xy}$
B. $\frac{3xy}{x+7}$
C. $\frac{xy}{3}$
D. $\frac{y+x}{3xy}$
E. $\frac{y+x}{3}$

114. Divide and simplify: $\frac{\sqrt{32b^3}}{\sqrt{8b}}$. Assume that $b \geq 0$.
A. $2\sqrt{b}$
B. $\sqrt{2b}$
C. $2b$
D. $\sqrt{2b^2}$
E. $b\sqrt{2b}$

115. Simplify: $\sqrt{\frac{x^2}{9}+\frac{x^2}{16}}$. Assume that $x \geq 0$.
A. $\frac{25x^2}{144}$
B. $\frac{5x}{12}$
C. $\frac{5x^2}{12}$
D. $\frac{x}{7}$
E. $\frac{7x}{12}$

116. Simplify: $\sqrt{36y^2 + 64x^2}$.
A. $6y + 8x$
B. $10xy$
C. $6y^2 + 8x^2$
D. $10x^2y^2$
E. Cannot be simplified

117. Simplify: $\sqrt{\frac{x^2}{64}-\frac{x^2}{100}}$. Assume that $x \geq 0$.
A. $\frac{x}{40}$
B. $-\frac{x}{2}$
C. $\frac{x}{2}$
D. $\frac{3x}{40}$
E. $\frac{3x}{80}$

118. Simplify: $\sqrt{\frac{y^2}{2}-\frac{y^2}{18}}$. Assume that $y \geq 0$.
A. $\frac{2y}{3}$
B. $\frac{y\sqrt{5}}{3}$
C. $\frac{10y}{3}$
D. $\frac{y\sqrt{3}}{6}$
E. Cannot be simplified

119. $\sqrt{a^2+b^2}$ is equal to which of the following?
A. $a + b$
B. $a - b$
C. $\sqrt{a^2} + \sqrt{b^2}$
D. $(a+b)(a-b)$
E. None of these

120. Given every pair (x, y) of negative numbers and resulting value $\frac{x}{|x|} + \frac{xy}{|xy|}$, what is the set of all numbers formed?
A. {0}
B. {−2}
C. {2}
D. {0, −2}
E. {0, 2}

121. When factored as completely as possible with respect to the integers, $16x^4 - 81y^{16} = ?$
A. $(4x^2 + 9y^4)(4x^2 - 9y^4)$
B. $(4x^2 + 9y^8)(4x^2 - 9y^8)$
C. $(4x^2 + 9y^4)(2x + 3y)(2x - 3y)$
D. $(4x^2 + 9y^8)(2x + 3y^4)(2x - 3y^4)$
E. $16x^4 - 81y^{16}$

Algebraic Equations and Inequalities

Pursuing the analogy between English and algebra as a language, the algebraic analogue of a complete sentence in English (with subject and verb) is an equation. An ***algebraic equation*** is a statement that two algebraic expressions are equivalent.

Examples:

English	Algebra
Ed is three years older than Paul...................................	$E = P + 3$
Paul is twice as old as Mary..	$P = 2M$
Ned has \$2 more than Ed..	$N = E + \$2$
Bill has three times as much money as does Ted..........	$B = 3T$

Solving Algebraic Formulas

An ***algebraic formula*** is an equation that typically involves a relationship between literal quantities. Problems that involve formulas often ask you to solve for a particular unknown (variable) using substitution. Algebraic formulas can take many different forms, including function math, scientific equations, geometric formulas, and story-problems. Regardless of the format, the concept is the same: Replace the variables for which values are given and solve for the unknown variable.

Examples:

1. For all real numbers x and y, $x \oplus y = 2x + y^2$. What is the value of $3 \oplus 7$?
   ➤ Substitute 3 for x and 7 for y in the given expression: $x \oplus y = 2x + y^2 \Rightarrow 3 \oplus 7 = 2(3) + (7)^2 = 6 + 49 = 55$.
2. The formula that relates Fahrenheit temperature to Celsius temperature is: $F = 1.8C + 32$, where F is Fahrenheit degrees (°F) and C is Celsius degrees (°C). What is the temperature, in Fahrenheit degrees, if the temperature is 25°C?
   ➤ Substitute 25 for C in the given equation and solve for F: $F = 1.8C + 32 = 1.8(25) + 32 = 45 + 32 = 77$°F.
3. The volume of a sphere is: $V = \frac{4\pi r^3}{3}$, where r is the radius of the sphere. Find the volume of a sphere with a radius of 6.
   ➤ Substitute 6 for r in the given formula and solve for V: $V = \frac{4\pi r^3}{3} = \frac{4\pi(6)^3}{3} = \frac{4\pi(216)}{3} = 4\pi \cdot 72 = 288\pi$.
4. If a person must pick one object from a group of x objects and then one object from a group of y objects, the number of possible combinations is xy. Jan must select 1 candy bar from 7 different candy bars and 1 pack of gum from 3 different packs of gum. What is the maximum number of combinations available to Jan?
   ➤ Substitute 7 for x and 3 for y in the given expression: # of combinations $= xy = (7)(3) = 21$.

Formulas that represent real-life situations often involve variables with units of measure, such as inches or gallons. You must ensure that all variables have similar units on both sides of the equation in order for the equality to remain true. To maintain consistency, it may be necessary to convert units using equivalent expressions (*e.g.*, 12 inches/foot, 1foot/12 inches, 60 minutes/hour, 1 hour/60 minutes). Thus, when dealing with quantities given in units of any type, it helps to explicitly write out the units in the expressions.

Example:

If string costs k cents per foot at the hardware store, how much will w feet and j inches of the string cost?

➤ Cost of string (¢) $= \frac{k \text{ cents}}{1 \text{ ft. of string}} \cdot$ length of string (ft.) $= \frac{k \text{ cents}}{1 \text{ ft.}} \cdot \left[w \text{ ft.} + \left(j \text{ in.} \cdot \frac{1 \text{ ft.}}{12 \text{ in.}}\right)\right] = \frac{k \text{ cents}}{1 \text{ ft.}} \cdot \left[w \text{ ft.} + \left(j \cancel{\text{in.}} \cdot \frac{1 \text{ ft.}}{12 \cancel{\text{in.}}}\right)\right] = \frac{k \text{ cents}}{1 \cancel{\text{ft.}}} \cdot \left(w + \frac{j}{12}\right)(\cancel{\text{ft.}})$. Therefore, the cost of the string, in cents, is: $k\left(w + \frac{j}{12}\right)$.

Basic Principle of Equations

The fundamental rule for working with any equation is: Whatever you do to one side of an equation, you must do exactly the same thing to the other side of the equation. This rule implies that you can add, subtract, multiply, and divide both sides of the equality by any value without changing the statement of equality. The only exception is that you cannot divide by zero. The following example illustrates the validity of this principle using an equation containing only real numbers.

Example:

$5 = 5$

➤ This is obviously a true statement. You can add any value to both sides of the equation, say 10, and the statement will remain true. Add 10: $5 + 10 = 5 + 10 \Rightarrow 15 = 15$. You can also subtract the same value from both sides, *e.g.*, 7: $15 - 7 = 15 - 7 \Rightarrow 8 = 8$. You can multiply both sides by the same value, *e.g.*, -2: $8 \cdot -2 = 8 \cdot -2 \Rightarrow -16 = -16$. Finally, you can divide both sides by the same value (except zero); *e.g.*, -4: $-16 \div -4 = -16 \div -4 \Rightarrow 4 = 4$.

This principle for manipulating equations applies to algebraic equations with variables, as the following example illustrates.

Example:

$5 + x = 5 + x$

➤ Add x: $5 + x + x = 5 + x + x \Rightarrow 5 + 2x = 5 + 2x$. Whatever x is, since it appears on both sides of the equation, both sides of the equation must still be equal. Now, subtract a value, *e.g.*, y: $5 + 2x - y = 5 + 2x - y$. Again, since y appears on both sides of the equation, the statement that the two expressions are equal remains true.

Do NOT multiply both sides of an equation by zero if the equation contains a variable. You may lose special characteristics of the variable. For example, the equation $2x = 8$ is true only if $x = 4$. However, the equation $0(2x) = 0(8)$ is true for any value of x.

Solving Linear Equations

Equations that have only variables of the first power are called equations of the first degree or ***linear equations***. While a linear equation can have any number of different variables, equations with one or two variables are most common on the exam.

The fundamental rule of equations is the key to solving linear equations. To solve for an unknown variable, identically manipulate both sides of the equation to isolate the variable on one side. Be sure to reduce the other side of the equation by combining similar terms.

Examples:

1. If $2x + 3 = x + 1$, then what is the value of x?
   ➤ To solve for x, manipulate the equation to isolate x. Subtract x from both sides: $2x + 3 - x = x + 1 - x \Rightarrow x + 3 = 1$. Next, subtract 3 from both sides: $x + 3 - 3 = 1 - 3 \Rightarrow x = -2$.
2. If $4x + 2 = 2x + 10$, then what is the value of x?
   ➤ Subtract $2x$ from both sides of the equation: $4x + 2 - 2x = 2x + 10 - 2x \Rightarrow 2x + 2 = 10$. Then, subtract 2 from both sides: $2x + 2 - 2 = 10 - 2 \Rightarrow 2x = 8$. Divide both sides by 2: $2x \div 2 = 8 \div 2 \Rightarrow x = 4$.
3. If $3y - 2x = 12$, then what is the value of y?
   ➤ Add $2x$ to both sides of the equation: $3y - 2x + 2x = 12 + 2x \Rightarrow 3y = 12 + 2x$. Divide both sides by 3: $y = \frac{2x}{3} + 4$.

So far, we have been very formal in following the fundamental rule for working with equations. The process is simplified using a shortcut called ***transposition***. Transposing is the process of moving a term or a factor from one side of the equation to the other by changing it into its mirror image. Perform these "inverse operations" until the variable is isolated. Note that this shortcut does not change the fundamental rule or its outcome: it simply bypasses the formal steps.

To transpose a term that is added or subtracted, move it to the other side of the equation and change its sign. Thus, a term with a positive sign on one side is moved to the other side and becomes negative, and vice versa. It is imperative when using transposition that you do not forget to change signs when terms change sides.

Examples:

1. $x + 5 = 10$
   ➤ Rather than going through the formal steps of subtracting 5 from both sides of the equality, simply transpose the 5: move it from the left side to the right side and change its sign from "+" to "–": $x = 10 - 5 \Rightarrow x = 5$.
2. $x - 5 = 10 \Rightarrow x = 10 + 5 \Rightarrow x = 15$
3. $3x = 5 + 2x \Rightarrow 3x - 2x = 5 \Rightarrow x = 5$

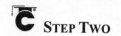

To transpose a multiplicative factor, move the factor to the opposite side of the equation and invert it; that is, replace it with its reciprocal.

Example:

$\frac{2x+5}{3} = 9$

➤ $2x$ and 5 are both divided by 3; in other words, they are both multiplied by $\frac{1}{3}$. Therefore, the $\frac{1}{3}$ must be transposed first. Move it to the opposite side of the equation and invert it: $2x + 5 = 9(3) = 27$. Now the 5 can be transposed: $2x = 27 - 5 = 22$. Finally, solve for x by transposing the 2: $x = 22 \bullet \frac{1}{2} = 11$.

Solving Simultaneous Equations

Ordinarily, if an equation has more than one variable, it is not possible to determine the unique numeric solution for any individual variable. For example, the equation $x + y = 10$ does not have one unique solution set for x and y: x and y could be 1 and 9, 5 and 5, −2 and 12, and so on. However, if there are as many equations as there are variables, the equations can be manipulated as a system to determine the value of each variable. This technique is called ***solving simultaneous equations*** because the equations are taken to be true at the same time, or simultaneously, in order to determine the variable value. On the exam, simultaneous equations are typically limited to two equations and two unknowns.

Example:

Given $x + y = 10$ and $x - y = 6$, solve for x and y.
➤ If we treat both of the equations as making true statements at the same time, then there is only one solution set for x and y, for there is only one pair of numbers that will satisfy both equations, $x = 8$ and $y = 2$.

It is easy to see the answer to the previous example, but solutions will not always be this obvious. How do you find the specific solution for a given set of equations? There are three methods for solving simultaneous equations: substitution, linear combination (elimination), and graphing using a calculator.

1. Substitution

The steps for ***substitution*** are as follows:

1. Pick one of the two given equations and define one variable in terms of the other.
2. Substitute the defined variable into the other equation and solve.
3. Substitute the solution back into either equation and solve for the remaining variable.

Examples:

1. If $2x + y = 13$ and $x - y = 2$, what are the values of x and y?
   ➤ Redefine one variable in terms of the other. Since y is already a single variable in both equations, define y in terms of x: $y = 13 - 2x$. Substitute $13 - 2x$ for y in the second equation and solve for x: $x - (13 - 2x) = 2 \Rightarrow 3x = 15 \Rightarrow x = 5$. Finally, solve for y by substituting 5 for x in either equation: $2x + y = 13 \Rightarrow 2(5) + y = 13 \Rightarrow y = 3$.
2. If $3x + 2y = 16$ and $2x - y = 6$, what are the values of x and y?
   ➤ Since y is a simple term in the second equation, define y in terms of x: $2x - y = 6 \Rightarrow y = 2x - 6$. Substitute this expression for y in the first equation and solve for x: $3x + 2(2x - 6) = 16 \Rightarrow 7x = 28 \Rightarrow x = 4$. Finally, solve for y by substituting 4 for x in either equation: $2x - y = 6 \Rightarrow 2(4) - y = 6 \Rightarrow y = 2$.
3. If $y = 7 + x$ and $3x + 2y = 4$, what are the values of x and y?
   ➤ Substitute $7 + x$ for y in the second equation and solve for x: $3x + 2y = 4 \Rightarrow 3x + 2(7 + x) = 4 \Rightarrow 5x = -10 \Rightarrow x = -2$. Substitute −2 for x in the first equation and solve for y: $y = 7 + x = 7 - 2 = 5$.

2. *Linear Combination (Elimination)*

The second method for solving simultaneous equations is ***linear combination*** or ***elimination***. Eliminate one of the two variables by adding or subtracting the two equations. If necessary, division of one equation by another may eliminate one of two variables. This is the case when solving equations containing variables with exponents.

Examples:

1. If $2x + y = 8$ and $x - y = 1$, what are the values of x and y?
   ➤ In this pair of simultaneous equations, there is a "$+y$" term in one equation and a "$-y$" term in the other. Since $+y$ and $-y$ added together yields zero, eliminate the y term by adding the two equations together. (Actually, you will be adding the left side of the second equation to the left side of the first equation and the right side of the second to the right side of the first, but it is easier to speak of the process as "adding equations.") $[2x + y = 8] + [(x - y = 1)] = [3x = 9] \Rightarrow x = 3$. Find the value of y by substituting 3 for x in either equation: $2x + y = 8 \Rightarrow 2(3) + y = 8 \Rightarrow y = 8 - 6 = 2$.
2. If $4x + 3y = 17$ and $2x + 3y = 13$, what are the values of x and y?
   ➤ In this pair, each equation has a $+3y$ term, which you can eliminate by subtracting the second equation from the first. $[4x + 3y = 17] - [2x + 3y = 13] = [2x = 4] \Rightarrow x = 2$. Solve for y by substituting 2 for x in either equation: $4x + 3y = 17 \Rightarrow 4(2) + 3y = 17 \Rightarrow 8 + 3y = 17 \Rightarrow 3y = 9 \Rightarrow y = 3$.
3. $x^5 = 6y$ and $x^4 = 2y$; x is a real number such that $x \neq 0$ and y is a real number. Solve for x.
   ➤ The system of equations is reduced to one equation and one variable by dividing the first equation by the second equation: $\frac{x^5}{x^4} = \frac{6y}{2y} \Rightarrow x = 3$.

If a system of equations has more variables than equations, then not every variable value can be determined. Instead, you will be asked to solve for one or more variables in terms of another variable.

Examples:

1. If $y = 2a$ and $3x + 8y = 28a$, find x in terms of a.
   ➤ Substitute $2a$ for y and solve for x: $3x + 8y = 28a \Rightarrow 3x + 8(2a) = 28a \Rightarrow 3x = 28a - 16a \Rightarrow x = \frac{12a}{3} = 4a$.
2. In terms of a, solve the following pair of equations for x and y: $3x - 4y = 10a$ and $5x + 2y = 8a$.
   ➤ First, solve for either x or y in terms of a alone. To find x in terms of a, multiply the second equation by 2 and add the result to the first equation. $[2(5x + 2y = 8a)] + [3x - 4y = 10a] = [13x = 26a] \Rightarrow x = 2a$. To find y in terms of a, substitute $2a$ for x in either equation: $5x + 2y = 8a \Rightarrow y = \frac{8a - 5(2a)}{2} \Rightarrow y = \frac{-2a}{2} = -a$.

3. *Graphing with a Calculator*

The ACT, PLAN, and EXPLORE allow calculators: A graphing calculator may be used to solve simultaneous equations quickly. There are several methods to solve a system of simultaneous equations using a calculator: (1) use a calculator's system solver program; (2) in each equation, define y in terms of x and graph these equations for y simultaneously to find the point of intersection, (x, y); (3) use inverse matrices, and (4) write a special program for certain types of problems.

Example:

Given $2x - y = 6$ and $3x + 2y = 16$, solve for x and y.

➤ A calculator graphs equations in y-form. Therefore, solve each equation for y before entering the equations into the graphing calculator. $2x - y = 6 \Rightarrow y = \frac{(6 - 2x)}{-1}$. $3x + 2y = 16 \Rightarrow y = \frac{(16 - 3x)}{2}$. Graph both equations—the point of intersection is (4, 2). Note that if your calculator has a system solver program, then rewriting the equations in y-form and explicitly graphing them is unnecessary.

Solving Quadratic Equations

Equations that involve variables of the second power (*e.g.*, x^2) are called ***quadratic equations***. Unlike a linear equation with a single variable, which has a single solution, a quadratic may have two solutions. By convention, quadratic equations are written so that the right side of the equation is equal to zero. The general form is: $\boldsymbol{ax^2 + bx + c = 0}$.

Example:

Solve for x: $x^2 + x - 2 = 0$.
➤ To solve the quadratic equation, factor the left side of the equation: $x^2 + x - 2 = 0 \Rightarrow (x + 2)(x - 1) = 0$. For the equality to hold true, $x + 2$ or $x - 1$ must equal zero. Therefore, $x = -2$ or 1, so this quadratic equation has two solutions.

This last example illustrates the ***zero product property***: if $xy = 0$, then $x = 0$ or $y = 0$.

Example:

$x^2 - 3x - 4 = 0$
➤ Factor the left side of the equation: $(x + 1)(x - 4) = 0$. Either $x + 1 = 0$, in which case $x = -1$, or $x - 4 = 0$, in which case $x = 4$. Therefore, the solution set for this quadratic equation is $\{-1, 4\}$.

However, not every quadratic equation has two different solutions.

Example:

$x^2 + 2x + 1 = 0$
➤ Factor the left side of the equation: $(x + 1)(x + 1) = 0$. Since the two factors are the same, the equation has one solution: -1.

For quadratic equations not in standard form, you must first group like terms and rearrange the equation into standard form.

Examples:

1. Solve for x: $2x^2 + 12 - 3x = x^2 + 2x + 18$.
➤ Rewrite the equation: $2x^2 + 12 - 3x = x^2 + 2x + 18 \Rightarrow (2x^2 - x^2) + (-3x - 2x) + (12 - 18) = 0 \Rightarrow x^2 - 5x - 6 = 0$. Factor the left side: $(x - 6)(x + 1) = 0$. Either $x - 6 = 0$ and $x = 6$, or $x + 1 = 0$ and $x = -1$. Therefore, $x = 6$ or -1.
2. Solve for x: $x(8 + x) = 2x + 36 + 6x$.
➤ Group like terms: $x(8 + x) = 2x + 36 + 6x \Rightarrow 8x + x^2 = 8x + 36 \Rightarrow x^2 = 36$. Since squaring a negative number yields a positive and squaring a positive number yields a positive, there are two answers for x. Thus, $x = 6$ or -6.

Some higher degree equations can also be solved if they can be written in quadratic form.

Example:

Solve for x: $x^4 - 13x^2 + 36 = 0$.
➤ Factor: $(x^2 - 9)(x^2 - 4) = 0$. Factor again: $(x + 3)(x - 3)(x + 2)(x - 2) = 0$. To find the four possible values of x, set each factor equal to zero and solve for x: $x + 3 = 0 \Rightarrow x = -3$; $x - 3 = 0 \Rightarrow x = 3$; $x + 2 = 0 \Rightarrow x = -2$; and $x - 2 = 0 \Rightarrow x = 2$. Therefore, the solution set is: $\{-3, 3, -2, 2\}$.

Alternatively, you can use the quadratic formula, $x = \frac{-b \pm \sqrt{b^2 - 4ac}}{2a}$, to solve quadratic equations.

Example:

Solve for x: $3 - x = 2x^2$.
➤ $3 - x = 2x^2 \Rightarrow 2x^2 + x - 3 = 0$. $a = 2$, $b = 1$, $c = -3$. $x = \frac{-b \pm \sqrt{b^2 - 4ac}}{2a} = \frac{-1 \pm \sqrt{1^2 - 4(2)(-3)}}{2(2)} = \frac{-1 \pm \sqrt{1 + 24}}{4} = \frac{-1 \pm 5}{4}$. $x = \{1, -\frac{3}{2}\}$.

Algebraic Inequalities

An ***inequality*** is very much like an equation except, as the name implies, it is a statement that two quantities are not equal. Four different symbols are used to make statements of inequality:

- $>$ greater than
- $<$ less than
- $\geq$ greater than or equal to
- $\leq$ less than or equal to

Examples:

$5 > 1$ .... 5 is greater than 1.
$2 > -2$ .... 2 is greater than -2.
$x > 0$............. x is greater than zero.
$x > y$............. x is greater than y.
$8 < 9$ .... 8 is less than 9.
$-4 < -1$ .... -4 is less than -1.
$x < 0$............. x is less than zero.
$y < x$............. y is less than x.
$x \geq 0$............. x is greater than or equal to zero. (x could be zero or any number larger than zero.)
$x \geq y$............. x is greater than or equal to y. (Either x is greater than y, or x and y are equal.)
$x \leq 0$............. x is less than or equal to zero. (x could be zero or any number less than zero.)
$x \leq y$............. x is less than or equal to y. (Either x is less than y, or x and y are equal.)

The fundamental rule for working with inequalities is similar to that for working with equalities: Treat each side of the inequality exactly the same. You can add or subtract the same value to each side of an inequality without changing the inequality, and you can multiply or divide each side of an inequality by any *positive* value without changing the inequality.

Example:

$5 > 2$ (Add 25 to both sides.)
$5 + 25 > 2 + 25 \Rightarrow$
$30 > 27$ (Subtract 6 from both sides.)
$30 - 6 > 27 - 6 \Rightarrow$
$24 > 21$ (Multiply both sides by 2.)
$24(2) > 21(2) \Rightarrow$
$48 > 42$ (Divide both sides by 6.)
$48 \div 6 > 42 \div 6 \Rightarrow$
$8 > 7$

However, if you multiply or divide an inequality by a *negative* number, the direction of the inequality is reversed. Therefore, remember to change the direction of the inequality when multiplying or dividing by a negative number.

Example:

$4 > 3$ (Multiply both sides by -2.)
$4(-2) < 3(-2) \Rightarrow$
$-8 < -6$

These properties hold true for inequalities containing variables, as the following two examples illustrate.

Examples:

1. For what values of x is $3(2-x)+7x>30$?
   ➤ Solve for x: $3(2-x)+7x>30 \Rightarrow 6-3x+7x>30 \Rightarrow 6+4x>30 \Rightarrow 4x>24 \Rightarrow x>6$.
2. For what values of x is $3(2-x)+x>30$?
   ➤ Solve for x: $3(2-x)+x>30 \Rightarrow 6-3x+x>30 \Rightarrow 6-2x>30 \Rightarrow -2x>24 \Rightarrow x<-12$.

Exponents in Equations and Inequalities

1. *Integer and Rational Exponents*

Algebraic equations and inequalities can include terms with integer and rational exponents. The rules of exponents apply when manipulating these terms.

Examples:

1. If $x=2$, then what is the value of $(x^{-2x})^{x^{-x}}$?
   ➤ Substitute $x=2$ into the given expression: $(x^{-2x})^{x^{-x}}=[(2)^{-2(2)}]^{2^{-2}}=[(2)^{-4}]^{1/2^2}=2^{(-4)(1/4)}=2^{-1}=\frac{1}{2}$.
2. Find the value of $2x^0+x^{2/3}+x^{-2/3}$ when $x=27$.
   ➤ Substitute $x=27$: $2x^0+x^{2/3}+x^{-2/3}=2(27)^0+(27)^{2/3}+(27)^{-2/3}=2(1)+(\sqrt[3]{27})^2+\frac{1}{27^{2/3}}=2+9+\frac{1}{9}=11\frac{1}{9}$.

2. *Algebraic Exponentials*

When solving equations that involve algebraic exponential terms, try to find a common base to use throughout the problem.

Example:

Solve for x: $4^{x+2}=8^{3x-6}$
➤ Since $4=2^2$ and $8=2^3$, the common base in this item is 2. Thus: $4^{x+2}=8^{3x-6} \Rightarrow (2^2)^{x+2}=(2^3)^{3x-6} \Rightarrow 2^{2x+4}=2^{9x-18}$.
Now, drop the common base and solve for x: $2x+4=9x-18 \Rightarrow 22=7x \Rightarrow x=\frac{22}{7}$.

3. *Exponential Growth*

Items that involve exponential growth test knowledge of exponential growth sequences, also called geometric sequences. In a geometric sequence, the ***ratio***, r, of any term to its preceding term is constant. If the terms of a geometric sequence are designated by $a_1, a_2, a_3 \ldots a_n$, then $\boldsymbol{a_n = a_1 r^{n-1}}$. Sequences that involve exponential growth have real-life applications, such as determining population growth over a specific period.

Examples:

1. Find the 5th term of the geometric sequence: 4, 12, 36....
   ➤ In this geometric sequence, the ratio between the terms is 3. Therefore, the 5th term is: $a_n=a_1r^{n-1} \Rightarrow a_5=4(3)^{5-1}=4(3)^4=4 \cdot 81=324$.
2. On June 1, 1990, the population of Grouenphast was 50,250. If the population is increasing at an annual rate of 8.4%, what is the approximate population of Grouenphast on June 1, 2010?
   ➤ An annual increase of 8.4% means that each year the population will be 108.4% of the previous year's population. Thus, the ratio between terms, r, is 1.084. The population on June 1, 1990 is the starting term: $a_1=50{,}250$. Since June 1, 2010 is 20 years later, the population at that time is the 21st term in the sequence: $n=21$. Therefore, the population on June 1, 2010 is: $a_n=a_1r^{n-1} \Rightarrow a_{21}=50{,}250(1.084)^{21-1}=50{,}250(1.084)^{20} \approx 252{,}186$.

The previous example involving growth over time suggests an alternate form of the geometric sequence equation called the ***exponential growth equation***: $a_t = a_0 r^{t/T}$. In this equation, a_t is the amount after time t; a_0 is the initial amount ($t = 0$), r is the proportionality constant, t is the total period of growth, and T is the time per cycle of growth. Note that this equation also applies to exponential decay, where the initial amount is larger than the amount after time t.

Example:

The number of rabbits in a certain population doubles every 3 months. Currently, there are 5 rabbits in the population. How many rabbits will there be 3 years from now?

➤ In this case, the total time of growth is 3 years. Since the population doubles every 3 months, the time per cycle of growth is one-fourth of a year. Using the formula for exponential growth: $a_t = a_0 r^{t/T} \Rightarrow a_3 = (5)(2)^{3/0.25} = (5)(2)^{12} = 20{,}450$. We can verify this solution by working out the values, allowing the population to double every 3 months.

Period (months)	0	3	6	9	12	15	18	21	24	27	30	33	36
Population Size	5	10	20	40	80	160	320	640	1,280	2,560	5,120	10,240	20,480

Rational Equations and Inequalities

Algebraic equations and inequalities may include rational (fractional) expressions. When manipulating rational expressions, follow the same rules as discussed with equations, inequalities, and algebraic fractions.

Example:

1. If $\frac{x}{x+6} = \frac{y^3-1}{(y+1)(y^2-y+1)+4}$, then $x = ?$

   ➤ $\frac{x}{x+6} = \frac{y^3-1}{y^3-y^2+y+y^2-y+1+4} = \frac{y^3-1}{y^3+5} = \frac{y^3-1}{y^3-1+6} = \frac{y^3-1}{(y^3-1)+6}$. Therefore, $x = y^3 - 1$.

2. Let x represent a positive whole number. Given the two inequalities, $\frac{1}{x} > \frac{1}{4}$ and $\frac{x-3}{(x^2-3x)} < \frac{1}{7}$, how many more values for x satisfy the second equality than satisfy the first inequality?

   ➤ For the first inequality: $\frac{1}{x} > \frac{1}{4} \Rightarrow x < 4$. Thus, the set of satisfying values for x is $\{1, 2, 3\}$. For the second inequality, $\frac{x-3}{x(x-3)} < \frac{1}{7}$, since it is not possible to divide by zero, $x \neq 3$. Reduce the equation: $\frac{x-3}{x(x-3)} < \frac{1}{7} \Rightarrow \frac{1}{x} < \frac{1}{7} \Rightarrow 7 > x$. Since $x < 7$ and $x \neq 3$, the set of satisfying values for the second inequality is $\{1, 2, 4, 5, 6\}$. Thus, two more whole numbers satisfy the second inequality than the first.

Radical Equations and Inequalities

Expressions in algebraic equations and inequalities may include radicals. The same principles for working with equations and inequalities apply when manipulating radicals.

Example:

$5\sqrt{x-4} - 28 = 12$ for what value of x?

➤ $5\sqrt{x-4} - 28 = 12 \Rightarrow 5\sqrt{x-4} = 40 \Rightarrow \sqrt{x-4} = 8 \Rightarrow x - 4 = 64 \Rightarrow x = 68$.

Absolute Value in Equations and Inequalities

Expressions in algebraic equations and inequalities may include absolute values. The same principles for working with equations and inequalities apply when manipulating absolute values.

Example:

1. What is the sum of all different integers that can be substituted for x such that $|x| + |x - 3| = 3$?
   ➤ The absolute value of any real number, including integers, is always zero or more. Therefore, try only $-3, -2, -1, 0, 1, 2, 3$. The last four work in the equality: $|0| + |0 - 3| = 0 + 3 = 3$; $|1| + |1 - 3| = 1 + 2 = 3$; $|2| + |2 - 3| = 2 + 1 = 3$; $|3| + |3 - 3| = 3 + 0 = 3$. Thus, $0 + 1 + 2 + 3 = 6$.

2. If x represents an integer, $|x - 3| + |x + 2| < 7$ for how many different values of x?
   ➤ Absolute values are always equal to or greater than zero. Thus, if $x = -4$, $|x - 3| = |-4 - 3| = 7$; there is no need to try any integers less than -3. Similarly, if $x = 5$, $|x + 2| = |5 + 2| = 7$, there is no need to try any integers greater than 4. Therefore, test only the integers between -3 and 4. Six integers satisfy the inequality: $-2, -1, 0, 1, 2, 3$. Alternatively, a graphing calculator could be used to solve this problem.

The ACT, PLAN, and EXPLORE allow calculators. A graphing calculator can be used to solve quadratic equations quickly. Depending on the type of calculator, you may need to write a quadratic formula program for your calculator.

EXERCISE 10

Algebraic Equations and Inequalities

DIRECTIONS: Choose the correct answer to each of the following items. Use a calculator when necessary. Answers are on page 922.

1. If $3x = 12$, then $x = ?$
   A. 2 B. 3 C. 4 D. 6 E. 10

2. If $2x + x = 9$, then $x = ?$
   A. 0 B. 1 C. 3 D. 6 E. 9

3. If $7x - 5x = 12 - 8$, then $x = ?$
   A. 0 B. 1 C. 2 D. 3 E. 4

4. If $3x + 2x = 15$, then $x = ?$
   A. 2 B. 3 C. 5 D. 6 E. 9

5. If $a - 8 = 10 - 2a$, then $a = ?$
   A. −2 B. 0 C. 2 D. 4 E. 6

6. If $p - 11 - 2p = 13 - 5p$, then $p = ?$
   A. −4 B. −1 C. 1 D. 2 E. 6

7. If $12x + 3 - 4x - 3 = 8$, then $x = ?$
   A. −5 B. −1 C. 0 D. 1 E. 5

8. If $5x - 2 + 3x - 4 = 2x - 8 + x + 2$, then $x = ?$
   A. −5 B. 0 C. 1 D. 3 E. 6

9. If $a + 2b - 3 + 3a = 2a + b + 3 + b$, then $a = ?$
   A. −1 B. 0 C. 2 D. 3 E. 6

10. If $4y + 10 = 5 + 7y + 5$, then $y = ?$
    A. −2 B. −1 C. 0 D. 4 E. 8

11. If $-4 - x = 12 + x$, then $x = ?$
    A. −8 B. −2 C. 1 D. 2 E. 4

12. If $\frac{x}{2} + x = 3$, then $x = ?$
    A. $\frac{1}{2}$ B. $\frac{2}{3}$ C. 1 D. 2 E. 3

13. If $\frac{2x}{3} + \frac{x}{4} + 4 = \frac{x}{6} + 10$, then $x = ?$
    A. $\frac{11}{12}$ B. $\frac{3}{2}$ C. 5 D. 8 E. 20

14. If $\frac{a}{2} - \frac{a}{4} = 1$, then $a = ?$
    A. $\frac{1}{2}$ B. $\frac{2}{3}$ C. 1 D. 2 E. 4

15. If $\frac{1}{p} + \frac{2}{p} + \frac{3}{p} = 1$, then $p = ?$
    A. $\frac{2}{3}$ B. $\frac{3}{4}$ C. 1 D. 2 E. 6

16. If $\frac{2x-6}{3} = 8$, then $x = ?$
    A. 1 B. 3 C. 6 D. 15 E. 18

17. If $\frac{5-x}{5} = 1$, then $x = ?$
    A. −5 B. −1 C. 0 D. 1 E. 5

18. If $\frac{2-x}{10} = 1$, then $x = ?$
    A. −8 B. −1 C. $-\frac{1}{5}$ D. 1 E. 5

19. If $\frac{5}{x+1} + 2 = 5$, then $x = ?$
    A. $-\frac{2}{7}$ B. $\frac{2}{3}$ C. $\frac{7}{2}$ D. 7 E. 10

20. If $\frac{x}{2} + \frac{x}{3} = \frac{1}{2} + \frac{1}{3}$, then $x = ?$
    A. $\frac{1}{3}$ B. $\frac{2}{3}$ C. 1 D. 2 E. 3

21. If $3x + y = 10$ and $x + y = 6$, then $x = ?$
A. 1
B. 2
C. 3
D. 4
E. 5

22. If $2x + y = 10$ and $x + y = 7$, then $y = ?$
A. 3
B. 4
C. 5
D. 6
E. 9

23. If $x + 3y = 5$ and $2x - y = 3$, then $x = ?$
A. 2
B. 4
C. 5
D. 6
E. 9

24. If $x + y = 2$ and $x - y = 2$, then $y = ?$
A. −2
B. −1
C. 0
D. 1
E. 2

25. If $a + b = 5$ and $2a + 3b = 12$, then $b = ?$
A. 1
B. 2
C. 3
D. 4
E. 6

26. If $5x + 3y = 13$ and $2x = 4$, then $y = ?$
A. 1
B. 2
C. 3
D. 4
E. 5

27. If $k - n = 5$, and $2k + n = 16$, then $k = ?$
A. −3
B. 0
C. 1
D. 5
E. 7

28. If $t = k - 5$ and $k + t = 11$, then $k = ?$
A. 2
B. 3
C. 8
D. 11
E. 14

29. If $a + 5b = 9$ and $a - b = 3$, then $a = ?$
A. 1
B. 4
C. 5
D. 7
E. 11

30. If $8 + x = y$ and $2y + x = 28$, then $x = ?$
A. 2
B. 4
C. 6
D. 12
E. 18

31. If $\frac{x+y}{2} = 4$ and $x - y = 4$, then $x = ?$
A. 1
B. 2
C. 4
D. 6
E. 8

32. If $\frac{x+y}{2} = 7$ and $\frac{x-y}{3} = 2$, then $x = ?$
A. 2
B. 4
C. 8
D. 10
E. 14

33. If $x + y + z = 10$ and $x - y - z = 4$, then $x = ?$
A. 2
B. 3
C. 6
D. 7
E. 12

34. If $x + 2y - z = 4$ and $2x - 2y + z = 8$, then $x = ?$
A. −2
B. 0
C. 4
D. 6
E. 8

35. If $x + y + z = 6$, $x + y - z = 4$, and $x - y = 3$, then $x = ?$
A. −2
B. 0
C. 4
D. 6
E. 8

36. If $x^2 - 5x + 4 = 0$, then $x = ?$
A. −2 or 1
B. 4 or 1
C. −1 or 2
D. −4 or −1
E. 4 or 2

37. If $x^2 - 3x - 4 = 0$, then $x = ?$
A. −4 or 1
B. −2 or 2
C. −1 or 2
D. 4 or −1
E. 6 or −1

38. If $x^2 + 5x + 6 = 0$, then $x = ?$
A. −3 or −2
B. −3 or 2
C. −1 or 6
D. 1 or −6
E. 6 or −2

39. If $x^2 - 3x + 2 = 0$, then $x = ?$
A. −2 or −1
B. −1 or 2
C. 1 or 2
D. 2 or 3
E. 3 or 5

40. If $x^2 + 3x + 2 = 0$, then which of the following values is (are) possible for x?
I. 1
II. −1
III. −2
A. I only
B. II only
C. III only
D. I and II only
E. II and III only

41. If $x^2 + 5x = -4$, then $x = ?$
A. −1 or −4
B. −1 or −2
C. 1 or 2
D. 1 or 4
E. 2 or 6

42. If $x^2 - 8 = 7x$, then $x = ?$
A. −8 and −1
B. −4 and 1
C. −1 and 8
D. 1 and 4
E. 1 and 8

43. If $k^2 - 10 = -3k$, then $k = ?$
A. −10 and −1
B. −10 and 1
C. −5 and 3
D. −3 and 5
E. 2 and −5

44. If $x^2 = 12 - x$, then $x = ?$
A. −4 and −3
B. −4 and 3
C. −3 and 4
D. −2 and 6
E. 1 and 6

45. If $3x^2 = 12x$, then $x = ?$
A. 0 or 3
B. 0 or 4
C. −2 or 2
D. 2 or 4
E. 3 or 12

46. If $4(5 - x) = 2(10 - x^2)$, then $x = ?$
A. 0 or 2
B. 2 or 4
C. −2 or 4
D. 0 or −2
E. 4 or 5

47. For what values of x is $3 + 4x < 28$?

A. $x < 4$ C. $x < 6.25$ E. $x \geq 0$
B. $x > 4$ D. $x > 6.25$

48. For what values of x is $5(3x - 2) \geq 50$?

A. $x \geq 4$ C. $x \geq 10$ E. $x > 8$
B. $x \leq 4$ D. $x \leq 10$

49. For what values of x is $8 - 3x > 35$?

A. $x > 0$ C. $x \geq 0$ E. $x \geq 9$
B. $x > -3$ D. $x < -9$

50. If $x^2 = 6x - 8$, then $x = ?$

A. −8 and −2 C. −2 and 2 E. 2 and 8
B. −4 and −2 D. 2 and 4

51. If $(x - 8)(x + 2) = 0$, then $x = ?$

A. −8 or −2 C. 4 or −2 E. 10 or −5
B. −4 or −2 D. 8 or −2

52. If $9 - 3(6 - x) = 12$, then $x = ?$

A. 4 or −2 C. 4 E. 7
B. 7 or −2 D. 6

53. If $\frac{x+5}{4} = 17$, then $x = ?$

A. 13 or 25 C. 63 E. 124
B. 54 D. 75 or −24

54. If $\frac{x}{2} - \frac{x-2}{3} = 0.4$, then $x = ?$

A. −1 or 1.4 C. 2 or −1.6 E. 2.6
B. −1.6 D. 2.4

55. If $0.02x + 1.44 = x - 16.2$, then $x = ?$

A. 18 C. 14 E. 10
B. 16 D. 12

56. If $3 - 2(x - 5) = 3x + 4$, then $x = ?$

A. $\frac{1}{2}$ or $\frac{1}{4}$ C. $\frac{9}{5}$ E. 5
B. $-\frac{9}{5}$ D. 1 or 3

57. If $x^2 - 9x = 22$, then $x = ?$

A. −11 or 2 C. 2 or 3 E. 11
B. 3 D. 11 or −2

58. If $(x + 8)(x + 1) = 78$, then $x^2 + 9x = ?$

A. 50 C. 60 E. 70
B. 55 D. 65

59. If $2x + 3y = 12$ and $x = -6$, then $y = ?$

A. 2 C. 8 E. 12
B. 4 D. 10

60. At what point does the line $5x + 2y = 20$ intersect the x-axis? (Hint: What must the y-coordinate be?)

A. (−4, 0) C. (0, 0) E. (4, 2)
B. (−2, 0) D. (4, 0)

61. If $3x + 5y = 10$, then $y = ?$

A. $-0.6x - 2$ C. $0.5x - 4$ E. $-0.6x + 2$
B. $-0.4x + 2$ D. $0.6x - 2$

62. If $x = ay + 3$, then $y = ?$

A. $\frac{x-2}{4a}$ C. $\frac{a}{x-3}$ E. $\frac{a}{3x}$
B. $\frac{x-3}{a}$ D. $\frac{x+a}{3}$

63. If $8x + 16 = (x + 2)(x + 5)$, then $x = ?$

A. 3 or −2 C. −2 E. 3
B. −3 D. 2 or 3

64. If $\frac{x+5}{0.2} = 0.3x$, then $x = ?$

A. $-\frac{125}{23}$ C. $-\frac{250}{47}$ E. $\frac{250}{47}$
B. −76 D. $\frac{47}{250}$

65. If $\frac{0.2+x}{3} = \frac{\frac{5}{6}}{4}$, then $x = ?$

A. $-\frac{40}{17}$ C. 0 E. $\frac{40}{17}$
B. $-\frac{17}{40}$ D. $\frac{17}{40}$

66. If x is an integer and $6 < x < 8$, then what is the value of x?

A. 4 C. 7 E. 10
B. 5 D. 9

67. If x is an integer and $5 \leq x \leq 7$, then which of the following values is (are) possible for x?

I. 5
II. 6
III. 7

A. II only D. II and III only
B. I and II only E. I, II, and III
C. I and III only

68. If x and y are integers, $2 < x < 4$, and $8 > y > 6$, then what is the value of xy?

A. 12 C. 21 E. 32
B. 16 D. 24

69. If x and y are integers, $5 > x \geq 2$, and $6 < y \leq 9$, then which of the following is the *minimum* value of xy?

A. 14 C. 20 E. 54
B. 18 D. 45

70. If $1 \leq x \leq 3$, then which of the following values is (are) possible for x?

I. $\frac{5}{2}$
II. $\frac{7}{2}$
III. $\frac{3}{2}$

A. I only
B. II only
C. I and II only
D. I and III only
E. I, II, and III

71. If $3^{8x+4} = 27^{2x+12}$, then $x = ?$

A. $\frac{1}{4}$
B. $\frac{1}{9}$
C. 4
D. 9
E. 16

72. If $(3 + x)x = 2x + x + 16$, then which of the following is (are) the possible value(s) for x?

A. 2
B. 4
C. 2 or −2
D. 4 or −4
E. 8 or −8

73. If $10x^2 = 30$ and $(6 + y)y = 6y + 52$, then $2x^2 + 2y^2 = ?$

A. 110
B. 96
C. 82
D. 72
E. 55

74. If $|x| = 5$, then $x = ?$

A. 5
B. 5 or − 5
C. Any real number less than 5
D. No real number
E. Any real number greater than zero

75. The commutative property states that if a final result involves two procedures or objects, then the final result is the same regardless of which procedure or object is taken first and which is taken second. Which of the following is an example of the commutative property of addition?

A. $xy = yx$
B. $5 + 4 = 4 + 5$
C. $2a + b = 2b + a$
D. $7 - 3 = 3 - 7$
E. $\frac{x}{y} = \frac{y}{x}$

76. The probability that an event will happen can be shown by the fraction $\frac{\textit{winning events}}{\textit{total events}}$ or $\frac{\textit{favorable events}}{\textit{total events}}$. From the 8 digit number 12,344,362, Helen selects a digit at random. What is the probability that she selected 4?

A. $\frac{1}{8}$
B. $\frac{1}{5}$
C. $\frac{1}{4}$
D. $\frac{1}{2}$
E. $\frac{4}{1}$

77. The perimeter of a regular hexagon is given by the formula $P = 6s$, where P is the perimeter and s is the length of one side. If one side of a regular hexagon has a length of 3, what is the perimeter?

A. 12
B. 15
C. 18
D. 21
E. 30

78. The simple interest earned on an investment is given by the formula $I = prt$, where I is the amount of interest, p is the amount invested, r is the yearly percentage rate of interest, and t is the number of years for the investment. What is the simple interest earned on an investment of $1,000 for 2 years at a yearly percentage rate of interest of 6%?

A. $6
B. $12
C. $60
D. $120
E. $600

79. If $x = 3a$ and $y = 5x + 6$, then $y = ?$

A. 21
B. $15a + 6$
C. $6a + 15$
D. $3a + 15$
E. $21a$

80. If $2(x + 3) = 18a + 10$, then $x = ?$

A. $9a + 2$
B. $9a + 5$
C. $16a + 4$
D. $9a + 3.5$
E. 11

81. The formula that relates Fahrenheit temperature to Celsius temperature is $F = 1.8C + 32$, where F is the temperature in Fahrenheit degrees and C is the temperature in Celsius degrees. What is the temperature, in Celsius degrees, if the temperature in Fahrenheit degrees is 41°?

A. 5
B. 7.2
C. 9
D. 10.8
E. 73

82. If x is a real number such that $x \neq 0$, y is a real number, $x^5 = 8y$, and $x^4 = y$, then which of the following is true?

A. $x = 7y$
B. $x = 8y$
C. $x = 8y^2$
D. $x = 7y^2$
E. $x = 8$

83. George must select 1 pencil from 6 different pencils and 1 pen from 5 different pens. How many different combinations can George make?

A. 5
B. 11
C. 30
D. 56
E. 65

84. The commutative property states that if a final result involves two procedures or objects, then the final result is the same regardless of which procedure or object is taken first and which is taken second. Which of the following is an example of the commutative property of multiplication?

A. $xy = yx$
B. $5 + 4 = 4 + 5$
C. $2a + b = 2b + a$
D. $7 - 3 = 3 - 7$
E. $\frac{x}{y} = \frac{y}{x}$

85. A geometric sequence is a sequence of numbers formed by continually multiplying by the same number; *e.g.*, {81, 27, 9, 3, ...} is a geometric sequence formed by continually multiplying by $\frac{1}{3}$. What is the next term in the geometric sequence of {2, 8, 32, 128, ...}?

A. 132 B. 256 C. 384 D. 512 E. 1,024

86. A sequence is formed by substituting consecutive whole numbers in the expression $x^3 + x^2 - 2x + 1$. What is the next term in the sequence of {1, 9, 31, 73, ...}?

A. 115 B. 125 C. 135 D. 137 E. 141

87. A letter is selected at random from the word "DAVID." What is the probability that the letter selected is "D"?

A. $\frac{1}{5}$
B. $\frac{1}{4}$
C. $\frac{1}{3}$
D. $\frac{2}{5}$
E. $\frac{3}{5}$

88. Which of the following values for c returns two distinct real solutions to the equation $x^2 - 8x + c = 0$?

A. -20 B. 17 C. 18 D. 19 E. 20

89. Which of the following values for b returns two distinct real solutions to the equation $x^2 + bx + 8 = 0$?

A. 6 B. 5 C. 4 D. $\sqrt{2}$ E. 1

90. The cost of buying a certain material is k cents per yard. What is the cost, in cents, of x yards and y inches of the material?

A. $kx + y$ B. $36x + y$ C. $x + 36y$ D. $xk + \frac{yk}{36}$ E. $xk + 36yk$

91. The volume of a cone is $\frac{\pi r^2 h}{3}$, where r is the radius of the cone base and h is the cone height. What is the volume, in cubic inches, of a cone of height 12 inches that has a base of radius 3 inches?

A. 144π B. 108π C. 72π D. 54π E. 36π

92. If $x^2 - 14k^2 = 5kx$, what are the 2 solutions for x in terms of k?

A. $2k$ and $7k$ B. $-2k$ and $7k$ C. k and $5k$ D. $-k$ and $5k$ E. k and $-5k$

93. An arithmetic sequence is a sequence of numbers formed by continually adding the same number; *e.g.*, {1, 3, 5, 7, 9, 11, ...} is an arithmetic sequence formed by continually adding 2. What is the ninth term in the arithmetic sequence of {1, 4, 7, 10, 13, ...}?

A. 16 B. 17 C. 19 D. 21 E. 25

94. One of the letters in the alphabet is selected at random. What is the probability that the letter selected is a letter found in the word "MATHEMATICS"?

A. $\frac{1}{26}$
B. $\frac{4}{13}$
C. $\frac{5}{13}$
D. $\frac{11}{26}$
E. $\frac{6}{13}$

95. $\frac{1}{a} + \frac{1}{b} = 7$ and $\frac{1}{a} - \frac{1}{b} = 3$. Find $\frac{1}{a^2} - \frac{1}{b^2}$.

A. 10 B. 7 C. 3 D. 21 E. 4

96. If $\frac{3x}{4} = 1$, then $\frac{2x}{3} = ?$

A. $\frac{1}{3}$ B. $\frac{1}{2}$ C. $\frac{2}{3}$ D. $\frac{8}{9}$ E. 2

97. If $x = \frac{y}{7}$ and $7x = 12$, then $y = ?$

A. 3 B. 5 C. 7 D. 12 E. 72

98. If $x = k + \frac{1}{2} = \frac{k+3}{2}$, then $x = ?$

A. $\frac{1}{3}$ B. $\frac{1}{2}$ C. 1 D. 2 E. $\frac{5}{2}$

99. If $7 - x = 0$, then $10 - x = ?$

A. -3 B. 0 C. 3 D. 7 E. 10

100. If $x = 7 - \sqrt{3}$ and $y = 7 + \sqrt{3}$, which of the following must be rational?

I. xy
II. $x + y$
III. $\frac{x}{y}$

A. I only
B. III only
C. I and III only
D. I and II only
E. I, II, and III

101. Find the value, in simplest form, of the fraction $\frac{2^{x+4}-2(2^x)}{2(2^{x+3})}$.

A. $\frac{1}{2}$
B. $\frac{1}{4}$
C. $\frac{3}{4}$
D. $\frac{5}{8}$
E. $\frac{7}{8}$

102. Let $y = 2^x$ and $w = 8^x$. For what value of x does $w = 2y$?

A. a rational number between 0 and 2
B. a whole number between 2 and 8
C. a irrational number between 2 and 8
D. no such value of x exists
E. more than one such value of x exists

103. Assume that the growth/decay formula is $y = kc^{t/T}$, in which y is the remaining amount after time t, k is the initial amount, c is the constant of proportionality, and T is the time per cycle of c. The half-life of a certain radioisotope is 9 days. Initially, there was 7.68 grams of the radioisotope. After how many days will less than 1 gram of the radioisotope be left?

A. 23
B. 27
C. 31
D. 32
E. 33

104. A population that starts at 16 and doubles every 30 months can be expressed as $16(2^{2x/5})$, where x is the number of elapsed years. What is the approximate population size after 105 months have elapsed?

A. 11
B. 27
C. 56
D. 181
E. 192

105. Let n be a member of the set {5, 6, 7, 8, 9, 10, 11, 12, 13, 14, 15, 16}. For how many different values of n is the following equation true?

$$\frac{1+2+\ldots+n}{2+4+\ldots+2n}=\frac{1}{2}$$

A. 0
B. 1
C. 6
D. 11
E. 12

106. Which of the following statements is always correct?

A. If $x < 0$, then $x^2 > -x$
B. If $x > 0$, then $(x+3)(x+2) > x^2+4x+3$
C. If $x > 0$, then $x^3+8 > (x+2)(x^2-2x+4)$
D. If $x = 8$, then $1+2+3+\ldots+x > x(x+1)$
E. If $x = 6$, then $\frac{2^x}{2^{x-1}} > 4$.

107. A prime number is defined as a whole number that is greater than 1 whose only divisors are 1 and the number itself. Examples of prime numbers are 13, 17, and 29. What is the smallest prime number that divides the sum of $3^3+5^5+7^7+11^{11}$?

A. 2
B. 3
C. 5
D. 7
E. 11

108. Let x represent a positive odd integer. The smallest value of x such that $(3^{1/4})(3^{3/4})(3^{5/4})\ldots(3^{x/4})$ is greater than 2^x is:

A. a multiple of 3
B. a multiple of 5 but not a multiple of 3
C. a multiple of 7 but not a multiple of either 3 or 5
D. 11
E. 13

109. If x represents a real number, how many different values of x satisfy the equation $x^{128} = 16^{32}$?

A. 0
B. 1
C. 2
D. more than 2, but infinite
E. infinite

110. How many of the following five numerical expressions represent whole numbers?

$$8^0, 9^{-2}, \left(\frac{1}{9}\right)^{-2}, \left(\frac{1}{8}\right)^{2/3}, \left(\frac{1}{16}\right)^{-1/4}$$

A. 0
B. 2
C. 3
D. 4
E. 4

111. If $y = 3^x$, $3^{x+2} = ?$

A. y^2
B. 2^y
C. $y+3$
D. $9y$
E. $y+9$

112. How many real values of x exist such that $x = \sqrt{x}+20$?

A. 0
B. 1
C. 2
D. more than 2, but not infinite
E. infinite

113. Let x be an element of {−6, −5, −4, −3, −2, −1, 0, 2, 4, 6, 8, 10, 12} and $x = 3k$, where k is an integer. Find the sum of all different values of x such that $\sqrt{2x+8}=\sqrt{y}$ for some value of y if y is an element of {−2, 0, 2, 4, 6, 8, 10, 12, 14, 16, 18, 20, 22, 24, 26, 28}.

A. 3
B. 6
C. 9
D. 12
E. 15

114. Let k be a positive whole number such that $11 < k < 15$. If $\sqrt{8x}+k = 18$, for how many different values of k will the solution set for x contain an even integer?

A. 0
B. 1
C. 2
D. 3
E. 4

Geometry

If you have ever taken a basic course in geometry, you probably remember having to memorize theorems and do formal proofs. Fortunately, you will not be asked to do any formal proofs on the exam, and the formulas you need to know are few and relatively simple. Most often, test items ask you to find the measure of an angle, the length of a line, or the area of a figure.

Geometric Notation

You should be familiar with basic geometric notation. The line segment with points P and Q as endpoints is represented by $\overline{PQ}$. PQ represents the length of $\overline{PQ}$. A line passing through points P and Q is represented by $\overleftrightarrow{PQ}$. $\overrightarrow{PQ}$ represents the ray beginning at point P and passing through point Q. Finally, the symbol "≅" is used to represent the term "congruent."

Example:

If $\overleftrightarrow{AB}$ does not contain point C, but it does contain point D, what is the maximum number of points in the intersection of $\overleftrightarrow{AB}$ and $\overleftrightarrow{CD}$?

➢ $\overleftrightarrow{AB}$ and $\overleftrightarrow{CD}$ are different lines, so the maximum number of points at which they can intersect is one point, point D.

Line and Angle Properties

For the purposes of this review and the test, the word ***line*** means a straight line:

The line above is designated line l. The portion of line l from point P to point Q is called "line segment $\overline{PQ}$."

When two lines intersect, they form an ***angle***, and their point of intersection is called the ***vertex*** of that angle.

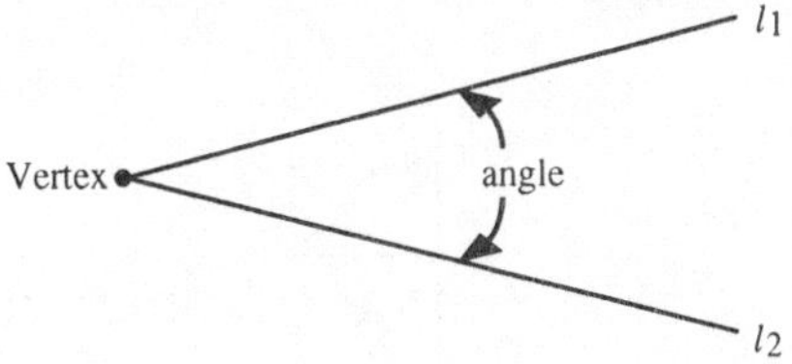

The size of an angle is measured in ***degrees***. Degrees are defined in reference to a circle. By convention, a circle is divided into 360 equal parts, or degrees.

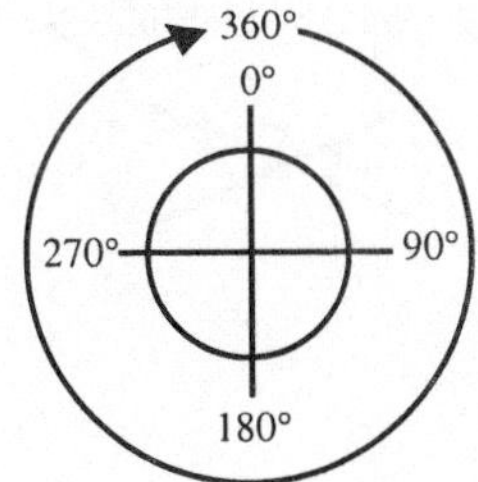

A 90° angle is also called a ***right angle***. A right angle is often indicated in the following way:

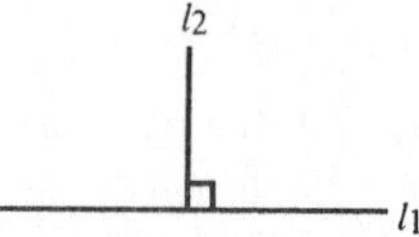

Two right angles form a straight line:

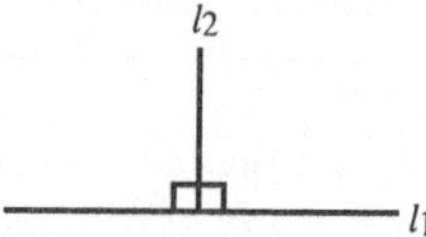

Since two right angles form a straight line, the degree measure of the angle of a straight line is 90° + 90° = 180°:

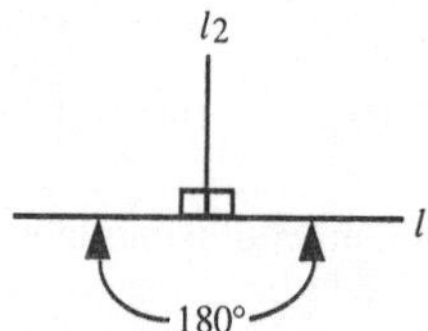

An angle that is less than 90° is called an ***acute angle***:

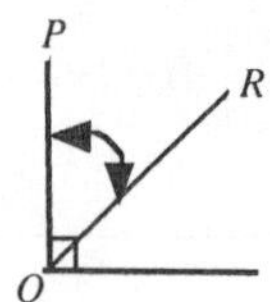

In the figure above, $\angle PQR$ is an acute angle.

An angle that is greater than 90° but less than 180° is called an ***obtuse angle***:

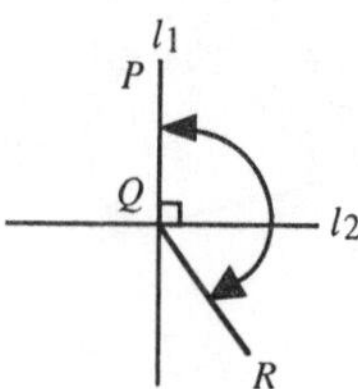

In the figure above, $\angle PQR$ is an obtuse angle.

When two lines intersect, the opposite (or vertical) angles created by their intersection are congruent, or equal:

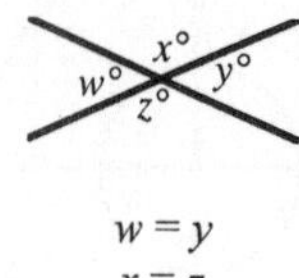

$w = y$
$x = z$

Two lines that do not intersect regardless of how far they are extended are ***parallel*** to each other. In the following figure, the symbol || indicates that l_1 and l_2 are parallel.

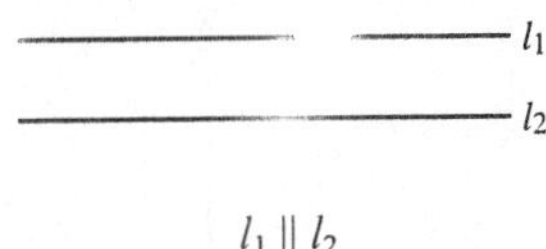

$l_1 \parallel l_2$

When parallel lines are intersected by a third line, a ***transversal***, the following angle relationships are created:

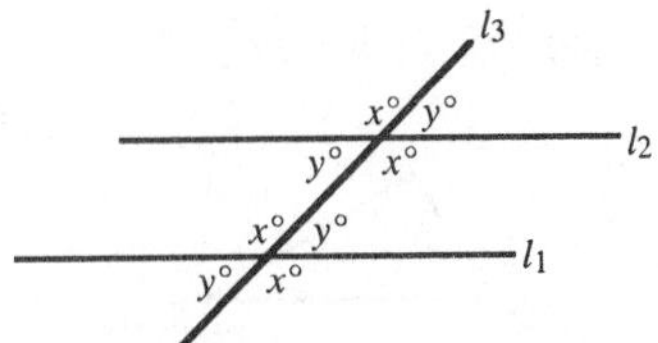

All angles labeled x are equal.
All angles labeled y are equal.
Any x plus any y totals 180.

Two lines that are ***perpendicular*** to the same line are parallel to each other:

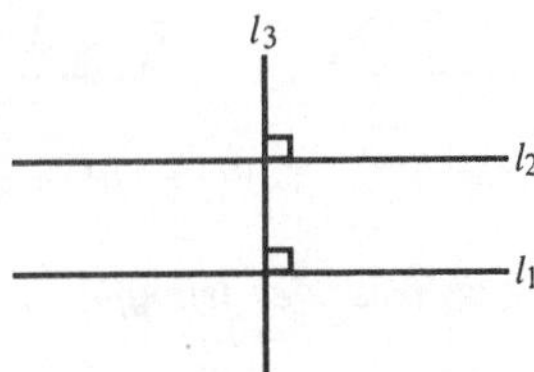

Since l_1 and l_2 are both perpendicular to l_3, we can conclude that l_1 and l_2 are parallel to each other.

Polygon Properties

- A ***polygon*** is a closed figure created by three or more lines.
- A ***triangle*** is any polygon with exactly three sides.
- A ***quadrilateral*** is any polygon with exactly four sides.
- A ***pentagon*** is any polygon with exactly five sides.
- A ***hexagon*** is any polygon with exactly six sides.

A polygon with more than six sides is usually referred to as a polygon with a certain number of sides; for example, a polygon with ten sides is called a ten-sided polygon. A ***regular polygon*** is a polygon with equal sides and equal angles (*e.g.*, a square). The sum of the degree measures of the ***exterior angles*** of a polygon is 360. The sum of the degree measures of the ***interior angles*** of a polygon can be expressed as $180(n-2)$, where n is the number of sides in the polygon.

Triangle Properties and Formulas

1. Properties of Triangles

A ***triangle*** is a three-sided figure. Within a given triangle, the larger an angle is, the longer the opposite side of the angle is; conversely, the longer a side is, the larger the opposite angle is.

Examples:

1. In the figure below, since $\overline{PR} > \overline{QR} > \overline{PQ}$, $\angle Q > \angle P > \angle R$.

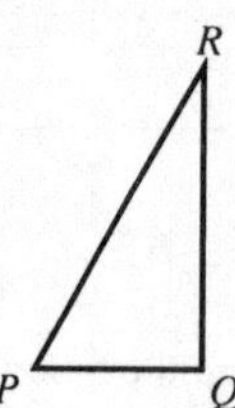

2. In the figure below, since $\angle P > \angle Q > \angle R$, $\overline{QR} > \overline{PR} > \overline{PQ}$.

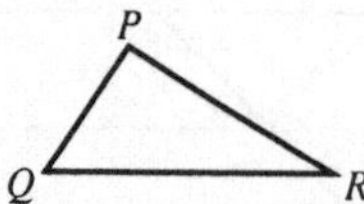

Within a given triangle, if two sides are equal, then the angles opposite the two sides are equal, and vice versa:

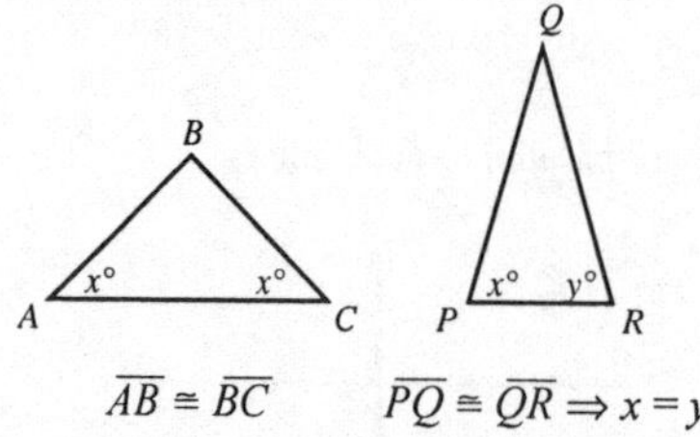

$\overline{AB} \cong \overline{BC}$ $\overline{PQ} \cong \overline{QR} \Rightarrow x = y$

A triangle with exactly two equal sides is called an ***isosceles triangle***. A triangle with exactly three equal sides is called an ***equilateral triangle***.

Example:

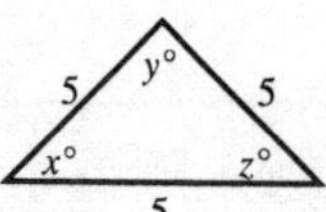

➤ An equilateral triangle has three equal sides and therefore three equal angles: $x = y = z$. Thus, each angle must be 60°.

A triangle with a right angle is called a ***right triangle***. The longest side of the right triangle, which is opposite the 90° angle, is called the ***hypotenuse***.

2. ***Pythagorean Theorem***

The sides of every right triangle fit a special relationship called the ***Pythagorean theorem***: the square of the hypotenuse is equal to the sum of the squares of the other two sides. This is easier to understand when it is summarized in a formula.

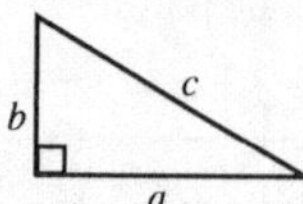

Pythagorean theorem: $c^2 = a^2 + b^2$

3. ***Formulas of Triangles***

The ***perimeter*** of a triangle is the sum of the lengths of the three sides:

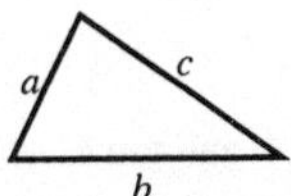

Perimeter $= P = a + b + c$

The ***altitude*** of a triangle is a line drawn from a vertex perpendicular to the opposite side. The formula for finding the ***area*** of a triangle is equal to one-half multiplied by the altitude and the base.

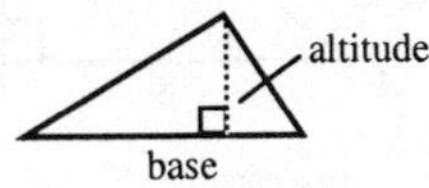

$$\textbf{Area} = \frac{ab}{2}$$

Example:

In the figure below, what is the area of the triangle?

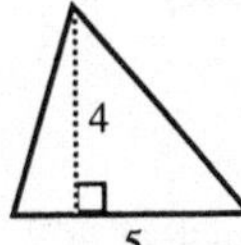

➤ $A_{\text{triangle}} = \frac{ab}{2} = \frac{4 \cdot 5}{2} = 10.$

30°-60°-90° and 45°-45°-90° Triangles

1. *Basic Trigonometric Identities*

Two right triangles deserve special mention: 30°-60°-90° and 45°-45°-90° triangles. These triangles have special properties that are derived from basic trigonometry. While trigonometry may be used as a method for finding the solution, items on these types of triangles can also be answered using an alternative method based on these special properties.

The basic trigonometric identities—***sine***, ***cosine***, and ***tangent***—relate the sides and angles of right triangles. These identities are defined in terms of hypotenuse, side opposite, and side adjacent. The ***hypotenuse*** is the side opposite the right angle. ***Side opposite*** refers to the side opposite a referenced angle. The ***side adjacent*** is the side next to the referenced angle other than the hypotenuse. The three basic trigonometric functions are defined as follows:

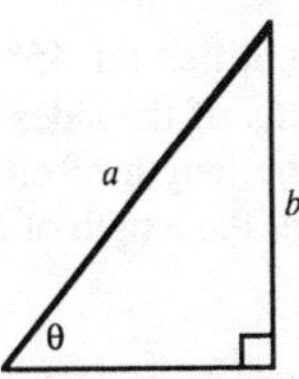

sine: $\sin\theta = \frac{\text{side Opposite } \angle\theta}{\text{Hypotenuse}} = \frac{b}{a}$

cosine: $\cos\theta = \frac{\text{side Adjacent } \angle\theta}{\text{Hypotenuse}} = \frac{c}{a}$

tangent: $\tan\theta = \frac{\text{side Opposite } \angle\theta}{\text{side Adjacent } \angle\theta} = \frac{b}{c}$

Note that the mnemonic "SOH-CAH-TOA" can be used to memorize the three definitions of sine, cosine, and tangent.

Example:

Find the values of sin A, sin C, cos A, cos C, tan A, and tan C in the triangle below.

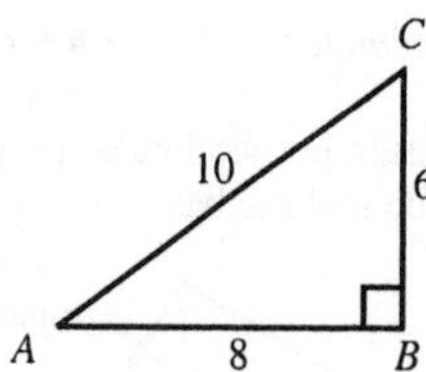

➤ $\sin A = \frac{\text{side opposite } \angle A}{\text{hypotenuse}} = \frac{6}{10} = \frac{3}{5}$, $\sin C = \frac{\text{side opposite } \angle C}{\text{hypotenuse}} = \frac{8}{10} = \frac{4}{5}$, $\cos A = \frac{\text{side adjacent } \angle A}{\text{hypotenuse}} = \frac{8}{10} = \frac{4}{5}$, $\cos C = \frac{\text{side adjacent } \angle C}{\text{hypotenuse}} = \frac{6}{10} = \frac{3}{5}$, $\tan A = \frac{\text{side opposite } \angle A}{\text{side adjacent } \angle A} = \frac{6}{8} = \frac{3}{4}$, $\tan C = \frac{\text{side opposite } \angle C}{\text{side adjacent } \angle C} = \frac{8}{6} = \frac{4}{3}$.

2. ***Trigonometry and the Pythagorean Theorem***

Using the basic trigonometric identities in conjunction with the Pythagorean theorem allows us to solve for the measure of any angle or side in a right triangle. Specifically, if we know the values of any two angles or sides, we can solve for any unknown angle or side. The following example illustrates this strategy.

Example:

In the right triangle below, $\sin x = \frac{3}{4}$. What is the length of $\overline{AC}$?

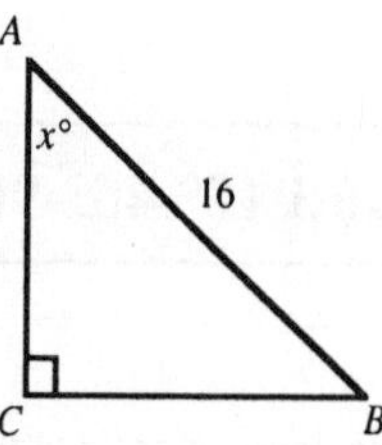

➤ Determine the length of $\overline{BC}$ from the given value for sin x: $\sin x = \frac{3}{4} = \frac{\text{side opposite } \angle x}{\text{hypotenuse}} = \frac{BC}{16} \Rightarrow BC = \frac{3(16)}{4} = 12$. Next, use the Pythagorean theorem to find the length of $\overline{AC}$: $(AB)^2 = (AC)^2 + (BC)^2 \Rightarrow 16^2 = (AC)^2 + 12^2 \Rightarrow (AC)^2 = 16^2 - 12^2 = 256 - 144 = 112 \Rightarrow AC = \sqrt{112} = \sqrt{16(7)} = 4\sqrt{7}$.

3. ***Special Properties of 45°-45°-90° Triangles***

The values of the sine, cosine, and tangent identities for 45°-45°-90° triangles, when applied to the Pythagorean theorem, provide us with a shortcut for relating the lengths of the sides of these special triangles. In a triangle with angles of 45°-45°-90°, the length of the hypotenuse is equal to the length of either side multiplied by the square root of two. Conversely, the length of each of the two sides is equal to one-half the length of the hypotenuse multiplied by the square root of two.

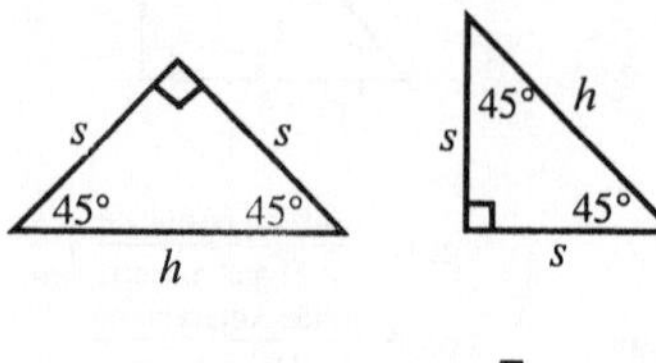

$$h = s\sqrt{2} \Leftrightarrow s = \frac{h\sqrt{2}}{2}$$

Examples:

1. In ΔABC, both $\angle A$ and $\angle C$ are 45°. If the length of $\overline{AB}$ is 3, what is the length of $\overline{AC}$?

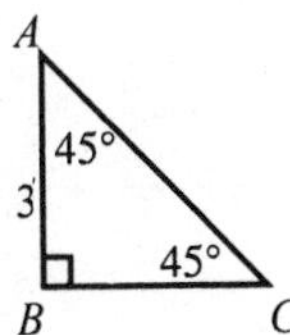

➤ $h = s\sqrt{2} \Rightarrow AC = AB(\sqrt{2}) = 3\sqrt{2}$.

2. In ΔLMN, both $\angle L$ and $\angle N$ are 45°. If the length of $\overline{LN}$ is 4, what is the length of $\overline{MN}$?

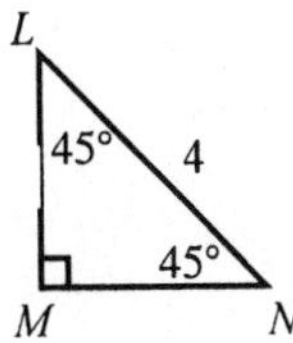

➤ $s = \frac{h\sqrt{2}}{2} \Rightarrow MN = LN\left(\frac{\sqrt{2}}{2}\right) = (4)\left(\frac{\sqrt{2}}{2}\right) = 2\sqrt{2}$.

3. In the figure below, FGHJ is a square. What is the value of sin $\angle$FHJ?

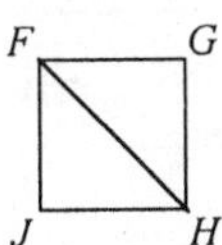

➤ In the square, diagonal $\overline{FH}$ bisects right angle $\angle GHJ$. Thus, $\angle FHJ = 45°$. Use the properties of 45°-45°-90° triangles: let $FJ = x$; then, $JH = x$, and $FH = x\sqrt{2}$. Thus, $\sin \angle FHJ = \frac{FJ}{FH} = \frac{x}{x\sqrt{2}} = \frac{1}{\sqrt{2}}$.

4. *Special Properties of 30°-60°-90° Triangles*

Similarly, the sides of 30°-60°-90° triangles also share special relationships based on the trigonometric functions and the Pythagorean theorem. In triangles with angles of 30°-60°-90°, the length of the side opposite the 30° angle is equal to one-half the length of the hypotenuse, and the length of the side opposite the 60° angle is equal to one-half the length of the hypotenuse multiplied by $\sqrt{3}$.

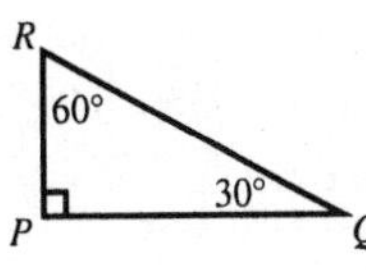

$$PR = \frac{QR}{2},\ PQ = \frac{QR\sqrt{3}}{2}$$

Examples:

1. In ΔABC, $\angle A = 60°$ and $\angle C = 40°$. If the length of $\overline{AC}$ is 6, what are the lengths of $\overline{AB}$ and $\overline{BC}$?

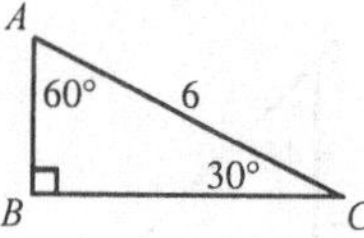

➤ $AB = \frac{AC}{2} = \frac{6}{2} = 3$. $BC = \frac{AC\sqrt{3}}{2} = \frac{6\sqrt{3}}{2} = 3\sqrt{3}$.

2. In ΔFGH, $\angle F = 60°$. If the length of $\overline{FH}$ is 14, what is the length of $\overline{FG}$?

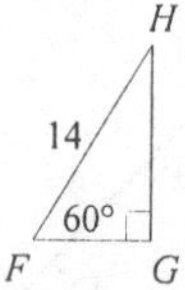

➤ The length of the side opposite the 30° angle, $\overline{FG}$, is equal to one-half the length of the side opposite the 90° angle, $\overline{FH}$: $FG = \frac{FH}{2} = \frac{14}{2} = 7$. Alternatively, use the trigonometry identities: $\sin 30° = \frac{FG}{FH} = \frac{FG}{14}$. Since $\sin 30° = \frac{1}{2}$, $\frac{1}{2} = \frac{FG}{14} \Rightarrow$ $FG = 7$.

Similar Triangles

"Real world" items such as blueprints, scale drawings, microscopes, and photo enlargements involve similar figures. ***Similar triangles*** are frequently encountered on the exams. The symbol for similarity is "~." If two triangles are similar, the corresponding sides have the same ratio, and their matching angles are ***congruent***; that is, they have the same number of degrees. The symbol for congruency is "≅."

Examples:

1. In the figure below, $\Delta ABC \sim \Delta DEF$. Find the length of $\overline{AC}$.

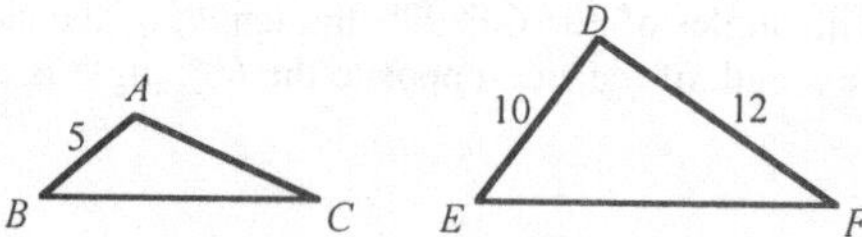

➤ The triangles are similar, so create a proportion relating the similar sides: $\frac{AC}{5} = \frac{12}{10} \Rightarrow 10(AC) = 5(12) = 60 \Rightarrow AC = 6$.

2. Right triangle PQR is similar to right triangle STV. The hypotenuse of ΔPQR is 12 units long and one of the legs is 6 units long. Find the smallest angle of ΔSTV.
➤ Any right triangle in which one leg is equal to one-half the hypotenuse must be a 30°-60°-90° triangle. Since the two triangles are similar, the matching angles are congruent. Therefore, the smallest angle of ΔSTV is 30°.

Quadrilateral Properties and Formulas

A ***quadrilateral*** is a closed, four-sided figure in two dimensions. Common quadrilaterals are the parallelogram, rectangle, and square. The sum of the four angles of a quadrilateral is 360°. A ***parallelogram*** is a quadrilateral in which both pairs of opposite sides are parallel. Opposite sides of a parallelogram are equal, or congruent. Similarly, opposite angles of a parallelogram are also equal, or congruent. Again, the symbol for congruency is "≅."

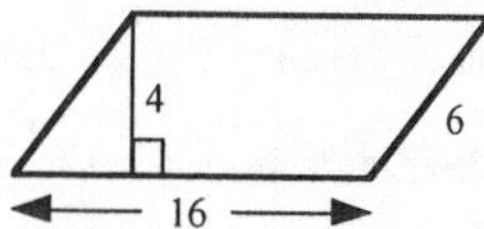

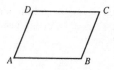

$\overline{DC} \cong \overline{AB}$; $\overline{DA} \cong \overline{CB}$
$\angle D \cong \angle B$; $\angle A \cong \angle C$

The area of a parallelogram is found by multiplying the base times its height. The height must be measured at a right angle.

Example:

In the figure below, find the area of the parallelogram.

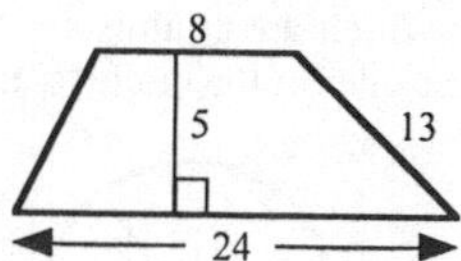

➢ The base of the parallelogram is 16 and the height is 4 (not 6). Remember, the height must be measured at a right angle to the base. Therefore, the area = 16 • 4 = 64.

A ***trapezoid*** is a quadrilateral with only two parallel sides. The area of a trapezoid is equal to one-half of the height times the sum of the two bases, which are the two parallel sides. Alternatively, a trapezoid can be broken down into triangles and rectangles, and the sum of these areas equals the trapezoid's area. The following example illustrates both methods.

Example:

In the figure below, find the area of the trapezoid.

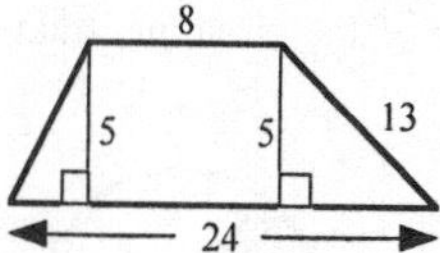

➢ The area of a trapezoid $= \frac{(b_1 + b_2)h}{2} = \frac{(8 + 24)(5)}{2} = 80$. However, if you do not remember the formula, simply break down the trapezoid into two triangles and a rectangle:

8
5 5 13
24

Use the Pythagorean theorem to find the base of the right-hand triangle: $x^2 + 5^2 = 13^2 \Rightarrow x = \sqrt{169 - 25} = \sqrt{144} = 12$. This implies that the base of the left-hand triangle is: 24 − 12 − 8 = 4. Thus, the left-hand triangle's area is: $\frac{4 \cdot 5}{2} = 10$; the right-hand triangle's area is: $\frac{12 \cdot 5}{2} = 30$; and the rectangle's area = 8 • 5 = 40. The trapezoid area is: 10 + 30 + 40 = 80.

FORMULAS FOR PARALLELOGRAMS AND TRAPEZOIDS

Parallelogram Area $= b \cdot h$

Trapezoid Area $= \frac{(b_1 + b_2)h}{2}$

A ***rectangle*** is any four-sided figure that has four right angles. Since the opposite sides of a rectangle are congruent, it is customary to speak of the two dimensions of a rectangle: width and length. A ***square*** is a rectangle with four congruent sides.

To find the ***perimeter*** of either a rectangle or a square, simply add the lengths of the four sides. To find the ***area*** of a rectangle, multiply the width times the length. In a square, the sides are all congruent, so there is no difference between length and width. To find the area of a square, just square the length of one side.

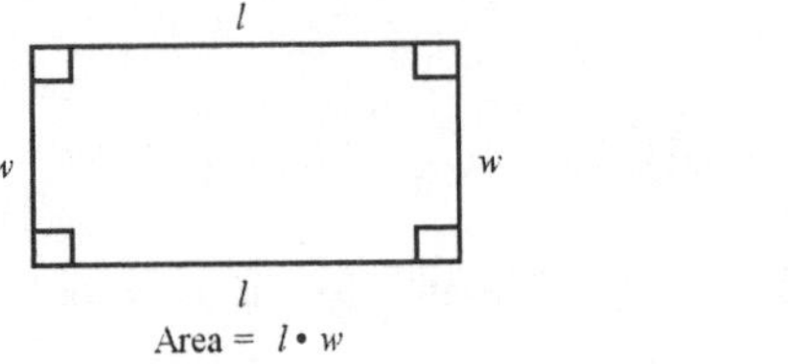

Area = $l \cdot w$

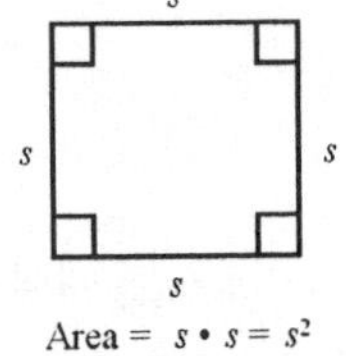

Area = $s \cdot s = s^2$

FORMULAS FOR RECTANGLES AND SQUARES

Rectangle Perimeter = 2(width) + 2(length)
= $2w + 2l = 2(w + l)$
Rectangle Area = $w \cdot l$

Square Perimeter = 4(side) = $4s$
Square Area = $s \cdot s = s^2$

Circle Properties and Formulas

1. ***Properties of Circles***

A ***circle*** is a closed plane curve, all points of which are equidistant from the center. A complete circle contains 360°, and a semicircle contains 180°. The distance from the center of the circle to any point on the circle is called the ***radius***:

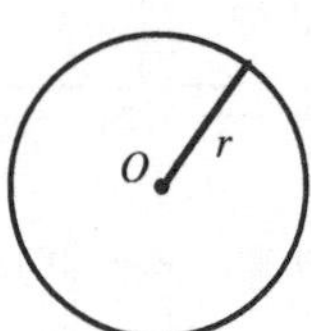

A line segment that passes through the center of the circle and that has endpoints on the circle is called the ***diameter***. The diameter of a circle is twice the radius.

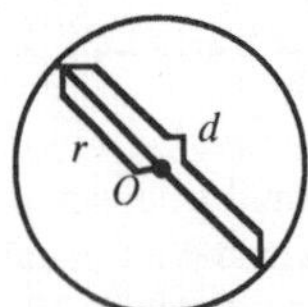

A ***chord*** is a line segment that connects any two points on a circle. A ***secant*** is a chord that [illegible], in either one or both directions. A ***tangent*** is a line that touches a circle at one and only one point. A line that is tangent to a circle is perpendicular to a radius drawn to the point of tangency. The ***circumference***, or perimeter, is the curved line that bounds the circle. An ***arc*** of a circle is any part of the circumference.

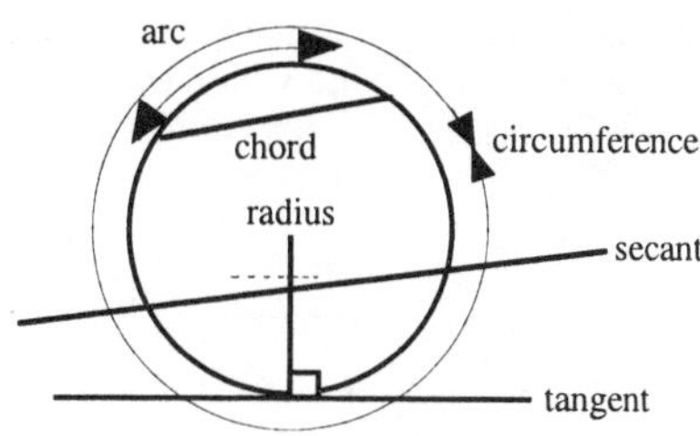

Example:

Two different circles lie in a flat plane. The circles may or may not intersect, but neither circle lies entirely within the other. What is the difference between the minimum and maximum number of lines that could be common tangents to both circles?

➤ Three cases are possible for the orientation of the two circles:

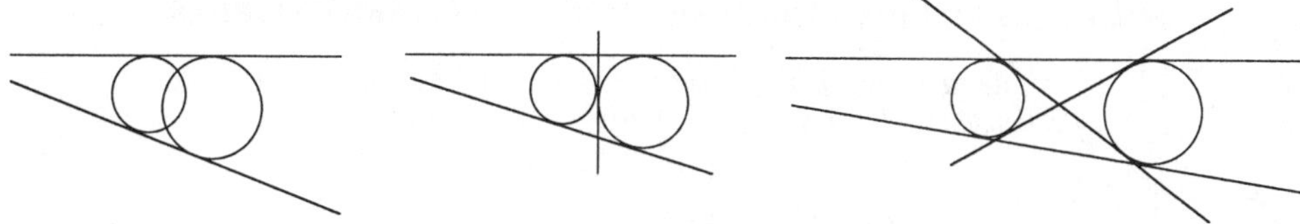

The difference between the minimum and maximum number of tangents that could be common to both circles is $4 - 2 = 2$.

A ***central angle***, such as $\angle AOB$ in the next figure, is an angle with a vertex at the center of the circle and with sides that are radii. A central angle is equal to, or has the same number of degrees as, its intercepted arc. An ***inscribed angle***, such as $\angle MNP$, is an angle with a vertex on the circle and with sides that are chords. An inscribed angle has half the number of degrees of its intercepted arc. $\angle MNP$ intercepts arc $\overline{MP}$ and has half the degrees of arc $\overline{MP}$.

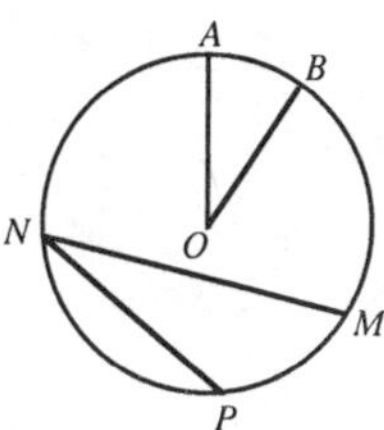

2. ***Formulas for Circles***

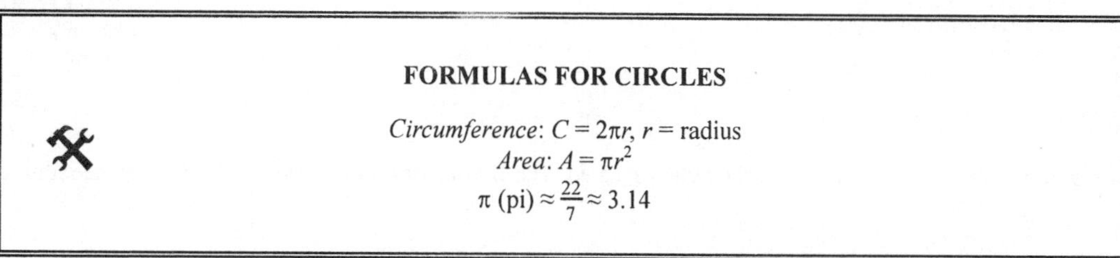

FORMULAS FOR CIRCLES

Circumference: $C = 2\pi r$, r = radius

Area: $A = \pi r^2$

π (pi) $\approx \frac{22}{7} \approx 3.14$

Surface Area and Volume of Solids

In a three-dimensional figure, the total space contained within the figure is called the ***volume***; it is expressed in ***cubic denominations*** (*e.g.*, cm.^{3}). The total outside surface is called the ***surface area***; it is expressed in ***square denominations*** (*e.g.*, cm.^{2}). In computing volume and surface area, express all dimensions in the same denomination.

A ***rectangular solid*** is a figure of three dimensions having six rectangular faces that meet each other at right angles. The three dimensions are length, width, and height. A ***cube*** is a rectangular solid whose edges are equal. A ***cylinder*** is a solid composed of two circular, parallel planes joined at the edges by a curved surface. The centers of the circular planes both lie in a line perpendicular to either plane.

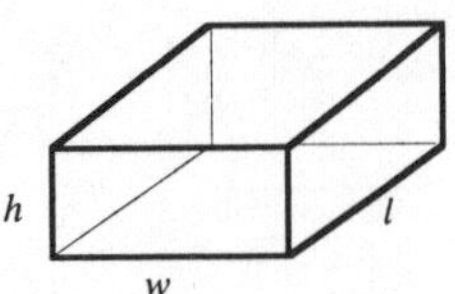

Volume = $w \cdot l \cdot h$

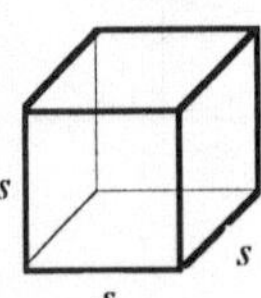

Cube Volume = s^3

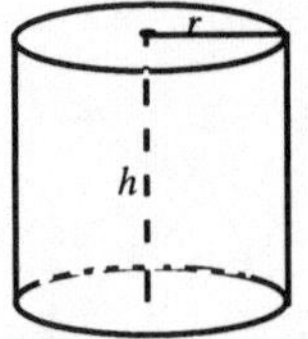

Cylinder Volume = $h\pi r^2$

FORMULAS FOR RECTANGULAR SOLIDS, CUBES, AND CYLINDERS

Rectangular Solid Volume = width • length • height = $w \cdot l \cdot h$

Rectangular Solid Surface Area = $2(w \cdot l) + 2(l \cdot h) + 2(h \cdot w)$

Cube Volume = $\text{side}^3 = s^3$

Cube Surface Area = $6s^2$

Cylinder Volume = height • end area = $h(\pi r^2)$

Cylinder Surface Area = $(2\pi r \cdot h) + 2(\pi r^2)$

Examples:

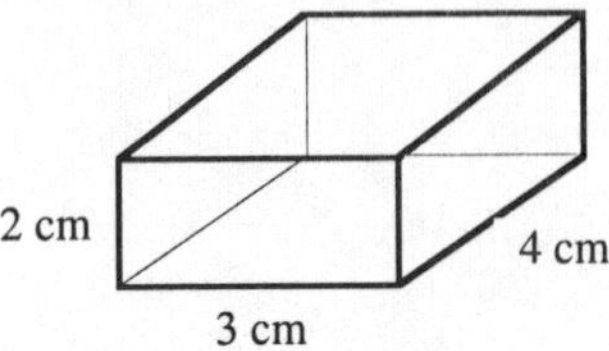

Volume = 3 cm • 4 cm • 2 cm = 24 cm^3
Surface Area = 2(3 cm • 4 cm)
+ 2(4 cm • 2 cm)
+ 2(2cm • 3 cm)
= 24 cm^2 + 16 cm^2 + 12 cm^2
= 52 cm^2

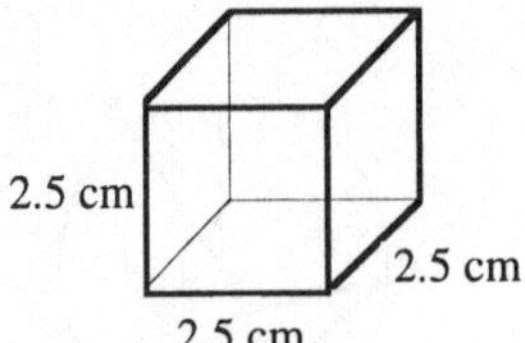

Volume = $(2.5 \text{ cm})^3 = 15.625 \text{ cm}^3$
Surface Area = $6(2.5 \text{ cm}^2) = 37.5 \text{ cm}^2$

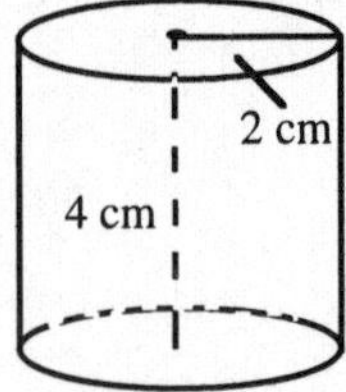

Volume = $4 \text{ cm} \cdot \pi(2 \text{ cm})^2 \approx 50.27 \text{ cm}^3$
Surface Area = $[2\pi(2 \text{ cm}) \cdot 4 \text{ cm}]$
$+ 2\pi(2 \text{ cm})^2$
$= \pi(16 \text{ cm}^2) + \pi(8 \text{ cm}^2)$
$= \pi(24 \text{ cm}^2)$
$\approx 75.4 \text{ cm}^2$

The ***surface area of a sphere*** is 4π multiplied by the radius squared. The ***volume of a sphere*** is $\frac{4\pi}{3}$ multiplied by the radius cubed.

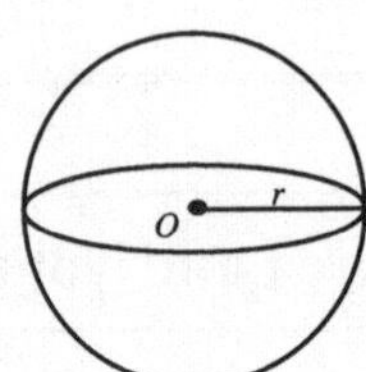

FORMULAS FOR SPHERES

Sphere Surface Area $= 4\pi r^2$

Sphere Volume $= \frac{4\pi r^3}{3}$

Geometric Probability

Some items on the exam may involve geometric probability. For example, if a point is to be chosen at random from the interior of a region, part of which is shaded, you might be asked to find the probability that the point chosen will be from the shaded portion of the region. Such an item might be presented in a specific context, such as throwing darts at a target.

Examples:

1. The figure below shows a circle inscribed in a square. The area of the square is 324. If a point is selected at random in the interior of the square, what is the approximate probability that the point also lies in the interior of the circle?

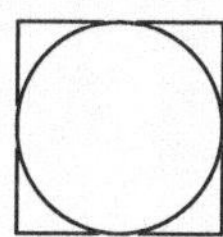

➢ Since the area of the square is 324, $A_{\text{square}} = s^2 \Rightarrow s = 18$. The side of the square is equal to the diameter of the circle, so the radius of the circle is $18 \div 2 = 9$. The area of the circle is: $A_{\text{circle}} = \pi r^2 = \pi(9)^2 = 81\pi$. Therefore, the probability that a point chosen at random in the interior of the square will also be in the interior of the circle is: $\frac{A_{\text{circle}}}{A_{\text{square}}} = \frac{81\pi}{324} = \frac{\pi}{4} \approx 0.785$.

2. The figure below shows a rectangle that is bounded by the two axes and two lines whose respective equations are $y = 8$ and $x = 6$. The shaded trapezoidal region is bounded on three sides by portions of three sides of the rectangle. The fourth unbounded side of the shaded trapezoidal region is a line segment that is a portion of the line whose equation is $2y = x + 4$. If a point is selected at random in the interior of the rectangle, what is the probability that the point also lies in the shaded region?

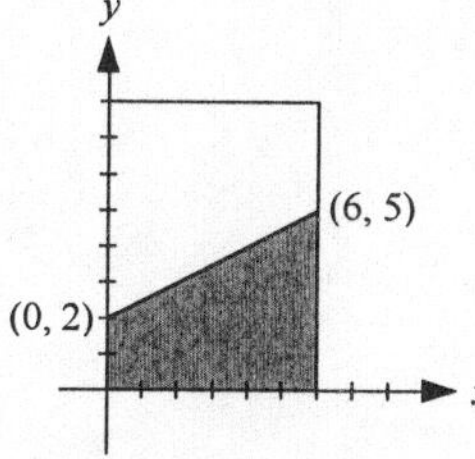

➢ For the line $2y = x + 4$, substitute values for x and solve for y. If $x = 0$, $2y = 0 + 4 \Rightarrow y = 2$. If $x = 6$, $2y = 6 + 4 \Rightarrow y = 5$. The parallel sides of the trapezoid have lengths of 2 and 5; the altitude of the trapezoid is 6. Therefore, the probability that the point will be in both the interior of the rectangle and the interior of the shaded region is:

$$\frac{A_{\text{shaded}}}{A_{\text{rectangle}}} = \frac{\frac{6(2+5)}{2}}{6 \cdot 8} = \frac{3 \cdot 7}{48} = \frac{21}{48} = \frac{7}{16}.$$

NOTE: The ACT, PLAN, and EXPLORE allow calculators. Therefore, it is important that you learn how to use a calculator and bring the same calculator with you to the exam. Use the "π" button to approximate and save valuable test time.

EXERCISE 11

Geometry

DIRECTIONS: Choose the correct answer to each of the following items. Use a calculator when necessary. Answers are on page 922.

1. In the figure below, $x = ?$

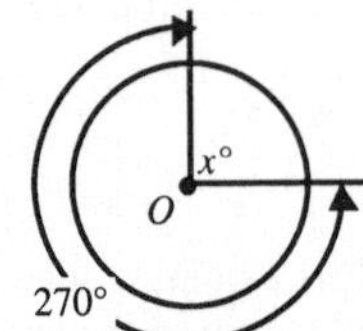

O is the center of the circle.

A. 30 C. 90 E. 270
B. 60 D. 120

2. In the figure below, $x = ?$

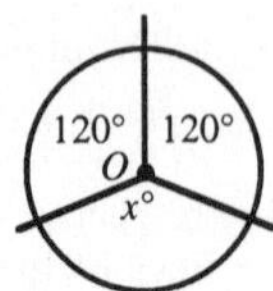

O is the cent e circle.

A. 45 E. 150
B. 60 . 120

3. In the figure below, $x = ?$

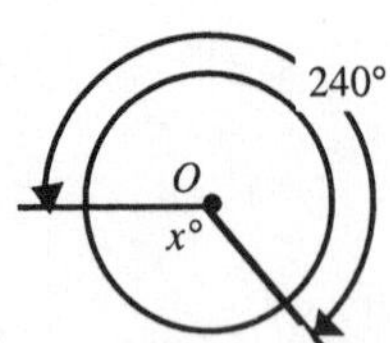

O is the center of the circle.

A. 60 C. 120 E. 180
B. 90 D. 150

4. In the figure below, $x = ?$

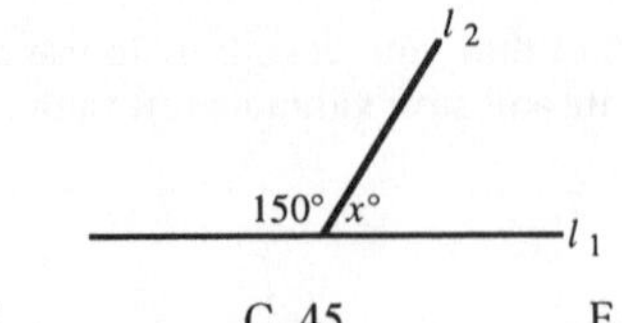

A. 15 C. 45 E. 120
B. 30 D. 90

5. In the figure below, $x = ?$

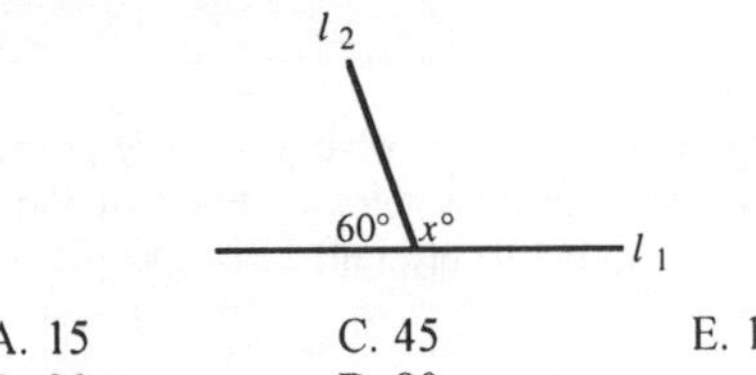

A. 15 C. 45 E. 120
B. 30 D. 90

6. In the figure below, $x = ?$

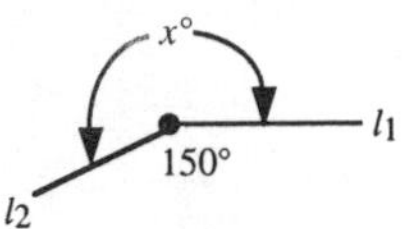

A. 210 C. 150 E. 120
B. 180 D. 135

7. In the figure below, $x = ?$

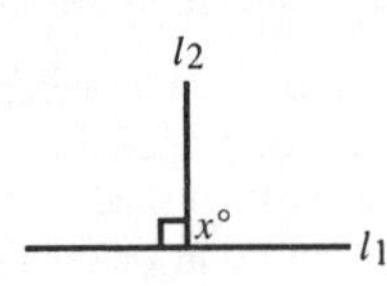

A. 15 C. 45 E. 90
B. 30 D. 60

8. In the figure below, $x = ?$

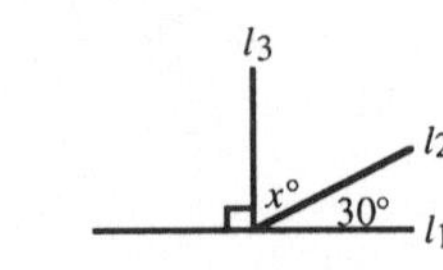

A. 15 C. 45 E. 90
B. 30 D. 60

9. In the figure below, $x = ?$

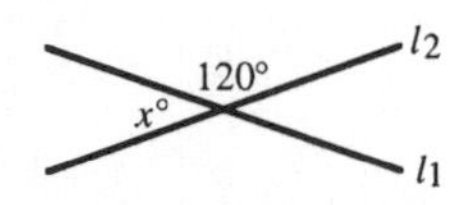

A. 45 C. 75 E. 120
B. 60 D. 90

10. In the figure below, $x = ?$

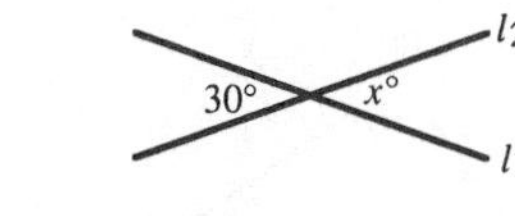

A. 30
B. 45
C. 55
D. 65
E. 80

11. Which of the following is (are) true of the figure below?

I. $\overline{AB} \cong \overline{BC}$
II. $\overline{BC} \cong \overline{AC}$
III. $\overline{AC} \cong \overline{AB}$

A. I only
B. II only
C. I and II only
D. I and III only
E. I, II, and III

Items #12-16 are based on the following figure.

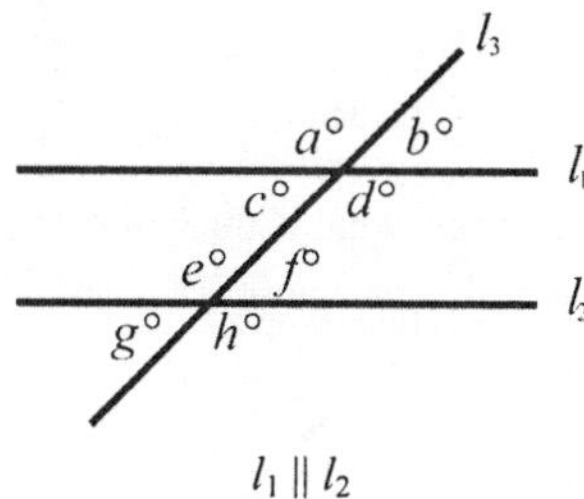

12. Which of the following is (are) necessarily true?
I. $a = b$
II. $b = c$
III. $g = h$

A. I only
B. II only
C. I and II only
D. II and III only
E. I, II, and III

13. Which of the following is (are) necessarily true?
I. $b = c$
II. $d = c$
III. $g = e$

A. I only
B. III only
C. I and III only
D. II and III only
E. I, II, and III

14. Which of the following is (are) necessarily true?
I. $c + d = 180$
II. $c + a = 180$
III. $b + g = 180$

A. I only
B. III only
C. I and II only
D. II and III only
E. I, II, and III

15. If $e = 120$, then $g = ?$

A. 60
B. 90
C. 120
D. 150
E. 180

16. If $h = 60$, then $d = ?$

A. 60
B. 90
C. 120
D. 150
E. 180

17. Which of the following is (are) true of the figure below?

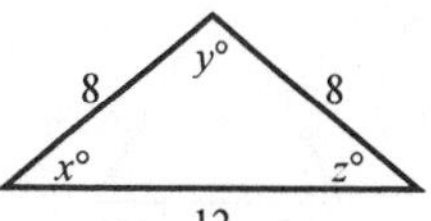

I. $x = y$
II. $y = z$
III. $z = x$

A. I only
B. II only
C. III only
D. I and II only
E. I, II, and III

18. Which of the following is (are) true of the figure below?

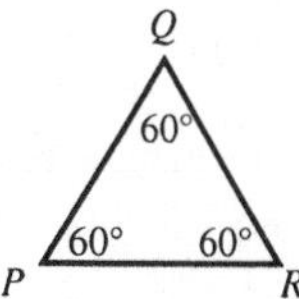

I. $\overline{PQ} \cong \overline{QR}$
II. $\overline{QR} \cong \overline{PR}$
III. $\overline{PR} \cong \overline{PQ}$

A. I only
B. III only
C. I and II only
D. II and III only
E. I, II, and III

19. Which of the following is (are) true of the figure below?

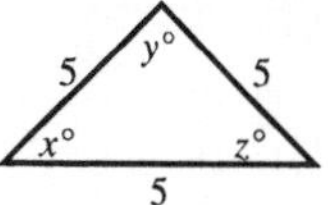

I. $x = y$
II. $y = z$
III. $z = x$

A. I only
B. I and II only
C. I and III only
D. II and III only
E. I, II, and III

20. What is the perimeter of the triangle below?

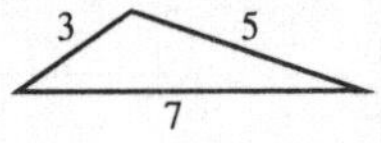

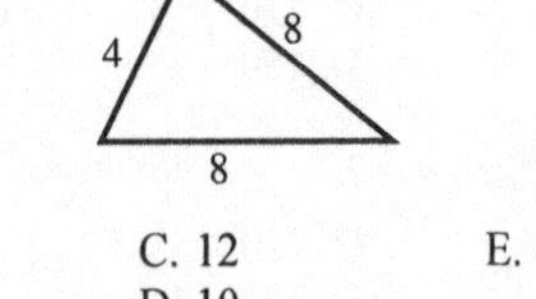

A. 3
B. 5
C. 15
D. 20
E. 30

21. What is the perimeter of the triangle below?

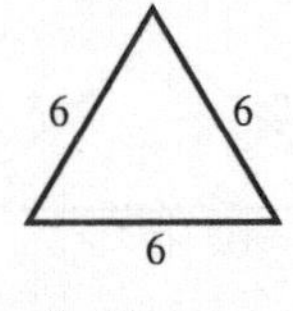

A. 20
B. 18
C. 12
D. 10
E. 8

22. What is the perimeter of the triangle below?

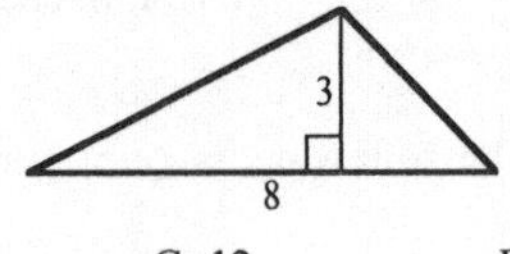

A. 6
B. 12
C. 18
D. 21
E. 24

23. What is the area of the triangle below?

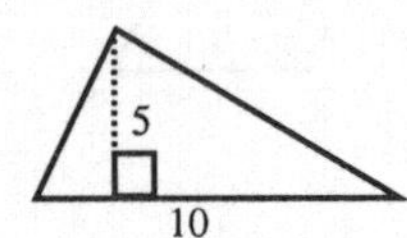

A. 3
B. 6
C. 12
D. 18
E. 24

24. What is the area of the triangle below?

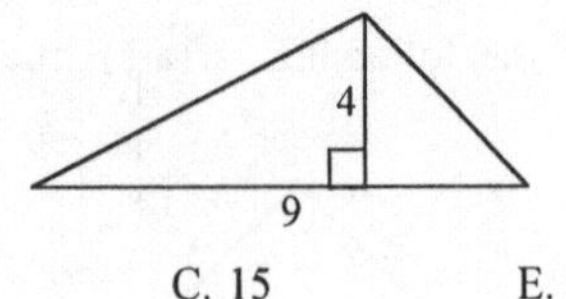

A. 5
B. 10
C. 12
D. 15
E. 25

25. What is the area of the triangle below?

A. 6
B. 12
C. 15
D. 18
E. 24

26. In the figure below, what is the length of $\overline{RS}$?

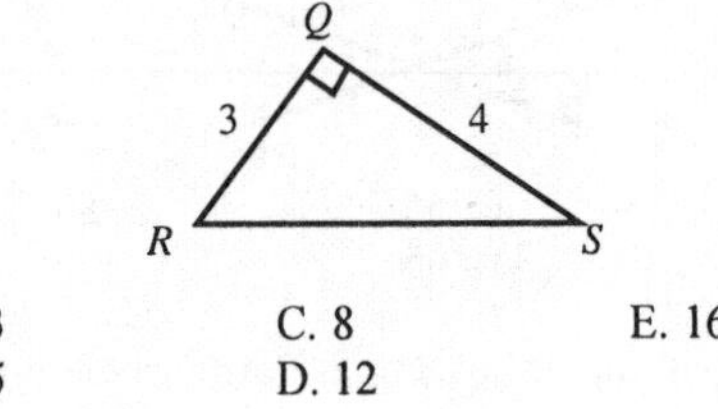

A. 3
B. 5
C. 8
D. 12
E. 16

27. In the figure below, what is the length of $\overline{AB}$?

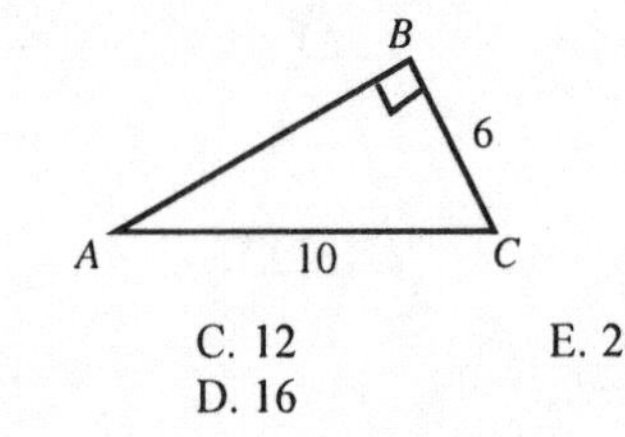

A. 4
B. 8
C. 12
D. 16
E. 24

28. In the figure below, what is the length of $\overline{PR}$?

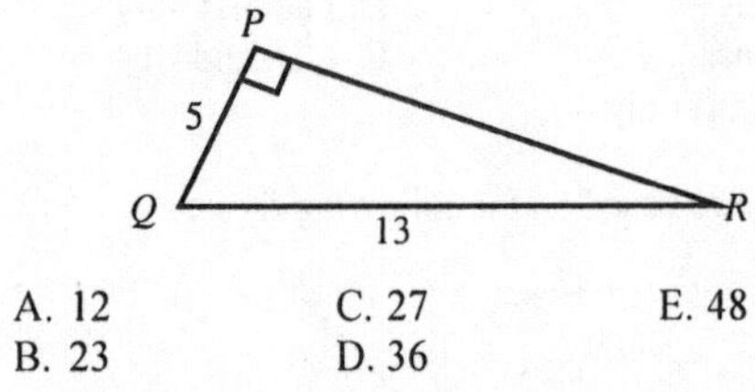

A. 12
B. 23
C. 27
D. 36
E. 48

29. In the figure below, what is the length of $\overline{AC}$?

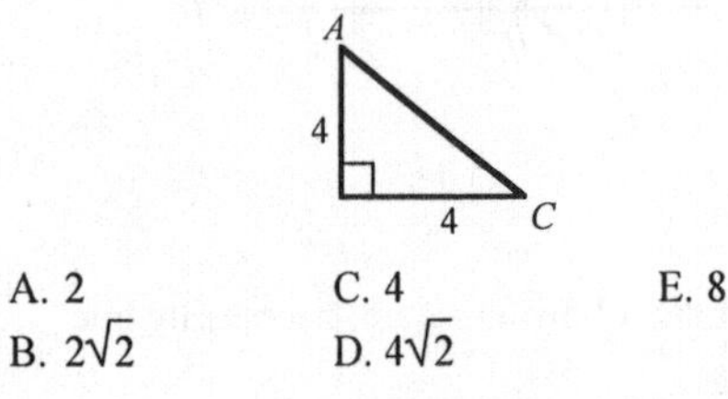

A. 2
B. $2\sqrt{2}$
C. 4
D. $4\sqrt{2}$
E. 8

30. In the figure below, what is the length of $\overline{JL}$?

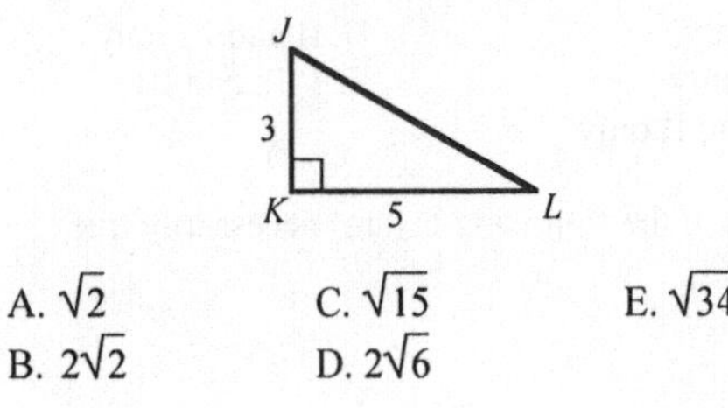

A. $\sqrt{2}$
B. $2\sqrt{2}$
C. $\sqrt{15}$
D. $2\sqrt{6}$
E. $\sqrt{34}$

31. What is the area of the parallelogram below?

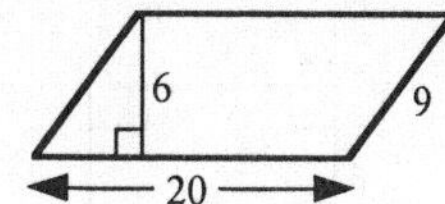

A. 180
B. 120
C. 58
D. 29
E. 15

32. What is the area of the parallelogram below?

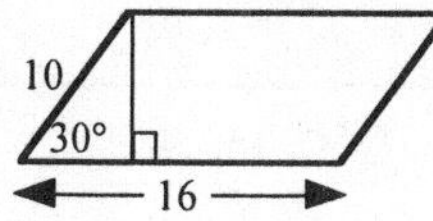

A. 160
B. 80
C. 52
D. 26
E. 16

33. What is the area of the parallelogram below?

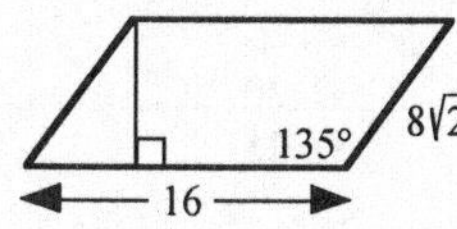

A. $128\sqrt{3}$
B. $128\sqrt{2}$
C. 128
D. $64\sqrt{2}$
E. 64

34. In the figure below, line segments $\overline{AC}$ and $\overline{BD}$ are diameters, and the measure of $\angle ABO$ is 70°. What is the measure of $\angle COD$?

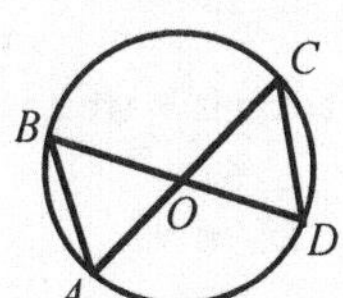

A. 110°
B. 70°
C. 40°
D. 35°
E. 30°

35. In the figure below, $\overline{AC}$ and $\overline{DE}$ bisect each other at point B. The measure of $\angle A$ is 20° and the measure of $\angle D$ is 86°. What is the measure of $\angle DBC$?

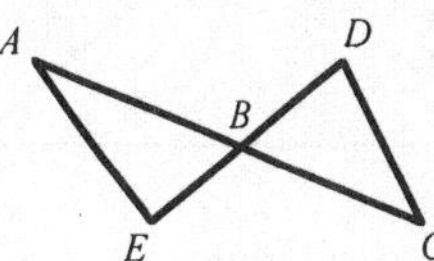

A. 106°
B. 74°
C. 66°
D. 45°
E. 33°

36. In ΔABC, the measure of $\angle A$ is 23° and the measure of $\angle B$ is 84°. What is the longest side of ΔABC?

A. $\overline{AC}$
B. $\overline{AB}$
C. $\overline{BC}$
D. $\overline{AC} \cong \overline{AB}$ (there is no longest side)
E. $\overline{AC} \cong \overline{BC}$ (there is no longest side)

37. In ΔABC, the measure of $\angle A$ is 40° and the measure of $\angle B$ is 70°. What is the longest side of ΔABC?

A. $\overline{AC}$
B. $\overline{AB}$
C. $\overline{BC}$
D. $\overline{AC} \cong \overline{AB}$ (there is no longest side)
E. $\overline{AC} \cong \overline{BC}$ (there is no longest side)

38. ΔABC has three sides with lengths $AB = 19$, $BC = 20$, and $AC = 21$. What is the smallest angle of ΔABC?

A. $\angle A$
B. $\angle B$
C. $\angle C$
D. $\angle A \cong \angle B$ (there is no smallest angle)
E. $\angle A \cong \angle B \cong \angle C$ (there is no smallest angle)

39. Each side of a cube is a square with an area of 49 square centimeters. What is the volume of the cube, in cubic centimeters?

A. 49
B. 7^3
C. 7^4
D. 49^7
E. 7^{49}

40. Each side of a cube is a square. The total surface area of all sides of this cube is 54 square inches. What is the volume of the cube, in cubic inches?

A. 54^3
B. $(\sqrt{54})^3$
C. 9^3
D. 27
E. 9

41. What is the area of the trapezoid below?

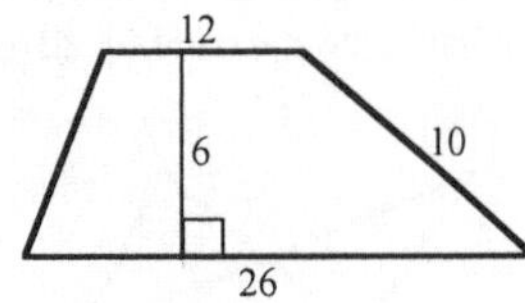

A. 260
B. 130
C. 130
D. 114
E. 58

42. What is the perimeter of the trapezoid below?

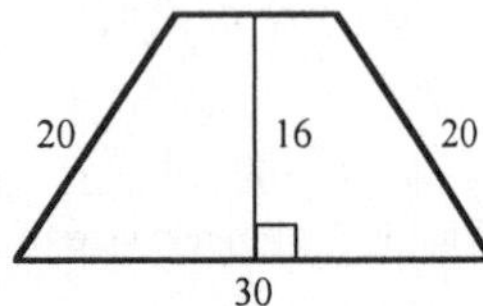

A. 70
B. 76
C. 80
D. 90
E. 100

43. The volume of a sphere is $V = \frac{4}{3}\pi r^3$, where r is the radius of the sphere. If the surface area of the sphere is 324π cm.^{2}, what is the sphere's volume, in cm.^{3}.

A. 243π
B. 324π
C. 729π
D. 972π
E. $1{,}296\pi$

44. What is the perimeter of the figure below?

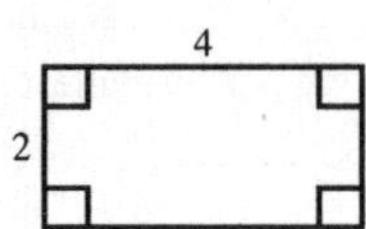

A. 6
B. 8
C. 10
D. 12
E. 16

45. What is the perimeter of the figure below?

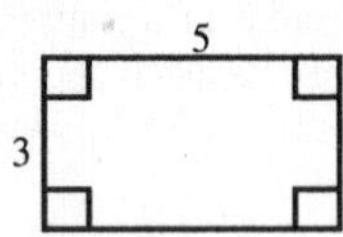

A. 8
B. 12
C. 14
D. 15
E. 16

46. What is the area of the figure below?

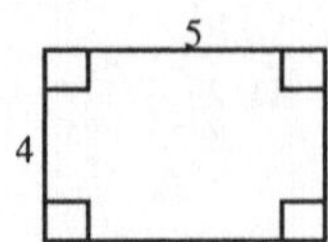

A. 10
B. 15
C. 16
D. 18
E. 20

47. What is the area of the figure below?

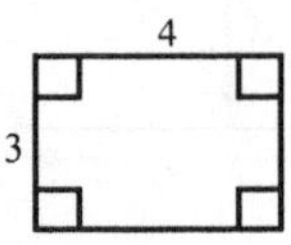

A. 6
B. 8
C. 12
D. 16
E. 24

48. What is the area of the figure below?

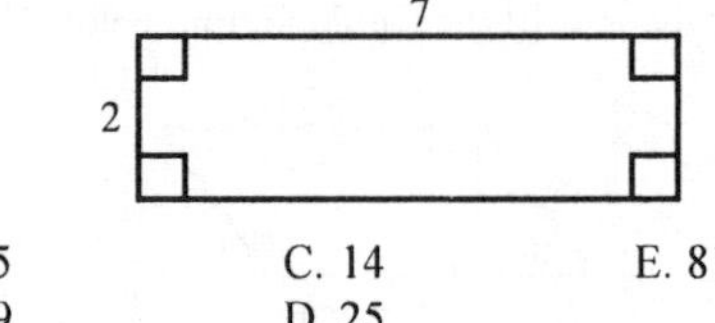

A. 5
B. 9
C. 14
D. 25
E. 81

49. In the figure below, $AB = 5$. What is the area of square $ABCD$?

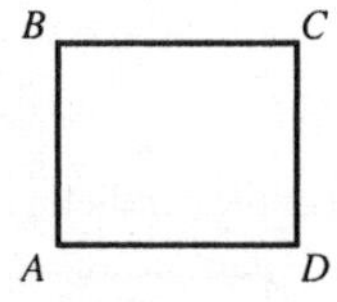

A. 5
B. 10
C. 20
D. 25
E. 40

50. If the radius of a circle is 2, what is the diameter?

A. 1
B. 2
C. 3
D. 4
E. 8

51. If the diameter of a circle is 10, what is the radius?

A. 2
B. 5
C. 8
D. 15
E. 20

52. If the radius of a circle is 3, what is the circumference?

A. 2π
B. 3π
C. 6π
D. 9π
E. 12π

53. If the radius of a circle is 5, what is the circumference?

A. 5π
B. 10π
C. 15π
D. 20π
E. 24π

54. If the diameter of a circle is 8, what is the circumference?

A. 8π
B. 6π
C. 4π
D. 2π
E. π

55. If the radius of a circle is 3, what is the area?

A. π
B. 3π
C. 6π
D. 9π
E. 12π

56. If the radius of a circle is 5, what is the area?

A. 25π
B. 21π
C. 18π
D. 2π
E. π

57. If the diameter of a circle is 8, what is the area?

A. 16π C. 10π E. 4π
B. 12π D. 8π

58. If the diameter of a circle is 12, what is the area?

A. 18π C. 30π E. 36π
B. 24π D. 32π

59. In the figure below, what are a and b?

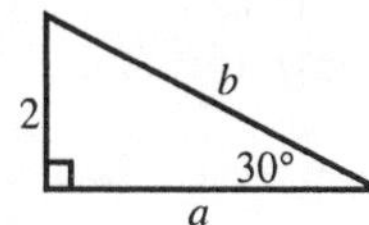

A. $a = \sqrt{3}, b = 2$ D. $a = 4, b = 2\sqrt{3}$
B. $a = 2\sqrt{3}, b = 4$ E. $a = 4, b = 4\sqrt{3}$
C. $a = 2, b = 2$

60. In the figure below, what are c and d?

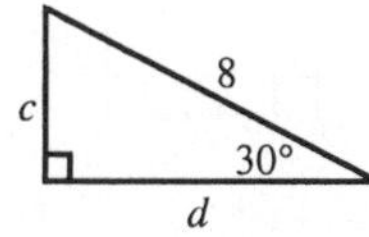

A. $c = 2, d = \sqrt{3}$ D. $c = 4\sqrt{2}, d = 2$
B. $c = 2\sqrt{2}, d = 3$ E. $c = 3, d = 2\sqrt{3}$
C. $c = 4, d = 4\sqrt{3}$

61. In the figure below, what are e and f?

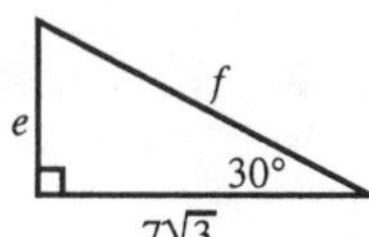

A. $e = 2, f = 6$ D. $e = 7, f = 10$
B. $e = \sqrt{2}, f = 8$ E. $e = 7, f = 14$
C. $e = 4, f = 3\sqrt{5}$

62. In the figure below, what are g and h?

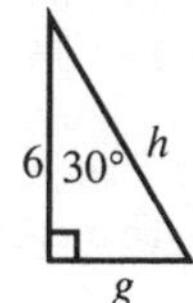

A. $g = \sqrt{3}, h = \sqrt{3}$ D. $g = 4, h = 4\sqrt{3}$
B. $g = 2\sqrt{2}, h = 2\sqrt{3}$ E. $g = 6, h = 7$
C. $g = 2\sqrt{3}, h = 4\sqrt{3}$

63. What is the altitude of an equilateral triangle with a perimeter of 24?

A. $2\sqrt{3}$ C. 6 E. 8
B. $4\sqrt{3}$ D. $4\sqrt{5}$

64. In the figure below, what are i and j?

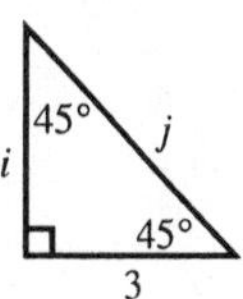

A. $i = 3, j = 3\sqrt{2}$ D. $i = 5, j = 3\sqrt{3}$
B. $i = 3, j = 3$ E. $i = 4, j = 5$
C. $i = 4\sqrt{2}, j = 4$

65. In the figure below, what are k and m?

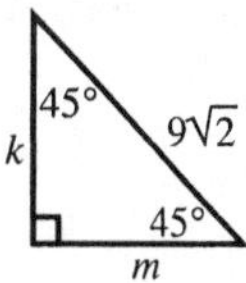

A. $k = 3, m = 3$ D. $k = 9, m = 9$
B. $k = 2\sqrt{3}, m = 3$ E. $k = 3, m = 9$
C. $k = 4, m = 6$

66. In the figure below, $AB = BC = \sqrt{6}$. What is the length of $\overline{AC}$? Note that the triangle is not drawn to scale.

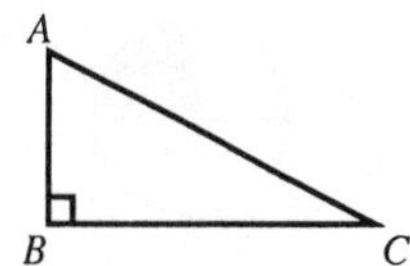

A. 2 C. 3 E. 4
B. $2\sqrt{3}$ D. $3\sqrt{2}$

67. If the perimeter of a square is equal to 40, what is the length of the diagonal?

A. $10\sqrt{2}$ C. 10 E. 14
B. $5\sqrt{3}$ D. $3\sqrt{5}$

68. In the figure below, what is p equal to?

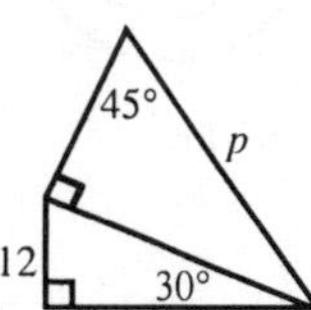

A. $2\sqrt{2}$ C. $10\sqrt{2}$ E. $24\sqrt{2}$
B. $2\sqrt{3}$ D. $20\sqrt{3}$

69. What is the number of degrees in the angle formed by the minute and hour hands of a clock at 2:20?

A. 90° C. 60° E. 30°
B. 70° D. 50°

70. What is the radius of a circle with an area of 49?

A. 7
B. 7π
C. $\frac{7}{\sqrt{\pi}}$
D. $\frac{7}{\pi}$
E. π^2

71. What is the area of a circle with a circumference of $\frac{22\pi}{3}$?

A. $\frac{484\pi}{9}$
B. $\frac{121\pi}{9}$
C. $\frac{121\pi}{3}$
D. $\frac{484\pi}{3}$
E. $\frac{556\pi}{4}$

72. A circle has an area of $36\pi^3$. What is the radius of the circle?

A. 6
B. 6π
C. $6\pi^2$
D. $6\pi^3$
E. $6\pi^4$

73. If the radius of a circle is 8, what is the circumference of the circle?

A. 4π
B. 8π
C. 12π
D. 14π
E. 16π

74. In the figure below, what is the value of the shaded area?

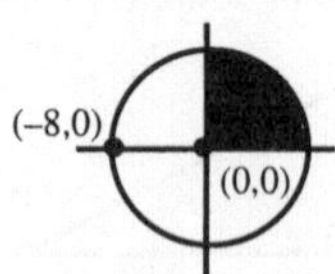

A. 16π
B. 32π
C. 64π
D. 66π
E. $16\pi^2$

75. In the figure below, the length of $\overline{OA}$ is 2 and the length of $\overline{OB}$ is 3. What is the area between the two circles?

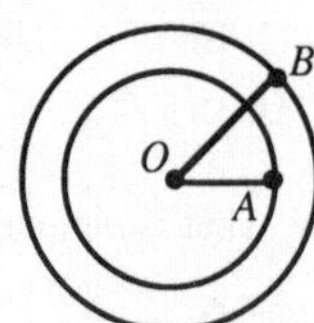

A. 4π
B. 5π
C. 6π
D. 7π
E. 8π

76. In the figure below, a circle with an area of 144π is inscribed in a square. What is the area of the shaded region?

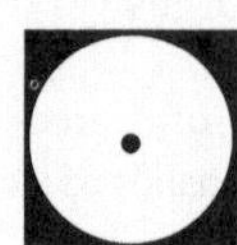

A. $576 - 144\pi$
B. $216 - 72\pi$
C. $144 - 24\pi$
D. $1,728 - 144\pi$
E. $256 - 24\pi$

77. A square has a perimeter of 40. A second square has an inscribed circle with an area of 64π. What is the ratio of the length of a side of the first square to the length of a side of the second square?

A. 5:8
B. 5:4
C. 5:16
D. $10:8\pi$
E. $12:\pi$

78. The area of a square is $64x^2y^{16}$. What is the length of a side of the square?

A. $8xy^8$
B. $8xy^4$
C. $8x^2y^{16}$
D. $16x^2y^{16}$
E. $20x^2y^4$

79. In the figure below, what is the area of square $BCDE$?

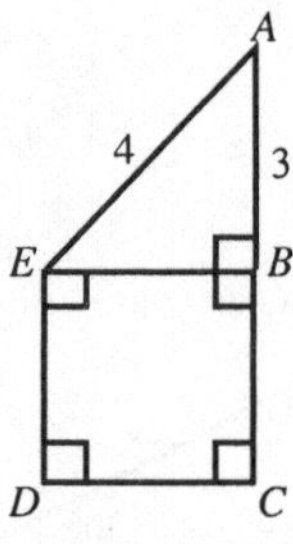

A. 5
B. 7
C. 12
D. 24
E. 49

80. What is the area of a right triangle with legs of lengths 4 and 5?

A. 6
B. 10
C. 12
D. 20
E. 24

81. In the figure below, assume O is the center of the circle. If $\angle OAB$ is 45°, then what is the area of the shaded segment?

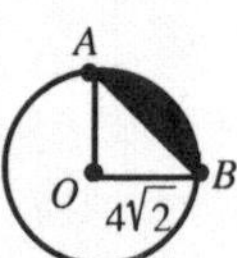

A. $32\pi - 16\sqrt{2}$
B. $32\pi - 8$
C. $4\pi - 8$
D. $8\pi - 16$
E. $8\pi - 8$

82. In the figure below, rectangle $ABCD$ has an area of 15. What is the length of the diagonal $\overline{AC}$?

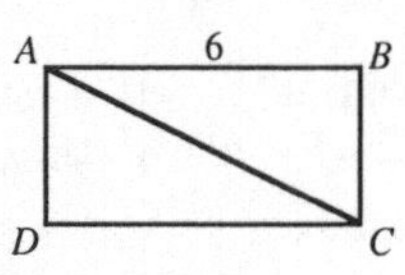

A. 4
B. 5
C. 6.5
D. 7
E. 7.5

83. Regarding the figure below, which one of the following statements is true?

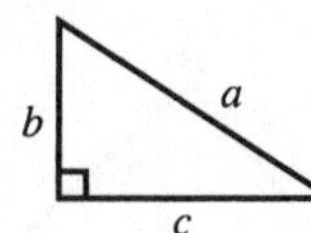

A. $a^2 + b^2 = c^2$ C. $b + c = a$ E. $a + c = b$
B. $a + b = c$ D. $b^2 + c^2 = a^2$

84. At 12 cents per square foot, how much will it cost to paint the rectangular slab in the figure below?

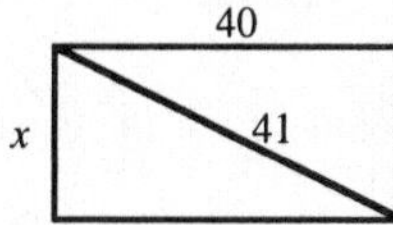

A. \$43.20 C. \$98.40 E. \$201.50
B. \$46.40 D. \$196.80

85. In the figure below, what is the length of $\overline{BC}$?

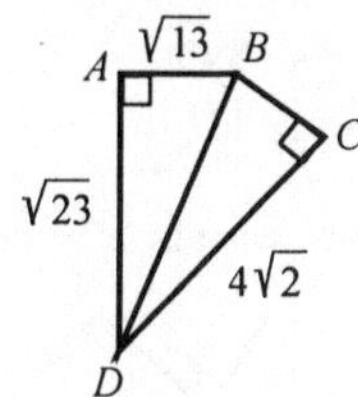

A. 1 C. 3 E. 5
B. 2 D. 4

86. If the diagonal of a square is $5\sqrt{2}$, what is the area of the square?

A. 10 C. 25 E. 35
B. 20 D. 30

87. What is the area of the rectangle in the figure below?

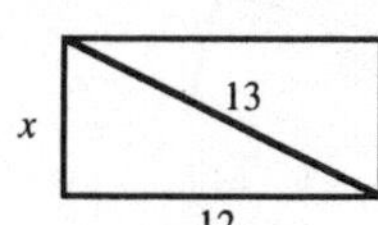

A. 156 C. 72 E. 60
B. 78 D. 66

88. In the figure below, what is x equal to?

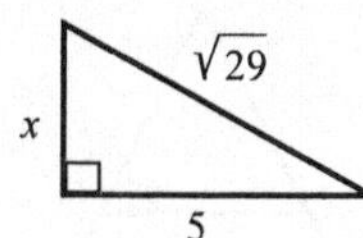

A. $\sqrt{29} - 5$ C. 24 E. $\sqrt{2}$
B. $\sqrt{24}$ D. 2

89. If $2\sqrt{3}$ is the diagonal of a square, then what is the perimeter of the square?

A. $4\sqrt{6}$ C. $6\sqrt{3}$ E. 14
B. 8 D. 12

90. In the figures below, what is the ratio of the perimeter of ΔABC to the perimeter of ΔDEF?

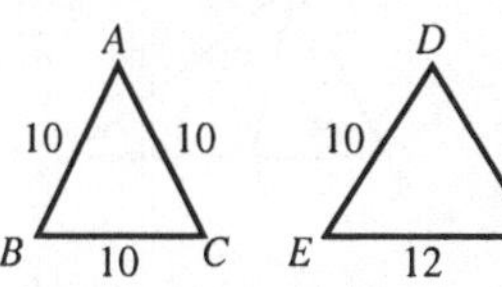

A. 1:1 C. 15:16 E. 7:3
B. 5:6 D. 6:5

91. In terms of π, what is the area of a circle whose radius is $2\sqrt{5}$?

A. π C. 10π E. 40π
B. 4π D. 20π

92. What is the radius of a circle whose area is 12π?

A. $\sqrt{3}$ C. $2\sqrt{3}$ E. 3
B. 1 D. 2

93. What is the radius of a circle if the distance to walk halfway around the rim of the circle is $\sqrt{6}\pi$?

A. $\sqrt{2}$ C. 2 E. 3
B. $\sqrt{3}$ D. $\sqrt{6}$

94. If the legs of a right triangle are 2 and 5, what is the hypotenuse?

A. $\sqrt{22}$ C. $5\sqrt{2}$ E. 6
B. $\sqrt{29}$ D. $\sqrt{35}$

95. If the hypotenuse of a right triangle is 37 and one leg is 35, what is the length of the other leg?

A. $4\sqrt{3}$ C. 12 E. 16
B. $6\sqrt{2}$ D. $14\sqrt{2}$

96. If $2\sqrt{12}$, $3\sqrt{6}$, and $4\sqrt{3}$ are the dimensions of a rectangular solid, what is the volume of the solid?

A. $216\sqrt{24}$ C. $144\sqrt{6}$ E. $\sqrt{24}$
B. $\sqrt{5,184}$ D. 5,184

97. What is the volume of a cylinder with an altitude of 10 and a circumference of $\sqrt{128\pi}$?

A. $\sqrt{1{,}280\pi}$ C. 640π E. $3{,}460\pi$
B. 320π D. $1{,}280\pi$

98. In the figure below, what is x equal to?

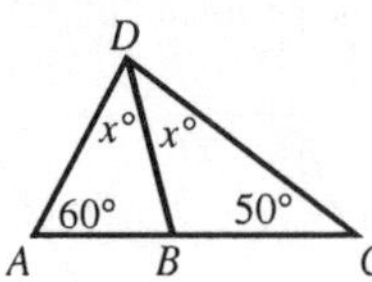

A. 30 C. 35 E. 70
B. 32 D. 40

99. If the ratio of the sides of a triangle are $x{:}x\sqrt{3}{:}2x$, and the length of the smallest side is 5, what is the length of the largest side?

A. 10 C. $8\sqrt{3}$ E. 20
B. 12 D. 15

100. In the figure below, what is the length of $\overline{JK}$?

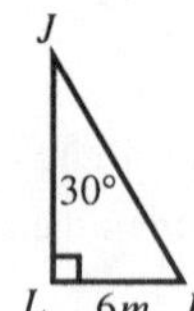

A. $6m\sqrt{3}$ C. $12m$ E. $14m$
B. $9m$ D. $12m\sqrt{3}$

101. In the figure below, ΔDEF is an isosceles triangle. What is the length of $\overline{DF}$?

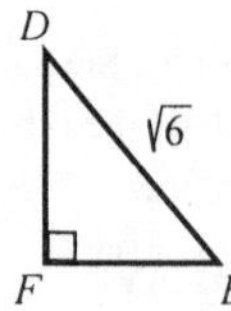

A. $2\sqrt{6}$ C. $\sqrt{3}$ E. $12\sqrt{2}$
B. $6\sqrt{2}$ D. 12

102. If the longest side of a 30°-60°-90° triangle is $2\sqrt{3}$, what is the area of the triangle?

A. 8 C. $1.5\sqrt{3}$ E. 1
B. 4 D. 2

103. In the figure below, what is the length of the diagonal $\overline{AC}$ of square $ABCD$?

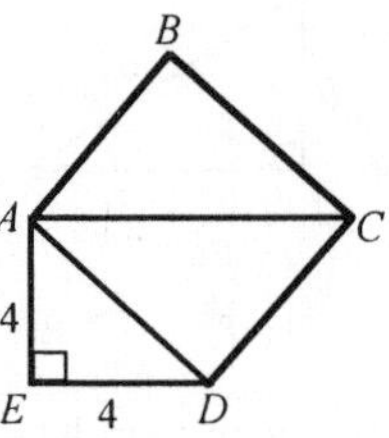

A. $4\sqrt{2}$ C. $8\sqrt{2}$ E. $32\sqrt{2}$
B. 8 D. 16

104. In the figure below, if arc $\overline{BC}$ equals 60°, then what is the area of ΔABC?

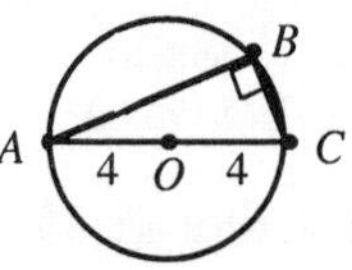

A. 16 C. $8\sqrt{3}$ E. $10\sqrt{2}$
B. $4\sqrt{3}$ D. 12

105. In the figure below, what is $2x° - 60°$ equal to?

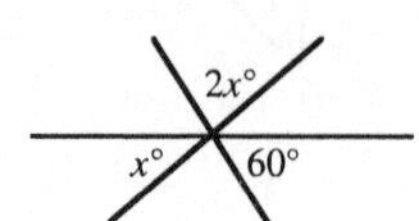

A. 80° C. 30° E. 10°
B. 40° D. 20°

106. In the figure below, a equals all of the following EXCEPT

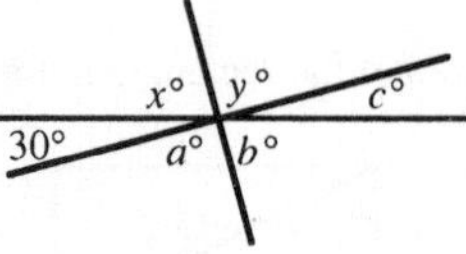

A. y C. $180 - b - c$ E. $180 - x - y$
B. $150 - x$ D. $150 - b$

107. In the figure below, $\overline{EC} \parallel \overline{AB}$ and $\overline{AD} \cong \overline{BD}$. What is the sum of the degree measures of $\angle A + \angle B + \angle BCE$?

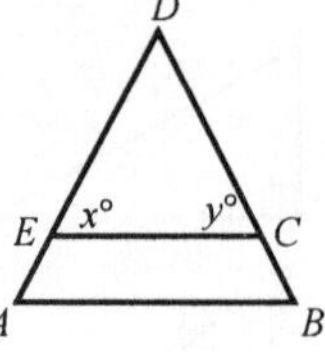

A. $x + y$ C. $180 + x$ E. $90 - y$
B. $3x$ D. $-2x$

108. In the figure below, if $\overline{AE} \parallel \overline{BD}$ and $\overline{BD} \cong \overline{DC}$, then what is $\angle BDC$ equal to?

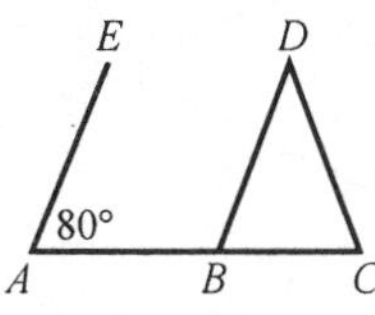

A. 10°
B. 15°
C. 18°
D. 20°
E. 24°

109. In the figure below, if $l_1 \parallel l_2$ and $\angle 7 = 117°$, which other angles must also equal 117°?

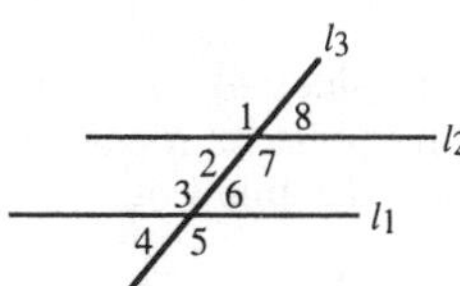

A. 1, 3, 5
B. 1, 2, 8
C. 2, 3, 6
D. 5, 6, 8
E. 1, 2, 3, 4

110. In the figure below, what is the value of x?

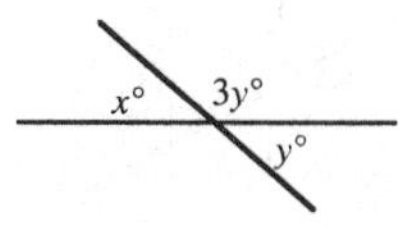

A. 30°
B. 45°
C. 60°
D. 65°
E. 80°

111. In the figure below, which of the following statements is true?

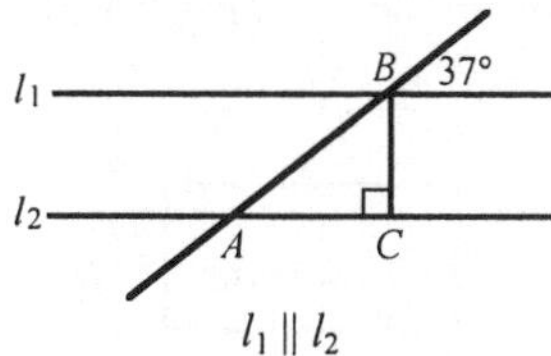

A. $\overline{AC} > \overline{BC}$
B. $\overline{AC} < \overline{BC}$
C. $\overline{AC} = \overline{BC}$
D. $\overline{AC} + \overline{BC} = \overline{AB}$
E. $\overline{AC} - \overline{BC} = \overline{AB}$

112. In the figure below, $\overline{OM} \parallel \overline{PJ}$, and $\overline{FG}$ and $\overline{EG}$ divide $\angle CGO$ into 3 congruent angles. What is the degree measure of $\angle EGC$?

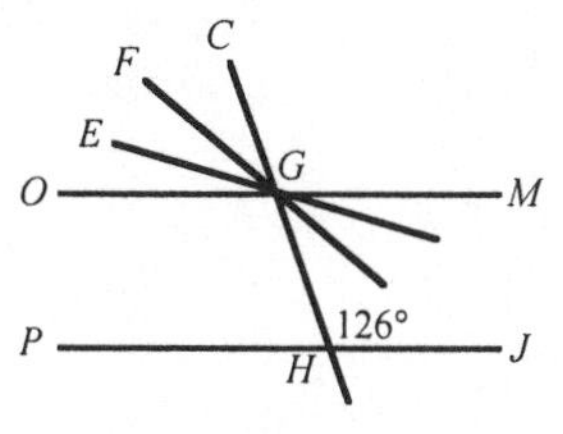

A. 18°
B. 36°
C. 42°
D. 54°
E. 63°

113. In the figure below, $\Delta ABE \sim \Delta ACD$. What is the length of $\overline{CD}$?

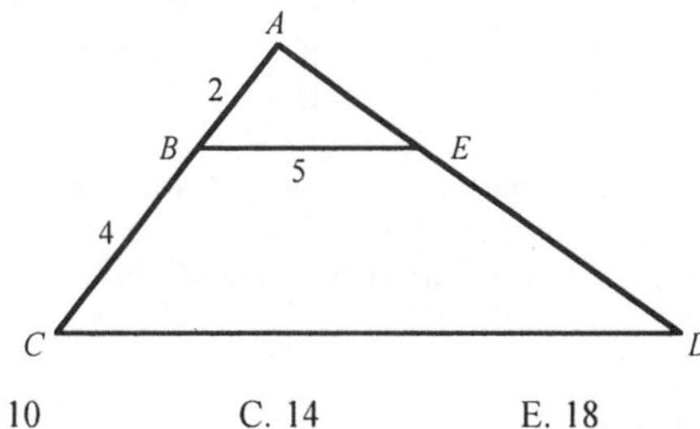

A. 10
B. 12
C. 14
D. 15
E. 18

114. A triangle with sides of 12, 14, and 20 is similar to a second triangle that has one side with a length of 40. What is the smallest possible perimeter of the second triangle?

A. 48
B. 92
C. 120
D. 160
E. 180

115. A right circular cylinder has a base whose diameter is $8x$; the height of the cylinder is $3y$. What is the volume of the cylinder?

A. $24xy$
B. $24\pi x^2y$
C. $48\pi xy$
D. $96\pi xy$
E. $48\pi x^2y$

116. If the perimeter of a rectangle is 68 yd. and the width is 48 ft., what is the length?

A. 10 yd.
B. 18 ft.
C. 20 ft.
D. 46 ft.
E. 54 ft.

117. What is the total length of fencing needed to enclose a rectangular area 46 ft. × 34 ft.?

A. $26\frac{1}{3}$ yd.
B. $26\frac{2}{3}$ yd.
C. 48 yd.
D. $52\frac{2}{3}$ yd.
E. $53\frac{1}{3}$ yd.

118. An umbrella 50" long can lie diagonally on the bottom of a trunk with a length and width that are which of the following, respectively?

A. 26", 30"
B. 30", 36"
C. 31", 31"
D. 40", 21"
E. 40", 30"

119. A road runs 1,200 ft. from point A to point B, and then makes a right angle going to point C, a distance of 500 ft. A new road is being built directly from A to C. How much shorter will the new road be than the old road?

A. 400 ft.
B. 609 ft.
C. 850 ft.
D. 1,000 ft.
E. 1,300 ft.

120. A certain triangle has sides of lengths 6", 8", and 10". A rectangle equal in area to that of the triangle has a width of 3". What is the perimeter, in inches, of the rectangle?

A. 11
B. 16
C. 22
D. 24
E. 30

121. A ladder 65 ft. long is leaning against a wall. Its lower end is 25 ft. away from the wall. How much farther away will it be if the upper end is moved down 8 ft.?

A. 60 ft. C. 14 ft. E. 8 ft.
B. 52 ft. D. 10 ft.

122. A rectangular bin 4 ft. long, 3 ft. wide, and 2 ft. high is solidly packed with bricks whose dimensions are 8 in. × 4 in. × 2 in. What is the number of bricks in the bin?

A. 54
B. 320
C. 648
D. 848
E Cannot be determined from the given information

123. If the cost of digging a trench is $2.12/yd.^{3}, what would be the cost of digging a trench $2 \times 5 \times 4$ yd.^{3}?

A. $21.20 C. $64.00 E. $104.80
B. $40.00 D. $84.80

124. A piece of wire is shaped to enclose a square, whose area is 121 square inches. It is then reshaped to enclose a rectangle whose length is 13 inches. What is the area of the rectangle, in square inches?

A. 64 C. 117 E. 234
B. 96 D. 144

125. What is the area of a 2-foot-wide walk around the outside of a garden that is 30 feet long and 20 feet wide?

A. 104 ft.^{2} C. 680 ft.^{2} E. 1,416 ft.^{2}
B. 216 ft.^{2} D. 704 ft.^{2}

126. The area of a circle is 49π. What is its circumference, in terms of π?

A. 14π C. 49π E. 147π
B. 28π D. 98π

127. In two hours, the minute hand of a clock rotates through an angle equal to which of the following?

A. 90° C. 360° E. 1,080°
B. 180° D. 720°

128. A box is 12 inches in width, 16 inches in length, and 6 inches in height. How many square inches of paper would be required to cover it on all sides?

A. 192 C. 720 E. 1,440
B. 360 D. 900

129. If the volume of a cube is 64 cubic inches, what is the sum of the lengths of its edges?

A. 48 in. C. 24 in. E. 12 in.
B. 32 in. D. 16 in.

130. In the figure below, $x = ?$

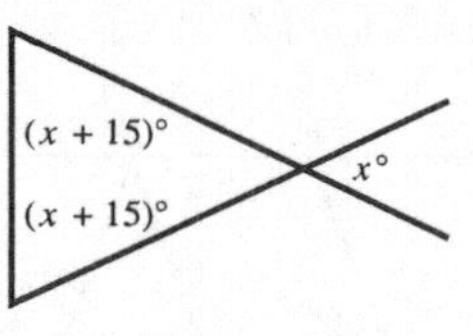

A. 20 C. 50 E. 90
B. 35 D. 65

131. What is the difference of the areas of two squares with sides of 5 and 4, respectively?

A. 3 C. 9 E. 91
B. 4 D. 16

132. A triangle with sides of 4, 6, and 8 has the same perimeter as an equilateral triangle with sides of length equal to which of the following?

A. 2 C. 3 E. 8
B. $\frac{3}{2}$ D. 6

133. In the figure below, $x = ?$

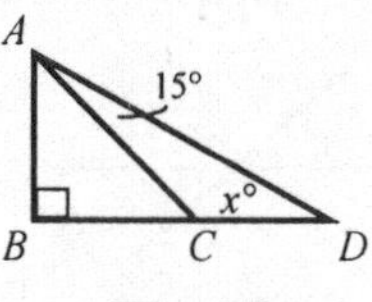

$\overline{AB} \cong \overline{BC}$

A. 15 C. 40 E. 75
B. 30 D. 60

134. If the area of the rectangle shown below is equal to 1, then $l = ?$

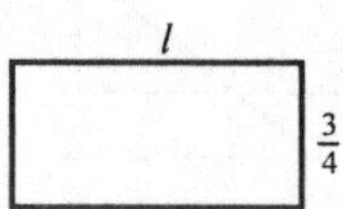

A. $\frac{4}{9}$ C. $\frac{4}{3}$ E. 2
B. 1 D. $\frac{9}{4}$

135. A semicircle is divided into three arcs with respective lengths 2π, 6π, and 14π. The semicircle is a part of a circle with which of the following radii?

A. 44
B. 33
C. 22
D. 11
E. 6

136. In the figure below, $x = ?$

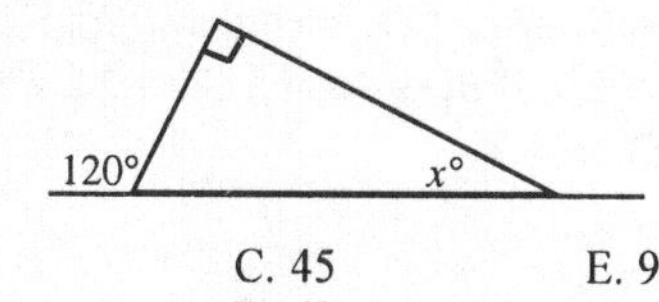

A. 15
B. 30
C. 45
D. 60
E. 90

137. In the figure below, $\angle A \cong \angle B$.

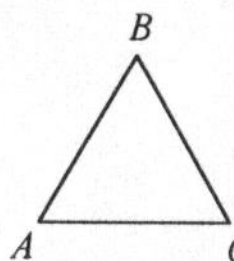

Which of the following statements must be true?

A. $\angle A \cong \angle B \cong \angle C$
B. $\angle A \ncong \angle C$
C. $\overline{AC} \cong \overline{BC}$
D. $\overline{BC} \cong \overline{AB}$
E. $\overline{AB} \cong \overline{AC}$

138. In the incomplete figure below, the circle and $\overrightarrow{AB}$ have how many points of intersection?

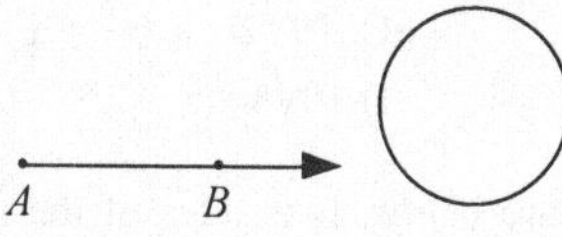

A. 0
B. 1
C. 2
D. 3
E. An infinite number

139. In the figure below, which is not necessarily drawn to scale, $\angle A \cong \angle C$ and $\angle B \cong \angle D$.

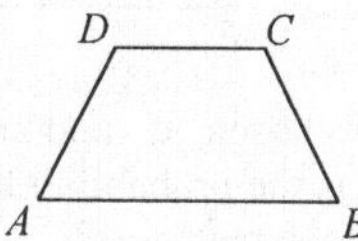

How many of the following four statements of congruence must be true?

$\angle A \cong \angle B$
$\overline{AB} \cong \overline{DC}$
$\overline{AD} \cong \overline{BC}$
$\overline{AB} \cong \overline{BC} \cong \overline{CD} \cong \overline{AD}$

A. 0
B. 1
C. 2
D. 3
E. 4

140. In the diagram below, $\overline{AD} \cong \overline{AE}$ and $\overline{AB} \cong \overline{BF} \cong \overline{CE} \cong \overline{CF} \cong \overline{DE}$.

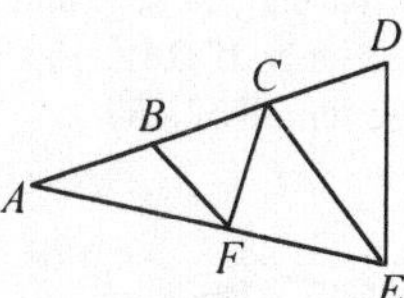

What is the number of degrees in $\angle DAE$?

A. 20
B. 24
C. 25
D. 30
E. 35

141. In the diagram below, $\angle ABC = 90°$, $AC = 10\sqrt{2}$, and $AB + BC = 3\sqrt{38}$. What is the area of ΔABC?

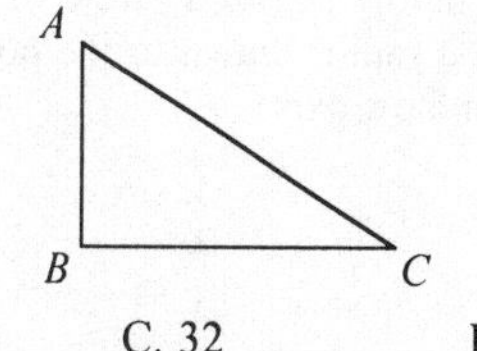

A. 19
B. 29
C. 32
D. 35.5
E. 40

142. In the figure below, ΔABC intersects a circle with center O. $\overline{AB}$ is tangent to the circle at A. If $AB = 8$ and $BO = 10$, what is the area of the circle?

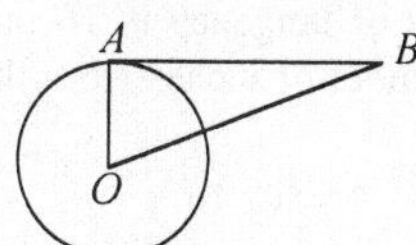

A. 4π
B. 6π
C. 36π
D. 64π
E. 100π

143. The figure below shows a circle with center O, two radii $\overline{OA}$ and $\overline{OB}$, and two tangents $\overline{AC}$ and $\overline{BC}$. What is the area of the shaded region?

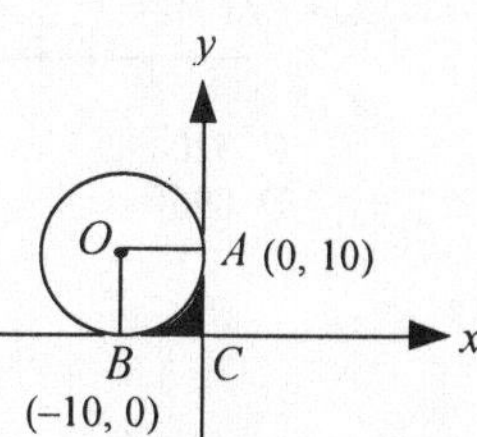

A. $100 - 100\pi$
B. $50 - 100\pi$
C. $50 - 50\pi$
D. $50 - 25\pi$
E. $100 - 25\pi$

144. The figure below shows two circles lying in the same plane with respective centers at O and P. $\overline{AB}$ is a common external tangent segment to the two circles at A and B, respectively. If $OA = 13$, $PB = 3$, and $OP = 26$, then what is the length of $\overline{AB}$?

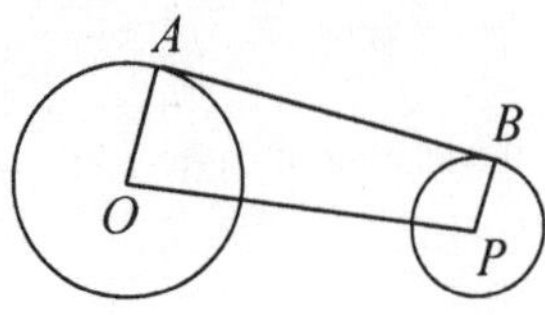

A. 26
B. 25
C. 24
D. 20
E. 18

145. The figure below shows a circle of area 144π square inches with a radius drawn to the point of tangency of the circle on the x-axis.

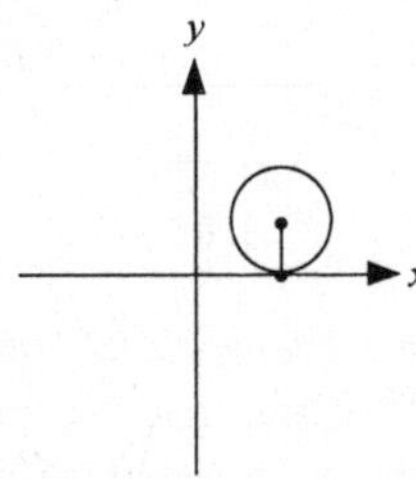

If this point of tangency is 16 inches from the origin, then the number of inches from the origin to the center of the circle is:

A. 12
B. $12\sqrt{2}$
C. 16
D. $16\sqrt{2}$
E. 20

146. In the figure below, $\overline{TP} \cong \overline{RA}$, and $\overline{TR} \parallel \overline{PA}$. $TR = 12$, $PA = 44$. If $\angle P = 45°$, what is the area of $TRAP$?

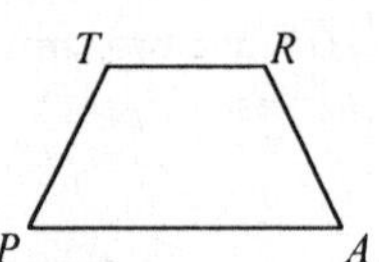

A. 448
B. 464
C. 520
D. 896
E. 1,792

147. In the figure below, B and E lie on $\overline{AC}$ and $\overline{AD}$, respectively, of ΔACD, such that $\overline{BE} \parallel \overline{CD}$. $\overline{BD} \perp \overline{AC}$, and $\overline{BC} \cong \overline{ED}$. If $BC = 10$ and $CD = 20$, what is the area of ΔABE?

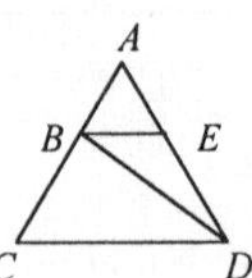

A. 100
B. $50\sqrt{3}$
C. 50
D. $25\sqrt{3}$
E. Cannot be determined from the given information

148. In the figure below, which is not necessarily drawn to scale, $\angle ABC = 90°$, $AB = 10$, and $\tan \angle ACB = 1$. What is the length of $\overline{AC}$?

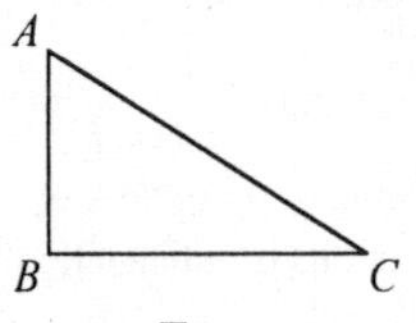

A. 10
B. 20
C. $10\sqrt{2}$
D. $10\sqrt{3}$
E. $20\sqrt{3}$

149. In the figure below, two sides of the rectangle $ABGF$ lie on two sides of the square $ACDE$. $AF = 9$, $BC = 8$, and $FE = 1$.

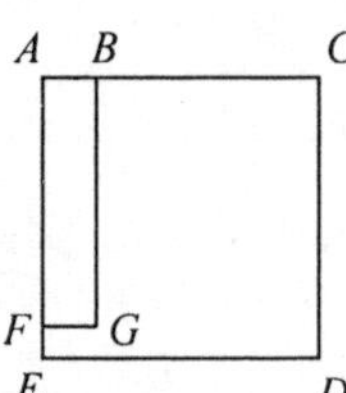

If a point is chosen at random in the interior of the square, what is the probability that the point also lies in the interior of the rectangle?

A. $\frac{1}{50}$
B. $\frac{3}{50}$
C. $\frac{7}{50}$
D. $\frac{9}{50}$
E. $\frac{11}{50}$

150. The figure below shows three acute angles and two obtuse angles.

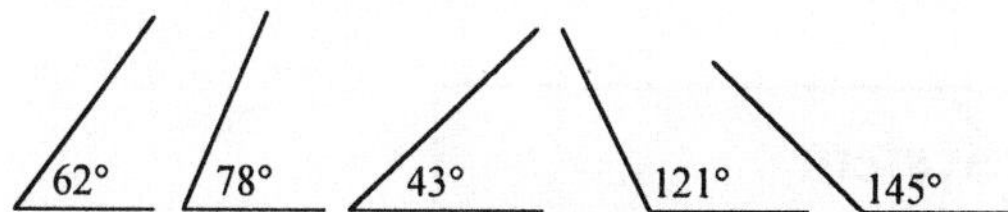

If two different angles are created randomly using the five angles shown, what is the probability that both angles are acute?

A. $\frac{1}{10}$
B. $\frac{1}{5}$
C. $\frac{2}{5}$
D. $\frac{3}{5}$
E. $\frac{3}{10}$

151. Last night, Dave and Kathy both arrived at Pizza Palace at two different random times between 10:00 p.m. and midnight. They had agreed to wait exactly 15 minutes for each other to arrive before leaving. What is the probability that Dave and Kathy were together at Pizza Palace last night between 10:00 p.m. and midnight?

A. $\frac{1}{8}$
B. $\frac{1}{4}$
C. $\frac{15}{64}$
D. $\frac{3}{8}$
E. $\frac{31}{64}$

Functions, Graphs, and Coordinate Geometry

Coordinate Axis System

The easiest way to understand the coordinate axis system is as an analog to the points of the compass. If we take a plot of land, we can divide it into quadrants:

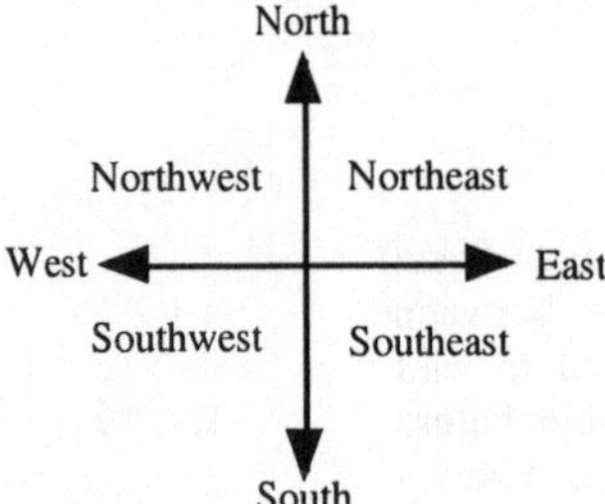

Now, if we add measuring units along each of the directional axes, we can actually describe any location on this piece of land by two numbers.

Example:

Point P is located at 4 units East and 5 units North. Point Q is located at 4 units West and 5 units North. Point R is located at 4 units West and 2 units South. Point T is located at 3 units East and 4 units South.

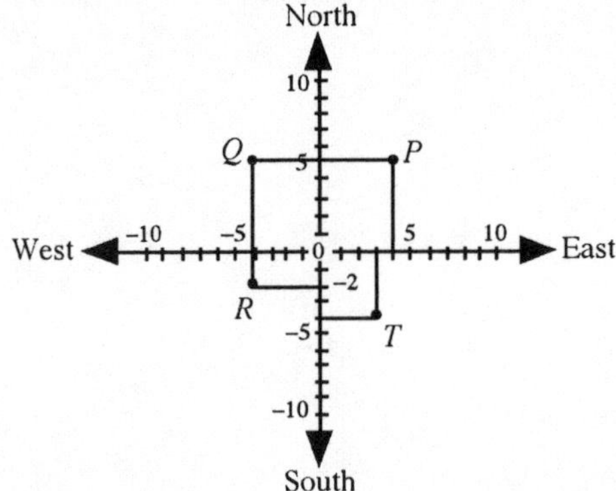

The coordinate system used in coordinate geometry differs from our map of a plot of land in that it uses x- and y-axes divided into negative and positive regions.

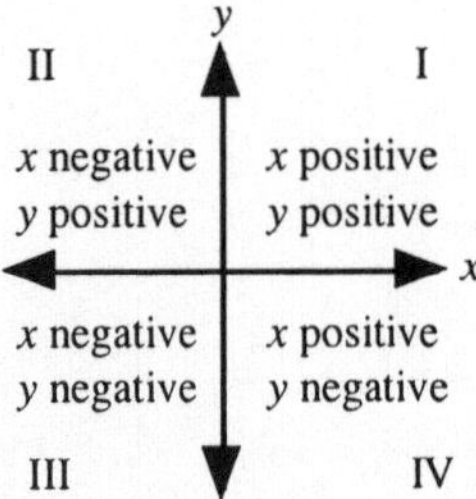

It is easy to see that ***Quadrant I*** corresponds to our Northeast quarter, in which the measurements on both the x- and y-axes are positive. ***Quadrant II*** corresponds to our Northwest quarter, in which the measurements on the x-axis are negative and the measurements on the y-axis are positive. ***Quadrant III*** corresponds to our Southwest quarter, in which both the x-axis measurements and the y-axis measurements are negative. Finally, ***Quadrant IV*** corresponds to our Southeast quarter, in which the x-values are positive while the y-values are negative.

Ordered Pairs

An ***ordered pair*** of coordinates has the general form **(x, y)**. The first element refers to the ***x-coordinate***: the distance left or right of the ***origin***, or intersection of the axes. The second element gives the ***y-coordinate***: the distance up or down from the origin.

Example:

Plot (3, 2).

➤ Move to the positive 3 value on the x-axis. Then, from there move up two units on the y-axis, as illustrated by the graph on the left. The graph on the right demonstrates an alternative method: the point (3, 2) is located at the intersection of a line drawn through the x-value 3 parallel to the y-axis and a line drawn through the y-value 2 parallel to the x-axis.

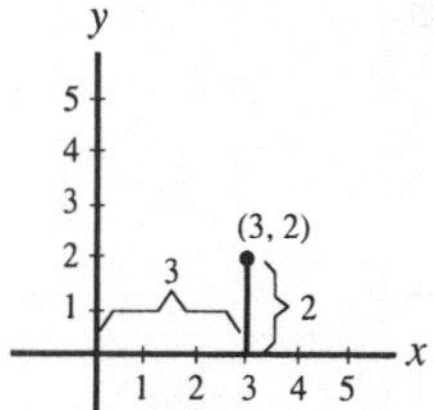

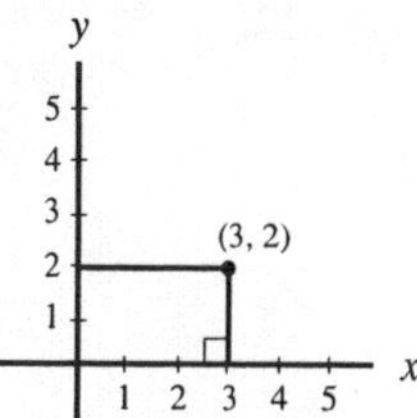

Properties of Functions

A function is a set of ordered pairs (x, y) such that for each value of x, there is exactly one value of y. By convention, we say that "y is a function of x," which is written as: $y = f(x)$ or $y = g(x)$, *etc.* The set of x-values for which the set is defined is called the ***domain*** of the function. The set of corresponding values of y is called the ***range*** of the function.

Example:

What are the domain and range of the function $y = |x|$?

➤ The function is defined for all real values of x. Hence the domain is the set of all real numbers. Since $y = |x|$ can only be a positive number or zero, the range of the function is given by the set of all real numbers equal to or greater than zero.

When we speak of $f(a)$, we mean the value of $y = f(x)$ when $x = a$ is substituted in the expression for $f(x)$. If $z = f(y)$ and $y = g(x)$, we say that $z = f[g(x)]$. Thus, z is in turn a function of x.

Examples:

1. If $f(x) = 2x^x - 3x$, find the value of $f(3)$.
   ➤ Substitute 3 for x in the given expression: $f(x) = 2x^x - 3x \Rightarrow f(3) = 2(3)^3 - 3(3) = 2(27) - 9 = 54 - 9 = 45$.
2. If $f(x) = 2x - 9^{1/x}$, what is $f(-2)$?
   ➤ $f(-2) = 2(-2) - 9^{-1/2} = -4 - \frac{1}{\sqrt{9}} = -4 - \frac{1}{3} = -\frac{13}{3}$.
3. If $z = f(y) = 3y + 2$ and $y = g(x) = x + 2$, then $z = ?$
   ➤ $z = f[g(x)] = 3[g(x)] + 2 = 3(x + 2) + 2 = 3x + 6 + 2 = 3x + 8$.

Plotting Equations

The coordinate axis system provides a framework for plotting equations. Simply plot several pairs of points for the given equation.

Examples:

1. Plot the equation $x = y$.
   ➤ This equation has an infinite number of solutions:

x	1	2	3	5	0	–3	–5	...
y	1	2	3	5	0	–3	–5	...

   Plot these pairs of x and y on the axis system. Draw a line through them to produce a plot of the original equation. The complete picture of the equation $x = y$ is a straight line including all the real numbers such that x is equal to y.

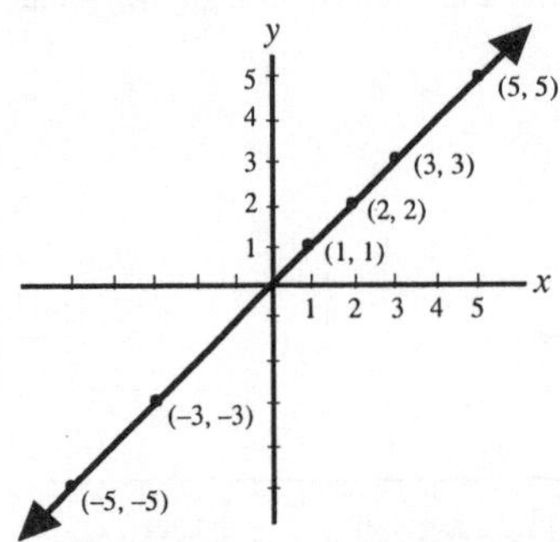

2. Plot the equation $y = 2x$.
   ➤ This equation has an infinite number of solutions:

x	–4	–2	–1	0	1	2	4	...
y	–8	–4	–2	0	2	4	8	...

   After entering the points on the graph, complete the picture. It is a straight line, but it rises more rapidly than does $x = y$.

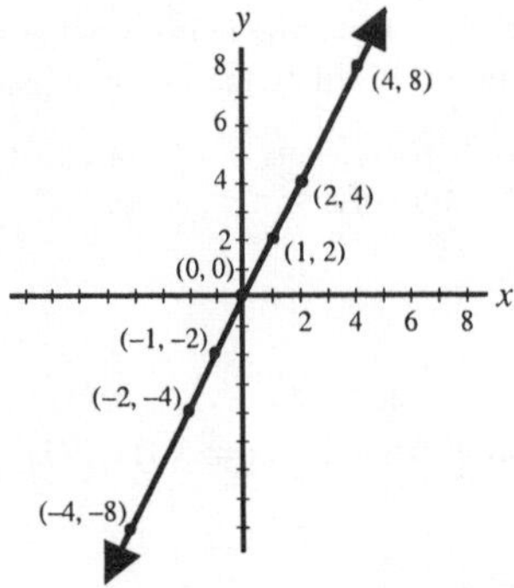

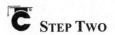

Midpoint of Line Segments

For a line segment between two points, (x_1, y_1) and (x_2, y_2), the ***midpoint*** $= \left(\frac{x_1+x_2}{2}, \frac{y_1+y_2}{2}\right)$. The x-coordinate of the midpoint is the average of the two x-axis endpoints and the y-coordinate of the midpoint is the average of the two y-axis endpoints.

Examples:

1. Find the midpoint between $(-5, 8)$ and $(11, 34)$.
   ➢ The midpoint is $\left(\frac{x_1+x_2}{2}, \frac{y_1+y_2}{2}\right) = \left(\frac{-5+11}{2}, \frac{8+34}{2}\right) = \left(\frac{6}{2}, \frac{42}{2}\right) = (3, 21)$.
2. One endpoint of a circle diameter is located at $(13, 1)$. If the center of the circle is $(15, 10)$, find the other endpoint.
   ➢ The midpoint of the diameter is $(15, 10)$, so $15 = \frac{x_1+x_2}{2} = \frac{13+x_2}{2}$ and $10 = \frac{y_1+y_2}{2} = \frac{1+y_2}{2}$. $x_2 = (15 \cdot 2) - 13 = 17$ and $y_2 = (10 \cdot 2) - 1 = 19$. Thus, $(x_2, y_2) = (17, 19)$.

Distance Between Two Points

To determine the distance between two points on a coordinate graph, consider points P and Q. For simplicity's sake, we will confine the discussion to the first quadrant, but the method generally works in all quadrants and even with lines covering two or more quadrants. Assign the value (x_1, y_1) to point P and (x_2, y_2) to point Q:

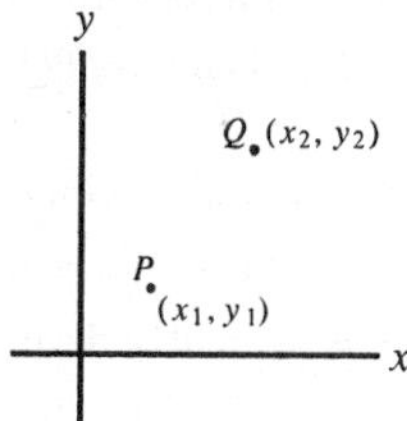

To find distance between points P and Q, construct a triangle:

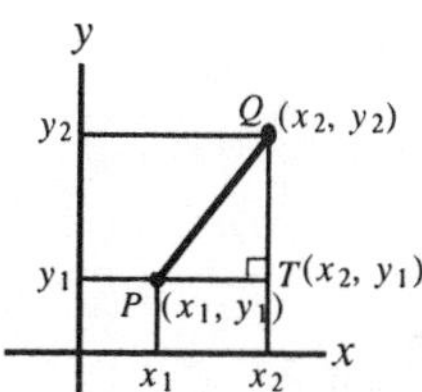

Point T now has the coordinates (x_2, y_1). To calculate the length of $\overline{PT}$, find the distance moved on the x-axis: $x_2 - x_1$ units. The y-coordinate does not change. Similarly, the length of $\overline{QT}$ will be $y_2 - y_1$ since the distance is purely vertical, moving up from y_1 to y_2, with no change in the x-value. Apply the Pythagorean theorem:

$$(PQ)^2 = (PT)^2 + (QT)^2 = (x_2 - x_1)^2 + (y_2 - y_1)^2$$
$$PQ = \sqrt{(x_2 - x_1)^2 + (y_2 - y_1)^2}$$

Example:

In the figure below, what is the length of $\overline{PQ}$?

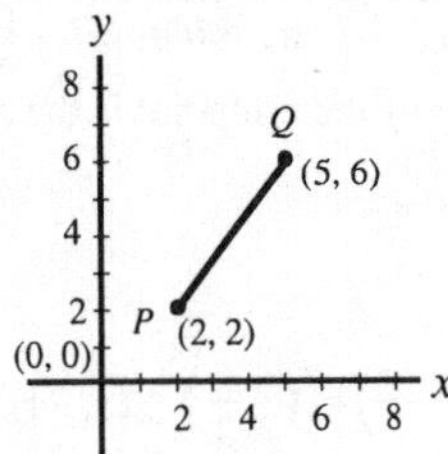

➤ Find the length of $\overline{PQ}$ by constructing a triangle:

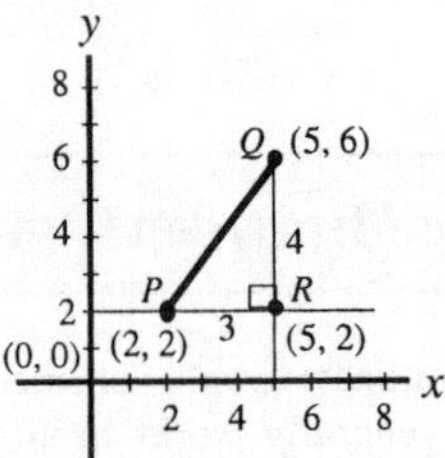

$\overline{QR}$ runs from (5, 6) to (5, 2), so it must be 4 units long. $\overline{PR}$ runs from (2, 2) to (5, 2), so it is 3 units long. Use the Pythagorean theorem: $(PQ)^2 = (QR)^2 + (PR)^2 = 4^2 + 3^2 = 16 + 9 = 25$. Therefore, $PQ = \sqrt{25} = 5$.

Therefore, you can find the length of any line segment drawn in a coordinate axis system between points (x_1, y_1) and (x_2, y_2) using this ***distance formula***: $d = \sqrt{(x_2 - x_1)^2 + (y_2 - y_1)^2}$. Notice that it does not actually matter which point is considered the start of the line and the end of the line, since the change in each coordinate is squared in the distance formula.

Example:

In the figure below, what is the distance between P and Q?

y
Q (10, 9)
P (2, 3)
x

➤ The distance between P and Q is: $\sqrt{(x_2 - x_1)^2 + (y_2 - y_1)^2} = \sqrt{(10 - 2)^2 + (9 - 3)^2} = \sqrt{64 + 36} = \sqrt{100} = 10$.

Linear Functions

1. *Slope-Intercept Form*

If x and y are related by a linear equation, then y is a ***linear function***. Except for a vertical line, every line equation is a linear function that can be represented in ***slope-intercept form***: $y = mx + b$. m is the slope of the line and b is the y-intercept. The y-intercept is the y-coordinate of the point where the line intersects the y-axis, or where $x = 0$. The ***slope***, m, of a line describes the steepness of the line. It is defined as the change in y-values divided by the change in x-values, or rise over run: ***slope*** $= m = \frac{y_2 - y_1}{x_2 - x_1} = \frac{rise}{run}$.

Examples:

1. Find the slope of the line containing (3, 2) and (8, 22).
   ➢ $m = \frac{y_2 - y_1}{x_2 - x_1} = \frac{22-2}{8-3} = \frac{20}{5} = 4$.
2. Find the slope of the line given by the equation $6x + 12y = 13$.
   ➢ $6x + 12y = 13 \Rightarrow 12y = -6x + 13 \Rightarrow y = \frac{-6x+13}{12} \Rightarrow y = -\frac{x}{2} + \frac{13}{12}$. Therefore, the slope is $-\frac{1}{2}$.
3. The points (−5, 12), (0, 7) and (10, −3) lie on a line. What is the y-intercept of this line?
   ➢ The x-coordinate of the second point is 0. Therefore, this point's y-coordinate, 7, is the y-intercept of the line.

2. *Parallel Lines*

The equation of a line that is parallel to the x-axis is $y = k$, where is a constant. The equation of a line that is parallel to the y-axis is $x = c$, where c is a constant. If two lines are parallel, their slopes are equal and vice versa.

Example:

Find the equation for a line that passes through the point (0, 12) and is parallel to the line $y = 7x - 15$.
➢ A line has slope-intercept form $y = mx + b$. If the line passes through the y-axis at (0, 12), then the y-intercept $b = +12$. If the two lines are parallel, then the slopes are equal and $m = +7$. Therefore, the line equation is $y = mx + b \Rightarrow y = 7x + 12$.

3. *Perpendicular Lines*

If two perpendicular lines have slopes m_1 and m_2, then $m_1 = -\frac{1}{m_2}$ and vice versa.

Example:

The equation of a line is $y = \frac{x}{4} + 10$. If a second line is perpendicular to the line, what is the slope of this line?

➢ If two lines are perpendicular to one another, their slopes are opposite reciprocals of one another. Thus, if a line has a slope of $\frac{1}{4}$, then the line perpendicular to it has a slope of −4.

Quadratic Functions

If y is expressed in the form $y = ax^2 + bx + c$, where $a \neq 0$ and b is any real number, y is a ***quadratic function***. Graphs of quadratic functions are called parabolas. The basic graph that you need to know is $f(x) = x^2$, as illustrated in the first of the following examples.

Examples:

1. Which of the following graphs depicts a quadratic function?

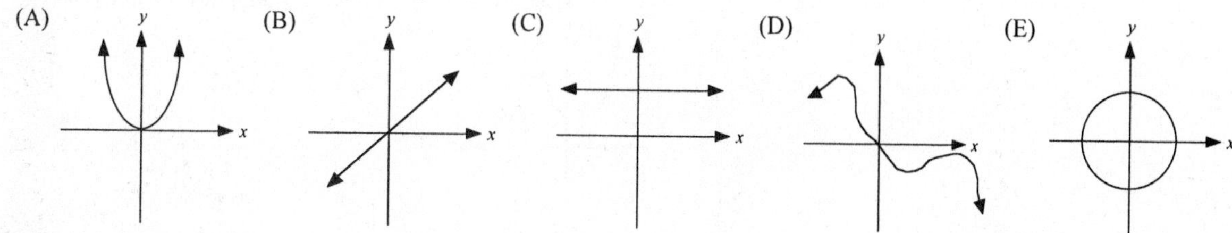

➢ All quadratic equations can be written in the form $y = ax^2 + bx + c$. (B) is a linear plot with the y-intercept equal to 0: $y = ax$. (C) is a constant value for y: $y = k$. (E) is a plot of a circle: $x^2 + y^2 = k$, where k is a constant. (D) is a complicated function without a standard form of equation. Only (A) is a quadratic equation: $y = ax^2$.

2. A quadratic function of the form $y = ax^2 + bx + c$ includes the following ordered pairs of (x, y): (1, 17), (5, 61), and (7, 95). What is the value of c for this quadratic function?

   ➤ Solve the system of three simultaneous equations that are generated by the three ordered pairs: $17 = a(1)^2 + b(1) + c$, $61 = a(5)^2 + b(5) + c$, and $95 = a(7)^2 + b(7) + c$. The quadratic function is $y = x^2 + 5x + 11$. Alternatively, the value of c can be determined by entering the three ordered pairs into a graphing calculator and using the quadratic regression feature.

Functions as Models

Functions can be mathematical models of real-life situations. For example, an item might present information about the projected sales of a product at various prices and ask for a mathematical model in the form of a graph or equation that represents projected sales as a function of price. Alternatively, you may be asked simply to identify graphs of linear and quadratic functions.

Example:

The line of best fit for $y = f(x)$ for the ordered pairs $(-4, -18)$, (1, 3), (2, 6), (3, 8), and (4, 14) is best represented by which of the following graphs?

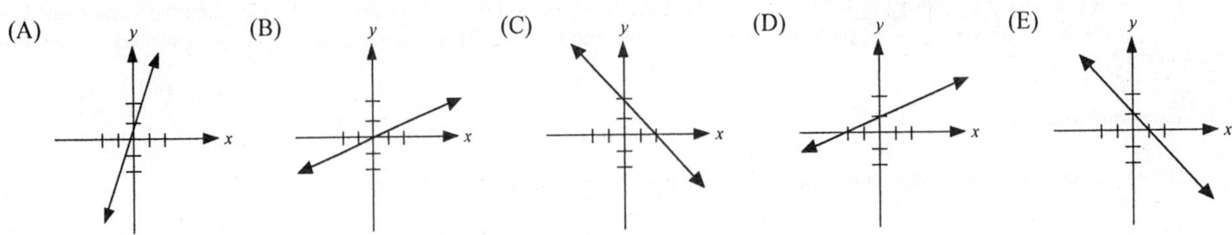

➤ The correct answer is (A). Both x and y increase in value for each ordered pair, so eliminate (C) and (E). You can eliminate (B) since the values of x and y in the given ordered pairs clearly indicate that $x \neq y$. Finally, eliminate (D) because when $x = 1$, $y = 3$, whereas in the graph of (D), $y < 3$ when $x = 1$.

Qualitative Behavior of Graphs

You should also understand how the graphs of functions behave qualitatively. Items on the exam might show the graph of a function in the xy-coordinate plane and ask for the number of values of x for which $f(x)$ equals a particular value. Alternatively, an item may present a graph with numerical values, requiring you to recognize the form of the graphed function.

Examples:

1. The figure below shows a graph of the function $y = x^2 + 2x + 6$. What is the smallest possible integer value of y?

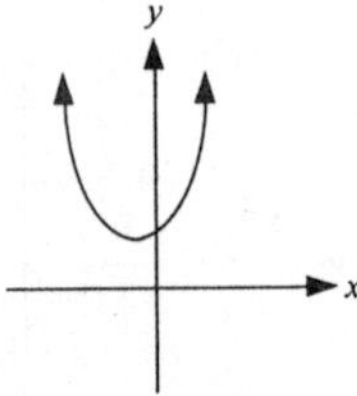

   ➤ The lowest point on the function occurs when $x < 0$. Find the symmetry by substitution: if $x = 1$, $y = 9$; if $x = 0$, $y = 6$; if $x = -1$, $y = 5$; if $x = -2$, $y = 6$; if $x = -3$, $y = 9$. The coordinates of these points are $(-3, 9)$, $(-2, 6)$, $(-1, 5)$, (0, 6), and (1, 9), respectively. Thus, the lowest point occurs at $(-1, 5)$. Alternatively, solve for the vertex using the properties of parabolas. The standard form of a parabola is: $y = a(x - h)^2 + k$, where the vertex is at (h, k). Write the equation in standard form: $y = (x^2 + 2x + 1) + 6 - 1 = (x + 1)^2 + 5 = [x - (-1)]^2 + 5$. Therefore, the vertex is at $(-1, 5)$.

2. What is the sum of all distinct integer y-values for the graph of the absolute value function in the figure below?

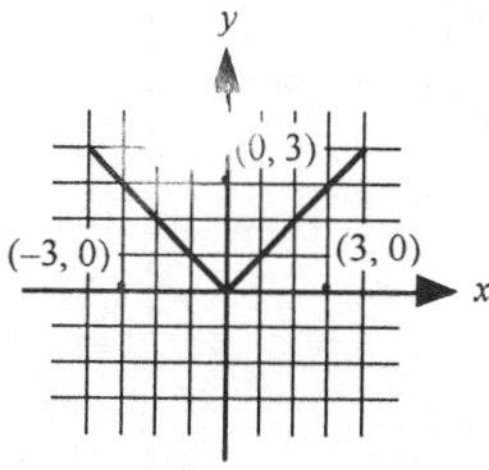

➤ Each negative y-value has a canceling positive y-value. Therefore, the answer is zero.

Transformation Effects on Graphs

When you alter a graph, you transform it. If you transform a graph without changing its shape, you translate it. Vertical and horizontal transformations are translations. Items on the exam may test knowledge of the effects of simple translations of graphs of functions. For example, the graph of a function $f(x)$ could be given and you might be asked items about the graph of the function $f(x + 2)$.

*1. **Vertical Translations***

To move a function up or down, you add or subtract outside the function. That is, $f(x) + b$ is $f(x)$ moved up b units, and $f(x) - b$ is $f(x)$ moved down b units.

Example:

In order to obtain the graph of $y = (x + 2)^2 + 6$ from the graph of $y = x^2 + 4x + 11$, how should the graph of $y = x^2 + 4x + 11$ be moved?

➤ Rewrite the original function in the form $f(x) + b$: $y = x^2 + 4x + 11 \Rightarrow y = x^2 + 4x + 4 + 7 = (x + 2)^2 + 7$. Therefore, to obtain the graph of $y = (x + 2)^2 + 6$ from the graph of $y = (x + 2)^2 + 7$, the graph must be moved one unit down.

*2. **Horizontal Translations***

To shift a function to the left or to the right, add or subtract inside the function. That is, $f(x + b)$ is $f(x)$ shifted b units to the left, and $f(x - b)$ is $f(x)$ shifted b units to the right.

Example:

The graph below is of the function $y = |x|$.

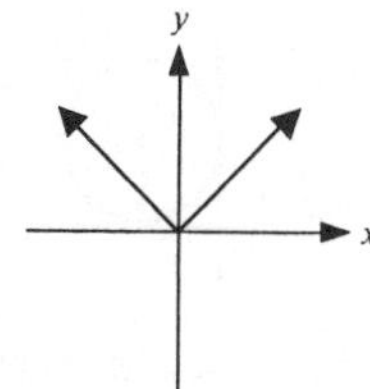

Which of the following is a graph of the function $y = |x + 3|$?

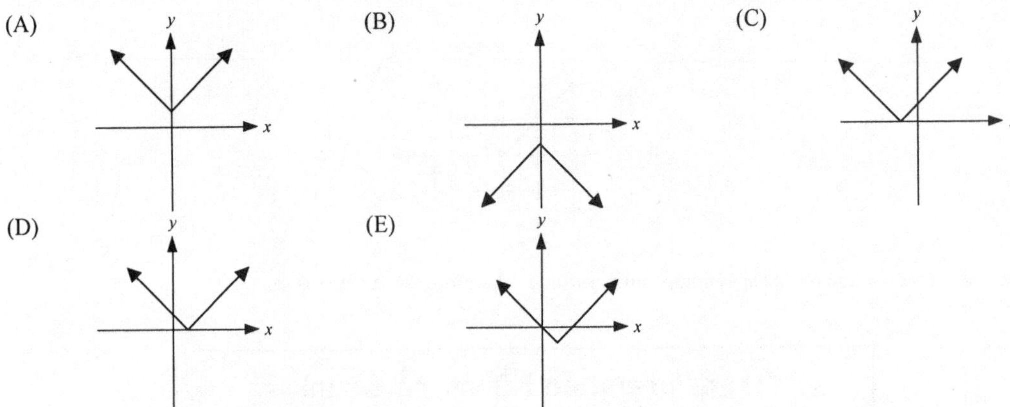

➤ By translation of the original graph from $y = |x|$ to $y = |x + 3|$, the original graph is moved three units to the left, (C). Alternatively, substitute values for x and y: $y = 0$ for $x = -3$. (C) is the only graph that contains the point $(-3, 0)$.

Graphing Geometric Figures

You can also use the coordinate system for graphing geometric figures. The following figure is a graph of a square whose vertices are at coordinates (0, 0), (4, 0), (4, 4), and (0, 4).

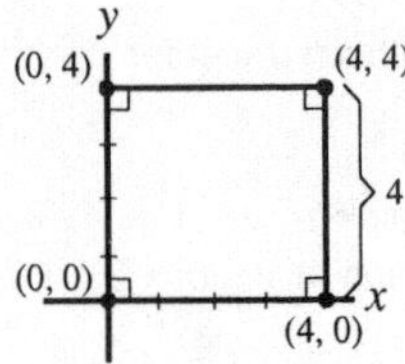

Each side of the square is equal to 4 since each side is 4 units long and parallel to either the x- or y-axis. Since every coordinate point is the perpendicular intersection of two lines, it is possible to measure distances in the coordinate system.

Examples:

1. In the figure below, what is the area of the circle?

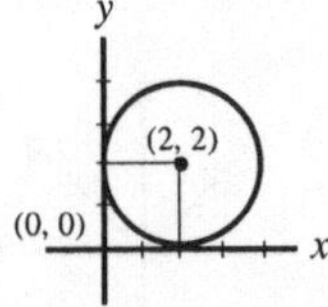

➤ To solve this problem, find the radius of the circle. The center of the circle is located at the intersection of $x = 2$ and $y = 2$, or the point (2, 2). Thus, the radius is 2 units long and the area is 4π.

2. ΔABC has coordinates A, B, and C equal to (5, 3), (19, 7), and (17, 25), respectively. By how much does the largest slope for any median of ΔABC exceed the largest slope for any altitude of ΔABC?

➤ The largest slope occurs for the steepest ascent for increasing values of x. Draw a figure of the given information in the coordinate plane:

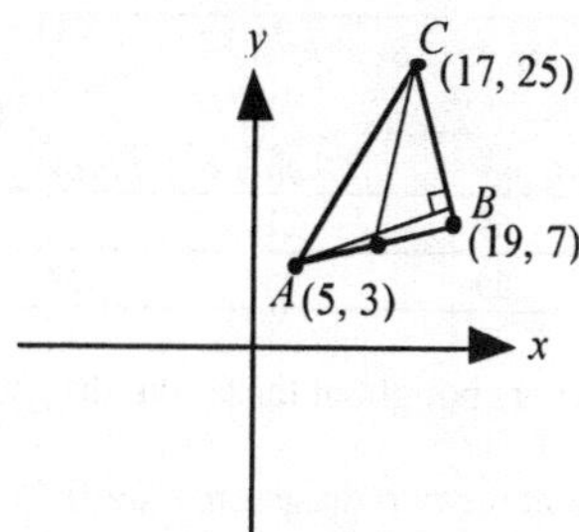

A median is drawn from one angle of a triangle to the midpoint of the opposite side. Of the three possible medians, the median that connects C to the midpoint of $\overline{AB}$ has the largest slope. The midpoint of $\overline{AB}$ is $\left(\frac{5+19}{2}, \frac{7+3}{2}\right) = (12, 5)$. Therefore, the slope of the median is $\frac{25-5}{17-12} = 4$. An altitude is drawn from one angle of a triangle to the opposite side at a right angle. Of the three possible altitudes, the altitude that connects A to $\overline{BC}$ has the largest slope. Since this altitude is perpendicular to $\overline{BC}$, its slope is the opposite reciprocal of the slope of $\overline{BC}$. The slope of $\overline{BC}$ is $\frac{25-7}{17-19} = \frac{18}{-2} = -9$, so the slope of the altitude $\frac{1}{9}$. Therefore, the amount by which the slope of the median is larger than the slope of the altitude is: $4 - \frac{1}{9} = \frac{36}{9} - \frac{1}{9} = \frac{35}{9}$.

Data Interpretation, Scatterplots, and Matrices

The test may ask about the line of best fit for a scatterplot. You would be expected to identify the general characteristics of the line of best fit by looking at the scatterplot. For example, an item may require you to identify that a line of best fit for a scatterplot has a slope that is positive but less than 1. You are not expected to use formal methods for finding the equation of a line of best fit.

Example:

The points in the scatter plot below show the relationship between 14 students' test scores on a mid-term test and a final test. What is the approximate average (arithmetic mean) of the scores on the final test for all students who scored above 90 on the midterm test?

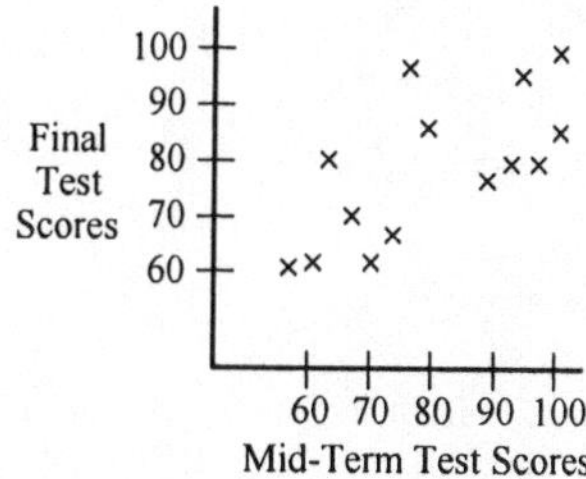

➤ Five students scored above 90 on the mid-term. Their marks are the five to the right on the scatterplot. The five corresponding scores on the final are approximately 80, 80, 85, 95, and 100. The average of these scores is approximately 88.

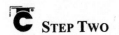

You are also expected to be able to interpret data displayed in tables, charts, and graphs.

Example:

The tables below show the number, type, and cost of candy bars bought during one week at two local drugstores.

	Number of Candy Bars Bought					
	Type A		*Type B*		*Type C*	
	Large	*Giant*	*Large*	*Giant*	*Large*	*Giant*
Drugstore *P*	60	20	69	21	43	17
Drugstore *Q*	44	18	59	25	38	13

	Cost per Candy Bar	
	Large	*Giant*
Type A	$0.45	$0.69
Type B	$0.45	$0.79
Type C	$0.55	$0.99

What is the total cost of all Type B candy bars bought at these two drugstores during the week?

➢ Total the cost of all Type B bars bought at the two drugstores: $69(0.45) + 21(0.79) + 59(0.45) + 25(0.79) = \$93.94$.

NOTE: The ACT, PLAN, and EXPLORE allow calculators. Therefore, it is important that you learn how to use a calculator and bring the same calculator with you to the exam.

EXERCISE 12

Functions, Graphs, and Coordinate Geometry

DIRECTIONS: Choose the correct answer to each of the following items. Use a calculator when necessary. Answers are on page 923.

1. Let $f(x) = \frac{x-2}{2x-13}$. If x represents a whole number, what is the largest value of x such that $f(x) < 0$?

   A. −1 B. 0 C. 1 D. 6 E. 8

2. If $f(x) = 8$ when $x = 2$ and $f(x) = 20$ when $x = 6$, then $f(x) = kx + w$. The value of $k + w$ is:

   A. 2 B. 4 C. 5 D. 8 E. 20

3. If $-5 < x < -1$, and $f(x) = |14 - |1 + 2x||$, then $f(x)$ equals:

   A. $13 - 2x$ B. $15 + 2x$ C. $13 + 2x$ D. $2x - 13$ E. $13 + 3x$

4. If $f(x) = \frac{kx}{3x+5}$, $x \neq -\frac{5}{3}$, k is a constant, and $f(x)$ satisfies the equation $f(f(x)) = x$ for all real values of x except for $x = -\frac{5}{3}$, what is the value of k?

   A. k cannot be uniquely determined.
   B. k does not equal any real value.
   C. $k = -\frac{5}{3}$
   D. $k = -\frac{3}{5}$
   E. $k = -5$

5. If $f(x) = 3 + 2^x$ and $g(x) = (2 + 3)^x$, then what is the value of $f(2) + g(3)$?

   A. 36 B. 132 C. 150 D. 225 E. 300

6. Which of the following graphs represents a relation of which the domain is the set of all real numbers and the range is the set of all non-negative real numbers?

   A.
   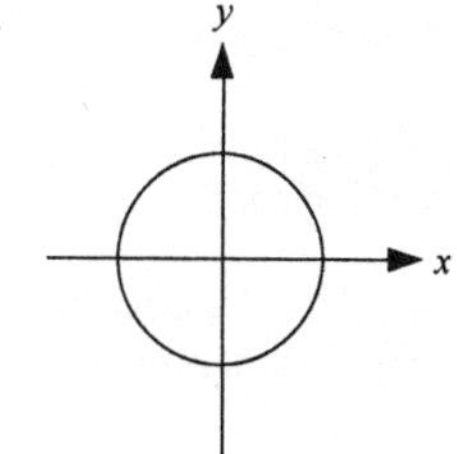

   B.
   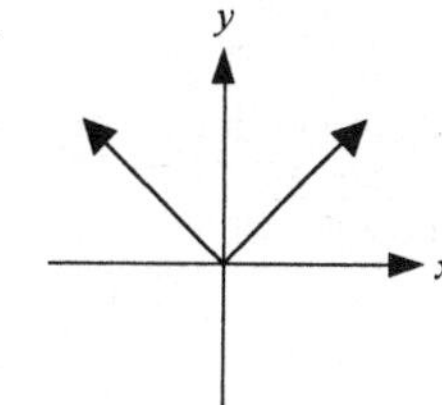

   C.
   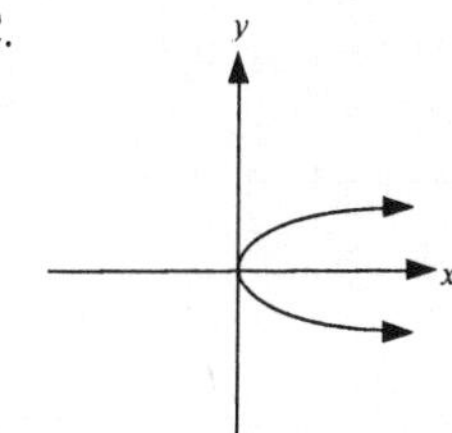

   D.
   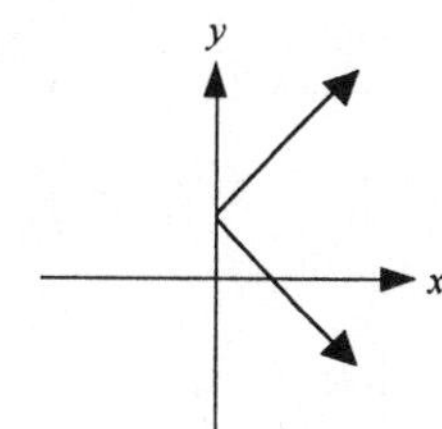

   E.
   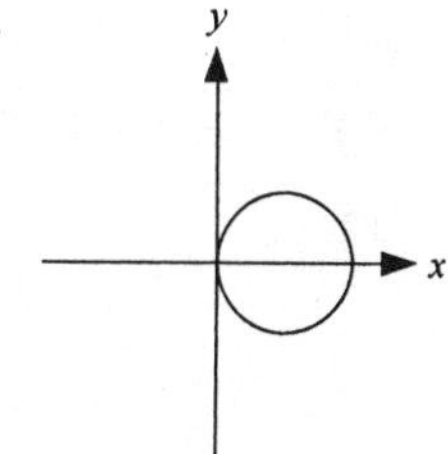

7. The range of the relation $\{(x, y) \mid y^2 = 4x\}$ is $\{0, 9, 16\}$. Which of the following is the domain?

A. {0, 20.25, 64}
B. {0, 3, 4}
C. {0, 36, 64}
D. {–4, –3, 0, 3, 4}
E. {0, 2.25, 4}

8. If $y = 2x + 1$ and the domain for x is the set of all non-negative integers, then the range for y is the set of which of the following?

A. non-negative integers
B. non-negative even integers
C. odd integers
D. positive odd integers
E. real numbers equal to or greater than 1

9. If $7x + 4y = 218$, and both x and y are positive integers, what is the sum of the two largest values in the range of y?

A. 433　C. 427　E. 95
B. 428　D. 101

10. How many whole numbers are not in the domain of values for x if $y = \frac{(x-1)(x-2)(x-3)}{x^2 - 11x + 30}$?

A. 1　C. 3　E. 5
B. 2　D. 4

11. Which of the lettered points on the number line below could represent the result when the coordinate of point F is divided by the coordinate of point X?

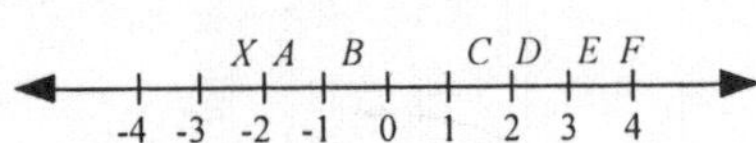

A. *A*　C. *C*　E. *E*
B. *B*　D. *D*

12. $\overline{AB}$ is the diameter of a circle whose center is point O. If the coordinates of point A are (2, 6) and the coordinates of point B are (6, 2), find the coordinates of point O.

A. (4, 4)　C. (2, –2)　E. (2, 2)
B. (4, –4)　D. (0, 0)

13. $\overline{AB}$ is the diameter of a circle whose center is point O. If the coordinates of point O are (2, 1) and the coordinates of point B are (4, 6), find the coordinates of point A.

A. $\left(3, 3\frac{1}{2}\right)$　C. $\left(0, -4\right)$　E. $\left(-1, -2\frac{1}{2}\right)$
B. $\left(1, 2\frac{1}{2}\right)$　D. $\left(2\frac{1}{2}, 1\right)$

14. Find the distance from the point whose coordinates are (4, 3) to the point whose coordinates are (8, 6).

A. 5　C. $\sqrt{7}$　E. 15
B. 25　D. $\sqrt{67}$

15. The vertices of a triangle are (2, 1), (2, 5), and (5, 1). What is the area of the triangle?

A. 12　C. 8　E. 5
B. 10　D. 6

16. The area of a circle whose center is at (0, 0) is 16π. The circle does NOT pass through which of the following points?

A. (4, 4)　C. (4, 0)　E. (0, –4)
B. (0, 4)　D. (–4, 0)

17. What is the slope of a line that passes through (0, –5) and (8, 27)?

A. 4　C. $\frac{8}{32}$　E. –4
B. 2　D. $-\frac{8}{32}$

18. The slope of a line that passes through points (3, 7) and (12, y) is $\frac{1}{3}$. What is the value of y?

A. 2　C. $6\frac{2}{3}$　E. 10
B. 4　D. $7\frac{1}{3}$

19. What is the slope of the line $y = 5x + 7$?

A. 7　C. 2　E. $\frac{1}{5}$
B. 5　D. $\frac{7}{5}$

20. A line passes through points (3, 8) and (w, $2k$). If $w \neq 3$, what is the slope of the line?

A. $\frac{8-2k}{3+w}$　C. $\frac{2k-8}{w-3}$　E. $\frac{3}{8}$
B. $\frac{2k+8}{w+3}$　D. $\frac{w-3}{2k-8}$

21. What is the equation of the line that passes through the point (0, 13) and is parallel to the line $4x + 2y = 17$?

A. $4x + 2y = 13$
B. $4x + 2y = -13$
C. $y = -2x + 13$
D. $y = 2x + 13$
E. Cannot be determined from the given information

22. A line passes through the point (0, −5) and is perpendicular to the line $y = -\frac{x}{2} + 5$. What is the equation of the line?

A. $y = -\frac{x}{2} - 5$
B. $y = 2x - 5$
C. $y = -2x - 5$
D. $y = -\frac{x}{2} + 13$
E. Cannot be determined from the given information

23. If point P has coordinates (−2, 2) and point Q has coordinates (2, 0), what is the distance from point P to point Q?

A. −4
B. $2\sqrt{5}$
C. $4\sqrt{5}$
D. 4
E. 6

24. If point R has coordinates (x, y) and point S has coordinates $(x + 1, y + 1)$, what is the distance between point R and point S?

A. $\sqrt{2}$
B. 2
C. $\sqrt{x^2 + y^2}$
D. $\sqrt{x^2 + y^2 + 2}$
E. $x + y + 1$

25. Will is standing 40 yards due north of point P. Grace is standing 60 yards due west of point P. What is the shortest distance between Will and Grace?

A. 20 yards
B. $4\sqrt{13}$ yards
C. $20\sqrt{13}$ yards
D. 80 yards
E. $80\sqrt{13}$ yards

26. On a coordinate graph, what is the distance between points (5, 6) and (6, 7)?

A. $\sqrt{2}$
B. 1
C. 2
D. 4
E. $6\sqrt{2}$

27. On a coordinate plane, point B is located 7 units to the left of point A. The x-coordinate of point A is x, and the y-coordinate of point A is y. What is the x-coordinate of point B?

A. $x - 7$
B. $x + 7$
C $y + 7$
D. $y - 7$
E. Cannot be determined from the given information

28. Point R is represented on the coordinate plane by (x, y). The vertical coordinate of point S is three times the vertical coordinate of point R and the two points have the same horizontal coordinate. The ordered pair that represents point S is:

A. $(3x, y)$
B. $(x, y + 3)$
C. $(x, y - 3)$
D. $(3x, 3y)$
E. $(x, 3y)$

29. A square is drawn in a coordinate plane. Which of the following transformations of the square will shift the square 7 units to the right and 5 units downward?

A. Add 7 to each x-coordinate and add 5 to each y-coordinate.
B. Multiply each x-coordinate by 7 and divide each y-coordinate by 5.
C. Add 7 to each x-coordinate and subtract 5 from each y-coordinate.
D. Subtract 7 from each x-coordinate and subtract 5 from each y-coordinate.
E. Subtract 7 from each x-coordinate and add 5 to each y-coordinate.

30. In the rectangular coordinate system below, if $x = 4.2$, then y equals which of the following?

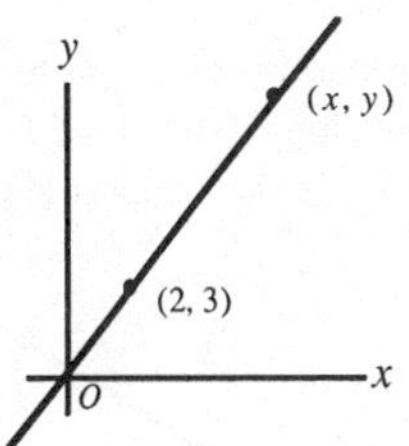

A. 2.8
B. 3.4
C. 4.8
D. 6.2
E. 6.3

31. Points $(x, -4)$ and $(-1, y)$ (not shown in the figure below) are in Quadrants III and II, respectively. If x and $y \neq 0$, in which quadrant is point (x, y)?

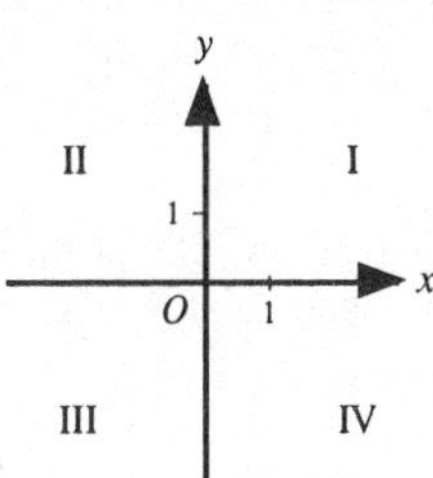

A. I
B. II
C. III
D. IV
E. Cannot be determined from the given information

32. If Sam lives 8 miles west of Jeni, and Molly lives 10 miles north of Jeni, approximately how many miles less would Molly walk if she walks directly to Sam's house, rather than first to Jeni's house and then to Sam's house?

A. 1
B. 2
C. 3
D. 4
E. 5

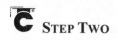

33. If point B (not shown in the figure below) lies below the x-axis at point (4, −4), what is the area of ΔABC?

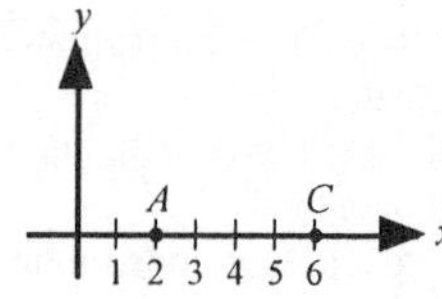

A. 2
B. 4
C. 6
D. 8
E. 16

34. On a coordinate graph, what is the distance between points (−1, 4) and (2, 8)?

A. 3
B. 4
C. 5
D. 6
E. 8

35. In the figure below, $\overline{AB}$ is the base of a water ski ramp and is 18 feet long. The slope (rise divided by run) of the ramp is m. If the ramp is y feet high, then what is the value of y?

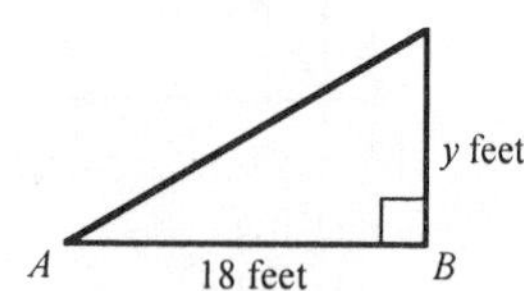

A. $\frac{m}{18}$
B. $18m$
C. $18 - m$
D. $m - 18$
E. $m + 18$

36. What is the midpoint between (−2, 15) and (8, 17)?

A. (6, 16)
B. (3, 16)
C. (5, 16)
D. (5, 32)
E. (6, 32)

37. In the figure below, $\overline{AB}$ is the diameter of a circle whose center is at point P. What are the coordinates for point B?

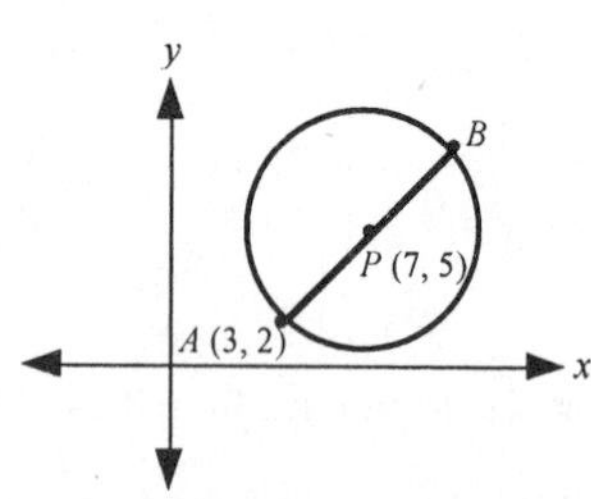

A. (10, 7)
B. (5, 2.5)
C. (12, 7)
D. (11, 8)
E. (11, 7)

38. If $f(x) = 17x + 14$, then $f(2) + f(3) + f(4)$ is:

A. 195
B. 153
C. 126
D. 102
E. 51

39. How many of the following graphs are graphs of linear functions?

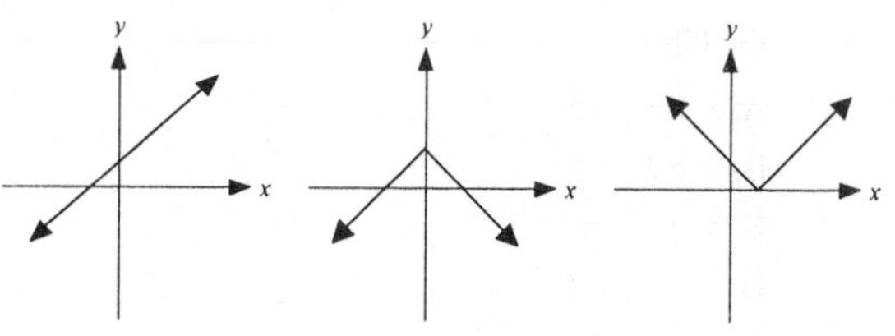

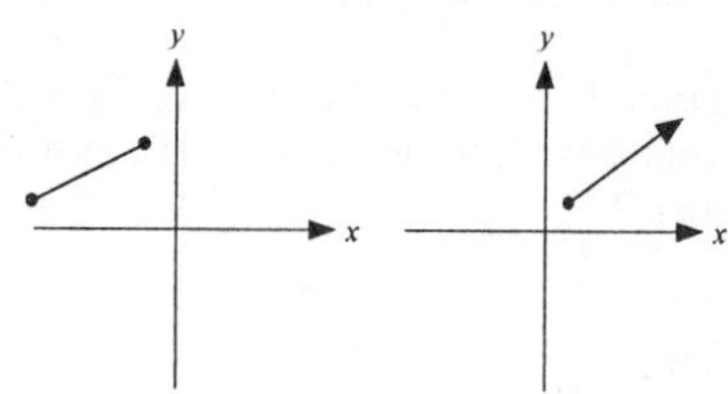

A. 1
B. 2
C. 3
D. 4
E. 5

40. $f(x)$ and $g(x)$ represent linear functions. If $f(x) = 5$ for $x = 1$, $g(x) = 3x + 8$, and $f(x) = g(x)$ for $x = 2$, then what is the value of $f(4)$?

A. 12
B. 16
C. 20
D. 24
E. 32

41. In each of the following four sets, the three ordered pairs belong to a linear function. In how many of the four sets is the value of the variable x less than zero?

{(0, 1), (−4, −7), (x, 0)}
{(0, 2), (−5, 52), (x, 12)}
{(2, −5), (−2, −17), (x, 13)}
{(6, 17), (8, 25), (x, 4)}

A. 0
B. 1
C. 2
D. 3
E. 4

42. If $y = mx + b$, $x = 5$ for $y = 20$, and $x = 9$ for $y = 32$, then $m + b$ is:

A. 76
B. 52
C. 14
D. 8
E. 3

43. Which of the following graphs depicts the quadratic functions $y = \frac{x^2}{2}$ and $y = -\frac{x^2}{2}$?

A.
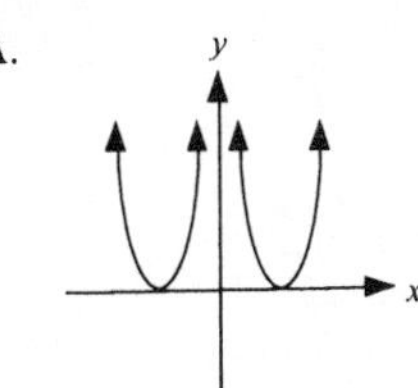

D.
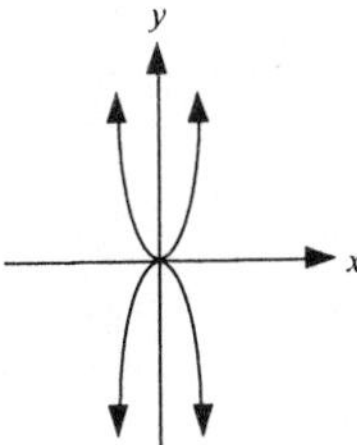

B.
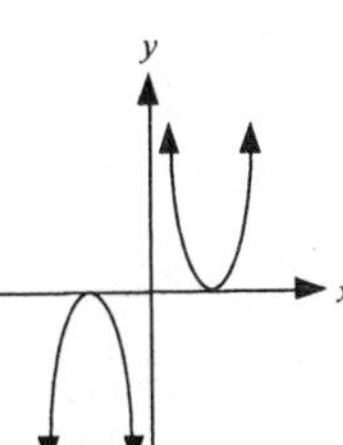

E.
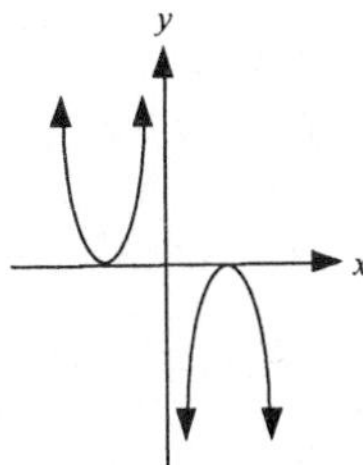

C.
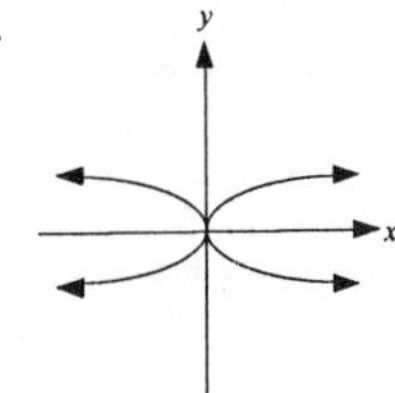

44. If $y = -2x^2 + 16x - 1$, what is the largest possible value for y?

A. −1
B. 13
C. 31
D. 32
E. Cannot be determined from the given information

45. The graph of $y = 4x^2$ intersects the graph of $y = x^2 + 3x$ at how many points?

A. 0 C. 2 E. 4
B. 1 D. 3

46. A student noted that the graph of the following ordered points for (x, y) appeared to approximate a parabolic curve: (1, 7), (−1, 0), (2, 12), (4, 29), (5, 42). Which of the following equations best represents the curve?

A. $y = x^2 + 6$
B. $y = x^2 + 3x + 2$
C. $y = 2x^2 + x + 4$
D. $y = x^2 - x + 8$
E. $y = 2x^2 + x + 4$

47. The graph of the following ordered pairs for (x, y) is approximately a straight line of the form $y = mx + b$: (1, 18), (2, 23), (3, 27), (4, 32), (5, 38). Which of the following best approximates the value of b?

A. 13 C. 20 E. 25
B. 18 D. 23

48. A scientist studying insect movement observes that in a day, each insect travels a particular geometric pattern and the distance traveled by each insect is directly proportional to the insect's length. The values for insect length and distance traveled in a day, in inches, for four insects are: (1, 1.57), (1.5, 2.36), (2, 3.14), and (3, 4.71). The geometric pattern traveled by the four insects is a:

A. square
B. equilateral triangle
C. circle
D. semicircle
E. regular polygon of five sides

49. The figure below shows two parallel lines with coordinates of points as shown. What is the slope of the line passing through point (0, 6)?

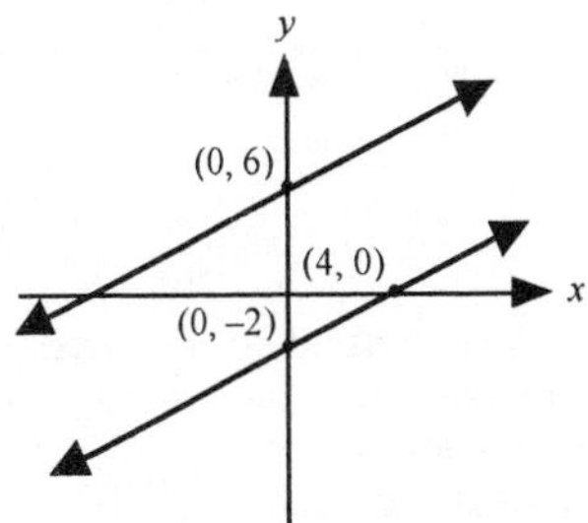

A. $\frac{1}{2}$ C. $\frac{1}{4}$ E. $\frac{1}{6}$
B. $\frac{1}{3}$ D. $\frac{1}{5}$

50. The center of a circle is located at (19, 7). One end of a diameter of the circle is located at (4, 6). The second end of the diameter is located at:

A. (11.5, 6.5) C. (34, 8) E. (38, 8)
B. (11.5, 13) D. (38, 14)

51. In the figure below, which is not necessarily drawn to scale, $ABCD$ is a square and $\angle FGH \cong \angle A$.

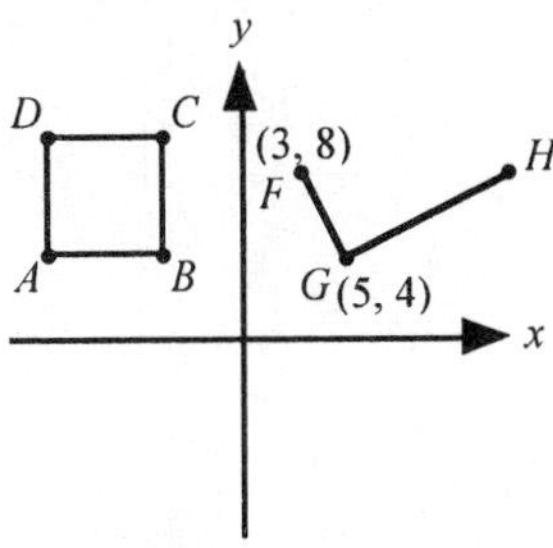

If points F and G have the coordinates as indicated in the figure, how many of the following four ordered pairs could possibly represent point H?

(8, 6), (9, 6), (11, 7), (13, 8)

A. 0 C. 2 D. 3
B. 1 E. 4

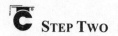

52. The line that passes through (1, 5) and (−2, 17) is parallel to the line that passes through (17, 6) and (13, y). What is the value of y?

A. 10 C. 16 E. 22
B. 14 D. 18

53. What is the distance from the point (−2, 5) to the point (7, −7)?

A. 9 C. 15 E. 24
B. 12 D. 18

54. The figure below shows a circle with an area of 9π.

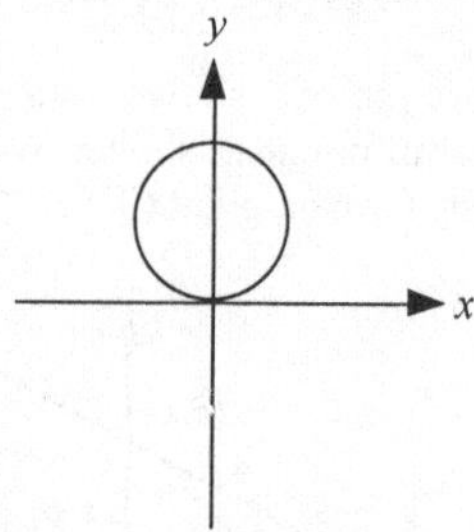

The circle is tangent to the x-axis at (0, 0) and the center of the circle lies on the y-axis. The constant function $y = k$ intersects the circle at exactly one point. If $k > 0$, what is the value of k?

A. 1 C. 3 E. 9
B. 2 D. 6

55. The figure below shows a graph of $y = \frac{12}{x^2 + 6x + 7}$. How many different integers for y are not a part of the graph of $y = \frac{12}{x^2 + 6x + 7}$?

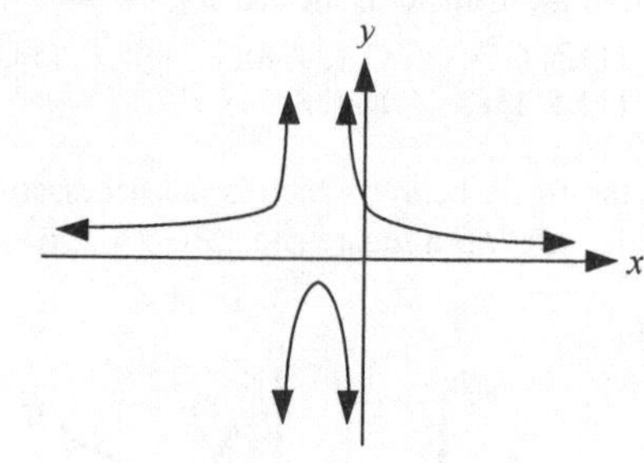

A. 2 C. 7 E. 13
B. 6 D. 12

56. The graph below shows two different parabola functions: $y = (x - 1)^2 + 4$ and $y - 2 = -(x + 5)^2$.

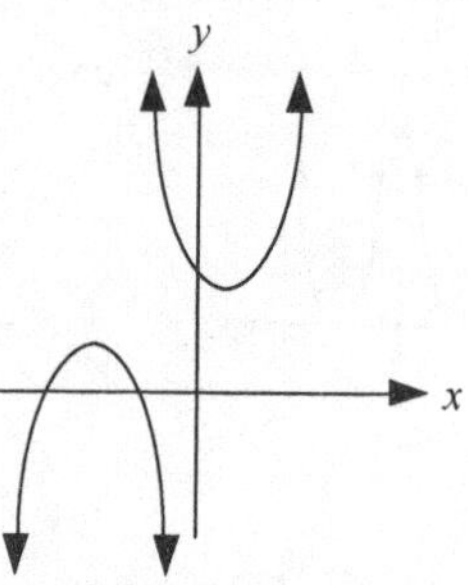

The values of y that are not on either of the parabolas are all values of y such that:

A. $-5 \leq y \leq 1$ C. $1 < y < 4$ E. $4 < y < 5$
B. $2 < y < 4$ D. $1 \leq y \leq 5$

57. The graph below is of the function $y = (x - 2)^2 + 3$.

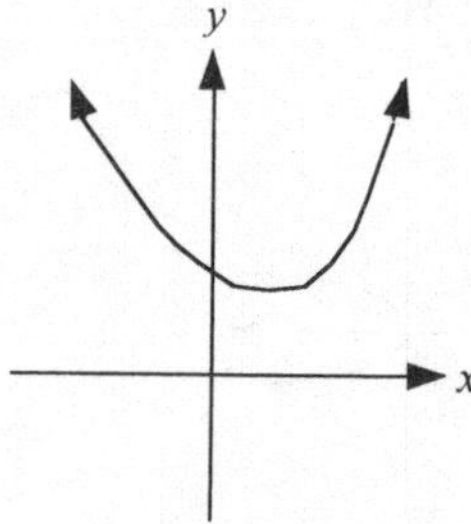

If a horizontal shift of four units to the left were performed on the original graph, at what point (x, y) would the transformed graph intersect the original graph?

A. (2, 7) C. (6, 3) E. (0, 3)
B. (2, −1) D. (−2, 3)

58. The graph of $y = 3x^2$ can be produced from the graph of $y = x^2$ by performing a vertical stretch by a factor of three. The graph of $y = 2x^2 + 12x + 1$ can be produced from the graph of $y = x^2$ by performing a vertical stretch by a factor of two, a horizontal shift of three units to the left, and a vertical shift of:

A. 17 units down.
B. 12 units down.
C. 1 unit down.
D. 1 unit up.
E. 12 units up.

59. The graph below shows a circle whose equation is $x^2 + y^2 = 16$.

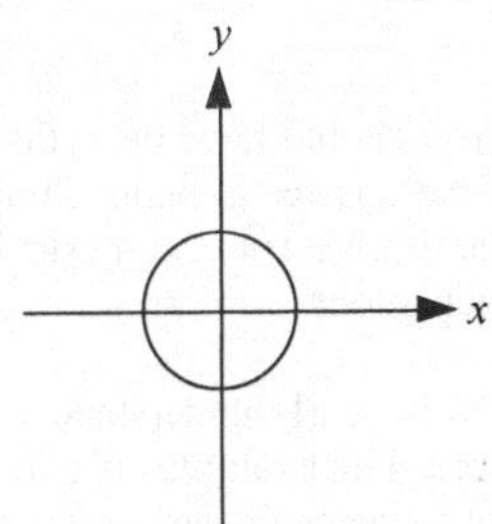

The graph is moved by the following transformations: four units to the right and two units up. Which of the following is the correctly transformed graph?

A.
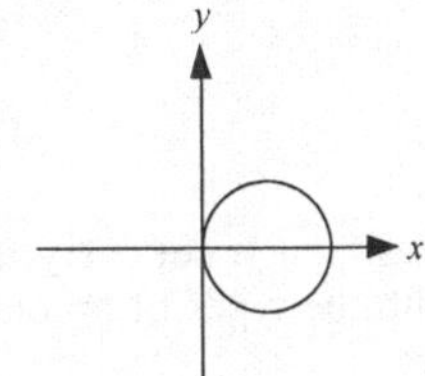

D.
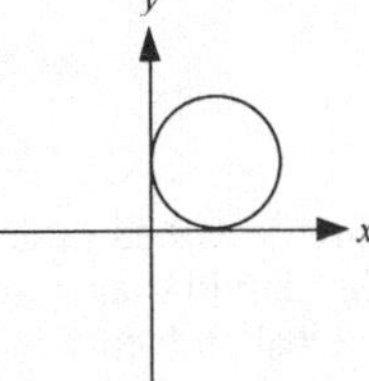

B.
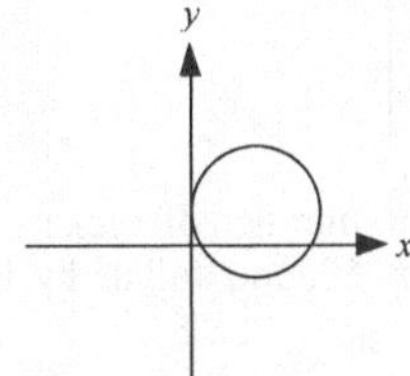

E.
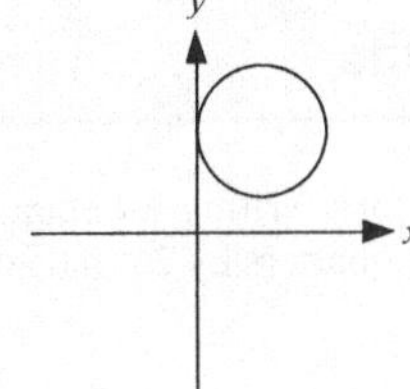

C.
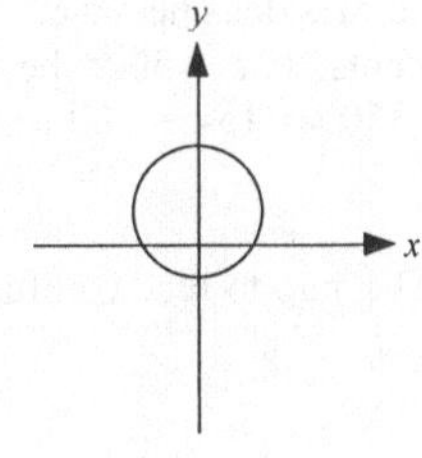

60. The stronger the relationship between two variables, the more closely the points on a scatter plot will approach some linear or curvilinear pattern. Which of the scatter plots below represents the strongest relationship between the two variables?

A.
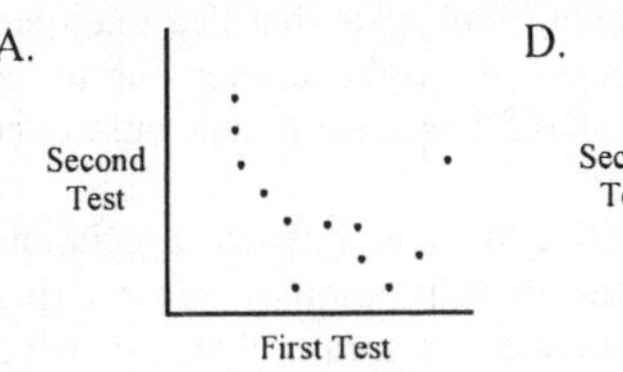

D.
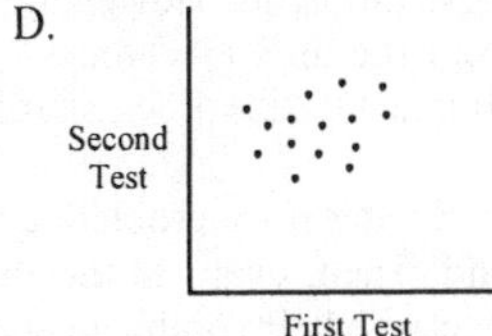

B.
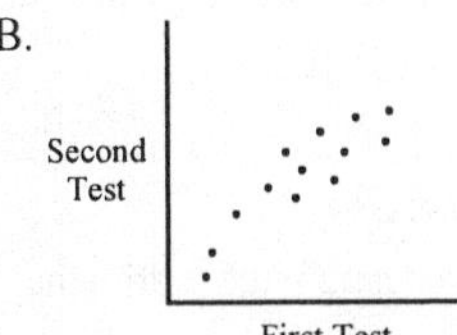

E.
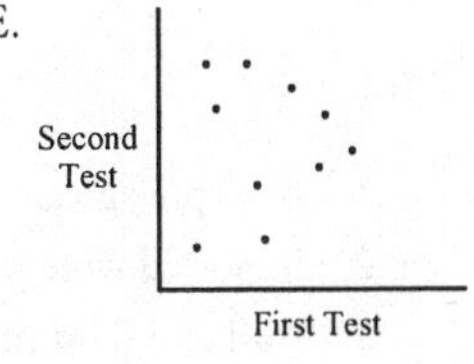

C.
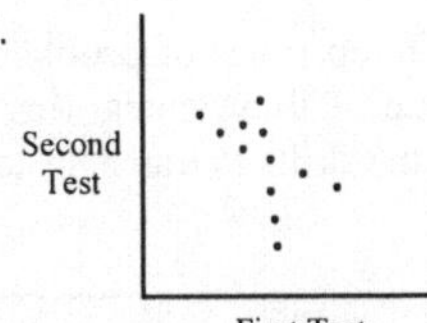

61. The following ordered pairs for (x, y) represent points on a graph: (5, 15), (10, 28), (11, 27), (25, 47), (40, 76), (50, 111), and (60, 129). Which of the following equations represents the line of best fit (the line that most closely approximates the set of points)?

A. $y = \frac{x}{3}$
B. $y = \frac{x}{3} - 2$
C. $y = 3x - 6$
D. $y = 2x + 3$
E. $y = 5x - 4$

Solving Story Problems

Story problems may test arithmetic, algebra, or geometry in the context of a "story." You should have everything you need to solve these problems. However, remember that if a math story item stumps you, you have the answer at hand. Simply work backwards from the answer choices—the right answer has to be one of the choices. Since quantitative (*i.e.*, numerical value) choices are arranged in size order, starting with the middle answer choice will result in the fewest calculations.

In solving story problems, the most important technique is to read accurately. Be sure you clearly understand what you are asked to find. Then, evaluate the item in common sense terms and to eliminate answer choices. For example, if two people are working together, their combined speed is greater than either individual speed, but not more than twice as fast as the fastest speed. Finally, be alert for the "hidden equation"—some necessary information so obvious that the item assumes that you know it.

Examples:

1. boys plus girls = total class
2. imported wine plus domestic wine = all wine
3. wall and floor make a right angle (Pythagorean theorem)

Some of the frequently encountered types of problem-solving problems are described in this section, although not every item you may encounter will fall into one of these categories. However, thoroughly familiarizing yourself with the types of problems that follow will help you to develop the skills to translate and solve all kinds of verbal problems.

Coin Problems

For coin ***problems***, change the value of all monies involved to cents before writing an equation. The number of nickels must be multiplied by 5 to give their value in cents; dimes must be multiplied by 10; quarters by 25; half-dollars by 50; and dollars by 100.

Example:

Richard has $3.50 consisting of nickels and dimes. If he has 5 more dimes than nickels, how many dimes does he have?
➤ Let x = the number of nickels; $x + 5$ = the number of dimes; $5x$ = the value of the nickels in cents; $10x + 50$ = the value of the dimes in cents; and 350 = the value of the money he has in cents. Thus: $5x + 10x + 50 = 350 \Rightarrow 15x = 300 \Rightarrow x = 20$. Therefore, Richard has 20 nickels and 25 dimes.

In an item such as this, you can be sure that 20 would be among the multiple-choice answers. You must be sure to read carefully what you are asked to find and then continue until you have found the quantity sought.

Number and Set Problems

Number problems can be story problems that require knowledge of the properties of numbers in order to solve the item. Typically, number problems involve ***consecutive integers*** or ***consecutive odd/even numbers***. Consecutive integers are one number apart and can be represented by x, $x + 1$, $x + 2$, *etc.* Consecutive even or odd integers are two numbers apart and can be represented by x, $x + 2$, $x + 4$, *etc.*

Example:

Three consecutive odd integers have a sum of 33. Find the average of these integers.
➤ Represent the integers as x, $x + 2$, and $x + 4$. Write an equation indicating the sum is 33: $3x + 6 = 33 \Rightarrow 3x = 27 \Rightarrow x = 9$. Thus, the integers are 9, 11, and 13. In the case of evenly spaced numbers such as these, the average is the middle number, 11. Since the sum of the three numbers was given originally, all we really had to do was to divide this sum by 3 to find the average, without ever knowing what the numbers were.

Set problems test understanding of relationships between different sets of numbers or ***elements***. A ***set*** is a collection of things; *e.g.*, the set of positive integers.

DEFINITIONS FOR WORKING WITH SETS

The ***number of elements*** in set P is: $n(P)$.

The ***union*** of two sets P and Q is the set of all elements in *either* P or Q, or both: $P \cup Q$.
The ***intersection*** of two sets P and Q is the set of all elements in *both* P and Q: $P \cap Q$.

The ***cardinal number theorem*** is used find the number of elements in a union of two sets.
$$n(P \cup Q) = n(P) + n(Q) - n(P \cap Q)$$

Examples:

1. Let $S = \{3, 5, x\}$. If exactly one subset of S contains two different elements whose sum is 12, what value(s) can x be?
   ➤ Since either $3 + x = 12$ or $5 + x = 12$, then $x = 9$ or $x = 7$.
2. In a class of 30 students, 15 students are learning French, 11 students are learning Spanish, and 7 students are learning neither French nor Spanish. How many students in the class are learning both French and Spanish?
   ➤ Use the cardinal number theorem: $n(F \cup S) = n(F) + n(S) - n(F \cap S) \Rightarrow 30 - 7 = 15 + 11 - n(F \cap S) \Rightarrow n(F \cap S) = 3$.

A ***Venn diagram*** may help to solve problems involving sets that overlap.

Example:

Two circles are drawn on a floor. 20 people are standing in circle A. 15 people are standing in circle B. 9 people are standing in both circles. Find the total number of people standing in the two circles.
➤ The item can be symbolized with a Venn diagram:

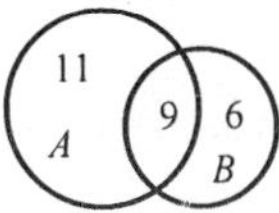

From the diagram, it can be seen that there are a total of $11 + 9 + 6$ or 26 people.

Age Problems

Age problems involve a comparison of ages at the present time, several years from now, or several years ago. A person's age x years from now is found by adding x to his present age. A person's age x years ago is found by subtracting x from his present age.

Example:

Michelle was 12 years old y years ago. What is her age b years from now?
➤ Michelle's present age is $12 + y$. In b years, her age will be $12 + y + b$.

Interest Problems

To calculate the annual amount of interest paid on an investment, multiply the principal invested by the rate (percent) of interest paid: ***Interest income = principal • rate***.

Example:

Mr. Krecker invests \$4,000, part at 6% and part at 7%; the first year return is \$250. Find the amount invested at 7%.

➢ Let x equal the amount invested at 7%. Thus, $4{,}000 - x$ equals the amount invested at 6%; $0.07x$ equals the income from the 7% investment; and $0.06(4{,}000 - x)$ equals the income from the 6% investment. Therefore: $0.07x + 0.06(4{,}000 - x) = 250 \Rightarrow 7x + 6(4{,}000 - x) = 25{,}000 \Rightarrow 7x + 24{,}000 - 6x = 25{,}000 \Rightarrow x = 1{,}000$ (\$1,000 invested at 7%).

Mixture Problems

You should be familiar with two kinds of ***mixture problems***. The first type is sometimes referred to as dry mixture, in which dry ingredients of different values, such as nuts or coffee, are mixed. The second type of mixture item deals with different priced tickets. For this type of problem, it is best to organize the data in a chart of three rows and three columns labeled as illustrated in the following problem.

Example:

A dealer wishes to mix 20 pounds of nuts selling for 45 cents per pound with some more expensive nuts selling for 60 cents per pound to make a mixture that will sell for 50 cents per pound. How many pounds of the more expensive nuts should he use?

➢ Create table summarizing the provided information:

	No. of lbs. ×	Price/lb. =	Total Value
Original	20	0.45	0.45(20)
Added	x	0.60	$0.60(x)$
Mixture	$20 + x$	0.50	$0.50(20 + x)$

The value of the original nuts plus the value of the added nuts must equal the value of the mixture: $0.45(20) + 0.60(x) = 0.50(20 + x) \Rightarrow 45(20) + 60(x) = 50(20 + x) \Rightarrow 900 + 60x = 1{,}000 + 50x \Rightarrow 10x = 100 \Rightarrow x = 10$. Therefore, he should use 10 lbs. of 60-cent nuts.

The second type of mixture item deals with percents and amounts rather than prices and value.

Example:

How much water must be added to 20 gallons of solution that is 30% alcohol to dilute it to a solution that is only 25% alcohol?

➢ Create a table summarizing the provided information:

	No. of gals. ×	% alcohol =	Amt. alcohol
Original	20	0.30	0.30(20)
Added	x	0	0
Mixture	$20 + x$	0.25	$0.25(20 + x)$

Note that the percent of alcohol in water is zero. Had pure alcohol been added to strengthen the solution, the percent would have been 100. Thus, the amount of alcohol added (none) plus the original amount must equal the amount of alcohol in the new solution: $0.30(20) = 0.25(20 + x) \Rightarrow 30(20) = 25(20 + x) \Rightarrow 600 = 500 + 25x \Rightarrow 100 = 25x \Rightarrow x = 4$ gallons.

Motion Problems

The fundamental relationship in all ***motion problems*** is ***distance = rate • time***. The problems at the level of this examination usually derive their equation from a relationship concerning distance. Most problems fall into one of three types.

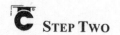

1. *Motion in Opposite Directions*

When two objects moving at the same speed start at the same time and move in opposite directions, or when two objects start at points at a given distance apart and move toward each other until they meet, then the distance the second travels will equal one-half the total distance covered. Either way, the total distance = $d_1 + d_2$:

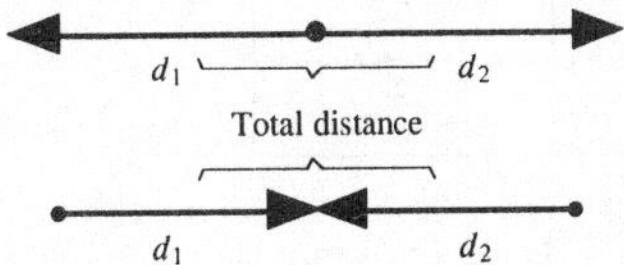

2. *Motion in the Same Direction*

This type of item is sometimes called the "catch-up" problem. Two objects leave the same place in the same direction at different times and at different rates, but one "catches up" to the other. In such a case, the two distances must be equal.

3. *Round Trip*

In this type of problem, the rate going is usually different from the rate returning. The times are also different. But if we go somewhere and then return to the starting point, the distances must be the same.

To solve any motion problem, it is helpful to organize the data in a box with columns for rate, time, and distance. A separate line should be used for each moving object. Remember that if the rate is given in *miles per hour*, the time must be in *hours* and the distance in *miles.*

Examples:

1. Two cars leave a restaurant at 1 p.m., with one car traveling east at 60 miles per hour and the other west at 40 miles per hour along a straight highway. At what time will they be 350 miles apart?

   ➢ Create a table summarizing the provided information:

	Rate ×	Time =	Distance
Eastbound	60	x	$60x$
Westbound	40	x	$40x$

   Notice that the time is unknown, since we must determine the number of hours traveled. However, since the cars start at the same time and stop when they are 350 miles apart, their times are the same: $60x + 40x = 350 \Rightarrow 100x = 350 \Rightarrow x = 3.5$. Therefore, in 3.5 hours, it will be 4:30 p.m.

2. Gloria leaves home for school, riding her bicycle at a rate of 12 m.p.h. Twenty minutes after she leaves, her mother sees Gloria's English paper on her bed and leaves to bring it to her. If her mother drives at 36 m.p.h, how far must she drive before she reaches Gloria?

   ➢ Create a table summarizing the provided information:

	Rate ×	Time =	Distance
Gloria	12	x	$12x$
Mother	36	$x-\frac{1}{3}$	$36\left(x-\frac{1}{3}\right)$

   The 20 minutes has been converted to $\frac{1}{3}$ of an hour. In this problem, the times are not equal, but the distances are: $12x = 36\left(x-\frac{1}{3}\right) = 36x - 12 \Rightarrow 12 = 24x \Rightarrow x = \frac{1}{2}$. Thus, if Gloria rode for $\frac{1}{2}$ hour at 12 m.p.h., the distance covered was 6 miles.

3. Nisha leaves home at 11 a.m. and rides to Andrea's house to return her bicycle. She travels at 12 miles per hour and arrives at 11:30 a.m. She turns right around and walks home. How fast does she walk if she returns home at 1 p.m.?

➢ Create a table summarizing the provided information:

	Rate $\times$	Time $=$	Distance
Going	12	$\frac{1}{2}$	6
Return	x	$1\frac{1}{2}$	$\frac{3x}{2}$

The distances are equal: $6 = \frac{3x}{2} \Rightarrow 12 = 3x \Rightarrow x = 4$ m.p.h.

Variation Problems

Variation in mathematics refers to the interrelationship of variables in such a manner that a change of value for one variable produces a corresponding change in another. There are three basic types of variation: ***direct***, ***inverse***, and ***joint***.

1. ***Direct Variation***

The expression "x varies directly with y" can be described by any of the following equations.

DIRECT VARIATION RELATIONSHIPS

$y = kx$, k is a constant $\qquad \frac{x_1}{y_1} = \frac{x_2}{y_2}$

Two quantities are said to vary directly if they change in the same direction. As one increases, the other increases and their ratio is equal to the positive constant.

For example, the amount you must pay for milk varies directly with the number of quarts of milk you buy. The amount of sugar needed in a recipe varies directly with the amount of butter used. The number of inches between two cities on a map varies directly with the number of miles between these cities.

Example:

If x varies directly as y^2, and $x = 12$ when $y = 2$, what is the value of x when $y = 3$?

➢ Notice that the variation involves the square of y. Therefore: $\frac{x_1}{y_1^2} = \frac{x_2}{y_2^2} \Rightarrow \frac{12}{2^2} = \frac{x}{3^2} \Rightarrow \frac{12}{4} = \frac{x}{9} \Rightarrow 3 = \frac{x}{9} \Rightarrow x = 27$.

2. ***Inverse Variation***

The expression "x varies inversely as y" can be described by any of the following equations.

INVERSE VARIATION RELATIONSHIPS

$xy = k$, k is a constant $\qquad \frac{x_1}{y_2} = \frac{x_2}{y_1}$

Two quantities vary inversely if they change in opposite directions. As one quantity increases, the other quantity decreases.

For example, the number of people hired to paint a house varies inversely with the number of days the job will take. A doctor's stock of flu vaccine varies inversely with the number of patients she injects. The number of days a given supply of cat food lasts varies inversely with the number of cats being fed.

Example:

The time t to empty a container varies inversely with the square root of the number of men m working on the job. If it takes 3 hours for 16 men to do the job, how long will it take 4 men working at the same rate to empty the container?

➤ $\frac{t_1}{\sqrt{m_2}} = \frac{t_2}{\sqrt{m_1}} \Rightarrow t_1\sqrt{m_1} = t_2\sqrt{m_2} \Rightarrow 3\sqrt{16} = t\sqrt{4} \Rightarrow t = 3 \cdot \frac{\sqrt{16}}{\sqrt{4}} = 3(\sqrt{4}) = 3 \cdot 2 = 6.$

3. ***Joint Variation***

The expression "x varies jointly as y and z" can be described by any of the following equations.

JOINT VARIATION RELATIONSHIPS

$\frac{x}{yz} = k$, k is a constant $\qquad \frac{x_1}{y_1z_1} = \frac{x_2}{y_2z_2} \qquad \frac{x_1}{x_2} = \left(\frac{y_1}{y_2}\right)\left(\frac{z_1}{z_2}\right)$

Example:

The area, A, of a triangle varies jointly as the base b and the height h. If $A = 20$ when $b = 10$ and $h = 4$, what is the value of A when $b = 6$ and $h = 7$?

➤ $\frac{A_1}{b_1h_1} = \frac{A_2}{b_2h_2} \Rightarrow \frac{20}{(10)(4)} = \frac{A_2}{(6)(7)} \Rightarrow A_2 = 21.$

Percent Problems

Many problem-solving items involve percents as they apply to certain types of business situations.

1. ***Percent Increase or Decrease***

Percent increase or decrease is found by putting the amount of increase or decrease over the original amount and changing this fraction to a percent.

Example:

A company normally employs 100 people. During a slow spell, it fired 20% of its employees. By what percent must it now increase its staff to return to full capacity?

➤ $20\% = \frac{1}{5} \cdot 100 = 20$. The company now has $100 - 20 = 80$ employees. If it then increases by 20 employees, the percent of increase is $\frac{20}{80} = \frac{1}{4}$, or 25%.

2. *Discounts*

A discount is expressed as a percent of the original price that will be deducted from that price to determine the sale price.

Examples:

1. Bill's Hardware offers a 20% discount on all appliances during a sale week. How much must Mrs. Russell pay for a washing machine marked at $280?
   ➤ $20\% = \frac{1}{5} \Rightarrow \frac{1}{5} \cdot \$280 = \$56$ discount $\Rightarrow \$280 - \$56 = \$224$ sale price. Alternatively, the following shortcut simplifies the solution: if there is a 20% discount, Mrs. Russell will pay 80% of the marked price: $80\% = \frac{4}{5} \Rightarrow \frac{4}{5} \cdot \$280 = \$224$ sale price.
2. A store offers a television set marked at $340 less consecutive discounts of 10% and 5%. Another store offers the same set with a single discount of 15%. How much does the buyer save buying at the better price?
   ➤ In the first store, the initial discount means the buyer pays 90%, or $\frac{9}{10}$ of $340, which is $306. The second discount must be figured on the first sale price. The additional 5% discount means the buyer pays 95% of $306, or $290.70. A 5% discount on $306 is less than an additional 5% discount on $340. Thus, the second store will have a lower sale price. In the second store, the buyer will pay 85% of $340, or $289—$1.70 less than the price at the first store.

3. *Commission*

Many salespeople earn money on a commission basis. In order to inspire sales, they are paid a percentage of the value of goods that they personally sell. This amount is called a commission.

Examples:

1. Mr. Saunders works at Brown's Department Store, where he is paid $80 per week in salary plus a 4% commission on all his sales. How much does he earn in a week in which he sells $4,032 worth of merchandise?
   ➤ Find 4% of $4,032 and add this amount to $80: $\$4{,}032 \cdot 0.04 = \$161.28 \Rightarrow \$161.28 + \$80 = \$241.28$.
2. Bill Olson delivers newspapers for a dealer and keeps 8% of all money collected. In one month, he was able to keep $16. How much did he forward to the dealer?
   ➤ First, find how much he collected by asking $16 is 8% of what number: $\$16 = 0.08x \Rightarrow \$1{,}600 = 8x \Rightarrow x = \$200$. Then, subtract the amount Bill kept ($16) from the total collected ($200). Therefore, Bill forwarded $184 to the dealer.

4. *Taxes*

Taxes are a percent of money spent or money earned.

Examples:

1. Dane County collects a 7% sales tax on automobiles. If the price of a used Ford is $5,832 before taxes, what will it cost when the sales tax is added in?
   ➤ Find 7% of $5,832 to determine the amount of tax and then add that amount to $5,832. This can be done in one step by finding 107% of $5,832: $\$5{,}832 \cdot 1.07 = \$6{,}240.24$.
2. If income is taxed at the rate of 10% for the first $10,000 of earned income, 15% for the next $10,000, 20% for the next $10,000, and 25% for all earnings over $30,000, how much income tax must be paid on a yearly income of $36,500?
   ➤ Find the income tax collected at each percentage rate and add them:

10% of first $10,000	= $1,000
15% of next $10,000	= $1,500
20% of next $10,000	= $2,000
+ 25% of $6,500	= $1,625
Total tax	= $6,125

EXERCISE 13

Solving Story Problems

DIRECTIONS: Choose the correct answer to each of the following items. Use a calculator when necessary. Answers are on page 923.

1. A suit is sold for \$68 while marked at \$80. What is the rate of discount?

   A. 15% C. $17\frac{11}{17}$% E. 24%
   B. 17% D. 20%

2. Lilian left home with \$60 in her wallet. She spent $\frac{1}{3}$ of that amount at the supermarket, and she spent $\frac{1}{2}$ of what remained at the drugstore. If Lilian made no other expenditures, how much money did she have when she returned home?

   A. \$10 C. \$20 E. \$50
   B. \$15 D. \$40

3. In the figure below, circle O and circle P are tangent to each other. If the circle with center O has a diameter of 8 and the circle with center P has a diameter of 6, what is the length of segment $\overline{OP}$?

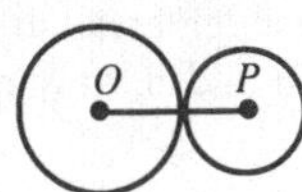

   A. 7 C. 14 E. 28
   B. 10 D. 20

4. A man buys a radio for \$70 after receiving a discount of 20%. What was the marked price?

   A. \$56 C. \$87.50 E. \$92
   B. \$84.50 D. \$90

5. Colin and Shaina wish to buy a gift for a friend. They combine their money and find they have \$4.00, consisting of quarters, dimes, and nickels. If they have 35 coins and the number of quarters is half the number of nickels, how many quarters do they have?

   A. 5 C. 20 E. 36
   B. 10 D. 23

6. Willie receives r% commission on a sale of s dollars. How many dollars does he receive?

   A. rs C. $100rs$ E. $\frac{rs}{100}$
   B. $\frac{r}{s}$ D. $\frac{r}{100s}$

7. Three times the smallest of three consecutive odd integers is 3 more than twice the largest. Find the largest integer.

   A. 9 C. 13 E. 17
   B. 11 D. 15

8. A refrigerator was sold for \$273, yielding a 30% profit on the cost. For how much should it be sold to yield only a 10% profit on the cost?

   A. \$210 C. \$235 E. \$241
   B. \$231 D. \$240

9. If 60 feet of uniform wire weigh 80 pounds, what is the weight, in pounds, of 2 yards of the same wire?

   A. $2\frac{2}{3}$ C. 80 E. 2,400
   B. 8 D. 120

10. What single discount is equivalent to two successive discounts of 10% and 15%?

    A. 25% C. 24% E. 22%
    B. 24.5% D. 23.5%

11. Robert is 15 years older than Stan. However, y years ago Robert was twice as old as Stan. If Stan is now b years old and $b > y$, find the value of $b - y$.

    A. 13 C. 15 E. 17
    B. 14 D. 16

12. The net price of a certain article is \$306 after successive discounts of 15% and 10% are taken off the marked price. What is the marked price?

    A. \$408 C. \$382.50 E. None of these
    B. \$400 D. \$234.09

13. A gear 50 inches in diameter turns a smaller gear 30 inches in diameter. If the larger gear makes 15 revolutions, how many revolutions does the smaller gear make in that time?

    A. 9 C. 20 E. 30
    B. 12 D. 25

14. If a merchant makes a profit of 20% based on the selling price of an article, what percent does he make on the cost?

    A. 15 C. 25 E. 45
    B. 20 D. 40

15. How many ounces of pure acid must be added to 20 ounces of a solution that is 5% acid to strengthen it to a solution that is 24% acid?

A. $2\frac{1}{2}$ C. 6 E. 10
B. 5 D. $7\frac{1}{2}$

16. If x men can do a job in h days, how long would y men take to do the same job?

A. $\frac{x}{h}$ C. $\frac{hy}{x}$ E. $\frac{x}{y}$
B. $\frac{xh}{y}$ D. xyh

17. A certain radio costs a merchant $72. At what price must he sell it if he is to make a profit of 20% of the selling price?

A. $86.40 C. $90 E. $148
B. $88 D. $144

18. A dealer mixes a pounds of nuts that cost b cents per pound with c pounds of nuts that cost d cents per pound. At what price should he sell a pound of the mixture if he wishes to make a profit of 10 cents per pound?

A. $\frac{ab+cd}{a+c}+10$ D. $\frac{b+d}{a+c}+0.10$
B. $\frac{ab+cd}{a+c}+0.10$ E. $\frac{b+d+10}{a+c}$
C. $\frac{b+d}{a+c}+10$

19. If a furnace uses 40 gallons of oil in a week, how many gallons, to the nearest gallon, does it use in 10 days?

A. 57 C. 28 E. 4
B. 44 D. 20

20. Nell invests $2,400 in the Security National Bank at 5%. How much additional money must she invest at 8% so that the total annual income will be equal to 6% of her entire investment?

A. $4,400 C. $3,000 E. $1,200
B. $3,600 D. $2,400

21. A baseball team has won 40 games out of 60 played. It has 32 more games to play. How many of these must the team win to make its record 75% for the season?

A. 28 C. 30 E. 34
B. 29 D. 32

22. A recipe requires 13 oz. of sugar and 18 oz. of flour. If only 10 oz. of sugar are used, how much flour, to the nearest ounce, should be used?

A. 11 C. 13 E. 15
B. 12 D. 14

23. Ivan left Austin to drive to Boxville at 6:15 p.m. and arrived at 11:45 p.m. If he averaged 30 miles per hour and stopped one hour for dinner, how many miles is Boxville from Austin?

A. 120 C. 180 E. 190
B. 135 D. 185

24. If prices are reduced 25% and sales increase 20%, what is the net effect on gross receipts?

A. They increase by 5%. D. They increase by 10%.
B. They decrease by 5%. E. They decrease by 10%.
C. They remain the same.

25. If a car can drive 25 miles on two gallons of gasoline, how many gallons will be needed for a trip of 150 miles?

A. 12 C. 16 E. 20
B. 13 D. 17

26. A plane traveling 600 miles per hour is 30 miles from Kennedy Airport at 4:58 p.m. At what time will it arrive at the airport?

A. 5:00 p.m. C. 5:02 p.m. E. 5:23 p.m.
B. 5:01 p.m. D. 5:20 p.m.

27. A salesperson earns a commission of 5% on all sales between $200 and $600, and 8% on all sales over $600. What is the commission earned in a week in which sales total $800?

A. $20 C. $48 E. $88
B. $36 D. $78

28. A school has enough bread to last 30 children 4 days. If 10 children are added, how many days will the bread last?

A. $\frac{1}{3}$ C. $2\frac{1}{3}$ E. 3
B. $1\frac{1}{3}$ D. $2\frac{2}{3}$

29. Mr. Bridges can wash his car in 15 minutes, while his son Dave takes twice as long to do the same job. If they work together, how many minutes will the job take them?

A. 5 C. 10 E. 30
B. $7\frac{1}{2}$ D. $22\frac{1}{2}$

30. At c cents per pound, what is the cost of a ounces of salami?

A. $\frac{c}{a}$ C. ac E. $\frac{16c}{a}$
B. $\frac{a}{c}$ D. $\frac{ac}{16}$

31. If 3 miles are equivalent to 4.83 kilometers, then 11.27 kilometers are equivalent to how many miles?

A. $2\frac{1}{3}$ C. 7 E. $7\frac{1}{2}$
B. 5 D. $7\frac{1}{3}$

32. If enrollment at City University grew from 3,000 to 12,000 in the last 10 years, what was the percent of increase in enrollment?

A. 25% C. 300% E. 400%
B. 125% D. 330%

33. At a certain printing plant, each of m machines prints 6 newspapers every s seconds. If all machines work together but independently without interruption, how many minutes will it take to print an entire run of 18,000 newspapers?

A. $\frac{180s}{m}$ C. $50ms$ E. $\frac{300m}{s}$
B. $\frac{50s}{m}$ D. $\frac{ms}{50}$

34. If p pencils cost d dollars, how many pencils can be bought for c cents?

A. $\frac{100pc}{d}$ C. $\frac{pd}{c}$ E. $\frac{cd}{p}$
B. $\frac{pc}{100d}$ D. $\frac{pc}{d}$

35. A car dealer who gives a customer a 20% discount on the list price of a car still realizes a net profit of 25% of cost. If the dealer's cost is $4,800, what is the usual list price of the car?

A. $6,000 C. $7,200 E. $8,001
B. $6,180 D. $7,500

36. The variable m varies directly as the square of t. If m is 7 when $t = 1$, what is the value of m when $t = 2$?

A. 28 C. 7 E. 2
B. 14 D. $3\frac{1}{2}$

37. 6 students in a class failed algebra, representing $16\frac{2}{3}\%$ of the class. How many students passed the course?

A. 48 C. 33 E. 28
B. 36 D. 30

38. If the value of a piece of property decreases by 10% while the tax rate on the property increases by 10%, what is the effect on taxes?

A. Taxes increase by 10%.
B. Taxes increase by 1%.
C. There is no change in taxes.
D. Taxes decrease by 1%.
E. Taxes decrease by 10%.

39. The variable m varies jointly as r and l. If m is 8 when r and l are each 1, what is the value of m when r and l are each 2?

A. 64 C. 16 E. 2
B. 32 D. 4

40. 95% of the residents of Coral Estates live in private homes. 40% of those live in air-conditioned homes. What percent of the residents of Coral Estates live in air-conditioned homes?

A. 3% C. 30% E. 38%
B. 3.8% D. 34%

41. Exactly three years before the year in which Anna was born, the year was $1980 - x$. In terms of x, what is the year of Anna's twentieth birthday?

A. $1977 + x$ C. $2003 - x$ E. $2006 + x$
B. $1997 + x$ D. $2003 + x$

42. Mr. Carlson receives a salary of $500 a month and a commission of 5% on all sales. What must be the amount of his sales in July so that his total monthly income is $2,400?

A. $48,000 C. $7,600 E. $2,000
B. $38,000 D. $3,800

43. John can wax his car in 3 hours. Jim can do the same job in 5 hours. How long will it take them if they work together?

A. $\frac{1}{2}$ hour C. 2 hours E. 8 hours
B. $1\frac{7}{8}$ hours D. $2\frac{7}{8}$ hours

44. In the junior class at Shawnee High School, 168 students took the SAT, 175 students took the ACT, 80 students took both, and 27 students did not take either one. What is the total number of students in the junior class at Shawnee High School?

A. 440 C. 290 E. 248
B. 343 D. 282

45. Let $R = \{3, 5, 6, 7, 9\}$. How many different subsets of R with 1, 2, 3, or 4 elements contain one or more odd numbers?

A. 31 C. 29 E. 27
B. 30 D. 28

46. A survey of 51 students was conducted concerning each student's favorite flavors of ice cream. Of the 51 students, 10 students liked only vanilla, 12 students liked only strawberry, and 15 students liked only chocolate. Every student liked at least one of the three flavors. 7 students liked both vanilla and strawberry, and 9 students liked both vanilla and chocolate. The largest possible number of students who could have liked both chocolate and strawberry is:

A. 2 C. 7 E. 14
B. 3 D. 12

47. Set X is the set of all positive integral multiples of 8: $X = \{8, 16, 24, 32, \ldots\}$. Set Y is the set of all positive integral multiples of 6: $Y = \{6, 12, 18, 24, \ldots\}$. The intersection of these two sets is the set of all positive integral multiples of:

A. 2
B. 4
C. 14
D. 24
E. 48

48. If y varies directly with x and the constant of variation is 3, then $y = 12.3$ when $x = 4.1$. If y varies directly with x and $y = 6.72$ when $x = 4.2$, then what is the constant of variation?

A. 3.1
B. 4.2
C. 2.52
D. 1.6
E. 2.50

49. Each of the following choices is comprised of three equations relating x and y. Identify the set of equations that demonstrates direct variation, inverse variation, and neither direct nor inverse variation, respectively?

A. $y = 3x$; $x^2 + y^2 = x + 5$; $y = \frac{4}{x}$
B. $y = 3x$; $x^2 + y^2 = x + 5$; $y = \frac{x}{4}$
C. $x = \frac{y}{3}$; $xy = 7$; $x^2 + y^2 = \frac{x}{5}$
D. $y = 3x$; $y = \frac{4}{x}$; $x = 5y$
E. $y = \frac{2x}{3}$; $x = 5y$; $x^2 + y^2 = x + 7$

50. At a constant temperature, the resistance of a wire varies directly with length and inversely with the square of the wire diameter. A piece of wire that is 0.1 inch in diameter and 50 feet long has a resistance of 0.1 ohm. What is the resistance, in ohms, of a wire of the same material that is 9000 feet long and 0.3 inches in diameter?

A. 0.3
B. 0.9
C. 2
D. 3
E. 9

51. Let y vary directly as x, and let w vary directly as the square of x. If $y = 10$ for $x = 1.25$ and $w = 8$ for $x = \sqrt{2}$, then for what positive value of x will $y = w$?

A. 1
B. $1\frac{1}{2}$
C. 2
D. 4
E. 5

52. The perimeter of a square varies directly as the length of one side of the square with a constant of variation of 4. The circumference of a circle varies directly as the circle's radius and a constant of variation equal to:

A. π
B. 2π
C. 1
D. 2
E. $\frac{1}{\pi}$

53. If x and y vary inversely, then for any ordered pair (x, y), the value of xy is a constant number. The ordered pairs $(-12, -3)$ and $(6, 6)$ represent an example of inverse variation for x and y. Which of the following graphs represents a possible inverse variation relationship between x and y?

A.
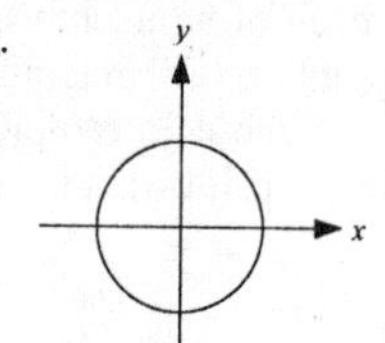

D.
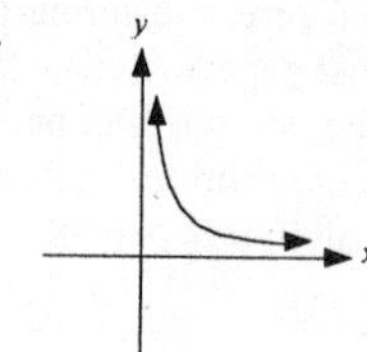

B.
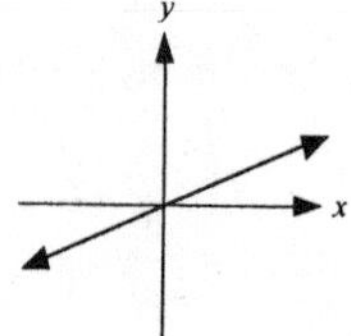

E.
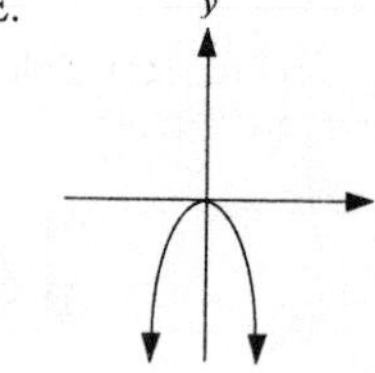

C.
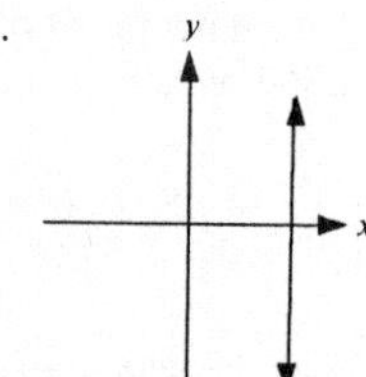

54. The formula for compound interest is $A = P\left(1 + \frac{r}{n}\right)^{nt}$, where A is the final amount, P is the initial investment, r is the annual percentage interest rate, t is the time period, and n is the number of times per year that the interest is compounded. If an initial investment of \$10,000 accrues compound interest at a percentage rate of 4.16% and is worth \$10,424.02, \$10,866.03, \$11,326.77, and \$11,807.06 after 1, 2, 3, and 4 years, respectively, then n is approximately equal to:

A. 1
B. 2
C. 4
D. 6
E. 12

Math Express Skills Review

TARGETED EDUCATIONAL SOLUTIONS.

Cambridge Course Concept Outline
MATH EXPRESS SKILLS REVIEW

Arithmetic Summary

1. **Real Numbers:** Real numbers are all the numbers on the number line, including integers, decimals, fractions, and radical numbers.

   e.g., $-\frac{1}{2}, 0, \frac{2}{3}, \sqrt{2}, \pi$

   A real number is *rational* if it can be written as the ratio of two integers where the denominator does not equal zero. Natural numbers, whole numbers, integers, common fractions, and repeating decimals are some examples of rational numbers.

   e.g., $-\frac{1}{2}, 0, 0.75, \frac{2}{3}$

   A real number is *irrational* if it cannot be written as the ratio of two integers. Irrational numbers have infinite non-repeating decimal representations.

   e.g., $\sqrt{2}, \pi$

   Properties of real numbers:
   $(+)(+) = (+)$
   $(-)(-) = (+)$
   $(+)(-) = (-)$
   $(-)^2 = (+)$
   $m + 0 = m$, where m is a real number
   $m \cdot 0 = 0$, where m is a real number

   e.g., 1. $\left(\frac{1}{2}\right)(4) = 2$
   2. $(-2)\left(-\frac{4}{5}\right) = \frac{8}{5}$
   3. $(2)(-4) = -8$
   4. $\left(-\frac{3}{4}\right)(4) = -3$
   5. $(-2)^2 = 4$
   6. $2 + 0 = 2$
   7. $(2)(0) = 0$

2. **Natural Numbers:** *Natural* numbers are the set of positive integers and are also referred to as counting numbers: 1, 2, 3, 4, 5, ...

3. **Whole Numbers:** *Whole* numbers are the numbers used for counting, plus the number zero: 0, 1, 2, 3, ...

   e.g., 0, 5, 56, 490

4. **Integers:** *Integers* are positive or negative whole numbers.

   e.g., $-568, -45, 0, 6, 67, \frac{16}{2}, 345$

5. **Positive and Negative Integers:** If the signs of the two numbers being added or subtracted are *different*, disregard the signs temporarily, subtract the smaller number from the larger number, and keep the sign attached to the larger number.

   e.g., $-3 + 2 = -1$
   $-4 + 6 = 2$

   If the signs of the two numbers being added or subtracted are the *same*, disregard the signs temporarily, add the two numbers, and keep the sign attached to each number.

   e.g., 1. $-5 - 3 = -8$
   2. $4 + 8 = 12$

6. **Even and Odd Integers:** An *even* integer is evenly divisible by 2, whereas an *odd* integer is not evenly divisible by 2. 0 is an even integer.

   e.g., Even integers: −50, −4, 0, 2, 34
   Odd integers: −45, −3, 9, 15

   Important properties of even and odd integers:

even + even = even	*e.g.*, $2 + 4 = 6$
even + odd = odd	$4 + 3 = 7$
odd + odd = even	$3 + 5 = 8$
odd + even = odd	$3 + 4 = 7$
even • even = even	$2 \cdot 4 = 8$
even • odd = even	$2 \cdot 3 = 6$
odd • odd = odd	$3 \cdot 5 = 15$
odd • even = even	$3 \cdot 2 = 6$

7. **Factor:** A *factor* is a number that divides evenly into another number.

   e.g., 1, 2, 3, 4, 6, and 12 are factors of 12

8. **Prime:** A *prime* number is any natural number (except 1) that is divisible only by 1 and itself.

   e.g., 2, 3, 5, 7, 11, 13, 17, and 19 are all prime numbers

9. **Prime Factors:** All natural numbers can be expressed as the product of prime numbers, which are called the *prime factors* of that number.

   e.g., 1. $3 = (3)(1)$
   2. $12 = (2)(2)(3)$

10. **Consecutive Integers:** *Consecutive* integers are in continuous sequence. If the first integer of a consecutive sequence is m, the sequence is m, $m + 1$, $m + 2$, *etc.*

    e.g., 1. {4, 5, 6, 7, ...}
    2. {−10, −9, −8, −7, ...}

    Consecutive *even* or *odd* integers are in continuous sequence of even or odd integers, respectively. An even or odd sequence is m, $m + 2$, $m + 4$, $m + 6$, *etc.*

    e.g., 1. {−4, −2, 0, 2, ...}
    2. {7, 9, 11, 13, ...}

11. **Miscellaneous Symbols:**

$= \Leftrightarrow$ is equal to
$\neq \Leftrightarrow$ is not equal to
$< \Leftrightarrow$ is less than
$> \Leftrightarrow$ is greater than
$\leq \Leftrightarrow$ is less than or equal to
$\geq \Leftrightarrow$ is greater than or equal to
$|x| \Leftrightarrow$ absolute value of x (always non-negative)

e.g., 1. $3 = 3$
2. $\frac{3}{4} \neq \frac{5}{6}$
3. $-3 < 6$
4. $5 > 4$
5. $m - 3 \leq -3$, for $m = \ldots, -3, -2, -1, 0$
6. $m + 3 \geq 3$, for $m = 0, 1, 2, 3, \ldots$
7. $|-5| = 5$

12. **Terms:** The *sum* or *total* is the result of adding numbers together. The *difference* is the result of subtracting one number from another. The *product* is the result of multiplying numbers together. The *quotient* is the result of dividing one number by another. The *remainder* is the number remaining after one number is divided into another number.

e.g., 1. The sum (or total) of 2 and 3 is 5: $2 + 3 = 5$.
2. The difference between 5 and 2 is 3: $5 - 2 = 3$.
3. The product of 2 and 3 is 6: $(2)(3) = 6$.
4. The quotient of 6 divided by 2 is 3: $6 \div 2 = 3$.
5. The remainder of 7 divided by 3 is 1: $7 \div 3 = 2$ plus a remainder of 1.

13. **Fractions:** When one whole integer is divided by another whole integer (other than zero) and the result is not a third whole integer, the result is a fraction, or ratio. The top number is called the *numerator*; the bottom number is called the *denominator.*

e.g., 2 divided by 3 results in a fraction, not a whole number: $2 \div 3 = \frac{2}{3}$.

Proper fractions have a numerator of lower value than the denominator and thus have a value less than 1.

e.g., $\frac{1}{2}$ and $\frac{3}{4}$ are both < 1.

Improper fractions have a numerator of greater value than the denominator, and thus have a value greater than 1.

e.g., $\frac{3}{2}$ and $\frac{4}{3}$ are both > 1.

A *mixed number* consists of both a whole number and a fraction written together.

e.g., 1. $2\frac{1}{2} = 2 + \frac{1}{2}$
2. $3\frac{4}{5} = 3 + \frac{4}{5}$

To add, subtract, multiply, or divide fractions, convert mixed numbers to improper fractions as follows:

a. The new denominator is the denominator of the fractional part of the mixed number.
b. The new numerator is the whole number of the mixed number multiplied by the denominator of the fractional part and then added to its numerator.

e.g., 1. $3\frac{1}{4} = \frac{(3 \cdot 4) + 1}{4} = \frac{13}{4}$
2. $6\frac{2}{5} = \frac{(6 \cdot 5) + 2}{5} = \frac{32}{5}$
3. $2\frac{12}{13} = \frac{(2 \cdot 13) + 12}{13} = \frac{38}{13}$

To convert an improper fraction to a mixed number, reverse the process as follows:

a. Divide the denominator into the numerator. The integer part of the quotient becomes the whole number part of the mixed number.
b. With the same denominator, create a fraction with the numerator equal to the remainder of the first step.

e.g., 1. $\frac{29}{5} = 29 \div 5 = 5$ with a remainder of $4 = 5\frac{4}{5}$.
2. $\frac{31}{6} = 31 \div 6 = 5$ with a remainder of $1 = 5\frac{1}{6}$.
3. $\frac{43}{13} = 43 \div 13 = 3$ with a remainder of $4 = 3\frac{4}{13}$.

14. **Reducing Fractions:** It is conventional to reduce all fractions to lowest terms. To reduce a fraction to lowest terms, eliminate redundant factors that are in both the numerator and the denominator. Either factor or divide out the redundant factors from both.

e.g., $\frac{8}{16} = \frac{1(8)}{2(8)} = \frac{1}{2}$, or $\frac{8}{16} = \frac{8 \div 8}{16 \div 8} = \frac{1}{2}$.

A fraction is expressed in *lowest terms* when there is no natural number (other than 1) that can be divided evenly into both the numerator and the denominator.

e.g., $\frac{8}{15}$ is in lowest terms, as there is no natural number (other than 1) that divides evenly into 8 and 15.

15. **Complex Fractions:** A *complex fraction* is a fraction in which either the numerator or the denominator, or both, contains fractions. There are two methods for simplifying complex fractions.

Method 1: Multiply the numerator by the reciprocal of the denominator and simplify.

e.g., $\frac{\frac{1}{2}}{\frac{3}{4}} = \left(\frac{1}{2}\right)\left(\frac{4}{3}\right) = \frac{4}{6} = \frac{2}{3}$

Method 2: Multiply both the numerator and the denominator by the least common denominator for the terms in the numerator and the denominator of the complex fraction and simplify.

e.g., $\frac{\frac{1}{2}}{\frac{3}{4}} \cdot \frac{(4)}{(4)} = \frac{\frac{4}{2}}{\frac{12}{4}} = \frac{2}{3}$

16. Common Denominators: A *common denominator* is a number that is a multiple of the denominators of two or more fractions.

e.g., Since 12 is an even multiple of both 3 and 4, it is a common denominator for $\frac{1}{3}$ and $\frac{1}{4}$.

Converting a fraction to another denominator is the reverse of reducing it to lowest terms. Multiplying the numerator and the denominator of a fraction by the same number is equal to multiplying it by 1—the value is unchanged.

e.g., 1. $\frac{1}{4}=\frac{(1)(3)}{(4)(3)}=\frac{3}{12}$

2. $\frac{2}{3}=\frac{(2)(4)}{(3)(4)}=\frac{8}{12}$

17. Adding Fractions: The procedure for adding fractions varies depending on whether or not the fractions already share the same denominator.

To add fractions with the same denominator, create a new fraction using the common denominator. The new numerator is the sum of the old numerators.

e.g., $\frac{3}{7}+\frac{2}{7}=\frac{5}{7}$

To add fractions with different denominators, find a common denominator and convert the fractions.

e.g., 1. $\frac{1}{3}+\frac{1}{5}=\frac{1(5)}{3(5)}+\frac{1(3)}{5(3)}=\frac{5}{15}+\frac{3}{15}=\frac{8}{15}$

2. $\frac{1}{3}+\frac{2}{7}=\frac{1(7)}{3(7)}+\frac{2(3)}{7(3)}=\frac{7}{21}+\frac{6}{21}=\frac{13}{21}$

To add a fraction and a whole number, treat the whole number as a fraction with a denominator of 1.

e.g., $2+\frac{1}{5}+\frac{1}{2}=\frac{2}{1}+\frac{1}{5}+\frac{1}{2}=\frac{2(10)}{1(10)}+\frac{1(2)}{5(2)}+\frac{1(5)}{2(5)}$
$=\frac{20}{10}+\frac{2}{10}+\frac{5}{10}=\frac{27}{10}$

To add a fraction and a mixed number, change the mixed number to an improper fraction and then add.

e.g., $2\frac{1}{3}+\frac{1}{3}=\frac{7}{3}+\frac{1}{3}=\frac{8}{3}=2\frac{2}{3}$

18. Subtracting Fractions: Follow the same procedure for addition, except subtract rather than add.

To subtract fractions with the same denominator, simply subtract the second numerator from the first.

e.g., $\frac{5}{7}-\frac{2}{7}=\frac{3}{7}$

To subtract fractions with different denominators, first find a common denominator.

e.g., $\frac{7}{8}-\frac{3}{5}=\frac{7(5)}{8(5)}-\frac{3(8)}{5(8)}=\frac{35}{40}-\frac{24}{40}=\frac{11}{40}$

19. "Flying-*X*" Method for Adding and Subtracting Fractions: It is not necessary to find the least common denominator when adding or subtracting fractions if you reduce the result to lowest terms. Any common denominator will work—simply use the *flying-x* method.

$$\frac{a}{b}+\frac{c}{d}=\frac{a}{b}\gtrless+\lessgtr\frac{c}{d}=\frac{ad+bc}{bd}$$

a. Multiply the denominators together to get a new denominator.

b Multiply the numerator of the first fraction by the denominator of the second.

c. Multiply the denominator of the first fraction by the numerator of the second.

d. The new numerator is the sum (or difference) of the results of steps 2 and 3.

e.g., 1. $\frac{2}{7}+\frac{1}{5}=\frac{2}{7}\gtrless+\lessgtr\frac{1}{5}=\frac{10+7}{35}=\frac{17}{35}$

2. $\frac{3}{5}+\frac{1}{3}=\frac{3}{5}\gtrless+\lessgtr\frac{1}{3}=\frac{9+5}{15}=\frac{14}{15}$

20. Multiplying Fractions: Multiplication of fractions does not require a common denominator. Just multiply numerators to create a new numerator, and multiply denominators to create a new denominator.

e.g., 1. $\frac{3}{4}\bullet\frac{1}{2}=\frac{(3)(1)}{(4)(2)}=\frac{3}{8}$

2. $\frac{2}{3}\bullet\frac{2}{5}=\frac{(2)(2)}{(3)(5)}=\frac{4}{15}$

21. Dividing Fractions: To divide by a fraction, take the reciprocal of the divisor (the fraction doing the dividing) and then multiply the two terms.

e.g., 1. $2\div\frac{1}{4}=2\bullet\frac{4}{1}=\frac{8}{1}=8$

2. $\frac{\frac{2}{3}}{\frac{5}{6}}=\frac{2}{3}\bullet\frac{6}{5}=\frac{12}{15}=\frac{4}{5}$

22. Converting Fractions to Decimals: If the fraction already has a denominator that is 10, 100, 1,000, *etc.*, the conversion is easy. The numerator of the fraction becomes the decimal. The placement of the decimal point is governed by the number of zeros in the denominator.

e.g., Express $\frac{127}{1{,}000}$ in decimal form.

In the numerator, count three places to the left of the 7—one for each zero in 1,000: $\frac{127}{1{,}000}=0.127$.

If there are fewer numbers in the numerator than there are decimal places, add zeros to the left of the number until there are enough decimal places.

e.g., $\frac{3}{100}=0.03$

To convert a proper fraction with a denominator other than 10, 100, etc., first convert the fraction to the equivalent form using a denominator such as 10, 100, *etc.* To determine which denominator to use, divide the denominator of the fraction into 10, then into 100, then into 1,000, until a denominator that is evenly divisible by the denominator of the original fraction is found.

e.g., 1. $\frac{2}{5}=\frac{(2)(2)}{(5)(2)}=\frac{4}{10}=0.4$

2. $\frac{1}{4}=\frac{(1)(25)}{(4)(25)}=\frac{25}{100}=0.25$

3. $\frac{3}{8}=\frac{(3)(125)}{(8)(125)}=\frac{375}{1{,}000}=0.375$

To convert proper fractions to decimals, dividing the denominator into the numerator is usually easier.

e.g., 1. $\frac{2}{5} = 5\overline{)2.0} = 0.4$ (quotient 0.4)

2. $\frac{3}{8} = 8\overline{)3.000} = 0.375$ (quotient 0.375)

To convert a mixed number into a decimal, convert the fractional part of the mixed number to a decimal as just discussed, and then place the whole number part of the mixed number to the left of the decimal point.

e.g., 1. $6\frac{1}{10} = 6.1$ (Convert $\frac{1}{10}$ to 0.1 and then place the 6 to the left of the decimal point.)

2. $3\frac{7}{8} = 3.875$ (Convert $\frac{7}{8}$ to 0.875 and then place the 3 to the left of the decimal point.)

To convert an improper fraction to a decimal, convert it to a mixed number and follow the procedure just outlined.

e.g., $\frac{9}{4} = 2\frac{1}{4} = 2.25$

23. Converting Decimals to Fractions: The numerator of the fraction is the digit(s) to the right of the decimal point. The denominator is a 1 followed by the same number of zeros as the number of decimal places to the right of the decimal point.

e.g., $0.005 = \frac{5}{1{,}000} = \frac{1}{200}$ (0.005 has three decimal places, so the new denominator is 1 followed by 3 zeros.)

If a decimal has numbers to both the right and left of the decimal point, the conversion to a fraction results in a mixed number. The whole part of the mixed number is the whole part of the decimal.

e.g., 1. $1.75 = 1 \text{ plus } \frac{75}{100} = 1 \text{ plus } \frac{3}{4} = 1\frac{3}{4}$

2. $357.125 = 357 \text{ plus } \frac{125}{1{,}000} = 357 \text{ plus } \frac{1}{8} = 357\frac{1}{8}$

Memorize these decimal equivalents:

$\frac{1}{2} = 0.5$	$\frac{1}{3} = 0.3\overline{3}$	$\frac{1}{4} = 0.25$	$\frac{1}{5} = 0.20$
$\frac{1}{6} = 0.16\overline{6}$	$\frac{1}{7} = 0.\overline{142857}$	$\frac{1}{8} = 0.125$	$\frac{1}{9} = 0.1\overline{1}$

Note: A bar over a digit or digits indicates that the digit or group of digits repeats.

24. Adding and Subtracting Decimals: To add or subtract decimals, line up the decimal points, fill in the appropriate number of zeros, and then add or subtract.

e.g., 0.25 + 0.1 + 0.825 = 0.25

0.1

+ 0.825

= 0.250

0.100

+ 0.825

1.175

25. Multiplying Decimals: To multiply decimals, first multiply as with whole numbers and then adjust the decimal point. Count the total number of decimal places in the numbers being multiplied, count that many places to the left from the right of the final number in the product, and put the decimal point there.

e.g., 1. (0.1)(0.2)(0.3) = 0.006 (1 • 2 • 3 = 6, and there are three decimal places in the multiplication.)

2. (0.10)(0.10)(0.10) = 0.001000 = 0.001 (10 • 10 • 10 = 1,000, and there are six decimal places in the problem.)

26. Dividing Decimals: When the divisor is a whole number, place a decimal point in the quotient immediately above the decimal point in the dividend. Keep dividing until there is no remainder, adding zeros as needed to the right of the divisor.

e.g., $2.5 \div 2 = 2\overline{)2.50}$ (quotient 1.25)

− 2

0 5

− 4

10

− 10

0

When the divisor is a *decimal,* "clear" the fractional part of the decimal by moving both the divisor and dividend decimal points the same number of spaces to the right.

e.g., $5 \div 2.5 = 2.5\overline{)5.0}$ (quotient 2.)

−5 0

0

27. Ratios: A *ratio* is a statement about the relationship between two quantities. The ratio of two quantities, *x* and *y*, can be expressed as $x \div y$, x/y, or $x{:}y$.

e.g., 1. $\frac{2}{5} = 2{:}5$

2. $\frac{\text{boys}}{\text{girls}}$ = boys:girls = ratio of boys to girls

3. $\frac{\text{miles}}{\text{hour}}$ = miles:hour = miles/hour = miles per hour

28. Proportions: A *proportion* is a statement of equality between two ratios.

e.g., $\frac{3}{4} = \frac{9}{12}$

With *direct variation,* ratios are directly related: The more of one quantity, the more of the other, and vice versa.

e.g., If 12 donuts cost \$3.60, how much do 4 donuts cost?

$\frac{\text{Total Cost for } X}{\text{Total Cost for } Y} = \frac{X}{Y} \Rightarrow \frac{\$3.60}{Y} = \frac{12}{4} \Rightarrow \$3.60(4) = 12Y$

$Y = 3.60(4) \div 12 = \$1.20$

With *inverse variation,* ratios are inversely related: An increase in one quantity is a decrease in the other. Use this method to solve inverse variation problems: first, set up an ordinary proportion, making sure that you group like quantities; then, take the reciprocal of the proportion's right side; and finally, cross-multiply and solve for the unknown.

e.g., Traveling at a constant rate of 150 m.p.h., a plane makes the trip from City P to City Q in four hours. How long will the trip take if the plane flies at a constant rate of 200 m.p.h.?
$\frac{\text{Speed } X}{\text{Speed } Y} = \frac{\text{Time } X}{\text{Time } Y} \Rightarrow \frac{150 \text{ mph}}{200 \text{ mph}} = \frac{4 \text{ hours}}{Y \text{ hours}} \Rightarrow \frac{150}{200} = \frac{Y}{4}$
$Y = 4(150) \div 200 = 3$ hours

29. **Percentage Conversions:** *To change any decimal to a percent,* move the decimal point two places to the right and add a percent sign. To change a percent to a decimal, reverse the process.

e.g.,
1. $0.275 = 27.5\%$
2. $0.03 = 3\%$
3. $0.02\% = 0.0002$
4. $120\% = 1.20$

To convert a fraction to a percent, first convert the fraction to a decimal. Reverse the process for converting percents to fractions.

e.g.,
1. $\frac{3}{4} = 0.75 = 75\% = 0.75 = \frac{75}{100} = \frac{3}{4}$
2. $\frac{5}{8} = 0.625 = 62.5\% = 0.625 = \frac{625}{1{,}000} = \frac{5}{8}$

30. **Common Percent Problems:** All percent problems have the same three components: *is*, *of*, and %. Depending on the form of the question, one of these three components is the unknown variable.

"What is x% of that?"
"This is what percent of that?"
"This is x% of what?

Percentage problems can be solved using several different methods. Two methods are outlined below.

Method 1: Write the statement as an equation, rewrite the percent as $\frac{\%}{100}$, and solve for the unknown.

e.g., 5 is 20% of what number?
$5 = \frac{20x}{100} \Rightarrow x = \frac{(5)(100)}{20} = 25$. Thus, 5 is 20% of 25.

Method 2: Since there are three parts to all percent problems (*is*, *of*, and %), use the following equation to solve for the unknown: $\frac{is}{of} = \frac{\%}{100}$.

e.g.,
1. 20 is what percent of 50?
   $\% = x$, $is = 20$, $of = 50$
   $\frac{is}{of} = \frac{\%}{100} \Rightarrow \frac{20}{50} = \frac{x}{100} \Rightarrow \frac{(20)(100)}{50} = 40\%$
2. What number is 20% of 25?
   $\% = 20$, $is = x$, $of = 25$
   $\frac{is}{of} = \frac{\%}{100} \Rightarrow \frac{x}{25} = \frac{20}{100} \Rightarrow x = \frac{(20)(25)}{(100)} = 5$

Another common percent item is *change in price*.

$$\% \text{ Price Change} = \frac{|\text{New Price} - \text{Old Price}|}{\text{Old Price}}$$

The absolute value allows for price decreases as well.

e.g., An item's price is increased from \$20 to \$25. What is the percent increase in the price?
$\frac{|\text{New Price} - \text{Old Price}|}{\text{Old Price}} = \frac{25-20}{20} = \frac{5}{20} = \frac{1}{4} = 25\%$

31. **Averages:** To calculate an *average* (or mean), add together the quantities to be averaged; then divide that sum by the number of quantities added.

e.g., The average of 3, 7, and 8 is 6: $3 + 7 + 8 = 18$ and $18 \div 3 = 6$.

If solving for a *missing element* of an average, set up the average equation and solve for the unknown.

e.g., The average score on four tests is 90. If three scores are 89, 92, and 94, what is the fourth score?
$\frac{89 + 92 + 94 + x}{4} = 90 \Rightarrow x = 85$

In *weighted averages*, greater weight is given to one element than to another.

e.g., Four books cost \$6.00 each and two books cost \$3.00 each. What is the average cost of a book?
$\frac{(4)(6) + (2)(3)}{4 + 2} = \frac{24 + 6}{6} = \frac{30}{6} = 5$

32. **Median:** The *median* is the middle value of a number set when arranged in ascending or descending order. The median of an even numbered set is the average of the two middle values, when the numbers are arranged in ascending or descending order.

e.g., The median of {8, 6, 34, 5, 17, 23} is: $\frac{8 + 17}{2} = 12.5$.

33. **Mode:** The value that appears most frequently in a set of numbers is the *mode*.

e.g., The mode of 4, 5, 3, 4, 5, 1, 2, 3, 6, 4, and 6, is 4.

34. **Counting Principle:** To determine the number of ways that particular events can occur, multiply the number of ways that each event can occur.

e.g.,
1. How many ways can you select one boy and one girl from a class of 15 girls and 13 boys?
   $(15)(13) = 195$ ways
2. In how many ways can 5 students sit in a row with 5 chairs?
   $(5)(4)(3)(2)(1) = 120$ ways
3. In how many ways can you fill three chairs given five students?
   $(5)(4)(3) = 60$ ways

35. **Probability Principle:** The probability that an event will happen can be found from the fraction $\frac{\text{winning events}}{\text{total events}}$ or $\frac{\text{favorable events}}{\text{total events}}$.

e.g., From the set {−4, −3, −2, 0, 1, 6, 8, 1002}, a number is selected at random. Find the probability that the selected number is an even integer.

There are 6 even integers (−4, −2, 0, 6, 8, 1002) out of a total of 8 integers, so the probability is: $\frac{6}{8}=\frac{3}{4}$.

Algebra Summary

1. **Basic Operations:**

Addition: $n + n = 2n$
$n + m = n + m$
Subtraction: $3n - 2n = n$
$n - m = n - m$
Multiplication: n times $m = (n)(m) = nm$
$(n)(0) = 0$
Division: n divided by $m = n \div m = \frac{n}{m}$
$n \div 0 =$ undefined

2. **Powers:** A *power* of a number indicates repeated multiplication.

e.g., 3 raised to the fifth power is (3)(3)(3)(3)(3) = 243.

3. **Exponents:** An *exponent* is a number that indicates the operation of repeated multiplication. Exponents are notated as superscripts. The number being multiplied is the *base*.

e.g., 1. $2^3 = (2)(2)(2) = 8$
2. $5^4 = (5)(5)(5)(5) = 625$

Exponent Rules:
1. $x^m \bullet x^n = x^{m+n}$
2. $x^m \div x^n = x^{m-n}$
3. $(x^m)^n = x^{mn}$
4. $(xy)^m = x^m y^m$
5. $\left(\frac{x}{y}\right)^m = \frac{x^m}{y^m}$
6. $x^1 = x$, for any number x
7. $x^0 = 1$, for any number x, such that $x \neq 0$
8. 0^0 is undefined.

e.g., 1. $(2^3)(2^2) = (2 \bullet 2 \bullet 2)(2 \bullet 2) = 2^{3+2} = 2^5$
$(3^2)(3^3)(3^5) = 3^{2+3+5} = 3^{10}$
2. $2^4 \div 2^2 = \frac{(2)(2)(2)(2)}{(2)(2)} = 2^{4-2} = 2^2$
$5^3 \div 5^5 = 5^{3-5} = 5^{-2} = \left(\frac{1}{5}\right)^2 = \frac{1}{25}$
3. $(2^2)^3 = (2 \bullet 2)^3 = (2 \bullet 2)(2 \bullet 2)(2 \bullet 2) = 2^{2 \bullet 3} = 2^6$
4. $(2 \bullet 3)^2 = (2 \bullet 3)(2 \bullet 3) = (2 \bullet 2)(3 \bullet 3) = 2^2 \bullet 3^2$
$= 4 \bullet 9 = 36$
$(2^3 \bullet 3^2)^2 = 2^{3 \bullet 2} \bullet 3^{2 \bullet 2} = 2^6 \bullet 3^4$
5. $\left(\frac{2}{3}\right)^2 = \frac{2^2}{3^2} = \frac{4}{9}$
$\left(\frac{3^3 \bullet 5^5}{3^2 \bullet 5^2}\right)^2 = (3^{3-2} \bullet 5^{5-2})^2 = (3^1 \bullet 5^3)^2 = (3^2)(5^6)$

A negative exponent signifies a fraction, indicating the *reciprocal* of the base.

e.g., 1. $x^{-1} = \frac{1}{x}$
2. $2x^{-1} = 2\left(\frac{1}{x}\right) = \frac{2}{x}$
3. $4^{-2} = \left(\frac{1}{4}\right)^2 = \frac{1}{16}$

4. **Roots:** The *root* of a number is a number that is multiplied a specified number of times to give the original number. Square root $= m^{1/2} = \sqrt{m}$. Cube root $= m^{1/3} = \sqrt[3]{m}$.

e.g., 1. $\sqrt{4} = 4^{1/2} = 2$
2. $\sqrt[3]{8} = 8^{1/3} = 2$
3. $\sqrt{125} = 125^{1/2} = (25 \bullet 5)^{1/2} = (25^{1/2})(5^{1/2}) =$
$(\sqrt{25})(\sqrt{5}) = 5\sqrt{5}$
4. $\sqrt{\frac{4}{9}} = \left(\frac{4}{9}\right)^{1/2} = \frac{4^{1/2}}{9^{1/2}} = \frac{\sqrt{4}}{\sqrt{9}} = \frac{2}{3}$

5. **Basic Algebraic Operations:** Algebraic operations are the same as for arithmetic, with the addition of unknown quantities. Manipulate operations in the same way, combining (adding and subtracting) only like terms. Like terms have the same variables with the same exponents.

e.g., 1. $x^2 - 3x + 5x - 3x^2 = -2x^2 + 2x$
2. $(x^2)(x^3) = x^{2+3} = x^5$
3. $4x^3y^4 \div 2xy^3 = 2x^2y$
4. $\frac{5}{x} + \frac{3}{x} = \frac{5+3}{x} = \frac{8}{x}$
5. $\left(\frac{x^2y^3}{z}\right)\left(\frac{x^3y^2}{wz}\right) = \frac{x^5y^5}{wz^2}$

6. **Multiplying Polynomials:** A *polynomial* is an algebraic expression with more than one term. A binomial is a polynomial consisting of exactly two terms. When multiplying two binomials, use the *FOIL* (*F*irst, *O*uter, *I*nner, *L*ast) *method*:

$(x + y)(x + y) = ?$
Multiply the *first* terms: $x \bullet x = x^2$
Multiply the *outer* terms: $x \bullet y = xy$
Multiply the *inner* terms: $y \bullet x = yx = xy$
Multiply the *last* terms: $y \bullet y = y^2$
Combine like terms: $(x + y)(x + y) = x^2 + 2xy + y^2$

e.g., $(x - y)(x - y) = ?$
First: $(x)(x) = x^2$
Outer: $(x)(-y) = -xy$
Inner: $(-y)(x) = -xy$
Last: $(-y)(-y) = y^2$
Combine: $x^2 - xy - xy + y^2 = x^2 - 2xy + y^2$

If the two polynomials are not binomials, do the following:

e.g., $(x+y)(x^2+2xy+y^2)$
$= x(x^2)+x(2xy)+x(y^2)+y(x^2)+y(2xy)+y(y^2)$
$= x^3+2x^2y+xy^2+x^2y+21xy^2+y^3$
$= x^3+3x^2y+3xy^2+y^3$

Memorize these common patterns:
$(x+y)^2=(x+y)(x+y)=x^2+2xy+y^2$
$(x-y)^2=(x-y)(x-y)=x^2-2xy+y^2$
$(x+y)(x-y)=x^2-y^2$

7. **Factoring:** *Factoring* is the reverse of multiplication. There are three factoring situations.

   a. If all of the terms in an expression contain a common factor, then it can be factored out of each term. Do this first, if possible.

   e.g., 1. $ab+ac+ad=a(b+c+d)$
   2. $x^2+x^3+x^4=x^2(1+x+x^2)$
   3. $3xy+xz+4x=x(3y+z+4)$

   b. Algebraic expressions are often one of three common patterns.

   e.g., 1. $x^2+2xy+y^2=(x+y)(x+y)=(x+y)^2$
   2. $x^2-2xy+y^2=(x-y)(x-y)=(x-y)^2$
   3. $x^2-y^2=(x-y)(x+y)$

   c. Occasionally, expressions do not fall into one of the two categories above. To factor the expression, which is usually in the form ax^2+bx+c, set up the following blank diagram: (   )(   ). Fill in the diagram by answering the following questions:

   - What factors produce the first term, ax^2?
   - What factors produce the last term, c?
   - Which of the possible factors, when added together, produce the middle term, bx?

   e.g., 1. $x^2+3x+2=(x+2)(x+1)$
   2. $x^2+4x-12=(x+6)(x-2)$

8. **Solving Linear Equations:** An equation that contains variables only of the first power is a linear equation. You can add, subtract, multiply, and divide both sides of an equation by the same value without changing the statement of equality. (You cannot multiply or divide by zero.) To find the value of a variable, isolate the variable on one side of the equation and solve.

   e.g., 1. $4x+2=2x+10$
   $4x+2-2x=2x+10-2x$
   $2x+2=10$
   $2x+2-2=10-2$
   $2x=8$
   $\frac{2x}{2}=\frac{8}{2}$
   $x=4$

   2. $\frac{2x+6}{2}=9$
   $x=\frac{9(2)-6}{2}=6$

9. **Solving Quadratic Equations:** Equations that involve variables of the second power are called quadratic equations and may have zero, one, or two real solutions.

   a. If possible, take the square root of both sides.

   e.g., $x^2=25 \Rightarrow x=\pm 5$

   b. Otherwise, arrange all terms on the left side of equation so that the right side of equation is zero: $ax^2+bx+c=0$. Factor the left side of the equation and set each binomial equal to zero. Solve for the unknown.

   e.g., 1. Solve for x: $x^2-2x=3$.
   $x^2-2x-3=0 \Rightarrow (x-3)(x+1)=0$
   $x=3$ or $x=-1$
   2. Solve for x: $x^2-3x=4$.
   $x^2-3x-4=0 \Rightarrow (x-4)(x+1)=0$
   $x=4$ or $x=-1$

   c. The quadratic formula, $x=\frac{-b\pm\sqrt{b^2-4ac}}{2a}$, may also be used to solve quadratic equations.

   e.g., Solve for x: $3-x=2x^2$.
   $3-x=2x^2 \Rightarrow 2x^2+x-3=0$
   $a=2;\ b=1;\ c=-3$.
   $x=\frac{-b\pm\sqrt{b^2-4ac}}{2a}=\frac{-1\pm\sqrt{1^2-4(2)(-3)}}{2(2)}=\frac{-1\pm\sqrt{1+24}}{4}$
   $=\frac{-1\pm 5}{4}=1$ or $-\frac{3}{2}$

   d. The ACT, PLAN, and EXPLORE allow calculators. A graphing calculator may be used to quickly solve quadratic equations if it has a quadratic formula program.

10. **Solving Simultaneous Equations:** Given two equations with two variables, the equations may be solved simultaneously for the values of the two variables. There are several methods for solving simultaneous equations.

Method 1—Substitution: Solve one equation for one variable and substitute this into the other equation to find the other variable. Plug back into the first equation.

e.g., If $2x - y = 6$ and $3x + 2y = 16$, solve for x and y.

Solve for y: $2x - y = 6$

$y = 6 - 2x = 2x - 6$

Substitute: $3x + 2y = 16$

$3x + 2(2x - 6) = 16$

$3x + 4x - 12 = 16$

$7x = 28$

$x = 4$

Substitute: $y = 2x - 6 = 2(4) - 6 = 2$

Method 2—Elimination: Make the coefficients of one variable equal and then add (or subtract) the two equations to eliminate one variable.

e.g., If $2x - y = 6$ and $3x + 2y = 16$, solve for x and y.

Combine: $2[2x - y = 6]$

$\underline{+\,3x + 2y = 16}$

$7x = 28 \Rightarrow x = 4$

Substitute: $2x - y = 6$

$2(4) - y = 6$

$y = 2$

Method 3—Graphing Calculator: The ACT, PLAN, and EXPLORE allow calculators: a graphing calculator may be used to quickly solve simultaneous equations. In each equation, solve for y in terms of x. Graph both equations simultaneously; the point of intersection, (x, y), is the solution. Some calculators may have a built-in program to solve simultaneous equations.

e.g., If $2x - y = 6$ and $3x + 2y = 16$, solve for x and y.

Solve each equation for y as a function of x.

$2x - y = 6$

$-y = 6 - 2x$

$y = \frac{(6 - 2x)}{-1}$

$3x + 2y = 16$

$2y = 16 - 3x$

$y = \frac{(16 - 3x)}{2}$

Graph both equations for y—the intersection is found at (4, 2).

Method 4—Calculator System Solver Program: A graphing calculator with a system solver program may also be used to solve simultaneous equations. Graphing the equations to find the point of intersection is not necessary using a system solver program.

11. **Inequalities:** The fundamental rule for working with inequalities is similar to that for working with equalities. The same value may be added or subtracted to each side of an inequality without changing the inequality. Each side may be multiplied or divided by the same *positive* value without changing the direction of the inequality.

e.g.,
1. $5 > 2$
   $5 + 25 > 2 + 25$
   $30 > 27$
2. $24 > 20$
   $24(2) > 20(2)$
   $48 > 40$
3. $24 > 20$
   $24 \div 4 > 20 \div 4$
   $6 > 5$

To multiply or divide by a *negative* number, reverse the direction of the inequality.

e.g.,
1. $4 > 2$
   $4(-2) < 2(-2)$
   $-8 < -4$
2. $4 > 2$
   $4 \div (-2) < 2 \div (-2)$
   $-2 < -1$

12. **Slope:** The *slope*, m, of a line describes its steepness. It is defined as the change in y-values divided by the change in x-values, or rise over run.

$$m = \frac{\Delta y}{\Delta x} = \frac{y_2 - y_1}{x_2 - x_1} = \frac{\text{rise}}{\text{run}}$$

e.g., The slope of the line that contains points (−3, 5) and (2, 7) is: $m = \frac{y_2 - y_1}{x_2 - x_1} = \frac{7 - 5}{2 - (-3)} = \frac{2}{5}$.

13. **Linear Equations:**

Slope-Intercept Form: $y = mx + b$; $m = \text{slope} = \frac{\Delta y}{\Delta x} = \frac{y_2 - y_1}{x_2 - x_1}$

Point-Slope Form: $y - y_1 = m(x - x_1)$

Standard Form: $Ax + By = C$; $m = -\frac{A}{B}$

14. **Distance Formula:** The distance between two points can be found using the *distance formula*:

$$d = \sqrt{(x_2 - x_1)^2 + (y_2 - y_1)^2}$$

where (x_1, y_1) and (x_2, y_2) are the given points.

e.g., The distance between (−1, 4) and (7, 3) is equal to: $d = \sqrt{(7 - (-1))^2 + (3 - 4)^2} = \sqrt{64 + 1} = \sqrt{65}$.

15. **Midpoint Formula:** The midpoint between two points, (x_1, y_1) and (x_2, y_2), is found using the *midpoint formula*:

$$\text{midpoint} = \left(\frac{x_1 + x_2}{2}, \frac{y_1 + y_2}{2}\right)$$

e.g., The midpoint between points (−3, 6) and (4, −9) is:

$$\left(\frac{x_1 + x_2}{2}, \frac{y_1 + y_2}{2}\right) = \left(\frac{-3 + 4}{2}, \frac{6 + -9}{2}\right) = \left(\frac{1}{2}, -\frac{3}{2}\right).$$

16. **Functions:** A function is a set of ordered pairs (x, y) such that for each value of x, there is exactly one value of y. The set of x-values for which the set is defined is called the domain of the function. The set of corresponding values of y is called the range of the function.

e.g., What is the domain and range for $f(x) = x^2$?

f represents the function. x represents values in the domain of the function. $f(x)$ represents values in the range of the function. Since x can be any real number, the domain is the set of all real numbers. We square the value of x to obtain $f(x)$. Squaring any real number yields a number of zero or more. Thus, the range is the set of all non-negative numbers.

Common Equations Summary

1. **Distance:** *Distance* = (*Rate*)(*Time*). Given two of the three values, any unknown may be solved for by rearranging the equation.

   e.g., After driving constantly for four hours, Olivia reached her destination—200 miles from where she started. What was her average rate of travel?

   Distance = (Rate)(Time)

   $\text{Rate} = \frac{\text{Distance}}{\text{Time}} = \frac{200 \text{ miles}}{4 \text{ hours}} = 50 \text{ mph}$

2. **Simple Interest:** $I_s = Prt$, where P is the principal, r is the rate, and t is the time period.

   e.g., With a principal of $1,200 and a rate of 10% per year, what was the interest earned over one month?

   $I_s = Prt = (\$1{,}200)\left(\frac{0.10}{\text{year}}\right)\left(\frac{1 \text{ year}}{12 \text{ months}}\right) = \$10$

3. **Compound Interest:** $I_c = P(1 + r)^n - P$, where P is the principal, r is the rate, and n is the number of periods.

   e.g., With a principal of $1,000 and a compound interest rate of 15% per year, how much compound interest was earned over 5 years?

   $$\begin{aligned} I_c &= P(1+r)^n - P \\ &= (\$1{,}000)(1+0.15)^5 - (\$1{,}000) \\ &\approx \$2{,}011 - \$1{,}000 = \$1{,}011 \end{aligned}$$

4. **Combined Work Rates:** $Rate_1 + Rate_2 = Rate_3$

   e.g., Machine I washes four loads in 60 minutes and Machine II washes one load in 30 minutes. How many loads will both machines working together wash in 20 minutes?

   $\frac{x \text{ loads}}{20 \text{ min.}} = \frac{4 \text{ loads}}{60 \text{ min.}} + \frac{1 \text{ load}}{30 \text{ min.}} = \frac{4 \text{ loads}}{60 \text{ min.}} + \frac{2 \text{ loads}}{60 \text{ min.}}$

   $x = 20\left(\frac{4}{60} + \frac{2}{60}\right) = \frac{6(20)}{60} = 2 \text{ loads}$

5. **Mixed Denominations:** When an item gives information that involves *mixed denominations* (*e.g.*, different prices for same item, tickets, colors, *etc.*), set up simultaneous equations and solve the system of equations for the desired unknown quantity.

   e.g., The store sold apples for $0.20 and oranges for $0.50 each. A total of 50 apples and oranges were bought for $19. How many apples and how many oranges were bought?

   x = # of apples; y = # of oranges

   $x + y = 50 \Rightarrow x = 50 - y$

   $$\begin{aligned} (0.20)x + (0.50)y &= 19 \\ 0.2(50 - y) + 0.5y &= 19 \\ 10 - 0.2y + 0.5y &= 19 \\ 0.3y &= 9 \\ y &= 30 \text{ oranges} \end{aligned}$$

   $x = 50 - y = 50 - 30 = 20$ apples

6. **Mixture of Concentrations or Values:** A *mixture item* is one in which two quantities of different items with different concentrations or values are mixed together and a new quantity (the sum of the two) and concentration or value are created.

   $$Q_1C_1 + Q_2C_2 = (Q_1 + Q_2)C_3$$

   e.g., How many liters of a juice that is 10% orange juice must be added to three liters of another juice that is 15% orange juice to produce a mixture that is 12% orange juice?

   $$\begin{aligned} Q_1C_1 + Q_2C_2 &= (Q_1 + Q_2)C_3 \\ Q(0.10) + (3)(0.15) &= (Q + 3)(0.12) \\ 0.1Q + 0.45 &= 0.12Q + 0.36 \\ 0.45 - 0.36 &= 0.12Q - 0.1Q \\ 0.09 &= 0.02Q \\ Q &= 4.5 \end{aligned}$$

7. **Markup, Cost, and Revenue:** $R = (1 + M)C$, where R is the revenue, M is the markup, and C is the cost.

   e.g., The revenue from an item is $120. With a markup in cost of 25%, what is the original cost?

   $C = \frac{R}{1 + M} = \frac{120}{1 + 0.25} = \$96$

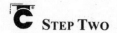

Geometry Summary

1. **Lines and Angles:**

   a. **Symbols:**

   $\overline{AB}$: line segment with endpoints A and B
   $\overrightarrow{AB}$: infinite ray from A through B
   $\overleftrightarrow{AB}$: infinite line through A and B
   $l_1 \parallel l_2$: parallel lines
   $\perp$: perpendicular
   ⊡: right angle

   b. **Facts About Lines and Angles:**

   Vertical angles are equal:

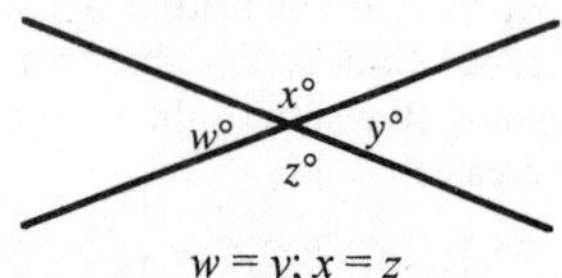

$w = y; x = z$

Two extended lines that do not intersect regardless of length are *parallel* to each other:

Parallel lines intersected by a third line, the transversal, create the following angles:

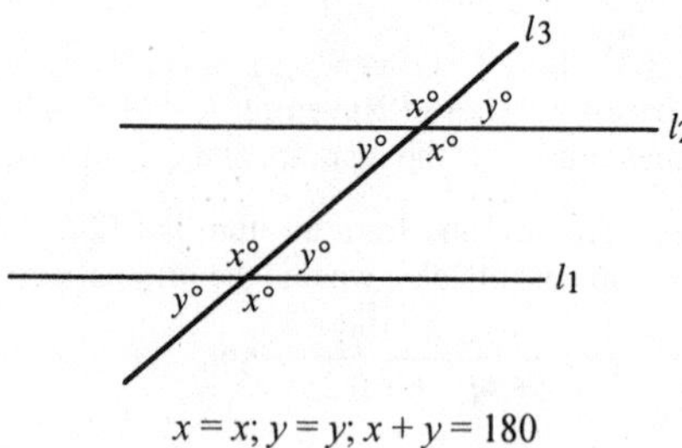

$x = x; y = y; x + y = 180$

Two lines *perpendicular* to the same line are parallel to each other:

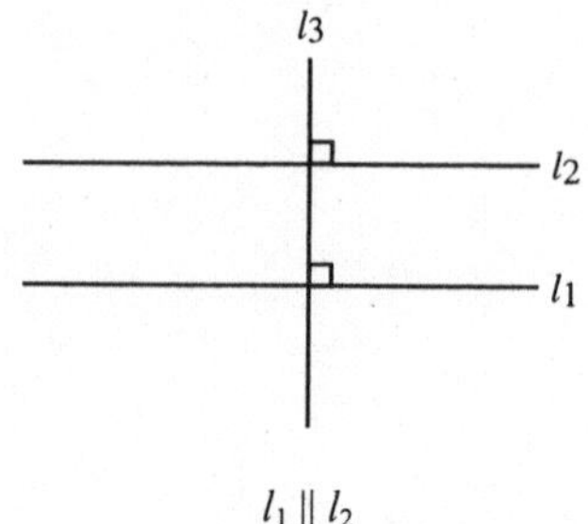

$l_1 \parallel l_2$

There are 180° in a *straight line*:

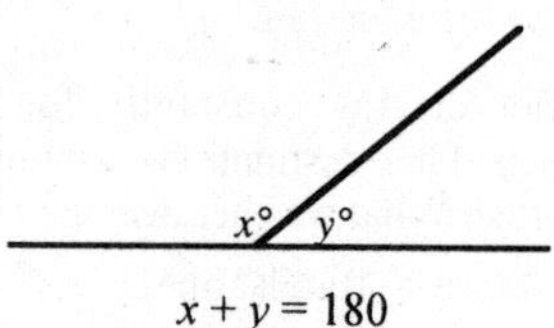

$x + y = 180$

There are 90° in a *right angle* and two right angles form a straight line:

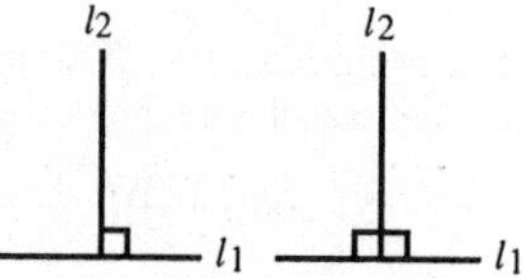

An angle less than 90° is an *acute angle*. In the following figure, $\angle PQR$ is an acute angle:

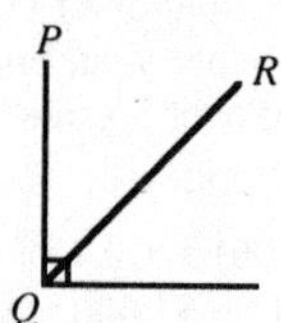

An angle greater than 90° is an *obtuse angle*. In the following figure, $\angle PQR$ is an obtuse angle:

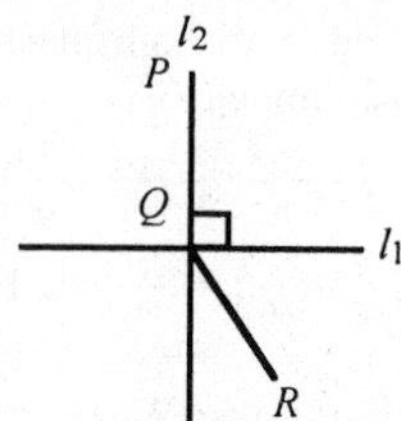

2. **Polygons:** A *polygon* is a closed figure created by three or more lines. The sum of the interior angles of any polygon is $180(n - 2)$, where n = the number of sides of the polygon. The sum of the measures of the exterior angles of a polygon is 360° for all polygons.

   A *triangle* is any polygon with exactly three sides.

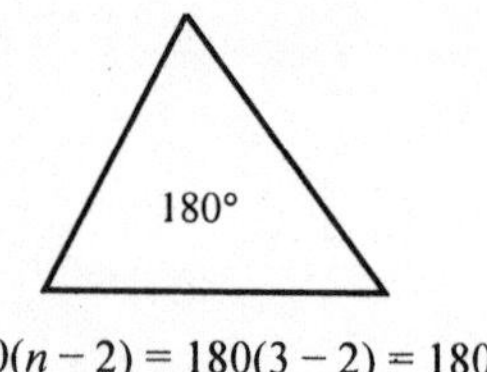

$180(n - 2) = 180(3 - 2) = 180$

A *quadrilateral* is any polygon with exactly four sides. Opposite sides of a *parallelogram* are equal and parallel.

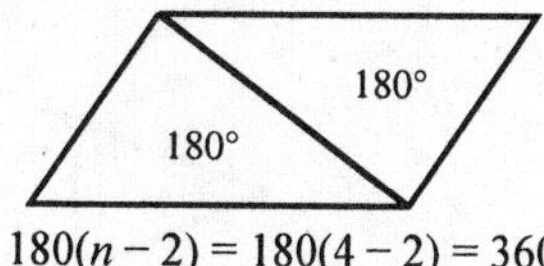

$$180(n-2) = 180(4-2) = 360$$

A *pentagon* is any polygon with exactly five sides.

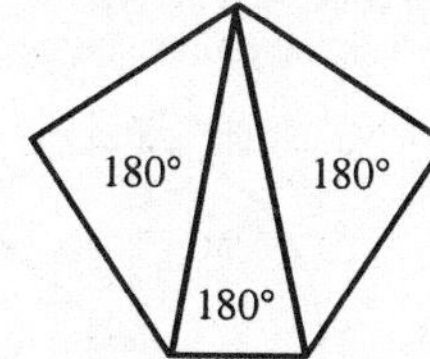

$$180(n-2) = 180(5-2) = 540$$

A *hexagon* is any polygon with exactly six sides.

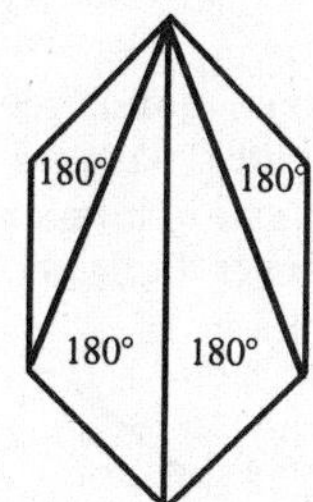

$$180(n-2) = 180(6-2) = 720$$

3. **Triangles:** A *triangle* is a 3-sided figure. Within a given triangle, the larger the angle, the longer the opposite side; conversely, the longer the side, the larger the opposite angle.

A triangle with two equal sides is an *isosceles* triangle. A triangle with three equal sides is an *equilateral* triangle.

Within a given triangle, if two sides are equal, their opposite angles are equal, and vice versa:

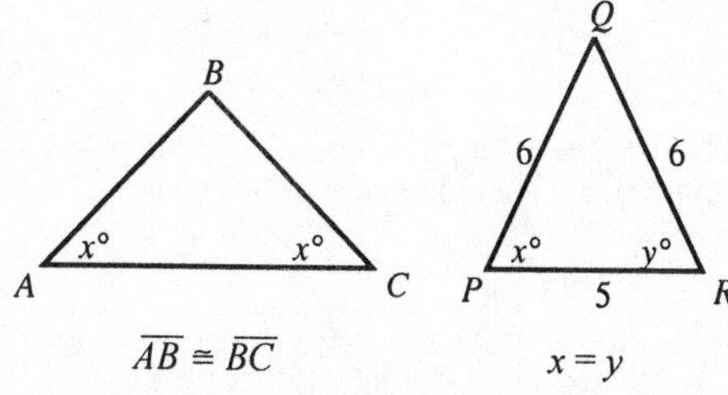

$\overline{AB} \cong \overline{BC}$ $\qquad$ $x = y$

The sides of every right triangle follow the *Pythagorean theorem*: the square of the hypotenuse is equal to the sum of the squares of the other two sides.

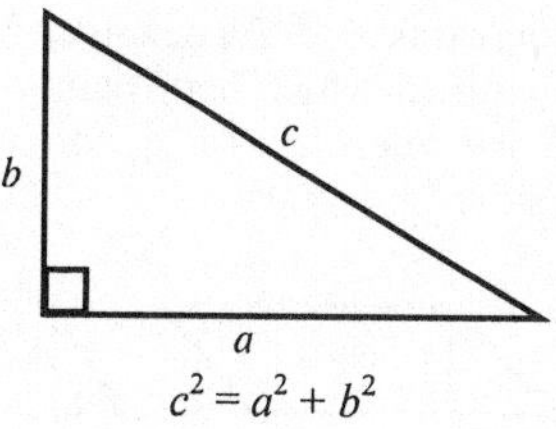

$$c^2 = a^2 + b^2$$

The *perimeter of a triangle* is the sum of the lengths of the three sides:

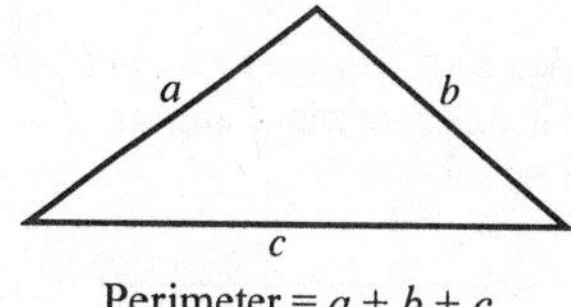

$$\text{Perimeter} = a + b + c$$

The *area of a triangle* is one-half times the base times the height:

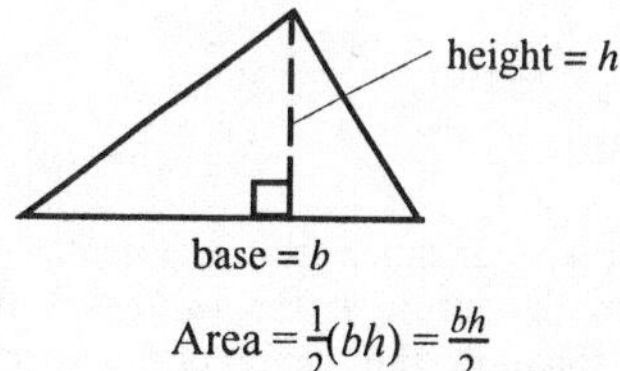

$$\text{Area} = \tfrac{1}{2}(bh) = \frac{bh}{2}$$

In a *45°-45°-90° triangle*, the length of the hypotenuse is equal to the length of either side multiplied by the square root of two:

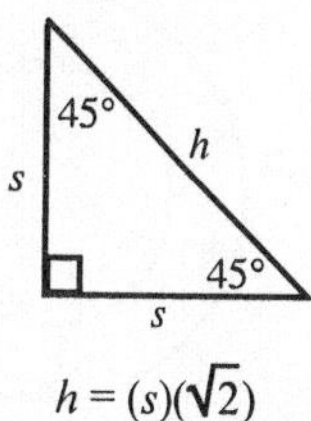

$$h = (s)(\sqrt{2})$$

In a *30°-60°-90° triangle*, the length of the side opposite the 30° angle is equal to one-half the length of the hypotenuse and the length of the side opposite the 60° angle is equal to one-half the length of the hypotenuse multiplied by $\sqrt{3}$:

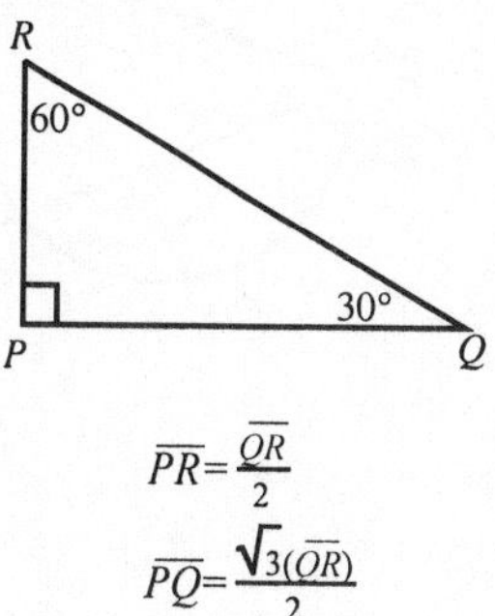

$$\overline{PR} = \frac{\overline{QR}}{2}$$

$$\overline{PQ} = \frac{\sqrt{3}(\overline{QR})}{2}$$

4. **Parallelograms and Trapezoids:** A *parallelogram* is a quadrilateral in which both pairs of opposite sides are parallel. A *trapezoid* is a quadrilateral with only two parallel sides.

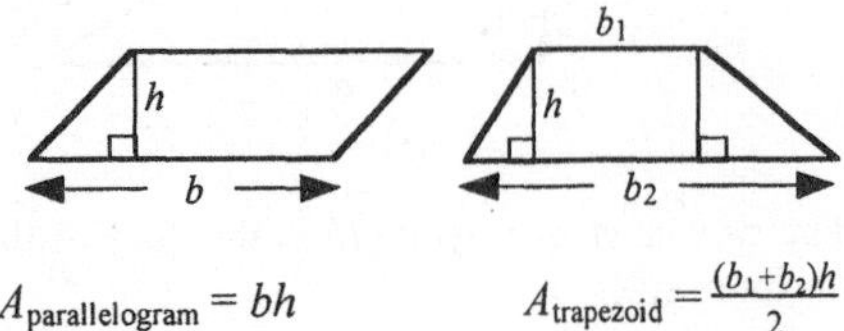

$A_{parallelogram} = bh$ $\qquad$ $A_{trapezoid} = \frac{(b_1+b_2)h}{2}$

5. **Rectangles and Squares:** A *rectangle* is any four-sided figure that has four right angles. A *square* is a rectangle with four equal sides:

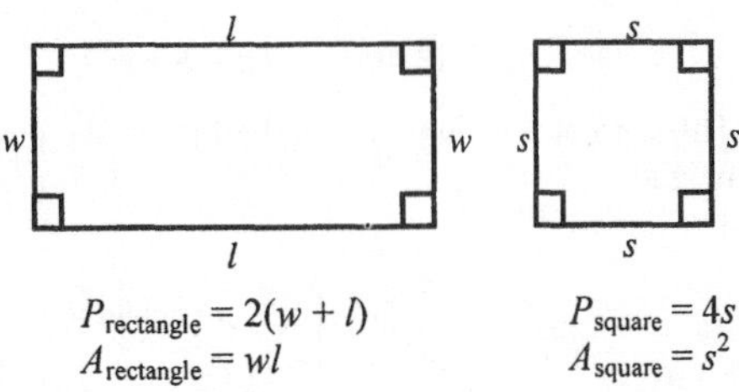

$P_{rectangle} = 2(w + l)$
$A_{rectangle} = wl$

$P_{square} = 4s$
$A_{square} = s^2$

6. **Circles:** The distance from the center of a circle to any point on the circle is the *radius*. A line segment that passes through the center of a circle and that has endpoints on the circle is called the *diameter*. The diameter of a circle is twice the radius. There are 360° of *arc* in a circle:

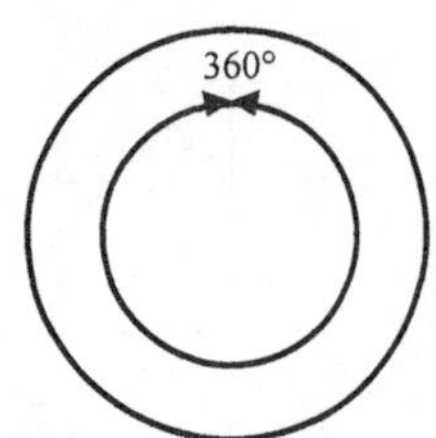

An angle inscribed in a circle intercepts an arc that is twice its measure:

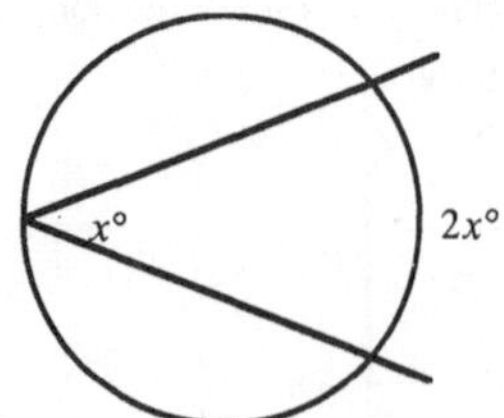

An angle whose vertex is at the center of a circle intercepts an arc of the same measure:

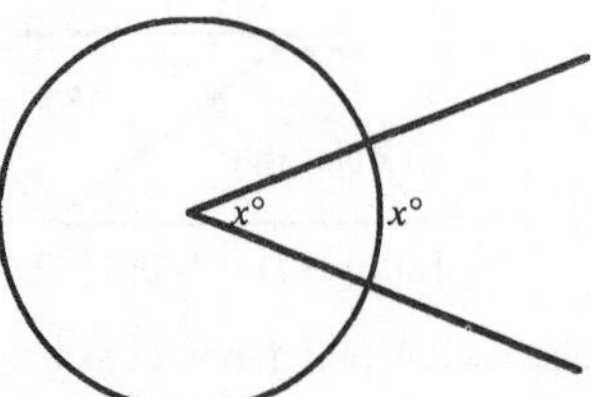

The *circumference of a circle* is the radius times 2π. The *area of a circle* is the radius squared times π.

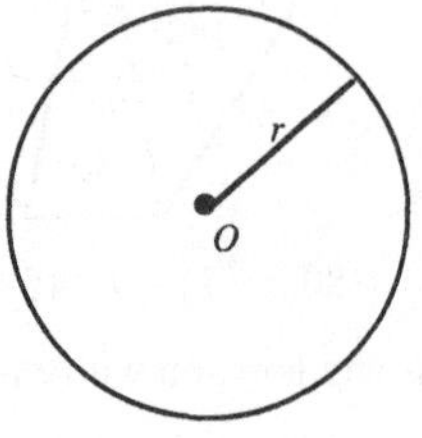

$C_{circle} = 2\pi r$; $A_{circle} = \pi r^2$

7. **Solid Geometry:** Solid geometry refers to three-dimensional figures. *Volume* is a three-dimensional quantity. The *volume of a rectangular solid* is the length times the width times the height:

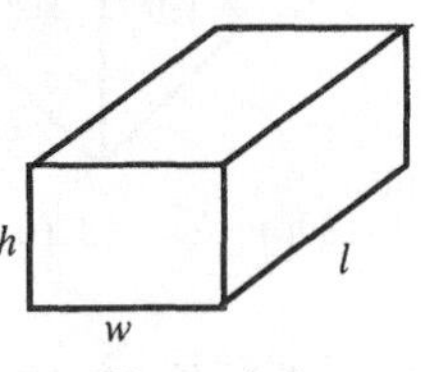

$V_{solid} = lwh$

The *volume of a cylinder* is the height times the radius squared times π.

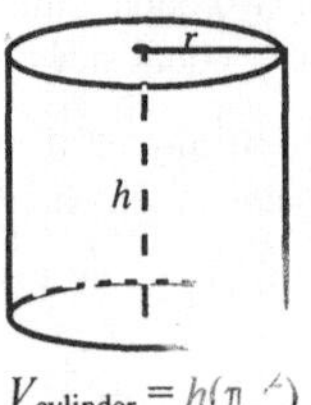

$V_{cylinder} = h(\pi r^2)$

The *volume of a right circular cone* is one-third of the height times the radius squared times π.

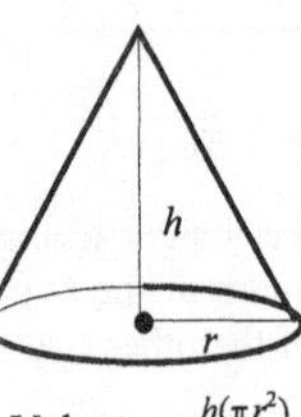

$\text{Volume} = \frac{h(\pi r^2)}{3}$

The *surface area of a sphere* is four times π times the radius squared. The *volume of a sphere* is four-thirds times π times the radius cubed.

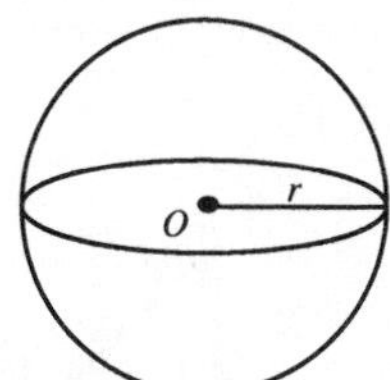

$A_{\text{sphere surface}} = 4\pi r^2$; $V_{\text{sphere}} = \frac{4\pi r^3}{3}$

Trigonometry Summary

1. **Basic Trigonometric Functions:** The three basic trigonometric functions are sine, cosine, and tangent. The functions can be viewed in relationship to a right triangle.

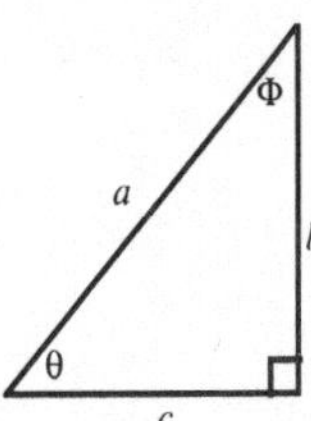

The *hypotenuse* is the side opposite the right angle. The *side opposite* is the side opposite the referenced angle. The *side adjacent* is the side next to the referenced angle, but not the hypotenuse.

Memorize these trigonometric definitions:

sine: $\sin\theta = \frac{\text{side Opposite } \angle\theta}{\text{Hypotenuse}} = \frac{b}{a}$

cosine: $\cos\theta = \frac{\text{side Adjacent } \angle\theta}{\text{Hypotenuse}} = \frac{c}{a}$

tangent: $\tan\theta = \frac{\text{side Opposite } \angle\theta}{\text{side Adjacent } \angle\theta} = \frac{b}{c}$

cosecant: $\csc\theta = \frac{1}{\sin\theta} = \frac{\text{Hypotenuse}}{\text{side Opposite } \angle\theta} = \frac{a}{b}$

secant: $\sec\theta = \frac{1}{\cos\theta} = \frac{\text{Hypotenuse}}{\text{side Adjacent } \angle\theta} = \frac{a}{c}$

cotangent: $\cot\theta = \frac{1}{\tan\theta} = \frac{\text{side Adjacent } \angle\theta}{\text{side Opposite } \angle\theta} = \frac{c}{b}$

SOH-CAH-TOA can be used to memorize the sine, cosine, and tangent ratios.

e.g., Find the values of sin *A*, cos *A*, tan *A*, csc *A*, sec *A*, cot *A*, sin *C*, cos *C*, tan *C*, csc *C*, sec *C*, and cot *C* in the triangle below.

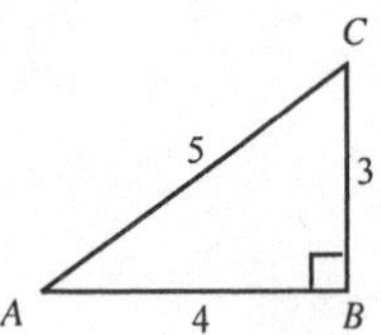

$\sin A = \frac{\text{side opp. } \angle A}{\text{hyp.}} = \frac{3}{5}$; $\sin C = \frac{\text{side opp. } \angle C}{\text{hyp.}} = \frac{4}{5}$

$\cos A = \frac{\text{side adj. } \angle A}{\text{hyp.}} = \frac{4}{5}$; $\cos C = \frac{\text{side adj. } \angle C}{\text{hyp.}} = \frac{3}{5}$

$\tan A = \frac{\text{side opp. } \angle A}{\text{side adj. } \angle A} = \frac{3}{4}$; $\tan C = \frac{\text{side opp. } \angle C}{\text{side adj. } \angle C} = \frac{4}{3}$

$\csc A = \frac{\text{hyp.}}{\text{side opp. } \angle A} = \frac{5}{3}$; $\csc C = \frac{\text{hyp.}}{\text{side opp. } \angle C} = \frac{5}{4}$

$\sec A = \frac{\text{hyp.}}{\text{side adj. } \angle A} = \frac{5}{4}$; $\sec C = \frac{\text{hyp.}}{\text{side adj. } \angle C} = \frac{5}{3}$

$\cot A = \frac{\text{side adj. } \angle A}{\text{side opp. } \angle A} = \frac{4}{3}$; $\cot C = \frac{\text{side adj. } \angle C}{\text{side opp. } \angle C} = \frac{3}{4}$

e.g., In the right triangle below, $\sin x = 0.75$. What is the length of $\overline{AC}$?

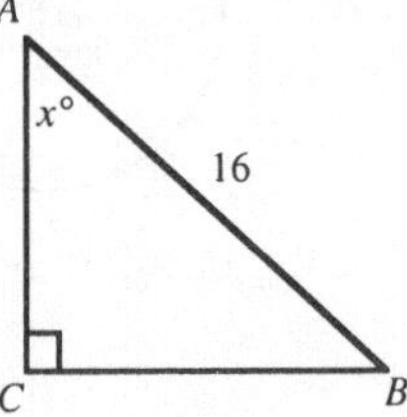

$\sin x = \frac{\text{side opposite } \angle x}{\text{hypotenuse}} \Rightarrow \frac{3}{4} = \frac{\overline{BC}}{16} \Rightarrow \overline{BC} = \frac{3(16)}{4} = 12.$

Therefore, using the Pythagorean theorem: $(\overline{AB})^2 = (\overline{AC})^2 + (\overline{BC})^2 \Rightarrow 16^2 = (\overline{AC})^2 + 12^2 \Rightarrow (\overline{AC})^2 = 256 - 144 = 112 \Rightarrow \overline{AC} = \sqrt{112} = \sqrt{16(7)} = 4\sqrt{7}.$

2. **Useful Trigonometric Relationships:**

$\sin x = \frac{1}{\csc x}$, $\cos x = \frac{1}{\sec x}$, $\tan x = \frac{1}{\cot x}$, $\tan x = \frac{\sin x}{\cos x}$,

$\sin^2 x + \cos^2 x = 1$; $1 + \cot^2 x = \csc^2 x$; $\tan^2 x + 1 = \sec^2 x$

Note: $\sin^2 x$ is the equivalent of $(\sin x)^2$.

e.g., If $\sin x = \frac{3}{5}$ and $\cos x = \frac{4}{5}$, what is the value of tan *x*, csc *x*, sec *x*, and cot *x*?

$\tan x = \frac{\sin x}{\cos x} = \frac{\frac{3}{5}}{\frac{4}{5}} = \frac{3}{4}$, $\csc x = \frac{1}{\sin x} = \frac{1}{\frac{3}{5}} = \frac{5}{3}$

$\sec x = \frac{1}{\cos x} = \frac{1}{\frac{4}{5}} = \frac{5}{4}$, $\cot x = \frac{1}{\tan x} = \frac{1}{\frac{3}{4}} = \frac{4}{3}$

e.g., If $\sin^2 x = \frac{1}{4}$, what is the value of $\cos^2 x$?

$\cos^2 x = 1 - \sin^2 x = 1 - \frac{1}{4} = \frac{3}{4}.$

3. **Graphing Using Trigonometry:** Frequently, trigonometry is used in graphing. Angles on a graph are customarily measured in a counterclockwise manner from the positive *x*-axis.

e.g., 1. In the figure below, the angle shown has a measure of 210°: 90° + 90° + 30° = 210°.

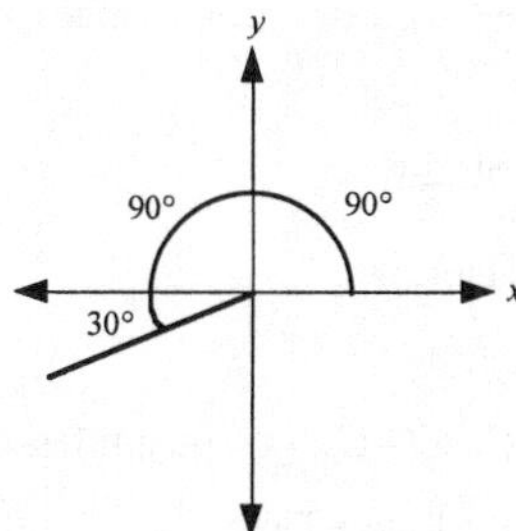

2. Without using a calculator, determine the values of cos 300° and sin 300°.

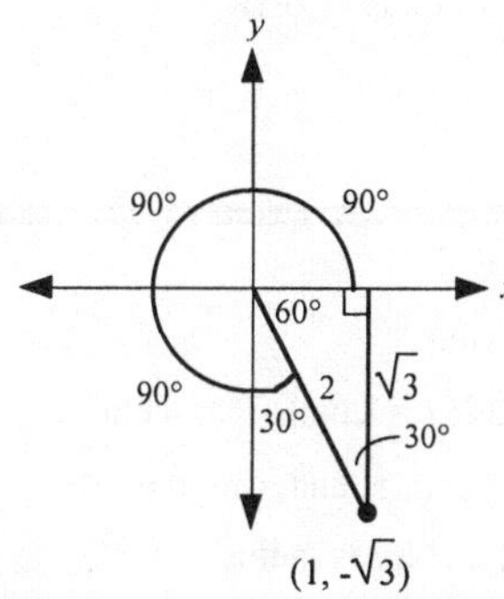

Notice that after drawing the angle, we create a right triangle by drawing a perpendicular from the end of the angle to the x-axis. The hypotenuse of any such triangle is always considered to be positive. However, the point at the end of the original angle may not always have positive coordinates. You may make up any length desired for one side of the triangle. Then, use geometry or trigonometry with the angles inside the triangle to get the remaining lengths. In this example, we let the hypotenuse equal 2 and used geometry or trigonometry to get 1 and $\sqrt{3}$ as shown on the figure. Notice that the point at the end of our original 300° angle has a positive x-coordinate, 1, and a negative y-coordinate, $-\sqrt{3}$. We must use those signed values. The 300° angle leaves us 60° from the closer x-axis. Thus, cos 300° uses the 60° angle: $\cos 300° = \frac{\text{side adj.}}{\text{hyp.}} = \frac{1}{2}$, and $\sin 300° = \frac{\text{side opp.}}{\text{hyp.}} = -\frac{\sqrt{3}}{2}$.

ARITHMETIC, ALGEBRA, AND COORDINATE GEOMETRY FORMULAS

Averages: $A = \frac{x_1 + x_2 + x_3 + \ldots + x_n}{n}$; $x_1, x_2, x_3 \ldots x_n$ = values, n = total numbers

Percentage Problems: $\frac{\text{is}}{\text{of}} = \frac{\%}{100}$

Price Percentage Change: $\Delta\% = \frac{|\text{New Price} - \text{Old Price}|}{\text{Old Price}}$

Distance Problems: Distance = Rate • Time

Combined Work Rate Problems: $\text{Rate}_3 = \text{Rate}_1 + \text{Rate}_2$

Mixture Problems: $(Q_1 + Q_2)C_3 = Q_1C_1 + Q_2C_2$; Q = quantities, C = concentrations

Simple Interest Problems: Interest = Principal • Rate • Time

Compound Interest Problems: $\text{Interest} = (\text{Principal})(1 + \text{Rate})^{\#\text{ of periods}} - \text{Principal}$

Revenue Problems: Revenue = (1 + Markup)(Cost)

Slope-Intercept Linear Equation: $y = mx + b$

Slope of a Line: $m = \frac{y_2 - y_1}{x_2 - x_1}$

GEOMETRY FORMULAS

Perimeter of a Square: $P_{\text{square}} = 4s$; s = side

Perimeter of a Rectangle: $P_{\text{rectangle}} = 2l + 2w$; l = length, w = width

Perimeter of a Triangle: $P_{\text{triangle}} = a + b + c$; a, b, and c are the sides

Circumference of a Circle: $C_{\text{circle}} = 2\pi r$; $\pi \approx 3.14$, r = radius

Area of a Square: $A_{\text{square}} = s^2$; s = length of side

Area of a Rectangle: $A_{\text{rectangle}} = lw$; l = length, w = width

Area of Parallelogram: $A_{\text{parallelogram}} = bh$; b = base, h = height

Area of Trapezoid: $A_{\text{trapezoid}} = \frac{(b_1 + b_2)h}{2}$; b = base, h = height

Area of a Triangle: $A_{\text{triangle}} = \frac{bh}{2}$; b = base, h = height

Area of a Circle: $A_{\text{circle}} = \pi r^2$; r = radius, $\pi \approx 3.14$

Volume of a Cube: $V_{\text{cube}} = s^3$; s = side

Volume of a Rectangle Solid: $V_{\text{solid}} = lwh$; l = length, w = width, h = height

Volume of a Cylinder: $V_{\text{cylinder}} = \pi r^2 h$; h = height, $\pi \approx 3.14$, r = radius

Volume of a Cone: $V_{\text{cone}} = \frac{\pi r^2 h}{3}$, h = height, $\pi \approx 3.14$, r = radius

Surface Area of a Sphere: $A_{\text{sphere surface}} = 4\pi r^2$; $\pi \approx 3.14$, r = radius

Volume of a Sphere: $V_{\text{sphere}} = \frac{4\pi r^3}{3}$; $\pi \approx 3.14$, r = radius

POLYGON FORMULAS

45°-45°-90° Triangle: $h = s\sqrt{2}$; h = hypotenuse, s = length of either leg

30°-60°-90° Triangle: $a = \frac{h}{2}$, a = side opposite ∠30°, h = hypotenuse

$b = \frac{\sqrt{3(h)}}{2}$; b = side opposite ∠60°, h = hypotenuse

Pythagorean Theorem (Right Triangles): $c^2 = a^2 + b^2$; c = hypotenuse, a and b = legs

Sum of Interior Angles of Polygon: $S = 180(n - 2)$; n = number of sides of the polygon

TRIGONOMETRY FORMULAS

$\sin A = \frac{\text{opp}}{\text{hyp}}$ $\cos A = \frac{\text{adj}}{\text{hyp}}$ $\tan A = \frac{\text{opp}}{\text{adj}}$ $\csc A = \frac{\text{hyp}}{\text{opp}}$ $\sec A = \frac{\text{hyp}}{\text{adj}}$ $\cot A = \frac{\text{adj}}{\text{opp}}$

$\sin^2 A + \cos^2 A = 1$ $1 + \cot^2 A = \csc^2 A$ $\tan^2 A + 1 = \sec^2 A$

GLOSSARY OF TERMS

Absolute Value—the value of a number when the sign is not considered
Acute Angle—an angle with a measure of less than 90°
Adjacent Angles—angles that share a common side and a common vertex
Area—the space within a closed plane figure, measured in square units
Binomial—an algebraic expression with two terms
Circle—the set of all points in a plane that are equidistant from a center point
Circumference—the distance around a circle
Coefficient—the number in front of a term
Complementary Angles—two angles with a sum of 90°
Composite Numbers—a number that can be divided evenly by more than itself and one
Cube (1)—a six-sided solid with all six faces being equal-sized squares
Cube (2)—the result when a number is multiplied by itself twice
Cube Root—a number that when raised to the third power will yield a second given number
Denominator—the bottom term of a fraction
Diameter—a line segment extending from one side of a circle to the opposite, through the center point
Difference—the result of subtraction
Domain—the set of all x-values for a function
Equilateral Triangle—a triangle with all three sides equal and all three angles being 60°
Evaluate—to determine the value of an expression
Exponent—used to indicate the operation of repeated multiplication
Factor—an integer that divides into another equally
Function—ordered pairs (x, y) with exactly one y-value for any x-value
Hypotenuse—the side opposite the right angle of a right triangle
Improper Fraction—a fraction where the numerator is larger than the denominator
Integers—the set of numbers divisible by one without producing a remainder
Irrational Numbers—any number that cannot be expressed as a fraction
Isosceles Triangle—a triangle with two equal sides and equal opposite angles
Least Common Denominator—the smallest natural number that can be divided evenly by all denominators in the equation
Legs—in a right triangle, the two sides that are not the hypotenuse
Mean—the sum of all items divided by the number of items
Median—in a set of numbers arranged in order, the middle value or the mean of the two middle values
Mixed Number—a term that has both a whole number part and a fractional part
Mode—the most commonly occurring value in a set of values
Monomial—an algebraic expression with only one term
Natural Numbers—the set of positive integers starting with 1
Numerator—the top term of a fraction
Obtuse Angle—an angle with a measure between 90° and 180°
Origin—the intersection between the x- and y-axes of a coordinate graph
Parallel Lines—lines that never intersect regardless of how far they are extended
Parallelogram—a four-sided closed figure with opposite sides that are parallel and of equal length
Percentage—a fraction with a denominator of 100
Perimeter—the total distance around the outside of a polygon
Perpendicular Lines—two lines that intersect at a 90°angle
Polygon—a multi-sided plane closed figure
Polynomial—an algebraic expression with two or more terms
Power—used to indicate repeated multiplication
Prime Numbers—numbers that are evenly divisible only by themselves and one
Product—the result of multiplication
Proper Fraction—a fraction where the denominator is larger than the numerator
Quadrants—the four sections of a coordinate graph
Quadrilateral—a four-sided plane closed figure
Quotient—the result of division
Radius—a line segment extending from the center of a circle to any point on the circle
Range (1)—the difference between the largest and smallest numbers in a set
Range (2)—the set of all y-values for a function
Rational Number—any number that can be expressed as a fraction
Real Numbers—the set of rational and irrational numbers
Rectangle—a four-sided plane closed figure with opposite sides equal and 90°angles
Right Triangle—a triangle with a 90°angle
Root—a number that when raised to a certain power will yield a second given number
Scientific Notation—a number written as the product of a real number between 1 and 10 and a power of 10
Set —a group of numbers, elements, objects, *etc.*
Square (1)—the result when a number is multiplied by itself
Square (2)—a four-sided plane closed figure with all four sides equal and 90°angles
Square Root—a number that when raised to the second power will yield a second given number
Sum—the result of addition
Supplementary Angles—two angles with a sum of 180°
Term—an expression, either numerical or literal
Triangle—a three-sided plane closed figure
Variable—a symbol that is used to stand for a number
Vertex—a point at which two rays or sides of a polygon meet to form an angle
Volume—the space inside a solid, measured in cubic units
Whole Numbers—the set of positive integers including zero
X-axis—the horizontal axis of a coordinate graph
Y-axis—the vertical axis of a coordinate graph

Reading Skills Review

TARGETED EDUCATIONAL SOLUTIONS.

Cambridge Course Concept Outline
READING SKILLS REVIEW

Careful Reading of Item Stems

After surveying thousands of students, we found that up to one-third of the time, an item was answered incorrectly because the student misinterpreted the item. In other words, students could have answered the item correctly had they understood what the test writers were really asking. You must read the item carefully and correctly, or you will get it wrong.

It may seem that this sort of error would only affect your ability to correctly answer Reading items. In fact, if you cannot read with enough precision to comprehend the exact item that is being asked, you are also limiting your potential to correctly answer English, Mathematics, and Science Reasoning items. An inability to focus on the actual question means that you would most likely have problems in all sections of the exam.

The following exercises are designed to reinforce careful reading of the item stems on the actual test. Although some of the items in this exercise may seem to require knowledge of basic verbal, math, and science concepts, it will not be necessary to "solve" an item. Do not be confused by distracting terminology or by an answer that "might" qualify as a correct restatement of the item stem. The correct answer choice to a Careful Reading item is the most specifically accurate, and therefore the *best*, restatement of the question that is being asked by the test-writers.

For each item in this section, you are asked to determine which of the given answer choices is the best restatement of the original item stem. The following Careful Reading item stems are representative of the four areas that are tested in this Skills Review.

Note: ✓ = correct, ✗ = wrong.

English:

What discussion would most likely precede this passage?
What topic is consistent with the main idea of the passage? ✓
What discussion is directly stated in the first paragraph of the passage? ✗

Mathematics:

After the area of a given figure is increased, what is the percent increase in the area of the figure?
What is the percentage change in area? ✓
What is the new total area after the increase in area? ✗

Reading:

According to the passage, all of the following are true EXCEPT:
Which of the following statements is not true? ✓
Which of the following statements is true? ✗

Science Reasoning:

What assumption is made to support the theory of the expanding universe?
The theory of the expanding universe is supported by which statement? ✓
The theory of the contracting universe is supported by which statement? ✗

EXERCISE 1

Careful Reading of English Item Stems

English items appear on the ACT, the PLAN, and the EXPLORE. The following exercise will help you focus on the exact question that is being asked by English item stems that correspond to passages on the ACT English Test. There is no need for you to see the entire selection as it would appear on the actual exam. When you have become proficient at careful reading, you will no longer waste valuable time on an individual item trying to determine the exact question that is being asked.

DIRECTIONS: Choose the *best* restatement of the item stem. Answers are on page 924.

1. Which of the following represents the most logical sequence for the paragraphs?

   (A) In what order should the paragraphs be arranged?
   (B) Which of the following sequences is illogical?
   (C) In what order should the paragraphs not be arranged?
   (D) Which paragraph would not be represented in the most logical sequence?

2. Is the author's quote of D.H. Lawrence in the last paragraph appropriate?

   (F) Is the quote made by the author appropriate to the passage?
   (G) Does D.H. Lawrence's quote belong in a different paragraph?
   (H) Is the quote made by D.H. Lawrence appropriate to the passage?
   (J) Does the author correctly quote D.H. Lawrence?

3. The author's intended audience is most likely

   (A) Who is most like the author's intended audience?
   (B) Whom does the author intend to address?
   (C) Which audience does the author most like?
   (D) Whom does the author not intend to address?

4. How might the author have developed the essay so that it was more interesting?

   (F) What would make the essay more interesting?
   (G) How could the author have written a less developed essay?
   (H) What would make the essay less interesting?
   (J) How could the author have written a more developed essay?

5. Which of the following best describes the overall character of the essay?

   (A) What is the main idea of the essay?
   (B) Which character in the essay best describes the overall theme?
   (C) What best describes the main character in the essay?
   (D) Which of the following best describes the characteristics of the essay in general?

6. Which of the following is most probably the author's opinion rather than a fact?

   (F) Which fact is not an opinion held by the author?
   (G) Which of the author's views could be argued as fact?
   (H) Which fact is presented by the author?
   (J) What is indicative of the author's viewpoint?

7. What would be the most logical continuation of the essay?

   (A) Logically, how might the author begin the essay?
   (B) Logically, how might the author end the essay?
   (C) Logically, how might the author continue the essay?
   (D) Logically, how might the author continue the first paragraph?

8. What might logically have preceded this essay?

   (F) What type of passage would logically come before this essay?
   (G) What is the precedent for a logically structured essay?
   (H) What type of passage would logically come after this essay?
   (J) What always precedes a logically structured essay?

9. This essay is most probably taken from a

   (A) What is this essay about?
   (B) How might this essay be continued?
   (C) What might be the source of this essay?
   (D) What might have preceded this essay?

10. What would strengthen the author's contention that con games rank first in heartlessness?

   (F) What weakens the author's argument that con games are not heartless?
   (G) What supports the author's argument that con games are not heartless?
   (H) What strengthens the author's argument that con games are the most heartless?
   (J) What weakens the author's argument that con games are the most heartless?

11. Which of the following would most strengthen the essay?

   (A) What would not make the essay weaker?
   (B) What would make the essay stronger?
   (C) What would not make the essay stronger?
   (D) What would make the essay weaker?

12. Is the final sentence of the passage an appropriate ending?

   (F) Would the final sentence be a more appropriate beginning?
   (G) Does the final sentence appropriately end the passage?
   (H) Is the fifth line an appropriate ending to the second paragraph?
   (J) Is the final sentence an appropriate statement?

13. What assumption is the essay's author making?

   (A) What does the author know to be true?
   (B) What does the author accept to be true?
   (C) What do you, as a reader, know to be true about the author?
   (D) What do you, as a reader, assume to be true about the essay?

14. Where might you find this essay published?

   (F) Where are most essays published?
   (G) Where would you publish this essay?
   (H) In what type of publication might this essay have been published?
   (J) Under what conditions might such an essay have been published?

15. Which of the following is not a strategy the author uses to make his/her point?

   (A) What does the author use to make the point?
   (B) What doesn't the author use to make the point?
   (C) What would not be effective in demonstrating the author's point?
   (D) What is the author's point?

16. Which of the following would most strengthen the author's argument that Shakespeare is the poet of human nature?

   (F) What least weakens the author's argument?
   (G) What most weakens the author's argument?
   (H) What doesn't least strengthen the author's argument?
   (J) What most strengthens the author's argument?

17. The author most likely wrote this essay for which of the following audiences?

   (A) Who most influenced the author?
   (B) Which audience would not read this essay?
   (C) For whom did the author write this essay?
   (D) Who most enjoyed the author's essay?

18. The author relies on which of the following to develop the passage?

   (F) What device is used to develop the passage?
   (G) What is the author's point of view?
   (H) What is the author's tone in the passage?
   (J) What conclusion does the author make in the passage?

19. The author probably quotes St. Augustine in order to

    (A) What is the author's view of St. Augustine?
    (B) Why does the author refer to St. Augustine?
    (C) Why does the author quote St. Augustine?
    (D) What is St. Augustine's quote?

EXERCISE 2

Careful Reading of Mathematics Item Stems

Math items appear on the ACT, the PLAN, and the EXPLORE. The following exercise will help you focus on the exact question that is being asked by Math item stems on the ACT Mathematics Test. It is not necessary to worry about your math skills; these skills are addressed in the Math Skills Review. When you have become proficient at careful reading, you will no longer waste valuable time on an individual item trying to determine the exact question that is being asked.

DIRECTIONS: Choose the *best* restatement of the item stem. Answers are on page 924.

1. If a machine produces 240 thingamabobs per hour, how many minutes are needed for the machine to produce 30 thingamabobs?

   (A) How many minutes does it take to make 270 thingamabobs?
   (B) How many minutes does it take to make 8 sets of 30 thingamabobs each?
   (C) How many minutes does it take to make 240 thingamabobs at 30 thingamabobs per hour?
   (D) How many minutes does it take to make 30 thingamabobs at 240 thingamabobs per hour?

2. After a 20-percent decrease in price, the cost of an item is *D* dollars. What was the price of the item before the decrease?

   (F) What was the original price of the item?
   (G) What was the price before the 80-percent decrease?
   (H) What was the price before the $20 decrease?
   (J) What was the price before the 80-percent increase?

3. If the price of candy increases from 5 pounds for $7 to 3 pounds for $7, how much *less* candy, in pounds, can be purchased for $3.50 at the new price than at the old price?

   (A) How much less candy can be purchased for $3.50 at the old price?
   (B) How much candy can be purchased for $3.50 at the new price?
   (C) How much less candy can be purchased for $3.50 at the new price?
   (D) How much candy can be purchased for $3.50 at the old price?

4. A jar contains 24 white marbles and 48 black marbles. What percent of the marbles in the jar are black?

   (F) What percent of the 72 marbles in the jar are white?
   (G) How many more black marbles than white marbles are in the jar?
   (H) What percent of all the marbles in the jar are not black?
   (J) Of the 72 white and black marbles in the jar, what percent are not white?

5. Twenty students attended Professor Rodriguez's class on Monday and twenty-five students attended on Tuesday. The number of students who attended on Tuesday was what percent of the number of students who attended on Monday?

   (A) 45 students are what percent of 20 students?
   (B) 45 students are what percent of 25 students?
   (C) 25 students are what percent of 20 students?
   (D) 20 students are what percent of 25 students?

6. Willie's monthly electric bills for last year were as follows: $40, $38, $36, $38, $34, $34, $30, $32, $34, $37, $39, and $40. What was the mode?

   (F) What number is the average of the series?
   (G) What number occurs least frequently?
   (H) What number occurs most frequently?
   (J) What number is the median of the series?

7. If 4.5 pounds of chocolate cost \$10, how many pounds of chocolate can be purchased for \$12?

   (A) At the given price, how much more chocolate can be purchased for \$12 than \$10?
   (B) At the given price, what is the cost of 12 pounds of chocolate?
   (C) At the given price, how many pounds can be purchased for \$12?
   (D) At the given price, how many pounds can be purchased for \$10?

8. At Star Lake Middle School, 45 percent of the students bought a yearbook. If 540 students bought yearbooks, how many students did NOT buy a yearbook?

   (F) How many students bought a yearbook?
   (G) How many students did not buy a yearbook if 45% bought yearbooks?
   (H) How many of the 540 students bought a yearbook if 45% bought yearbooks?
   (J) How many of the 540 students did not buy a yearbook?

9. Walking at a constant rate of 4 miles per hour, it took Jill exactly 1 hour to walk home from school. If she walked at a constant rate of 5 miles per hour, how many minutes did the trip take?

   (A) How long was the trip if Jill walked at a rate of 1 mile per hour when it takes 4 hours to walk home at a rate of 5 miles per hour?
   (B) How long was the trip if Jill walked at a rate of 4 miles per hour when it takes 1 hour to walk home at a rate of 5 miles per hour?
   (C) How long was the trip if Jill walked at a rate of 5 miles per hour when it takes 1 hour to walk home at a rate of 4 miles per hour?
   (D) How long was the trip if Jill walked at a rate of 5 miles per hour when it takes 4 hours to walk home at a rate of 1 mile per hour?

10. If the sum of 5 consecutive integers is 40, what is the smallest of the 5 integers?

   (F) What is the smallest of 5 integers that equal 40 when added together?
   (G) What is the smallest of 10 consecutive integers that equal 40 when added together?
   (H) What is the largest of 5 consecutive integers that equal 40 when added together?
   (J) What is the smallest of 5 consecutive integers that equal 40 when added together?

11. Which of the following equations correctly describes the relationship between the values x and y in the table?

   (A) According to the table, what is the relationship between x and y as expressed in an equation?
   (B) How much larger than x is y?
   (C) How much smaller than x is y?
   (D) According to the table, what is the relationship between x and z?

12. The quadratic equation $x^2 - 3x = 4$ can be solved by factoring. Which of the following states the complete solution?

   (F) What is the complete solution to the quadratic equation $x^2 - 4x = 3$?
   (G) What is the complete solution to the quadratic formula?
   (H) What is the complete solution to the quadratic equation $x^2 - 3x = 4$?
   (J) What is one of the values of x for the given quadratic equation?

13. In a card game, a player had 5 successful turns in a row, and after each one, the number of points added to his total score was double what was added the preceding turn. If the player scored a total of 465 points, how many points did he score on the first turn?

   (A) How many points did he score on the fifth turn?
   (B) How many total points did he score after all five turns?
   (C) How many points did he score after the first turn?
   (D) On the first turn, how many points did the player score?

14. At a certain firm, d gallons of fuel are needed per day for each truck. At this rate, g gallons of fuel will supply t trucks for how many days?

   (F) How many t trucks will g gallons supply for d days?
   (G) d gallons will supply t trucks for how many days if g gallons of fuel are needed per day for each truck?
   (H) g gallons will supply t trucks for how many days if d gallons of fuel are needed per day for each truck?
   (J) g gallons and d gallons together will supply t trucks for how many days?

15. A merchant increased the price of a \$25 item by 10 percent. If she then reduces the new price by 10 percent, the final result is equal to which of the following?

(A) What is the final price of a \$25 item after its price has been decreased by 10% and the resulting price is then increased by 10%?
(B) What is 10% of ten \$25 items?
(C) What is the final price of a \$25 item after its price has been increased by 10% and the resulting price is then decreased by 10%?
(D) How much is 20% of a \$25 item?

16. If a train travels *m* miles in *h* hours and 45 minutes, what is its average speed in miles per hour?

(F) How long does it take the train to travel 45 miles?
(G) What is the average speed if a train travels *h* miles in *m* hours and 45 minutes?
(H) What is the average speed, in miles per hour, if a train travels 45 miles in *h* hours and *m* minutes?
(J) What is the average speed if a train travels *m* miles in *h* hours and 45 minutes?

17. In a right isosceles triangle, the hypotenuse is equal to which of the following?

(A) What is the hypotenuse of a right triangle?
(B) What is the hypotenuse of a right triangle in which two sides are equal?
(C) What is the hypotenuse of an isosceles triangle in which all three sides are equal?
(D) What is the hypotenuse of a 30°-60°-90° triangle?

18. If a line intersects two points that are plotted at (3, 6) and (7, 9), what is its slope?

(F) What are the slopes of two lines that include points (3, 6) and (7, 9), respectively?
(G) What is the slope of a line that includes points (3, 6) and (7, -9)?
(H) What is the slope of a line that includes points (6, 3) and (9, 7)?
(J) What is the slope of a line that includes points (3, 6) and (7, 9)?

19. The average of 8 numbers is 6; the average of 6 other numbers is 8. What is the average of all 14 numbers?

(A) What is the average of the 8 numbers?
(B) What is the average of all 14 numbers?
(C) What is the average of 8 numbers plus the other average of 6 numbers?
(D) What is the average of the other 6 numbers?

20. If the fourth term in a geometric sequence is 125 and the sixth term is 3,125, what is the second term of the sequence?

(F) What is the second term in the periodic sequence?
(G) What value is represented between the first and third terms in the geometric sequence?
(H) What geometric term represents the process that is necessary to determine the value of the given sequence?
(J) What is the difference between 3,125 and 125?

EXERCISE 3

Careful Reading of Reading Item Stems

Reading items appear on the ACT, the PLAN, and the EXPLORE. The following exercise will help you focus on the exact question that is being asked by Reading item stems that correspond to passages on the ACT Reading Test. There is no need for you to see the entire selection as it would appear on the actual exam. When you have become proficient at careful reading, you will no longer waste valuable time on an individual item trying to determine the exact question that is being asked.

DIRECTIONS: Choose the *best* restatement of the item stem. Answers are on page 924.

1. What is the main idea of the passage?

   (A) What is the central theme of the passage?
   (B) Which specific detail is mentioned in the first paragraph of the passage?
   (C) Which idea is always stated in the last paragraph of the passage?
   (D) Which idea is a supporting detail in the passage?

2. According to the passage, which of the following was true of the presidential election of 1796?

   (F) What did not happen in the presidential election of 1796?
   (G) What does the passage say about the presidential election of 1792?
   (H) What could have happened in the presidential election of 1796?
   (J) What actually happened in the presidential election of 1796?

3. According to the passage, Hamilton's plan did not include which of the following?

   (A) What was the focus of Hamilton's plan?
   (B) Who opposed Hamilton's plan?
   (C) What was not a part of Hamilton's plan?
   (D) Which of Hamilton's plans did not succeed?

4. The tone of this passage can best be described as

   (F) What is the main point made by the author?
   (G) What is the author's definition of tone?
   (H) How does this passage make you feel?
   (J) How does the author feel about the topic of the passage?

5. According to the passage, all of the following are true of the Republicans EXCEPT

   (A) What is true of the Republicans?
   (B) What is true ONLY of the Republicans?
   (C) What is not true of the Republicans?
   (D) What is not true ONLY of the Republicans?

6. It can be inferred from the passage that the term "Monocrats" means

   (F) What does the term "Monocrats" mean?
   (G) What does the author infer about Monocrats?
   (H) Why does the author use the term "Monocrats" in the passage?
   (J) Where does the author refer to Monocrats in the passage?

7. Unlike the sublittoral zone, the littoral zone has which of the following features?

   (A) What is a definition of the sublittoral zone?
   (B) How does the littoral zone differ from the sublittoral zone?
   (C) Which characteristic isn't true of either zone?
   (D) How are the two zones similar to each other?

8. It can be inferred that Miss Hephzibah views the day's coming events with

   (F) What events occur on this particular day?
   (G) Is Miss Hephzibah inferring how the day's events will occur?
   (H) How does Miss Hephzibah feel about the day's coming events?
   (J) What does Miss Hephzibah infer about the day's coming events?

9. Mrs. Gay's primary quality seems to be her

   (A) How does Mrs. Gay seem to others?
   (B) What does Mrs. Gay's primary quality seem to be?
   (C) Are the quality views of Mrs. Gay not primarily consistent?
   (D) What doesn't the primary quality of Mrs. Gay seem to be?

10. According to the passage, the Republican Party appealed primarily to:

   (F) What was the Republican Party's primary appeal?
   (G) Who won the Republican Party primary?
   (H) Who appealed primarily to the Republican Party?
   (J) Who liked the Republican Party?

11. According to the author, most authorities regard the Biarni narrative as

   (A) How do all authorities regard the Biarni narrative?
   (B) How do most authorities regard the Biarni narrative?
   (C) How does the author regard the Biarni narrative?
   (D) How does the author agree with the authorities in regarding the Biarni narrative?

12. According to the passage, radar will have difficulty locating an airplane under which of the following conditions?

   (F) What is the ideal condition for radar to function properly?
   (G) Under which condition is it impossible to use radar for detecting airplanes?
   (H) Under which condition should airplanes not be permitted to fly?
   (J) Under which condition will radar have difficulty detecting airplanes?

13. The relationship between the frequency and wavelength of a wave is

   (A) What is the wave's relationship to its frequency?
   (B) The frequency and wavelength of a wave have what sort of relationship?
   (C) What is the relationship between a wave and its wavelength?
   (D) How frequently do wavelengths exhibit a relationship to their respective waves?

14. Since radio waves will not penetrate the ionosphere but microwaves will, would you expect x-rays to penetrate the ionosphere?

   (F) Do x-rays penetrate the ionosphere?
   (G) Do microwaves penetrate the ionosphere?
   (H) Do radio waves penetrate the ionosphere?
   (J) Since radio waves penetrate the ionosphere when microwaves do, would you expect x-rays to do the same?

15. Which factor would be most important in order for radar to detect and track storms?

   (A) Which is the only important factor in order for radar to detect and track storms?
   (B) Which factor is deemed least important for radar to detect and track storms?
   (C) The ability of radar to detect and track storms depends most upon which of the following factors?
   (D) What is the most important factor for radar to function properly?

16. Which of the following points out a serious weakness in the passage's reasoning?

   (F) What would least strengthen the reasoning?
   (G) What would most strengthen the reasoning?
   (H) What would least weaken the reasoning?
   (J) What would most weaken the reasoning?

17. Each of the following could help explain the apparent contradiction EXCEPT

   (A) What is the contradiction?
   (B) Why is the contradiction apparent?
   (C) What does not help explain the contradiction?
   (D) What helps explain the contradiction?

18. Which of the following would most weaken the conclusion?

(F) What would strengthen the conclusion?
(G) What is the weakness of the conclusion?
(H) What is the weakest conclusion?
(J) What would most weaken the conclusion?

19. The passage makes which of the following assumptions?

(A) Which assumption is made by the author?
(B) What is the passage about?
(C) Which of the choices is an assumption?
(D) Which assumption is not made by the author?

20. If the statements are true, which of the following could also be true?

(F) What is not true of the statements?
(G) What could be true of the statements?
(H) What is true all of the time?
(J) What could be true if the statements are true?

21. Which of the following would be the most logical continuation of the passage?

(A) Which ending is the best ending of the passage?
(B) What is the best way to continue the passage?
(C) What is the logical ending of the passage?
(D) What would be the most illogical continuation of the passage?

22. The speaker implies that

(F) What does the speaker say is implied?
(G) What does the speaker say that could be implied?
(H) What does the speaker imply in the passage?
(J) What doesn't the speaker imply in the passage?

23. The passage assumes that

(A) What assumption can be made by the reader of the passage?
(B) What is the conclusion of the passage?
(C) What is the main idea of the passage?
(D) What does the author assume in the passage?

24. Which of the following, if true, would best help to explain the apparent contradiction?

(F) Which truth best explains the contradiction?
(G) What is the contradiction?
(H) Why is the contradiction apparently true?
(J) Which contradiction is true?

25. The argument relies primarily on

(A) Which statement primarily supports the argument?
(B) What is the passage primarily about?
(C) Is the argument of the passage primarily about reliance?
(D) What is the primary argument?

26. Which of the following statements is logically inconsistent with the passage?

(F) Which statement is inconsistently logical?
(G) Which statement is both logical and consistent with the passage?
(H) Which statement is both illogical and inconsistent with the passage?
(J) Which statement does not logically fit within the passage's structure?

27. The main point of the passage is

(A) What is the main point of the second paragraph?
(B) What is the main idea of the passage?
(C) Which point is a specific detail in the passage?
(D) Which of the following points is not mentioned in the passage?

EXERCISE 4

Careful Reading of Science Reasoning Item Stems

Science items appear on the ACT, the PLAN, and the EXPLORE. The following exercise will help you focus on the exact question that is being asked by Science item stems that correspond to passages on the ACT Science Reasoning Test. There is no need for you to see the entire selection as it would appear on the actual exam. It is also not necessary to worry about your science skills; these skills are addressed in the Science Skills Review. When you have become proficient at careful reading, you will no longer waste valuable time on an individual item trying to determine the exact question that is being asked.

DIRECTIONS: Choose the *best* restatement of the item stem. Answers are on page 924.

1. Which of the following would be good animals to use for the experiment?

   (A) Which animals are best suited for the experiment?
   (B) Which experiment would be most appropriate to determine whether animals are good or bad?
   (C) What subject other than animals would be best suited for the experiment?
   (D) Which procedure would necessarily follow an experiment on animals?

2. What was the control for temperature in Experiment 5?

   (F) What did Experiments 1 through 5 use as the control for temperature?
   (G) What was used to control the temperature in Experiment 5?
   (H) What was the temperature in Experiment 5?
   (J) What did Experiment 5 use as the control for temperature?

3. Which of the following conclusions is consistent with the data presented in the table?

   (A) The information provided in the table conforms with which determination?
   (B) Which conclusions are consistent with the data presented in the table?
   (C) The data provided in the table is not consistent with which conclusion?
   (D) Which element of data in the table is most consistent with the following conclusion?

4. Which statement is supported by the results of Experiment 1 alone?

   (F) The results of Experiment 1 exclusively support which statement?
   (G) Which statement is exclusively supported by the results of Experiment 1?
   (H) Without the results of Experiment 1, the results of which experiment would support the statement?
   (J) Which statement about Experiment 1 is supported by the results of the other experiments?

5. Which hypothesis best explains the observation that the agar plates never appear clear beyond a 2-inch area surrounding the soaked paper disks?

   (A) The observation that the agar plates appear clear beyond a 2-inch area surrounding the soaked paper disks is best explained by which hypothesis?
   (B) The condition of the agar plates within a 2-inch area surrounding the soaked paper disks is best explained by which hypothesis?
   (C) The condition of the agar plates beyond a 2-inch area surrounding the soaked paper disks is best explained by which hypotheses?
   (D) The condition of the agar plates beyond a 2-inch area surrounding the soaked paper disks is best explained by which hypothesis?

6. Which of the following changes in the experiments would have permitted a test of the hypothesis that the quality of a fossil imprint depends on the pressure applied?

(F) A test of the hypothesis that the quality of a fossil imprint does not depend on the pressure applied would have been permitted by which changes in the experiments?
(G) A test of the hypothesis that the quality of a fossil imprint depends on the pressure applied would not have been permitted by which changes in the experiments?
(H) A test of the hypothesis that the quantity of a fossil imprint depends on the pressure applied would have been permitted by which changes in the experiments?
(J) A test of the hypothesis that the quality of a fossil imprint depends on the pressure applied would have been permitted by which changes in the experiments?

7. A scientist seeking to explain why Theory 2 has more predictive power than Theory 1 might argue that

(A) What might a scientist argue to explain why Theory 2 has more predictive power than Theory 1?
(B) What might a scientist argue to explain why Theory 2 has less predictive power than Theory 1?
(C) What might a scientist argue to explain why Theory 1 has less predictive power than Theory 2?
(D) What might a scientist argue to explain why Theory 1 has more predictive power than Theory 2?

8. Which of the following is the strongest argument that Scientist 1 could use to counter Scientist 2's suggested mechanism for the origin of life?

(F) In order to support Scientist 2's suggested mechanism for the origin of life, which of Scientist 1's arguments is the strongest?
(G) What is Scientist 2's suggested mechanism for the origin of life?
(H) In order to counter Scientist 1's suggested mechanism for the origin of life, which of Scientist 2's arguments is the strongest?
(J) In order to counter Scientist 2's suggested mechanism for the origin of life, which of Scientist 1's arguments is the strongest?

9. According to the graph, female moths are most sensitive to sounds between

(A) Within what range of sounds do female moths exhibit the least sensitivity?
(B) Within what range of sounds do female moths exhibit the highest sensitivity?
(C) Within what range of sounds do male moths exhibit the highest sensitivity?
(D) Within what range of sounds do male moths exhibit the least sensitivity?

10. It is thought that some species of birds "learn" to fly. This belief is based on observations of young birds fluttering and flapping their wings at the nest until they reach the age when flight is possible. In Species *X*, nestlings were kept in harmless, but tight, plastic tubes in which they could not carry out such "practice movements." They were released when they reached the age of flight. Viewpoint 1 predicts that the birds will fly

(F) What does Viewpoint 1 predict about all birds' ability to fly?
(G) Regarding Species *X*, what does Viewpoint 1 predict about their ability to fly?
(H) Regarding all species of birds other than Species *X*, what does Viewpoint 1 predict about their ability to fly?
(J) What does Viewpoint 1 predict about Species *X* that Viewpoint 2 also predicts?

11. What is the minimum number of points where two circumferences from two seismic stations, both measuring the same earthquake, can meet?

(A) Two circumferences can meet at what maximum number of points?
(B) What is the minimum number of earthquakes that two seismic stations can measure?
(C) Two circumferences can meet at what minimum number of points?
(D) What is the minimum number of seismic stations required to measure an earthquake?

12. Was the site most recently above or below water?

(F) Was the site below water?
(G) Was the site recently above water?
(H) Will the site be above water or below water?
(J) As of late, was the site below water or above water?

13. What assumption is made to relate the fossil record to the environment?

(A) What relates the fossil record to the environment?
(B) What assumption about the fossil record can also be made about the environment?
(C) The fossil record is related to the environment based on what assumption?
(D) What assumption can be made about the relationship between fossil records and the environment?

14. With which explanation of the similar biochemistry of all life on Earth would Scientist 2 most likely agree?

(F) How would Scientist 1 most likely explain the similar biochemistry of all life on Earth?
(G) How would Scientist 2 most likely explain the similar biochemistry of all life on Earth?
(H) How would Scientist 2 most likely explain the dissimilar biochemistry of all life on Earth?
(J) Why does Scientist 2 not agree with the explanation that the biochemistry of all life on Earth is similar?

15. According to the diagram, the trophic level with the largest relative biomass is the

(A) Which diagram depicts the trophic level with the largest relative biomass?
(B) How much is the largest relative biomass that is represented by the given trophic levels?
(C) According to the diagram, which trophic level has the largest biomass in relationship to the other trophic levels?
(D) According to the diagram, why is the trophic level with the largest relative biomass greater than the others?

16. In Experiment 1, gravity accelerates the stone as it falls from the cliff, causing it to pick up speed as it drops. Which of the following series of pictures most resembles how the stone appears as it drops?

(F) The falling stone in Experiment 2 most resembles which group of pictures?
(G) Which group of pictures most resembles the stone as it appears before it is dropped from the cliff in Experiment 1?
(H) Which group of pictures most resembles the decelerating stone as if falls from the cliff in Experiment 1?
(J) The falling stone in Experiment 1 most resembles which group of pictures?

Coding of Item Stems

Most students are pressed for time on the Reading items. You can save time by looking for the correct answers to items as you read the passage for the first time. Reading a passage and answering several corresponding items at the rate of less than one item per minute requires a very different skill than what you would typically use when reading a book, newspaper, or magazine.

For Reading items, you must not only read the item correctly, but you must also correctly identify the item-type. Every Reading item, regardless of the corresponding passage format, will be from one of seven basic types. You can avoid memorizing information that is not needed to answer an item by focusing only on information that is needed to answer the question that is being asked by that specific item-type. Remember that many more questions could be asked on any given passage than are actually asked. If you do not identify the correct item-type, then there is a good chance that you will not use the appropriate strategy for finding the correct answer. You must therefore know the characteristics of the correct answer that are associated with each item-type.

Reading items are designed to test three levels of reading comprehension: appreciation of the general theme, understanding of specific points, and evaluation of the text. This section will help you to immediately recognize both the item-type and the level of reading comprehension that are being tested based on the wording of the item stem.

SEVEN TYPES OF READING ITEMS

(1) **Main Idea** – What is the unifying theme?

(2) **Explicit Detail** – What is explicitly mentioned?

(3) **Vocabulary** – How are certain words used?

(4) **Development** – How are the ideas constructed and arranged?

(5) **Implied Idea** – What can be inferred?

(6) **Application** – How can the information be applied to new situations?

(7) **Voice** – What does the writer reveal through attitude, tone, or voice?

Refer to the Core Lesson section of the Reading Lesson in Step Three of the *Cambridge ACT • PLAN • EXPLORE Victory Student Textbook* for a more detailed description of the seven item-types.

Each of the three levels of reading comprehension is represented by at least one of the aforementioned seven types of Reading items as follows:

Comprehension Level	Item-Type
General Theme	Main Idea
Specific Points	Explicit Detail Vocabulary Development
Evaluation	Implied Idea Application Voice

GENERAL THEME

The first level of reading, appreciation of the general theme, is the most basic. Main Idea items and items about the overall development of the selection test whether you understand the passage at the most general level. The first sentence of a paragraph—often the topic sentence—may provide a summary of the content of that paragraph. Also, the last sentence of a paragraph usually provides concluding material that may also be helpful in understanding the general theme of the passage.

SPECIFIC POINTS

The second level of reading, understanding specific points, takes you deeper into the selection. Explicit Detail items, items about the meanings of words, and items about the logical role of details all test your ability to read carefully. Since this is an "open-book" test, you can always return to the selection. Therefore, if something is highly technical or difficult to understand, do not dwell on it for too long—come back to the item later if necessary.

EVALUATION

The third level of reading, evaluation of the text, takes you even deeper into the selection. Implied Idea, Application, and Voice items requires, in addition to an understanding of the material, a judgment or an evaluation of what you have read. This is why these items are usually the most difficult.

When taking the test, approach the Reading items in the following way: First, preview the item; second, identify the item-type; third, code each item according to its respective level of reading comprehension; and finally, think of the characteristics of the correct answer before you begin to read the passage. Read each passage slowly and carefully as you search for clues that will help answer each item. Also, do not "speed-read" or skim through the passage. The faster you read the passage, the less likely you are to pick the correct answer choice. Most answer choices require careful reading, analysis, and an application of the facts to the exact question that is being asked.

EXERCISE 5

Coding of Item Stems

DIRECTIONS: Code each item stem according to one of the three levels of reading comprehension: General Theme (GT), Specific Points (SP), and Evaluation (E). Answers are on page 924.

1. According to the passage, tears and laughter have all of the following in common EXCEPT

2. The author implies that animals lack the ability to

3. The word "ludicrous" in line # most nearly means

4. The author develops the passage primarily by

5. In the second paragraph, the author

6. Which of the following titles best describes the content of the selection?

7. The author is primarily concerned with discussing the

8. The passage states that the open government statute is intended to accomplish all of the following EXCEPT

9. The passage most strongly supports which of the following conclusions about a decision that is within the authority of the executive director of an agency?

10. In the final paragraph, the author discusses

11. The author makes all of the following points about the rules governing the commission EXCEPT

12. It can be inferred from the passage that the executive director is authorized to make certain purchases costing less than $5,000 in order to

13. Which of the following statements about a "review and comment" session can be inferred from the selection?

14. According to the passage, all of the following are true of metamorphic rock EXCEPT

15. As described by the selection, the sequence of events leading to the present landscape was

16. The author regards the explanation he gives as

17. The author provides information that defines which of the following terms?

18. The author would most likely agree with which of the following statements?

19. The passage supports which of the following conclusions about the writings of Yevgeny Zamyatin?

20. The author's treatment of James Burnham's writing can best be described as

21. The statement that Burnham inverted the logical priority of the individual over the state means that Burnham believed that

22. The author criticized Burnham for

23. According to Burnham, in the completely autocratic state, history will have come to an end because

24. It can be inferred from the passage that the physical features of a galaxy that do not belong to a rich cluster are determined primarily by the

25. The author implies that the currently accepted theories on galaxy formation are

26. According to the passage, a cluster with a central, supergiant galaxy will

27. According to the passage, the outcome of a collision between galaxies depends on which of the following?

28. According to the passage, as a galaxy falls inward toward the center of a cluster, it

29. According to the passage, a star such as our Sun would probably not be found in a cluster such as Virgo because

30. The phrase "Nature never became a toy to the wise spirit" means which of the following?

31. The author implies that the difference between farms and the landscape is primarily a matter of

32. The author uses the word "property" in the phrase "property in the horizon" (line #) to mean

33. The phrase "color of the spirit" in line # means

34. The main purpose of this passage is to

35. Which of the following best explains the distinction between a life circumstance and a life event?

36. The author uses all of the following techniques EXCEPT

37. Which of the following best explains the relationship between the first paragraph and the second paragraph of the passage?

38. The passage provides information that defines which of the following terms?

39. According to the passage, Wineland was characterized by which of the following geographical features?

40. It can be inferred from the passage that scholars who doubt the authenticity of the Biarni narrative make all of the following objections EXCEPT

41. The author mentions the two high mountains in order to show that it is unlikely to be true that

42. All of the following are mentioned as similarities between Leif Erikson's voyage and Biarni's voyage EXCEPT

43. It can be inferred that the author regards the historicity of the Biarni narrative as

Vocabulary

Students often believe that if they do not know what a certain word means, then they will not be able to correctly answer an item that requires them to understand the meaning of that word. This section helps you focus on recognizing word parts, becoming more familiar with challenging vocabulary words, and using context clues to determine what difficult words mean. In addition to understanding context, this section emphasizes the importance of understanding the logical structure of a sentence and applying that understanding to anticipate appropriate words in succeeding on vocabulary-related items.

Word Parts List

While memorizing vocabulary words is not the key to succeeding on vocabulary-related items, greater familiarity with the Word Parts List can only improve your chances of answering items correctly.

Prefix(es)	*Meaning(s)*	*Example(s)*
a	**in, on, of, to**	**abed—in bed**
a, ab, abs	**from, away**	**abrade—wear off** **absent—away, not present**
a, an	**lacking, not**	**asymptomatic—showing no symptoms** **anaerobic—able to live without air**
ad, ac, af, ag, al, an ap, ar, as, at	**to, toward**	**accost—approach and speak to** **adjunct—something added to** **aggregate—bring together**
ambi, amphi	**around, both**	**ambidextrous—using both hands equally** **amphibious—living both in water and on land**
ana	**up, again, anew, throughout**	**analyze—loosen up, break up into parts** **anagram—word spelled from letters of other word**
ante	**before**	**antediluvian—before the Flood, extremely old**
anti	**against**	**anti-war—against war**
arch	**first, chief**	**archetype—first model**
auto	**self**	**automobile—self-moving vehicle**
bene, ben	**good, well**	**benefactor—one who does good deeds**
circum	**around**	**circumnavigate—sail around**
com, co, col, con, cor	**with, together**	**concentrate—bring closer together** **cooperate—work together** **collapse—fall together**
contra, contro, counter	**against**	**contradict—speak against** **counterclockwise—against the clock**
de	**away from, down, opposite of**	**detract—draw away from**
di	**twice, double**	**dichromatic—having two colors**
dia	**across, through**	**diameter—measurement across**
dis, di	**not, away from**	**dislike—to not like** **digress—turn away from the subject**
dys	**bad, poor**	**dyslexia—poor reading**
equi	**equal**	**equivalent—of equal value**
ex, e, ef	**from, out**	**expatriate—one living outside native country** **emit—send out**
extra	**outside, beyond**	**extraterrestrial—from beyond the earth**
fore	**in front of, previous**	**forecast—tell ahead of time** **foreleg—front leg**
homo	**same, like**	**homophonic—sounding the same**
hyper	**too much, over**	**hyperactive—overly active**
hypo	**too little, under**	**hypothermia—having too little body heat**
in, il, ig, im, ir	**not**	**innocent—not guilty** **ignorant—not knowing** **irresponsible—not responsible**
in, il, im, ir	**on, into, in**	**impose—place on** **invade—go into**

intra, intro	within, inside	intrastate—within a state
mal, male	bad, wrong, poor	maladjusted—poorly adjusted
		malevolent—ill-wishing
mis	badly, wrongly	misunderstand—understand incorrectly
mis, miso	hatred	misogyny—hatred of women
mono	single, one	monorail—train that runs on a single rail
neo	new	Neolithic—of the New Stone Age
non	not	nonentity—a nobody
ob	over, against, toward	obstruct—stand against
omni	all	omnipresent—present in all places
pan	all	panorama—a complete view
peri	around, near	periscope—device for seeing all around
poly	many	polygonal—many-sided
post	after	postmortem—after death
pre	before, earlier than	prejudice—judgment in advance
pro	in favor of, forward, in front of	proceed—go forward
		pro-war—in favor of war
re	back, again	rethink—think again
		reimburse—pay back
retro	backward	retrospective—looking backward
se	apart, away	seclude—keep away
semi	half	semiconscious—half conscious
sub, suc, suf, sug, sus	under, beneath	subscribe—write underneath
		suspend—hang down
		suffer—undergo
super	above, greater	superfluous—beyond what is needed
syn, sym, syl, sys	with, at the same time	synthesis—a putting together
		sympathy—a feeling with
tele	far	television—machine for seeing far
trans	across	transport—carry across a distance
un	not	uninformed—not informed
vice	acting for, next in rank to	vice president—second in command

Suffix(es)	*Meaning(s)*	*Example(s)*
able, ble	able, capable	acceptable—able to be accepted
acious, cious	characterized by, having the quality of	spacious—having the quality of space
age	sum, total	mileage—total number of miles
al	of, like, suitable for	theatrical—suitable for theater
ance, ancy	act or state of	disturbance—act of disturbing
ant, ent	one who	defendant—one who defends himself
ary, ar	having the nature of, concerning	military—relating to soldiers
		polar—state of being raised
cy	act, state, or position of	presidency—position of president
		ascendancy—state of being raised up
dom	state, rank, that which belongs to	wisdom—state of being wise
ence	act, state, or quality of	dependence—state of depending
er, or	one who, that which	doer—one who does
		conductor—that which conducts
escent	becoming	obsolescent—becoming obsolete
fy	to make	pacify—make peaceful
ic, ac	of, like	demonic—of or like a demon
il, ile	having to do with, like, suitable for	civil—having to do with citizens
		tactile—having to do with touch
ion	act or condition of	operation—act of operating
ious	having, characterized by	anxious—characterized by anxiety
ish	like, somewhat	foolish—like a fool
ism	belief or practice of	racism—belief in racial superiority
ist	one who does, makes, or is concerned with	scientist—one concerned with science
ity, ty, y	character or state of being	amity—friendship
		jealousy—state of being jealous

ive	of, relating to, tending to	destructive—tending to destroy
logue, loquy	speech or writing	monologue—speech by one person colloquy—conversation
logy	speech, study of	geology—study of the earth
ment	act or state of	abandonment—act of abandoning
mony	a resulting thing, condition, or state	patrimony—trait inherited from one's dad
ness	act or quality	kindness—quality of being kind
ory	having the quality of a place or thing for	compensatory—quality of compensation lavatory—place for washing
ous, ose	full of, having	glamorous—full of glamour
ship	skill, state of being	horsemanship—skill in riding ownership—state of being an owner
some	full of, like	frolicsome—playful
tude	state or quality of	rectitude—state of being morally upright
ward	in the direction of	homeward—in the direction of home
y	full of, like, somewhat	wily—full of wiles

Root(s)	*Meaning(s)*	*Example(s)*
acr	bitter	acrid, acrimony
act, ag	do, act, drive	action, react, agitate, agent
acu	sharp, keen	acute, acumen
agog	leader	pedagogue, demagogic
agr	field	agronomy, agriculture
ali	other	alias, alienate, inalienable
alt	high	altitude, contralto
alter, altr	other, change	alternative, altercation, altruism
am, amic	love, friend	amorous, amiable
anim	mind, life, spirit	animism, animate, animosity
annu, enni	year	annual, superannuated, biennial
anthrop	man	anthropoid, misanthropy
apt, ept	fit	apt, adapt, ineptitude
aqu	water	aquatic, aquamarine
arbit	judge	arbiter, arbitrary
arch	chief	anarchy, matriarch
arm	arm, weapon	army, armature, disarm
art	skill, a fitting together	artisan, artifact, articulate
aster, astr	star	asteroid, disaster, astral
aud, audit, aur	hear	auditorium, audition, auricle
aur	gold	aureate, aureomycin
aut	self	autism, autograph
bell	war	anti-bellum, belligerent
brev	short	brevity, abbreviation, abbreviate
cad, cas, cid	fall	cadence, casualty, accident
cand	white, shining	candid, candle, incandescent
cant, chant	sing, charm	cantor, recant, enchant
cap, capt, cept, ceipt, cept, cip	take, seize, hold	capable, captive, accept, incipient
capit	head	capital, decapitate, recapitulate
cede, ceed, cess	go, yield	secede, exceed, process, intercession
cent	hundred	century, percentage, centimeter
cern, cert	perceive, make certain, decide	concern, certificate, certain
chrom	color	monochrome, chromatic
chron	time	chronometer, anachronism
cide, cis	cut, kill	genocide, incision, suicide
cit	summon, impel	cite, excite, incitement
civ	citizen	uncivil, civilization
clam, claim	shout	clamorous, proclaim, claimant
clar	clear	clarity, clarion, declare
clin	slope, lean	inclination, recline
clud, clus, clos	close, shut	seclude, recluse, closet
cogn	know	recognize, incognito
col, cul	prepare	colony, cultivate, agriculture

corp	body	incorporate, corpse
cosm	order, world	cosmetic, cosmos, cosmopolitan
crac, crat	power, rule	democrat, theocracy
cre, cresc, cret	grow	increase, crescent, accretion
cred	trust, believe	credit, incredible
crux, cruc	cross	crux, crucial, crucifix
crypt	hidden	cryptic, cryptography
cur, curr, curs	run, course	occur, current, incursion
cura	care	curator, accurate
dem	people	demographic, demagogue
dent	tooth	dental, indentation
derm	skin	dermatitis, pachyderm
di, dia	day	diary, quotidian
dic, dict	say, speak	indicative, edict, dictation
dign	worthy	dignified, dignitary
doc, doct	teach, prove	indoctrinate, docile, doctor
domin	rule	predominate, domineer, dominion
dorm	sleep	dormitory, dormant
du	two	duo, duplicity, dual
duc, duct	lead	educate, abduct, ductile
dur	hard, lasting	endure, obdurate, duration
dyn	force, power	dynamo, dynamite
equ	equal	equation, equitable
erg, urg	work, power	energetic, metallurgy, demiurge
err	wander	error, aberrant
ev	time, age	coeval, longevity
fac, fact, fect, fic	do, make	facility, factual, perfect, artifice
fer	bear, carry	prefer, refer, conifer, fertility
ferv	boil	fervid, effervesce
fid	belief, faith	infidelity, confidant, perfidious
fin	end, limit	finite, confine
firm	strong	reaffirm, infirmity
flect, flex	bend	reflex, inflection
flor	blossom	florescent, floral
flu, fluct, flux	flow	fluid, fluctuation, influx
form	shape	formative, reform, formation
fort	strong	effort, fortitude
frag, fract	break	fragility, infraction
fug	flee	refuge, fugitive
gam	marry	exogamy, polygamous
ge, geo	earth	geology, geode, perigee
gen	birth, kind, race	engender, general, generation
gest	carry, bear	gestation, ingest, digest
gon	angle	hexagonal, trigonometry
grad, gress	step, go	regress, gradation
gram, graph	writing	cryptogram, telegraph
grat	pleasing, agreeable	congratulate
grav	weight, heavy	grave (situation), gravity
greg	flock, crowd	gregarious, segregate
habit, hibit	have, hold	habitation, inhibit, h[illegible]
heli	sun	helium, heliocentric, aphelion
her, hes	stick, cling	adherent, cohesive
hydr	water	dehydration, hydrofoil
iatr	heal, cure	pediatrics, psychiatry
iso	same, equal	isotope, isometric
it	journey, go	itinerary, exit
ject	throw	reject, subjective, projection
jud	judge	judicial, adjudicate
jug, junct	join	conjugal, juncture, conjunction
jur	swear	perjure, jurisprudence
labor	work	laborious, belabor

leg	law	legal, illegitimate
leg, lig, lect	choose, gather, read	illegible, eligible, select, lecture
lev	light, rise	levity, alleviate
liber	free	liberal, libertine
liter	letter	literate, alliterative
lith	rock, stone	Neolithic, lithograph
loc	place	locale, locus, allocate
log	word, study	logic, biology, dialogue
loqu, locut	talk, speech	colloquial, loquacious, interlocutor
luc, lum	light	translucent, pellucid, illumine
lud, lus	play	allusion, ludicrous, interlude
magn	large, great	magnificent, magnitude
mal	bad, ill	malodorous, malady
man, manu	hand	manifest, manicure, manuscript
mar	sea	maritime, submarine
mater, matr	mother	matrilocal, maternal
medi	middle	intermediary, medieval
ment	mind	demented, mental
merg, mers	plunge, dip	emerge, submersion
meter, metr, mens	measure	chronometer, metronome, geometry
micr	small	microfilm, micron
min	little	minimum, minute
mit, miss	send	remit, admission, missive
mon, monit	warn	admonish, monument, monitor
mor	custom	mores, immoral
mor, mort	death	mortify, mortician
morph	shape	amorphous, anthropomorphic
mov, mob, mot	move	removal, automobile, motility
mut	change	mutable, transmute, mutation
nasc, nat	born	native, natural, nascent, innate
necr	dead, die	necropolis, necrosis
neg	deny	renege, negative
nom, noun, nown,	name, order, rule	anonymous, antinomy, misnomer
nam, nym, nomen, nomin	name	nomenclature, cognomen, nominate
nomy	law, rule	astronomy, antinomy
nov	new	novice, innovation
ocul	eye	binocular, oculist
onym	name	pseudonym, antonym
oper	work	operate, cooperation, inoperable
ora	speak, pray	oracle, oratory
orn	decorate	adorn, ornate
orth	straight, correct	orthodox, orthopedic
pan	all	panacea, pantheon
pater, patr	father	patriot, paternity
path, pat, pass	feel, suffer	telepathy, patient, compassion
ped	child	pedagogue, pediatrics
ped, pod	foot	pedestrian, impede, tripod
pel, puls	drive, push	impel, propulsion
pend, pens	hang	pendulous, suspense
pet, peat	seek	petition, impetus, repeat
phil	love	philosopher, Anglophile
phob	fear	phobic, agoraphobia
phon	sound	phonograph, symphony
phor	bearing	semaphore, metaphor
phot	light	photograph, photoelectric
pon, pos	place, put	component, repose, postpone
port	carry	report, portable, deportation
pot	power	potency, potential
press	press	pressure, impression
prim, proto, prot	first	primal, proton, protagonist
psych	mind	psychic, metempsychosis

Root	Meaning	Examples
quer, quir, quis, ques	ask, seek	query, inquiry, inquisitive, quest
reg, rig, rect	straight, rule	regulate, dirigible, corrective
rid, ris	laugh	deride, risible, ridiculous
rog	ask	rogation, interrogate
rupt	break	erupt, interruption, rupture
sanct	holy	sacrosanct, sanctify, sanction
sci, scio	know	nescient, conscious, omniscience
scop	watch, view	horoscope, telescopic
scrib, script	write	scribble, proscribe, description
sed, sid, sess	sit, seat	sediment, sedate, session
seg, sect	cut	segment, section, intersect
sent, sens	feel, think	nonsense, sensitive, sentient
sequ, secut	follow	sequel, consequence, consecutive
sol	alone	solitary, solo, desolate
solv, solu, solut	loosen	dissolve, soluble, absolution
somn	sleep	insomnia, somnolent
son	sound	sonorous, unison
soph	wise, wisdom	philosophy, sophisticated
spec, spic, spect	look	specimen, conspicuous, spectacle
spir	breathe	spirit, conspire, respiration
stab, stat	stand	unstable, status, station
stead	place	instead, steadfast
string, strict	bind	astringent, stricture, restrict
stru, struct	build	construe, structure, destructive
sum, sumpt	take	presume, consumer, assumption
tang, ting, tact, tig	touch	tangent, contingency, contact
tax, tac	arrange, arrangement	taxonomy, tactic
techn	skill, art	technique, technician
tele	far	teletype, telekinesis
tempor	time	temporize, extemporaneous
ten, tain, tent	hold	tenant, tenacity, retention
tend, tens, tent	stretch	contend, extensive, intent
tenu	thin	tenuous, attenuate
test	witness	attest, testify
the	god	polytheism, theologist
tom	cut	atomic, appendectomy
tort, tors	twist	tortuous, torsion, contort
tract	pull, draw	traction, attract, protract
trib	assign, pay	attribute, tribute, retribution
trud, trus	thrust	obtrude, intrusive
turb	agitate	perturb, turbulent, disturb
umbr	shade	umbrella, penumbra
urb	city	urbane, suburb, urban
vac	empty	vacuous, evacuation
vad, vas	go	invade, evasive
val, vail	strength, worth	valid, avail, prevalent
ven, vent	come	advent, convene, prevention
ver	true	aver, veracity, verity
verb	word	verbose, adverb, verbatim
vert, vers	turn	revert, perversion, versatile
vest	dress	vestment
vid, vis	see	video, evidence, vision, revise
vinc, vict	conquer	evince, convict, victim
viv, vit	life	vivid, revive, vital
vo, voc, vok, vow	call	vociferous, provocative, equivocate
vol	wish	involuntary, volition
volv, volut	roll, turn	involve, convoluted, revolution

vulg .... common .... divulge, vulgarity
zo .... animal .... zoologist, Paleozoic

Vocabulary List

The following list is composed of words that students may find challenging on standardized tests. The list is divided into two difficulty levels. Familiarity with the Vocabulary List can only improve your chances of answering items correctly.

—Difficulty Level 1—

abacus—a frame with beads or balls used for doing or teaching arithmetic
abash—disconcert; to make embarrassed and ill at ease
abate—to deduct; to make less
abduction—to carry off by force
aberration—a deviation from the normal or the typical
abeyance—temporary suspension
abhor—detest; to shrink from in disgust or hatred
abhorrence—loathing; detestation
abide—to stay; stand fast; remain
abjure—recant; to give up (opinions) publicly
abominate—loathe; to dislike very much
abrade—to scrape or rub off
abridge—shorten; to reduce in scope or extent
abrogate—cancel; call off
abscond—to go away hastily and secretly
absolve—acquit; to pronounce free from guilt or blame
abstinence—the act of voluntarily doing without pleasures
abstruse—hard to understand; deep; recondite
absurdity—nonsense
abyss—chasm; a deep fissure in the earth; bottomless gulf
acclaim—to greet with loud applause or approval
accretion—growth in size by addition or accumulation
acerbic—sharp, bitter, or harsh in temper and language
acquisition—something or someone acquired or added
acrimony—asperity; bitterness or harshness of temper, manner, or speech
acute—shrewd; keen or quick of mind
adapt—adjust; to make fit or suitable by changing
adjunct—connected or attached in a secondary or subordinate way
adorn—ornament; to put decorations on something
adroit—expert; clever; skillful in a physical or mental way
adulterate—not genuine; to make inferior or impure
adversary—opponent; a person who opposes or fights against another
advocate—a person who pleads another's cause
aesthete—a person who artificially cultivates artistic sensitivity or makes a cult of art and beauty
aesthetic—artistic; sensitive to art and beauty
affable—gentle and kindly
affinity—connection; close relationship
afflict—to cause pain or suffering to; distress very much
affluent—plentiful; abundant; flowing freely
aggrandize—to make seem greater
alias—assumed name
allegiance—loyalty or devotion
alleviate—to reduce or decrease; lighten or relieve
allocate—allot; to distribute in shares or according to a plan
alloy—the relative purity of gold or silver; fineness
allude—to refer in a casual or indirect way
altercation—an angry or heated argument
amalgamate—unite; combine
ambiguous—not clear; having two or more possible meanings
ambivalence—simultaneously conflicting feelings toward a person or thing
amble—to go easily and unhurriedly
ameliorate—improve; to make or become better
amenable—willing to follow advice or suggestion; answerable
amiable—good-natured; having a pleasant and friendly disposition
amicable—peaceable; showing good will
amphibious—can live both on land and in water
anagram—a word or phrase made from another by rearranging its letters
analogy—partial resemblance; similarity in some respects between things otherwise unlike
anarchy—the complete absence of government
anathema—a thing or person greatly detested
anatomist—a person who analyzes in great detail
anecdote—a short, entertaining account of some happening
anhydrous—without water
animosity—hostility; a feeling of strong dislike or hatred
annexation—attachment; adding on
anomalous—abnormal; deviating from the regular arrangement, general rule, or usual method
anthology—a collection of poems, stories, songs, or excerpts
antidote—a remedy to counteract a poison
antigen—a protein, toxin, or other substance to which the body reacts by producing antibodies
antipathy—strong or deep-rooted dislike
anvil—an iron or steel block on which metal objects are hammered into shape
apathetic—feeling little or no emotion; unmoved
apocryphal—not genuine; spurious; counterfeit; of doubtful authorship or authenticity
appease—to satisfy or relieve
appraise—to set a price for; decide the value of
apprehension—an anxious feeling of foreboding; dread
apprentice—novice; any learner or beginner
arabesque—a complex and elaborate decorative design
arbitrary—unreasonable; unregulated; despotic
arbitrate—to decide a dispute
arboreal—of or like a tree
arcane—hidden or secret
ardor—passion; emotional warmth
arduous—difficult to do; laborious; onerous

arid—dry and barren; lacking enough water for things to grow
aromatic—smelling sweet or spicy; fragrant or pungent
arouse—to awaken, as from sleep
articulate—expressing oneself easily and clearly
artisan—craftsman; a worker in a skilled trade
aspiration—strong desire or ambition
assail—assault; to attack physically and violently
assay—an examination or testing
assert—to state positively; declare; affirm
assimilate—to absorb and incorporate into one's thinking
astound—amaze; to bewilder with sudden surprise
astute—cunning; having or showing a clever or shrewd mind
atrocity—brutality; a very displeasing or tasteless thing
auditor—a hearer or listener
augment—enlarge; to make greater, as in size, quantity, or strength
auspicious—successful; favored by fortune
austere—forbidding; having a severe or stern look or manner
avid—eager and enthusiastic
avow—to declare openly or admit frankly

ballad—a romantic or sentimental song
banal—commonplace; dull or stale because of overuse
bane—ruin; death; deadly harm
barrage—a heavy, prolonged attack of words or blows
barren—empty; devoid
barrio—in Spanish-speaking countries, a district or suburb of a city
bask—to warm oneself pleasantly, as in the sunlight
baste—to sew with long, loose stitches
beacon—any light for warning or guiding
bedazzle—to dazzle thoroughly
bedizen—to dress or decorate in a cheap, showy way
belated—tardy; late or too late
belligerent—at war; showing a readiness to fight or quarrel
beneficent—doing good
benevolence—a kindly, charitable act or gift
benign—good-natured; kindly
bequeath—to hand down; pass on
berate—to scold or rebuke severely
bewilder—puzzle; to confuse hopelessly
bias—a mental leaning or inclination; partiality; bent
bilge—the bulge of a barrel or cask
bilk—to cheat or swindle; defraud
blandishment—a flattering act or remark meant to persuade
blatant—disagreeably loud or boisterous
blithe—carefree; showing a gay, cheerful disposition
boisterous—rowdy; noisy and unruly
bolster—a long, narrow cushion or pillow; to support
boon—blessing; welcome benefit
boor—a rude, awkward, or ill-mannered person
bourgeois—a person whose beliefs, attitudes, and practices are conventionally middle-class
brazen—like brass in color, quality, or hardness; impudent
breach—a breaking or being broken
breadth—width; lack of narrowness
brevity—the quality of being brief
buttress—a projecting structure built against a wall to support or reinforce it

cadet—a student at a military school; younger son or brother
cadge—to beg or get by begging
cajole—to coax with flattery and insincere talk
calk—a part of a horseshoe that projects downward to prevent slipping
callous—unfeeling; lacking pity or mercy
camaraderie—loyal, warm, and friendly feeling among comrades
candid—honest or frank
capacious—roomy; spacious
caprice—whim; a sudden, impulsive change
capricious—erratic; flighty; tending to change abruptly
caption—a heading or title, as of an article
carping—tending to find fault
cartographer—a person whose work is making maps or charts
castigate—to punish or rebuke severely
catalyst—a person or thing acting as the stimulus in bringing about or hastening a result
catapult—a slingshot or type of launcher
catastrophe—any great and sudden disaster or misfortune
caustic—corrosive; that which can destroy tissue by chemical action
cavern—a cave
cerebral—intellectual; appealing to the intellect rather than the emotions
charlatan—a person who pretends to have expert knowledge or skill
chary—careful; cautious
chasten—to punish; to refine; to make purer in style
chide—to scold
chivalrous—gallant; courteous; honorable
circuitous—roundabout; indirect; devious
circumlocution—an indirect way of expressing something
circumspect—cautious; careful
circumvent—entrap; to surround or encircle with evils
citizenry—all citizens as a group
clairvoyant—having the power to perceive that which is outside of the human senses
clamor—a loud outcry; uproar
clamorous—noisy; loudly demanding or complaining
clandestine—kept secret or hidden
cleave—split; to divide by a blow
cliché—an expression or idea that has become trite
coalesce—to grow together; to unite or merge
coddle—to treat tenderly
codicil—an appendix or supplement
coerce—enforce; to bring about by using force
coeval—of the same age or period
cognizance—perception or knowledge
cognizant—aware or informed
coherent—clearly articulated; capable of logical, intelligible speech and thought
colloquial—conversational; having to do with or like conversation
combustion—the act or process of burning
commend—praise; to express approval of
commensurate—proportionate; corresponding in extent or degree
commingle—intermix; blend; to mingle together
commodity—anything bought and sold

communicable—that which can be communicated
compassion—deep sympathy; sorrow for the sufferings of others
compatible—that which can work well together, get along well together, combine well
compelling—captivating; irresistibly interesting
competent—well qualified; capable; fit
complacency—quiet satisfaction; contentment
complacent—self-satisfied; smug
complaisant—willing to please; obliging
compliance—a tendency to give in readily to others
compliant—yielding; submissive
comprehensive—able to understand fully
comprise—to include; contain
compulsion—that which compels; driving force
computation—calculation; a method of computing
concession—an act or instance of granting or yielding
conciliatory—tending to reconcile
concise—brief and to the point; short and clear
concoct—devise; invent; plan
condemn—censure; disapprove of strongly
condescension—a patronizing manner or behavior
condolence—expression of sympathy with another in grief
condone—forgive; pardon; overlook
conduit—a channel conveying fluids; a tube or protected trough for electric wires
confiscate—to seize by authority
conformity—action in accordance with customs, rules, and prevailing opinion
congregation—a gathering of people or things
congruent—in agreement; corresponding; harmonious
conjoin—to join together; unite; combine
conjunction—a joining together or being joined together
consensus—an opinion held by all or most
conspire—to plan and act together secretly
consternation—great fear or shock that makes one feel helpless or bewildered
constituent—component; a necessary part or element
consummate—supreme; complete or perfect in every way
contemn—scorn; to view with contempt
contemporaneous—existing or happening in the same period of time
contemptuous—scornful; disdainful
contentious—always ready to argue; quarrelsome
contentment—the state of being satisfied
context—the whole situation, background, or environment relevant to a particular event, personality, creation, *etc.*
contrite—penitent; feeling sorry for sins
contumacious—disobedient; obstinately resisting authority
conventional—customary; of, sanctioned by, or growing out of custom or usage
conversion—a change from one belief, religion, doctrine, opinion, *etc.* to another
convey—to make known
conviction—a strong belief
convoluted—extremely involved; intricate; complicated
copious—very plentiful; abundant
coronation—act or ceremony of crowning a sovereign
corpuscle—a very small particle
corroborate—confirm; to make more certain the validity of
countenance—facial expression; composure
coup—a sudden, successful move or action
covert—concealed; hidden; disguised
covet—to want ardently; long for with envy
crass—tasteless; insensitive; coarse
craven—very cowardly; abjectly afraid
credence—belief, especially in the reports or testimony of another
credulity—a tendency to believe too readily
crescendo—any gradual increase in force, intensity
criterion—a standard on which judgment can be based
critique—a critical analysis or evaluation
cryptic—mysterious; having a hidden or ambiguous meaning
culmination—climax; the highest point
culpable—deserving blame; blameworthy
cultivate—to promote development or growth
cumulative—accumulated; increasing in effect, size, quantity, *etc.*
cunning—skillful or clever
curator—a person in charge of a museum, library, *etc.*
cynical—sarcastic; sneering

daunt—intimidate; to make afraid or discouraged
dearth—any scarcity or lack
debacle—an overwhelming defeat
debase—cheapen; to make lower in value, quality, character, or dignity
debilitate—to make weak or feeble
decelerate—to reduce speed; slow down
decipher—decode; to make out the meaning of
decisive—showing determination or firmness
decry—denounce; to speak out against strongly and openly
deference—courteous regard or respect
defiance—open, bold resistance to authority or opposition
defiant—openly and boldly resisting
defunct—no longer living or existing; dead or extinct
defuse—to render harmless
degenerate—having sunk below a former or normal condition
delegate—to send from one place to another; appoint; assign
deleterious—injurious; harmful to health or well-being
delineate—describe; to depict in words
delirium—uncontrollably wild excitement or emotion
demagogue—a leader who gains power using popular prejudices and false claims; a leader of the common people in ancient times
demise—a ceasing to exist; death
demure—affectedly modest or shy; coy
denouement—the outcome, solution, unraveling, or clarification of a plot in a drama, story
denounce—to condemn strongly
despotic—of or like a despot; autocratic; tyrannical
destitute—living in complete poverty
desuetude—disuse; the condition of not being used
detonate—to explode violently and noisily
detumescence—a gradual shrinking of a swelling
devastate—to make helpless; overwhelm
devious—not straightforward or frank
diction—manner of expression in words
diminutive—very small; tiny
disabuse—to rid of false ideas or misconceptions
discern—make out clearly

discombobulate—upset the composure of
discomfit—make uneasy
disconcert—embarrass; confuse
discord—disagreement; conflict
discordant—disagreeing; conflicting
discourteous—impolite; rude; ill-mannered
discrepancy—difference; inconsistency
disinter—bring to light
disparage—show disrespect for; belittle
dissident—not agreeing
distillate—the essence; purified form
distraught—extremely troubled
divergence—separating; branching off
divergent—deviating; different
diverse—different; dissimilar
diversion—distraction of attention
divination—the art of foretelling future events; clever conjecture
doggerel—trivial, awkward, satirical verse
dogma—a doctrine; tenet; belief
dolt—a stupid, slow-witted person; blockhead
dormant—as if asleep; quiet; still
dross—waste matter; worthless stuff; rubbish
drub—to defeat soundly in a fight or contest
dubious—feeling doubt; hesitating; skeptical
dulcet—sweet-sounding; melodious
duress—constraint by threat; imprisonment

eccentricity—irregularity; oddity
eclectic—selecting from various systems, doctrines, or sources
efficacious—having the intended result; effective
effusive—expressing excessive emotion
embellish—decorate by adding detail; ornament
embodiment—concrete expression of an idea
emend—correct or improve
eminent—rising above other things or places
emissary—a person sent on a specific mission
emollient—softening; soothing
empathy—ability to share in another's emotions, thoughts, or feelings
emulate—imitate
enamor—fill with love and desire; charm
encroach—trespass or intrude
endow—provide with some talent or quality
enigma—riddle; a perplexing and ambiguous statement
enmity—hostility; antagonism
enthrall—captivate; fascinate
enumerate—count; determine the number of
epigram—a short poem with a witty point
epithet—a descriptive name or title
epitome—a person or thing that shows typical qualities of something
equipoise—state of balance or equilibrium
equivocal—having two or more meanings
equivocate—to be deliberately ambiguous
eradicate—wipe out; destroy; to get rid of
erroneous—mistaken; wrong
espionage—the act of spying
espouse—support or advocate
euphoria—feeling of vigor or well-being
evocation—calling forth
ewe—female sheep
exalt—elevate; to praise; glorify
exasperate—irritate or annoy very much; aggravate
excoriate—denounce harshly
exemplary—serving as a model or example
expunge—erase or remove completely
extant—still existing; not extinct
extol—praise highly
extrapolate—arrive at conclusions or results
exuberance—feeling of high spirits

faddish—having the nature of a fad
fallacious—misleading or deceptive
famine—hunger; a withering away
feckless—weak; ineffective
feint—a false show; sham
feral—untamed; wild
fervent—hot; burning; glowing
fervid—impassioned; fervent
finite—having measurable or definable limits; not infinite
fissure—a long, narrow, deep cleft or crack
flippant—frivolous and disrespectful; saucy
florid—highly decorated; gaudy; showy; ornate
flout—show scorn or contempt
forage—search for food or provisions
forbearance—patience
forbid—not permit; prohibit
forensics—debate or formal argumentation
forge—a furnace for heating metal to be wrought; to advance
forlorn—without hope; desperate
formidable—causing fear or dread
forthright—straightforward; direct; frank
fortify—strengthen
fracas—a noisy fight or loud quarrel; brawl
fractious—hard to manage; unruly
fraught—emotional; tense; anxious; distressing
frenetic—frantic; frenzied
frieze—ornamental band formed by a series of decorations
froward—not easily controlled; stubbornly willful
fulsome—offensively flattering
futile—ineffectual; trifling or unimportant

genial—cheerful; friendly; sympathetic
germinate—start developing or growing
glib—done in a smooth, offhand fashion
goad—driving impulse; spur
gouge—scrape or hollow out
gourmand—a glutton; one who indulges to excess
gregarious—fond of the company of others; sociable
gristle—cartilage found in meat
grouse—complain; grumble
grovel—behave humbly or abjectly

hackney—make trite by overuse
hapless—unfortunate; unlucky; luckless
haste—the act of hurrying; quickness of motion
haughty—proud; arrogant
heed—take careful notice of
hence—thereafter; subsequently
herbaceous—like a green leaf in texture, color, shape

heroine—girl or woman of outstanding courage and nobility
hew—chop or cut with an ax or knife; hack; gash
hierarchy—an arrangement in order of rank, grade, class
hindsight—ability to see, after the event, what should have been done
hirsute—hairy; shaggy; bristly
homogeneous—of the same race or kind
hone—to perfect; sharpen; yearn
hoodwink—mislead or confuse by trickery
hue—a particular shade or tint of a given color
humble—not proud; not self-assertive; modest
humdrum—lacking variety; dull; monotonous
humility—absence of pride or self-assertion
hybrid—anything of mixed origin; unlike parts
hypocrisy—pretending to be what one is not
hypothesis—unproved theory

idealist—visionary or dreamer
idiosyncrasy—personal peculiarity or mannerism
idol—object of worship; false god
idolatrous—given to idolatry or blind adoration
idolatry—worship of idols
immaculate—perfectly clean; unsoiled
impart—make known; tell; reveal
impeccable—without defect or error; flawless
impede—obstruct or delay
impenitent—without regret, shame, or remorse
imperturbable—cannot be disconcerted, disturbed, or excited; impassive
impervious—not affected
impetuous—moving with great, sudden energy
impinge—to make inroads or encroach
impious—lacking respect or dutifulness
implacable—unable to be appeased or pacified; relentless
implicate—to involve or concern
imposture—fraud; deception
inadvertent—not attentive or observant; heedless
incantation—chanted words or formula
incarcerate—imprison; confine
incessant—continual; never ceasing
incinerate—burn up; cremate
incongruous—lacking harmony or agreement
incontrovertible—not disputable or debatable
incorrigible—unable to be corrected, improved, or reformed
incumbent—lying, resting on something; imposed as a duty
indignation—righteous anger
indignity—unworthiness or disgrace
indiscernible—imperceptible
indiscriminate—confused; random
indispensable—absolutely necessary or required
indomitable—not easily discouraged, defeated, or subdued
industrious—diligent; skillful
ineffable—too overwhelming to be expressed in words
inefficacious—unable to produce the desired effect
infallible—incapable of error; never wrong
infamy—bad reputation; notoriety; disgrace
ingratiate—to achieve one's good graces by conscious effort
inimical—hostile; unfriendly
innate—existing naturally rather than through acquisition
innocuous—harmless; not controversial, offensive, or stimulating
inquisitor—harsh or prying questioner
insipid—not exciting or interesting; dull
insouciant—calm and untroubled; carefree
insularity—detachment; isolation
intelligible—clear; comprehensible
intemperate—lacking restraint; excessive
interstellar—between or among the stars
inveterate—habitual; of long standing; deep-rooted
irascible—easily angered; quick-tempered

jaunty—gay and carefree; sprightly; perky
jubilant—joyful and triumphant; elated; rejoicing
jurisprudence—a part or division of law

kernel—the most central part; a grain

lackluster—lacking energy or vitality
lambaste—scold or denounce severely
lament—mourn; grieve
languid—without vigor or vitality; drooping; weak
laudable—praiseworthy; commendable
laudatory—expressing praise
legion—a large number; multitude
lethargic—abnormally drowsy or dull; sluggish
limerick—nonsense poem of five anapestic lines
limn—describe
lionize—treat as a celebrity
listless—spiritless; languid
literati—scholarly or learned people
lithe—bending easily; flexible; supple
litigant—a party to a lawsuit
liturgy—ritual for public worship in any of various religions or churches
livid—grayish-blue; extremely angry
loquacious—fond of talking
loquacity—talkativeness
lucid—transparent
lummox—a clumsy, stupid person

magnanimous—noble in mind
magnitude—greatness; importance or influence
malevolence—malice; spitefulness; ill will
malfeasance—wrongdoing or misconduct
malinger—pretend to be ill to escape duty or work; shirk
masque—dramatic composition
maverick—a person who takes an independent stand
maxim—statement of a general truth
mazurka—a lively Polish folk dance
meager—thin; lean; emaciated
medieval—characteristic of the Middle Ages
mellifluous—sounding sweet and smooth; honeyed
menace—threaten harm or evil
mercenary—motivated by a desire for money or other gain
merriment—gaiety and fun
metamorphose—transform
metaphor—a figure of speech containing an implied comparison
methodology—system of procedures
meticulous—extremely careful about details
minatory—menacing; threatening
miser—a greedy, stingy person

mitigate—make less rigorous or less painful; moderate
mnemonic—helping, or meant to help, the memory
modicum—small amount
monarch—hereditary head of a state
mordant—biting; cutting; caustic; sarcastic
morose—ill-tempered; gloomy
myriad—indefinitely large number
mythical—imaginary; fictitious

narcissism—self-love
negate—make ineffective
nexus—a connected group or series
nib—point of a pen
nocturnal—active during the night
noisome—having a bad odor; foul-smelling
nomad—one who has no permanent home, who moves about constantly
nostalgia—longing for things of the past
notoriety—prominence or renown, often unfavorable
novice—apprentice; beginner
nuance—a slight or delicate variation

obliterate—erase; efface
obsequious—compliant; dutiful; servile
obsolete—no longer in use or practice
obstinate—unreasonably determined to have one's own way; stubborn
obtuse—not sharp or pointed; blunt
occult—secret; esoteric
odium—disgrace brought on by hateful action
officious—ready to serve; obliging
ominous—threatening; sinister
omnipotent—unlimited in power or authority
onerous—burdensome; laborious
opulent—very wealthy or rich
oration—a formal public speech
orator—eloquent public speaker
ornate—heavily ornamented or adorned
orthodox—strictly conforming to the traditional
oscillate—to be indecisive in purpose or opinion; vacillate
ossify—settle or fix rigidly
ostracism—rejection or exclusion by general consent
overwrought—overworked; fatigued

paean—a song of joy, triumph, praise
palliate—relieve without curing; make less severe
pallid—faint in color; pale
palpable—tangible; easily perceived by the senses
pantomime—action or gestures without words as a means of expression
paradigm—example or model
paradox—a statement that seems contradictory
paramount—ranking higher than any other
parch—dry up with heat
pariah—outcast
parody—a poor or weak imitation
pathology—conditions, processes, or results of a particular disease
peccadillo—minor or petty sin; slight fault
pellucid—transparent or translucent; clear
penchant—strong liking or fondness
penitent—truly sorry for having sinned and willing to atone
peremptory—intolerantly positive or assured
peril—exposure to harm or injury; danger
peripheral—outer; external; lying at the outside
pervade—to become prevalent throughout
petrous—of or like rock; hard
petulant—peevish; impatient or irritable
philistine—a person smugly narrow and conventional in views and tastes
pinion—confine or shackle
placate—stop from being angry; appease
platitude—commonplace, flat, or dull quality
plethora—overabundance; excess
poignant—emotionally touching or moving
poseur—a person who assumes attitudes or manners merely for their effect upon others
postulate—claim; demand; require
pragmatic—busy or active in a meddlesome way; practical
preclude—shut out; prevent
precocious—exhibiting premature development
predilection—preconceived liking; partiality or preference
presage—sign or warning of a future event; omen
prescience—foreknowledge
preside—exercise control or authority
prig—annoyingly pedantic person
proclivity—natural or habitual inclination
procure—obtain; secure
profane—show disrespect for sacred things; irreverent
profuse—generous, often to excess
proliferate—to reproduce (new parts) in quick succession
prolific—turning out many products of the mind
prolix—wordy; long-winded
propagate—reproduce; multiply
propinquity—nearness of relationship; kinship
propriety—properness; suitability
prosaic—matter of fact; ordinary
prose—ordinary speech; dull
protuberance—projection; bulge
provocative—stimulating; erotic
prudence—careful management
pugnacious—eager and ready to fight; quarrelsome
pundit—actual or self-professed authority
punitive—inflicting, concerned with, or directed toward punishment

quaff—drink deeply in a hearty or thirsty way
quell—crush; subdue; put an end to
querulous—full of complaint; peevish
quotidian—everyday; usual or ordinary

ramify—divide or spread out into branches
rancor—deep spite or malice
rapacious—taking by force; plundering
rasp—rough, grating tone
ratify—approve or confirm
raucous—loud and rowdy
reciprocate—cause to move alternately back and forth
recluse—secluded; solitary
recompense—repay; compensate
regale—delight with something pleasing or amusing
relegate—exile or banish

relinquish—give up; abandon
remedial—providing a remedy
reparation—restoration to good condition
replete—well-filled or plentifully supplied
reprieve—give temporary relief to, as from trouble or pain
reprobate—disapprove of strongly
repugnant—contradictory; inconsistent
requiem—musical service for the dead
resplendent—dazzling; splendid
restitution—return to a former condition or situation
reticent—habitually silent; reserved
rhapsodize—to describe in an extravagantly enthusiastic manner
rogue—a rascal; scoundrel
rubric—a category or section heading, often in red; any rule or explanatory comment
ruffian—brutal, violent, lawless person
ruse—trick or artifice

sacred—holy; of or connected with religion
salutary—healthful; beneficial
salutation—greeting, addressing, or welcoming by gestures or words
salve—balm that soothes or heals
sanctimonious—pretending to be very holy
sanction—support; encouragement; approval
savant—learned person; eminent scholar
scrupulous—having principles; extremely conscientious
scurvy—low; mean; vile; contemptible
semaphore—system of signaling
seminal—of reproduction; germinal; originative
serene—calm; peaceful; tranquil
servile—humbly yielding or submissive; of a slave or slaves
shroud—covers, protects, or screens; veil; shelter
signatory—joined in the signing of something
sinister—wicked; evil; dishonest
sinuous—not straightforward; devious
slake—make less intense by satisfying
snide—slyly malicious or derisive
sodden—filled with moisture; soaked
solace—comfort; consolation; relief
soluble—able to be dissolved
somber—dark and gloomy or dull
soporific—pertaining to sleep or sleepiness
sporadic—occasional; not constant or regular
spurious—not true or genuine; false
squalid—foul or unclean
stealth—secret, furtive, or artfully sly behavior
stigma—mark or sign indicating something not considered normal or standard
stint—restrict or limit
stolid—unexcitable; impassive
stymie—situation in which one is obstructed or frustrated
subliminal—on the threshold of consciousness; under the surface
submission—resignation; obedience; meekness
suffice—be adequate
sully—soil; stain; tarnish by disgracing
sunder—break apart; separate; split
superfluous—excessive
supine—sluggish; listless; passive
surfeit—too great an amount or supply; excess
surreptitious—acting in a secret, stealthy way
symbiosis—relationship of mutual interdependence
syntax—orderly or systematic arrangement of words

tactile—perceived by touch; tangible
tangible—having actual form and substance
tawdry—cheap and showy; gaudy; sleazy
tedium—tediousness
tempt—persuade; induce; entice
tenet—principle, doctrine, or belief held as a truth
tenuous—slender or fine; not dense
terrestrial—worldly; earthly
throng—crowd
timorous—subject to fear; timid
toupee—a man's wig
tractable—easily worked; obedient; malleable
tranquil—calm; serene; peaceful
transcend—exceed; surpass; excel
transgress—go beyond a limit
translucent—partially transparent or clear
transmute—transform; convert
treacherous—untrustworthy or insecure
treachery—perfidy; disloyalty; treason
trepidation—fearful uncertainty; anxiety
trite—no longer having originality
troubadour—minstrel or singer
truncate—cut short
tumultuous—wild and noisy; uproarious
turgid—swollen; distended
turmoil—commotion; uproar; confusion
tyranny—very cruel and unjust use of power or authority

uncanny—inexplicable; preternaturally strange; weird
underling—one in a subordinate position; inferior
unfeigned—genuine; real; sincere
unfetter—free from restraint; liberate
unification—state of being unified
unintelligible—unable to be understood; incomprehensible
unity—oneness; singleness
univocal—unambiguous
unscrupulous—not restrained by ideas of right and wrong
untenable—incapable of being occupied
untoward—inappropriate; improper
unwitting—not knowing; unaware
upbraid—rebuke severely or bitterly
uproarious—loud and boisterous
usury—interest at a high rate
utilitarian—stressing usefulness over beauty
utopia—idealized place

vacillate—sway to and fro; waver; totter
vacuum—completely empty space
vagabond—wandering; moving from place to place
vagrant—a person who lives a wandering life
valiant—brave
vapid—tasteless; flavorless; flat
variegate—vary; diversify
veer—change direction; shift
vehement—acting or moving with great force
venerate—show feelings of deep respect; revere

vengeance—revenge
vestige—a trace of something that once existed
vex—distress; afflict; plague
vicarious—serving as a substitute
villainous—evil; wicked
vitiate—spoil; corrupt
vivacious—full of life and animation; lively
vocation—trade; profession; occupation
volatile—flying or able to fly
voluble—talkative
voluminous—large; bulky; full
voracious—ravenous; gluttonous

waft—float, as on the wind
wane—grow dim or faint
wary—cautious; on one's guard
welter—to become soaked; stained; bathed
wheedle—coax; influence or persuade by flattery
whet—make keen; stimulate
wile—sly trick
wither—shrivel; wilt
witty—cleverly amusing
wrath—intense anger; rage; fury
wrench—sudden, sharp twist or pull

yacht—small vessel for pleasure cruises or racing
yearn—to have longing or desire
yielding—submissive; obedient

zeal—intense enthusiasm
zenith—highest point; peak

—Difficulty Level 2—

abstemious—exercising moderation; self-restraint
aggregation—gathered together; accumulated
alacrity—cheerful promptness; eagerness
ambient—surrounding
amorphous—shapeless; formless
antediluvian—before the flood; antiquated
apostate—fallen from the faith
arrogate—to claim or seize as one's own
ascetic—practicing self-denial; austere
ascribe—attribute to a cause
asperity—having a harsh temper; roughness
assuage—lessen; soothe
assiduous—diligent
attenuation—a thinning out
august—great dignity or grandeur
aver—affirm; declare to be true

bacchanalian—drunken
baleful—menacing; deadly
beguile—to deceive; cheat; charm; coax
beleaguer—besiege or attack; harass
bellicose—belligerent; pugnacious; warlike
belie—misrepresent; be false to
bombastic—pompous; puffed up with conceit; using inflated language
bovine—resembling a cow; placid or dull
bucolic—rustic; pastoral
burgeon—grow forth; send out buds

cacophony—harsh or discordant sound; dissonance
calumny—slander
capitulate—surrender
cathartic—purgative; inducing a figurative cleansing
cavil—disagree; nit-pick; make frivolous objections
celerity—swiftness
chassis—framework and working parts of an automobile
chimerical—fantastically improbable; highly unrealistic
churlish—rude; surly
circumscribe—limit
cogent—convincing
collusion—conspiring in a fraudulent scheme
comely—attractive; agreeable
compendium—brief, comprehensive summary
concord—harmony
confluence—flowing or coming together
consecrate—induct into a religious office; declare sacred
consonance—agreement; harmony
contrite—penitent; repentant; feeling sorry for sins
contumely—insult; contemptuous treatment
conundrum—riddle; difficult problem
cosset—pamper
cupidity—excessive desire for money; avarice
cursory—hasty; done without care

decimate—destroy a great number
defer—yield; delay
demur—to take exception; object
denigrate—blacken someone's reputation or character
derision—ridicule
desiccate—dry up; drain
desultory—aimless; unmethodical; unfocused
diaphanous—translucent; see-through
diatribe—speech full of bitterness
didactic—intended primarily to instruct
diffidence—modesty; shyness; lack of confidence
dilatory—given to delay or procrastination
dilettante—aimless follower of the arts; amateur; dabbler
din—loud confusing noise
disaffection—lack of trust; to cause discontent
disarming—deprive of resentment; peaceable or friendly; win over
discursive—rambling; passing from one topic to another
disingenuous—deceitful; lacking in candor; not frank
disparate—basically different; unrelated
disputatious—argumentative
disquietude—uneasiness; anxiety
dissemble—conceal true motives; pretend
dissolute—loose in morals or conduct
dissonant—lacking in harmony; discordant
dogmatic—adhering to a tenet
dolorous—sorrowful; having mental anguish
duplicity—deception by pretending to feel and act one way while acting another; bad faith; double dealing

ebullient—greatly excited
edify—instruct; correct morally
efface—erase; obliterate as if by rubbing it out
efficacy—power to produce desired effect
effrontery—shameless boldness; impudence; temerity
egregious—notorious; shocking
encomium—glowing praise
encumber—hinder
endemic—prevailing among a specific group
enervate—weaken; debilitate
engender—cause; produce
ensconce—settle in; hide; conceal
ephemeral—fleeting; short-lived
equanimity—calmness; composure
erudite—learned; scholarly
eschew—shun
esoteric—hard to understand
etymology—study of word parts
evanescent—tending to vanish like vapor
evince—show clearly
exacerbate—worsen; embitter
exculpate—clear from blame
execrable—detestable
exegesis—explanation, especially of biblical passages
exhort—urge
exigency—urgent situation
expatriate—one choosing to live abroad

facile—easily accomplished; ready or fluent
fatuous—foolish or inane
fealty—loyalty; allegiance
felicitous—well chosen; apt; suitable
ferment—agitation; commotion
fetid—malodorous

filial—pertaining to a son or daughter
flaccid—flabby
foment—stir up; instigate
fortuitous—accidental; by chance
fulminate—to thunder; explode
fungible—capable of being used in place of something else

gainsay—contradict; speak or act against
galvanize—stimulate by shock; stir up; revitalize
gambol—romp; to skip about
garrulous—loquacious; wordy; talkative
gossamer—sheer, like cobwebs
gratuitous—given freely; unwarranted
guile—slyness and cunning

hackles—hairs on back and neck
halcyon—calm; peaceful
harbinger—one that announces or foreshadows what is coming; precursor; portent
hummock—small hill
hedonist—one who believes pleasure is sole aim in life
hegemony—dominance, especially of one nation over another
heinous—atrocious; hatefully bad
hermetic—obscure and mysterious; relating to the occult
hubris—arrogance; excessive self-conceit
humus—substance formed by decaying vegetable matter

iconoclastic—attacking cherished traditions
ignominious—dishonorable; disgraceful
imbroglio—complicated situation
immolate—offer as a sacrifice
immutable—unchangeable
impalpable—imperceptible; intangible
impecunious—without money
importune—repeatedly urge
impuissance—powerlessness; feebleness
impunity—freedom from punishment or harm
inchoate—recently begun; rudimentary
incipient—becoming apparent; beginning
incisive—sharply expressive
inculcate—impress on the mind by admonition
incursion—temporary invasion
indelible—not able to be removed or erased
indemnify—make secure against loss
indigent—poor
indite—write; compose
indolent—lazy
ineluctable—irresistible; not to be escaped
inexorable—not to be moved by entreaty; unyielding; relentless
iniquitous—wicked; immoral
insidious—deceitful; treacherous
internecine—mutually destructive
interpolate—insert between other things
intractable—stubborn
intransigence—refusal to compromise
intrepid—brave
inure—make accustomed to something difficult
invective—abuse
inveigh—condemn; censure

jaundice—prejudice; envious; yellow
jettison—throw overboard
jocose—given to joking
jocund—merry
juggernaut—irresistible, crushing force
juxtapose—place side by side

ken—range of knowledge
kinetic—producing motion
kismet—fate
knell—tolling of a bell
knoll—little round hill

lachrymose—producing tears
laconic—using few words
largess—liberal giving; generous gift
lascivious—lustful
lassitude—weariness; debility
latent—potential but undeveloped; dormant
laxity—carelessness
legerdemain—sleight of hand
licentious—amoral; lewd and lascivious
Lilliputian—extremely small
limpid—clear
lugubrious—mournful, often to an excessive degree

maelstrom—whirlpool
maladroit—clumsy; bungling
malediction—curse
malleable—capable of being shaped
malignant—growing worse
maraud—rove in search of plunder
martinet—one who issues orders
masticate—chew
maudlin—effusively sentimental
megalomania—mania for doing grandiose things
melee—fight
mendacity—untruthfulness
mendicant—beggar
mercurial—volatile; changeable; fickle
meretricious—flashy; tawdry
miasma—a poisonous atmosphere
misanthrope—a person who hates mankind
miscreant—villain
mollify—soothe
monolithic—consisting of a single character; uniform; unyielding
moribund—dying
myopic—nearsighted; lacking foresight
munificent—generous

nadir—lowest point
nascent—incipient; coming into being
nebulous—unclear; vague; hazy; cloudy
necromancy—black magic; dealing with the dead
nefarious—wicked
nostrum—questionable medicine
nubile—marriageable
nugatory—futile; worthless

obdurate—stubborn; unyielding

obfuscate—make obscure; confuse
obloquy—slander; disgrace; infamy
obstreperous—unruly; boisterous; noisy
obviate—make unnecessary
occlude—shut; close
odious—hateful; vile
oligarchy—government by a privileged few
opprobrium—infamy; vilification
ostensible—apparent; showing outwardly; professed

panegyric—formal praise
paragon—model of perfection
parlance—language; idiom
parlay—exploit successfully
parsimonious—stingy
paucity—scarcity
pecuniary—obsessed by money
pedantic—bookish
pejorative—negative in connotation; having a tendency to make worse; disparaging
penurious—marked by penury; stingy
perdition—eternal damnation; complete ruin
perfidy—treacherous; betrayal of trust
perfunctory—indifferent; done merely as a duty; superficial
pernicious—fatal; very destructive or injurious
perspicacious—having insight; penetrating; astute
perspicuous—plainly expressed
phlegmatic—calm; not easily disturbed
piebald—of different colors; mottled; spotted
piety—devoutness; reverence for God
pillory—criticize or ridicule
piquancy—something that stimulates taste; tartness
pithy—essential; brief and to the point
polemic—controversy; argument in support of a point of view
polyglot—speaking several languages
portent—sign; omen; something that foreshadows a coming event
precipitous—abrupt or hasty
probity—honesty; integrity
prodigal—wasteful; reckless with money
prodigious—marvelous; enormous
profligate—dissolute; reckless; loose in morals; wanton
profundity—intellectual depth
promulgate—proclaim; make public; put into effect
propitious—favorable; timely
proscribe—outlaw; ostracize; banish
protract—prolong in time or space; extend; lengthen
puerile—childish; lacking in maturity
pungent—stinging; sharp in taste; caustic
pusillanimous—cowardly

quiescent—at rest; dormant; temporarily inactive
quixotic—idealistic but impractical

raconteur—someone who is skilled at telling stories or anecdotes
raffish—vulgar; crude
raiment—clothing
recalcitrant—stubborn; refractory; reluctant; unwilling; refusing to submit
recidivism—habitual return to crime
recondite—abstruse; profound; secret
recumbent—reclining; lying down
redolent—suggestive of an odor; fragrant
redoubtable—formidable; causing fear
refractory—stubborn; obstinate
remand—order back; return to service
remonstrate—object; protest
remunerative—compensating; rewarding for service
repine—complain; mourn; fret
ribald—wanton; profane or coarse; joking or mocking

sagacious—perceptive; shrewd; having insight
salacious—lustful; lecherous; lascivious
salient—standing out conspicuously; prominent
salubrious—healthful
sanguine—having a ruddy complexion; cheerful; hopeful
sardonic—sneering; sarcastic; cynical
sartorial—tailored
saturnine—sullen; sardonic; gloomy
sedition—resistance to authority
sedulous—diligent; persevering
sententious—terse; concise; aphoristic
sophistry—seemingly plausible but fallacious reasoning
specious—seeming reasonable but incorrect
spendthrift—one who spends money extravagantly
splenetic—bad-tempered; irritable
static—showing a lack of motion
stentorian—powerful in sound; extremely loud
stringent—vigorous; rigid; binding
succor—aid; assistance; comfort
supercilious—contemptuous; arrogant
sycophant—one who seeks favor by flattering; a parasite

taciturn—quiet; habitually silent
tangential—peripheral; only slightly connected
temerity—foolish or rash boldness
temporal—not lasting forever; limited by time
tenacity—holding fast
toady—servile flatterer; a "yes man"
tome—large book
torpor—lack of activity; lethargy
tortuous—winding; full of curves
traduce—to speak falsely
transcendent—exceeding usual limits; incomparable; beyond ordinary existence; peerless
trenchant—effective; thorough; cutting; keen
truculent—threatening; aggressively self-assertive; savage
turbid—muddy
turpitude—depravity

ubiquitous—being everywhere; omnipresent
unctuous—oily; suave
undulating—moving with a wavelike motion
unequivocal—plain; obvious

vacuity—emptiness
vainglorious—boastful
vanguard—forerunner; advance forces
venal—capable of being bribed
venial—forgivable; trivial

veracious—truthful
verbose—wordy
verdant—green; lush in vegetation
verisimilitude—appearance of truth
veritable—actual; being truly so
vicissitude—change of fortune
viscid—having a cohesive and sticky fluid
vitriolic—corrosive; sarcastic
vituperative—abusive; scolding
vociferous—clamorous; noisy
vouchsafe—bestow condescendingly; guarantee

waggish—mischievous; humorous; tricky
wanton—excessively merry; frolicsome; having no regard for others
winnow—sift; separate good parts from bad
winsome—agreeable; gracious
wizen—wither; shrivel

xenophobia—fear or hatred of foreigners

zealous—fervent; enthusiastic
zephyr—gentle breeze; west wind

EXERCISE 6

Vocabulary: Passages

DIRECTIONS: The following is a vocabulary exercise. After reading the passage, choose the *best* answer to each item. Answer all items on the basis of what is either *explicitly stated* or *implied* in the passage. Answers are on page 924.

Items #1-10 are based on the following passage.

The following passage is an excerpt from a history of the political career of Thomas Jefferson, the author of the "Declaration of Independence."

"Heartily tired" from the brutal, almost daily conflicts that erupted over questions of national policy between himself and Alexander Hamilton, Thomas Jefferson resigned his position as Secretary of State in 1793. Although his Federalist opponents were convinced that this was merely a strategic withdrawal to allow him an opportunity to plan and promote his candidacy for the Presidency should Washington step down in 1796, Jefferson insisted that this retirement from public life was to be final.

But even in retirement, the world of politics pursued him. As the election grew nearer and it became apparent that Washington would not seek a third term, rumors of Jefferson's Presidential ambitions grew in intensity. Reacting to these continuous insinuations in a letter to James Madison, Jefferson allowed that while the idea that he coveted the office of chief executive had been originated by his enemies to impugn his political motives, he had been forced to examine his true feelings on the subject for his own peace of mind. In so doing he concluded that his reasons for retirement—the desire for privacy, and the delight of family life—coupled with his now failing health were insuperable barriers to public service. The "little spice of ambition" he had in his younger days had long since evaporated and the question of his Presidency was forever closed.

Jefferson did not actively engage in the campaign on his own behalf. The Republican party, anticipating modern campaign tactics, created grass roots sentiment for their candidate by directing their efforts toward the general populace. In newspapers, Jefferson was presented as the uniform advocate of equal rights among the citizens while Adams was portrayed as the champion of rank, titles, heredity, and distinctions. Jefferson was not certain of the outcome of the election until the end of December. Under the original electoral system established by the Constitution, each Presidential elector cast his ballot for two men without designating between them as to office. The candidate who received the greater number of votes became the President; the second highest, the Vice President. Jefferson foresaw on the basis of his own calculations that the electoral vote would be close. He wrote to Madison that in the event of a tie, he wished for the choice to be in favor of Adams. In public life, the New Englander had always been senior to Jefferson; and so, he explained, the expression of public will being equal, Adams should be preferred for the higher honor. Jefferson, a shrewd politician, realized that the transition of power from the nearly mythical Washington to a lesser luminary in the midst of the deep and bitter political divisions facing the nation could be perilous, and he had no desire to be caught in the storm that had been brewing for four years and was about to break. "This is certainly not a moment to covet the helm," he wrote to Edward Rutledge. When the electoral vote was tallied, Adams emerged the victor. Rejoicing at his "escape," Jefferson was completely satisfied with the decision. Despite their obvious and basic political differences, Jefferson genuinely respected John Adams as a friend and compatriot. Although Jefferson believed that Adams had deviated from the course set in 1776, in Jefferson's eyes he never suffered diminution; and Jefferson was quite confident that Adams would not steer the nation too far from its Republican tack. Within two years, Jefferson's views would be drastically altered as measures such as the Alien and Sedition Acts of 1798 convinced him of the need to wrest control of the government from the Federalists.

1. In line 1, the word "heartily" most nearly means:
   (A) sincerely
   (B) vigorously
   (C) zealously
   (D) completely

2. In line 9, the word "public" most nearly means
   (F) communal
   (G) open
   (H) official
   (J) people

3. In line 9, the word "final" most nearly means
   (A) last
   (B) closing
   (C) ultimate
   (D) conclusive

4. In line 15, the word "allowed" most nearly means:
   (F) permitted
   (G) admitted
   (H) tolerated
   (J) granted

5. In line 26, the word "anticipating" most nearly means:
   (A) expecting
   (B) presaging
   (C) awaiting
   (D) inviting

6. In line 30, the word "uniform" most nearly means:
   (F) standard
   (G) unchanging
   (H) militant
   (J) popular

7. In line 31, the word "champion" most nearly means:
   (A) victor
   (B) opponent
   (C) colleague
   (D) defender

8. In line 42, the word "senior" most nearly means:
   (F) older in age
   (G) higher in rank
   (H) graduate
   (J) mentor

9. In line 46, the word "luminary" most nearly means:
   (A) bright object
   (B) famous person
   (C) office holder
   (D) candidate

10. In line 58, the word "diminution" most nearly means:
    (F) foreshortening
    (G) shrinkage
    (H) abatement
    (J) degradation

EXERCISE 7

Vocabulary: Context Clues

DIRECTIONS: Select an appropriate completion for each blank in the following paragraph from the corresponding numbered lists provided below. Answers are on page 924.

Today, the Surgeon General announced the findings of a new ——(1) that concludes that smoking represents a serious ——(2) to non-smokers as well as to ——(3). According to the Surgeon General, disease risk due to ——(4) of tobacco smoke is not limited to the ——(5) who is smoking, but it can also extend to those who ——(6) tobacco smoke in the same room. Simple ——(7) of smokers and non-smokers within the same airspace may reduce, but does not ——(8), exposure of non-smokers to environmental smoke. A spokesperson for the tobacco industry ——(9) the report, saying the available ——(10) does not support the conclusion that environmental tobacco smoke is a hazard to non-smokers. On the other hand, the Coalition for Smoking on Health, an anti-smoking organization, ——(11) the report and called for ——(12) government action to ensure a smoke-free environment for all non-smokers.

1. (A) movie
   (B) election
   (C) report
   (D) advertisement

2. (F) consciousness
   (G) hazard
   (H) remedy
   (J) possibility

3. (A) cigarettes
   (B) fumes
   (C) alcoholics
   (D) smokers

4. (F) observation
   (G) criticism
   (H) improvement
   (J) inhalation

5. (A) individual
   (B) doctor
   (C) campaign
   (D) reporter

6. (F) create
   (G) breathe
   (H) enjoy
   (J) ban

7. (A) encouragement
   (B) prohibition
   (C) separation
   (D) intermingling

8. (F) imagine
   (G) increase
   (H) prepare
   (J) eliminate

9. (A) purchased
   (B) prepared
   (C) understood
   (D) criticized

10. (F) alibi
    (G) publicity
    (H) evidence
    (J) reaction

11. (A) praised
    (B) rejected
    (C) prolonged
    (D) denied

12. (F) minimal
    (G) immediate
    (H) reactionary
    (J) uncontrolled

DIRECTIONS: Each of the following items contains one blank. Write down a few *possible* words that you anticipate could be used to complete the sentence. Answers are on page 925.

13. Stress is the reaction an individual feels when he believes the demands of a situation —— his ability to meet them.

____
____
____

14. The —— of his career, capturing the coveted "Most Valuable Player" award, came at a time of deep personal sadness.

____
____
____

15. Martin's opponent is a(n) —— speaker who is unable to elicit a reaction from a crowd on even the most emotional of issues.

____
____
____

16. The cold weather caused —— damage to the Florida citrus crop, prompting growers to warn that the reduced yield is likely to result in much higher prices.

____
____
____

17. The report is so —— that it covers all of the main points in detail and at least touches on everything that is even remotely connected with its topic.

____
____
____

18. The Constitution sets up a system of checks and balances among the executive, the legislative, and the judicial branches to ensure that no one branch can establish —— control over the government.

____
____
____

19. The females of many common species of birds have dull coloring that —— them when they are sitting on a nest in a tree or other foliage.

____
____
____

20. She was one of the most —— criminals of the 1930s, her name a household word and her face in every post office.

____
____
____

21. Although he had not been physically injured by the explosion, the violence of the shock left him temporarily ——.

____
____
____

22. Good teachers know that study habits learned as a youngster stay with a student for life, so they try to find ways to —— enthusiasm for studies.

____
____
____

DIRECTIONS: Each of the following items contains one blank. Analyze each item by underlining a few words or phrases that provide clues for the completion of the sentences. Write down a few *possible* words that you anticipate could be used to complete the sentence. Answers are on page 925.

23. The survivors had been drifting for days in the lifeboat, and in their weakness, they appeared to be —— rather than living beings.

24. The guillotine was introduced during the French Revolution as a(n) ——, an alternative to other less humane means of execution.

25. Because of the —— nature of the chemical, it cannot be used near an open flame.

26. The Mayor's proposal for a new subway line, although a(n) ——, is not a final solution to the city's transportation needs.

27. In a pluralistic society, policies are the result of compromise, so political leaders must be —— and must accommodate the views of others.

28. The committee report vigorously expounded the bill's strengths but also acknowledged its ——.

29. Because there is always the danger of a power failure and disruption of elevator service, high-rise buildings, while suitable for younger persons, are not recommended for ——.

30. For a child to be happy, his day must be very structured; when his routine is ——, he becomes nervous and irritable.

31. The current spirit of —— among different religions has led to a number of meetings that their leaders hope will lead to better understanding.

32. Our modern industrialized societies have been responsible for the greatest destruction of nature and life; indeed, it seems that more civilization results in greater ——.

Science Skills Review

TARGETED EDUCATIONAL SOLUTIONS.

Cambridge Course Concept Outline
SCIENCE SKILLS REVIEW

Introduction

The purpose of most science sections of standardized tests is to examine your ability to read and understand scientific information. Rather than testing your knowledge of science facts, the items will measure your science reasoning and problem-solving skills. These science tests emphasizes the ability to reason using the skills of a scientist, not the recall of scientific content or specific mathematical skills that are used in science.

Studying and completing the activities in the Science Skills Review will enhance your science reasoning abilities. This review will examine how an experiment is set up, provide guidelines for organizing data collected by observation and experimentation, and present a list of terms that are often found in the passages and corresponding items.

Science Reasoning Passages

The scientific skills that are measured on the science reasoning tests, such as the ACT, are tested by items that ask about scientific information presented in three different types of passages: Research Summary, Data Representation, and Conflicting Viewpoints. The scientific information in all three types of passages is obtained through observation and experimentation.

1. ***Research Summary Passages***

   The ***Research Summary*** passages consist of descriptions of how specific experiments were carried out and a summary of the experimental results. In the Research Summary passages, you may be required to identify the differences in the design of the experiments, predict the outcome based on the results of an experiment, or predict the outcome of an experiment if the design is changed. You may also be required to identify a hypothesis that is being tested, select a hypothesis supported by the results of an experiment, determine the conclusion supported by the given results of an experiment, or select an experiment that could be conducted in order to test another hypothesis.

2. ***Data Representation Passages***

   The ***Data Representation*** passages present scientific information in the form of graphs, tables, and figures. In Data Representation passages, you may be asked to select a conclusion that can be supported by the data, determine the relationship between two variables, or select an explanation for a given experimental result. You may also be required to determine if a conclusion is consistent with the information given, apply the given data to a new situation, or determine what the slope of a line on a graph represents.

3. ***Conflicting Viewpoints Passages***

   The ***Conflicting Viewpoints*** passages present differing hypotheses, theories, or viewpoints of two or three scientists. In the Conflicting Viewpoints passages, you may be required to determine each scientist's position, select the evidence that supports the viewpoints of one or more of the scientists, or determine the similarities and differences of the various scientists' viewpoints. You may also be asked to determine the strengths and weaknesses of the viewpoints, figure out how new information would affect one or more of the viewpoints, or predict evidence that would support a scientist's viewpoint.

Presentation of Additional Information

While more commonly found in Data Representation passages, any Science Reasoning passage may include information that is organized in the form of charts, diagrams, figures, graphs, illustrations, and tables like those found in science journals and textbooks. Typically, on the test, you will be asked to read, interpret, and analyze data presented in these forms.

Science Reasoning Vocabulary

The following list is composed of terms that are commonly found in the passages and corresponding items. Understanding the definitions and uses of these terms will help you to understand the passage or item in which they are used better.

absolute: existing independent of any other cause
accuracy: freedom from mistake; exactness; the relationship between the gradation on a measuring device and the actual standard for the quantity being measured
adverse: acting against or in an opposite direction
analogous: similar or comparable in certain respects
analyze: to study the relationship of the parts of something by analysis
application: ability to put to a practical use; having something to do with the matter at hand
approximately: nearly; an estimate or figure that is almost exact
argument: a reason for or against something
assumption: something accepted as true
comprehend: to understand fully
concentration: the ratio of the amount of solute to the amount of solvent or solution
conclusion: a final decision based on facts, experience, or reasoning
confirm: to make sure of the truth of something
consequence: something produced by a cause or condition
consistent: in agreement; firm; changeless
constant: remaining steady and unchanged
contradiction: a statement in opposition to another
control group: experimental group in which conditions are controlled
controlled experiment: one in which the condition suspected to cause an effect is compared to one without the suspected condition
controlled variable: a factor in an experiment that remains constant
correlation: a close connection between two ideas or sets of data
criticism: a finding of fault; disapproval
definitive: most nearly complete or accurate
demonstrate: to explain by use of examples or experiments
dependence: a state of being controlled by something else
dependent variable: result or change that occurs due to the part of an experiment being tested (positioned on the vertical *y*-axis)
diminish: to make smaller or less; decrease in size
direct relationship: the connection between two variables that show the same effect (*i.e.*, both increase or both decrease)
effective: producing or able to produce a desired condition
estimation: forming a calculation based on incomplete data
ethical: following accepted rules of behavior
evaluation: the result of a finding; estimating the value of something
evidence: that which serves to prove or disprove something
examine: to look at or check carefully
expectation: the extent of a chance that something will occur
experiment: a test made to find something out
experimental design: the plan for a controlled experiment
experimental group: the experimental part in which all conditions are kept the same except for the condition being tested
explanation: a statement that makes something clear
extrapolation: estimating a value for one characteristic that is beyond the range of a given value of another characteristic
figure: a picture that explains
fundamental: a basic part
generalization: something given as a broad statement or conclusion
hypothesis: testable explanation of a question or problem
illustrate: to make clear by using examples
imply: to suggest rather than to say plainly
inconsistent: not in agreement
incorporate: to join or unite closely into a single body
independent variable: in a controlled experiment, the variable that is being changed (positioned on the horizontal *x*-axis)
indication: the act of pointing out or pointing to something
indicator: any device that measures, records, or visibly points out; any of various substances used to point out, such as, a cause, treatment, or outcome on an action
ingredient: any of the components of which something is made
interpolation: estimating a value that falls between two known values; a "best-fit line" on a graph
interpretation: the act of telling the meaning of; explanation
inverse (indirect) relationship: the connection between two variables that shows the opposite effect (*i.e.*, when the value of one variable increases, the value of the other variable deceases)
investigate: to study by close and careful observation
irregular: not continuous or coming at set times
issue: something that is questioned
judgment: an opinion formed by examining and comparing
justify: to prove or show to be right or reasonable
legend: a title, description, or key accompanying a figure or map
maximum: as great as possible in amount or degree
measurement: the act of finding out the size or amount of something
mechanism: the parts or steps that make up a process or activity
minimum: as small as possible in amount or degree
model: a pattern or figure of something to be made
modify: to make changes in something
observation: the act of noting and recording facts and events
opinion: a belief based on experience and on seeing certain facts
optimum: the best or most favorable degree, condition, or amount
pattern: a model, guide, or plan used in making things; definite direction, tendency, or characteristics
perform: to carry out; accomplish
phenomenon: an observable fact or event
precision: the quality of being exactly stated; exact arrangement
predict: to figure out and tell beforehand
preference: a choosing of or liking for one thing rather than another
probability: the quality of being reasonably sure but not certain of something happening or being true
procedure: the way in which an action or actions is carried out
proponent: one who supports a cause
proportional: any quantities or measurements having the same fixed relationship in degree or number
reasonable: showing or containing sound thought
refute: to prove wrong by argument or evidence
relationship: the state of being connected
replicate: to copy or reproduce
revise: to look over again; to correct or improve
simulation: the act or process of simulating a system or process
study: a careful examination and investigation of an event
suggest: to offer as an idea
summarize: to state briefly
support: to provide evidence
theory: a general rule offered to explain experiences or facts
translate: to change from one state or form to another
treatment: to expose to some action
underlying: to form the support for something
unit: a fixed quantity used as a standard of measurement
validity: based on evidence that can be supported
value: the quantity or amount for which a symbol stands
variable: that which can be changed
viewpoint: opinion; judgment

Basics of Experimental Design

The Science Reasoning passages describe scientific methods that may be unfamiliar to you, but are commonly used by scientists to interpret and analyze scientific information. You need to be familiar with these basics of experimental design in order to understand the complete meaning of the passages and items.

Types of Research

Scientists regularly attempt to identify and solve problems by investigating the world around them. Different scientists may use different approaches to conduct their investigations. ***Qualitative***, or descriptive, research is based generally on observable data only.

Example:

A field biologist may observe coral reefs in order to determine if the loss of this habitat would threaten the extinction of many species that live in the coral reefs.

Quantitative research is based on the collection of numerical data—usually by counting or measuring.

Example:

A laboratory biologist may investigate the factors that affect the flow of substances across cell membranes. Numerical data is collected by measuring the change in mass of a cellophane bag that is filled with a sugar solution and then placed in a beaker of pure water.

Forming and Testing Hypotheses

Scientists normally ***form a hypothesis*** and then test it through observation, experimentation, and/or prediction. A hypothesis is defined as a possible explanation of a question or problem that can be formally tested. A hypothesis can be thought of as a prediction about why something occurs or about the relationship between two or more variables.

Scientists describe an experiment as a procedure that ***tests a hypothesis*** by the process of collecting information under controlled conditions. Based on the experimental results, scientists can determine whether or not the hypothesis is correct or must be modified and re-tested. Testing hypotheses through experiments is at the core of scientific investigations and studies.

An important part of testing a hypothesis is identifying the ***variables*** that are part of an experiment. A variable is any condition that can change in an experiment. Controlled experimentation is carried out by keeping all the variables constant, except the one under study. The variable under study is called the ***independent variable*** and is determined by the experimenter. This variable can be changed independently of the other variables, and it is the only variable that can affect the outcome of an experiment by causing a change that can be observed or measured. The changed conditions are called the ***dependent variables*** because they are the result of, or dependent upon, the changes in the independent variable.

Scientists attempt to test only one independent variable at a time so that he or she knows which condition produced the effect. ***Controlled variables***, or controls, are conditions that could affect the outcome of an experiment but do not, because they are held constant. Controls are used to eliminate the possibility that conditions other than those that are a part of an experiment may affect the outcome of the experiment.

The statement of a testable hypothesis must be structured so that it will demonstrate how a change in the independent variable can cause an observed or measured change in the dependent variable. A hypothesis may be typically structured as follows: the independent variable will describe how the variable under study is changed; the dependent variable will describe the effect of those changes.

Example:

In a controlled experiment, in order to determine the effect of a high protein diet on the growth rate of rats, the independent variable would be the exposure to a high protein diet, while the dependent variable would be the effect on the growth rate. A possible hypothesis for this experiment may be stated as follows: When the amount of protein is increased in the diet of rats, then their growth rate will increase.

Design of Controlled Experiments

The design of controlled experiments involves two groups: the ***control group*** and the ***experimental group***. In the control group, all variables are kept the same. In the experimental group, all conditions are kept the same as the control group except the condition that is being tested, the independent variable.

The control group and the experimental group must be as similar as possible at the beginning of a controlled experiment. The only difference in the design of the two groups is the addition of the independent variable that is tested in the experimental group. It is common in a controlled experiment to have more than one experimental group to represent the possible variations in the conditions of the independent variable. All other variables that could affect the outcome of the experiment are held constant.

> *Example:*
>
> In the previous experiment about the effect of a high protein diet on the growth rate of rats, a large test population of commonly similar rats would be randomly divided into two smaller groups of equal number—the control group and the experimental group.

The rats in the above experiment are randomly divided to ensure that both groups are representative samples of the original population. If the test group is not representative of the original population, other uncontrolled conditions could affect the outcome of the experiment. If there are any uncontrolled conditions in either group, it could be argued that any experimental results would be due to differences in the composition of the different test groups instead of a result of the independent variable.

Continuing the development of the experiment, we see that the establishment of certain conditions makes this a controlled experiment.

> *Example:*
>
> The rats in the control group are exposed to the same environmental conditions as the rats in the experimental group, except for the amount of protein in their diet. The control group rats are given a diet with the normal amount of protein. The rats in the experimental group are exposed to a high protein diet (independent variable), in addition to exposure to the same environmental conditions as the control group. (It would be possible to have more than one experimental group with each having a greater amount of protein.) The other conditions that could change, such as the temperature, amount of food and water, and amount of living space, are held constant for both groups of rats.

These conditions are the controls necessary for this experiment to be considered a controlled experiment. The data collected can be used to determine if the hypothesis is correct, and it will ultimately lead to the forming of a conclusion. The figure below illustrates the design of this experiment.

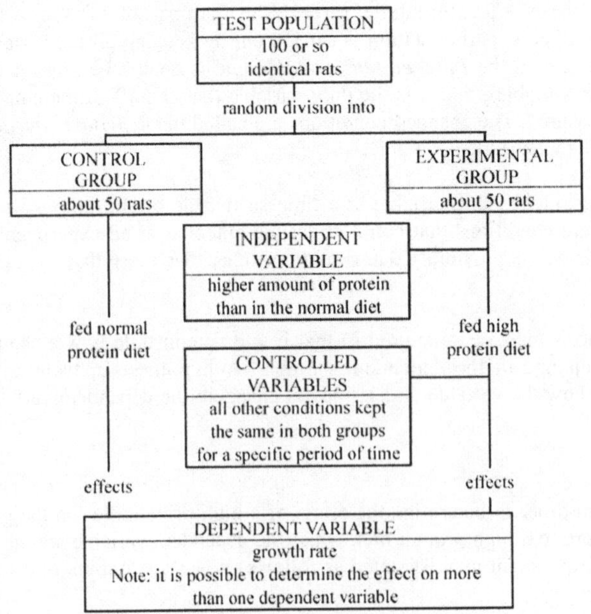

EXERCISE 1

Basics of Experimental Design

DIRECTIONS: Read the description of the following controlled experiment and answer the accompanying items. Answers are on page 927.

An experiment was carried out to determine the effect of temperature on the heart rate of frogs. In the experiment, 100 frogs were removed from a large 25° C enclosure and separated randomly into four equal groups: A, B, C, and D. Each group was maintained in a separate container at a different constant temperature: Group A at 5° C; Group B at 15° C; Group C at 25° C; and Group D at 35° C. All other conditions, such as the size, type, age, and number of the frogs, as well as the size of the container and the amount of light, were the same for all groups of frogs.

1. The purpose of the experiment is to: ______________

____

______________________________.

2. The independent variable is: ______________

____

______________________________.

3. The dependent variable is: ______________

____

______________________________.

4. Write a possible hypothesis by filling in the blanks in the following sentence.

When the ____________ (independent variable) is ______________ (describe how it is changed),

then the ____________ (dependent variable) will ______________ (describe the effect).

5. The controlled variables are: ______________

____

______________________________.

6. The control group(s) is (are): ______________

____

______________________________.

7. The experimental group(s) is (are): ______________

____

______________________________.

Data Organization in Controlled Experiments

After collecting data, a scientist must determine the most appropriate way to present the information so that it can be easily interpreted and analyzed. The two most common ways that scientists report their data are tables and graphs. These pictorial representations are easy ways to show where a pattern, trend, or relationship exists. The tables and graphs can be organized in a variety of ways, but there are some generally accepted basic guidelines.

Tables

Generally, ***tables*** are a series of vertical columns, subdivided horizontally into rows. The number of columns and rows depends on the kind and amount of data collected. In the most basic tables, there is a column for both the independent variable and the dependent variable. In complex tables, the columns may be subdivided to represent additional variations in the conditions of the independent and dependent variables. The rows include the data from repeated trials under the same experimental setup. When recording data in a table, the values of the independent variable are arranged in an ordered manner—numerical values are arranged from the largest to the smallest or from the smallest to the largest. When relevant, units of measurement for the variables are included. A heading or title is included to communicate the purpose of the experiment.

Relationships between variables may be direct, indirect (inverse), or constant. A ***direct relationship*** occurs when one variable increases as the other increases, or when one variable decreases as the other decreases. An ***indirect***, or inverse, ***relationship*** occurs when one variable increases as the other decreases. A ***constant relationship*** occurs when a change in one variable has no effect on the other variable.

Example:

The table below makes it easy to see that there is a direct relationship between the temperature and the heart rate of frogs.

The Effect of Temperature on Frog Heart Rates

Group	*Temperature (°C)* (independent variable)	*Average Heart Rate (per minute)* (dependent variable)
A	5	10
B	15	20
C	25	30
D	35	40

As the temperature increases, so does the heart rate of the frog. If the heart rate had decreased as the temperature increased, then there would have been an indirect relationship between the two variables. If the heart rate had remained the same as the temperature was increased or decreased, then the relationship would have been considered constant.

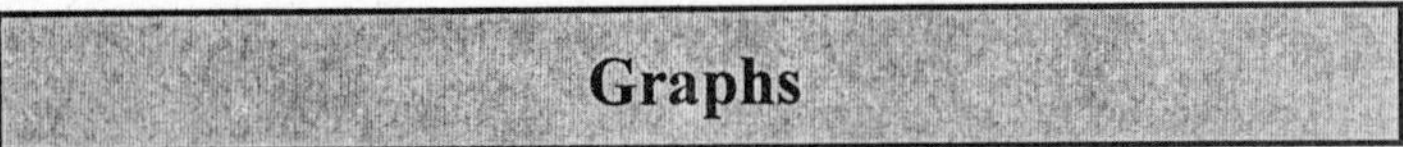

Graphs

Scientists often collect large amounts of data while performing experiments. It may not be possible to clearly present the data in the form of a table. The arrangement of the data in a table may not easily or adequately show a pattern, trend, or relationship. Usually, a well-constructed ***graph*** can communicate experimental results more clearly than a data table. Generally, when the values of the variables are arranged in a graph, the patterns, trends, and relationships are more apparent than when those same values are arranged in a table. Three of the most useful kinds of graphs are line, bar, and circle (pie) graphs.

1. Line Graphs

A ***line graph*** has four basic parts: ***horizontal axis*** (*A*), ***vertical axis*** (*B*), ***line*** (*C*), and ***heading or title*** (*D*). A line graph is used to show the relationship between two variables. The variables being compared are positioned on the two axes of the graph.

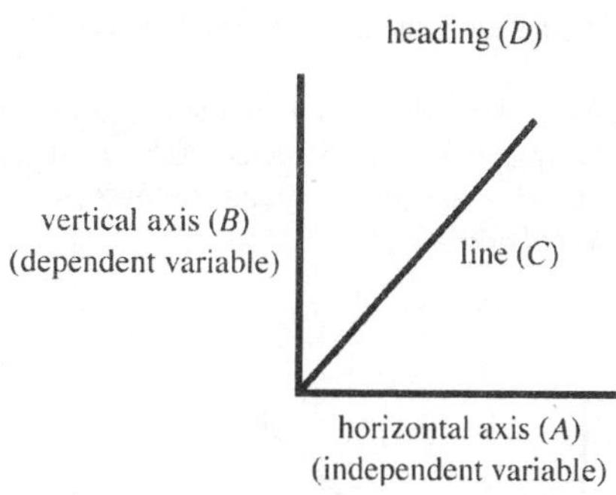

The ***independent variable*** is always positioned on the horizontal axis, called the ***x-axis***. The experimenter can change the value of the independent variable and those values are marked off along the horizontal axis.

The ***dependent variable*** is always positioned on the vertical axis, the ***y-axis***. The dependent variable, such as the rate of a chemical reaction, is any change that results from changing the value of the independent variable. Values of the dependent variable are marked off along the vertical axis.

The data that describe the relationship between the variables appear on the graph as dots, connected to form a line or curve. Each dot, or plot, represents the relationship that exists between a measurement on the vertical axis and a measurement on the horizontal axis. The slope of the line that is created by the connected points represents the relationship between the two variables. If more than one line appears on the same graph, each line represents different independent variable conditions. Additionally, the lines may be curved rather than straight. However, typically, this does not affect the general relationship illustrated.

Finally, as with a table, the heading or title communicates the purpose of the experiment.

Example:

The slopes of the lines in the following three graphs illustrate the typical kinds of relationships between variables shown in a line graph.

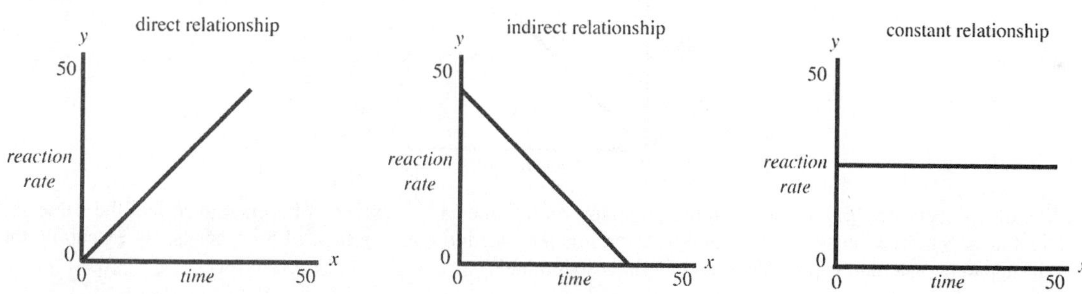

The first graph illustrates a direct relationship—as time increases, the reaction rate increases. The second graph illustrates an indirect relationship—as time increases, the reaction rate decreases. The third graph illustrates a constant relationship—as time increases, the rate of reaction remains the same; that is, time had no effect on the rate of reaction.

Example:

The following graphs illustrate variations on the graphs from the previous example.

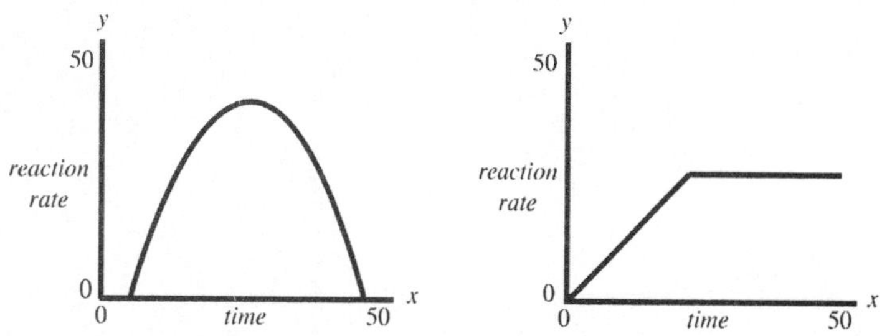

The first graph indicates that as time increases, the reaction rate increases to an ***optimum***, or best rate, and then decreases.

The second graph indicates that as time increases, the reaction rate increases, and then becomes constant.

Since the collection of experimental data is often subject to error, data points plotted on a line may not be directly connected. The graph may show only scattered points so that a smooth line may not be constructed. As a result, another type of line graph is required to illustrate an estimate of a value that falls among the known values on the graph. A "***best-fit***" line, a line that comes close to all of the points, must be constructed. This process is called ***interpolation***.

Example:

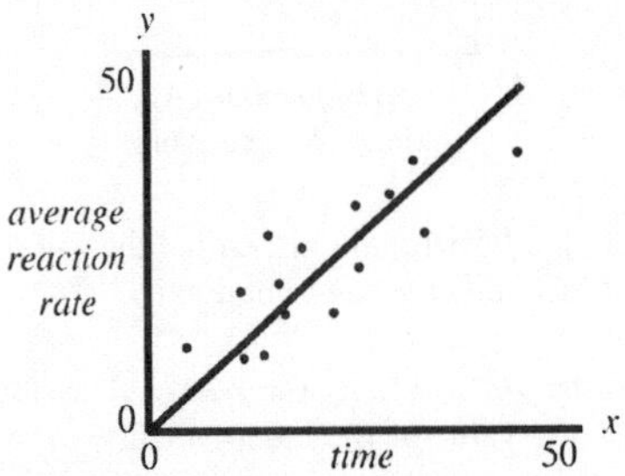

The scattered points in the graph above illustrate data collected from several reactions over an increasing period of time. To determine the relationship between average reaction rate and time, a line is drawn so that an approximately equal number of points fall on either side of the line. This graph indicates a direct relationship between the reaction rate and time.

Sometimes, it is necessary for a scientist to estimate a value for one variable based on a given value of another variable that is beyond the limits of the available data shown on the graph. The scientist must then extend the line on the graph based on the data given. The process is called ***extrapolation***.

Example:

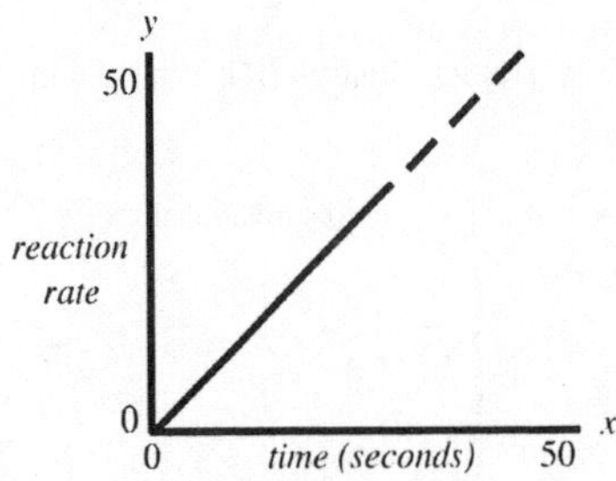

If the line is relatively straight, as shown in the graph above, the line can be extended far enough so that the values called for can be included. Suppose the scientist wanted to determine the reaction rate at a time of 50 seconds. By extending the line to follow the apparent pattern, it is possible to predict the reaction rate.

When using the technique of extrapolation, a scientist must be careful not to make the possible false assumption that the relationship will continue unchanged indefinitely. It is possible that beyond a certain time, an unexpected change in the independent variable will result in an unpredicted change in the dependent variable. When the graph line is a curve, it is necessary to use one's best judgment to extend the line to follow the apparent pattern.

Example:

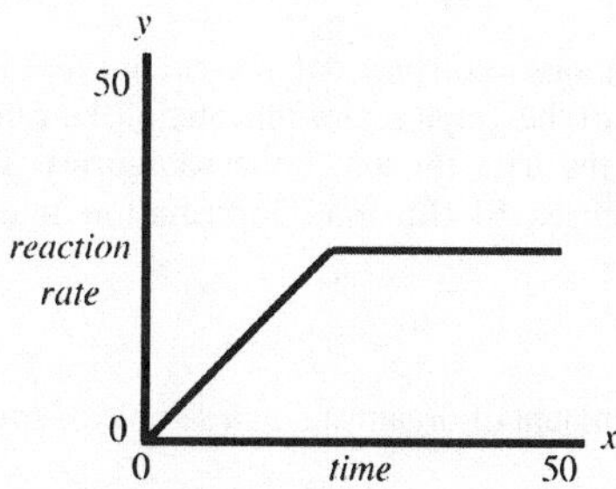

In the graph above, if the data collection had stopped after about 15 units of time, the scientist may have inaccurately predicted that the reaction rate would continue to increase.

2. ***Bar Graphs***

A ***bar graph*** is similar to a line graph, but it is better for making simple comparisons. This type of graph is typically used to display data that does not continuously change. Bar graphs present related data side by side so the data can be easily compared.

The basic setup of a bar graph is similar to a line graph in that there is a horizontal *x*-axis and a vertical *y*-axis. The independent ***variable*** is positioned on the *x*-axis and the dependent variable is on the *y*-axis. Thick bars rather than data points show relationships among data. The bars representing the values of the independent variable, on the *x*-axis, are drawn up to an imaginary point where they would intersect with the values of the dependent variable on the *y*-axis if these values were extended. Generally, the taller the bar, the greater the value it represents.

Note that bar graphs may be configured horizontally, as well as vertically. In a horizontal configuration, the longer the bar, the greater the value it represents. A heading describing the presented data accompanies the graph.

Example:

The following bar graph shows the percentage of the human population having each of the four blood types.

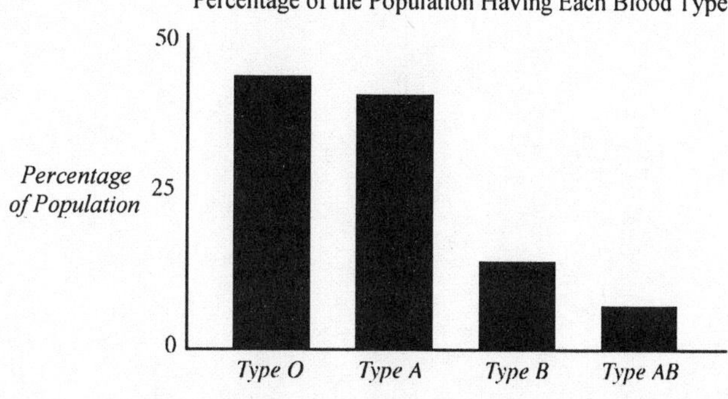

The independent variable is the different blood types found in the population. The dependent variable is the percentage of each blood type. The graph shows that the most common blood type is Type O, while the least common is Type AB.

3. *Circle Graphs*

Circle graphs use a circle divided into sections to display data. A circle graph is sometimes called a pie chart because it looks like a pie cut up into pieces. Each section of the graph represents one of the categories of a particular subject. The whole circle represents 100%, or all of the parts, of the data for all of the categories. The bigger the section, the larger the value it represents. Circle graphs are typically used to illustrate information that is collected by observation rather than by experimentation.

Example:
The following circle graph represents the amount of organisms in a sample of soil.

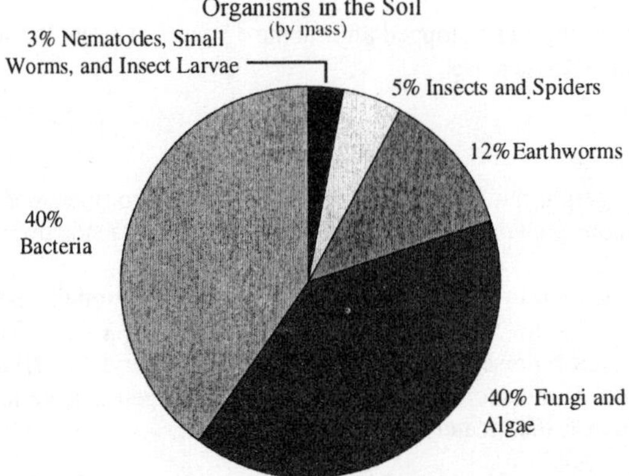

As indicated in the graph, bacteria, fungi, and algae are the most common organisms in the soil. Each group makes up 40% of the total amount of organisms.

EXERCISE 2

Data Organization in Controlled Experiments

DIRECTIONS: Read the descriptions of the following controlled experiments and answer the accompanying items. Answers are on page 927.

EXPERIMENT I

A laboratory investigation was performed to determine the length of time necessary to digest starch (carbohydrates). Ten grams of potato were added to 15 milliliters of an enzyme solution and placed in a test tube. The percentage of starch digested was recorded over a 24-hour period, as can be seen in the table below. A line graph is also provided to illustrate the relationship between the variables.

Carbohydrate Digestion over a 24-Hour Period	
Time (hours)	*Percentage of Carbohydrates Digested*
0	0
4	5
8	15
12	50
16	75
20	85
24	90

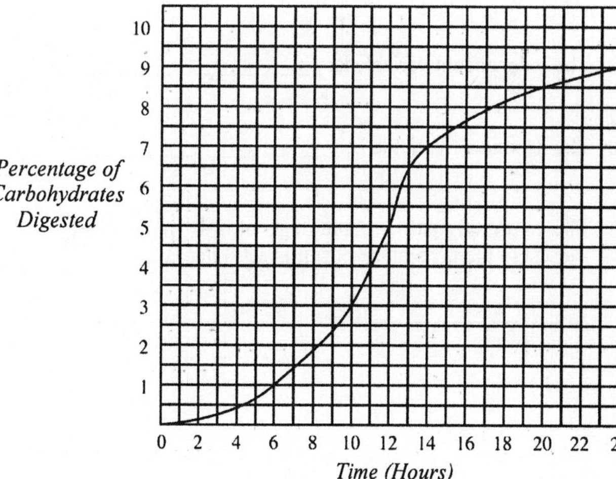

1. The independent variable is: ______________________ ______________________ ______________________.

2. The dependent variable is: ______________________ ______________________ ______________________.

3. The independent variable is on the _______ axis.

4. The dependent variable is on the ________ axis.

5. The slope of the line indicates that generally as the amount of time (increases, decreases, stays constant), the percentage of carbohydrates digested (increases, decreases, stays constant).

6. According to the data, during which four-hour period did the greatest amount of carbohydrate digestion occur?

   A. 0-4 hours
   B. 4-8 hours
   C. 8-12 hours
   D. 20-24 hours

EXPERIMENT II

The following graph illustrates the results of an investigation comparing the salt content in the urine of two mammals (humans and kangaroo rats) with the salt content of seawater.

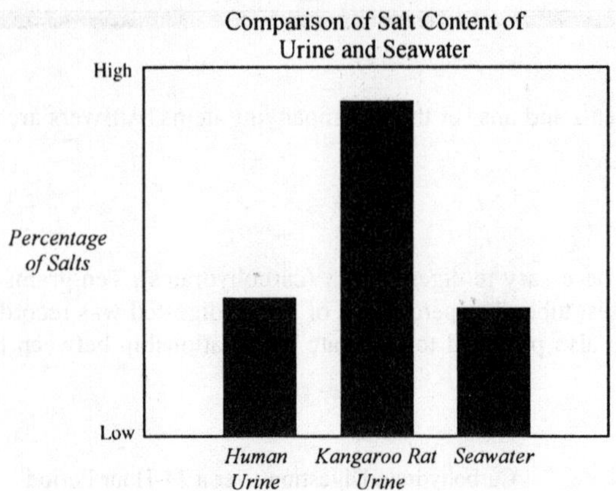

7. The independent variable is: ____________________.

8. The dependent variable is: ____________________.

9. The mammal with a percentage of salt in its urine closest to the percentage of salt in seawater is:

   ____.

Presentation of Conflicting Viewpoints

In laboratory experiments, scientists study the characteristics of matter or energy and attempt to find factors that will affect these characteristics. In typical experiments, scientists get to manipulate or change the independent variable. The independent variable, sometimes called the "causal variable," is assumed to cause any resulting change in the dependent variable.

Many problems (dependent variables) studied by scientists cannot be studied in the lab. An example might be the cause of cancer in humans. Scientists cannot put humans in a lab and treat them with substances that cause cancer. Instead, they must look at groups of individuals who get cancer and groups that do not get cancer, and determine the "secret" independent variable that caused the problem from the collected data. "Cause" is a strong word in science, and it generally leads to arguments among scientists. Differences in opinions lead us to ***conflicting viewpoints***.

Conflicting Viewpoints passages can always be recognized because they are labeled with names such as Scientist I and Scientist II. The scientists may be labeled with more specificity, for example, a chemistry passage may have Chemist I arguing with Chemist II about a chemistry problem; however, the argument is usually over the independent variable.

> *Example:*
>
> Ask yourself the question, "Do cigarettes cause cancer?" Scientists from tobacco companies and doctors are certainly in disagreement over this issue. There is a warning on cigarette packaging; however, it does not say that cigarettes cause cancer. You may know many people who smoke who are cancer-free. Likewise, there are individuals that get lung cancer who never smoke.

Your job in reading these passages is to identify the problem (dependent variable) and determine the conflict of opinion over the cause (independent variable). Each scientist will provide you with data; some data will support only their respective position, and some data will support multiple positions. Some data may attempt to discredit the data of the other scientist. You need to sort out these matters.

EXERCISE 3

Presentation of Conflicting Viewpoints

DIRECTIONS: Read the descriptions of the following conflicting viewpoints and answer the accompanying items. Answers are on page 927.

Two detectives are called to the scene of a crime at about 5:00 AM. The neighbors called the police when they heard a noise at 4:30 AM; however, they thought it was a firecracker rather than a gun. The victim is a 25-year-old female with a gunshot wound to the head. There is a large bruise on the back of her head. The door to the apartment was locked and there is no sign of forced entry. Nothing appears to have been taken. There is a gun lying on the floor near the left hand of the woman. A check of the serial number found that the woman had recently purchased the weapon. There was a blood-soaked pillow just above the woman's head. The police could not find a suicide note. There did not appear to be any other physical evidence at the scene. Neighbors that were interviewed said that the woman had recently been divorced and that she had been noticeably upset by the divorce.

Detective I: Detective I believes that the death was a homicide and asks that the ex-husband be picked up for questioning.

Detective II: Detective II believes that the death was a suicide and asks that the ex-husband be notified.

1. The dependent variable (the problem) is: __________

____

____.

2. The conflicting viewpoint is: ________________

____

____.

3. The independent variable causing the conflict is: ____

____

____.

4. Fill in the following table:

Data	More Consistent with Detective I	More Consistent with Detective II	Equally Consistent with Both Detectives I and II
Gun Owned by Woman			
Bloody Pillow			
Bruise on Head			
Firecracker-Like Noise			
No Forced Entry			
Locked Door			
No Suicide Note			
Divorced Victim			
Despondent Victim			

EXERCISE 4

Science Reasoning Passages

DIRECTIONS: Each passage is followed by several items. After reading a passage, choose the best answer to each item. You may refer to the passages as often as necessary. Answers are on page 928.

PASSAGE I

Germination is the beginning of the growth of a seed after a period of inactivity. The following experiments were designed to compare the amount of time it takes for seeds of different vegetables to germinate.

Experiment 1: Radish seeds, soaked in water for 24 hours, were germinated at 25° C for 10 days. The results are shown in Graph 1.

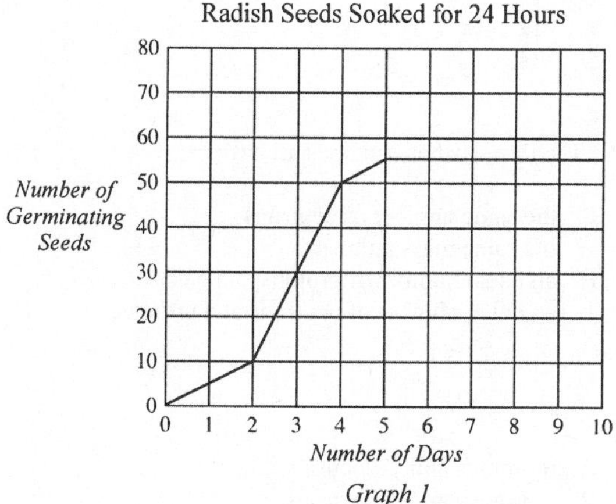

Graph 1

Experiment 2: Bean seeds, soaked in water for 24 hours, were germinated at 25° C for 10 days. The results are shown in Graph 2.

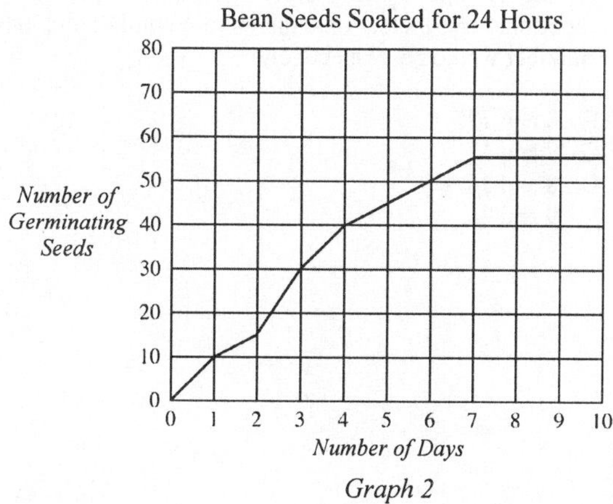

Graph 2

1. Graphs 1 and 2 show that after 3 days:

   A. more radish seeds have germinated.
   B. more bean seeds have germinated.
   C. equal numbers of radish seeds and bean seeds have germinated.
   D. no radish seeds or bean seeds have germinated.

2. A generalization that can be made about the data is that:

   F. 24 hours is the best soaking period for both radish seeds and bean seeds.
   G. radish seeds germinate more rapidly than bean seeds.
   H. the bean seeds had a steady rate of germination.
   J. most bean seeds of this kind require 7 days to germinate.

3. Which factor is the independent variable in this experiment?

   A. The period of the soaking
   B. The dishes in which the seeds were planted
   C. The rate of germination
   D. The kind of seeds used

4. To test the hypothesis that ultraviolet radiation affects bean seed germination, which of the following experimental designs would be the best to use?

   F. Plant 20 normal bean seeds, note results; then plant 20 bean seeds that have been exposed to ultraviolet radiation, and compare results.
   G. Plant 20 bean seeds that have been exposed to ultraviolet radiation; at the same time, plant 20 normal bean seeds, and compare the results.
   H. Use 20 radish seeds and 20 bean seeds that have been exposed to ultraviolet violation, and compare the results.
   J. Plant 50 bean seeds that have been exposed to ultraviolet radiation, and note the effects of the radiation.

PASSAGE II

A scientist wanted to determine the effects of different doses of an experimental drug called PCH. This drug was believed to help control weight gain. To test this hypothesis, four experimental groups, each with 100 rats, were given a daily dose with only sugar or a daily dose with sugar and a different amount of the drug. The rats were all fed the same kind and amount of food. After one year, the percentage of rats gaining weight was determined. The results of this experiment are presented in the following table.

Group	Contents of Dose	% of Rats Gaining Weight
1	5 grams of sugar	19%
2	5 grams of sugar 1 gram of PCH	21%
3	5 grams of sugar 5 grams of PCH	19%
4	5 grams of sugar 10 grams of PCH	20%

5. Which was the control group in this experiment?

A. 1
B. 2
C. 3
D. 4

6. As the dose of PCH increases, the percentage of rats gaining weight:

F. increases.
G. decreases.
H. remains constant.
J. varies.

7. In order to interpret the results of this experiment, it would be most useful to know the:

A. characteristics of the rats in each group.
B. chemical composition of PCH.
C. kind of sugar used in the doses.
D. kind of food fed to the rats.

8. From the data showing the percentage of rats gaining weight, it could be concluded that:

F. PCH was effective in helping control the weight gain of the rats.
G. sugar was required for the PCH to be effective.
H. sugar alone was responsible for the weight gain of the rats.
J. PCH had no significant effect in helping control the weight gain of the rats.

PASSAGE III

Atoms are considered the basic building blocks of matter. The atom consists of a positively charged center, or nucleus, surrounded by negatively charged electrons. The major kinds of particles in the nucleus are positively charged protons and neutrally charged neutrons. The number of protons, called the atomic number, identifies the element. The mass number of the atom represents the total number of protons and neutrons. Not all of the atoms of an element are identical. The different atoms of an element are called isotopes. The three carbon-isotopes are shown in the following table.

Name	Protons	Neutrons	Electrons	Mass Number
Carbon-12	6	6	6	12
Carbon-13	6	7	6	13
Carbon-14	6	8	6	14

9. The atomic number of the element carbon is:

A. 6.
B. 7.
C. 12.
D. 34.

10. The three carbon-isotopes all have:

F. the same number of neutrons.
G. the same mass number.
H. an equal number of protons and electrons.
J. an equal number of neutrons and protons.

11. Carbon-13 has:

A. 6 protons and 7 electrons.
B. 7 protons and 6 electrons.
C. 6 protons and 7 neutrons.
D. 13 protons.

12. If the isotope of an element contains 8 protons, 9 neutrons, and 8 electrons, the atomic number and mass number would be, respectively:

F. 8 and 17.
G. 9 and 17.
H. 8 and 26.
J. 9 and 26.

PASSAGE IV

Sodium chloride (table salt) is a crystal made up of rows of sodium (Na) ions and chloride (Cl) ions. Ions are atoms that are electrically charged. When sodium chloride is dissolved in water, it separates into its ions. The sodium ions and chloride ions are released from their positions in the crystal pattern and they move about freely. Other crystalline substances, such as sugar, do not produce ions when dissolved in water. When substances react with water to form ions, they are said to be ionized. The charged ions in the water are responsible for the conduction of electricity. Substances that conduct an electrical current when dissolved are called electrolytes. Substances that do not conduct an electric current are called non-electrolytes.

To study the electrical conductivity, an apparatus that measures the ability of substances to conduct electricity was used.

Experiment 1: Solid sodium chloride was tested and found to be a non-conductor. Pure water was also tested and found to be a non-conductor. When a teaspoon of sodium chloride was added to water, the solution was found to be a good conductor of electricity. Sugar did not conduct electricity as a solid or when dissolved in water.

Experiment 2: When a few crystals of sodium chloride were added to water, the solution showed a weak conduction of electricity. As additional sodium chloride was added, the ability of the solution to conduct electricity increased.

13. Experiment 1 indicates that sodium chloride conducts electricity when it:

    A. dissolves in alcohol.
    B. is tested as a solid.
    C. dissolves in water.
    D. is combined with sugar.

14. Which of the following graphs represents the relationship between the amount of sodium chloride dissolved in water and its conductivity?

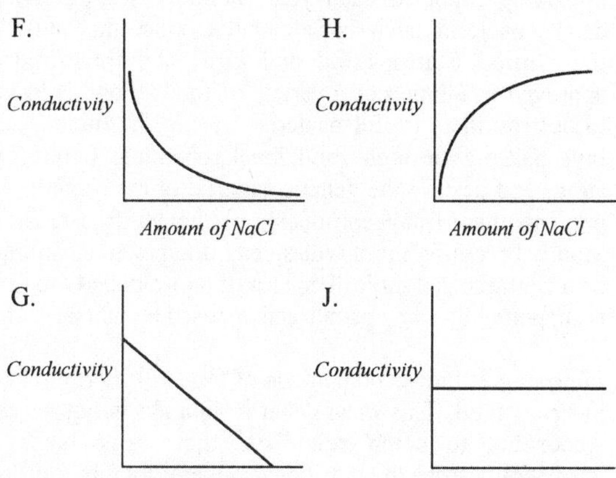

15. In order for a substance to be a conductor of electricity, the substance must have:

    A. rapidly moving molecules.
    B. charged particles that are free to move.
    C. ions in a crystalline form.
    D. been dissolved in a solvent.

16. Which of the following is NOT a characteristic of sugar?

    F. Solid sugar is an electrolyte.
    G. Solid sugar is a non-electrolyte.
    H. Solid sugar dissolves in water.
    J. Sugar solutions do not conduct electricity.

PASSAGE V

In the United States, there are millions of cases of food poisoning reported each year. Food poisoning is due to deadly bacteria, such as Salmonella. Since the mid-1980's, the United States Food and Drug Administration has approved irradiation of a variety of foods. Food is irradiated to destroy the harmful bacteria. During irradiation, gamma rays passing through food break chemical bonds among atoms and destroy the genetic material of the bacteria, which prevents them from reproducing. Although the irradiation of food is becoming more widespread, the practice continues to be a controversial topic. The idea of an irradiated food supply is supported by some people and opposed by others.

Viewpoint 1: Proper preparation of food kills harmful bacteria in or on food. This means that irradiation is not necessary. According to some scientists, there is evidence that irradiation lessens the nutritional value of food by causing the loss of vitamins. Foods exposed to gamma rays have lost such vitamins as A, C, and E. One study found that animals that were fed irradiated food lost weight. Pregnant animals often miscarry, most likely due to reduced amounts of vitamin E in the irradiated food. Some chemicals in the food may be changed, resulting in the production of toxic by-products. While these unidentified toxic substances occur in small amounts, no one is certain what effect they will have as they accumulate in the body over a lifetime of consuming irradiated food.

Viewpoint 2: Food irradiation has significant value in destroying the bacteria that infect the food. Irradiated food has a much longer shelf life than traditionally treated food. Irradiation destroys nutrients but no more than is normally destroyed by cooking food. Food irradiated with 10,000 rads or less of gamma rays show little or no nutrient loss. According to the FDA, food exposed to greater than 10,000 rads exhibits nutrient loss that is generally no more than the loss that occurs in frozen and canned food. FDA scientists also admit that some by-products of the alteration of chemicals in the food are cancer-causing agents. However, they occurred in very small amounts in irradiated food. Most of these by-products turned out to be identical to naturally occurring food substances.

17. One of the principal differences between the viewpoints concerns:

    A. loss of nutritional value of food caused by irradiation.
    B. the effectiveness of food irradiation in destroying harmful bacteria.
    C. the accumulation of by-products of food irradiation in the body.
    D. the effect of gamma rays on the breakdown of vitamin A.

18. According to Viewpoint 1:

    F. the by-products of food irradiation are cancer-causing.
    G. the irradiation of food increases the nutritional value of food.
    H. the by-products of food irradiation are identical to naturally occurring food substances.
    J. the irradiation of food lessens the nutritional value of food.

19. These viewpoints are similar because they both suggest that food irradiation:

    A. is necessary to destroy harmful bacteria in food.
    B. is not necessary to destroy harmful bacteria in food.
    C. can lessen the nutritional value of food.
    D. can improve the nutritional value of food.

20. Which experimental information would NOT support Viewpoint 1?

    F. Food exposed to gamma rays loses much of vitamins A, C, and E.
    G. Food exposed to gamma rays does not lose much of vitamins A, C, and E.
    H. Toxic by-products of food alteration by gamma rays are accumulated in the body over a period of time.
    J. Irradiated food has a shelf life twice that of non-irradiated food.

PASSAGE VI

Nuclear reactors release great amounts of nuclear energy through controlled chain reactions. For this reason, nuclear power has been considered a source of abundant energy. Nuclear power, however, poses several problems. The most serious problem is the radioactive waste produced by the use of nuclear energy. The waste is very dangerous and remains so for thousands of years. How and where to dispose of this waste safely is a dilemma that has not been resolved. In 1987, the U.S. Congress authorized the Department of Energy to study Yucca Mountain in the southern desert of Utah as a place to bury the highly radioactive nuclear fuel rods from nuclear power plants.

Geologist 1: The most feasible and safe method for disposing of highly radioactive material is to store it underground. Yucca Mountain was chosen because it is believed that the mountain rock could keep the radioactive waste isolated for thousands of years. This proposed site is located underneath a thick layer of volcanic ash. It is above the ground water of aquifers in order to reduce the danger of seepage. The area is very remote and almost uninhabited. It is located in an area with low rainfall, thus less water enters the ground. It is also an area where the ground is mostly composed of volcanic tuff that slows down the filtration of water into the ground. The volcanic activity near Yucca Mountain is mild, with minimal chance for a large eruption. The chance of a severe earthquake is also remote.

Geologist 2: Burial of radioactive waste is the best disposal method. Yucca Mountain, however, is not the best site because it is hydrologically and geologically active. Burial at this site poses the risk of radioactive materials leaking out and contaminating surrounding soil and ground water. If a leak did occur, ground water contamination would be a major problem. Many of the surrounding cities, including parts of Las Vegas, receive some of their water from the aquifers in the area. The area around Yucca Mountain has numerous faults and even a small volcano nearby. Any significant geological activity could disturb waste containers. If earthquakes or volcanic eruptions occurred, the radioactive material at the site could be carried to the surface, threatening the entire region.

21. According to Geologist 1:

    A. radioactive waste should not be buried underground.
    B. the geologic structure of Yucca Mountain would minimize geological activity.
    C. earthquake or volcanic activity is likely to occur near Yucca Mountain.
    D. the radioactive waste should be buried somewhere other than Yucca Mountain.

22. Both geologists agree that:

    F. the radioactive waste should be buried somewhere other than Yucca Mountain.
    G. hydrological and geological activity near Yucca Mountain is minimal.
    H. the best way to store radioactive waste is to bury it underground.
    J. the radioactive waste is likely to leak into ground water.

23. Which of the following would provide the strongest evidence for the position of Geologist 2?

    A. The site is both geologically stable and safe from the entry of water.
    B. Construction at the site has been found to be destructive to animal habitats.
    C. The rock formations of Yucca Mountain will keep the waste sufficiently isolated for thousands of years.
    D. There is a periodic upwelling of ground water at Yucca Mountain.

24. Which of the following would provide the strongest evidence for the position of Geologist 1?

    F. The rock formations of Yucca Mountain were formed by rainwater seeping downward, not by groundwater seeping upward.
    G. There is a large aquifer underneath Yucca Mountain.
    H. The Yucca Mountain site is affected by 32 known earthquake faults.
    J. Rainwater containing nuclear chemicals has reached the site level.

Writing Skills Review

TARGETED EDUCATIONAL SOLUTIONS.

Cambridge Course Concept Outline
WRITING SKILLS REVIEW

Planning an Essay

Understand the Assignment

1. Let the Prompt Be Your Topic

When presented with a prompt, always read it several times until you are completely familiar with the material. Sometimes it may be helpful to underline key words or phrases that are important.

Usually, the prompt is intended to be your topic and an inspiration to writing. If you pay careful attention to the language of the prompt, it can actually help you to get started.

Consider this sample essay prompt:

> *Human beings are often cruel, but they also have the capacity for kindness and compassion. In my opinion, an example that demonstrates this capacity is ——.*
>
> **Assignment:** Complete the statement above with an example from current affairs, history, literature, or your own personal experience. Then write a well-organized essay explaining why you regard that event favorably.

This topic explicitly invites you to choose an example of kindness or compassion from history, current events, literature, or even personal experience. Thus, you could write about the end of a war (history), a mission of humanitarian aid (current events), the self-sacrifice of a fictional character (literature), or even about the day that your family helped a stranded motorist (personal experience). Remember that what you have to say is not as important as how you say it.

2. Develop a Point of View

Sometimes an essay prompt will invite you to present your opinion on an issue. When you encounter such prompts, you must decide whether you are in agreement or disagreement with the statement given.

3. Write Only on the Assigned Topic

While the types of prompts may differ among assignments or tests, the directions all agree on this point: You must write on the assigned topic. The assigned topic is often "open-ended," so you should have no problem coming up with something to write.

Organize Your Thoughts

1. Limit the Scope of Your Essay

The requirements of your writing assignment should determine the length and scope of your essay. Always remember to define the coverage of an essay before setting pen to paper; this will improve the focus of an essay so that the essay sets out to accomplish only the assigned task, whether it is to defend a controversial position or to define a definition. The more limited and specific your topic, the more successful your essay is likely to be: You will be able to supply the specific details that add depth and sophistication to an essay. You will also reduce the possibility of straying onto a tangent point or under-developing a specific claim.

2. *Develop a Thesis*

A thesis statement solidifies the scope, purpose, and direction of an essay in a clear and focused statement. This thesis statement usually includes your claims or assertions and the reasoning and evidence that support them. If possible, try to formulate the thesis of your composition in a single sentence during the pre-writing stage. When developing a thesis, keep in mind the following ideas:

IMPORTANT POINTS FOR DEVELOPING A THESIS

1. The thesis must not be too broad or too narrow.
2. The thesis must be clear to both you and the essay reader.
3. Everything in the essay must support your thesis.
4. Use specific details and examples rather than generalizations to support your thesis.

3. *Identify Key Points*

Identify the two or three (perhaps four) important points that you want to make. Then, decide on the order of presentation for those points.

4. *Write an Outline*

Once you gain a clear understanding of the assignment and its requirements, it is then important to organize the major points of your essay in a written outline. The purpose of outline is to develop a logical structure to your arguments and to streamline the focus of your essay. An outline should include your thesis statement, the key points of your argument, and the concluding statement of your essay. A sample outline structure is presented below for your reference.

SAMPLE OUTLINE

I. Introduction
   A. Thesis Statement

II. First Key Point.
   A. Subpoint 1
   B. Subpoint 2
   C. Subpoint 3

III. Second Key Point
   A. Subpoint 1
   B. Subpoint 2

IV. Third Key Point
   A. Subpoint 1
   B. Subpoint 2
   C. Subpoint 3

V. Conclusion
   A. Restatement of Thesis

Composition

Organize Ideas into Paragraphs

It is the hallmark of a good writer to use paragraphs effectively. Paragraphs are important because they provide a structure through which the writer can convey meaning. To illustrate this point with an analogy, imagine a grocery store in which items are not organized into sections. In this store, there is no fresh produce section, no canned goods section, no baked goods section, and no frozen foods section. Consequently, a single bin holds bunches of bananas, cans of beans, loaves of bread, and frozen turkeys; this disorganization characterizes every bin, shelf, rack, and refrigerated case in the store, making shopping in our imaginary store very difficult. Likewise, essays without paragraphs, or with poorly organized paragraphs, are very difficult—if not impossible—to understand.

Decide on how many paragraphs you are going to write. Your essay should contain two to four important points that develop or illustrate your thesis. Each important point should be treated in its own paragraph.

Do not write simply to fill up pages and make it seem that you have many ideas. This approach can result in repetition and wordiness, which is a sign of disorganization and unclear thinking. Write enough to sufficiently demonstrate your writing ability and to prove your thesis. Five paragraphs (an introduction paragraph, three main body paragraphs, and a concluding paragraph) are usually sufficient.

Write the Essay

Many students get frustrated before they even begin to write. They sit and stare at the blank page and complain that they are "blocked": They can't think of anything to write. The secret to successfully beginning an essay is to simply start writing after you have completed the pre-writing stage, even if the first few sentences of the essay may need revision. Follow this simple essay structure:

BASIC ESSAY STRUCTURE

Introduction:	State what you are going to elaborate in the essay. State your position clearly. State the elements that you will be using to support your position.
Body:	Each paragraph in the body of your essay will be devoted to one of the supporting elements that are introduced in the introduction. Elaborate on the element in the paragraph by using examples.
Conclusion:	Summarize your position and the reasons for your position.

1. The Introduction

You have already analyzed the question in your pre-writing stage. Now, you will use the introduction (first paragraph) to write clear and concise sentences, describing the topic that you are writing about and indicating to the reader what you plan to say in your essay to back up your position or to illustrate, with examples, the main point. The general idea of the introduction is to indicate to the reader the direction that your essay will take. However, do not spend too much time on the introduction. This is not the place to expound on the ideas and examples.

When writing your introduction, keep in mind these points:

WRITING INTRODUCTORY PARAGRAPHS

1. Always remain focused on the essay prompt. Never stray from the intended essay thesis.
2. Avoid being cute or funny, ironic or satiric, overly emotional or too dramatic. Set the tone or attitude in your first sentence. Your writing should be sincere, clear, and straightforward.
3. Do not repeat the question word for word. A paraphrase in your own words is far better than just copying the words of the exam question.
4. In your first paragraph, tell the reader the topic of your essay and the ideas that will guide the essay's development and organization. A clear topic sentence accomplishes this task.
5. Each sentence should advance your topic and be interesting to your reader.

An effective introduction often refers to the subject of the essay, explains the value of the topic, or attracts the attention of the reader by giving a pertinent illustration. Ineffective beginnings often contain unrelated material, ramble, and lack clarity.

2. The Body

The heart of the essay is the development, or the middle paragraph(s). Here, the writer must attempt, in paragraph form, to support the main idea of the essay through illustrations, details, and examples. The developmental paragraphs must serve as a link in the chain of ideas and contribute directly to the essay's central thought. All the sentences of the development must explain the essential truth of the thesis or topic sentence without digression.

Each paragraph should start with a transitional statement or phrase that describes the relationship of the paragraph to the previous paragraphs. The length of any one of these body paragraphs can be variable, but each paragraph should only cover one main idea with adequate detail. You may do this through a style that is descriptive, narrative, or expository, using a factual or an anecdotal approach. Whatever approach you choose and whatever style you adopt, your writing must be coherent, logical, unified, and well-ordered.

When writing your essay, avoid the following common mistakes:

AVOID THESE COMPOSITION ERRORS

1. Don't use sentences that are irrelevant and contain extraneous material.
2. Don't use sentences that have no sequence of thought or logical development of ideas.
3. Don't use sentences that do not relate to the topic sentence or do not flow from the preceding sentence.

3. Transitions

The good writer makes use of transitional words or phrases to connect thoughts, to provide for a logical sequence of ideas, and to link paragraphs. On the next page is a list of some of these transitions and the logical relationships that they indicate.

TRANSITIONAL WORDS AND PHRASES FOR ESSAY DEVELOPMENT

Addition:	also moreover again both...and finally	in addition similarly and	first, second, third furthermore not only...but (also)	besides likewise
Alternation:	or	nor	either...or	neither...nor
Cause/effect/ purpose:	therefore since so that as a result	as for so	consequently accordingly as a consequence	because hence for this purpose
Conditions:	if	as if (as though)	once...then	unless
Contrast:	however but even though though	still on the other hand yet	all the same on the contrary instead	although nevertheless otherwise
Space:	here there in the middle	opposite to to the left/right	next to wherever	where nearby
Support:	for example in general	such as	for instance	in fact
Summary:	as shown above in brief	to sum up in conclusion	in other words in summary	in short in general
Time:	later since (clause) then as soon as when	after (noun) until (clause) during at the present time before (clause)	meanwhile while (clause) after (clause) in (month, year)	finally before (noun) whenever eventually

4. *The Conclusion*

The successful writer must know when and how to end an essay. To effectively conclude your essay, you should draw together comments in a strong, clear concluding paragraph. This paragraph should give the reader the feeling that the essay has made its point, that the thesis has been explained, or that a point of view has been established. This can be accomplished in about three to six sentences in one of the following ways:

EFFECTIVE METHODS FOR CONCLUDING AN ESSAY

1. Restate the main idea.
2. Summarize the material covered in the essay.
3. Conclude with a clear statement of your opinion on the issue(s) involved and discussed in the essay.

There are good techniques, and there are some very ineffective methods for drawing a composition to a close. Avoid the following mistakes:

INEFFECTIVE METHODS FOR CONCLUDING AN ESSAY
1. DO NOT apologize for your inability to discuss all the issues in the allotted time.
2. DO NOT complain that the topic did not interest you or that you don't think it was fair to be asked to write on so broad a topic.
3. DO NOT introduce material that you will not develop, ramble on about non-pertinent matters, or use material that is trite or unrelated.

Keep in mind that a good conclusion is related to the thesis of the essay and is an integral part of the essay. It may be a review or a restatement, or it may lead the reader to do his or her own thinking, but the conclusion must be strong, clear, and effective.

An effective concluding paragraph may restate the thesis statement, summarize the main idea of the essay, draw a logical conclusion, or offer a strong opinion of what the future holds. An ineffective final paragraph often introduces new material in a scanty fashion, apologizes for the ineffectiveness of the material presented, or is illogical or unclear.

Principles of Good Writing

While writing, keep the three principles of good writing in mind: write grammatically, punctuate and spell correctly, and write concisely, clearly, and legibly. Following these conventions will allow you to communicate your ideas clearly and effectively, improving the overall quality of your essay.

1. *Write Grammatically*

The principles of grammar covered in the Grammar and Mechanics Skills Review should be used when writing your essay. At a minimum, you should be sure of the following when writing your essay:

CORRECT GRAMMAR IS A MUST FOR EFFECTIVE ESSAYS
1. Does each sentence have a conjugated (main) verb that agrees with its subject?
2. Does each pronoun have a referent (antecedent) with which it agrees?
3. Do similar elements in each sentence have parallel form?
4. Do the modifiers make sense?
5. Does each sentence say what it means to say in a direct and concise way?

Your checklist should also include the other writing principles reviewed in the Grammar and Mechanics Skills Review.

2. *Punctuate and Spell Correctly*

In addition to writing grammatically, concisely, and formally (without using slang and other low-level usage language), you must punctuate and spell correctly. Refer to the Grammar and Mechanics Skills Review for an in-depth punctuation and spelling review.

Since you are in charge of writing the essay, you can choose to avoid punctuation and spelling errors. If you are unsure about how to punctuate a particular construction or spell a particular word, choose an alternative.

3. *Write Concisely, Clearly, and Legibly*

Simple, direct sentences are less likely to get you into trouble than complex, convoluted ones. In writing an essay for a standardized test, any sentence that is more complicated than a sentence with two independent clauses joined by a conjunction such as "and" or "but" or a sentence with one dependent and one independent clause joined by a conjunction such as "while" or "although" is an invitation to error. Unless you are confident in your ability to keep all of the elements of a more complicated sentence under control, use a simpler method of expression.

Additionally, avoid using unnecessary and wordy phrases, such as those illustrated in the chart below:

AVOID THESE UNNECESSARY AND WORDY PHRASES

Instead of:	*Say:*
In my opinion, I believe that	I believe that
In the event of an emergency	In an emergency
On the possibility that it may	Since it may
close to the point of	close to
have need for	need
with a view to	to
in view of the fact that	because
give consideration to	consider
mean to imply	imply
disappear from view	disappear
in this day and age	today
the issue in question	issue

Also, while neatness is not graded, it is almost certainly true that an illegible essay will not receive a good grade. Even if you cannot perform calligraphy, you should at least be able to write legibly.

Revision

Proofread Your Essay

Proofreading is an essential part of the writing process. The first draft of an essay usually will not be free of errors. This means that you will need to reread the essay and correct any grammatical errors or logical inconsistencies in your paper. There are two categories of errors that generally manifest in essays: structural errors and mechanics and usage errors.

1. *Proofread for Structural Errors*

When proofreading, first consider the structural elements of an essay, as these are of primary importance in establishing your argument. The three most important structural factors that should be considered when editing an essay are unity, coherence, and support. Essays are judged by how well they meet these three basic requirements. To improve your essay, ask yourself the following questions:

UNITY, COHERENCE, AND SUPPORT ARE VITAL FOR AN EFFECTIVE ESSAY

1. Do all of the details in the essay support and develop the main thesis?
2. Do all of the illustrations relate to the main point and add to the general effectiveness of the essay?
3. Have irrelevant ideas been deleted?
4. Does the essay show a sense of organization?
5. Is the material presented logically?
6. Does the essay include transitional words or phrases that allow the reader to move easily from one idea to the next?
7. Does the essay use details that make it interesting and vivid?
8. Is the main idea supported with concrete and specific illustrations?
9. Does the essay contain sufficient supporting details to clarify and persuade?

2. *Proofread for Mechanics and Usage Errors*

Next, look for any mechanics and usage errors. Although these errors are less important than structural errors, they may distract the reader from the substance of your arguments, decreasing the overall ease and readability of your essay. As you proofread, you may also consider altering a word or adjusting a phrase to make your essay more effective.

COMMON WRITING ERRORS ELIMINATED BY PROOFREADING

1. Omission of words—especially "the," "a," and, "an"
2. Omission of final letters on words
3. Careless spelling errors
4. Incorrect use of capital letters
5. Faulty punctuation

Scoring Rubric

The following rubric (scoring guide) summarizes how your essay will likely be graded by the essay reader:

ESSAY SCORE QUALIFICATIONS

Score	Essay Qualities
Outstanding	• demonstrates *clear and consistent competence* though it may have occasional errors • effectively and insightfully addresses the writing task • is well-organized and fully developed • uses appropriate and innovative examples to support ideas • demonstrates a superior grasp of grammar and style, varies sentence structure, and uses a wide range of vocabulary
Superior	• demonstrates *reasonably consistent competence* with occasional errors or lapses in quality • effectively addresses the writing task • is generally well-organized and adequately developed • uses appropriate examples to support ideas • demonstrates a competent grasp of grammar and style, employs some syntactic variety, and uses appropriate vocabulary
Good	• demonstrates *adequate competence* with occasional errors and lapses in quality • addresses the writing task • is organized and somewhat developed • uses examples to support ideas • demonstrates an adequate but inconsistent grasp of grammar and style with minor errors in grammar and diction • displays minimal sentence variety
Average	• demonstrates *developing competence* • may contain one or more of the following weaknesses: inadequate organization or development; inappropriate or insufficient details to support ideas; and an accumulation of errors in grammar, diction, or sentence structure
Below Average	• demonstrates *some incompetence* • is flawed by one or more of the following weaknesses: poor organization; thin development; little or inappropriate detail to support ideas; and frequent errors in grammar, diction, and sentence structure
Weak	• demonstrates *incompetence* • is seriously flawed by one or more of the following weaknesses: very poor organization, very thin development, and usage or syntactical errors so severe that meaning is somewhat obscured

EXERCISE 1

Sample Essay 1

DIRECTIONS: You have 30 minutes to plan and write an essay on the topic assigned below. DO NOT WRITE ON ANY OTHER TOPIC. AN ESSAY ON ANOTHER TOPIC IS NOT ACCEPTABLE. Think carefully about the issue presented in the following excerpt and the assignment below. Sample essays and analyses are on page 929.

Teachers evaluate the work of students by grading exams, homework, and other assignments, as well as class participation. The end-of-term report card with its letter or numerical grades is a time-honored tradition. Now, some teachers and administrators suggest that students be given the opportunity to grade teachers. They point out that students are in a unique position to assess the effectiveness of their teachers, because they spend so much time with the teachers in the classroom. Some of those favoring this idea propose that students complete forms, ranking teachers according to relevant criteria, such as "Preparedness" and "Ability to Communicate." Other teachers and administrators oppose this idea and argue that students lack the experience and perspective to determine what makes an effective teacher. They also express concern that the evaluation forms could be used by students to retaliate against teachers for personal reasons. In your opinion, should students be given the opportunity to grade their teacher?

Assignment: In your essay, take a position on this issue. You may address either of the two points described above, or you may offer an entirely different perspective on the issue. Be sure to use specific reasons and examples to support your analysis.

3

Step Three: Problem-Solving, Concepts, and Strategies

Step Three Highlights:

Review the most commonly-tested concepts for each ACT, PLAN, and EXPLORE section.

Learn everything you need to know about the five test sections: English, Mathematics, Reading, Science Reasoning, and Writing.

Discover the powerful alternative test-taking strategies that will give you an edge when taking the ACT, PLAN, or EXPLORE.

Measure progress on tested concepts with quizzes and advanced "upper-quartile" items.

Step Three Overview:

This section of the textbook contains many items that look like those found on the real ACT, PLAN, and EXPLORE. When compared with items on the real test, these problems have the same content, represent similar difficulty levels, and are solved by using the same problem-solving and alternative test-taking strategies. You will go over these items with your instructor in class. Use the "Notes and Strategies" sheets located throughout this section to record the alternative test-taking strategies taught during these lessons.

English

TARGETED EDUCATIONAL SOLUTIONS.

Cambridge Course Concept Outline
ENGLISH

CORE LESSON

The items in this section accompany the Core Lesson of the English Lesson. You will work through the items with your instructor in class. Note that many of the items in this section are intended to illustrate particular concepts and do not reflect the format of the official tests. Answers are on page 933.

DIRECTIONS: Items #1-108 consist of two types of items: (1) When four separate parts of a sentence are underlined, identify the underlined part that contains an error. Some of these sentences may not contain any errors; in such a case, choose "No error." No sentence contains more than one error, and no sentence contains an error that is not underlined. (2) When a single part of a sentence is underlined or the entire sentence is underlined, identify the re-phrasing that best expresses the meaning of the underlined material. (A) is always NO CHANGE, which indicates that the underlined material is correct as written.

1. The professor were traveling (A) in Europe when (B) she received (C) notice of her (D) promotion. No error (E)

2. The professor voted Teacher of the Year (A) by the students were traveling (B) in Europe when (C) she received notice of her (D) promotion. No error (E)

3. Most teachers, unless they have (A) an appointment to a prestigious university, earns (B) relatively less as (C) a teacher than they might (D) in business. No error (E)

4. Many nutritionists now believe (A) that (B) a balanced diet and not large doses of vitamins are (C) the best (D) guarantee of health. No error (E)

5. Television comedies in which (A) there is (B) at least one really detestable (C) character captures (D) the interest of viewers. No error (E)

6. The opposition to smoking in public places <u>are prompting many state legislatures to consider</u> banning smoking in such locations.

   (A) NO CHANGE
   (B) is prompting many state legislatures to consider
   (C) are prompting many state legislatures considering
   (D) is prompting many state legislatures considering
   (E) is prompting many state legislatures' consider

7. Diplomats sent to an unstable region or a genuinely hostile territory usually <u>is assigned an aide or chauffeur who function</u> also as a bodyguard.

   (A) NO CHANGE
   (B) are assigned an aide or chauffeur who function
   (C) are assigned an aide or chauffeur who functions
   (D) is assigned an aide or chauffeur that function
   (E) are assigned an aide or chauffeur which functions

8. Though (A) this is the wealthiest country in the world, within a few (B) blocks of the White House there is (C) scores of homeless people who live (D) on the streets. No error (E)

9. Just a few miles from the factories and
A
skyscrapers stand a medieval castle which looks
B C
exactly as it did in the 12th century. No error
D E

10. John, his wife, and the rest of his family plans
A
to attend the award dinner to be given by the
B C
company for the employees with the most
D
seniority. No error
E

11. Either the governor or one of his close aides
prefer not to have the Senator seated at the head
A B C
table where he would be conspicuous. No error
D E

12. Surrounded by layers of excelsior, none of the
A
crystal goblets were broken when the workers
B C
dropped the crate. No error
D E

13. During her rise to fame, she betrayed many of her friends, and because of it, very few people trust her.

(A) NO CHANGE
(B) and in spite of it
(C) and because of her friends
(D) and even though
(E) and because of her behavior

14. In New York City, they are brusque and even
A
rude but quick to come to one another's
B C
assistance in a time of crisis. No error
D E

15. Ten years ago, the United States imported ten
A
times as much French wine as Italian wine, but
B
today Americans are drinking more of it.
C D
No error
E

16. Although a police officer used to be a symbol of
A
authority, today they receive little respect
B C
from most people. No error
D E

17. The Abbot was an effective administrator
A
who attempted to assign each monk a task
B
particularly suited to their talents and training.
C D
No error
E

NOTES AND STRATEGIES

18. After three years of college education, a person should be allowed to (A) apply to graduate school, because (B) by that time you are (C) ready to choose (D) a profession. No error (E)

19. If (A) one wishes to apply for (B) a scholarship, you (C) must submit a completed (D) application by March 1. No error (E)

20. The judges were (A) unable to make a final decision on a single winner, so they (B) divided the first prize between (C) John and he (D). No error (E)

21. Although Peter had been looking (A) forward to (B) the debate for weeks, a sore throat prevented him (C) taking part (D). No error (E)

22. The company's mission statement took into consideration the significant changes that were made in the field of technology.

(A) NO CHANGE
(B) significantly changes
(C) significant changed
(D) significantly changed
(E) significantly to change

23. When asked about the chance that the defenders might concentrate their forces at the beachhead, the general responded tart that he was fully aware of all the possibilities.

(A) NO CHANGE
(B) tartly that he was full
(C) tart that he was full
(D) tart that he fully was
(E) tartly that he was fully

24. When the door burst open, Kevin looked up angry from his desk.

(A) NO CHANGE
(B) was looking up angry
(C) looked up angrily
(D) looks up angrily
(E) looked angry up

25. The director explained that the scene required Edmund to look distraughtly on hearing the news of his sister's death.

(A) NO CHANGE
(B) looking distraughtly
(C) to have looked distraughtly
(D) to have looked distraught
(E) to look distraught

26. Some psychologists maintain that a child who (A) has seen (B) violence on television is (C) more likely to react violent (D) in situations of stress. No error (E)

27. The recent created (A) commission has done (B) nothing to address the problem except to approve (C) the color of its (D) stationary. No error (E)

28. The track meet begins at 10:00 am, so the team needs to depart from the school at a reasonable early hour.

(A) NO CHANGE
(B) at a reasonably early hour
(C) during a reasonable early hour
(D) while a reasonably early hour
(E) at a reasonably hour that is early

29. Not hardly a sound could be heard in the
A B
auditorium when the speaker approached the dais
C D
to announce the result of the contest. No error
E

30. Although she had been hired by the magazine
A
to write book reviews, she knew scarcely nothing
B C D
about current fiction. No error
E

31. The reason Harriet fired her secretary is because he
A B
was frequently late and spent too much time on
C D
personal phone calls. No error
E

32. The reason the manager changed catchers was because he hoped that the opposing side would put in a left-handed pitcher.

(A) NO CHANGE
(B) The reason that catchers were changed by the manager was because
(C) The reason the manager changed catchers which
(D) The manager changed catchers because
(E) The manager changed catchers, the reason being

33. I read in a magazine where scientists believe that
A B
they have discovered a new subatomic particle.
C D
No error
E

34. The great pianist Vladimir Horowitz plays the
A
music of the Romantic Era better than any pianist
B C D
in history. No error
E

35. Like Neil Simon, many of Tennessee Williams' plays reflect a culture familiar to the playwright.

(A) NO CHANGE
(B) Many of Tennessee Williams' plays, like Neil Simon's
(C) Many of Tennessee Williams' plays, like Neil Simon
(D) Many of Neil Simon and Tennessee Williams' plays
(E) As with the plays of Neil Simon, many of Tennessee Williams' plays

36. Educators are now expressing their concern that
A B
American school children prefer watching
C
television to books. No error
D E

37. The novels of Nathaniel Hawthorne contain
A
characters who are every bit as sinister and
B C
frightening as the master of cinematic suspense,
D
Alfred Hitchcock. No error
E

38. A Japanese firm has developed (A) a computer so small that users can carry (B) it in their (C) briefcase (D). No error (E)

39. Carlos has a very (A) pleasant personality and he is a talented musician; therefore, (B) he gets (C) good grades in (D) school. No error (E)

40. John had already been (A) granted three extensions of the deadline; moreover, (B) the dean refused (C) to grant him another (D). No error (E)

41. A poll of students shows that (A) Helen is the top choice for (B) student body president. Helen, however, (C) is (D) likely to win the election. No error (E)

42. The producers realized the concert has been a success as they heard the cheers and applause of the audience.

(A) NO CHANGE
(B) has been a success hearing
(C) was a success hearing
(D) had been a success when they heard
(E) succeeded in that they heard

43. After the broken glass and other debris were cleaned up, we realized that the thief had took not only the necklace but a valuable ring as well.

(A) NO CHANGE
(B) had taken
(C) was took
(D) was taken
(E) were took

44. Everyone was very surprised when Sylvia brought her grandfather to music class and asked him to perform several Spanish songs on the guitar.

(A) NO CHANGE
(B) because Sylvia bringing
(C) while Sylvia brought
(D) that Sylvia brang
(E) for Sylvia to bring

45. The sheriff called off the search for the escaped convict because he doubted that the convict can successfully cross the river because the current was so swift.

(A) NO CHANGE
(B) the convict successfully crossed the river because the current was so swift
(C) the convict successfully crossed the river being that the current was so swift
(D) the convict would have been successful in crossing the river, the current being so swift
(E) a successful attempt to cross the river was made by the convict because the current was so swift

46. Elaine is the favorite to win the final event because she had always run well at the 100-meter distance.

(A) NO CHANGE
(B) has always run
(C) have always run
(D) always ran
(E) will always run

47. My computer crashed several times before I finally figured out that I had loaded on a corrupted copy of the program.

(A) NO CHANGE
(B) had finally figured out that I loaded
(C) had finally figured out that I had loaded
(D) finally had figured out that I loaded
(E) figured out finally that I would load

48. At the current rate of consumption, we have exhausted our supply of firewood before the weather turns warm.

(A) NO CHANGE
(B) had exhausted
(C) exhausted
(D) will exhaust
(E) will have exhausted

49. The will is going to be read at 3:00 pm, so the lawyer has asked that all family members are present in the office at that time.

(A) NO CHANGE
(B) are presently
(C) are going to be present
(D) be present
(E) being present

50. A dangerous situation could arise if the override switch were left open and the water drops below 50% of capacity.

(A) NO CHANGE
(B) dropped
(C) allowed to drop
(D) allowed dropping
(E) allows to drop

51. The teacher began to discuss the homework
A
assignment when he will be interrupted by the
B C D
sound of the fire alarm. No error
E

52. The conductor announced that the concert would
A
resume as soon as the soloist replaces the broken
B C
string on her violin. No error
D E

53. Many patients begin to show symptoms again
A B
after they stopped taking the drug. No error
C D E

54. The winter was so severe that several of Hillary's
A B
prize rose bushes had sustained serious damage
C D
from the frost. No error
E

NOTES AND STRATEGIES

55. In contrast of the prevailing opinion, the
A
editorial lays the blame for the strike on the
B C
workers and their representatives. No error
D E

56. Although ballet and modern dance are both

concerned in movement in space to musical
A
accompaniment, the training for ballet is more
B C
rigorous than that for modern dance. No error
D E

57. By midnight the guests still had not been served
A
anything to eat, so they were ravishing. No error
B C D E

58. The raise in the number of accidents attributable
A B
to drunk drivers has prompted a call for stiffer
C D
penalties for driving while intoxicated. No error
E

59. The idea of trying completing the term paper by
A B
Friday caused Ken to cancel his plans for the
C D
weekend. No error
E

60. Psychologists think that many people eat
A
satisfying a need for affection that is not
B C
otherwise fulfilled. No error
D E

61. John, having took his seat at the head of the
A
table, announced that the dinner would feature
B C D
specialties from Thailand. No error
E

62. The armor plating on the new tank protects more vulnerable areas than the armor on the old tank, it costs about three times as much to manufacture and install.

(A) NO CHANGE
(B) areas than the armor on the old tank, because it costs
(C) areas than the armor on the old tank, and it costs
(D) areas than the armor on the old tank which costs
(E) areas than the armor on the old tank, it costs

63. The filibuster continued late into the night some Senators slept sitting upright in the chairs while others slumped over their desks.

(A) NO CHANGE
(B) As the filibuster continued late into the night, some
(C) Because of the filibuster continuing late into the night, some
(D) The filibuster continued late into the night with
(E) The filibuster, which continued late into the night, some

64. The weather forecast predicted heavy rain, the baseball game was postponed until the following day.

(A) NO CHANGE
(B) rain while the
(C) rain, so the
(D) rain the
(E) rain or the

65. The devastation caused by the flood was so complete, it was impossible to tell that the pile of debris had once been a house.

(A) NO CHANGE
(B) so complete, and it
(C) so complete that it
(D) so completely, it
(E) so that it

66. The audience, dazzled by the sequined costumes and brilliant lights and applauded wildly.

(A) NO CHANGE
(B) The audience, dazzled by the sequined costumes and brilliant lights, applauded wildly.
(C) The audience was dazzled by the sequined costumes and brilliant lights applauding wildly.
(D) The audience, applauding wildly and dazzled by the sequined costumes and brilliant lights.
(E) Dazzled by the sequined costumes and brilliant lights, the applauding audience.

67. Most of the delegates, who were from smaller villages and rural areas and so opposed any plans to improve conditions in the large cities.

(A) NO CHANGE
(B) Most of the delegates from smaller villages and rural areas and so opposed any plans to improve conditions in the large cities.
(C) The delegates, most of whom were from smaller villages and rural areas and so opposed any plans to improve conditions in the large cities.
(D) The delegates who opposed any plans to improve conditions in the large cities and were from smaller villages and rural areas.
(E) Most of the delegates, who were from smaller villages and rural areas, opposed any plans to improve conditions in the large cities.

68. The driving snow made the roadway slippery and reduced visibility to no more than a few feet, and fortunately there were no accidents despite the heavy volume of traffic.

(A) NO CHANGE
(B) but fortunately there were no
(C) and fortunately there were some
(D) while fortunately there were no
(E) so fortunately there were no

69. The land surrounding Las Vegas is characterized by parched red dunes and flats with dry ravines, but it is almost entirely lacking in vegetation.

(A) NO CHANGE
(B) and they are
(C) and it is
(D) but they are
(E) but are

70. To abandon their homes, leave behind their
A
families, and traveling across the ocean required
B C
great courage on the part of the immigrants
who moved to America. No error
D E

71. The review praised the wit, charm, and
A
interpreting of the recitalist but never once
B C
mentioned her voice. No error
D E

72. To acknowledge that one has something to learn
A B
is taking the first step on the road to true
C D
wisdom. No error
E

73. The students are <u>critical of</u> the dean because he <u>is</u> either <u>unfamiliar or</u> doesn't care about the urgent <u>need for</u> new student housing on campus. <u>No error</u>
(A: critical of; B: is; C: unfamiliar or; D: need for; E: No error)

74. Baseball <u>has and</u> probably always will be the sport <u>that</u> <u>symbolizes</u> for people <u>in</u> other countries the American way of life. <u>No error</u>
(A: has and; B: that; C: symbolizes; D: in; E: No error)

75. <u>Letters were received by the editor of the newspaper that complained of its editorial policy.</u>

(A) NO CHANGE
(B) Letters were received by the editor of the newspaper having complained of its editorial policy.
(C) The editor of the newspaper received letters complaining of the newspaper's editorial policy.
(D) Letters were received by the editor in which there were complaints to the editor of the newspaper about its editorial policy.
(E) Letters were received by the editor complaining of the newspaper's editorial policy by the editor.

76. Riding in a coach and wearing the crown jewels, <u>the crowd cheered the royal couple</u>.

(A) NO CHANGE
(B) cheering for the royal couple was done by the crowd
(C) the royal couple was cheered by the crowd
(D) the royal couple's cheering was done by the crowd
(E) the royal couple, who was being cheered by crowd

77. <u>Wrapped in several thicknesses of newspaper, packed carefully in a strong cardboard carton, and bound securely with tape, the worker made sure that the fragile figurines would not be broken.</u>

(A) NO CHANGE
(B) Wrapped in several thicknesses of newspaper, packed carefully in a strong cardboard carton, and then binding the carton securely with tape, the worker made sure that the fragile figurines would not be broken.
(C) The figurines, having been securely wrapped in several thicknesses of newspaper, packed carefully in a strong cardboard carton which was then securely bound with tape, the worker made sure would not be broken.
(D) The worker, wrapping the figurines in several thicknesses of newspaper, packing them carefully in a strong cardboard carton, and securely binding the carton with tape, made sure that they would not be broken.
(E) To make sure that the figurines would not be broken, the worker wrapped them in several thicknesses of newspaper, packed them carefully in a strong cardboard carton, and securely bound the carton with tape.

78. Mary Lou was awarded the gold medal because she <u>scored</u> <u>more points than any child participating</u> in the field day.

(A) NO CHANGE
(B) more points than any other child participating
(C) most points than any child participating
(D) more points than any child who had participated
(E) more points as any child participating

79. <u>Appearing</u> in his first American tour, the British singer's album rose to the top of the charts.

(A) NO CHANGE
(B) While appearing
(C) While he was appearing
(D) When appearing
(E) Upon appearing

80. I think that Dore's illustrations of Dante's *Divine Comedy* are excellent; but my favorite drawing is "Don Quixote in His Library."

(A) NO CHANGE
(B) are excellent, but my favorite drawing is "Don Quixote in His Library."
(C) are excellent and my favorite drawing is "Don Quixote in His Library."
(D) are excellent in that my favorite drawing is "Don Quixote in His Library."
(E) are excellent even though "Don Quixote in His Library" is my favorite drawing.

81. Practically (A) all nitrates are crystalline and readily (B) soluble, and (C) they are characterized by marked decrepitation when (D) heated on charcoals by a blowpipe. No error (E)

82. The door was (A) ajar, (B) and the house had been (C) ransacked (D). No error (E)

83. Since many diseases and insects cause serious damage to crops, (A) special national legislation has been passed to provide for the quarantine of imported plants; (B) and under provisions of various acts, (C) inspectors are placed at ports of entry to prevent smugglers from bringing in plants that might be (D) dangerous. No error (E)

84. A full train crew consists of a motorman, a brakeman, a conductor, and two ticket takers.

(A) NO CHANGE
(B) A full train crew consists of a motorman, a brakeman, a conductor and two ticket takers.
(C) A full train crew consists of a motorman, brakeman, conductor, and two ticket takers.
(D) A full train crew consists of, a motorman, a brakeman, a conductor, and two ticket takers.
(E) A full train crew consists of a motorman a brakeman a conductor and two ticket takers.

85. The procedure requires that you open the outer cover plate, (A) remove the thermostat, (B) replace the broken switch, (C) and then (D) replace the thermostat. No error (E)

86. After (A) Peter finished painting the bird feeder (B) he and (C) Jack hung it (D) from a limb of the oak tree. No error (E)

87. When (A) Pat explained to his mother that ten was the highest mark given (B) on the entrance test (C) she breathed (D) a sigh of relief. No error (E)

88. Tim hopes to score well on the exam because he plans to go to an Ivy League school.

(A) NO CHANGE
(B) Tim hopes to score well on the exam and he plans to go to an Ivy League school.
(C) Tim hopes to score well on the exam, because he plans to go to an Ivy League school.
(D) Tim hopes to score well on the exam, and he plans to go to an Ivy League school.
(E) Tim hopes to score well on the exam he plans to go to an Ivy League school.

89. In this impoverished region with its arid soil a typical diet may contain only 800 calories per day.

(A) NO CHANGE
(B) In this impoverished region with its arid soil; a typical diet may contain only 800 calories per day.
(C) In this impoverished region, with its arid soil, a typical diet may contain only 800 calories per day.
(D) In this impoverished region with its arid soil, a typical diet may contain only 800 calories per day.
(E) In this impoverished region with its arid soil: a typical diet may contain only 800 calories per day.

90. Begun (A) in 1981 and completed in 1985 (B) the bridge provided (C) the first link between (D) the island and the mainland. No error (E)

91. To slow the bleeding Van tied a tourniquet around the lower portion of the leg.

(A) NO CHANGE
(B) To slow the bleeding—Van tied a tourniquet around the lower portion of the leg.
(C) To slow the bleeding, Van tied a tourniquet around the lower portion of the leg.
(D) To slow the bleeding, Van tied a tourniquet, around the lower portion of the leg.
(E) Van tied a tourniquet, to slow the bleeding, around the lower portion of the leg.

92. Niagara Falls, (A) which (B) forms part of the border between the United States and Canada, (C) was the site of a saw mill built by the French in 1725 (D). No error (E)

93. Secretary of State Acheson, (A) however, (B) made a reasoned (C) defense of (D) the treaty. No error (E)

94. Until the end of the 18th century, (A) the only musicians in Norway, (B) were simple unsophisticated peasants who (C) traveled about (D). No error (E)

95. Prizes will be (A) awarded in each event, (B) and the participant, who compiles the greatest overall total, (C) will receive (D) a special prize. No error (E)

96. Since learning of the dangers of caffeine, (A) neither (B) my wife nor (C) I have consumed any beverage, (D) containing caffeine. No error (E)

97. After months of separation, Gauguin finally joined Van Gogh in Arles in October of 1888, Gauguin left a few weeks later.

(A) NO CHANGE
(B) in Arles; Gauguin, however, leaving a few weeks later
(C) in Arles, while Gauguin left a few weeks later
(D) in Arles, it was three weeks later when Gauguin was gone
(E) in Arles, in October of 1888, but left a few weeks later

98. He grew up on a farm in Nebraska; he is now the captain of a Navy ship.

(A) NO CHANGE
(B) He grew up on a farm in Nebraska, he is now the captain of a Navy ship.
(C) He grew up on a farm in Nebraska he is now the captain of a Navy ship.
(D) He grew up on a farm; in Nebraska he is now the captain of a Navy ship.
(E) He grew up on a farm in Nebraska but he is now the captain of a Navy ship.

99. The Smithtown players cheered the referee's decision; the Stonybrook players booed it.

(A) NO CHANGE
(B) The Smithtown players cheered the referee's decision the Stonybrook players booed it.
(C) The Smithtown players cheered the referee's decision, the Stonybrook players booed it.
(D) The Smithtown players cheered the referee's decision: the Stonybrook players booed it.
(E) The Smithtown players cheered the referee's decision, but the Stonybrook players booed it.

100. When John entered the room; everyone stood up.
A B C D
No error
E

101. Clem announced that the prize would be donated
A B C
to Harbus House; a well-known charity. No error
D E

102. The nineteenth-century composers Wagner and Mahler did more than just write music, they conducted their own works.

(A) NO CHANGE
(B) music, in that they conducted
(C) music; they conducted
(D) music, with their conducting of
(E) music; as conductors, they did

103. The seemingly tranquil lane has been the scene of
A
many crimes including: two assaults, three
B C
robberies, and one murder. No error
D E

104. In addition to test scores, college admissions
A
officers take into consideration many other
factors such as: grades, extracurricular activities,
B C D
and letters of recommendation. No error
D E

105. Peter notified Elaine. The guidance counselor, that he had been accepted.

(A) NO CHANGE
(B) Peter notified Elaine the guidance counselor, that he had been accepted.
(C) Peter notified Elaine, the guidance counselor that he had been accepted.
(D) Peter notified Elaine, the guidance counselor, that he had been accepted.
(E) Peter notified Elaine that the guidance counselor had been accepted.

106. Peanuts—blanched or lightly roasted, add an interesting texture and taste to garden salads.

(A) NO CHANGE
(B) Peanuts—blanched or lightly roasted—add an interesting texture and taste to garden salads.
(C) Peanuts: blanched or lightly roasted, add an interesting texture and taste to garden salads.
(D) Peanuts, blanched or lightly roasted—add an interesting texture and taste to garden salads.
(E) Peanuts blanched or lightly roasted; add an interesting texture and taste to garden salads.

107. The optimist <u>feels that</u> his glass is <u>one-half</u> <u>full;</u> the pessimist feels that his glass is one-half <u>empty</u>. <u>No error</u>

A: feels that — B: one-half — C: full; — D: empty — E: No error

108. <u>The first chapter of *The Scarlet Letter* is "The Custom House."</u>

(A) NO CHANGE
(B) The first chapter of *The Scarlet Letter* is "The Custom House".
(C) The first chapter of *The Scarlet Letter* is The Custom House.
(D) The first chapter of *The Scarlet Letter* is *The Custom House.*
(E) The first chapter of *The Scarlet Letter* is "The Custom House."

DIRECTIONS: Punctuate the following paragraph.

109. On Monday Mark received a letter of acceptance from State College He immediately called his mother herself a graduate of State College to tell her about his acceptance When he told her he had also been awarded a scholarship she was very excited After hanging up Mark's mother decided to throw a surprise party for Mark She telephoned his brother his sister and several of his friends Because the party was supposed to be a surprise she made them all promise not to say anything to Mark Mark however had a similar idea a party for his mother to celebrate his acceptance at her alma mater He telephoned his brother his sister and several of his parents' friends to invite them to a party at his house on Saturday night and he made them all promise to say nothing to his mother On Saturday night both Mark and his mother were surprised

DIRECTIONS: The following passages are early drafts of essays. Some parts of the passages need to be rewritten. Read each passage and answer the items that follow. Some items are about particular sentences or parts of sentences and ask you to improve sentence structure and word choice. Other items refer to parts of the passage or the entire passage and ask you to consider organization and development. In making your decisions, follow the conventions of standard written English.

<u>Items 110-114</u> are based on the following essay, which is a response to an assignment to write about an issue that is facing America and what might be done to resolve it.

[1] In my mind, one of the most pressing issues facing America today is healthcare. [2] One aspect of the problem is lack of access to a doctor. [3] Many people just cannot afford to pay for a visit to a doctor. [4] They avoid going to the doctor until they are really sick. [5] If they were treated in the first place, they wouldn't get so sick. [6] This practice not only causes human suffering but is wasteful. [7] Health insurance for surgery is also an issue. [8] Many people do not get adequate health insurance with their jobs and cannot afford to pay for it. [9] The inability to pay for health insurance also creates an unfair distribution of healthcare in America.

[10] An even more important aspect of the healthcare problem in America is the choices that people make for themselves. [11] Take smoking for example. [12] Scientific evidence proves that smoking causes lung cancer and other diseases. [13] Yet, many people continue to smoke, and young people continue to start smoking. [14] There are other health problems such as being overweight and using drugs that may also come from private choices.

[15] Some government assistance is needed for those who cannot afford medical care or health insurance. [16] The most important thing is for people to be concerned with their own health. [17] If we take care of ourselves by eating better, exercising more, and avoiding destructive choices, we will all live longer, healthier, and happier lives.

110. The author considers inserting the following factual statement between sentences 13 and 14:

Nicotine, which is found in tobacco, is one of the most addictive chemicals known to science.

Would this statement add to the development of the paragraph?

(A) Yes, because the paragraph identifies smoking as a serious problem.
(B) Yes, because the sentence explains why young people start to smoke.
(C) No, because scientific evidence is irrelevant to the author's point.
(D) No, because the addictive mechanism behind smoking is not relevant.
(E) No, because essays should emphasize positive points, not negative ones.

111. Which of the following revisions to sentence 15 best clarifies the author's position?

(A) NO CHANGE
(B) Some government assistance is needed for those who cannot afford medical care or health insurance and people need to be concerned with their own health.
(C) The most important thing is for people to be concerned with their own health and for them to ask for government assistance.
(D) Even though some government assistance is needed for those who cannot afford medical care or health insurance, the most important thing is for people to be concerned with their own health.
(E) OMIT sentence 15

112. In context, which of the following best describes the main purpose of the essay?

(A) To expose faulty reasoning
(B) To evaluate a theory set forth earlier
(C) To provide specific illustrations
(D) To propose a solution to a problem
(E) To persuade the reader to change an opinion

113. In writing this passage, the author was most probably addressing

(A) a convention of surgeons
(B) a group of concerned citizens
(C) a meeting of insurance executives
(D) a conference of tobacco executives
(E) an assembly of noted scientists

114. What should be done to sentence 7 to strengthen the organization of the essay?

(A) NO CHANGE
(B) Begin a new paragraph
(C) Switch sentence 6 with sentence 7
(D) Switch sentence 7 with sentence 8
(E) OMIT sentence 7

Item 115 is based on the following essay, which is a response to an assignment to write about a chore for which you have a responsibility and why you like or dislike doing the chore.

Each year, my family plants a vegetable garden. Both my parents work, and with this it is the job of the children to tend the garden.

Work starts several weeks before the growing season actually begins. We put little pots of soil containing seeds that must sprout before they are planted outdoors on the sun porch. Then, my father prepares the ground with a rototiller. The danger of frost is past, it is time to plant.

For the first few weeks, we water the seed beds regularly and pull weeds by hand. Once the plants are established, the leaves of the good plants block the sunlight so weeds can't grow. However, there are other jobs such as staking tomatoes and tending to running vines.

Then the blossoms appear and are pollinated by bees and other insects. As small vegetables appear, the blossoms drop off. They continue to grow and later in the summer begin to ripen. Up to this point, tending the garden has been a chore, but now it becomes a pleasure. Each afternoon, we pick the ripe ones and wash them so that they are ready for cooking. I suppose that I feel proud that I have helped to feed my family. I have to admit that I enjoy the taste of the freshly picked vegetables.

115. Which of the following best describes the overall organization of the passage?

(A) Chronological development
(B) Explanation of two sides of an issue
(C) Generalization of a statement with illustrations
(D) Posing a question and then answering it
(E) Citing an authority and then drawing a conclusion

116. Angela is hoping to save enough for a trip to Europe, during which the small village where her grandparents were born will be visited.

(A) NO CHANGE
(B) the small village where her grandparents had been born will be visited
(C) she will visit the small village where her grandparents were born
(D) there will be a visit to the small village where her grandparents were born
(E) a visit to the small village where her grandparents were born will be included

117. Finally and at long last the old dog opened his eyes and noticed the intruder.

(A) NO CHANGE
(B) Finally
(C) So finally
(D) Yet at long last
(E) Finally and long lastingly

118. The speaker declared that alternative ways of utilizing waterfront land ought to be explored.

(A) NO CHANGE
(B) alternatives of use for
(C) alternative utilizations of
(D) alternative ways of utilization of
(E) alternate uses of

119. Since only (A) the ruling party is allowed to (B) vote, its (C) members are able to maintain the existing (D) status quo. No error (E)

120. Each year, the geese make their annual migration from Northern Canada to their winter habitats in the United States. No error
(A: make; B: annual; C: migration; D: their winter habitats; E: No error)

121. Although the committee met for over two weeks and issued a 50-page report, its findings were of little importance or consequence. No error
(A: Although; B: its findings; C: of little; D: importance or; E: No error)

122. Along with an end to featherbedding and no-show jobs, the new head of the Transit Authority has eliminated many other inefficient employment practices.

(A) NO CHANGE
(B) In addition to eliminating featherbedding and no-show jobs
(C) Not only did he end featherbedding and no-shows jobs,
(D) Besides featherbedding and no-show jobs coming to an end
(E) Together with the ending of featherbedding and no-show jobs

123. Being that the hour was late, we agreed to adjourn the meeting and reconvene at nine o'clock the following morning. No error
(A: Being that; B: was; C: agreed; D: reconvene; E: No error)

DIRECTIONS: In the passage that follows, certain words and phrases are underlined and numbered. In the right-hand column, you will find alternatives for the underlined part. In most cases, you are to choose the one that best expresses the idea, makes the statement appropriate for standard written English, or is worded most consistently with the style and tone of the passage as a whole. If you think the original version is best, choose "NO CHANGE." In some cases, you will find an item about the underlined part in the right-hand column. You are to choose the best answer to the question that is posed.

You will also find items about a section of the passage, or about the passage as a whole. These items do not refer to an underlined portion of the passage, but rather are identified by a number or numbers in a box.

For each item, choose the alternative you consider best. Read the passage through once before you begin to answer the items that accompany it. For many of the items, you must read several sentences beyond the item to determine the answer. Answers are on page 933.

Appalachia's European Settlers

The first Europeans who adopted Appalachia as home, followed [124] the trails pounded out by those earliest mountain engineers: the [125] buffalo, elk, deer, and other wild game. (Later, they found the great traces forged by the Indian tribes on their trading and fighting forays.) [126] Gradually, these first Europeans hewed out passages that become part of [127] America's history, and portions of which may still be discovered along today's interstates and back roads. Their very names connect us to [128] the past in the region: The Great Warrior's Trail, Boone's Trace (which became the Wilderness Road), and the Cumberland Gap.

124. A. NO CHANGE
B. home followed
C. home: followed
D. home; followed

125. F. NO CHANGE
G. engineers, the
H. engineers the
J. engineers. The

126. A. NO CHANGE
B. Great traces forged by the Indian tribes, however, were later found on their trading and fighting forays.
C. (Finding later, great traces forged by the Indian tribes, on their trading and fighting forays.)
D. Later, they found the great traces forged by the Indian tribes on their trading and fighting forays.

127. F. NO CHANGE
G. will become a part of
H. became part of
J. became part

128. A. NO CHANGE
B. connecting us to
C. connected us to
D. connect us

Geographic isolation greatly influenced the region's culture. From the beginning, numerous ethnic groups contributed to Appalachian settlement. During the late 1600s and into the next century, Germans from the Rhineland settled in the Great Appalachian Valley. Building fat barns and tight houses on the fertile fields of Pennsylvania, Maryland, Virginia, and North Carolina. They were the "Pennsylvania Dutch." The German settlers made important contributions. One of the important contributions made by German settlers to frontier life was the Pennsylvania rifle—also called the Kentucky rifle and the Long rifle. A weapon born of necessity and economy, its extended barrel assured greater accuracy and precision than could be achieved with the old muskets, and its smaller bore required less powder and lead for each shot (precious commodities). Such rifles were highly prized possessions, and their manufacture was one of the central industries of pioneer Appalachia.

129. F. NO CHANGE
G. Geographically isolated
H. Isolated geographically
J. Isolated geography

130. A. NO CHANGE
B. Valley, building
C. Valley: building
D. Valley,

131. For the sake of the logic and coherence of this paragraph, the underlined sentence should be:
F. left as it is now.
G. placed in parentheses.
H. placed in quotation marks.
J. omitted.

132. A. NO CHANGE
B. accuracy as well as precision
C. accuracy plus precision
D. accuracy

133. The most appropriate placement of the underlined phrase in this sentence would be:
F. where it is now.
G. after the word "powder."
H. after the word "lead."
J. after the word "each."

CHALLENGE ITEMS

The passages and items in this section reflect both the format and difficulty range of passages and items on the ACT English Test, though difficult material is emphasized. Answers are on page 933.

DIRECTIONS: In the passages that follow, certain words and phrases are underlined and numbered. In the right-hand column, you will find alternatives for the underlined part. In most cases, you are to choose the one that best expresses the idea, makes the statement appropriate for standard written English, or is worded most consistently with the style and tone of the passage as a whole. If you think the original version is best, choose "NO CHANGE." In some cases, you will find a question that asks about the underlined part. For these, choose the best answer to the question that is posed.

You will also find questions about a section of the passage, or about the passage as a whole. These items do not refer to an underlined portion of the passage, but rather are identified by a number or numbers in a box.

For each item, choose the alternative that you consider to be the best. Read the passage through once before you begin to answer the items that accompany it. For many of the items, you must read several sentences beyond the item to determine the answer.

PASSAGE I

Significance of Symbolism in Medieval Art

Art of the Middle Ages is first and foremost a sacred script, the symbols and meanings of which are well settled (1). A circular halo placed vertically behind the head of a figure signifies sainthood, meanwhile (2) the halo impressed with a cross signifies divinity.

A tower (3) with a window indicates a village, and should an angel be watching from the battlements, that city is thereby identified as Jerusalem. Mathematics is also an important element of this iconography. "The Divine Wisdom," wrote Saint

1. A. NO CHANGE
   B. is well settled
   C. are settled well
   D. would be settled

2. F. NO CHANGE
   G. sainthood, because
   H. sainthood because
   J. sainthood, while

3. A. NO CHANGE
   B. (Do NOT begin a new paragraph) A tower
   C. Towers
   D. Having a tower

Augustine, "reveals itself everywhere in numbers." A doctrine [4] derived from the Neoplatonists who [5] revived the teachings of Pythagoras. And numbers require symmetry. At Chartres, a stained-glass window shows the four prophets Isaac, Ezekiel, Daniel, and Jeremiah carrying on their shoulders the four evangelists Matthew, Mark, Luke, and John.

4. F. NO CHANGE
   G. numbers," which
   H. numbers." This doctrine was
   J. numbers" which

5. A. NO CHANGE
   B. Neoplatonists that
   C. Neoplatonist's that
   D. Neoplatonist's who

Every painting [6] is also an allegory, showing us

6. F. NO CHANGE
   G. (Do NOT begin a new paragraph) Every painting
   H. However, every painting
   J. (Do NOT begin a new paragraph) However, every painting

one thing and inviting us to see another. In this respect, the artist was [7] asked to imitate God, who had

7. A. NO CHANGE
   B. Furthermore, the artist was
   C. The artist, however, was
   D. Generally, artists are

hidden a profound meaning behind [8] the literal and who wished nature to be a moral lesson to man. In a painting of the final judgment, the foolish virgins can

8. F. NO CHANGE
   G. meaning which was behind
   H. meaning being behind
   J. meaning behind and in back of

be seen by us [9] at the left hand of Jesus and the wise on the right, and we understand that this symbolizes

9. A. NO CHANGE
   B. by all of us
   C. by each of us
   D. OMIT the underlined portion.

those who are lost and those that have been saved [10].

10. F. NO CHANGE
    G. those who have been saved
    H. those who are saved
    J. the saved

Within such a system, [11] even the most mediocre

11. A. NO CHANGE
    B. (Do NOT begin a new paragraph) Within such a system,
    C. (Do NOT begin a new paragraph) Inside of such a system,
    D. (Do NOT begin a new paragraph) To be inside such a system,

talent was elevated by the genius of centuries, and [12] the first artist of the Renaissance broke with the tradition

12. F. NO CHANGE
    G. with
    H. however
    J. since

at great risk. Even when they are great, medieval artists are no more than the equals of the old masters who passively followed the sacred rules. When they are not outstanding, they scarcely [13] avoid banality and insignificance in their religious works.

13. A. NO CHANGE
    B. always
    C. ever
    D. OMIT the underlined portion.

Items 14-16 ask about the preceding passage as a whole.

14. The author most likely wrote this essay for which of the following?
    F. A scholarly art journal
    G. A book tracing the history of mathematics
    H. A history of the Catholic Church
    J. A book surveying the history of Western art

15. The author relies on which of the following to develop the passage?
    A. Examples
    B. Extensive quotations from other authorities
    C. Statistics
    D. Personal experience

16. The author probably quotes Saint Augustine in order to:
    F. ridicule his position.
    G. emphasize the importance of numbers and symmetry.
    H. prove the importance of Church teaching.
    J. illustrate Augustine's knowledge of art.

PASSAGE II

Pursuit of the Bottomless Pit

A persistent and universal symbol in the mythology of virtually every culture, is [17] that of a bottomless pit or an engulfing whirlpool. It was the maw of the abyss: and those [18] venturing too close were dragged inward toward chaos by an irresistible force. Socrates (a Greek philosopher who committed suicide) [19] talked of a chasm that pierced the world straight through from side to side. Ulysses also encountering it, [20] as did a mythical Cherokee who escaped, but not before he was drawn down to the narrowest circle of the maelstrom where he could peer into the netherworld of the dead. Many primitive cultures bury their dead with tools in the belief that The tools will be useful to them in the afterlife. [21]

On the other hand, the search [22] for a solution to one of astronomys' [23] most persistent and perplexing riddles, black holes, could be viewed by one [24] as a

17. A. NO CHANGE
    B. culture is
    C. culture are
    D. cultures are

18. F. NO CHANGE
    G. abyss, and those
    H. abyss meanwhile those
    J. abyss due to the fact that

19. A. NO CHANGE
    B. (a philosopher from Greece who committed suicide)
    C. (a Greek philosopher who had committed suicide)
    D. OMIT the underlined portion.

20. F. NO CHANGE
    G. also encountered it,
    H. also encountered them,
    J. encountered them also,

21. For the sake of the logic and coherence of this paragraph, the underlined sentence should be:
    A. left as it is now.
    B. placed before the word "Ulysses."
    C. placed at the end of the passage.
    D. omitted.

22. F. NO CHANGE
    G. The search
    H. (Do NOT begin a new paragraph) The search
    J. Also, the search

23. A. NO CHANGE
    B. astronomy's
    C. astronomy
    D. astronomys

24. F. NO CHANGE
    G. by one astronomer
    H. by those
    J. OMIT the underlined portion

continuation of the search for [25] the whirlpool that is the maw of the abyss, a depth our telescopes cannot reach and from which nothing will have returned [26].

What is incredible to contemplate, and what sets us [27] apart from the ancients, is that we think we have a fair idea not only as to [28] how they are formed, but also how large they are and so forth. A combination of theory and observation have led to [29] the growing suspicion among astrophysicists that the nucleus of virtually every galaxy harbors a massive black hole.

25. A. NO CHANGE
    B. continuing the search of
    C. continuation to the search for
    D. continuation for the search for

26. F. NO CHANGE
    G. will return
    H. returns
    J. returning

27. A. NO CHANGE
    B. setting us
    C. and that sets us
    D. and we are set

28. F. NO CHANGE
    G. about
    H. not about
    J. OMIT the underlined portion.

29. A. NO CHANGE
    B. has led to
    C. has led
    D. led

NOTES AND STRATEGIES

PASSAGE III

Tradition Preservation During Meiji Restoration

Instead of casting aside traditional values during the Meiji Restoration of 1888, those who strove to dismantle feudalism and to modernize the country chose to preserve three traditions as the foundations <u>on which they could build a modern Japan upon</u> [30].

The <u>older</u> [31] tradition and basis of the entire Japanese value system was <u>respect for and even worshipping</u> [32] the Emperor. During the early centuries of Japanese history, the Shinto cult, in which <u>the Imperial family traced its ancestry to the Sun Goddess,</u> [33] became the people's sustaining faith. <u>Being later subordinated</u> [34] to imported Buddhism and Confucianism, Shintoism was perpetuated in Ise and Izumo, the great shrines of the Imperial family, until the Meiji modernizers established it as a quasi state religion to unify the people and restore the Emperor as the symbol of national unity and the object of loyalty <u>to the Japanese</u> [35].

30. F. NO CHANGE
    G. on which they could be building a modern Japan upon
    H. upon which they could build a modern Japan
    J. upon which they someday could probably build a modern Japan

31. A. NO CHANGE
    B. oldest
    C. old
    D. OMIT the underlined portion.

32. F. NO CHANGE
    G. respecting and even worshipping
    H. respect for and even worship of
    J. respect and even worship

33. A. NO CHANGE
    B. the Imperial family got its ancestry traced back to the Sun Goddess
    C. the Imperial family's ancestry was traced back to the Sun Goddess
    D. the Sun Goddess was considered to be the ancestor of the Imperial family

34. F. NO CHANGE
    G. Later subordinated
    H. Later subordinated,
    J. Subordinated later,

35. A. NO CHANGE
    B. the Japanese had
    C. by the Japanese
    D. for the Japanese

Another tradition that was enduring [36] was the hierarchical system of social relations based on feudalism. Confucianism prescribed a pattern by [37] ethical conduct between groups of people within a fixed hierarchy. Four of the five Confucian relationships (those between ruler and subject, husband and wife, father and son, and elder brother and younger brother) [38] were [39] vertical since they [40] required loyalty and obedience from the inferior toward the superior and benevolence and protection from the superior to the inferior [41]. Only the fifth relationship, that [42] between friend and friend—was horizontal. A [43] third tradition was respect

36. F. NO CHANGE
G. Another tradition
H. (Do NOT begin a new paragraph) Another tradition
J. The other tradition

37. A. NO CHANGE
B. patterns by
C. a pattern for
D. patterns with

38. Is the author's use of parentheses appropriate?
F. Yes, because the examples are irrelevant to the passage.
G. Yes, because although the information is relevant, the material is not part of the main development of the passage.
H. No, because the examples are relevant to the meaning of the sentence.
J. No, because the material is essential to the reader's understanding of the passage.

39. A. NO CHANGE
B. was
C. are
D. could be

40. F. NO CHANGE
G. vertical, they
H. vertical, since it
J. vertical, being they

41. A. NO CHANGE
B. and also benevolence and protection from the superior to the inferior
C. with the benevolence and protection being from the superior to the inferior
D. and from the superior to the inferior, the benevolence and prote[illegible]

42. F. NO CHANGE
G. relationship that
H. relationship—that
J. relationship

43. A. NO CHANGE
B. Furthermore, a
C. (Begin a new paragraph) A
D. (Begin a new paragraph) Also a

for learning, another basic idea of Confucius. In traditional Japan, study was the absolute duty of man. It was a religious mandate as well as a social duty and was a means of promoting a harmonious and stable society. The individual's behavior was strictly prescribed by law and custom. Only the Samurai had the right to retaliate with force if they were displeased. But his primary duty was to the lord.

44. F. NO CHANGE
    G. Confucius idea
    H. idea of Confucianism
    J. Confucianism idea

45. A. NO CHANGE
    B. mandate as well as being
    C. mandate as well,
    D. mandate,

46. F. NO CHANGE
    G. An individual behavior
    H. Behavior by individual's
    J. The individuals behavior

47. A. NO CHANGE
    B. But their
    C. Being that their
    D. Because their

Item 48 asks about the preceding passage as a whole.

48. The best description of the development of this essay would be:
    F. argument and rebuttal.
    G. a personal narrative.
    H. a three-part exposition.
    J. question and answer.

TIMED-PRACTICE QUIZZES

This section contains three English ACT quizzes. Complete each quiz under timed conditions. Answers are on page 933.

DIRECTIONS: In the passages that follow, certain words and phrases are underlined and numbered. In the right-hand column, you will find alternatives for the underlined part. In most cases, you are to choose the one that best expresses the idea, makes the statement appropriate for standard written English, or is worded most consistently with the style and tone of the passage as a whole. If you think the original version is best, choose "NO CHANGE." In some cases, you will find a question that asks about the underlined part. For these, choose the best answer to the question that is posed.

You will also find questions about a section of the passage, or about the passage as a whole. These items do not refer to an underlined portion of the passage, but rather are identified by a number or numbers in a box.

For each item, choose the alternative that you consider to be the best. Read the passage through once before you begin to answer the items that accompany it. For many of the items, you must read several sentences beyond the item to determine the answer.

A. QUIZ I (32 items; 20 minutes)

PASSAGE I

Shakespeare's Mirror of Life

No writer can please many readers and please them for a long time excepting by[1] the accurate representation of human nature. Shakespeare, however,[2] is above all writers, the poet of human nature, the writer who holds up to his readers a faithful and true[3] mirror of manners and life.

Shakespeare's characters are not modified by the customs of particular places unknown to the rest of the world, by peculiarities of study or professions known to just a few, or[4] by the latest fashions or popular opinions.

1. A. NO CHANGE
   B. except by
   C. except for
   D. excepting

2. F. NO CHANGE
   G. moreover
   H. therefore
   J. furthermore

3. A. NO CHANGE
   B. faithful
   C. faithfully true
   D. true and real

4. F. NO CHANGE
   G. about by only a few, and
   H. to just a few, but
   J. to only a few, since

Shakespeare's characters are each[5] genuine representations of common humanity. Hamlet and Othello act and speak[6] according to the general passions and principles that affect all of us. In the writings of other poets, whoever they may be,[7] a character is too often an individual; in that of Shakespeare,[8] it is commonly a species. Other dramatists can gain attention only by using exaggerated characters. Shakespeare has no heroes; his[9] scenes only[10] are occupied by persons who act and speak as the reader thinks he or she would of spoken[11] or acted on the same occasion. This, therefore, is the praise of Shakespeare that[12] his drama is the mirror of life. [13]

5. A. NO CHANGE
   B. every
   C. all
   D. each one a

6. F. NO CHANGE
   G. acting and speaking
   H. acted and spoke
   J. acted and spoken

7. A. NO CHANGE
   B. whoever they may be
   C. whomever they may be,
   D. OMIT the underlined portion.

8. F. NO CHANGE
   G. the one of Shakespeare,
   H. those of Shakespeare's,
   J. those of Shakespeare,

9. A. NO CHANGE
   B. has no heroes: his
   C. has no heroes his
   D. has no heroes, his

10. The most appropriate placement of the underlined phrase in this sentence would be:
    F. where it is now.
    G. after the word "act."
    H. before the word "act."
    J. after the word "occupied."

11. A. NO CHANGE
    B. would have speaked
    C. would have spoken
    D. would speak

12. F. NO CHANGE
    G. Shakespeare,
    H. Shakespeare. That
    J. Shakespeare: that

13. Is the final sentence an appropriate ending?
    A. Yes, because it makes a final point about Shakespeare that was not previously mentioned and will leave the reader with something to think about.
    B. Yes, because it is a summary of what was said in the introductory paragraph and will give the reader a sense of closure.
    C. No, because it is irrelevant to the essay and will leave the reader confused.
    D. No, because it is so repetitious that it will make the reader impatient.

Items 14-17 ask about the preceding passage as a whole.

14. What assumption is the essay's author making?
    F. Everyone believes Shakespeare is a good writer.
    G. No one has ever heard of Shakespeare.
    H. An accurate representation of human nature is important for great art.
    J. We could not understand Shakespeare's characters in the twentieth century.

15. Where might you find this essay published?
    A. In a book of literary criticism
    B. In a journal for Renaissance scholars
    C. In a Shakespeare biography
    D. In a sociology textbook

16. Which of the following is NOT a strategy the author uses to make his/her point?
    F. Comparison
    G. Argument
    H. Examples
    J. Personal anecdote

17. Which of the following would most strengthen the author's argument that Shakespeare is the poet of human nature?
    A. A discussion of Shakespeare's poetry
    B. An analysis of the characters Hamlet and Othello
    C. Biographical background on Shakespeare
    D. A description of Shakespeare's Globe Theater

PASSAGE II

Diary of a Black Hole

[1]

In the course of billions of years, millions of stars may sometimes occasionally [18] be concentrated into a region, or regions, only a few light years across, and in these crowded conditions colliding [19] with one another. Some of these collisions would occur [20] at high speeds, in which case the stars are partially or completely torn apart. Other collisions are gentle bumps, but the stars coalesce. [21] The bigger the star becomes, the more likely [22] it is to be hit again and the faster it grows until it reaches instability, collapses on itself, and forms a black hole. [23]

[2]

When most of the stars and gas in the core of a galaxy has been [24] swallowed up by the black hole, the nucleus of the galaxy settles down to a relative [25] quiet existence. This is probably the state of the nucleus of our own galaxy, but every hundred million years or

18. F. NO CHANGE
    G. sometimes, occasionally
    H. occasionally
    J. off and on

19. A. NO CHANGE
    B. colliding
    C. and in these crowded conditions, they collide
    D. which causes them to collide

20. F. NO CHANGE
    G. will occur
    H. to occur
    J. occur

21. A. NO CHANGE
    B. bumps, since the stars
    C. bumps, and the stars coalesce
    D. bumps, with the stars coalescing

22. F. NO CHANGE
    G. becomes the more
    H. becomes the more,
    J. becomes; the more

23. A. NO CHANGE
    B. and a black hole is formed
    C. and when this happens a black hole is formed
    D. and thus a black hole is formed at this very moment

24. F. NO CHANGE
    G. have been
    H. will have been
    J. would have been

25. A. NO CHANGE
    B. to a relatively
    C. for a relative and
    D. relatively

so it may flare upto[26] a brightness 100 times its present level when a globular cluster or especially large gas cloud of enormous size[27] spirals into the nucleus.

[3]

Once formed, a central "seed" black hole grows mainly through the accretion of gas accumulated in the nucleus; gas[28] obtained from disrupted stars, from supernova explosions, or from stars torn apart by the gravitational field of the black hole. Perhaps an entire galaxy can collide with another galaxy, and the result would be[29] the transfer of large amounts of gas from one galaxy to each other[30].

26. F. NO CHANGE
    G. up
    H. up to
    J. OMIT the underlined portion.

27. A. NO CHANGE
    B. of great enormity
    C. which is huge
    D. OMIT the underlined portion.

28. F. NO CHANGE
    G. nucleus and gas
    H. nucleus. Gas
    J. nucleus gas

29. A. NO CHANGE
    B. galaxy to result in
    C. galaxy. Such a collision could result in
    D. galaxy with the results that

30. F. NO CHANGE
    G. to the other
    H. an other
    J. and another

Items 31 and 32 ask about the preceding passage as a whole.

31. Which of the following represents the most logical sequence for the paragraphs?
    A. 1, 2, 3
    B. 1, 3, 2
    C. 2, 3, 1
    D. 3, 1, 2

32. The author's intended audience is most likely:
    F. astronomers.
    G. young children.
    H. high school students.
    J. physicists.

B. QUIZ II (29 items; 20 minutes)

PASSAGE I

The Influence of the Southwest on Artists

Georgia O'Keeffe, <u>who's</u>[1] death <u>at age ninety-eight</u>[2] closed one of the most fertile chapters of American <u>creativity and flourished</u>[3] as a maverick in her life and work. <u>Since other</u>[4] painters spent a season or two in the country trying to come to terms with the scenes and settings of the Southwest—O'Keeffe stayed a lifetime. When the canvases of other <u>artists, working in the region</u>[5] faded from view and <u>then were neglected in the chronicle of American visual history</u>[6], her stylized images made an <u>indelible and permanent</u>[7] impression on countless eyes.

Between 1900 and 1945, the region now called New Mexico both fascinated <u>and also it perplexed</u>[8] two

1. A. NO CHANGE
   B. which
   C. that
   D. whose

2. F. NO CHANGE
   G. at the old age of ninety-eight
   H. at the age of ninety-eight years
   J. when she was ninety-eight years old

3. A. NO CHANGE
   B. creativity, and flourished
   C. creativity—flourished
   D. creativity, flourished

4. F. NO CHANGE
   G. Because other
   H. In that other
   J. Other

5. A. NO CHANGE
   B. artists working in the region,
   C. artists working in the region
   D. artists, who worked in the region

6. F. NO CHANGE
   G. got neglected then in the chronicle of American visual history
   H. were also then neglected in the American visual history chronicle
   J. then they were also totally neglected in the chronicle of American visual history

7. A. NO CHANGE
   B. indelible
   C. indelible—and permanent—
   D. indelible but permanent

8. F. NO CHANGE
   G. and perplexed
   H. while perplexing
   J. but perplexed

generations of American artists. Despite successes, [9] many of those artists wearied of the industrial world of the east. The vast expanse of the West offered a promise for inspiration. [10] For these artists, life and art, so separate in New York and Paris, seemed inextricably bounded [11] in Southwestern cultures. Painters of every persuasion were convinced [12] that sampling this mysterious phenomenon will strengthen [13] and enrich their own work. Most were touched by what D.H. Lawrence called the "spirit of the place." Besides the scenic beauty bathed in clear golden light. The [14] rich traditions of New Mexico's Indian and Hispanic people who were living there [15] became frequent subjects of the artists who traveled to Taos and Santa Fe.

9. A. NO CHANGE
   B. Despite successes
   C. In spite of their successes
   D. Ensuring successes,

10. F. NO CHANGE
    G. America's West, with its vast expanse, offered an inspiring promise.
    H. America's vast expanse of the West offered a promise for inspiration.
    J. Offering a promise of inspiration to the artists was the vast expanse of the American West.

11. A. NO CHANGE
    B. inextricably bound
    C. inextricable bounding
    D. inextricably bounding

12. F. NO CHANGE
    G. could be convinced
    H. will be convinced
    J. are convincing

13. A. NO CHANGE
    B. would strengthen
    C. strengthens
    D. strengthening

14. F. NO CHANGE
    G. light, the
    H. light the
    J. light: the

15. A. NO CHANGE
    B. who lived there
    C. living there
    D. OMIT the underlined portion.

Items 16 and 17 ask about the preceding passage as a whole.

16. Is the author's quote of D. H. Lawrence in the last paragraph appropriate?
    F. Yes, because the author is talking about how this spirit inspired artists, and the quote strengthens his argument.
    G. No, because the author has already made his point about the spirit, and the quote is redundant.
    H. No, because the author does not make it clear that Lawrence is an authority on the subject.
    J. Yes, because it is always a good idea to end an article with a quotation.

17. How might the author have developed the essay so that it was more interesting?
    A. The author could have told an anecdote about D. H. Lawrence.
    B. The author could have eliminated all mention of Georgia O'Keeffe.
    C. The author could have discussed the settling of New Mexico.
    D. The author could have been more specific about the other artists who went to the Southwest.

PASSAGE II

Chippewa Chief Demands Timber Payment

Early in November 1850, the work of a logging detail from Fort Gaines in the Minnesota Territory was interrupted by a party of Chippewa warriors who demanded payment for the timber. <u>The loggers refused, so</u> [18] the Indians, <u>acting at the direction of Chief Hole-in-the-Day</u> [19] confiscated the government's oxen. The loggers had established their camp on Chippewa lands <u>without his authorizing it</u> [20]. <u>Therefore</u> [21], in a move designed to force reimbursements for the timber, Hole-in-the-Day <u>was ordering</u> [22] his braves to seize the oxen.

Captain John Todd, the commanding officer at Fort Gaines, demanded <u>that the cattle had to be returned to them</u> [23]. The chief's reply was firm, <u>and at the same time, it was friendly</u> [24]. In his message to Captain Todd, Hole-in-the-Day explained that he had <u>delayed to seize</u> [25] the cattle until he could meet Todd in council and had sent a messenger to the officer requesting a conference at Crow Wing.

18. F. NO CHANGE
    G. The loggers refused—
    H. The loggers refused:
    J. The loggers refused so

19. A. NO CHANGE
    B. that acted at the direction of Chief Hole-in-the-Day,
    C. acting at the direction of Chief Hole-in-the-Day,
    D. (acting at the direction of Chief Hole-in-the-Day),

20. F. NO CHANGE
    G. without his authorization
    H. without their authorizing it
    J. without his authorization of it

21. A. NO CHANGE
    B. Henceforth
    C. Since
    D. On the contrary

22. F. NO CHANGE
    G. gave orders that
    H. orders
    J. ordered

23. A. NO CHANGE
    B. the return of the cattle
    C. the cattle's returning
    D. that they return the cattle

24. F. NO CHANGE
    G. but, at the same time, it was friendly
    H. yet friendly
    J. at the same time—friendly

25. A. NO CHANGE
    B. delayed to have seized
    C. delayed to seized
    D. delayed seizing

When Todd did not come, he <u>acted, additionally</u> [26] he later decided that since the army had not paid for timber cut the previous winter, he intended to keep the oxen until the tribe <u>was reimbursed by</u> [27] all the timber taken for the fort. Hole-in-the-Day concluded by saying, "Do not think hard of me, but I do as others would—the timber is mine." [28]

26. F. NO CHANGE
    G. acted but additionally
    H. acted. Additionally,
    J. acted additionally,

27. A. NO CHANGE
    B. reimbursed for
    C. reimbursed
    D. was reimbursed for

28. Is the author's use of the quote in the final paragraph appropriate?
    F. Yes, because it neatly summarizes the main point of the essay.
    G. No, because the chief's thoughts were irrelevant to the events.
    H. Yes, but the author should have included a quotation from Captain Todd.
    J. No, because quotations have no place in expository writing.

Item 29 asks about the preceding passage as a whole.

29. Which of the following best describes the overall character of the essay?
    A. Description of a scene
    B. Narration of events
    C. Comparison of two theories
    D. Argument for a change

C. QUIZ III (31 items; 20 minutes)

PASSAGE I

The Con Game is No Game

Most people have a certain crime that one believes[1] should be ranked as the worst of all crimes. For some, its'[2] murder; for others, it may be selling drugs to children. I believe, moreover,[3] that the worst of all crimes may be the confidence scheme.

The confidence scheme may seem an odd[4] choice for the worst crime since con games are usually nonviolent. Although,[5] it is a crime that ranks in heartlessness. Con artists are the most devious, the most harmful, and the most disruptive members of society because they break[6] down the most important bonds of the social order, honesty and trust[7].

The con games themselves are simplistic almost infantile[8]. They work on account of a con artist can[9] win complete confidence, talk fast enough to

1. A. NO CHANGE
   B. that they believe
   C. which one believes
   D. that you believe

2. F. NO CHANGE
   G. they are
   H. it's
   J. its

3. A. NO CHANGE
   B. however
   C. further
   D. therefore

4. F. NO CHANGE
   G. obvious
   H. irrelevant
   J. apt

5. A. NO CHANGE
   B. nonviolent, though
   C. nonviolent, but
   D. nonviolent, and

6. F. NO CHANGE
   G. it breaks
   H. of its breaking
   J. of them breaking

7. A. NO CHANGE
   B. order, honesty, and trust
   C. order: honesty and trust
   D. order: honesty, and trust

8. F. NO CHANGE
   G. simplistic; almost infantile
   H. simplistic, almost infantile
   J. simplistic, yet almost infantile

9. A. NO CHANGE
   B. on account of a con artist's ability to
   C. owing to a con artist's ability to
   D. because a con artist can

keep the victim slightly confused, <u>and dangling</u> [10] enough temptation to suppress any suspicion or skepticism. The primary targets of these criminals <u>will be</u> [11] the elderly and <u>women. (And they prefer to work in large crowds.)</u> [12]

10. F. NO CHANGE
    G. and dangles
    H. and has dangled
    J. and dangle

11. A. NO CHANGE
    B. to be
    C. are
    D. is

12. F. NO CHANGE
    G. women, and the con artists prefer to work in large crowds.
    H. women, preferring, of course, to work in large crowds.
    J. women (who prefer to work in large crowds).

Items 13-15 ask about the preceding passage as a whole.

13. Which of the following is most probably the author's opinion rather than a fact?
    A. Con artists are the most disruptive members of society.
    B. Most con games are nonviolent.
    C. Most of the targets are the elderly and women.
    D. Most con games are simple.

14. What would be the most logical continuation of the essay?
    F. A description of some confidence games
    G. An account of the elderly as crime victims in society
    H. An account of the author's experience with con artists
    J. An explanation of crowd psychology

15. What would strengthen the author's contention that con games rank first in heartlessness?
    A. Statistics to show the number of people who were taken in by the con artist
    B. A discussion of the way the police handle the problem
    C. An example that shows how the con artist breaks down honesty and trust
    D. An example to illustrate that con games are nonviolent and simple

PASSAGE II

Elizabeth I's Intellect Ruled Supreme

Elizabeth I had a sensuous and indulgent nature that she inherited from her mother, Anne Boleyn (who was beheaded by Henry VIII).[16] Splendor and pleasure is[17] the very air she breathed. She loved gaiety, laughter, and wit. Her vanity remained even, to old age. The[18] vanity of a coquette.

The statesmen who she outwitted[19] believed, almost to the end, that Elizabeth I was little more than a frivolous woman who was very vain.[20] But the Elizabeth whom they saw was far from being[21] all of Elizabeth. The willfulness of Henry and the triviality of Anne played over the surface of a nature so hard like[22] steel—a purely intellectual temperament. Her vanity and caprice carried no weight whatsoever[23] in state affairs. The coquette of the presence chamber had became[24] the coolest and hardest of politicians at the council board.

16. F. NO CHANGE
    G. (having been beheaded by Henry VIII)
    H. beheaded by Henry VIII
    J. OMIT the underlined portion.

17. A. NO CHANGE
    B. is,
    C. were
    D. were,

18. F. NO CHANGE
    G. remains, even to old age, the
    H. remains, even to old age the
    J. remained, even to old age, the

19. A. NO CHANGE
    B. that she outwitted
    C. whom she outwitted
    D. who she was outwitting

20. F. NO CHANGE
    G. and she was also very vain
    H. known for her great vanity
    J. OMIT the underlined portion.

21. A. NO CHANGE
    B. to be
    C. having been
    D. OMIT the underlined portion.

22. F. NO CHANGE
    G. as hard as
    H. so hard as
    J. as hard like

23. A. NO CHANGE
    B. no matter what
    C. whatever, at all
    D. whatever, despite everything

24. F. NO CHANGE
    G. became
    H. used to become
    J. becomes

It was this part that gave her marked superiority over[25] the statesmen of her time. No more nobler a group[26] of ministers ever gathered round the council board than those of Elizabeth, but she was the instrument of none. She listened and she weighed, but her policy, as a whole, was her own. It was the policy of good sense, not genius, she[27] endeavored to keep her throne, to keep England out of war, and she wanted[28] to restore civil and religious order.

25. A. NO CHANGE
B. superiority in regard to
C. superiority about
D. superior quality to

26. F. NO CHANGE
G. nobler a group,
H. nobler a group
J. more nobler of a group,

27. A. NO CHANGE
B. not genius she
C. not genius. She
D. —not genius, she

28. F. NO CHANGE
G. wanting
H. and wanting
J. and

Items 29-31 ask about the preceding passage as a whole.

29. What might logically have preceded this essay?
A. Some biographical background on Elizabeth I
B. A discussion of the wives of Henry VIII
C. A discussion of the politics of Tudor England
D. A discussion of the policies of Elizabeth's ministers

30. This essay is most probably taken from a:
F. scholarly work on Renaissance England.
G. biography of Elizabeth I.
H. diary kept by one of Elizabeth's ministers.
J. political science textbook.

31. Which of the following would most strengthen the essay?
A. Knowing who the ministers were and what their policies were
B. Examples of Elizabeth's dual nature
C. A discussion of Henry VIII's policies
D. A discussion of the role of the woman in Tudor England

TARGETED EDUCATIONAL SOLUTIONS.

Strategy Summary Sheet
ENGLISH

SUMMARY OF TEST MECHANICS: The ACT English Test contains five passages, each accompanied by approximately 15 items. The ACT English Test is 45 minutes long with a total of 75 multiple-choice items. The PLAN Reading Test is 30 minutes long with 50 multiple-choice items. The EXPLORE Reading Test is 30 minutes long with 40 multiple-choice items.

The ACT English section features two content areas, each containing three sub-categories. These six sub-categories represent the six English item-types. The multiple-choice English items are designed to measure an examinee's ability to identify effective expressions in standard written English, to recognize faults in usage and structure, and to choose effective revisions in sentences and paragraphs. They test common writing problems, such as consistency, logical expression, clarity, and precision. They do not ask examinees to define or use grammatical terms, nor do they test spelling or capitalization. Summarized below are the distributions of the items among the two English content areas for the ACT, the PLAN, and the EXPLORE.

NUMBER OF ITEMS PER CONTENT AREA

		ACT *(75 items)*	PLAN *(50 items)*	EXPLORE *(40 items)*
Usage/Mechanics:	Grammar and Usage	12	9	8
	Sentence Structure	18	14	11
	Punctuation	10	7	6
Rhetorical Skills:	Strategy	12	6	5
	Organization	11	7	5
	Style	12	7	5

ITEM-TYPES:

1. GRAMMAR AND USAGE

Grammar and Usage items test student knowledge of grammar. Topics include: subject-verb agreement, pronoun and antecedent agreement, correct placement of modifiers and the modified word, verb formation, pronoun case, correct use of comparative and superlative adjectives and adverbs, and idiomatic use of the English language.

2. SENTENCE STRUCTURE

Sentence Structure items test understanding of the relationships between and among clauses. This type of item might ask examinees to determine the logical placement of modifiers in a sentence or detect errors in shifts of construction.

3. PUNCTUATION

Punctuation items test student knowledge of the conventions of punctuation, emphasizing the relationship of punctuation to meaning, avoiding ambiguity, indicating appositives, *etc.* This type of item will often ask examinees to evaluate a portion of the sentence for correct punctuation.

4. STRATEGY

Strategy items are concerned with topic development in terms of focus and purpose. This type of item tests the ability to develop a given topic by selecting expressions that are appropriate to the passage's audience and purpose; accurately judging the effect of adding or deleting supporting material; and choosing effective opening, transitional, and closing statements.

5. ORGANIZATION

Organization items test the ability to organize and develop an essay by judging the relevance of statements in context. This type of item will ask examinees to make decisions about the order of sentences or paragraphs in context.

6. STYLE

Style items are concerned with word choice, tone, clarity, and economy. This type of item tests how well an examinee selects appropriate words and revises existing elements in a sentence to maintain the level of style and tone in an essay. These item-types also deal with ambiguous pronoun references, wordiness, and redundancy issues.

GENERAL STRATEGY:

1. After memorizing the directions, they can be safely ignored; therefore, do not waste valuable test time by re-reading instructions.
2. Read the entire selection for comprehension of the overall meaning. Look for possible errors. Mentally note how to correct possible errors.
3. Study the answer choices, looking for one that matches your anticipated answer.
4. Compare the answer choices. What makes them different from one another?
5. Do not choose answer choices that introduce new errors or change the meaning of the selection.
6. Use the Checklist for Possible Writing Errors, presented below, when searching for errors.

STRATEGY FOR USAGE/MECHANICS CONTENT AREA:

1. Check for grammatical errors.

   a. Look for obvious subject-verb agreement problems. The test-writers may try to obscure agreement by inserting material between the subject and the verb, inverting the sentence structure so that the verb precedes the subject, or introducing compound subjects.

   b. Check for proper pronoun usage. Remember that all pronouns must have antecedents. The pronoun must clearly refer to the antecedent and must agree in case, number, and person.

   c. Be alert to the proper usage of adjectives and adverbs. Note that adjectives modify nouns, while adverbs modify verbs. Also, adjectives and not adverbs follow linking verbs. Lastly, watch out for adjectives posing as adverbs. Sometimes, adjectives can be transformed into adverbs by adding "ly," so it is important to identify whether the modifier is an adjective or an adverb.

d. Watch for double negatives. Even though double negatives are sometimes used colloquially, they are not grammatically correct.

e. Check for proper noun clause introductions. A noun clause is a group of words that functions as the subject of a sentence and must be introduced with "that." Note that "because" and "why" should not be used to introduce noun clauses.

f. Watch for illogical comparisons. Comparisons can only be made between similar objects. Be alert to the use of the comparative form of an adjective (for comparing two objects) and the superlative form of an adjective (for comparing three or more objects). Remember that some adjectives and adverbs express the highest degree of quality; therefore, they cannot be improved upon.

g. Check for improper verb and mood shifts. The same verb tense and mood should be used within a sentence or paragraph unless there's a valid reason for a change. Also, be alert to the improper usage of verb tenses in general. Make sure that the verb tense within a sentence or a paragraph is logical.

h. Make sure that the choice of verb tense in a sentence reflects the sequence and the duration of the events described.

i. Check for idiomatic expression errors such as wrong prepositions, improper word choice, and gerund-infinitive switching.

2. Check for sentence structure errors.

a. Check to see if the sentence is a run-on.

b. Be aware of comma splice errors in sentences.

c. Check to see if the sentence is a fragment.

d. Make sure the sentence contains logical coordinating conjunctions.

e. Watch for faulty parallelism in a sentence. Note that whenever elements of a sentence perform similar or equal functions, they should have the same form.

f. Be alert for sentence structures in which two otherwise separate ideas are joined together by a later element, or split constructions. Check that any interrupted thought is correctly completed. A simple way to check for this type of error is to read the sentence without the intervening material—the sentence should make sense, be grammatically correct, and represent a complete thought.

g. Look for misplaced modifiers. Modifiers should be placed as close as possible to what they modify. Errors in placement of modifiers create ambiguous and illogical constructions.

h. Be alert to misplacements or omissions of certain elements of a sentence. These errors lead to unintended meanings. Makes sure the intended meaning of the sentence follows from its logical structure.

3. Check for punctuation errors.

a. Check to see if the comma is used correctly in the sentence. The following list summarizes the most important uses and misuses of commas.

i. Use a comma before coordinating conjunctions.

   ii. Use commas for clarity.

   iii. Use commas to separate coordinate adjectives, words in a series, and nouns in direct address.

   iv. Use commas to separate quotations and introductory phrases.

   v. Use pairs of commas to set off appositive, parenthetical, and non-restrictive elements.

   vi. A comma should not be used to separate a subject from its verb.

   vii. Commas should not be used to set off restrictive or necessary clauses or phrases.

   viii. A comma should not be used in place of a conjunction.

b. Check for correct semicolon usage. The following list summarizes the appropriate uses of semicolons.

   i. Use a semicolon to separate two complete ideas.

   ii. Use a semicolon to separate a series of phrases with commas and a series of numbers.

   iii. Use a semicolon to separate independent clauses.

   iv. Do not use semicolons to separate dependent clauses.

c. Check for correct colon usage. The following list summarizes the rules for colon usage.

   i. A colon should be placed after the salutation in a business letter.

   ii. Use a colon to separate hours from minutes.

   iii. Colons are used to precede lists of three of more items or long quotations.

   iv. A colon should be used to introduce a question.

   v. Do not use colons to introduce or to call attention to elaboration or explanation if that is already signaled by expressions such as "like," "for example," or "such as."

d. Check for correct end-stop punctuation. Make sure that any material that includes a period is a complete sentence.

e. Check for correct usage of dashes. The following presents the rules for situations requiring the use of a dash.

   i. Use a dash for emphasis or to set off an explanatory group of words.

   ii. Use a dash before a word or group of words that indicates a summation or reversal of what preceded it.

   iii. Use a dash to mark a sudden break in thought that leaves a sentence unfinished.

f. Check for correct hyphen usage. Remember that hyphens are used with a compound modifier preceding a noun and with fractions that serve as adjectives or adverbs.

g. Check the selection for quotation errors. Quotation marks are used to enclose the actual words of a speaker or writer, to emphasize words used in a special or unusual sense, and to set off titles of short themes or parts of a larger work. Quotation marks are not used for indirect quotations or to justify a poor choice of words.

h. Check to see if a punctuation mark is need to clarify the selection.

STRATEGY FOR RHETORICAL SKILLS CONTENT AREA:

1. Check to see if the strategy used by the writer is appropriate.
   a. Make sure that all supporting material is appropriate to the selection.
   b. Be alert to opening, transitional, and concluding sentences. Check to see if they are effective or if they need improvement.
   c. Read the selection for the main ideas and identify the main purpose of the entire passage.
   d. Look for diction, purpose, and tone clues that identify the writer's audience.
2. Check for organization errors.
   a. Determine whether the development of the paragraph is appropriate. Each paragraph should have only one main idea.
   b. Be aware of the two levels of organization.
      i. Check for sentence-level structure errors, such as grammar, idiomatic usage, and clarity of expression.
      ii. Check for paragraph-level structure errors. Look for the basic pattern of development. Make sure that the organization of the paragraphs is logical and coherent. Look for proper introductory, transitional, and concluding statements.
3. Check for stylistic problems.
   a. Make sure that the sentences are concise and to the point.
      i. Look for awkward sentences or weak passive verbs.
      ii. Look for needlessly wordy sentences.
   b. Check for ambiguous sentences. Such sentences run two or more ideas together and require further clarification to separate and connect the disparate ideas.
   c. Check for low-level usage language.

CHECKLIST FOR POSSIBLE WRITING ERRORS:

1. *Verbs:* Does the sentence have a main verb? Do all verbs agree with their subjects? Are they in the correct tense?
2. *Pronouns:* Do all pronouns have clearly identifiable referents? Do they agree with their referents? Are they in the proper case?
3. *Adjectives and Adverbs:* Do all adjectives correctly modify nouns? Do all adverbs correctly modify verbs or adjectives? Is the use of a specific adjective or adverb appropriate?
4. *Prepositions:* Are all prepositions used idiomatically?
5. *Conjunctions:* Are all conjunctions consistent with the logic of the sentence?
6. *Modifier:* If the sentence has a modifier, is it close to what it modifies? Is the idea clearly and logically presented?

7. *Comparisons:* If the sentence makes a comparison, are like things being compared? Is the idea clearly and logically presented?

8. *Parallelism:* If the sentence includes a series of ideas, are the ideas presented in the same form?

9. *Diction:* Do the words mean what the sentence intends for them to mean?

10. *Conciseness:* Does the sentence use more words than necessary?

11. *Directness:* Can the sentence be worded more directly?

ADDITIONAL STRATEGIES FROM IN-CLASS DISCUSSION: ______________________________

Mathematics

TARGETED EDUCATIONAL SOLUTIONS.

Cambridge Course Concept Outline
MATHEMATICS

CORE LESSON

The items in this section accompany the Core Lesson of the Mathematics Lesson. They demonstrate the Mathematics concepts and skills that are tested by the ACT, the PLAN, and the EXPLORE. You will work through the items with your instructor in class. You may use any available space in the section for scratch work. Answers are on page 934.

DIRECTIONS: Solve each item and choose the correct answer choice. Then, fill in the corresponding oval on the bubble sheet.

Allocate time wisely. Try to solve as many items as possible, returning to skipped items if time permits.

Calculator use is permitted on this test; however, some items are best solved without the use of a calculator.

Note: Unless otherwise stated, assume all of the following.

1. Illustrative figures are NOT necessarily drawn to scale.
2. The word *average* indicates arithmetic mean.
3. The word *line* indicates a straight line.
4. Geometric figures lie in a plane.

---

1. If the price of fertilizer has been decreased from 3 pounds for \$2 to 5 pounds for \$2, how many more pounds of fertilizer can be purchased for \$10 than could have been purchased before?

   (A) 2
   (B) 8
   (C) 10
   (D) 12
   (E) 15

2. Five students formed a political club to support a candidate for local office. They project that club membership will double every three weeks. Which of the following can be used to find the number of members that the club projects to have after twelve weeks?

   (F) $5(2^{2/3})$
   (G) $5(2^{3/2})$
   (H) $5(2^{12/3})$
   (J) $5(2^{3/12})$
   (K) $5 + 5(2^4)$

3. If $\frac{2x-5}{3} = -4x$, then $x =$

   (A) -1
   (B) $-\frac{5}{14}$
   (C) 0
   (D) $\frac{5}{14}$
   (E) 1

4. A vending machine dispenses k cups of coffee, each at a cost of c cents, every day. During a period d days long, what is the amount of money in dollars taken in by the vending machine from the sale of coffee?

   (F) $\frac{100kc}{d}$
   (G) kcd
   (H) $\frac{dk}{c}$
   (J) $\frac{kcd}{100}$
   (K) $\frac{kc}{100d}$

5. If $f(x) = 2x - 3$ and $g(x) = x^2 - 2$, then $f(g(2)) =$

(A) –1
(B) 0
(C) 1
(D) 4
(E) 7

6. If $|x + 3| = 5$, then $x =$

(F) –8 or 2
(G) –2 or 8
(H) –8
(J) –2
(K) 2 or 8

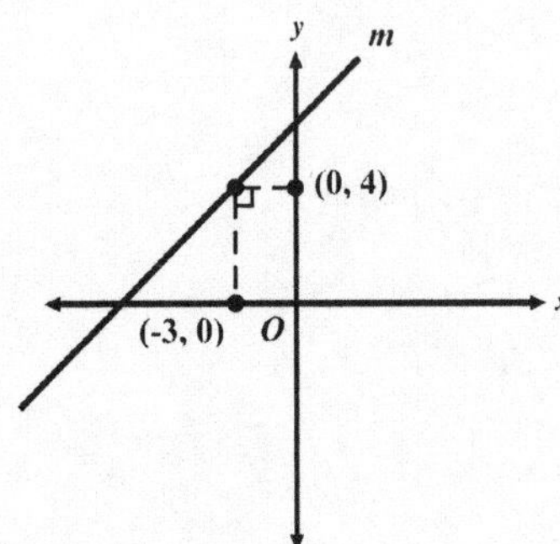

7. In the figure above, line m has a slope of 1. What is the y-intercept of the line?

(A) –5
(B) –3
(C) 0
(D) 3
(E) 7

8. If a circle has a radius of 1, what is its area?

(F) $\frac{\pi}{2}$
(G) π
(H) 2π
(J) 4π
(K) π^2

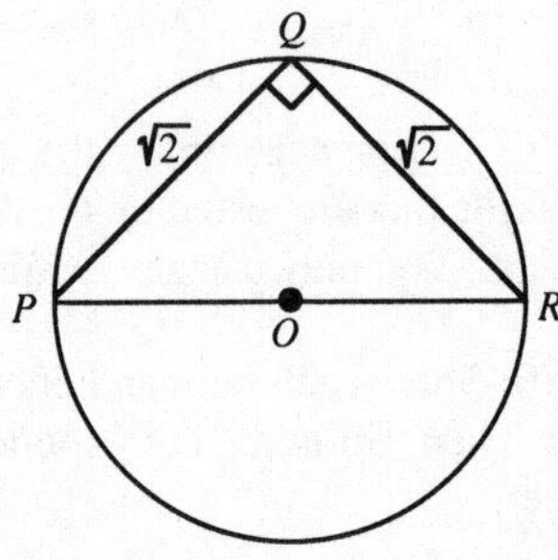

9. In the figure above, ΔPQR is inscribed in a circle with center O. What is the area of the circle?

(A) $\frac{\pi}{2}$
(B) $\frac{\pi}{\sqrt{2}}$
(C) π
(D) $\pi\sqrt{2}$
(E) 2π

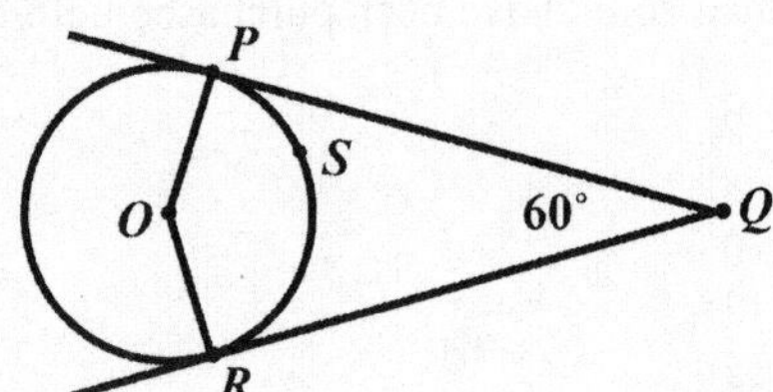

10. In the figure above, $\overrightarrow{QP}$ is tangent to circle O at point P, and $\overrightarrow{QR}$ is tangent to circle O at point R. What is the degree measure of the minor arc PSR?

(F) 30
(G) 60
(H) 90
(J) 120
(K) 180

11. In the figure below, $\sin A = ?$

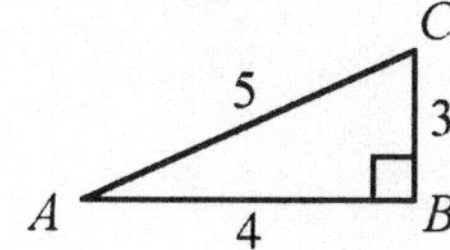

(A) $\frac{3}{4}$
(B) $\frac{3}{5}$
(C) $\frac{4}{5}$
(D) $\frac{5}{3}$
(E) $\frac{5}{4}$

12. What is the average of 8.5, 7.8, and 7.7?

(F) 8.3
(G) 8.2
(H) 8.1
(J) 8.0
(K) 7.9

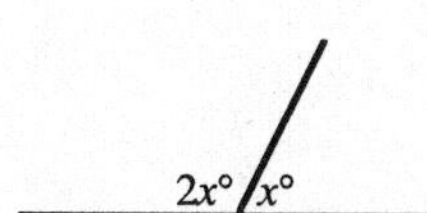

13. In the figure above, $x =$

(A) 15
(B) 30
(C) 45
(D) 60
(E) 120

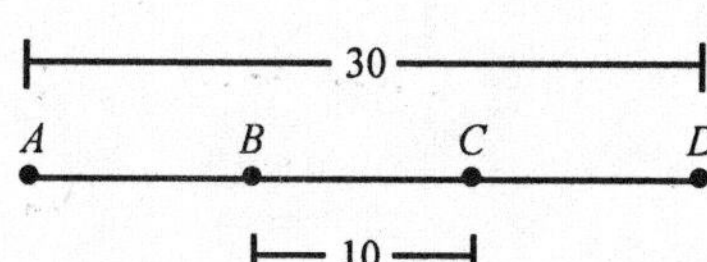

Note: Figure not drawn to scale.

14. In the figure above, what is the length of $\overline{AB} + \overline{CD}$?

(F) 5
(G) 10
(H) 15
(J) 20
(K) 40

Items 15-16 refer to the following figure.

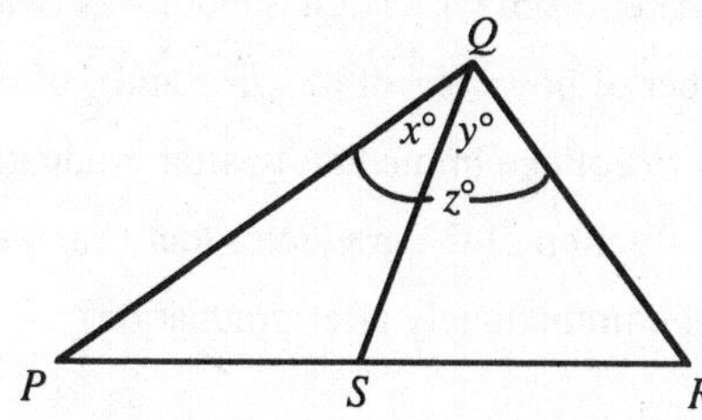

Note: Figure not drawn to scale.

15. Which of the following must be true?

I. $PS < SR$
II. $z = 90$
III. $x > y$

(A) I only
(B) I and II only
(C) I and III only
(D) I, II, and III
(E) Neither I, II, nor III

16. Which of the following must be true?

I. $PR > PS$
II. $z > x$
III. $x + y = z$

(F) I only
(G) I and II only
(H) I and III only
(J) I, II, and III
(K) Neither I, II, nor III

17. In a certain year, the number of girls who graduated from City High School was twice the number of boys. If $\frac{3}{4}$ of the girls and $\frac{5}{6}$ of the boys went to college immediately after graduation, what fraction of the graduates that year went to college immediately after graduation?

(A) $\frac{5}{36}$
(B) $\frac{16}{27}$
(C) $\frac{7}{9}$
(D) $\frac{29}{36}$
(E) $\frac{31}{36}$

18. A jar contains black and white marbles. If there are ten marbles in the jar, then which of the following could NOT be the ratio of black to white marbles?

(F) 9:1
(G) 7:3
(H) 1:1
(J) 1:4
(K) 1:10

19. If n is a negative number, which of the following is the <u>least</u> in value?

(A) $-n$
(B) $n-n$
(C) $n+n$
(D) n^2
(E) n^4

NOTES AND STRATEGIES

20. If a machine produces 240 thingamabobs per hour, how many minutes are needed for the machine to produce 30 thingamabobs?

(F) 6
(G) 7.5
(H) 8
(J) 12
(K) 12.5

21. Of the 120 people in a room, $\frac{3}{5}$ are women. If $\frac{2}{3}$ of the people are married, what is the maximum number of women in the room who could be unmarried?

(A) 80
(B) 72
(C) 48
(D) 40
(E) 32

22. Three friends are playing a game in which each person simultaneously displays one of three hand signs: a clenched fist, an open palm, or two extended fingers. How many unique combinations of the signs are possible?

(F) 3
(G) 9
(H) 10
(J) 12
(K) 27

23. If $\frac{1}{3}$ of the number of girls in a school equals $\frac{1}{5}$ of the total number of students, what is the ratio of girls to boys in the school?

(A) 5:3
(B) 3:2
(C) 2:5
(D) 1:3
(E) 1:5

24. Peter walked from point P to point Q and back again, a total distance of 2 miles. If he averaged 4 miles per hour on the trip from P to Q and 5 miles per hour on the return trip, what was his average walking speed for the entire trip?

(F) $2\frac{2}{9}$
(G) 4
(H) $4\frac{4}{9}$
(J) $4\frac{1}{2}$
(K) 5

25. After a 20 percent decrease in price, the cost of an item is D dollars. What was the price of the item before the decrease?

(A) $0.75D$
(B) $0.80D$
(C) $1.20D$
(D) $1.25D$
(E) $1.5D$

26. On a certain trip, a motorist drove 10 miles at 30 miles per hour, 10 miles at 40 miles per hour, and 10 miles at 50 miles per hour. What portion of her total driving time was spent driving 50 miles per hour?

(F) $1\frac{13}{51}$
(G) $\frac{5}{7}$
(H) $\frac{5}{12}$
(J) $\frac{1}{3}$
(K) $\frac{12}{47}$

27. What is the maximum number of non-overlapping sections that can be created when a circle is crossed by three straight lines?

(A) 3
(B) 4
(C) 5
(D) 6
(E) 7

28. At Glenridge High School, 20 percent of the students are seniors. If all of the seniors attended the school play, and 60 percent of all the students attended the play, what percent of the <u>non-seniors</u> attended the play?

(F) 20%
(G) 40%
(H) 50%
(J) 60%
(K) 100%

Water Usage in Cubic Feet

29. The water meter at a factory displays the reading above. What is the <u>minimum</u> number of cubic feet of water that the factory must use before four of the five digits on the meter are again the same?

(A) 10,000
(B) 1,000
(C) 999
(D) 666
(E) 9

30. A telephone call from City X to City Y costs \$1.00 for the first three minutes and \$0.25 for each additional minute thereafter. What is the <u>maximum</u> length of time, in minutes, that a caller could talk for \$3.00?

(F) 8
(G) 10
(H) 11
(J) 12
(K) 13

31. In the figure below, $m + n + o + p + q + r = ?$

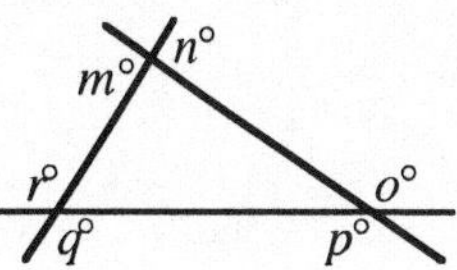

(A) 360
(B) 540
(C) 720
(D) 900
(E) Cannot be determined from the given information

32. $\frac{8}{9} - \frac{7}{8} =$

(F) $\frac{1}{72}$
(G) $\frac{1}{8}$
(H) $\frac{1}{7}$
(J) $\frac{15}{72}$
(K) $\frac{15}{7}$

33. $\sqrt{1 - \left(\frac{2}{9} + \frac{1}{36} + \frac{1}{18}\right)} =$

(A) $\frac{1}{5}$
(B) $\sqrt{\frac{2}{3}}$
(C) $\frac{5}{6}$
(D) 1
(E) $\sqrt{3}$

34. $\frac{1}{2} \bullet \frac{2}{3} \bullet \frac{3}{4} \bullet \frac{4}{5} \bullet \frac{5}{6} \bullet \frac{6}{7} \bullet \frac{7}{8} =$

(F) $\frac{1}{56}$
(G) $\frac{1}{8}$
(H) $\frac{28}{37}$
(J) $\frac{41}{43}$
(K) $\frac{55}{56}$

35. $86(37) - 37(85) =$

(A) 0
(B) 1
(C) 37
(D) 85
(E) 86

36. Which of the following is a prime factorization of 120?

(F) (2)(2)(15)
(G) (2)(3)(4)(5)
(H) (2)(2)(3)(10)
(J) (2)(2)(2)(3)(5)
(K) (2)(2)(3)(3)(5)

37. $-4.01(3.2) + 0.2(0.4) = ?$

(A) -12.752
(B) -4.536
(C) 0.432
(D) 1.251
(E) 12.783

38. $\frac{0.2521 \cdot 8.012}{1.014}$ is approximately equal to

(F) 0.25
(G) 0.5
(H) 1.0
(J) 1.5
(K) 2.0

39. Which of the following fractions is the largest?

(A) $\frac{111}{221}$
(B) $\frac{75}{151}$
(C) $\frac{333}{998}$
(D) $\frac{113}{225}$
(E) $\frac{101}{301}$

40. If $z = \frac{x+y}{x}$, $1 - z =$

(F) $\frac{1-x+y}{x}$
(G) $\frac{x+y-1}{x}$
(H) $\frac{1-x-y}{x}$
(J) $-\frac{y}{x}$
(K) $1-x-y$

41. $0.125 \cdot 0.125 \cdot 64 = ?$

(A) 0.625
(B) 0.125
(C) 0.5
(D) 1
(E) 8

42. $\frac{0.111 \cdot 0.666}{0.166 \cdot 0.125}$ is approximately equal to which of the following?

(F) 6.8
(G) 4.3
(H) 3.6
(J) 1.6
(K) 0.9

43. If the senior class has 360 students, of whom $\frac{5}{12}$ are women, and the junior class has 350 students, of whom $\frac{4}{7}$ are women, how many more women are there in the junior class than in the senior class?

(A) $(360-350)(\frac{4}{7}-\frac{5}{12})$
(B) $\frac{(360-350)(\frac{4}{7}-\frac{5}{12})}{2}$
(C) $(\frac{4}{7}\cdot\frac{5}{12})(360-350)$
(D) $(\frac{4}{7}\cdot 350)-(\frac{5}{12}\cdot 360)$
(E) $(\frac{5}{12}\cdot 360)-(\frac{4}{7}\cdot 350)$

44. If the price of candy increases from 5 pounds for \$7 to 3 pounds for \$7, how much less candy (in pounds) can be purchased for \$3.50 at the new price than at the old price?

(F) $\frac{2}{7}$
(G) 1
(H) $1\frac{17}{35}$
(J) 2
(K) $3\frac{34}{35}$

45. If n is any integer, which of the following is always an odd integer?

(A) $n-1$
(B) $n+1$
(C) $n+2$
(D) $2n+1$
(E) $2n+2$

46. Which of the following expressions represents the product of two consecutive integers?

(F) $2n+1$
(G) $2n+n$
(H) $2n^2$
(J) n^2+1
(K) n^2+n

47. If n is any integer, which of the following expressions <u>must</u> be even?

I. $2n$
II. $2n+n$
III. $2n \bullet n$

(A) I only
(B) II only
(C) III only
(D) I and II only
(E) I and III only

NOTES AND STRATEGIES

48. If n is the first number in a series of three consecutive even numbers, which of the following expressions represents the sum of the three numbers?

(F) $n+2$
(G) $n+4$
(H) $n+6$
(J) $3n+6$
(K) $6(3n)$

49. If n is an odd number, which of the following expressions represents the third odd number following n?

(A) $n+3$
(B) $n+4$
(C) $n+6$
(D) $3n+3$
(E) $4n+4$

50. If n is any odd integer, which of the following expressions must also be odd?

I. $n+n$
II. $n+n+n$
III. $n \cdot n \cdot n$

(F) I only
(G) II only
(H) III only
(J) II and III only
(K) I, II, and III

51. If n is a negative number, which of the following expressions must be positive?

I. $2n$
II. n^2
III. n^5

(A) I only
(B) II only
(C) III only
(D) I and II only
(E) II and III only

52. If $0 < x < 1$, which of the following expressions is the largest?

(F) x
(G) $2x$
(H) x^2
(J) x^3
(K) $x+1$

53. If $-1 < x < 0$, which of the following expressions is the largest?

(A) -1
(B) x
(C) $2x$
(D) x^3
(E) $x-1$

54. If set $S = \{2, 3, 4\}$ and set P is the set of all products of different elements in set S, then set $P =$

(F) $\{6, 8, 12\}$
(G) $\{6, 8, 18\}$
(H) $\{6, 8, 12, 24\}$
(J) $\{6, 8, 12, 18, 24\}$
(K) $\{6, 8, 12, 18, 24, 36\}$

55. If set X is the set of all integers between 1 and 24, inclusive, that are evenly divisible by 3, and set Y is the set of all integers between 1 and 24, inclusive, that are evenly divisible by 4, what is the set of all elements in both sets X and Y?

(A) $\{12\}$
(B) $\{3, 4\}$
(C) $\{12, 24\}$
(D) $\{4, 12, 24\}$
(E) $\{3, 4, 12, 24\}$

56. If x is an element of set X, in which set X is the set of integers evenly divisible by 3 such that $6 < x < 11$, and y is an element of set Y, where set Y is the set of integers evenly divisible by 4 such that $7 < y < 12$, what is the intersection of sets X and Y?

(F) {}
(G) {8}
(H) {9}
(J) {12}
(K) {8, 12}

57. If set S is the set of all positive odd integers and set T is the set of all positive even integers, then the union of sets S and T (the set of all elements that are in either set or both sets) is the set of

(A) positive integers
(B) integers
(C) even integers
(D) odd integers
(E) real numbers

58. In a certain school, each of the 72 music students must participate in the marching band, the orchestra, or both. If only music students participate, 48 students total participate in the marching band, and 54 students total participate in the orchestra, how many students participate in both programs?

(F) 6
(G) 18
(H) 24
(J) 30
(K) 36

59. $|-2| + 3 - |-4| =$

(A) –5
(B) –4
(C) –1
(D) 1
(E) 9

60. $|5| - |-5| + |-3| =$

(F) –8
(G) –3
(H) 3
(J) 8
(K) 13

61. $|-3| \cdot |-4| \cdot -5 =$

(A) –60
(B) –30
(C) –7
(D) 20
(E) 60

62. $(3 + i)(4 - 3i) = ?$

(F) $12 + 3i^2$
(G) $12 - 3i^2$
(H) $9 - 5i^2$
(J) $9 - 5i$
(K) $15 - 5i$

63. $\frac{1}{2-i} = ?$

(A) -2
(B) -1
(C) $\frac{2+i}{5}$
(D) $\frac{2-i}{5}$
(E) $\frac{2+i}{3}$

64. A jar contains 24 white marbles and 48 black marbles. What percent of the marbles in the jar are black?

(F) 10%
(G) 25%
(H) $33\frac{1}{3}$%
(J) 60%
(K) $66\frac{2}{3}$%

65. A group of 3 friends shared the cost of a tape recorder. If Andy, Barbara, and Donna each paid \$12, \$30, and \$18, respectively, then Donna paid what percent of the cost of the tape recorder?

(A) 10%
(B) 30%
(C) $33\frac{1}{3}\%$
(D) 50%
(E) $66\frac{2}{3}\%$

66. Twenty students attended Professor Rodriguez's class on Monday and 25 students attended on Tuesday. The number of students who attended on Tuesday was what percent of the number of students who attended on Monday?

(F) 5%
(G) 20%
(H) 25%
(J) 80%
(K) 125%

67. If the population of a town was 20,000 in 1990 and 16,000 in 2000, what was the percentage decline in the town's population?

(A) 50%
(B) 25%
(C) 20%
(D) 10%
(E) 5%

Items 68-70 refer to the following table.

CAPITAL CITY FIRES	
Year	*Number of Fires*
1992	100
1993	125
1994	140
1995	150
1996	135

68. The number of fires in 1992 was what percentage of the number of fires in 1993?

(F) 25%
(G) $66\frac{2}{3}\%$
(H) 80%
(J) 100%
(K) 125%

69. The number of fires in 1996 was what percentage of the number of fires in 1995?

(A) 90%
(B) 82%
(C) 50%
(D) 25%
(E) 10%

70. What was the percent decrease in the number of fires from 1995 to 1996?

(F) 10%
(G) 25%
(H) 50%
(J) 82%
(K) 90%

71. A groom must divide 12 quarts of oats between two horses. If Dobbin is to receive twice as much as Pegasus, how many quarts of oats should the groom give to Dobbin?

(A) 4
(B) 6
(C) 8
(D) 9
(E) 10

72. If the ratio of John's allowance to Lucy's allowance is 3:2, and the ratio of Lucy's allowance to Bob's allowance is 3:4, what is the ratio of John's allowance to Bob's allowance?

(F) 1:6
(G) 2:5
(H) 1:2
(J) 3:4
(K) 9:8

73. If 4.5 pounds of chocolate cost $10, how many pounds of chocolate can be purchased for $12?

(A) $4\frac{3}{4}$
(B) $5\frac{2}{5}$
(C) $5\frac{1}{2}$
(D) $5\frac{3}{4}$
(E) 6

NOTES AND STRATEGIES

74. At Star Lake Middle School, 45 percent of the students bought a yearbook. If 540 students bought yearbooks, how many students did not buy a yearbook?

(F) 243
(G) 540
(H) 575
(J) 660
(K) 957

75. In the equation $y = kx$, k is the constant of variation. If y is equal to 6 when $x = 2.4$, what is the constant of variation?

(A) 0.4
(B) 2.5
(C) 3.4
(D) 3.6
(E) 14.4

76. A train traveling at a constant speed, k, takes 90 minutes to go from point P to point Q, a distance of 45 miles. What is the value of k, in miles per hour?

(F) 20
(G) 30
(H) 45
(J) 60
(K) 75

77. The cost of picture framing depends on the outer perimeter of the frame. If a 15" × 15" picture frame costs $35 more than a 10" × 10" picture frame, what is the cost of framing, in dollars per inch?

(A) $3.50
(B) $2.75
(C) $2.25
(D) $1.75
(E) $1.50

78. Walking at a constant speed of 4 miles per hour, it took Jill exactly 1 hour to walk home from school. If she walked at a constant speed of 5 miles per hour, how many minutes did the trip take?

(F) 48
(G) 54
(H) 56
(J) 72
(K) 112

79. Ms. Peters drove from her home to the park at an average speed of 30 miles per hour and returned home along the same route at an average speed of 40 miles per hour. If her driving time from home to the park was 20 minutes, how many minutes did it take Ms. Peters to drive from the park to her home?

(A) 7.5
(B) 12
(C) 15
(D) 24
(E) 30

80. Which of the following is the larger of two numbers the product of which is 600 and the sum of which is five times the difference between the two?

(F) 10
(G) 15
(H) 20
(J) 30
(K) 50

81. If $\frac{1}{3}$ of a number is 3 more than $\frac{1}{4}$ of the number, then what is the number?

(A) 18
(B) 24
(C) 30
(D) 36
(E) 48

82. If $\frac{3}{5}$ of a number is 4 more than $\frac{1}{2}$ of the number, then what is the number?

(F) 20
(G) 28
(H) 35
(J) 40
(K) 56

83. If both 16 and 9 are divided by n, the remainder is 2. What is n?

(A) 3
(B) 4
(C) 5
(D) 6
(E) 7

84. The sum of the digits of a three-digit number is 16. If the tens digit of the number is 3 times the units digit, and the units digit is $\frac{1}{4}$ of the hundreds digit, then what is the number?

(F) 446
(G) 561
(H) 682
(J) 862
(K) 914

85. If the sum of five consecutive integers is 40, what is the smallest of the five integers?

(A) 4
(B) 5
(C) 6
(D) 7
(E) 8

86. If $a^3 + b = 3 + a^3$, then $b =$

(F) 3^3
(G) $3\sqrt{3}$
(H) 3
(J) $\sqrt[3]{3}$
(K) $-\sqrt{3}$

87. Which of the following expressions is equivalent to $4a + 3b - (-2a - 3b)$?

(A) $2a$
(B) $12ab$
(C) $2a + 6b$
(D) $6a + 6b$
(E) $8a + 9b$

88. If $x = 2$, what is the value of $x^2 + 2x - 2$?

(F) −2
(G) 0
(H) 2
(J) 4
(K) 6

89. If $x = 2$, then $\frac{1}{x^2} + \frac{1}{x} - \frac{x}{2} =$

(A) $-\frac{3}{4}$
(B) $-\frac{1}{4}$
(C) 0
(D) $\frac{1}{4}$
(E) $\frac{1}{2}$

90. If $\frac{1}{3}x = 10$, then $\frac{1}{6}x =$

(F) $\frac{1}{15}$
(G) $\frac{2}{3}$
(H) 2
(J) 5
(K) 30

91. If $p = 1$, $q = 2$, and $r = 3$, then $\frac{(q \cdot r)(r - q)}{(q - p)(p \cdot q)} =$

(A) −3
(B) −1
(C) 0
(D) 3
(E) 6

92. $\frac{9(x^2y^3)^6}{(3x^6y^9)^2} =$

(F) 1
(G) 3
(H) x^2y^3
(J) $3x^2y^3$
(K) $x^{12}y^{12}$

93. $2(4^{-1/2}) - 2^0 + 2^{3/2} + 2^{-2} =$

(A) $-2\sqrt{2} - \frac{1}{4}$
(B) $2\sqrt{2} - \frac{1}{4}$
(C) $2\sqrt{2}$
(D) $2\sqrt{2} + \frac{1}{4}$
(E) $2\sqrt{2} + \frac{5}{4}$

94. Which of the following expressions is equivalent to $\frac{x^2 - y^2}{x + y}$?

(F) $x^2 - y^2$
(G) $x^2 + y^2$
(H) $x^2 + y$
(J) $x + y^2$
(K) $x - y$

95. Which of the following expressions is equivalent to $\frac{x^2 - x - 6}{x + 2}$?

(A) $x^2 - \frac{x}{2} - 3$
(B) $x^2 - 2$
(C) $x - 2$
(D) $x - 3$
(E) x

96. Which of the following is the factorization of $6x^2 + 4x - 2$?

(F) $(6x + 1)(x - 3)$
(G) $(6x + 3)(x - 1)$
(H) $(3x - 1)(2x - 2)$
(J) $(2x + 2)(3x - 1)$
(K) $(2x + 4)(3x - 2)$

97. In a geometric sequence of positive numbers, the fourth term is 125 and the sixth term is 3,125. What is the second term of the sequence?

(A) 1
(B) 5
(C) 10
(D) 25
(E) 50

98. City University projects that a planned expansion will increase the number of enrolled students every year for the next five years by 50 percent. If 400 students enroll in the first year of the plan, how many students are expected to enroll in the fifth year of the plan?

(F) 200
(G) 600
(H) 675
(J) 1,350
(K) 2,025

99. Jimmy's uncle deposited \$1,000 into a college fund account and promised that at the start of each year, he would deposit an amount equal to 10% of the account balance. If no other deposits or withdrawals were made and no additional interest accrued, what was the account balance after three additional annual deposits were made by Jimmy's uncle?

(A) \$1,030
(B) \$1,300
(C) \$1,331
(D) \$1,500
(E) \$1,830

100. A tank with a capacity of 2,400 liters is filled with water. If a valve is opened that drains 25 percent of the contents of the tank every minute, what is the volume of water (in liters) that remains in the tank after 3 minutes?

(F) 1,800
(G) 1,350
(H) 1,012.5
(J) 600
(K) 325.75

NOTES AND STRATEGIES

101. If $(2 + 3)(1 + x) = 25$, then $x =$

(A) $\frac{1}{5}$
(B) $\frac{1}{4}$
(C) 1
(D) 4
(E) 5

102. If $\frac{12}{x+1} - 1 = 2$, and $x \neq -1$, then $x =$

(F) 1
(G) 2
(H) 3
(J) 11
(K) 12

103. If $\frac{x}{x+2} = \frac{3}{4}$, and $x \neq -2$, then $x =$

(A) 6
(B) 4
(C) 3
(D) 2
(E) 1

104. If $\frac{x}{x-2} - \frac{x+2}{2(x-2)} = 8$, and $x \neq 2$, which of the following is the complete solution set for x?

(F) {}
(G) {–2}
(H) {2}
(J) {4}
(K) {8}

105. If $\frac{3}{x-2} > \frac{1}{6}$, which of the following defines the possible values for x?

(A) $x < 20$
(B) $x > 0$
(C) $x > 2$
(D) $0 < x < 20$
(E) $2 < x < 20$

106. If $\sqrt{2x+1} - 1 = 4$, then $x =$

(F) –5
(G) –1
(H) 1
(J) 12
(K) 24

107. Which of the following is the complete solution set for $\sqrt{3x-2} - 3 = -4$?

(A) {}
(B) {–1}
(C) {1}
(D) {–1, 1}
(E) {1, 2}

108. If $\sqrt{2x-5} = 2\sqrt{5-2x}$, then $x =$

(F) 1
(G) 2
(H) $\frac{5}{2}$
(J) 10
(K) 15

109. Which of the following is the complete solution set for $\sqrt{x^2+9} = 5$?

(A) {–4, 4}
(B) {–4}
(C) {0}
(D) {4}
(E) {}

110. If $4^{x+2} = 64$, then $x =$

(F) 1
(G) 2
(H) 3
(J) 4
(K) 5

111. If $8^x = 2^{x+3}$, then $x =$

(A) 0
(B) 1
(C) $\frac{2}{3}$
(D) 3
(E) $\frac{3}{2}$

112. If $3^{2x} = \frac{1}{81}$, then $x =$

(F) -2
(G) $-\frac{3}{2}$
(H) $-\frac{2}{3}$
(J) $\frac{2}{3}$
(K) $\frac{3}{2}$

113. If $5^3 = (\sqrt{5})^{-2x}$, then $5^x =$

(A) $\frac{1}{125}$
(B) $\frac{1}{25}$
(C) $\frac{1}{5}$
(D) 5
(E) 25

114. Which of the following is the complete solution set for $\left|\frac{2x+1}{3}\right| = 5$?

(F) $\{-8, -7\}$
(G) $\{-8, 7\}$
(H) $\{-7, 8\}$
(J) $\{7\}$
(K) $\{8\}$

115. Which of the following is the complete solution set for $|x + 6| = 3x$?

(A) $\{-3, \frac{3}{2}\}$
(B) $\{-\frac{3}{2}, 3\}$
(C) $\{\frac{3}{2}, 3\}$
(D) $\{3\}$
(E) $\{\}$

116. Which of the following is the complete solution set for $|2x - 1| > 3$?

(F) All real numbers
(G) The null set
(H) All real numbers less than -1 or greater than 2
(J) All real numbers less than -2 or greater than 1
(K) All real numbers less than -3

117. If $|3x - 6| > 9$, then which of the following must be true?

(A) $-3 < x < 2$
(B) $-2 < x < 3$
(C) $x < -3$ or $x > 2$
(D) $x < -1$ or $x > 5$
(E) $x < -1$ or $x > 9$

118. Which of the following identifies exactly those values of x that satisfy $|-2x + 4| < 4$?

(F) $x > -4$
(G) $x < 4$
(H) $x > 0$
(J) $0 < x < 4$
(K) $-4 < x < 0$

119. If $f(x) = x^2 + x$, what is the value of $f(-2)$?

(A) -8
(B) -2
(C) 2
(D) 8
(E) 12

120. Given: $y = f(x) = \left(\frac{6x^2 - 2^{-x}}{|x|}\right)^{-1/2}$ for all integers. If $x = -1$, what is the value of y?

(F) 2
(G) $\frac{1}{2}$
(H) $\frac{1}{4}$
(J) $-\frac{1}{2}$
(K) –2

121. If $f(x) = x + 3$ and $g(x) = 2x - 5$, what is the value of $f(g(2))$?

(A) –2
(B) 0
(C) 2
(D) 4
(E) 10

122. If $f(x) = 3x + 2$ and $g(x) = x^2 + x$, what is the value of $g(f(-2))$?

(F) 15
(G) 12
(H) 6
(J) 3
(K) –2

123. If $f(x) = 2x^2 + x$ and $g(x) = f(f(x))$, what is the value of $g(1)$?

(A) 3
(B) 18
(C) 21
(D) 39
(E) 55

124. If $f(x) = 3x + 4$ and $g(x) = 2x - 1$, for what value of x does $f(x) = g(x)$?

(F) –5
(G) –2
(H) 0
(J) 3
(K) 7

125. If $\bigtriangledown\!x = x^2 - x$ for all integers, then $\bigtriangledown\!{-2} =$

(A) –6
(B) –2
(C) 0
(D) 4
(E) 6

126. If $\bigtriangledown\!x = x^2 - x$ for all integers, then $\bigtriangledown\!(\bigtriangledown\!3) =$

(F) 27
(G) 30
(H) 58
(J) 72
(K) 121

127. If $f(x) = 3x - 2$ and $-5 < x < 5$, which of the following defines the range of $f(x)$?

(A) $-17 < f(x) < 13$
(B) $-13 < f(x) < 17$
(C) $-5 < f(x) < 12$
(D) $0 < f(x) < 17$
(E) $3 < f(x) < 13$

128. If $f(x) = \frac{x+2}{x-1}$, for which of the following values of x is $f(x)$ undefined?

(F) –2
(G) –1
(H) $\frac{1}{2}$
(J) 1
(K) 2

129. If $f(x) = \frac{2-2x}{x}$, which of the following defines the range of $f(x)$?

(A) All real numbers
(B) All real numbers except –2
(C) All real numbers except 0
(D) All real numbers except 2
(E) All real numbers greater than 2

NOTES AND STRATEGIES

130. If $|4x - 8| < 12$, which of the following defines the possible values of x?

(F) $-8 < x < -4$
(G) $-4 < x < 8$
(H) $-1 < x < 5$
(J) $1 < x < 5$
(K) $4 < x < 8$

131. The cost of making a call using a phone-card is \$0.15 for dialing and \$0.04 per minute of connection time. Which of the following equations could be used to find the cost, y, of a call x minutes long?

(A) $y = x(0.04 + 0.15)$
(B) $y = 0.04x + 0.15$
(C) $y = 0.04 + 0.15x$
(D) $y = 0.15 - 0.04x$
(E) $y = 0.04 - 0.15x$

132. If $x + y = 3$, then $2x + 2y =$

(F) $-\frac{2}{3}$
(G) $\frac{1}{2}$
(H) $\frac{2}{3}$
(J) 6
(K) Cannot be determined from the given information

133. If $2x + y = 8$ and $x - y = 1$, then $x = ?$

(A) -2
(B) -1
(C) 0
(D) 1
(E) 3

134. If $7x = 2$ and $3y - 7x = 10$, then $y =$

(F) 2
(G) 3
(H) 4
(J) 5
(K) 6

135. If $2x + y = 8$ and $x - y = 1$, then $x + y =$

(A) -1
(B) 1
(C) 2
(D) 3
(E) 5

136. If $4x + 5y = 12$ and $3x + 4y = 5$, then $7(x + y) =$

(F) 7
(G) 14
(H) 49
(J) 77
(K) 91

x	-2	-1	0	1	2
y	$\frac{10}{3}$	$\frac{8}{3}$	2	$\frac{4}{3}$	$\frac{2}{3}$

137. Which of the following equations correctly describes the relationship between the values x and y in the table above?

(A) $3x + 2y = 6$
(B) $3x - 2y = 3$
(C) $3x + 3y = -6$
(D) $6x + 4y = 7$
(E) $2x + 3y = 6$

138. Which of the following is the solution set for $2x^2 - 2x = 12$?

(F) $\{-3, -2\}$
(G) $\{-2, 3\}$
(H) $\{\frac{2}{3}, 3\}$
(J) $\{\frac{3}{2}, 2\}$
(K) $\{2, 3\}$

139. If $x^2 - 3x = 4$, then which of the following shows all possible values of x?

(A) $\{4, 1\}$
(B) $\{4, -1\}$
(C) $\{-4, 1\}$
(D) $\{-4, -1\}$
(E) $\{-4, 1, 4\}$

140. If $x^2 - y^2 = 0$ and $x + y = 1$, then $x - y =$

(F) -1
(G) 0
(H) 1
(J) 2
(K) 4

141. Which of the following is the solution set for $3x^2 + 3x = 6$?

(A) $\{1, -2\}$
(B) $\{1, 2\}$
(C) $\{\frac{1}{2}, 1\}$
(D) $\{\frac{1}{2}, \frac{1}{3}\}$
(E) $\{-1, -2\}$

142. Which of the following is the solution set for $2x^2 - 3x = 2$?

(F) $\{\frac{1}{2}, 2\}$
(G) $\{-\frac{1}{2}, 2\}$
(H) $\{-\frac{1}{2}, -2\}$
(J) $\{2, -2\}$
(K) $\{2, 4\}$

143. Diana spent $\frac{1}{2}$ of her weekly allowance on a new book and another \$3 on lunch. If she still had $\frac{1}{6}$ of her original allowance left, how much is Diana's allowance?

(A) \$24
(B) \$18
(C) \$15
(D) \$12
(E) \$9

144. In a certain game, a player had five successful turns in a row, and after each one, the number of points added to his total score was double what was added the preceding turn. If the player scored a total of 465 points, how many points did he score on the first play?

(F) 15
(G) 31
(H) 93
(J) 155
(K) 270

145. At a certain firm, d gallons of fuel are needed per day for each truck. At this rate, g gallons of fuel will supply t trucks for how many days?

(A) $\frac{dt}{g}$
(B) $\frac{gt}{d}$
(C) dgt
(D) $\frac{t}{dg}$
(E) $\frac{g}{dt}$

146. Y years ago, Paul was twice as old as Bob. If Bob is now 18 years old, how old is Paul today in terms of Y?

(F) $36 + Y$
(G) $18 + Y$
(H) $18 - Y$
(J) $36 - Y$
(K) $36 - 2Y$

147. After filling the car's fuel tank, a driver drove from point P to point Q and then to point R. She used $\frac{2}{5}$ of the fuel driving from P to Q. If she used another 7 gallons to drive from Q to R and still had $\frac{1}{4}$ of a tank left, how many gallons does the tank hold?

(A) 12
(B) 18
(C) 20
(D) 21
(E) 35

148. If pencils cost x cents each, how many pencils can be purchased for y dollars?

(F) $\frac{100}{xy}$
(G) $\frac{xy}{100}$
(H) $\frac{100y}{x}$
(J) $\frac{y}{100x}$
(K) $100xy$

149. A merchant increased the original price of an item by 10 percent. If she then reduces the new price by 10 percent, the final price, in terms of the original price, is equal to which of the following?

(A) a decrease of 11 percent
(B) a decrease of 1 percent
(C) no net change
(D) an increase of 1 percent
(E) an increase of 11 percent

150. Harold is twice as old as Jack, who is three years older than Dan. If Harold's age is five times Dan's age, how old (in years) is Jack?

(F) 2
(G) 4
(H) 5
(J) 8
(K) 10

151. A tank with capacity T gallons is empty. If water flows into the tank from Pipe X at the rate of X gallons per minute, and water is pumped out by Pipe Y at the rate of Y gallons per minute, and X is greater than Y, in how many minutes will the tank be filled?

(A) $\frac{T}{Y-X}$
(B) $\frac{T}{X-Y}$
(C) $\frac{T-X}{Y}$
(D) $\frac{X-Y}{60T}$
(E) $\frac{60T}{XY}$

152. Machine X produces w widgets in five minutes. Machine X and Machine Y, working at the same time, produce w widgets in two minutes. How long will it take Machine Y working alone to produce w widgets?

(F) 2 minutes, 30 seconds
(G) 2 minutes, 40 seconds
(H) 3 minutes, 20 seconds
(J) 3 minutes, 30 seconds
(K) 3 minutes, 40 seconds

153. If a train travels m miles in h hours and 45 minutes, what is its average speed in miles per hour?

(A) $\frac{m}{h+\frac{3}{4}}$
(B) $\frac{m}{1\frac{3}{4}h}$
(C) $m\left(h+\frac{3}{4}\right)$
(D) $\frac{m+45}{h}$
(E) $\frac{h}{m+45}$

154. On a playground, there are x seesaws. If 50 children are all riding on seesaws, two to a seesaw, and five seesaws are <u>not</u> in use, what is the value of x?

(F) 15
(G) 20
(H) 25
(J) 30
(K) 35

155. In the figure below, what is the length of $\overline{PQ}$?

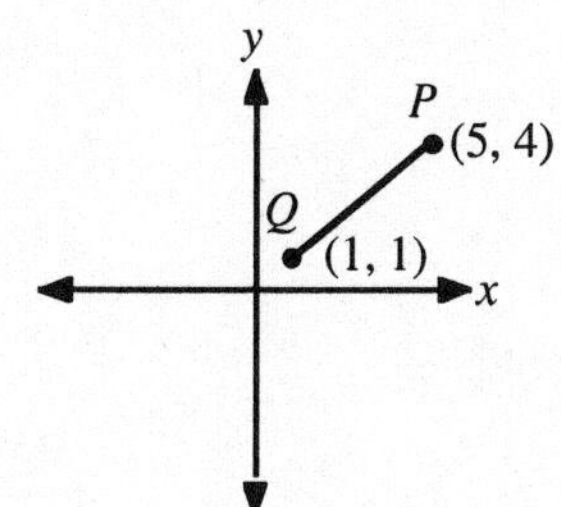

(A) $\sqrt{2}$
(B) $\sqrt{3}$
(C) 3
(D) 4
(E) 5

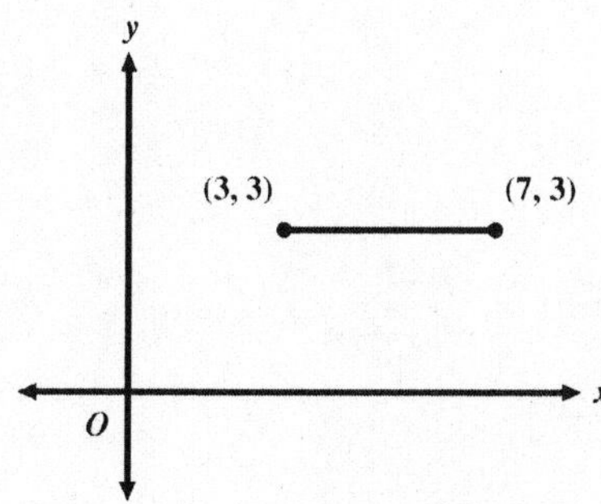

156. In the figure above, the line segment joining points (3, 3) and (7, 3) forms one side of a square. Which of the following CANNOT be the coordinates of another vertex of the square?

(F) (3, –1)
(G) (3, 7)
(H) (7, –3)
(J) (7, –1)
(K) (7, 7)

NOTES AND STRATEGIES

157. Which of the following is a graph of the line that passes through the points (–5, 3), (–1, 1), and (3, –1)?

(A) (D)

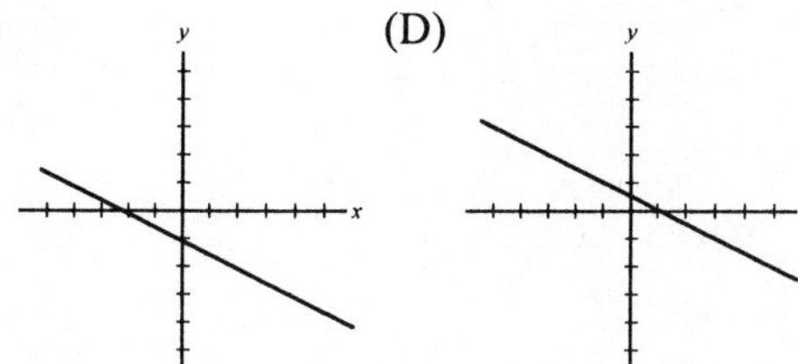

(B) (E)

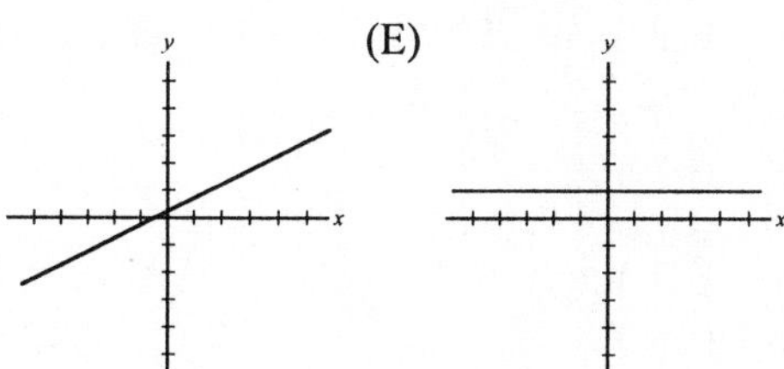

(C)

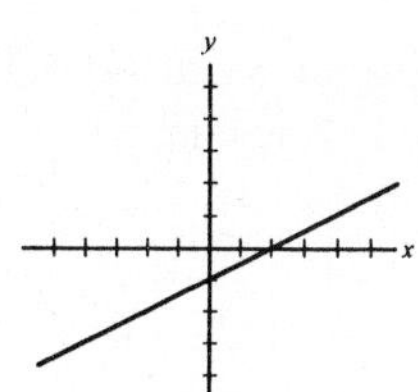

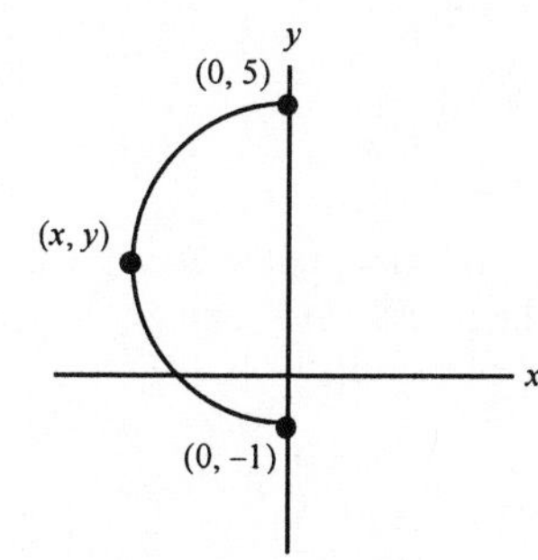

158. In the figure above, what are the coordinates, (x, y), of the point on the semicircle that is farthest from the y-axis?

(F) (–4, –4)
(G) (–3, –3)
(H) (–2, –3)
(J) (–3, 2)
(K) (3, 2)

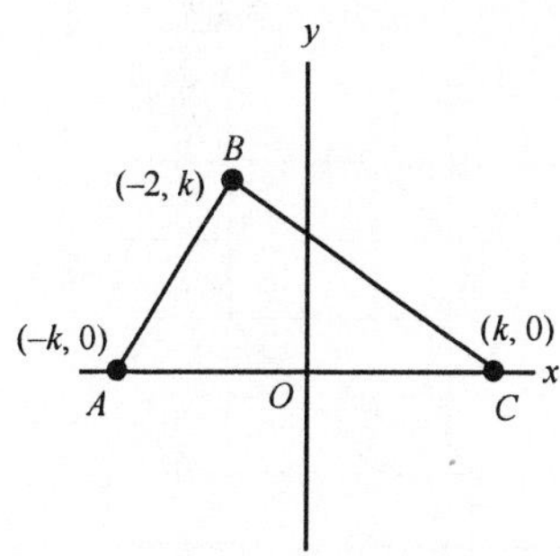

159. In the figure above, the area of ΔABC is 8. What is the value of k?

(A) 2
(B) $2\sqrt{2}$
(C) 4
(D) $4\sqrt{2}$
(E) 8

160. In the figure below, what is the slope of the line?

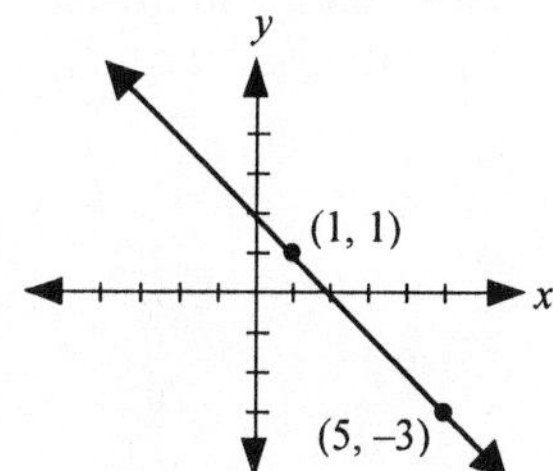

(F) -3
(G) -2
(H) -1
(J) 1
(K) 2

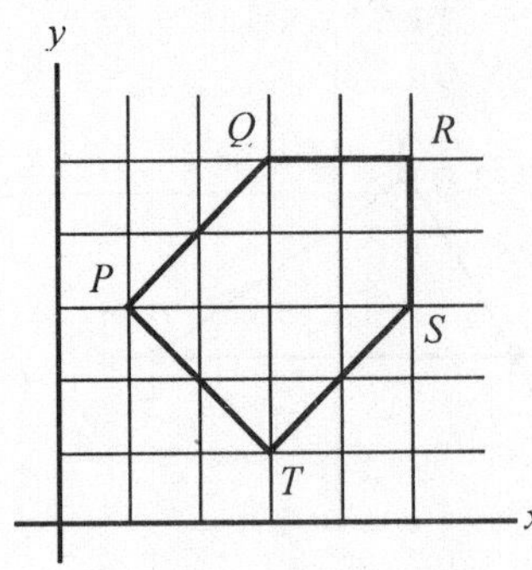

161. In the figure above, which two sides of polygon *PQRST* have the same slope?

(A) $\overline{PQ}$ and $\overline{QR}$
(B) $\overline{PQ}$ and $\overline{RS}$
(C) $\overline{PQ}$ and $\overline{ST}$
(D) $\overline{QR}$ and $\overline{RS}$
(E) $\overline{RS}$ and $\overline{ST}$

162. Line l is the graph of the equation $y = \frac{3x}{2} + 2$. The graph of which of the following equations is perpendicular to line l at (0, 2)?

(F) $y = \frac{3x}{2} - 2$
(G) $y = \frac{2x}{3} - 2$
(H) $y = -\frac{2x}{3} + 2$
(J) $y = -\frac{3x}{2} + 3$
(K) $y = -3x + 4$

163. If Set $A = \{(-2, 3); (-1, -1); (-4, -5)\}$, and Set $B = \{(3, 4); (4, 3); (2, -1)\}$, how many lines can be drawn with a positive slope that include exactly one point from Set A and one point from Set B?

(A) 2
(B) 3
(C) 4
(D) 5
(E) 6

164. A line includes the points (2, 3) and (3, 6). What is the equation of the line?

(F) $y = 2x - 3$
(G). $y = 3x - 3$
(H) $y = \frac{3x - 3}{2}$
(J) $y = 3 + 3$
(K) $y = x - 3$

165. Which of the following is the equation for the line with slope of 2 that includes point (0, 2)?

(A) $y = x - 1$
(B) $y = 2x - 1$
(C) $y = 2x - 2$
(D) $y = 2x + 2$
(E) $y = x + 1$

166. Which of the following is the equation for the line that includes points (–1, 1) and (7, 5)?

(F) $y = \frac{x}{2} + 2$
(G) $y = \frac{x}{2} + \frac{3}{2}$
(H) $y = \frac{x}{2} + \frac{2}{3}$
(J) $y = 2x + \frac{3}{2}$
(K) $y = 2x + 2$

167. If the graph of a line in the coordinate plane includes the points (2, 4) and (8, 7), what is the y-intercept of the line?

(A) 6
(B) 4
(C) 3
(D) –1
(E) –3

168. If the slope and y-intercept of a line are –2 and 3, respectively, then the line passes through which of the following points?

(F) (–5, –10)
(G) (–5, 10)
(H) (–2, 3)
(J) (3, 4)
(K) (4, –5)

169. What is the distance between the points (–3, –2) and (3, 3)?

(A) $\sqrt{3}$

(B) $2\sqrt{3}$

(C) 5

(D) $\sqrt{29}$

(E) $\sqrt{61}$

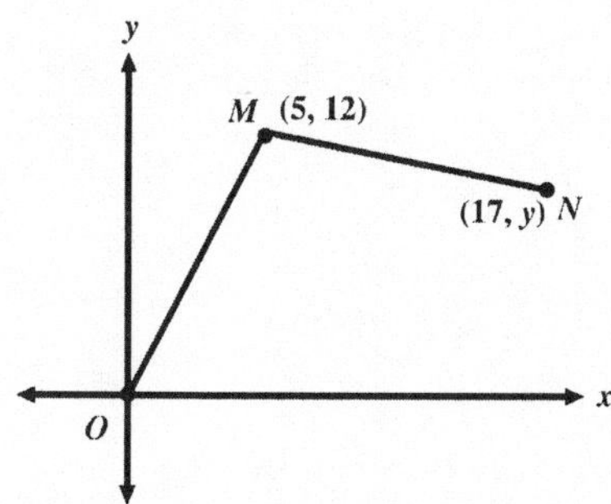

170. In the coordinate plane above, $\overline{MO} \cong \overline{MN}$ and $\overline{MO} \perp \overline{MN}$. What is the value of y?

(F) 5
(G) 7
(H) 12
(J) 13
(K) 17

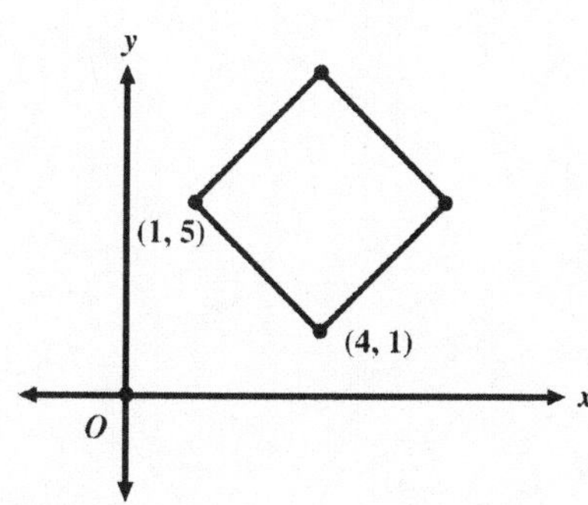

171. In the figure above, what is the area of the square region?

(A) 4

(B) 8

(C) $8\sqrt{2}$

(D) 16

(E) 25

172. In the coordinate plane, what is the midpoint of the line segment with endpoints (–3, –5) and (5, 7)?

(F) (1, 1)

(G) (1, 6)

(H) $(3, \frac{7}{2})$

(J) (4, 6)

(K) (8, 12)

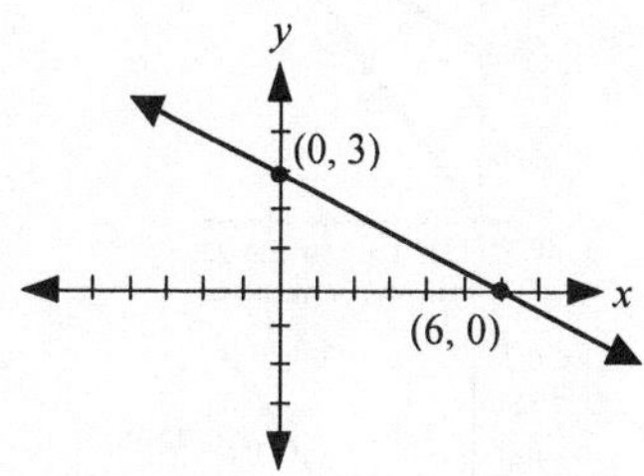

173. The figure above is the graph of which of the following equations?

(A) $x + 2y = 6$

(B) $2x + y = 6$

(C) $x + \frac{y}{2} = 6$

(D) $\frac{x}{2} + y = 2$

(E) $x - 3y = 2$

174. A school rented the ballroom of a hotel for a dance. The cost of the rental is $1,500 plus $5.00 per person who attends. Each person who attends will pay an admission charge of $12.50. If x represents the number of people who attend, which of the graphs can be used to determine how many people must attend for the admission charges to cover exactly the cost of renting the ballroom?

(F)

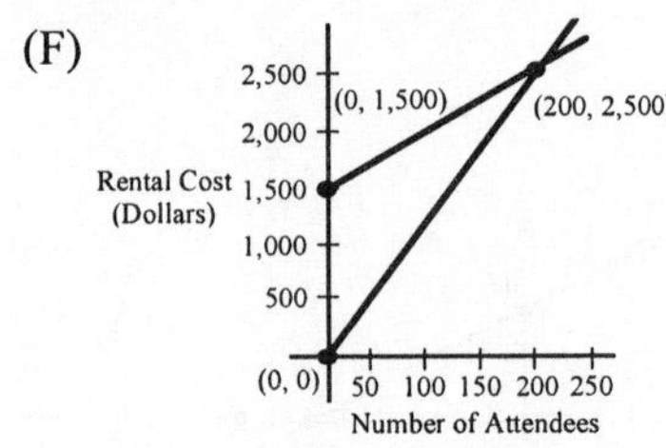

(G)

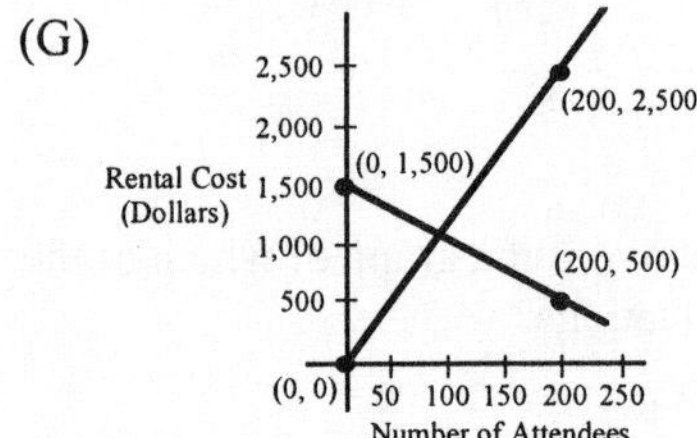

(H)

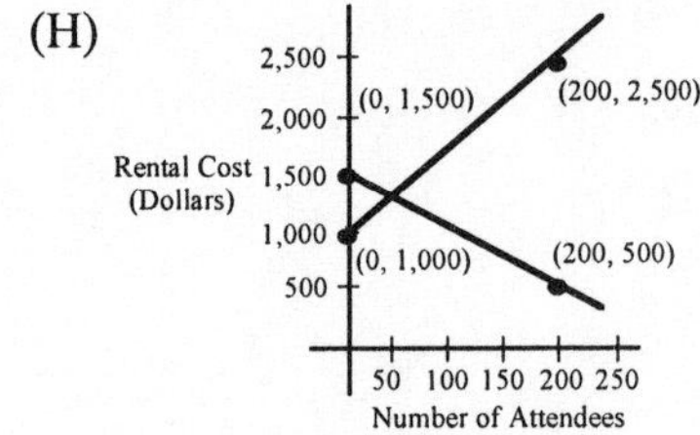

(J)

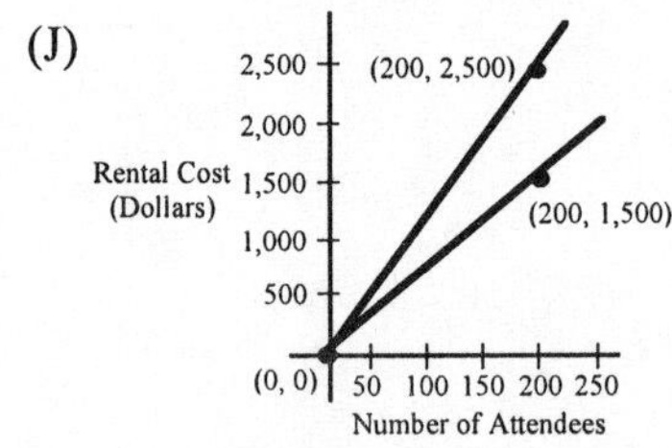

(K)

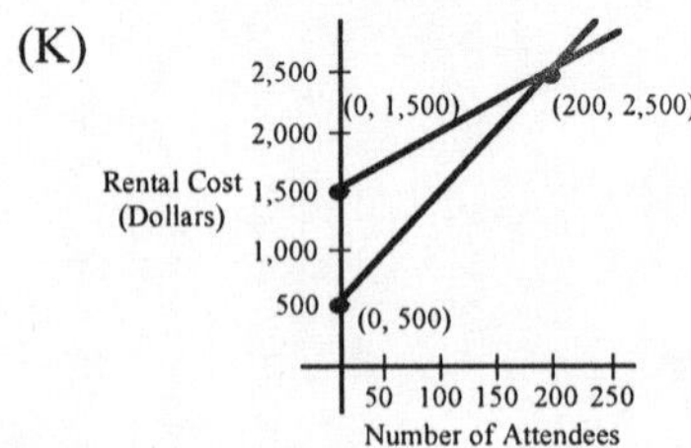

NOTES AND STRATEGIES

175. Which of the following is the graph of the inequality $y \geq 2x$?

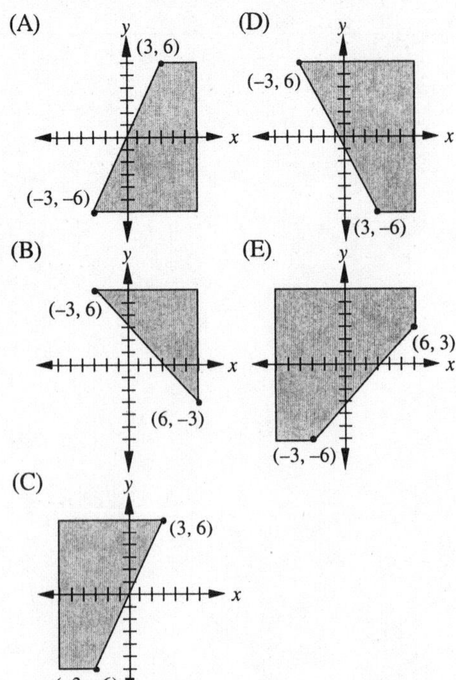

176. Which of the following is the graph of the equation $(x-1)^2 + y^2 = 4$?

(F)

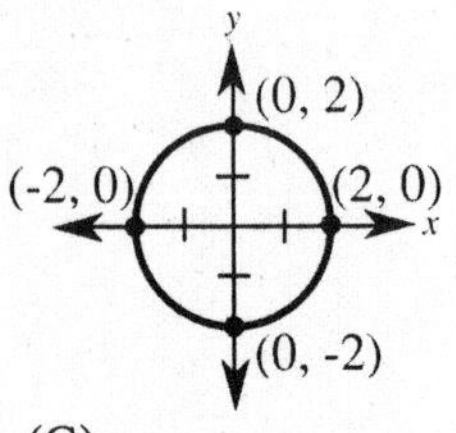

(0, 2) (-2, 0) (2, 0) (0, -2)

(G)

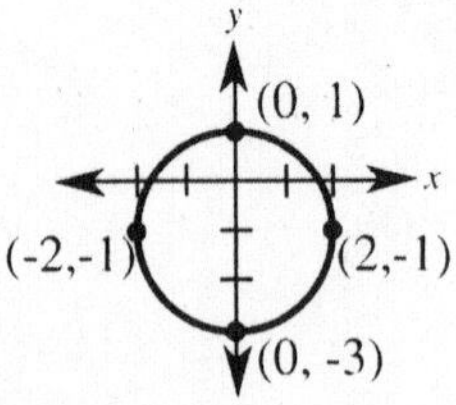

(0, 1) (-2,-1) (2,-1) (0, -3)

(H)

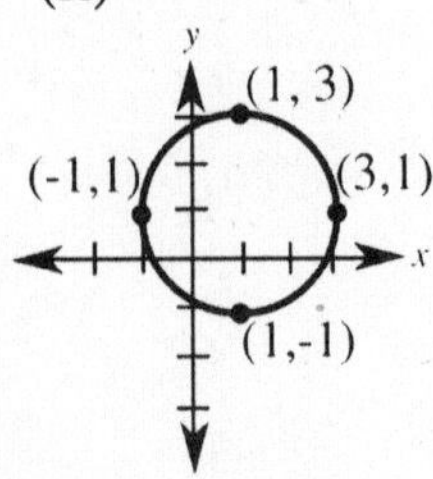

(J)

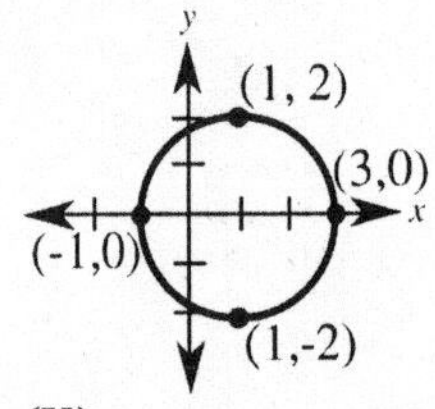

(K)

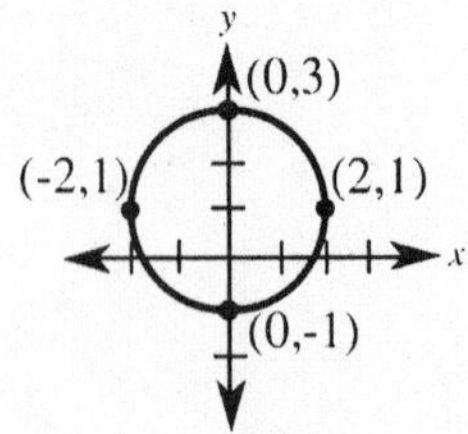

177. Which of the following is the graph of the equation $\frac{x^2}{9} + \frac{y^2}{16} = 1$?

(A)

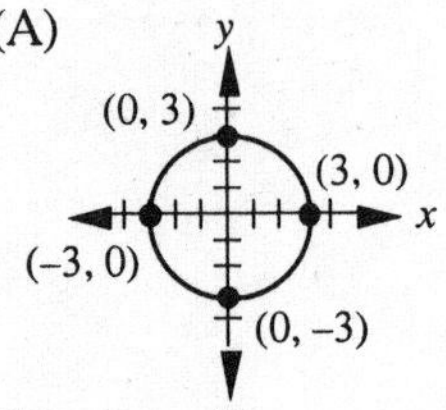

(0, 3) (3, 0) (–3, 0) (0, –3)

(B)

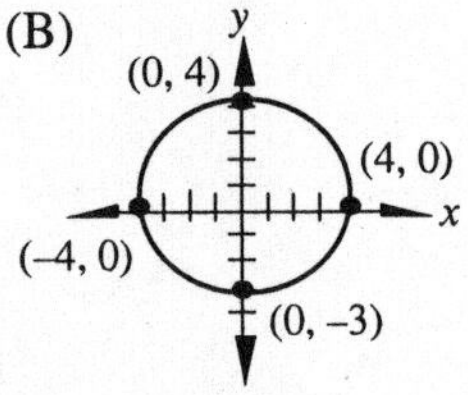

(0, 4) (4, 0) (–4, 0) (0, –3)

(C)

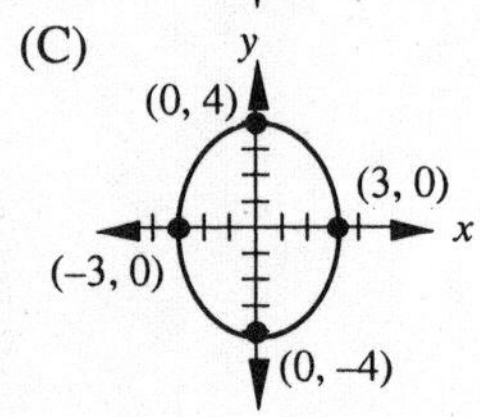

(D)

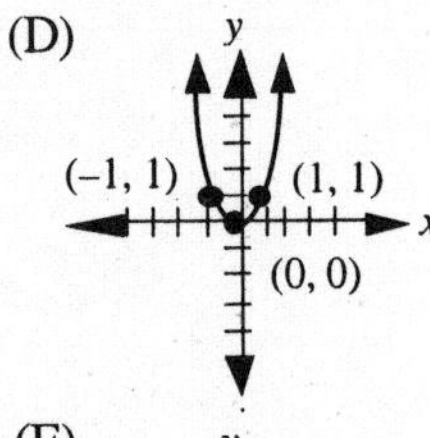

(E)

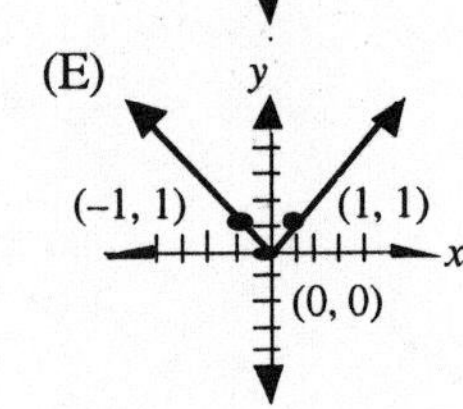

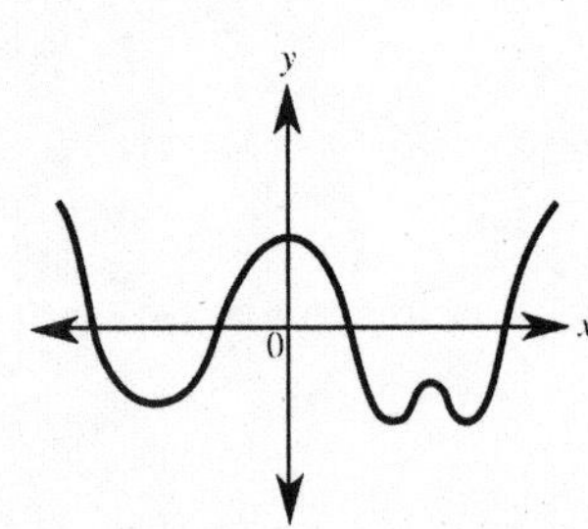

178. The figure above shows the graph of a function $g(x)$. How many times does the graph cross the x-axis?

(F) 1
(G) 2
(H) 3
(J) 4
(K) 5

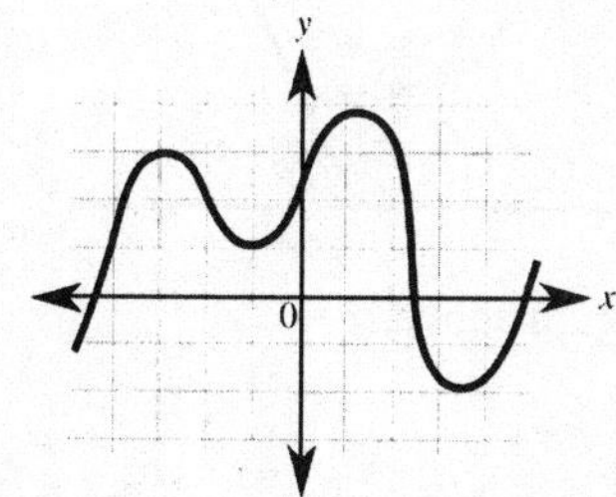

179. The figure above shows the graph of $f(x)$ in the coordinate plane. For the portion of the graph shown, for how many values of x is $f(x) = 3$?

(A) 0
(B) 1
(C) 2
(D) 3
(E) 4

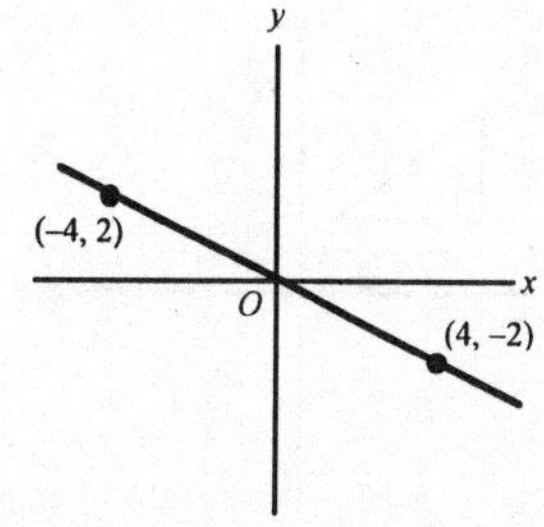

180. The figure above represents the graph of $y = f(x)$ in the coordinate plane. Which of the following is the graph of $y' = f(x - 1)$?

(F)

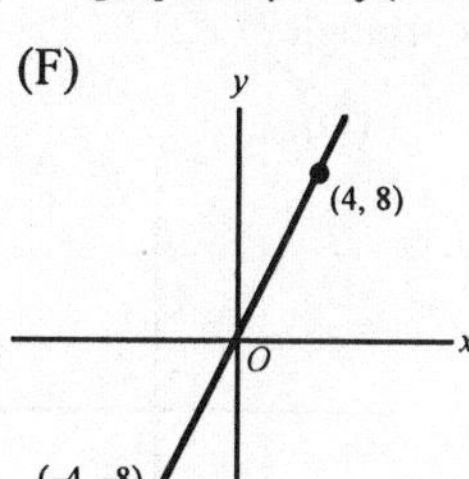

(J)

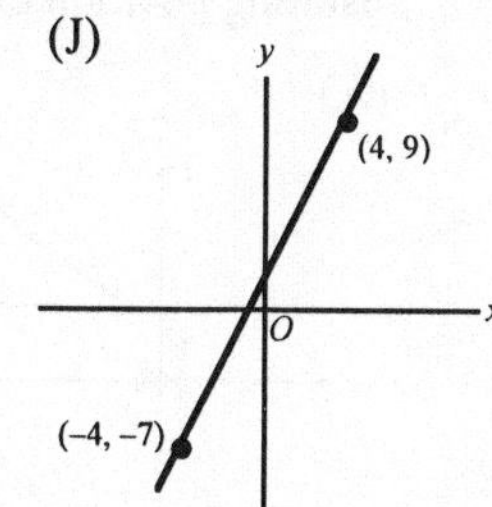

(G)

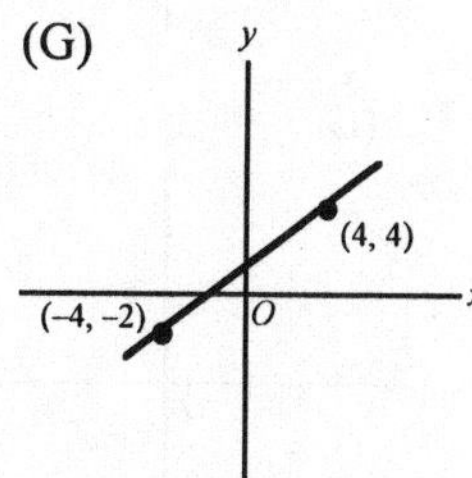

(K)

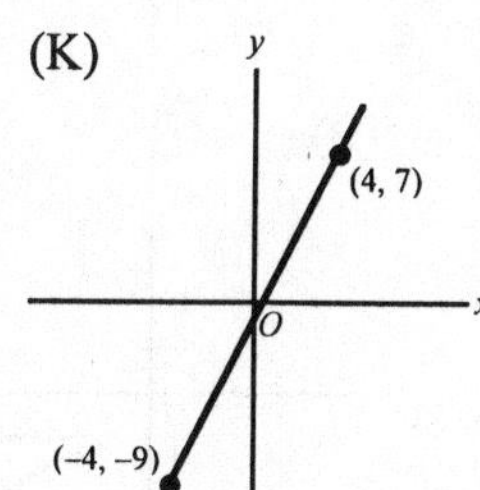

(H)

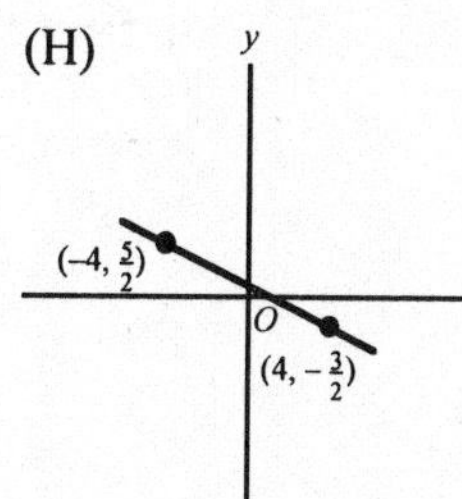

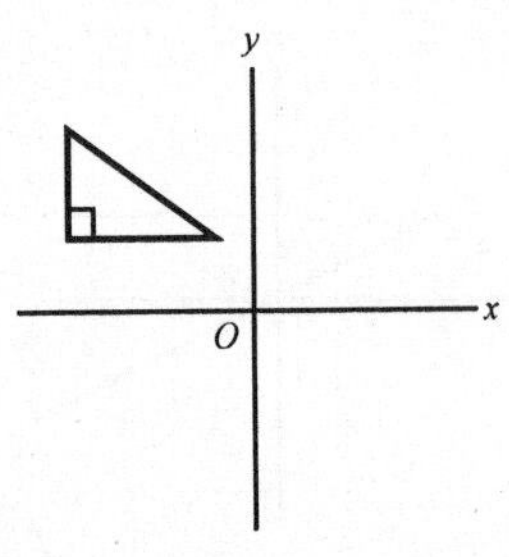

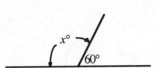

181. If the triangle in the figure above is reflected across the y-axis and then reflected across the x-axis, which of the following graphs shows the resulting position of the triangle?

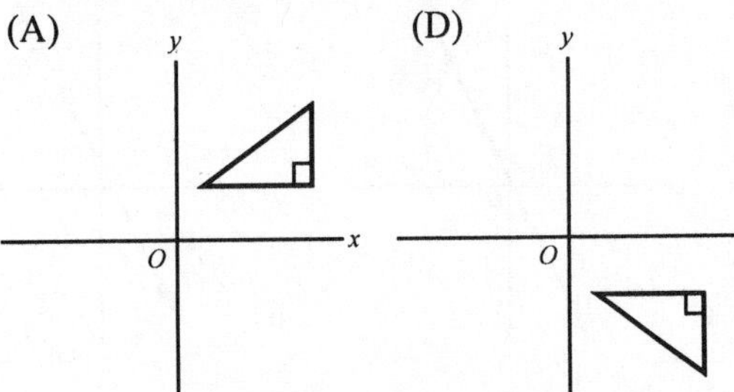

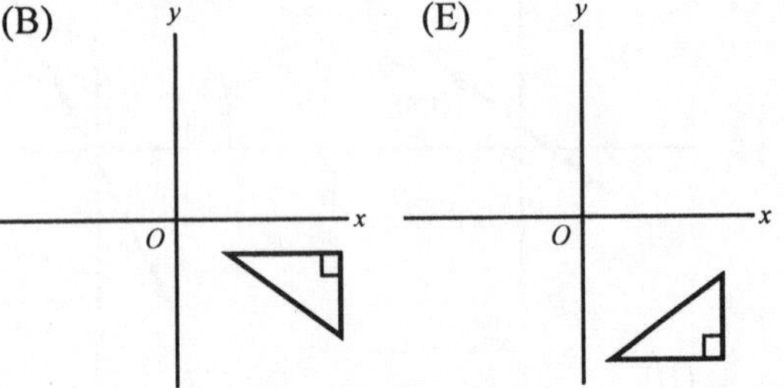

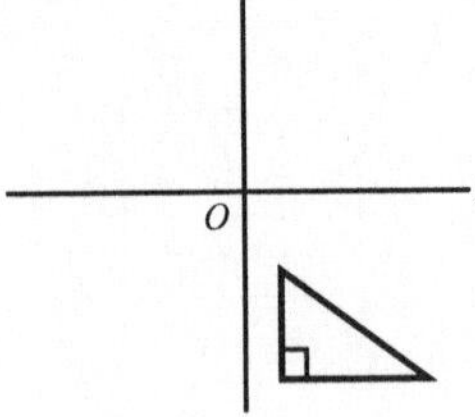

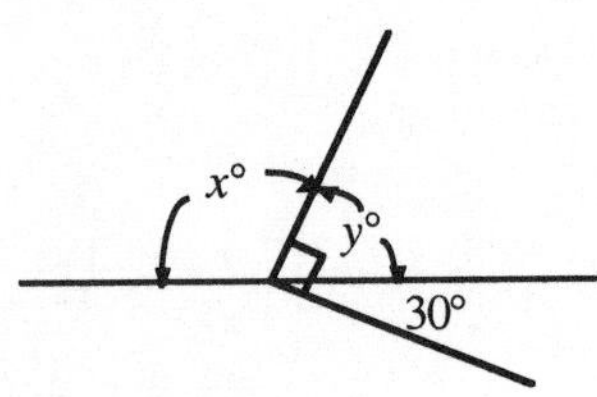

182. In the figure above, $x =$

(F) 45
(G) 60
(H) 75
(J) 90
(K) 120

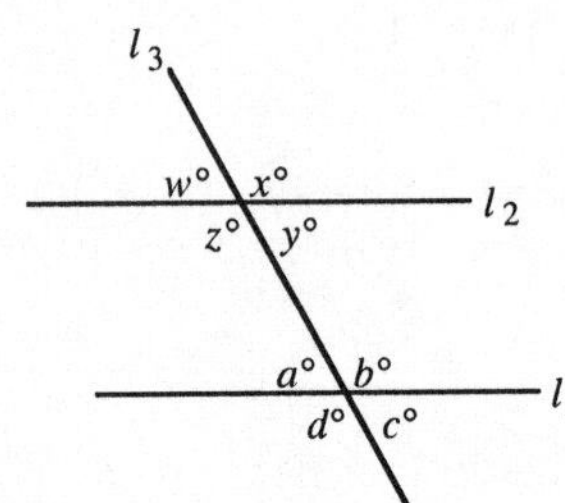

183. In the figure above, $x =$

(A) 45
(B) 60
(C) 90
(D) 105
(E) 120

184. In the figure above, l_1 is parallel to l_2. Which of the following <u>must</u> be true?

(F) $w = a$
(G) $y + b = 180$
(H) $w = a$ and $y + b = 180$
(J) $y + b = 180$ and $x +$ … 0
(K) $w = a, y + b = 180$ … $+ d = 180$

NOTES AND STRATEGIES

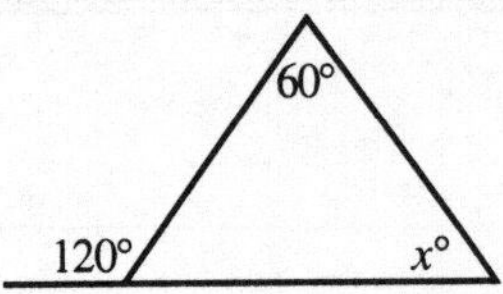

185. In the figure above, $x = ?$

(A) 30
(B) 45
(C) 60
(D) 75
(E) 90

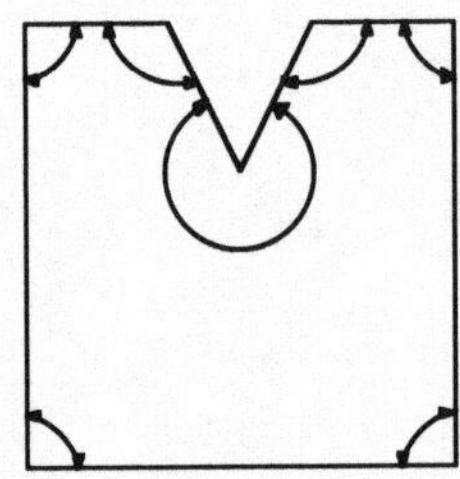

186. In the figure above, what is the sum of the indicated angles?

(F) 540
(G) 720
(H) 900
(J) 1,080
(K) 1,260

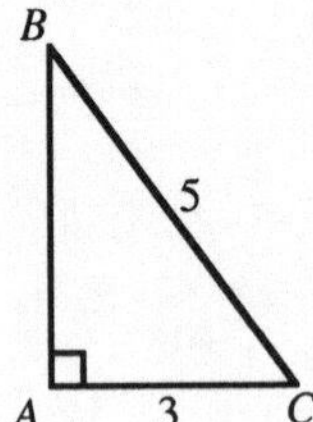

187. In the figure above, what is the length of $\overline{AB}$?

(A) 2
(B) $2\sqrt{3}$
(C) 4
(D) $4\sqrt{2}$
(E) 8

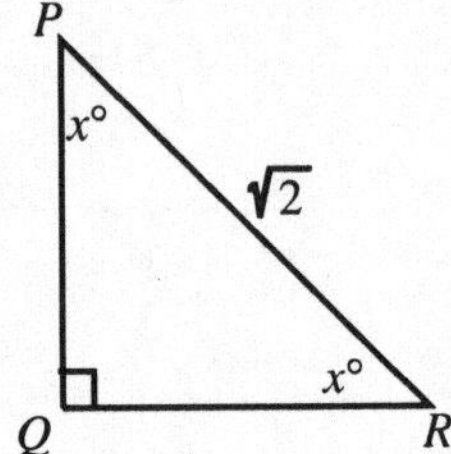

188. In the figure above, what is the length of $\overline{PQ}$?

(F) 1
(G) $\sqrt{2}$
(H) $2\sqrt{2}$
(J) 4
(K) 5

189. In a right isosceles triangle, the hypotenuse is equal to which of the following?

(A) Half the length of either of the other sides
(B) The length of either of the other sides multiplied by $\sqrt{2}$
(C) Twice the length of either of the other sides
(D) The sum of the lengths of the other two sides
(E) The sum of the lengths of the other two sides multiplied by $\sqrt{2}$

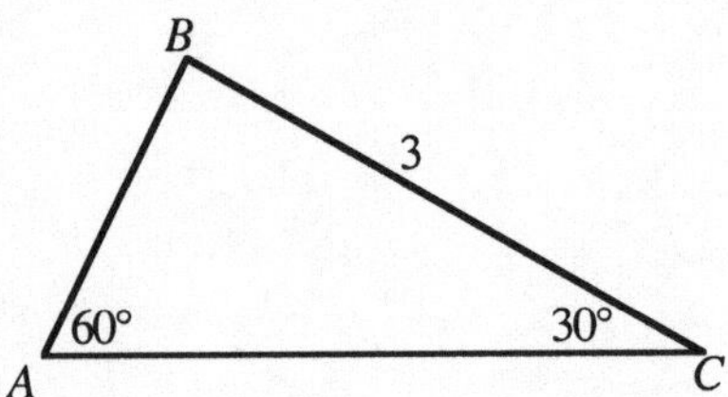

190. In the triangle above, what is the length of $\overline{AC}$?

(F) 2
(G) $\sqrt{3}$
(H) $2\sqrt{3}$
(J) $3\sqrt{3}$
(K) 6

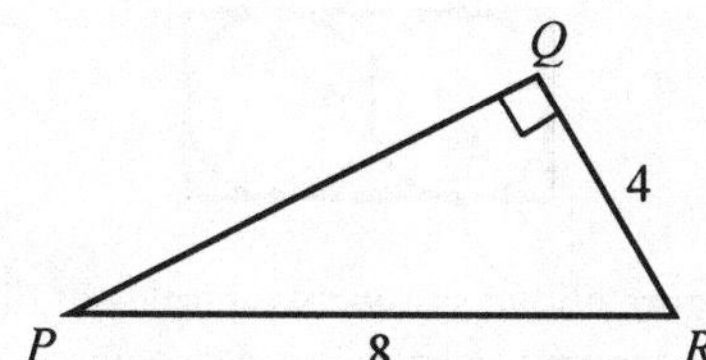

191. In the figure above, the perimeter of ΔPQR =

(A) $12 + \sqrt{3}$
(B) $12 + 2\sqrt{3}$
(C) $12 + 4\sqrt{3}$
(D) 28
(E) 56

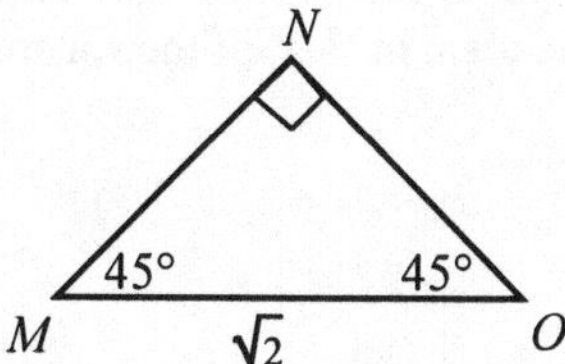

192. In the figure above, what is the area of ΔMNO?

(F) $\frac{1}{2}$
(G) $\frac{\sqrt{2}}{2}$
(H) 1
(J) $\sqrt{2}$
(K) 2

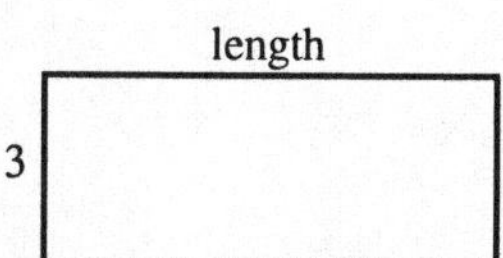

193. If the area of the rectangle above is 18, what is the perimeter?

(A) 9
(B) 12
(C) 18
(D) 24
(E) 30

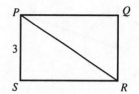

194. In the figure above, $PQRS$ is a rectangle. If $\overline{PR}$ = 5 centimeters, what is the area, in square centimeters, of the rectangle?

(F) 2
(G) 3
(H) 4
(J) 8
(K) 12

195. If the width of a rectangle is increased by 10% and the length of the rectangle is increased by 20%, by what percent does the area of the rectangle <u>increase</u>?

(A) 2%
(B) 10%
(C) 15%
(D) 32%
(E) 36%

196. If the area of a circle is equal to 9π inches, which of the following is (are) true?

I. The radius is 3 inches.
II. The diameter is 6 inches.
III. The circumference is 6π inches.

(F) I only
(G) II only
(H) III only
(J) I and II only
(K) I, II, and III

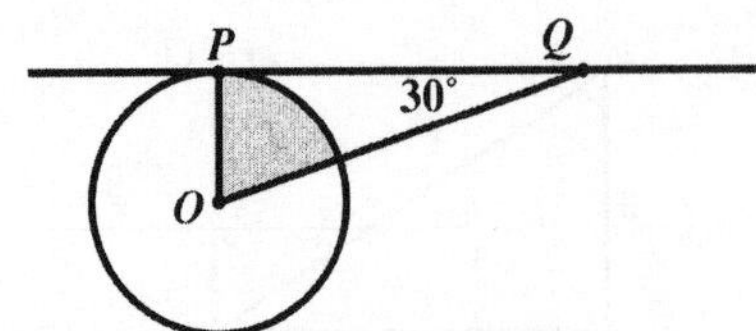

197. In the figure above, O is the center of the circle, and $\overleftrightarrow{PQ}$ is tangent to the circle at P. If the radius of circle O has a length of 6, what is the area of the shaded portion of the figure?

(A) π
(B) 3π
(C) 6π
(D) 9π
(E) 12π

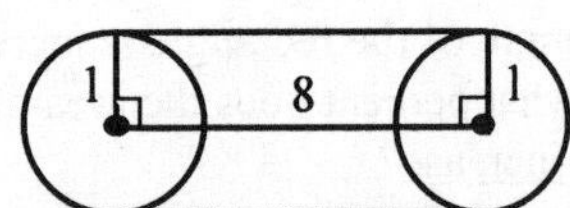

Note: Figure not drawn to scale.

198. The figure above shows two pulleys connected by a belt. If the centers of the pulleys are 8 feet apart and the pulleys each have a radius of 1 foot, what is the length, in feet, of the belt?

(F) 4π
(G) 8π
(H) $8 + \pi$
(J) $16 + \pi$
(K) $16 + 2\pi$

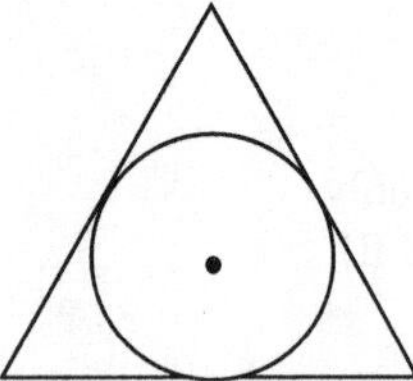

199. In the figure above, a circle is inscribed in an equilateral triangle. If the radius of the circle is 1, what is the perimeter of the triangle?

(A) $\sqrt{3}$
(B) $2\sqrt{3}$
(C) $3\sqrt{3}$
(D) 6
(E) $6\sqrt{3}$

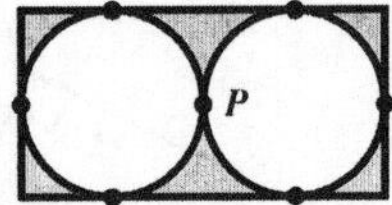

200. The figure above shows two circles of diameter 2 that are tangent to each other at point P. The line segments form a rectangle and are tangent to the circles at the points shown. What is the area of the shaded portion of the figure?

(F) $8 - 2\pi$
(G) $8 - \pi$
(H) $4 - 2\pi$
(J) $4 - \pi$
(K) 2π

201. If a circle of radius 1 foot is inscribed in a square, what is the area, in feet, of the square?

(A) $\frac{\sqrt{2}}{2}$
(B) 1
(C) $\sqrt{2}$
(D) 2
(E) 4

202. An isosceles right triangle is inscribed in a semicircle with a radius of 1 inch. What is the area, in square inches, of the triangle?

(F) $\frac{\sqrt{2}}{3}$
(G) $\frac{1}{2}$
(H) 1
(J) $\sqrt{2}$
(K) $2\sqrt{2}$

NOTES AND STRATEGIES

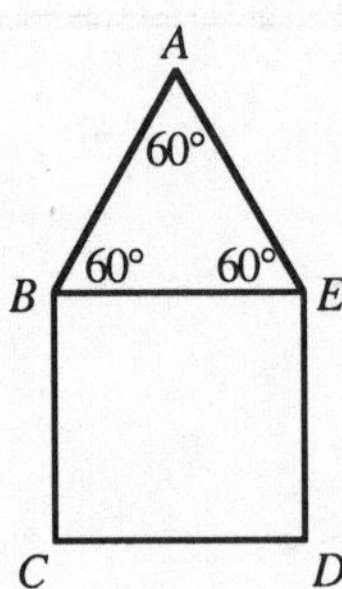

203. In the figure above, $BCDE$ is a square with an area of 4. What is the perimeter of ΔABE?

(A) 3
(B) 4
(C) 6
(D) 8
(E) 12

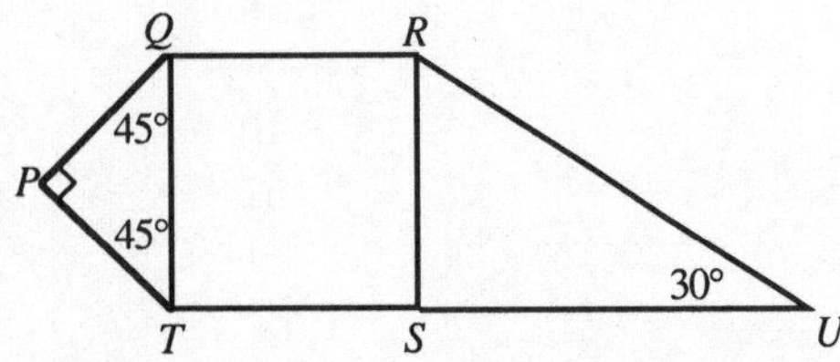

204. In the figure above, if $QRST$ is a square and the length of $\overline{PQ}$ is $\sqrt{2}$, what is the length of $\overline{RU}$?

(F) $\sqrt{2}$
(G) $2\sqrt{2}$
(H) $\sqrt{6}$
(J) 4
(K) $4\sqrt{3}$

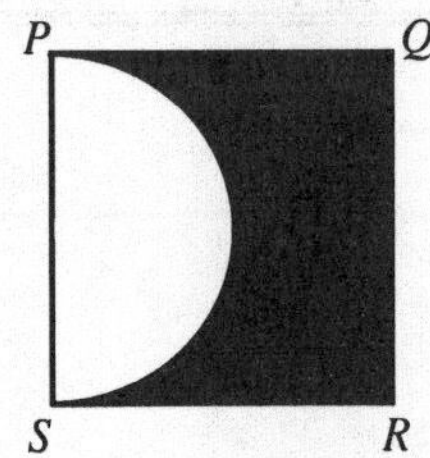

205. In the figure above, $PQRS$ is a square, and $\overline{PS}$ is the diameter of a semicircle. If the length of $\overline{PQ}$ is 2, what is the area of the shaded portion of the diagram?

(A) $4-2\pi$
(B) $4-\pi$
(C) $4-\frac{\pi}{2}$
(D) $8-\pi$
(E) $8-\frac{\pi}{2}$

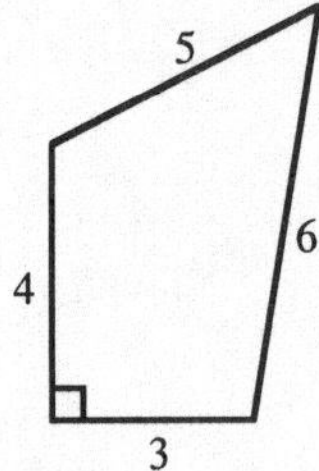

206. If the lengths of the sides, in inches, are as marked on the figure above, what is the area, in square inches, of the quadrilateral?

(F) 6
(G) $6+\sqrt{3}$
(H) 12
(J) 18
(K) 24

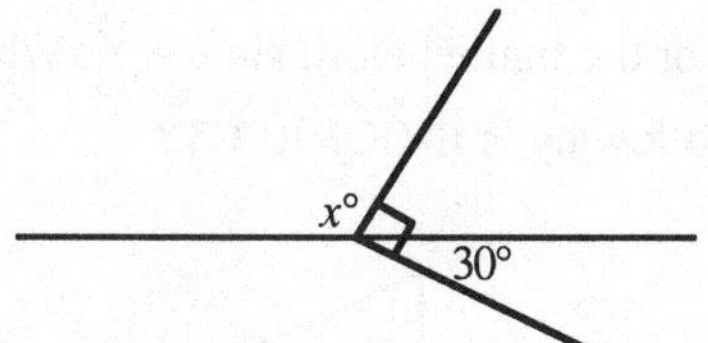

207. In the figure above, $x =$

(A) 30
(B) 65
(C) 120
(D) 150
(E) 170

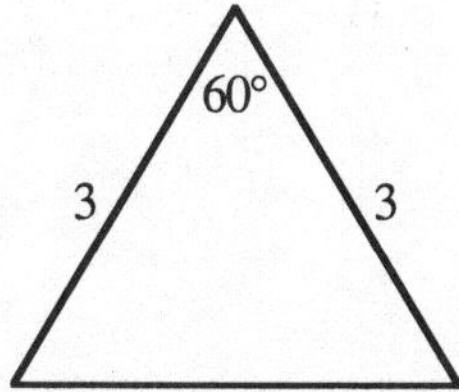

208. The perimeter of the triangle shown above is

(F) $3\sqrt{2}$
(G) 6
(H) 7.5
(J) 9
(K) 15

209. In the figure below, $x = ?$

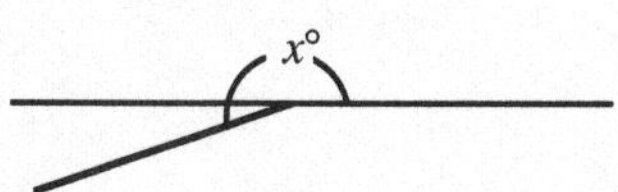

(A) 120
(B) 150
(C) 180
(D) 210
(E) 240

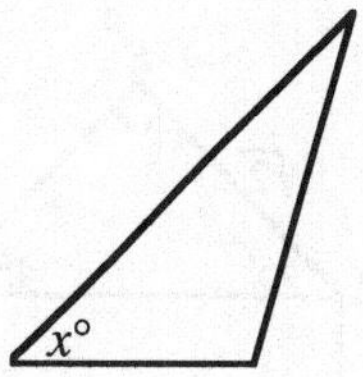

210. In the figure above, $x =$

(F) 30
(G) 45
(H) 60
(J) 75
(K) 90

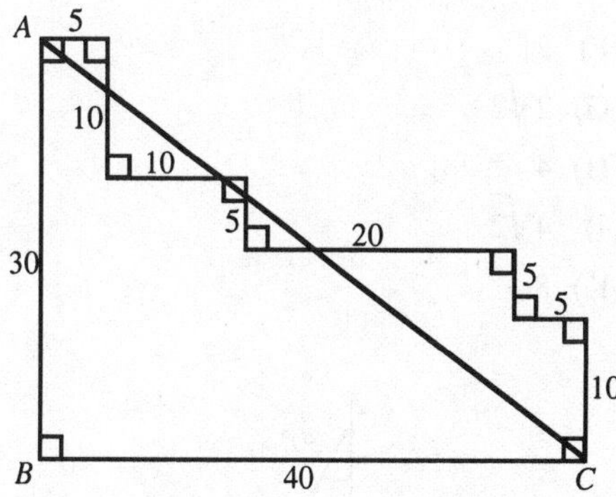

211. In the figure above, what is the length of $\overline{AC}$?

(A) $30\sqrt{2}$
(B) 50
(C) 75
(D) $60\sqrt{2}$
(E) 100

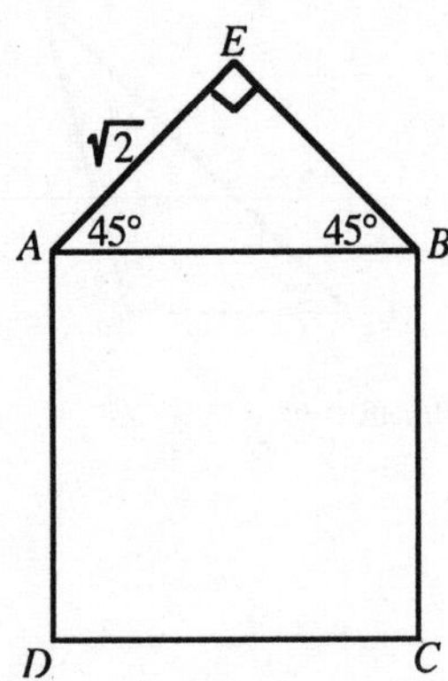

212. In the figure above, what is the area of square *ABCD*?

(F) 2
(G) $2\sqrt{2}$
(H) 4
(J) $4\sqrt{2}$
(K) 8

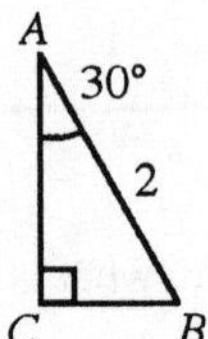

213. In the triangle above, the measure of $\angle BAC$ is 30° and the length of $\overline{AB}$ is 2. Which of the following best approximates the length of $\overline{AC}$?

(A) 0.8
(B) 1.0
(C) 1.7
(D) 1.9
(E) 2.3

214. For the figure below, $\sin\theta = \frac{12}{13}$. Which of the following is INCORRECT?

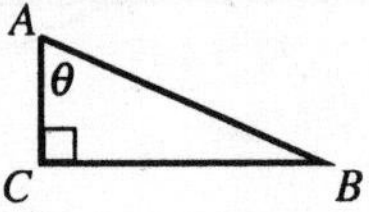

(F) $\cos\theta = \frac{5}{13}$
(G) $\tan\theta = \frac{12}{5}$
(H) $\cot\theta = \frac{5}{12}$
(J) $\sec\theta = \frac{13}{5}$
(K) $\csc\theta = \frac{12}{13}$

215. In the right triangle below, the length of $\overline{AB}$ is 5 centimeters and $\angle A$ measures 30°. What is the length, in centimeters, of $\overline{BC}$? (sin 30° = 0.5.)

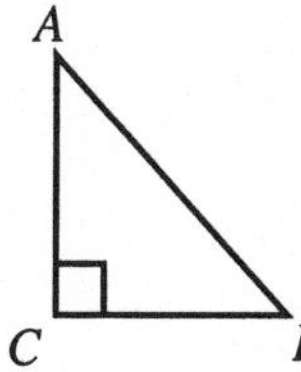

(A) 4
(B) $3\frac{1}{2}$
(C) $2\frac{3}{4}$
(D) $2\frac{1}{2}$
(E) 2

216. If sin 60° is equal to $\frac{\sqrt{3}}{2}$, what is the value of $\sin^2 30° + \cos^2 30°$?

(F) $\frac{\sqrt{3}+1}{2}$
(G) $\sqrt{5}$
(H) $\frac{\sqrt{5}}{2}$
(J) $\frac{3}{4}$
(K) 1

217. Which of the following is equivalent to $\frac{\sin A}{\cos A}$?

(A) tan A
(B) cot A
(C) sec A
(D) csc A
(E) $\frac{1}{\tan A}$

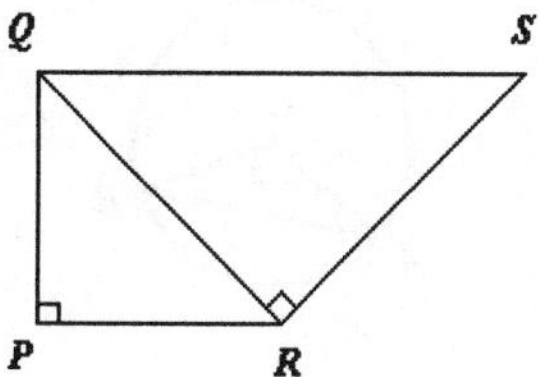

218. In the figure above, ΔPQR and ΔPRS are isosceles right triangles. If $QP = 3$, what is the length of $\overline{QS}$? ($\sin 45° = \frac{\sqrt{2}}{2}$.)

(F) $\sqrt{2}$
(G) $2\sqrt{2}$
(H) 4
(J) 6
(K) 8

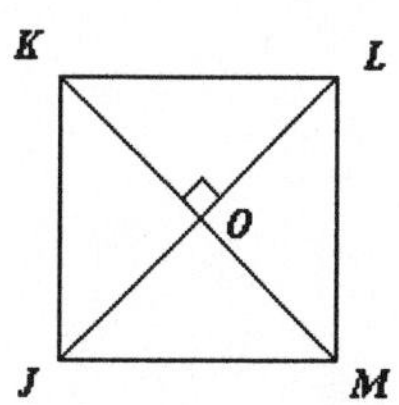

219. If the area of the square $JKLM$ in the figure above is 4, what is the sum of the lengths of the diagonals $\overline{JL}$ and $\overline{KM}$? ($\sin 45° = \frac{\sqrt{2}}{2}$.)

(A) $\frac{\sqrt{2}}{2}$
(B) $2 + \frac{\sqrt{2}}{2}$
(C) $4\sqrt{2}$
(D) $4 + 4\sqrt{2}$
(E) $8\sqrt{2}$

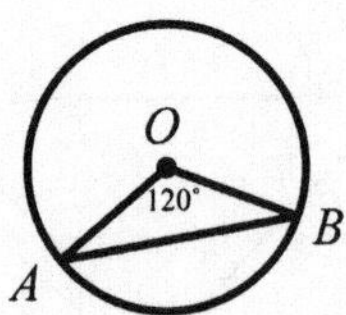

220. In the figure above, O is the center of the circle with radius 10. What is the area of ΔAOB? ($\sin 30° = \frac{1}{2}$; $\sin 60° = \frac{\sqrt{3}}{2}$.)

(F) $10\sqrt{3}$
(G) 10
(H) 25
(J) $25\sqrt{3}$
(K) 50

221. If the average of 35, 38, 41, 43, and x is 37, what is x?

(A) 28
(B) 30
(C) 31
(D) 34
(E) 36

222. The average weight of 6 packages is 50 pounds per package. Another package is added, making the average weight of the 7 packages 52 pounds per package. What is the weight, in pounds, of the additional package?

(F) 2
(G) 7
(H) 52
(J) 62
(K) 64

223. The average of 10 test scores is 80. If the high and low scores are dropped, the average is 81. What is the average of the high and low scores?

(A) 76
(B) 78
(C) 80
(D) 81
(E) 82

224. In Latin 101, the final exam grade is weighted two times as heavily as the mid-term grade. If Leo received a score of 84 on his final exam and 90 on his mid-term, what was his course average?

(F) 88
(G) 87.5
(H) 86.5
(J) 86
(K) 85

225. In a group of children, three children are 10 years old and two children are 5 years old. What is the average age, in years, of the children in the group?

(A) 6
(B) 6.5
(C) 7
(D) 7.5
(E) 8

226. The number of employment applications received by All-Star Staffing each month during 2002 was as follows: 8, 3, 5, 3, 4, 3, 1, 0, 3, 4, 0, and 7. What is the median number of applications received in 2002?

(F) 3
(G) 4
(H) 5
(J) 6
(K) 7

227. William's monthly electric bills for last year were as follows: \$40, 38, 36, 38, 34, 34, 30, 32, 34, 37, 39, and 40. What is the mode of the bills?

(A) \$33
(B) \$34
(C) \$35
(D) \$36
(E) \$37

228. If Set $A = \{1, 2, 3, 4, 5, 6\}$ and Set $B = \{1, 2, 3, 4, 5, 6\}$, what is the probability that the sum of one number from Set A and one number from Set B will total 7?

(F) $\frac{1}{12}$ 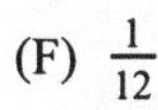

(G) $\frac{5}{36}$

(H) $\frac{1}{6}$

(J) $\frac{1}{5}$

(K) $\frac{1}{3}$

The Dark Night	History of Canada	RING MORE THAN ONCE	A Bright Morning	Chemistry	George Washington
Mary Smith	Carol Kim	Mary Smith	T. Jackson	Victor Brown	C. Adams
•Mystery•	•Textbook•	•Mystery•	•Mystery•	•Textbook•	•Biography•

229. If a book is selected at random from the collection shown above, which of the following has the greatest probability of being selected?

(A) A book by Mary Smith
(B) A textbook
(C) A mystery
(D) A book written by either Carol Kim or Victor Brown
(E) A biography

230. If a jar contains r red marbles, b blue marbles, and g green marbles, which of the following expresses the probability that a marble drawn at random will NOT be red?

(F) $\frac{-r}{r+b+g}$

(G) $\frac{r}{r+b+g}$

(H) $\frac{b+g-r}{b+g+r}$

(J) $\frac{r}{b+g}$

(K) $\frac{b+g}{b+g+r}$

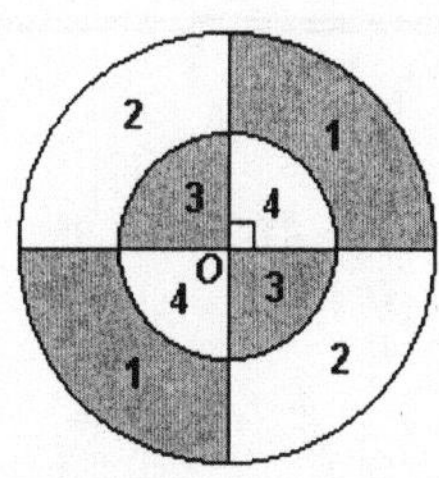

231. The figure above shows a dartboard consisting of two concentric circles with center O. The radius of the larger circle is equal to the diameter of the smaller circle. What is the probability that a randomly thrown dart striking the board will score a "3."

(A) $\frac{1}{16}$

(B) $\frac{1}{8}$

(C) $\frac{1}{4}$

(D) $\frac{1}{2}$

(E) $\frac{3}{4}$

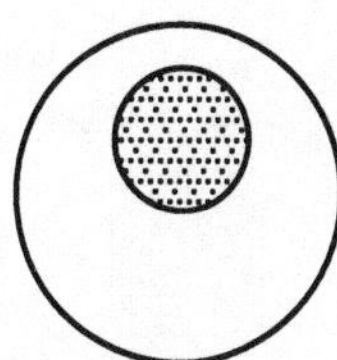

Note: Figure not drawn to scale.

232. An underwater salvage team is searching the ocean floor for a lost signal device using a large circular search pattern and a smaller circular search pattern with a radius equal to one-third that of the larger pattern. If the device is known to be inside the boundary of the larger search area, what is the probability that it is NOT located in the shaded portion of the figure?

(F) $\frac{1}{9}$

(G) $\frac{1}{6}$

(H) $\frac{1}{3}$

(J) $\frac{1}{2}$

(K) $\frac{8}{9}$

NOTES AND STRATEGIES

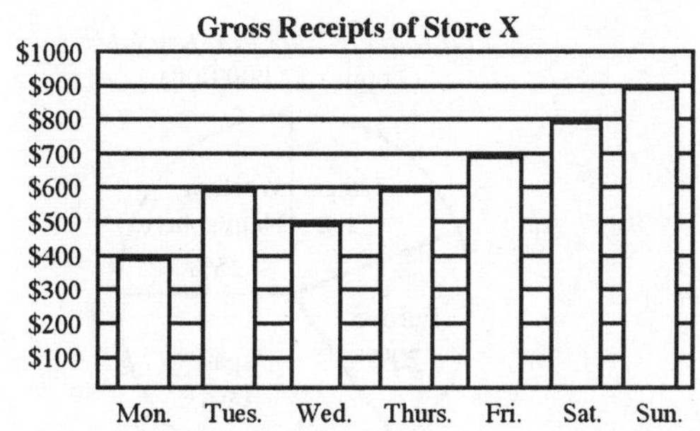

233. During the week shown in the graph above, what was the greatest increase in sales from one day to the next?

(A) $50
(B) $100
(C) $150
(D) $200
(E) $250

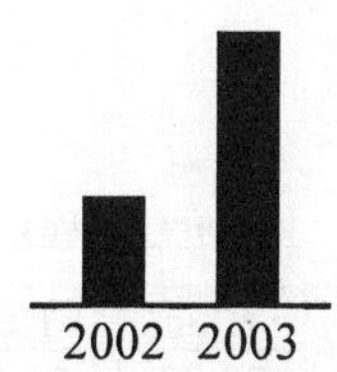

234. If the graph above represents expenditures by Corporation X in two different years, what was the approximate ratio of expenditures in 2002 to those in 2003?

(F) $\frac{1}{5}$
(G) $\frac{2}{5}$
(H) $\frac{1}{2}$
(J) $\frac{2}{3}$
(K) 2

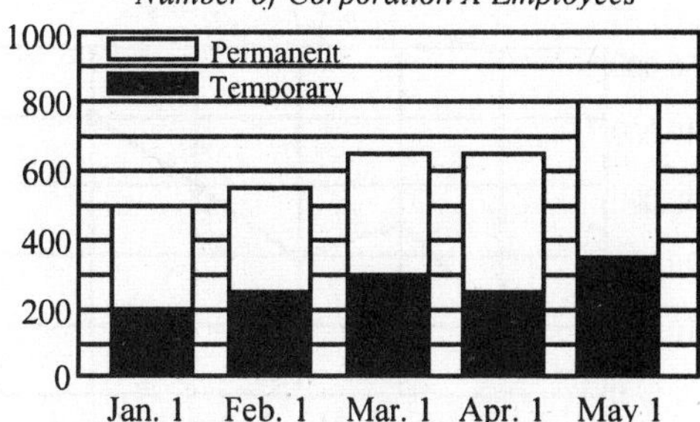

235. Based on the data presented above, what was the difference, if any, between the number of permanent workers employed by Corporation X on March 1st and the number of permanent workers employed by Corporation X on April 1st?

(A) 0
(B) 50
(C) 100
(D) 150
(E) 200

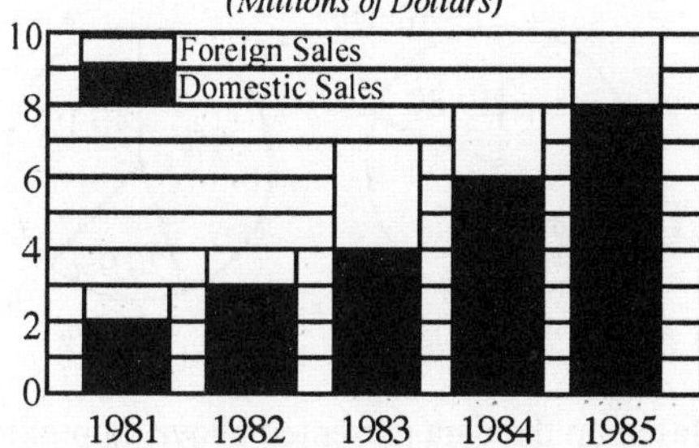

236. Based on the data presented above, what was the difference in the value of foreign sales by Company T between 1983 and 1985?

(F) $1,000,000
(G) $2,000,000
(H) $3,000,000
(J) $5,000,000
(K) $6,000,000

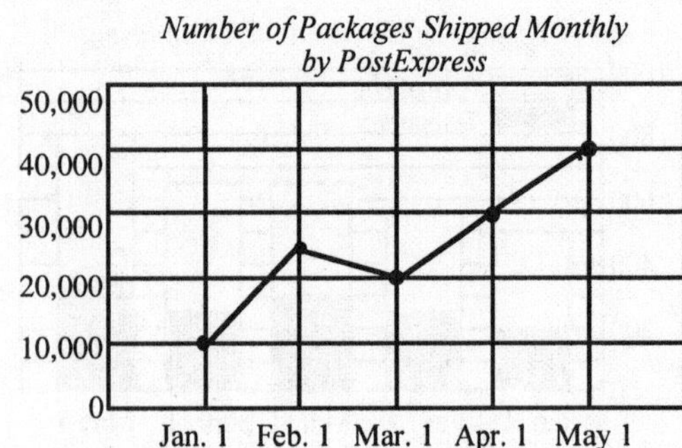

237. Based on the data presented above, what was the approximate total number of packages shipped by PostExpress for the months January, February, and March, inclusive?

(A) 40,000
(B) 55,000
(C) 60,000
(D) 70,000
(E) 85,000

GOVERNMENT EXPENDITURES
$1,000,137 = 100%

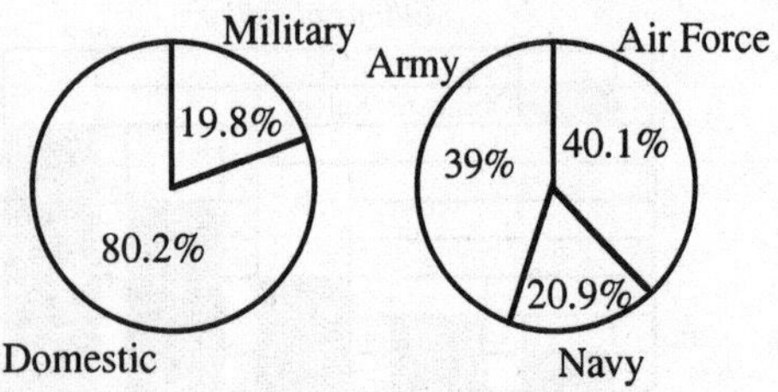

238. Based on the data presented above, approximately how much money was spent on the Air Force?

(F) $39,704
(G) $79,409
(H) $96,123
(J) $198,027
(K) $401,054

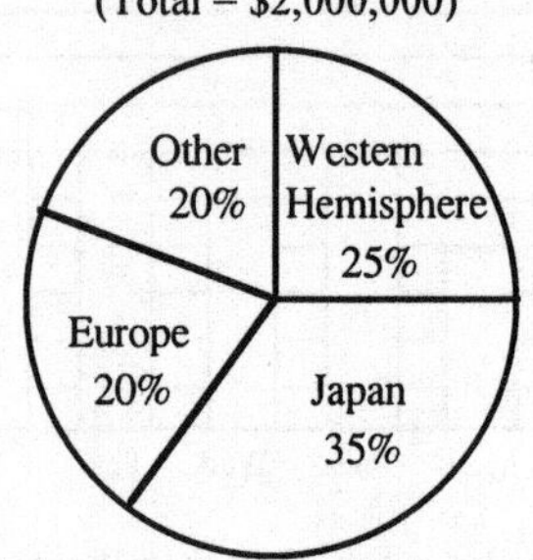

239. Based on the data presented above, what was the dollar value of foreign sales to Europe by PetProducts in 2002?

(A) $200,000
(B) $400,000
(C) $1,200,000
(D) $1,600,000
(E) $2,000,000

T-shirt Prices

	Blue	Red	White
Small	$5.00	$6.00	$7.00
Large	$5.75	$6.50	$7.25
Extra Large	$6.50	$7.25	$8.00

240. Based on the data presented above, what is the total cost of 5 large blue t-shirts, 8 small red t-shirts, and 4 extra large white t-shirts?

(F) $56.00
(G) $88.25
(H) $105.50
(J) $108.75
(K) $135.00

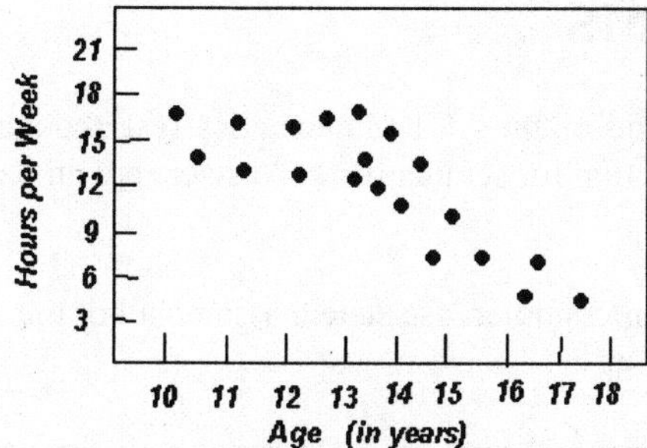

241. The above scatterplot shows the video-game playing habits of 20 students. The graph most strongly supports the conclusion that the number of hours per week spent playing video-games

(A) is constant from age 10 to age 18
(B) increases as age increases from 10 to 18
(C) decreases as age increases from 10 to 18
(D) is constant for ages 10 through 14 and then decreases
(E) is constant for ages 10 through 14 and then increases

CHALLENGE ITEMS

The items in this section reflect both the format and difficulty range of items on the ACT Mathematics Test, though difficult items are emphasized. You may use any available space in the section for scratch work. Answers are on page 934.

DIRECTIONS: Solve each item and choose the correct answer choice. Then, fill in the corresponding oval on the bubble sheet.

Allocate time wisely. Try to solve as many items as possible, returning to skipped items if time permits.

Calculator use is permitted on this test; however, some items are best solved without the use of a calculator.

Note: Unless otherwise stated, assume all of the following.

1. Illustrative figures are NOT necessarily drawn to scale.
2. The word *average* indicates arithmetic mean.
3. The word *line* indicates a straight line.
4. Geometric figures lie in a plane.

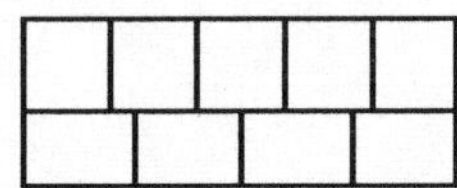

1. Nine playing cards from the same deck are placed as shown in the figure above to form a large rectangle of area 180 sq. in. How many inches are there in the perimeter of this large rectangle?

   (A) 29
   (B) 58
   (C) 64
   (D) 116
   (E) 210

2. If each of the dimensions of a rectangle is increased by 100%, by what percent is the area increased?

   (F) 100%
   (G) 200%
   (H) 300%
   (J) 400%
   (K) 500%

3. What is 10% of $\frac{1}{3}x$ if $\frac{2}{3}x$ is 10% of 60?

   (A) 0.1
   (B) 0.2
   (C) 0.3
   (D) 0.4
   (E) 0.5

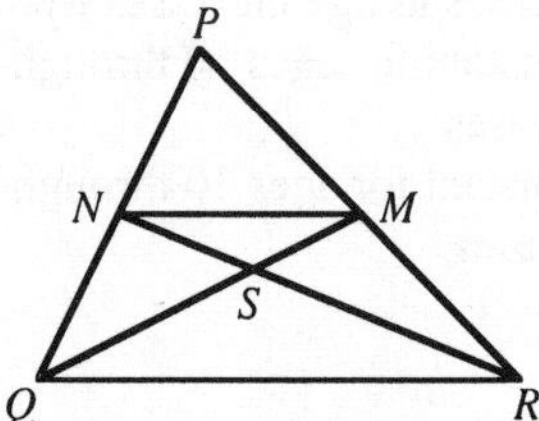

4. In the figure above, M and N are midpoints of sides $\overline{PR}$ and $\overline{PQ}$, respectively, of ΔPQR. What is the ratio of the area of ΔMNS to that of ΔPQR?

   (F) 2:5
   (G) 2:9
   (H) 1:4
   (J) 1:8
   (K) 1:12

NOTES AND STRATEGIES

5. A cube has an edge that is 4 inches long. If the edge is increased by 25%, by what percent is the volume increased?

(A) 25%
(B) 48%
(C) 73%
(D) 95%
(E) 122%

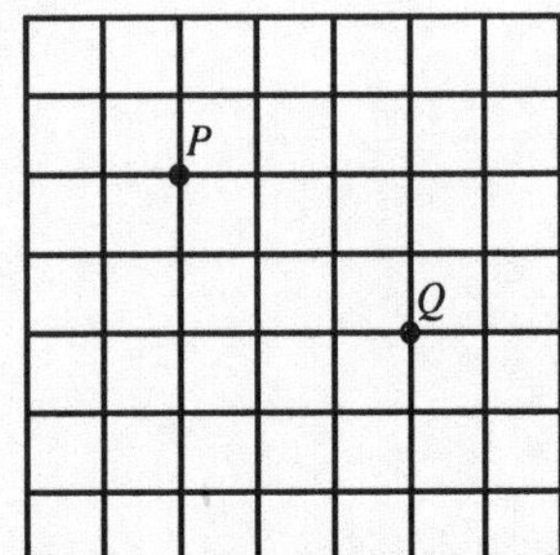

6. In the graph above, the axes and the origin are not shown. If point P has coordinates (3, 7), what are the coordinates of point Q, assuming each box is one square unit?

(F) (5, 6)
(G) (1, 10)
(H) (6, 9)
(J) (6, 5)
(K) (5, 10)

7. The average of 8 numbers is 6; the average of 6 other numbers is 8. What is the average of all 14 numbers?

(A) 6
(B) $6\frac{6}{7}$
(C) 7
(D) $7\frac{2}{7}$
(E) $8\frac{1}{7}$

8. The front wheels of a wagon are 7 feet in circumference and the back wheels are 9 feet in circumference. When the front wheels have made 10 more revolutions than the back wheels, what distance, in feet, has the wagon gone?

(F) 126
(G) 180
(H) 189
(J) 315
(K) 630

9. Doreen can wash her car in 15 minutes, while her younger brother Dave takes twice as long to do the same job. If they work together, how many minutes will the job take them?

(A) 5
(B) $7\frac{1}{2}$
(C) 10
(D) $22\frac{1}{2}$
(E) 30

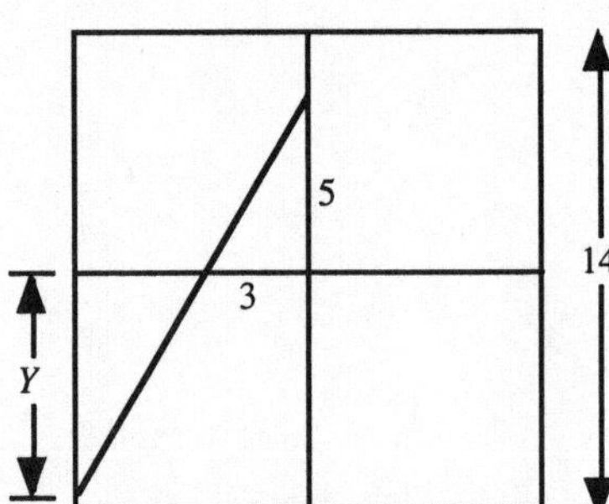

10. In the figure above, the sides of the large square are each 14 inches long. Joining the midpoints of each opposite side forms 4 smaller squares. What is the value of Y, in inches?

(F) 5
(G) 6
(H) $6\frac{5}{8}$
(J) $6\frac{2}{3}$
(K) 6.8

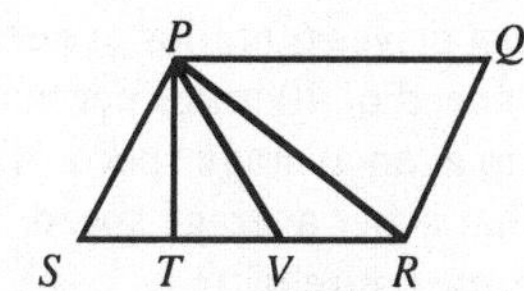

Note: Figure not drawn to scale.

11. In the figure above, $PQRS$ is a parallelogram, and $\overline{ST} = \overline{TV} = \overline{VR}$. If $\angle PTS = 90°$, what is the ratio of the area of ΔSPT to the area of the parallelogram?

(A) $\frac{1}{6}$
(B) $\frac{1}{5}$
(C) $\frac{2}{7}$
(D) $2\frac{1}{3}$
(E) Cannot be determined from the given information

12. If $p > q$ and $r < 0$, which of the following is (are) true?

I. $pr < qr$
II. $p + r > q + r$
III. $p - r < q - r$

(F) I only
(G) II only
(H) I and III only
(J) I and II only
(K) I, II, and III

13. A pound of water is evaporated from 6 pounds of seawater that is 4% salt. What is the percentage of salt in the remaining solution?

(A) 3.6%
(B) 4%
(C) 4.8%
(D) 5.2%
(E) 6%

14. John is now three times Pat's age. Four years from now, John will be x years old. In terms of x, how old is Pat now?

(F) $\frac{x+4}{3}$
(G) $3x$
(H) $x + 4$
(J) $x - 4$
(K) $\frac{x-4}{3}$

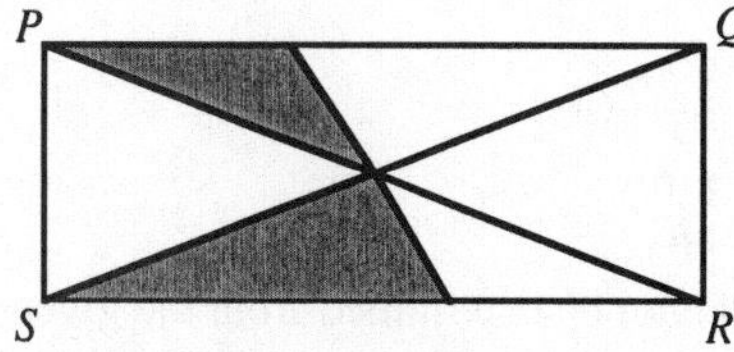

15. In the figure above, what percent of the area of rectangle $PQRS$ is shaded?

(A) 20
(B) 25
(C) 30
(D) $33\frac{1}{3}$
(E) 35

16. A cylindrical container has a diameter of 14 inches and a height of 6 inches. Since one gallon equals 231 cubic inches, what is the approximate capacity, in gallons, of the tank?

(F) $\frac{2}{3}$
(G) $1\frac{1}{7}$
(H) $2\frac{2}{7}$
(J) $2\frac{2}{3}$
(K) 4

17. A train running between two towns arrives at its destination 10 minutes late when it goes 40 miles per hour and 16 minutes late when it goes 30 miles per hour. What is the distance, in miles, between the two towns?

(A) $8\frac{6}{7}$
(B) 12
(C) 192
(D) 560
(E) 720

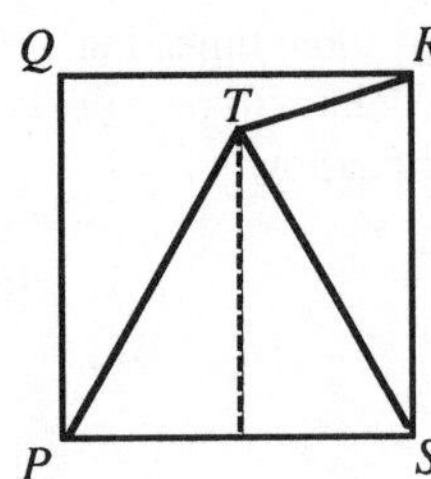

18. In the figure above, $PQRS$ is a square and PTS is an equilateral triangle. What is the degree measure of $\angle TRS$?

(F) 60
(G) 75
(H) 80
(J) 90
(K)Cannot be determined from the given information

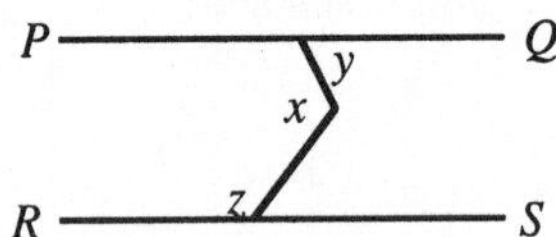

19. In the figure above, line $\overline{PQ}$ is parallel to line $\overline{RS}$, $y = 60°$, and $z = 130°$. What is the degree measure of $\angle x$?

(A) 90
(B) 100
(C) 110
(D) 120
(E) 130

20. Paul can paint a fence in 2 hours and Fred can paint the same fence in 3 hours. If Paul and Fred work together, how many hours will it take them to paint the fence?

(F) 5
(G) $2\frac{1}{2}$
(H) $1\frac{1}{5}$
(J) 1
(K) $\frac{5}{6}$

21. A motorist drives 60 miles to her destination at an average speed of 40 miles per hour and makes the return trip at an average speed of 30 miles per hour. What is her average speed, in miles per hour, for the entire trip?

(A) 17
(B) $34\frac{2}{7}$
(C) 35
(D) $43\frac{1}{3}$
(E) 70

22. An ice cream truck drives down Willy Street 4 times a week. The truck carries 5 different flavors of ice cream bars, each of which comes in 2 different designs. If the truck runs Monday through Thursday, and Monday was the first day of the month, by what day of the month could Zachary, buying 1 ice cream bar each time the truck drives down the street, purchase all of the different varieties of ice cream bars?

(F) 11th
(G) 16th
(H) 21st
(J) 24th
(K) 30th

23. If $N! = N(N-1)(N-2)\ldots[N-(N-1)]$, what does $\frac{N!}{(N-2)!}$ equal?

(A) $N^2 - N$
(B) $N^5 + N^3 - N^2 + \frac{N}{N^2}$
(C) $N + 1$
(D) 1
(E) 6

NOTES AND STRATEGIES

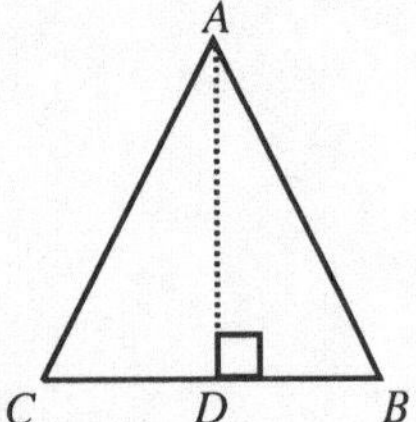

24. In the figure above, ABC is an equilateral triangle with a perpendicular line drawn from point A to point D. If the triangle is "folded over" on the perpendicular line so that points B and C meet, the perimeter of the new triangle is approximately what percent of the perimeter of the triangle before the fold?

(F) 100%
(G) 78%
(H) 50%
(J) 32%
(K) Cannot be determined from the given information

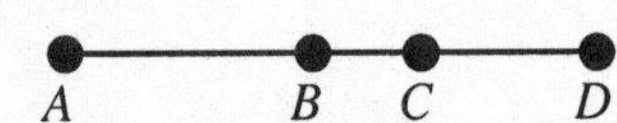

Note: Figure not drawn to scale.

25. In the figure above, segment $\overline{AB}$ is three times longer than segment $\overline{BC}$, and segment $\overline{CD}$ is two times longer than segment $\overline{BC}$. If segment $\overline{BC}$ is removed from the line and the other two segments are joined to form one line, what is the ratio of the original length of $\overline{AD}$ to the new length of $\overline{AD}$?

(A) 3:2
(B) 6:5
(C) 5:4
(D) 7:6
(E) 11:10

26. If $(x + 1)(x - 2)$ is positive, then

(F) $x < -1$ or $x > 2$
(G) $x > -1$ or $x < 2$
(H) $-1 < x < 2$
(J) $-2 < x < 1$
(K) $x = -1$ or $x = 2$

Annual Sale of Cassettes ABC SOUND STORES	
Year	*Number Sold*
1995	7,000
1996	9,000
1997	12,000
1998	16,000
1999	20,000
2000	24,000

27. In the above table, which yearly period had the smallest percent increase in sales?

(A) 1995-96
(B) 1996-97
(C) 1997-98
(D) 1998-99
(E) 1999-00

28. If s, t, and u are different positive integers and $\frac{s}{t}$ and $\frac{t}{u}$ are positive integers, which of the following CANNOT be a positive integer?

(F) $\frac{s}{u}$
(G) $s \cdot t$
(H) $\frac{u}{s}$
(J) $(s + t)u$
(K) $(s - u)t$

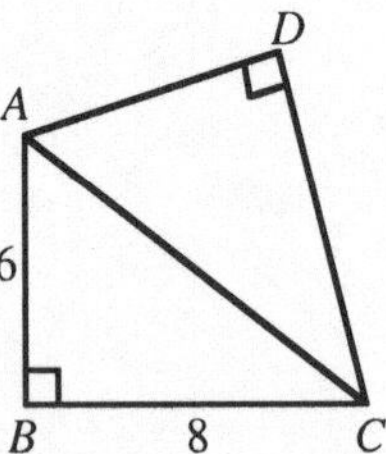

Note: Figure not drawn to scale.

29. In the figure above, $\overline{AD} = \overline{DC}$. What is the value of $\overline{AD} + \overline{DC}$?

(A) $18\sqrt{2}$
(B) 18
(C) $10\sqrt{2}$
(D) 10
(E) $6\sqrt{2}$

30. For the figure below, which of the following statements is true?

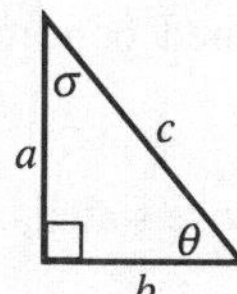

(F) $\sin\theta = \frac{b}{c}$
(G) $\tan\sigma = \frac{a}{b}$
(H) $\cos\theta = \frac{c}{a}$
(J) $\sin\theta = \cos\sigma$
(K) $\cot\sigma = \tan\sigma$

31. In the figure below, if $\arcsin s = 2(\arcsin d)$, then $x = ?$

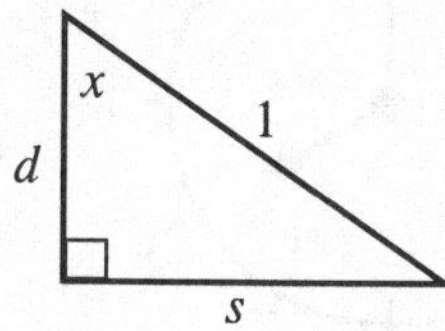

(A) 15
(B) 30
(C) 45
(D) 60
(E) 75

32. In the figure below, if $\overline{AC}$ is the diameter of the circle, B is a point on the circle, and $\sin\theta = \frac{1}{2}$, then $\sin\phi = ?$

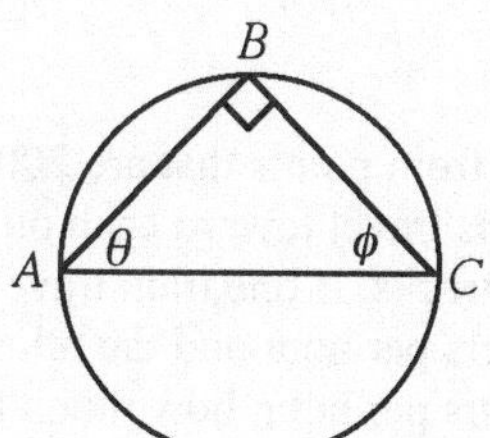

(F) $\frac{\sqrt{2}}{3}$
(G) $\frac{\sqrt{3}}{3}$
(H) $\frac{\sqrt{3}}{2}$
(J) $\frac{2\sqrt{2}}{3}$
(K) $\frac{2\sqrt{3}}{2}$

33. The figure below is a possible graph of which of the following equations?

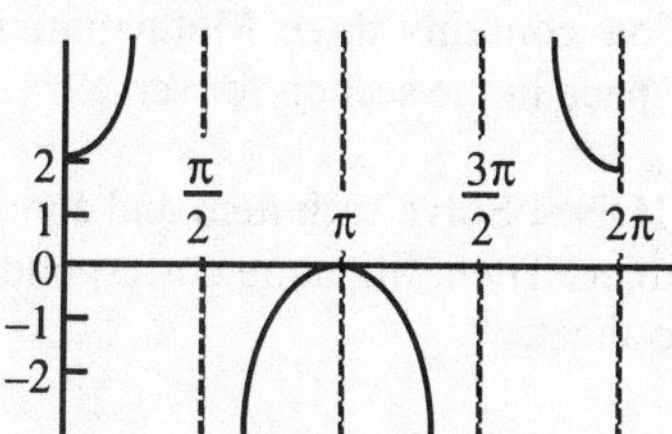

(A) $y = 2\sin x$
(B) $y = \sin x + 2$
(C) $y = \csc x + 1$
(D) $y = \csc x - 1$
(E) $y = \sec x + 1$

34. If θ is an acute angle and $\cos\theta = \frac{b}{c}$, $b > 0$ and $c > 0$ and $b \neq c$, then $\sin\theta$ is equal to which of the following?

(F) $\frac{b}{\sqrt{b^2 - c^2}}$
(G) $\frac{c}{\sqrt{b^2 - b^2}}$
(H) $\frac{\sqrt{b^2 - c^2}}{b}$
(J) $\frac{\sqrt{b^2 - c^2}}{c}$
(K) $\frac{\sqrt{c^2 - b^2}}{c}$

TIMED-PRACTICE QUIZZES

This section contains three Mathematics quizzes. Complete each quiz under timed conditions. You may use any available space in the section for scratch work. Answers are on page 934.

DIRECTIONS: Solve each item and choose the correct answer choice. Then, fill in the corresponding oval on the bubble sheet.

Allocate time wisely. Try to solve as many items as possible, returning to skipped items if time permits.

Calculator use is permitted on this test; however, some items are best solved without the use of a calculator.

Note: Unless otherwise stated, assume all of the following.

1. Illustrative figures are NOT necessarily drawn to scale.
2. The word *average* indicates arithmetic mean.
3. The word *line* indicates a straight line.
4. Geometric figures lie in a plane

A. QUIZ I (16 items; 20 minutes)

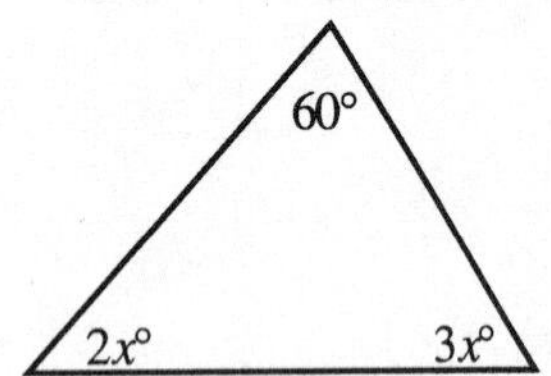

1. In the triangle above, $x =$

(A) 24
(B) 20
(C) 16
(D) 12
(E) 10

2. A normal dozen contains 12 items, and a baker's dozen contains 13 items. If x is the number of items that could be measured either in a whole number of normal dozens or in a whole number of baker's dozens, what is the minimum value of x?

(F) 1
(G) 12
(H) 13
(J) 25
(K) 156

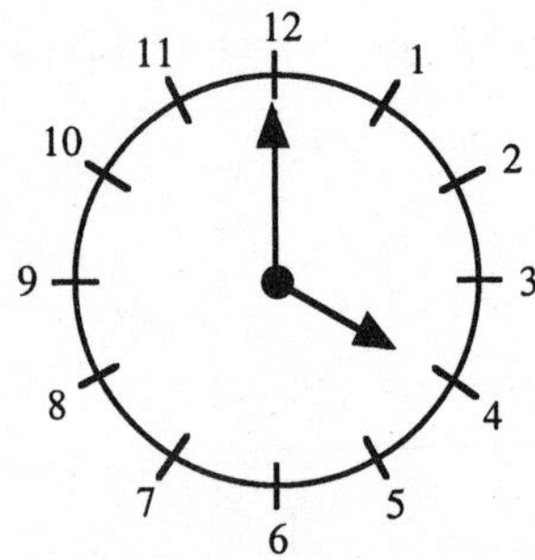

3. In the figure above, what is the degree measure of the smaller of the two angles formed by the hour and minute hands of the clock?

(A) 45
(B) 60
(C) 90
(D) 120
(E) 240

4. Starting from points that are 200 kilometers apart, two trains travel toward each other along two parallel tracks. If one train travels at 70 kilometers per hour and the other travels at 80 kilometers per hour, how much time, in hours, will elapse before the trains pass each other?

(F) $\frac{3}{4}$
(G) 1
(H) $\frac{4}{3}$
(J) $\frac{3}{2}$
(K) 2

5. A student begins heating a certain substance with a temperature of 50° C over a Bunsen burner. If the temperature of the substance will rise 20° C for every 24 minutes it remains over the burner, what will be the temperature, in degrees Celsius, of the substance after 18 minutes?

(A) 52
(B) 56
(C) 60
(D) 65
(E) 72

6. If the ratio of men to women in a meeting is 8 to 7, what fractional part of the people at the meeting is women?

(F) $\frac{1}{56}$
(G) $\frac{1}{15}$
(H) $\frac{1}{7}$
(J) $\frac{7}{15}$
(K) $\frac{8}{7}$

7. The object of a popular board game is to use clues to identify a suspect and the weapon used to commit a crime. If there are 3 suspects and 6 weapons, how many different solutions to the game are possible?

(A) 2
(B) 3
(C) 9
(D) 12
(E) 18

8. The average weight of three boxes is $25\frac{1}{3}$ pounds. If each box weighs at least 24 pounds, what is the <u>greatest</u> possible weight, in pounds, of any one of the boxes?

(F) 25
(G) 26
(H) 27
(J) 28
(K) 29

9. If n subtracted from $\frac{13}{2}$ is equal to n divided by $\frac{2}{13}$, what is the value of n?

(A) $\frac{2}{3}$
(B) $\frac{13}{15}$
(C) 1
(D) $\frac{13}{11}$
(E) 26

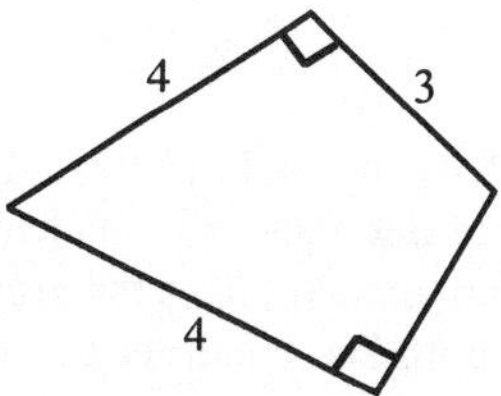

10. In the figure above, what is the area of the quadrilateral?

(F) 18
(G) 15
(H) 12
(J) 9
(K) 8

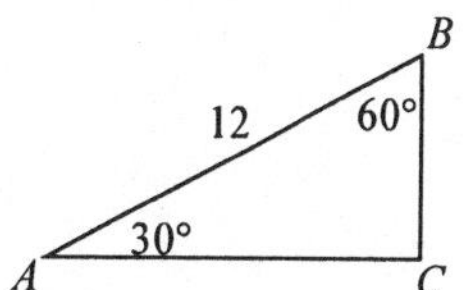

11. In the figure above, what is the length of $\overline{BC}$? ($\sin 30° = \frac{1}{2}$.)

(A) 2
(B) 3
(C) $3\sqrt{3}$
(D) 6
(E) $6\sqrt{3}$

12. After being dropped from a height of h meters, a ball bounces 3 meters high on the third bounce and $\frac{4}{3}$ meters high on the fifth bounce. What is the value, in meters, of h?

(F) $\frac{27}{8}$
(G) $\frac{9}{2}$
(H) $\frac{27}{4}$
(J) $\frac{81}{8}$
(K) $\frac{27}{2}$

13. Set $A = \{-2, -1, 0\}$, and Set $B = (-1, 0, 1\}$. If a is an element of Set A and b is an element of Set B, for how many pairs (a, b) is the product ab a member of both Set A and Set B?

(A) 0
(B) 2
(C) 4
(D) 6
(E) 9

14. Which of the following is the complete solution set for $|2x + 4| = 12$?

(F) $\{-8, 4\}$
(G) $\{-4, 8\}$
(H) $\{0, 8\}$
(J) $\{4, 8\}$
(K) $\{6, 8\}$

15. If $f(x) = \frac{(x-1)^2}{(-2-x)}$, for what value of x is $f(x)$ undefined?

(A) −2
(B) −1
(C) 0
(D) 1
(E) 2

16. For the figure below, which of the following statements is INCORRECT?

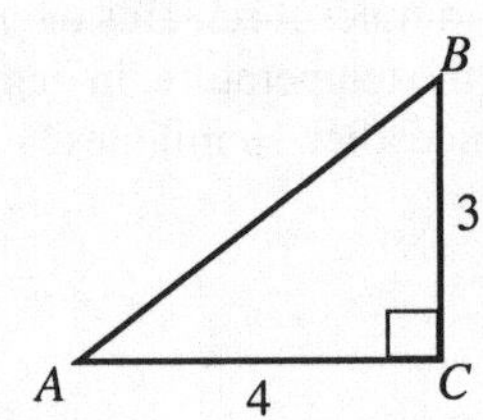

(F) $\sin A = \frac{3}{5}$

(G) $\cos A = \frac{4}{5}$

(H) $\tan A = \frac{3}{4}$

(J) $\cot A = \frac{5}{3}$

(K) $\sec A = \frac{5}{4}$

B. QUIZ II (21 items; 25 minutes)

1. The figure above is a plan that shows a solid set of steps to be constructed from concrete blocks of equal size. How many blocks are needed to construct the steps?

(A) 12
(B) 15
(C) 18
(D) 21
(E) 24

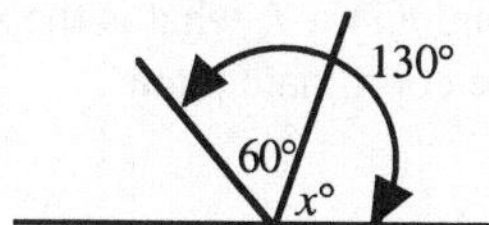

2. In the figure above, what is the value of x?

(F) 70
(G) 60
(H) 50
(J) 40
(K) 30

3. If $2^{x+1} = 4^{x-1}$, what is the value of x?

(A) 1
(B) 2
(C) 3
(D) 4
(E) 5

4. Of the actors in a certain play, five actors are in Act I, 12 actors are in Act II, and 13 actors are in Act III. If 10 of the actors are in exactly two of the three acts and all of the other actors are in just one act, how many actors are in the play?

(F) 17
(G) 20
(H) 24
(J) 30
(K) 38

5. In the figure above, $\overline{AB} \cong \overline{BC} \cong \overline{CA}$. What is the value of y?

(A) 20
(B) 60
(C) 80
(D) 100
(E) 120

6. Under certain conditions, a bicycle traveling k meters per second requires $\frac{k^2}{20} + k$ meters to stop. If $k = 10$, how many meters does the bicycle need to stop?

(F) 10
(G) 12
(H) 15
(J) 20
(K) 30

7. What is the slope of a line that passes through the origin and $(-3, -2)$?

(A) $\frac{3}{2}$
(B) $\frac{2}{3}$
(C) 0
(D) $-\frac{2}{3}$
(E) $-\frac{3}{2}$

8. An album contains x black-and-white photographs and y color photographs. If the album contains 24 photographs, then which of the following CANNOT be true?

(F) $x = y$
(G) $x = 2y$
(H) $x = 3y$
(J) $x = 4y$
(K) Cannot be determined from the given information

9. If $2a = 3b = 4c$, then what is the average (arithmetic mean) of a, b, and c, in terms of a?

(A) $\frac{13a}{18}$
(B) $\frac{13a}{9}$
(C) $\frac{8a}{3}$
(D) $\frac{4a}{3}$
(E) $2a$

10. If $x = 6 + y$ and $4x = 3 - 2y$, what is the value of x?

(F) 4
(G) $\frac{11}{3}$
(H) $\frac{5}{2}$
(J) $-\frac{2}{3}$
(K) $-\frac{7}{2}$

11. If $\frac{2}{3}$ is written as a decimal to 101 places, what is the sum of the first 100 digits to the right of the decimal point?

(A) 66
(B) 595
(C) 599
(D) 600
(E) 601

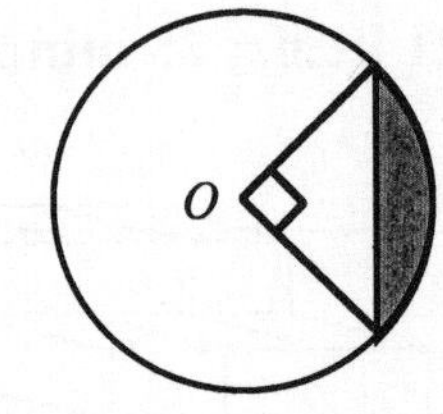

12. In the figure above, O is the center of the circle with radius 1. What is the area of the shaded region?

(F) $\frac{3\pi}{4} + \frac{1}{2}$
(G) $\frac{3\pi}{4} - \frac{1}{2}$
(H) $\frac{\pi}{4} + \frac{1}{2}$
(J) $\frac{\pi}{4} - \frac{1}{2}$
(K) $\pi - 1$

13. If $f(3) = 5$ and $f(7) = 7$, what is the slope of graph of $f(x)$ in the coordinate plane?

(A) -2
(B) $-\frac{1}{2}$
(C) 1
(D) $\frac{1}{2}$
(E) 2

14. In a list of the first 100 positive integers, the digit 9 appears how many times?

(F) 9
(G) 10
(H) 11
(J) 19
(K) 20

15. If $\frac{x}{x+3} = \frac{3}{4}$, and $x \neq -3$, then $x =$

(A) 3
(B) 4
(C) 5
(D) 7
(E) 9

16. Which of the following is the complete solution set for $\sqrt{2x+3}+2=5$?

(F) {}
(G) {–1}
(H) {3}
(J) {–1, 3}
(K) {1, 2}

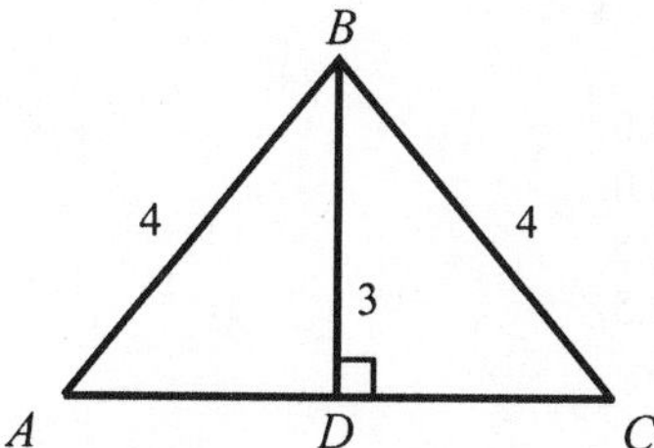

17. In the figure above, what is the length of $\overline{AC}$? ($\sin \angle ABD = \frac{\sqrt{7}}{4}$.)

(A) 5
(B) $2\sqrt{7}$
(C) $4\sqrt{3}$
(D) 7
(E) $3\sqrt{7}$

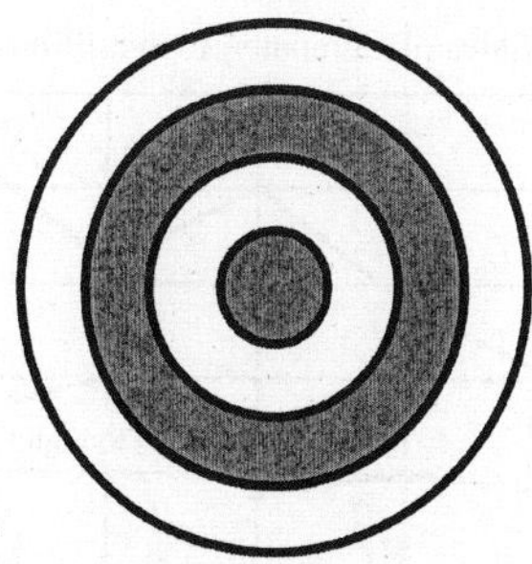

18. A dartboard has four concentric circles with the center as indicated in the figure above. If the diameter of each circle except for the smallest is twice that of the next smaller circle, what is the probability that a randomly thrown dart will strike the shaded portion of the figure?

(F) $\frac{3}{16}$
(G) $\frac{1}{4}$
(H) $\frac{13}{64}$
(J) $\frac{17}{64}$
(K) $\frac{1}{2}$

19. If $f(3) = 4$ and $f(-3) = 1$, what is the y-intercept of the graph of $f(x)$ in the coordinate plane?

(A) $-\frac{5}{2}$
(B) $-\frac{2}{5}$
(C) 0
(D) $\frac{2}{5}$
(E) $\frac{5}{2}$

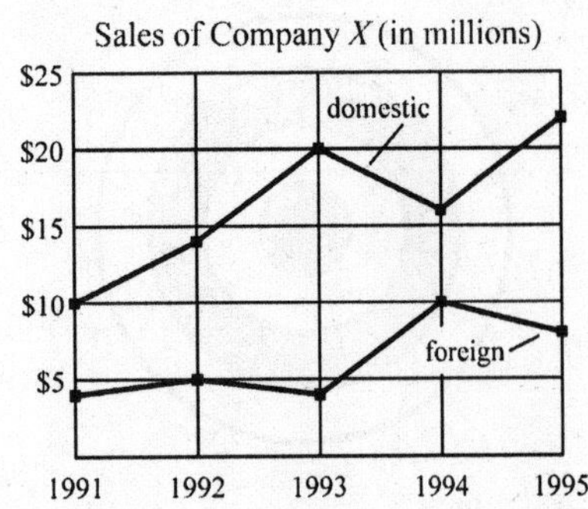

20. Which of the following pie graphs best represents the division of total sales between foreign and domestic sales for 1994?

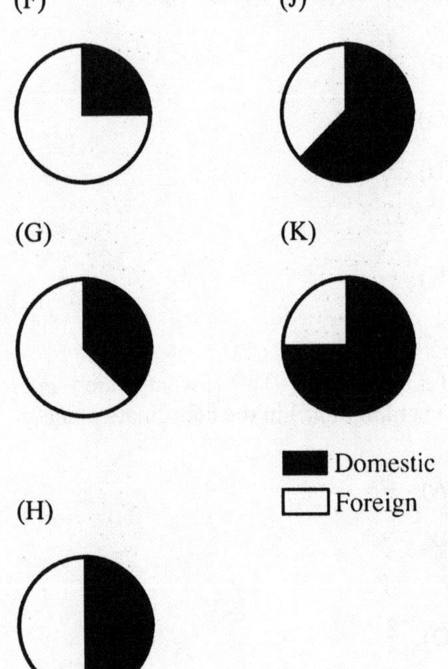

21. In the figure below, the length of $\overline{AC}$ is 5 units. Which of the following is the best approximation for the number of units in the length of $\overline{BC}$ ($\tan 22° \approx 0.4$.)?

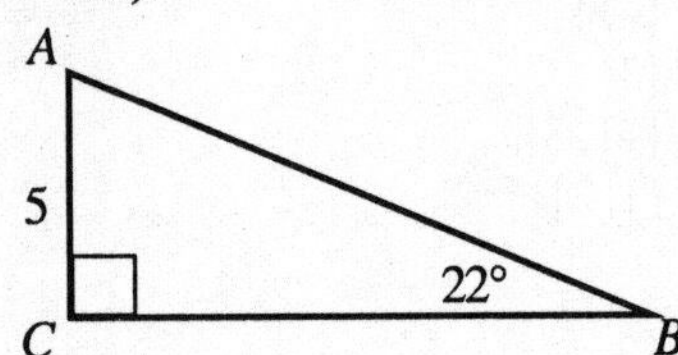

(A) 2.0
(B) 3.0
(C) 7.5
(D) 12.5
(E) 16

C. QUIZ III (26 items; 25 minutes)

1. What is the average (arithmetic mean) of all integers 6 through 15 (including 6 and 15)?

   (A) 6
   (B) 9
   (C) 10.5
   (D) 11
   (E) 21

2. Which of the following numbers is the largest?

   (F) 0.08
   (G) 0.17
   (H) 0.171
   (J) 0.1077
   (K) 0.10771

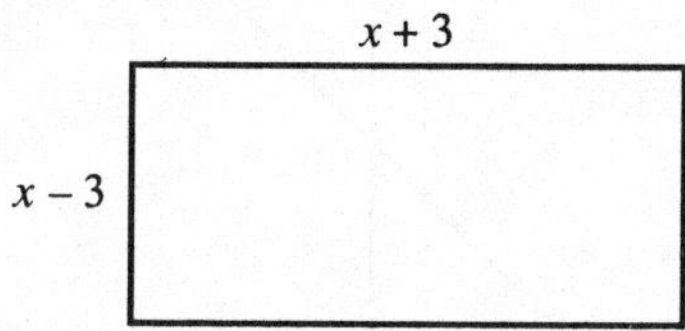

3. If the rectangle above has an area of 72, then $x =$

   (A) 3
   (B) 4
   (C) 6
   (D) 8
   (E) 9

4. Machine X produces 15 units per minute and Machine Y produces 12 units per minute. In one hour, Machine X will produce how many more units than Machine Y?

   (F) 90
   (G) 180
   (H) 240
   (J) 270
   (K) 360

Team Expenses

Category	Amount
Transportation	\$240
Lodging	\$360
Meals	\$120

5. Which of the following pie charts represents the data shown above?

   (A) 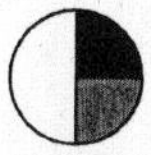
   (B) 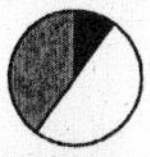
   (C) 
   (D) 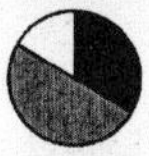
   (E)

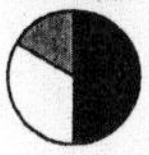

6. On the first day after being given an assignment, a student read $\frac{1}{2}$ the number of pages assigned, and on the second day, the student read 3 more pages. If the student still has 6 additional pages to read, how many pages were assigned?

   (F) 15
   (G) 18
   (H) 24
   (J) 30
   (K) 36

7. The average (arithmetic mean) of Pat's scores on three tests was 80. If the average of her scores on the first two tests was 78, what was her score on the third test?

   (A) 82
   (B) 84
   (C) 86
   (D) 88
   (E) 90

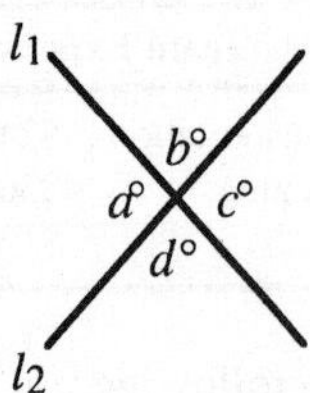

8. In the figure above, $a + c - b$ is equal to which of the following?

(F) $2a - d$
(G) $2a + d$
(H) $2d - a$
(J) $2a$
(K) 180

9. If $3a + 6b = 12$, then $a + 2b =$

(A) 1
(B) 2
(C) 3
(D) 4
(E) 6

10. Two circles with radii r and $r + 3$ have areas that differ by 15π. What is the radius of the <u>smaller</u> circle?

(F) 4
(G) 3
(H) 2
(J) 1
(K) $\frac{1}{2}$

11. If x, y, and z are integers, $x > y > z > 1$, and $xyz = 144$, what is the <u>greatest</u> possible value of x?

(A) 8
(B) 12
(C) 16
(D) 24
(E) 36

12. For all integers, $x \spadesuit y = 2x + 3y$. Which of the following must be true?

I. $3 \spadesuit 2 = 12$
II. $x \spadesuit y = y \spadesuit x$
III. $0 \spadesuit (1 \spadesuit 2) = (0 \spadesuit 1) \spadesuit 2$

(F) I only
(G) I and II only
(H) I and III only
(J) II and III only
(K) I, II, and III

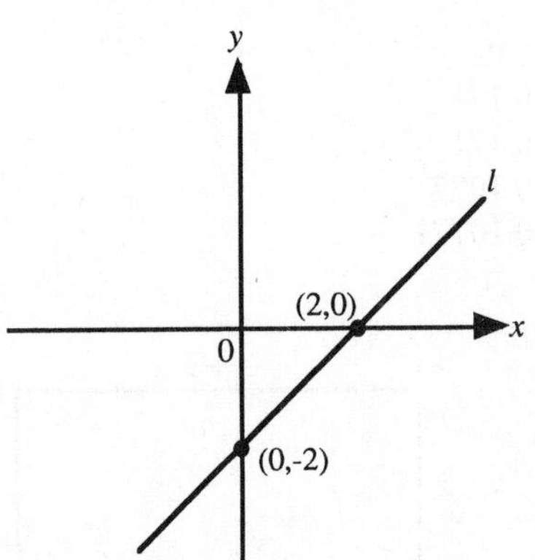

13. In the figure above, what is the slope of line l?

(A) 1
(B) $\frac{1}{2}$
(C) 0
(D) $-\frac{1}{2}$
(E) -1

14. If Yuriko is now twice as old as Lisa was 10 years ago, how old is Lisa today if Yuriko is now n years old?

(F) $\frac{n}{2} + 10$
(G) $\frac{n}{2} - 10$
(H) $n - 10$
(J) $2n + 10$
(K) $2n - 10$

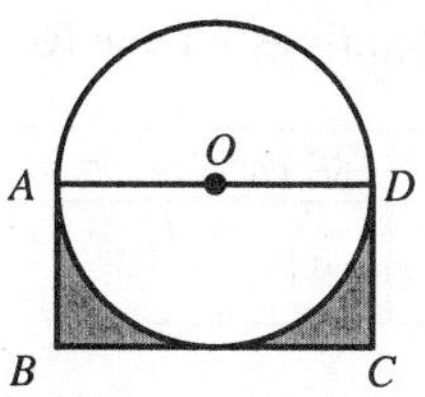

15. In the figure above, $ABCD$ is a rectangle with sides $\overline{AB}$, $\overline{BC}$, and $\overline{CD}$ touching the circle with center O. If the radius of the circle is 2, what is the area of the shaded region?

(A) $\frac{3\pi}{2}$
(B) $\frac{3\pi}{4}$
(C) $8 - 2\pi$
(D) $2 - \pi$
(E) $\pi - 1$

16. The sum of two positive consecutive integers is n. In terms of n, what is the value of the larger of the two integers?

(F) $\frac{n-1}{2}$
(G) $\frac{n+1}{2}$
(H) $\frac{n}{2} + 1$
(J) $\frac{n}{2} - 1$
(K) $\frac{n}{2}$

	Old Scale	*New Scale*
Minimum Score	0	120
Minimum Passing Score	60	?
Maximum Score	100	180

17. The table above shows a teacher how to convert scores for a test from the Old Scale to the New Scale. What is the Minimum Passing Score on the New Scale?

(A) 108
(B) 136
(C) 156
(D) 164
(E) 208

18. If a polygon with all equal sides is inscribed in a circle, then the measure in degrees of the minor arc created by adjacent vertices of the polygon could be all of the following EXCEPT

(F) 30
(G) 25
(H) 24
(J) 20
(K) 15

19. A jar contains 5 blue marbles, 25 green marbles, and x red marbles. If the probability of drawing a red marble at random is $\frac{1}{4}$, what is the value of x?

(A) 25
(B) 20
(C) 15
(D) 12
(E) 10

20. $\frac{1}{10^{25}} - \frac{1}{10^{26}} =$

(F) $\frac{9}{10^{25}}$
(G) $\frac{9}{10^{26}}$
(H) $\frac{1}{10^{25}}$
(J) $-\frac{9}{10^{25}}$
(K) $-\frac{1}{10}$

21. When the 10-gallon tank of an emergency generator is filled to capacity, the generator operates without interruption for 20 hours, consuming fuel at a constant rate. Which of the graphs below represents the fuel consumption of the generator over time?

(A) 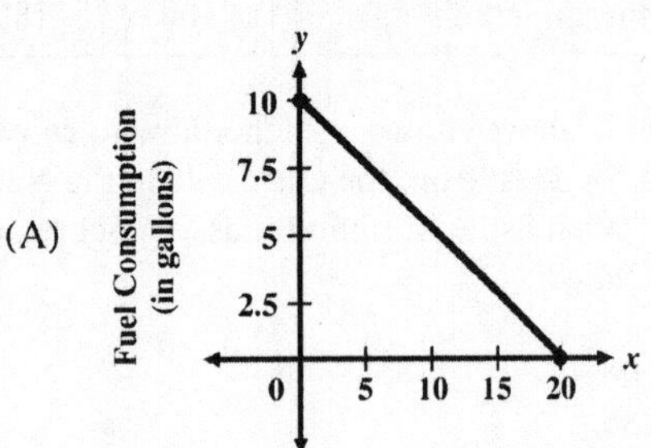

(B) 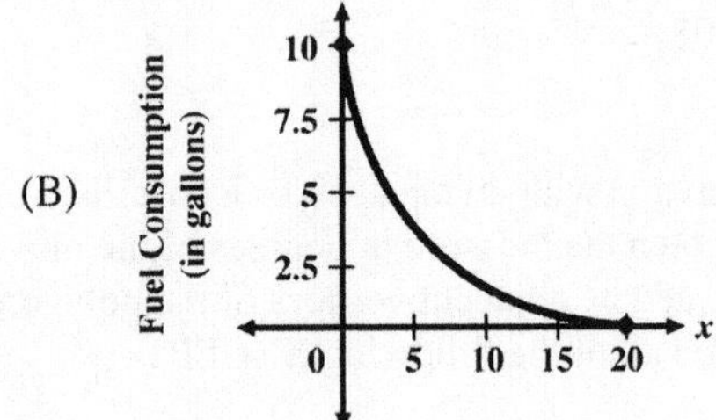

(C) 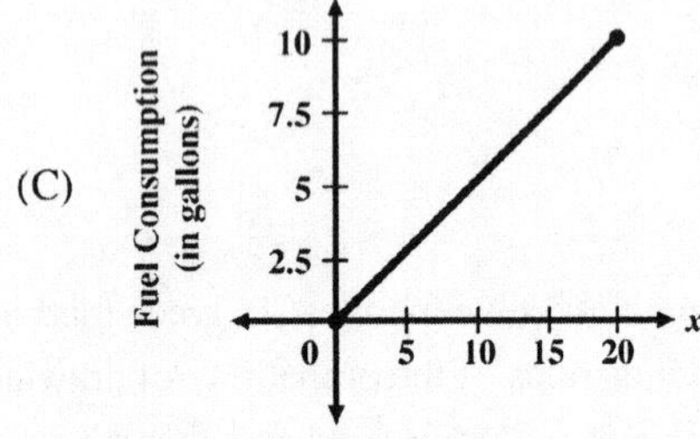

(D) 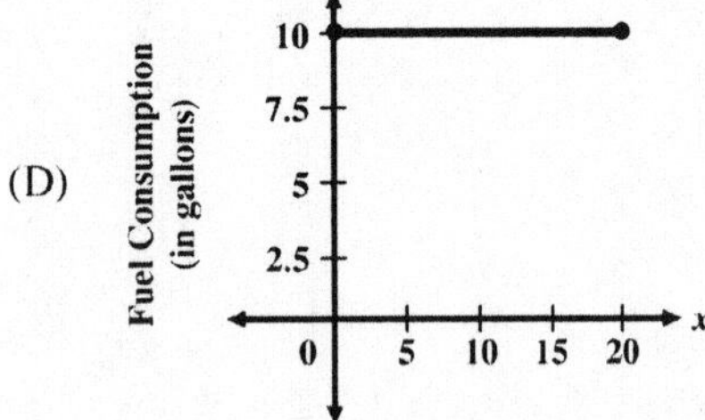

(E) 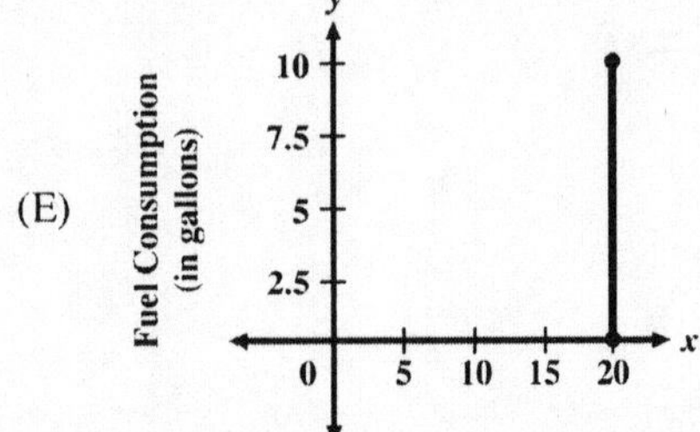

Floor Readings for the Red River

Time	1:00 pm	2:00 pm	3:00 pm	4:00 pm
Inches above Normal	0.5	1.5	?	13.5

22. The table above shows readings of water levels for the Red River at various times. If readings of the rise of the water level followed a geometric progression, the water level at 3:00 was how many inches above normal?

(F) 4
(G) 4.5
(H) 4.75
(J) 5
(K) 5.25

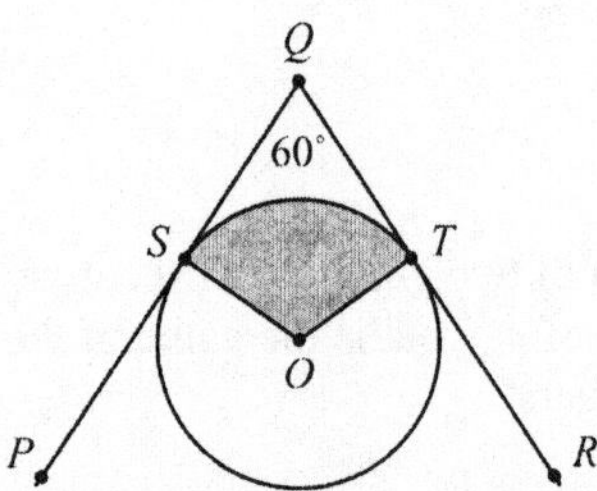

23. In the figure above, $\overline{PQ}$ is tangent to circle O at point S and $\overline{QR}$ is tangent to circle O at point T. If the radius of circle O is 2, what is the area of the shaded portion of the figure?

(A) $\frac{\pi}{3}$
(B) $\frac{2\pi}{3}$
(C) π
(D) $\frac{4\pi}{3}$
(E) 2π

Items 24-25 refer to the following table.

ANNUAL EXPENDITURES FOR THE JONES FAMILY
(percent of disposable income)

Category	2002	2003
Rent	23.0%	19.3%
Food	17.6%	18.2%
Clothing	14.2%	15.1%
Automobile	11.3%	12.3%
Utilities	10.9%	10.2%
Savings	6.2%	5.1%
Entertainment	5.2%	5.3%
Medical and Dental Care	4.0%	3.7%
Charitable Contributions	3.2%	3.9%
Household Furnishings	2.9%	3.1%
Other	1.5%	3.8%
+	100.0%	100.0%
Total Expenditures:	$34,987.00	$40,012.00

24. Approximately how much money did the Jones family spend on medical and dental care in 2002?

(F) $1,200
(G) $1,400
(H) $1,520
(J) $2,250
(K) $4,000

25. If the categories in the table are rank ordered from one to eleven in each year, for how many categories would the rank ordering change from 2002 to 2003?

(A) 2
(B) 3
(C) 4
(D) 5
(E) 6

26. In the figure below, the length of $\overline{AB}$ is 2 units. Which of the following is the best approximation for the number of units in the length of $\overline{BC}$? ($\cos 45° \approx 0.7$.)

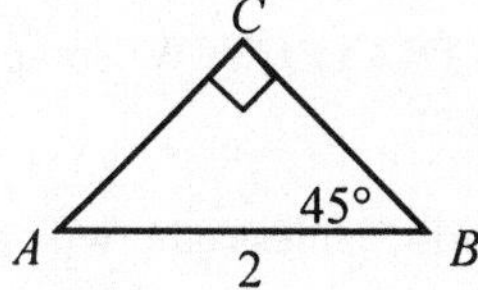

(F) 0.7
(G) 1.2
(H) 1.4
(J) 2.9
(K) 3.4

TARGETED EDUCATIONAL SOLUTIONS.

Strategy Summary Sheet
MATHEMATICS

STRUCTURE OF MATHEMATICS: The ACT Mathematics Test is 60 minutes long and is comprised of 60 Multiple-Choice items. The PLAN Mathematics Test has a total of 40 items and is 40 minutes long; the EXPLORE Mathematics Test has a total of 30 items and is 30 minutes long. While there is no definite ladder of difficulty (increasing difficulty with increasing item number), more advanced concepts tend to be tested towards the end of the test. The following is a summary of the approximate distributions of the Mathematics Test items on the ACT, the PLAN, and the EXPLORE (ACT summary is approximate):

NUMBER OF ITEMS PER CONTENT AREA

	ACT *(60 items)*	PLAN *(40 items)*	EXPLORE *(30 items)*
Arithmetic (Pre-Algebra)	14	14	10
Algebra	19	8	9
Coordinate Geometry	9	11	–
Geometry (Plane)	14	7	7
Trigonometry	4	–	–
Statistics and Probability	–	–	4

GENERAL STRATEGY: When approaching a Mathematics item, there are several things for which you should pay careful attention:

1. *Figures:* Unless otherwise specifically noted, the figures included as illustrations are drawn to scale.

2. *Answer Choices:* Most answer choices are arranged in the order of ascending or descending value and many incorrect answer choices correspond to conceptual errors.

3. *Signal Words:* Typically, signal words are capitalized, underlined, or sometimes italicized. Whenever an answer is asked for in specified units, those units will be underlined (or italicized). While the specific formatting of these signal words may vary, the importance they lend to correctly understanding the item is critical. When an item stem contains a thought-reverser, it is usually capitalized. Pay careful attention to any thought-reversers—"NOT," "CANNOT," and "EXCEPT"—as they reverse the intended meaning of an item.

4. *Ladder of Difficulty:* Difficult Mathematics items tend to be clustered near the end of the section. When solving items that are high on the ladder of difficulty, be wary of simplistic answers and the "Cannot be determined..." response. Remember to pace yourself—difficult, time-consuming items have the same value as the easy items.

5. *Preview Item Stems:* Read the item stem first (usually it is located at the end of the item material.) Only then should examinees read the details of the item, keeping this item stem in mind.

6. *Confirm Solutions:* Double-check the solution by confirming that it answers the particular question that is being asked. When applicable, this confirmation includes verifying that the solution is given in the units specified by the item stem.

If you are unable to either find an elegant (quick) solution or solve the item directly based on subject knowledge, the following alternative solutions strategies can be extremely helpful:

1. *"Test-the-Test" Strategy*: The correct answer to any item is always one of five given choices. Sometimes, the easiest and quickest way to solve an item is to test each of the answer choices. The "test-the-test" strategy can mean plugging answer choices back into the item, starting with the middle answer choice, to test the validity of an expression, or checking each answer choice against any stated conditions. "Test-the-test" typically applies to items with numerical solutions or variables and values that meet stated conditions.

2. *"Plug-and-Chug" Strategy*: This strategy is similar to the "test-the-test" strategy in that the item stem and answer choices (rather than direct mathematical solution strategies) are used to isolate the correct answer. The difference is that rather than testing the validity of each answer choice against the item stem conditions, the item stem and/or answer choices are evaluated by plugging in chosen numbers: "plug-and-chug." This strategy is especially helpful when solving Algebra items.

3. *"Eliminate-and-Guess" Strategy*: If unable to determine the correct answer directly by using mathematical methods or indirectly by using either the "test-the-test" or "plug-and-chug" strategy, eliminate as many answer choices as possible and then guess from the remaining answer choices. For difficult mathematics items, eliminate answer choices that can be reached either by a single step or by copying a number from the item.

CHECKLIST OF CONCEPTS AND SKILLS:

ARITHMETIC

___ Simplifying: Fractions, Collecting Terms
___ Factoring
___ Approximation
___ The "Flying-X" Method
___ Decimal/Fraction Equivalents
___ Properties of Numbers (Odd, Even, Negative, Positive, Consecutive)
___ Sets (Union, Intersection, Elements)
___ Absolute Value
___ Percents (Change, Original Amount, Price Increase)
___ Ratios (Two-Part, Three-Part, Weighted)
___ Proportions (Direct, Indirect)

ALGEBRA

___ Evaluation of Expressions (Rational, Radical)
___ Exponents (Integer, Rational, Negative)
___ Factoring
___ Sequence
___ Solving Single Variable Equations and Inequalities
___ Absolute Value
___ Function (Picture) Math
___ Domain and Range
___ Solving Equations (Multi-Variable, Linear, Quadratic, Simultaneous)
___ Story Problems: Work (Joint Effort), Averages

COORDINATE GEOMETRY

___ Coordinate Plane
___ Slope of a Line
___ Slope-Intercept Form of a Linear Equation
___ Distance Formula
___ Graphing Linear Equations
___ Graphing First-Degree Inequalities
___ Graphing Quadratic Equations
___ Permutations of Equations and Graphs

GEOMETRY

___ Lines and Angles (Perpendicular, Parallel, Intersecting, Big Angle/Little Angle Theorem)
___ Triangles (Equilateral, Isosceles, Acute, Obtuse, Perimeter, Area, Altitudes, Angles, Bisectors, Pythagorean Theorem)
___ Quadrilaterals (Squares, Rectangles, Rhombuses, Parallelograms, Trapezoids, Perimeter, Area)
___ Polygons (Sum of Interior Angles)
___ Circles (Chords, Tangents, Radius, Diameter, Circumference, Area)
___ Solids (Cubes, Cylinders, Spheres, Volumes, Surface Areas)
___ Complex Figures

TRIGONOMETRY

___ Trigonometric Functions
___ Trigonometric Values
___ Trigonometric Relationships

STATISTICS AND PROBABILITY

___ Averages (Simple, Weighted), Median, and Mode
___ Probability
___ Graphs (Bar, Cumulative, Line)
___ Pie Charts
___ Tables (Matrices)
___ Scatterplots

ADDITIONAL STRATEGIES FROM IN-CLASS DISCUSSION: ______________________________

Reading

TARGETED EDUCATIONAL SOLUTIONS.

Cambridge Course Concept Outline
READING

CORE LESSON

The passages and items in this section accompany the Core Lesson of the Reading Lesson. You will work through the items with your instructor in class. Use the included Notes and Strategies pages to record the problem-solving strategies that are discussed in class.

The first passage begins on the following page.

DIRECTIONS: Each passage below is followed by one or more items based on its content. Answer the items on the basis of what is stated or implied in the corresponding passage. Answers are on page 936.

Items 1-15 are based on the following passage.

SOCIAL SCIENCE: This passage discusses the presidential election of 1796.

To broaden their voting appeal in the Presidential election of 1796, the Federalists selected Thomas Pinckney, a leading South Carolinian, as running mate for the New Englander John Adams. But Pinckney's Southern friends chose to ignore their party's intentions and regarded Pinckney as a Presidential candidate, creating a political situation that Alexander Hamilton was determined to exploit. Hamilton had long been wary of Adams' stubbornly independent brand of politics and preferred to see his running mate, who was more pliant and over whom Hamilton could exert more control, in the President's chair.

The election was held under the system originally established by the Constitution. At that time, there was but a single tally, with the candidate receiving the largest number of electoral votes declared President and the candidate with the second largest number declared Vice President. Hamilton anticipated that all the Federalists in the North would vote for Adams and Pinckney equally in an attempt to ensure that Jefferson would not be either first or second in the voting. Pinckney would be solidly supported in the South while Adams would not. Hamilton concluded if it were possible to divert a few electoral votes from Adams to Pinckney, Pinckney would receive more than Adams, yet both Federalists would outpoll Jefferson.

Various methods were used to persuade the electors to vote as Hamilton wished. In the press, anonymous articles were published attacking Adams for his monarchical tendencies and Jefferson for being overly democratic, while pushing Pinckney as the only suitable candidate. In private correspondence with state party leaders, the Hamiltonians encouraged the idea that Adams' popularity was slipping, that he could not win the election, and that the Federalists could defeat Jefferson only by supporting Pinckney.

Had sectional pride and loyalty not run as high in New England as in the deep South, Pinckney might well have become Washington's successor. New Englanders, however, realized that equal votes for Adams and Pinckney in their states would defeat Adams; therefore, eighteen electors scratched Pinckney's name from their ballots and deliberately threw away their second votes to men who were not even running. It was fortunate for Adams that they did, for the electors from South Carolina completely abandoned him, giving eight votes to Pinckney and eight to Jefferson.

In the end, Hamilton's interference in Pinckney's candidacy lost him even the Vice Presidency. Without New England's support, Pinckney received only 59 electoral votes, finishing third to Adams and Jefferson. He might have been President in 1797, or as Vice President a serious contender for the Presidency in 1800; instead, stigmatized by a plot he had not devised, he served a brief term in the United States Senate and then dropped from sight as a national influence.

1. The main purpose of the passage is to:

(A) propose reforms of the procedures for electing the President and Vice President.
(B) condemn Alexander Hamilton for interfering in the election of 1796.
(C) describe the political events that led to John Adams' victory in the 1796 Presidential election.
(D) contrast the political philosophy of the Federalists to that of Thomas Jefferson.

2. Which of the following titles best describes the content of the passage?

(F) The Failure of Alexander Hamilton's Plan for Thomas Pinckney to Win the 1796 Presidential Election
(G) The Roots of Alexander Hamilton's Distrust of John Adams and New England's Politics
(H) Important Issues in the 1796 Presidential Campaign as Presented by the Federalist Candidates
(J) The Political Careers of Alexander Hamilton, John Adams, and Thomas Pinckney

3. According to the passage, which of the following was true of the Presidential election of 1796?

   (A) Thomas Jefferson received more electoral votes than did Thomas Pinckney.
   (B) John Adams received strong support from the electors of South Carolina.
   (C) Alexander Hamilton received most of the electoral votes of New England.
   (D) Thomas Pinckney was selected by Federalist party leaders to be the party's Presidential candidate.

4. According to the passage, Hamilton's plan included all of the following EXCEPT:

   (F) articles published in newspapers to create opposition to John Adams.
   (G) South Carolina's loyalty to Thomas Pinckney.
   (H) private contact with state officials urging them to support Thomas Pinckney.
   (J) John Adams' reputation as a stubborn and independent New Englander.

5. The passage supplies information that answers which of the following questions?

   (A) How many electoral votes were cast for John Adams in the 1796 Presidential election?
   (B) Under the voting system originally set up by the Constitution, how many votes did each elector cast?
   (C) Who was Jefferson's running mate in the 1796 Presidential election?
   (D) What became of Alexander Hamilton after his plan to have Thomas Pinckney elected President failed?

6. In line 11, the word "pliant" most nearly means:

   (F) assertive.
   (G) public.
   (H) national.
   (J) yielding.

7. Why does the author refer to the election procedure established by the original Constitution?

   (A) To prove to the reader that New England as a whole had more electoral votes than the state of South Carolina
   (B) To persuade the reader that Thomas Pinckney's defeat could have been avoided
   (C) To alert the reader that the procedure used in 1796 was unlike that presently used
   (D) To encourage the reader to study Constitutional history

8. The overall development of the passage can best be described as:

   (F) refuting possible explanations for certain phenomena.
   (G) documenting a thesis with specific examples.
   (H) offering an explanation of a series of events.
   (J) making particular proposals to solve a problem.

9. The passage implies that some electors voted for John Adams because they were:

   (A) in favor of a monarchy.
   (B) persuaded to do so by Hamilton.
   (C) afraid South Carolina would not vote for Pinckney.
   (D) anxious to have a President from their geographical region.

10. Which of the following can be inferred from the passage?

   (F) Thomas Pinckney had a personal dislike for Jefferson's politics.
   (G) The Federalists regarded themselves as more democratic than Jefferson.
   (H) The Hamiltonians contacted key Southern leaders to persuade them to vote for Adams.
   (J) Electors were likely to vote for candidates from their own geographical region.

11. It can be inferred that had South Carolina not cast any electoral votes for Jefferson, the outcome of the 1796 election would have been a:

(A) larger margin of victory for John Adams.
(B) victory for Thomas Jefferson.
(C) Federalist defeat in the Senate.
(D) victory for Thomas Pinckney.

12. The electors who scratched Pinckney's name from their ballots behaved most like which of the following people?

(F) A newspaper publisher who adds a special section to the Sunday edition to review the week's political events
(G) A member of the clergy who encourages members of other faiths to meet to discuss solutions to the community's problems
(H) An artist who saves preliminary sketches of an important work even after the work is finally completed
(J) A general who orders his retreating troops to destroy supplies they must leave behind so the enemy cannot use the supplies

13. Hamilton's strategy can best be summarized as:

(A) divide and conquer.
(B) retreat and regroup.
(C) feint and counterattack.
(D) hit and run.

14. The tone of the passage can best be described as:

(F) witty.
(G) comical.
(H) scholarly.
(J) frivolous.

15. The author's attitude toward Hamilton's plan can be described as:

(A) angry.
(B) approving.
(C) analytical.
(D) regretful.

NOTES AND STRATEGIES

Items 16-20 are based on the following passage.

SOCIAL SCIENCE: This passage is adapted from an essay on citizenship in a social science textbook.

The liberal view of democratic citizenship that developed in the 17th and 18th centuries was fundamentally different from that of the classical Greeks. The pursuit of private interests with as little interference as possible from government was seen as the road to human happiness and progress rather than the public obligations and involvement in the collective community that were emphasized by the Greeks. Freedom was to be realized by limiting the scope of governmental activity and political obligation and not through immersion in the collective life of the *polis*. The basic role of the citizen was to select governmental leaders and keep the powers and scope of public authority in check. On the liberal view, the rights of citizens against the state were the focus of special emphasis.

Over time, the liberal democratic notion of citizenship developed in two directions. First, there was a movement to increase the proportion of members of society who were eligible to participate as citizens—especially through extending the right of suffrage—and to ensure the basic political equality of all. Second, there was a broadening of the legitimate activities of government and a use of governmental power to redress imbalances in social and economic life. Political citizenship became an instrument through which groups and classes with sufficient numbers of votes could use the state's power to enhance their social and economic well-being.

Within the general liberal view of democratic citizenship, tensions have developed over the degree to which government can and should be used as an instrument for promoting happiness and well-being. Political philosopher Martin Diamond has categorized two views of democracy as follows. On the one hand, there is the "libertarian" perspective that stresses the private pursuit of happiness and emphasizes the necessity for restraint on government and protection of individual liberties. On the other hand, there is the "majoritarian" view that emphasizes the "task of the government to uplift and aid the common man against the malefactors of great wealth." The tensions between these two views are very evident today. Taxpayer revolts and calls for smaller government and less government regulation clash with demands for greater government involvement in the economic marketplace and the social sphere.

16. The author's primary purpose is to:

(F) study ancient concepts of citizenship.
(G) contrast different notions of citizenship.
(H) criticize modern libertarian democracy.
(J) describe the importance of universal suffrage.

17. It can be inferred from the passage that the Greek word "polis" means:

(A) family life.
(B) military service.
(C) marriage.
(D) political community.

18. The author cites Martin Diamond in the last paragraph because the author:

(F) regards Martin Diamond as an authority on political philosophy.
(G) wishes to refute Martin Diamond's views on citizenship.
(H) needs a definition of the term "citizenship."
(J) is unfamiliar with the distinction between libertarian and majoritarian concepts of democracy.

19. According to the passage, all of the following are characteristics that would distinguish the liberal idea of government from the Greek idea of government EXCEPT:

(A) the emphasis on the rights of private citizens.
(B) the activities that government may legitimately pursue.
(C) the obligation of citizens to participate in government.
(D) the size of the geographical area controlled by a government.

20. A majoritarian would be most likely to favor legislation that would:

(F) eliminate all restrictions on individual liberty.
(G) cut spending for social welfare programs.
(H) provide greater protection for consumers.
(J) lower taxes on the wealthy and raise taxes on the average worker.

Items 21-24 are based on the following passage.

SOCIAL SCIENCE: This passage is adapted from an article about John Dewey and his theories of education.

The place of public education within a democratic society has been widely discussed and debated through the years. Perhaps no one has written more widely on the subject in the United States than John Dewey, sometimes called "the father of public education," whose theories of education have a large social component; that is, he places an emphasis on education as a social act and the classroom or learning environment as a replica of society.

Dewey defined various aspects or characteristics of education. First, it was a necessity of life inasmuch as living beings needed to maintain themselves through a process of renewal. Therefore, just as humans needed sleep, food, water, and shelter for physiological renewal, they also needed education to renew their minds, assuring that their socialization kept pace with physiological growth.

A second aspect of education was its social component, which was to be accomplished by providing the young with an environment that would provide a nurturing atmosphere to encourage the growth of their, as yet, undeveloped social customs.

A third aspect of public education was the provision of direction to youngsters, who might otherwise be left in uncontrolled situations without the steadying and organizing influences of school. Direction was not to be of an overt nature, but rather indirect through the selection of the school situations in which the youngster participated.

Finally, Dewey saw public education as a catalyst for growth. Since the young came to school capable of growth, it was the role of education to provide opportunities for that growth to occur. The successful school environment is one in which a desire for continued growth is created—a desire that extends throughout one's life beyond the end of formal education. In Dewey's model, the role of education in a democratic society is not seen as a preparation for some later stage in life, such as adulthood. Rather, education is seen as a process of growth that never ends, with human beings continuously expanding their capacity for growth. Neither did Dewey's model see education as a means by which the past was recapitulated. Instead, education was a continuous reconstruction of experiences, grounded very much in the present environment.

Since Dewey's model places a heavy emphasis on the social component, the nature of the larger society that supports the educational system is of paramount importance. The ideal larger society, according to Dewey, is one in which the interests of a group are all shared by all of its members and in which interactions with other groups are free and full. According to Dewey, education in such a society should provide members of the group a stake or interest in social relationships and the ability to negotiate change without compromising the order and stability of the society.

Thus, Dewey's basic concept of education in a democratic society is based on the notion that education contains a large social component designed to provide direction and assure children's development through their participation in their school group.

21. Which of the following best states the main idea of this passage?

    (A) The role of education is extremely complex.
    (B) Dewey's notion of education contains a significant social component.
    (C) Dewey's model of education is not relevant today.
    (D) Direction provided in education must not be overt.

22. The phrase "a continuous reconstruction of experiences" (lines 44-45) used in reference to education means that education is:

    (F) based in life experiences.
    (G) a never-ending process.
    (H) a meaning-based endeavor.
    (J) an individual pursuit.

23. The passage implies that:

    (A) true education fosters the desire for lifelong learning.
    (B) a truly educated person understands physics.
    (C) Dewey was a radical philosopher.
    (D) education must cease at some point.

24. The tone of this passage can best be described as:

    (F) humorous.
    (G) serious.
    (H) dramatic.
    (J) informal.

Items 25-39 are based on the following passage.

SOCIAL SCIENCE: This passage is adapted from an article on Aleut language and culture.

The Aleuts, residing on several islands of the Aleutian Chain, the Pribilof Islands, and the Alaskan Peninsula, have possessed a written language since 1825, when the Russian missionary Ivan Veniaminov selected appropriate characters of the Cyrillic alphabet to represent Aleut speech sounds, recorded the main body of Aleut vocabulary, and formulated grammatical rules. The Czarist Russian conquest of the proud, independent sea hunters was so devastatingly thorough that tribal traditions, even tribal memories, were almost obliterated. The slaughter of the majority of an adult generation was sufficient to destroy the continuity of tribal knowledge, which was dependent upon oral transmission. Consequently, the Aleuts developed a fanatical devotion to their language as their only cultural heritage.

The Russian occupation placed a heavy linguistic burden on the Aleuts. Not only were they compelled to learn Russian to converse with their overseers and governors, but they had to learn Old Slavonic to take an active part in church services as well as to master the skill of reading and writing their own tongue. In 1867, when the United States purchased Alaska, the Aleuts were unable to break sharply with their immediate past and substitute English for any one of their three languages.

To communicants of the Russian Orthodox Church, knowledge of Slavonic remained vital, as did Russian, the language in which one conversed with the clergy. The Aleuts came to regard English education as a device to wean them from their religious faith. The introduction of compulsory English schooling caused a minor renaissance of Russian culture as the Aleut parents sought to counteract the influence of the schoolroom. The harsh life of the Russian colonial rule began to appear more happy and beautiful in retrospect.

Regulations forbidding instruction in any language other than English increased its unpopularity. The superficial alphabetical resemblance of Russian and Aleut linked the two tongues so closely that every restriction against teaching Russian was interpreted as an attempt to eradicate the Aleut tongue. From the wording of many regulations, it appears that American administrators often had not the slightest idea that the Aleuts were clandestinely reading and writing in their own tongue or that they even had a written language of their own. To too many officials, anything in Cyrillic letters was Russian and something to be stamped out. Bitterness bred by abuses and the exploitations that the Aleuts suffered from predatory American traders and adventurers kept alive the Aleut resentment against the language spoken by Americans.

Gradually, despite the failure to emancipate the Aleuts from a sterile past by relating the Aleut and English languages more closely, the passage of years has assuaged the bitter misunderstandings and caused an orientation away from Russian toward English as their second language, but Aleut continues to be the language that molds their thought and expression.

25. The author is primarily concerned with describing:

(A) the Aleuts' loyalty to their language and American failure to understand the language.
(B) Russian and American treatment of Alaskan inhabitants both before and after 1867.
(C) how the Czarist Russian occupation of Alaska created a written language for the Aleuts.
(D) American government attempts to persuade the Aleuts to use English as a second language.

26. The author is primarily concerned with:

(F) describing the Aleuts' loyalty to their language and American failure to understand the language.
(G) criticizing Russia and the United States for their mistreatment of the Aleuts.
(H) praising the Russians for creating a written language for the Aleuts.
(J) condemning Russia for its mistreatment of the Aleuts during the Czarist Russian occupation.

27. Which of the following titles best fits the passage?

(A) Aleut Loyalty to Their Language: An American Misunderstanding
(B) Failure of Russian and American Policies in Alaska
(C) Russia's Gift to the Aleuts: A Written Language
(D) Mistreatment of Aleuts During Russian Occupation

28. According to the passage, which of the following was the most important reason for the Aleuts' devotion to their language?

(F) Invention of a written version of their language
(G) Introduction of Old Slavonic for worship
(H) Disruption of oral transmission of tribal knowledge
(J) Institution of compulsory English education

29. In line 17, the word "linguistic" infers relation to:

(A) orthodoxy.
(B) commerce.
(C) language.
(D) laws.

30. In line 33, the word "renaissance" most nearly means:

(F) resurgence.
(G) rejection.
(H) repeal.
(J) reassessment.

31. In line 45, the word "clandestinely" most nearly means:

(A) secretly.
(B) reliably.
(C) openly.
(D) casually.

32. In line 54, the word "sterile" most nearly means:

(F) germ-free.
(G) unproductive.
(H) fortunate.
(J) ill-timed.

33. In line 56, the word "assuaged" most nearly means:

(A) failed.
(B) created.
(C) intensified.
(D) eased.

34. The passage is developed primarily by:

(F) testing the evidence supporting a theory.
(G) describing causes and effects of events.
(H) weighing the pros and cons of a plan.
(J) projecting the future consequences of a decision.

35. Why does the author mention that the Russians killed the majority of adult Aleuts?

(A) To call attention to the immorality of foreign conquest
(B) To urge Russia to make restitution to the children of those killed
(C) To stir up outrage against the Russians for committing such atrocities
(D) To explain the extreme loyalty that Aleuts feel to their language

36. Which of the following statements about the religious beliefs of the Aleuts can be inferred from the passage?

(F) Prior to the Russian occupation they had no religious beliefs.
(G) American traders and adventurers forced them to abandon all religious beliefs.
(H) At no time in their history have the Aleuts had an organized religion.
(J) The Russians forced Aleuts to become members of the Russian Orthodox Church.

37. The passage implies that:

(A) the Cyrillic alphabet was invented for the Aleut language
(B) all of the Cyrillic characters were used in writing the Aleut language
(C) Russian and the Aleut language have some similar speech sounds
(D) English is also written using the Cyrillic alphabet

38. Distributing which of the following publications would be most likely to encourage Aleuts to make more use of English?

(F) Russian translations of English novels
(G) English translations of Russian novels
(H) An English-Russian bilingual text devoted to important aspects of Aleutian culture
(J) An Aleut-English bilingual text devoted to important aspects of Aleutian culture

39. The author's attitude toward the Aleuts can best be described as one of:

(A) understanding and sympathy
(B) callousness and indifference
(C) condemnation and reproof
(D) ridicule and disparagement

NOTES AND STRATEGIES

EXTENDED LESSON

The passages and items in this section accompany the Extended Lesson of the Reading Lesson. You will work through the items with your instructor in class. Answers are on page 936.

DIRECTIONS: Each passage below is followed by one or more items based on its content. Answer the items on the basis of what is stated or implied in the corresponding passage.

Items 1-8 are based on the following passage.

NATURAL SCIENCE: This passage is adapted from a science magazine article about galaxies.

Galaxies come in a variety of sizes and shapes: majestic spirals, ruddy disks, elliptically shaped dwarfs and giants, and a menagerie of other, more bizarre forms. Most currently, popular theories suggest that conditions prior to birth—mass of the protogalactic cloud, its size, its rotation—determine whether a galaxy will be large or small, spiral or elliptical; but about ten percent of all galaxies are members of rich clusters of thousands of galaxies. The gravitational forces of fields of nearby galaxies constantly distort galaxies in the crowded central region of rich clusters. In addition, rich clusters of galaxies are pervaded by a tenuous gas with a temperature of up to 100 million degrees. Galaxies are blasted and scoured by a hot wind created by their motion through the gas. In crowded conditions such as these, environment becomes a more important determinant of the size and shape of a galaxy than heredity. In fact, if our galaxy had happened to form well within the core of a cluster such as Virgo, the Sun would probably never have formed, because the Sun, a second- or third-generation star located in the disk of the galaxy, was formed from leftover gas five billion years or so after the initial period of star formation. By that time, in a rich cluster, the galaxy may well have already been stripped of its gas.

As a galaxy moves through the core of a rich cluster, it is not only scoured by hot gas; it encounters other galaxies as well. If the collision is one-on-one at moderate to high speeds of galaxies of approximately the same size, both galaxies will emerge relatively intact, if a little distorted and ragged about the edges. If, however, a galaxy coasts by a much larger one in a slow, grazing collision, the smaller one can be completely disrupted and assimilated by the larger.

Under the right conditions, these cosmic cannibals can consume 50 to 100 galaxies. The accumulative effect of these collisions is to produce a dynamic friction on the large galaxy, slowing it down. As a result, it gradually spirals in toward the center of the cluster. Eventually, the gravitational forces that bind the stars to the infalling galaxy are overwhelmed by the combined gravity of the galaxies in the core of the cluster—just as the ocean is pulled away from the shore at ebb tide by the Moon, the stars are pulled away from their infalling parent galaxy. If there is a large galaxy at the center of the cluster, it may ultimately capture these stars. With the passage of time, many galaxies will be torn asunder in the depths of this gravitational maelstrom and be swallowed up in the ever-expanding envelope of the central cannibal galaxy.

Galactic cannibalism also explains why there are few if any bright galaxies in these clusters other than the central supergiant galaxy. That is because the bright galaxies, which are the most massive, experience the greatest dynamical friction. They are the first to go down to the gravitational well and be swallowed up by the central galaxies.

Over the course of several billion years, 50 or so galaxies may be swallowed up, leaving only the central supergiant and the 51st, the 52nd, *etc.*, brightest galaxies. Given time, all the massive galaxies in the cluster will be absorbed, leaving a sparse cluster of a supergiant galaxy surrounded by clouds of small, dim galaxies.

1. In line 3, the word "menagerie" most nearly means:

   (A) odd mixture.
   (B) open environment.
   (C) uniform collection.
   (D) flat area.

2. It can be inferred from the passage that the physical features of a galaxy that does not belong to a rich cluster are determined primarily by the:

   (F) size and rotation of the protogalactic cloud.
   (G) intensity of light emanating from the galaxy.
   (H) temperature of the interstellar gas.
   (J) age of the protogalactic cloud.

3. The author implies that the currently accepted theories on galaxy formation are:

(A) completely incorrect and misguided.
(B) naive and out-of-date.
(C) speculative and unsupported by observation.
(D) substantially correct but in need of modification.

4. According to the passage, a cluster with a central, supergiant galaxy will:

(F) contain no intermediately bright galaxies.
(G) have 50-100 galaxies of all sizes and intensities.
(H) consist solely of third- and fourth-generation stars.
(J) produce only spiral and disk-shaped galaxies.

5. According to the passage, the outcome of a collision between galaxies depends on which of the following?

(A) The relative velocities of the galaxies
(B) The relative ages of the galaxies
(C) The relative sizes of the galaxies
(D) The relative velocities and sizes of the galaxies

6. According to the passage, as a galaxy falls inward toward the center of a cluster, it:

(F) collides with the central core and emerges relatively intact.
(G) absorbs superheated gases from the interstellar medium.
(H) is broken apart by the gravitational forces of the core.
(J) is transformed by collisions into a large, spiral galaxy.

7. The passage provides information that will answer which of the following questions?

(A) What is the age of our sun?
(B) What proportion of all galaxies are found in clusters?
(C) Approximately how many galaxies would be found in a rich cluster?
(D) What type of galaxy is ours?

8. The tone of the passage can best be described as:

(F) light-hearted and amused.
(G) objective but concerned.
(H) detached and unconcerned.
(J) cautious but sincere.

Items 9-13 are based on the following passage.

NATURAL SCIENCE: This passage reviews the basic physical chemistry of atoms and radioactive decay.

An atom consists of a nucleus (containing protons and neutrons) surrounded by electrons. Each proton has a positive charge of +1, and each electron has a negative charge of -1. A neutron has no charge. The number of protons in their nuclei determines the identities of the different elements. For example, hydrogen atoms have only one proton, while oxygen atoms have eight protons. The total number of protons in the nucleus is the "atomic number" of that element. The total number of protons and neutrons in the nucleus is the "atomic mass" of the atom. Different atoms of the same element may contain a different number of neutrons, and so have different atomic masses. (But they will have the same number of protons and the same atomic number.) Atoms of the same element with different atomic masses are called isotopes of that element.

Certain elements are radioactive—they emit various types of radiation from their atomic nuclei. Two common types of radiation are alpha particles and beta particles. An alpha particle, which is the equivalent of a helium nucleus, consists of two protons and two neutrons. It is written ${}^{4}_{2}\text{He}$ (the superscript 4 is the mass number of the particle, and the subscript 2 is its atomic number). A beta particle is an electron traveling at high speed. It is written ${}^{0}_{-1}\text{e}$. Both types of radiation are emitted at a very high speed and can easily penetrate other substances.

When atoms of a substance emit radiation, they are said to undergo radioactive decay. The result is a different element with a different atomic number and a different mass number. For example, when a radium atom emits an alpha particle, it decays into an atom of radon. This reaction is shown in the following equation:

$${}^{226}_{88}\text{Ra} \rightarrow {}^{4}_{2}\text{He} + {}^{222}_{86}\text{Rn}$$

Note that the equation is balanced. That is, the atomic number of the original atom on the left side of the equation equals the sum of the atomic numbers of the products on the right side of the equation. Similarly, the mass number of the original atom equals the sum of the mass numbers of the products. Every nuclear reaction balances in this same manner.

Some types of nuclear radiation take place very slowly; other types are very rapid. The rate of radiation is measured in half-lives. A half-life is the time required for one-half the amount of a given radioactive substance to decay.

9. As radium emits alpha particles, the mass of radium will:

(A) increase.
(B) decrease.
(C) stay the same.
(D) either increase or decrease, depending on the conditions.

10. In nuclear chemistry notation, two isotopes, or forms, of cobalt are written ${}^{59}_{27}\text{Co}$ and ${}^{60}_{27}\text{Co}$. The difference between the two isotopes is:

(F) an alpha particle.
(G) a beta particle.
(H) a proton.
(J) a neutron.

11. An alpha particle has:

(A) no electric charge.
(B) a positive electric charge.
(C) a negative electric charge.
(D) a variable electric charge.

12. A beta particle has:

(F) no electric charge.
(G) a positive electric charge.
(H) a negative electric charge.
(J) a variable electric charge.

13. When an atom emits a beta particle, the atomic mass number will:

(A) increase.
(B) decrease.
(C) stay the same.
(D) either increase or decrease, depending on the conditions.

NOTES AND STRATEGIES

Items 14-23 are based on the following passage.

NATURAL SCIENCE: This passage discusses the development of basic inheritance theories and the role of DNA in genetic mutation processes.

In 1866, Gregor Mendel published the results of his studies on the breeding of different races of pea plants. Through his experiments, Mendel discovered a pattern of inheritance and subsequently developed the concept of a "unit of inheritance."

Mendel started with a pure stock of pea plants that had recognizably different characteristics. He artificially cross-pollinated the different races of plants and noted the characteristics of the different offspring over several generations. Mendel concluded that a pair of discrete "factors" governed each trait and that they segregated upon the formation of the gametes. This pair of factors is now known as the maternally and paternally derived alleles on homologous chromosomes that first come together at fertilization and later segregate during meiosis.

Subsequent studies have shown that new genes could appear as mutations of existing genes and that crossing over and recombination could redistribute maternal and paternal characteristics. Genes can occur in a linear sequence, and groups of genes that segregate together are called "linkage groups." The chromosome is the carrier of the linear array of genes and the physical basis of the linkage groups.

It was originally thought that proteins were the genetic carrier. In contrast to nucleic acids, proteins were known to mediate complex reactions and to be composed of a variety of different building blocks. There are approximately 20 different amino acids in a protein, but only 4 different nucleotides in a nucleic acid molecule. It was not until 1944 that Avery *et al.* noted that deoxyribonucleic acid (DNA) was the genetic carrier, not protein. Avery and his co-workers conducted experiments on the transformation in pneumococcus. Two strains of the bacteria had been isolated: one produced colonies having a smooth (S) appearance and was able to cause pneumonia in a suitable host; the other grew into rough (R) colonies because of a defect in its capsule and was non-virulent. When a cell-free extract of the S bacteria was added to the medium in which the R strain was growing, a few of the R bacteria grew into smooth colonies and were virulent. They had become transformed. From the time of transformation, the progeny of that cell continued to have the properties of the S strain. The transformation was a stable genetic change. Avery and his co-workers purified the contents of cells in detergent after their disruption and found that among the contents of the cells, only the purified DNA was capable of causing the transformation. As a result of these and future experiments, it was determined that in order for transformation to occur, DNA fragments entered the recipient cell intact and substituted in the bacterial chromosome for the original DNA, which was eliminated. This process resulted in the creation of a genetically different microorganism.

DNA is a very long, fibrous molecule with a backbone composed of alternate sugar and phosphate groups joined by 3'-5'-phosphodiester linkages. Attached to each sugar is one of four possible nitrogenous bases. There are two types of bases: the pyrimidines, cytosine (C) and thymine (T); and the purines, adenine (A) and guanine (G). The amount of purine equals the amount of pyrimidine, and, more specifically, the amount of adenine equals the amount of thymine, and the amount of guanine equals the amount of cytosine.

In 1953, Watson and Crick proposed that DNA was made of two chains of nucleotides coiled around a common axis, with the sugar-phosphate backbone on the outside and the bases pointing in toward the axis, and that the two chains were held together by hydrogen bonds. The hydrogen bonds occur between each base of one chain and an associated base on the other chain. Based on the 20-angstrom width of the fiber, a pyrimidine from one chain is always paired with a purine from the other chain. Adenine is the only purine capable of bonding to thymine and guanine is the only purine capable of bonding to cytosine.

Watson and Crick proposed that the information in DNA was coded for by the linear sequence of the base pairs. They theorized that a mutation could be accounted for by a chance mistake in the formation of the sequence during duplication. Another major aspect of the Watson and Crick model was the proposed complementarity between hydrogen-bonded nucleotides. For example, adenine is complementary to thymine, AGC is complementary to TCG, and one chain is complementary to the other. If the base sequence of one chain is known, then the base sequence of the complementary chain can be derived. The concept of complementarity of nucleic acids in DNA and RNA chains is the basis of most research in which these classes of molecules are involved.

14. Mendel conducted his studies using the method known as:

(F) cloning.
(G) genetic mapping.
(H) cross-pollination.
(J) transformation.

15. Mendel's findings were important because they indicated that:

I. DNA fragments can replace original DNA.
II. specific units, handed down from one generation to the next, govern traits in organisms.
III. proteins are composed of approximately 20 different amino acids.

(A) I only
(B) II only
(C) I and III only
(D) I, II, and III

16. Contrary to earlier beliefs, Avery *et al.* discovered that:

(F) there are only four nucleotides in DNA.
(G) pneumonia can be passed from host to host.
(H) genes can mutate.
(J) DNA, not protein, carries genetic information.

17. If you witnessed R strain pneumococcus infected with S extract and saw a few R strain pneumococcus transformed to S strain, you would expect:

(A) the remaining R strain pneumococcus to transform later.
(B) only the new S strain cells to survive.
(C) offspring of those transformed cells to be S strain as well.
(D) a few S strain pneumococcus to transform to R strain.

18. The author uses the word "non-virulent" (line 39) to mean:

(F) harmless.
(G) toxic.
(H) bacterial.
(J) sweet.

19. In contrast to the paragraphs before, the fifth paragraph is intended primarily to:

(A) give historical genetic research information .
(B) describe the results of Mendel's experiments.
(C) speculate on the future of genetic research.
(D) provide a definition for an essential element in genetic research.

20. A chain of DNA with the pattern CAG would bond with a chain with the pattern:

(F) GAC.
(G) TGA.
(H) GTC.
(J) Cannot be determined from the given information

21. Which of the following is (are) classified as a purine?

I. cytosine
II. guanine
III. thymine

(A) I only
(B) II only
(C) III only
(D) I and II only

22. Watson and Crick's contribution to the study of genetics was:

I. information about the transfer of genes across membranes.
II. the notion that pairs of genes could work together.
III. a suggestion about the structure of DNA.

(F) I only
(G) II only
(H) III only
(J) I, II, and III

23. The concept of complementarity in DNA is apparently important because:

    (A) it contradicts the notion that proteins are the basis for genetic transformation.
    (B) hydrogen bonds connect the nucleotides.
    (C) if maternally and paternally derived alleles were not complementary, life could not exist.
    (D) if you know one chain's sequence, you can determine that of the other.

Items 24-30 are based on to the following passage.

SOCIAL SCIENCE: This passage is adapted from a policy article about attempts to change the healthcare system.

Considerable advances have been made in healthcare services since World War II. These include better access to healthcare (particularly for the poor and minorities), improvements in physical plants, and increased numbers of physicians and other health personnel. All have played a part in the recent improvement in life expectancy. But there is mounting criticism of the large remaining gaps in access, unbridled cost inflation, the further fragmentation of service, excessive indulgence in wasteful high-technology "gadgeteering," and breakdowns in doctor-patient relationships. In recent years, proposed panaceas and new programs, small and large, have proliferated at a feverish pace and disappointments have multiplied at almost the same rate. This has led to an increased pessimism—"everything has been tried and nothing works"—that sometimes borders on cynicism or even nihilism.

It is true that the automatic "pass through" of rapidly spiraling costs to government and insurance carriers produced for a time a sense of unlimited resources and allowed a mood to develop whereby every practitioner and institution could "do his own thing" without undue concern for the "Medical Commons." The practice of full-cost reimbursement encouraged capital investment and now the industry is overcapitalized. Many cities have hundreds of excess hospital beds; hospitals have proliferated a superabundance of high-technology equipment; and structural ostentation and luxury were the order of the day. In any given day, one-fourth of all community beds are vacant; expensive equipment is underused or, worse, used unnecessarily. Capital investment brings rapidly rising operating costs.

Yet, in part, this pessimism derives from expecting too much of healthcare. Care is often a painful experience accompanied by fear and unwelcome results; although there is room for improvement, it will always retain some unpleasantness and frustration. Moreover, the capacities of medical science are limited. Humpty Dumpty cannot always be put back together again. Too many physicians are reluctant to admit their limitations to patients; too many patients and families are unwilling to accept such realities. Nor is it true that everything has been tried and nothing works, as shown by the prepaid group practice plans at the Kaiser Foundation and Puget Sound. However, typically such undertakings have been drowned by a veritable flood of public and private moneys that have supported and encouraged the continuation of conventional practices and subsidized their shortcomings on a massive, almost unrestricted scale. Except for the most idealistic and dedicated, there were no incentives to seek change or to practice self-restraint or frugality. In this atmosphere, it is not fair to condemn as failures all attempted experiments; it may be more accurate to say that many never had a fair trial.

24. In line 14, the word "feverish" most nearly means:

(F) diseased.
(G) rapid.
(H) controlled.
(J) timed.

25. According to author, the "pessimism" mentioned in line 34 is partly attributable to the fact that:

(A) there has been little real improvement in healthcare services.
(B) expectations about healthcare services are sometimes unrealistic.
(C) large segments of the population find it impossible to get access to healthcare services.
(D) advances in technology have made healthcare service unaffordable.

26. The author cites the prepaid plans (lines 45-46) as:

(F) counterexamples to the claim that nothing has worked.
(G) examples of healthcare plans that were overfunded.
(H) evidence that healthcare services are fragmented.
(J) proof of the theory that no plan has been successful.

27. It can be inferred that the sentence "Humpty Dumpty cannot always be put back together again" means that:

(A) the cost of healthcare services will not decline.
(B) some people should not become doctors.
(C) medical care is not really essential to good health.
(D) medical science cannot cure every ill.

28. With which of the following descriptions of the system for the delivery of healthcare services would the author most likely agree?

(F) It is biased in favor of doctors and against patients.
(G) It is highly fragmented and completely ineffective.
(H) It has not embraced new technology rapidly enough.
(J) It is generally effective but can be improved.

29. Which of the following best describes the logical structure of the selection?

(A) The third paragraph is intended as a refutation of the first and second paragraphs.
(B) The second and third paragraphs are intended as a refutation of the first paragraph.
(C) The second and third paragraphs explain and put into perspective the points made in the first paragraph.
(D) The first paragraph describes a problem, and the second and third paragraphs present two horns of a dilemma.

30. The author's primary concern is to:

(F) criticize physicians and healthcare administrators for investing in technologically advanced equipment.
(G) examine some problems affecting delivery of healthcare services and assess the severity of those problems.
(H) defend the medical community from charges that healthcare has not improved since World War II.
(J) analyze the reasons for the healthcare industry's inability to provide quality care to all segments of the population.

Items 31-35 are based on to the following passage.

SOCIAL SCIENCE: This passage discusses the contest over the vice presidency in the 1792 election.

In 1792, there was no contest for the presidency. George Washington received the unanimous vote of the electors, Federalist and Republican alike. But the struggle over the vice presidency hinted at the rekindling of old divisions and antagonisms sparked by Alexander Hamilton's system. Southern planters who in 1789 had been ready, in fact eager, to cooperate with the moneyed men of the North, parted with them when they realized that the policies designed to benefit Northern merchants and bankers brought no profit to them as landed aristocrats. Even more, they saw themselves paying for a system that contributed to another section's prosperity. Although in 1792 they were willing to continue with Washington, they were not as willing to go along with Vice President John Adams, who represented the commerce, shipbuilding, fisheries, and banking institutions of New England and the North. If the Federalists were to have the first office, then the followers of Jefferson—who had already come to call themselves Republicans in contradistinction to the unpopular term anti-Federalist, insisted that they were to command the second office.

Appealing to the shopkeepers, artisans, laboring men, and farmers of the North based on their sympathy with the French Revolution, and to the Southern planters with their agrarian bias, the Republicans waged a gallant but losing campaign for the second office. However, the campaign served notice to the overconfident Federalists that when the Republicans became better organized nationally, they would have to be more seriously considered. This did not take long. In 1793, England went so far as to declare war with republican France over the guillotining of Louis XVI, and in 1794, John Jay's treaty terminating the United States' difficulties with Britain seemed to suggest a sympathetic policy toward monarchical and conservative England, instead of republican, liberty-loving France. The treaty intensified party spirit and gave the Republicans a sense of mission that legitimized their existence. The contest was now between the Republican "lovers of liberty" and the Monocrats.

31. Which of the following titles best describes the content of the passage?

(A) The Origins of Jefferson's Republican Party
(B) Jefferson's Defeat in the 1792 Election
(C) The Legacy of Hamilton's Political System
(D) Political Differences Between the Rich and the Poor

32. According to the passage, all of the following are true of the Republicans EXCEPT:

(F) they opposed the monied interests of the North.
(G) they were led by Thomas Jefferson.
(H) they disapproved of the French Revolution.
(J) they and the Federalists supported the same candidate for president in 1792.

33. It can be inferred from the passage that the term "Monocrats" (line 42) was:

(A) used by John Jay in his treaty to refer to France's King Louis XVI.
(B) invented by the Federalists to refer to the aristocratic landowners of the South.
(C) coined by the Republicans to disparage the Federalists' support of England.
(D) employed by Republicans to describe their leader, Thomas Jefferson.

34. The passage implies that Thomas Jefferson was unsuccessful in his 1792 bid for the vice presidency because the Republican Party:

(F) did not have a presidential candidate.
(G) was not as well organized as the Federalists.
(H) refused to support John Adams.
(J) appealed to workers in the North.

35. The tone of the passage can best be described as:

(A) enthusiastic and impassioned.
(B) scholarly and neutral.
(C) opinionated and dogmatic.
(D) argumentative and categorical.

Items 36-44 are based on to the following passage.

SOCIAL SCIENCE: This passage is adapted from the speech "Is it a Crime for a Citizen of the United States to Vote?" by Susan B. Anthony.

Friends and fellow citizens: I stand before you tonight under indictment for the alleged crime of having voted at the last presidential election without having a lawful right to vote. It shall be my work this evening to prove to you that in thus voting, I not only committed no crime, but, instead, simply exercised *my citizen's rights*, guaranteed to me and all United States citizens by the National Constitution, beyond the power of any State to deny. The preamble of the Federal Constitution says: "We, the people of the United States, in order to form a more perfect union, establish justice, insure *domestic* tranquility, provide for the common defense, promote the general welfare, and secure the blessings of liberty to ourselves and our posterity, do ordain and establish this Constitution for the United States of America."

It was we, the people, not we, the white male citizens; but we, the whole people, who formed the Union. And we formed it, not to give the blessings of liberty, but to secure them; not to the half of ourselves and the half of our posterity but to the whole people—women as well as men. And it is a downright mockery to talk to women of their enjoyment of the blessings of liberty while they are denied the use of the only means of securing them provided by this democratic-republican government—the ballot.

For any State to make sex a qualification that must ever result in the disfranchisement of one entire half of the people is a violation of the supreme law of the land. By it the blessings of liberty are forever withheld from women and their female posterity. To them this government has no just powers derived from the consent of the governed. To them this government is not a democracy. It is not a republic. It is a hateful oligarchy of sex. An oligarchy of learning, where the educated govern the ignorant, might be endured; but this oligarchy of sex, which makes father, brothers, husband, sons, the oligarchs or rulers over the mother and sisters, the wife and daughters of every household—which ordains all men sovereigns, all women subjects, carries dissension, discord and rebellion into every home of the nation.

Webster's Dictionary defines a citizen as a person in the United States, entitled to vote and hold office.

The only question left to be settled now is, Are women persons? And I hardly believe any of our opponents will have the hardihood to say we are not. Being persons, then, women are citizens; and no State has a right to make any law, or to enforce any old law, that shall abridge their privileges or immunities. Hence, every discrimination against women in the constitutions and laws of the several States is today null and void.

36. The nineteenth century feminist leader Susan B. Anthony fought long and hard to guarantee women the right to vote. In this speech, she talks as if she were a:

(F) defendant on trial.
(G) chairperson of a committee.
(H) legislator arguing for a new law.
(J) judge ruling at a trial.

37. Anthony broadens her appeal to her audience by showing how her case could affect all:

(A) existing laws.
(B) United States citizens.
(C) women.
(D) uneducated persons.

38. Anthony quotes the preamble to the Constitution (lines 10-16) in order to:

(F) impress the audience with her intelligence.
(G) utilize a common legalistic trick.
(H) point out which part of the preamble needs to be changed.
(J) add force to her argument.

39. According to Anthony, who formed the Union?

(A) Only one-half of the people
(B) The whole people
(C) White male citizens only
(D) White female citizens

40. When Anthony says that the blessings of liberty are forever withheld from women and their female posterity, she means that:

(F) all classes of women are discriminated against.
(G) women of the past have been victimized.
(H) female children of the poor will be the only ones affected.
(J) women of the present and the future will suffer.

41. Anthony argues that a government that denies women the right to vote is not a democracy because its powers do not come from:

(A) the Constitution of the United States.
(B) the rights of the states.
(C) the consent of the governed.
(D) the vote of the majority.

42. According to this speech, an "oligarchy of sex" would cause:

(F) women to rebel against the government.
(G) men to desert their families.
(H) problems to develop in every home.
(J) the educated to rule the ignorant.

43. In this speech, a citizen is defined as a person who has the right to vote and also the right to:

(A) acquire wealth.
(B) speak publicly.
(C) hold office.
(D) pay taxes.

44. Anthony argues that state laws that discriminate against women are:

(F) being changed.
(G) null and void.
(H) helpful to the rich.
(J) supported by the Constitution.

Items 45-53 are based on the following passage.

HUMANITIES: This passage is adapted from an article that discusses literary genre.

When we speak casually, we call *Nineteen Eighty-Four* a novel, but to be more exact we should call it a political fable. This requirement is not refuted by the fact that the book is preoccupied with an individual, Winston Smith, who suffers from a varicose ulcer, or by the fact that it takes account of other individuals, including Julia, Mr. Charrington, Mrs. Parsons, Syme, and O'Brien. The figures claim our attention, but they exist mainly in their relation to the political system that determines them. It would indeed be possible to think of them as figures in a novel, though in that case they would have to be imagined in a far more diverse set of relations. They would no longer inhabit or sustain a fable, because a fable is a narrative relieved of much contingent detail so that it may stand forth in an unusual degree of clarity and simplicity. A fable is a structure of types, each of them deliberately simplified lest a sense of difference and heterogeneity reduce the force of the typical. Let us say, then, that *Nineteen Eighty-Four* is a political fable, projected into a near future and incorporating historical references mainly to document a canceled past.

Since a fable is predicated upon a typology, it must be written from a certain distance. The author cannot afford the sense of familiarity that is induced by detail and differentiation. A fable, in this respect, asks to be compared to a caricature, not to a photograph. It follows that in a political fable there is bound to be some tension between a political sense dealing in the multiplicity of social and personal life, and a fable sense committed to simplicity of form and feature. If the political sense were to prevail, the narrative would be drawn away from fable into the novel, at some cost to its simplicity. If the sense of fable were to prevail, the fabulist would station himself at such a distance from any imaginary conditions in the case that his narrative would appear unmediated, free or bereft of conditions. The risk would be considerable: a reader might feel that the fabulist has lost interest in the variety of human life and fallen back upon an unconditioned sense of its types, that he has become less interested in lives than in a particular idea of life. The risk is greater still if the fabulist projects his narrative into the future: The reader cannot question by appealing to life conditions already known. He is asked to believe that the future is another country and that "they just do things differently there."

In a powerful fable, the reader's feeling is likely to be mostly fear: He is afraid that the fabulist's vision of any life that could arise may be accurate. The fabulist's feeling may be more various. A fable such as *Nineteen Eighty-Four* might arise from disgust, despair, or world-weariness induced by evidence that nothing, despite one's best efforts, has changed and that it is too late now to hope for the change one wants.

45. In line 15, the word "contingent" most nearly means:

(A) dependent.
(B) essential.
(C) boring.
(D) unnecessary.

46. In drawing an analogy between a fable and a caricature (lines 26-27), the author would most likely regard which of the following pairs of ideas as also analogous?

(F) The subject of a caricature and the topic of a fable
(G) The subject of a caricature and the main character in *Nineteen Eighty-Four*
(H) The subject of a fable and the artist who draws the caricature
(J) The artist who draws the caricature and a novelist

47. Which of the following would be the most appropriate title for the passage?

(A) A Critical Study of the Use of Characters in *Nineteen Eighty-Four*
(B) *Nineteen Eighty-Four*: Political Fable Rather Than Novel
(C) *Nineteen Eighty-Four*: Reflections on the Relationship of the Individual to Society
(D) The Use of Typology in the Literature of Political Fables

48. According to the passage, which of the following are characteristics of a political fable?

(F) It is widely popular at its time of development.
(G) The reader is unlikely to experience fear as his reaction to the political situation described.
(H) Its time frame must treat events that occur at some point in the future.
(J) Its characters are defined primarily by their relationship to the social order.

49. Which of the following best explains why the author mentions that Winston Smith suffers from a varicose ulcer?

(A) To demonstrate that a political fable must emphasize type over detail
(B) To show that Winston Smith has some characteristics that distinguish him as an individual
(C) To argue that Winston Smith is no more important than any other character in *Nineteen Eighty-Four*
(D) To illustrate one of the features of the political situation described in *Nineteen Eighty-Four*

50. The "tension" that the author mentions in line 29 refers to the:

(F) necessity of striking a balance between the need to describe a political situation in simple terms and the need to make the description realistic.
(G) reaction the reader feels because he is drawn to the characters of the fable as individuals but repulsed by the political situation.
(H) delicate task faced by a literary critic who must interpret the text of a work while attempting to describe accurately the intentions of the author.
(J) danger that too realistic a description of a key character will make the reader feel that the fable is actually a description of his own situation.

51. The author's attitude toward *Nineteen Eighty-Four* can best be described as:

(A) condescending.
(B) laudatory.
(C) disparaging.
(D) scholarly.

52. The author uses the phrase "another country" to describe a political fable in which:

(F) political events described in a fable occur in a place other than the country of national origin of the author.
(G) a lack of detail makes it difficult for a reader to see the connection between his own situation and the one described in the book.
(H) too many minor characters create the impression of complete disorganization, leading the reader to believe he is in a foreign country.
(J) the author has allowed his personal political convictions to infect his description of the political situation.

53. The author's primary concern is to:

(A) define and clarify a concept.
(B) point out a logical inconsistency.
(C) trace the connection between a cause and an effect.
(D) illustrate a general statement with examples.

Items 54-58 are based on the following passage.

HUMANITIES: This passage discusses the impact of Southwestern environment and culture on twentieth century artists.

Georgia O'Keeffe, whose death at age 98 closed one of the most fertile chapters of American artistic creativity, flourished as a maverick in her life and work. While other painters spent a season or two in the country trying to come to terms with the scenes and settings of the Southwest, O'Keeffe stayed a lifetime. When the canvases of other artists working in the region faded from view, and then were neglected in the chronicle of American visual history, her stylized images, skeletal, floral, and geological motifs made an indelible impression on countless eyes.

Between 1900 and 1945, the region now called New Mexico both fascinated and perplexed two generations of American artists—luminaries such as Stuart Davis, Marsden Hartley, and John Sloan, whose reputations were built largely on depictions of gritty, modern life in Eastern urban centers. Despite successes, many of these artists wearied of the industrial world of the East. The vast expanse of the American West offered a promise for inspiration. It was an ancient yet new world to their eyes—an enchanted land far removed from urban conventions.

For these artists, life and art, so separate in New York and Paris, seemed inextricably bound in Southwestern cultures. Painters of every persuasion were convinced that sampling this mysterious phenomenon would strengthen and enrich their own work. Most were touched by what D.H. Lawrence called the "spirit of the place." Besides the scenic possibilities bathed in clear golden light, the rich traditions of New Mexico's Native American and Latino people—their dress, crafts, adobe pueblos, plaza life, rituals, and simple dignity—became frequent subjects of the artists who traveled to Taos and Santa Fe.

Some of the artists were traditionalists—local color realists; some were modernists—like O'Keeffe, avant-garde painters of the abstract. Their varied talents coupled with the attractions of the land gave New Mexico's art centers a status unrivaled among other American summer colonies and contributed to their heyday in the early twentieth century.

54. This passage deals primarily with:

(F) the life of Georgia O'Keeffe.
(G) the major trends of American modern art.
(H) the mystery and spirit of the Southwest.
(J) artists in the American Southwest.

55. The author implies that the Southwest attracted artists for all of the following reasons EXCEPT:

(A) the quality of life was different from that of large urban centers.
(B) the inhabitants and culture provided interesting subject matter.
(C) New Mexico was the only state to support young, avant-garde painters.
(D) the region offered unusual geological features and landscapes.

56. The author implies that most of the artists who painted in the Southwest:

(F) originally studied in Paris.
(G) lived there only temporarily.
(H) painted only landscapes.
(J) received considerable recognition.

57. The author mentions which of the following facts about Georgia O'Keeffe?

I. She resided permanently in the Southwest.
II. She enjoyed considerable and lasting fame.
III. She created modern, abstract paintings.

(A) I only
(B) II only
(C) I and III only
(D) I, II, and III

58. Stuart Davis, Marsden Hartley, and John Sloan were painters who painted mainly in:

(F) Paris.
(G) New Mexico.
(H) cities in the Eastern United States.
(J) Rome.

NOTES AND STRATEGIES

Items 59-66 are based on the following passage.

HUMANITIES: This passage is adapted from an essay by Oliver Goldsmith that appeared in *The Citizen of the World.*

Were we to estimate the learning of the English by the number of books that are every day published among them, perhaps no country, not even China itself, could equal them in this particular. I have reckoned not less than twenty-three new books published in one day, which, upon computation, makes eight thousand three hundred and ninety-five in one year. Most of these are not confined to one single science, but embrace the whole circle. History, politics, poetry, mathematics, metaphysics, and the philosophy of nature are all comprised in a manual not larger than that in which our children are taught the letters. If then, we suppose the learned of England to read but an eighth part of the works which daily come from the press (and surely none can pretend to learning upon less easy terms), at this rate every scholar will read a thousand books in one year. From such a calculation, you may conjecture what an amazing fund of literature a man must be possessed of, who thus reads three new books every day, not one of which but contains all the good things that ever were said or written.

And yet I know not how it happens, but the English are not, in reality, so learned as would seem from this calculation. We meet but few who know all arts and sciences to perfection; whether it is that the generality are incapable of such extensive knowledge, or that the authors of those books are not adequate instructors. In China, the Emperor himself takes cognizance of all the doctors in the kingdom who profess authorship. In England, every man may be an author that can write; for they have by law a liberty, not only of saying what they please, but also of being as dull as they please.

Yesterday, I testified my surprise, to the man in black, where writers could be found in sufficient number to throw off the books I daily saw crowding from the press. I at first imagined that their learned seminaries might take this method of instructing the world. But, to obviate this objection, my companion assured me that the doctors of colleges never wrote, and that some of them had actually forgotten their reading. "But if you desire," continued he, "to see a collection of authors, I fancy I can introduce you to a club, which assembles every Saturday at seven...." I accepted his invitation; we walked together, and entered the house some time before the usual hour for the company assembling.

My friend took this opportunity of letting me into the characters of the principal members of the club....

"The first person," said he, "of our society is Doctor Nonentity, a metaphysician. Most people think him a profound scholar, but, as he seldom speaks, I cannot be positive in that particular; he generally spreads himself before the fire, sucks his pipe, talks little, drinks much, and is reckoned very good company. I'm told he writes indexes to perfection: he makes essays on the origin of evil, philosophical inquiries upon any subject, and draws up an answer to any book upon 24 hours' warning...."

59. Goldsmith's disdainful attitude toward English authors is best explicated in:

(A) lines 1-4.
(B) lines 12-17.
(C) lines 30-33.
(D) lines 42-44.

60. Goldsmith believes that:

(F) we can tell how knowledgeable English authors are by counting the number of books they publish.
(G) the number of books published in England is not up to standards set in China.
(H) the number of books published in England says nothing about English scholarship.
(J) every English scholar reads a thousand books a year.

61. Why does Goldsmith calculate the number of books published in England?

(A) To impress his readers with English erudition
(B) To make the point that anyone can be an author
(C) As defense for his argument that England is better than China
(D) As a comparison with publication quotas in other lands

62. The tone of the second paragraph may best be described as:

(F) self-satisfied.
(G) awestruck.
(H) affectionate.
(J) sardonic.

63. Goldsmith first assumes that English writers come from:

(A) foreign lands.
(B) seminaries.
(C) China.
(D) clubs.

64. The word "obviate" (line 39) means:

(F) clarify.
(G) obscure.
(H) turn.
(J) negate.

65. Goldsmith's opinion of the first member of the club is illuminated by which of the following?

I. His conversation with the character
II. The given name for the character
III. His friend's description of the character

(A) I only
(B) II only
(C) I and III only
(D) II and III only

66. One of Goldsmith's major objections to English authors is to their:

(F) deficiency in language skills.
(G) inclination to drink.
(H) tendency to write about everything at once.
(J) inability to retain information.

NOTES AND STRATEGIES

Items 67-71 are based on the following passage.

PROSE FICTION: This passage is adapted from Nathaniel Hawthorne's *The House of the Seven Gables*.

It still lacked a half hour of sunrise when Miss Hepzibah—we will say awoke, it being doubtful whether the poor old lady had so much as closed her eyes during the brief night of midsummer—but, at all events, arose from her solitary pillow, and began the adornment of her person. She was alone in the old house—quite a house by itself, indeed—with locks, bolts, and oaken bars on all the intervening doors. Inaudible, consequently, were poor Miss Hepzibah's gusty sighs, inaudible the creaking joints of her stiffened knees, as she knelt down by the bedside. And inaudible too, by mortal ear, that almost agony of prayer—now whispered, now a groan, now a struggling silence—wherewith she sought the Divine assistance through the day! Evidently this is to be the day of more than ordinary trial to Miss Hepzibah, who for above a quarter of a century gone by has dwelt in strict seclusion, taking no part in the business of life, and just as little in its intercourse and pleasures.

Here comes Miss Hepzibah. Forth she steps into the dusky, time-darkened passage a tall figure, clad in black silk, with a long and shrunken waist, feeling her way towards the stair like a nearsighted person, which in truth she is.

Her scowl—as the world persisted in calling it—her scowl had done Miss Hepzibah every ill office, in establishing her character as an ill-tempered old maid; nor does it appear improbable that, by often gazing at herself in a dim looking glass, and perpetually encountering her own frown within its ghostly sphere, she had been led to interpret the expression almost unjustly as the world did. But her heart never frowned.

67. According to the passage, Miss Hepzibah is all of the following EXCEPT:

(A) elderly.
(B) reclusive.
(C) religious.
(D) vain.

68. The author's portrait of Miss Hepzibah is:

(F) critical and disparaging.
(G) loving and intimate.
(H) sarcastic and mocking.
(J) interested and sympathetic.

69. It can be inferred that Miss Hepzibah views the day's coming events with:

(A) apprehension.
(B) confidence.
(C) eagerness.
(D) boredom.

70. Which of the following correctly describes the scene as set by the passage?

I. The season is summer.
II. The weather is threatening.
III. The time is morning.

(F) I only
(G) III only
(H) I and II only
(J) I and III only

71. In the last paragraph, the author implies that Miss Hepzibah is:

(A) old and wicked.
(B) affable and outgoing.
(C) good-hearted but misunderstood.
(D) sincere but blasphemous.

Items 72-81 are based on the following passage.

PROSE FICTION: This passage is adapted from the short story "Mrs. Gay's Prescription" by Louisa May Alcott.

The poor little woman looked as if she needed rest but was not likely to get it; for the room was in a chaotic state, the breakfast table presented the appearance of having been devastated by a swarm of locusts, the baby began to fret, little Polly set up her usual whine of "I want sumpin to do," and a pile of work loomed in the corner waiting to be done.

"I don't see how I ever shall get through it all," sighed the despondent matron as she hastily drank a last cup of tea, while two great tears rolled down her cheeks, as she looked from one puny child to the other, and felt the weariness of her own tired soul and body more oppressive than ever.

"A good cry" was impending, when there came a brisk ring at the door, a step in the hall, and a large, rosy woman came bustling in, saying in a cheery voice as she set a flower-pot down upon the table, "Good morning! Nice day, isn't it? Came in early on business and brought you one of my Lady Washingtons, you are so fond of flowers."

"Oh, it's lovely! How kind you are. Do sit down if you can find a chair; we are all behind hand today, for I was up half the night with poor baby, and haven't energy enough to go to work yet," answered Mrs. Bennet, with a sudden smile that changed her whole face, while baby stopped fretting to stare at the rosy clusters, and Polly found employment in exploring the pocket of the newcomer, as if she knew her way there.

"Let me put the pot on your stand first, girls are so careless, and I'm proud of this. It will be an ornament to your parlor for a week," and opening a door Mrs. Gay carried the plant to a sunny bay window where many others were blooming beautifully.

Mrs. Bennet and the children followed to talk and admire, while the servant leisurely cleared the table.

"Now give me that baby, put yourself in the easy chair, and tell me all about your worries," said Mrs. Gay, in the brisk, commanding way which few people could resist.

"I'm sure I don't know where to begin," sighed Mrs. Bennet, dropping into the comfortable seat while baby changed bearers with great composure.

"I met your husband and he said the doctor had ordered you and these chicks off to Florida for the winter. John said he didn't know how he should manage it, but he meant to try."

"Isn't it dreadful? He can't leave his business to go with me, and we shall have to get Aunt Miranda to come and see to him and the boys while I'm gone, and the boys can't bear her strict, old-fashioned ways, and I've got to go that long journey all alone and stay among strangers, and these heaps of fall work to do first, and it will cost an immense sum to send us, and I don't know what is to become of me."

Here Mrs. Bennet stopped for breath, and Mrs. Gay asked briskly, "What is the matter with you and the children?"

"Well, baby is having a hard time with his teeth and is croupy, Polly doesn't get over scarlet fever well, and I'm used up; no strength or appetite, pain in my side and low spirits. Entire change of scene, milder climate, and less work for me, is what we want, the doctor says. John is very anxious about us, and I feel regularly discouraged."

"I'll spend the day and cheer you up a bit. You just rest and get ready for a new start tomorrow; it is a saving of time to stop short now and then and see where to begin next. Bring me the most pressing job of work. I can sew and see to this little rascal at the same time."

72. The phrase "little woman" (line 1) refers to:

(F) Lady Washington.
(G) a servant.
(H) Mrs. Bennet.
(J) Mrs. Gay.

73. When Alcott compares the breakfast table to something "devastated by a swarm of locusts" (lines 4-5), she means:

(A) that it is a mess left by an uncaring mob.
(B) that children are no more meaningful than insects to Mrs. Bennet.
(C) to illustrate the horror of Mrs. Bennet's life.
(D) that the Bennets are pests.

74. Had Mrs. Gay not arrived when she did, the author leads us to suspect that:

(F) Mrs. Bennet would have gone back to bed.
(G) the children would have continued to cry.
(H) Mrs. Bennet would have accomplished little all day.
(J) sickness would have overtaken the entire family.

75. The phrase "rosy clusters" (lines 26-27) refers to:

(A) Mrs. Gay's cheeks.
(B) Mrs. Bennet's cheeks.
(C) candies from Mrs. Gay's pockets.
(D) flowers.

76. In lines 29-33, the author:

(F) reveals Mrs. Bennet's only talent.
(G) uses the sunny parlor as a symbol of hope.
(H) contrasts Mrs. Gay's sunniness with Mrs. Bennet's dullness.
(J) contrasts Mrs. Bennet's plants with her children.

77. When Mrs. Bennet says that she's "used up" (line 60), she means that she:

(A) has no energy.
(B) is abused.
(C) is exploited.
(D) has spent all her money.

78. The word "pressing" (line 68) means:

(F) heavy.
(G) ardent.
(H) forceful.
(J) important.

79. The disposition of Mrs. Bennet's friend is indicated by:

I. her name.
II. her speech.
III. her clothing.

(A) I only
(B) III only
(C) I and II only
(D) I and III only

80. The author implies that Mrs. Bennet's real problem is:

(F) her inability to cope.
(G) a touch of fever.
(H) the cold winter weather.
(J) a lack of common sense.

81. Mrs. Gay's primary quality seems to be her:

(A) lethargy.
(B) anxiety.
(C) dignity.
(D) practical nature.

Items 82-91 are based on the following passage.

PROSE FICTION: This passage is adapted from the memoir series "Old Times on the Mississippi" by Mark Twain that appeared in *Atlantic Monthly.*

At the end of what seemed a tedious while, I had managed to pack my head full of islands, towns, bars, "points," and bends; and a curiously inanimate mass of lumber it was, too. However, inasmuch as I could shut my eyes and reel off a good long string of these names without leaving out more than ten miles of river in every fifty, I began to feel that I could make her skip those little gaps. But of course my complacency could hardly get started enough to lift my nose a trifle into the air, before Mr. Bixby would think of something to fetch it down again. One day he turned on me suddenly with this settler:

"What is the shape of Walnut Bend?"

He might as well have asked me my grandmother's opinion of protoplasm. I reflected respectfully, and then said I didn't know it had any particular shape. My gunpowdery chief went off with a bang, of course, and then went on loading and firing until he was out of adjectives.

I had learned long ago that he only carried just so many rounds of ammunition, and was sure to subside into a very placable and even remorseful old smoothbore as soon as they were all gone. That word "old" is merely affectionate; he was not more than thirty-four. I waited. By and by he said:

"My boy, you've got to know the *shape* of the river perfectly. It is all there is left to steer by on a very dark night. Everything else is blotted out and gone. But mind you, it hasn't the same shape in the night that it has in the daytime."

"How on earth am I ever going to learn it, then?"

"How do you follow a hall at home in the dark? Because you know the shape of it. You can't see it."

"Do you mean to say that I've got to know all the million trifling variations of shape in the banks of this interminable river as well as I know the shape of the front hall at home?"

"On my honor, you've got to know them *better* than any man ever did know the shapes of the halls in his own house."

"I wish I was dead!"

"Now I don't want to discourage you, but…"

"Well, pile it on me; I might as well have it now as another time."

"You see, this has got to be learned; there isn't any getting around it. A clear starlight night throws such heavy shadows that, if you didn't know the shape of a shore perfectly, you would claw away from every bunch of timber, because you would take the black shadow of it for a solid cape; and you see you would be getting scared to death every fifteen minutes by the watch. You would be fifty yards from shore all the time when you ought to be within fifty feet of it. You can't see a snag in one of those shadows, but you know exactly where it is, and the shape of the river tells you when you are coming to it. Then there's your pitch-dark night; the river is a very different shape on a pitch-dark night from what it is on a starlit night. All shores seem to be straight lines, then, and mighty dim ones, too; and you'd *run* them for straight lines, only you know better. You boldly drive your boat right into what seems to be a solid straight wall (you knowing very well that in reality there is a curve there), and that wall falls back and makes way for you. Then there's your gray mist. You take a night when there's one of these grisly, drizzly, gray mists, and then there isn't any particular shape to a shore. A gray mist would tangle the head of the oldest man that ever lived. Well, then different kinds of *moonlight* change the shape of the river in different ways."

82. In line 12, the word "settler" is used to mean:

(F) a pioneer.
(G) a perch on the railing.
(H) a remark that decides the issue.
(J) a humbling problem.

83. When the narrator compares Bixby's question to asking his "grandmother's opinion of protoplasm" (line 15), he means that:

(A) the question is inane.
(B) the speaker is very old.
(C) he does not know the answer.
(D) his grandmother would be able to respond.

84. Comparing the chief to a gun (lines 17-19) points out the chief's:

(F) accuracy.
(G) peppery temper.
(H) love of hunting.
(J) violent past.

85. When Twain writes that Mr. Bixby "carried just so many rounds of ammunition," he means that:

(A) Bixby used a pistol to settle arguments.
(B) Bixby loaded and fired his gun at random.
(C) Bixby was an impossible employer.
(D) Bixby's hot temper would soon subside.

86. The narrator's reaction to Mr. Bixby's insistence on the need to know the river at night is:

(F) despair.
(G) elation.
(H) puzzlement.
(J) anger.

87. In the phrase "pile it on me" (line 43), "it" refers to:

(A) clothing.
(B) information.
(C) the river.
(D) the shoreline.

88. The word "cape" (line 50) means:

(F) cloak.
(G) robe.
(H) peninsula.
(J) waterway.

89. Mr. Bixby is shown to be extremely:

(A) knowledgeable.
(B) rude.
(C) condescending.
(D) fearful.

90. What is the purpose of including the lengthy explanation provided in the last paragraph of the selection?

I. To show how well Bixby speaks
II. To show how much a riverboat captain must know
III. To show the many modes of the river

(F) I only
(G) II only
(H) I and III only
(J) II and III only

91. According to the passage, which of the following is true?

(A) A riverboat should always be within 50 feet of the shore.
(B) On a clear, starlit night, the shoreline is easy to see.
(C) On a pitch-dark night, the pilot cannot discern the curve of the shoreline.
(D) The river's shape gives no hint of underwater snags.

NOTES AND STRATEGIES

CHALLENGE ITEMS

This section contains advanced-level Reading items. Answers are on page 936.

DIRECTIONS: Each passage below is followed by items based on its content. Answer the items on the basis of what is stated or implied in each passage.

Items 1-8 are based on the following passage.

SOCIAL SCIENCE: This passage discusses systems for reporting and investigating adverse drug effects.

A fundamental principle of pharmacology is that all drugs have multiple actions. Actions that are desirable in the treatment of disease are considered therapeutic, while those that are undesirable or pose risks to the patient are called "effects." Adverse drug effects range from the trivial, for example, nausea or dry mouth, to the serious, such as massive gastrointestinal bleeding or thromboembolism; and some drugs can be lethal. Therefore, an effective system for the detection of adverse drug effects is an important component of the healthcare system of any advanced nation. Much of the research conducted on new drugs aims at identifying the conditions of use that maximize beneficial effects and minimize the risk of adverse effects. The intent of drug labeling is to reflect this body of knowledge accurately so that physicians can properly prescribe the drug or, if it is to be sold without prescription, so that consumers can properly use the drug.

The current system of drug investigation in the United States has proved very useful and accurate in identifying the common side effects associated with new prescription drugs. By the time a new drug is approved by the Food and Drug Administration, its side effects are usually well described in the package insert for physicians. The investigational process, however, cannot be counted on to detect all adverse effects because of the relatively small number of patients involved in pre-marketing studies and the relatively short duration of the studies. Animal toxicology studies are, of course, done before marketing in an attempt to identify any potential for toxicity, but negative results do not guarantee the safety of a drug in humans, as evidenced by such well known examples as the birth deformities due to thalidomide.

This recognition prompted the establishment in many countries of programs to which physicians report adverse drug effects. The United States and other countries also send reports to an international program operated by the World Health Organization. These programs, however, are voluntary reporting programs and are intended to serve a limited goal: alerting a government or private agency to adverse drug effects detected by physicians in the course of practice. Other approaches must be used to confirm suspected drug reactions and to estimate incidence rates. These other approaches include conducting retrospective control studies, for example, the studies associating endometrial cancer with estrogen use, and systematically monitoring hospitalized patients to determine the incidence of acute common side effects, as typified by the Boston Collaborative Drug Surveillance Program.

Thus, the overall drug surveillance system of the United States is composed of a set of information bases, special studies, and monitoring programs, each contributing in its own way to our knowledge about marketed drugs. The system is decentralized among a number of governmental units and is not administered as a coordinated function. Still, it would be inappropriate at this time to attempt to unite all of the disparate elements into a comprehensive surveillance program. Instead, the challenge is to improve each segment of the system and to take advantage of new computer strategies to improve coordination and communication.

1. In line 63, the word "disparate" most nearly means:

   (A) useless.
   (B) expensive.
   (C) temporary.
   (D) unconnected.

2. The author's primary concern is to discuss:

   (F) methods for testing the effects of new drugs on humans.
   (G) the importance of having accurate information about the effects of drugs.
   (H) procedures for determining the long-term effects of new drugs.
   (J) attempts to curb the abuse of prescription drugs.

3. The author implies that a drug with adverse side effects:

   (A) will not be approved for use by consumers without a doctor's prescription.
   (B) must wait for approval until lengthy studies prove the effects are not permanent.
   (C) should be used only if its therapeutic value out-weighs its adverse effects.
   (D) should be withdrawn from the marketplace pending a government investigation.

4. Which of the following can be inferred from the passage?

   (F) The decentralization of the overall drug surveillance system results in it being completely ineffective in any attempts to provide information about adverse drug effects.
   (G) Drugs with serious adverse side effects are never approved for distribution.
   (H) Some adverse drug effects are discovered during testing because they are very rare.
   (J) Some adverse drug effects cannot be detected prior to approval because they take a long time to develop.

5. The author introduces the example of thalidomide in the last sentence of the second paragraph to show that some:

   (A) drugs do not have the same actions in humans that they do in animals.
   (B) drug testing procedures are ignored by careless laboratory workers.
   (C) drugs have no therapeutic value for humans.
   (D) drugs have adverse side effects as well as beneficial actions.

6. It can be inferred that the estrogen study mentioned in the last sentence of the third paragraph:

   (F) uncovered long-term side effects of a drug that had already been approved for sale by the Food and Drug Administration.
   (G) discovered potential side effects of a drug that was still awaiting approval for sale by the Food and Drug Administration.
   (H) revealed possible new applications of a drug that had previously been approved for a different treatment.
   (J) is an example of a study that could be more efficiently conducted by a centralized authority than by volunteer reporting.

7. The author is most probably leading up to a discussion of some suggestions about how to:

   (A) centralize authority for drug surveillance in the United States.
   (B) centralize authority for drug surveillance among international agencies.
   (C) coordinate better the sharing of information among the drug surveillance agencies.
   (D) eliminate the availability and sale of certain drugs now on the market.

8. The author makes use of which of the following devices in the passage?

   (F) Definition of terms
   (G) Examples
   (H) Analogy
   (J) Definition of terms and example

Items 9-15 are based on the following passage.

NATURAL SCIENCE: This passage is adapted from a science magazine article that discusses lightning.

Lightning is an electrical discharge of immense proportions. Some 80% of lightning occurs within clouds; about 20% is cloud-to-ground lightning; and an extremely small percentage is cloud-to-sky lightning.

Cloud-to-ground lightning begins when complex meteorological processes cause a tremendous electrostatic charge to build up within a cloud. Typically, the bottom of the cloud is negatively charged. When the charge reaches 50 to 100 million volts, air is no longer an effective insulator, and lightning occurs within the cloud itself. Ten to 30 minutes after the onset of intracloud lightning, negative charges called stepped leaders emerge from the bottom of the cloud, moving toward the earth in 50-meter intervals at speeds of 100 to 200 kilometers per second and creating an ionized channel. As the leaders near the Earth, their strong electric field causes streamers of positively charged ions to develop at the tips of pointed objects that are connected directly or indirectly to the ground. These positively charged streamers flow upward.

When the distance, known as the striking distance, between a stepped leader and one of the streamers reaches 30 to 100 meters, the intervening air breaks down completely and the leader is joined to the Earth via the streamer. Now a pulse of current known as a return stroke ranging from thousands to hundreds of thousands of amperes moves at one tenth to one third the speed of light from the Earth through the object from which the streamer emanated and up the ionized channel to the charge center within the cloud. An ionized channel remains in the air and additional negative charges called dart leaders will quickly move down this path resulting in further return strokes. This multiplicity causes the flash to flicker. The entire event typically lasts about one second.

The return stroke's extremely high temperature creates the visible lightning and produces thunder by instantly turning moisture into steam. Most direct damage results from the heavy return stroke current because it produces high temperatures in the channel, or from arcing at the point of ground contact. If the lightning current is carried by an enclosed conductor (*e.g.*, within a jacketed cable, through a concrete wall, or beneath a painted surface), entrapped moisture is turned into high-pressure steam that can cause a cable, wall, or painted object to explode. Arcing frequently ignites combustibles.

Lightning causes hundreds of millions of dollars in property losses annually and the majority of forest fires. Lightning is also the leading weather-related killer in the U.S., causing from 100 to 200 deaths each year.

9. In line 12, the word "intracloud" most nearly means:

   (A) between clouds.
   (B) within a cloud.
   (C) from cloud to sky.
   (D) from ground to cloud.

10. The selection defines the striking distance as the distance between:

   (F) the ground and the cloud.
   (G) a stepped leader and a dart leader.
   (H) a dart leader and a return stroke.
   (J) a streamer and a stepped leader.

11. According to the selection, the flickering appearance of a lightning strike is created by:

   (A) the stepped movement of leaders.
   (B) multiple return strokes.
   (C) water being vaporized.
   (D) arcing at ground contact.

12. What topic might the author logically address in a continuation of the passage?

   (F) Precautions to minimize lightning damage
   (G) Other weather phenomena that cause injury
   (H) Basic principles governing electricity
   (J) Identifying different types of clouds

13. According to the passage, which of the following is NOT true of stepped leaders?

   (A) They develop 10 to 30 minutes after intracloud lightning.
   (B) As they traverse the distance from cloud to ground, they create an ionized channel.
   (C) Their powerful positive charge causes streamers to develop in grounded objects.
   (D) They emerge from the bottom of the cloud and move downward in intervals of 50 meters.

14. The passage answers which of the following questions?

    (F) How does lightning produce the associated thunder?
    (G) How far above the ground is the bottom of the typical lightning-producing cloud?
    (H) How frequently will lightning strike a given object?
    (J) How long does it take a cloud to build up an electrostatic charge?

15. The author's primary concern is to:

    (A) warn about the dangers posed by lightning strikes.
    (B) describe the sequence of events that make up a lightning strike.
    (C) discuss fundamental scientific laws pertaining to electricity.
    (D) support the commonly held view that lightning strikes the ground.

Items 16-24 are based on the following passage.

SOCIAL SCIENCE: This passage discusses the history of hospitals.

Public general hospitals originated in the almshouse infirmaries established as early as colonial times by local governments to care for the poor. Later, in the late eighteenth and early nineteenth centuries, the infirmary separated from the almshouse and became an independent institution supported by local tax money. At the same time, private charity hospitals began to develop. Both private and public hospitals mainly provided food and shelter for the impoverished sick, since there was little that medicine could actually do to cure illness, and the middle class was treated at home by private physicians.

Late in the nineteenth century, private charity hospitals began trying to attract middle-class patients. Although the depression of 1890 stimulated the growth of charitable institutions and an expanding urban population became dependent on assistance, there was a decline in private contributions to these organizations that forced them to look to local government for financial support. Since private institutions had also lost benefactors, they began to charge patients. In order to attract middle-class patients, private institutions provided services and amenities that distinguished between paying and nonpaying patients, making the hospital a desirable place for private physicians to treat their own patients. As paying patients became more necessary to the survival of the private hospital, the public hospitals slowly became the only place for the poor to get treatment. By the end of the nineteenth century, cities were reimbursing private hospitals for their care of indigent patients and the public hospitals remained dependent on the tax dollars.

The advent of private hospital health insurance, which provided middle-class patients with the purchasing power to pay for private hospital services, guaranteed the private hospital a regular source of income. Private hospitals restricted themselves to revenue-generating patients, leaving the public hospitals to care for the poor. Although public hospitals continued to provide services for patients with communicable diseases and outpatient and emergency services, the Blue Cross plans developed around the needs of the private hospitals and the inpatients they served. Thus, reimbursement for ambulatory care has been minimal under most Blue Cross plans, and provision of outpatient care has not been a major function of the private hospital, in part because private patients can afford to pay for the services of private physicians. Additionally, since World War II, there has been a tremendous influx of federal money into private medical schools and the hospitals associated with them. Further, large private medical centers with expensive research equipment and programs have attracted the best administrators, physicians, and researchers. Because of the greater resources available to the private medical centers, public hospitals have increasing problems attracting highly qualified research and medical personnel. With the mainstream of health care firmly established in the private medical sector, the public hospital has become a "dumping ground."

16. In line 31, the word "indigent" most nearly means:

(F) without the means to pay.
(G) having emergency medical needs.
(H) lacking health insurance.
(J) reimbursed by the government.

17. According to the passage, the very first private hospitals:

(A) developed from almshouse infirmaries.
(B) provided better care than public infirmaries.
(C) were established mainly to service the poor.
(D) were supported by government revenues.

18. It can be inferred that the author believes the differences that currently exist between public and private hospitals are primarily the result of:

(F) political considerations.
(G) economic factors.
(H) ethical concerns.
(J) legislative requirements.

19. It can be inferred that the growth of private health insurance:

(A) relieved local governments of the need to fund public hospitals.
(B) guaranteed that the poor would have access to medical care.
(C) forced middle-class patients to use public hospitals.
(D) reinforced the distinction between public and private hospitals.

20. Which of the following would be the most logical topic for the author to introduce in the next paragraph?

    (F) A plan to improve the quality of public hospitals
    (G) An analysis of the profit structure of health insurance companies
    (H) A proposal to raise taxes on the middle class
    (J) A discussion of recent developments in medical technology

21. The author's primary concern is to:

    (A) describe the financial structure of the healthcare industry.
    (B) demonstrate the importance of government support for healthcare institutions.
    (C) criticize wealthy institutions for refusing to provide services to the poor.
    (D) identify the historical causes of the division between private and public hospitals.

22. The author cites all of the following as factors contributing to the decline of public hospitals EXCEPT:

    (F) Government money was used to subsidize private medical schools and hospitals to the detriment of public hospitals.
    (G) Public hospitals are not able to compete with private institutions for top-flight managers and doctors.
    (H) Large private medical centers have better research facilities and more extensive research programs than public hospitals.
    (J) Blue Cross insurance coverage does not reimburse subscribers for medical expenses incurred in a public hospital.

23. The author's attitude toward public hospitals can best be described as:

    (A) contemptuous and prejudiced.
    (B) apprehensive and distrustful.
    (C) concerned and understanding.
    (D) enthusiastic and supportive.

24. The author implies that any outpatient care provided by a hospital is:

    (F) paid for by private insurance.
    (G) provided in lieu of treatment by a private physician.
    (H) supplied primarily by private hospitals.
    (J) a source of revenue for public hospitals.

NOTES AND STRATEGIES

Items 25-32 are based on the following passage.

SOCIAL SCIENCE: This passage discusses a historical argument that emerged following U.S. military unification.

The National Security Act of 1947 created a national military establishment headed by a single Secretary of Defense. The legislation had been a year-and-a-half in the making—beginning when President Truman first recommended that the armed services be reorganized into a single department. During that period, the President's concept of a unified armed service was torn apart and put back together several times; the final measure to emerge from Congress was a compromise. Most of the opposition to the bill came from the Navy and its numerous civilian spokesmen, including Secretary of the Navy James Forrestal. In support of unification (and a separate air force that was part of the unification package) were the Army air forces, the Army, and, most importantly, the President of the United States.

Passage of the bill did not end the bitter interservice disputes. Rather than unify, the act served only to federate the military services. It neither halted the rapid demobilization of the armed forces that followed World War II nor brought to the new national military establishment the loyalties of officers steeped in the traditions of the separate services. At a time when the balance of power in Europe and Asia was rapidly shifting, the services lacked any precise statement of United States foreign policy from the National Security Council on which to base future programs. The services bickered unceasingly over their respective roles and missions, already complicated by the Soviet nuclear capability that, for the first time, made the United States subject to devastating attack. Not even the appointment of Forrestal as First Secretary of Defense allayed the suspicions of naval officers and their supporters that the role of the U.S. Navy was threatened with permanent eclipse. Before the war of words died down, Forrestal himself was driven to resignation and then suicide.

By 1948, the United States military establishment was forced to make do with a budget approximately 10 percent of what it had been at its wartime peak. Meanwhile, the cost of weapons procurement was rising geometrically as the nation came to put more and more reliance on the atomic bomb and its delivery systems. These two factors inevitably made adversaries of the Navy and the Air Force as the battle between advocates of the B-36 and the supercarrier so amply demonstrates. Given severe fiscal restraints on the one hand, and on the other the nation's increasing reliance on strategic nuclear deterrence, the conflict between these two services over roles and missions was essentially a contest over slices of an ever-diminishing pie.

Yet if in the end neither service was the obvious victor, the principle of civilian dominance over the military clearly was. If there had ever been any danger that the United States military establishment might exploit, to the detriment of civilian control, the goodwill it enjoyed as a result of its victories in World War II, that danger disappeared in the interservice animosities engendered by the battle over unification.

25. In line 20, the word "demobilization" most nearly means:

(A) shift to a unified military.
(B) realignment of allies.
(C) change from war to peace.
(D) adoption of new technology.

26. According to the passage, the interservice strife that followed unification occurred primarily between the:

(F) Army and Army air forces.
(G) Army and Navy.
(H) Army air forces and Navy.
(J) Air Force and Navy.

27. It can be inferred from the passage that Forrestal's appointment as Secretary of Defense was expected to:

(A) placate members of the Navy.
(B) result in decreased levels of defense spending.
(C) outrage advocates of the Army air forces.
(D) win Congressional approval of the unification plan.

28. According to the passage, President Truman supported which of the following?

(F) Elimination of the Navy
(G) A unified military service
(H) Establishment of a separate air force
(J) A unified military service and establishment of a separate air force

29. With which of the following statements about defense unification would the author most likely agree?

(A) Unification ultimately undermined United States military capability by inciting interservice rivalry.
(B) The unification legislation was necessitated by the drastic decline in appropriations for the military services.
(C) Although the unification was not entirely successful, it had the unexpected result of ensuring civilian control of the military.
(D) In spite of the attempted unification, each service was still able to pursue its own objectives without interference from the other branches.

30. According to the selection, the political situation following the passage of the National Security Act of 1947 was characterized by all of the following EXCEPT:

(F) a shifting balance of power in Europe and in Asia.
(G) fierce interservice rivalries.
(H) lack of strong leadership by the National Security Council.
(J) a lame-duck President who was unable to unify the legislature.

31. The author cites the resignation and suicide of Forrestal in order to:

(A) underscore the bitterness of the interservice rivalry surrounding the passage of the National Security Act of 1947.
(B) demonstrate that the Navy eventually emerged as the dominant branch of service after the passage of the National Security Act of 1947.
(C) suggest that the nation would be better served by a unified armed service under a single command.
(D) provide an example of a military leader who preferred to serve his country in war rather than in peace.

32. The author is primarily concerned with:

(F) discussing the influence of personalities on political events.
(G) describing the administration of a powerful leader.
(H) criticizing a piece of legislation.
(J) analyzing a political development.

NOTES AND STRATEGIES

Items 33-40 are based on the following passage.

SOCIAL SCIENCE: This passage is adapted from an article about early American education ideology.

The founders of the American Republic viewed their revolution primarily in political rather than economic or social terms. Furthermore, they talked about education as essential to the public good—a goal that took precedence over knowledge as occupational training or as a means to self-fulfillment or self-improvement. Over and over again, the Revolutionary generation, both liberal and conservative in outlook, asserted its conviction that the welfare of the Republic rested upon an educated citizenry and that schools, especially free public schools, would be the best means of educating the citizenry in civic values and the obligations required of everyone in a democratic republican society. All agreed that the principal ingredients of a civic education were literacy and the inculcation of patriotic and moral virtues, some others adding the study of history and the study of principles of the republican government itself.

The founders, as was the case with almost all their successors, were long on exhortation and rhetoric regarding the value of civic education, but they left it to the textbook writers to distill the essence of those values for schoolchildren. Texts in American history and government appeared as early as the 1790s. The textbook writers turned out to be largely of conservative persuasion, more likely Federalist in outlook than Jeffersonian, and they almost universally agreed that political virtue must rest upon moral and religious precepts. Since most textbook writers were New Englanders, this meant that the texts were infused with Protestant, and above all Puritan, outlooks.

In the first half of the Republic, civic education in the schools emphasized the inculcation of civic values and made little attempt to develop participatory political skills. That was a task left to incipient political parties, town meetings, churches, and the coffee or ale houses where men gathered for conversation. Additionally, as a reading of certain Federalist papers of the period would demonstrate, the press probably did more to disseminate realistic as well as partisan knowledge of government than the schools. The goal of education, however, was to achieve a higher form of *unum* for the new Republic. In the middle half of the nineteenth century, the political values taught in the public and private schools did not change substantially from those celebrated in the first fifty years of the Republic. In the textbooks of the day, their rosy hues if anything became golden. To the resplendent values of liberty, equality, and a benevolent Christian morality were now added the middle-class virtues—especially of New England—of hard work, honesty, integrity, the rewards of individual effort, and obedience to parents and legitimate authority. But of all the political values taught in school, patriotism was preeminent; and whenever teachers explained to schoolchildren why they should love their country above all else, the idea of liberty assumed pride of place.

33. In line 5, the phrase "took precedence over" most nearly means:

(A) set an example for.
(B) formulated a policy of.
(C) enlightened someone on.
(D) had greater importance than.

34. The passage deals primarily with the:

(F) content of textbooks used in early American schools.
(G) role of education in late eighteenth- and early to mid-nineteenth-century America.
(H) influence of New England Puritanism on early American values.
(J) origin and development of the Protestant work ethic in modern America.

35. According to the passage, the founders of the Republic regarded education primarily as:

(A) a religious obligation.
(B) a private matter.
(C) an unnecessary luxury.
(D) a political necessity.

36. The author states that textbooks written in the middle part of the nineteenth century:

(F) departed radically in tone and style from earlier textbooks.
(G) mentioned for the first time the value of liberty.
(H) treated traditional civic virtues with even greater reverence.
(J) were commissioned by government agencies.

37. Which of the following would LEAST likely have been the subject of an early American textbook?

(A) Basic rules of English grammar
(B) The American Revolution
(C) Patriotism and other civic virtues
(D) Vocational education

38. The author's attitude toward the educational system discussed in the passage can best be described as:

(F) cynical and unpatriotic.
(G) realistic and analytical.
(H) pragmatic and frustrated.
(J) disenchanted and bitter.

39. The passage provides information that would be helpful in answering which of the following questions?

(A) Why was a disproportionate share of early American textbooks written by New England authors?
(B) Was the Federalist party primarily a liberal or conservative force in early American politics?
(C) How many years of education did the founders believe were sufficient to instruct young citizens in civic virtue?
(D) What were the names of some of the Puritan authors who wrote early American textbooks?

40. The author implies that an early American Puritan would likely insist that:

(F) moral and religious values are the foundation of civic virtue.
(G) textbooks should instruct students in political issues of vital concern to the community.
(H) textbooks should give greater emphasis to the value of individual liberty than to the duties of patriotism.
(J) private schools with a particular religious focus are preferable to public schools with no religious instruction.

Items 41-46 are based on the following passage.

SOCIAL SCIENCE: This passage discusses the interrelationship of the United States economy and international commerce.

International commerce is woven thoroughly into the fabric of the American economy. Exports and imports amounted to more than 11 percent of the U.S. gross domestic product (GDP) in 1991, up dramatically from 7.5 percent just 5 years before. More than 7 million American jobs are related to exports, and millions more depend on the overall economic activity generated by export trade. Export-related jobs pay more—almost 17 percent more than the average American job.

Exports are vital to the economic health of many key sectors of the manufacturing economy. For instance, makers of computers, aerospace and heavy earthmoving equipment, and farm implements are increasingly dependent on export markets. For these exports, slow growth abroad translates to declining vitality at home. The same picture is true of agriculture, where roughly one in four farm acres is now harvested for the export market. International sales of business-related services—construction, finance, insurance, and engineering, among others—amount to tens of billions of dollars each year.

In the early years of the post-World War II era, the United States stood virtually alone as the industrial and technological leader of the world. At that time, the U.S. produced almost half of the world's GDP, including much of the world's manufactured goods, and had roughly 80 percent of the world's hard currency reserves. Today, while the U.S. remains the world's leading economy, its share of world GDP has shrunk to about 24 percent, and its share of world manufacturers is even lower. Experts agree that, relative to the size of the economy and the diversity of its industrial and technological base, the U.S. has lagged far behind its export potential.

Meanwhile, the potential for growth in U.S. exports is enormous. Markets in Europe and Japan are huge and relatively stable. There is growing promise in Asia's $5.7 trillion economy and Latin America's $1 trillion economy. These markets are generating a rapidly growing demand for infrastructure investment, aircraft, and high-technology capital goods—all areas in which the U.S. has real or potential strengths. In addition, new entrants into the world economy, such as Central and Eastern Europe and the countries of the former Soviet Union, show real promise as potential markets for U.S. exports.

Growing world markets, however, do not automatically translate into U.S. export sales. The fierce competition for international markets comes primarily from the more innovative firms in Europe and Japan. In particular, Japanese companies have set the pace with a mix of aggressive business practices and a virtually economy-wide commitment to quality, rapid time to market, ongoing innovation, and customer satisfaction. American companies are beginning to try to meet the competition abroad, as well as to view their success as a benchmark for improvement, whether that best is in Chicago, Frankfurt, or Osaka.

The new realities of international competition yield lessons for the U.S. government as well. Persistent economic diplomacy and high-level advocacy, competitive and well-focused export financing, and improved efforts at information-gathering have become necessary components of an export promotion policy. Many foreign governments have been more aggressive and more focused than the U.S. government in working with their firms to secure export sales. Senior government officials, up to and including the President or Prime Minister, often will travel to support the sale of their home country's goods and services. The U.S. government needs to begin to measure its export strategy against the flexibility and effectiveness of the competition. Exports are central to growth, jobs, and a rising standard of living for all Americans. Our role in building a better America at home and acting as an economic leader abroad is dependent on our ability to develop a coherent, aggressive, and effective national export strategy.

41. Which of the following U.S. economic sectors has declined most seriously since World War II?

(A) Agriculture
(B) Manufacturing
(C) High-technology products
(D) Business-related services

42. Which of the following best expresses the central point of the passage?

(F) Exports drive the U.S. economy.
(G) U.S. exports have declined since shortly after World War II.
(H) Exports are so important to the U.S. economy that steps should be taken to increase U.S. exports worldwide.
(J) The U.S. government should encourage U.S. corporations to expand into markets in Asia and Latin America.

43. Which of the following areas is NOT mentioned in the passage as a potential market for U.S. goods abroad?

(A) Asia
(B) Latin America
(C) Central Europe
(D) Northern Africa

44. The passage suggests that both U.S. corporations and the U.S. government should:

(F) discourage imports in favor of exports.
(G) focus on improving the quality of American products.
(H) try to meet the competition abroad.
(J) take steps to reduce the economy's dependence on exports.

45. With which of the following explanations for the decline in the United States' share of world GDP would the author be most likely to agree?

I. Other countries are relatively uninterested in purchasing the goods and services the U.S. has to offer.
II. Other governments have done more to encourage their countries' exports than has the U.S. government.
III. Companies in some other countries have been more enterprising in producing high-quality goods and services.

(A) II only
(B) I and II only
(C) I and III only
(D) II and III only

46. According to the passage, an increase in U.S. exports abroad would generate:

(F) more high-paying jobs for American workers.
(G) increased profits for American farmers.
(H) greater diversity in American industry.
(J) resentment among foreign competitors.

Items 47-55 are based on the following passage.

NATURAL SCIENCE: This passage details lake regions, the conditions under which the regions occur, and how various interactions between these regions create different types of lakes.

Lakes arise from sources that are almost entirely geologic in nature. Once they have formed, lakes are doomed. Because of the concave nature of the lake basin, there is a trend toward demise as the basin fills in with sediment. A lake lives through youthful stages to maturity, senescence, and death when the basin is finally full. This procedure does not always follow a direct course. Periods of rejuvenation occasionally occur in some lakes. Eventually, marshes, swampy meadows, and forests appear where lakes once existed. Large lakes may be far from death as a result of shoaling, but climatic changes or geologic events that result in drying out or drainage eventually lead to their ends.

The littoral zone of a lake is the region of the shallows. The shallows are subject to fluctuating temperatures and erosion of the shoreline through wave action and the effects of weather. The shallows are usually well lit and serve as home to rooted aquatic plants. The littoral region is the region from the shoreline to the depth where the weeds disappear. Sometimes, wave action is so extreme that most aquatic vegetation is absent and only algae are present, marking the outer regions of the littoral region. The littoral benthos is the bottom region of the littoral region. This region contains many species and taxonomic groups. A high diversity and high annual production set this community apart from other regions of the lake.

The sublittoral zone extends from the outer region of the littoral region. Sediments in the sublittoral zone are finer grained than those of the littoral zone. Although this region is dimly lit, it is usually well oxygenated. The sublittoral zone community contains fewer species than does the littoral zone. This is due mainly to the reduced number of habitats.

In some lakes, the old shells of gastropods and pelecypods that inhabit the littoral zone are found accumulated in the sublittoral zone. These shell zones are thought to mark the place where weather interactions and currents have carried and dropped these remains.

The profundal zone is defined as the region of a lake where summer temperature stratification is apparent. Under such conditions a deep cold region is formed where currents are at a minimum and where light is greatly reduced. The temperature is mostly uniform throughout this region, and under some conditions, oxygen is almost completely absent, but CO_2 and methane are prevalent. The hydrogen ion concentration is high because of the presence of carbonic acid. This stratum of water is characterized by the existence of decayed matter rather than by the production of organic matter.

As solar radiation passes down from the surface of the lake, it disappears exponentially, and the heating wavelengths are usually absorbed very fast. At the end of the yearly heating period, one might expect the temperature stratum to resemble the light curve; however, due to weather conditions—for example, wind—the temperature profiles of lakes are altered. The temperature difference is readily explained by the wind mixing the upper layers of water and distributing downward the heat that has been absorbed by the surface layers of water.

Direct stratification occurs when dense cold water lies beneath lighter warm layers of water. Direct stratification divides a lake into three regions. The upper warm region, mixed completely by wind to produce a region that is almost at a uniform temperature throughout, is called the epilimnion. At the bottom is a colder, heavier region of water, which is unaffected by wind action and therefore remains stagnant. This region is called the hypolimnion. Separating these two regions is the thermocline, a region of water where temperature drops quickly with increasing depth.

Dimictic lakes are lakes that have two mixing periods: vernal and autumnal. The typical dimictic lake stratifies directly during the warm months. When the cold months arrive, the surface water starts to cool, which eventually destroys the stratification and initiates complete circulation. During the fall mixing, chilling of the entire water mass continues until the water mass achieves a uniform temperature of about 4 degrees Celsius.

Polymictic lakes are lakes that have many mixing periods or which have continuous circulation throughout the year. Polymictic lakes are influenced more by fluctuations in temperature from day to night than by seasonal changes.

Meromictic lakes circulate at times, but incompletely. The entire water mass does not participate in the mixing. A dense region of water at the bottom remains stagnant and anaerobic. The three regions of a meromictic lake have their own names. The bottom layer, which is basically stagnant and contains a greater concentration of dissolved substances, is called the monimolimnion. The upper layer is mixed by the wind, is more dilute, and shows seasonal changes. This region is called the mixolimnion. Between the monimolimnion and the mixolimnion is a region where salinity increases quickly with depth. This region is called the chemocline.

47. The author uses "doomed" in line 3 to indicate that:

I. he regrets the event.
II. the lakes have a limited future.
III. people will destroy the lakes.

(A) I only
(B) II only
(C) II and III only
(D) I, II, and III

48. Unlike the sublittoral zone, the littoral zone:

(F) has fine-grained sediment.
(G) contains many varied habitats.
(H) contains aquatic vegetation.
(J) is well oxygenated.

49. Why is aquatic vegetation absent in some lakes?

(A) Extreme wave action might uproot plants.
(B) Some lakes have no littoral or sublittoral regions.
(C) Algae take over the littoral region.
(D) The lakes are fully mature.

50. The remains of gastropods are deposited in the sublittoral zone by:

I. currents.
II. wind.
III. animals.

(F) I only
(G) II only
(H) I and II only
(J) I and III only

51. The profundal zone is marked by:

(A) shells of organisms, low vegetation, and high diversity.
(B) solar radiation and a vernal mixing period.
(C) increased temperatures in summer and production of organic matter.
(D) cold temperatures, low light, and a lack of oxygen.

52. In October, you would expect a northern dimictic lake to:

(F) be warmer on the surface than it was in May.
(G) cool from the surface to achieve a uniform temperature.
(H) begin to stratify directly.
(J) slowly freeze across the surface.

53. A polymictic lake might be coldest:

(A) at night.
(B) in autumn.
(C) after sunrise.
(D) in spring.

54. The chemocline in a meromictic lake is equivalent to:

(F) the littoral zone in a senescent lake.
(G) the profundal zone in a dimictic lake.
(H) the thermocline in a dimictic lake.
(J) the epilimnion in a polymictic lake.

55. Which of the following conclusions CANNOT be drawn from this passage?

(A) Deep lakes are unaffected by weather.
(B) Lakes have geologic derivations.
(C) Lakes vary in temperature.
(D) All lakes will eventually die.

NOTES AND STRATEGIES

Items 56-62 are based on the following passage.

HUMANITIES: This passage discusses home and building construction in the Appalachian region of North America.

For nearly a century, the houses and other artificial structures of the Appalachian region have played a prominent role in its representation in books, magazines, and film. From nineteenth century magazine illustrations of single-room log cabins to twentieth century television programs focusing on unpainted, one- or two-room company houses, the dominant image of the region has been the dilapidated, weather-beaten Appalachian home. While some of these presentations are authentic, some are contrived, and nearly all are selective. Interpreters of Appalachian culture have tended to focus on extremes and, as a result, have misrepresented Appalachian life. A survey of the New River Gorge area in West Virginia revealed a much more diverse landscape than has been described in the past. While project researchers did locate log cabins and abandoned coal towns, they also found considerable architectural variety. Contrary to past reports, the New River Gorge cultural landscape reflects the history of a community that designed, built, and used its buildings according to individual tastes and principles.

The territory is dotted with homes that have had the original appearances altered to suit the occupant. These individually styled facades may appear quirky to the outsider, but their meaning is revealed through an understanding of the local history. Coal companies originally constructed many of the homes for their workers. Whole towns of box houses (cheap, fast to build, and temporary) were constructed at one time. While the floor plans varied, the basic construction technique did not. Vertical boards attached to sills and plates formed both the interior and exterior walls, as well as the buildings' weight-bearing supports. Today, West Virginians commonly call box houses "Jinn Linns." One local resident related a story concerning the origin of the term. Jenny Lynn, a coal camp resident, decided to distinguish her home from the other identical box houses in her camp by nailing narrow strips over the spaces between the vertical boards, creating the board and batten siding now characteristic of these houses. Soon, many others followed her example and eventually named the house type after her.

Unlike Jenny Lynn, most coal camp residents were required to maintain their box houses according to strict company standards or risk eviction. As the coal boom declined, however, companies began selling the homes to their tenants. Having obtained the freedom to maintain their homes according to their own standards, residents altered facades or added rooms or porches, resulting in the variety of box houses visible in the region today. Others decided to leave the company camps altogether. Many purchased modern prefabricated houses, for example, the Lustron, an all-steel factory-made home manufactured in Ohio between 1948 and 1950. The Lustron was a one-story, gable-roof ranch house with an exterior and interior skin of enameled steel panels bolted to a structural-steel frame and a concrete slab foundation. Unlike the Jinn Linn, the home was durable, easy to maintain, and strong.

Innovative construction materials are also produced locally. Bluish cinder blocks and "red dog" blocks, both by-products of the coal industry, have been used to construct homes, churches, gymnasiums, and barns throughout the Gorge. These and other colorful materials, including glazed tile, are often used in striking combinations, and an unusual amount of care is given to decorative detail. For example, yellow and red bricks and stones are often used for window and door trims, quoins, and belt courses (projecting horizontal strips around the outside of a building).

The complex balance between formal design and personal expression is a striking feature of the New River Gorge landscape. Like the quilts made in the region, much of the architecture is pieced together from locally made and recycled materials. Materials rarely used in combination in other areas are carefully pieced together into a landscape filled with personal meaning.

56. The author uses the word "selective" (line 11) when describing the popular representations of Appalachian architecture to indicate that they:

(F) present only one facet of Appalachian architecture.
(G) focus on public buildings rather than on private homes.
(H) show only the most [illegible]ve side of Appalachian architecture.
(J) represent the percepti[illegible] only of the residents themselv[illegible]

57. With which of the following aspects of New River Gorge houses described in the passage would the interpreters mentioned in line 11 be most surprised?

(A) Their uniformity
(B) Their unusually large size
(C) The ease with which they were built and maintained
(D) The attention given to decorative detail in constructing them

58. Which of the following best expresses the author's main point in telling the story of Jenny Lynn (lines 37-44)?

(F) Residents of the coal camps modified their originally identical homes to suit their own preferences.
(G) The person who most influenced architecture in the New River Gorge was Jenny Lynn.
(H) Box houses are the most common type of house in the New River Gorge because they were inexpensive to construct.
(J) Coal companies had a great deal of control over the architecture of the New River Gorge.

59. Which of the following is NOT a difference between Lustron houses and Jinn Linn houses?

(A) Lustron houses were tougher than were Jinn Linn houses.
(B) Lustron houses were easier to keep up than were Jinn Linn houses.
(C) Lustron houses were made of steel while Jinn Linn houses were made of wood.
(D) Lustron houses came in several different floor plans while Jinn Linn houses always had the same plan.

60. According to the passage, Lustron houses were:

(F) less expensive than box houses.
(G) more common in Ohio than in West Virginia.
(H) ready-made in one place to be put up elsewhere.
(J) extremely popular among former coal-camp residents.

61. In what way is the architecture of the New River Gorge like the quilts made there?

I. Both use designs or plans that originally come from outside the region.
II. Both are made from available materials used in innovative ways.
III. Both express the personal tastes of the makers or users.

(A) I and II only
(B) II only
(C) II and III only
(D) I, II, and III

62. Which of the following aspects of Appalachian architecture does the author appear to value most highly?

(F) Its beauty
(G) Its diversity
(H) Its practicality
(J) Its durability

TIMED-PRACTICE QUIZZES

This section contains six quizzes. Complete each quiz under timed conditions. Answers are on page 936.

DIRECTIONS: Each passage below is followed by one or more items based on its content. Answer the items on the basis of what is stated or implied in the corresponding passage.

A. QUIZ I (8 items; 15 minutes)

Items 1-8 are based on the following passage.

SOCIAL SCIENCE: This passage discusses the economic structure of current healthcare policy.

The healthcare economy is replete with unusual and even unique economic relationships. One of the least understood involves the peculiar roles of producer or "provider" and purchaser or "consumer" in the typical doctor-patient relationship. In most sectors of the economy, the seller attempts to attract a potential buyer with various inducements of price, quality, and utility, and the buyer makes the decision. Where circumstances permit the buyer no choice because there is effectively only one seller and the product is relatively essential, government usually asserts monopoly and places the industry under price and other regulations. Neither of these conditions prevails in most of the healthcare industry.

In the healthcare industry, the doctor-patient relationship is the mirror image of the ordinary relationship between producer and consumer. Once an individual has chosen to see a physician—and even then there may be no real choice—it is the physician who usually makes all significant purchasing decisions: whether the patient should return "next Wednesday," whether x-rays are needed, whether drugs should be prescribed, *etc.* It is a rare and sophisticated patient who will challenge such professional decisions or raise in advance questions about price, especially when the ailment is regarded as serious.

This is particularly significant in relation to hospital care. The physician must certify the need for hospitalization, determine what procedures will be performed, and announce when the patient may be discharged. The patient may be consulted about some of these decisions, but in the main it is the doctor's judgments that are final. Little wonder, then, that in the eyes of the hospital, the physician is the real "consumer." Consequently, the medical staff represents the "power center" in hospital policy and decision-making, not the administration.

Although usually there are in this situation four identifiable participants—the physician, the hospital, the patient, and the payer (generally an insurance carrier or government)—the physician makes the essential decisions for all of them. The hospital becomes an extension of the physician; the payer generally meets most of the bona fide bills generated by the physician/hospital; and for the most part the patient plays a passive role. In routine or minor illnesses, or just plain worries, the patient's options are, of course, much greater with respect to use and price. In illnesses that are of some significance, however, such choices tend to evaporate, and it is for these illnesses that the bulk of the healthcare dollar is spent. We estimate that about 75 to 80 percent of healthcare expenditures are determined by physicians, not patients. For this reason, economy measures directed at patients or the public are relatively ineffective.

1. In line 1, the phrase "replete with" most nearly means:

   (A) filled with.
   (B) restricted by.
   (C) enriched by.
   (D) damaged by.

2. The author's primary purpose is to:

   (F) speculate about the relationship between a patient's ability to pay and the treatment received.
   (G) criticize doctors for exercising too much control over patients.
   (H) analyze some important economic factors in healthcare.
   (J) urge hospitals to reclaim their decision-making authority.

3. It can be inferred that doctors are able to determine hospital policies because:

   (A) it is doctors who generate income for the hospital.
   (B) most of a patient's bills are paid by health insurance.
   (C) hospital administrators lack the expertise to question medical decisions.
   (D) a doctor is ultimately responsible for a patient's health.

4. According to the author, when a doctor tells a patient to "return next Wednesday," the doctor is in effect:

   (F) taking advantage of the patient's concern for his health.
   (G) instructing the patient to buy more medical services.
   (H) warning the patient that a hospital stay might be necessary.
   (J) advising the patient to seek a second opinion.

5. The author is most probably leading up to:

   (A) a proposal to control medical costs.
   (B) a discussion of a new medical treatment.
   (C) an analysis of the causes of inflation in the United States.
   (D) a study of lawsuits against doctors for malpractice.

6. The tone of the passage can best be described as:

   (F) whimsical.
   (G) cautious.
   (H) analytical.
   (J) inquisitive.

7. With which of the following statements would the author be likely to agree?

   (A) Few patients are reluctant to object to the course of treatment prescribed by a doctor or to question the cost of the services.
   (B) The payer, whether an insurance carrier or the government, is less likely to acquiesce to demands for payment when the illness of the patient is regarded as serious.
   (C) Today's patients are more informed as to what services and procedures they will need from their healthcare providers.
   (D) The more serious the illness of a patient, the less likely it is that the patient will object to the course of treatment prescribed or to question the cost of services.

8. The author's primary concern is to:

   (F) define a term.
   (G) clarify a misunderstanding.
   (H) refute a theory.
   (J) discuss a problem.

B. QUIZ II (7 items; 15 minutes)

Items 1-7 are based on the following passage.

NATURAL SCIENCE: This passage discusses human social evolution and adaptation.

Man, so the truism goes, lives increasingly in a man-made environment. This puts a special burden on human immaturity, for it is plain that adapting to such variable conditions must depend very heavily on opportunities for learning, or whatever the processes are that are operative during immaturity. It must also mean that during immaturity, man must master knowledge and skills that are neither stored in the gene pool nor learned by direct encounter, but that are contained in the culture pool—knowledge about values and history, skills as varied as an obligatory natural language or an optional mathematical one, as mute as levers or as articulate as myth telling.

Yet, it would be a mistake to leap to the conclusion that because human immaturity makes possible high flexibility, therefore anything is possible for the species. Human traits were selected for their survival value over a four- to five-million-year period with a great acceleration of the selection process during the last half of that period. There were crucial, irreversible changes during that final man-making period: the recession of formidable dentition, a 50-percent increase in brain volume, the obstetrical paradox—bipedalism and strong pelvic girdle, larger brain through a smaller birth canal—an immature brain at birth, and creation of what Washburn has called a "technical-social way of life," involving tool and symbol use.

Note, however, that hominidization consisted principally of adaptations to conditions in the Pleistocene.

These preadaptations, shaped in response to earlier habitat demands, are part of man's evolutionary inheritance. This is not to say that close beneath the skin of man is a naked ape, that civilization is only a veneer. The technical-social way of life is a deep feature of the species adaptation. But we would err if we assumed *a priori* that man's inheritance placed no constraint on his power to adapt. Some of the preadaptations can be shown to be presently maladaptive. Man's inordinate fondness for fats and sweets no longer serves his individual survival well. Furthermore, the human obsession with sexuality is plainly not fitted for survival of the species now, however well it might have served to populate the upper Pliocene and the Pleistocene. Nevertheless, note that the species responds typically to these challenges by technical innovation rather than by morphological or behavioral change. Contraception dissociates sexuality from reproduction. Of course, we do not know what kinds and what range of stresses are produced by successive rounds of such technical innovation. Dissociating sexuality and reproduction, for example, surely produces changes in the structure of the family, which in turn redefine the role of women, which in turn alters the authority pattern affecting the child, *etc.* Continuing and possibly accelerating change seems inherent in such adaptation. This, of course, places an enormous pressure on man's uses of immaturity, preparing the young for unforeseeable change—the more so if there are severe restraints imposed by human preadaptations to earlier conditions of life.

1. The primary purpose of the passage is to:

   (A) refute some misconceptions about the importance of human immaturity.
   (B) introduce a new theory of the origins of the human species.
   (C) describe the evolutionary forces that formed the physical appearance of modern humans.
   (D) discuss the importance of human immaturity as an adaptive mechanism.

2. It can be inferred that the obstetrical paradox is puzzling because:

   (F) it occurred very late during the evolution of the species.
   (G) evolutionary forces seemed to work at cross purposes to each other.
   (H) technological innovations have made the process of birth easier.
   (J) an increase in brain size is not an ordinary evolutionary event.

3. Which of the following statements can be inferred from the passage?
   (A) Human beings are today less sexually active than were our ancestors during the Pleistocene era.
   (B) During the Pleistocene era, a fondness for fats and sweets was a trait that contributed to survival of humans.
   (C) Mathematics was invented by human beings during the latter half of the Pleistocene era.
   (D) The use of language and tools is a trait that is genetically transmitted from one generation to the next.

4. As used in line 32, the term "preadaptations" refers to traits that:
   (F) were useful to earlier human beings but have since lost their utility.
   (G) appeared in response to the need to learn a natural language and the use of tools.
   (H) humans currently exhibit but that developed in response to conditions of an earlier age.
   (J) are disadvantageous to creatures whose way of life is primarily technical and social.

5. The author mentions contraception to demonstrate that:
   (A) human beings may adapt to new conditions by technological invention rather than by changing their behavior.
   (B) sexual promiscuity is no longer an aid to the survival of the human species.
   (C) technological innovation is a more important adaptive mechanism than either heredity or direct encounter.
   (D) conditions during the upper Pliocene and Pleistocene eras no longer affect the course of human evolution.

6. With which of the following statements would the author LEAST likely agree?
   (F) The technical-social way of life of humans is an adaptive mechanism that arose in response to environmental pressures.
   (G) The possibility of technical innovation makes it unlikely that the physical appearance of humans will change radically in a short time.
   (H) Technological innovations can result in changes in the social structures in which humans live.
   (J) The fact that humans have a technical-social way of life makes the species immune from evolutionary pressures.

7. The author is most probably addressing which of the following audiences?
   (A) Medical students in a course on human anatomy
   (B) College students in an introductory course on archaeology
   (C) Psychologists investigating the uses of human immaturity
   (D) Biologists trying to trace the course of human evolution

C. QUIZ III (8 items; 15 minutes)

Items 1-8 are based on the following passage.

SOCIAL SCIENCE: This passage is adapted from an article that discusses Japanese culture and civilization.

The uniqueness of the Japanese character is the result of two, seemingly contradictory forces: the strength of traditions, and selective receptivity to foreign achievements and inventions. As early as the 1860s, there were counter movements to the traditional orientation. Yukichi Fukuzawa, the most eloquent spokesman of Japan's "Enlightenment," claimed "The Confucian civilization of the East seems to me to lack two things possessed by Western civilization: science in the material sphere and a sense of independence in the spiritual sphere." Fukuzawa's great influence is found in the free and individualistic philosophy of the Education Code of 1872, but he was not able to prevent the government from turning back to the canons of Confucian thought in the Imperial Rescript of 1890. Another interlude of relative liberalism followed World War I, when the democratic idealism of President Woodrow Wilson had an important impact on Japanese intellectuals and, especially, students; but more important was the Leninist ideology of the 1917 Bolshevik Revolution. Again, in the early 1930s, nationalism and militarism became dominant, largely because of failing economic conditions.

Following the end of World War II, substantial changes were undertaken in Japan to liberate the individual from authoritarian restraints. The new democratic value system was accepted by many teachers, students, intellectuals, and old liberals, but it was not immediately embraced by the society as a whole. Japanese traditions were dominated by group values, and notions of personal freedom and individual rights were unfamiliar.

Today, democratic processes are evident in the widespread participation of the Japanese people in social and political life; yet, there is no universally accepted and stable value system. Values are constantly modified by strong infusions of Western ideas, both democratic and Marxist. School textbooks espouse democratic principles, emphasizing equality over hierarchy and rationalism over tradition; but in practice these values are often misinterpreted and distorted, particularly by youth who translate the individualistic and humanistic goals of democracy into egoistic and materialistic ones.

Most Japanese people have consciously rejected Confucianism, but vestiges of the old order remain. An important feature of relationships in many institutions such as political parties, large corporations, and university faculties is the *oyabun-kobun* or parent-child relation. A party leader, supervisor, or professor, in return for loyalty, protects those subordinate to him and takes general responsibility for their interests throughout their entire lives, an obligation that sometimes even extends to arranging marriages. The corresponding loyalty of the individual to his patron reinforces his allegiance to the group to which they both belong. A willingness to cooperate with other members of the group and to support without qualification the interests of the group in all its external relations is still a widely respected virtue. The *oyabun-kobun* creates ladders of mobility that an individual can ascend, rising as far as abilities permit, so long as he maintains successful personal ties with a superior in the vertical channel, the latter requirement usually taking precedence over a need for exceptional competence. Consequently, there is little horizontal relationship between people even within the same profession.

1. As used in line 46, the word "vestiges" most nearly means:

   (A) institutions.
   (B) superiors.
   (C) traces.
   (D) subordinates.

2. Which of the following is most like the relationship of the *oyabun-kobun* described in the passage?

   (F) A political candidate and the voting public
   (G) A gifted scientist and his protégé
   (H) Two brothers who are partners in a business
   (J) A judge presiding at the trial of a criminal defendant

3. According to the passage, Japanese attitudes are NOT influenced by which of the following?

   (A) Democratic ideals
   (B) Elements of modern Western culture
   (C) Remnants of an earlier social structure
   (D) Confucianism

4. The author implies that:

   (F) decisions about promotions within the vertical channel are often based on personal feelings.
   (G) students and intellectuals do not understand the basic tenets of Western democracy.
   (H) Western values have completely overwhelmed traditional Japanese attitudes.
   (J) respect for authority was introduced into Japan following World War II.

5. In developing the passage, the author does which of the following?

   (A) Introduces an analogy
   (B) Defines a term
   (C) Presents statistics
   (D) Cites an authority

6. It can be inferred that the Imperial Rescript of 1890:

   (F) was a protest by liberals against the lack of individual liberty in Japan.
   (G) marked a return in government policies to conservative values.
   (H) implemented the ideals set forth in the Education Code of 1872.
   (J) was influenced by the Leninist ideology of the Bolshevik Revolution.

7. Which of the following is the most accurate description of the organization of the passage?

   (A) A sequence of inferences in which the conclusion of each successive step becomes a premise in the next argument
   (B) A list of generalizations, most of which are supported by only a single example
   (C) A chronological analysis of historical events leading up to a description of the current situation
   (D) A statement of a commonly accepted theory that is then subjected to a critical analysis

8. Which of the following best states the central thesis of the passage?

   (F) The value system of Japan is based upon traditional and conservative values that have, in modern times, been modified by Western and other liberal values.
   (G) Students and radicals in Japan have used Leninist ideology to distort the meaning of democratic, Western values.
   (H) The notions of personal freedom and individual liberty did not find immediate acceptance in Japan because of the predominance of traditional group values.
   (J) Modern Japanese society is characterized by hierarchical relationships in which a personal tie to a superior is often more important than merit.

D. QUIZ IV (10 items; 15 minutes)

Items 1-10 are based on the following passage.

SOCIAL SCIENCE: This passage discusses the presidential election of 1796 between Thomas Jefferson and John Adams.

"Heartily tired" from the brutal, almost daily, conflicts that erupted over questions of national policy between himself and Alexander Hamilton, Thomas Jefferson resigned his position as Secretary of State in 1793. Although his Federalist opponents were convinced that this was merely a strategic withdrawal to allow him an opportunity to plan and promote his candidacy for the presidency should Washington step down in 1796, Jefferson insisted that this retirement from public life was to be final.

But even in retirement, the world of politics pursued him. As the election grew nearer and it became apparent that Washington would not seek a third term, rumors of Jefferson's presidential ambitions grew in intensity. Reacting to these continuous insinuations in a letter to James Madison, Jefferson admitted that while his enemies to impugn his political motives had originated the idea that he coveted the office of chief executive, he had been forced to examine his true feelings on the subject for his own peace of mind. In so doing he concluded that his reasons for retirement—the desire for privacy, and the delight of family life—coupled with his now failing health were insuperable barriers to public service. The "little spice of ambition" he had in his younger days had long since evaporated and the question of his presidency was forever closed.

Jefferson did not actively engage in the campaign on his own behalf. The Republican Party, presaging modern campaign tactics, created a grass roots sentiment for their candidate by directing their efforts toward the general populace. In newspapers, Jefferson was presented as "the uniform advocate of equal rights among the citizens" while Adams was portrayed as the "champion of rank, titles, heredity, and distinctions."

Jefferson was not certain of the outcome of the election until the end of December. Under the original electoral system established by the Constitution, each presidential elector cast his ballot for two men without designating between them as to office. The candidate who received the greater number of votes became the president; the second highest, the vice president. Based on his own calculations, Jefferson foresaw that the electoral vote would be close. He wrote to Madison that in the event of a tie, he wished for the choice to be in favor of Adams. The New Englander had always been his senior in public office, he explained, and the expression of public will being equal, he should be preferred for the higher honor. Jefferson, a shrewd politician, realized that the transition of power from the nearly mythical Washington to a lesser luminary in the midst of the deep and bitter political divisions facing the nation could be perilous, and he had no desire to be caught in the storm that had been brewing for four years and was about to break. "This is certainly not a moment to covet the helm," he wrote to Edward Rutledge. When the electoral vote was tallied, Adams emerged as the victor. Rejoicing at his "escape," Jefferson was completely satisfied with the decision. Despite their obvious and basic political differences, Jefferson genuinely respected John Adams as a friend and compatriot. Although he believed that Adams had deviated from the course set in 1776, Jefferson never felt a diminution of confidence in Adams' integrity and was confident he would not steer the nation too far off its Republican tack. Within two years, Jefferson's views would be drastically altered as measures such as the Alien and Sedition Acts of 1798 convinced him of the need to wrest control of the government from the Federalists.

1. The phrase "heartily tired" (line 1) is most probably a quotation from:

   (A) Alexander Hamilton.
   (B) Thomas Jefferson.
   (C) George Washington.
   (D) John Adams.

2. The "escape" mentioned in line 57 refers to the fact that Jefferson:

   (F) was no longer Secretary of State.
   (G) would not be burdened with the problems of the presidency.
   (H) fled the country following the election.
   (J) was hoping that the votes would be recounted.

3. According to the passage, the Republican Party appealed primarily to:

   (A) wealthy landowners.
   (B) ordinary people.
   (C) prosperous merchants.
   (D) high society.

4. The author states that all of the following were reasons Jefferson resigned as Secretary of State EXCEPT:

(F) Jefferson disliked Madison.
(G) Jefferson wanted to spend time with his family.
(H) Jefferson was weary of the demands of public service.
(J) Jefferson wished for greater privacy.

5. The author is primarily concerned with revealing the:

(A) feud between Alexander Hamilton and Thomas Jefferson.
(B) difference between the Federalists and the Republicans.
(C) strategies used by early American political parties.
(D) character and personality of Thomas Jefferson.

6. The author relies on which of the following in developing the selection?

I. Personal correspondence
II. Newspapers
III. Voter registration rolls

(F) I only
(G) II only
(H) I and II only
(J) I and III only

7. One reason for Jefferson's retirement was his disagreement with:

(A) Alexander Hamilton.
(B) George Washington.
(C) James Madison.
(D) Edward Rutledge.

8. In the context of the passage, the phrase "covet the helm" (line 55) means:

(F) to aspire to be President.
(G) to desire to purchase a boat.
(H) to wish to be left in peace.
(J) to hope to become wealthy.

9. The passage suggests that two years after the 1796 election, Jefferson would:

(A) ally himself with Alexander Hamilton.
(B) ally himself with John Adams.
(C) disagree with John Adams.
(D) disagree with Edward Rutledge.

10. The newspaper depicted Jefferson and Adams as:

(F) conservative and liberal, respectively.
(G) liberal and conservative, respectively.
(H) conservatives.
(J) liberals.

E. QUIZ V (10 items; 15 minutes)

Items 1-10 are based on the following passage.

HUMANITIES: This passage discusses the voyages to North American continents by Leif Ericsson and Biarni and debates the veracity of the varied accounts.

In the summer of 999, Leif Ericsson voyaged to Norway and spent the following winter with King Olaf Tryggvason. Substantially the same account is given by both the Saga of Eric the Red and the Flat Island Book. Of Leif's return voyage to Greenland the latter says nothing, but according to the former it was during this return voyage that Leif discovered America. The Flat Island Book, however, tells of another and earlier landfall by Biarni, the son of a prominent man named Heriulf, and makes this Leif's inspiration for the voyage to the new land. In short, like Leif, Biarni and his companions sight three countries in succession before reaching Greenland, and to come upon each new land takes one "doegr" more than the last until Biarni comes to land directly in front of his father's house in the last-mentioned country.

Most later writers have rejected this narrative, and they may be justified. Possibly, Biarni was a companion of Leif when he voyaged from Norway to Greenland via America, or it may be that the entire tale is but a garbled account of that voyage and Biarni another name for Leif. It should be noted, however, that the stories of Leif's visit to King Olaf and Biarni's to that king's predecessor are in the same narrative in the Flat Island Book, so there is less likelihood of duplication than if they were from different sources. Also, Biarni landed on none of the lands he passed, but Leif apparently landed on one, for he brought back specimens of wheat, vines, and timber. Nor is there any good reason to believe that the first land visited by Biarni was Wineland. The first land was "level and covered with woods," and "there were small hillocks upon it." Of forests, later writers do not emphasize them particularly in connection with Wineland, though they are often noted incidentally; and of hills, the Saga says of Wineland only "wherever there was hilly ground, there were vines."

Additionally, if the two narratives were from the same source, we should expect a closer resemblance of Helluland. The Saga says of it: "They found there hellus" (large flat stones). According to the Biarni narrative, however, "this land was high and mountainous." The intervals of one, two, three, and four "doegr" in both narratives are suggestive, but mythic formulas of this kind may be introduced into narratives without altogether destroying their historicity. It is also held against the Biarni narrative that its hero is made to come upon the coast of Greenland exactly in front of his father's home. But it should be recalled that Heriulfsness lay below two high mountains that served as landmarks for navigators.

I would give up Biarni more readily were it not that the story of Leif's voyage, contained in the supposedly more reliable Saga, is almost as amazing. But Leif's voyage across the entire width of the North Atlantic is said to be "probable" because it is documented in the narrative of a preferred authority, while Biarni's is "improbable" or even "impossible" because the document containing it has been condemned.

1. The author's primary concern is to demonstrate that:

   (A) Leif Ericsson did not visit America.
   (B) Biarni might have visited America before Leif Ericsson.
   (C) Biarni did not visit Wineland.
   (D) Leif Ericsson visited Wineland first.

2. The passage provides information that defines which of the following terms?

   I. Doegr
   II. Hellus
   III. Heriulfsness

   (F) I only
   (G) II only
   (H) I and II only
   (J) II and III only

3. It can be inferred from the passage that scholars who doubt the authenticity of the Biarni narrative make all of the following objections EXCEPT:

(A) Biarni might have accompanied Leif Ericsson on the voyage to America, and that is why a separate, erroneous narrative was invented.
(B) the similarity of the voyages described in the Saga and in the Flat Island Book indicates that there was but one voyage, not two voyages.
(C) it seems very improbable that a ship, having sailed from America to Greenland, could have found its way to a precise point on the coast of Greenland.
(D) both the Saga of Eric the Red and the Flat Island Book make use of mythic formulas, so it is probable that the same person wrote them both.

4. The author mentions the two high mountains (lines 50-51) in order to show that it is:

(F) reasonable for Biarni to land precisely at his father's home.
(G) possible to sail from Norway to Greenland without modern navigational equipment.
(H) likely that Biarni landed on America at least 100 years before Leif Ericsson.
(J) probable that Leif Ericsson followed the same course as Biarni.

5. All of the following are mentioned as similarities between Leif Ericsson's voyage and Biarni's voyage EXCEPT:

(A) both visited Norway.
(B) on the return voyage, both visited three different lands.
(C) both returned to Greenland.
(D) both sighted Wineland.

6. It can be inferred that the author regards the historicity of the Biarni narrative as:

(F) conclusively proved.
(G) almost conclusively proved.
(H) possibly true.
(J) highly unlikely.

7. In the final paragraph, the author suggests that some authorities who regard the Saga as authentic are guilty of which of the following errors in reasoning?

(A) Oversimplification
(B) Logical contradiction
(C) False analogy
(D) Circular reasoning

8. According to the passage, Heriulf is:

(F) Leif Ericsson's son.
(G) one of Leif Ericsson's sailors.
(H) Biarni's father.
(J) King Olaf Tryggvason's son.

9. According to the author, most authorities regard the Biarni narrative as:

(A) conclusively demonstrated.
(B) probably true.
(C) probably untrue.
(D) an attempted fraud.

10. Biarni's home was in:

(F) Norway.
(G) Greenland.
(H) Wineland.
(J) Flat Island.

E. QUIZ VI (10 items; 15 minutes)

Items 1-10 are based on the following passage.

NATURAL SCIENCE: This passage reviews the basic physics of electromagnetic waves and radar specifically.

Whether used to control airplane traffic, detect speeding automobiles, or track a hurricane, radar is a very useful tool. Developed during World War II, this technology allows for remote sensing, that is, locating objects that are not seen directly. The word "radar" is a contraction of "radio detection and ranging." It works in much the same way as an echo. When you shout toward a cliff or a large building, part of the sound bounces back. In radar, waves of electromagnetic radiation are sent out. When they strike an object, they bounce back and are picked up by a receiver. The returning signal indicates the direction of the object; the time it takes for the signal to return indicates the distance to the object. Radar waves detect objects by their varying densities. They are not deflected by atmospheric layers and therefore always travel in a straight line—in all weather, both day and night.

Radar waves are electromagnetic waves, as are light waves, electric waves, x-rays, cosmic rays, and radio waves. All electromagnetic waves travel at 300,000 kilometers per second—the speed of light. Waves differ from each other in the number of times they vibrate per second; this variable is known as frequency and is usually expressed as cycles per second. Waves also differ in their size, or wavelength. The speed, frequency, and wavelength of a wave are related by the wave equation in which:

$$\text{speed} = \text{frequency} \cdot \text{wavelength}$$

This shows that the product of the frequency and wavelength of any given wave is always a constant—the speed of light. To find the wavelength of a wave, knowing the frequency, this formula is used:

$$\text{wavelength} = \frac{\text{speed}}{\text{frequency}}$$

For example, if a radio station broadcasts waves at 600,000 cycles per second (cps), the wavelength would be calculated this way:

$$\begin{aligned}\text{wavelength} &= 300{,}000 \text{ km per sec}/600{,}000 \text{ cps}\\ &= 0.5 \text{ km} = 500 \text{ m}\end{aligned}$$

If the frequency of the wave is doubled to 1,200,000 cycles per second, its wavelength would be cut in half to 250 meters. Since frequencies are so high, the unit "megahertz" is usually used; 1 megahertz = 1,000,000 cycles per second.

Wavelengths within the electromagnetic spectrum vary greatly. Radar has wavelengths that measure from approximately one centimeter (0.01 meters) up to one meter. Each kind of wave has a range of wavelengths. The table compares some sample wavelengths of several kinds of electromagnetic waves.

Type of Wave (meters)	*Sample Wavelength*
cosmic rays	0.0000000000000001
x-rays	0.0000000001
ultraviolet rays	0.00000001
visible light	0.000001
infrared heat	0.0001
microwaves	0.001
radar	0.1
television	1.0
radio	100
long radio waves	10,000
electric power	1,000,000

1. Radio waves and radar waves have the same:

   (A) frequency.
   (B) wavelength.
   (C) cycles per second.
   (D) speed.

2. A radar signal having a frequency of 3,000 megahertz would have a wavelength of:

   (F) 0.001 km.
   (G) 0.01 km.
   (H) 10 m.
   (J) 0.1 m.

3. A radar set could not locate an airplane if it were flying:

   (A) faster than the speed of sound.
   (B) above a heavy storm.
   (C) above the atmosphere.
   (D) below the horizon.

4. It is possible to find the distance to an object from a radar set because the:

(F) wavelength of radar is known.
(G) frequency of radar is known.
(H) speed of radar is 300,000 kilometers per second.
(J) set operates at 10 megahertz.

5. The relationship between the frequency and wavelength of a wave is:

(A) constant.
(B) directly proportional.
(C) exponential.
(D) inverse.

6. An antenna picks up a signal that has a wavelength of about one meter. It is likely to be:

(F) in the visible spectrum.
(G) an ultraviolet ray.
(H) a television signal.
(J) an x-ray.

7. Radio waves will not penetrate the ionosphere, but microwaves will. Would you expect x-rays to penetrate the ionosphere?

(A) Yes, because they have a shorter wavelength than microwaves and radio waves.
(B) Yes, because they have a lower frequency than microwaves and radio waves.
(C) No, because they travel more slowly than microwaves.
(D) No, because they have fewer cycles per second than microwaves or radio waves.

8. Compared to cosmic rays, the frequency value of visible light waves is:

(F) higher.
(G) lower.
(H) the same.
(J) Cannot be determined from the given information

9. Which factor would be most important in order for radar to detect and track storms?

(A) Radar signals travel in straight lines.
(B) The densities of moist air masses are different from those of dry air masses.
(C) The atmosphere does not deflect radar signals.
(D) Radar signals travel much faster than storm tracks.

10. Like a radar reflection, an echo can be used to determine the distance of an object. This must be because:

(F). sound is a form of radar.
(G) sound travels at a relatively fixed rate.
(H) sound waves have different frequencies.
(J) sound waves are invisible.

TARGETED EDUCATIONAL SOLUTIONS.

Strategy Summary Sheet
READING

STRUCTURE OF READING: The ACT Reading Test contains four 500-600 word reading passages—one from each of the four content areas: Natural Science, Social Science, Humanities, and Prose Fiction. The ACT Reading Test is 35 minutes long with 40 items. The PLAN Reading Test is 20 minutes long with 25 items. The EXPLORE Reading Test is 30 minutes long with 30 items. Each passage is followed by 10 items. Items on the Reading Test are Multiple-Choice with four answer choices. Summarized below are the distributions of the passages and items among the four content areas for the ACT, PLAN, and EXPLORE.

NUMBER OF ITEMS PER CONTENT AREA

	ACT (40 items)	PLAN (25 items)	EXPLORE (30 items)
Natural Science	10	–	–
Social Science	10	8	10
Humanities	10	9	10
Prose Fiction	10	8	10

ITEM-TYPES: Knowing the seven item-types can help you to quickly identify what an item is asking.

1. *Main Idea*: Main Idea items ask about the central theme that unifies the passage(s).

   EXAMPLES: *Which of the following is the main point of the passage?*
   The primary purpose of the passage is to....

2. *Explicit Detail*: Explicit Detail items ask about details that are specifically mentioned in the passage. This type of item differs from a Main Idea item in that explicit details are points provided by the author in developing the main idea of the passage. Explicit Detail items provide "locator words" that identify the required information in the passage.

   EXAMPLES: *The author mentions which of the following?*
   According to the passage,...?

3. *Vocabulary*: Vocabulary items test the understanding of a word or phrase in context. The nature of the Vocabulary items indicates two points. First, the correct answer choice will make sense when it is substituted for the referenced word. Second, the correct answer choice may not be the most commonly used meaning of the word; in fact, if it were, then what would be the point of including the item on the test? Thus, the general strategy for this type of item is to favor the less commonly used meaning.

   EXAMPLES: *The word —— in line ## means....*
   In line ##, what is the best definition of —— ?

4. *Development*: Development items ask about the overall structure of the passage or about the logical role played by a specific part of the passage.

   EXAMPLES: *The author develops the passage primarily by....*
   The author mentions...in order to....

5. *Implied Idea*: Rather than ask about what is specifically stated in the passage, Implied Idea items ask about what can be logically inferred from what is stated in the passage. For example, the passage might explain that a certain organism (*X*) is found only in the presence of another organism (*Y*). An accompanying Implied Idea item might ask the following question: "If organism *Y* is not present, what can be inferred?" Since the passage implies that in the absence of *Y*, *X* cannot be present, the answer would be "*X* is not present." Since this type of item generally builds on a specific detail, "locator words" for identifying information in the passage are often provided in the item stem.

   EXAMPLES: *The passage implies that....*
   The author uses the phrase "..." to mean....

6. *Application*: Application items are similar to Implied Idea items, but they go one step further: Examinees must apply what they have learned from the passage to a new situation.

   EXAMPLES: *With which of the following statements would the author most likely agree?*
   The passage is most probably taken from which of the following sources?

7. *Voice*: Voice items ask about the author's attitude toward a specific detail or the overall tone of the passage.

   EXAMPLES: *The tone of the passage can best be described as....*
   The author regards...as....

GENERAL STRATEGY: This is not an exact science. Practice is essential to mastering the following techniques:

1. *Read the first two sentences of each passage in the test section.* There is usually an introductory paragraph for excerpted passages that identifies the author and provides a brief description of the selection. Read this introductory material to gauge interest, and read the first two sentences of each passage to determine its difficulty-level. Label each passage as either "Easy" or "Hard" based on your initial understanding of the material and your level of interest. Analyze the easier passages first.

2. *Preview the first and last sentences of each paragraph.* Begin with a preview of the first and last sentences of each paragraph.

3. *Preview the item stems for a given passage.* Code each item stem as one of the following three levels of reading comprehension:

   a. *Level 1—Appreciation of the General Theme*: The first level of reading, appreciation of the general theme, is the most basic. Main Idea items and items about the overall development of the selection test whether you understand the passage at the most general level. The first sentence of a paragraph—often the topic sentence—may provide a summary of the content of that paragraph. Also, the last sentence of a paragraph usually provides concluding material that may also be helpful in understanding the general theme of the passage.

      EXAMPLE: Main Idea items

   b. *Level 2—Understanding of Specific Points*: The second level of reading, understanding specific points, takes you deeper into the selection. Explicit Detail items, items about the meanings of words, and items about the logical role of details all test your ability to read carefully. Since this is an "open-book" test, you can always return to the selection. Therefore, if something is highly technical or difficult to understand, do not dwell on it for too long—come back later if necessary.

EXAMPLES: Explicit Detail items
Vocabulary items
Development items

c. *Level 3—Evaluation of the text*: The third level of reading, evaluation of the text, takes you even deeper into the selection. Implied Idea, Application, and Voice items ask not just for understanding, but require a judgment or an evaluation of what you have read. This is why these items are usually the most difficult.

EXAMPLES: Implied Idea items
Application items
Voice items

4. *Read the passage.* Ask what the author is attempting to describe, especially in the case of Evaluation items. Also, read the first sentence in each paragraph prior to reading the entire selection. This step is optional, depending on the ease of the selection, your personal preference, and the time available. Bracket difficult material, either mentally or with some sort of a mark, and then simply revisit it if necessary or if time permits. Instead of wasting time re-reading, attempt to understand the context in which the author introduces a particular concept.

5. *Circle the answers to the items in the test booklet, and transcribe the answers to all the items for a passage to the answer sheet after finishing each passage.* Circle the answers to the items in the test booklet. This approach helps increase accuracy and makes checking your work easier and more efficient. For each selection, transcribe the answers to the answer sheet together as a group. Only when the time limit approaches should you transcribe the answers individually.

ADDITIONAL STRATEGIES FROM IN-CLASS DISCUSSION: ______

Science Reasoning

TARGETED EDUCATIONAL SOLUTIONS.

Cambridge Course Concept Outline
SCIENCE REASONING

I. CORE LESSON (p. 603)

A. ITEM-TYPES
1. COMPREHENSION
2. ANALYSIS
3. APPLICATION

B. GENERAL STRATEGIES
1. PLAN YOUR ATTACK—EASIEST PASSAGES FIRST
2. DO NOT PREVIEW ITEM STEMS BEFORE READING PASSAGE
3. UNDERLINE KEY WORDS AND PHRASES
4. PAY ATTENTION TO WHAT IS THERE, NOT WHAT ISN'T THERE
5. PAY ATTENTION TO DIFFERENCES
6. WATCH FOR ASSUMPTIONS
7. LOOK FOR TRENDS
8. TRANSCRIBE ANSWERS IN GROUPS
9. ANSWER THE QUESTION THAT IS BEING ASKED
10. WORK OUT THE ANSWER FIRST
11. MAKE NOTES TO CLARIFY VIEWPOINTS

C. DATA REPRESENTATION REVIEW AND STRATEGIES
1. GRAPHS
   a. STRAIGHT LINES
   b. PARABOLIC CURVES
   c. GRAPH READING STRATEGIES (Items #1-3, p. 603)
2. TABLES
   a. UNDERSTANDING NATURE OF DATA (Items #4-5, p. 604)
   b. RECOGNIZING TRENDS (Items #6-8, p. 604)
   c. DRAWING CONCLUSIONS (Item #9, p. 604)
3. TYPICAL DATA REPRESENTATION ITEMS (Items #10-14, p. 606)
4. DATA REPRESENTATION STRATEGIES (Items #15-19, p. 608)

D. RESEARCH SUMMARY REVIEW AND STRATEGIES
1. UNDERSTANDING DESIGN OF EXPERIMENT
2. PREDICTING RESULTS
3. EVALUATING DATA
4. TYPICAL RESEARCH SUMMARY ITEMS (Items #20-30, p. 610)
5. RESEARCH SUMMARY STRATEGIES (Items #31-36, p. 612)

E. CONFLICTING VIEWPOINTS REVIEW AND STRATEGIES
1. PREDICTING RESULTS
2. "SPOTTING THE ASSUMPTIONS"
3. "PICKING THE BEST ARGUMENT"
4. TYPICAL CONFLICTING VIEWPOINTS ITEMS (Items #37-47, p. 613)
5. CONFLICTING VIEWPOINTS STRATEGIES (Items #48-54, p. 616)

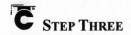

CORE LESSON

The passages and items in this section accompany the Core Lesson of the Science Reasoning Lesson. You will work through the items with your instructor in class. Answers are on page 937.

DIRECTIONS: Each passage is followed by several items. After reading a passage, choose the best answer to each item. You may refer to the passages as often as necessary. You are NOT permitted the use of a calculator.

Passage I

The kinetic energy of an object with mass *m* (measured in grams) after a fall from a height *h* (measured in centimeters) was recorded for different heights. A graph was made representing the kinetic energy versus height.

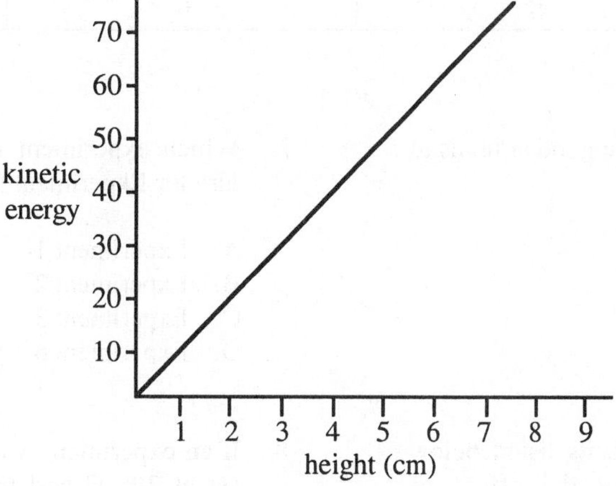

1. If the kinetic energy is given in units of g • cm^2/s^2, what units must the slope have?

   A. g • cm/s
   B. g • cm/s^2
   C. s • cm/g
   D. s^2/(g • cm)

2. It is discovered that if we redo the experiment with an object with twice the mass, the kinetic energy obtained for every height is doubled. The slope of the new set of experiments can be obtained by doing what to the old slope?

   F. Multiplying by 2
   G. Dividing by 2
   H. Squaring
   J. Taking the square root

3. What would be the kinetic energy in g • cm^2/s^2 of an object of mass *m* if it were dropped from a height of 4.5 cm?

   A. 4.5
   B. 9.0
   C. 45
   D. 90

Passage II

A scientist investigated the variables that affect the age at which a female of the animal species *taedi periculum* first gives birth. Some of the results of this study are summarized in the table below.

Experiment	*Temperature (° C)*	*Average food intake (grams)*	*Age when first gave birth (months)*
1	25	15	7
2	25	30	6
3	25	45	4
4	35	15	5
5	35	30	3
6	35	45	3

4. Which of the following would be good animals to use for the experiment?

   F. Adult females
   G. Newborn females
   H. Newborn males
   J. Adult males

5. Which of the pairs of experiments listed below would be useful for studying the effect of temperature on the age of first birth?

   A. 1 and 2
   B. 1 and 5
   C. 1 and 4
   D. 2 and 6

6. If all other variables are kept constant, which of the following will result in an increase in the age at which the animals give birth?

   F. Increase in temperature from 25° C to 35° C
   G. Increase in food from 15 grams to 45 grams
   H. Decrease in food from 30 grams to 15 grams
   J. Increase in temperature from 25° C to 30° C

7. Which experiment was the control for temperature for Experiment 5?

   A. Experiment 1
   B. Experiment 2
   C. Experiment 3
   D. Experiment 6

8. If an experiment was set up with the temperature set at 30° C and the food intake at 30 grams, which of the following would be a reasonable prediction of the age in months of the animals when they first gave birth?

   F. 7.5
   G. 6.0
   H. 4.5
   J. 2.5

9. Which of the following conclusions is consistent with the data presented in the table?

   A. The weight of the firstborn is proportional to the food intake.
   B. The weight of the firstborn is related to the temperature.
   C. The age of the mother at time of first offspring's birth increases with decreasing food intake.
   D. The age of the mother at time of first offspring's birth decreases with decreasing food intake.

NOTES AND STRATEGIES

Passage III

The chart below shows the average blood pressure and relative total surface area associated with the different types of human blood vessels.

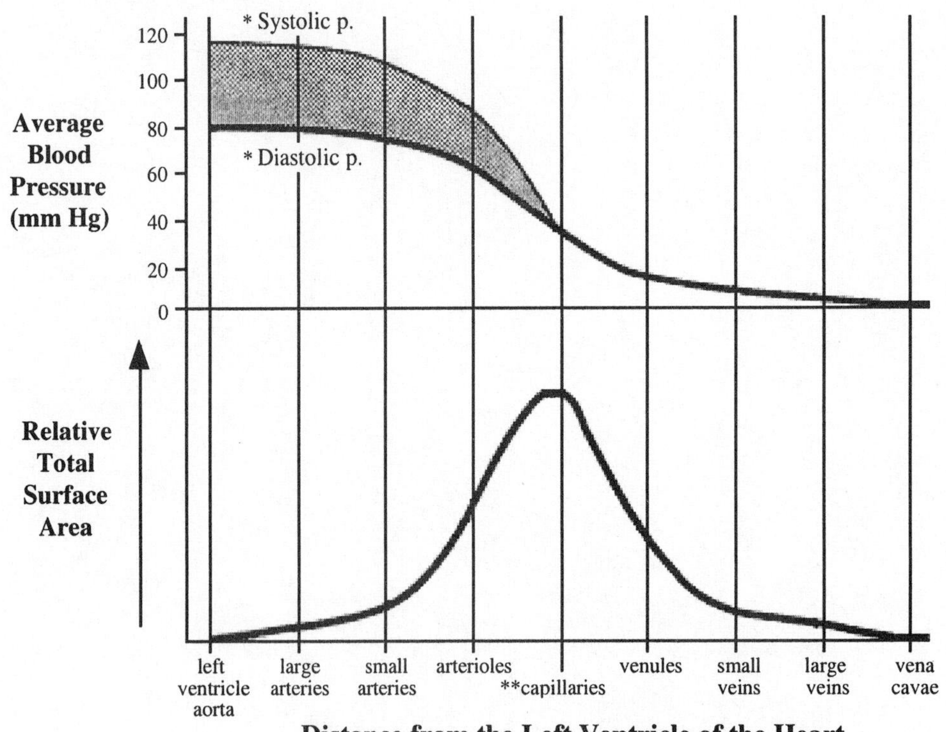

*Pulse is the difference between systolic and diastolic pressure.
**Blood velocity is lowest in the capillaries (averaging 3 cm/sec.).

10. According to the diagram, pulse pressure can be detected:

    F. in large arteries only.
    G. in large arteries as well as in large veins.
    H. in blood vessels between the aorta and the capillaries.
    J. primarily in the arterioles, capillaries, and venules.

11. Based on the information in the diagram, which of the following conclusions about average blood pressure is correct?

    A. The average blood pressure decreases continuously as it gets further away from the left ventricle.
    B. The average blood pressure remains approximately the same as it passes through the different blood vessels of the body.
    C. Starting at the aorta, average blood pressure first increases and then decreases.
    D. The average blood pressure is highest in the blood vessels with the greatest relative total surface area.

12. Which of the following correctly states the relationship between the relative total surface area of different blood vessels and their average blood pressure?

F. As relative total surface area decreases, average blood pressure increases.
G. As relative total surface area decreases, average blood pressure decreases.
H. As relative total surface area decreases, average blood pressure may increase or decrease.
J. Average blood pressure always changes in the opposite direction as the relative total surface area changes.

13. Which of the following conclusions can be drawn from the information provided in the diagram?

A. As the distance of blood vessels from the left ventricle increases, their relative total surface area decreases.
B. As the distance of blood vessels from the left ventricle increases, their pulse pressure increases.
C. Blood vessels with the greatest relative total surface area have the highest pulse pressure.
D. Blood vessels closest to and farthest away from the left ventricle have the smallest relative total surface area.

14. A physician examining a newly discovered tribe of people deep in the Amazon jungles found that the relative total surface area of their capillaries was greater than that previously reported for any other group of people. If the physician were to predict the average velocity of blood through the capillaries of these people, which of the following values would be most reasonable?

F. 2 cm/sec
G. 3 cm/sec
H. 4 cm/sec
J. 5 cm/sec

Passage IV

Ocean water contains "salt"—actually a mixture of ions, primarily sodium, chloride, potassium, calcium, magnesium, bicarbonate, and sulfate. The solid-line graph below indicates the percentage of these ions ("salinity") in a slab of ice that lies over seawater on a cold ocean surface. The arrow and dashed line indicate the salinity of the water beneath the ice.

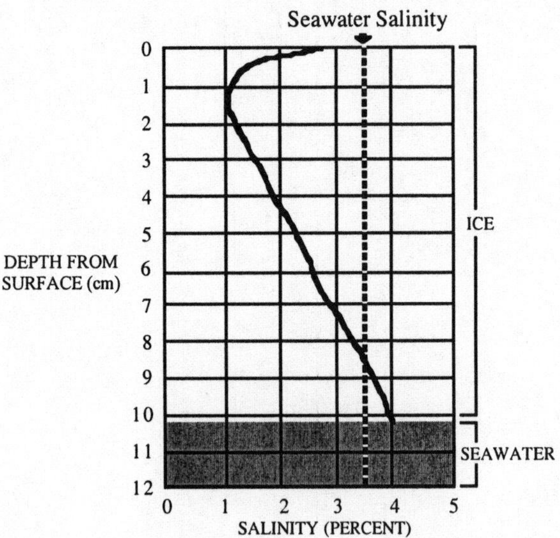

15. According to this figure, the salt content of the ice above the ocean water:

A. equals 0.
B. is constant at all depths.
C. generally decreases with greater depth.
D. generally increases with greater depth.

16. Compared to the ocean water below it, the salinity of the ice is:

F. generally lower.
G. about the same.
H. generally higher.
J. unable to be determined.

17. The salinity of the ice at the surface of the slab is equal to the salinity of:

A. the ice at a depth of approximately 1.5 cm.
B. the ice at a depth of approximately 7.0 cm.
C. the ice at a depth of approximately 9.0 cm.
D. the water beneath the ice.

18. An experimenter wants to take a sample of ice that is one half the salinity of the seawater below. At what depth should he sample?

F. Between 1 and 2 cm
G. Between 4 and 5 cm
H. Either between 0 and 1 cm or between 3 and 4 cm
J. Between 5 and 6 cm

19. The investigator takes a 1-gram sample of ice from a depth of 10 cm, and wishes to take a sample of ice from 1.3 cm depth that will contain the same weight of total salts. How large a sample is needed?

A. 0.25 grams
B. 1.0 grams
C. 4.0 grams
D. 10 grams

NOTES AND STRATEGIES

Passage V

To test the hypothesis that all antibiotics are equally effective in preventing bacterial growth, the following three experiments were carried out using clear plastic plates filled with nutrient agar (a mixture of ingredients that supports the growth of bacteria).

Experiment 1: Three plates (A, B, and C) of agar were set up, each with an equal amount of bacterial culture (Bacterium X) spread over the agar surface and with a paper disk placed in the center. Plate A's disk was soaked in Antibiotic I; Plate B's disk was soaked in Antibiotic II; Plate C's disk was soaked in plain water. After incubation overnight at 37° C (body temperature), Plates A and B had a clear area, 2" in diameter surrounding the paper disk, but beyond this 2" region, the plates were cloudy. Plate C was entirely cloudy, including the area adjacent to the paper disk. When bacteria reproduce successfully, colonies form on the agar, giving it a cloudy appearance.

Experiment 2: Identical procedures were followed except that Plates A, B, and C were incubated overnight at 22° C (room temperature). After incubation, Plate A had a clear area, 2" in diameter, surrounding the paper disk. Plates B and C were entirely cloudy.

Experiment 3: Identical procedures were followed except that the concentrations of Antibiotic I (Plate A) and Antibiotic II (Plate B) were made twice as strong. After incubation overnight at 22° C, Plates A and B both had clear, 2" areas around the paper disk, while Plate C remained entirely cloudy.

20. After incubation, a clear area around a previously soaked paper disk represents a region where:

    F. agar had washed away.
    G. decomposition had occurred due to high incubation temperatures.
    H. bacterial growth did not occur.
    J. bacteria grew best.

21. Which of the following results would indicate that the antibiotics being tested have nothing to do with the control of bacterial growth?

    A. A clear, 2" region was always observed around the disks soaked in water.
    B. All results remained the same at the two experimental temperatures and at the two antibiotic concentration levels.
    C. Plates A and B always remained clear.
    D. The disks soaked in water were not used in the experiments at all.

22. Which statement is supported by the results of Experiment 1 alone?

    F. Antibiotic I, Antibiotic II, and water are equally effective as inhibitors (preventers) of bacterial growth at 37° C.
    G. Dry paper disks can be effective in controlling bacterial growth at 37° C.
    H. The concentration of an antibiotic may influence its effectiveness in controlling bacterial growth at 37° C.
    J. Both Antibiotics I and II can inhibit bacterial growth at 37° C.

23. The results of both Experiment 2 and Experiment 3 lead to which of the following conclusions?

    A. Antibiotics I and II have similar effects on bacterial growth, regardless of concentrations.
    B. Antibiotic II and water have similar effects on bacterial growth, regardless of concentrations.
    C. The effectiveness of Antibiotic I at 22° C depends on its concentration.
    D. The effectiveness of Antibiotic II at 22° C depends on its concentration.

24. Which hypothesis best explains the observation that the agar plates never appear clear beyond a 2" area surrounding the soaked paper disks?

    F. The bacteria cannot grow well within 2" of any moist paper disks.
    G. The antibiotics cannot seep through the agar beyond a distance of 2".
    H. At the experimental incubation temperatures used, the two antibiotics interfere with each other's effectiveness.
    J. The paper disks can absorb nutrients out of the agar from the distance of 2".

25. If either Antibiotic I or II could be prescribed for internal use to prevent the spread of Bacterium X infections, which recommendation, based on the experimental results, is appropriate if the cost due to the amount of antibiotic used per dose is the most critical factor (the antibiotics are equal in cost for equal concentrations)?

    A. Either Antibiotic I or II can be taken at equal cost.
    B. Antibiotic I would be less expensive.
    C. Antibiotic II would be less expensive.
    D. Neither Antibiotic I nor II would be effective in preventing the spread of Bacterium X.

Passage VI

To investigate the hypothesis that the quality of the detail of a fossil depends on the size of the particles that make up the rock surrounding the fossil, three experiments were performed using a particular type of leaf with many fine veins.

Experiment 1: A leaf was placed on a flat bed made of paste from extra-fine plaster and then completely covered with more of the same paste. A glass cover with a 5-lb weight was placed on top of the paste for one hour, until the plaster set. The plaster was then baked for 30 minutes at 25° C. When the cast was opened, the imprint of the leaf showed all of the veins, including the finest ones.

Experiment 2: A leaf was placed on a flat bed made of paste from fine-grade plaster and then completely covered with more of the same paste. A glass cover with a 5-lb weight was placed on top of the plaster for one hour, until the plaster set. The plaster was then baked for 30 minutes at 25° C. When the cast was opened, all the main veins were visible, but only isolated traces of the finer veins were found.

Experiment 3: A leaf was placed on a flat bed made of paste from coarse-grain plaster and then completely covered with more of the same paste. A glass cover with a 5-lb weight was placed on top of the plaster for one hour, until the plaster set. The plaster was then baked for 30 minutes at 25° C. When the cast was opened, only the thickest veins were visible, and some of the leaf edge was difficult to discern.

26. Should the investigator have used a different type of leaf in each experiment?

F. Yes: different types of structure could be studied.
G. Yes: in real life, many different types of fossils are found.
H. No: the leaf served as a controlled variable.
J. No: the nature of the leaf is not important.

27. When a fossil is formed, the sediment that surrounds it is normally compressed by the tons of earth deposited over it. What part of the model simulates this compressing element?

A. The 5-lb weight
B. The glass
C. The upper layer of paste
D. The baking oven

28. A fourth experiment was set up the same way as the previous three, except the paste was made by mixing equal amounts of very coarse sand with the extra-fine plaster. The investigator is likely to discover:

F. no change from Experiment 1 because only the plaster counts.
G. no change because the same kind of leaf is used.
H. the imprint is better than Experiment 1 because the sand provides air pockets.
J. the imprint is worse than Experiment 1 because the average particle size is bigger.

29. Which of the following hypotheses is supported by the results of Experiment 1 alone?

A. The finer the sediment the greater the detail of the resulting fossil.
B. Hardened sediment can preserve the imprint of a specimen.
C. All fossils must have been baked at high temperatures.
D. Only organic material can leave imprints in sediment.

30. Which of the following changes in the experiments would have permitted a test of the hypothesis that the quality of a fossil imprint depends on the pressure applied?

F. Repeat the experiments except for using a 10-lb weight in Experiment 2, and a 20-lb weight in Experiment 3.
G. Choose one of the plasters, and run experiments using the same plaster in all trials while varying the weights.
H. Rerun all the experiments without the glass.
J. Vary the depth of the leaf in each new trial, because in nature increased pressure means the fossil is at a greater depth.

Passage VII

Erosion refers to processes that wear down rocks and soil, as well as processes that transport the worn-away materials to other locations. Although these processes usually cause effects gradually (over geologic time), laboratory models can be designed to investigate which environmental factors affect erosion rate.

Three experimental sandboxes were set up that were identical in size (10 ft. • 15 ft.), had identical types of soil and rocks, and were filled to equal depths (3 ft.). The sandboxes were kept for two weeks in large environmental chambers, each maintained at a constant temperature, with a continuous wind flow of 5 mph.

Sandbox 1: One half was kept bare (just soil and rocks), while the other half had a variety of grasses and weeds planted among the soil and rocks. After two weeks, the bare half had small channels (ruts) running along its length that averaged 1 inch in width. The planted half had few channels, and those that were found averaged less than 1 inch wide.

Sandbox 2: The conditions were identical to those of Sandbox 1, with the addition that both halves were subjected to light, 15-minute showers of water every twelve hours. After two weeks, the bare half had channels averaging 4 inches wide, while the planted half had fewer channels averaging 2 inches wide.

Sandbox 3: The conditions were identical to those of Sandbox 2, but the entire box was mechanically raised to rest at an angle of 15° to simulate a steep slope. After two weeks, the bare half had channels averaging 7 inches wide, while channels in the planted half were less common and averaged 4 inches in width.

31. Results from all three sandboxes indicate that:

    A. different types of soils and rocks are affected differently by environmental factors.
    B. under all tested conditions, plants reduce erosion.
    C. changing wind and temperature conditions can affect erosion patterns.
    D. water from short periods of rain has little or no effect on erosion patterns.

32. Which of the following claims does the design and results of the experiments NOT support?

    F. Light winds have no erosive effect.
    G. Slopes have more erosion than level surfaces.
    H. Water has major erosive effects.
    J. The effects of changing temperature remain unanswered.

33. Sudden cloudbursts are known to cause more erosion than longer periods of mild rains. How could the present experiments be changed to examine this idea?

    A. Raise the angle in Sandbox 3 to produce a steeper slope.
    B. Add the "rain conditions" from Sandbox 2 to the conditions in Sandbox 1.
    C. Include light, 15-minute showers every six hours instead of every twelve hours.
    D. Every twelve hours allow the same total volume of water to fall in a 5-minute span rather than in a 15-minute span.

34. Should the investigator have used different soil types in each sandbox experiment?

    F. Yes, because different soils may erode differently.
    G. Yes, because a different group of plants could have been used in each sandbox as well.
    H. No, because some soils can be washed completely away within the 2-week experiment.
    J. No, because the soil type was a controlled variable in all three experiments.

35. Sandbox 3 specifically demonstrates the role of which particular variable in the set of experiments?

    A. Rain
    B. Wind
    C. Gravity
    D. Temperature

36. If another sandbox were set up, which of the following conditions would probably cause wider and deeper channels in the soil of the new sandbox than those in Sandbox 3?

    I. Steeper angles for the sandbox
    II. A greater volume of water during the 15-minute showers every twelve hours
    III. Removal of plants from soil

    F. I only
    G. I and II only
    H. II and III only
    J. I, II, and III

Passage VIII

Theory 1: Early in the twentieth century, many chemists believed that the stability of the molecule methane, CH_4, could be explained by the "octet" rule, which states that stability occurs when the central atom, in this case carbon, is surrounded by eight "valence," or outer, electrons. Four of these originally came from the outer electrons of the carbon itself, and four came from the four surrounding hydrogen atoms (the hydrogen atom was considered an exception to the rule since it was known to favor a closed shell of two electrons as helium has.) According to the octet rule, neither CH_3 nor CH_5 should exist as stable compounds, and this prediction has been borne out by experiment.

Theory 2: While the octet rule predicted many compounds accurately, it also had shortcomings. Ten electrons, for example, surround the compound PC_{15}. The greatest shock to the octet rule concerned noble gases such as krypton and xenon, which have eight electrons surrounding them in their atomic states, and therefore should not form compounds since no more electrons would be needed to make an octet. The discovery in 1960 that xenon could form compounds such as XeF_4 forced consideration of a new theory, which held that (a) compounds formed when electrons were completely paired, either in bonds or in non-bonded pairs; (b) the total number of shared electrons around a central atom varied, and could be as high as twelve; (c) the shapes of compounds were such as to keep the pairs of electrons as far from each other as possible.

For example, since six electrons in the atomic state surround sulfur, in the compound SF_6 it acquired six additional shared electrons from the surrounding fluorines for a total of twelve electrons. The shape of the compound is "octahedral," as shown below, since this conformation minimizes the overlap of bonding pairs of electrons.

37. According to Theory 1, the compound CH_2Cl_2:

A. should have eight electrons surrounding the carbon atom.
B. cannot exist since the original carbon atom does not have eight electrons.
C. should have eight electrons surrounding each hydrogen atom.
D. requires more electrons for stability.

38. According to Theory 1, the compound XeF_4:

F. exists with an octet structure around the xenon.
G. should not exist since more than eight electrons surround the xenon.
H. will have similar chemical properties to CH_4.
J. exists with the xenon surrounded by twelve electrons.

39. The atom boron has three outer electrons, and in bonding to boron, a fluorine atom donates one electron. The BF_3 molecule is known to exist. Which of the following is true?

A. BF_3 obeys Theory 1.
B. The existence of BF_3 contradicts Theory 2.
C. According to Theory 2, the structure of BF_3 is a pyramid:

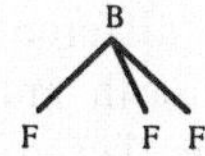

D. According to Theory 2, the structure of BF_3 is triangular and planar:

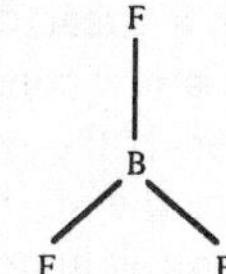

40. A scientist seeking to explain why Theory 2 has more predictive power than Theory 1 might argue that:

F. eight electrons shall represent a "closed shell."
G. while eight electrons represent a "closed shell" for some atoms, for others the closed shell may be six, ten, or twelve.
H. it is incorrect to assume that a given atom always has the same number of electrons around it.
J. CH_4 is not as important a compound as XeF_4.

41. Theory 2 could be threatened by evidence of:

A. the existence of SF_4.
B. the existence of XeF_5.
C. molecules with stable octets.
D. the existence of SF_6.

Passage IX

Scientist 1: The atmosphere of the Earth was at one time almost totally lacking in oxygen. One piece of evidence supporting this assertion is the very fact that life got started at all. The first chemical reactions that are necessary for the origin of life, the formation of amino acids, require ultraviolet light. Most of the ultraviolet light coming from the Sun is now absorbed by oxygen in the atmosphere. If there were as much oxygen in the atmosphere then as there is now, there would have been too little ultraviolet light available to enable life to begin. Also, the oldest bacteria, the ones that have the shortest DNA, are almost all anaerobes—they either do not need oxygen or die if exposed to oxygen. Most of the oxygen that exists now entered the atmosphere later from volcanic fumes.

Scientist 2: The prevailing opinion is that the atmosphere, though thicker now than it was in the past, is not essentially different in composition. The argument that the Earth must originally have been deficient in oxygen is flawed. First of all, the presence of iron and other oxides in the rocks from this time indicates that there was oxygen available. Secondly, the requirement for a great deal of ultraviolet light holds only if there is a low concentration of the starting materials in the water. If the water in some prehistoric lake began to freeze, the starting materials would be concentrated in a small volume of unfrozen water. The high concentration of the starting materials would offset the so-called deficiency of ultraviolet light, and life could begin.

42. According to the hypothesis of Scientist 1, which of the following would have been among the last living things to evolve?

    F. Anaerobes
    G. Plants
    H. Insects
    J. Viruses

43. According to the information presented by Scientist 1, if his theory of the origin of oxygen in the atmosphere is correct, the total amount of oxygen in the air over the next million years, on the average, should:

    A. decrease, then increase.
    B. increase, then decrease.
    C. increase.
    D. decrease.

44. Underlying the argument of Scientist 2 is the assumption that the oxygen in the oxides in the rocks was:

    F. always tied up in the rocks.
    G. involved in biological reactions.
    H. all gaseous during the early days of the atmosphere.
    J. proportional to the oxygen in the atmosphere at the time.

45. Underlying Scientist 1's suggestion that the evolutionary record supports the idea of an oxygen deficiency on the early Earth is the assumption that the oldest living things:

    A. have the shortest DNA.
    B. have the most fragmented DNA.
    C. have changed radically.
    D. must have died out.

46. Which of the following is the strongest argument Scientist 1 could use to counter Scientist 2's suggested mechanism for the origin of life?

    F. There was not enough ultraviolet light available.
    G. Chemical reactions occurred differently then.
    H. The temperature at the surface of the Earth at that time was always above 35° C because of geothermal heat release.
    J. Most lakes would not have covered large enough areas to guarantee that all the essential building blocks were present.

47. To refute Scientist 1's hypothesis, Scientist 2 might best show that:

    A. the amount of oxides in rocks has changed little over the past four billion years.
    B. there are ways of making the biologically important molecules without ultraviolet light.
    C. there are complex anaerobic bacteria.
    D. the atmospheric pressure has not changed over the Earth's history.

NOTES AND STRATEGIES

Passage X

In the 1940s, 1950s, and 1960s, the growing field of animal behavior maintained an ongoing debate about the origin of observed behavior in many different animal species. Two extreme viewpoints were at the center of this "Nature vs. Nurture" debate.

Viewpoint 1 (Nature): Many behaviors or instincts are literally programmed by one or more genes. Genes serve as "blueprints" that enable an individual to carry out a particular stereotyped behavior (Fixed Action Pattern) as soon as the appropriate stimulus (releaser) is observed. Other individuals do not have to be observed performing the behavior. The releasing stimulus need never have been seen before. At first view of the releaser and every time thereafter, the Fixed Action Pattern will be carried out to completion in the exact same way—even if the releaser is removed before the Fixed Action Pattern is finished! Examples include: a) the pecking of baby gulls at the red spot on their mother's bill (which causes the mother gull to regurgitate food), b) song birds producing their species song without ever having heard it before, and c) a male stickle-back fish defending its territory by attacking anything red because other breeding males always have red underbellies.

Viewpoint 2 (Nurture): Many behaviors are determined by experience and/or learning during an individual's lifetime. Genes provide the limits of the "blank slate" that each individual starts out as, but then various experiences will determine the actual behavior patterns within the individual genetic range of possibilities. In other words, behavior can be modified. Examples include: a) positive ("reward") reinforcement and punishment causing a behavior to increase and decrease (respectively), and b) songbirds producing their species song only after having heard it performed by other individuals of their species.

48. The red spot on a mother gull's bill is called a(n):

    F. Fixed Action Pattern.
    G. instinct.
    H. releaser.
    J. stereotyped response.

49. To refute the strict "genetic blueprint" ideas of Viewpoint 1, a scientist could show that:

    A. baby gulls peck at a stick with a red spot.
    B. baby gulls will peck at mother gulls' red spot as soon as they hatch out of their eggs.
    C. baby gulls pecking at the red spot happens exactly the same way each time.
    D. baby gulls' accuracy in pecking at mother gulls' red spot improves with practice.

50. A food-seeking blue jay captured a distinctively colored butterfly that had a bad-tasting substance in its tissues. After spitting out the butterfly, it never again tried to capture a similarly colored butterfly. This incident seems to support:

    F. Viewpoint 1.
    G. Viewpoint 2.
    H. both viewpoints.
    J. neither viewpoint (the incident is irrelevant).

51. Which of the following supports Viewpoint 1?

    A. A rat reaches the end of a maze by the same route, but finishes faster after each trip.
    B. Monkey A watches other monkeys wash sweet potatoes before they eat them; then, he washes sweet potatoes before he eats them.
    C. A male stickleback fish attacks a picture of a red mailbox held in front of his aquarium.
    D. A bird performs its species song after hearing the song only once.

52. If baby chickens peck at grains of food on the ground when hungry, but not as much after they have recently eaten, then this:

    F. supports Viewpoint 1.
    G. supports Viewpoint 2.
    H. does not refer to behavior.
    J. is irrelevant to the Nature vs. Nurture debate.

53. It is thought that some species of birds "learn" to fly. This belief is based on observations of young birds fluttering and flapping their wings at the nest until they reach the age when flight is possible. In Species X, nestlings were kept in harmless, but tight plastic tubes in which they could not carry out such "practice movements." They were released when they reached the age of flight. Viewpoint 1 predicts that the birds will fly:

    A. after fluttering their wings for a time.
    B. after watching other birds flutter their wings.
    C. after watching other birds flutter and fly.
    D. immediately.

54. A songbird can sing its species song after it hears other birds of its own species singing. Yet, if it hears the song from another species, the bird will not sing the "foreign" song. This suggests that:

    F. genetic "programming" and experience play a role in this species' ability to sing its song.
    G. this species' song is a Fixed Action Pattern.
    H. song development in this species is strictly a learned behavior with no genetic component.
    J. genes appear to be far more important than experience in this example.

CHALLENGE ITEMS

The passages and items in this section reflect both the format and difficulty range of passages and items on the ACT Science Reasoning Test, though difficult items are emphasized. Answers are on page 937.

DIRECTIONS: Each passage is followed by several items. After reading a passage, choose the best answer to each item. You may refer to the passages as often as necessary. You are NOT permitted the use of a calculator.

Passage I

The graph of the thin line below shows the hearing sensitivity of female moths. The auditory characteristics of certain sounds important to moth survival are also included.

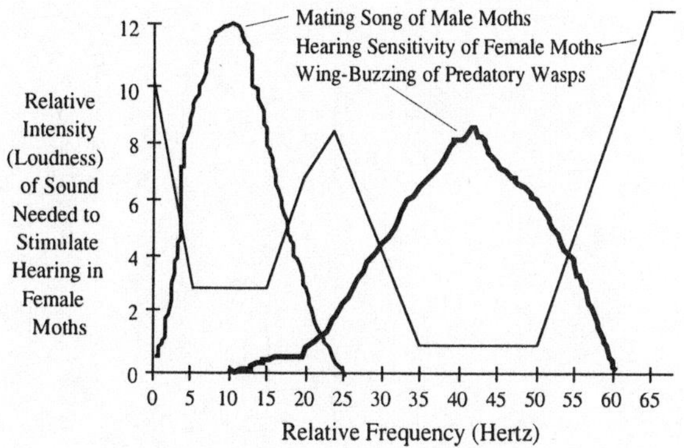

1. According to the graph, female moths are most sensitive to sounds between:

   A. 0-5 Hertz.
   B. 5-15 Hertz.
   C. 20-25 Hertz.
   D. 35-50 Hertz.

2. The nervous system of female moths may be set up to allow them to respond differently to sounds of different frequencies. Based on the information in the graph, which statement best describes the appropriate responses of female moths?

   F. Approach sounds between 5-15 Hertz, withdraw from sounds between 35-50 Hertz
   G. Approach sounds between 35-50 Hertz, withdraw from sounds between 5-15 Hertz
   H. Approach sounds between 5-15 Hertz and 35-50 Hertz
   J. Withdraw from sounds between 5-15 Hertz and 35-50 Hertz

3. Which of the following statements is supported by the information in the graph?

   A. The wing-buzzing sounds of wasps occur at a narrower range of frequencies than the range of the male moth mating song.
   B. The frequency range of the male moth mating song is narrower than the range of wasp wing-buzzing sounds.
   C. Female moths cannot hear sounds with relative intensities less than 3.
   D. Male moths are less sensitive to sounds than predatory wasps.

4. Which of the following statements accurately describes the relationship between the male moth mating song and female moth hearing sensitivity?

   F. The frequency range of the male song coincides with the frequency range at which females are maximally sensitive to any sound.
   G. Females need not be maximally sensitive at the frequency range of the male song because of the extremely high intensity of the song.
   H. Females cannot hear the male song if its intensity level is less than 10.
   J. The male song does not extend to an intensity level above 10.

5. If a new species of wasp were introduced into the moths' environment, which of the following wing-buzzing characteristics would make it the most successful predator of female moths?

   A. Extremely high intensity at relative frequencies between 35-50 Hertz
   B. An intensity level of 7-8 at relative frequencies between 20-25 Hertz
   C. Low intensity at relative frequencies above 60 Hertz
   D. Extremely high intensity at relative frequencies above 60 Hertz

6. A "new male" comes to town having a mating song with a frequency range between 20-25 Hertz and an intensity level of 4. What are his chances of finding a mate?

   F. Excellent
   G. Poor
   H. Good, if no wasps are present
   J. Cannot be determined from the given information

Passage II

A chemistry student wishes to study weight relationships between compounds before and after they take part in reactions. Two experiments were conducted to investigate two different reactions. The reactions are shown below, together with the amount (grams) of each substance before and after each reaction has proceeded. Equations are balanced to show the number of each type of atom before and after the reactions.

Experiment 1						
	NaBr +	$AgNO_3$	⇒	AgBr +	$NaNO_3$
Initial Wt.	103	170		0	0
Final Wt.	0	0		188	85

Experiment 2						
	Na_2CO_3 +	2HCl	⇒	2NaCl +	H_2O (g) +	CO_2
Initial Wt.	106	72		0	0	(?)
Final Wt.	0	0		117	18	(?)

(The student has measured the quantities he could, but was unable to weigh the CO_2 because it is a gas. Since it is a gas, he assumes it has negligible weight.)

7. In Experiment 1, the data indicate that after the reaction has proceeded:

   A. all of the Na originally present has been converted to Ag.
   B. there are fewer molecules of $NaNO_3$ than there were molecules of $AgNO_3$ at the outset.
   C. no NaBr remains.
   D. no AgBr remains.

8. Which of the following is (are) conserved in the reaction in Experiment 1?

   I. mass
   II. number of atoms
   III. amount of $AgNO_3$

   F. I only
   G. I and II only
   H. I and III only
   J. I, II, and III

9. In Experiment 2, the mass of the weighed products is:

   A. 0.
   B. less than the mass of reactants.
   C. equal to the mass of reactants.
   D. greater than the mass of reactants.

10. Experiment 2 differs from Experiment 1 in that:

    F. the number of atoms is not conserved.
    G. the reaction does not go to completion.
    H. there are no ionic compounds involved.
    J. gas is evolved.

11. Assuming the student is right in neglecting the weight of one of the products in Experiment 2, he can conclude from the data that:

    A. mass is consumed as the reaction proceeds.
    B. mass is produced as the reaction proceeds.
    C. energy is consumed as the reaction proceeds.
    D. mass is conserved as the reaction proceeds.

12. The student is advised of a means to weigh the CO_2 gas produced in the reaction, and finds this weight to be 43 grams. The student can now state that the two experiments:

    F. lead to similar conclusions: neither mass nor atoms are conserved.
    G. lead to similar conclusions: both mass and atoms are conserved.
    H. lead to different conclusions: the number of molecules is not the same for the reactants as for the products.
    J. lead to different conclusions: gases have negligible weight.

Passage III

Jean Baptiste Lamarck hypothesized the process of biological evolution before Charles Darwin was born. Some aspects of Lamarck's ideas and Darwin's ideas are presented below.

Lamarckism: Observations of the fossil record led Lamarck to believe that several lines of descent led to nature's broad diversity of organisms. Old fossils and recent fossils showed patterns leading to the characteristics of modern species. He believed that newer forms were more complex and more "perfectly" adapted to their environment. New adaptations could arise as the environment changed. Body organs that were used to cope with the environment became stronger and larger, while those not used deteriorated. For example, giraffes stretching their necks to reach higher leaves would develop longer necks. In addition, such changes in structure could then be passed on to offspring (these acquired characteristics could be inherited).

Darwinism: Based on the fossil and geologic record, Darwin also came to believe that various modern species were related through descent from common ancestors. He also noted that the great diversity of organisms that he observed during his travels were all very well adapted to their environments. The adaptations, however, did not come about through "coping" or usage. Instead, individuals from a population can each show slight genetic or "heritable" differences (variability) in a trait. If such differences, by chance alone, give the individual some reproductive advantage (he or she can successfully produce more offspring than other members of the population), then more individuals with that trait will make up the next generation. Through this "natural selection" of individuals with characteristics that give them a slight advantage in their particular environment, species appear to become very well suited to their natural world. However, "perfection" is not a useful term since the environment is constantly changing. The adaptations that are advantageous "today" may not be advantageous "tomorrow" under different conditions.

13. A major difference between Lamarck and Darwin relates to their views on:

A. the diversity of organisms in the natural world.
B. the significance of fossils.
C. the importance of adaptations to the environment.
D. the way adaptations come about.

14. Which viewpoint supports the idea that present-day species are descended from earlier forms?

F. Lamarckism
G. Darwinism
H. Both viewpoints
J. Neither viewpoint

15. Which statement might be used by a Darwinist to explain the extinction of a species?

A. The environment changed, and not enough individuals had traits or adaptations well suited to the new conditions.
B. The environment changed, and body parts could not be manipulated enough to adapt to new conditions.
C. As the environment changed, the individuals present were not "perfect" enough.
D. As the environment changed, there was no "natural selection."

16. Darwin might dispute the Lamarckian idea of inheriting acquired characteristics by pointing out that:

F. giraffes with short necks may do just as well as those with long necks.
G. giraffes that break a leg and walk around on three legs all their lives still do not produce three-legged offspring.
H. giraffes had shorter necks millions of years ago.
J. giraffes that break a leg would not be able to reach the highest leaves.

17. Many species of moles live underground, in the dark. These species often have small, almost dysfunctional eyes. Which of the following statement(s) would a Lamarckian thinker use to explain this phenomenon?

    I. Moles without eyesight are better adapted for survival underground and therefore produce more offspring.
    II. Disuse of eyes in the dark led to their deterioration in mole species.
    III. Eye deterioration can be transferred to a mole's genes, which are then passed on to the next generation.

    A. I only
    B. II only
    C. II and III only
    D. I, II, and III

18. Which factor is vital to Darwin's ideas, but not to those of Lamarck?

    F. The fossil record
    G. An examination of modern species
    H. The inheritance of adaptations
    J. Chance

19. A few individuals in a population have an adaptation that enables them to tolerate extremely cold temperatures. In their lifetimes, the environment never reaches such extremes. If all other traits are the same among individuals, what would a Darwinist predict about the number of offspring left in the next generation by these individuals, compared to the number left by other members of the population?

    A. These individuals will leave approximately the same number of offspring.
    B. These individuals will leave more offspring.
    C. These individuals will leave fewer offspring.
    D. These individuals will probably not leave any offspring.

Passage IV

Graph I shows the relationship between the relative rates of activity of enzymes A and B and temperature. Graph II shows the relationship between the relative rates of activity of enzymes A and B and pH.

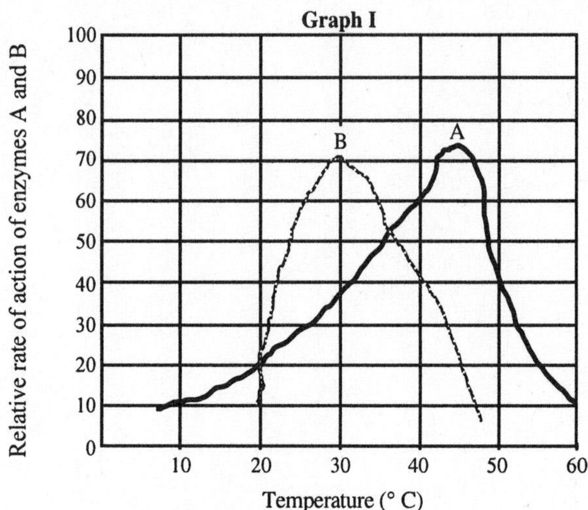

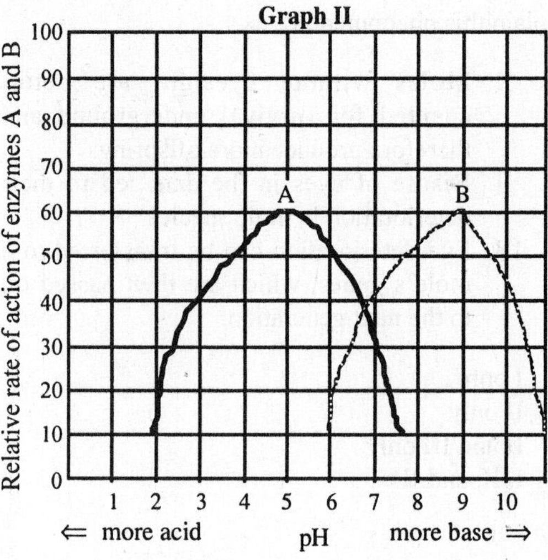

20. Under which conditions is enzyme A most effective?

F. 40° C and a pH of 5
G. 45° C and a pH of 5
H. 45° C and a pH of 9
J. 50° C and a pH of 9

21. The optimum environment for enzyme B is:

A. acidic.
B. basic.
C. either acidic or basic.
D. neutral.

22. At which one of the following temperatures do A and B exhibit the same relative rate of action?

F. 6.9° C
G. 10° C
H. 37° C
J. 47° C

23. At which pH do both A and B exhibit the same relative rate of action?

A. 6.9
B. 10
C. 37
D. 47

24. At what temperature does A have half the activity of B?

F. 20° C
G. 25° C
H. 42° C
J. 53° C

25. At what temperature does B have half the activity of A?

A. 20° C
B. 30° C
C. 42° C
D. 53° C

26. Over which of the following pH ranges will both A and B be active?

F. 1 to 3
G. 3 to 6
H. 6 to 8
J. 8 to 10

27. At what pH will both A and B be at their maximum activity?

A. 2
B. 5
C. 8.5
D. No such pH

Passage V

A series of three experiments was designed to investigate the interrelationships between various factors known to influence gases: temperature (Kelvin), pressure (atmospheres), volume (liters), and the number of moles of gas.

Experiment 1: A gas at 200 K and a volume of 0.30 liters was found to have a pressure of 0.40 atm. After the temperature was raised to 400 K while keeping the volume the same, the pressure was found to be 0.80 atm.

Experiment 2: A gas at 200 K had a pressure of 0.50 atm. when its volume was 1 liter. Its volume was then increased to 2 liters at constant temperature. The resulting pressure was 0.25 atm.

Experiment 3: Two moles of a gas were found to occupy 44.8 liters at 1 atm. pressure and 273 K. Four moles of the same gas are added to the system with temperature and pressure held constant, resulting in a new volume of 134.4 liters.

28. Which of the following hypotheses is (are) supported by the results of Experiment 1?

    I. The pressure of the gas is proportional to its volume at constant temperature.
    II. The volume of the gas is proportional to its temperature at constant pressure.
    III. The pressure of a gas is proportional to its temperature at constant volume.

    F. I only
    G. I and II only
    H. III only
    J. II and III only

29. The results of Experiment 2 support the hypothesis that if the temperature of a gas is held constant, then the pressure:

    A. increases as the volume increases.
    B. decreases as the volume increases.
    C. does not depend strongly on the volume.
    D. Cannot be determined from the given information

30. The result of Experiment 3 supports the hypothesis that if both the pressure and the temperature of a gas are held constant, then the volume:

    F. varies inversely with the number of moles of gas.
    G. varies directly with the number of moles of gas.
    H. is raised to a maximum value of 134.4 liters when additional gas is added.
    J. does not depend on the number of moles of gas.

31. An experimenter put 0.08 moles of gas into a 4-liter flask at 273 K and 0.448 atm. pressure. She allowed 0.02 moles of the gas to escape, and she put the remaining gas into a smaller flask that caused the pressure to remain at 0.448 atm. pressure, while the temperature was kept constant as well. According to Experiment 3, the volume of the smaller flask must be:

    A. 0.06 liter.
    B. 0.448 liters.
    C. 3 liters.
    D. Cannot be determined from the given information

32. Six moles of a gas originally at 0.1 atm. pressure and 273 K occupy a volume of 13.4 liters. The temperature is then changed to 300 K and the volume changed to 10.0 liters. To predict the final pressure on the six moles of gas, a student should use the results of:

    I. Experiment 1.
    II. Experiment 2.
    III. Experiment 3.

    F. I only
    G. II only
    H. I and II only
    J. I and III only

33. The final pressure of the gas described in the previous question will be:

    A. less than 0.1 atm. pressure.
    B. equal to 0.1 atm. pressure.
    C. greater than 0.1 atm pressure.
    D. Cannot be determined from the given information

Passage VI

How did life originate on the planet Earth? Two opposing views are presented.

Scientist 1: The idea that Earth could have given rise to life independently is mistaken. Life on this planet must have come from elsewhere for several reasons. First of all, complex life appears very suddenly in the geological record. Secondly, all life on Earth has a very similar biochemistry. If life originated on Earth, one would expect regional variations in biochemistry, similar to the variations in species spread over large areas. Finally, the time when life first appeared in the geological record was also a time when large numbers of meteorites struck the Earth. The meteorites must have caused life to appear on the Earth. The simplest hypothesis is that the meteorites brought life with them.

Scientist 2: Life need not have been imported from outer space. The chemicals required for life existed on the surface of the Earth at the time life first appeared. The fact that all life has a similar biochemistry can be explained by considering that any group of chemicals that won the race to life would probably have used the "almost-living" as food. Since we can offer explanations for what happened without relying on a meteorite of unknown composition that might have fallen to Earth, we should stick to hypotheses that have fewer unknowns.

34. Which of the following is an assumption of Scientist 1?

F. Complex life forms can develop quickly.
G. Meteorites burn up as soon as they hit the Earth's atmosphere.
H. There is a cause-and-effect relationship between meteors falling and the origin of life.
J. The changes on the Earth's surface due to the presence of life attracted meteor showers.

35. Which of the following, if true, strengthens Scientist 2's argument the most?

A. Only 5% more meteors than normal fell on the Earth during the time life began.
B. Only 5% of the meteorites studied contained organic molecules.
C. A simulation of early Earth chemistry showed the spontaneous formation of complex biomolecules.
D. Meteorites containing amoebas have been found.

36. Which of the following, if true, strengthens Scientist 1's argument the most?

F. Only 5% more meteors than normal fell on the Earth during the time life began.
G. Only 5% of the meteorites studied contained organic molecules.
H. A simulation of early Earth chemistry showed the spontaneous formation of complex biomolecules.
J. Meteorites containing amoebas have been found.

37. With which explanation of the similar biochemistry of all life on Earth would Scientist 1 most likely agree?

A. A single chemical pathway to life exists.
B. Life arose from a single source.
C. Life is not varied.
D. Meteors are simple.

38. With which explanation of the similar biochemistry of all life on Earth would Scientist 2 most likely agree?

F. A single chemical pathway to life exists.
G. Life arose from a single source.
H. Life is not varied.
J. Meteors are simple.

39. Which scientist would be likely to disagree with the idea that life on different planets could have different biochemistries?

A. Scientist 1
B. Scientist 2
C. Both scientists
D. Neither scientist

40. Which of the following questions would be the most difficult for Scientist 1 to defend his theory against?

F. Why was there more meteorite activity earlier in Earth's history?
G. Why have other meteors not brought other life based on a different biochemistry?
H. Why did complex life emerge suddenly?
J. Why should meteor activity have any connection to the origin of life?

41. Could Scientist 2 believe that life exists on other planets without affecting his hypothesis?

A. Yes, as long as he believes that life elsewhere has a different biochemistry.
B. Yes, because wherever the chemicals required for life exist, life can begin.
C. No, because then he has to admit that meteorites brought life from these planets.
D. No, because then he has to admit that meteorites that came from pieces of similar planets brought life to the Earth.

Passage VII

A seismographic station can detect how far away an earthquake occurred, but it cannot determine the direction of the earthquake. Any given station can therefore report that the epicenter of an Earthquake occurred somewhere on the circumference of a circle. The map below shows the data recorded for an earthquake at three different seismic stations (A, B, and C). Intersections of the three seismic stations' curves are marked by Roman numerals.

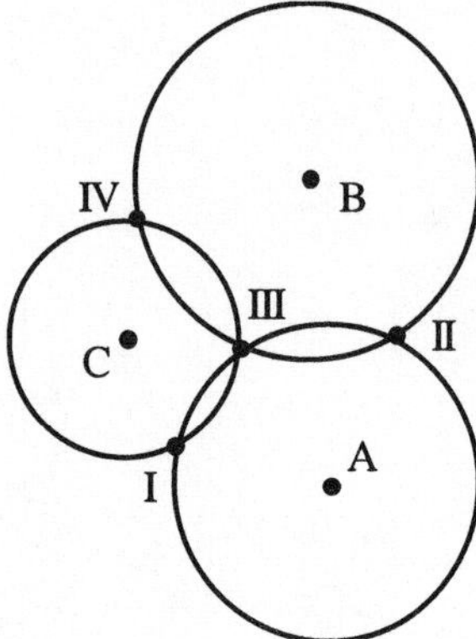

42. Which station was closest to the earthquake epicenter?

F. A
G. B
H. C
J. Cannot be determined from the given information

43. Given the information from stations A and B only, which site(s) is (are) possible for the earthquake epicenter?

A. I only
B. III only
C. II and III only
D. I and III only

44. Given the information from stations A and C only, which site(s) is (are) possible for the earthquake epicenter?

F. I only
G. III only
H. II and III only
J. I and III only

45. Given the information from all three stations, which site(s) is (are) possible for the epicenter?

A. I only
B. III only
C. I and III only
D. II and III only

46. If a fourth seismic station gave a report, at what point must its curve meet A's curve?

F. I
G. II
H. III
J. IV

47. If a fourth seismic station gave a report, at what point must its curve meet C's curve?

A. I
B. II
C. III
D. IV

48. What is the minimum number of points where two circumferences from two seismic stations, both measuring the same Earthquake, can meet?

F. 1
G. 2
H. 3
J. Infinite

Passage VIII

To investigate the factors affecting the rate at which starch is broken down to sugar by the digestive enzyme salivary amylase, two experiments were performed. In both experiments, starch (in the form of a cracker) was mixed in a beaker with the enzyme, and the samples were removed every three minutes. Dipping special sugar indicators in the sample revealed the presence of starch in a sample (indicating that the cracker had not yet been completely digested).

Experiment 1: To test the effects of different pH levels on enzyme activity rate, one cracker and a standard amount of enzyme were placed in three beakers, each containing buffers of different pH. This procedure was repeated using standard amounts of water in place of the enzyme. All tests were carried out at optimal temperature. Starch and sugar levels (starch/sugar) from selected samples are shown in Table 1.

Table 1

CONTENTS OF BEAKERS	APPROXIMATE pH LEVELS	LEVELS OF STARCH/SUGAR			
		After 3 min.	*After 9 min.*	*After 15 min.*	*After 60 min.*
cracker + enzyme + buffer	5	high/none	high/none	high/low	moderate/moderate
	7	moderate/moderate	low/high	none/high	none/high
	9	high/none	high/none	high/low	moderate/moderate
cracker + water + buffer	5	high/none	high/none	high/none	high/none
	7	high/none	high/none	high/none	high/none
	9	high/none	high/none	high/none	high/none

Experiment 2: To test the effects of temperature on enzyme activity rate, one cracker and a standard amount of enzyme were placed in 3 beakers, each kept at different temperatures. This was also repeated using standard amounts of water in place of the enzyme. All tests were carried out at optimal pH. Starch and sugar levels (starch/sugar) from selected samples are shown in Table 2.

Table 2

CONTENTS OF BEAKERS	TEMPERATURES	LEVELS OF STARCH/SUGAR			
		After 3 min.	*After 9 min.*	*After 15 min.*	*After 60 min.*
cracker + enzyme	25° C	high/none	high/none	high/low	moderate/moderate
	37° C	moderate/moderate	low/high	none/high	none/high
	45° C	high/none	high/none	high/low	moderate/moderate
cracker + water	25° C	high/none	high/none	high/none	high/none
	37° C	high/none	high/none	high/none	high/none
	45° C	high/none	high/none	high/none	high/none

49. Under what conditions does salivary amylase appear to work best?

A. Any pH level greater than 5 and any temperature greater than 25° C
B. Any pH level greater than 5 and any temperature less than 45° C
C. pH level of 9 and temperature equals 37° C
D. pH level of 7 and temperature equals 37° C

50. The ingredient used as a control for both experiments is the:

F. cracker.
G. water.
H. enzyme.
J. starch/sugar level.

51. Which of the following hypotheses is supported by the results of Experiment 1?

A. At the appropriate pH, water can break down starch, but at a slower rate than salivary amylase can.
B. At any one-time interval, no differences in the effects of the three buffers on salivary amylase activity should be detectable.
C. Salivary amylase can show activity at each of the three pH levels tested.
D. The duration of time in which starch and enzyme remain in the beakers should have no effect on the amount of sugar produced.

52. Which of the following experimental designs would test the hypothesis that enzyme concentration can affect the rate of starch digestion?

F. Using the same pH, temperature, and enzyme levels in all beakers, test additional samples at 90 minutes, 120 minutes, and 240 minutes.
G. Using different pH, temperature, and enzyme levels in all beakers, test additional samples at 90 minutes, 120 minutes, and 240 minutes.
H. Using the same pH and temperatures in all beakers, test additional samples with the enzyme at $\frac{1}{2}$ • strength, 2 • strength, and 4 • strength.
J. Using the same pH, temperature, and enzyme levels in all beakers, test additional samples after stirring for 3 minutes, 9 minutes, 15 minutes, and 60 minutes.

53. In Experiment 2, an additional beaker was tested at 70° C (cracker + enzyme). After 60 minutes, the sample showed high levels of starch and no sugar. Which of the following best explains this result?

A. All the starch was destroyed at this high temperature.
B. The enzyme does not work at all at this high temperature.
C. Starch cannot be detected at this high temperature.
D. Iodine and sugar indicators cannot function properly at this high temperature.

54. On the basis of the results of Experiment 1, what would probably occur if Experiment 2 were carried out at a pH level of 5?

F. Digestion of starch to sugar would slowly begin in the beakers containing crackers plus water.
G. Overall, digestion of starch to sugar would probably take place less efficiently.
H. Overall, digestion of starch to sugar would probably take place more efficiently.
J. Results would not change.

Passage IX

What will the end of the universe be like? Two opposing views are presented.

Scientist 1: The universe will die out with a whimper because the energy of the big bang that created the universe will spread itself out over larger and larger regions of space. Since there is only so much energy in the universe, every cubic foot must hold, on the average, less energy as time goes on. In the end everything will get so cold that all motion will stop. That will be the true end of time.

Scientist 2: The idea that the universe will spread itself too thin and freeze is seriously flawed. Such theories do not take into account the gravitational attractions of the bits of matter in the universe for each other. Gravity can act as a cosmic glue to keep the universe from dissolving into nothingness.

55. Which of the following is a major assumption of Scientist 1?

    A. All matter consists of atoms.
    B. There is a limited amount of energy in the universe.
    C. Gravity does not exist in interstellar space.
    D. The universe is contracting.

56. Which of the following facts, if true, does not help Scientist 2's hypothesis?

    F. It is shown that the galaxies are moving away from each other with a constant speed.
    G. It is shown that the galaxies are moving towards each other with a constant speed.
    H. It is shown that the galaxies are moving towards each other with a constant acceleration.
    J. It is shown that the galaxies are not moving at all relative to each other.

57. It has been calculated that if the universe has a mass greater than or equal to m, then the universe will eventually collapse on itself. Scientist 1 would likely say that the mass of the universe:

    A. is equal to m.
    B. is less than or equal to m.
    C. is greater than m.
    D. is less than m.

58. If Scientist 2 claims that the universe is contracting, what would he expect the average temperature of the universe to be in ten billion years?

    F. Higher than now
    G. Lower than now
    H. Same as now
    J. No comparison is possible

59. What must be true about the energy content of the universe if Scientist 1 is correct?

    A. It is increasing.
    B. It is decreasing.
    C. It is a constant.
    D. It increased at the moment of the big bang, and decreased afterwards.

60. What would happen if the forces moving the galaxies farther out were exactly balanced by the forces pulling them together?

    F. The galaxies would stop moving.
    G. The galaxies would move in a straight line with constant speed.
    H. The galaxies would move in a straight line with constant acceleration.
    J. The galaxies would move back and forth in a straight line.

Passage X

A scientist investigated the number of fossils per cubic foot through several feet in a quarry. The results are presented below.

Layer	Fish	Shells	Plants	Land Reptile
1 (TOP)	0	0	3	1
2	0	1	8	2
3	1	10	4	0
4	5	18	1	0
5	7	20	0	0

61. When was the site most likely above water?

A. During the formation of Layers 1 and 2
B. During the formation of Layers 2 and 3
C. During the formation of Layers 1 and 4
D. During the formation of Layer 3

62. Was the site most recently above or below water?

F. Above
G. Below
H. Borderline
J. Cannot be determined from the given information

63. What assumption is made to relate the fossil record to the environment?

A. No assumption
B. That fossils do not affect the environment
C. That the fossils are mostly from plants and animals that lived in the region
D. That only animal fossils are important

64. No trilobite fossils were found. This proves:

F. that no trilobites were in the region.
G. that the layers were formed before trilobites existed.
H. that the layers were formed after the trilobites died out.
J. nothing about the presence of the trilobite in the region.

65. A nautilus shell was found in Layer 3. This proves that:

A. Layer 3 formed while the nautilus still existed.
B. Layer 3 is newer than Layer 2.
C. Layer 3 is older than Layer 2.
D. the nautilus once lived on land.

66. Where will the newest layer form?

F. Under Layer 4
G. Over Layer 1
H. Across all the layers
J. Layers no longer form

Passage XI

Using electrical circuits, three experiments were performed to investigate the relationship between voltage (olts), resistance (ohms) (total resistance equals sum of individual resistances), and current (amperes.) Each experiment was set up with the following circuit design:

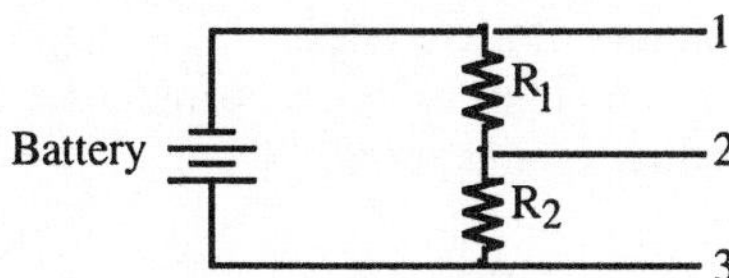

Experiment 1: Using a 6-volt battery (far left), and two 1,000-ohm resistors (R_1 and R_2), the measured voltages between points 1 and 2 and between points 2 and 3 were 3 volts each.

Experiment 2: When the battery voltage was increased to 12 volts, and the resistors were kept the same (1,000 ohms each), the measured voltages between points 1 and 2 and between points 2 and 3 were 6 volts each.

Experiment 3: Using the original 6-volt battery, R_1 was replaced with a 2,000-ohm resistor. The voltages measured between points 1 and 2 and between points 2 and 3 were 4 volts and 2 volts, respectively.

67. Judging from the results in Experiment 1 and Experiment 2, if the battery voltage were changed to 1.5 volts, what voltage would be expected between point 1 and point 2?

    A. 0.75 volts
    B. 1.5 volts
    C. 3.0 volts
    D. 6.0 volts

68. The experimenter studies the measurement made in the previous question, as well as those made earlier in Experiments 1, 2, and 3, and hypothesizes that:

    F. voltage measured across a resistor is inversely proportional to the value of that resistor.
    G. voltage measured across a resistor is directly proportional to the value of that resistor.
    H. voltage measured across a resistor is not related to the value of that resistor.
    J. voltage measured across a resistor equals the battery voltage.

69. When the experimenter recorded the current in the circuit of Experiment 1, it measured 0.003 amperes. In Experiment 3, however, the current measured 0.002 amperes. These results show that current and total resistances are:

    A. directly proportional.
    B. inversely proportional.
    C. equal.
    D. unrelated.

70. Which of the following formulas for the current in the circuit best summarizes the above results? (The battery voltage is given by V_b and the total resistance is given by R.)

    F. V_bR
    G. $\frac{R}{V_b}$
    H. $\frac{V_b}{R}$
    J. $V_b + R$

71. A new circuit is set up, similar in design to those in the experiments. The battery voltage and the size of the resistors are unknown, but the current measures 0.001 amperes. If the battery voltage is doubled and one of the two resistors is replaced with one having a smaller value, which answer most accurately describes the new current?

    A. It will be smaller than 0.001.
    B. It will be unchanged.
    C. It will be greater than 0.001.
    D. Cannot be determined from the given information

72. Which of the following single changes to Experiment 2 would produce a current of 0.004 amperes?

    F. Decrease the voltage to 8 volts.
    G. Increase the resistance to 3,000 ohms.
    H. Neither change will create a current of 0.004 amperes.
    J. Either change will create a current of 0.004 amperes.

Passage XII

How old is the Earth? Two opposing views are presented.

Scientist 1: The Earth is approximately five billion years old. We know this to be true because of radioactive dating. Some chemical elements are unstable and will fall apart into smaller pieces over time. This disintegration occurs over a period of time that is very regular for the particular element. In general, we talk about the half-life of the element, which is the time necessary for one-half of the material to disintegrate. This time is constant whether we have an ounce or a ton of the material. So, by measuring the relative amounts of the material left and the disintegration products, we can form an accurate idea of how old the Earth is by determining how many half-lives have occurred.

Scientist 2: The argument that supports the hypothesis that the Earth is only five billion years old is seriously flawed. What the argument fails to take into account is that the Earth is the constant recipient of a shower of cosmic debris in the form of meteorites. These meteorites replenish the stock of radioactive material on the surface of the Earth, making it seem as though the Earth has gone through fewer half-lives than it really has. Therefore, all estimates of the age of the Earth based on radioactive dating are too low.

73. Which of the following is a major assumption of Scientist 1?

    A. The Earth has life that recycles carbon-14.
    B. The Earth is five billion years old.
    C. The radioactive material was formed at the same time as the Earth.
    D. There is no longer any radioactivity on the Earth.

74. Which of the following is a major assumption of Scientist 2?

    F. The meteorites that land on the Earth are radioactive.
    G. Few meteorites have landed on the Earth.
    H. The Earth is more than five billion years old.
    J. The Earth is highly radioactive.

75. Which of the following, if true, would best refute Scientist 2's argument?

    A. Recent meteorites have been found to be radioactive.
    B. The Earth has a greater amount of radioactive material on the surface than in the mantle.
    C. The Earth's orbit intersects the orbits of a number of meteorites.
    D. Few meteorites have been found to contain radioactive material.

76. Which of the following would be most likely if Scientist 2's hypothesis were correct?

    F. The amount of radioactive material and its disintegration products on the Earth has decreased over time.
    G. The amount of radioactive material and its disintegration products has increased over time.
    H. The amount of radioactive material and its disintegration products has stayed essentially the same over time.
    J. The Earth will reach a critical mass and explode.

77. Which of the following would be most likely if Scientist 1's hypothesis were correct?

    A. The amount of radioactive material and its disintegration products has decreased over time.
    B. The amount of radioactive material and its disintegration products has increased over time.
    C. The amount of radioactive material and its disintegration products has stayed essentially the same over time.
    D. The Earth will reach a critical mass and explode.

78. Which of the following conditions, if true, would prevent an estimation of the Earth's age by Scientist 1's method?

    F. No radioactive disintegration has occurred.
    G. Only some of the radioactive material has disintegrated.
    H. Eighty percent of the radioactive material has disintegrated.
    J. All of the radioactive material has disintegrated.

NOTES AND STRATEGIES

TIMED-PRACTICE QUIZZES

This section contains three Science Reasoning quizzes. You will work through the items with your instructor in class. Answers are on page 937.

DIRECTIONS: Each passage is followed by several items. After reading a passage, choose the best answer to each item. You may refer to the passages as often as necessary. You are NOT permitted the use of a calculator.

A. QUIZ I (10 items; 9 minutes)

Passage I

The ecological pyramid below shows the relative biomass[†] of organisms at each trophic feeding level of a marine food chain.

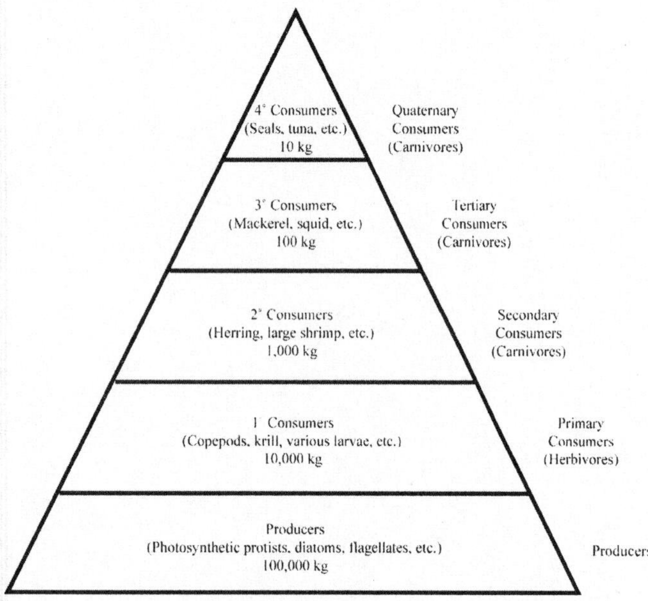

[†]*Biomass:* Total dry weight of organisms (useable chemical energy stored in organic matter) at each trophic level at any given time.

1. According to the diagram, the trophic level with the largest relative biomass is the:

   A. 4° consumers.
   B. 3° and 2° consumers.
   C. 1° consumers.
   D. producers.

2. From the information in the diagram, one can conclude that at any given time:

   F. 10 seals may be found for every mackerel.
   G. the relative dry weight of all carnivores combined is far greater than that of the herbivores alone.
   H. only 1% of all producers live long enough to be eaten by a mackerel.
   J. the relative dry weight of every consumer trophic level is usually less than that of the trophic level on which they feed.

3. Organisms from which trophic level are most likely to be found near the water surface where light can penetrate?

   A. 4° consumers
   B. 2° consumers
   C. 3° consumers
   D. producers

4. If there were an additional trophic level of carnivores (5° consumers), its relative biomass at any given time would be approximately:

   F. 11 kg.
   G. 1,000,000 kg.
   H. 1 kg.
   J. 111 kg.

5. The best explanation for biomass being measured as dry weight is:

   A. if water weight were included, efficiency ratios at each trophic level would be unpredictable.
   B. body fluids contribute little to the mass of marine organisms.
   C. water molecules contain little or no usable chemical energy.
   D. each trophic level contains a different amount of water.

Passage II

The table below shows various characteristics of different layers of the atmosphere.

Approximate Altitude (km)	*Layers of the Atmosphere*	*Approximate Mean Temperature (° C)*	*Clouds*
60,000			
6,000			
	THERMOSPHERE		
600		1200	
80		–90	
	MESOSPHERE		
50		–3	
	STRATOSPHERE		Cirrus
12		–50	
			Cirrostratus
5	TROPOSPHERE		Altostratus
0		18	Nimbostratus

6. Which statement accurately describes the relationship between the approximate altitude and the approximate mean temperature of the layers of the atmosphere?

   F. As altitude increases, temperature increases.
   G. As altitude increases, temperature decreases.
   H. As altitude increases, temperature first decreases then continuously increases.
   J. As altitude increases, temperature first decreases, then increases, then decreases, and then increases.

7. Based on the information in the table, the atmospheric layer with the narrowest range of altitude is the:

   A. thermosphere.
   B. troposphere.
   C. mesosphere.
   D. stratosphere.

8. The type of cloud(s) most likely to consist of ice crystals is (are):

   F. nimbostratus only.
   G. nimbostratus and altostratus.
   H. cirrus and cirrostratus.
   J. cirrostratus only.

9. The absorption of solar heat energy increases as the gases of the atmosphere become rarefied. The layer of the atmosphere that appears most rarefied is the:

   A. thermosphere.
   B. mesosphere.
   C. stratosphere.
   D. troposphere.

10. According to the table, which atmospheric layer shows a decrease in temperature of approximately 3° C for every 1-kilometer increase in altitude?

    F. thermosphere
    G. mesosphere
    H. stratosphere
    J. troposphere

B. QUIZ II (10 items; 9 minutes)

Passage I

The chart below shows in outline form a common means of analyzing a sample solution for various cations (positive ions). Ions above the horizontal arrows are those that are suspected to be present in the sample solution; the substances in the boxes are the reagents added as tests (0.3 M H^+ is acidic, NH_4OH is alkaline); the products shown next to the arrows pointing downward are solid precipitates resulting from the tests. Tests for specific ions need not always start from the beginning of the sequence.

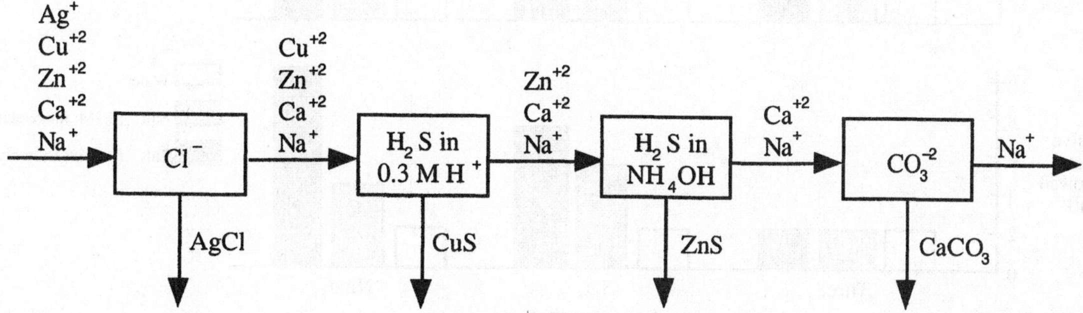

1. According to the chart, which precipitate indicates if silver (Ag) is present in the sample?

   A. AgCl
   B. Ag
   C. CuS
   D. ZnS

2. If a solution containing silver (Ag) nitrate and cupric (Cu) nitrate is tested according to this scheme, an experimenter will:

   F. first observe AgCl on treatment with Cl^-, and next observe CuS on treatment with H_2S.
   G. first observe CuS on treatment with Cl^-, and next observe AgCl on treatment with H_2S.
   H. first observe $CaCO_3$ on treatment with CO_3^{-2}, and next observe AgCl on treatment with Cl^-.
   J. observe no reactions, since the scheme does not test for nitrate.

3. What is the minimum number of tests necessary to confirm the composition of an unknown solution that contains no other positive ions except Cu^{+2} or Zn^{+2}, but not both?

   A. 1
   B. 2
   C. 3
   D. 4

4. Which statement is most correct concerning the separation of Cu^{+2} from Zn^{+2} in the same solution?

   F. Completely different test reagents are used in each of the two steps.
   G. The same test reagents are used in each of the two steps.
   H. The same test reagents are used, but the first step must be in an alkaline environment while the second step must be in an acidic environment.
   J. The same test reagents are used, but the first step must be in an acidic environment while the second step must be in an alkaline environment.

5. A clear solution is found, by a method not discussed here, to contain chloride ion (Cl^-). From the information given here, what ion could not be present in the solution?

   A. Carbonate (CO^{-2})
   B. Cupric (Cu^{+2})
   C. Silver (Ag^+)
   D. Zinc (Zn^{+2})

Passage II

The chart below shows the flavor preferences of white-tailed deer when offered various fluids to drink at different ages.

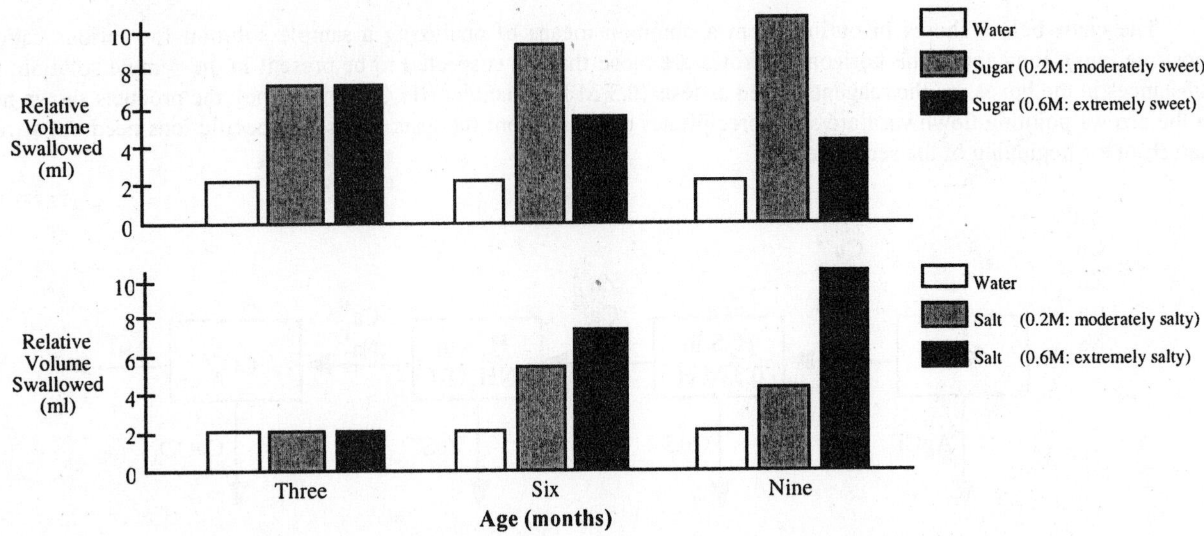

6. Which category on the chart shows no preference between water and the experimental flavor?

   F. Three months of age/sugar
   G. Six months of age/salt
   H. Three months of age/salt
   J. Nine months of age/sugar

7. Which statement about white-tailed deer is supported by the information in the chart?

   A. As age increases, the preference for all tested sugars increases.
   B. As age increases, the preference for all tested salts increases.
   C. As age increases, differences between sugars cannot be detected, and differences between salts cannot be detected.
   D. As age increases, differences between sugars can be detected, and differences between salts can be detected.

8. The flavor preference that fluctuates most irregularly with age is:

   F. moderately salty.
   G. moderately sweet.
   H. extremely salty.
   J. extremely sweet.

9. Based on the trends shown in the chart, which of the following predictions is most reasonable for one-year-old white-tailed deer?

   A. Moderately sweet and moderately salty will be most preferred.
   B. Extremely sweet and extremely salty will be most preferred.
   C. Moderately sweet and extremely salty will be most preferred.
   D. Extremely sweet and moderately salty will be most preferred.

10. Which of the following conclusions about water is NOT consistent with the data in the chart?

   F. Water is never preferred over any tested flavors.
   G. Before the age of six months, white-tailed deer cannot taste the difference between water and sugar or between water and salt.
   H. At the age of three months, both salty fluids are equal to the water swallowed.
   J. As age increases, the volume of water swallowed remains the same.

C. QUIZ III (11 items; 9 minutes)

Passage I

The table below shows the first three ionization energies for the atoms hydrogen through potassium. The first ionization energy, E_1, is the energy (in kilocalories per mole of atoms) that must be added in order to remove the first electron. E_2 is the energy required to remove a second electron once the first has been removed, and E_3 is the energy needed to remove a third electron. If an atom lacks a second or third electron, no value is given in the table.

IONIZATION ENERGIES OF THE ELEMENTS (kcal/mole)

Atomic No.	*Element*	E_1	E_2	E_3
1	H	313.6	-	-
2	He	566.8	1254	-
3	Li	124.3	1744	2823
4	Be	214.9	419.9	3548
5	B	191.3	580.0	874.5
6	C	259.6	562.2	1104
7	N	335.1	682.8	1094
8	O	314.0	810.6	1267
9	F	401.8	806.7	1445
10	Ne	497.2	947.2	1500
11	Na	118.5	1091	1652
12	Mg	176.3	346.6	1848
13	Al	138.0	434.1	655.9
14	Si	187.9	376.8	771.7
15	P	241.8	453.2	695.5
16	S	238.9	540	807
17	Cl	300.0	548.9	920.2
18	Ar	363.4	637	943.3
19	K	100.1	733.6	1100

1. For a given element, the ionization energies increase in the order:

   A. E_3, E_2, E_1.
   B. E_2, E_1, E_3.
   C. E_1, E_2, E_3.
   D. Order varies.

2. A student suspects that there may be an atom for which the second ionization energy is roughly twice that of the first, and the third is roughly twice that of the second. Which of the following atoms best fits this relationship?

   F. Be
   G. C
   H. Ne
   J. Ar

3. As atomic number increases, the trend in the values of E_2 is:

   A. generally upward.
   B. generally downward.
   C. upward for a few values, then suddenly downward, followed by another increase, *etc.*
   D. downward for a few values, then suddenly upward, followed by a decrease again, *etc.*

4. If the chart were continued to the element having atomic number 20, its value for E_1 would be expected to be closest to:

   F. 20.
   G. 90.
   H. 140.
   J. 730.

5. An experimenter has at her disposal a means of providing an atom with any energy up to 200 kcal/mole. From how many different atoms could she remove one electron?

   A. 7
   B. 8
   C. 11
   D. 12

Passage II

A physics student performed two sets of experiments designed to examine the factors that influence the motion of falling objects.

Experiment 1: A stone was dropped from a steep cliff while a camera, mounted on a tripod on the ground, took photographs at 1-second intervals. Back in the laboratory, the same procedure was repeated in the absence (nearly) of air inside a huge vacuum chamber.

Experiment 2: The experiments were repeated (on the cliff and inside the vacuum chamber) using a stone and a cork with identical masses dropped at the same time. At the cliff, the stone hit the ground first. In the vacuum chamber, both objects hit the ground together.

6. Assuming that air acts to resist the downward acceleration of the stone, how will the total time required to reach the ground in the vacuum chamber compare to the time required to reach the ground from the cliff?

F. Longer time in air than in vacuum chamber
G. Longer time in vacuum chamber than in air
H. Same time in each
J. Cannot be determined from the given information

7. If part of Experiment 1 were repeated on the moon, where the pull of gravity is one sixth that of the Earth, the stone's downward speed would increase as it falls (*i.e.*, it would accelerate) but the rate of increase in speed would only be one sixth as great as on the Earth. When the photos taken at 1-second intervals on the moon are compared to the photos taken on Earth, the series of moon pictures of the stone will be:

A. closer together.
B. farther apart.
C. identical.
D. closer at some times and farther apart at others.

8. In Experiment 2, the observed results can be explained by the hypothesis that:

F. heavier objects fall more rapidly than lighter ones.
G. a cork of the same mass as a stone is smaller than the stone, and it encounters more air resistance.
H. a cork of the same mass as a stone is larger than the stone, and it encounters more air resistance.
J. the gravitational acceleration of objects toward the ground diminishes when air is not present.

9. In Experiment 1, gravity accelerates the stone as it falls from the cliff, causing it to pick up speed as it drops. Which of the following series of pictures most resembles how the stone appears as it drops?

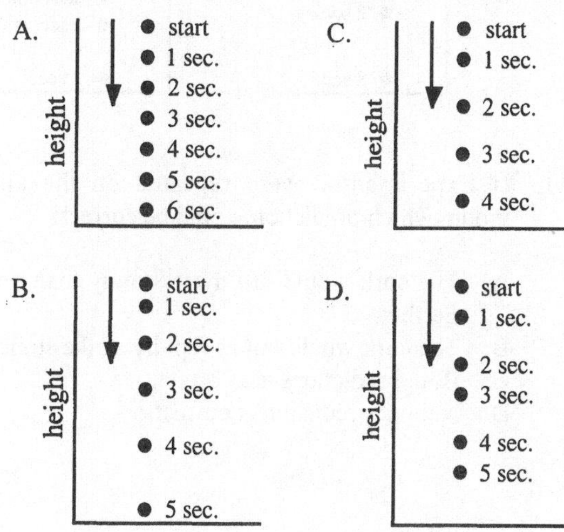

10. The experimenter devises a means of suspending the Earth's gravity for short periods of time. Armed with this technique, he drops the stone (on Earth, in air, under conditions of normal gravity), and then suspends gravity 2 seconds after the stone has been falling and leaves it off for the next minute. Recalling that gravity causes the stone's downward speed to increase continually, choose the "photo" that best illustrates, in 1-second intervals, this experiment.

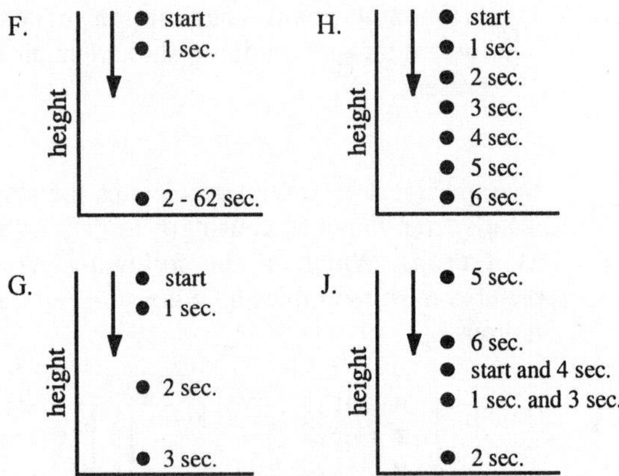

11. If Experiment 2 were repeated on the airless moon, which prediction would be correct?

A. The cork would fall more slowly than on the Earth.
B. The cork would fall as rapidly as the stone.
C. Both predictions are correct.
D. Neither prediction is correct.

TARGETED EDUCATIONAL SOLUTIONS.

Strategy Summary Sheet
SCIENCE REASONING

STRUCTURE OF SCIENCE REASONING: The ACT Science Reasoning Test is 35 minutes long with 40 Multiple-Choice items. (The PLAN is 30 items in 25 minutes; the EXPLORE is 28 items in 30 minutes). There will be about seven reading passages divided among biology, physics, chemistry, and earth/physical sciences. While there is no general ladder of difficulty (increasing difficulty with increasing item number), the items within an item group tend to get harder towards the end of the group of items. There will be six to eight groups with five to seven items each, preceded by a scientific discussion. The approximate distribution of the Science Reasoning items is as follows:

NUMBER OF ITEMS PER CONTENT AREA

	ACT *(40 items)*	**PLAN** *(30 items)*	**EXPLORE** *(28 items)*
Data Representation	15	17	12
Research Summary	18	6	10
Conflicting Viewpoints	7	7	6

GENERAL STRATEGY: This section tests your reasoning skills, not your scientific knowledge. Most of the passages have all of the information you will need to answer the items. In some cases, background information at the level of your high school general science courses is required, but do not assume data that is not given. The following are basic general Science Reasoning strategies:

- ***Pacing is important.*** Remember that within the 35-minute limit, you will have to read and think about seven reading passages and the accompanying item sets. In other words, you will have an average of just five minutes per passage. You will need to work quickly to answer every item.

- Before reading any passage, ***quickly glance over the passages and code them according to passage-type*** in order to determine the order in which you will attack the passages. Identifying and coding each passage should take no more than five seconds.

- ***Do not preview the item stems.*** Previewing the Science Reasoning item stems will only confuse you and slow you down, since they tend to be confusing without having first read the passage.

- It is important to only ***read the passage thoroughly once***, rather than to skim over it several times. The material can be difficult to understand, thus it is important to read thoughtfully and carefully. ***Be an active reader.*** Use your pencil to underline key words and points of information. That way, you will be able to locate them easily when answering the items.

- When a reading passage includes tables or graphs, make sure you ***read and understand the labels*** on axes, columns, and rows. You need to know what information is being presented and what units of measure are being used.

- Tables and graphs present results, often of observations or experiments. Items will usually ask you to spot patterns in the data, so ***look for trends*** such as upward movement, downward movement, inverse variation, *etc.*

- Many passages will contain much more information than you need to answer a particular item. In your search for a logical conclusion, ***do not be misled by data that does not relate to the item at hand.***

- The experiments described in Research Summary items are based on scientific assumptions. However, if an assumption is faulty, the experiment may not prove what it claims to prove, and conclusions drawn from it may be invalid. Therefore, for items that ask about the validity of a scientific conclusion, ***consider the validity of underlying assumptions***.

- The arguments presented in Conflicting Viewpoint items are also based on scientific assumptions. Again, ***if the assumption is wrong, the entire argument is open to challenge.*** Assumptions that are based on scientific fact add strength to an argument; faulty assumptions weaken an argument.

- Offering the assumptions that you started with as proof of your argument is called circular reasoning, and this type of proof is not acceptable. For that reason, any conclusions discussed in Science Reasoning passages or offered as answer choices must be based on additional evidence (*e.g.*, experiments) to be valid. ***Beware of any conclusions that are nothing more than a restatement of an underlying premise.***

- All of the information that you need to answer the items is provided in the passage—do not imply any information that is not given or relate previous experience to the passage. ***Pay attention to material noted with an asterisk.***

- ***Transcribe your answers from the test booklet to the answer sheet in groups*** (by passage). However, when you get to the last passage, transcribe each answer as it is determined.

STRATEGIES FOR EACH TYPE OF PASSAGE:

1. ***Data Representation Passages:*** When given data in the form of a graph or a chart, pay particular attention to the scale, units, legend, and other noted information.

2. ***Research Summary Passages:*** When given multiple experiments, identify the controls and variables. Note that the controls must remain the same and that variables can only change one at a time in all experiments.

3. ***Conflicting Viewpoints Passages:*** When given two points of view on a topic, identify the main points of difference and the logical value of each argument. After you understand the nature of the passage, attack the items.

STRATEGIES FOR EACH ITEM-TYPE:

1. ***Comprehension Items:*** Recognize basic concepts. Read carefully. Make sure that your answers consider appropriate scales and units. Also, note the difference between absolute and percentage changes.

2. ***Analysis Items:*** Identify relationships and trends. Pay particular attention to direct and inverse relationships.

3. ***Application Items:*** Draw conclusions, predict outcomes, and synthesize new information. In answering Application items, beware of the following terms: "all," "none," "always," and "never." Remember that a single case of contradictory evidence is all that is necessary to disprove an absolute theory.

ADDITIONAL STRATEGIES FROM IN-CLASS DISCUSSION:

Writing

TARGETED EDUCATIONAL SOLUTIONS.

Cambridge Course Concept Outline
WRITING

CORE LESSON

The items in this section accompany the Core Lesson of the Writing Lesson. You will work through the items with your instructor in class.

DIRECTIONS: Read the following prompt and corresponding assignment, which are written as they would appear on the ACT. Then, use the space that is provided below to create an <u>outline</u> for an essay that responds to the assignment. Include a thesis, as well as a topic sentence and a list of several examples for each part of your essay.

1. *Residents of rural areas often wonder why people would voluntarily choose to live in a large city and insist that rural life—with its open spaces, relative freedom from worries about crime, and healthful living conditions—is preferable. Conversely, residents of urban areas say that city life—with access to public transportation, cultural amenities, and many entertainment opportunities—is preferable. Which do you find more compelling, the belief that the quality of life is greater in urban areas or the belief that the quality of life is greater in rural areas?*

   In your essay, take a position on this question. You may write about either one of the two points of view given, or you may present a different point of view on this question. Use specific reasons and examples to support your position.

DIRECTIONS: Read the following prompt and corresponding assignment, which are written as they would appear on the ACT. Then, use the space that is provided below to write an essay that responds to the assignment. Use the essay outline from the previous item as a guide.

2. *Residents of rural areas often wonder why people would voluntarily choose to live in a large city and insist that rural life—with its open spaces, relative freedom from worries about crime, and healthful living conditions—is preferable. Conversely, residents of urban areas say that city life—with access to public transportation, cultural amenities, and many entertainment opportunities—is preferable. Which do you find more compelling, the belief that the quality of life is greater in urban areas or the belief that the quality of life is greater in rural areas?*

   In your essay, take a position on this question. You may write about either one of the two points of view given, or you may present a different point of view on this question. Use specific reasons and examples to support your position.

TIMED-PRACTICE QUIZZES

This section contains three Writing quizzes. Complete each quiz under timed conditions.

A. QUIZ I (1 item; 30 minutes)

DIRECTIONS: Plan and write an essay on the topic assigned below. DO NOT WRITE ON ANY OTHER TOPIC. AN ESSAY ON ANOTHER TOPIC IS NOT ACCEPTABLE. Think carefully about the issue presented in the following prompt and corresponding assignment below.

1. *Some schools and districts have eliminated study hall for their students. The primary drive behind this elimination is to allow students to take additional electives and substantive subjects. Though students might have slightly more work to complete at home, they will leave school much more well-rounded with their added knowledge. Proponents of study hall argue that study hall provides an environment that is conducive to learning for students who suffer from time constraints at home. Some students may not have the luxury to complete homework assignments at home due to work or heavy extracurricular activities. In addition, proponents of study hall argue that the core classes are more important than elective courses in developing a student's future prospects; therefore, it is important to provide a quiet learning environment for students who cannot complete core class assignments at home. In your opinion, should schools and districts eliminate study hall for their students?*

   In your essay, take a position on this question. You may write about either one of the two points of view given, or you may present a different point of view on this question. Use specific reasons and examples to support your position.

B. QUIZ II (1 item; 30 minutes)

DIRECTIONS: Plan and write an essay on the topic assigned below. DO NOT WRITE ON ANY OTHER TOPIC. AN ESSAY ON ANOTHER TOPIC IS NOT ACCEPTABLE. Think carefully about the issue presented in the following prompt and corresponding assignment below.

1. *In some countries, upon graduating from or leaving high school, young people are required to perform 24 months of compulsory service. A choice is offered between military service and an alternative, community service. Some people think universal compulsory service is a good idea because young people learn valuable lessons from the experience. Other people think that such a required service engenders resentment so that no important civic lesson is learned. In your opinion, should all young people be required to participate in some form of universal compulsory service?*

   In your essay, take a position on this question. You may write about either one of the two points of view given, or you may present a different point of view on this question. Use specific reasons and examples to support your position.

C. QUIZ III (1 item; 30 minutes)

DIRECTIONS: Plan and write an essay on the topic assigned below. DO NOT WRITE ON ANY OTHER TOPIC. AN ESSAY ON ANOTHER TOPIC IS NOT ACCEPTABLE. Think carefully about the issue presented in the following prompt and corresponding assignment below.

1. *Some schools, notably military academies, have honor codes that not only prohibit cheating but require students to inform authorities of any acts of cheating by classmates of which they may be aware. Some teachers and administrators think that all schools should have honor codes because the codes teach the virtue of personal integrity and reinforce a sense of responsibility among students toward one another. Other teachers and administrators argue that honor codes are often ineffective and further that they require students to make impossible choices between loyalty to friends and the demands of the honor code. In your opinion, should schools adopt honor codes that cover all students?*

   In your essay, take a position on this question. You may write about either one of the two points of view given, or you may present a different point of view on this question. Use specific reasons and examples to support your position.

TARGETED EDUCATIONAL SOLUTIONS.

Strategy Summary Sheet
WRITING

STRUCTURE OF THE ESSAY: The ACT includes an optional Writing Test that measures an examinee's proficiency at composition and is administered after all four multiple-choice sections of the ACT. The Writing Test includes one writing prompt that defines an issue and describes two opposing viewpoints on that issue. Students will have 30 minutes to write an essay supporting a position on the issue presented in the prompt.

GENERAL STRATEGY FOR THE ESSAY:

1. Begin with the prompt.
2. Write only on the assigned topic. Writing on any other topic will result in a score of 0.
3. Do not try to do too much. Try to mentally limit the scope of your topic.
4. Organize your thoughts and write an outline before beginning the essay. Do not spend more than two minutes writing the outline.
    a. Familiarize yourself with the essay prompt and assignment.
    b. Develop a point of view.
    c. Develop a thesis.
    d. Identify two to four important points.
    e. Decide on the order of presentation of the major points.
5. Organize ideas into paragraphs.
    a. Introduction
    b. Two to Four Body Paragraphs
    c. Conclusion
6. Write grammatically.
7. Write clearly, concisely, and legibly.
8. Punctuate and spell correctly.
9. Spend at least four minutes proofreading your essay.

ADDITIONAL STRATEGIES FROM IN-CLASS DISCUSSION:

Step Four: Practice Test Reinforcement

Step Four Highlights:

Complete the four, full-length ACT tests to reinforce everything you've learned in your course.

Work through the tests either all at once or by section to highlight specific skills and concepts.

Step Four Overview:

In this section, you will have the opportunity to apply everything that you have learned throughout the Cambridge Course. Each of the four practice tests has been arranged in an order and with a frequency that approximates the real ACT. Completing these practice tests will help reinforce the test content, help you become more comfortable with timing and pacing, reduce your test anxiety, and give you the chance to practice using alternative test-taking strategies. If you're working on these on your own, complete the first two tests without timing restrictions to practice the application of the concepts you've learned this far. Then, complete the second two tests with the appropriate timing to practice your pacing.

Practice Test I

TARGETED EDUCATIONAL SOLUTIONS.

Cambridge Course Concept Outline
PRACTICE TEST I

When completing Practice Test I, use the Bubble Sheet on page 669, unless otherwise directed by your instructor.

BUBBLE SHEET

Name ______________________ Student ID Number ______________________

Date ____________ Instructor ______________________ Course/Session Number ____________

TEST 1—ENGLISH

1 (A) (B) (C) (D)	16 (F) (G) (H) (J)	31 (A) (B) (C) (D)	46 (F) (G) (H) (J)	61 (A) (B) (C) (D)
2 (F) (G) (H) (J)	17 (A) (B) (C) (D)	32 (F) (G) (H) (J)	47 (A) (B) (C) (D)	62 (F) (G) (H) (J)
3 (A) (B) (C) (D)	18 (F) (G) (H) (J)	33 (A) (B) (C) (D)	48 (F) (G) (H) (J)	63 (A) (B) (C) (D)
4 (F) (G) (H) (J)	19 (A) (B) (C) (D)	34 (F) (G) (H) (J)	49 (A) (B) (C) (D)	64 (F) (G) (H) (J)
5 (A) (B) (C) (D)	20 (F) (G) (H) (J)	35 (A) (B) (C) (D)	50 (F) (G) (H) (J)	65 (A) (B) (C) (D)
6 (F) (G) (H) (J)	21 (A) (B) (C) (D)	36 (F) (G) (H) (J)	51 (A) (B) (C) (D)	66 (F) (G) (H) (J)
7 (A) (B) (C) (D)	22 (F) (G) (H) (J)	37 (A) (B) (C) (D)	52 (F) (G) (H) (J)	67 (A) (B) (C) (D)
8 (F) (G) (H) (J)	23 (A) (B) (C) (D)	38 (F) (G) (H) (J)	53 (A) (B) (C) (D)	68 (F) (G) (H) (J)
9 (A) (B) (C) (D)	24 (F) (G) (H) (J)	39 (A) (B) (C) (D)	54 (F) (G) (H) (J)	69 (A) (B) (C) (D)
10 (F) (G) (H) (J)	25 (A) (B) (C) (D)	40 (F) (G) (H) (J)	55 (A) (B) (C) (D)	70 (F) (G) (H) (J)
11 (A) (B) (C) (D)	26 (F) (G) (H) (J)	41 (A) (B) (C) (D)	56 (F) (G) (H) (J)	71 (A) (B) (C) (D)
12 (F) (G) (H) (J)	27 (A) (B) (C) (D)	42 (F) (G) (H) (J)	57 (A) (B) (C) (D)	72 (F) (G) (H) (J)
13 (A) (B) (C) (D)	28 (F) (G) (H) (J)	43 (A) (B) (C) (D)	58 (F) (G) (H) (J)	73 (A) (B) (C) (D)
14 (F) (G) (H) (J)	29 (A) (B) (C) (D)	44 (F) (G) (H) (J)	59 (A) (B) (C) (D)	74 (F) (G) (H) (J)
15 (A) (B) (C) (D)	30 (F) (G) (H) (J)	45 (A) (B) (C) (D)	60 (F) (G) (H) (J)	75 (A) (B) (C) (D)

TEST 2—MATHEMATICS

1 (A) (B) (C) (D) (E)	13 (A) (B) (C) (D) (E)	25 (A) (B) (C) (D) (E)	37 (A) (B) (C) (D) (E)	49 (A) (B) (C) (D) (E)
2 (F) (G) (H) (J) (K)	14 (F) (G) (H) (J) (K)	26 (F) (G) (H) (J) (K)	38 (F) (G) (H) (J) (K)	50 (F) (G) (H) (J) (K)
3 (A) (B) (C) (D) (E)	15 (A) (B) (C) (D) (E)	27 (A) (B) (C) (D) (E)	39 (A) (B) (C) (D) (E)	51 (A) (B) (C) (D) (E)
4 (F) (G) (H) (J) (K)	16 (F) (G) (H) (J) (K)	28 (F) (G) (H) (J) (K)	40 (F) (G) (H) (J) (K)	52 (F) (G) (H) (J) (K)
5 (A) (B) (C) (D) (E)	17 (A) (B) (C) (D) (E)	29 (A) (B) (C) (D) (E)	41 (A) (B) (C) (D) (E)	53 (A) (B) (C) (D) (E)
6 (F) (G) (H) (J) (K)	18 (F) (G) (H) (J) (K)	30 (F) (G) (H) (J) (K)	42 (F) (G) (H) (J) (K)	54 (F) (G) (H) (J) (K)
7 (A) (B) (C) (D) (E)	19 (A) (B) (C) (D) (E)	31 (A) (B) (C) (D) (E)	43 (A) (B) (C) (D) (E)	55 (A) (B) (C) (D) (E)
8 (F) (G) (H) (J) (K)	20 (F) (G) (H) (J) (K)	32 (F) (G) (H) (J) (K)	44 (F) (G) (H) (J) (K)	56 (F) (G) (H) (J) (K)
9 (A) (B) (C) (D) (E)	21 (A) (B) (C) (D) (E)	33 (A) (B) (C) (D) (E)	45 (A) (B) (C) (D) (E)	57 (A) (B) (C) (D) (E)
10 (F) (G) (H) (J) (K)	22 (F) (G) (H) (J) (K)	34 (F) (G) (H) (J) (K)	46 (F) (G) (H) (J) (K)	58 (F) (G) (H) (J) (K)
11 (A) (B) (C) (D) (E)	23 (A) (B) (C) (D) (E)	35 (A) (B) (C) (D) (E)	47 (A) (B) (C) (D) (E)	59 (A) (B) (C) (D) (E)
12 (F) (G) (H) (J) (K)	24 (F) (G) (H) (J) (K)	36 (F) (G) (H) (J) (K)	48 (F) (G) (H) (J) (K)	60 (F) (G) (H) (J) (K)

TEST 3—READING

1 (A) (B) (C) (D)	9 (A) (B) (C) (D)	17 (A) (B) (C) (D)	25 (A) (B) (C) (D)	33 (A) (B) (C) (D)
2 (F) (G) (H) (J)	10 (F) (G) (H) (J)	18 (F) (G) (H) (J)	26 (F) (G) (H) (J)	34 (F) (G) (H) (J)
3 (A) (B) (C) (D)	11 (A) (B) (C) (D)	19 (A) (B) (C) (D)	27 (A) (B) (C) (D)	35 (A) (B) (C) (D)
4 (F) (G) (H) (J)	12 (F) (G) (H) (J)	20 (F) (G) (H) (J)	28 (F) (G) (H) (J)	36 (F) (G) (H) (J)
5 (A) (B) (C) (D)	13 (A) (B) (C) (D)	21 (A) (B) (C) (D)	29 (A) (B) (C) (D)	37 (A) (B) (C) (D)
6 (F) (G) (H) (J)	14 (F) (G) (H) (J)	22 (F) (G) (H) (J)	30 (F) (G) (H) (J)	38 (F) (G) (H) (J)
7 (A) (B) (C) (D)	15 (A) (B) (C) (D)	23 (A) (B) (C) (D)	31 (A) (B) (C) (D)	39 (A) (B) (C) (D)
8 (F) (G) (H) (J)	16 (F) (G) (H) (J)	24 (F) (G) (H) (J)	32 (F) (G) (H) (J)	40 (F) (G) (H) (J)

TEST 4—SCIENCE REASONING

1 (A) (B) (C) (D)	9 (A) (B) (C) (D)	17 (A) (B) (C) (D)	25 (A) (B) (C) (D)	33 (A) (B) (C) (D)
2 (F) (G) (H) (J)	10 (F) (G) (H) (J)	18 (F) (G) (H) (J)	26 (F) (G) (H) (J)	34 (F) (G) (H) (J)
3 (A) (B) (C) (D)	11 (A) (B) (C) (D)	19 (A) (B) (C) (D)	27 (A) (B) (C) (D)	35 (A) (B) (C) (D)
4 (F) (G) (H) (J)	12 (F) (G) (H) (J)	20 (F) (G) (H) (J)	28 (F) (G) (H) (J)	36 (F) (G) (H) (J)
5 (A) (B) (C) (D)	13 (A) (B) (C) (D)	21 (A) (B) (C) (D)	29 (A) (B) (C) (D)	37 (A) (B) (C) (D)
6 (F) (G) (H) (J)	14 (F) (G) (H) (J)	22 (F) (G) (H) (J)	30 (F) (G) (H) (J)	38 (F) (G) (H) (J)
7 (A) (B) (C) (D)	15 (A) (B) (C) (D)	23 (A) (B) (C) (D)	31 (A) (B) (C) (D)	39 (A) (B) (C) (D)
8 (F) (G) (H) (J)	16 (F) (G) (H) (J)	24 (F) (G) (H) (J)	32 (F) (G) (H) (J)	40 (F) (G) (H) (J)

DIRECTIONS

Practice Test I consists of five sections: English, Mathematics, Reading, Science Reasoning, and Writing. Calculator use is only permitted on the Mathematics Test.

The items in each test are numbered and the answer choices lettered. The provided bubble sheet has numbered rows that correspond to the items on the test. Each row contains lettered ovals to match the answer choices for each item on the test. Each numbered row on the bubble sheet has a corresponding item on the test.

For each item, first decide on the best answer choice. Then, locate the row number that corresponds to the item. Next, find the oval in that row that matches the letter of the chosen answer. Then, use a soft lead pencil to fill in the oval. Do not use a ballpoint pen.

Mark only one answer for each item. If you change your mind about the answer choice, thoroughly erase the first mark before marking your new answer.

Note that only responses marked on your bubble sheet will be scored. Your score on each test will be based only on the number of items that are correctly answered during the time allowed for that test. Guessing is not penalized. Therefore, it is to your best advantage to answer every item on the test, even if you must guess.

You may work on each test only during the time allowed for that test. If you finish a test before time is called, use the time to review your answer choices or work on items about which you are uncertain. You may not return to a test on which time has already been called and you may not preview another test. You must lay down your pencil immediately when time is called at the end of each test. You may not for any reason fill in or alter ovals for a test after time expires for that test. Violation of these rules will result in immediate disqualification from the exam.

1 1 1 1 1 1 1 1 1 1 1 1

ENGLISH TEST

45 Minutes—75 Items

DIRECTIONS: In the following passages, certain words and phrases are underlined. The items in the right hand column provide alternatives for the underlined parts. In most cases, you are to choose the alternative that best expresses the idea of the sentence in context, corrects grammatical errors, and/or is best suited to the tone and style of the passage. If the original best accomplishes this, then choose "NO CHANGE." In some cases, you will be asked questions regarding an underlined part. You are to choose the best answer to the question.

You will also find items on this test that refer to a section of the passage or to the passage as a whole. These items DO NOT refer to an underlined portion of the passage. Rather, they are identified by a number or numbers in a box.

For each item, choose the best alternative and fill in the corresponding oval on your bubble sheet. You should read the passage before answering the accompanying items. For many of the items, you must read several sentences beyond the item to determine the answer. Be sure that you have read far enough ahead before you answer.

Answers are on page 941.

PASSAGE I

Basic Principles of Nuclear Weapons

The challenge to start to begin to make (1) timely progress toward removing the threat of nuclear war is today the most important challenge in international relations. Three general principles guide our defense and negotiating policies toward such a goal, principles based on the technical realities of nuclear war.

First, nuclear weapons are fundamentally different than (2) non-nuclear weapons. These weapons of mass destruction that could do a lot of harm (3) have a

1. **A.** NO CHANGE
   B. to begin making
   C. to begin the making of
   D. of beginning the making of

2. **F.** NO CHANGE
   G. different than fundamentally
   H. different from fundamentally
   J. fundamentally different from

3. **A.** NO CHANGE
   B. (and they could also do a great deal of harm)
   C. (owing to the fact that they could do a lot of harm)
   D. OMIT the underlined portion.

GO ON TO THE NEXT PAGE.

long and deadly radioactive memory, the unknowns of nuclear conflict dwarf the predictable consequences.
4

The number of deaths resulting from injuries and the unavailability of medical care and the economic
5

damage as a result from disruption and disorganization
6

would be even more devastating than the direct loss of life and property. [8]
7

Second, the sole purpose of nuclear weapons
9

must be to deter nuclear war, it is neither a substitute for maintaining adequate conventional military forces
10

to meet vital national security goals but an effective defense against the almost total mutual annihilation and devastation that results from a full-scale nuclear war. Third, arms control is an essential part of our national security. Thus far, we have had no effective controls on offensive nuclear weaponry, and it is clear that each step forward in the arms race toward more
11
12

4. F. NO CHANGE
   G. memory. The
   H. memory the
   J. memory and the

5. A. NO CHANGE
   B. from injuries and also from the unavailability of medical care
   C. from the unavailability of injuries and medical care
   D. both from injuries and also from the unavailability of medical care as well

6. F. NO CHANGE
   G. as a result to
   H. resulting from
   J. with a result of

7. A. NO CHANGE
   B. is even more devastating than
   C. are even more devastating as
   D. might be more devastating even as

8. Which of the following would be an appropriate final sentence for this paragraph?
   F. And so I believe nuclear weapons to be a challenge.
   G. Nuclear war could have no winners.
   H. Nuclear conflict is very dangerous.
   J. Nuclear conflict would be rather wasteful.

9. A. NO CHANGE
   B. solely, the purpose
   C. the solely purpose
   D. the purpose solely

10. F. NO CHANGE
    G. war. They are
    H. war they are
    J. war; it is

11. A. NO CHANGE
    B. and
    C. nor
    D. including

12. F. NO CHANGE
    G. Third
    H. (Begin a new paragraph) Third
    J. (Begin a new paragraph) Third,

GO ON TO THE NEXT PAGE.

and improved weapons has made less our security.[13]

13. A. NO CHANGE
B. has lessened
C. have lessened
D. have made less of

Before deploying additional weapons, they must develop[14] a coherent arms control strategy.

14. F. NO CHANGE
G. the development is necessary of
H. it is necessary to develop
J. it is necessarily to be developed,

Items 15 and 16 ask about the preceding passage as a whole.

15. Which of the following best describes the overall structure of the essay?
A. A three-part argument
B. A two-part narrative
C. A three-part comparison
D. A four-part argument

16. Which of the following is the thesis of this essay?
F. Nuclear weapons are fundamentally different from non-nuclear weapons.
G. The sole purpose of nuclear weapons must be to deter nuclear war.
H. There are three principles that guide our effort to remove the threat of nuclear war.
J. Nuclear war is a frightening possibility.

PASSAGE II

Education for a New Republic

The founders of the Republic viewing their[17] revolution primarily in political terms rather as[18] in economic terms. Therefore,[19] they viewed the kind of education needed for the new Republic largely in

17. A. NO CHANGE
B. having viewed its
C. viewed its
D. viewed their

18. F. NO CHANGE
G. rather than
H. but
J. OMIT the underlined portion.

19. A. NO CHANGE
B. Since
C. However
D. On the contrary

GO ON TO THE NEXT PAGE.

political terms instead of <u>as a means to</u> [20] academic excellence or individual self-fulfillment. <u>Talking about</u> [21] education as a bulwark for liberty, equality, popular consent, and devotion to the public <u>good goals</u> [22] that <u>took precedence over</u> [23] the uses of knowledge for self-improvement or occupational preparation. Over and over again, the Revolutionary generation, both liberal and conservative in <u>outlook—assert their</u> [24] faith that the welfare of the Republic rested upon an educated citizenry.

All agreed that the principal ingredients of a civic education <u>was</u> [25] literacy and inculcation of patriotic and moral <u>virtues some</u> [26] others added the study of history and the study of the principles of the republican government itself. The founders, as was the case of almost all their successors, were long on exhortation and rhetoric regarding the value of civic <u>education; since</u> [27] they left it to the textbook writers to distill the essence of those values for school children. Texts in American history and government appeared as early as the 1790s. The textbook writers <u>turned out being</u> [28] very largely of conservative persuasion, more likely Federalist in outlook than Jeffersonian, and

20. F. NO CHANGE
    G. as a means or a way to
    H. to
    J. as

21. A. NO CHANGE
    B. Talking
    C. With the talking about
    D. They talked about

22. F. NO CHANGE
    G. good. Goals
    H. good, goals
    J. good; goals

23. A. NO CHANGE
    B. precede
    C. precede over
    D. took precedence on

24. F. NO CHANGE
    G. outlook, asserted its
    H. outlook; asserted its
    J. outlook asserts their

25. A. NO CHANGE
    B. being
    C. were
    D. were like

26. F. NO CHANGE
    G. virtues—some
    H. virtues, some
    J. virtues; some

27. A. NO CHANGE
    B. education. And
    C. education. Since
    D. education, but

28. F. NO CHANGE
    G. turned out to be
    H. turning out to be
    J. having turned out to be

GO ON TO THE NEXT PAGE.

universally almost agreed that political virtue must rest
29
upon moral and religious precepts. Since most textbook writers were New Englanders, this meant that the texts had a decidedly Federalist slant.

29. **A.** NO CHANGE
B. almost, agreed universally
C. almost universally agreed
D. almost universally, agreed

In the first half of the Republic, civic education in the schools emphasized the inculcation of civic values, put less emphasis on political knowledge, and no attempt to develop political skills. The
30
development of political skills was left to the local parties, town meetings, churches, coffeehouses, and ale houses where men gathered to talk. [31]

30. **F.** NO CHANGE
G. made no attempt to develop
H. none at all on the development of
J. none was put at all on developing

31. Which of the following correctly describes how the last paragraph of the essay functions?
A. It contradicts much of what was said before.
B. It continues the logical development of the essay.
C. It reiterates what was said in the first paragraph.
D. It is a transitional paragraph to introduce a new topic.

Item 32 asks about the preceding passage as a whole.

32. This essay would most likely be published in a:
F. history textbook.
G. political science journal.
H. journal for educators.
J. biography of Jefferson.

PASSAGE III

Women and World War I

[1]

The contribution of women on the home front
33
during World War I was varied. It included a large

33. **A.** NO CHANGE
B. Women, their contribution
C. The contribution of woman
D. Woman's contribution

GO ON TO THE NEXT PAGE.

range of activities–from knitting and the operation of [34] drill presses–and engaged a cross section of the female population, from housewives to society girls. World War I marked the first time [35] in the history of the United States that a systematic effort was made, through organizations like the League for Women's Service, to utilize [36] the capabilities of women in all regions of the country.

[2]

While much of this volunteer work falls within [37] the established bounds of women's club work, many women entered areas of industrial work previously reserved by [38] the male population. Women put on the uniforms of elevator operators, streetcar conductors, postmen, and industrial workers. However, they were employed [39] in aircraft and munitions plants as well as in shipbuilding yards and steel mills.

[3]

Much of the work fell into the traditional realm of volunteer activity knitting [40] garments for the boys overseas, canning for Uncle Sam, planting Victory gardens, *etc.* Through these activities, every homemaker could demonstrate their [41] patriotism while still fulfilling her role as homemaker. Women with

34. **F.** NO CHANGE
G. from knitting with the operation of
H. from knitting and operating
J. from knitting to operating

35. **A.** NO CHANGE
B. has marked the first time
C. is the first time it is marked
D. was marked, the first time

36. **F.** NO CHANGE
G. being able to utilize
H. utilizing
J. and utilize

37. **A.** NO CHANGE
B. fell within
C. having fallen within
D. fell in

38. **F.** NO CHANGE
G. having previously been reserved
H. previously reserved for
J. reserved previous to then

39. **A.** NO CHANGE
B. workers. They were employed
C. workers, but they were employed
D. workers. Since they were employed

40. **F.** NO CHANGE
G. activity—knitting
H. activity: knitting
J. activity, knitting

41. **A.** NO CHANGE
B. be demonstrating
C. have demonstrated their
D. demonstrate her

GO ON TO THE NEXT PAGE.

more time volunteered to hostess at canteens: make [42] bandages, and organize food and clothing drives. The Women's Land Army, dressed in bloomer uniforms and armed with such slogans as "The Woman with the Hoe Must Defend the Man with the Musket," was dispatched [43] to assist farmers in processing crops.

[4]

Women performed ably during the war and laid the foundation [44] for more specialized jobs, increased wages, better working conditions, and a more competitive job status in the labor market.

42. **F.** NO CHANGE
G. canteens make
H. canteens, make
J. canteens; make

43. **A.** NO CHANGE
B. Musket," which was then dispatched
C. Musket," and it was dispatched
D. Musket," and it got dispatched

44. **F.** NO CHANGE
G. the foundation was laid
H. the foundation was lain
J. laying the foundation

Items 45 and 46 ask about the preceding passage as a whole.

45. Which of the following represents the most logical order for the paragraphs?

A. 1, 4, 3, 2
B. 1, 3, 4, 2
C. 1, 3, 2, 4
D. 2, 4, 3, 1

46. Is the use of the sample slogan appropriate to the essay?

F. Yes, because it helps the reader to understand one of the points being made.
G. Yes, because all general statements should be illustrated with an example.
H. No, because it does not help the reader to understand the point being made.
J. No, because it is needlessly distracting.

GO ON TO THE NEXT PAGE.

PASSAGE IV

Democracy in Japan

Following the end of World War II, substantial changes undertaken (47) in Japan to liberate the individual from authoritarian restraints. The new democratic value system was acceptable by (48) many teachers, students, intellectuals, and old liberals, and (49) it was not immediately embraced by the society as a whole. Japanese traditions were dominated by group values, (50) and notions of personal freedom and individual rights being (51) unfamiliar.

Today, the triumph of (52) democratic processes is clear (53) evident in the widespread participation of the Japanese in social and political life. Furthermore, (54) there is no universally accepted and stable value system, values being (55) constantly modified by strong infusions of Western ideas. School textbooks expound

47. A. NO CHANGE
B. will be undertaken
C. have been undertaken
D. were undertaken

48. F. NO CHANGE
G. accepted by
H. excepted by
J. excepted to

49. A. NO CHANGE
B. liberals, since
C. liberals, but
D. liberals; consequently

50. F. NO CHANGE
G. Dominated by group values were the Japanese traditions
H. Group values were always dominating the Japanese traditions
J. Dominating Japanese traditions were group values

51. A. NO CHANGE
B. were
C. was
D. are

52. F. NO CHANGE
G. (Do NOT begin a new paragraph) Today the triumph, of
H. Today, the triumph, of
J. (Do NOT begin a new paragraph) Today, owing to the fact that

53. A. NO CHANGE
B. is
C. is clear and also
D. are clearly

54. F. NO CHANGE
G. Therefore,
H. So,
J. Yet,

55. A. NO CHANGE
B. system with that values are
C. system since that values are
D. system since values are

GO ON TO THE NEXT PAGE.

democratic principles, and so emphasizing [56] equality over hierarchy and rationalism over tradition, but in practice, these values are often sometimes distorted, [57] particularly by the youth that translated [58] the individualistic and humanistic goals of democracy into egoistic and materialistic ones. [59]

56. F. NO CHANGE
    G. principles, emphasizing
    H. principles and the emphasis of
    J. principles with the emphasis that

57. A. NO CHANGE
    B. had been misinterpreted and distorted often
    C. often misinterpreted and distorted
    D. are often misinterpreted and distorted

58. F. NO CHANGE
    G. that translate
    H. who translate
    J. translate

59. What type of discussion might logically follow this last paragraph?
    A. A discussion of goals of Japanese youth
    B. A discussion of democratic principles
    C. A discussion of Western education
    D. A discussion of World War II

PASSAGE V

Zoological Nature

From the beginning, humankind always has shared [60] some sort of link with the animal world. The earliest and most primitive was surely that of hunter and prey—with humans possibly playing the fatal role of victim. Later, of course, humans reversed the roles as they became more skillful and intelligenter. [61] The later domestication of certain animals and also [62] the discovery of agriculture, made for a more settled and stable existence and was an essential step in the not-so-

60. F. NO CHANGE
    G. have always shared
    H. is always sharing
    J. has always shared

61. A. NO CHANGE
    B. so intelligent
    C. and more intelligent
    D. but intelligent

62. F. NO CHANGE
    G. animals, also
    H. animals, along with
    J. animals; along with

GO ON TO THE NEXT PAGE.

orderly and very chaotic (63) process of becoming civilized. However, the intellectual distance between regarding an animal as the source of dinner or of material comfort and to consider them (64) a worthy subject for study is considerable.

Not until Aristotle did the animal world become a subject for serious scientific study. Although he seemingly writes on (65) every subject, Aristotle's work (66) in zoology—studying animals as animals—is considered his most successful. He seemed to have had a natural affinity for and curiosity about all the living creatures of the world, and (67) he took special interest in marine life.

Aristotle's zoological writings reveal him to be a remarkably astute observer of the natural world, wedding his (68) observations to what might be called speculative reason. He was therefore a theorist as well. His overall theory was simple. In (69) the works of Nature," he said, "purpose and not accident is predominant." A thing is known then when we know what it is for. He linked and combined (70) theory and practice by saying that interpretation of an observed phenomenon must always be made in light of its purpose (71). His zoological theory was thus a

63. **A.** NO CHANGE
B. (and very chaotic)
C. yet very chaotic
D. OMIT the underlined portion.

64. **F.** NO CHANGE
G. considering it
H. considering them
J. then to consider them

65. **A.** NO CHANGE
B. he wrote (seemingly) on
C. writing seemingly on
D. he wrote on seemingly

66. **F.** NO CHANGE
G. subject; Aristotles work
H. subject Aristotles' work
J. subject: Aristotle's work

67. **A.** NO CHANGE
B. so
C. but
D. because

68. **F.** NO CHANGE
G. who was wedded to
H. in that he wedded
J. with the wedding of

69. **A.** NO CHANGE
B. simple—in
C. simple. "In
D. simply. "In

70. **F.** NO CHANGE
G. combining
H. to combine
J. OMIT the underlined portion.

71. **A.** NO CHANGE
B. always keeping its purpose in mind
C. without ever forgetting what its purpose is
D. given an understanding of what its purpose is

GO ON TO THE NEXT PAGE.

reflection of the essentially teleological nature of his overall philosophy. 72

72. Is the quote from Aristotle in the last paragraph appropriate?
   - F. Yes, because it is important to quote the works of people you are talking about.
   - G. Yes, because it is a succinct statement of Aristotle's theory.
   - H. No, because the quote is irrelevant to what the author is talking about in that paragraph.
   - J. No, because it is wrong to quote when you can express the idea in your own words.

Items 73-75 ask about the preceding passage as a whole.

73. The author probably had which of the following audiences in mind for this essay?
   - A. Zoologists
   - B. Students who are studying Aristotle
   - C. The average person interested in science
   - D. Teachers of marine biology

74. What is the actual thesis of this essay?
   - F. People have always liked animals.
   - G. Animals and people reversed roles.
   - H. Aristotle was interested in the natural world.
   - J. The animal world became a source of serious study because of Aristotle.

75. How does the first paragraph of this essay function?
   - A. It poses questions to be answered.
   - B. It provides general background for the rest of the passage.
   - C. It introduces an argument.
   - D. It provides an anecdote related to the rest of the passage.

END OF TEST 1.

STOP! DO NOT TURN THE PAGE UNTIL TOLD TO DO SO.

2 2 2 2 2 2 2 2 2 2 2 2

MATHEMATICS TEST

60 Minutes—60 Items

DIRECTIONS: Solve each item and choose the correct answer choice. Then, fill in the corresponding oval on the bubble sheet.

Allocate time wisely. Try to solve as many items as possible, returning to skipped items if time permits.

Calculator use is permitted on this test; however, some items are best solved without the use of a calculator.

Note: Unless otherwise stated, assume all of the following.

1. Illustrative figures are NOT necessarily drawn to scale.
2. The word *average* indicates arithmetic mean.
3. The word *line* indicates a straight line.
4. Geometric figures lie in a plane.

Answers are on page 941.

DO YOUR FIGURING HERE.

1. If $\frac{1}{x}+\frac{1}{x}=8$, then $x=$?

A. $\frac{1}{4}$
B. $\frac{1}{2}$
C. 1
D. 2
E. 4

2. If $x=2$ and $y=-1$, then $3x-4y=$?

F. -5
G. -1
H. 0
J. 2
K. 10

3. In a certain school, there are 600 boys and 400 girls. If 20 percent of the boys and 30 percent of the girls are on the honor roll, how many of the students are on the honor roll?

A. 120
B. 175
C. 240
D. 250
E. 280

GO ON TO THE NEXT PAGE.

4. If p, q, r, s, and t are whole numbers, the expression $t(r(p + q) + s)$ must be an even number when which of the 5 numbers is even?

F. p
G. q
H. r
J. s
K. t

5. A student conducting a lab experiment finds that the population of flies in a bottle increases by a certain multiple from week to week. If the pattern shown in the table continues, how many flies can the student expect to find in the bottle in week 5?

Results of Biology Project Conducted by Student X					
Week	1	2	3	4	5
# of Flies in Bottle	3	12	48	192	?

A. 195
B. 240
C. 384
D. 564
E. 768

6. At a school assembly, 3 students are each scheduled to give a short speech. In how many different orders can the speeches be scheduled?

F. 12
G. 9
H. 6
J. 4
K. 3

DO YOUR FIGURING HERE.

GO ON TO THE NEXT PAGE.

7. If points P and Q lie in the xy-plane and have the coordinates shown below, what is the midpoint of $\overline{PQ}$?

DO YOUR FIGURING HERE.

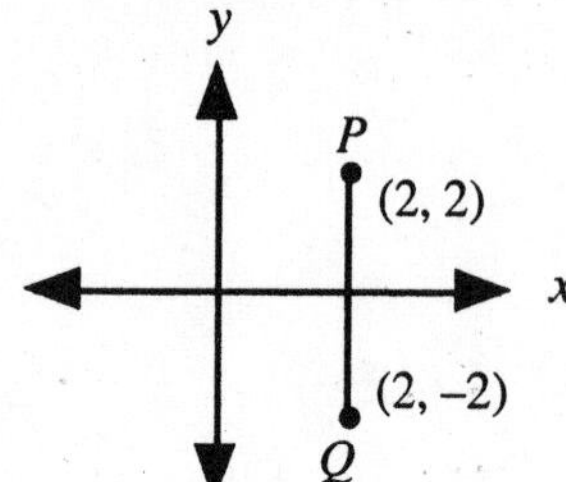

A. (-2, 0)
B. (-2, 2)
C. (0, 2)
D. (2, 0)
E. (2, 2)

8. If $xy = |xy|$ and $xy \neq 0$, which of the following CANNOT be true?

F. $x > y > 0$
G. $y > x > 0$
H. $x > 0 > y$
J. $0 > x > y$
K. $0 > y > x$

9. In the scale drawing of the floor of a rectangular room *shown* below, the scale used was 1 centimeter = 4 meters. What is the actual area, in square meters, of the floor of the room?

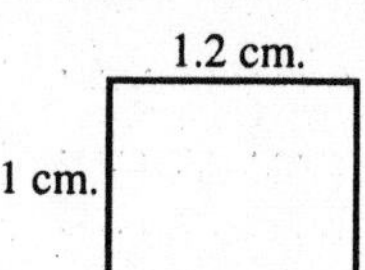

A. 9.6
B. 13.6
C. 15
D. 19.2
E. 38.4

10. If $30{,}000 \cdot 20 = 6 \cdot 10^n$, then $n = ?$

F. 4
G. 5
H. 6
J. 7
K. 8

GO ON TO THE NEXT PAGE.

11. Karen purchased 4 pounds of candy, which was a mix of chocolates and caramels. If chocolates cost \$3 per pound and caramels cost \$2 per pound, and if Karen spent a total of \$10.00, how many pounds of chocolates did she buy?

A. 1
B. 2
C. 2.5
D. 3
E. 3.5

DO YOUR FIGURING HERE.

12. The average of Al's scores on 3 tests was 80. If the average of his scores on the first 2 tests was also 80, what was his score on the third test?

F. 90
G. 85
H. 80
J. 75
K. 72

13. A book contains 10 photographs, some in color and some in black-and-white. Each of the following could be the ratio of color to black-and-white photographs EXCEPT:

A. 9:1
B. 4:1
C. 5:2
D. 3:2
E. 1:1

14. If $\frac{4}{5} = \frac{x}{4}$, then $x = ?$

F. 5
G. $\frac{16}{5}$
H. $\frac{5}{4}$
J. $\frac{4}{5}$
K. $\frac{5}{16}$

GO ON TO THE NEXT PAGE.

15. In the figure below, 3 equilateral triangles have a common vertex. How many degrees is $x+y+z$?

DO YOUR FIGURING HERE.

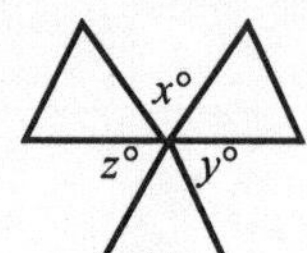

A. 60
B. 90
C. 120
D. 180
E. 240

16. Peter spent $\frac{1}{4}$ of his allowance on Monday and $\frac{1}{3}$ of the remainder on Tuesday. What part of the allowance does Peter still have?

F. $\frac{1}{12}$
G. $\frac{1}{4}$
H. $\frac{1}{2}$
J. $\frac{3}{4}$
K. $\frac{11}{12}$

17. If 100 identical bricks weigh p pounds, then how many pounds do 20 bricks weigh in terms of p?

A. $\frac{p}{20}$
B. $\frac{p}{5}$
C. $20p$
D. $\frac{5}{p}$
E. $\frac{20}{p}$

18. If the distances between points P, Q, and R are equal, which of the following could be true?

I. P, Q, and R are points on a circle with center O.
II. P and Q are points on a circle with center R.
III. P, Q, and R are vertices of an equilateral triangle.

F. I only
G. I and II only
H. I and III only
J. II and III only
K. I, II, and III

GO ON TO THE NEXT PAGE.

19. In the table below, the percent *increase* in the price of the item was greatest during which of the following periods?

Year	1950	1955	1960	1965	1970	1975
Price	$2	$4	$7	$12	$20	$30

A. 1950-1955
B. 1955-1960
C. 1960-1965
D. 1965-1970
E. 1970-1975

20. Which of the following is a factorization of $x^2 + 4x - 12$?

F. $(x - 6)(x + 2)$
G. $(x - 4)(x + 3)$
H. $(x - 2)(x + 6)$
J. $(x + 2)(x + 6)$
K. $(x + 3)(x + 4)$

21. Two cartons weigh $3x - 2$ and $2x - 3$. If the average weight of the cartons is 10, the heavier carton weighs how much more than the lighter carton?

A. 2
B. 4
C. 5
D. 6
E. 10

22. A group of 15 students took a test that was scored from 0 to 100. If 10 students scored 75 or more on the test, what is the lowest possible value for the average score of all 15 students?

F. 25
G. 50
H. 70
J. 75
K. 90

DO YOUR FIGURING HERE.

GO ON TO THE NEXT PAGE.

DO YOUR FIGURING HERE.

23. For all real numbers x, 16^x is equal to which of the following expressions?

A. x^{16}
B. 2^{3x}
C. 4^{2x}
D. 8^{2x}
E. 8^{4x}

24. If the figure below is a square, what is the perimeter of the figure?

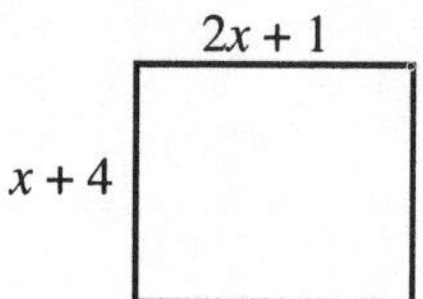

F. 28
G. 16
H. 9
J. 3
K. 2

25. If a certain rectangle has a length that is 2 times its width, what is the ratio of the area of the rectangle to the area of an isosceles right triangle with a hypotenuse equal to the width of the rectangle?

A. $\frac{1}{8}$
B. $\frac{1}{4}$
C. $\frac{1}{2}$
D. $\frac{4}{1}$
E. $\frac{8}{1}$

26. In the coordinate plane, what is the shortest distance between the point with (x, y) coordinates $(1, 3)$ and the line with the equation $x = -2$?

F. 1
G. 3
H. 4
J. 6
K. 9

GO ON TO THE NEXT PAGE.

27. If 5 pounds of coffee cost $12, how many pounds of coffee can be purchased for $30?

A. 7.2
B. 10
C. 12.5
D. 15
E. 18

DO YOUR FIGURING HERE.

28. If the 2 triangles below are equilateral, what is the ratio of the perimeter of the smaller to that of the larger?

F. $\frac{1}{36}$
G. $\frac{1}{15}$
H. $\frac{1}{9}$
J. $\frac{1}{4}$
K. $\frac{1}{3}$

29. If $f(x) = -3x^3 + 3x^2 - 4x + 8$, then $f(-2) = ?$

A. 16
B. 22
C. 28
D. 36
E. 52

30. A merchant pays $120 wholesale for a dress and then adds a 30% markup. Two weeks later, the dress is put on sale at 40% off the retail price. What is the sale price of the dress?

F. $102.40
G. $97.30
H. $93.60
J. $89.40
K. $87.00

GO ON TO THE NEXT PAGE.

DO YOUR FIGURING HERE.

31. If $\frac{1}{3}$ of a number is 2 more than $\frac{1}{5}$ of the number, then which of the following equations can be used to find the number x?

A. $\frac{1}{3}x + 2 = -\frac{1}{5}x$
B. $\frac{1}{3}x - 2 = -\frac{1}{5}x$
C. $\frac{1}{3}x - \frac{1}{5}x = 2$
D. $\frac{1}{3}x - \frac{1}{5}x = -2$
E. $5(\frac{1}{3}x + 2) = 0$

32. In the figure below, the triangle is equilateral and has a perimeter of 12 centimeters. What is the perimeter, in centimeters, of the square?

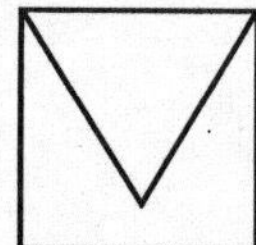

F. 9
G. 12
H. 16
J. 20
K. 24

33. If one solution of the equation $12x^2 + kx = 6$ is $\frac{2}{3}$, then $k = ?$

A. 1
B. $\frac{3}{2}$
C. 2
D. 5
E. 9

34. If a 6-sided polygon has 2 sides of length $x - 2y$ each and 4 sides of length $2x + y$ each, what is its perimeter?

F. $6x - 6y$
G. $6x - y$
H. $5x$
J. $6x$
K. $10x$

GO ON TO THE NEXT PAGE.

35. At the first stop on her route, a driver unloaded $\frac{2}{5}$ of the packages in her van. After she unloaded another 3 packages at her next stop, $\frac{1}{2}$ of the original number of packages in the van remained. How many packages were in the van before the first delivery?

DO YOUR FIGURING HERE.

A. 10
B. 18
C. 25
D. 30
E. 36

36. For all x and y, $12x^3y^2 - 8x^2y^3 = ?$

F. $4x^2y^2(2xy)$
G. $4x^2y^2(3xy)$
H. $4x^2y^2(3x - 2y)$
J. $2x^2y^2(4x - y)$
K. $x^3y^3(12xy - 8xy)$

37. $\frac{1}{1+\frac{1}{x}}$ equals which of the following expressions?

A. $x + 1$
B. $\frac{1}{x+1}$
C. $\frac{x}{x+1}$
D. $\frac{x+1}{x}$
E. $x^2 + x$

38. If S is 150% of T, what percent of $S + T$ is T?

F. $33\frac{1}{3}\%$
G. 40%
H. 50%
J. 75%
K. 80%

GO ON TO THE NEXT PAGE.

39. In ΔPQR, the lengths of $\overline{PQ}$ and $\overline{QR}$ are equal, and the measure of $\angle Q$ is 3 times that of $\angle P$. What is the measure of $\angle R$?

A. 24°
B. 30°
C. 36°
D. 45°
E. 60°

DO YOUR FIGURING HERE.

40. If the cost of b books is d dollars, which of the following equations can be used to find the cost, C, in dollars, of x books at the same rate?

F. $C = xd$
G. $C = \frac{dx}{b}$
H. $C = \frac{bd}{x}$
J. $C = bx$
K. $C = \frac{bx}{d}$

41. An article is on sale for 25% off its regular price of \$64. If the merchant must also collect a 5% sales tax on this reduced price, what is the total cost of the article including sales tax?

A. \$42.10
B. \$44.20
C. \$49.60
D. \$50.40
E. \$56.70

42. If $\frac{x}{z} = k$ and $\frac{y}{z} = k - 1$, then $x = ?$

F. $y - 1$
G. $y + 1$
H. $y + z$
J. $z - y$
K. $\frac{y}{z}$

GO ON TO THE NEXT PAGE.

43. If x is 25 percent of y, then y is what percent of x?

A. 400%
B. 300%
C. 250%
D. 125%
E. 75%

DO YOUR FIGURING HERE.

44. If x is an integer that is a multiple of both 9 and 5, which of the following *must* be true?

I. x is equal to 45.
II. x is a multiple of 15.
III. x is odd.

F. I only
G. II only
H. III only
J. II and III only
K. I, II, and III

45. If each edge of a cube is 2 units long, what is the distance from any vertex to the cube's center?

A. $\frac{\sqrt{2}}{2}$
B. $\sqrt{3}$
C. $2\sqrt{2}$
D. $2\sqrt{3}$
E. $\frac{3}{2}$

GO ON TO THE NEXT PAGE.

DO YOUR FIGURING HERE.

46. The figure below shows 2 circular cylinders, C and C'. If $r = kr'$ and $h = kh'$, what is the ratio of $\frac{\text{Volume of } C}{\text{Volume of } C'}$. (Volume of a cylinder = $\pi r^2 h$.)

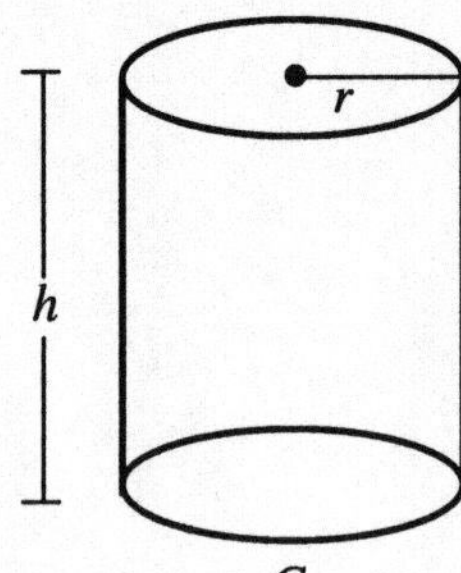

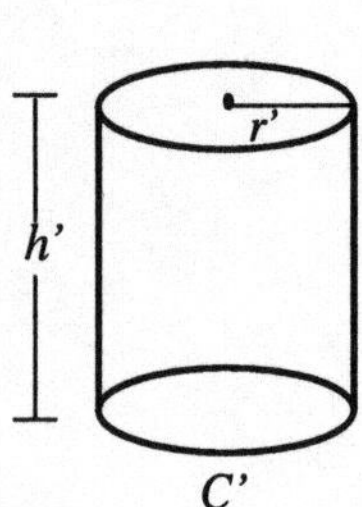

F. $\frac{1}{\pi}$

G. π

H. $k\pi$

J. $\frac{1}{k^3}$

K. k^3

47. In the figure below, if the triangle has an area of 1 square unit, what is the area of the circle, in square units?

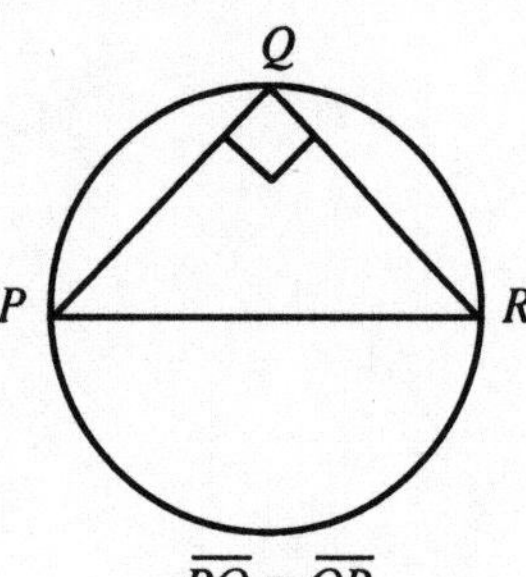

$\overline{PQ} = \overline{QR}$

A. π

B. 2π

C. $2\sqrt{3}\pi$

D. 4π

E. $4\sqrt{3}\pi$

GO ON TO THE NEXT PAGE.

48. In the figure below, the radius of the circles is 1 inch. What is the perimeter, in inches, of the shaded part of the figure?

DO YOUR FIGURING HERE.

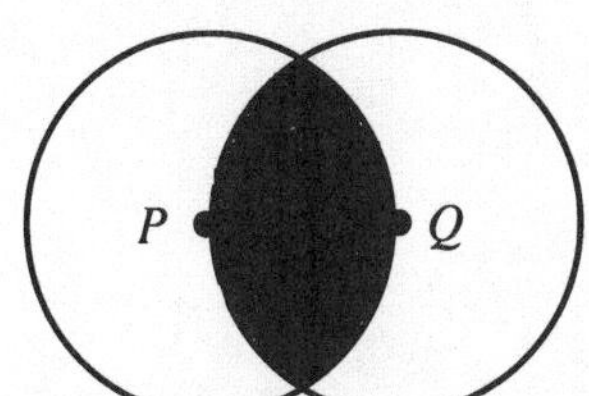

F. $\frac{4\pi}{3}$

G. π

H. $\frac{2\pi}{3}$

J. $\frac{\pi}{3}$

K. $\frac{\pi}{6}$

49. A student's final grade in a certain course is the average of his scores on 10 tests graded on a scale of 0 to 100, inclusive. For the first 6 tests, the student's scores averaged 83. If x is the student's final grade for the course, then which of the following is true?

A. $8.3 \leq x \leq 83.0$
B. $49.8 \leq x \leq 83.0$
C. $49.8 \leq x \leq 89.8$
D. $54.7 \leq x \leq 89.8$
E. $83.0 \leq x \leq 89.8$

50. What is the multiplicative inverse of the complex number $2 - i$?

F. $2 + i$

G. $i - 2$

H. $\frac{2+i}{3}$

J. $\frac{2-i}{3}$

K. $\frac{2+i}{5}$

GO ON TO THE NEXT PAGE.

DO YOUR FIGURING HERE.

51. $\log_3\sqrt{3} = ?$

A. -1

B. $\frac{1}{3}$

C. $\frac{1}{2}$

D. $\frac{2}{3}$

E. 2

52. If $f(x) = (x - 1)^2 + 2$, then what value for x creates the minimum value for $f(x)$?

F. -3
G. -2
H. 0
J. 1
K. 2

53. If, for all n, $2^n + 2^n + 2^n + 2^n = x(2^{n+1})$, then $x = ?$

A. 2
B. 4
C. 2^n
D. 2^{2n}
E. 2^{n+1}

54. If $f(k) = k^2 + 2k + 1$, then what is the set of all k for which $f(k) = f(-k)$?

F. {0}
G. {1}
H. {2}
J. {1, 2}
K. All real numbers

55. What is $\lim_{x \to 1} \frac{x^2 - 1}{x - 1}$?

A. -1
B. 0
C. 1
D. 2
E. The limit does not exist.

GO ON TO THE NEXT PAGE.

56. If $0 \leq x \leq \pi$ and $\cos x = -1$, then $\cos \frac{x}{2} = ?$

DO YOUR FIGURING HERE.

F. $-\frac{\sqrt{3}}{2}$

G. $-\frac{1}{2}$

H. 0

J. $\frac{1}{2}$

K. $\frac{\sqrt{3}}{2}$

57. Which of the following defines the range of the function $f(x) = \frac{1-x}{x}$?

A. All real numbers
B. All real numbers except -1
C. All real numbers except 0
D. All real numbers except 1
E. All real numbers greater than -1

58. Which of the following graphs represents the equations $x = 3(\sin \theta)$ and $y = 2(\cos \theta)$?

F.

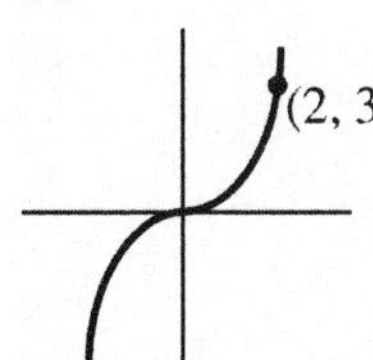

J.

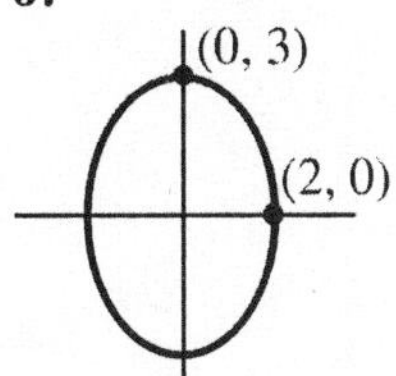

G.

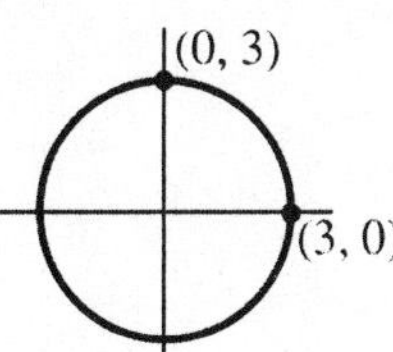

K.

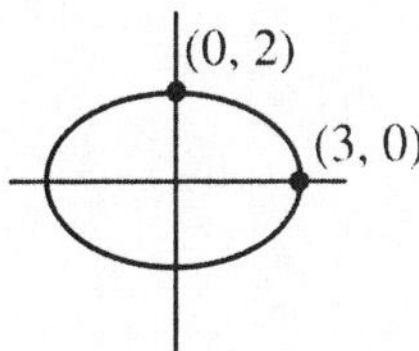

H.

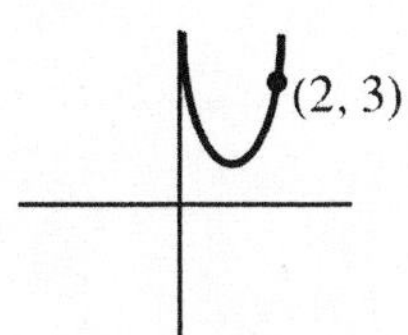

GO ON TO THE NEXT PAGE.

59. For all θ such that $0° < \theta° < 90°$, which of the following is equal to $\sin \theta \cdot \csc \theta$?

DO YOUR FIGURING HERE.

A. 1
B. $\sqrt{2}$
C. $\tan \theta$
D. $\cot \theta$
E. $\sec \theta$

60. In ΔABC below, the measures of $\angle ABC$, $\angle BCA$, and $\angle CAB$ are 90°, 40°, and 50°, respectively. If $\overline{AB}$ is 3 units long, how many units long is $\overline{BC}$?

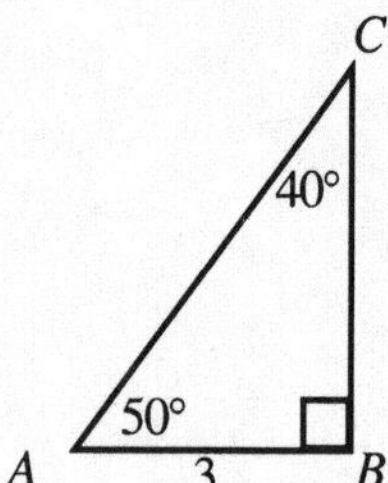

F. 4
G. 5
H. sin 10°
J. 3(tan 50°)
K. 3(tan 40°)

END OF TEST 2.
STOP! DO NOT TURN THE PAGE UNTIL TOLD TO DO SO.
DO NOT RETURN TO THE PREVIOUS TEST.

3 3 3 3 3 3 3 3 3 3 3 3

READING TEST

35 Minutes—40 Items

DIRECTIONS: The passages presented in the test are each followed by a set of items. Read the passage and choose the best answer for each item. Fill in the corresponding oval on your bubble sheet. You may refer to the passage as often as necessary to answer the passage items.

Answers are on page 942.

Passage I

SOCIAL SCIENCE: This passage discusses Frederick Turner's hypothesis of the American Frontier.

In July of 1893, Frederick Jackson Turner, a historian from the University of Wisconsin, presented a paper to a group of historians convening in Chicago during the Columbian Exposition. Entitled "The Significance of the American Frontier in History," Turner's paper drew little immediate reaction. Yet no theory of history has had a greater influence on the direction and methodology of inquiry and the issues of debate in American history. Later historians took issue with some of Turner's interpretations; some of his own students were among those whose research proved certain of his views wrong. Yet these debates merely serve to illustrate the importance of Turner's hypothesis.

Turner's was an overarching hypothesis about how the settlement of the frontier had shaped the American experience and character. As with all general hypotheses in any field of study, it gave a coherent interpretation to many facts that had been largely ignored by historians up to that time.

Turner used statistical evidence from the 1880 census as the basis for a startling conclusion: Prior to 1880 there had been a frontier to be settled. By 1890, Turner pointed out, there was no longer any area of wilderness completely untouched by settlements. The frontier had disappeared. The passing of the frontier, Turner concluded, was a historic moment.

Turner further claimed that the frontier experience had produced a distinctively American character, which was not explainable simply as the predictable behavioral traits molded by English political institutions. Frontier settlers developed inquisitiveness, inventiveness, energy, and a great passion for freedom. These attributes defined a new American character—one evidenced in nationalism, independence, and democracy. This new sense of national identity derived from the fact that people from every section of the country mixed at the Western frontier. Economic independence could be traced to the fact that the settlers no longer depended on England for goods but had become self-sufficient. In addition, the frontier settlers, whose basic social unit was the family, enjoyed freedom from direct governmental interference. Frontier life thus reinforced the fundamental ideals of populist democracy.

In addition, Turner argued that the frontier fostered democracy in the cities of the East. The availability of free land at the frontier provided a "safety-valve" against possible social unrest: those discontented with social inequities and economic injustice could strike out and settle the free land available in frontier territories.

Turner's thesis was thus original in both what it said and in the methodology that Turner used in formulating it. Up to the time of Turner's essay, history had been essentially the history of politics. A Midwesterner, Turner challenged this traditional approach of Eastern historians by incorporating techniques of the social sciences, showing how factors of geography, economics, climate, and society influenced the development of the American West. Although now common among historians, at the time this interdisciplinary approach was novel.

GO ON TO THE NEXT PAGE.

1. Turner's essay challenged the views of:

A. frontier writers such as Mark Twain.
B. other American historians of his time.
C. sociologists.
D. European critics of America.

2. Turner's methods were original in that he:

F. utilized research techniques from a variety of other academic fields.
G. insulted other historians.
H. refused to encourage further research.
J. ignored the need for a unifying view.

3. Turner's evidence for the disappearance of the American frontier drew on:

A. interviews with settlers.
B. his reading of Karl Marx.
C. diaries.
D. the census of 1880.

4. Turner's essay affected:

F. the reputations of American historians in Europe.
G. future settlements in the West.
H. the way in which population was counted.
J. the subsequent focus of inquiry in American history.

5. One fact that would cast a doubtful light on Turner's view that the West was settled by individuals looking for escape from the pressures of Eastern city life would be if:

A. many Western towns had few inhabitants.
B. few people settled in mountain country.
C. much of the land in the West and Midwest was actually bought by wealthy land speculators from the East.
D. many people chose to settle along the banks of the Mississippi.

6. Which of the following, if true, would prove that Turner's "safety-valve" theory was false?

F. Population movements showed that more people actually left the farms for the cities than left cities to move to the frontier.
G. Much of the West had a desert climate.
H. The transcontinental railroad was completed in 1869.
J. The numbers of buffalo dropped markedly during the late nineteenth century.

7. A theory would best be defined as:

A. a foolish notion founded on questionable data.
B. an idle speculation that may have no basis in fact.
C. a hypothesis that explains a large number of isolated facts.
D. a somewhat questionable view of factual data.

8. America's frontier line moved essentially from:

F. the South to the East.
G. the West to the East.
H. the East to the West.
J. the North to the South.

9. The economic independence of Americans arose, Turner said, from the fact that:

A. Americans rarely bought anything.
B. many pioneers had few relatives left in Europe.
C. Americans were buying American goods rather than English goods.
D. few settlers ever voted in local elections.

10. Which of the following quotations captures the approach of historians at the time when Turner read his paper?

F. "This history of the world is but the biography of great men."
G. "History is past politics and politics is present history."
H. "Those who do not heed the lessons of history are doomed to repeat them."
J. "Anybody can make history. Only a great man can write it."

GO ON TO THE NEXT PAGE.

Passage II

HUMANITIES: In this passage, the author expresses his opinion regarding the role of philosophy.

The service of philosophy towards the human spirit is to startle it into sharp and eager observation. Every moment, and for that moment only, some form grows perfect in hand or face; some tone on the hills or the sea is choicer than the rest. Not the fruit of experience, but experience itself is the end. Only a counted number of pulses are given to us of a variegated, dramatic life. How shall we pass most quickly from point to point and be present always at the focus where the greatest number of vital forces unite in their purest energy?

To burn always with this hard, gemlike flame, to maintain this ecstasy, is success in life. It is only the roughness of the eye that makes any two persons, things, or situations seem alike. While all melts under our feet, we may well catch at any exquisite passion, or any knowledge that seems by a lifted horizon to set the spirit free for a moment, or any stirring of the senses, strange dyes, strange colors, curious odors, or work of the artist's hands or the faces of one's friends. Not to discriminate every moment some passionate attitude in those about us, and in the brilliancy of their gifts some tragic dividing of forces of their ways is, on this short day of the frost and sun, to sleep before evening. With this sense of the splendor of our experience and of its awful brevity, gathering all we are into one desperate effort to see and touch, we shall hardly have time to make theories about the things we see and touch.

We are all under sentence of death but with a sort of indefinite reprieve; we have an interval and then our place knows us no more. Some spend this interval in listlessness, others in high passions, the wisest—at least among the "children of this world"—in art and song. Our one chance lies in expanding this interval—in getting as many pulsations as possible into the given time. Great passions may give us this quickened sense of life, ecstasy, sorrow, and love, the various forms of enthusiastic activity. Of this wisdom, the poetic passion, the desire of beauty, the love of art for art's sake has most; for art comes to you professing frankly to give nothing but the highest quality to your moments as they pass, and simply for the sake of those moments.

11. Which of the following best describes the overall structure of the passage?

A. The author raises a question and then provides an answer.
B. The author presents a theory, which he then proves.
C. The author studies a widely held belief and then rejects it.
D. The author defines a term and then provides examples.

12. In the passage, the author uses the word "pulsations" (line 35) to mean:

F. children.
G. lives.
H. death.
J. experiences.

13. According to the author, the function of art is to:

A. depict reality accurately.
B. stimulate strong emotions.
C. encourage social reform.
D. express the artist's feelings.

14. With which of the following statements would the author most likely agree?

F. A person's lifetime is merely preparation for what comes after death.
G. Only an artist can truly enjoy life.
H. The original experience is more important than the memory of it.
J. A perceptive person understands that all experience is repetitious.

15. The tone of the passage can best be described as:

A. impassioned.
B. scholarly.
C. informative.
D. speculative.

GO ON TO THE NEXT PAGE.

16. In the context of this passage, the phrase "short day of the frost and sun" (lines 23-24) refers to:

    F. the transient effect of poetry.
    G. a brief moment of passion.
    H. the life of a person.
    J. stimulation of the senses.

17. The phrase "awful brevity" (line 26) means that:

    A. philosophy is not really useful.
    B. art may not satisfy everyone.
    C. life is short.
    D. passion is the greatest virtue.

18. The "children of this world" (line 33) are NOT:

    F. passionate.
    G. wise.
    H. lovers of art and song.
    J. listless.

19. According to the author, the greatest passion is the love of:

    A. beauty.
    B. one's spouse.
    C. wealth.
    D. security.

20. The phrase "then our place knows us no more" (lines 30-31) means that we:

    F. move to another town.
    G. have children.
    H. die.
    J. divorce.

GO ON TO THE NEXT PAGE.

Passage III

NATURAL SCIENCE: This passage explains how energy becomes usable through photosynthesis.

Every living cell must acquire energy in a usable form. According to the First Law of Thermodynamics, energy, which is the capacity for doing work, can be converted from one form into another without any net gain or loss. An organism must have an outside source of usable energy. The Second Law of Thermodynamics states that every energy transformation reduces the free (usable) energy of the system. Living cells primarily use chemical energy derived from complex organic compounds.

Photosynthesis is the process by which green plants transform sunlight into a usable energy source. Green plants utilize the energy of light to combine carbon dioxide with water to form organic material (sugar) and oxygen.

$$6CO_2 + 12H_2O + \text{light} \xrightarrow{\text{chlorophyll}} 6O_2 + C_6H_{12}O_6 + 6H_2O$$

Photosynthesis is a reduction reaction. Reduction is the addition of one or more electrons to an atom or molecule. Oxidation is the removal of electrons from an atom or molecule. Reduction stores energy, while oxidation releases it. Biological systems rely on the addition or removal of an electron from hydrogen. Photosynthesis is based on two key processes. Light energy is trapped and stored, and hydrogen atoms are transformed from water to carbon dioxide to form carbohydrate.

Photosynthesis takes place within the chloroplasts. The pigments within the chloroplasts are precisely arranged within the membranes of flattened sacs called thylakoids. Thylakoids often lie close together in sacks called grana. The light reactions of photosynthesis take place within the thylakoid membranes, while the dark reactions take place in the colorless matrix (stroma) surrounding the thylakoids.

Different wavelengths of light, especially red and blue light, are trapped by various pigment molecules contained within chloroplasts. When a photon of light strikes a pigment molecule and is absorbed, the energy is transferred to an electron, which is raised to a high-energy state. A specialized form of chlorophyll passes the energized electron to an acceptor molecule, X, which has a high affinity for electrons. X passes the electron to a series of acceptor molecules, each at a slightly lower energy level. After being passed from molecule to molecule, the electron may return to the chlorophyll from which it started. Some of the energy released as the electron is passed down the energy gradient is used to synthesize the compound *ATP* from *ADP* and inorganic phosphate.

ATP is a universal energy packet used by cells to do work. ATP is synthesized from ADP and inorganic phosphate in a process called phosphorylation. Phosphorylation is a very high energy demanding process. *Cyclic photophosphorylation* occurs when the energy used for ATP synthesis comes from light-energized electrons as they are returned to the chlorophyll molecules from which they originated.

Another process that occurs in green plants is noncyclic photophosphorylation. In this reaction, some electrons are passed from the chlorophyll to a different type of acceptor molecule called $NAPD_{ox}$, which retains the electron and is therefore reduced to become $NAPD_{re}$.

The ATP and $NAPD_{re}$ produced in the light reaction are used to reduce carbon dioxide to carbohydrate in a series of reactions called the *Calvin cycle* (dark reaction). Basically, a five-carbon sugar, ribulose diphosphate (RuDP), is combined with CO_2. This process is called carboxyilation. The products are then phosphorylated by ATP and reduced by $NAPD_{re}$ to form PGAL, a three-carbon sugar.

Under certain conditions, the very same enzyme that under more agreeable conditions would facilitate its carboxyilation oxidizes RuDP. This process, called photorespiration, is seemingly a wasteful process since no ATP is created. Photorespiration predominates over photosynthesis when CO_2 levels are low and O_2 levels are high.

Some tropical angiosperm plants have a unique leaf structure known as *Kranz* anatomy (C_4 plants). In Kranz plants, the bundle-sheath cells have numerous chloroplasts (other plants usually do not), and the mesophyll cells are clustered in a ring-like arrangement around the bundle sheath. These plants can carry out photosynthesis under conditions of high temperature and concentrated light, when loss of water induces closure of the stomata. When the stomata close, the concentration of CO_2 in the air spaces inside the leaf falls, and the concentration of O_2 rises. Under these conditions most plants (C_3) would experience a net loss of CO_2 because of photorespiration. Kranz plants (C_4) do not because of their specialized way of initially fixing CO_2. They combine CO_2 with a three-carbon compound in the mesophyll cells to form a four-carbon compound that passes into the bundle-sheath cells, where the CO_2 is regenerated. Therefore, Kranz plants can maintain a CO_2 level in the bundle-sheath cells that allows carboxyilation of RuDP in the Calvin cycle to predominate over its oxidation in photorespiration.

GO ON TO THE NEXT PAGE.

21. According to this passage, "the capacity for doing work" is the definition of:

A. photosynthesis.
B. energy.
C. oxidation.
D. thermodynamics.

22. In the equation in line 16, $C_6H_{12}O_6$ apparently names:

F. oxygen.
G. carbon dioxide.
H. a sugar.
J. photosynthesis.

23. Which of these could be considered the reverse of reduction?

A. Oxidation
B. Photosynthesis
C. Transformation
D. Phosphorylation

24. Which of the following conclusions is (are) suggested by the third paragraph?

I. Photosynthesis involves the addition of electrons.
II. Photosynthesis involves action on hydrogen.
III. Photosynthesis is a form of energy release.

F. I only
G. II only
H. III only
J. I and II only

25. The fifth paragraph deals mainly with:

A. defining terms related to plant growth.
B. comparing one reduction reaction to another.
C. explaining the process of photosynthesis.
D. expressing the author's opinion.

26. Which of the following statements is NOT true about ATP?

F. It mixes with phosphate to make ADP.
G. It is created through phosphorylation.
H. It serves a purpose in the Calvin cycle.
J. It is used by cells to do work.

27. The Calvin cycle involves:

A. the combination of carbon dioxide and a five-carbon sugar, with a three-carbon sugar as the result.
B. the combination of oxygen and a three-carbon sugar, with a five-carbon sugar as the result.
C. a mix of ATP and sugar to create carbon dioxide.
D. a reduction of carbohydrate to form carbon dioxide.

28. By "more agreeable conditions" (line 73), the author probably means:

F. conditions that produce higher levels of oxygen.
G. conditions that produce higher levels of CO_2.
H. conditions with higher temperatures.
J. conditions with longer growing periods.

29. Which of the following statements names a difference between photorespiration and photosynthesis?

I. Photorespiration involves RuDP.
II. In photosynthesis, ATP is synthesized.
III. Photorespiration is a reduction reaction.

A. I only
B. I and II only
C. II and III only
D. I, II, and III

30. Unlike the preceding paragraphs, the final paragraph discusses:

F. plants that do not photosynthesize.
G. living matter other than plants.
H. plants with an unusual structure.
J. plants that transform carbon dioxide into carbohydrate.

GO ON TO THE NEXT PAGE.

Passage IV

PROSE FICTION: In this passage, a young country man, alone in town for the first time, tries to find a relative, Major Molineux.

It was near nine o'clock of a moonlight evening, when a boat crossed the ferry with a single passenger, who had obtained his conveyance at that unusual hour by the promise of extra fare. He was a youth of barely eighteen years, evidently country-bred, and now upon his first visit to town. The youth finally drew from his pocket a little province bill of five shillings, which, in depreciation in that sort of currency, satisfied the ferryman's demand with the addition of a sex-angular piece of parchment, valued at three pence. He then walked forward into the town with as light a step as if his day's journey had not already exceeded thirty miles and with as eager an eye as if he were entering London city, instead of the little metropolis of a New England colony. However, before Robin had proceeded far, it occurred to him that he knew not whither to direct his steps; so he paused, and looked up and down the narrow street, scrutinizing the small and mean wooden buildings that were scattered on either side.

"This low hovel cannot be my kinsman's dwelling," thought he, "nor yonder old house; and truly I see none hereabouts that might be worthy of him. It would have been wise to inquire my way of the ferryman and doubtless he would have gone with me, and earned a shilling from the Major for his pains. But the next man I meet will do as well."

He resumed his walk, and was glad to perceive that the street now became wide, and the houses were more respectable in their appearance. He soon discerned a figure moving on moderately in advance, and he hastened his steps to overtake it. Robin laid hold of the skirt of the man's old coat, just when the light from the open door and windows of a barber's shop fell upon both their figures.

"Good evening to you, honored sir," said he, making a low bow, and still retaining hold of the skirt. "I pray you tell me whereabouts is the dwelling of my kinsman, Major Molineux."

The citizen answered him in a tone of excessive anger and annoyance. "Let go my garment, fellow! I tell you, I know not the man you speak of. What! I have the authority, I have—hem, hem—authority; and if this be the respect you show for your betters, your feet shall be brought acquainted with the stocks by daylight, tomorrow morning!"

Robin released the old man's skirt, and hastened away, pursued by an ill-mannered roar of laughter from the barber's shop. He was at first considerably surprised by the result of his question, but, being a shrewd youth, he soon thought himself able to account for the mystery.

"This is some country representative," was his conclusion, "who has never seen the inside of my kinsman's door, and lacks the breeding to answer a stranger civilly. Ah, Robin, Robin! Even the barber's boys laugh at you for choosing such a guide! You will be wiser in time, friend Robin."

31. In the final paragraph, the young man is talking to:

A. the Major.
B. the man in the coat.
C. himself.
D. the barbers.

32. The total cost of the young man's passage on the ferryboat was:

F. five shillings.
G. three pence.
H. five shillings less three pence.
J. five shillings plus three pence.

33. The young man believes that his relative is a:

A. barber.
B. wealthy person.
C. constable.
D. builder.

34. The incidents described in the passage take place:

F. in the late morning.
G. in the early afternoon.
H. in the late afternoon.
J. at night.

35. The passage suggests that thirty miles is:

A. a long distance to travel in one day.
B. easily traveled in a single day.
C. easily traveled in an hour.
D. a long ferryboat ride.

GO ON TO THE NEXT PAGE.

36. The young man believes that the barbers laughed at him because:

    F. his clothes clearly show that he is from the country.
    G. he asked a question of a stranger who obviously would not know the answer.
    H. he badly needs a haircut and a shave.
    J. the stranger he questioned is actually the man he is looking for.

37. The scenes in the passage are most likely set in which of the following time periods?

    A. Eighteenth century
    B. Nineteenth century
    C. Early twentieth century
    D. Present time

38. The young man approaches the stranger in the coat:

    F. respectfully.
    G. rudely.
    H. coyly.
    J. stealthily.

39. The young man is the only passenger on the ferryboat because:

    A. he paid the ferryman extra for a private charter.
    B. no one else was traveling at that hour.
    C. the Major had sent the boat especially for him.
    D. the ferryman was a good friend of the young man.

40. Just after he gets off the ferry, the young man finds himself in a:

    F. poorer neighborhood.
    G. wealthy neighborhood.
    H. forest.
    J. large city.

END OF TEST 3.
STOP! DO NOT TURN THE PAGE UNTIL TOLD TO DO SO.
DO NOT RETURN TO A PREVIOUS TEST.

4 4 4 4 4 4 4 4 4 4 4 4

SCIENCE REASONING TEST

35 Minutes—40 Items

DIRECTIONS: The passages presented in the test are each followed by a set of items. Read the passage and choose the best answer for each item. Fill in the corresponding oval on your bubble sheet. You may refer to the passage as often as necessary to answer the passage items.

Warning: Calculator use is not permitted on this test.

Answers are on page 942.

Passage I

The chart below shows several physical properties of compounds called alkanes, which are long "chains" of carbons to which hydrogen atoms are attached. As an example, the compound propane, which has three carbons, has the structural formula:

$$CH_3—CH_2—CH_3$$

PHYSICAL PROPERTIES OF STRAIGHT-CHAIN ALKANES

Name	*# of Carbons*	*Boiling Point (° C)*	*Melting Point (° C)*	*Density*
methane	1	-162	-183	0.47
ethane	2	-89	-183	0.57
propane	3	-42	-188	0.50
butane	4	0	-138	0.58
pentane	5	36	-130	0.56
hexane	6	69	-95	0.66
heptane	7	98	-91	0.68
octane	8	126	-57	0.70
nonane	9	151	-54	0.72
decane	10	174	-30	0.74

1. The general trends shown in the chart are:

   A. as the number of carbons increases, all properties increase in value (with occasional exceptions).
   B. as the number of carbons increases, boiling points and melting points decrease, while density increases.
   C. as the number of carbons increases, density decreases and other properties increase.
   D. as the number of carbons increases, all properties decrease.

2. The change in boiling point is greatest:

   F. from methane to ethane.
   G. from propane to butane.
   H. from butane to pentane.
   J. from nonane to decane.

3. For alkanes with more than one carbon, the change in melting point from one alkane to the next:

   A. tends to be greater f[illegible] an even number of carbons to the nex[illegible] number.
   B. tends to be grea[illegible] an odd number of carbons to the next even number.
   C. is similar, whether from an even number of carbons to the next odd number, or from an odd number of carbons to the next even number.
   D. Cannot be determined from the given info[illegible]nati[illegible]

GO ON TO THE NEXT PAGE.

4. Considering the alkane properties listed, if alkane *X* has a higher boiling point than alkane *Y*, then without exception, it must also have a:

F. higher melting point.
G. higher density.
H. higher number of carbons.
J. longer name.

5. The greatest percentage increase in density occurs from:

A. ethane to propane.
B. propane to butane.
C. pentane to hexane.
D. hexane to heptane.

GO ON TO THE NEXT PAGE.

Passage II

A student performs a set of physics laboratory experiments, in which objects of different masses glide "frictionlessly" along a smooth surface, collide, and then continue to glide. The momentum of each object is defined as its "mass • velocity." The momentum of a system of objects is the sum of the individual momentums.

Experiment 1: The light mass moves toward the stationary, heavy mass, and both stick together and continue to move. Table 1 shows the relevant information.

Table 1

	Object 1	*Object 2*
Mass	2 kg	5 kg
Initial velocity	4 m/sec	0 m/sec
Final velocity	1.14 m/sec	1.14 m/sec

Experiment 2: The student performs a similar experiment in which the objects do not stick together, but collide "elastically"—that is, rebound from each other with no loss in energy. Table 2 shows the results.

Table 2

	Object 1	*Object 2*
Mass	2 kg	5 kg
Initial velocity	4 m/sec	0 m/sec
Final velocity	-1.71 m/sec	2.29 m/sec

(Note that positive velocities indicate motion to the right, negative velocities indicate motion to the left.)

6. In Experiment 1, the momentum of Object 1 before the collision is:

   F. 0 kg • m/sec.
   G. 2 kg • m/sec.
   H. 4 kg • m/sec.
   J. 8 kg • m/sec.

7. After the collision in Experiment 1, the momentum of the combined masses is:

   A. much less than the initial total momentum of the two masses.
   B. about equal to the initial total momentum of the two masses.
   C. much greater than the initial total momentum of the two masses.
   D. Cannot be determined from the given information

8. After the collision in Experiment 2:

   F. both objects are moving to the right.
   G. both objects are moving to the left.
   H. Object 1 is moving to the left and Object 2 to the right.
   J. Object 1 is moving to the right and Object 2 to the left.

9. In Experiment 2, if Object 2 were replaced by another object that was far more massive than Object 1, its final velocity would be closest to:

   A. 4.0 m/sec.
   B. 2.3 m/sec.
   C. -1.7 m/sec.
   D. 0 m/sec.

10. Under the conditions described in the previous item, the final velocity of Object 1 would be closest to:

    F. –2 m/sec.
    G. -1.7 m/sec.
    H. 0 m/sec.
    J. 2 m/sec.

11. Kinetic energy is defined as $\frac{1}{2}(mv^2)$. During the collision described in Experiment 1, the kinetic energy of Object 1:

    A. increases.
    B. remains the same.
    C. decreases.
    D. Cannot be determined from the given information.

GO ON TO THE NEXT PAGE.

Passage III

The table below shows how an increase (+) or a decrease (-) in one or more plant hormones and environmental factors can affect various plant activities. The activities listed on the left occur when the combinations of conditions to the right exist at the same time. Hormones (H) are numbered; *e.g.*, H_1, H_2, *etc.*

Activities	H_1	H_2	H_3	H_4	H_5	*Day Length*	*Temperature*
Plant growth	+ +		+ +				
No plant growth (1)	+ +		+ +	+ +			
No plant growth (2)	+ +		+ +		+ +		
Seed germination			+ +				
Flowering			+ +		+ +	(+ + *or* - -)†	+ +
Flower drop-off	- -	+ +					
Fruit drop-off	- -	+ +					
Leaf drop-off	- -	+ +					- -

†Different species of plants require different combinations of light and darkness to stimulate flowering.

12. Based on the information in the table, a drop in temperature will help cause:

F. flowering.
G. loss of leaves, fruit, and flowers.
H. loss of leaves only.
J. seed germination.

13. The hormones that can inhibit (prevent) plant growth are:

A. 1 and 3.
B. 1, 3, and 4.
C. 1, 3, and 5.
D. 4 and 5.

14. Which conclusion is correct about the various factors affecting plant activities?

F. Hormone 3 influences more plant activities than any other factor.
G. Seed germination is influenced by the fewest factors, whereas flowering is influenced by the most.
H. For Hormone 1 to have an effect on any plant activity, it must be changing in the opposite direction of at least one other hormone.
J. Temperature changes can affect all plant activities.

GO ON TO THE NEXT PAGE.

15. Which activity would most likely be affected by changing a houseplant's growing conditions from twelve hours of light per twelve hours of darkness to constant light?

I. Plant growth
II. Loss of leaves
III. Flowering

A. I only
B. II only
C. III only
D. I and III only

16. Which statement best describes the relationship between Hormone 1 and Hormone 2?

F. Hormone 2 must change in the opposite direction of Hormone 1 for plant growth to occur.
G. When Hormone 1 and Hormone 2 affect a plant activity together, no other factors influence that activity.
H. As Hormone 1 increases, Hormone 2 always decreases; and as Hormone 1 decreases, Hormone 2 always increases.
J. Hormone 2 only affects plant activities when Hormone 1 is also involved.

GO ON TO THE NEXT PAGE.

Passage IV

In order to examine the factors that affect the flow of substances across cell membranes, three experiments were carried out. In each experiment, semi-permeable bags (bags with small pores that allow some substances to pass through, but not others) were partially filled with a fluid, tied, and then weighed (first weighing). The bags were then submerged into a large beaker of water, and at 10-minute intervals, removed from the beaker of water and re-weighed.

Experiment 1: A bag containing a 30% red dye solution (30% red dye and 70% water) weighed 100 grams. The bag was then submerged in a beaker of pure water. After 20 minutes, the bag weighed 110 grams. The beaker water remained clear.

Experiment 2: A second bag containing 40% red dye solution (40% red dye and 60% water) weighed 100 grams before being submerged in a beaker of pure water. After only 10 minutes, the bag weighed 110 grams. The beaker water remained clear.

Experiment 3: A third bag containing only pure water and weighing 100 grams was submerged in a beaker of 50% red dye solution (50% red dye and 50% water). After 20 minutes, the bag weighed 70 grams. The bag water remained clear.

17. In Experiment 1, a gain in bag weight suggests that:

A. material passed out from bag to beaker faster than it passed in from beaker to bag.
B. material passed in from beaker to bag faster than it passed out from bag to beaker.
C. material passed in and out of the bag at approximately the same rate.
D. material did not move at all.

18. Which of the following hypotheses is supported by the results of all three experiments?

F. Red dye can leave the bag but not enter.
G. Red dye can enter the bag but not leave.
H. Red dye can enter or leave the bag.
J. Red dye cannot enter or leave the bag.

19. Which of the following represents the best approximation for the weight of the bag in Experiment 2 after 20 minutes?

A. 90 grams
B. 100 grams
C. 110 grams
D. 120 grams

20. Which of the following questions is the entire set of experiments designed to answer?

F. How does concentration of red dye affect rate and direction of water flow?
G. How does concentration of water affect rate and direction of red dye flow?
H. How does rate of red dye flow affect direction of water movement?
J. How does direction of red dye movement affect rate of water flow?

21. A control experiment was set up to confirm the investigation's conclusion. A bag containing pure water and weighing 100 grams was submerged in a beaker of pure water. What is expected to occur?

A. The bag will slowly gain weight.
B. The bag will slowly lose weight.
C. The bag will remain approximately the same weight.
D. The bag will eventually become empty, and the water level in the beaker will rise.

22. Assuming that salts cannot freely pass across a cell's membrane, what would happen to human red blood cells (approximately 1% salt and 99% water) submerged in sea water (approximately 5% salt and 95% water)?

F. The cells would shrink due to a loss of water.
G. The cells would shrink due to a loss of salt.
H. The cells would swell up due to a gain of water.
J. The cells would swell up due to a gain of salt.

GO ON TO THE NEXT PAGE.

Passage V

The chart below shows various physical characteristics of different types of soil.

PHYSICAL CHARACTERISTICS OF SOIL				
Types of Soil	*Diameter of Particles (μm)*	*Relative Ability*† *to Hold Positively Charged Minerals* (Ca^{+2}, K^{+}, Mg^{+2})	*Relative Ability*† *to Maintain Air Spaces*	*Relative Ability*† *to Retain Water*
Clay	less than 2	1	4	1
Silt	2-20	2	3	2
Sand	20-200	3	2	3
Coarse Sand	200-2,000	4	1	4

†Relative abilities are rated from 1, indicating the best (most able), to 4, indicating the worst (least able).

23. The soil type that is LEAST able to hold substances such as magnesium (Mg^{+2}) is:

A. sand.
B. coarse sand.
C. silt.
D. clay.

24. Based on the information in the chart, which of the following statements best describes the relationship between a soil's particle size and its other physical characteristics?

F. As particle size increases, the ability to hold positively charged minerals increases.
G. As particle size decreases, the ability to retain water decreases.
H. As particle size decreases, the ability to maintain air spaces increases.
J. As particle size increases, the ability to retain water decreases.

25. The size of particles in the soil type that is neither best nor worst at any of the listed abilities must be:

A. less than 20 micrometers.
B. more than 20 micrometers.
C. between 2 and 200 micrometers.
D. between 2 and 2,000 micrometers.

26. Loam is a type of soil that is mostly clay, but it also contains some sand and silt particles. Which prediction is most likely to be accurate about the ability of loam to support plant growth?

F. Plants will grow well because loam primarily has small particles that can hold minerals and retain water, yet it also has enough large particles to provide air spaces containing oxygen.
G. Plants will grow well because loam primarily has large particles that can provide air spaces containing oxygen, yet it also has enough small particles that can hold minerals and retain water.
H. Plants will not grow well because although loam is excellent at maintaining air spaces for oxygen, it will not hold enough minerals or water.
J. Plants will not grow well because although loam has enough minerals and air spaces for oxygen, it cannot retain enough water.

27. Based on the information provided in the chart, which of the following conclusions about soil types is NOT correct?

A. Soils best at retaining water are also best at holding positively charged minerals.
B. No two soil types have the exact same combination of relative abilities.
C. Clay and coarse sand are the soil types that are most different in every physical characteristic.
D. At each listed ability, a different type of soil is best.

GO ON TO THE NEXT PAGE.

Passage VI

Theory 1: The rate of a chemical reaction is defined as the number of moles of a specified reactant consumed in one second. Reactants must collide in order for a reaction to occur, so it might seem that rates would depend upon the concentration of reactants—the more reactants that are present, the greater the likelihood of a collision. In fact, this is the case; a concrete example makes this clear. For the reaction: $2NO + O_2 \Rightarrow 2NO_2$, the rate is proportional to the amount of NO and O_2 present. This fact is expressed as the following "rate law": rate = $k[NO]^2[O_2]^1$, where k is the rate constant, and the exponents reflect the coefficients in front of the reactants in the reaction. The relationship between numbers of reactant molecules and exponents in the rate law is a general one.

Theory 2: Theory 1 is very often true, for it expresses the reasonable insight that the greater the concentration of reactants, the greater the likelihood of a reaction. It has a great shortcoming, however, in its assumption that all reactions proceed in one fell swoop rather than in several skirmishes.

For example, let letters A, B, and C stand for molecules. In the reaction $A + 2B \Rightarrow C$, Theory 1 predicts a rate law as follows: rate = $k[A][B]^2$. However, if the reaction actually proceeds in two stages, the first one would be $A + B \Rightarrow AB$ and the second one would be $AB + B \Rightarrow C$.

Thus, Theory 2 implies that one must understand the details of the reaction, including the relative speeds of the sub-reactions, in order to predict a rate law. Theory 1 is not completely wrong, just incomplete.

28. Theory 1 relates:

F. reaction rate to the concentration of products.
G. reaction rate to the concentration of reactants.
H. the relative amounts of products to one other.
J. reaction rate to the individual rates of various stages of the reaction.

29. According to a proponent of Theory 2, Theory 1:

A. can never give a correct prediction for a rate law.
B. will give a correct result if the reactant coefficients are all equal to 1.
C. will give a correct result for a single-stage reaction.
D. is in error because it claims that collisions are required for reactions to occur.

30. According to Theory 1, the rate of the reaction $3M + 2N \Rightarrow 4P$ will be given by:

F. $k[M][N]$.
G. $k[M]^3[N]^2$.
H. $k[M]^3[N]^2[P]^4$.
J. $k([M]^3 + [N]^2)$.

31. A chemist studies the rate of the reaction $2NO_2 + F_2 \Rightarrow 2NO_2F$. According to Theory 1, the rate of the reaction is proportional to:

A. the first power of NO_2 and the first power of F_2.
B. the second power of NO_2 and the second power of NO_2F.
C. the second power of NO_2 and the second power of F_2.
D. the second power of NO_2 and the first power of F_2.

32. Supporters of Theory 2 would best be able to defend their positions if:

F. they could show that the reaction occurs in more than one stage.
G. they slowed the reaction down by cooling the reactants.
H. they sped the reaction up with additional heat.
J. they eliminated all collisions.

33. According to Theory 2, if in a two-stage reaction Stage 1 is much slower than Stage 2, then the overall reaction rate will be:

A. primarily determined by the rate of Stage 1.
B. primarily determined by the rate of Stage 2.
C. undeterminable unless all collisions are counted.
D. undeterminable unless the rate law is measured experimentally.

34. When discussing the rates of reactions that have more than one stage, Theory 2 would not be necessary if:

F. all stages went quickly.
G. all stages had different rates.
H. the sum of the rates of each stage always equaled the rate of the reaction as a whole.
J. the sum of the rates of each stage was never equal to the rate of the reaction as a whole.

GO ON TO THE NEXT PAGE.

Passage VII

Closely related species of butterflies are often found living in very different environments. A pair of experiments was performed in which butterfly species previously captured in either desert areas or mountain areas were tested in laboratory incubators to determine the conditions at which they could carry out important life functions such as mating, oviposition (egg-laying), and pupation (the stage in which the stationary cocoon undergoes its final development into an adult).

Experiment 1: Under conditions of 100% relative humidity (maximum moisture content of the air), 100 desert butterflies (Species D) and 100 mountain butterflies (Species M) were tested at temperature intervals of 2° C (from 0° C to 40° C) to determine if they could mate, oviposit, and pupate. Each species achieved at least 90% success at the following ranges of temperatures:

Table 1

TEMPERATURE RANGES (° C)			
	Mating	*Oviposition*	*Pupation*
Species D	10-34	14-34	4-38
Species M	6-30	10-28	4-34

Experiment 2: The experiment was repeated at 0% relative humidity (minimum moisture content of the air). The species achieved at least 90% success at the following ranges of temperatures:

Table 2

TEMPERATURE RANGES (° C)			
	Mating	*Oviposition*	*Pupation*
Species D	10-34	14-34	4-38
Species M	6-24	10-22	4-28

35. Results of Experiments 1 and 2 indicate that the life function with the narrowest range of temperature at which both species achieve 90% success is:

A. mating.
B. oviposition.
C. pupation.
D. different in Experiment 1 than it is in Experiment 2.

36. Which condition has the most detrimental effects on Species M for mating, oviposition, and pupation?

F. Moist air at low temperatures
G. Moist air at high temperatures
H. Dry air at low temperatures
J. Dry air at high temperatures

37. A third experiment was conducted at 100% relative humidity in which the temperature range for caterpillar survival (another life function) was tested in Species D and Species M. Species D achieved 90% success at 12-36 (° C), while Species M achieved 90% success at 8-30 (° C). Which temperature range is a good prediction of survival in Species D under dry conditions?

A. 8° C-30° C
B. 8° C-24° C
C. 12° C-36° C
D. 12° C-30° C

38. If an investigator wanted to set up an experiment to determine the effects of light and dark on mating ability in Species D and Species M at 100% relative humidity, which set of conditions would provide the most complete results?

F. Test both species at 6° C in the light and 6° C in the dark.
G. Test both species at 20° C in the light and 20° C in the dark.
H. Test both species at 34° C in the light and 34° C in the dark.
J. Test both species at 34° C in the light and 30° C in the dark.

39. Which hypothesis is NOT supported by the results of Experiment 1 and Experiment 2?

A. For all tested life functions, dry conditions only affect Species M at the high end of its temperature ranges.
B. For all tested life functions, dry conditions have no effects on the temperature ranges of the desert species.
C. Species D does better than Species M at high temperatures in all tested life functions.
D. Species M does better than Species D at low temperatures for pupation.

GO ON TO THE NEXT PAGE.

40. Which of the following statements best explains the broad range of temperatures for pupation observed in both butterfly species?

F. Since the cocoon is stationary, it must be able to survive changing temperature conditions until the adult butterfly emerges.
G. Deserts can get very hot and mountains can get very cold.
H. Mountain butterflies would not survive long in the desert, and desert butterflies would not survive long in the mountains.
J. The stationary cocoon must be able to survive under light and dark conditions until the adult butterfly emerges.

END OF TEST 4.
STOP! DO NOT TURN THE PAGE UNTIL TOLD TO DO SO.
DO NOT RETURN TO A PREVIOUS TEST.

5 5 5 5 5 5 5 5 5 5 5 5

WRITING TEST (OPTIONAL)

30 Minutes—1 Essay Prompt

DIRECTIONS: This is a test of your writing skills. Before you begin planning and writing your essay, read the writing prompt carefully to understand the instructions. Your essay will be evaluated on the evidence it provides of your ability to express judgments by taking a position on the issue in the writing prompt; to maintain a focus on the topic throughout the essay; to develop a position by using logical reasoning and supporting ideas; to organize ideas in a logical way; and to use language clearly and effectively according to the conventions of standard written English.

If you finish before time is called, you may review your work. Lay your pencil down immediately when time is called.

Writing Test Prompt

Some educators and parents advocate changing from the traditional nine-month school year to a twelve-month program. They point out that the nine-month school year was first adopted when students were needed to work on family farms during the summer months, a need that no longer exists. They also state that year round school would improve academic achievement because it would eliminate the need to review each previous year's work at the beginning of a new school year and allow teachers to cover material in greater detail. Other teachers and parents are opposed to such a change. They point out that summer is the traditional time for family vacations and that in addition to giving students a needed break from academic work, the summer vacation is the time for part-time jobs, summer camp, and special trips, all of which are also learning experiences. Do you think that schools should change from a nine-month school year to a twelve-month school year?

In your essay, take a position on this issue. You may address either of the two points described above, or you may offer an entirely different perspective on the issue. Be sure to use specific reasons and examples to support your analysis.

END OF TEST 5.
STOP! DO NOT RETURN TO ANY OTHER TEST.

Practice Test II

TARGETED EDUCATIONAL SOLUTIONS.

Cambridge Course Concept Outline
PRACTICE TEST II

When completing Practice Test II, use the Bubble Sheet on page 725, unless otherwise directed by your instructor.

BUBBLE SHEET

Name ____________________ Student ID Number ____________________

Date ____________________ Instructor ____________________ Course/Session Number ____________________

TEST 1—ENGLISH

1 A B C D	16 F G H J	31 A B C D	46 F G H J	61 A B C D
2 F G H J	17 A B C D	32 F G H J	47 A B C D	62 F G H J
3 A B C D	18 F G H J	33 A B C D	48 F G H J	63 A B C D
4 F G H J	19 A B C D	34 F G H J	49 A B C D	64 F G H J
5 A B C D	20 F G H J	35 A B C D	50 F G H J	65 A B C D
6 F G H J	21 A B C D	36 F G H J	51 A B C D	66 F G H J
7 A B C D	22 F G H J	37 A B C D	52 F G H J	67 A B C D
8 F G H J	23 A B C D	38 F G H J	53 A B C D	68 F G H J
9 A B C D	24 F G H J	39 A B C D	54 F G H J	69 A B C D
10 F G H J	25 A B C D	40 F G H J	55 A B C D	70 F G H J
11 A B C D	26 F G H J	41 A B C D	56 F G H J	71 A B C D
12 F G H J	27 A B C D	42 F G H J	57 A B C D	72 F G H J
13 A B C D	28 F G H J	43 A B C D	58 F G H J	73 A B C D
14 F G H J	29 A B C D	44 F G H J	59 A B C D	74 F G H J
15 A B C D	30 F G H J	45 A B C D	60 F G H J	75 A B C D

TEST 2—MATHEMATICS

1 A B C D E	13 A B C D E	25 A B C D E	37 A B C D E	49 A B C D E
2 F G H J K	14 F G H J K	26 F G H J K	38 F G H J K	50 F G H J K
3 A B C D E	15 A B C D E	27 A B C D E	39 A B C D E	51 A B C D E
4 F G H J K	16 F G H J K	28 F G H J K	40 F G H J K	52 F G H J K
5 A B C D E	17 A B C D E	29 A B C D E	41 A B C D E	53 A B C D E
6 F G H J K	18 F G H J K	30 F G H J K	42 F G H J K	54 F G H J K
7 A B C D E	19 A B C D E	31 A B C D E	43 A B C D E	55 A B C D E
8 F G H J K	20 F G H J K	32 F G H J K	44 F G H J K	56 F G H J K
9 A B C D E	21 A B C D E	33 A B C D E	45 A B C D E	57 A B C D E
10 F G H J K	22 F G H J K	34 F G H J K	46 F G H J K	58 F G H J K
11 A B C D E	23 A B C D E	35 A B C D E	47 A B C D E	59 A B C D E
12 F G H J K	24 F G H J K	36 F G H J K	48 F G H J K	60 F G H J K

TEST 3—READING

1 A B C D	9 A B C D	17 A B C D	25 A B C D	33 A B C D
2 F G H J	10 F G H J	18 F G H J	26 F G H J	34 F G H J
3 A B C D	11 A B C D	19 A B C D	27 A B C D	35 A B C D
4 F G H J	12 F G H J	20 F G H J	28 F G H J	36 F G H J
5 A B C D	13 A B C D	21 A B C D	29 A B C D	37 A B C D
6 F G H J	14 F G H J	22 F G H J	30 F G H J	38 F G H J
7 A B C D	15 A B C D	23 A B C D	31 A B C D	39 A B C D
8 F G H J	16 F G H J	24 F G H J	32 F G H J	40 F G H J

TEST 4—SCIENCE REASONING

1 A B C D	9 A B C D	17 A B C D	25 A B C D	33 A B C D
2 F G H J	10 F G H J	18 F G H J	26 F G H J	34 F G H J
3 A B C D	11 A B C D	19 A B C D	27 A B C D	35 A B C D
4 F G H J	12 F G H J	20 F G H J	28 F G H J	36 F G H J
5 A B C D	13 A B C D	21 A B C D	29 A B C D	37 A B C D
6 F G H J	14 F G H J	22 F G H J	30 F G H J	38 F G H J
7 A B C D	15 A B C D	23 A B C D	31 A B C D	39 A B C D
8 F G H J	16 F G H J	24 F G H J	32 F G H J	40 F G H J

DIRECTIONS

Practice Test II consists of five sections: English, Mathematics, Reading, Science Reasoning, and Writing. Calculator use is only permitted on the Mathematics Test.

The items in each test are numbered and the answer choices lettered. The provided bubble sheet has numbered rows that correspond to the items on the test. Each row contains lettered ovals to match the answer choices for each item on the test. Each numbered row on the bubble sheet has a corresponding item on the test.

For each item, first decide on the best answer choice. Then, locate the row number that corresponds to the item. Next, find the oval in that row that matches the letter of the chosen answer. Then, use a soft lead pencil to fill in the oval. Do not use a ballpoint pen.

Mark only one answer for each item. If you change your mind about the answer choice, thoroughly erase the first mark before marking your new answer.

Note that only responses marked on your bubble sheet will be scored. Your score on each test will be based only on the number of items that are correctly answered during the time allowed for that test. Guessing is not penalized. Therefore, it is to your best advantage to answer every item on the test, even if you must guess.

You may work on each test only during the time allowed for that test. If you finish a test before time is called, use the time to review your answer choices or work on items about which you are uncertain. You may not return to a test on which time has already been called and you may not preview another test. You must lay down your pencil immediately when time is called at the end of each test. You may not for any reason fill in or alter ovals for a test after time expires for that test. Violation of these rules will result in immediate disqualification from the exam.

1 1 1 1 1 1 1 1 1 1 1 1

ENGLISH TEST

45 Minutes—75 Items

DIRECTIONS: In the following passages, certain words and phrases are underlined. The items in the right hand column provide alternatives for the underlined parts. In most cases, you are to choose the alternative that best expresses the idea of the sentence in context, corrects grammatical errors, and/or is best suited to the tone and style of the passage. If the original best accomplishes this, then choose "NO CHANGE." In some cases, you will be asked questions regarding an underlined part. You are to choose the best answer to the question.

You will also find items on this test that refer to a section of the passage or to the passage as a whole. These items DO NOT refer to an underlined portion of the passage. Rather, they are identified by a number or numbers in a box.

For each item, choose the best alternative and fill in the corresponding oval on your bubble sheet. You should read the passage before answering the accompanying items. For many of the items, you must read several sentences beyond the item to determine the answer. Be sure that you have read far enough ahead before you answer.

Answers are on page 943.

PASSAGE I

The Philosophy of Botany

[1]

Botany is surely the more gentler of[1] sciences. The careful observation of a flower is a calm, ostentatious[2] action—the peaceful contemplation of a beautiful object. Reduced to its essentials, it[3] requires no laboratory but the natural world,[4] a few tools and the naked eye. Botany in its most scientific or purest form consists about[5] seeking to know more about the plant simply for the sake of that knowledge. Plants

1. **A.** NO CHANGE
   B. the most gentle of
   C. the gentler of
   D. the gentlest in the

2. **F.** NO CHANGE
   G. unobtrusive
   H. violent
   J. chaotic

3. **A.** NO CHANGE
   B. essentials; it
   C. essentials; botany
   D. essentials, botany

4. **F.** NO CHANGE
   G. but you do need the natural world
   H. and the natural world is needed
   J. but the natural world is necessary

5. **A.** NO CHANGE
   B. consists of
   C. consists in
   D. consist of

GO ON TO THE NEXT PAGE.

have not always been regarded as worthy of knowing (6) or studying in and of themselves, not on their merits as sources of food or drugs but as life-forms. In fact, the history of botany can be viewed in terms of repeated rediscoveries of this one theme—that plants are worthy of study in and of themselves (7), quite apart from any use they might have for mankind.

6. **F.** NO CHANGE
G. for knowledge
H. of knowledge
J. to know

7. **A.** NO CHANGE
B. by themselves
C. themselves
D. by and for themselves

[2]

[8] The practical motives behind plant study should not be disparaging—the (9) bulk of our medical history, for instance, is made up of accounts of herbal remedies. Nonetheless (10), the study of the medicinal properties of plants contained a self-limiting mechanism: if a plant seemed to have no utilitarian value, it was disregarded, and no further study of it is made (11). The Renaissance attitude towards nature changed this overly practical bent and initiated the scientific study of plants.

8. Beginning Paragraph 2 with which of the following might make the transition from Paragraph 1 to Paragraph 2 clearer?
F. However,
G. Since
H. Heretofore
J. Hence

9. **A.** NO CHANGE
B. disparaged—the bulk
C. disparaging, the bulk
D. disparaged; the bulk

10. **F.** NO CHANGE
G. Consequently
H. Thus
J. Moreover

11. **A.** NO CHANGE
B. had been made
C. were made
D. was made

[3]

Botany, as a pure science, has certain characteristics and makes certain assumptions that prove thought provoking and interesting. One of its

GO ON TO THE NEXT PAGE.

unspoken or[12] basic assumptions is an implicit respect and regard for all living things. The botanist who studies a plant's structure or tries to have understood their[13] functions confronts nature on its own terms. Investigations of how a plant thrives or reproduces, or studies of the purposefulness of a flower's coloration and structure, are almost implicitly egalitarian and tautological. The botanist studies the flower because they exist, but[14] because it exists, it is worthy of study.

12. F. NO CHANGE
G. because
H. and thus
J. yet

13. A. NO CHANGE
B. to understand its
C. understanding their
D. having understood its

14. F. NO CHANGE
G. it exists, but
H. it exists and
J. it exists, and

Item 15 asks about the preceding passage as a whole.

15. The last sentence of the essay is actually a restatement of which of the following ideas?

A. The study of the medicinal properties of plants has a self-limiting mechanism.
B. The botanist who tries to understand a plant's function confronts nature on its own terms.
C. Botany is a gentle science.
D. The study of plants and flowers is egalitarian and tautological.

PASSAGE II

Poverty in America

The main characteristic of poverty is, of course,[16] lack of money. A family is defined as poor when its

16. The use of the phrase "of course" is:

F. appropriate because someone who is poor obviously lacks money.
G. appropriate because it is not obvious that someone who is poor lacks money.
H. questionable since someone might be poor in spirit.
J. appropriate because it disrupts the flow of the sentence.

GO ON TO THE NEXT PAGE.

annual income falls below a certain dollar amount,[17] calculated by the U.S. Federal Government to be the minimum a family of their[18] size would need to maintain a minimally decent standard of living. In certain areas of rural America, consequently,[19] poverty is the rule rather than the exception. As many as 50 percent of the families may earn less than[20] the poverty level, and some may manage to subsist somehow on amounts even less than half the official poverty level income. [21]

Although[22] lack of money is the defining characteristic of poverty, poverty is more than simply lack of money. Poverty is an entire complex of symptoms. Low levels of formal schooling among adults parallel[23] low-income levels. Additionally, in families below the poverty level, the number of children and aged who depend on those who work is in general higher than the national average for all families. As a consequence,[24] fewer workers support a greater number of non-workers than in other, more prosperous families.

Often, the schooling provided in low-income

17. **A.** NO CHANGE
    B. falls and is under a certain dollar amount,
    C. is under a certain specified dollar amount,
    D. OMIT the underlined portion.

18. **F.** NO CHANGE
    G. there
    H. its
    J. it's

19. **A.** NO CHANGE
    B. and therefore, as a result of this,
    C. moreover, due to this fact,
    D. OMIT the underlined portion.

20. **F.** NO CHANGE
    G. lower than
    H. less as
    J. lower as

21. The first paragraph provides which of the following?
    A. A definition
    B. An argument
    C. A comparison
    D. A narrative

22. **F.** NO CHANGE
    G. (Do NOT begin a new paragraph) Although
    H. Since
    J. (Do NOT begin a new paragraph) Since

23. **A.** NO CHANGE
    B. go along with
    C. are a lot like
    D. very often go together with

24. **F.** NO CHANGE
    G. However,
    H. Surprisingly,
    J. Fortunately,

GO ON TO THE NEXT PAGE.

areas are as inadequate like incomes. In particular, rural children get poorer schooling than city children, and many rural poor are severely handicapped by it. The general rural average is only 8.8 years of school completed. Moreover, low educational levels seem to just keep repeating and repeating themselves. If the head of a rural poor family have little schooling, the children are often handicapped in their efforts to get an education. It is especially difficult for people who are handicapped educationally to acquire new skills, get new jobs, or otherwise adjust to an increasingly urbanized society. This is as true on the farm rather than in urban industry, since modern farming of the present day requires skills that poor educated people lack. Lacking in education, the rural poor either take low-paying jobs on the farm or elsewhere in rural areas or swell the ranks of the unemployed or under-employed.

25. A. NO CHANGE
B. is—like family income, inadequate
C. is so inadequate as family income
D. is, like family income, inadequate

26. F. NO CHANGE
G. education
H. their education
J. their lack of education

27. A. NO CHANGE
B. be self-perpetuating of themselves
C. be self-perpetuating
D. cause the same thing to happen all over again

28. F. NO CHANGE
G. have had
H. has had
J. was to have

29. A. NO CHANGE
B. rather as
C. as they are
D. as it is

30. F. NO CHANGE
G. of the present
H. presently
J. OMIT the underlined portion.

31. A. NO CHANGE
B. poorly educated
C. educated poor
D. poor education

Item 32 asks about the preceding passage as a whole.

32. The author does NOT use which of the following in the development of the essay?

F. Definitions
G. Explanation
H. Statistics
J. Personal experience

GO ON TO THE NEXT PAGE.

PASSAGE III

School Dropouts

One out of every four children who entered the fifth grade in the fall of 1966 fail to graduate (33) with his or her class. The total number that should of (34) graduated was 4.1 million, but approximately 900,000 fell by the wayside.

Those who do not make it are called school drop-outs. (Official statistics define a dropout as a person who has not yet attained the age of 16 and leaves school before graduation for any reason except transfer.) School officials who work with dropouts who leave school (35) say a student will usually starting thinking (36) about dropping out about two years before he or she ceases to attend school: roughly (37) at age 14. Absenteeism, class cutting, lack of motivation, and lack of interest in school is often (38) early signs of the potential dropout. Also, (39) many students drop out mentally very early in their school career, despite their physical presence until graduation.

The dropout is most often a boy who mostly, frequently (40) leaves school at the age of 16 while in the

33. A. NO CHANGE
B. failed to graduate
C. failed graduation
D. fails to graduate

34. F. NO CHANGE
G. that should of been
H. who should of
J. who should have

35. A. NO CHANGE
B. who have left school
C. who are leaving school
D. OMIT the underlined portion.

36. F. NO CHANGE
G. usually will be starting thinking
H. starts usually thinking
J. usually starts to think

37. A. NO CHANGE
B. school but roughly
C. school and roughly
D. school, roughly

38. F. NO CHANGE
G. is oftentimes
H. are often
J. were often

39. A. NO CHANGE
B. dropout also
C. dropout many
D. dropout but also

40. F. NO CHANGE
G. frequently and often
H. frequently
J. sometimes often

GO ON TO THE NEXT PAGE.

tenth grade. He is most likely than those [41] who stay in school to score low on an intelligence test and is likely to be failing in school at the time of him dropping out [42].

Yet most dropouts are really not less bright [43] than students who remain in school until graduation. The dropout typically comes from the lower-income class and most often leaves school for financial reasons. His absences from school increasing noticeably [44] during the eighth grade and he participates little or none [45] in extra-curricular activities. The reasons a student drops out of school goes deeper as [46] a mere desire to be rid of school. Dropping out is a symptom; the roots of the problem are usually below the surface. [47]

41. **A.** NO CHANGE
    B. more likely than those
    C. most likely as one
    D. more likely than one

42. **F.** NO CHANGE
    G. he drops out
    H. of his having dropped out
    J. he dropped out

43. **A.** NO CHANGE
    B. really they are no less bright than are the students who remain
    C. are, than the students who remain, really no less bright
    D. than the students who remain are really no less bright

44. **F.** NO CHANGE
    G. increase so that
    H. increase noticeably
    J. increased to the point where it was noticed

45. **A.** NO CHANGE
    B. and not at all
    C. or not much
    D. or not at all

46. **F.** NO CHANGE
    G. go more deeply than
    H. go deeper as
    J. go deeper than

47. A logical continuation of the essay would be a discussion of:
    A. the financial reasons a student might leave school.
    B. a student's lack of motivation.
    C. possible extracurricular activities.
    D. why students might drop out of school.

Item 48 asks about the preceding passage as a whole.

48. Is the use of the official definition of dropout in the second paragraph appropriate?
    F. Yes, because without a definition, the article would not be understandable.
    G. Yes, because the nature of a "dropout" is one of the central themes of the passage.
    H. No, because the definition has nothing to do with what the author is discussing in the second paragraph.
    J. No, because the author then redefines the

GO ON TO THE NEXT PAGE.

PASSAGE IV

Wind Machines

The idea of generating electricity with wind power is not new. But the kind of attention that idea is getting today, in terms of research and development, are both new and encouraging to planners looking for renewable energy sources satisfying growing national demands. An effort is being made in the United States to use one of humankind's oldest energy sources to solve one of its most modern problems, to find reliable and cost-effective ways to harness the wind to produce electricity.

Wind machines are not the simple devices that they may be appearing to be, and the lessons they teach seldom come easy. On the other hand, the potential reward to a nation that needs more energy from a renewable source is beyond calculation. Rewards for using wind power have been gathered by civilizations and cultures since early in recorded history.

No record survives of the earliest wind machine. It may have been built in China more than three thousand years ago. It may have been built on the windy plains of Afghanistan. History hints at some

49. **A.** NO CHANGE
B. development, is
C. developing, is
D. development are

50. **F.** NO CHANGE
G. that would have satisfied
H. to satisfy
J. with the satisfaction of

51. **A.** NO CHANGE
B. their
C. it's
D. your

52. **F.** NO CHANGE
G. problems: to find
H. problems, finding
J. problems. To find

53. **A.** NO CHANGE
B. they may be
C. it may seem to be
D. they may appear to be

54. **F.** NO CHANGE
G. Therefore,
H. As a consequence
J. This means that

55. **A.** NO CHANGE
B. has been gathering
C. is gathering
D. will have been gathered

56. **F.** NO CHANGE
G. may have been
H. was being built
J. has been building

GO ON TO THE NEXT PAGE.

sort of wind power used in the Pharaoh's Egypt for the drawing of water 57 for agriculture, long before the birth of Christ. Hammurabi may have taken time out from developing a legal code about 2,000 BC to sponsor development of some sort of wind machine. The earliest confirmed wind machines are in that same region. Persian writers described gardens irrigated through the means of 58 wind-driven water lifts several 59 centuries before the birth of Christ.

Ultimately, we can only guess at the origin of the windmill 60.

Persian machines were horizontal devices, 61 carousel-like contraptions that revolved around a center pole and caught the wind with bundles of reeds.

The carousel is perhaps the more simple design for capturing 62 the wind; it cares nothing for the direction of the breeze, but revolves no matter where on the compass the wind may originate. From the Middle East, wind-machine technology may have been carried to Europe by returning Crusaders. Accurate records do not exist, but soon after the Crusades, windmills appeared in northern Europe and soon were found on

57. **A.** NO CHANGE
B. to draw water
C. in order that water be drawn
D. in order to draw water

58. **F.** NO CHANGE
G. irrigated by means of
H. which were then irrigated by means of
J. irrigated by

59. **A.** NO CHANGE
B. lifts several,
C. lifts but several
D. lifts and several

60. **F.** NO CHANGE
G. the origin of the windmill can only be guessed at
H. the origin of the windmill can only be guessed at by us
J. the origin of the windmill could only be guessed at

61. **A.** NO CHANGE
B. (Do NOT begin a new paragraph) Persian machines were horizontal devices,
C. Since Persian machines were
D. It was discovered that Persian machines were horizontal devices,

62. **F.** NO CHANGE
G. most simplest design for capturing
H. simpler design to capture
J. simplest design for capturing

GO ON TO THE NEXT PAGE.

the British Isles.

For a while, windmills flourished in Europe, but with the advent of steam power, they come close to [63] extinction for the wind is real iffy. [64] It can fail to blow just when it is needed the most, or it can rage into a gale [65] when it is not needed at all.

63. A. NO CHANGE
B. came close to
C. are coming closer to
D. come close upon

64. F. NO CHANGE
G. likely to blow sometimes and not to others
H. here today and gone tomorrow isn't
J. capricious

65. The author's use of the phrase "rage into a gale" is:

A. appropriate because it creates a vivid image.
B. appropriate because it minimizes the importance of weather.
C. inappropriate because images are out of place in scientific writing.
D. inappropriate because wind is sometimes calm.

PASSAGE V

The Development of Television Programming

Television and its programs do not just happen. It is [66] planned products of a huge, wealthy, and highly competitive commercial enterprise. The television industry, which includes stations, networks, production companies, actors, and writers, are [67] responsible for selecting, creating, and distributing programs. The three most popular programs are the episodic series, the [68] made-for-television movie, and the mini-series.

In the 1970s, the episodic series, both dramatic

66. F. NO CHANGE
G. They are
H. They would be
J. It was

67. A. NO CHANGE
B. writers, is
C. writers are
D. writers—is

68. F. NO CHANGE
G. episodic series the
H. episodic, series the
J. episodic series the,

GO ON TO THE NEXT PAGE.

and comic, was the most (69) popular of these. With the advent (70) of cable and pay television and of video disks and tapes, the television movie is rapidly gaining in (71) popularity. The past ten years have seen (72) several changes in television drama. The action-adventure police drama has lost and the situation comedy has grew (73) in popularity. Topics previously considered taboo emerged. Unmarried (74) couples living together, divorces, and single parents. Even topics that are politically controversy (75) can now be the focus of programs.

69. A. NO CHANGE
B. was the more
C. were the most
D. were the more

70. F. NO CHANGE
G. Including the advent
H. Notwithstanding the advent
J. With the beginning of the advent

71. A. NO CHANGE
B. has rapidly gained in
C. is rapidly gaining
D. will rapidly gain in

72. F. NO CHANGE
G. see
H. will see
J. would be seeing

73. A. NO CHANGE
B. has grown
C. grew
D. grow

74. F. NO CHANGE
G. emerged, unmarried
H. emerged unmarried
J. emerged: unmarried

75. A. NO CHANGE
B. politically controversial
C. politics controversy
D. political controversy

END OF TEST 1.
STOP! DO NOT TURN THE PAGE UNTIL TOLD TO DO SO.

2 2 2 2 2 2 2 2 2 2 2 2

MATHEMATICS TEST

60 Minutes—60 Items

DIRECTIONS: Solve each item and choose the correct answer choice. Then, fill in the corresponding oval on the bubble sheet.

Allocate time wisely. Try to solve as many items as possible, returning to skipped items if time permits.

Calculator use is permitted on this test; however, some items are best solved without the use of a calculator.

Note: Unless otherwise stated, assume all of the following.

1. Illustrative figures are NOT necessarily drawn to scale.
2. The word *average* indicates arithmetic mean.
3. The word *line* indicates a straight line.
4. Geometric figures lie in a plane.

Answers are on page 943.

1. $121{,}212 + (2 \cdot 10^4) = ?$

A. 312,212
B. 141,212
C. 123,212
D. 121,412
E. 121,232

2. If $6x + 3 = 21$, then $2x + 1 = ?$

F. 1
G. 2
H. 3
J. 6
K. 7

3. At a recreation center, it costs \$3 per hour to rent a ping pong table and \$12 per hour to rent a lane for bowling. For the cost of renting a bowling lane for 2 hours, it is possible to rent a ping pong table for how many hours?

A. 4
B. 6
C. 8
D. 18
E. 36

DO YOUR FIGURING HERE.

GO ON TO THE NEXT PAGE.

DO YOUR FIGURING HERE.

4. If j, k, l, and m are natural numbers and $j < k < l < m$, which of the following could be true?

F. $k = k + l$
G. $j = l + m$
H. $j + k = l + m$
J. $j + k + m = l$
K. $j + m = k + l$

5. Which of the following is greater than $\frac{1}{2}$?

A. $\frac{6}{11}$
B. $\frac{9}{19}$
C. $\frac{7}{15}$
D. $\frac{4}{9}$
E. $\frac{3}{7}$

6. Out of a group of 360 students, exactly 18 are on the track team. What percent of the students are on the track team?

F. 5%
G. 10%
H. 12%
J. 20%
K. 25%

7. In the figure below, 3 lines intersect as shown. Which of the following *must* be true?

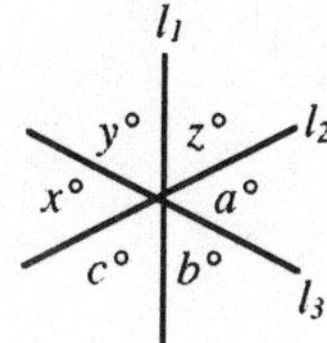

I. $a = x$
II. $y + z = b + c$
III. $x + a = y + b$

A. I only
B. II only
C. I and II only
D. I and III only
E. I, II, and III only

GO ON TO THE NEXT PAGE.

8. In the figure below, $x = ?$

DO YOUR FIGURING HERE.

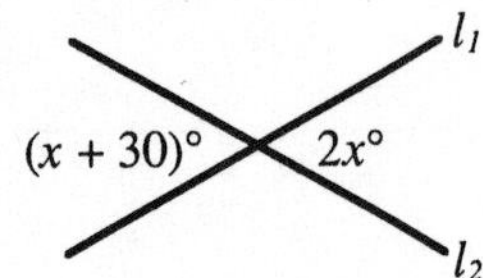

F. 15
G. 30
H. 45
J. 60
K. 90

9. Which of the following is the prime factorization of 60?

A. (2)(3)(10)
B. (3)(4)(5)
C. (2)(2)(3)(5)
D. (2)(2)(3)(6)
E. (3)(3)(3)(5)

10. The average height of 4 buildings is 20 meters. If 3 of the buildings are each 16 meters tall, what is the height, in meters, of the fourth building?

F. 32
G. 28
H. 24
J. 22
K. 18

11. In the figure below, what is the value of x?

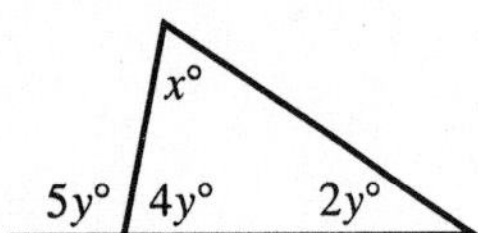

A. 15
B. 20
C. 30
D. 45
E. 60

GO ON TO THE NEXT PAGE.

12. In the figure below, what is the length of $\overline{PQ}$?

DO YOUR FIGURING HERE.

F. 0.09
G. 0.11
H. 0.12
J. 0.13
K. 0.16

13. What is the perimeter of the rectangle below?

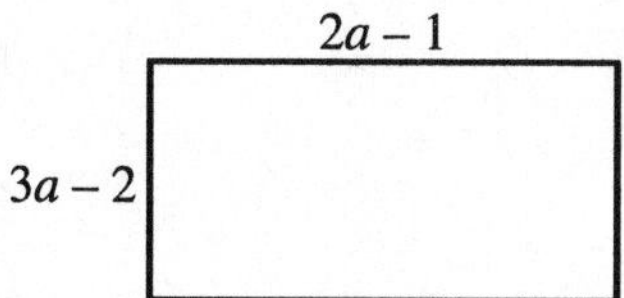

A. $10a - 6$
B. $10a - 3$
C. $6a - 3$
D. $5a - 6$
E. $5a - 3$

14. If the average of x, x, x, 56, and 58 is 51, then $x = ?$

F. 43
G. 47
H. 49
J. 51
K. 53

15. For how many integers x is $-2 \leq 2x \leq 2$?

A. 1
B. 2
C. 3
D. 4
E. 5

GO ON TO THE NEXT PAGE.

DO YOUR FIGURING HERE.

16. For all real numbers x, 8^x equals which of the following?

F. $8x$
G. x^8
H. 2^{2x}
J. $x^{2/3}$
K. 2^{3x}

17. What is the sum of the areas of 2 squares with sides of 2 and 3 unit lengths, respectively?

A. 1
B. 5
C. 13
D. 25
E. 36

18. If the rectangular solid shown below has a volume of 54 cubic inches, what is the value of x, in inches?

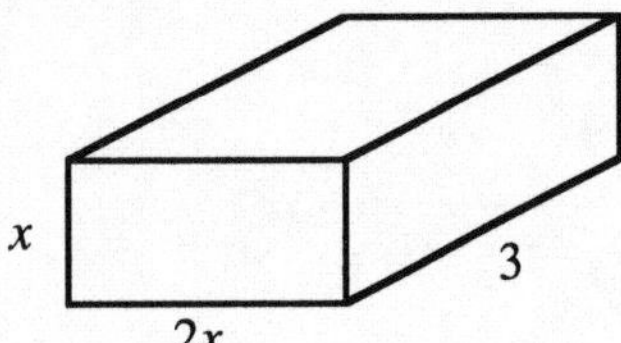

F. 2
G. 3
H. 6
J. 9
K. 12

19. If x is 80 percent of y, then y is what percent of x?

A. $133\frac{1}{3}\%$
B. 125%
C. 120%
D. 90%
E. 80%

20. From which of the following statements can it be deduced that $m > n$?

F. $m + 1 = n$
G. $2m = n$
H. $m + n > 0$
J. $m - n > 0$
K. $mn > 0$

GO ON TO THE NEXT PAGE.

DO YOUR FIGURING HERE.

21. If $f(x) = x^2 + x$, then what is the value of $f(f(2))$?

A. 42
B. 38
C. 32
D. 18
E. 4

22. The circle below with center O has a radius with a length of 2. If the total area of the shaded regions is 3π, then $x = ?$

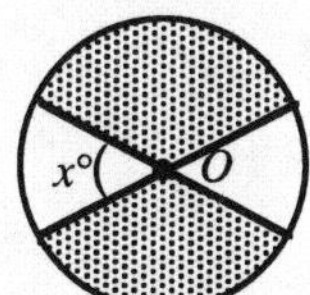

F. 270
G. 180
H. 120
J. 90
K. 45

23. If a bar of metal alloy consists of 100 grams of tin and 150 grams of lead, what percent of the entire bar, by weight, is tin?

A. 10%
B. 15%
C. $33\frac{1}{3}\%$
D. 40%
E. $66\frac{2}{3}\%$

24. If $\frac{1}{x} + \frac{1}{y} = \frac{1}{z}$, then $z = ?$

F. $\frac{1}{xy}$
G. xy
H. $\frac{x+y}{xy}$
J. $\frac{xy}{x+y}$
K. $\frac{2xy}{x+y}$

GO ON TO THE NEXT PAGE.

25. $|-5| + |-12| - |-2| + (-6) = ?$

DO YOUR FIGURING HERE.

A. 2
B. 3
C. 6
D. 9
E. 14

26. If the average of $2x$, $2x + 1$, and $2x + 2$ is $x - 1$, which of the following equations could be used to find x?

F. $6x + 3 = x - 1$
G. $6x + 3 = 3(x - 1)$
H. $3(6x + 3) = x - 1$
J. $(6x + 3) + (x - 1) = 3$
K. $(6x + 3)(x - 1) = 3$

27. Members of a civic organization purchase boxes of candy for $1 each and sell them for $2 each. If no other expenses are incurred, how many boxes of candy must they sell to earn a net profit of $500?

A. 250
B. 500
C. 1,000
D. 1,500
E. 2,000

28. $(-2)^2 - (-2)^3 = ?$

F. 16
G. 12
H. 2
J. -2
K. -8

29. The sum, the product, and the average of 3 different integers are equal. If 2 of the integers are x and $-x$, the third integer is:

A. $\frac{x}{2}$
B. $2x$
C. -1
D. 0
E. 1

GO ON TO THE NEXT PAGE.

30. In a school with a total enrollment of 360, 90 students are seniors. What percent of all students enrolled in the school are seniors?

F. 25%
G. $33\frac{1}{3}\%$
H. 50%
J. $66\frac{2}{3}\%$
K. 75%

31. The perimeter of the square below is:

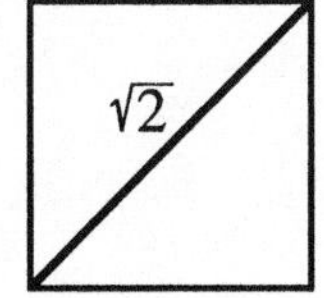

A. 1
B. $\sqrt{2}$
C. 4
D. $4\sqrt{2}$
E. 8

32. If 2 straight lines intersect as shown, what is the value of x?

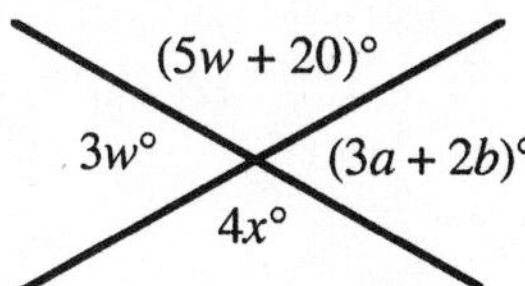

F. 15
G. 30
H. 45
J. 60
K. 75

DO YOUR FIGURING HERE.

GO ON TO THE NEXT PAGE.

DO YOUR FIGURING HERE.

33. The figure below is a scale drawing of the floor of a dining hall. If 1 centimeter on the drawing represents 5 meters, what is the area, in square meters, of the floor?

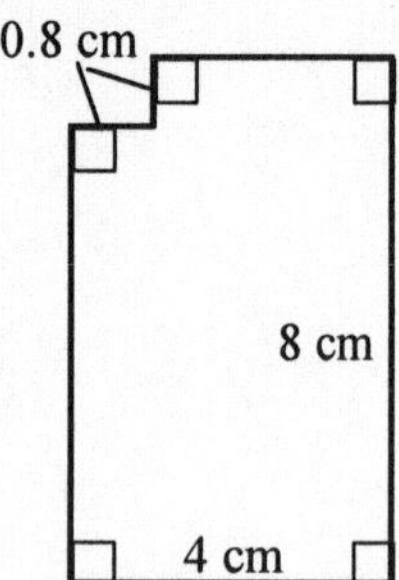

A. 144
B. 156
C. 784
D. 796
E. 844

34. A triangle has one side with a length of 4 and another side with a length of 11. What are the *greatest* and *least* possible integer values for the length of the remaining side?

F. 7 and 4
G. 11 and 4
H. 14 and 8
J. 15 and 7
K. 16 and 7

35. Which of the following is the solution set for the equation $-x^2 = 3 - 4x$?

A. {-3, -1}
B. {-3, 1}
C. {1, 3}
D. {1, 4}
E. {3, 5}

36. A school club spends $\frac{2}{5}$ of its budget for one project and $\frac{1}{3}$ of what remains for another project. If the club's entire budget is \$300, how much of the budget is left after the 2 projects?

F. \$60
G. \$90
H. \$120
J. \$180
K. \$240

GO ON TO THE NEXT PAGE.

37. If the cost of n nails is c cents, which of the following equations could be used to determine d, the cost in dollars, of x nails?

A. $d = 100cnx$

B. $d = 100\frac{cx}{n}$

C. $d = \frac{100nx}{c}$

D. $d = \frac{nx}{100c}$

E. $d = \frac{cx}{100n}$

38. If $a^2b^3c < 0$, which of the following inequalities *must* be true?

F. $b^3 < 0$
G. $b^2 < 0$
H. $b < 0$
J. $c < 0$
K. $bc < 0$

39. If the figure below is an equilateral triangle, what is its perimeter?

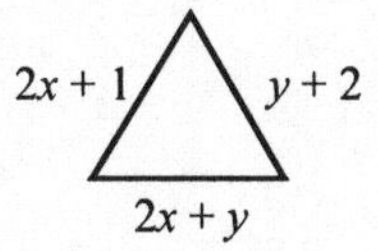

2x + 1
y + 2
2x + y

A. 1
B. 3
C. 9
D. 12
E. 15

40. In the coordinate plane, what is the distance between the point with (x, y) coordinates $(2, 1)$ and the point with (x, y) coordinates $(5, 5)$?

F. $\sqrt{3}$
G. $2\sqrt{3}$
H. $3\sqrt{2}$
J. 5
K. 6

DO YOUR FIGURING HERE.

GO ON TO THE NEXT PAGE.

41. $\sqrt{45} - \sqrt{20} + \sqrt{5} = ?$

DO YOUR FIGURING HERE.

A. 0
B. $2 - \sqrt{5}$
C. $2 + \sqrt{5}$
D. $2\sqrt{5}$
E. 10

42. What is the least positive integer x for which $12 - x$ and $15 - x$ will yield non-zero results with opposite signs?

F. 3
G. 4
H. 11
J. 12
K. 13

43. The solution set to the pair of equations $mx + ny = 15$ and $nx + my = 13$ is $x = 3$ and $y = 1$. What are the values of m and n?

A. $m = 5; n = 3$
B. $m = 4; n = 3$
C. $m = 3; n = 4$
D. $m = 3; n = 5$
E. $m = 2; n = 6$

44. In the figure below, line segments intersecting each other at 90° join equally spaced points. If the total length of all line segments in the figure is 24, what is the area of the shaded part?

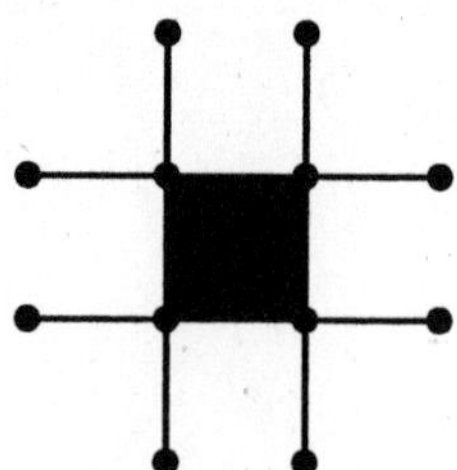

F. 1
G. 4
H. 8
J. 12
K. 16

GO ON TO THE NEXT PAGE.

45. All of the following are true for all real numbers EXCEPT:

DO YOUR FIGURING HERE.

A. $|a| = |-a|$
B. $|a - b| = |b - a|$
C. $|a - b| = -|b - a|$
D. $|a + b| \leq |a| + |b|$
E. $|a - b| \leq |a| + |b|$

46. Arccos $(\cos \frac{\pi}{2}) = ?$

F. 0
G. $\frac{\pi}{4}$
H. $\frac{\pi}{2}$
J. π
K. $\frac{3\pi}{2}$

47. ΔABC has coordinates A (-1, -2), B (0, 4), and C (3, -1). Which of the following provides the coordinates of $\Delta A'B'C'$, respectively, the image of ΔABC after a reflection in the line $y = -x$?

A. (2, 1), (-4, 0), (1, -3)
B. (1, 2), (0, -4), (-3, 1)
C. (2, 1), (4, 0), (1, -3)
D. (3, 2), (5, 1), (2, -2)
E. (4, 0), (3, -1), (-1, -2)

48. If $\sin x = \cos x$, then x terminates only in the:

F. first quadrant
G. second quadrant
H. first or third quadrants
J. second or third quadrants
K. second or fourth quadrants

49. If the line $x = k$ is tangent to the circle $(x - 2)^2 + (y + 1)^2 = 4$, then which of the following is the point of tangency?

A. (-6, -1) or (2, -1)
B. (-2, -1) or (6, -1)
C. (0, -1) or (4, -1)
D. (0, 1) or (4, 1)
E. (2, 1) or (6, 1)

GO ON TO THE NEXT PAGE.

DO YOUR FIGURING HERE.

50. What is the last term in the expansion $(2x + 3y)^4$?

F. y^4
G. $9y^4$
H. $27y^4$
J. $81y^4$
K. $(xy)^4$

51. Which of the following could be a graph of the equation $y = ax^2 + bx + c$, where $b^2 - 4ac = 0$?

A.
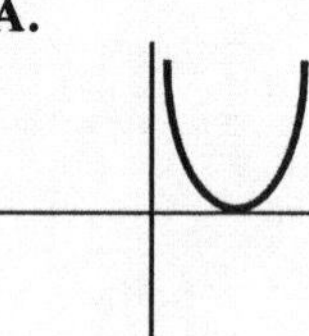

D.
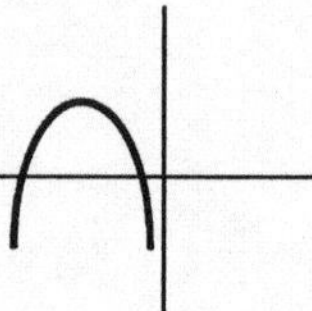

B.
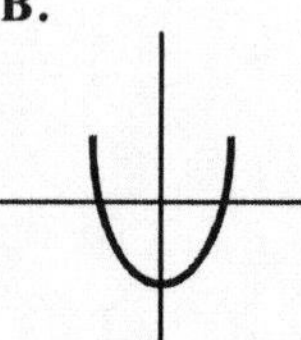

E.
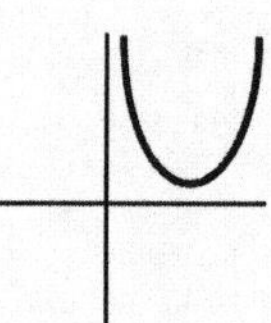

C.
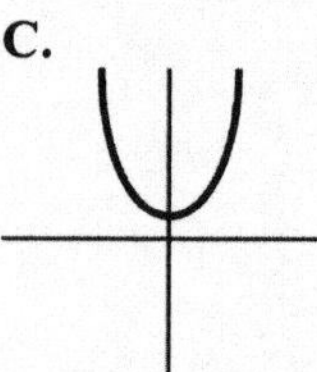

52. For any acute angle θ, which of the following is equal to $\frac{\sin\theta}{\cos\theta}$?

F. 0.5
G. 1
H. $\tan\theta$
J. $\cot\theta$
K. $\sec\theta$

53. An angle that measures $\frac{3}{2}\pi$ radians measures how many degrees?

A. 60
B. 90
C. 120
D. 180
E. 270

GO ON TO THE NEXT PAGE.

54. What is the solution set for $|2x - 1| = 3$?

DO YOUR FIGURING HERE.

F. All real numbers
G. The empty set
H. {-1}
J. {2}
K. {-1, 2}

55. The end points of a line have coordinates of (2, 5) and (2, -4). What are the coordinates of the midpoint of the line?

A. (0, 1)
B. $(2, \frac{1}{2})$
C. (2, 1)
D. (2, 9)
E. (4, 9)

56. What is the slope of the line with the equation $2x + 3y - 2 = 0$?

F. $-\frac{3}{2}$
G. $-\frac{2}{3}$
H. $\frac{2}{3}$
J. 4
K. 6

57. $\frac{1}{\sqrt{3} - 1} = ?$

A. $\frac{\sqrt{3} - 1}{4}$
B. $\frac{\sqrt{3} - 1}{3}$
C. $\frac{\sqrt{3} - 1}{2}$
D. $\frac{\sqrt{3} + 1}{2}$
E. $\sqrt{3 + 1}$

GO ON TO THE NEXT PAGE.

DO YOUR FIGURING HERE.

58. $(-2)^2 - 2^{-2} = ?$

F. -5

G. -3

H. 3

J. $3\frac{3}{4}$

K. $4\frac{1}{4}$

59. $\frac{-3+\sqrt{5}}{2}$ is 1 root of the equation $x^2 + 3x + 1 = 0$. What is the other root?

A. $\frac{3+\sqrt{5}}{2}$

B. $\frac{3-\sqrt{5}}{2}$

C. $\frac{-3-\sqrt{5}}{2}$

D. $3+\frac{\sqrt{5}}{2}$

E. $3-\frac{\sqrt{5}}{2}$

60. The figure below represents which of the following equations?

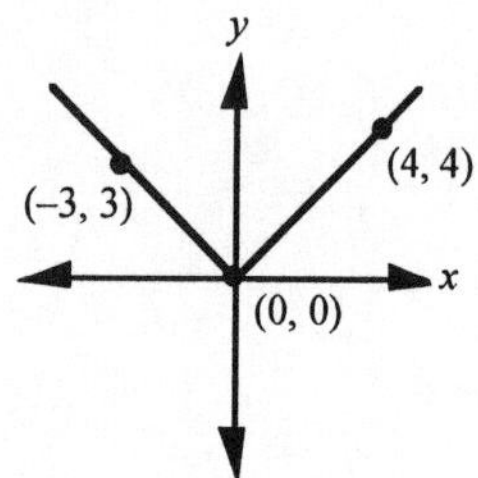

F. $y = x$

G. $y = -x$

H. $y = |x|$

J. $y = 2x$

K. $y = x^2$

END OF TEST 2.
STOP! DO NOT TURN THE PAGE UNTIL TOLD TO DO SO.
DO NOT RETURN TO THE PREVIOUS TEST.

3 3 3 3 3 3 3 3 3 3 3 3

READING TEST

35 Minutes—40 Items

DIRECTIONS: The passages presented in the test are each followed by a set of items. Read the passage and choose the best answer for each item. Fill in the corresponding oval on your bubble sheet. You may refer to the passage as often as necessary to answer the passage items.

Answers are on page 944+.

Passage I

PROSE FICTION: In this passage, the narrator shares his exasperation with and sympathy for an employee.

Turkey was a short, pursy Englishman, of about my own age—that is, somewhere not far from sixty. In the morning, one might say, his face was of a fine florid hue, but after twelve o'clock, meridian—his dinner hour—it blazed like a grate full of Christmas coals; and continued blazing—but, as it were, with a gradual wane—till six o'clock p.m., or thereabouts; after which, I saw no more of the proprietor of the face, which, gaining its meridian with the Sun, seemed to set with, to rise, culminate, and decline the following day, with the like regularity and undiminished glory. There are many singular coincidences I have known in the course of my life, not the least among which was the fact that, exactly when Turkey displayed his fullest beams from his red and radiant countenance, just then, too, at that critical moment, began the daily period when I considered his business capacities as seriously disturbed for the remainder of the twenty-four hours.

Not that he was absolutely idle, or averse to business then; far from it. The difficulty was he was apt to be altogether too energetic. There was a strange, inflamed, flurried, flighty recklessness of activity about him. He would be incautious in dipping his pen into his inkstand. All his blots upon my documents were dropped there after twelve o'clock, meridian. Indeed, not only would he be reckless, and sadly given to making blots in the afternoon, but, some days, he went further, and was rather noisy. At such times, too, his face flamed with augmented blazonry, as if cannel coal had been heaped upon anthracite. He made an unpleasant racket with his chair; spilled his sand box; in mending his pens, impatiently split them all to pieces, and threw them on the floor in a sudden passion; stood up, and leaned over his table, boxing the papers about in a most indecorous manner, very sad to behold in an elderly man like him.

Nevertheless, as he was in many ways a most valuable person to me, and all the time before twelve o'clock, meridian, was the quickest, steadiest creature, too, accomplishing a great deal of work in a style not easily to be matched—for these reasons, I was willing to overlook his eccentricities, though, indeed, occasionally, I remonstrated with him. I did this very gently, however, because, though the civilest, nay, the blandest and most reverential of men in the morning, in the afternoon he was disposed, upon provocation, to be slightly rash with his tongue—in fact, insolent. Now, valuing his morning services as I did, and resolved not to lose them—yet, at the same time, made uncomfortable by his inflamed ways after twelve o'clock—and being a man of peace, unwilling by my admonitions to call forth unseemly retorts from him, I took upon me, one Saturday noon (he was always worse on Saturdays) to hint to him, very kindly, that perhaps, now that he was growing old, it might be well to abridge his labors; in short, he need not come to my chambers after twelve o'clock, but, dinner over, had best go home to his lodgings, and rest himself till teatime. But no; he insisted upon his afternoon devotions. His countenance became intolerably fervid, as he oratorically assured me—gesticulating with a long ruler at the other end of the room—that if his services in the morning were useful, how indispensable, then, in the afternoon?

"With submission, sir," said Turkey, on this occasion, "I consider myself your right-hand man. In the morning I but marshal and deploy my columns; but in the afternoon I put myself at their head, and gallantly charge the foe, thus"—and he made a violent thrust with the ruler.

GO ON TO THE NEXT PAGE.

"But the blots, Turkey," intimated I.

"True; but, with submission sir, behold these hairs! I am getting old. Surely, sir, a blot or two of a warm afternoon is not to be severely urged against gray hairs. Old age—even if it blot the page—is honorable. With submission, sir, we *both* are getting old."

This appeal to my fellow-feeling was hardly to be resisted. At all events, I saw that go he would not. So, I made up my mind to let him stay, resolving, nevertheless, to see to it that, during the afternoon, he had to do with my less important papers.

1. The narrator is Turkey's:

A. older brother.
B. physician.
C. employer.
D. co-worker.

2. The passage suggests that Turkey is a:

F. copyist.
G. painter.
H. fencing instructor.
J. sales clerk.

3. A logical explanation for Turkey's behavior is that he:

A. becomes fatigued.
B. is growing old.
C. drinks alcohol.
D. dislikes the narrator.

4. The "fellow-feeling" mentioned in the final paragraph is based on the fact that:

F. Turkey is the narrator's right-hand man.
G. Turkey and the narrator are the same age.
H. the narrator also makes ink blots.
J. the ink blots are not very serious.

5. The narrator's final resolution of the problem is to:

A. find a replacement for Turkey.
B. give Turkey Saturdays off.
C. give Turkey afternoons off.
D. give Turkey less important work after noon.

6. According to the narrator, Turkey's face is reddest:

F. in early morning.
G. at noon.
H. in midafternoon.
J. in early evening.

7. It can be inferred that when cannel coal is heaped on anthracite, a fire:

A. burns more intensely.
B. burns less intensely.
C. goes out altogether.
D. begins to sputter and spit.

8. The narrator's attitude toward Turkey's afternoon behavior is one of:

F. amusement.
G. discomfort.
H. indifference.
J. outrage.

9. The narrator finds Turkey's work in the mornings to be:

A. entirely satisfactory.
B. frequently unsatisfactory.
C. almost always unsatisfactory.
D. inconsistent.

10. Which of the following does NOT characterize Turkey's behavior in the afternoon?

F. Frenzied activity
G. Excessive carelessness
H. Idleness
J. Verbal insolence

GO ON TO THE NEXT PAGE.

Passage II

SOCIAL SCIENCE: This passage discusses punishment for individuals who have violated the law.

Justice in society must include both a fair trial to the accused and the selection of an appropriate punishment for those proved guilty. Because justice is regarded as one form of equality, we find in its earlier expressions the idea of a punishment equal to the crime. Recorded in the Old Testament is the expression "an eye for an eye, and a tooth for a tooth." That is, the individual who has done wrong has committed an offense against society. To atone for this offense, society must get even. Only inflicting an equal injury upon him can do this. This conception of retributive justice is reflected in many parts of the legal codes and procedures of modern times. It is illustrated when we demand the death penalty for a person who has committed murder.

The German idealist, Hegel, supported this philosophy of punishment. He believed that society owed it to the criminal to administer a punishment equal to the crime committed. The criminal has by his own actions denied his true self, and it is necessary to do something to restore the self that has been denied. To the murderer, nothing less than giving up his own life will pay his debt. The exaction of the death penalty is a right the state owes the criminal, and it should not deny him his due.

Modern jurists have tried to replace retributive justice with the notion of corrective justice. The aim of the latter is not to abandon the concept of equality but to find a more adequate way to express it. It tries to preserve the ideal of equal opportunity for each individual to realize the best that is in him. The criminal is regarded as being socially ill and in need of treatment that will enable him to become a normal member of society. Before treatment can be administered, the causes that led to antisocial behavior must be found. If the causes can be removed, provisions must be made to have this done.

Only those criminals who are incurable should be permanently separated from the rest of society. This does not mean that criminals will escape punishment or be quickly returned to take up careers of crime. It means that justice is to heal the individual, not simply to get even with him. If severe punishment is the only adequate means for accomplishing this, it should be administered. However, the individual should be given every opportunity to assume a normal place in society. His conviction of crime must not deprive him of the opportunity to make his way in the society of which he is a part.

11. The best title for this selection is:

  A. Fitting Punishment to the Crime.
  B. Approaches to Just Punishment.
  C. Improvement in Legal Justice.
  D. Attaining Justice in the Courts.

12. Hegel would view the death sentence for murder as:

  F. inadequate justice.
  G. the best way for society to get revenge.
  H. the most efficient method of removing a known danger.
  J. an inalienable right of the murderer.

13. The passage implies that the basic difference between retributive justice and corrective justice is:

  A. the type of crime that was committed.
  B. the severity of the punishment.
  C. the reason for the sentence.
  D. the outcome of the trial.

14. The punishment that would be most inconsistent with the views of corrective justice is:

  F. forced brain surgery.
  G. solitary confinement.
  H. life imprisonment.
  J. the electric chair.

15. The Biblical expression "an eye for an eye, and a tooth for a tooth" was presented in order to:

  A. justify the need for punishment as a part of law.
  B. give moral backing to retributive justice.
  C. show that humanity has long been interested in justice as a form of equality.
  D. indicate the lack of social development during Biblical times.

GO ON TO THE NEXT PAGE.

16. The concept of retributive justice still reflected in many modern legal codes is:

F. giving the accused a fair trial.
G. rehabilitating the criminal.
H. separating incurable criminals from the rest of society.
J. inflicting equal injury on the criminal.

17. A major goal of modern jurists is to:

A. ensure that criminals do not escape punishment.
B. preserve the notion of equality.
C. restore states' rights.
D. select an appropriate punishment for a crime.

18. Under the notion of corrective justice, assuming "a normal place in society" (line 46) most likely means:

F. acting in one's best interests.
G. denying one's true self.
H. curing antisocial behavior.
J. accepting punishment.

19. The author's tone in the passage is best described as:

A. argumentative.
B. sympathetic.
C. explanatory.
D. conciliatory.

20. According to the author, criminals cannot be treated until:

F. they have been punished properly for their crime.
G. they have received a fair trial.
H. a legal code for treatment has been established.
J. the causes of antisocial behavior have been found.

GO ON TO THE NEXT PAGE.

Passage III

HUMANITIES: This passage describes events leading to and the effects of World War I.

The event that touched off World War I occurred in Sarajevo, the capital of the Austro-Hungarian province of Bosnia, on June 28, 1914. There the Archduke Francis Ferdinand, the Hapsburg heir to the throne of the Austro-Hungarian Empire, was shot and killed by a young Serbian nationalist seeking revenge against the Austrians for their annexation of Bosnia. Austria issued an ultimatum to Serbia. The Serbians acquiesced, in an attempt to stave off war. Austria, however, was intent on exacting retribution and in July of that year declared war on Serbia.

For almost a century, since the Congress of Vienna in 1815, European diplomats had prevented any real threat to the delicate balance of power achieved by the Congress. This time, though, they seemed powerless to stop the movement toward war. The assassination provoked a fateful series of failed diplomatic attempts that led suspicious Russia to mobilize its armed forces as Serbia's ally. Austria sought and received the mobilization aid of its ally Germany. The other members of the Triple Entente, France and Great Britain, soon joined their ally Russia against Austria. In 1917, the United States was drawn into the battle as an ally of France and Great Britain.

World War I was unlike any other war fought before or since. The profound shock it generated dramatically affected the progression of life in Europe and America and changed the course of world politics. Moreover, the war shocked millions of people throughout Europe into confronting the terrible losses and the grim and brutal realities of modern war. The few wars that had been fought since 1815 were distant colonial wars. Europeans had always been victorious, and the battles seemed nothing more than skirmishes that offered chances to experience adventure and to demonstrate bravery and heroism. The trenches and battlefields of Europe introduced millions of young men and women to a world of pain and death that they had never imagined.

The war altered the collective social sensibility of the people of Europe. It destroyed the spirit of optimism that had prevailed in the nineteenth century. Civilized, polite behavior now seemed archaic and utterly hypocritical. Moreover, the impression that there appeared to be no sane way to end the carnage only added to the sense of futility. The war changed relationships between members of the same social class. Before the war, the upper classes of Europe felt a common bond that united them across national borders. After the war, national boundaries defined social consciousness in a way that destroyed the solidarity of class.

World War I produced several dramatic changes in the political landscape of Europe. The breakup of the Austro-Hungarian, Russian, and German empires led to the reemergence of the state of Poland and the formation of other independent nation states in Europe. The war acted as a catalyst for European revolutionaries. The Russian Revolution of 1917 set the stage for the Bolshevik seizure of power, the exercise of total power by the Communist party; and the rise of Stalin as the absolute dictator of the Russian state (renamed the Union of Soviet Socialist Republics). World War I bore bitter fruit in Central and Southern Europe as well. The rise of Nazism in Germany and fascism in Italy led many historians to conclude that World War II, which was begun by Nazi Germany in 1939, was in actuality the continuation of the Great War that destroyed the social fabric of Europe in 1914.

21. The precipitating cause of World War I was:

A. an assassination.
B. a coronation.
C. a rebellion.
D. a plebiscite.

22. The event occurred in the city of:

F. Sarajevo in Bosnia.
G. Vienna in Austria.
H. Trieste in Italy.
J. Budapest in Hungary.

23. Before World War I, a balance of power had existed for:

A. nearly 15 years.
B. almost a quarter century.
C. almost 100 years.
D. nearly 10 years.

GO ON TO THE NEXT PAGE.

24. The chief reason European countries other than Austria and Serbia were drawn into the conflict was that they:

    F. were members of the two alliance systems to which the combatants belonged.
    G. feared the Hapsburgs.
    H. wanted to ensure freedom of the seas.
    J. wanted the land of neighboring countries.

25. Mobilization for war resulted swiftly when:

    A. the United States declared war.
    B. attempts at diplomacy failed.
    C. Russia refused to help Serbia.
    D. Italy joined the conflict.

26. The way in which class relationships changed as a result of the outbreak of World War I suggests that:

    F. nationalism might have weakened had the war never occurred.
    G. the middle classes had no real love of country.
    H. the upper classes had eagerly anticipated war.
    J. everyone sanctioned the war.

27. The forces of militant nationalism that were unleashed during World War I culminated in the breakup of the Russian Empire and the German Empire. The political regimes that came to power in Germany and the Soviet Union before World War II were:

    A. democracies that isolated themselves from world politics.
    B. ruthless dictatorships dedicated to world conquest.
    C. weak states allied with the United States.
    D. members of a Europe-wide common market.

28. The sense of futility felt throughout Europe during and after World War I would be evident in a study of:

    F. American investment policies.
    G. statistics concerning foreign language study in America.
    H. European literature of the 1920s, 1930s, and 1940s.
    J. the number of transatlantic voyages between 1920 and 1930.

29. World War I and its aftermath suggest the idea that:

    A. nationalism has little to do with world conflict.
    B. war feeds on nationalist sympathies.
    C. the cause of peace is best aided by reinvigorating the spirit of nationalism.
    D. diplomacy never works.

30. Archduke Francis Ferdinand, as the heir to the Austro-Hungarian Empire, was a member of the:

    F. Hohenzollern family.
    G. Hanover family.
    H. Hapsburg family.
    J. Stuart family.

GO ON TO THE NEXT PAGE.

Passage IV

NATURAL SCIENCE: This selection discusses the information gathered about the planet Uranus by the Voyager 2 spacecraft.

When the Voyager 2 spacecraft flew past Uranus and its moons in 1986, it gathered startling new information about these extraordinary celestial objects. Uranus had long been known to be different from all the other planets in one important respect: It lies tipped over on its side and instead of spinning like a top, it rolls like a ball along the path of its orbit. Its geographic poles, instead of being on the top and bottom of the planet as Earth's are, are located on either side, one facing the Sun and one facing away—as if they were the ends of a gigantic axle. Voyager found another oddity: Uranus' magnetic poles, instead of lying close to the geographic poles as Earth's do, are located not far from the planet's equator, 60° away from the geographic poles. Still another discovery is that the clouds in the Uranian atmosphere move in the same direction as the planet rotates; that is, from top to bottom and back to top, rather than horizontally, as Earth's clouds move.

The Uranian moons proved to have equally striking features. Miranda, the moon nearest the planet, bears tremendous markings where terrains of completely different types appear to have been wedged together. On Ariel, the next moon out, the landscape has been stretched apart, creating huge faults where the ground has broken apart and sunk inward. However, there is no evidence of any geological activity. Umbriel, the third moon, seems to be "painted" with some dark substance. On one side of Umbriel is a large, round bright marking called the "donut." It is presumably some type of impact crater. Each of Uranus' other seven moons is equally odd and unique in its own way. Furthermore, between the orbit of Miranda and Uranus' surface are up to one hundred charcoal-colored rings, ringlets, and bands of dust, and between some of these rings are still more tiny moonlets.

The moons and rings of Uranus are odd in still another way. Like the clouds in the planet's atmosphere, they circle Uranus in the same direction as the planet rotates. That is, they orbit over the top and bottom of the planet rather than around the sides, as Earth's moon does.

31. Because of the odd way in which Uranus rotates, one geographic pole:

A. alternates between daylight and darkness.
B. receives only indirect sunlight.
C. varies between heat from the Sun and cold.
D. is always in darkness.

32. The warmest spot on Uranus would most likely be located at:

F. one of the magnetic poles.
G. the equator.
H. one of the geographic poles.
J. a spot midway between a geographic pole and the equator.

33. On Uranus, a surface location that receives sunlight:

A. will alternate between daylight and darkness.
B. will always be in daylight.
C. will occasionally be in darkness.
D. must be near one of the magnetic poles.

34. The Uranian equator extends:

F. around the planet horizontally, as Earth's does.
G. around the planet through the geographic poles.
H. around the planet from top to bottom.
J. around the planet through the magnetic poles.

35. An observer at the Uranian equator would most likely experience:

A. a regular succession of days and nights.
B. constant, indirect sunlight.
C. a regular succession of warmth and cold.
D. only darkness.

GO ON TO THE NEXT PAGE.

36. Auroras are sky phenomena that generally appear near a planet's magnetic poles. On Earth, auroras can be seen at extreme north or south latitudes. On Uranus, auroras would most likely:

F. be visible near the planet's geographic poles.
G. never be visible.
H. be visible not far from the planet's equator.
J. be visible from everywhere on the planet's surface.

37. On Earth, atmospheric circulation patterns are largely controlled by the varying amounts of sunlight received at different latitudes. On Uranus:

A. atmospheric circulation functions in an identical way.
B. there is no atmospheric circulation.
C. the atmosphere circulates from one geographic pole to the other.
D. some other factor besides sunlight controls atmospheric circulation.

38. It has been suggested that the moon Miranda was shattered into pieces by a collision with some other object. Gravity then caused the pieces to reassemble; however, great "seam" marks most likely remained because:

F. the gravitational forces involved were weak.
G. the lack of atmosphere meant that no erosion ever took place.
H. the second object remained nearby, exerting gravitational pull.
J. the force of the collision was so great.

39. The great faults observed on the moon Ariel could have been caused by:

A. moonquakes.
B. continental drift.
C. the gravitational pull of other nearby moons.
D. volcanic activity.

40. Uranus has how many moons?

F. 3
G. 7
H. 10
J. 12

END OF TEST 3.
STOP! DO NOT TURN THE PAGE UNTIL TOLD TO DO SO.
DO NOT RETURN TO A PREVIOUS TEST.

4 4 4 4 4 4 4 4 4 4 4 4

SCIENCE REASONING TEST

35 Minutes—40 Items

DIRECTIONS: The passages presented in the test are each followed by a set of items. Read the passage and choose the best answer for each item. Fill in the corresponding oval on your bubble sheet. You may refer to the passage as often as necessary to answer the passage items.

Warning: Calculator use is not permitted on this test.

Answers are on page 944.

Passage I

The table below shows selected elements from the periodic table, together with atomic radii in angstrom units (Å) and electronegativities (second number). When two atoms form a covalent bond, the approximate bond length may be calculated by adding together the two atomic radii.

H 0.37 Å 2.20						
Li 1.35 Å 0.98	Be 0.90 Å 1.57	B 0.80 Å 2.04	C 0.77 Å 2.55	N 0.70 Å 3.04	O 0.66 Å 3.44	F 0.64 Å 3.98
Na 1.54 Å 0.93	Mg 1.30 Å 1.31	Al 1.25 Å 1.61	Si 1.17 Å 1.90	P 1.10 Å 2.19	S 1.04 Å 2.58	Cl 0.99 Å 3.16
K 1.96 Å 0.82						Br 1.14 Å 2.96
Rb 2.11 Å 0.82						I 1.33 Å 2.66

The electronegativity has important chemical significance. If two atoms form a bond, the difference in the two electronegativities indicates the degree to which the bond is covalent (indicated by a small difference) or ionic (indicated by a large difference).

1. What occurs when moving down the table's columns?

   A. Radii decrease; electronegativities decrease.
   B. Radii increase; electronegativities increase.
   C. Radii decrease; electronegativities increase.
   D. Radii increase; electronegativities decrease.

2. The greatest electronegativity in the table is:

   F. fluorine (F).
   G. chlorine (Cl).
   H. rubidium (Rb).
   J. hydrogen (H).

3. The bond length in the P-Cl bond is:

   A. 0.11 angstroms.
   B. 0.97 angstroms.
   C. 2.09 angstroms.
   D. 5.35 angstroms.

4. The bond between which of the following is likely to have the most covalent character?

   F. Sodium (Na) and iodine (I)
   G. Magnesium (Mg) and oxygen (O)
   H. Sulfur (S) and oxygen (O)
   J. Carbon (C) and nitrogen (N)

5. The table indicates that bonds of greatest ionic character generally occur:

   A. between elements by each other in a row.
   B. between elements that are near each other in a column but far apart along a row.
   C. between elements that are far apart along a column but close in a row.
   D. between elements far apart along a column and far apart in a row.

GO ON TO THE NEXT PAGE.

6. The element cesium (Cs) lies directly below rubidium (Rb) in the Periodic Table. The electronegativity difference in CsF is likely to be:

   F. less than 3.16.
   G. equal to 3.16.
   H. greater than 3.16.
   J. Cannot be determined from the given information

GO ON TO THE NEXT PAGE.

Passage II

A set of experiments was carried out to investigate the relative sizes of the planets of our solar system and the relative distances from the Sun. Table 1 was given to all students performing the experiments.

Experiment 1: Using a compass, ruler, and paper (11 in. × 14 in.), students were asked to compare the sizes of the planets. Calling the size of Earth 1.00 (Earth diameter = 5 in.), a circle was made by inserting the point of the compass in the center of the paper. The circle had a radius of 2.5 in. to produce a circle with a diameter of 5 in. representing the Earth. All other planets were drawn to scale based on the size of their diameters relative to one Earth diameter (Table 1).

Table 1

Planet	*Approximate Diameter (in Earth diameters)*	*Approximate Distance from the Sun (A.U.)*
Mercury	0.38	0.40
Venus	0.95	0.70
Earth	1.00	1.00
Mars	0.54	1.50
Jupiter	11.20	5.20
Saturn	9.50	9.50
Uranus	3.70	19.20
Neptune	3.50	30.00
Pluto	0.47	40.00

Experiment 2: Using the equipment from Experiment 1, students were also asked to compare planetary distances from the Sun. The Earth is 93 million miles from the Sun. This distance is called 1.00 Astronomical Unit (1 A.U. = 0.5 inches), and it was used as a reference distance when the other planets were drawn at their proper distances (Table 1) from the Sun (a planet twice as far as the Earth is from the Sun would be drawn 2 A.U., or 1.0 inches, from the Sun).

7. In Experiment 1, the two planets represented by circles most similar in size on the paper are:

   A. Earth and Venus.
   B. Mars and Pluto.
   C. Uranus and Neptune.
   D. Mercury and Pluto.

8. In Experiment 2, if the paper were held the "long way" and the left-hand paper edge represented the Sun, which planet(s) would not fit on the paper?

   F. Uranus, Neptune, and Pluto
   G. Neptune and Pluto
   H. Pluto only
   J. All planets would fit on the paper.

9. Which of the following statements is supported by the data in Table 1?

   A. The larger the planet, the greater is its distance from the Sun.
   B. The smaller the planet, the greater is its distance from the Sun.
   C. Only planets larger than the Earth are farther away from the Sun.
   D. There is no consistent pattern between a planet's size and its distance from the Sun.

10. A planet's "year" is how long it takes to orbit the Sun and it is related to the distance of that planet from the Sun. If asteroids are found 2.8 A.U. from the Sun, an "asteroid year" should be:

   F. longer than a "Mars year" but shorter than a "Jupiter year."
   G. longer than an "Earth year" but shorter than a "Mars year."
   H. longer than an "Earth year" but shorter than a "Neptune year."
   J. longer than a "Neptune year" but shorter than a "Uranus year."

11. In Experiment 1, how large would a circle representing the Sun be if its diameter is approximately 110 times greater than that of the Earth?

   A. It would have a radius of approximately 550 inches.
   B. It would have a diameter of approximately 550 inches.
   C. It would have a radius of approximately 55 inches.
   D. It would have a diameter of approximately 55 inches.

12. A third experiment was conducted in which the mass of each planet was described relative to the mass of the Earth (Jupiter had the greatest mass, Saturn had the next largest mass, Mercury and Pluto had the smallest masses). If the planets were placed in an order based on how they compared to Earth for the variables measured in all three experiments, which two orders would be expected to be most similar?

   F. Diameter and distance from the Sun
   G. Mass and distance from the Sun
   H. Diameter and mass
   J. All three orders would be similar.

GO ON TO THE NEXT PAGE.

Passage III

It is known that during photosynthesis, leaf pigments absorb light energy that eventually results in the production of glucose and other carbohydrates to be used by the green plant. Oxygen gas (O_2) is also produced during the process. Various factors affecting the rate of photosynthesis were investigated by counting the number of oxygen bubbles produced under the conditions described in the following three experiments.

Experiment 1: A sample of leaf extract (a mixture of pigments previously separated from other leaf components) from the pond plant *Elodea* was placed in a beaker containing water and a standard concentration of carbon dioxide (CO_2) (both are necessary ingredients for photosynthesis). Light of varying intensity was used to illuminate the beaker, and the number of oxygen bubbles emitted by the plant each minute was recorded. The results are illustrated in Figure 1.

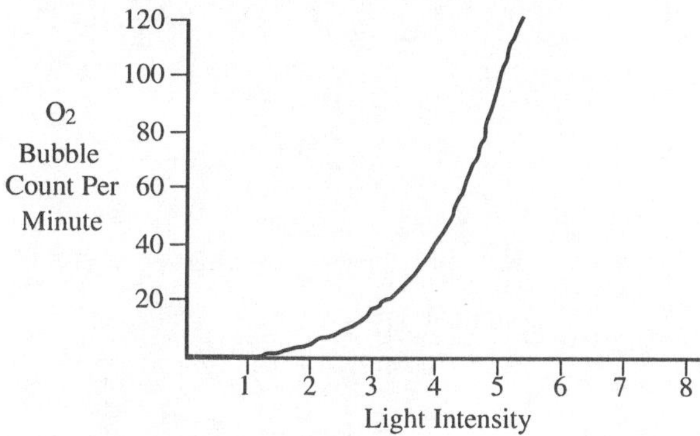

Figure 1

Experiment 2: An identical experiment was conducted in which the concentration of leaf extract was reduced four-fold (the mixture was one-fourth as concentrated as in Experiment 1). The results are shown in Figure 2.

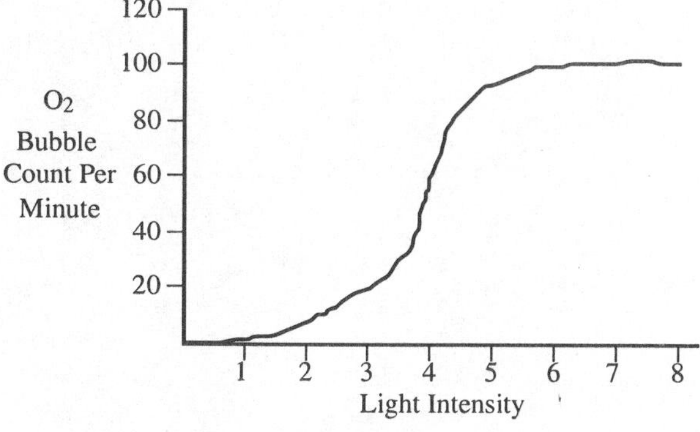

Figure 2

Experiment 3: Visible light consists of many different colors, or light wavelengths. Only those wavelengths that are absorbed by leaf pigments can provide the energy to maintain photosynthesis in the leaf. Different light wavelengths were used separately to illuminate two samples of leaf extract, each containing a different *Elodea* leaf pigment. Oxygen (O_2) bubbles were counted again as a measure of the rate of photosynthesis. Figure 3 summarizes the results.

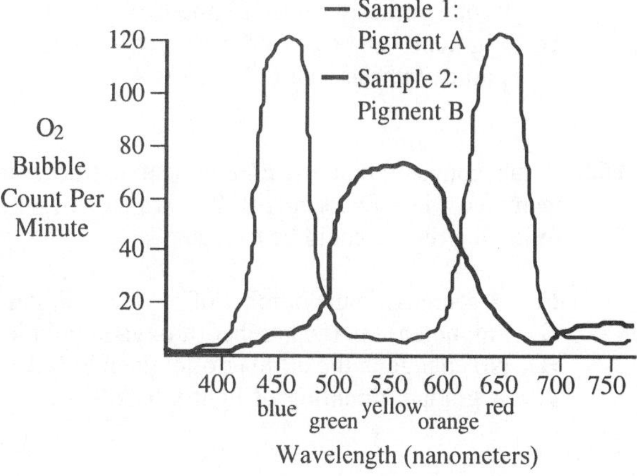

Figure 3

13. When running Experiment 1, which of the following changes in CO_2 should be made in order to determine its effect on the rate of photosynthesis?

A. Repeat the experiment using the same concentration of CO_2 in the beaker of water, but with different species of green plants.
B. Repeat the experiment using first no CO_2 and then varying concentrations of carbon dioxide in the beaker of water.
C. Repeat the experiment using different levels of water in the beaker containing a standard concentration of CO_2.
D. Repeat the experiment using additional light intensities.

14. The results in Experiments 1 and 2 demonstrate that in order to maintain a continued increase in the photosynthesis rate:

F. adequate amounts of light are needed.
G. adequate amounts of carbon dioxide are needed.
H. adequate amounts of oxygen are needed.
J. adequate amounts of leaf pigments are needed.

GO ON TO THE NEXT PAGE.

15. Based on the information in Figure 3, which of the following statements is correct?

A. Pigment A primarily absorbs light at 450 and 650 nanometers, while Pigment B absorbs light at 500-575 nanometers.
B. Pigment B primarily absorbs light at 450 and 650 nanometers, while Pigment A primarily absorbs light at 500-575 nanometers.
C. Pigment A can influence the rate of photosynthesis, while Pigment B cannot.
D. Pigment B can influence the rate of photosynthesis, while Pigment A cannot.

16. If the concentration of *Elodea* leaf extract was increased in Experiment 2, which of the following results could be expected?

F. A decrease in the number of oxygen bubbles
G. An increase in the number of oxygen bubbles
H. No change in the number of oxygen bubbles
J. A gradual dimming of light intensity

17. In Experiments 1 and 2, approximately how many oxygen bubbles/minute were produced at a light intensity level of 4?

A. 20-30
B. 30-40
C. 40-50
D. Between 0 and 10

18. According to the information in Figure 3, if an additional experiment were conducted, which condition would be LEAST effective in maintaining photosynthetic rate in *Elodea*?

F. Using blue light only
G. Using red light only
H. Using yellow light only
J. Using orange light only

GO ON TO THE NEXT PAGE.

Passage IV

The accompanying figure shows how the world records for various footraces have improved during a portion of this century. Speeds are given in both meters/minute and minutes/mile.

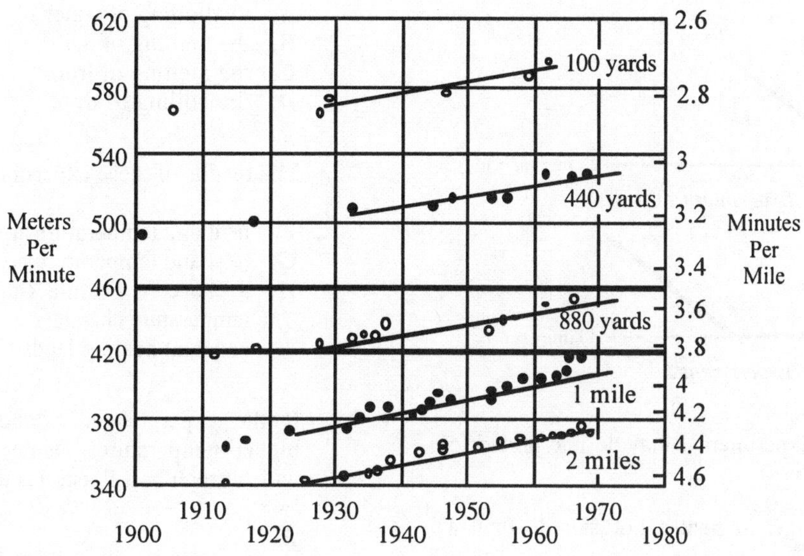

Modified from H.W. Ryder, H.J. Carr, and P. Herget, "Future performance in footracing," *Sci. Amer.* 234 (6): 109-114, 1976.

19. In what race and in what year was the greatest speed in meters/minute achieved?

A. The 440-yard dash in 1900
B. The 100-yard dash in 1930
C. The 100-yard dash in 1962
D. The 1-mile run in 1947

20. The trend in the graphs of meters/minute for the various distances shows:

F. roughly a linear increase.
G. roughly a linear decrease.
H. a linear increase for short distances and a linear decrease for long distances.
J. no systematic pattern.

21. For 1960, the ratio of minutes/mile values for the 1-mile run to that for the 440-yard dash is roughly:

A. 3/4
B. 4/5
C. 5/4
D. 4/3

22. The increase in speed, in meters/minute, for the 2-mile run from 1925 to 1967 is roughly:

F. 0.3
G. 10
H. 30
J. 100

23. If the trends shown can be expected to hold for later years, then the value of minutes per mile for the 880-yard run in 1980 is expected to be:

A. 3.5
B. 3.8
C. 420
D. 460

GO ON TO THE NEXT PAGE.

Passage V

Two experiments were performed in which constant amounts of heat were added continuously to samples over a defined period of time. The temperatures of the samples were monitored while the heat was added. The results from the two experiments are shown below.

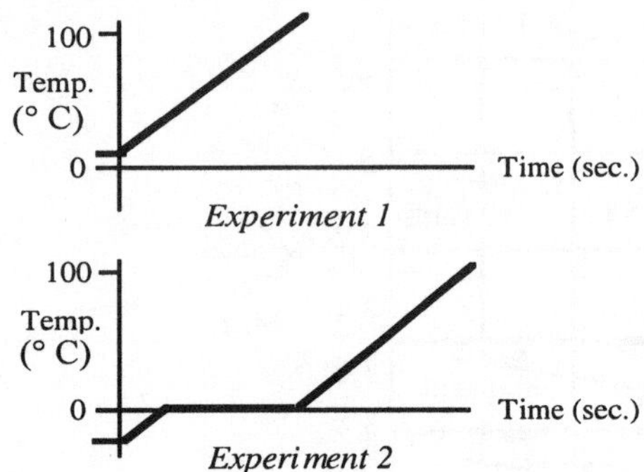

24. The results of Experiment 1 may be interpreted to show that:

    F. it takes longer to heat a hot sample than a cold one.
    G. the temperature of the sample rises proportionately with time as heat is applied.
    H. temperature is not related to heat.
    J. temperature and time measure the same thing.

25. Experiment 2 differs from Experiment 1 in that:

    A. only the starting temperature is different in the two experiments.
    B. the graph in Experiment 2 is not a straight line; there must have been experimental error.
    C. Experiment 2 has a lower starting temperature and a time period when the temperature does not rise.
    D. in Experiment 2, the heat went off for a while in the middle of the experiment.

26. The experimenter wants to explain the flat part of the graph from Experiment 2. It could represent:

    F. a period when the clock was turned off.
    G. a period when the heat was turned off.
    H. a period when heat was added but some process that did not occur in the first experiment (such as absorption of heat), caused the temperature to remain constant.
    J. a period when less heat was added.

27. The "phase" of the sample changes (an example of a phase change is the melting of a solid, or the boiling of a liquid) in conjunction with the flat part of the graph in Experiment 2. From the temperature data given, the phase change might be:

    A. the boiling of water.
    B. the melting of ice.
    C. the melting of iron.
    D. the boiling of iron.

28. The results of these experiments demonstrate that:

    F. heat and temperature are basically the same.
    G. heat and temperature are not the same.
    H. a pause in heating can lead to a pause in temperature change.
    J. constant heating leads to constant change.

29. If the experimenter extends Experiment 2 to higher temperatures, using water as a sample, which graph best illustrates the expected results?

    A.

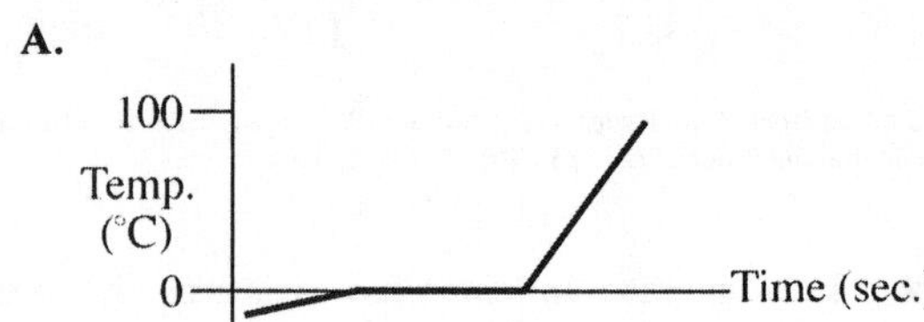

B.

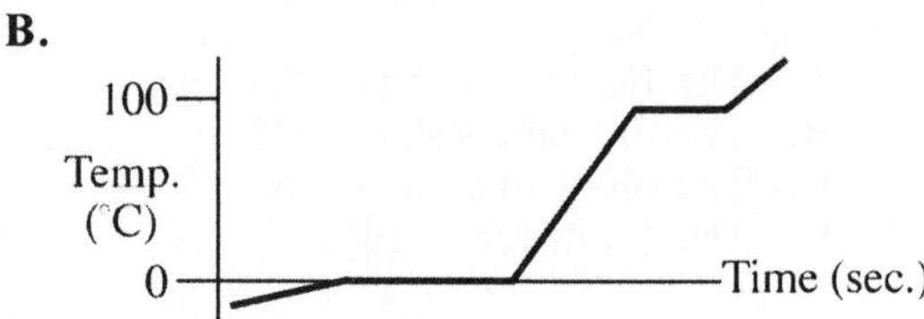

C.

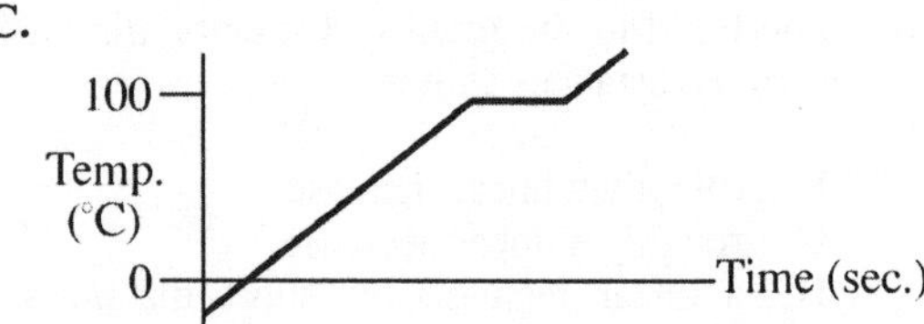

D.

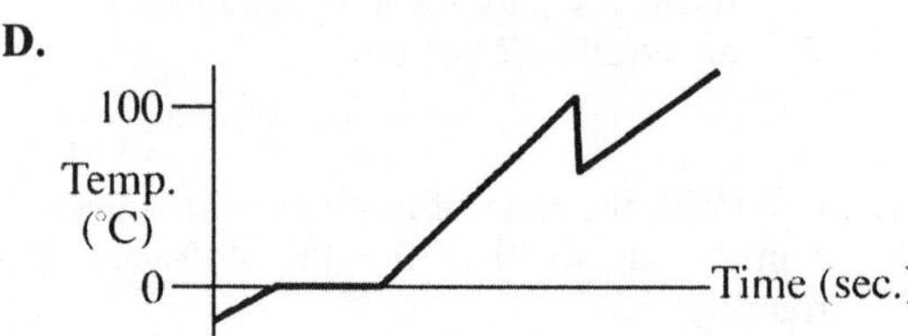

GO ON TO THE NEXT PAGE.

Passage VI

The following chart shows the generalized sequence of early developmental stages (terms in boxes) observed in most vertebrates.

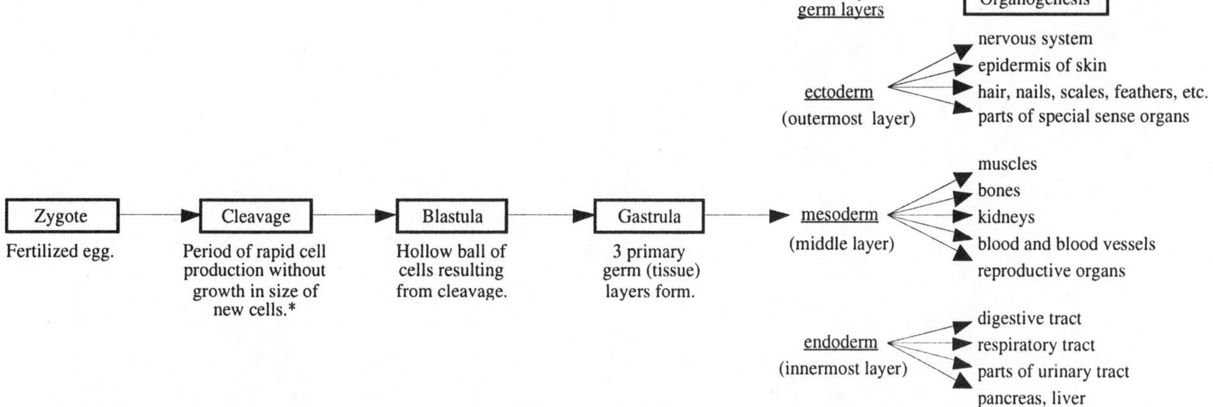

*New cells form as the zygote and its subsequent daughter cells divide and re-divide.

30. According to the chart, the stage of development when the three primary tissue layers form is:

F. cleavage.
G. blastula.
H. gastrula.
J. organogenesis.

31. Differentiation refers to a period of cell maturation during which time cells become specialized in structure and function. At which stage of development would most differentiation be expected to occur?

A. Cleavage
B. Blastula
C. Gastrula
D. Organogenesis

32. Based on the information in the diagram, which conclusion is NOT correct?

F. Vertebrates develop three primary germ layers.
G. Most bones develop from the innermost primary germ layer.
H. Diverse structures such as scales, feathers, and hair always develop from the same primary germ layer.
J. Before an organism can form different primary tissue layers, it must go through a stage in which it is in the form of a hollow ball of cells.

33. If a species of monkey were found to have extraordinary vision due to special receptor cells that were highly sensitive to different colors of light, from which primary germ layer(s) would you predict such cells to develop?

A. Endoderm
B. Mesoderm
C. Ectoderm
D. A combination of endoderm and mesoderm

GO ON TO THE NEXT PAGE.

34. On the basis of the information provided, the stage of development that probably has the smallest cells is:

F. zygote.
G. cleavage.
H. gastrula.
J. adult.

GO ON TO THE NEXT PAGE.

Passage VII

The following are two theories regarding the proportions of chemicals that will react to form products.

Theory 1: Although a chemical reaction is more than simple mixing, the two are similar in that any amounts of reactants may be brought together to form chemical products that contain the same elements as the reactants. For example, in the reaction "hydrogen + oxygen ⇒ water" we may use 1 mole of hydrogen and 1 mole of oxygen, or 2 to 1, or 1 to 2, *etc.* The reaction will adjust to the proportions given.

Theory 2: Only certain proportions of reactants will combine chemically. For example, when hydrogen and oxygen are reacted, the amounts that will combine will be *exactly* 2 grams of hydrogen for every 32 grams of oxygen. We can show, using molecular weights, that these weights of reactants (which correspond to 2 moles of hydrogen and 1 mole of oxygen), imply the following reaction:

$$2H_2 + O_2 \Rightarrow 2H_2O$$

From this statement about the proportions of hydrogens and oxygens that react with each other, we can conclude that two hydrogen molecules must react with a single oxygen molecule to form two molecules of water.

35. Theory 1 does NOT predict which of the following?

A. 2 moles of zinc may react completely with 2 moles of sulfur.
B. 2 moles of zinc may react completely with 3 moles of sulfur.
C. 7 moles of zinc may react completely with 4 moles of sulfur.
D. If 3 moles of zinc were mixed with 4 moles of sulfur, 1 mole of sulfur would be left unreacted.

36. According to Theory 1, how many moles of water would be produced by the reaction of 2 moles of hydrogen and 1 mole of oxygen?

F. 1
G. 2
H. 4
J. Cannot be determined from the given information

37. An experimenter finds that when 170 grams of $AgNO_3$ is reacted with 58.5 grams of NaCl to form products, none of the original reactants remain in appreciable amounts. When the original amount of $AgNO_3$ is increased to 175 grams, then all of the NaCl is used up, but 5 grams of $AgNO_3$ remains. This result is:

A. consistent with Theory 1.
B. consistent with Theory 2.
C. consistent with both Theory 1 and Theory 2.
D. not consistent with either theory.

38. According to Theory 2, how might the remaining 5 grams of $AgNO_3$ be used up?

F. Add more of the reactant NaCl.
G. Remove some of the reactant NaCl.
H. Add even more of the reactant $AgNO_3$.
J. There is no mechanism for using the 5 grams of $AgNO_3$.

39. An experimenter wishes to determine which theory better fits her data for an experiment in which iron (Fe) is chemically combined with oxygen (O). She finds that 2 moles of Fe will react completely with 2 moles of O; she also finds that 2 moles of Fe will react completely with 3 moles of O. At this point she is confident that Theory 1, which is in opposition to the idea of "definite proportions," is correct. What further experiment might she do to test the success of Theory 1 over Theory 2?

A. Add 1 mole of Fe to 1 mole of O.
B. Add 2 moles of Fe to 4 moles of O.
C. Add 3 moles of Fe to 4.5 moles of O.
D. Add 4 moles of Fe to 4 moles of O.

40. According to Theory 1, the product of the reaction of hydrogen and oxygen:

F. is H_2O.
G. could be anything.
H. must contain hydrogen and oxygen, but lacks a specific formula.
J. has a definite proportion of hydrogen to oxygen.

END OF TEST 4.
STOP! DO NOT TURN THE PAGE UNTIL TOLD TO DO SO.
DO NOT RETURN TO A PREVIOUS TEST.

5 5 5 5 5 5 5 5 5 5 5 5

WRITING TEST (OPTIONAL)

30 Minutes—1 Essay Prompt

DIRECTIONS: This is a test of your writing skills. Before you begin planning and writing your essay, read the writing prompt carefully to understand the instructions. Your essay will be evaluated on the evidence it provides of your ability to express judgments by taking a position on the issue in the writing prompt; to maintain a focus on the topic throughout the essay; to develop a position by using logical reasoning and supporting ideas; to organize ideas in a logical way; and to use language clearly and effectively according to the conventions of standard written English.

If you finish before time is called, you may review your work. Lay your pencil down immediately when time is called.

Writing Test Prompt

The founders of this country viewed public education as a way to instill civic virtues such as patriotism, honesty, hard work, and personal responsibility. Some people think that school's today do not place enough emphasis on these virtues and say that schools should require a course in civics as part of each year of the high school curriculum. Only by producing a population, they say, that knows the value of these virtues will it be possible to maintain a secure and prosperous nation. Other people think that the purpose of public schools is purely educational and that the schools should not attempt to teach civic virtues. They note that while people tend to agree that patriotism, honesty, hard work, and responsibility are virtuous, people disagree on what these ideas mean in specific circumstance. They point out, for example, that many people think it is unpatriotic to protest when the country is at war while others think that it is patriotic to oppose an unjust or unwise war. Consequently, this group says that teaching about these virtues should be left to family, religion, and other civic organizations. Do you think that schools should teach civic virtues such as patriotism, honesty, hard work, and personal responsibility?

In your essay, take a position on this issue. You may address either of the two points described above, or you may offer an entirely different perspective on the issue. Be sure to use specific reasons and examples to support your analysis.

END OF TEST 5.
STOP! DO NOT RETURN TO ANY OTHER TEST.

Practice Test III

TARGETED EDUCATIONAL SOLUTIONS.

Cambridge Course Concept Outline
PRACTICE TEST III

When completing Practice Test III, use the Bubble Sheet on page 779, unless otherwise directed by your instructor.

BUBBLE SHEET

Name ______________________ Student ID Number ______________________

Date ______________ Instructor ______________________ Course/Session Number ______________

TEST 1—ENGLISH

1 A B C D	16 F G H J	31 A B C D	46 F G H J	61 A B C D
2 F G H J	17 A B C D	32 F G H J	47 A B C D	62 F G H J
3 A B C D	18 F G H J	33 A B C D	48 F G H J	63 A B C D
4 F G H J	19 A B C D	34 F G H J	49 A B C D	64 F G H J
5 A B C D	20 F G H J	35 A B C D	50 F G H J	65 A B C D
6 F G H J	21 A B C D	36 F G H J	51 A B C D	66 F G H J
7 A B C D	22 F G H J	37 A B C D	52 F G H J	67 A B C D
8 F G H J	23 A B C D	38 F G H J	53 A B C D	68 F G H J
9 A B C D	24 F G H J	39 A B C D	54 F G H J	69 A B C D
10 F G H J	25 A B C D	40 F G H J	55 A B C D	70 F G H J
11 A B C D	26 F G H J	41 A B C D	56 F G H J	71 A B C D
12 F G H J	27 A B C D	42 F G H J	57 A B C D	72 F G H J
13 A B C D	28 F G H J	43 A B C D	58 F G H J	73 A B C D
14 F G H J	29 A B C D	44 F G H J	59 A B C D	74 F G H J
15 A B C D	30 F G H J	45 A B C D	60 F G H J	75 A B C D

TEST 2—MATHEMATICS

1 A B C D E	13 A B C D E	25 A B C D E	37 A B C D E	49 A B C D E
2 F G H J K	14 F G H J K	26 F G H J K	38 F G H J K	50 F G H J K
3 A B C D E	15 A B C D E	27 A B C D E	39 A B C D E	51 A B C D E
4 F G H J K	16 F G H J K	28 F G H J K	40 F G H J K	52 F G H J K
5 A B C D E	17 A B C D E	29 A B C D E	41 A B C D E	53 A B C D E
6 F G H J K	18 F G H J K	30 F G H J K	42 F G H J K	54 F G H J K
7 A B C D E	19 A B C D E	31 A B C D E	43 A B C D E	55 A B C D E
8 F G H J K	20 F G H J K	32 F G H J K	44 F G H J K	56 F G H J K
9 A B C D E	21 A B C D E	33 A B C D E	45 A B C D E	57 A B C D E
10 F G H J K	22 F G H J K	34 F G H J K	46 F G H J K	58 F G H J K
11 A B C D E	23 A B C D E	35 A B C D E	47 A B C D E	59 A B C D E
12 F G H J K	24 F G H J K	36 F G H J K	48 F G H J K	60 F G H J K

TEST 3—READING

1 A B C D	9 A B C D	17 A B C D	25 A B C D	33 A B C D
2 F G H J	10 F G H J	18 F G H J	26 F G H J	34 F G H J
3 A B C D	11 A B C D	19 A B C D	27 A B C D	35 A B C D
4 F G H J	12 F G H J	20 F G H J	28 F G H J	36 F G H J
5 A B C D	13 A B C D	21 A B C D	29 A B C D	37 A B C D
6 F G H J	14 F G H J	22 F G H J	30 F G H J	38 F G H J
7 A B C D	15 A B C D	23 A B C D	31 A B C D	39 A B C D
8 F G H J	16 F G H J	24 F G H J	32 F G H J	40 F G H J

TEST 4—SCIENCE REASONING

1 A B C D	9 A B C D	17 A B C D	25 A B C D	33 A B C D
2 F G H J	10 F G H J	18 F G H J	26 F G H J	34 F G H J
3 A B C D	11 A B C D	19 A B C D	27 A B C D	35 A B C D
4 F G H J	12 F G H J	20 F G H J	28 F G H J	36 F G H J
5 A B C D	13 A B C D	21 A B C D	29 A B C D	37 A B C D
6 F G H J	14 F G H J	22 F G H J	30 F G H J	38 F G H J
7 A B C D	15 A B C D	23 A B C D	31 A B C D	39 A B C D
8 F G H J	16 F G H J	24 F G H J	32 F G H J	40 F G H J

DIRECTIONS

Practice Test III consists of five sections: English, Mathematics, Reading, Science Reasoning, and Writing. Calculator use is only permitted on the Mathematics Test.

The items in each test are numbered and the answer choices lettered. The provided bubble sheet has numbered rows that correspond to the items on the test. Each row contains lettered ovals to match the answer choices for each item on the test. Each numbered row on the bubble sheet has a corresponding item on the test.

For each item, first decide on the best answer choice. Then, locate the row number that corresponds to the item. Next, find the oval in that row that matches the letter of the chosen answer. Then, use a soft lead pencil to fill in the oval. Do not use a ballpoint pen.

Mark only one answer for each item. If you change your mind about the answer choice, thoroughly erase the first mark before marking your new answer.

Note that only responses marked on your bubble sheet will be scored. Your score on each test will be based only on the number of items that are correctly answered during the time allowed for that test. Guessing is not penalized. Therefore, it is to your best advantage to answer every item on the test, even if you must guess.

You may work on each test only during the time allowed for that test. If you finish a test before time is called, use the time to review your answer choices or work on items about which you are uncertain. You may not return to a test on which time has already been called and you may not preview another test. You must lay down your pencil immediately when time is called at the end of each test. You may not for any reason fill in or alter ovals for a test after time expires for that test. Violation of these rules will result in immediate disqualification from the exam.

1 1 1 1 1 1 1 1 1 1 1 1

ENGLISH TEST

45 Minutes—75 Items

DIRECTIONS: In the following passages, certain words and phrases are underlined. The items in the right hand column provide alternatives for the underlined parts. In most cases, you are to choose the alternative that best expresses the idea of the sentence in context, corrects grammatical errors, and/or is best suited to the tone and style of the passage. If the original best accomplishes this, then choose "NO CHANGE." In some cases, you will be asked questions regarding an underlined part. You are to choose the best answer to the question.

You will also find items on this test that refer to a section of the passage or to the passage as a whole. These items DO NOT refer to an underlined portion of the passage. Rather, they are identified by a number or numbers in a box.

For each item, choose the best alternative and fill in the corresponding oval on your bubble sheet. You should read the passage before answering the accompanying items. For many of the items, you must read several sentences beyond the item to determine the answer. Be sure that you have read far enough ahead before you answer.

Answers are on page 945. Explanations begin on page 947.

PASSAGE I

Trade in the Northwest Territory

[1]

In 1849, San Francisco became the first official port of entry on the Pacific Coast. In 1851, on account of (1) the rapid growth of lumbering activity and a corresponding expansion of population in the Northwest Territory, the government established the Puget Sound District of the Bureau of Customs. Nonetheless, (2) smuggling grew rapidly, fostered by the tempting proximity of British havens and the natural cover afforded by vast forested areas and by the coves and inlets of countless heavy (3) timbered islands.

1. A. NO CHANGE
   B. since
   C. because of
   D. for

2. F. NO CHANGE
   G. Therefore,
   H. Consequently,
   J. On the contrary,

3. A. NO CHANGE
   B. countless, heavy
   C. countless, heavily
   D. countlessly heavy

GO ON TO THE NEXT PAGE.

[2]

Such fears were well foundationed[4]. In 1851, U.S. customs officers seize[5] the Hudson Bay Company's steamer *Beaver* for a technical violation of the revenue laws[6]. This incident signaled an end to the era of unrestricted trade in the Pacific Northwest and drove some traders on both sides of the international border into illicit commercial arrangements. British wool, blankets, and liquor were the principle articles[7] of this trade. In fact,[8] so much British wool was smuggled into the San Juan Islands selling[9] as domestic wool by American sheepmen one[10] naive textbook writer credited San Juan sheep with a world's record annual production of 150 pounds of wool per animal.

[3]

Although[11] American settlers in the Northwest Territory welcomed[12] the assertion of national control to the forty-ninth parallel, they were less amenable to restrictions on the trade with Vancouver Island. They wanted the duty-free rum and woolens offered by the

4. **F.** NO CHANGE
G. well founded
H. founded well
J. well found

5. **A.** NO CHANGE
B. seized
C. were seizing
D. have seized

6. **F.** NO CHANGE
G. on account of violating the revenue laws
H. for technically being in violation of the revenue laws
J. in that they were in technical violation of the revenue laws

7. **A.** NO CHANGE
B. were the principal articles
C. was the principle article
D. was the principal article

8. **F.** NO CHANGE
G. Furthermore,
H. Moreover,
J. On the contrary,

9. **A.** NO CHANGE
B. and sold
C. and would be sold
D. to sell

10. **F.** NO CHANGE
G. sheepmen, one
H. sheepmen that one
J. sheepmen, and a

11. **A.** NO CHANGE
B. Since
C. Therefore
D. Thus

12. **F.** NO CHANGE
G. welcoming
H. would welcome
J. were welcomed by

GO ON TO THE NEXT PAGE.

British but were fearing[13] that the imposition and enforcement of permanent tariffs on goods from British North America might be resulting in the losing[14] of British markets for American products.

13. A. NO CHANGE
B. and were fearing
C. and was fearful
D. but feared

14. F. NO CHANGE
G. might result in the losing
H. might result in the loss
J. results in the loss

Items 15 and 16 ask about the preceding passage as a whole.

15. Which of the following represents the most logical order of the three paragraphs?

A. 1, 2, 3
B. 1, 3, 2
C. 2, 3, 1
D. 3, 1, 2

16. Which of the following does NOT represent a technique used in the development of the essay?

F. Narrative
G. Example
H. Statistics
J. Quotations

PASSAGE II

Mapping the Cosmos

One of the beauties of astronomy is that one does not have to be an expert to enjoy it[17]. Anyone can step outside on a clear, moonless night, gaze at thousands of stars shining across the vast interstellar spaces, and then one can become[18] intoxicated by a heady mix of grandeur and existential chill. The same questions come to mind time and again, how[19] far away are the stars? How many are there? Are they strewn endlessly through space, or are we a part of an island universe of

17. A. NO CHANGE
B. is the not having to be an expert to enjoy it
C. is that the enjoying of it does not have to be done by an expert
D. is that one doesn't necessarily have to be an expert in order to derive some enjoyment from it

18. F. NO CHANGE
G. spaces—and became
H. spaces, and become
J. spaces and becomes

19. A. NO CHANGE
B. again and how
C. again how
D. again. How

GO ON TO THE NEXT PAGE.

suns ending 20 abruptly somewhere out there in the black ocean of space?

It has been the sometimes heroic and often frustrating task of astronomers since the dawn of science to chart 21 our position in the cosmic ocean. In the twentieth century, significant progress had been made 22 in constructing an accurate map of the cosmos. We know, for example, that our solar system is part of a much larger system of hundreds of billions of stars. As such, this 23 system is the Milky Way Galaxy, a huge disk of stars and gas. We also know that ours is not the only galaxy in the universe. As far as the largest telescopes in the world can see, there are galaxies in every direction. The 24 nearest galaxies to our own are the Magellanic Clouds; the "crown jewels" 25 of the southern skies.

Since they are so near, they offer a laboratory in which astronomers can study the evolution of stars and galaxies. The nearest large galaxy to the Milky Way is the Andromeda Galaxy, which is about two million light years away. It is a giant spiral galaxy, much like 26 our own in size, shape, and number and type of stars. This nearby sister galaxy provides to us 27 an opportunity to get a bird's eye view of a galaxy much like our

20. **F.** NO CHANGE
G. that ends
H. that end
J. ended

21. **A.** NO CHANGE
B. charting
C. having charted
D. who charted

22. **F.** NO CHANGE
G. has been made
H. is made
J. will be made

23. **A.** NO CHANGE
B. Obviously, this
C. Doubtless, this
D. This

24. **F.** NO CHANGE
G. These
H. (Begin a new paragraph here rather than after "skies") The
J. (Begin a new paragraph here rather than after "skies") As the

25. **A.** NO CHANGE
B. Clouds, the crown jewels
C. Clouds which is the "crown jewels"
D. Clouds, the "crown jewels"

26. **F.** NO CHANGE
G. much as
H. like much
J. much the same like

27. **A.** NO CHANGE
B. provides us
C. provide us
D. providing to us

GO ON TO THE NEXT PAGE.

own—<u>in effect, to see ourselves as others do</u>.[28]

28. F. NO CHANGE
G. to see ourselves the way other people tend to see us
H. so that we would be seeing ourselves the way other people would be seeing us
J. so that in this way we would see ourselves as others do

Item 29 asks about the preceding passage as a whole.

29. Which of the following is NOT one of the reasons the author poses a series of questions in the first paragraph?
A. To give the reader a sense of the "grandeur and existential chill"
B. To stimulate the reader's interest in astronomy
C. To give specific examples of questions about the cosmos that are still unanswered
D. To alert the reader that answers to these questions will follow later in the passage

---

PASSAGE III

A Brief History of the Mercury Space Program

The first astronauts entered the Mercury program in April 1959. They were volunteer, military <u>pilots, graduated</u>[30] of test pilot schools. Each <u>were required having</u>[31] a bachelor's degree in engineering (or its equivalent) and at least 1,500 hours of jet time. Of the first group of sixty candidates called to Washington to hear about the program, more than 80 percent volunteered. Only seven <u>got</u>[32] chosen. (Officials

30. F. NO CHANGE
G. pilots graduates
H. pilots; graduates
J. pilots, graduates

31. A. NO CHANGE
B. was required to have
C. required having
D. had been required to have

32. F. NO CHANGE
G. were
H. had been
J. has been

GO ON TO THE NEXT PAGE.

assumed that no more than seven men would have the opportunity to fly.) [33] These men were true

pioneers, they[34] volunteered at a time when the plans for space travel were only on paper and no one knew what the chance of success was.

Scientists[35] were able to learn from each failure.

Fortunately they had these failures[36] early in the program. The astronauts and the animal passengers as well were flown without mishap when their time came for them[37].

[3]

The most spectacular failure in the Mercury [38] program came to be known as the "tower flight." The escape tower, the parachutes, and the peroxide fuel were all deployed on the launching pad in front of the

33. Is the second use of parentheses in the first paragraph appropriate?
   A. Yes, because the information explains something the author said but is not vital to the understanding of the passage.
   B. Yes, because the information contained in the parentheses is irrelevant to the passage.
   C. No, because the material is vital to the understanding of the author's main argument.
   D. No, because an entire sentence should never be placed in parentheses.

34. F. NO CHANGE
   G. pioneers but
   H. pioneers yet
   J. pioneers. They

35. Which of the following phrases would best replace the word "Scientists" to provide a transition from the first to the second paragraph?
   A. It was lucky that the men volunteered because scientists
   B. There were failures as well as successes in the Mercury program, but scientists
   C. Since the chances for success were unknown, scientists
   D. Since the volunteers were also engineers, scientists

36. F. NO CHANGE
   G. Fortunately, they had these failures occurring
   H. These failures occurred fortunately
   J. Fortunately, these failures occurred

37. A. NO CHANGE
   B. the time for them finally came
   C. their time finally came for them
   D. their time came

38. Is the use of the word "spectacular" in the first sentence of the third paragraph appropriate?
   F. Yes, because the author is using the word in an ironic sense.
   G. Yes, because the author obviously disapproves of the Mercury program.
   H. No, because the reader might be misled about goals of the Mercury program.
   J. No, because the failure cited was caused by a simple defect.

GO ON TO THE NEXT PAGE.

domestic and international press. A relatively simple [39] ground-circuit defect in the Redstone launch vehicle caused the main rocket engine to ignite and then shutting [40] down immediately after liftoff from the launching pad. The "flight" lasted only a second and covered a distance of inside only two inches. [41]

One of the requirements [42] of the Mercury program was that an animal had to precede man into space [43]. The flight of Ham, the chimpanzee, was a major milestone in the program. Again, there were some problems. The pickup of the spacecraft was delayed, and water had leaked into [44] the capsule. Ham, however, was eventually rescued unharmed [45].

Sending a man into zero gravity was among the greatest medical experiments of all time. Fortunately, all astronauts found the weightlessness to be no problem. All returning [46] to Earth with no medical difficulties whatsoever. In this area, the only question left unanswered by the Mercury program was how long

39. A. NO CHANGE
B. relative and simple
C. relative simple
D. simple relatively

40. F. NO CHANGE
G. and then will shut
H. and then they shut
J. and then to shut

41. The author put the word "flight" in quotation marks because:
A. the article is quoting from another source.
B. there was no real flight at all.
C. the word is a technical term used by astronauts.
D. the word is often repeated in the passage.

42. F. NO CHANGE
G. (Do NOT begin a new paragraph) One of the requirements
H. (Do NOT begin a new paragraph) One requirement
J. (Do NOT begin a new paragraph) A requirement

43. A. NO CHANGE
B. had to be the one to precede man in space
C. was going to have to go into space before man
D. needed to be the one to go into space before man did

44. F. NO CHANGE
G. water leaked into
H. water leaks in
J. leaking water into

45. A. NO CHANGE
B. (Place before the word "was")
C. (Place before the word "eventually")
D. (Place before the word "rescued")

46. F. NO CHANGE
G. return
H. returned
J. will return

GO ON TO THE NEXT PAGE.

man will tolerate weightlessness. It seemed like,
47 48
however, that longer flights would require only that

47. A. NO CHANGE
B. will be able to tolerate
C. was able to tolerate
D. could tolerate

48. F. NO CHANGE
G. seemed,
H. seemed as,
J. seemed to be,

astronauts to have suitable methods of exercise and
49
nutrition. [50]

49. A. NO CHANGE
B. have
C. had had
D. are sure to have

50. Which of the following might be an appropriate concluding sentence for the essay?
F. Although the Mercury program had some failures, it was on the whole a successful part of the space program.
G. Although the Mercury program had some successes, it was on the whole a failure.
H. Many people have objected that it is immoral to use animals in testing programs.
J. Science fiction writers have often written about space travel.

PASSAGE IV

Advances in Modern Medicine

It was not until the nineteenth century that
medicine was able, in any broad and real way, to help
51
the suffering individual. During this century, technical
advances aided the diagnostician and also the surgeon,
52
and the beginnings of an understanding of the
fundamental mechanisms of disease had been emerging.
53
All aspects of medicine—from the research laboratory
to the operating table—was enjoying the benefits of
54
the rigorous application of the scientific method.

51. A. NO CHANGE
B. way of help
C. way to help
D. way, of helping

52. F. NO CHANGE
G. as well as
H. with
J. as opposed to

53. A. NO CHANGE
B. was emerging
C. were emerging
D. emerged

54. F. NO CHANGE
G. were enjoying
H. is enjoying
J. enjoys

GO ON TO THE NEXT PAGE.

By the end of the nineteenth century, a person's chances were fairly good that a doctor could not only give a name to his medical complaint <u>yet probably had</u> [55] an elementary understanding of what it was and how it progressed. With somewhat more luck, the doctor could select the proper treatment <u>and he could also mitigate</u> [56] the symptoms if not cure the disease altogether.

55. A. NO CHANGE
B. but probably had
C. consequently probably has
D. but, probably would have

56. F. NO CHANGE
G. but could mitigate
H. and mitigate
J. and can mitigate

This transition to modern medicine depended on three important advances. First, it required an understanding of the true nature and origin of disease. Second, it required that an organized body of standard medical practice <u>be available to</u> [57] guide physicians in diagnosis and treatment of disease. Last, <u>it presupposes</u> [58] a degree of medical technology never before available.

57. A. NO CHANGE
B. was available to
C. is available for
D. be available as

58. F. NO CHANGE
G. it is presupposed
H. it presupposed
J. they presuppose

<u>Among the more dramatic</u> [59] nineteenth century medical advances were those in the field of human physiology. [60] In 1822, an obscure American army

59. A. NO CHANGE
B. (Do NOT begin a new paragraph) Among the more dramatic
C. Since
D. (Do NOT begin a new paragraph) Since

60. Which of the following correctly describes the function of the first sentence of this paragraph?
F. It introduces a topic that has nothing to do with the material discussed in the first three paragraphs.
G. It introduces material that will contradict what was discussed in the first three paragraphs.
H. It provides a transition that sets up a contrast to the material that came before.
J. It provides a transition that moves from a general discussion to a more specific, but related topic.

GO ON TO THE NEXT PAGE.

camp surgeon practicing medicine near where the Canadian frontier is [61] was transformed almost overnight into a specialist on the mechanism of human digestion. The physician, William Beaumont, was called to treat a young trapper, accidentally shot in the stomach. Beaumont's operating skill [62] saved the boy's life but the patient was left with an abnormal opening leading to the stomach. To Beaumont's credit, he recognized this unique opportunity to study the human digestive process, but [63] for the next ten years he conducted hundreds of experiments with the reluctant cooperation of his not-so-willing patient.

From his experiments, Beaumont was able to describe the physiology of digestion, demonstrating the characteristics of gastric motility and describe [64] the properties of gastric juice. He determined that the stomach contained hydrochloric acid and that it broke down food by a chemical process and not by maceration or putrefaction. Beaumont's pioneering work made him a famous man. The young trapper did not fare as well; he was forced to tour medical schools as "the man with the window in his stomach."

61. **A.** NO CHANGE
B. near where the Canadian frontier is,
C. near where the Canadian frontier was
D. near the Canadian frontier

62. **F.** NO CHANGE
G. (Begin a new paragraph) Beaumont's operating skill
H. The skill of Beaumont at operating
J. (Begin a new paragraph) The skill of Beaumont at operating

63. **A.** NO CHANGE
B. process, and
C. process,
D. process. But

64. **F.** NO CHANGE
G. to describe
H. that describe
J. and describing

GO ON TO THE NEXT PAGE.

PASSAGE V

All About Babies

Newborn babies are not the passive creatures most people assume him to be [65]. Recent research shows that the newborn comes well-endowed of [66] charm and full potential for social graces. His eyes are equipped with surprisingly good vision. Shortly after birth, he begins to watch his mother's face, which he soon comes to recognize. He also learns to know her voice and will turn toward her when he hears it. This [67] is about the time when affection begins. The infant's cry alerts the mother and causes a biological including [68] an emotional reaction. The infant's ability to cling and cuddle communicates a pleasurable warmth to the mother, and the infant's odor is pleasant and uniquely its own. The newborn also smiles. The human infant, unfortunately, [69] is in possession of [70] a collection of attributes that are guaranteeing [71] its attractiveness.

Although there is some argument about whether the child sparks the development of love or whether or not [72] a special physiological state of the mother prompts her to interact with the new infant. But most [73] researchers agree that the newborn does mold or trigger adult behavior. The neonate organizes the mother's

65. **A.** NO CHANGE
B. he was
C. them to be
D. it is

66. **F.** NO CHANGE
G. for
H. with
J. by

67. **A.** NO CHANGE
B. it, this
C. it this
D. it

68. **F.** NO CHANGE
G. and
H. with
J. but

69. **A.** NO CHANGE
B. on the other hand
C. nevertheless
D. in fact

70. **F.** NO CHANGE
G. possessed
H. possesses
J. are in possession of

71. **A.** NO CHANGE
B. guaranteed
C. guarantees
D. guarantee

72. **F.** NO CHANGE
G. or whether
H. and whether if
J. or whether if

73. **A.** NO CHANGE
B. infant: but most
C. infant. Most
D. infant, most

GO ON TO THE NEXT PAGE.

behavior by crying and by eye-to-eye contact. The newborn is not a passive creature at all.

Items 74 and 75 ask about the preceding passage as a whole.

74. Which of the following best describes the function of the last sentence of the essay?

F. It introduces a new topic for the reader to investigate.
G. It contradicts everything that was said before.
H. It reiterates the main theme of the passage.
J. It establishes the author as an authority.

75. Which of the following best describes the overall development of the essay?

A. A comparison and contrast using anecdotes
B. A narrative using examples
C. A description using statistics
D. An argument using examples

END OF TEST 1.
STOP! DO NOT TURN THE PAGE UNTIL TOLD TO DO SO.

2 2 2 2 2 2 2 2 2 2 2 2

MATHEMATICS TEST

60 Minutes—60 Items

DIRECTIONS: Solve each item and choose the correct answer choice. Then, fill in the corresponding oval on the bubble sheet.

Allocate time wisely. Try to solve as many items as possible, returning to skipped items if time permits.

Calculator use is permitted on this test; however, some items are best solved without the use of a calculator.

Note: Unless otherwise stated, assume all of the following.

1. Illustrative figures are NOT necessarily drawn to scale.
2. The word *average* indicates arithmetic mean.
3. The word *line* indicates a straight line.
4. Geometric figures lie in a plane.

Answers are on page 945. Explanations begin on page 952.

DO YOUR FIGURING HERE.

1. A barrel contained 5.75 liters of water and 4.5 liters evaporated. How many liters of water remain in the barrel?

A. 0.75
B. 1.25
C. 1.75
D. 2.25
E. 13.25

2. Which of the following expressions correctly describes the mathematical relationship below?

3 less than the product of 4 times x

F. $4x - 3$
G. $3x - 4$
H. $4(x - 3)$
J. $3(4x)$
K. $\frac{4x}{3}$

3. If $\frac{3}{4}$ of x is 36, then $\frac{1}{3}$ of $x = ?$

A. 9
B. 12
C. 16
D. 24
E. 42

GO ON TO THE NEXT PAGE.

4. In the figure below, what is the value of $x + y$?

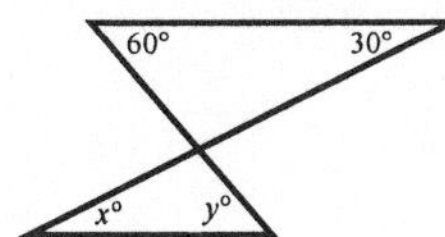

F. 45
G. 60
H. 75
J. 90
K. 120

5. If n is a multiple of 3, which of the following expressions is also a multiple of 3?

A. $2 + n$
B. $2 - n$
C. $2n - 1$
D. $2n + 1$
E. $2n + 3$

6. Which of the following is NOT equal to the ratio of 2 whole numbers?

F. $(\frac{1}{5})^2$
G. 5%
H. $\frac{1}{5}$
J. 0.25
K. $\frac{\sqrt{5}}{1}$

7. If the area of a square is 16 square inches, what is the perimeter, in inches?

A. 2
B. 4
C. 8
D. 16
E. 32

8. If $12 + x = 36 - y$, then $x + y = ?$

F. -48
G. -24
H. 3
J. 24
K. 48

DO YOUR FIGURING HERE.

GO ON TO THE NEXT PAGE.

DO YOUR FIGURING HERE.

9. What is the greatest factor of the expression $3x^2y^3z + 6x^3yz^3 + 2xy^2z^2$?

A. $3x^2y^2z^2$
B. $2x^2y^2z^2$
C. $x^3y^3z^3$
D. xyz
E. xz

10. Depending on the value of k, the expression $3k + 4k + 5k + 6k + 7k$ may or may not be divisible by 7. Which of the terms, when eliminated from the expression, guarantees that the resulting expression is divisible by 7 for every positive integer k?

F. $3k$
G. $4k$
H. $5k$
J. $6k$
K. $7k$

11. If $\frac{1}{3} < x < \frac{3}{8}$, which of the following is a possible value of x?

A. $\frac{3}{16}$
B. $\frac{17}{48}$
C. $\frac{9}{24}$
D. $\frac{5}{12}$
E. $\frac{1}{2}$

12. If $x^2 - y^2 = 3$ and $x - y = 3$, then $x + y = ?$

F. 0
G. 1
H. 2
J. 3
K. 9

13. If n is a positive integer, which of the following *must* be an even integer?

A. $n + 1$
B. $3n + 1$
C. $3n + 2$
D. $n^2 + 1$
E. $n^2 + n$

GO ON TO THE NEXT PAGE.

DO YOUR FIGURING HERE.

14. If the area of a square inscribed in a circle is 16 square centimeters, what is the area of the circle, in square centimeters?

    F. 2π
    G. 4π
    H. 8π
    J. 16π
    K. 32π

15. Ellen bought a tape recorder on sale for 25 percent off the usual price of $120. If the store also collected an 8-percent sales tax on the sale price of the tape recorder, how much did Ellen pay for the tape recorder, including sales tax?

    A. $106.30
    B. $101.40
    C. $97.20
    D. $95.10
    E. $88.44

16. A certain mixture of gravel and sand consists of 2.5 kilograms of gravel and 12.5 kilograms of sand. What percent of the mixture, by weight, is gravel?

    F. 10%
    G. $16\frac{2}{3}\%$
    H. 20%
    J. 25%
    K. $33\frac{1}{3}\%$

GO ON TO THE NEXT PAGE.

17. The figure below is the top-view of a folding room divider, hinged at P and Q. If sections PR and QS are moved as shown until R and S meet, what will be the enclosed area, in square feet? (Ignore the thickness of the hinges and the screen's sections.)

DO YOUR FIGURING HERE.

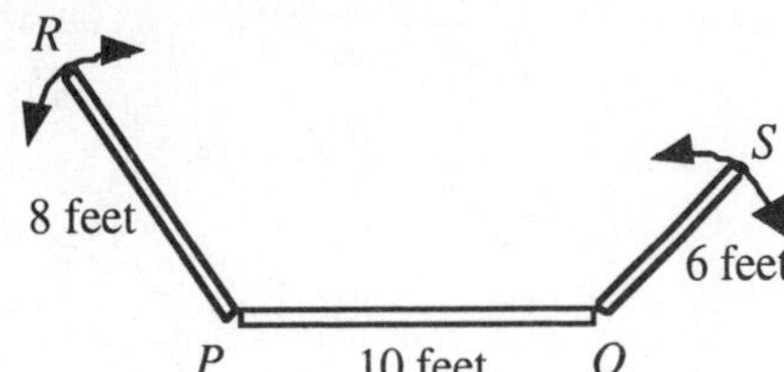

A. 6
B. 12
C. 6π
D. 24
E. 12π

18. Motorcycle A averages 40 kilometers per liter of gasoline while Motorcycle B averages 50 kilometers per liter. If the cost of gasoline is \$2 per liter, what will be the difference in the cost of operating the 2 motorcycles for 300 kilometers?

F. \$3
G. \$6
H. \$12
J. \$15
K. \$20

19. If $f(x) = x^2 - 2x + 1$, then what is $f(f(3))$?

A. 3
B. 9
C. 14
D. 27
E. 39

20. For a positive integer k, which of the following equals $6k + 3$?

F. $\frac{1}{2}(k + 1)$
G. $\frac{1}{k} + 4$
H. $2k + 1$
J. $3(k + 1)$
K. $3(2k + 1)$

GO ON TO THE NEXT PAGE.

DO YOUR FIGURING HERE.

21. Mailing a letter costs x cents for the first ounce and y cents for every additional ounce or fraction of an ounce. What is the cost, in cents, to mail a letter weighing a whole number of ounces, w?

A. $w(x + y)$
B. $x(w - y)$
C. $x(x - 1) + y(w - 1)$
D. $x + wy$
E. $x + y(w - 1)$

22. $|-3| \cdot |2| \cdot |-\frac{1}{2}| + (-4) = ?$

F. -1
G. 0
H. 1
J. $\frac{3}{2}$
K. 4

23. In the figure below, the area of the square $OPQR$ is 2 square inches, what is the area of the circle with center O?

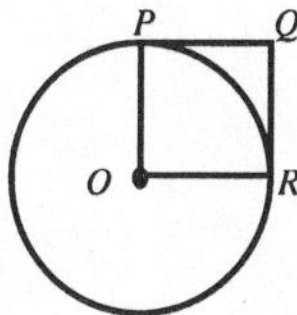

A. $\frac{\pi}{4}$
B. $\pi\sqrt{2}$
C. 2π
D. $2\sqrt{2}\pi$
E. 4π

24. Which of the following *must* be an odd number?

I. The product of a prime number and a prime number
II. The sum of a prime number and a prime number
III. The product of an odd number and another odd number

F. I only
G. III only
H. I and II only
J. II and III only
K. I, II, and III

GO ON TO THE NEXT PAGE.

DO YOUR FIGURING HERE.

25. What is the area of the shaded portion of the figure below, expressed in terms of a and b?

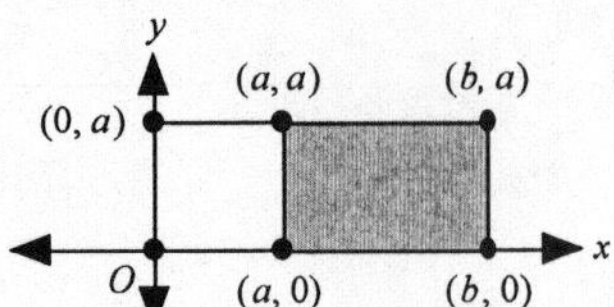

A. $a(b-a)$
B. $a(a-b)$
C. $b(a-b)$
D. $b(b-a)$
E. ab

26. $\sqrt{(43-7)(29+7)} = ?$

F. $3\sqrt{3}$
G. 6
H. 36
J. 42
K. 1,296

27. A concrete mixture contains 4 cubic yards (yd.^{3}) of cement for every 20 yd.^{3} of grit. If a mason orders 50 yd.^{3} of cement, how much grit (in yd.^{3}) should he order if he is to use all of the cement?

A. 250
B. 200
C. 100
D. 80
E. 10

28. In the figure below, $\overline{QT} = \overline{QR}$. If $x° = 120°$, then $y = ?$

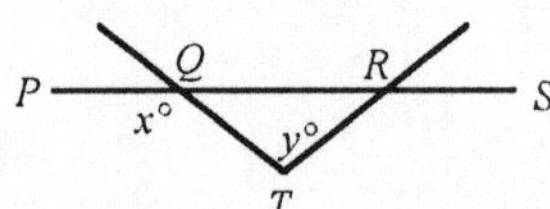

F. 30
G. 60
H. 75
J. 90
K. 120

GO ON TO THE NEXT PAGE.

DO YOUR FIGURING HERE.

29. If $\frac{x}{y} = -1$, then $x + y = ?$

A. 2
B. 1
C. 0
D. -1
E. -2

30. According to the table below, which fabric costs the LEAST per square yard?

Fabric	Cost
F	3 yards for $8
G	2 yards for $6
H	4 yards for $9
J	5 yards for $7
K	6 yards for $4

F. F
G. G
H. H
J. J
K. K

31. In ΔPQR below, if $\overline{PQ} \parallel \overline{ST}$, then $y = ?$

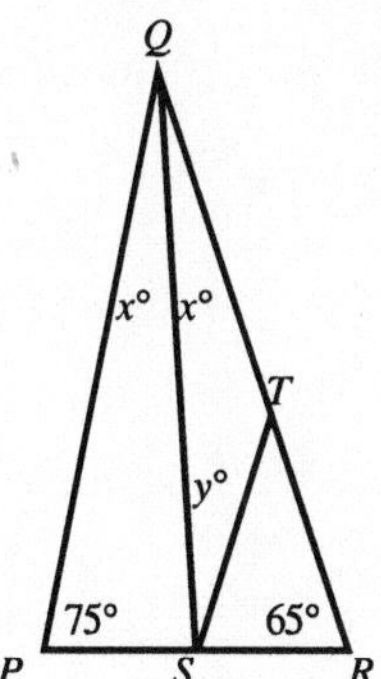

A. 20
B. 40
C. 45
D. 50
E. 55

32. $\frac{10^3(10^5 + 10^5)}{10^4} = ?$

F. 10^4
G. 10^6
H. $2(10^2)$
J. $2(10^4)$
K. $2(10^9)$

GO ON TO THE NEXT PAGE.

33. What is the solution set for the following equation: $x^2 - 5x + 4 = 0$?

DO YOUR FIGURING HERE.

A. {-4, -1}
B. {-3, -1}
C. {-1, 3}
D. {1, 4}
E. {2, 3}

34. The average of seven different positive integers is 12. What is the greatest that any one integer could be?

F. 19
G. 31
H. 47
J. 54
K. 63

35. If $x = b + 4$ and $y = b - 3$, then in terms of x and y, $b = ?$

A. $x + y - 1$

B. $x + y + 1$

C. $x - y - 1$

D. $\frac{x + y + 1}{2}$

E. $\frac{x + y - 1}{2}$

36. If $5x = 3y = z$, and x, y, and z are positive integers, all of the following must be an integer EXCEPT:

F. $\frac{z}{xy}$
G. $\frac{z}{5}$
H. $\frac{z}{3}$
J. $\frac{z}{15}$
K. $\frac{x}{3}$

GO ON TO THE NEXT PAGE.

DO YOUR FIGURING HERE.

37. What is the width of a rectangle with an area of $48x^2$ and a length of $24x$?

A. 2
B. $2x$
C. $24x$
D. $2x^2$
E. $3x^2$

38. If $x = \frac{1}{y+1}$ and $y \neq -1$, then $y = ?$

F. $x + 1$
G. x
H. $\frac{x+1}{x}$
J. $\frac{x-1}{x}$
K. $\frac{1-x}{x}$

39. In the figure below, if the area of the triangle is 54, then $x = ?$

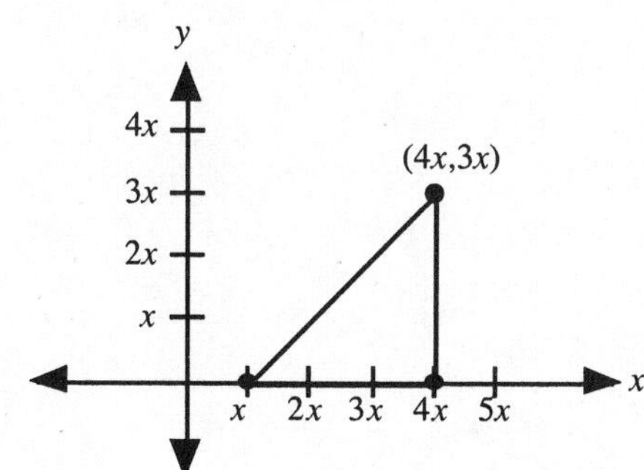

A. $3\sqrt{3}$
B. $2\sqrt{3}$
C. 3
D. 2
E. $\sqrt{2}$

GO ON TO THE NEXT PAGE.

DO YOUR FIGURING HERE.

40. A drawer contains 4 green socks, 6 blue socks, and 10 white socks. If socks are pulled out of the drawer at random and not replaced, what is the minimum number of socks that must be pulled out of the drawer to *guarantee* that 2 of every color have been pulled out of the drawer?

F. 6
G. 7
H. 11
J. 12
K. 18

41. In the figure below, the circle with center O has a radius that is 4 units long. If the area of the shaded region is 14π square-units, what is the value of x?

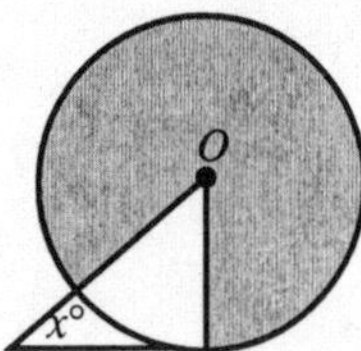

A. 90
B. 75
C. 60
D. 55
E. 45

42. In the figure below, a circle is inscribed in a square that is in turn inscribed in a larger circle. What is the ratio of the area of the larger circle to that of the smaller circle?

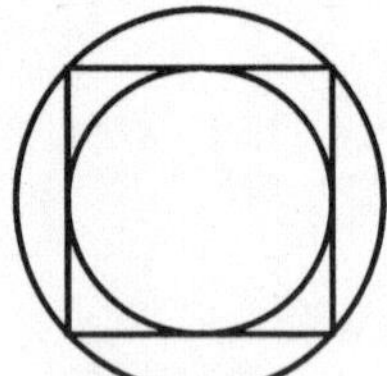

F. 8:1
G. 4:1
H. $2\sqrt{2}$:1
J. 2:1
K. $\sqrt{2}$:1

GO ON TO THE NEXT PAGE.

43. $2^0 + 2^3 - 2^{-2} = ?$

DO YOUR FIGURING HERE.

A. 4
B. $6\frac{1}{4}$
C. 7
D. $8\frac{3}{4}$
E. $9\frac{3}{4}$

44. The graph of $y = x^2 - 3$ is a parabola with the axis of symmetry given by the equation $x = 0$. Which of the following are the (x, y) coordinates of the point on the parabola that is symmetric, with respect to the axis of symmetry, to the point with coordinates (-1, -2)?

F. (-2, -1)
G. (-1, 2)
H. (0, -3)
J. (1, -2)
K. (1, 2)

45. If 2 lines with equations $y = m_1x + b_1$ and $y = m_2x + b_2$ are perpendicular, which of the following *must* be true?

A. $m_1 = m_2$
B. $m_1m_2 = 1$
C. $m_1m_2 = -1$
D. $b_1 = b_2$
E. $b_1b_2 = -1$

46. The figure below has lengths as marked, in units. What is the area, in square units, of the figure?

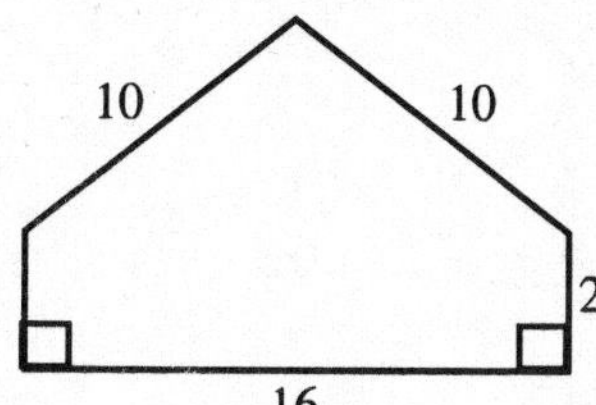

F. 36
G. 48
H. 56
J. 64
K. 80

GO ON TO THE NEXT PAGE.

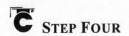

47. For all $x > 0$ and $y > 0$, the radical expression $\frac{\sqrt{x}}{2\sqrt{x} - \sqrt{y}}$ is equivalent to:

DO YOUR FIGURING HERE.

A. $\frac{2\sqrt{x} - \sqrt{y}}{2}$
B. $\frac{2\sqrt{x} + \sqrt{y}}{4xy}$
C. $\frac{2x + \sqrt{xy}}{2x - y}$
D. $\frac{2x + \sqrt{xy}}{4x - y}$
E. $\frac{4x + \sqrt{xy}}{4x - y}$

48. In the figure below, if $l_1 \parallel l_2$, then $x = ?$

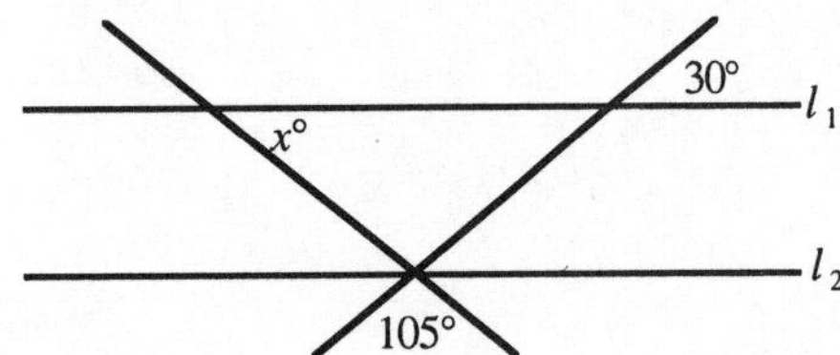

F. 20
G. 30
H. 45
J. 65
K. 130

49. The graph of $y = 2(\cos 2x) + 2$ intersects the y-axis where $y = ?$

A. 0
B. 2
C. 3
D. 4
E. 5

GO ON TO THE NEXT PAGE.

50. In the figure below, *PQRS* is a square, and each of the 4 circles has a radius of r. What fractional part of the area of the square is shaded?

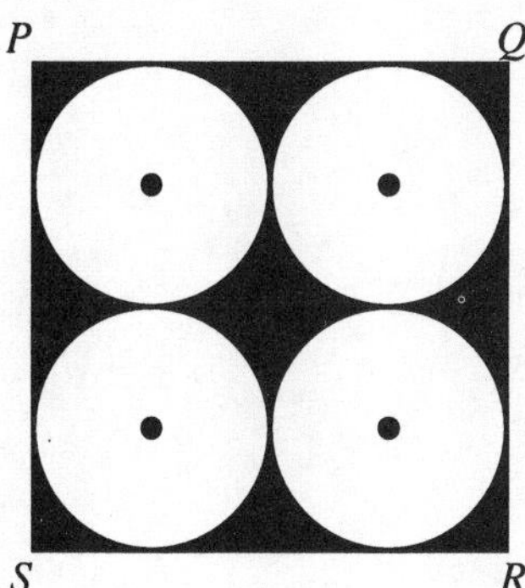

F. $\frac{\pi-4}{2}$
G. $\frac{4-\pi}{4}$
H. $\frac{\pi}{4}$
J. $\frac{4}{\pi}$
K. π

DO YOUR FIGURING HERE.

51. If $0° < \theta° < 90°$, $\frac{\sin^2\theta + \cos^2\theta}{\sin\theta}$ is equivalent to:

A. $\sin\theta$
B. $\cos\theta$
C. $\csc\theta$
D. $\tan\theta$
E. $\cot\theta$

52. In the figure below, *ABC* is a right triangle. If $\sin 35° \approx 0.57$ and $\tan 55° \approx 1.4$, which of the following is the best approximation of the length of $\overline{AC}$?

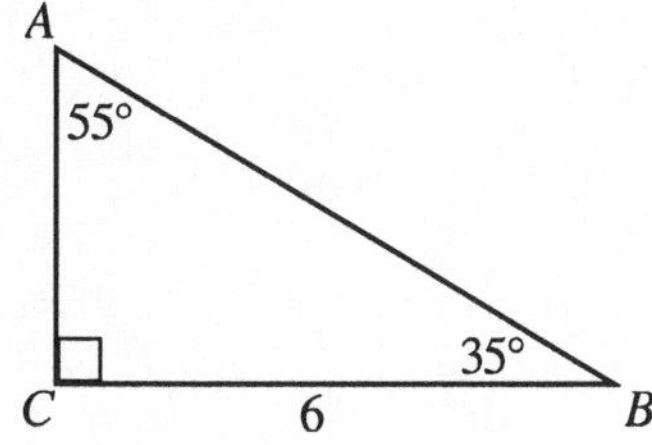

F. 3.42
G. 4.28
H. 8.57
J. 10.50
K. 12.25

GO ON TO THE NEXT PAGE.

DO YOUR FIGURING HERE.

53. What are the values for which $\frac{x(x+3)}{(x-1)(x+2)}$ is undefined?

A. -3 only
B. -2 only
C. 1 only
D. -2 and 1 only
E. -3, -2, and 1

54. What is the maximum value of $3y$ for x and y satisfying the system of inequalities below?

$$x \geq 0$$
$$y \geq 0$$
$$x + y \leq 6$$

F. -3
G. 0
H. 6
J. 12
K. 18

GO ON TO THE NEXT PAGE.

55. Which of the following graphs in the standard (x, y) coordinate plane correctly shows the points on the graph of $y = |x^2 - 3|$ for $x = -1, 0,$ and 1?

DO YOUR FIGURING HERE.

A.

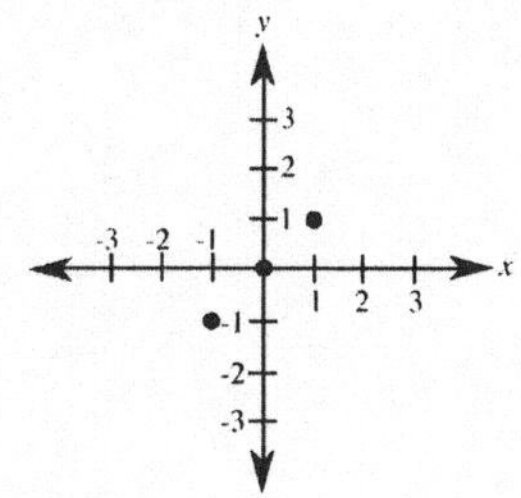

B.

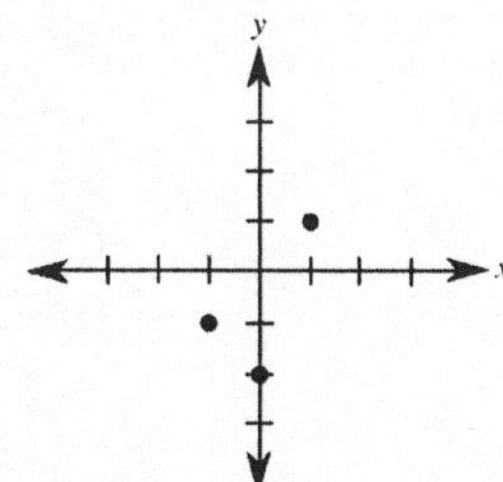

C.

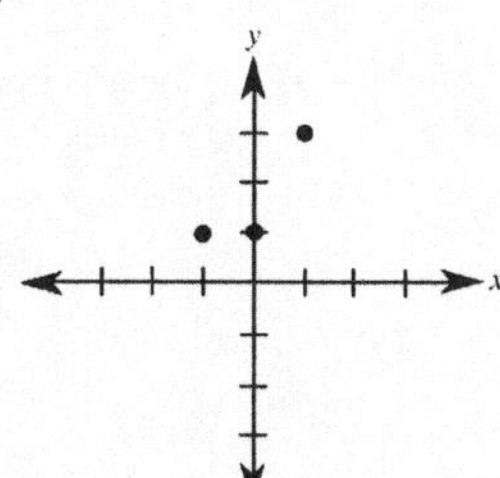

D.

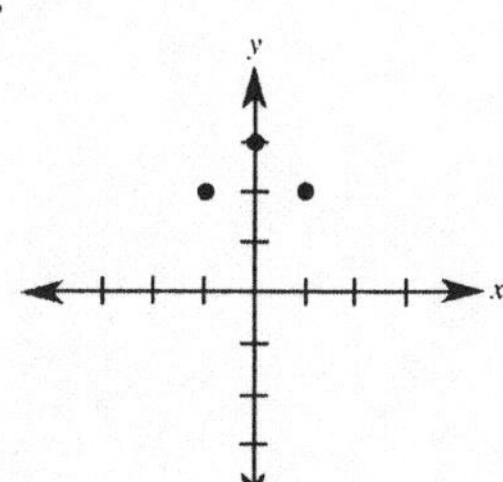

E.

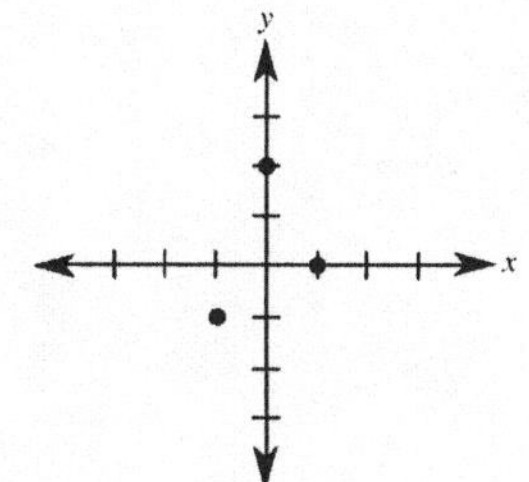

GO ON TO THE NEXT PAGE.

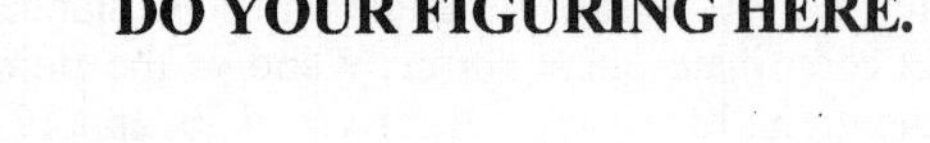

56. The figure below is a graph of which of the following equations?

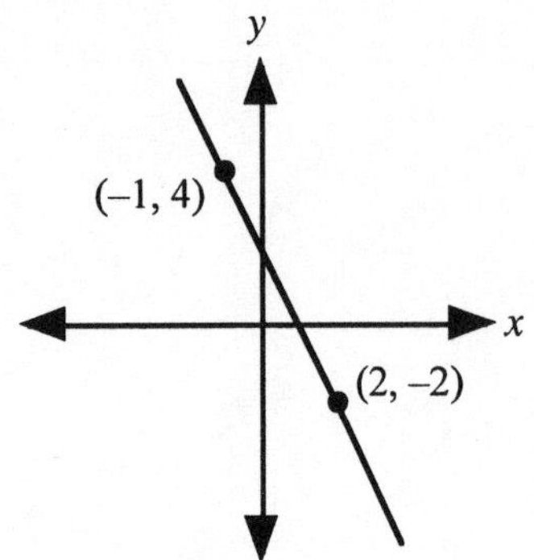

F. $y = -3x + 5$

G. $y = -2x + 2$

H. $y = -\frac{3}{2}x - 2$

J. $y = \frac{2}{3}x + 3$

K. $y = x + 2$

57. The roots of equation $ax^2 + bx + c = 0$ are $\frac{-3 + \sqrt{5}}{2}$ and $\frac{-3 - \sqrt{5}}{2}$. Which of the following could be the equation?

A. $x^2 + 3x + 1 = 0$
B. $x^2 - 3x + 1 = 0$
C. $x^2 + 3x - 1 = 0$
D. $x^2 - 3x - 1 = 0$
E. $-x^2 + 3x + 1 = 0$

58. The relation defined by the set of ordered pairs {(0, 3), (2, 1), (3, 0), (-1, 2), (0, 5), and (-2, 5)} is NOT a function. Deleting which of the ordered pairs will make the resulting set a function?

F. (0, 3)
G. (2, 1)
H. (3, 0)
J. (-1, 2)
K. (-2, 5)

GO ON TO THE NEXT PAGE.

DO YOUR FIGURING HERE.

59. Trapezoid $ABCD$ has lengths, in units, and angle measures as marked in the figure below. What is the area of the trapezoid $ABCD$?

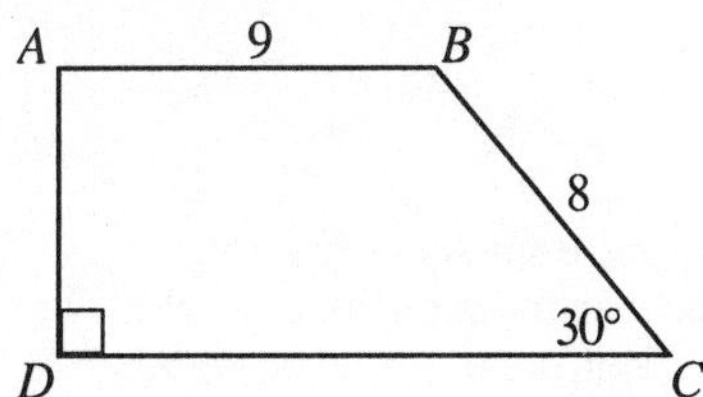

A. $18 + 8\sqrt{2}$
B. $18 + 8\sqrt{3}$
C. $36 + 8\sqrt{2}$
D. $36 + 8\sqrt{3}$
E. 42

60. What is $\tan\theta$ if $\sin\theta = \frac{3}{5}$ and $\cot\theta = \frac{4}{3}$?

F. $\frac{9}{20}$
G. $\frac{3}{4}$
H. $\frac{7}{8}$
J. $\frac{5}{3}$
K. $\frac{20}{9}$

END OF TEST 2.
STOP! DO NOT TURN THE PAGE UNTIL TOLD TO DO SO.
DO NOT RETURN TO THE PREVIOUS TEST.

3 3 3 3 3 3 3 3 3 3 3 3

READING TEST

35 Minutes—40 Items

DIRECTIONS: The passages presented in the test are each followed by a set of items. Read the passage and choose the best answer for each item. Fill in the corresponding oval on your bubble sheet. You may refer to the passage as often as necessary to answer the passage items.

Answers are on page 946. Explanations begin on page 960.

Passage I

HUMANITIES: This passage explores the contributions of Josquin des Prez to Western music.

Until Josquin des Prez (1440-1521), Western music was liturgical, designed as an accompaniment to worship. Like the intricately carved gargoyles perched atop medieval cathedrals beyond sight of any human, music was composed to please God before anybody else; its dominant theme was reverence. Emotion was there, but it was the grief of Mary standing at the foot of the Cross, the joy of the faithful hailing Christ's resurrection. Even the secular music of the Middle Ages was tied to predetermined patterns that sometimes seemed to stand in the way of individual expression.

While keeping one foot firmly planted in the divine world, Josquin stepped with the other into the human world. He scored magnificent masses, but also newly expressive motets such as the lament of David over his son Absalom or the "Deploration d'Ockeghem," a dirge on the death of Ockeghem, the greatest master before Josquin, a motet written all in black notes, and one of the most profoundly moving scores of the Renaissance. Josquin was the first composer to set psalms to music. But alongside *Benedicite omnia opera Domini Domino* ("Bless the Lord, all ye works of the Lord") he put *El Grillo* ("The cricket is a good singer who manages long poems") and *Allegez moy* ("Solace me, sweet pleasant brunette"). Martin Luther praised Josquin, for his music blends respect for tradition with a rebel's willingness to risk the horizon. What Galileo was to science, Josquin was to music. While preserving their allegiance to God, both asserted a new importance for man.

Why then should Josquin languish in relative obscurity? The answer has to do with the separation of concept from performance in music. In fine art, concept and performance are one; both the art lover and the art historian have thousands of years of paintings, drawings, and sculptures to study and enjoy. Similarly with literature: Poetry, fiction, drama, and criticism survive on the printed page or in manuscript for judgment and admiration by succeeding generations. But musical notation on a page is not art, no matter how lofty or excellent the composer's conception; it is, crudely put, a set of directions for producing art.

Being highly symbolic, musical notation requires training before it can even be read, let alone performed. Moreover, because the musical conventions of other days are not ours, translation of a Renaissance score into modern notation brings difficulties of its own. For example, the Renaissance notation of Josquin's day did not designate the tempo at which the music should be played or sung. It did not indicate all flats or sharps; these were sounded in accordance with musician rules, which were capable of transforming major to minor, minor to major, diatonic to chromatic sound, and thus affect melody, harmony, and musical expression. A Renaissance composition might include several parts—but it did not indicate which were to be sung or played, or whether instruments were to be used at all.

Thus, Renaissance notation permits several interpretations and an imaginative musician may give an interpretation that is a revelation. But no matter how imaginative, few modern musicians can offer any interpretation of Renaissance music. The public for it is small, limiting the number of musicians who can afford to learn, rehearse, and perform it. Most of those who attempt it at all are students organized in *collegia musica* whose memberships have a distressing habit of changing every semester, thus preventing directors from maintaining the year-in, year-out continuity required to achieve excellence of performance. Finally, the instruments used in Renaissance times—krummhorns, recorders, rausch-pfeifen, shawms, sackbuts, organettos—must be specially procured.

GO ON TO THE NEXT PAGE.

1. The primary purpose of the passage is to:

   A. introduce the reader to Josquin and account for his relative obscurity.
   B. describe the main features of medieval music and show how Josquin changed them.
   C. place Josquin's music in an historical context and show its influence on later composers.
   D. enumerate the features of Josquin's music and supply critical commentary.

2. The passage contains information that would help answer all of the following items EXCEPT:

   F. What are the titles of some of Josquin's secular compositions?
   G. What are the names of some Renaissance musical instruments?
   H. Who was the greatest composer before Josquin?
   J. What are the names of some of Josquin's most famous students?

3. It can be inferred from the passage that modern musical notation has which of the following characteristics?

   I. The tempo at which a composition is to be played is indicated in the notation.
   II. Whether a note is sharp or a flat is indicated in the notation.
   III. The notation indicates which parts of the music are to be played by which instruments.

   A. I only
   B. II only
   C. I and III only
   D. I, II, and III

4. The author would most likely agree with which of the following statements?

   F. Music is a better art form than painting or sculpture.
   G. Music can be said to exist only when it is being performed.
   H. Josquin was the greatest composer of the Middle Ages.
   J. Renaissance music is superior to music produced in modern times.

5. The passage leads most logically to a proposal to:

   A. establish more *collegia musica.*
   B. study Josquin's compositional techniques in greater detail.
   C. include Renaissance music in college studies.
   D. provide funds for musicians to study and play Josquin.

6. The author cites all of the following as reasons for Josquin's relative obscurity EXCEPT:

   F. the difficulty one encounters in attempting to read his musical notation.
   G. the inability of modern musicians to play instruments of the Renaissance.
   H. the difficulty of procuring unusual instruments needed to play the music.
   J. the lack of public interest in Renaissance music.

7. The author's attitude toward Galileo can best be described as:

   A. admiring.
   B. critical.
   C. accepting.
   D. analytical.

8. Which of the following statements about liturgical music is consistent with the selection?

   F. It is lacking in any emotion.
   G. It is written to entertain people.
   H. It is intended to be reverential.
   J. It treats primarily nonreligious themes.

9. Which of the following is NOT an example of fine art as that term is used in the passage?

   A. A ballet
   B. A novel
   C. A poem
   D. A mural

10. Josquin des Prez is important in the history of music because he:

   F. wrote motets using only black notes.
   G. wrote only nonliturgical music.
   H. wrote both liturgical and nonliturgical music.
   J. invented new musical instruments for his music.

GO ON TO THE NEXT PAGE.

Passage II

PROSE FICTION: In this passage, the character Miss Mix experiences an exciting robbery and learns a great deal about her employer, Mr. Rawjester.

My pupil was a bright little girl, who spoke French with a perfect accent. She said to me: "Miss Mix, did you ever have the *grande passion*? Did you ever feel a fluttering here?" and she placed her hand upon her small chest. "There is to be company here tomorrow," she added, rattling on with childish naiveté, "and papa's sweetheart—Blanche Marabout—is to be here. You know they say she is to be my mamma."

What thrill was this shot through me? But I rose calmly, and administering a slight correction to the child, left the apartment.

Blunderbore House, for the next week, was the scene of gaiety and merriment. That portion of the mansion closed with a grating was walled up, and the midnight shrieks no longer troubled me.

But I felt more keenly the degradation of my situation. I was obliged to help Lady Blanche at her toilette and help her to look beautiful. For what? To captivate him? Oh-no, no—but why this sudden thrill and faintness? Did he really love her? I had seen him pinch and swear at her. But I reflected that he had thrown a candlestick at my head, and my foolish heart was reassured.

It was a night of festivity, when a sudden message obliged Mr. Rawjester to leave his guests for a few hours. "Make yourselves merry, idiots," he said, under his breath, as he passed me. The door closed and he was gone.

A half-hour passed. In the midst of the dancing a shriek was heard, and out of the swaying crowd of fainting women and excited men, a wild figure strode into the room. One glance showed it to be a highwayman, heavily armed, holding a pistol in each hand.

"Let no one pass out of this room!" he said, in a voice of thunder. "The house is surrounded and you cannot escape. The first one who crosses yonder threshold will be shot like a dog. Gentlemen, I'll trouble you to approach in single file, and hand me your purses and watches."

Finding resistance useless, the order was ungraciously obeyed.

"Now, ladies, please to pass up your jewelry and trinkets."

This order was still more ungraciously complied with. As Blanche handed to the bandit captain her bracelet, she endeavored to conceal a diamond necklace, the gift of Mr. Rawjester, in her bosom. But, with a demoniac grin, the powerful brute tore it from its concealment.

It was now my turn. With a beating heart, I made my way to the robber chieftain and sank at his feet. "Oh, sir, I am nothing but a poor governess, pray let me go."

"Oh, ho! A governess? Give me your last month's wages, then. Give me what you have stolen from your master!" and he laughed fiendishly.

I gazed at him quietly, and said, in a low voice, "I have stolen nothing from you, Mr. Rawjester!"

"Ah, discovered! Hush! Listen, girl!" he hissed in a fiercer whisper, "utter a syllable to frustrate my plans and you die—aid me, and—" but he was gone.

In a few moments the party, with the exception of myself, were gagged and locked in the cellar. The next moment, torches were applied to the rich hangings, and the house was in flames. I felt a strong hand seize me, and bear me out in the open air and place me upon the hillside, where I could overlook the burning mansion. It was Mr. Rawjester.

"Burn!" he said, as he shook his fist at the flames. Then sinking on his knees before me, he said hurriedly:

"Mary Jane, I love you; the obstacles to our union are or will be soon removed. In yonder mansion were confined my three crazy wives. One of them, as you know, attempted to kill me! Ha! This is vengeance! But will you be mine?"

I fell, without a word, upon his neck.

11. The name of the narrator is:

   A. Blanche Blunderbore.
   B. Blanche Mix.
   C. Mary Jane Mix.
   D. Mary Jane Rawjester.

GO ON TO THE NEXT PAGE.

12. Mr. Rawjester leaves the party in order to:

F. obtain more refreshments for his guests.
G. attend to an urgent business matter.
H. disguise himself and return to the party as a robber.
J. check on the whereabouts of his daughter.

13. The degradation the narrator describes in the fourth paragraph (lines 17-19) comes from:

A. having to help the fiancée of the man she loves.
B. having to tutor a small child who speaks French.
C. her inability to earn more money.
D. her inability to sleep through the night without being disturbed.

14. What is the narrator's position at Blunderbore house?

F. The master's wife
G. The master's mistress
H. The child's governess
J. Blanche Marabout's sister

15. Mr. Rawjester's attitude towards his guests is one of:

A. warmth.
B. revulsion.
C. indifference.
D. admiration.

16. The child believes that:

F. Blanche Marabout is her natural mother.
G. Blanche Marabout is to marry her father.
H. the narrator is her natural mother.
J. her father dislikes the narrator.

17. It can be inferred that the narrator:

A. denounces Mr. Rawjester to his guests.
B. cooperates with Mr. Rawjester.
C. defends herself against Mr. Rawjester's attack.
D. gives the highwayman her month's wages.

18. The purpose of the visit of the highwayman is to:

F. obtain valuable jewelry.
G. kidnap the narrator.
H. kill the child.
J. deflect suspicion from Mr. Rawjester.

19. Blanche was unable to hide the diamond necklace because:

A. the highwayman had given it to her and knew she had it.
B. the narrator told the highwayman where it was hidden.
C. some of the other guests insisted that she give it up.
D. the child whispered its location to the highwayman.

20. The exchange between the narrator and the highwayman that takes place in the house was heard:

F. only by those two persons.
G. by the child.
H. by Blanche.
J. by every guest in the room.

GO ON TO THE NEXT PAGE.

Passage III

SOCIAL SCIENCE: This passage discusses legislation for the regulation of corporate takeovers.

American financial markets are regulated by the federal government through the Securities and Exchange Commission and by various state agencies. In recent years, there has been considerable discussion of the need for more regulation because of the increased number of corporate takeovers. Many observers of the economic scene argue that much of this activity has had harmful effects not only on stockholders but also on the economy as a whole.

Many corporate takeovers are hostile; that is, an outside group or company tries to seize control of an existing company whose management opposes the takeover. Most hostile takeovers begin with a tender offer in which the outside raiders offer to buy a sufficient amount of the company's outstanding stock at a stated price—usually well above the current market price. Another takeover strategy is to orchestrate a proxy battle in which a vote of shareholders of record on a specific date is taken to approve or reject a new slate of directors put forth by the raiders. The raiders generally argue that the new directors will make the company more profitable and thereby enhance the value of the stock for the existing stockholders.

Regardless of the takeover strategy employed, most raiders must purchase a significant portion of the company's stock at a price above its current market value. Outsiders usually finance such large purchases of stock through the sale of bonds that pay a very high rate of interest. The raiders argue that the debt to be incurred can easily be paid off by selling parts of the targeted company or by drawing on the additional profits that the new management insists it can make.

In 1986 and 1987, charges emerged that individuals within Wall Street firms specializing in raising capital for corporate takeovers were, in fact, selling inside information about future takeover attempts. Some of the individuals involved have already been sentenced to jail terms. In addition, such scandals have added to pressure on Congress and the Securities and Exchange Commission to provide more effective regulation of the financial aspects of attempted corporate takeovers.

Critics of hostile corporate takeovers believe that the managers of the company to be taken over usually engage in short-term activities that have very negative long-term effects. In order to avoid hostile takeovers, managers of companies generally take measures to make the takeovers less desirable. For instance, they may insert a *golden parachute clause* in employment contracts. This clause requires a company to pay very large bonuses to any management members who are fired after a takeover. Another tactic, the *poison pill,* restructures the financial base of the corporation so that an attempted takeover would make the company less profitable. Yet another anti-raid tactic is to pay *greenmail* to the raiders; that is, the target of the takeover pays the raiders, who have acquired a significant percentage of the stock at a premium, to sell those shares back to the targeted company at a much higher price. This prevents the takeover, but it usually adds a substantial sum to the company's debt.

Supporters of corporate raiders counter-argue that, in fact, it is the threat of a takeover that makes managers more efficient. For instance, it may cause managers to sell parts of the corporation that they are not managing well in order to raise the money to fend off the takeover. In addition, those who believe that takeovers are good argue that the existing shareholders always do better in a hostile takeover since they invariably get a higher price for each share of stock than the current market value.

21. Which statement expresses the main idea of this passage?

A. The government is regulating the financial aspects of corporate takeovers adequately.
B. There has been recent debate over the need for additional government regulation of corporate takeovers.
C. Hostile corporate takeovers are beneficial to the targeted corporation.
D. Trading insider secrets has become a common problem in hostile corporate takeovers.

22. A corporation's board of directors votes to approve a new company policy. According to the plan, each member of the board and of upper management would receive severance of two to five years' pay if the new owner fired the member after a corporate takeover. This action would be considered:

F. a poison pill.
G. a golden parachute.
H. greenmail.
J. a hostile takeover.

GO ON TO THE NEXT PAGE.

23. What is the most important difference between a hostile and a non-hostile takeover?

A. In a hostile takeover, stockholders must pay greenmail to the existing directors.
B. In a non-hostile takeover, raiders sell bonds with high interest rates.
C. In a hostile takeover, the existing management is opposed to the takeover.
D. In a non-hostile takeover, existing management uses golden parachutes.

24. According to the passage, which of the following parties in a hostile takeover will likely incur new debt?

F. The raiders, because they need money to buy large blocks of stock
G. The Securities and Exchange Commission, because it must oversee the transactions more closely
H. The stockholders, because they must furnish additional funds works
J. The critics of hostile takeovers, because they make less money in the stock market

25. According to the passage, a poison pill strategy involves:

A. paying the raiders high prices to buy back the company's stock from them.
B. paying high bonuses to the members of the old management who are fired by the new management.
C. more regulation by the Securities and Exchange Commission.
D. restructuring the financial base of the company so that it will be less profitable or valuable to the raiders.

26. According to the passage, supporters of corporate takeovers believe that:

F. the shareholders always lose money because a takeover profits only the raiders.
G. fear of being targeted for a takeover makes managers more efficient.
H. insider trading should be made legal.
J. a proxy fight is the best way to win control.

27. According to the passage, in a proxy fight:

A. the raiders sell bonds to buy the targeted company's stock.
B. the raiders offer to buy stock at a higher-than-market price.
C. insider information is traded illegally.
D. a stockholders' meeting is called to vote for approval or rejection of a new board of directors put forth by the raiders.

28. The management of a business recently targeted for takeover decides to sell two of its unprofitable subsidiaries to raise cash and cut expenses. Supporters of corporate takeovers would say that this action:

F. is an example of how the greenmail strategy works.
G. is an example of how a golden parachute strategy works.
H. is an example of how the fear of a takeover makes managers more efficient.
J. is an example of how the poison pill strategy works.

29. The Securities and Exchange Commission is a:

A. state regulatory agency that polices financial markets.
B. federal regulatory agency that polices financial markets.
C. source of funding for hostile takeovers.
D. board of business executives who promote fair business practices.

30. Some individuals working on Wall Street have been sentenced to jail terms for:

F. attempting to greenmail other companies.
G. forcing companies to swallow a poison pill.
H. selling inside information about takeover attempts.
J. agreeing to pay greenmail to corporate raiders.

GO ON TO THE NEXT PAGE.

Passage IV

NATURAL SCIENCE: This passage discusses supernova explosions and their effects.

About twice every century, the light reaches us from one of the massive stars in our galaxy that blew apart millions of years ago in a supernova explosion that sends massive quantities of radiation and matter into space and generates shock waves that sweep through the arms of the galaxy. The shock waves heat the interstellar gas, evaporate small clouds, and compress larger ones to the point at which they collapse under their own gravity to form new stars. The general picture that has been developed for the supernova explosion and its aftermath goes something like this. Throughout its evolution, a star is much like a leaky balloon; it keeps its equilibrium figure through a balance of internal pressure against the tendency to collapse under its own weight. The pressure is generated by nuclear reactions in the core of the star that must continually supply energy to balance the energy that leaks out in the form of radiation. Eventually, the nuclear fuel is exhausted, and the pressure drops in the core. With nothing to hold it up, the matter in the center of the star collapses inward, creating higher and higher densities and temperatures, until the nuclei and electrons are fused into a super-dense lump of matter known as a neutron star.

As the overlying layers rain down on the surface of the neutron star, the temperature rises until, with a blinding flash of radiation, the collapse is reversed. A thermonuclear shock wave runs through the now expanding stellar envelope, fusing lighter elements into heavier ones and producing a brilliant visual outburst that can be as intense as the light of 10 billion suns. The shell of matter thrown off by the explosion plows through the surrounding gas, producing an expanding bubble of hot gas, with gas temperatures in the millions of degrees. This gas will emit most of its energy at x-ray wavelengths, so it is not surprising that x-ray observatories have provided some of the most useful insights into the nature of the supernova phenomenon. More than twenty supernova remnants have now been detected in x-ray studies.

Recent discoveries of meteorites with anomalous concentrations of certain isotopes indicate that a supernova might have precipitated the birth of our solar system more than four and a half billion years ago. Although the cloud that collapsed to form the Sun and the planets was composed primarily of hydrogen and helium, it also contained carbon, nitrogen, and oxygen, elements essential for life as we know it. Elements heavier than helium are manufactured deep in the interior of stars and would, for the most part, remain there if it were not for the cataclysmic supernova explosions that blow giant stars apart. Additionally, supernovas produce clouds of high-energy particles called cosmic rays. These high-energy particles continually bombard the Earth and are responsible for many of the genetic mutations that are the driving force of the evolution of species.

31. According to the passage, we can expect to observe a supernova in our galaxy about:

A. twice each year.
B. 100 times each century.
C. once every 50 years.
D. once every other century.

32. According to the passage, all of the following are true of supernovas EXCEPT:

F. they are extremely bright.
G. they are an explosion of some sort.
H. they are emitters of large quantities of x-rays.
J. they are caused by the collision of large galaxies.

33. The author employs which of the following to develop the first paragraph?

A. Analogy
B. Deduction
C. Generalization
D. Example

34. It can be inferred from the passage that the "meteorites" mentioned by the author (line 41):

F. contain dangerous concentrations of radioactive materials.
G. give off large quantities of x-rays.
H. include material not created in the normal development of our solar system.
J. are larger than the meteors normally found in a solar system like ours.

GO ON TO THE NEXT PAGE.

35. The author implies that:

A. it is sometimes easier to detect supernovas by observation of the x-ray spectrum than by observation of visible wavelengths of light.
B. life on Earth is endangered by its constant exposure to radiation forces that are released by a supernova.
C. recently discovered meteorites indicate that the Earth and other planets of our solar system survived the explosion of a supernova several billion years ago.
D. lighter elements are formed from heavier elements during a supernova as the heavier elements are torn apart.

36. According to the passage, what is the first event in the sequence that leads to the occurrence of a supernova?

F. An ordinary star begins to emit tremendous quantities of x-rays.
G. A superheated cloud of gas envelops a neutron star.
H. An imbalance between light and heavy elements causes an ordinary star to collapse.
J. An ordinary star exhausts its supply of nuclear fuel and begins to collapse.

37. According to the passage, a neutron star is:

A. a gaseous cloud containing heavy elements.
B. an intermediate stage between an ordinary star and a supernova.
C. the residue that is left by a supernova.
D. the core of an ordinary star that houses the thermonuclear reactions.

38. The author is primarily concerned with:

F. speculating about the origins of our solar system.
G. presenting evidence proving the existence of supernovas.
H. discussing the nuclear reaction that occurs in the core of a star.
J. describing a theory about the causes of supernovas.

39. How long ago was our galaxy formed?

A. 100 million years
B. 1 billion years
C. 2 billion years
D. Over 4.5 billion years

40. What is the connection between supernovas and the evolution of species on Earth?

F. There is no connection.
G. Cosmic radiation from supernovas retards evolution.
H. Cosmic radiation from supernovas drives evolution.
J. Evolution makes possible future supernovas.

END OF TEST 3.
STOP! DO NOT TURN THE PAGE UNTIL TOLD TO DO SO.
DO NOT RETURN TO A PREVIOUS TEST.

4 4 4 4 4 4 4 4 4 4 4 4

SCIENCE REASONING TEST

35 Minutes—40 Items

DIRECTIONS: The passages presented in the test are each followed by a set of items. Read the passage and choose the best answer for each item. Fill in the corresponding oval on your bubble sheet. You may refer to the passage as often as necessary to answer the passage items.

Warning: Calculator use is not permitted on this test.

Answers are on page 946. Explanations begin on page 962.

Passage I

Before making their historic first powered flight, the Wright Brothers made extensive lift tests in 1901 using a glider. Their data differed from that obtained twelve years earlier by the German, Otto Lilienthal.

Results of both tests (Wright: thin line; Lilienthal: thick line) are shown below. "Lift" is the force that pulls the wing away from the Earth, in a direction perpendicular to the flight path, and the "angle of incidence" is the angle that the flight path makes with the horizon.

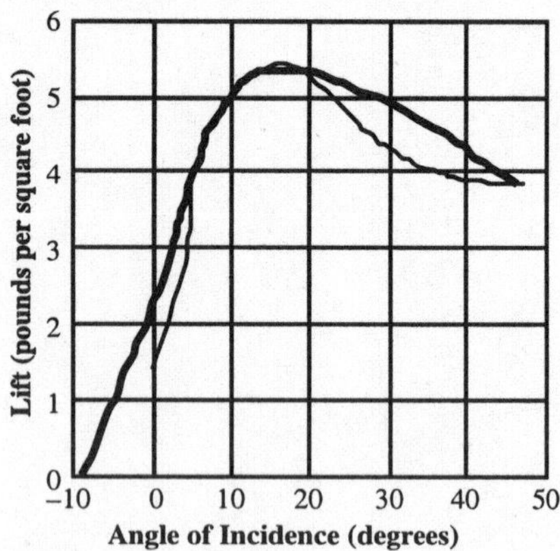

Modified from Culick, F.E.C, "The Wright 'Flyer' was the outcome of an intensive program of research." *Sci. Amer. 241* (1): 86-100, 1979.

1. The two curves differ chiefly in that:

   A. the Wright's data were more accurate.
   B. lift was generally greater in the Wright's experiments.
   C. lift was generally greater in Lilienthal's experiments.
   D. the peak value for lift was greater in Lilienthal's experiments.

2. In the Wright's experiments, the greatest lift occurred at an angle of incidence of about:

   F. 5.5 degrees.
   G. 0 degrees.
   H. 16 degrees.
   J. 46 degrees.

3. At an angle of incidence of 50 degrees, by how much would you expect the two experiments to show a difference in lift?

   A. 0-1 pounds/sq. ft.
   B. 1-2 pounds/sq. ft.
   C. 2-3 pounds/sq. ft.
   D. 3-4 pounds/sq. ft.

4. The two sets of experiments differed most in lift at which of the following angles?

   F. 10 degrees
   G. 15 degrees
   H. 30 degrees
   J. 40 degrees

GO ON TO THE NEXT PAGE.

5. The widest range of angles, in degrees, over which the Lilienthal values for lift continuously exceeded the Wright's values was:

   A. 10.
   B. 19.
   C. 25.
   D. 43.

GO ON TO THE NEXT PAGE.

Passage II

Two experiments were performed to determine the effects of temperature on the rate of cellular respiration* in germinating peas.

*Summary Equation: $C_6H_{12}O_6$ (glucose) + $6O_2$ (oxygen) ⇒ $6CO_2$ (carbon dioxide) + $6H_2O$ (water)

Experiment 1: A simple respirometer was used, primarily consisting of a large test tube partially filled with germinating peas. The peas were covered with a layer of cotton and a small amount of potassium hydroxide (KOH), a substance that can absorb and remove carbon dioxide from the tube. The remainder of the tube, with its starting volume of air sealed inside (200 ml.), was closed to the outside with a rubber stopper. Attached was a meter designed to detect and measure any changes in gas volume in the tube during the experiment. The experiment was conducted at room temperature (22° C), and the respirator was monitored for 15 minutes. At the end of 15 minutes, the volume of gas inside the tube had *decreased* to 120 ml.

Experiment 2: An identical experiment was conducted at 30° C. At this temperature, the volume of gas inside the tube after 15 minutes had decreased from 200 ml (starting volume) to 60 ml.

6. Separate control experiments were performed alongside Experiments 1 and 2. The control contained plastic beads (the same size as peas) instead of germinating peas. All other conditions were identical. Any decrease in gas volume inside the control tube would suggest that:

   F. plastic beads utilize oxygen at approximately the same rate as germinating peas.
   G. plastic beads produce carbon dioxide at about the same rate as germinating peas.
   H. plastic beads carry out all aspects of cellular respiration at approximately the same rate as germinating peas.
   J. factors having nothing to do with cellular respiration must be responsible.

7. In both experiments, the decrease in volume in the tube was mainly due to a change in the volume of what specific gas?

   A. Oxygen
   B. Carbon dioxide
   C. Potassium hydroxide
   D. All of the above

8. If potassium hydroxide (KOH) were not included in the tubes, what would happen to the volume of gas during each experiment?

   F. Final volumes would be higher than starting volumes.
   G. Final volumes would decrease faster than what was observed in Experiments 1 and 2.
   H. Final volumes would approximately be the same as starting volumes.
   J. Results would not be different from what was observed in Experiments 1 and 2.

9. Experiment 2 showed a greater decrease in gas volume in the tube because:

   A. at higher temperatures, peas use oxygen slower.
   B. at higher temperatures, peas produce carbon dioxide faster.
   C. at higher temperatures, peas use oxygen faster.
   D. at lower temperatures, peas use oxygen slower than they produce carbon dioxide.

10. An additional set of experiments with germinating peas is conducted in the dark at 22° C and 30° C. All other conditions are identical to those in Experiments 1 and 2. After 15 minutes, if the final gas volume inside the tube at 22° C is 120 ml, and the final gas volume inside the tube at 30° C is 60 ml, which hypothesis best explains the results?

    F. Darkness affects cellular respiration in germinating peas the same way that a rise in temperature affects cellular respiration in germinating peas.
    G. Light/dark conditions have little or no effect on cellular respiration in germinating peas.
    H. Cellular respiration in germinating peas occurs faster in the light than in the dark.
    J. Cellular respiration in germinating peas occurs faster in the dark than in the light.

11. The summary equation in the passage shows that during cellular respiration, germinating peas must consume glucose. In Experiments 1 and 2, glucose molecules:

    A. were in the peas.
    B. were not available.
    C. were consumed at equal rates.
    D. were available but not consumed at all.

GO ON TO THE NEXT PAGE.

Passage III

Two different views of the Earth's past are presented below.

Scientist 1: The history of our planet has been marked by sudden spectacular events that have no counterpart in the natural processes observed today (Catastrophism). Today's valleys formed during periods of downward slippage by fragments of the Earth's crust. Mountains rose due to gigantic upheavals of land during the Earth's beginnings. The three major types of rock formed when one worldwide ocean precipitated out great masses of different materials during three sudden and separate events. Substances such as granite were precipitated first (today's igneous rocks), while materials in the flat upper layers precipitated last (today's sedimentary rocks). This was followed by the disappearance of much of this great ocean's water (perhaps by evaporation during years of intensive heat). Distinct assemblages of animal and plant fossils, found in successive rock layers of a region, can be explained by local catastrophic events, such as massive fires or floods. Old forms were wiped out, and eventually new forms replaced them as foreign species immigrated from other geographic areas.

Scientist 2: Processes now in operation are adequate to account for changes in the Earth's past (Principle of Uniform Change). Although today's processes seem to have negligible effects on the landscape, great changes can result from ongoing processes, if given long enough periods of time. Valleys form as flowing water cuts through the sides and bottom of the land and rock they pass across. Rocks and mountains can be formed, destroyed and reformed by processes still going on today such as volcanic activity, heat and pressure under the Earth's surfaces, erosion, weathering, and even shifts and movements that can lift massive areas below the land and ocean surfaces to high elevations. Different fossil types in successive layers of rocks represent the changes in form that can take place among related organisms as a result of evolutionary processes over vast periods of time.

12. One major difference between the views of Scientist 1 and Scientist 2 relates to:

F. where fossils are found.
G. when the processes that shape the Earth take place.
H. the size of mountain ranges.
J. whether water played a role in forming any of the Earth's characteristics.

13. Which of the following provides the strongest evidence against Scientist 1's point about mountain formation?

A. The beginnings of the Earth are not well documented.
B. Floods and fires have never been massive enough to eliminate fossils from all mountain areas.
C. Volcanic activity, weathering, and erosion are believed to be less common today than in years past.
D. Fossils of recent sea creatures can be found in rocks on mountain peaks.

14. Based on the differences between Scientist 1 and Scientist 2 stated above, which description is most accurate concerning their views about the time span needed for the Earth's geologic characteristics to form?

F. Scientist 1 makes references to time span and suggests a longer Earth history than Scientist 2.
G. Scientist 2 makes no references to time span, but implies a shorter Earth history than Scientist 1.
H. Scientist 2 makes references to time span and suggests a longer Earth history than does Scientist 1.
J. Neither scientist refers to time span or implies any difference in length of Earth history.

15. According to Scientist 1, which of the major types of rocks should be found at the lowest levels?

A. Igneous (granite)
B. Metamorphic (marble)
C. Sedimentary (limestone)
D. Cannot be determined from the given information

GO ON TO THE NEXT PAGE.

16. According to the views of Scientist 1, the number of major rock types will most likely:

F. remain unchanged.
G. decrease.
H. increase.
J. Cannot be determined from the given information

17. To refute Scientist 2's point of view about strictly uniform processes of change, Scientist 1 could argue that:

A. the streams of today are not measurably effective in cutting through the sides and bottoms of rock they pass across.
B. fossils are not found everywhere today.
C. at some early point in time, the actual formation of the Earth had to involve very different processes from those now in evidence.
D. no mountain ranges have formed in our lifetime.

18. Which argument does NOT support the views of Scientist 2?

F. There are many regions of lava where no volcanoes are present today.
G. There are three major types of rock that exist today.
H. Many rivers today are flowing far below their former channels.
J. Distinctive fossils in upper layers of rock show similarities to those in lower layers, yet they are never found in any other geographic areas.

GO ON TO THE NEXT PAGE.

Passage IV

Cold-blooded animals (poikilotherms) cannot regulate their body temperatures internally. Their body temperature varies as the environmental temperature varies. Consequently, the rates of many bodily processes also vary as outside temperatures change (as environmental temperatures increase, body temperature as well as the rates of bodily processes also may increase). Warm-blooded animals (homeotherms), on the other hand, can maintain their body temperatures internally. Therefore, the rates of their bodily processes can remain relatively stable when environmental temperatures change.

Experiments were set up to determine how the bodily process heart rate may be affected by different temperatures in two species of live laboratory animals.

Experiment 1: Ten individuals from Species A and ten individuals from Species B were kept in 20 separate containers at room temperature (22° C) for 30 minutes. Their heart rates (heart beats/minute) were recorded every 10 minutes. Average heart rates for the entire experiment were then calculated for each species. Results were as follows: Species A had an average heart rate of 150 beats/minute, while Species B averaged 100 beats/minute.

Experiment 2: Identical procedures were used to repeat the original experiment except that the containers holding the individuals of each species were placed in an incubator set at 35° C. At the end of 30 minutes, the average heart rate for both species was 148 beats/minute.

19. How many values were used to calculate the average heart beats for each species in each of these experiments?

A. 1
B. 10
C. 20
D. 30

20. Which of the following hypotheses is supported by the results of both experiments?

F. Species A is most likely poikilothermic.
G. Species B is most likely poikilothermic.
H. Both species are most likely poikilothermic.
J. Neither species is poikilothermic.

21. Which of the following statements best explains why ten individuals of each species were used in the experiments?

A. In case a few died, there would still be others available for testing.
B. If only one individual was used, it would be lonely.
C. An average value for ten individuals reduces the chance of getting an extreme value for any one individual.
D. If only one individual was chosen from each species, it would be difficult to show differences.

22. If a third experiment were conducted at 6° C, which set of results for average heart rates (in beats/minute) is closest to what might be expected?

F. Species A = 146; Species B = 146
G. Species A = 50; Species B = 146
H. Species A = 50; Species B = 50
J. Species A = 146; Species B = 50

23. Which statement is accurate concerning Species A and Species B?

A. At 22° C, Species A has a higher average heart rate than Species B.
B. Species A has a larger average size than Species B.
C. As environmental temperature increases, average heart rate increases more for Species A than Species B.
D. As environmental temperature decreases, average heart rate increases more for Species A than Species B.

24. If the average body temperature for ten individuals of each species were recorded during Experiments 1 and 2, which results would be expected?

F. Species A: Temperature stays the same in both experiments. Species B: Temperature increases in Experiment 2.
G. Species A: Temperature increases in Experiment 2. Species B: Temperature stays the same in both experiments.
H. Both Species: Temperature increases in Experiment 2.
J. Both Species: Temperature stays the same in both experiments.

GO ON TO THE NEXT PAGE.

Passage V

The chart below shows a set of "energy levels" that an electron in molecule X can occupy. The value of the energy in each level is shown to the right.

Energy Levels

E_5---------2.07
E_4---------1.75
E_3---------1.52
E_2---------1.20
E_1---------0.60

An electron can move from one level to the next (transition) in two ways:

(a) the molecule can absorb a particle of light, called a "photon," of just the right energy to lift the electron to a higher level. For example, an electron in level 4 can be raised to level 5 if the molecule absorbs a photon whose energy is 0.32.

(b) the molecule can emit, or give off, a photon of just the right energy necessary to lower an electron to another level. For example, an electron in level 4 can move to level 3 if the molecule emits a photon whose energy is 0.23.

25. A sample containing many X molecules absorbs light, each photon of which carries 0.60 units of energy. As the light is absorbed:

A. an electron moves from level 1 to level 2.
B. an electron moves from level 2 to level 4.
C. an electron moves from level 2 to level 1.
D. an electron moves from level 4 to level 2.

26. A sample of molecule X emits light, each photon of which carries 0.32 units of energy. Which of the following statements best explains this observation?

F. An electron moved from level 3 to level 2.
G. An electron moved from level 2 to level 3.
H. An electron moved from level 5 to level 4.
J. An electron moved from level 3 to level 2 or from level 5 to level 4.

27. A sample of molecule X emits light whose photons each carry 0.92 units of energy. As the light is emitted:

A. an electron moves from level 5 to level 2.
B. an electron moves from level 1 to level 5.
C. an electron moves from level 1 to level 3.
D. an electron moves from level 3 to level 1.

28. Suppose that in a sample of molecule X, all of the electrons are in level 1. Based on the information in the chart, photons of how many different energies could be absorbed by the sample?

F. 1
G. 2
H. 3
J. 4

29. Assume that each of the molecules in a sample of molecule X has only 1 electron, whose level is not known. Light is passed through the sample, and photons, each of energy 0.23, are absorbed. A very short time later, photons of the same energy are emitted. It is likely that:

A. electrons are being promoted from level 1 to level 2.
B. electrons are moving from level 4 to level 3, and then back again to level 4.
C. electrons are moving from level 3 to level 4, then back again to level 3.
D. electrons are moving from level 5 to level 4.

30. If photons whose individual energies are each 2.07 encounter a sample of molecule X, then:

F. electrons will be promoted from level 1 to level 5.
G. electrons will be promoted from all levels to level 5.
H. electrons will drop from level 5 to level 1.
J. no electron transitions will occur.

GO ON TO THE NEXT PAGE.

Passage VI

A student performs a set of three experiments in which a light beam passes through water and air. The "refraction angles" are the angles that the light beam makes with a vertical line. In the water, this angle is called θ_1. When the beam leaves the water and passes into air, a second angle, θ_2, can be measured. Figure 1 illustrates θ_1 and θ_2.

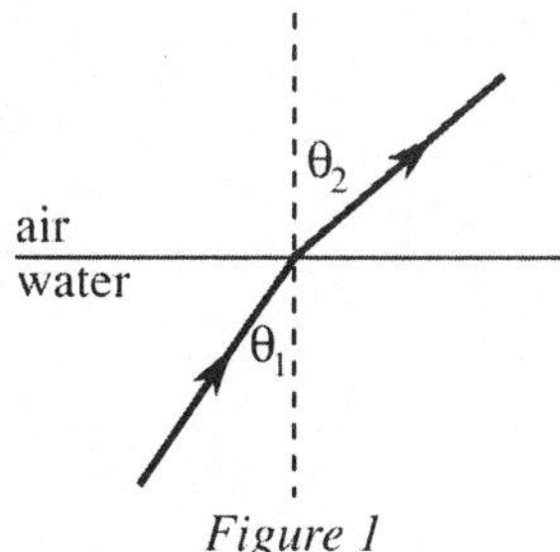

Figure 1

Experiment 1: The entry angle, θ_1, and the exit angle, θ_2, are both equal to zero.

Experiment 2: The angles observed are shown in Figure 2.

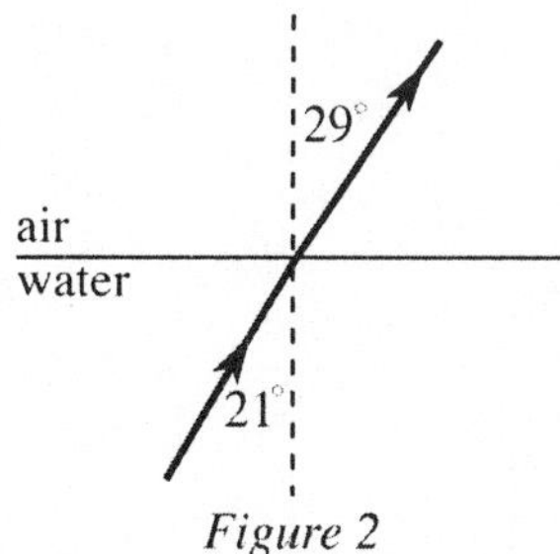

Figure 2

Experiment 3: The angles observed are shown in Figure 3.

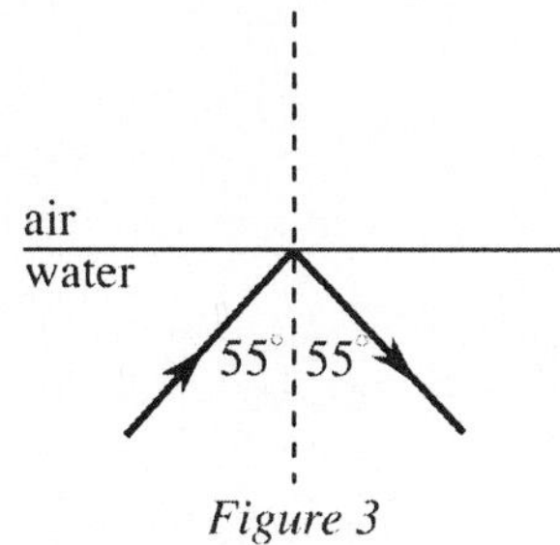

Figure 3

31. Which of the following diagrams could represent the observations of Experiment 1?

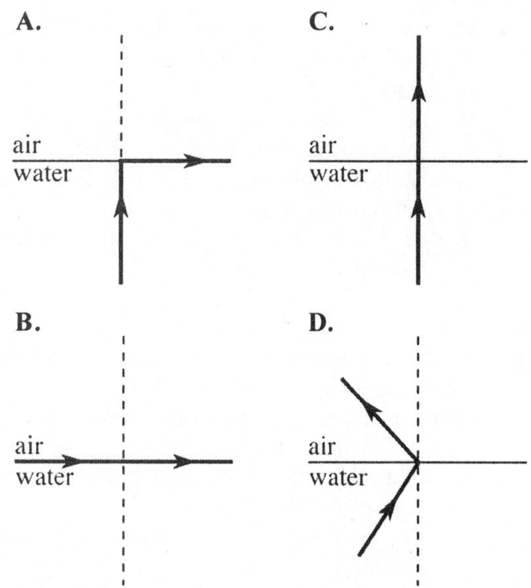

32. The student attempts to draw a conclusion from Experiments 1 and 2 that may apply to all other measurements as well. Which of the following is justified by the data?

F. Refraction angles in water are greater than those in air.
G. Refraction angles in water are less than those in air.
H. Refraction angles are equal in air and in water.
J. Refraction angles in water are equal to or less than those in air.

33. In Experiment 3, the beam travels through the water and:

A. is reflected back down from the surface of the water.
B. enters the air.
C. is absorbed completely.
D. is reflected back on itself.

GO ON TO THE NEXT PAGE.

34. An observer in the air attempts to see the beam of light in Experiments 2 and 3. She will:

- **F.** be able to observe the light in each experiment, provided she is in the right place.
- **G.** be unable to observe the light in either experiment, regardless of position.
- **H.** be able to observe the light in Experiment 2 but not Experiment 3.
- **J.** be able to observe the light in Experiment 3 but not Experiment 2.

35. A student attempts to summarize the results of all three experiments. Which of the following is most consistent with the observations?

- **A.** The angle of refraction in water is less than that in air.
- **B.** The angle of refraction in air is less than that in water.
- **C.** The angle of refraction in water is less than or equal to that in air, but at high angles in the water, the light is reflected back into the water.
- **D.** The angle of refraction in water is less than or equal to that in air.

GO ON TO THE NEXT PAGE.

Passage VII

The table below presents the results of a study in which butterflies of different size and color were captured in flight for marking with a chemical, and then recaptured in flight a few weeks later.

SIZE	WHITE # marked	WHITE Recaptured	TAN # marked	TAN Recaptured	DARK BROWN # marked	DARK BROWN Recaptured
Small (less than 20 mm)	35	30	40	10	20	10
Medium (20-40 mm)	30	15	40	20	20	10
Large (greater than 40 mm)	50	25	60	30	30	10

36. For all sizes of butterflies, the color that seems most difficult to capture for marking is:

F. white.
G. tan.
H. dark brown.
J. Both tan and dark brown are almost equally difficult

37. The specific type of butterfly that is easiest to recapture after being marked is:

A. between 10-20 mm and tan.
B. greater than 40 mm and tan.
C. greater than 40 mm and dark brown.
D. less than 20 mm and white.

38. Based on the information in the table, which statement best represents the relationship between a butterfly's size and its tendency to be captured for marking?

F. The larger the butterfly, the harder it is to be captured for marking.
G. The larger the butterfly, the easier it is to be captured for marking.
H. Medium-sized butterflies are consistently the easiest to capture for marking.
J. The smaller the butterfly, the easier it is to be captured for marking.

39. The chemical used to mark all the butterflies was found to be poisonous to one specific type because it was being absorbed through the wings. Based on the data in the table, which type of butterfly appears most likely to have suffered from the effects of the marking chemical?

A. Greater than 40 mm and white
B. Less than 20 mm and tan
C. Greater than 40 mm and dark brown
D. Less than 20 mm and white

40. Which conclusion is correct concerning the information in the table?

F. For tan butterflies, the proportion of individuals that are recaptured always stays the same.
G. For medium-sized butterflies, the proportion of individuals that are recaptured always stays the same.
H. For small-sized butterflies, the proportion of individuals recaptured always stays the same.
J. For all sizes of butterflies, the darker the color the easier it is to recapture an individual.

END OF TEST 4.
STOP! DO NOT TURN THE PAGE UNTIL TOLD TO DO SO.
DO NOT RETURN TO A PREVIOUS TEST.

5 5 5 5 5 5 5 5 5 5 5 5

WRITING TEST (OPTIONAL)

30 Minutes—1 Essay Prompt

DIRECTIONS: This is a test of your writing skills. Before you begin planning and writing your essay, read the writing prompt carefully to understand the instructions. Your essay will be evaluated on the evidence it provides of your ability to express judgments by taking a position on the issue in the writing prompt; to maintain a focus on the topic throughout the essay; to develop a position by using logical reasoning and supporting ideas; to organize ideas in a logical way; and to use language clearly and effectively according to the conventions of standard written English.

If you finish before time is called, you may review your work. Lay your pencil down immediately when time is called.

Sample essays begin on page 964.

Writing Test Prompt

Doctors and government leaders have become increasingly concerned about what is called the "obesity epidemic" in America. Many people are overweight, and researchers now believe that childhood eating habits have a major effect on whether an adult will be overweight. Some people now argue that schools should eliminate all "junk food" from the cafeteria offerings, remove all vending machines that sell soda pop and sugary snacks, and prohibit students from bringing into the school cafeteria from outside foods that are considered unhealthy. Other people oppose this idea. They say that the choice of what to eat should be left to individuals and families. Those parents who do not want their children eating "junk food" can take steps to regulate their diet; other parents can determine how often their children may eat such food and how much of it. Do you think that schools should take steps to ensure that only healthful foods are served and consumed on school premises?

In your essay, take a position on this issue. You may address either of the two points described above, or you may offer an entirely different perspective on the issue. Be sure to use specific reasons and examples to support your analysis.

END OF TEST 5.
STOP! DO NOT RETURN TO ANY OTHER TEST.

Practice Test IV

TARGETED EDUCATIONAL SOLUTIONS.

Cambridge Course Concept Outline
PRACTICE TEST IV

When completing Practice Test IV, use the Bubble Sheet on page 835, unless otherwise directed by your instructor.

BUBBLE SHEET

Name ______________________ Student ID Number ______________________

Date ______________ Instructor ______________________ Course/Session Number ______________

TEST 1—ENGLISH

1 Ⓐ Ⓑ Ⓒ Ⓓ	16 Ⓕ Ⓖ Ⓗ Ⓙ	31 Ⓐ Ⓑ Ⓒ Ⓓ	46 Ⓕ Ⓖ Ⓗ Ⓙ	61 Ⓐ Ⓑ Ⓒ Ⓓ
2 Ⓕ Ⓖ Ⓗ Ⓙ	17 Ⓐ Ⓑ Ⓒ Ⓓ	32 Ⓕ Ⓖ Ⓗ Ⓙ	47 Ⓐ Ⓑ Ⓒ Ⓓ	62 Ⓕ Ⓖ Ⓗ Ⓙ
3 Ⓐ Ⓑ Ⓒ Ⓓ	18 Ⓕ Ⓖ Ⓗ Ⓙ	33 Ⓐ Ⓑ Ⓒ Ⓓ	48 Ⓕ Ⓖ Ⓗ Ⓙ	63 Ⓐ Ⓑ Ⓒ Ⓓ
4 Ⓕ Ⓖ Ⓗ Ⓙ	19 Ⓐ Ⓑ Ⓒ Ⓓ	34 Ⓕ Ⓖ Ⓗ Ⓙ	49 Ⓐ Ⓑ Ⓒ Ⓓ	64 Ⓕ Ⓖ Ⓗ Ⓙ
5 Ⓐ Ⓑ Ⓒ Ⓓ	20 Ⓕ Ⓖ Ⓗ Ⓙ	35 Ⓐ Ⓑ Ⓒ Ⓓ	50 Ⓕ Ⓖ Ⓗ Ⓙ	65 Ⓐ Ⓑ Ⓒ Ⓓ
6 Ⓕ Ⓖ Ⓗ Ⓙ	21 Ⓐ Ⓑ Ⓒ Ⓓ	36 Ⓕ Ⓖ Ⓗ Ⓙ	51 Ⓐ Ⓑ Ⓒ Ⓓ	66 Ⓕ Ⓖ Ⓗ Ⓙ
7 Ⓐ Ⓑ Ⓒ Ⓓ	22 Ⓕ Ⓖ Ⓗ Ⓙ	37 Ⓐ Ⓑ Ⓒ Ⓓ	52 Ⓕ Ⓖ Ⓗ Ⓙ	67 Ⓐ Ⓑ Ⓒ Ⓓ
8 Ⓕ Ⓖ Ⓗ Ⓙ	23 Ⓐ Ⓑ Ⓒ Ⓓ	38 Ⓕ Ⓖ Ⓗ Ⓙ	53 Ⓐ Ⓑ Ⓒ Ⓓ	68 Ⓕ Ⓖ Ⓗ Ⓙ
9 Ⓐ Ⓑ Ⓒ Ⓓ	24 Ⓕ Ⓖ Ⓗ Ⓙ	39 Ⓐ Ⓑ Ⓒ Ⓓ	54 Ⓕ Ⓖ Ⓗ Ⓙ	69 Ⓐ Ⓑ Ⓒ Ⓓ
10 Ⓕ Ⓖ Ⓗ Ⓙ	25 Ⓐ Ⓑ Ⓒ Ⓓ	40 Ⓕ Ⓖ Ⓗ Ⓙ	55 Ⓐ Ⓑ Ⓒ Ⓓ	70 Ⓕ Ⓖ Ⓗ Ⓙ
11 Ⓐ Ⓑ Ⓒ Ⓓ	26 Ⓕ Ⓖ Ⓗ Ⓙ	41 Ⓐ Ⓑ Ⓒ Ⓓ	56 Ⓕ Ⓖ Ⓗ Ⓙ	71 Ⓐ Ⓑ Ⓒ Ⓓ
12 Ⓕ Ⓖ Ⓗ Ⓙ	27 Ⓐ Ⓑ Ⓒ Ⓓ	42 Ⓕ Ⓖ Ⓗ Ⓙ	57 Ⓐ Ⓑ Ⓒ Ⓓ	72 Ⓕ Ⓖ Ⓗ Ⓙ
13 Ⓐ Ⓑ Ⓒ Ⓓ	28 Ⓕ Ⓖ Ⓗ Ⓙ	43 Ⓐ Ⓑ Ⓒ Ⓓ	58 Ⓕ Ⓖ Ⓗ Ⓙ	73 Ⓐ Ⓑ Ⓒ Ⓓ
14 Ⓕ Ⓖ Ⓗ Ⓙ	29 Ⓐ Ⓑ Ⓒ Ⓓ	44 Ⓕ Ⓖ Ⓗ Ⓙ	59 Ⓐ Ⓑ Ⓒ Ⓓ	74 Ⓕ Ⓖ Ⓗ Ⓙ
15 Ⓐ Ⓑ Ⓒ Ⓓ	30 Ⓕ Ⓖ Ⓗ Ⓙ	45 Ⓐ Ⓑ Ⓒ Ⓓ	60 Ⓕ Ⓖ Ⓗ Ⓙ	75 Ⓐ Ⓑ Ⓒ Ⓓ

TEST 2—MATHEMATICS

1 Ⓐ Ⓑ Ⓒ Ⓓ Ⓔ	13 Ⓐ Ⓑ Ⓒ Ⓓ Ⓔ	25 Ⓐ Ⓑ Ⓒ Ⓓ Ⓔ	37 Ⓐ Ⓑ Ⓒ Ⓓ Ⓔ	49 Ⓐ Ⓑ Ⓒ Ⓓ Ⓔ
2 Ⓕ Ⓖ Ⓗ Ⓙ Ⓚ	14 Ⓕ Ⓖ Ⓗ Ⓙ Ⓚ	26 Ⓕ Ⓖ Ⓗ Ⓙ Ⓚ	38 Ⓕ Ⓖ Ⓗ Ⓙ Ⓚ	50 Ⓕ Ⓖ Ⓗ Ⓙ Ⓚ
3 Ⓐ Ⓑ Ⓒ Ⓓ Ⓔ	15 Ⓐ Ⓑ Ⓒ Ⓓ Ⓔ	27 Ⓐ Ⓑ Ⓒ Ⓓ Ⓔ	39 Ⓐ Ⓑ Ⓒ Ⓓ Ⓔ	51 Ⓐ Ⓑ Ⓒ Ⓓ Ⓔ
4 Ⓕ Ⓖ Ⓗ Ⓙ Ⓚ	16 Ⓕ Ⓖ Ⓗ Ⓙ Ⓚ	28 Ⓕ Ⓖ Ⓗ Ⓙ Ⓚ	40 Ⓕ Ⓖ Ⓗ Ⓙ Ⓚ	52 Ⓕ Ⓖ Ⓗ Ⓙ Ⓚ
5 Ⓐ Ⓑ Ⓒ Ⓓ Ⓔ	17 Ⓐ Ⓑ Ⓒ Ⓓ Ⓔ	29 Ⓐ Ⓑ Ⓒ Ⓓ Ⓔ	41 Ⓐ Ⓑ Ⓒ Ⓓ Ⓔ	53 Ⓐ Ⓑ Ⓒ Ⓓ Ⓔ
6 Ⓕ Ⓖ Ⓗ Ⓙ Ⓚ	18 Ⓕ Ⓖ Ⓗ Ⓙ Ⓚ	30 Ⓕ Ⓖ Ⓗ Ⓙ Ⓚ	42 Ⓕ Ⓖ Ⓗ Ⓙ Ⓚ	54 Ⓕ Ⓖ Ⓗ Ⓙ Ⓚ
7 Ⓐ Ⓑ Ⓒ Ⓓ Ⓔ	19 Ⓐ Ⓑ Ⓒ Ⓓ Ⓔ	31 Ⓐ Ⓑ Ⓒ Ⓓ Ⓔ	43 Ⓐ Ⓑ Ⓒ Ⓓ Ⓔ	55 Ⓐ Ⓑ Ⓒ Ⓓ Ⓔ
8 Ⓕ Ⓖ Ⓗ Ⓙ Ⓚ	20 Ⓕ Ⓖ Ⓗ Ⓙ Ⓚ	32 Ⓕ Ⓖ Ⓗ Ⓙ Ⓚ	44 Ⓕ Ⓖ Ⓗ Ⓙ Ⓚ	56 Ⓕ Ⓖ Ⓗ Ⓙ Ⓚ
9 Ⓐ Ⓑ Ⓒ Ⓓ Ⓔ	21 Ⓐ Ⓑ Ⓒ Ⓓ Ⓔ	33 Ⓐ Ⓑ Ⓒ Ⓓ Ⓔ	45 Ⓐ Ⓑ Ⓒ Ⓓ Ⓔ	57 Ⓐ Ⓑ Ⓒ Ⓓ Ⓔ
10 Ⓕ Ⓖ Ⓗ Ⓙ Ⓚ	22 Ⓕ Ⓖ Ⓗ Ⓙ Ⓚ	34 Ⓕ Ⓖ Ⓗ Ⓙ Ⓚ	46 Ⓕ Ⓖ Ⓗ Ⓙ Ⓚ	58 Ⓕ Ⓖ Ⓗ Ⓙ Ⓚ
11 Ⓐ Ⓑ Ⓒ Ⓓ Ⓔ	23 Ⓐ Ⓑ Ⓒ Ⓓ Ⓔ	35 Ⓐ Ⓑ Ⓒ Ⓓ Ⓔ	47 Ⓐ Ⓑ Ⓒ Ⓓ Ⓔ	59 Ⓐ Ⓑ Ⓒ Ⓓ Ⓔ
12 Ⓕ Ⓖ Ⓗ Ⓙ Ⓚ	24 Ⓕ Ⓖ Ⓗ Ⓙ Ⓚ	36 Ⓕ Ⓖ Ⓗ Ⓙ Ⓚ	48 Ⓕ Ⓖ Ⓗ Ⓙ Ⓚ	60 Ⓕ Ⓖ Ⓗ Ⓙ Ⓚ

TEST 3—READING

1 Ⓐ Ⓑ Ⓒ Ⓓ	9 Ⓐ Ⓑ Ⓒ Ⓓ	17 Ⓐ Ⓑ Ⓒ Ⓓ	25 Ⓐ Ⓑ Ⓒ Ⓓ	33 Ⓐ Ⓑ Ⓒ Ⓓ
2 Ⓕ Ⓖ Ⓗ Ⓙ	10 Ⓕ Ⓖ Ⓗ Ⓙ	18 Ⓕ Ⓖ Ⓗ Ⓙ	26 Ⓕ Ⓖ Ⓗ Ⓙ	34 Ⓕ Ⓖ Ⓗ Ⓙ
3 Ⓐ Ⓑ Ⓒ Ⓓ	11 Ⓐ Ⓑ Ⓒ Ⓓ	19 Ⓐ Ⓑ Ⓒ Ⓓ	27 Ⓐ Ⓑ Ⓒ Ⓓ	35 Ⓐ Ⓑ Ⓒ Ⓓ
4 Ⓕ Ⓖ Ⓗ Ⓙ	12 Ⓕ Ⓖ Ⓗ Ⓙ	20 Ⓕ Ⓖ Ⓗ Ⓙ	28 Ⓕ Ⓖ Ⓗ Ⓙ	36 Ⓕ Ⓖ Ⓗ Ⓙ
5 Ⓐ Ⓑ Ⓒ Ⓓ	13 Ⓐ Ⓑ Ⓒ Ⓓ	21 Ⓐ Ⓑ Ⓒ Ⓓ	29 Ⓐ Ⓑ Ⓒ Ⓓ	37 Ⓐ Ⓑ Ⓒ Ⓓ
6 Ⓕ Ⓖ Ⓗ Ⓙ	14 Ⓕ Ⓖ Ⓗ Ⓙ	22 Ⓕ Ⓖ Ⓗ Ⓙ	30 Ⓕ Ⓖ Ⓗ Ⓙ	38 Ⓕ Ⓖ Ⓗ Ⓙ
7 Ⓐ Ⓑ Ⓒ Ⓓ	15 Ⓐ Ⓑ Ⓒ Ⓓ	23 Ⓐ Ⓑ Ⓒ Ⓓ	31 Ⓐ Ⓑ Ⓒ Ⓓ	39 Ⓐ Ⓑ Ⓒ Ⓓ
8 Ⓕ Ⓖ Ⓗ Ⓙ	16 Ⓕ Ⓖ Ⓗ Ⓙ	24 Ⓕ Ⓖ Ⓗ Ⓙ	32 Ⓕ Ⓖ Ⓗ Ⓙ	40 Ⓕ Ⓖ Ⓗ Ⓙ

TEST 4—SCIENCE REASONING

1 Ⓐ Ⓑ Ⓒ Ⓓ	9 Ⓐ Ⓑ Ⓒ Ⓓ	17 Ⓐ Ⓑ Ⓒ Ⓓ	25 Ⓐ Ⓑ Ⓒ Ⓓ	33 Ⓐ Ⓑ Ⓒ Ⓓ
2 Ⓕ Ⓖ Ⓗ Ⓙ	10 Ⓕ Ⓖ Ⓗ Ⓙ	18 Ⓕ Ⓖ Ⓗ Ⓙ	26 Ⓕ Ⓖ Ⓗ Ⓙ	34 Ⓕ Ⓖ Ⓗ Ⓙ
3 Ⓐ Ⓑ Ⓒ Ⓓ	11 Ⓐ Ⓑ Ⓒ Ⓓ	19 Ⓐ Ⓑ Ⓒ Ⓓ	27 Ⓐ Ⓑ Ⓒ Ⓓ	35 Ⓐ Ⓑ Ⓒ Ⓓ
4 Ⓕ Ⓖ Ⓗ Ⓙ	12 Ⓕ Ⓖ Ⓗ Ⓙ	20 Ⓕ Ⓖ Ⓗ Ⓙ	28 Ⓕ Ⓖ Ⓗ Ⓙ	36 Ⓕ Ⓖ Ⓗ Ⓙ
5 Ⓐ Ⓑ Ⓒ Ⓓ	13 Ⓐ Ⓑ Ⓒ Ⓓ	21 Ⓐ Ⓑ Ⓒ Ⓓ	29 Ⓐ Ⓑ Ⓒ Ⓓ	37 Ⓐ Ⓑ Ⓒ Ⓓ
6 Ⓕ Ⓖ Ⓗ Ⓙ	14 Ⓕ Ⓖ Ⓗ Ⓙ	22 Ⓕ Ⓖ Ⓗ Ⓙ	30 Ⓕ Ⓖ Ⓗ Ⓙ	38 Ⓕ Ⓖ Ⓗ Ⓙ
7 Ⓐ Ⓑ Ⓒ Ⓓ	15 Ⓐ Ⓑ Ⓒ Ⓓ	23 Ⓐ Ⓑ Ⓒ Ⓓ	31 Ⓐ Ⓑ Ⓒ Ⓓ	39 Ⓐ Ⓑ Ⓒ Ⓓ
8 Ⓕ Ⓖ Ⓗ Ⓙ	16 Ⓕ Ⓖ Ⓗ Ⓙ	24 Ⓕ Ⓖ Ⓗ Ⓙ	32 Ⓕ Ⓖ Ⓗ Ⓙ	40 Ⓕ Ⓖ Ⓗ Ⓙ

DIRECTIONS

Practice Test IV consists of five sections: English, Mathematics, Reading, Science Reasoning, and Writing. Calculator use is only permitted on the Mathematics Test.

The items in each test are numbered and the answer choices lettered. The provided bubble sheet has numbered rows that correspond to the items on the test. Each row contains lettered ovals to match the answer choices for each item on the test. Each numbered row on the bubble sheet has a corresponding item on the test.

For each item, first decide on the best answer choice. Then, locate the row number that corresponds to the item. Next, find the oval in that row that matches the letter of the chosen answer. Then, use a soft lead pencil to fill in the oval. Do not use a ballpoint pen.

Mark only one answer for each item. If you change your mind about the answer choice, thoroughly erase the first mark before marking your new answer.

Note that only responses marked on your bubble sheet will be scored. Your score on each test will be based only on the number of items that are correctly answered during the time allowed for that test. Guessing is not penalized. Therefore, it is to your best advantage to answer every item on the test, even if you must guess.

You may work on each test only during the time allowed for that test. If you finish a test before time is called, use the time to review your answer choices or work on items about which you are uncertain. You may not return to a test on which time has already been called and you may not preview another test. You must lay down your pencil immediately when time is called at the end of each test. You may not for any reason fill in or alter ovals for a test after time expires for that test. Violation of these rules will result in immediate disqualification from the exam.

1 1 1 1 1 1 1 1 1 1 1 1

ENGLISH TEST

45 Minutes—75 Items

DIRECTIONS: In the following passages, certain words and phrases are underlined. The items in the right hand column provide alternatives for the underlined parts. In most cases, you are to choose the alternative that best expresses the idea of the sentence in context, corrects grammatical errors, and/or is best suited to the tone and style of the passage. If the original best accomplishes this, then choose "NO CHANGE." In some cases, you will be asked questions regarding an underlined part. You are to choose the best answer to the question.

You will also find items on this test that refer to a section of the passage or to the passage as a whole. These items DO NOT refer to an underlined portion of the passage. Rather, they are identified by a number or numbers in a box.

For each item, choose the best alternative and fill in the corresponding oval on your bubble sheet. You should read the passage before answering the accompanying items. For many of the items, you must read several sentences beyond the item to determine the answer. Be sure that you have read far enough ahead before you answer.

Answers are on page 967. Explanations begin on page 969.

PASSAGE I

An American Christmas

As befits a nation made up of immigrants from all over the Christian world, Americans have no distinctive Christmas symbols, but [1] we have taken the symbols of all the nations and made them our own. The Christmas tree, the holly and the ivy, the mistletoe, the exchange of gifts, the myth of Santa Claus, the carols of all nations, the plum pudding, and the wassail bowl are all elements in the American Christmas of the early twenty-first century as we know it today [2]. Though we have no Christmas symbols of our own, the American Christmas still has a distinctive aura by virtue of two character [3] elements.

The first of these is when [4], as might be expected in a nation as dedicated to the carrying on of business

1. A. NO CHANGE
   B. symbols but
   C. symbols; but
   D. symbols: but

2. F. NO CHANGE
   G. as it is known today
   H. known as it is today
   J. OMIT the underlined portion.

3. A. NO CHANGE
   B. characters
   C. characterized
   D. characteristic

4. F. NO CHANGE
   G. is that
   H. is which
   J. is where

GO ON TO THE NEXT PAGE.

as the American nation, the dominant role of the Christmas festivities has become[5] to serve as a stimulus to retail business. The themes of Christmas advertising begin to appear as early as September, and the open season on Christmas shopping begins in November. 50 years ago,[6] Thanksgiving Day was regarded like it was[7] the opening day of the season for Christmas shopping; today, the season opens immediately after Halloween. Thus, virtually a whole month has been added to the Christmas season—for[8] shopping purposes.

Second, the Christmas season of festivities has insensibly combined with the New Years[9] celebration into one lengthened period of Saturnalia. This starts with office parties a few days before Christmas continues[10] on Christmas Eve, now the occasion in America of one of two large-scale revels that mark the season, and continues in spirited euphoria until New Year's Eve, the second of the large-scale revels. New Year's Day is spent resting, possibly regretting somebody's[11] excesses, and watching a football "bowl"[12] game.

5. A. NO CHANGE
B. have become
C. having become
D. becomes

6. F. NO CHANGE
G. 50 year ago
H. Fifty years ago
J. One time ago

7. A. NO CHANGE
B. like as
C. as
D. like

8. F. NO CHANGE
G. season. For
H. season, for
J. season: for

9. A. NO CHANGE
B. New Year's
C. New Years'
D. New Year

10. F. NO CHANGE
G. Christmas, continues
H. as Christmas continues
J. Christmas as continues

11. A. NO CHANGE
B. everyone's
C. someone's
D. one's

12. Is the use of quotation marks appropriate?
F. No, because the essay has no dialogue.
G. No, because commas would be more appropriate.
H. Yes, because quotation marks are used to set off words used out of context.
J. Yes, because quotation marks are used around titles of books, plays, and poems.

GO ON TO THE NEXT PAGE.

PASSAGE II

The Myth of a Criminal Physique

[1]

Can you spot a criminal by his physical characteristics? [13] When the science of criminology was founded in the nineteenth century, an imaginative Italian observer decided that criminals are born that way and are distinctly (14) by certain physical marks. They are, he claimed, "a special species, a subspecies having distinct physical and mental characteristics. In general, all criminals have long, large, protruding ears, abundant hair, a thin beard, prominent front sinuses, a protruding chin, and large cheekbones." Rapists, he argued, have "brilliant eyes, delicate faces" and murderers may be distinguished by "cold, glassy eyes, nose always large and frequently aquiline; jaws strong; cheekbones large, hair curly, dark and abundant." [15]

13. Is the use of a question appropriate to begin Paragraph 1?

A. No, because questions are not used in formal writing.
B. No, because the question is not answered.
C. Yes, because it varies sentence structure and interests the reader.
D. Yes, because an essay should always begin with a question.

14. **F.** NO CHANGE
G. distinguish
H. distinguished
J. distinguishing

15. Is the use of quotation marks in this paragraph appropriate?

A. No, because it contains no dialogue.
B. No, because too much physical detail is confusing.
C. Yes, because it discusses a theory of criminology.
D. Yes, because quotation marks are used around direct quotations.

GO ON TO THE NEXT PAGE.

[2]

But the myth does not die easily. During the 1930s, a German criminologist, Gustav Aschaffenburg, declared that stout, squat people with large abdomens are more like to be occasional offenders, while slender builds and slight muscular development are common among habitual offenders. In the 1940s, according to writer Jessica Mitford, a group of Harvard sociologists who study sociology, decided that criminals are most likely to be "mesomorphs," muscular types with large trunks who walk assertively, talk noisily, and behave aggressively. Watch out for those kind of characteristics.

[3]

Around about the turn of the century, a British physician made a detailed study of the faces of three thousand convicts and compared them with a like number of English college students, measuring the noses ears eyebrows and chins of both groups. He could find no correlation among physical types and criminal behavior.

16. F. NO CHANGE
G. easy
H. easiest
J. easier

17. A. NO CHANGE
B. likely
C. likely apt
D. possible

18. F. NO CHANGE
G. whom study sociological changes
H. who studied sociology
J. OMIT the underlined portion.

19. A. NO CHANGE
B. those sort of
C. them kind of
D. those

20. F. NO CHANGE
G. At about
H. Around
J. OMIT the underlined portion.

21. A. NO CHANGE
B. compare
C. compares
D. comparing

22. F. NO CHANGE
G. noses ears and eyebrows and chins
H. noses; ears; eyebrows and chins
J. noses, ears, eyebrows, and chins

Items 23 and 24 ask about the preceding passage as a whole.

23. This essay was probably excerpted from:
A. a general sociology textbook.
B. a technical monograph on criminology.
C. a news magazine.
D. a biography of Gustav Aschaffenburg.

GO ON TO THE NEXT PAGE.

24. Choose the order of paragraph numbers that will make the essay's structure most logical.
   F. NO CHANGE
   G. 3, 2, 1
   H. 1, 3, 2
   J. 2, 3, 1

PASSAGE III

Scientific Advances Pose Global Risks

[1]

The history of modern pollution problems show (25) that most have resulted from negligence and ignorance. We have an appalling tendency to interfere with nature before all of the possible consequences of our actions have been studied into completeness (26). We produce and distribute radioactive substances, synthetic chemicals, and many other potent compounds before fully comprehending their effects (27) on living organisms. Synthetic means manmade. Many of today's fashions are made with synthetic fibers. (28) Our education is dangerously incomplete.

[2]

It will be argued that the purpose of science is to move into unknown territory; (29) to explore, and to discover. It can be said that similar risks have been taken before, and that these risks are necessary to

25. A. NO CHANGE
   B. shown
   C. shows
   D. showed

26. F. NO CHANGE
   G. a lot
   H. for completeness
   J. in depth

27. A. NO CHANGE
   B. effectiveness
   C. affect
   D. affects

28. F. NO CHANGE
   G. Synthetic fibers are manmade.
   H. Many of today's fashions are made with synthetic fibers.
   J. OMIT the underlined portion.

29. A. NO CHANGE
   B. territory:
   C. territory,
   D. territory

GO ON TO THE NEXT PAGE.

technological progress. [30]

[3]

These arguments overlook an important element. (31) In the past, risks taken in the name of scientific progress were restricted to a small place and brief period of time. The effects of the processes we now strive to master are not either (32) localized nor brief. Air pollution covers vast urban areas. Ocean pollutants have been discovered in nearly every part of the world. Synthetic chemicals spread over huge stretches of forest and farmland may remain in the soil for decades and years to come. (33) Radioactive pollutants will be found in the biosphere for generations. The size and persistent (34) of these problems have grown with the expanding power of modern science.

[4]

One might also argue that the hazards of modern pollutants are small comparison for (35) the dangers associated with other human activity. No estimate of the actual harm done by smog, fallout, or chemical residues can obscure the reality that the risks are being taken before being fully understood.

[5]

The importance of these issues lies in the failure

30. The writer could most effectively bolster the essay at this point by:
F. including an example of one of the risks argued by some to be necessary for technological progress.
G. adding rhetorical emphasis with the sentence "The risks are necessary."
H. briefly describing an unknown territory.
J. defining the word "science."

31. A. NO CHANGE
B. a important
C. importance
D. important

32. F. NO CHANGE
G. either
H. not neither
J. neither

33. A. NO CHANGE
B. for decades.
C. for years to come in decades.
D. for decades and years.

34. F. NO CHANGE
G. persistence
H. persevering
J. persisting

35. A. NO CHANGE
B. consideration for
C. comparing with
D. compared to

GO ON TO THE NEXT PAGE.

of science to predict and <u>control. Human</u> [36] intervention into natural processes. The true measure of the danger is represented by the hazards we will encounter if we enter the new age of technology without first evaluating our responsibility to the environment.

36. F. NO CHANGE
G. control human
H. control; human
J. control and human

Items 37 and 38 ask about the preceding passage as a whole.

37. Choose the order of paragraph numbers that will make the essay's structure most logical.
A. NO CHANGE
B. 2, 4, 3, 1, 5
C. 1, 3, 2, 4, 5
D. 5, 1, 2, 3, 4

38. This essay was probably intended for readers who:
F. lack an understanding of the history of technology.
G. are authorities on pollution and its causes.
H. are interested in becoming more aware of our environmental problems and the possible solutions to these problems.
J. have worked with radioactive substances.

PASSAGE IV

The Changing Scientific Workplace

[1]

Many researchers can be of greatest service to a company by <u>staying around</u> [39] in the laboratory. A single outstanding discovery <u>may of had</u> [40] a far greater impact on the company's five-year profit picture than the activities of even the <u>most able</u> [41] administrator. It is simply good sense—and good economics—to allow

39. A. NO CHANGE
B. remaining
C. remaining around
D. staying up

40. F. NO CHANGE
G. maybe
H. might of had
J. may have

41. A. NO CHANGE
B. most ablest
C. more ablest
D. most abled

GO ON TO THE NEXT PAGE.

qualified researchers to continue their work. Granting these researchers maximum freedom to explore their scientific ideas is also eminently good sense.

[2]

In recent years however this theory has fallen into wide disrepair. Companies find that many researchers continue to be highly productive throughout their careers. There is every reason to allow these researchers to continue their pioneering work.

[3]

Some years ago, the theory was rampant that after the age of about 40, the average researcher began losing their creative spark. The chance of one making a major discovery was believed to drop off sharply. Hence, there really wasn't much point to encouraging a person of 45 or 50 to do research. [45]

[4]

Companies are also convinced that the traditional guideposts in establishing salaries are not completely valid. In former years of long ago, the size of a man's paycheck was determined primarily by the size of his annual budget. On this basis, the researcher—however brilliant—who had perhaps one assistant and never spent much money made an extremely poor showing. Companies now realize that the two very important

42. **F.** NO CHANGE
G. years, however
H. years, however,
J. years however,

43. **A.** NO CHANGE
B. argument
C. ill repute
D. disrepute

44. **F.** NO CHANGE
G. its
H. his or her
J. theirs

45. If, at this point in the essay, the writer wanted to increase the information about creative contributions from researchers, which of the following additions would be most relevant to the passage as a whole?
A. A bibliography of books about retirement
B. A description of a few of the contributions older researchers have made to science
C. A list of today's most prominent researchers
D. A brief description of a model retirement benefits plan

46. **F.** NO CHANGE
G. a long time ago
H. long ago,
J. OMIT the underlined portion.

GO ON TO THE NEXT PAGE.

criteria that must also be considerable [47] are a man's actual contributions to the company and his creative potential.

[5]

In today's era of scientific manpower shortages, companies have more reason than ever to encourage scientists to do the work for which they are most qualified. They also have greater reason than ever to provide within the laboratory the environment in which [48] the creative processes of research can be carried out most effectively.

47. A. NO CHANGE
B. be considered
C. most considerable
D. considerable of

48. F. NO CHANGE
G. about which
H. of which
J. into which

Items 49 and 50 ask about the preceding passage as a whole.

49. Choose the order of paragraph numbers that will make the essay's structure most logical.

A. NO CHANGE
B. 1, 2, 4, 3, 5
C. 1, 2, 3, 5, 4
D. 3, 2, 1, 4, 5

50. Is the author's use of the dash appropriate in the essay?

F. No, because a dash is never used in formal writing.
G. No, because commas would have been as effective for emphasis.
H. Yes, because the dash gives emphasis to the sudden break in thought or interruption in the sentence in which it was used.
J. Yes, because using a dash adds excitement to the essay.

PASSAGE V

An Argument in Favor of Scientific Contributions

[1]

What are those of us whom [51] have chosen careers

51. A. NO CHANGE
B. who
C. whose
D. what

GO ON TO THE NEXT PAGE.

in science and engineering able to do about meeting our current problems? 52

[2]

Second, we can identify the many areas in which science and technology, more considerately used, can be of greatest 53 service in the future than in the past to improve the quality of life. While we can make many speeches and pass many laws, the quality of our environment will be improved only threw 54 better knowledge and better application of that knowledge.

[3]

Third, we can recognize that much of the dissatisfaction we suffer today results from our very successes of former years in the past 55. We have been so eminently successful in attaining material goals that we are deeply dissatisfied of the fact that 56 we cannot attain other goals more rapidly. We have achieved a better life for most people, but we are unhappy that we have not spread it to all people. We have illuminated many sources of environmental deterioration, because of 57 we are unhappy that we have not conquered all of them. It is our raising 58 expectations rather than our failures that now cause our distress.

[4]

First, we can help destroy the false impression that science and engineering have caused the current

52. F. NO CHANGE
G. problems.
H. problems!
J. problems;

53. A. NO CHANGE
B. great
C. more great
D. greater

54. F. NO CHANGE
G. through
H. though
J. from

55. A. NO CHANGE
B. of the past
C. being in the past
D. OMIT the underlined portion.

56. F. NO CHANGE
G. in the fact that
H. about
J. that

57. A. NO CHANGE
B. despite
C. but
D. also

58. F. NO CHANGE
G. arising
H. rising
J. raised

GO ON TO THE NEXT PAGE.

world troubles. Quite the contrary, [59] science and engineering have made vast contributions to better living for more people. [60]

[5]

Although many of our current problems must be cured more by social, political, and economic instruments rather than by science and technology, science and technology must still be the tools to make further advances in [61] such things as clean air, clean water, better transportation, better housing, better medical care, more adequate welfare programs, purer food, conservation of resources, and many other areas.

59. **A.** NO CHANGE
B. Contrary to,
C. Contrasted with,
D. OMIT the underlined portion.

60. Suppose, at this point, that the writer wanted to add more information about the benefits of science and engineering. Which of the following additions would be most relevant?
F. A list of the colleges with the best science and engineering degree programs
G. Specific examples of contributions from the areas of science and engineering that have improved the standard of living
H. A brief explanation of the current world troubles
J. The names of several famous scientists and engineers

61. **A.** NO CHANGE
B. advances, in
C. advances. In
D. advances—in

Items 62 and 63 ask about the preceding passage as a whole.

62. This essay was probably written for readers who:
F. are college graduates.
G. are interested in an environmental services career.
H. are in a career or contemplating a career in science or engineering.
J. are frustrated with the current world problems.

63. Choose the order of paragraph numbers that will make the essay's structure most logical.
A. NO CHANGE
B. 1, 4, 2, 3, 5
C. 5, 4, 2, 3, 1
D. 4, 2, 3, 1, 5

GO ON TO THE NEXT PAGE.

PASSAGE VI

Youth Market of Europe

With increasing prosperity, West European youth am having a fling that is creating distinctive consumer and cultural patterns.
64

The result has been the increasing emergence in Europe of that phenomenon well known in America as the "youth market." This here is a market in which enterprising businesses cater to the demands of teenagers and older youths in all their rock mania and pop-art forms. The evolving European youth market has both similarities and differences from the American youth market.
65
66

The markets basis is essentially the same—more spending power and freedom to use it in the hands of teenagers and older youths. Young consumers also make up an increasing high proportion of the population.
67
68

Youthful tastes in the United States and Europe include a similar range of products—records and record players, tapes and CDs, VCRs and DVD players, leather jackets, "trendy" clothing, cosmetics, and soft drinks, generally it now is difficult to tell in which direction transatlantic teenage influences are flowing.
69
70

As in the United States, where "teen" and "teenager" have become merchandising terms,

64. F. NO CHANGE
G. youths is
H. youth be
J. youth is

65. A. NO CHANGE
B. here idea
C. here thing
D. OMIT the underlined portion.

66. F. NO CHANGE
G. similarity
H. similarities to
J. similar

67. A. NO CHANGE
B. markets'
C. market's
D. market

68. F. NO CHANGE
G. increasingly high
H. increasing higher
J. high increasing

69. A. NO CHANGE
B. drinks. Generally,
C. drinks, in general
D. drinks generally

70. F. NO CHANGE
G. Trans-Atlantic
H. trans-Atlantic
J. Trans-atlantic

GO ON TO THE NEXT PAGE.

Europeans also have adapted similar terminology. In Flemish and Dutch it is "tiener" for teenagers. The French have simply adopted the English word "teenagers." In West Germany the key word in advertising addressed to teenagers is "freizeit," meaning "holidays" or "time off."

71. A. NO CHANGE
B. picked up
C. added
D. adopted

The most obvious difference among the youth market in Europe and that in the United States is in size. In terms of volume and variety of sales, the market in Europe is only a shadow of its American counterpart, but it is a growing shadow.

72. F. NO CHANGE
G. betwixt
H. amongst
J. between

Items 73-75 ask about the preceding passage as a whole.

73. Is the author's use of quotation marks appropriate in this essay?

A. No, because quotation marks are used to set off a direct quote.
B. No, because the essay has no dialogue.
C. Yes, because quotation marks are used to set off words used in a special sense.
D. Yes, because quotation marks indicate a conversation.

74. This essay was probably written for readers who:

F. are interested in new trends in the consumer patterns of the world's youth.
G. are parents of teenagers.
H. are teenagers.
J. are interested in the different cultural patterns of West Germany.

75. Is the use of the dash appropriate in this essay?

A. Yes, because the dash is used to set off interruptions, additions, and illustrations.
B. No, because the dash is never used in formal writing.
C. Yes, because the dash adds flair to the essay.
D. Yes, because the dash is more effective than brackets or parentheses.

END OF TEST 1.
STOP! DO NOT TURN THE PAGE UNTIL TOLD TO DO SO.

2 2 2 2 2 2 2 2 2 2 2 2

MATHEMATICS TEST

60 Minutes—60 Items

DIRECTIONS: Solve each item and choose the correct answer choice. Then, fill in the corresponding oval on the bubble sheet.

Allocate time wisely. Try to solve as many items as possible, returning to skipped items if time permits.

Calculator use is permitted on this test; however, some items are best solved without the use of a calculator.

Note: Unless otherwise stated, assume all of the following.

1. Illustrative figures are NOT necessarily drawn to scale.
2. The word *average* indicates arithmetic mean.
3. The word *line* indicates a straight line.
4. Geometric figures lie in a plane.

Answers are on page 967. Explanations begin on page 972.

DO YOUR FIGURING HERE.

1. What is the additive inverse of $-\frac{2}{3}$?

A. $-\frac{3}{2}$
B. 0
C. $\frac{2}{3}$
D. 1
E. $\frac{3}{2}$

2. In the figure below, if $\angle AOC$ is a central angle and equals 70°, what is the measure of $\angle ABC$?

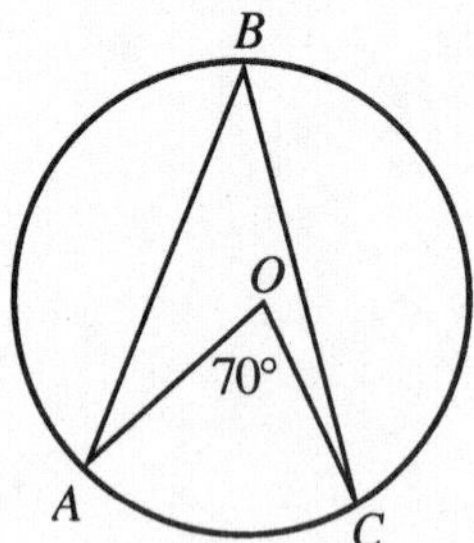

F. 22°
G. 35°
H. 50°
J. 70°
K. 140°

GO ON TO THE NEXT PAGE.

DO YOUR FIGURING HERE.

3. Which of the following is an element of the solution set of the equation $x^2 + 6x + 8 = 0$?

A. -8
B. -2
C. 4
D. 6
E. 8

4. In the figure below $l_1 \parallel l_2$. If $\angle x = 70°$ and $\angle y = 105°$, what is the measure of $\angle r$?

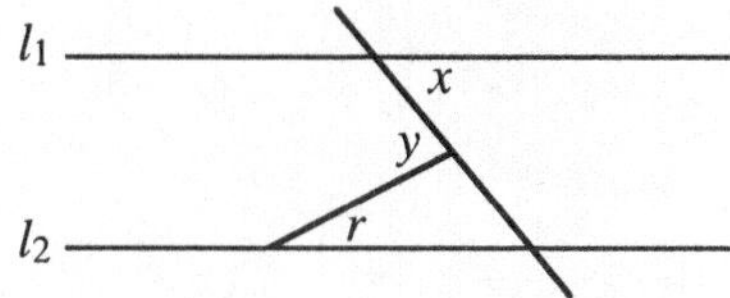

F. 35°
G. 45°
H. 85°
J. 145°
K. 175°

5. $A = \frac{2gr}{g+r}$. What is the value of g, when $r = 1$ and $A = 4$?

A. -2
B. $\frac{4}{7}$
C. $\frac{8}{5}$
D. 2
E. 4

6. The figure below represents which of the following equations?

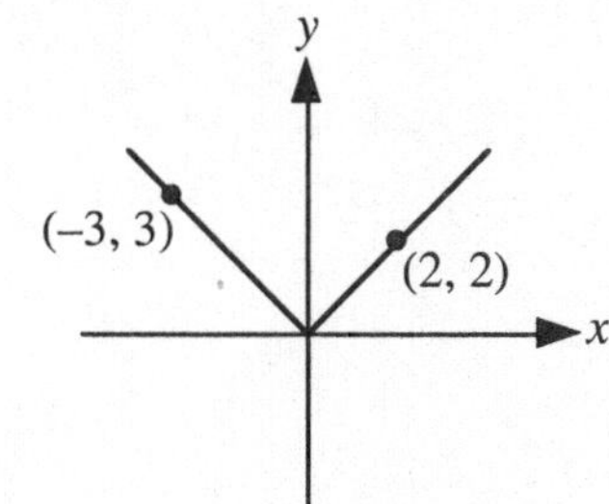

F. $y = x$
G. $y = -x$
H. $y = |x|$
J. $|y| = x$
K. $y = x^2$

GO ON TO THE NEXT PAGE.

DO YOUR FIGURING HERE.

7. Which of the following is an illustration of the distributive property?

   A. $(12 \cdot 25)(4) = 12(25 \cdot 4)$
   B. $7n + 2 - 3n = 7n - 3n + 2$
   C. $(17)(b^2)(5) = (17)(5)(b)^2$
   D. $ab + ac = ba + ca$
   E. $x(x + 2) = x^2 + 2x$

8. Joshua buys a television that costs $600. If the sales tax is 7%, what is the total cost of the purchase?

   F. $4.20
   G. $42.00
   H. $420.00
   J. $604.20
   K. $642.00

9. What is the value of $-x^2 - 2x^3$ when $x = -1$?

   A. -3
   B. -1
   C. 0
   D. 1
   E. 3

10. What is the average of $n + 3$, $2n - 1$, and $3n + 4$?

   F. $\frac{5n+6}{3}$
   G. $2n + 2$
   H. $3n + 3$
   J. $\frac{6n+7}{3}$
   K. $6n + 6$

11. If $x = 9$, what is the value of $x^0 + x^{1/2} + x^{-2}$?

   A. $3\frac{1}{81}$
   B. $4\frac{1}{81}$
   C. $5\frac{7}{18}$
   D. $76\frac{1}{2}$
   E. $77\frac{1}{2}$

GO ON TO THE NEXT PAGE.

DO YOUR FIGURING HERE.

12. $4\sqrt{3} + 3\sqrt{27} = ?$

F. $7\sqrt{30}$
G. $10\sqrt{3}$
H. $13\sqrt{3}$
J. 63
K. 108

13. Jessica Dawn received marks of 87, 93, and 86 on 3 successive tests. What grade must she receive on a fourth test in order to have an average grade of 90?

A. 90
B. 91
C. 92
D. 93
E. 94

14. In terms of x, what is the total number of cents in $4x$ dimes?

F. $0.04x$
G. $0.4x$
H. $4x$
J. $40x$
K. $400x$

15. Which of the following is shown by the graph below?

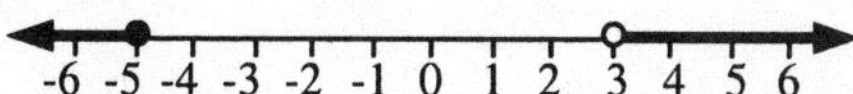

A. $-5 \leq x < 3$
B. $-5 < x$ or $x < 3$
C. $-5 \leq x$ or $x > 3$
D. $-5 \leq x \leq 3$
E. $-5 \geq x$ or $x > 3$

GO ON TO THE NEXT PAGE.

DO YOUR FIGURING HERE.

16. $2\frac{2}{5} - 1\frac{7}{8} = ?$

F. $\frac{11}{40}$
G. $\frac{19}{40}$
H. $\frac{21}{40}$
J. $\frac{7}{13}$
K. $1\frac{5}{40}$

17. In a circle with a radius of 6, what is the measure (in degrees) of an arc whose length is 2π?

A. 20°
B. 30°
C. 60°
D. 90°
E. 120°

18. If $\frac{2x}{3\sqrt{2}} = \frac{3\sqrt{2}}{x}$, what is the positive value of x?

F. 9
G. 3
H. $2\sqrt{3}$
J. $\sqrt{6}$
K. $\sqrt{3}$

19. If $f(x) = 2x - x^2$ and $g(x) = x - 4$, what is the value of $g(f(2))$?

A. -8
B. -4
C. -2
D. 0
E. 3

20. What is the solution set of the equation $|5 - 2x| = 7$?

F. {6, -1}
G. {6}
H. {-1}
J. {1}
K. The empty set

GO ON TO THE NEXT PAGE.

DO YOUR FIGURING HERE.

21. Which of the following is equivalent to $\frac{3-\frac{3}{x}}{x-1}$?

A. $\frac{1}{x-1}$
B. $\frac{1}{3}$
C. $x+1$
D. 3
E. $\frac{3}{x}$

22. What is the slope of the line that passes through the points (-3, 5) and (4, 7)?

F. $\sqrt{53}$
G. $\frac{7}{2}$
H. 2
J. $\frac{1}{2}$
K. $\frac{2}{7}$

23. In the figure below, diameter $\overline{AB}$ is perpendicular to chord $\overline{CD}$ at E. If chord $\overline{CD}$ = 8 inches and line $\overline{OE}$ = 3 inches, what is the length of the radius of the circle, in inches?

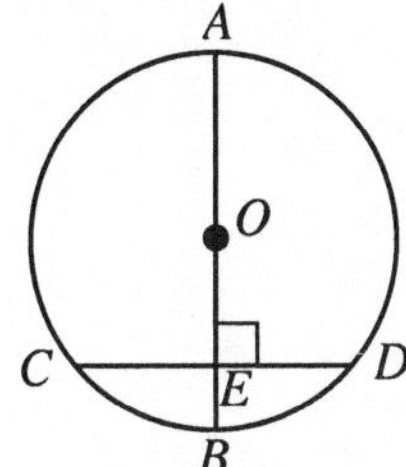

A. $\sqrt{3}$
B. $\sqrt{5}$
C. $\sqrt{7}$
D. $\sqrt{15}$
E. 5

GO ON TO THE NEXT PAGE.

DO YOUR FIGURING HERE.

24. The diagonals of parallelogram $ABCD$ intersect at point E. If $\overline{DB} = 4x + 2$ and $\overline{DE} = x + 4$, what is the value of x?

F. 3
G. 2
H. 1
J. $\frac{2}{3}$
K. 0

25. If the measure of the central angle of a sector of a circle is 120°, what is the area, in square units, of the sector if the radius is 6 units long?

A. 4π
B. 6π
C. 8π
D. 10π
E. 12π

26. If the statement "If two triangles are red, then they are equal in area" is true, then which of the following *must* be true?

F. If the two triangles are not equal in area, then they are not red.
G. If the two triangles are equal in area, then they are red.
H. If the two triangles are equal in area, then they are not red.
J. If the two triangles are not red, then they are not equal in area.
K. If the two triangles are red, then they are not equal in area.

27. If $\frac{a}{b} = \frac{r}{t}$, then which of the following is NOT necessarily true?

A. $\frac{a}{r} = \frac{b}{t}$
B. $\frac{a}{t} = \frac{b}{r}$
C. $\frac{a+b}{b} = \frac{r+t}{t}$
D. $\frac{b}{a} = \frac{t}{r}$
E. $at = br$

GO ON TO THE NEXT PAGE.

28. If $-2x + 5 = 2 - (5 - 2x)$, then $x = ?$

DO YOUR FIGURING HERE.

F. 6
G. 5
H. 4
J. 3
K. 2

29. $\frac{(1 + \sin x)(1 - \sin x)}{(1 + \cos x)(1 - \cos x)}$ is equivalent to which of the following?

A. $\cos x$
B. $\tan x$
C. $\tan^2 x$
D. $\cos^2 x$
E. $\cot^2 x$

30. In the figure below, ΔACB is a right triangle. $\overline{CE}$ is the median to hypotenuse $\overline{AB}$, and $\overline{AB} = 14$ centimeters. What is the length, in centimeters, of $\overline{CE}$?

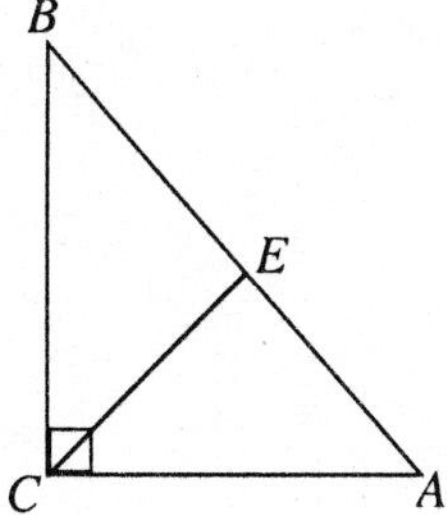

F. 5
G. 6
H. 7
J. 8
K. Cannot be determined from the given information

31. If y varies directly as x, and $y = 10$ when $x = \frac{1}{5}$, what is the value of y when $x = \frac{1}{2}$?

A. 1
B. 4
C. 7
D. 16
E. 25

GO ON TO THE NEXT PAGE.

32. $\frac{(-1)(2)(-3)(4)(-5)}{(5)(-4)(3)(-2)(1)} = ?$

DO YOUR FIGURING HERE.

F. -2
G. -1
H. 1
J. 2
K. 3

33. In the diagram below, chords $\overline{AB}$ and $\overline{CD}$ of circle O intersect at E. If $\overline{AE} = 6$ units long, $\overline{EB} = 4$ units long, $\overline{CE} = x$, and $\overline{ED} = 6x$, then how many units long is x?

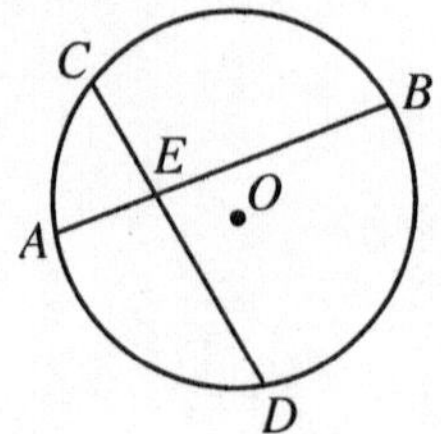

A. 1
B. $1\frac{3}{7}$
C. 2
D. 4
E. 6

34. The measure of the vertex angle of an isosceles triangle is 50°. What is the measure, in degrees, of each base angle?

F. 40°
G. 50°
H. 65°
J. 75°
K. 130°

GO ON TO THE NEXT PAGE.

35. Using the table below, what is the median of the following data?

DO YOUR FIGURING HERE.

Score	Frequency
20	4
30	4
50	7

A. 20
B. 30
C. 40
D. 50
E. 60

36. Which of the following number lines represents the solution set of $x^2 - 2x - 3 > 0$?

F.
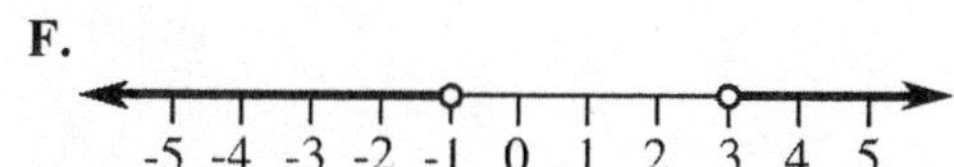
G.
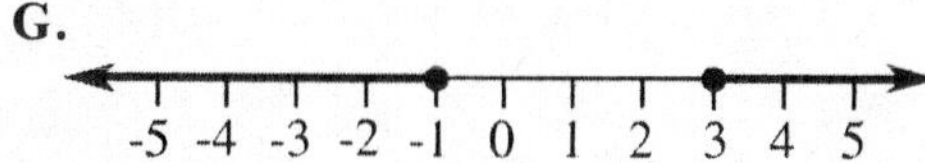
H.
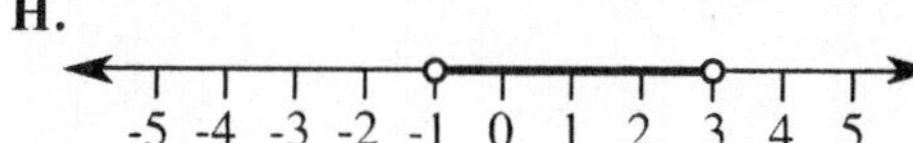
J.
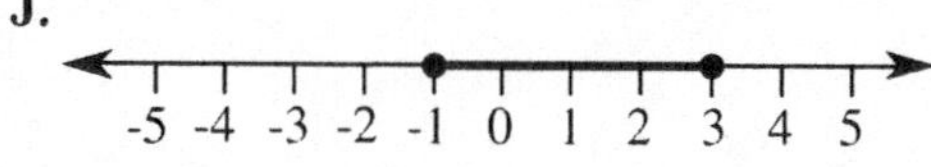
K.
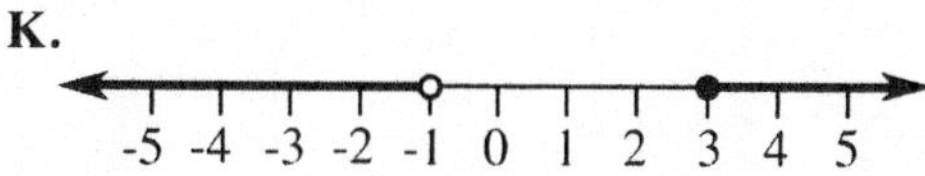

37. The expression $\sin x + \frac{\cos^2 x}{\sin x}$ is equal to which of the following?

A. 1

B. $\sin x$

C. $\cos x$

D. $\frac{1}{\sin x}$

E. $\frac{1}{\cos x}$

GO ON TO THE NEXT PAGE.

DO YOUR FIGURING HERE.

38. The value of $(2.5 \cdot 10^5)^2$ is equal to which of the following?

F. $6.25 \cdot 10^7$
G. $6.25 \cdot 10^{10}$
H. $2.5 \cdot 10^7$
J. $2.7 \cdot 10^{10}$
K. $5 \cdot 10^7$

39. If $A * B$ is defined as $\frac{AB - B}{-B}$, what is the value of $-2 * 2$?

A. -3
B. -1
C. 0
D. 1
E. 3

40. If 1 of the roots of the equation $x^2 + kx - 12 = 0$ is 4, what is the value of k?

F. -1
G. 0
H. 1
J. 3
K. 7

41. In the figure below, D is a point on $\overline{AB}$ and E is a point on $\overline{BC}$ such that $\overline{DE} \parallel \overline{AC}$. If $\overline{DB} = 4$ units long, $\overline{AB} = 10$ units long, and $\overline{BC} = 20$ units long, how many units long is $\overline{EC}$?

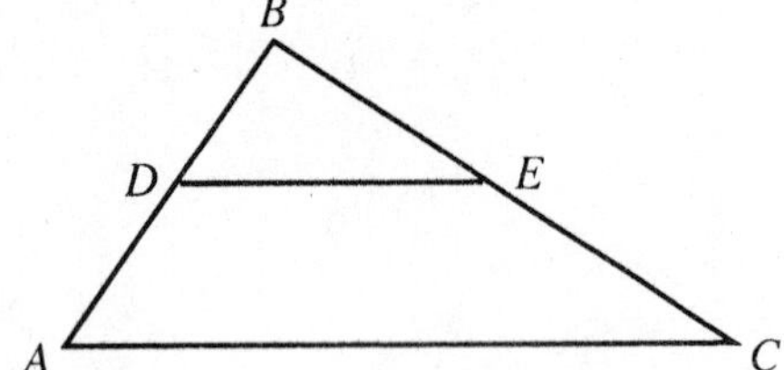

A. 4
B. 6
C. 8
D. 10
E. 12

GO ON TO THE NEXT PAGE.

42. $(x + 2)(x - 4) - (x + 4)(x - 2) = ?$

DO YOUR FIGURING HERE.

F. 0
G. $2x^2 + 4x - 16$
H. $-4x$
J. $4x$
K. $-4x - 16$

43. If the sum of the measures of the interior angles of a polygon equals the sum of the measures of the exterior angles, how many sides does the polygon have?

A. 3
B. 4
C. 5
D. 6
E. 7

44. If the perimeter of an equilateral triangle is 12 inches, what is its area, in square inches?

F. $2\sqrt{3}$
G. $4\sqrt{3}$
H. 8
J. $6\sqrt{3}$
K. $36\sqrt{3}$

45. If the ratio of 2 complementary angles is 8:1, what is the measure, in degrees, of the smaller angle?

A. 10
B. 20
C. 30
D. 40
E. 80

GO ON TO THE NEXT PAGE.

46. Given a square, a rectangle, a trapezoid, and a circle, if one figure is selected at random, what is the probability that the figure has four right angles?

DO YOUR FIGURING HERE.

F. 1

G. $\frac{3}{4}$

H. $\frac{1}{2}$

J. $\frac{1}{4}$

K. 0

47. A man travels 320 miles in 8 hours. If he continues at the same rate, how many miles will he travel in the next 2 hours?

A. 6
B. 40
C. 80
D. 120
E. 240

48. $\frac{\sin x}{\cos x} + \frac{\cos x}{\sin x} = ?$

F. 1

G. $\sin x$

H. $\frac{1}{\sin x \cos x}$

J. $\tan x$

K. $\frac{\sin x + \cos x}{\sin x \cos x}$

49. The average temperatures for 5 days were 82°, 86°, 91°, 79°, and 91°. What is the mode of these temperatures?

A. 79°
B. 82°
C. 85.8°
D. 86°
E. 91°

GO ON TO THE NEXT PAGE.

50. A booklet contains 30 pages. If 9 pages in the booklet have drawings, what percentage of the pages in the booklet have drawings?

DO YOUR FIGURING HERE.

F. 30%

G. 9%

H. 3%

J. 1%

K. $\frac{3}{10}$%

51. Which of the following represents $-7t + 6t^2 - 3$ when it is completely factored?

A. $(3t - 1)(2t + 3)$
B. $(3t + 1)(2t - 3)$
C. $(6t - 1)(t + 3)$
D. $(6t + 1)(t - 3)$
E. $(2t - 1)(3t + 3)$

52. What is the solution set of $2^{x^2 + 2x} = 2^{-1}$?

F. {1}
G. {-1}
H. {1, -1}
J. {2}
K. The empty set

53. Jessica is 3 years younger than Joshua. If x represents Joshua's age now, what was Jessica's age four years ago in terms of x?

A. $x - 1$
B. $x - 3$
C. $x - 4$
D. $x - 6$
E. $x - 7$

54. In a drama club, x students contributed y dollars each to buy an \$18 gift for their advisor. If three more students had contributed, each student could have contributed one dollar less to buy the same gift. Which of the following sets of equations expresses this relationship?

F. $xy = 18$ and $(x + 3)(y - 1) = 18$
G. $xy = 18$ and $(x - 3)(y + 1) = 18$
H. $xy = 18$ and $(x + 3)(y + 1) = 18$
J. $xy = 18$ and $(x - 3)(y - 1) = 18$
K. $xy = 18$ and $(x + 1)(y - 3) = 18$

GO ON TO THE NEXT PAGE.

DO YOUR FIGURING HERE.

55. $\frac{1}{2}\sqrt{112}-\sqrt{28}+2\sqrt{63}=?$

A. $6\sqrt{7}$
B. $7\sqrt{7}$
C. $8\sqrt{7}$
D. $9\sqrt{7}$
E. $10\sqrt{7}$

56. What is the value of x for the following set of simultaneous equations?

$$\frac{1}{x}+\frac{1}{y}=\frac{1}{4}$$
$$\frac{1}{x}-\frac{1}{y}=\frac{3}{4}$$

F. 4

G. 2

H. $\frac{1}{2}$

J. $\frac{1}{4}$

K. -4

57. Which set could represent the lengths of the sides of a triangle?

A. {1, 3, 6}
B. {2, 4, 7}
C. {2, 10, 12}
D. {4, 6, 8}
E. {4, 4, 10}

58. What is the solution set, in terms of a and b, for the following system of equations?

$$ax+y=b$$
$$2ax+y=2b$$

F. $\{-\frac{b}{a}, 1\}$

G. $\{-a, b\}$

H. $\{\frac{b}{a}, 0\}$

J. $\{\frac{b}{a}, \frac{a}{b}\}$

K. $\{\frac{2a}{b}, \frac{2b}{a}\}$

GO ON TO THE NEXT PAGE.

59. In the figure below, $\sin\theta = \frac{r}{4}$. What is the value of $\cos\theta$?

DO YOUR FIGURING HERE.

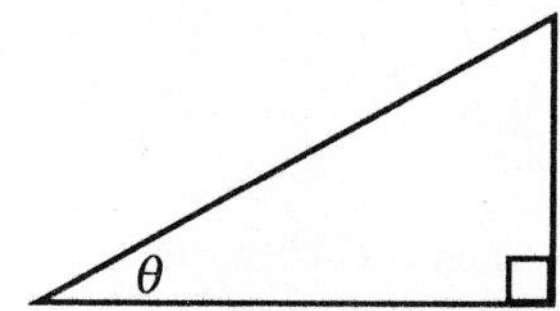

A. $\frac{\sqrt{16-r^2}}{4}$
B. $\frac{4-r}{4}$
C. $\frac{16-r^2}{2}$
D. $\frac{4-r}{2}$
E. $\frac{16-r^2}{r}$

60. If 3 copier machines can copy 300 sheets in 3 hours, assuming the same rate, how long, in hours, will it take 6 such copiers to copy 600 sheets?

F. 2
G. 3
H. 4
J. 6
K. 9

END OF TEST 2.
STOP! DO NOT TURN THE PAGE UNTIL TOLD TO DO SO.
DO NOT RETURN TO THE PREVIOUS TEST.

3 3 3 3 3 3 3 3 3 3 3 3

READING TEST

35 Minutes—40 Items

DIRECTIONS: The passages presented in the test are each followed by a set of items. Read the passage and choose the best answer for each item. Fill in the corresponding oval on your bubble sheet. You may refer to the passage as often as necessary to answer the passage items.

Answers are on page 968. Explanations begin on page 978.

Passage I

NATURAL SCIENCE: This passage discusses the production of electromagnetic radiation.

Whenever a changing electric field is produced, electromagnetic radiation is also produced. If you run a comb through your hair, you disturb electrons (negatively charged subatomic particles) in both hair and comb, producing static electricity. Every electron is surrounded by an electric field. Any sudden change in the electron's motion gives rise to *electromagnetic radiation.* If you were to run a comb through your hair while standing near an AM radio, you would produce radio static. These previous examples illustrate an important principle: Whenever you change the motion of an electron, you generate electromagnetic waves.

If you apply this principle to a heated object, you must first determine what is meant by heat. When an object is hot, its atoms are vibrating rapidly. The hotter an object becomes, the faster the atoms vibrate. The vibrating atoms collide with the electrons in the material. Each time the motion of an electron is disturbed, it emits a photon. Therefore, you should expect a heated object to emit electromagnetic radiation. This type of radiation, called *black body radiation,* is very common and is responsible for the light emitted from an incandescent light bulb.

A *spectrum* is an array of electromagnetic radiation in order of wavelength. The spectrum of visible light, such as what you see when you look at a rainbow, is most familiar, but the visible spectrum is just a small segment of the much larger electromagnetic spectrum.

The average wavelength of visible light is about 0.0005 mm. Because this unit is so small (50 light waves could be lined up end to end across the thickness of ordinary plastic wrap), wavelengths are measured in *Angstroms.* One Angstrom (Å) is 10^{-10} m. The wavelength of visible light ranges from 4,000 Å to 7,000 Å. Light near the short wavelength end of the visible spectrum (4,000 Å) looks violet, and light near the long wavelength end (7,000 Å) looks red (Figure 1). Beyond the red end of the visible spectrum lies infrared radiation, where wavelengths range from 7,000 Å to 1 mm. At wavelengths shorter than violet, there is ultraviolet radiation. These wavelengths range from 4,000 Å down to about 100 Å. At wavelengths shorter than these are x-rays and gamma rays. Long wavelength radiation (7,000 Å to 1 mm) can be observed in "heat lamps," where our skin senses infrared wavelengths as heat. These lower-energy infrared photons can warm you, but because of their low energy, they cannot give you a tan. In contrast are the short wavelengths, which contain a high amount of energy. These wavelengths can be dangerous. Small doses can give you a suntan, larger doses produce sunburns, and extreme doses might produce skin cancers.

When a filament is heated, two types of collisions take place among the electrons. Gentle collisions produce low-energy photons with long wavelengths, and violent collisions produce high-energy photons with short wavelengths. A graph of the energy emitted at different wavelengths produces a curve like that in Figure 2. The curve indicates that gentle collisions and violent collisions occur infrequently. Most collisions lie somewhere in between, producing photons of intermediate wavelengths.

The *wavelength of maximum* (λ_{max}) is the wavelength at which an object emits the maximum amount of energy. The wavelength of maximum depends on the object's temperature. As an object is heated, the average collision becomes more violent, producing high-energy, shorter-wavelength photons. The hotter the object is, the shorter the λ_{max} is (Figure 2). Physics shows that λ_{max} in Angstroms equals 30 million divided by the temperature in degrees Kelvin.

GO ON TO THE NEXT PAGE.

$$\lambda_{max} = \frac{30 \cdot 10^6}{T}$$

This is a very important point in astronomy, since with this equation it is possible to determine the temperature of a star from its light. It is also possible to estimate the temperature of a star from the color of light it emits. For a hot star λ_{max} lies in the ultraviolet spectrum and most of the radiation cannot be seen, but in the visible range the star emits more blue than red. Thus, a hot star looks blue. In contrast, a cooler star radiates its maximum energy in the infrared. In the visible range of the spectrum it radiates more red than blue and therefore looks red.

The total amount of radiation emitted at all wavelengths depends on the number of collisions per second. If an object's temperature is high, there are many collisions and it emits more light than a cooler object of the same size. Energy is measured in units called *ergs*. The total radiation given off by 1 cm^2 of the object in ergs per second equals a constant number, represented by s ($5.67 \cdot 10^{-5}$ ergs/cm^2 sec degree^4) times the temperature raised to the fourth power.

$$E = sT^4 \text{ (ergs/sec/cm}^2\text{)}$$

It can be seen from this equation that doubling an object's temperature would cause the object to radiate 2^4, or 16, times more energy.

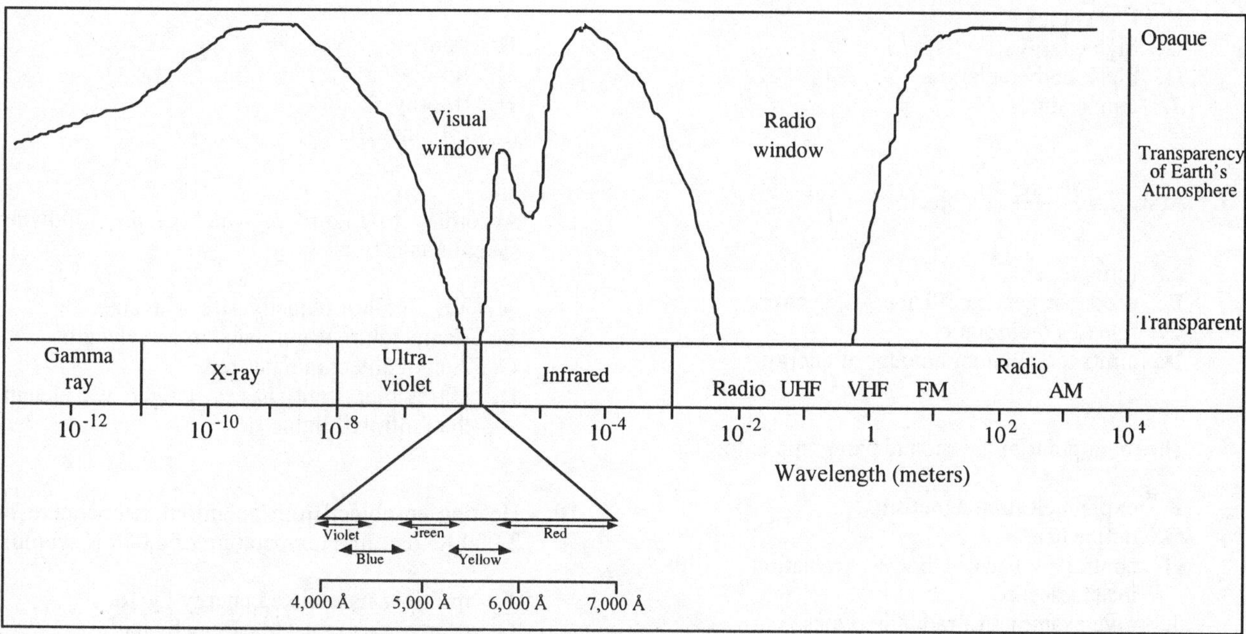

Figure 1: The electromagnetic spectrum includes all wavelengths of electromagnetic radiation. Earth's atmosphere is relatively opaque at most wavelengths. Visual and radio windows allow light and some radio waves to reach Earth's surface.

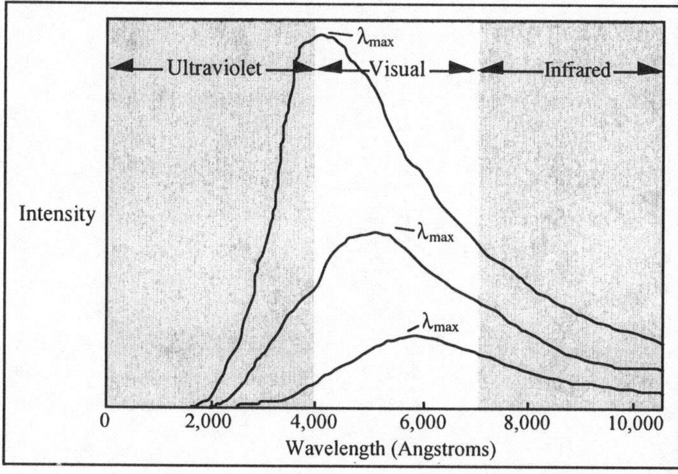

Figure 2: The intensity of radiation emitted by a heated body depends on wavelength. λ_{max} designates the wavelength of maximum intensity. Hotter objects radiate more energy and have shorter λ_{max} than cooler objects. A hot object radiates more blue light than red and therefore looks blue. A cool object radiates more red than blue and therefore looks red.

GO ON TO THE NEXT PAGE.

1. An x-ray has a wavelength shorter than that of:

   I. ultraviolet radiation.
   II. infrared radiation.
   III. 500 Å.

   A. I only
   B. III only
   C. I and III only
   D. I, II, and III

2. A short wavelength can be more dangerous than a long wavelength due to its:

   F. low energy.
   G. high energy.
   H. black body radiation.
   J. temperature.

3. At $\lambda_{max} = \frac{30 \cdot 10^6}{T}$ an object:

   A. turns blue.
   B. produces gentle collisions of electrons.
   C. releases radio static.
   D. emits a maximum amount of energy.

4. The main point of the second paragraph is to:

   F. explain electromagnetism.
   G. define heat.
   H. contrast black body radiation with incandescence.
   J. give examples of radiation types.

5. According to Figure 1, which of the following wavelengths would fall within the visible spectrum?

   A. 500 Å
   B. 1,000 Å
   C. 5,000 Å
   D. 10,000 Å

6. In the equation shown in line 94, what is *T*?

   F. Time
   G. Wavelength
   H. Number of photons emitted
   J. Temperature

7. An astronomer views two stars of different temperatures. Which is hotter?

   A. The one that is larger
   B. The one that is smaller
   C. The one that is redder
   D. The one that is bluer

8. Lines 86-87 refer to "collisions per second," meaning collisions of:

   I. photons.
   II. electrons.
   III. photons with electrons.

   F. I only
   G. II only
   H. III only
   J. I, II, and III

9. According to Figure 2, which of the following statements is true?

   A. λ_{max} of a hot object varies with size.
   B. Temperature is unrelated to wavelength.
   C. A cool object radiates red.
   D. Ultraviolet light has a longer wavelength than infrared light.

10. Heating an object from an initial temperature of 2,000 K to a final temperature of 4,000 K would:

    F. multiply its radiated energy by 16.
    G. decrease its radiated energy by half.
    H. have no effect on the energy released.
    J. cause it to radiate more red light.

GO ON TO THE NEXT PAGE.

Passage II

PROSE FICTION: This passage is adapted from the short story "Paul's Case" by Willa Cather.

It was Paul's afternoon to appear before the faculty of Pittsburgh High School to account for his various misdemeanors. He had been suspended a week ago, and his father had called at the Principal's office and confessed his perplexity about his son. Paul entered the faculty room suave and smiling. His clothes were a trifle outgrown, and the tan velvet on the collar of his open overcoat was frayed and worn; but for all that there was something of the dandy in him, and he wore an opal pin in his neatly knotted black four-in-hand, and a red carnation in his buttonhole. This latter adornment the faculty somehow felt was not properly significant of the contrite spirit befitting a boy under the ban of suspension.

Paul was tall for his age and very thin, with high, cramped shoulders and a narrow chest. His eyes were remarkable for a certain hysterical brilliancy, and he continually used them in a conscious, theatrical sort of way, peculiarly offensive in a boy. The pupils were abnormally large, as though he was addicted to belladonna, but there was a glassy glitter about them, which that drug does not produce.

When questioned by the Principal as to why he was there Paul stated, politely enough, that he wanted to come back to school. This was a lie, but Paul was quite accustomed to lying; he found it, indeed, indispensable for overcoming friction. His teachers were asked to state their respective charges against him, which they did with such a rancor and aggrievement as evinced that this was not a usual case. Disorder and impertinence were among the offenses named, yet each of his instructors felt that it was scarcely possible to put into words the real cause of the trouble, which lay in a sort of hysterically defiant manner of the boy's, in the contempt which they all knew he felt for them, and which he seemingly made not the least effort to conceal. Once, when he had been making a synopsis of a paragraph at the blackboard, his English teacher had stepped to his side and attempted to guide his hand. Paul had started back with a shudder and thrust his hands violently behind him. The astonished woman could scarcely have been more hurt and embarrassed had he struck at her. The insult was so involuntary and definitely personal as to be unforgettable. In one way or another he had made all his teachers, men and women alike, conscious of the same feeling of physical aversion. In one class he habitually sat with his hand shading his eyes; in another he always looked out of the window during the recitation; in another he made a running commentary on the lecture, with humorous intention.

His teachers felt this afternoon that his whole attitude was symbolized by his shrug and his flippant red carnation flower, and they fell upon him without mercy, his English teacher leading the pack. He stood through it smiling, his pale lips parted over his white teeth. (His lips were continuously twitching, and he had a habit of raising his eyebrows that was contemptuous and irritating to the last degree.) Older boys than Paul had broken down and shed tears under that baptism of fire, but his set smile did not once desert him, and his only sign of discomfort was the nervous trembling of the fingers that toyed with the buttons of his overcoat, and an occasional jerking of the other hand that held his hat. Paul was always smiling, always glancing about him, seeming to feel that people might be watching him and trying to detect something. This conscious expression, since it was as far as possible from boyish mirthfulness, was usually attributed to insolence or "smartness."

11. This short story is subtitled "A Study in Temperament," which suggests that Cather wants to examine:

A. a certain type of character.
B. reactions under pressure.
C. how people change over time.
D. people and their settings.

12. The introductory phrases "something of the dandy" (line 9), "hysterical brilliancy" (line 17), and "peculiarly offensive" (line 19):

I. describe Paul's reaction to his peers.
II. show the narrator's distaste for Paul.
III. reveal Paul as an unpleasant character.

F. I only
G. III only
H. I and II only
J. II and III only

13. Cather makes it clear in the first paragraph that the faculty of the high school:

A. is perplexed by Paul's actions.
B. finds Paul's demeanor inappropriate.
C. cannot understand Paul's words.
D. wants only the best for Paul.

GO ON TO THE NEXT PAGE.

14. The words "hysterical" and "hysterically," as used in lines 17 and 34, seem to imply:

F. delirium.
G. raving.
H. uncontrolled behavior.
J. frothing.

15. Cather implies that the most serious flaw Paul has is his:

A. inability to complete his work.
B. flippant sense of humor.
C. drug use.
D. failure to hide his contempt for others.

16. To keep the reader from sympathizing with the faculty, Cather compares them metaphorically to:

F. rabbits.
G. wolves.
H. dictators.
J. comedians.

17. Cather uses the phrase "baptism of fire" in line 61 to denote the:

A. challenge faced by students in a faculty inquisition.
B. youthfulness of Paul and his fellow students.
C. obstacles adolescents confront while growing up.
D. fury with which Paul faced the faculty.

18. "Smartness" (line 70) is used to mean:

F. wit.
G. intelligence.
H. impudence.
J. reasonableness.

19. Which adjective does NOT describe Paul as he is presented in this story?

A. Defiant
B. Proud
C. Flippant
D. Candid

20. By the end of the selection, we find that the faculty:

F. resent and loathe Paul.
G. admire and trust Paul.
H. struggle to understand Paul.
J. are physically revolted by Paul.

GO ON TO THE NEXT PAGE.

Passage III

HUMANITIES: This passage is adapted from Thomas Bulfinch's *Mythology*.

Minerva was the goddess of wisdom, but on one occasion she did a very foolish thing; she entered into competition with Juno and Venus for the prize of beauty. It happened thus: At the nuptials of Peleus and Thetis all the gods were invited with the exception of Eris, or Discord. Enraged at her exclusion, the goddess threw a golden apple among the guests, with the inscription, "For the fairest." Thereupon Juno, Venus, and Minerva each claimed the apple. Jupiter, not willing to decide in so delicate a matter, sent the goddesses to Mount Ida, where the beautiful shepherd Paris was tending his flocks, and to him was committed the decision. The goddesses accordingly appeared before him. Juno promised him power and riches, Minerva glory and renown in war, and Venus the fairest of women for his wife, each attempting to bias his decision in her own favour. Paris decided in favour of Venus and gave her the golden apple, thus making the two other goddesses his enemies. Under the protection of Venus, Paris sailed to Greece, and was hospitably received by Menelaus, king of Sparta. Now Helen, the wife of Menelaus, was the very woman whom Venus had destined for Paris, the fairest of her sex. She had been sought as a bride by numerous suitors, and before her decision was made known, they all, at the suggestion of Ulysses, one of their number, took an oath that they would defend her from all injury and avenge her cause if necessary. She chose Menelaus, and was living with him happily when Paris became their guest. Paris, aided by Venus, persuaded her to elope with him, and carried her to Troy, whence arose the famous Trojan War, the theme of the greatest poems of antiquity, those of Homer and Virgil.

Menelaus called upon his brother chieftains of Greece to fulfill their pledge, and join him in his efforts to recover his wife. They generally came forward, but Ulysses, who had married Penelope, and was very happy in his wife and child, had no disposition to embark in such a troublesome affair. He therefore hung back and Palamedes was sent to urge him. When Palamedes arrived at Ithaca, Ulysses pretended to be mad. He yoked an ass and an ox together to the plough and began to sow salt. Palamedes, to try him, placed the infant Telemachus before the plough, whereupon the father turned the plough aside, showing plainly that he was no madman, and after that could no longer refuse to fulfill his promise. Being now himself gained for the undertaking, he lent his aid to bring in other reluctant chiefs, especially Achilles. This hero was the son of that Thetis at whose marriage the apple of Discord had been thrown among the goddesses. Thetis was herself one of the immortals, a sea-nymph, and knowing that her son was fated to perish before Troy if he went on the expedition, she endeavored to prevent his going. She sent him away to the court of King Lycomedes, and induced him to conceal himself in the disguise of a maiden among the daughters of the king. Ulysses, hearing he was there, went disguised as a merchant to the palace and offered for sale female ornaments, among which he had placed some arms. While the king's daughters were engrossed with the other contents of the merchant's pack, Achilles handled the weapons and thereby betrayed himself to the keen eye of Ulysses, who found no great difficulty in persuading him to disregard his mother's prudent counsels and join his countrymen in the war.

21. By describing Jupiter as "not willing to decide in so delicate a matter" (lines 9-10), the author implies that:

A. Jupiter is usually heavy-handed.
B. any decision is bound to offend someone.
C. Jupiter is overly sensitive.
D. the problems are so obscure that no one can judge them.

22. The word "disposition" (line 39) is used to mean:

F. inclination.
G. nature.
H. integrity.
J. value.

23. All of the following assertions are examples of the author's inserting himself into the narrative EXCEPT:

A. Minerva did a foolish thing.
B. The poems of Homer and Virgil were great.
C. Helen was the fairest of her sex.
D. The greatest poems of antiquity were about the Trojan War.

24. The sowing of salt (line 43) is intended to show:

F. Ulysses' attempt to be found insane.
G. the difficulty of cultivating in rocky soil.
H. how the tears of the gods created the sea.
J. Ulysses' talent as a soldier rather than a farmer.

GO ON TO THE NEXT PAGE.

25. When Palamedes tries Ulysses (lines 44-48), he:

A. finds him guilty.
B. judges him.
C. tests him.
D. attempts to help him.

26. The author reveals that Thetis is a sea-nymph in order to explain:

F. why she married Peleus.
G. why she dislikes the idea of war.
H. the effect of the apple of Discord.
J. her ability to predict the future.

27. Among the chieftains of Greece apparently are:

A. Juno, Venus, and Minerva.
B. Paris and Lycomedes.
C. Ulysses, Achilles, and Menelaus.
D. Eris and Thetis.

28. Why does Ulysses display arms among the ornaments?

F. To trick Achilles into revealing himself
G. As a declaration of war
H. To mislead the daughters of the king
J. To complete his disguise as a merchant

29. This passage foreshadows which of the following events?

I. The death of Achilles
II. The advent of war
III. The downfall of Paris

A. I only
B. II only
C. I and II only
D. II and III only

30. A reasonable title for this narrative might be:

F. "Achilles and Ulysses"
G. "The Apple of Discord Leads to War"
H. "Beauty and the Beast"
J. "The Pettiness of the Gods"

GO ON TO THE NEXT PAGE.

Passage IV

SOCIAL SCIENCE: This passage discusses the history of African Americans in Congress.

Only with the enforcement of the Reconstruction Act of 1867 and the ratification of the Fifteenth Amendment to the Constitution—nearly 70 years after the ratification of the U.S. Constitution—did African Americans first win seats in Congress. Hiram Revels of Mississippi became the first African American to serve in Congress when he took his seat in the Senate on February 25, 1870. Joseph Rainey of South Carolina became the first African American member of the House of Representatives later in 1870. In the next 80 years, nearly seventy African Americans served in Congress.

African Americans throughout the South became politically active soon after emancipation and the close of the Civil War. State conventions and local political societies such as the Union League provided an opportunity for freed African Americans to articulate their vision of full participation in the political and economic life of the former slave states. Out of this broad-based political mobilization emerged a generation of African American leaders who nearly unanimously adhered to the Republican Party because it had championed the rights of African Americans. African Americans elected to Congress during Reconstruction found the national legislature an effective forum for the advocacy of political equality. Following the end of federal Reconstruction in 1877, African Americans continued to win election to Congress and they carried on the struggle for civil rights and economic opportunity. The African American congressional representatives of the late nineteenth century were the most prominent indication of the persistence of political organization on a local level in the South.

During the 1890s and early 1900s, no African American won election to Congress, in part because of restrictive state election codes in some southern states. During World War I and in the following decade, however, African American migration to northern cities established the foundation for political organization in urban centers. Oscar DePriest's election in 1928 as a representative from Chicago began a slow but steady succession of political victories in the North. Over the next three decades African Americans won congressional seats in New York City, Detroit, and Philadelphia. In the wake of the civil rights movement and the enforcement of the Voting Rights Act of 1965, African Americans regained seats in the South. Since the 1930s, nearly all African American representatives have been Democrats.

Since the nineteenth century, African American members of Congress have served as advocates for all African Americans as well as representatives for their constituencies. During Reconstruction and the late nineteenth century, African American representatives called on their colleagues to protect the voting rights of African Americans. These members of Congress, many of them former slaves, also called for expanded educational opportunities and land grants for freed African Americans. In the mid-twentieth century, African American representatives turned to the needs of urban communities and urged federal programs for improved housing and job training. As the most prominent African American office-holders of the time, these representatives served as defenders of the civil rights movement and proponents of legislation to end segregation. In 1971, the establishment of the Congressional Black Caucus offered a formal means of representing the combined interests of African Americans. The caucus has demonstrated a special concern for the protection of civil rights; the guarantee of equal opportunity in education, employment, and housing; and a broad array of foreign and domestic policy issues.

African Americans in Congress have been further united by their shared experience in the African American community. Many of the early Black representatives were born in slavery. The political and economic opportunities of Reconstruction offered these representatives the hope that African Americans might achieve genuine equality in American society, while the opposition of some white Southerners reminded them of the need for federal protection of the liberties won in the aftermath of the Civil War.

Since the victories of the civil rights movement in the 1960s, African American men and women have won election to Congress from increasingly diverse regions of the country. Whether from largely urban districts, suburban areas, or more recently from rural Mississippi, these members of Congress have maintained their common concern with economic issues that affect African Americans and with the protection of civil rights.

The collected biographies of African Americans who served in the House and Senate provide an important perspective on the history of the Congress and the role of African Americans in American politics. Their stories offer eloquent testimony to the long struggle to extend the ideals of the founders to encompass all citizens of the United States.

GO ON TO THE NEXT PAGE.

31. According to the passage, the first African American to serve in the House of Representatives was:

A. Hiram Revels.
B. Joseph Rainey.
C. from Chicago.
D. a former slave.

32. The passage suggests that, in contrast to African Americans elected to Congress during and shortly after Reconstruction, African Americans selected to Congress today are more likely to:

F. come from urban areas in the North.
G. be members of the Republican Party.
H. work for full political equality for all African Americans.
J. come from districts in which the majority is African American.

33. One difference between African American congressional representatives in the nineteenth century and those in the mid-twentieth century was:

A. the political party to which they were likely to belong.
B. their commitment to education for African Americans.
C. the strength of their ties to the African American community as a whole.
D. the extent to which they represented all African Americans and not just their constituents.

34. When the African American representatives "turned to" certain issues in the mid-twentieth century (line 60), they:

F. became antagonistic toward those issues.
G. reversed their positions on those issues.
H. devoted themselves to those issues.
J. referred to those issues.

35. According to the passage, one reason African Americans began to be elected to Congress from cities in the northern United States after the 1930s was that:

A. more African Americans lived in northern cities at that time than had been the case previously.
B. African Americans in northern cities had better political organizations than did African Americans in the rural South.
C. African American politicians in the North were more likely to be members of the Democratic Party than were those in the South.
D. African American politicians in the North were more likely to focus on voting rights for African Americans than were those in the South.

36. Which one of the following is NOT mentioned in the passage as a common concern of African American congressional representatives?

F. Enforcing voting rights for African Americans
G. Increasing educational opportunities for African Americans
H. Ensuring opportunities for employment for African Americans
J. Protecting people of African descent in other countries

37. One reason cited in the passage for the election of African Americans to Congress from both southern states after Reconstruction and northern states after World War I is the:

A. success of the civil rights movement.
B. passage and enforcement of the Fifteenth Amendment.
C. strength of local African American political organizations.
D. predominance of African Americans in certain districts.

GO ON TO THE NEXT PAGE.

38. According to the passage, the Congressional Black Caucus:

F. focused its attention almost exclusively on domestic issues.
G. was the first organization founded exclusively for African American congressional representatives.
H. was intended to replace local African American political organizations with one large national organization.
J. provided a forum in which African American representatives could deal with issues of concern to all African Americans.

39. The last paragraph suggests that this passage might serve as:

A. a call to political involvement on the part of African Americans.
B. an introduction to biographies of African American members of Congress.
C. the conclusion of a history of African Americans in the United States.
D. part of a longer work on the history of the United States Congress.

40. The author expresses admiration toward the African American congressional representatives discussed in the passage for their:

F. political acumen.
G. attempts to ensure the rights of all Americans.
H. single-minded devotion to the struggle for civil rights.
J. focus on providing economic opportunity for African Americans.

END OF TEST 3.
STOP! DO NOT TURN THE PAGE UNTIL TOLD TO DO SO.
DO NOT RETURN TO A PREVIOUS TEST.

4 4 4 4 4 4 4 4 4 4 4 4

SCIENCE REASONING TEST

35 Minutes—40 Items

DIRECTIONS: The passages presented in the test are each followed by a set of items. Read the passage and choose the best answer for each item. Fill in the corresponding oval on your bubble sheet. You may refer to the passage as often as necessary to answer the passage items.

Warning: Calculator use is not permitted on this test.

Answers are on page 968. Explanations begin on page 980.

Passage I

The solubility of materials in liquids depends not only on the nature of the solute and the solvent, but also on temperature. A graph showing the solubilities of several substances in water is presented below.

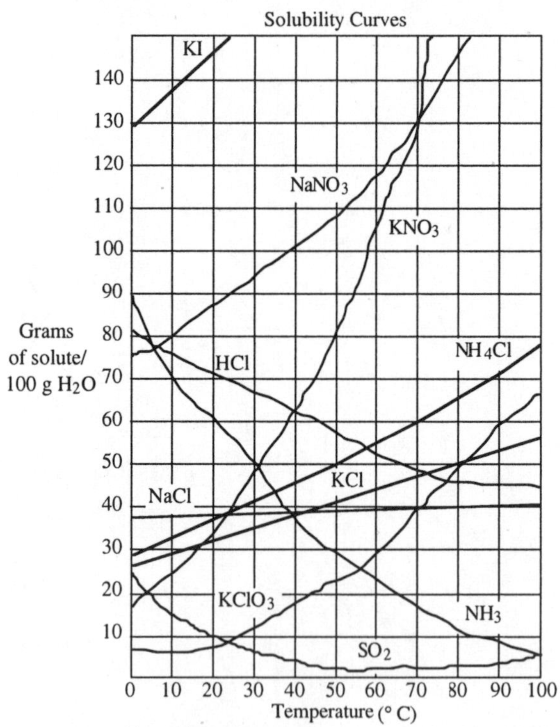

Note: NH_3 is a gas.

1. Which of the following has the most temperature sensitive solubility throughout the range shown?

   A. $NaNO_3$
   B. KNO_3
   C. NaCl
   D. NH_3

2. The solubility of sodium (Na) salts is:

   F. high because sodium is an alkali metal.
   G. low because sodium combines with anions to make salts.
   H. dependent on what salt it forms.
   J. always greater than 20 grams per 100 grams of water.

3. A 250 ml alcoholic solution of KNO_3 at 50° C contains how many grams KNO_3 at saturation?

   A. 80
   B. 200
   C. 30
   D. Cannot be determined from the given information

GO ON TO THE NEXT PAGE.

4. A solution containing equal amounts of $NaNO_3$ and KNO_3 is allowed to cool until a white powder begins to appear at the bottom of the flask. That powder is:

   F. KNO_3.
   G. $NaNO_3$.
   H. a mixture of both.
   J. Cannot be determined from the given information

5. The solubility curve of NH_3 suggests an explanation of why:

   A. divers get the bends (nitrogen bubbles in the blood) if they rise too quickly.
   B. soda goes flat.
   C. warm lemonade is sweeter than cold lemonade.
   D. hot air balloons rise.

GO ON TO THE NEXT PAGE.

Passage II

Part of our understanding of Earth comes from a consideration of its physical properties. A table of selected properties is presented below.

Property	*Value*
Mass	$6 \cdot 10^{24}$ kg
Diameter	$6 \cdot 10^{6}$ m
Orbital Radius	$1.5 \cdot 10^{11}$ m
Period of Revolution	365.3 days
Period of Rotation	24 hours

Below is a table comparing the other planets of the solar system to Earth.

	Earth	*Jupiter*	*Mars*	*Mercury*	*Neptune*	*Pluto*	*Saturn*	*Uranus*	*Venus*
Diameter	1	10	0.55	0.38	4.3	?	9.4	4.1	0.98
Mass	1	320	0.10	0.58	17	?	95	14	0.83
Surface Gravity	1	2.7	0.40	0.40	1.2	?	1.2	1.1	0.90
Volume	1	1,320	0.15	0.58	42	0.729	760	50	0.90
Average Distance to Sun	1	5.3	1.5	0.40	30	40	10	19	0.70
Period of Revolution	1	12	2	0.25	165	248	30	84	0.60
Period of Rotation	1	0.40	1	60	0.50	0	0.40	0.50	240

The following are a few basic equations: (1) density = $\frac{\text{mass}}{\text{volume}}$, (2) distance = rate • time, and (3) volume of a sphere = $\frac{4}{3}\pi r^3$ where r is the radius of the sphere.

6. Based on the table above, what is the approximate ratio of the period of revolution in days to the period of rotation in days for Mercury?

F. 240
G. $\frac{3}{2}$
H. $\frac{2}{3}$
J. $\frac{1}{240}$

7. Which planet is as dense as the planet Earth?

A. Mercury
B. Venus
C. Mars
D. None

8. Which planet orbits the sun at the slowest rate?

F. Mercury
G. Jupiter
H. Neptune
J. Pluto

9. Analysis of the tables above shows that surface gravity most likely depends on:

A. mass alone.
B. distance and mass.
C. density alone.
D. density of the planet and proximity to the sun.

10. Assuming that both Earth and Pluto are spherical, the diameter of Pluto is:

F. 0.729 • the radius of Earth.
G. 0.9 • the radius of Earth.
H. 1.8 • the radius of Earth.
J. 2.7 • the radius of Earth.

GO ON TO THE NEXT PAGE.

11. How many meters separate the orbits of the farthest apart planetary neighbors?

 A. 40 • Earth's orbital radius
 B. 11 • Earth's orbital radius
 C. 10 • Earth's orbital radius
 D. 9 • Earth's orbital radius

GO ON TO THE NEXT PAGE.

Passage III

Four groups of 1,000 men each were placed on strict diets that contained different intakes of cholesterol. The men stayed on the diet for 40 years, and their history of illness over that time is recorded below.

	Death rate, standardized/1,000			
		Men taking in a daily average of		
Illness	*No cholesterol*	0–5 grams	6–20 grams	20+ grams
Cancer				
Colon	0.01	0.03	0.04	0.02
Prostate	2.02	0.06	1.03	4.01
Lung	0.03	0.06	0.40	0.20
Coronary				
Thrombosis	5.02	1.01	4.00	10.05
Arrest	6.00	0.98	5.09	11.00
Cardiovascular	5.96	0.65	4.97	9.08
Cerebral Clot	4.01	0.02	0.50	4.01
Depression	5.01	0.30	0.30	0.30

12. Which of the following statements is best supported by the data?

F. A man ingesting no cholesterol is approximately twice as likely to die of prostate cancer as a man ingesting 10 grams per day.
G. Any ingestion of cholesterol decreases the risk of dying from all three forms of cancer listed here.
H. Ingestion of cholesterol seems unrelated to the probability of coronary disease.
J. Cerebral clots are the most prevalent form of death among the group consuming the most cholesterol.

13. What might one conclude about the relationship between cholesterol ingestion and depression based on the information above?

A. Cholesterol causes depression.
B. Ingestion of cholesterol has no effect on the occurrence of depression.
C. Small amounts of cholesterol are most effective in combating depression.
D. Large and small amounts of cholesterol are equally effective in reducing the depression death rate.

14. For which of the following diseases does the highest cholesterol diet increase the probability of death most, compared relatively to the non-cholesterol diets?

F. Cerebral clots
G. Coronary arrest
H. Cardiovascular disease
J. Coronary thrombosis

15. For which of the following groups of diseases does a daily intake of 0-5 grams of cholesterol reduce the probability of death?

A. Cerebral clot, coronary thrombosis, and lung cancer
B. Cerebral clot, depression, and colon cancer
C. Depression, coronary arrest, and prostate cancer
D. Depression, coronary thrombosis, and colon cancer

GO ON TO THE NEXT PAGE.

16. What might be involved in determining a standardized death rate for men?

    F. Ignoring deaths that do not conform to the average results
    G. Adjusting death rates according to discrepancies in age
    H. Assuming that the natural death rate is 0 deaths per 1,000 men
    J. Comparing data with a similar experiment involving women

GO ON TO THE NEXT PAGE.

Passage IV

The resistance (R) of a material is directly proportional to the resistivity (r) of the material, resistivity is measured in ohm-meters. The voltage (V, measured in volts) in a circuit is directly proportional to both the resistance (R, measured in ohms) and the current (I, measured in amperes). Resistors in series act as one resistor according to the formula:

$$R_s = R_1 + R_2 + R_3 + \ldots$$

and resistors in parallel act as one resistor according to the formula:

$$\frac{1}{R_p} = \frac{1}{R_1} + \frac{1}{R_2} + \frac{1}{R_3} + \ldots$$

The resistivities of several materials are listed below.

Substance	*Resistivity, r (ohm-meters)*
Aluminum	$2.63 \cdot 10^{-8}$
Copper	$1.72 \cdot 10^{-8}$
Germanium	$6.00 \cdot 10^{-1}$
Silicon	$2.30 \cdot 10^{3}$
Silver	$1.47 \cdot 10^{-8}$
Sulfur	$1.00 \cdot 10^{15}$

17. According to the information provided, the best formula for the voltage in a circuit, where voltage is V, current is I, and resistance is R is:

A. $V = \frac{I}{R}$.
B. $V = I + R$.
C. $V = IR$.
D. $V = I - R$.

18. According to the information provided, how would the voltage in a circuit with a silver resistor compare to the voltage in a circuit with a germanium resistor of the same size? (Current is the same in both circuits.)

F. The voltage in the silver circuit would be greater.
G. The voltage in the germanium circuit would be greater.
H. The voltage would be the same in both circuits.
J. Cannot be determined from the given information

19. Two resistors with $R = 2$ are placed in series. How does the voltage in the circuit compare with the voltage in a circuit with only one resistor, $R = 2$? (Assume current remains constant.)

A. The voltage is doubled.
B. The voltage is halved.
C. The voltage is the same.
D. The voltage is zero.

20. A resistor with $R = 4$ is put in parallel with an identical resistor, $R = 4$. What is R_p?

F. 0
G. $\frac{1}{2}$
H. 1
J. 2

21. Power is defined as $P = I^2R$. If R is a constant, then power would increase —— with an increase in the current. (Fill in the blank space with the best answer choice.)

A. logarithmically
B. directly
C. exponentially
D. inversely

22. In order to keep the current in a circuit constant, if one increases the voltage, one must:

F. lengthen the circuit.
G. shorten the circuit.
H. decrease the resistance.
J. increase the resistance.

GO ON TO THE NEXT PAGE.

Passage V

In order to discover the steps by which a chemical reaction occurs, the dependence of the initial rate of reaction on the concentration of the reactants is determined. Three experiments exploring the mechanism of a reaction are presented below.

Experiment 1: Compound *A* is injected into a rapidly stirred solution of *B* in hexamethyl phosphoramide. As *A* and *B* react, they form a compound that has a characteristic absorption at 520 nanometers. The concentration of product, and therefore the rate of reaction, can be calculated by measuring the strength of the absorption. Results are presented below:

Trial	Concentration A	Concentration B	Rate
1	4	4	60
2	2	2	30
3	4	2	30
4	4	8	120

Experiment 2: Compound *A* is injected into a rapidly mixed solution of *B* in carbon tetrachloride. The product of the reaction is identical to the product in Experiment 1. The course of the reaction is followed by spectrophotometric methods as in Experiment 1.

Trial	Concentration A	Concentration B	Rate
1	3	3	27
2	6	6	108
3	6	3	54
4	12	6	216

Experiment 3: Compound *A* is injected in a swirling solution of *B* in a 1:1-by-volume mixture of carbon tetrachloride and hexamethyl phosphoramide. The formation of product, as before, is followed by spectrophotometry.

Trial	Concentration A	Concentration B	Rate
1	9	9	54
2	9	4.5	27
3	4	4.5	18
4	4	9	36

23. Which of the following statements best describes the effect of Concentration *A* on the rate of reaction in Experiment 1?

A. Rate increases with increasing *A*.
B. Rate increases by the square of *A*'s concentration.
C. Rate increases by the square root of *A*'s concentration.
D. Rate is independent of *A*'s concentration.

24. Which of the following statements best describes the effect of Concentration *A* on the rate of reaction in Experiment 2?

F. Rate increases with increasing *A*.
G. Rate increases by the square of *A*'s concentration.
H. Rate increases by the square root of *A*'s concentration.
J. Rate is independent of *A*'s concentration.

25. Which of the following statements best describes the effect of Concentration *A* on the rate in Experiment 3?

A. Rate increases with increasing *A*.
B. Rate increases by the square of *A*'s concentration.
C. Rate increases by the square root of *A*'s concentration.
D. Rate is independent of *A*'s concentration.

26. What is the likeliest explanation for the results obtained in Experiment 3?

F. A mechanism intermediates between the ones found in Experiments 1 and 2.
G. Some of the molecules react by Experiment 1's mechanism, others by Experiment 2's mechanism.
H. A different mechanism is responsible.
J. There is an averaging of the mechanisms.

27. What is the best conclusion that can be drawn from this set of experiments?

A. Rate is increased by changing solvents.
B. Reactions may depend on solvent effects as well as on the nature of the reactants.
C. Mechanisms can always be changed by use of an appropriate solvent.
D. Reactions depend on solvent effects as well as on the nature of the reactants.

GO ON TO THE NEXT PAGE.

Passage VI

Acceleration is defined as the change in the velocity of an object divided by the length of time during which that change took place. Contrary to popular belief, Galileo did not base his conclusion of the acceleration of gravity on experiments done with cannonballs dropped from the Leaning Tower of Pisa. Instead, he used the motion of objects moving down an inclined plane to develop his theory. In the following sets of experiments, a student studies the motion of bodies on an inclined plane.

For all of the following experiments, time is measured in seconds, distance in meters, and velocity in meters per second. The distance (d) an object travels at a constant acceleration (a) in time (t), assuming it starts from rest, is given by the equation: $d = \frac{1}{2}at^2$.

Experiment 1: A student set up a smooth wooden board at an angle of 30° from horizontal. The board had a length of 10 meters. Using a stroboscope, the student was able to determine the position of a 100-gram steel ball that was rolled down the incline. Velocity was determined by means of a radar gun. The results are presented below:

Time	*Distance (m)*	*Velocity (m/sec)*
0	0	0
0.5	0.44	1.75
1.0	1.75	3.5
1.5	3.94	5.25
2.0	7.00	7.00

Experiment 2: The same 10-meter wooden board was used in Experiment 2. The angle used was again 30°. The object used this time was a 100-gram sled made of the same material as the ball in Experiment 1. The stroboscope and the radar gun were used to determine its position and velocity as it slid down the inclined plane. The results are presented below:

Time	*Distance (m)*	*Velocity (m/sec)*
0	0	0
0.5	1.13	2.45
1.0	2.45	4.90
1.5	5.51	7.35
2.0	9.80	9.80

Experiment 3: The same board at the same angle was used in the third experiment as in the previous two. In this experiment, a 100-gram box made of the same material as the ball and the sled was used. The same recording devices were used, and the results are presented below:

Time	*Distance (m)*	*Velocity (m/sec)*
0	0	0
1.0	0.33	0.66
2.0	1.31	1.32
3.0	2.97	1.98
4.0	5.28	2.64
5.0	8.25	3.30

Experiment 4: The board in the previous experiments was carefully oiled. Once again, the board was placed at an angle of 30° from horizontal. Each of the objects was then allowed to move down the inclined plane, and the time required to reach the bottom of the plane is recorded below:

Object	*Time*
sled	2.02
ball	2.39
box	4.08

28. Which object in the first three experiments has the greatest acceleration?

F. Ball
G. Sled
H. Box
J. Ball and sled are equal.

29. The acceleration of the ball relative to that of the sled is due to the ball's:

A. rolling.
B. friction.
C. rolling and friction.
D. being the same mass as the sled, and therefore having the same acceleration.

GO ON TO THE NEXT PAGE.

30. The acceleration of the ball relative to that of the box is due to:

F. the ball's rolling only.
G. the ball's friction only.
H. the ball's rolling and the box's friction.
J. the ball's having the same mass as the box, and therefore having the same acceleration.

31. Based on these four experiments, the ratio of the acceleration of the ball to the acceleration of the sled is:

A. 1.
B. $\frac{5}{7}$.
C. dependent on the amount of friction.
D. dependent on time.

32. Based on these four experiments, the ratio of the acceleration of the ball to the acceleration of the box is:

F. 1.
G. $\frac{5}{7}$.
H. dependent on the amount of friction.
J. dependent on time.

GO ON TO THE NEXT PAGE.

Passage VII

What was the fate of Neanderthal man? Two differing views are presented below.

Scientist 1: Neanderthals were very similar to modern humans in appearance. It is true that Neanderthals were somewhat more muscular than modern humans and that the way the muscles seem to have been arranged on the skeleton was, in a few minor ways, different. This we are able to deduce from the places on the surviving bones that mark where the ligaments were once attached. For example, the neck and wrists of Neanderthals were far thicker than is natural to modern humans. Some of the facial structure was also different, especially the protrusion of the brow. But differences between the appearance of Neanderthals and modern humans have been exaggerated since they are based on the skeleton of one individual who was later discovered to have been suffering from severe arthritis. It is not unlikely that, because of the low population density and the nomadic lifestyle that spread the few individuals over ever-larger areas, Neanderthal and early modern humans interbred and eventually merged into one species. The notion that some sort of "war" broke out between these different species (or, more likely, subspecies) of humans is an attempt to look out of early human eyes with a modern perspective.

Scientist 2: Whenever two species compete for the same niche there is a conflict. In this conflict the loser either moves to a different niche or dies out. It is unusual for two species to interbreed. The difference between early modern humans and Neanderthals physically may not appear great to an anatomist, but to the average man on the street, or prehistoric man in the forest, the differences are not subtle. And it was these individuals, not the anatomists, who had to decide whether or not to mate. Even if early modern humans and Neanderthals did mate, the result—us—would look more like a mix of the two rather than like modern humans. Early modern humans and Neanderthals, because they were so close to each other physically, must have been deadly enemies. The population was thinly dispersed at that time because the resources available would not support a greater population density. There literally was not room enough on the planet for the two species. They could not combine because they were so different in appearance, so only one answer remained. We survived because we killed our cousin.

33. Underlying the hypothesis of Scientist 1 is the assumption that:

   A. early modern humans and Neanderthals did not compete for the same kinds of food.
   B. early modern humans and Neanderthals were genetically close.
   C. early modern humans and Neanderthals did not necessarily live in the same area.
   D. early modern humans and Neanderthals often fought.

34. Underlying the hypotheses of both scientists is the assumption that:

   F. early modern humans and Neanderthals understood the consequences of their actions.
   G. early modern humans and Neanderthals both lived in exactly the same type of environment.
   H. early modern humans and Neanderthals both lived in the same geographical regions.
   J. early modern humans were more intelligent than Neanderthals.

35. If an isolated community of Neanderthals was discovered, whose hypothesis would be more damaged?

   A. Scientist l's because his theory does not allow for such a community to survive
   B. Scientist 2's because the descendants of early modern humans inhabit all the Earth and therefore there should be no community of Neanderthals
   C. Both hypotheses are disproved.
   D. Neither hypothesis is affected.

36. Which of the following, if true, would most support the hypothesis of Scientist 2?

   F. The camps of early modern humans are often close to the camps of Neanderthals.
   G. The camps of early modern humans are never close to Neanderthal camps.
   H. Bones of Neanderthals and early modern humans are often found near each other.
   J. Chipped Neanderthal bones are found with early modern human weapons.

GO ON TO THE NEXT PAGE.

37. The fact that lions and tigers fight when brought together even though they can be interbred supports which hypothesis to the greater extent?

A. Scientist 1's hypothesis, because it proves two species can interbreed
B. Scientist 1's hypothesis, because two species still exist that share the same niche
C. Scientist 2's hypothesis, because it suggests that two species that can interbreed may not do so under natural conditions
D. Scientist 2's hypothesis, because lions and tigers fight when brought together

38. According to the hypothesis of Scientist 2, what should be the result of interbreeding lions and tigers?

F. The offspring should be infertile.
G. The offspring will resemble one parent only.
H. The offspring will possess a mixture of traits.
J. Scientist 2's hypothesis makes no conjectures on the point because lions and tigers would not interbreed.

39. What other assumption do both Scientist 1 and Scientist 2 make about Neanderthals and early modern humans?

A. That early modern humans were directly involved in the disappearance of Neanderthals
B. That early modern humans were the more intelligent of the two
C. That Neanderthals differed little from early modern humans
D. That early modern humans only inhabited regions that were hospitable for Neanderthals

40. If a burial site containing over one hundred early modern humans and Neanderthal remains was discovered, and if two Neanderthal skeletons were found with early modern human spearpoints in them, which hypothesis would be the most strengthened?

F. Scientist 1's hypothesis, because spearpoints need not have been what killed the two Neanderthals
G. Scientist 2's hypothesis, because two Neanderthals were killed by early modern humans and no early modern humans were killed by Neanderthals
H. Scientist 2's hypothesis, because the spearpoints prove that the early modern humans had more developed weapons
J. Scientist 1's hypothesis, because only a couple of the individuals buried together died violently

END OF TEST 4.
STOP! DO NOT TURN THE PAGE UNTIL TOLD TO DO SO.
DO NOT RETURN TO A PREVIOUS TEST.

5 5 5 5 5 5 5 5 5 5 5 5

WRITING TEST (OPTIONAL)

30 Minutes—1 Essay Prompt

DIRECTIONS: This is a test of your writing skills. Before you begin planning and writing your essay, read the writing prompt carefully to understand the instructions. Your essay will be evaluated on the evidence it provides of your ability to express judgments by taking a position on the issue in the writing prompt; to maintain a focus on the topic throughout the essay; to develop a position by using logical reasoning and supporting ideas; to organize ideas in a logical way; and to use language clearly and effectively according to the conventions of standard written English.

If you finish before time is called, you may review your work. Lay your pencil down immediately when time is called.

Sample essays begin on page 983.

Writing Test Prompt

Some people believe that schools do not emphasize enough the concept of public service. They point out that volunteer service is a tradition in America and mention organizations such as the Girl and Boy Scouts, volunteer fire departments and rescue squads, and Big Brother and Sister. They believe that high schools should encourage volunteerism by offering students academic credit for such activities. They state that allowing academic credit would release students from studies to do volunteer work and further that such service would strengthen the sense of community. Other people say that volunteer service should be voluntary and that release time from school is a form of compensation for students. Students who receive such compensation would not really be doing volunteer work. Opponents of release time point out that students have opportunities to volunteer after school, on weekends, and during the summer months.

In your essay, take a position on this issue. You may address either of the two points described above, or you may offer an entirely different perspective on the issue. Be sure to use specific reasons and examples to support your analysis.

END OF TEST 5.
STOP! DO NOT RETURN TO ANY OTHER TEST.

Step Five: Post-Assessment and Review

Step Five Highlights:

See how far you have come and measure your improvement with this second, official test.

Put into action all of the content knowledge and test-taking strategies you've learned.

Redirect your study plan with a new snapshot of your performance.

Make sure that you're able to work through the test quickly without losing accuracy.

Step Five Overview:

It's time to measure your progress. You will put into action everything that you've learned during this second "dress rehearsal." After taking this final exam, you will be able to compare your pre- and post-test scores and see how much you have improved. You will have a chance to identify any remaining areas of weakness so that you know where to focus your studies prior to the actual test.

Step Five: Post-Assessment and Review

Step Five Overview

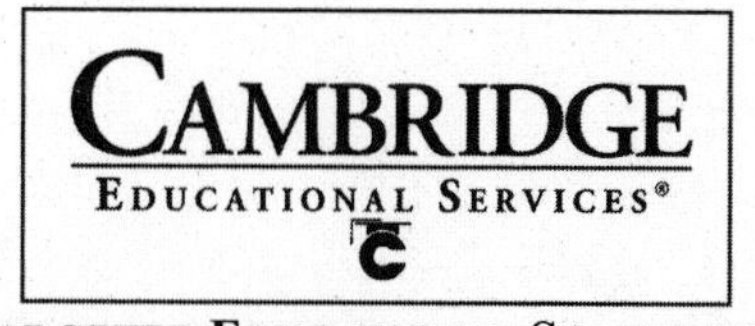

TARGETED EDUCATIONAL SOLUTIONS.

Cambridge Course Concept Outline
POST-ASSESSMENT AND REVIEW

The Bubble Sheet on page 895 is for use when taking the ACT, PLAN, or EXPLORE Post-Test.

POST-TEST BUBBLE SHEET

Start with number 1 for each new section. If a section has fewer items than answer spaces, leave the extra answer spaces blank. Be sure to erase any errors or stray marks completely.

Name ____________________ Student ID Number ____________________

Date ____________ Instructor ____________________ Course/Session Number ____________

TEST 1—ENGLISH

1 A B C D	16 F G H J	31 A B C D	46 F G H J	61 A B C D
2 F G H J	17 A B C D	32 F G H J	47 A B C D	62 F G H J
3 A B C D	18 F G H J	33 A B C D	48 F G H J	63 A B C D
4 F G H J	19 A B C D	34 F G H J	49 A B C D	64 F G H J
5 A B C D	20 F G H J	35 A B C D	50 F G H J	65 A B C D
6 F G H J	21 A B C D	36 F G H J	51 A B C D	66 F G H J
7 A B C D	22 F G H J	37 A B C D	52 F G H J	67 A B C D
8 F G H J	23 A B C D	38 F G H J	53 A B C D	68 F G H J
9 A B C D	24 F G H J	39 A B C D	54 F G H J	69 A B C D
10 F G H J	25 A B C D	40 F G H J	55 A B C D	70 F G H J
11 A B C D	26 F G H J	41 A B C D	56 F G H J	71 A B C D
12 F G H J	27 A B C D	42 F G H J	57 A B C D	72 F G H J
13 A B C D	28 F G H J	43 A B C D	58 F G H J	73 A B C D
14 F G H J	29 A B C D	44 F G H J	59 A B C D	74 F G H J
15 A B C D	30 F G H J	45 A B C D	60 F G H J	75 A B C D

TEST 2—MATHEMATICS

1 A B C D E	13 A B C D E	25 A B C D E	37 A B C D E	49 A B C D E
2 F G H J K	14 F G H J K	26 F G H J K	38 F G H J K	50 F G H J K
3 A B C D E	15 A B C D E	27 A B C D E	39 A B C D E	51 A B C D E
4 F G H J K	16 F G H J K	28 F G H J K	40 F G H J K	52 F G H J K
5 A B C D E	17 A B C D E	29 A B C D E	41 A B C D E	53 A B C D E
6 F G H J K	18 F G H J K	30 F G H J K	42 F G H J K	54 F G H J K
7 A B C D E	19 A B C D E	31 A B C D E	43 A B C D E	55 A B C D E
8 F G H J K	20 F G H J K	32 F G H J K	44 F G H J K	56 F G H J K
9 A B C D E	21 A B C D E	33 A B C D E	45 A B C D E	57 A B C D E
10 F G H J K	22 F G H J K	34 F G H J K	46 F G H J K	58 F G H J K
11 A B C D E	23 A B C D E	35 A B C D E	47 A B C D E	59 A B C D E
12 F G H J K	24 F G H J K	36 F G H J K	48 F G H J K	60 F G H J K

TEST 3—READING

1 A B C D	9 A B C D	17 A B C D	25 A B C D	33 A B C D
2 F G H J	10 F G H J	18 F G H J	26 F G H J	34 F G H J
3 A B C D	11 A B C D	19 A B C D	27 A B C D	35 A B C D
4 F G H J	12 F G H J	20 F G H J	28 F G H J	36 F G H J
5 A B C D	13 A B C D	21 A B C D	29 A B C D	37 A B C D
6 F G H J	14 F G H J	22 F G H J	30 F G H J	38 F G H J
7 A B C D	15 A B C D	23 A B C D	31 A B C D	39 A B C D
8 F G H J	16 F G H J	24 F G H J	32 F G H J	40 F G H J

TEST 4—SCIENCE REASONING

1 A B C D	9 A B C D	17 A B C D	25 A B C D	33 A B C D
2 F G H J	10 F G H J	18 F G H J	26 F G H J	34 F G H J
3 A B C D	11 A B C D	19 A B C D	27 A B C D	35 A B C D
4 F G H J	12 F G H J	20 F G H J	28 F G H J	36 F G H J
5 A B C D	13 A B C D	21 A B C D	29 A B C D	37 A B C D
6 F G H J	14 F G H J	22 F G H J	30 F G H J	38 F G H J
7 A B C D	15 A B C D	23 A B C D	31 A B C D	39 A B C D
8 F G H J	16 F G H J	24 F G H J	32 F G H J	40 F G H J

Step Six: Personal Study Plan

Step Six Highlights:

With the post-test data, create a focused study plan with the help of your instructor so you know where to review.

Don't waste time on areas you've already mastered; target the remaining areas of weakness to maximize your ACT score.

See what parts of the textbook you need to spend more time on: skills review, test-taking strategies, or pacing with practice tests.

Make sure you understand all the ACT-specific information on guessing, item-types, and content before the real test.

Step Six Overview:

Based on the results of the post-test, you will collaborate with your instructor to develop a personalized study plan. While each plan is different, you may be asked to return to items you've already reviewed but have not yet mastered in Steps Two, Three, or Four. If there are any items you have not yet completed, this is the time to return to those areas. You may need to review specific test-taking strategies; to focus on pacing, timing, and guessing; or to focus on other weaknesses. This plan will target your weaknesses in order to help you reach your true potential and ability.

TARGETED EDUCATIONAL SOLUTIONS.

Cambridge Course Concept Outline
PERSONAL STUDY PLAN

In this step, you will design a study plan to maximize your performance on the official exam. Between the date that your course ends and the date of the official exam, you will want to maintain your skills, target a final set of challenging concepts, and all around ready yourself for victory on the ACT, PLAN, or EXPLORE.

On the pages that follow, you will find some useful tips for planning the final segment in your ACT, PLAN, or EXPLORE study.

PERSONAL STUDY PLAN

Up until this point, you have spent a great deal of time preparing for the test both in class and on your own. After receiving the results of your final assessment (Step Five) and finishing your ACT • PLAN • EXPLORE preparation course, you will most likely have some spare time before the day of the official test. Spend this time wisely to make the best effort in preparation for the exam. This Personal Study Plan section is included as a short guide on how to use that remaining time to your best advantage.

A personal study plan is critical in order to reinforce and maintain the skills that you have learned throughout the course. Depending on whether several weeks or several days remain before the official exam date, you will want to plan your study differently. If there are several weeks remaining before the day of the test, you should plan to review more material than if there are only a few days remaining. If only a few days remain, a quick summary review is a better choice.

Many topics that are related to creating your personal study plan have already been covered in the Overcoming Test Anxiety section (Step One) of this textbook. It is important for you to review the material in that section when designing your study plan. In particular, you should balance a plan that will leave you confident of your preparation, but also calm and rested for the day of the exam.

The largest problem that most students face on the official exam is not a lack of subject knowledge but poor management of time. If you have not yet done so, take the four practice tests included in Step Four of this book. These practice tests not only serve to reinforce skills and strategies, but they also emphasize the importance of time management since they are to be administered with time restrictions. These time restrictions are put in place to simulate the experience of the actual test. Therefore, when taking the practice tests, hold rigorously to the allotted times. It is always worthwhile to return to a practice test to address skipped or unfinished items, but you should do so only at the conclusion of the allotted time.

Besides helping your pacing and preparedness, the practice tests are also an excellent guide to targeting your study plan. Look out for things that you know you could do better if you had the opportunity to peek at your notes. These are likely targets for review as you approach the day of the exam. Listing a few concrete topics for review sets a firm starting ground for your study plan.

The most significant aspect of a personal study plan is that it is a written plan. A written study plan is more concrete than one that you simply draw on from memory. So, when creating a personal study plan, write out a day-by-day schedule for reviewing all of the materials that are necessary to succeed on the test. This written format will provide a clear and dependable guide for study. The schedule should be prioritized according to the time that you will devote to each of the different subject areas based on the amount of time that you have remaining before the day of the official exam. Plan to review all of the materials equally several weeks before test day. Then, when the test date approaches, start focusing on the subject areas that are giving you the most difficulty. Divide your time proportionally among the test sections based on your assessment of the difficulty of the subject areas. Although subject area preparation is extremely important, the amount of time that you have remaining before the exam will determine how strongly you should focus on reviewing certain subject area material. In the final days before the test, you will not be able to learn a great deal of new material. Therefore, unless there is a long span of time between the end of your review course and the date of the exam, you should focus on practicing the skills that you have already learned (*e.g.*, time management, use of calculators, the process of elimination strategy, *etc.*).

The following sample schedules are provided for your reference. Remember that these schedules are only examples and that you should devise your own schedule to target the areas that you find most challenging. After you have designed a basic study plan, ask your teacher for insight. Your teacher may be able to suggest further strategies or a subtle re-allotment of your time.

If you are satisfied with your writing scores but have not attained your goals for the mathematics section, you might consider designing a study plan that emphasizes mathematics. Your plan for the week might appear as follows:

DAY OF THE WEEK	ASSIGNMENT	WHERE TO FIND IT
SATURDAY	Last class day. Formulate your study plan with your instructor.	
SUNDAY	Review coordinate geometry rules and memorize volume formulas.	Math Skills Review
MONDAY	Revisit punctuation rules, especially the use of colons, semicolons, and dashes.	Grammar and Mechanics Skills Review
TUESDAY	Review the Algebra formulas in the Math Express Skills Review.	Math Express Skills Review
WEDNESDAY	Take a Mathematics quiz or practice test.	Step Three or Step Four
THURSDAY	Review Mathematics explanations for Practice Tests III and IV.	Answers and Explanations
FRIDAY	Day off. Relax. Use test anxiety reduction strategies. Get a good night's sleep.	Overcoming Test Anxiety (Step One)
SATURDAY	Test day. Eat a healthy breakfast.	

On the other hand, if you are more comfortable with the mathematics portions of the test, you may want to review both the grammar and reading portions. While you may consider returning to vocabulary that you have already learned, it is probably too late to begin memorizing new word lists. Rather, a focus on concepts is a better use of your time. A plan that emphasizes reading and writing might appear as follows:

DAY OF THE WEEK	ASSIGNMENT	WHERE TO FIND IT
SATURDAY	Last class day. Formulate your study plan with your instructor.	
SUNDAY	Review coordinate geometry rules and memorize volume formulas.	Math Skills Review
MONDAY	Revisit punctuation rules, especially the use of colons, semicolons, and dashes.	Grammar and Mechanics Skills Review
TUESDAY	Review vocabulary and word roots.	Reading Skills Review
WEDNESDAY	Take a Writing quiz or practice test.	Step Three or Step Four
THURSDAY	Review Reading explanations for Practice Tests III and IV.	Answers and Explanations
FRIDAY	Day off. Relax. Use test anxiety reduction strategies. Get a good night's sleep.	Overcoming Test Anxiety (Step One)
SATURDAY	Test day. Eat a healthy breakfast.	

Once you have determined your rubric for study, stick to it without fail. Such discipline will surely reward you on the day of the test. However, do not study too much. An hour or two of studying each day will be more productive than a severe study schedule that leaves you physically and mentally exhausted when the time comes to take the actual exam. Think of this process as training for a sport. While it is necessary to practice every day, it is counterproductive to overexert yourself and to practice too much.

Answers and Explanations

Answers and Explanations:
Step Two

GRAMMAR AND MECHANICS SKILLS REVIEW ANSWER KEY

EXERCISE 1—PARTS OF SPEECH (p. 39)

1. ambulance = noun
   traffic = noun
   it = pronoun
   hurried = verb
   hospital = noun

2. movers = noun
   unloaded = verb
   and = conjunction
   it = pronoun
   in = preposition

3. dark = modifier
   clouds = noun
   blocked = verb
   our = pronoun
   and = conjunction

4. dinner = noun
   cleared = verb
   table = noun
   and = conjunction
   sat = verb

5. room = noun
   was filled = verb
   with = preposition
   authors = noun
   Polish = modifier

6. first = modifier
   shows = noun
   were = verb
   earlier = modifier
   programs = noun

7. waiter = noun
   arrived = verb
   Victor = noun
   ordered = verb
   and = conjunction

8. inspector = noun
   finally = modifier
   approved = verb
   and = conjunction
   allowed = verb

9. notified = verb
   in = preposition
   water = noun
   would be = verb
   hours = noun

10. band = noun
    finished = verb
    crowd = noun
    burst = verb
    loud = modifier

11. telephoned = verb
    her = pronoun
    would be = verb
    their = pronoun
    date = noun

12. cat = noun
    was sleeping = verb
    warmth = noun
    of = preposition
    sun = noun

13. train = noun
    pulled = verb
    called = verb
    name = noun
    and = conjunction

14. we = pronoun
    children = noun
    were = verb
    in = preposition
    rear = noun

15. they = pronoun
    leave = verb
    teach = verb
    hikers = noun
    and = conjunction

16. covered = verb
    steaming = modifier
    melted = modifier
    sticky = modifier
    syrup = noun

17. weekend = noun
    made = verb
    special = modifier
    brilliant = modifier
    beautiful = modifier

18. eventful = modifier
    wrote = verb
    but = conjunction
    his = pronoun
    unopened = modifier

19. barely = modifier
    make out = verb
    bus = noun
    as = conjunction
    it = pronoun

20. offered = verb
    us = pronoun
    or = conjunction
    were = verb
    delicious = modifier

21. C
22. D
23. B
24. A
25. A
26. B
27. C
28. B
29. B
30. A
31. B
32. B
33. C
34. B
35. B
36. C

EXERCISE 2—COMMON GRAMMATICAL ERRORS (p. 53)

1. A
2. D
3. D
4. C
5. C
6. D
7. B
8. B
9. A
10. C
11. C
12. D
13. B
14. B
15. B
16. D
17. A
18. D
19. B
20. B
21. D
22. D
23. D
24. C
25. A

26. The adverb "slowly" is the correct answer choice.

27. The adverb phrase "really well" is the correct answer choice.

28. The adjective "polite" is the correct answer choice.

29. The adverb "well" is the correct answer choice.

30. The adjective "good" is the correct answer choice.

31. The adjective "terrible" is the correct answer choice.

32. The adjective "awful" is the correct answer choice.

33. The adverb "terribly" is the correct answer choice.

34. The adverb "well" is the correct answer choice.

35. The adverb "well" is the correct answer choice.

36. The adverb "hard" is the correct answer choice.

37. The adverb "fast" is the correct answer choice.

38. The adjective "near" is the correct answer choice.

39. The adverb "slowly" is the correct answer choice.

40. The adjective "healthy" is the correct answer choice.

41. The adjective "heavy" is the correct answer choice.

EXERCISE 3—ANALYZING SENTENCE STRUCTURE (p. 64)

1. The plural subject "many people" requires the plural form "receive."
2. The plural subject "books" requires the plural form "were."
3. The plural subject "stores" requires the plural form "offer."
4. The plural subject "bottles" requires the plural form "remain."
5. The singular subject "tourist" requires the singular form "is."
6. The plural subject "several different species" requires the plural form "were."
7. The plural subject "young boys" requires the plural form "were."
8. The plural subject "several barrels" requires the plural form "have."
9. The plural subject "sponsors" requires the plural form "hope."
10. The plural subject "Dawn, Harriet, and Gloria" requires the plural form "are."
11. The singular subject "the mayor" requires the singular form "worries."
12. The plural subject "acts" requires the plural form "have been."
13. The plural subject "rock musicians" requires the plural form "lose."
14. The plural subject "the leaves" requires the plural form "fall."
15. The plural subject "The computer and the printer" requires the plural form "have."
16. The singular subject "Theresa" requires the singular form "was."
17. The singular subject "the film critic" requires the singular form "writes."
18. The plural subject "ingredients" requires the plural form "have."
19. The singular subject "The computer" requires the singular form "was."
20. The singular subject "support" requires the singular form "has."
21. The plural subject "Bill and Jean" requires the plural form "are."

22. The plural subject "several students" requires the plural form "were."

23. The singular pronoun "his or her" is the correct answer choice.

24. The singular pronoun "her" is the correct answer choice.

25. The singular subject "music" requires the singular form "is."

26. The plural pronoun "their" is the correct choice.

27. The subject of this sentence ("Either Mrs. Martinez or Carlos") is a disjunctive subject, so the singular form "goes" is required.

28. "Have" is the correct answer choice.

29. "Could" is the correct answer choice.

30. "Became" is the correct answer choice.

31. D
32. B
33. E
34. B
35. A
36. C
37. D
38. E
39. C
40. D
41. C
42. E
43. A
44. E
45. B
46. E
47. B
48. E
49. A
50. C
51. A
52. E
53. C
54. B
55. D
56. C
57. E
58. C
59. C
60. B
61. A
62. D
63. C
64. D
65. B
66. A
67. A
68. C
69. B
70. C
71. C
72. C
73. D
74. C
75. B
76. D
77. B
78. C
79. C
80. B
81. C

82. "When at school, he studies, goes to the library, and works on the computer."

83. "In order to get eight hours of sleep, the student prefers sleeping in late in the morning to going to bed early in the evening."

84. "I still need to pass Math 252 and English 301 and return two overdue books before I am allowed to graduate."

85. The original is correct.

86. The original is correct.

87. The original is correct.

88. "Our instructor suggested that we study the assignment carefully, go to the library to research the topic extensively, and conduct a survey among 20 subjects."

89. "The increase of attrition among community college students is caused by a lack of family support and a limited income while attending school."

90. "Many non-smokers complained about the health risks associated with second-hand smoke; as a result, smoking is banned in the library and the cafeteria, and smokers have to leave the building to light a cigarette."

91. "After talking to financial aid and seeing your advisor, return to the registrar's office."

92. "Professor Walker helped not only me, but many of my classmates as well."

93. "In his communications class, he can work either in groups or in pairs."

94. "I prefer that other geography class because of the clear explanations and numerous exercises in the textbook, as well as Mrs. Patrick's vivid teaching style."

95. "The question is whether to study tonight or to get up earlier tomorrow morning."

96. "Reasons for the latest tuition increase are the upgraded computers, the new library, and the 6.5% inflation."

EXERCISE 4—PROBLEMS OF LOGICAL EXPRESSION (p. 76)

1. C	5. B	9. C	13. B	17. B	21. C	25. A	29. A
2. B	6. A	10. E	14. C	18. A	22. D	26. D	
3. C	7. B	11. A	15. A	19. C	23. D	27. D	
4. E	8. E	12. B	16. D	20. A	24. B	28. D	

30. "The life of my generation is easier than that of my parents."

31. "My two daughters enjoy different TV shows; the older one watches game shows, while the younger one prefers talk shows."

32. "Her present instructor is the best of all the ones she has had so far."

33. "In the technology lab, I choose the computer with the greatest memory."

34. "According to the counselor, taking these classes in this order is much more beneficial than the other way around."

35. "Our school is unique in many aspects."

36. "The fraternity he joined is better than all other fraternities."

37. The original is correct.

38. The original is correct.

39. "Which of these three sections is best?"

40. "I am spending more time on the assignments in my management class than on those in all my other classes combined."

41. "You will receive your grades no later than tomorrow at 2 p.m."

42. "There is no need for further negotiation."

43. "She is doing so badly in her art class that she could not do any worse."

44. "This exercise seems more difficult than all of the others."

45. "Going to school, he tripped on a crack in the pavement."

46. "Only Mary failed the test; everyone else in her class passed."

47. "Did you see the film on television about the five people on the boat?"

48. "The police officer, in his patrol car, ordered the man to stop."

49. "When you picked up the phone, the noise became muted."

50. "While I was swimming, a fish nibbled on my toe."

51. The original is correct.

52. "Of all his admirers, only his wife loved him."

53. "When we entered the class, the blackboard came into view."

54. "The baby was in a stroller pushed by his mother."

55. "She likes tennis, golf, and swimming."

56. "He could not deliver the supplies because the roads had not yet been plowed."

57. "If you want to succeed, you must be willing to work hard."
"If one wants to succeed, one must be willing to work hard."

58. "Jeff is taller than any other boy in his class."

59. "To get to school, we walked nearly two miles."

60. "The heroine was unbelievably naive."

61. The original is correct.

62. "Leaning out the window, she could see the garden below."

63. "The hotel room that we had reserved was clean and comfortable."

64. "This book is heavier than that one."

EXERCISE 5—IDIOMS AND CLARITY OF EXPRESSION (p. 92)

1. The adjective "principal" is the correct answer choice.
2. The verb "accept" is the correct answer choice.
3. The noun "weather" is the correct answer choice.
4. The preposition "into" is the correct answer choice.
5. The verb "advise" is the correct answer choice.
6. The conjunction "than" is the correct answer choice.
7. The phrase "all ready" is the correct answer choice.
8. The noun "stationery" is the correct answer choice.
9. The noun "effect" is the correct answer choice.
10. The verb "sit" is the correct answer choice.
11. The verb "lie" is the correct answer choice.
12. The adverb "altogether" is the correct answer choice.
13. The past tense verb "passed" is the correct answer choice.
14. The noun "dessert" is the correct answer choice.
15. The verb "lose" is the correct answer choice.
16. The verb "affect" is the correct answer choice.
17. The contraction "you're" is the correct answer choice.
18. "Used" is the correct answer choice.
19. The verb "rise" is the correct answer choice.
20. "Supposed" is the correct answer choice.
21. The possessive pronoun "its" is the correct answer choice.

22. The adjective "conscious" is the correct answer choice.

23. The verb "seem" is the correct answer choice.

24. The plural noun "allusions" is the correct answer choice.

25. The noun "complement" is the correct answer choice.

26. The adjective "later" is the correct answer choice.

27. The noun "build" is the correct answer choice.

28. The past tense verb "knew" is the correct answer choice.

29. The adjective "personal" is the correct answer choice.

30. The noun "course" is the correct answer choice.

31. The adjective "cloth" is the correct answer choice.

32. The verb "elude" is the correct answer choice.

33. The adverb "no" is the correct answer choice.

34. The prefix "ante" is the correct answer choice.

35. The noun "morale" is the correct answer choice.

36. The adjective "capital" is the correct answer choice.

37. The verb "faze" is the correct answer choice.

38. "Excess" is the correct answer choice.

39. The verb "proceed" is the correct answer choice.

40. The noun "forte" is the correct answer choice.

41. The verb "disperse" is the correct answer choice.

42. The adverb "formally" is the correct answer choice.

43. The adjective "averse" is the correct answer choice.

44. The noun "incidence" is the correct answer choice.

45. The adjective "dual" is the correct answer choice.

46. The verb "expend" is the correct answer choice.

47. The noun "discomfort" is the correct answer choice.

48. The noun "idol" is the correct answer choice.

49. The verb "emigrate" is the correct answer choice.

50. The noun "clique" is the correct answer choice.

51. The noun "prophecy" is the correct answer choice.

52. The noun "lightning" is the correct answer choice.

53. The adjective "whatever" is the correct answer choice.

54. The adjective "imminent" is the correct answer choice.

55. The verb "adapt" is the correct answer choice.

56. The noun "epitaphs" is the correct answer choice.

57. The preposition "among" is the correct answer choice.

58. The noun "benefit" is the correct answer choice.

59. The adverb "a lot" is the correct answer choice.

60. The noun "number" is the correct answer choice.

61. The adverb "almost" is the correct answer choice.

62. The adjective "all right" is the correct answer choice.

63. The verb "annoy" is the correct answer choice.

64. The singular noun "alumnus" is the correct answer choice.

65. The adverb "alongside" is the correct answer choice.

66. The conjunction "since" is the correct answer choice.

67. The adjective "eager" is the correct answer choice.

68. The verb "meet" is the correct answer choice.

69. The adverb "awhile" is the correct answer choice.

70. The adverb "about" is the correct answer choice.

71. "Couple of" is the correct answer choice.

72. "You and me" is the correct answer choice.

73. The adjective "continuous" is the correct answer choice.

74. "Seems unable" is the correct answer choice.

75. The verb "assume" is the correct answer choice.

76. The adjective "uninterested" is the correct answer choice.

77. "Just as" is the correct answer choice.

78. The conjunction "that" is the correct answer choice.

79. The pronoun "one another" is the correct answer choice.

80. The conjunction "whether" is the correct answer choice.

81. The plural noun "human beings" is the correct answer choice.

82. The verb "finalize" is the correct answer choice.

83. The past tense verb "flouted" is the correct answer choice.

84. The adjective "healthful" is the correct answer choice.

85. The noun "slander" is the correct answer choice.

86. "Regard" is the correct answer choice.

87. The adverb "regardless" is the correct answer choice.

88. The verb "lend" is the correct answer choice.

89. The singular verb "is" is the correct answer choice.

90. The preposition "off" is the correct answer choice.

91. The verb "stop" is the correct answer choice.

92. The conjunction "that" is the correct answer choice.

93. The verb "manage" is the correct answer choice.

94. The singular pronoun "his or her" is the correct answer choice.

95. "Any other" is the correct answer choice.

96. The conjunction "but" is the correct answer choice.

97. "Try to" is the correct answer choice.

98. "Whoever" is the correct answer choice.

99. The preposition "for" is the correct answer choice.

100. C	104. B	108. C	112. B	116. D	120. C	124. D	128. C
101. A	105. C	109. A	113. C	117. B	121. D	125. D	129. C
102. B	106. A	110. B	114. A	118. B	122. D	126. D	
103. B	107. C	111. A	115. B	119. A	123. C	127. C	

EXERCISE 6—PUNCTUATION (p. 108)

1. He was not aware that you had lost your passport.

2. Did you report the loss to the proper authorities?

3. I suppose you had to fill out many forms.

4. What a nuisance!

5. I hate doing so much paper work!

6. Did you ever discover where the wallet was?

7. I imagine you wondered how it was misplaced.

8. Good for you!

9. At least you now have your passport.

10. What will you do if it happens again?

11. I don't know if they are coming, though I sent them an invitation weeks ago.

12. Neurology is the science that deals with the anatomy, physiology, and pathology of the nervous system.

13. Nursery lore, like everything human, has been subject to many changes over long periods of time.
 Nursery lore—like everything human—has been subject to many changes over long periods of time.

14. Bob read Joyce's Ulysses to the class; everyone seemed to enjoy the reading.

15. In order to provide more living space, we converted an attached garage into a den.

16. Because he is such an industrious student, he has many friends.

17. I don't recall who wrote *A Midsummer Night's Dream*.

18. In the writing class, students learned about coordinating conjunctions—and, but, so, or, yet, for, and nor.

19. "Those who do not complain are never pitied" is a familiar quotation by Jane Austen.

20. Howard and his ex-wife are on amicable terms.

21. Her last words were, "call me on Sunday," and she jumped on the train.

22. He is an out-of-work carpenter.

23. This is what is called a "pregnant chad."

24. "Come early on Monday," the teacher said, "to take the exit exam."

25. The dog, man's best friend, is a companion to many.
 The dog—man's best friend—is a companion to many.

26. The winner of the horse race is, to the best of my knowledge, Silver.
 The winner of the horse race is—to the best of my knowledge—Silver.

27. Every time I see him, the dentist asks me how often I floss.

28. The officer was off-duty when he witnessed the crime.

29. *Anna Karenina* is my favorite movie.

30. Red, white, and blue are the colors of the American flag.

31. Stop using "stuff" in your essays; it's too informal.

32. She was a self-made millionaire.

33. The Smiths, who are the best neighbors anyone could ask for, have moved out.
 The Smiths—who are the best neighbors anyone could ask for—have moved out.

34. My eighteen-year-old daughter will graduate this spring.

35. Dracula lived in Transylvania.

36. The students were told to put away their books.

37. Begun while Dickens was still at work on *Pickwick Papers*, *Oliver Twist* was published in 1837 and is now one of the author's most widely read works.

38. Given the great difficulties of making soundings in very deep water, it is not surprising that few such soundings were made until the middle of this century.

39. Did you finish writing your thesis prospectus on time?

40. The root of modern Dutch was once supposed to be Old Frisian, but the general view now is that the characteristic forms of Dutch are at least as old as those of Old Frisian.

41. Moose, once scarce because of indiscriminate hunting, are protected by law, and the number of moose is once again increasing.

    Moose—once scarce because of indiscriminate hunting—are protected by law, and the number of moose is once again increasing.

42. He ordered a set of books, several records, and a film almost a month ago.

43. Perhaps the most interesting section of New Orleans is the French Quarter, which extends from North Rampart Street to the Mississippi River.

44. Writing for a skeptical and rationalizing age, Shaftesbury was primarily concerned with showing that goodness and beauty are not determined by revelation, authority, opinion, or fashion.

45. We tried our best to purchase the books, but we were completely unsuccessful even though we went to every bookstore in town.

46. A great deal of information regarding the nutritional requirements of farm animals has been accumulated over countless generations by trial and error; however, most recent advances have come as the result of systematic studies at schools of animal husbandry.

47. *Omoo*, Melville's sequel to *Typee*, appeared in 1847 and went through five printings in that year alone.

    Omoo—Melville's sequel to *Typee*—appeared in 1847 and went through five printings in that year alone.

48. "Go to Florence for the best gelato in all of Italy," said the old man to the young tourist.

49. Although the first school for African Americans was a public school established in Virginia in 1620, most educational opportunities for African Americans before the Civil War were provided by private agencies.

50. As the climate of Europe changed, the population became too dense for the supply of food obtained by hunting, and other means of securing food, such as the domestication of animals, were necessary.

    As the climate of Europe changed, the population became too dense for the supply of food obtained by hunting, and other means of securing food—such as the domestication of animals—were necessary.

51. In Faulkner's poetic realism, the grotesque is somber, violent, and often inexplicable; in Caldwell's writing, it is lightened by a ballad-like, humorous, sophisticated detachment.

52. The valley of the Loire, a northern tributary of the Loire at Angers, abounds in rock villages; they occur in many other places in France, Spain, and northern Italy.

    The valley of the Loire—a northern tributary of the Loire at Angers—abounds in rock villages; they occur in many other places in France, Spain, and northern Italy.

53. The telephone rang several times; as a result, his sleep was interrupted.

54. He has forty-three thousand dollars to spend; however, once that is gone, he will be penniless.

55. Before an examination, do the following: review your work, get a good night's sleep, eat a balanced breakfast, and arrive on time to take the test.

EXERCISE 7—CAPITALIZATION AND SPELLING (p. 114)

1. You should capitalize "Thanksgiving."
2. You should not capitalize "flower."
3. You should not capitalize "airplane."
4. You should capitalize "Ohio."
5. You should capitalize "France."
6. You should capitalize "Muhammad Ali."
7. You should not capitalize "magician."
8. You should not capitalize "tin can."
9. You should capitalize "Rocky Mountains."
10. You should capitalize "Governor Davis."
11. You should not capitalize "pine tree."
12. You should not capitalize "overcoat."
13 You should not capitalize "television."
14. You should capitalize "Michael Jordan."
15. You should not capitalize "arsonist."
16. You should not capitalize "uncle."
17. You should not capitalize "token."
18. You should not capitalize "hamburger."
19. You should capitalize "Halloween."
20. You should not capitalize "morning."
21. You should capitalize "Central Park."
22. You should not capitalize "ten o'clock."
23. You should capitalize "January."
24. You should not capitalize "afternoon."
25. You should capitalize "Monday."
26. The correct spelling is "field."
27. The correct spelling is "conceit."
28. The correct spelling is "sleigh."
29. The correct spelling is "vein."
30. The correct spelling is "ceiling."

31. The correct spelling is "niece."

32. The correct spelling is "scientific."

33. The correct spelling is "seizure."

34. The correct spelling is "conscientious."

35. The correct spelling is "ancient."

36. The correct spelling is "fibbing."

37. The correct spelling is "begging."

38. The correct spelling is "controllable."

39. The correct spelling is "commitment."

40. The correct spelling is "colorful."

41. The correct spelling is "stopping."

42. The correct spelling is "biggest."

43. The correct spelling is "quitting."

44. The correct spelling is "robbing."

45. The correct spelling is "gladly."

46. The correct spelling is "bridal."

47. The correct spelling is "forcible."

48. The correct spelling is "forceful."

49. The correct spelling is "imaginary."

50. The correct spelling is "hopeless."

51. The correct spelling is "truly."

52 The correct spelling is "removing."

53. The correct spelling is "lifelike."

54. The correct spelling is "likely."

55. The correct spelling is "serviceable."

56. The misspelled word is "consceince." "Conscience" is the correct spelling.

57. The misspelled word is "aviater." The correct spelling is "aviator."

58. The misspelled word is "alltogether." The correct spelling is "altogether."

59. The misspelled word is "desireable." The correct spelling is "desirable."

60. The misspelled word is "independance." The correct spelling is "independence."

61. The misspelled word is "billian." The correct spelling is "billion."

62. The misspelled word is "naturaly." The correct spelling is "naturally."

63. The misspelled word is "speach." The correct spelling is "speech."

64. The misspelled word is "transfered." The correct spelling is "transferred."

65. The misspelled word is "reciept." The correct spelling is "receipt."

66. The misspelled word is "calender." The correct spelling is "calendar."

67. The misspelled word is "affidavid." The correct spelling is "affidavit."

68. The misspelled word is "diptheria." The correct spelling is "diphtheria."

69. The misspelled word is "prevelent." The correct spelling is "prevalent."

70. The misspelled word is "bookeeper." The correct spelling is "bookkeeper."

71. The misspelled word is "repetetious." The correct spelling is "repetitious."

72. The misspelled word is "donkies." The correct spelling is "donkeys."

73. The misspelled word is "wirey." The correct spelling is "wiry."

74. The misspelled word is "propagander." The correct spelling is "propaganda."

75. The misspelled word is "specificaly." The correct spelling is "specifically."

76. The misspelled word is "innoculate." The correct spelling is "inoculate."

77. The misspelled word is "amethist." The correct spelling is "amethyst."

78. The misspelled word is "laringytis." The correct spelling is "laryngitis."

79. The misspelled word is "cinamon." The correct spelling is "cinnamon."

80. The misspelled word is "resind." The correct spelling is "rescind."

81. The misspelled word is "irresistably." The correct spelling is "irresistibly."

82. The misspelled word is "brocoli." The correct spelling is "broccoli."

83. The misspelled word is "mayonaise." The correct spelling is "mayonnaise."

84. The misspelled word is "jeoperdy." The correct spelling is "jeopardy."

85. The misspelled word is "mocassin." The correct spelling is "moccasin."

MATH SKILLS REVIEW ANSWER KEY

EXERCISE 1—WHOLE NUMBERS (p. 129)

1. B	9. E	17. C	25. A	33. C	41. A	49. A	57. C
2. B	10. B	18. B	26. D	34. E	42. C	50. B	58. C
3. B	11. C	19. B	27. B	35. B	43. C	51. B	59. D
4. C	12. D	20. C	28. B	36. A	44. A	52. A	60. C
5. C	13. D	21. C	29. A	37. D	45. E	53. C	61. A
6. D	14. C	22. C	30. D	38. B	46. A	54. C	62. D
7. C	15. D	23. E	31. D	39. D	47. B	55. C	63. A
8. E	16. C	24. A	32. C	40. B	48. A	56. E	64. E

EXERCISE 2—FRACTIONS (p. 138)

1. E	10. C	19. B	28. A	37. C	46. C	55. E	64. E
2. D	11. B	20. E	29. B	38. B	47. B	56. C	65. D
3. B	12. C	21. B	30. C	39. B	48. A	57. E	66. A
4. C	13. B	22. B	31. D	40. A	49. A	58. A	67. C
5. C	14. E	23. D	32. B	41. B	50. A	59. D	68. D
6. D	15. E	24. B	33. D	42. A	51. D	60. D	69. D
7. A	16. A	25. C	34. A	43. A	52. C	61. E	70. C
8. C	17. C	26. C	35. A	44. B	53. A	62. A	71. C
9. E	18. C	27. E	36. C	45. A	54. A	63. B	

EXERCISE 3—SIGNED NUMBERS (p. 146)

1. E	9. D	17. C	25. A	33. E	41. C	49. B	57. B
2. D	10. D	18. C	26. D	34. D	42. A	50. A	58. D
3. D	11. E	19. A	27. D	35. A	43. C	51. A	59. B
4. A	12. E	20. B	28. B	36. D	44. B	52. C	60. E
5. B	13. D	21. A	29. C	37. D	45. D	53. A	
6. A	14. C	22. B	30. E	38. B	46. B	54. A	
7. C	15. D	23. D	31. A	39. B	47. D	55. C	
8. A	16. C	24. A	32. A	40. C	48. C	56. E	

EXERCISE 4—DECIMALS (p. 155)

1. C	10. A	19. B	28. A	37. D	46. D	55. A	64. B
2. C	11. B	20. A	29. B	38. A	47. B	56. C	65. C
3. B	12. B	21. C	30. D	39. B	48. B	57. C	66. C
4. B	13. B	22. E	31. E	40. B	49. B	58. B	67. A
5. B	14. C	23. A	32. C	41. A	50. C	59. D	68. D
6. E	15. A	24. A	33. A	42. A	51. A	60. B	
7. B	16. B	25. C	34. A	43. B	52. C	61. D	
8. A	17. B	26. B	35. E	44. B	53. E	62. C	
9. E	18. D	27. D	36. D	45. A	54. B	63. C	

EXERCISE 5—PERCENTS (p. 163)

1. E
2. A
3. B
4. B
5. C
6. A
7. C
8. B
9. A
10. A
11. B
12. B
13. A
14. A
15. A
16. C
17. B
18. D
19. C
20. C
21. C
22. D
23. E
24. D
25. D
26. B
27. C
28. A
29. C
30. A
31. B
32. E
33. D
34. B
35. D
36. C
37. D
38. B
39. A
40. A
41. D
42. A
43. E
44. A
45. B
46. D
47. A
48. B
49. A
50. A
51. C
52. C
53. B
54. B
55. B
56. B
57. C
58. B
59. C
60. D
61. D
62. C
63. B
64. B
65. B
66. B
67. E
68. C
69. D
70. B
71. B
72. D
73. C
74. C
75. D
76. D
77. D
78. C
79. C
80. C
81. D
82. C
83. C
84. C
85. A
86. D
87. D
88. C
89. D
90. E
91. C
92. D
93. E
94. A
95. B
96. C
97. E
98. D
99. A
100. D
101. D
102. C
103. B
104. A
105. C
106. C
107. E
108. C
109. E
110. D
111. D
112. E
113. D
114. B
115. D
116. E
117. C
118. E
119. A
120. C
121. D
122. D
123. C
124. B
125. B
126. D
127. A
128. A

EXERCISE 6—MEAN, MEDIAN, AND MODE (p. 172)

1. A
2. D
3. C
4. B
5. C
6. E
7. A
8. C
9. E
10. A
11. E
12. B
13. B
14. A
15. C
16. D
17. E
18. A
19. D
20. D
21. D
22. E
23. E
24. B
25. B
26. C
27. B
28. E
29. B
30. B
31. C
32. D
33. D
34. A
35. C
36. C
37. D
38. B
39. D
40. A
41. B
42. B
43. E
44. D
45. B
46. C

EXERCISE 7—RATIOS AND PROPORTIONS (p. 178)

1. B
2. A
3. D
4. C
5. A
6. A
7. D
8. B
9. B
10. D
11. D
12. C
13. B
14. C
15. D
16. D
17. E
18. D
19. D
20. E
21. C
22. B
23. C
24. C
25. B
26. C
27. D
28. B
29. E
30. C
31. D
32. C
33. B
34. A
35. D
36. C
37. B
38. B
39. C
40. A
41. D
42. B
43. C
44. B
45. D
46. B
47. A
48. C
49. B
50. E

EXERCISE 8—EXPONENTS AND RADICALS (p. 189)

1. E
2. D
3. E
4. B
5. C
6. E
7. C
8. A
9. A
10. A
11. B
12. C
13. C
14. B
15. B
16. C
17. E
18. D
19. C
20. C
21. C
22. A
23. E
24. A
25. D
26. A
27. C
28. B
29. C
30. C
31. A
32. A
33. D
34. B
35. B
36. C
37. D
38. B
39. C
40. E
41. D
42. B
43. D
44. A
45. B
46. A
47. D
48. C
49. B
50. A
51. D
52. E

EXERCISE 9—ALGEBRAIC OPERATIONS (p. 200)

1. A	17. D	33. C	49. A	65. D	81. D	97. B	113. D
2. E	18. D	34. D	50. D	66. B	82. D	98. C	114. C
3. C	19. B	35. A	51. D	67. B	83. C	99. C	115. B
4. C	20. C	36. E	52. A	68. A	84. D	100. A	116. E
5. E	21. C	37. E	53. D	69. B	85. B	101. E	117. D
6. B	22. B	38. E	54. D	70. C	86. A	102. C	118. A
7. A	23. A	39. C	55. E	71. B	87. C	103. E	119. E
8. E	24. C	40. D	56. B	72. B	88. B	104. C	120. A
9. B	25. B	41. B	57. D	73. A	89. C	105. A	121. D
10. B	26. C	42. B	58. C	74. A	90. D	106. C	
11. C	27. C	43. C	59. A	75. A	91. A	107. A	
12. C	28. C	44. D	60. D	76. C	92. E	108. D	
13. E	29. C	45. D	61. A	77. E	93. D	109. B	
14. A	30. C	46. E	62. D	78. D	94. B	110 B	
15. E	31. B	47. E	63. A	79. A	95. D	111. A	
16. D	32. A	48. C	64. D	80. C	96. A	112. E	

EXERCISE 10—ALGEBRAIC EQUATIONS AND INEQUALITIES (p. 215)

1. C	16. D	31. D	46. A	61. E	76. C	91. E	106. B
2. C	17. C	32. D	47. C	62. B	77. C	92. B	107. A
3. C	18. A	33. D	48. A	63. A	78. D	93. E	108. A
4. B	19. B	34. C	49. D	64. C	79. B	94. B	109. C
5. E	20. C	35. C	50. D	65. D	80. A	95. D	110. C
6. E	21. B	36. B	51. D	66. C	81. A	96. D	111. D
7. D	22. B	37. D	52. E	67. E	82. E	97. D	112. B
8. B	23. A	38. A	53. C	68. C	83. C	98. E	113. E
9. D	24. C	39. C	54. B	69. A	84. A	99. C	114. B
10. C	25. B	40. E	55. A	70. D	85. D	100. D	
11. A	26. A	41. A	56. C	71. E	86. E	101. E	
12. D	27. E	42. C	57. D	72. D	87. D	102. A	
13. D	28. C	43. E	58. E	73. A	88. A	103. B	
14. E	29. B	44. B	59. C	74. B	89. A	104. D	
15. E	30. B	45. B	60. D	75. B	90. D	105. E	

EXERCISE 11—GEOMETRY (p. 234)

1. C	14. C	27. B	40. D	53. B	66. B	79. B	92. C
2. D	15. A	28. A	41. D	54. A	67. A	80. B	93. D
3. C	16. A	29. D	42. B	55. D	68. E	81. D	94. B
4. B	17. C	30. E	43. D	56. A	69. D	82. C	95. C
5. E	18. E	31. B	44. D	57. A	70. C	83. D	96. C
6. A	19. E	32. B	45. E	58. E	71. B	84. A	97. B
7. E	20. C	33. C	46. E	59. B	72. B	85. B	98. C
8. D	21. A	34. C	47. C	60. C	73. E	86. C	99. A
9. B	22. C	35. B	48. C	61. E	74. A	87. E	100. C
10. A	23. C	36. A	49. D	62. C	75. B	88. D	101. C
11. B	24. E	37. D	50. D	63. B	76. A	89. A	102. C
12. B	25. D	38. C	51. B	64. A	77. A	90. C	103. B
13. A	26. B	39. B	52. C	65. D	78. A	91. D	104. C

105. D	111. A	117. E	123. D	129. A	135. C	141. D	147. D
106. E	112. B	118. E	124. C	130. C	136. B	142. C	148. C
107. C	113. D	119. A	125. B	131. C	137. C	143. E	149. D
108. D	114. B	120. C	126. A	132. D	138. C	144. C	150. E
109. A	115. E	121. C	127. D	133. B	139. C	145. E	151. C
110. B	116. E	122. C	128. C	134. C	140. A	146. A	

EXERCISE 12—FUNCTIONS, GRAPHS, AND COORDINATE GEOMETRY (p. 259)

1. D	9. E	17. A	25. C	33. D	41. C	49. A	57. E
2. C	10. B	18. E	26. A	34. C	42. D	50. C	58. A
3. B	11. A	19. B	27. A	35. B	43. D	51. D	59. B
4. E	12. A	20. C	28. E	36. B	44. C	52. E	60. B
5. B	13. C	21. C	29. C	37. D	45. C	53. C	61. D
6. B	14. A	22. B	30. E	38. A	46. B	54. D	
7. A	15. D	23. B	31. B	39. C	47. A	55. A	
8. D	16. A	24. A	32. E	40. E	48. D	56. B	

EXERCISE 13—SOLVING STORY PROBLEMS (p. 273)

1. A	8. B	15. B	22. D	29. C	36. A	43. B	50. C
2. C	9. B	16. B	23. B	30. D	37. D	44. C	51. C
3. A	10. D	17. C	24. E	31. C	38. D	45. C	52. B
4. C	11. C	18. A	25. A	32. C	39. B	46. D	53. D
5. B	12. B	19. A	26. B	33. B	40. E	47. D	54. E
6. E	13. D	20. E	27. B	34. B	41. C	48. D	
7. D	14. C	21. B	28. E	35. D	42. B	49. C	

READING SKILLS REVIEW ANSWER KEY

EXERCISE 1—CAREFUL READING OF ENGLISH ITEM STEMS (p. 306)

1. A	4. F	7. C	10. H	13. B	16. J	19. C
2. H	5. D	8. F	11. B	14. H	17. C	
3. B	6. J	9. C	12. G	15. B	18. F	

EXERCISE 2—CAREFUL READING OF MATHEMATICS ITEM STEMS (p. 309)

1. D	4. J	7. C	10. J	13. D	16. J	19. B
2. F	5. C	8. G	11. A	14. H	17. B	20. G
3. C	6. H	9. C	12. H	15. C	18. J	

EXERCISE 3—CAREFUL READING OF READING ITEM STEMS (p. 312)

1. A	5. C	9. B	13. B	17. C	21. B	25. A
2. J	6. F	10. J	14. F	18. J	22. H	26. J
3. C	7. B	11. B	15. C	19. A	23. D	27. B
4. J	8. H	12. J	16. J	20. J	24. F	

EXERCISE 4—CAREFUL READING OF SCIENCE REASONING ITEM STEMS (p. 315)

1. A	3. A	5. D	7. A	9. B	11. C	13. C	15. C
2. J	4. G	6. J	8. J	10. G	12. J	14. G	16. J

EXERCISE 5—CODING OF ITEM STEMS (p. 320)

1. SP	7. GT	13. E	19. E	25. E	31. E	37. SP	43. E
2. E	8. SP	14. SP	20. E	26. SP	32. SP	38. SP	
3. SP	9. E	15. SP	21. E	27. SP	33. E	39. SP	
4. SP	10. SP	16. E	22. SP	28. SP	34. GT	40. E	
5. SP	11. SP	17. SP	23. SP	29. SP	35. E	41. SP	
6. GT	12. E	18. E	24. E	30. E	36. SP	42. SP	

EXERCISE 6—VOCABULARY: PASSAGES (p. 342)

1. D	3. D	5. B	7. D	9. B
2. H	4. G	6. G	8. G	10. J

EXERCISE 7—VOCABULARY: CONTEXT CLUES (p. 344)

1. C	3. D	5. A	7. C	9. D	11. A
2. G	4. J	6. G	8. J	10. H	12. G

13. exceed, surpass

14. climax, high point, zenith

15. boring, dull, uninspiring

16. serious, severe, large-scale

17. complete, comprehensive

18. complete, total, authoritarian

19. hides, camouflages, conceals

20. wanted, infamous, notorious

21. dazed, confused, disoriented

22. generate, spark, increase

23. The survivors had been drifting for days in the lifeboat, and in their weakness, they appeared to be _____ rather than living beings.

    The blank must be filled with a word that means the opposite of something that is alive. "Dead," "spirits," and "ghosts" are possible completions. Notice that the missing word can either be an adjective (*e.g.*, "dead"), modifying the noun "beings," or a noun (*e.g.*, "spirits"), paralleling the phrase "living beings."

24. The guillotine was introduced during the French Revolution as a(n) _____, an alternative to other less humane means of execution.

    The blank must be filled with a noun that extends the idea of something that is an "alternative to" a "less humane" practice. "Reform" and "improvement" are possible completions.

25. Because of the _____ nature of the chemical, it cannot be used near an open flame.

    The blank must be filled with an adjective that extends the idea of a chemical that "cannot be used near an open flame." "Flammable," which means "easily capable of burning," is one obvious completion.

26. The Mayor's proposal for a new subway line, although a(n) _____, is not a final solution to the city's transportation needs.

    The blank must be filled with a noun that both extends the idea of something that is "new" and reverses the idea of something that is "final." "Start" and "beginning" are possible completions.

27. In a pluralistic society, policies are the result of compromise, so political leaders must be _____ and must accommodate the views of others.

    The blank must be filled with an adjective that extends the idea of a "compromise" and parallels the idea of accommodation. "Tolerant" and "understanding" are possible completions.

28. The committee report vigorously expounded the bill's strengths but also acknowledged its _____.

    The blank must be filled with a plural noun that means the opposite of "strengths." "Weaknesses" and "shortcomings" are possible completions.

29. Because there is always the danger of a power failure and disruption of elevator service, high-rise buildings, while suitable for younger persons are not recommended for _____.

The sentence suggests that high-rise buildings are suitable for "younger persons" but not for a different group of people. So, the blank must be filled with a word or phrase that means the opposite of "younger persons." "The elderly" and "senior citizens" are possible completions.

30. For a child to be happy, his day must be very structured; when his routine is _____, he becomes nervous and irritable.

The "if-then" logical structure of the sentence indicates that if the child is to be happy, his day must be structured. However, the word clue, nervous and irritable, after the semicolon suggests that the parallel structure in the second clause of the sentence must be the reverse of the first. If "structured" activity makes a child "happy," then unstructured activity would make a child "nervous and irritable." So, the blank must be filled with a verb that suggests the idea of unstructured activity. "Disrupted" and "interrupted" are possible completions.

31. The current spirit of _____ among different religions has led to a number of meetings that their leaders hope will lead to better understanding.

The blank must be filled with a noun that satisfies the following construction: The spirit of _____ has led to understanding. "Cooperation" and "accord" are possible completions.

32. Our modern industrialized societies have been responsible for the greatest destruction of nature and life; indeed, it seems that more civilization results in greater _____. (annihilation, death)

The blank must be filled with a noun that extends the idea of the "destruction of nature and life," thereby satisfying the following construction: If "modern industrialized societies" are "responsible for" the "destruction of nature and life," then "more civilization" "results in greater" _____. "Annihilation" and "death" are possible completions.

SCIENCE SKILLS REVIEW ANSWER KEY

EXERCISE 1—BASICS OF EXPERIMENTAL DESIGN (p. 357)

1. The purpose of the experiment is to determine the effect of temperature on the heart rate of frogs.
2. The independent variable is temperature. (The experimenter determined the temperature before the experiment started.)
3. The dependent variable is heart rate.
4. When the temperature is increased, then the heart rate of the frogs will decrease.
5. The controlled variables are size, type, age, and number of frogs, as well as container size and amount of light.
6. The control group is Group C. (Group C refers to the frogs in the container that is approximately the same temperature as the enclosure from which the frogs were removed).
7. The experimental groups are Groups A, B, and D.

EXERCISE 2—DATA ORGANIZATION IN CONTROLLED EXPERIMENTS (p. 363)

1. The independent variable is the amount of time (in hours) over which the experiment was conducted.
2. The dependent variable is the percentage of carbohydrate digested.
3. The independent variable is on the horizontal axis.
4. The dependent variable is on the vertical axis.
5. The slope of the line indicates that generally as the amount of time increases, the percentage of carbohydrates digested increases.
6. The correct answer is (C).
7. The independent variable is the source of salt.
8. The dependent variable is the percentage of salt.
9. The mammal with a percentage of salt in its urine closest to the percentage of salt in seawater is the human.

EXERCISE 3—PRESENTATION OF CONFLICTING VIEWPOINTS (p. 366)

1. The dependent variable (the problem) is the discovery of a dead woman.
2. The conflicting viewpoint is whether the death was a homicide or a suicide.
3. The independent variable causing the conflict is the lack of evidence indicating who shot the gun.

4.

Data	More Consistent with Detective I	More Consistent with Detective II	Equally Consistent with Both Detectives I and II
Gun Owned by Woman		✓	
Bloody Pillow			✓
Bruise on Head	✓		
Firecracker-Like Noise			✓
No Forced Entry			✓
Locked Door		✓	
No Suicide Note	✓		
Divorced Victim	✓		
Despondent Victim		✓	

EXERCISE 4—SCIENCE REASONING PASSAGES (p. 367)

1. C	4. G	7. A	10. H	13. C	16. F	19. C	22. H
2. G	5. A	8. J	11. C	14. H	17. A	20. G	23. D
3. D	6. J	9. A	12. F	15. B	18. J	21. B	24. F

WRITING SKILLS REVIEW

EXERCISE 1—SAMPLE ESSAY 1 (p. 386)

Sample Response 1—Below Average Response

In my opinion, students should not get to evaluate teachers because it wouldn't mean anything and it would just be a chance for some students to dump on teachers they don't like.

Teachers give students grades for a reason. Teachers know more than the students do because they've been to college. So when a teacher gives a test, that teacher knows the right answer and can mark the papers accordingly. This system makes sense. Students have not been to college. They don't have experience teaching classes. Most, if not all, students couldn't make up an exam to test a teacher's ability to teach. They wouldn't know which questions to ask on the exam and wouldn't know what the right answers are. So students really don't know how to grade a teacher on ability to teach.

Also, some, maybe even many, students would use the evaluation to take pot shots at teachers they don't like or have a grudge about. This would be specially dangerous if students got together to say the same thing. If only one student says a teacher is rude, then no one might care. If half the class says a teacher is rude, the principal would figure where theres' smoke theres' fire.

The evaluations could also be unfair to hard teachers. No students like to have a lot of homework, but homework is important. It's a given fact that some teachers give more homework that others. So would students give low marks to the teachers who gave the most homework? That seems like it might happen.

Even if there were an evaluation form with categories, this would still be a problem. Everyone could agree to mark low on "Preparedness" and "Ability to Communicate." That way, there wouldn't be any question asked about retribution. The students would be using the form.

Student evaluations of teachers is not a good idea. The whole thing won't help and it could really hurt some good teachers.

Position on issue:

The writer conveys the position in the first sentence. Although the position is clearly stated, the prose used is not an effective manner in which to start the essay.

Topic Development and Essay Organization:

This essay is pretty rough, but it does contain some relevant ideas. The writer explains that the evaluations would have limited utility and further that the system could be abused. The second point is developed in greater detail than the first. The writer argues that students might conspire against an unpopular teacher and that the evaluations might be used to retaliate against taskmasters. The final point in this development—that the evaluation form itself might mask this phenomenon—is particularly interesting.

The essay lacks coherent structure. The writer fails to outline her ideas in the introductory paragraphs and does not use helpful transitional phrases.

Language usage, sentence structure, and punctuation:

The essay suffers from informal language and glaring grammar errors.

Summary and conclusions:

The prose is not polished. Nonetheless it is an honest effort and addresses the topic. This essay would likely be a "3." Some readers might not score it quite that high, and it would be surprising if it were given a "4."

Sample Response 2—Above Average Response

Parents, educators, and government leaders are increasingly concerned about the quality of education in our schools. Recently, the government instituted a policy of comprehensive testing to ensure that all students are getting a quality education and that no child is left behind. The theory is that these tests show what students have learned. If the students in a particular school don't score high enough, then that school is deemed to be failing its students. At that point, special programs are made available to provide additional instruction and tutoring to the school's students. The additional opportunities are supposed to help students learn and then perform better on the tests.

If you think about the structure of education, you'll see that it involves teachers and students in a school setting. Teachers have always evaluated students. Periodically, teachers give us tests, and we get report cards to tell our parents how we are doing in school. The new government testing is designed to find out whether schools are doing a good job. But in all of this, no one is testing the teachers. I think that if everyone is serious about improving the quality of education, then it would be a good idea to have students give their teachers report cards.

From a school improvement standpoint, teacher evaluations would help administrators learn which teachers are doing a good job and which teachers are not. When a student performs poorly in math, everyone assumes that it is the student who is at fault. And with the new testing program, if the average math score is low, then it must be the school that is failing. But it might also be the case that a single bad teacher is the real cause. A teacher who can't make math concepts clear to students could easily have an entire class with students getting poor marks on their report cards. Parents will lecture their children but never realize that the whole class has the same problem. The school may get blamed for not providing a quality education, but maybe there are other classes in the school that don't have this problem. In other words, student evaluations could be a valuable tool for identifying the real problem.

Another advantage of student evaluations would be improving the quality of teaching. Let's say, for example, that a particular teacher speaks softly and is hard to hear. Students might not want to say anything about the teacher. If only one or two students complain, they may be considered trouble-makers. But if the entire class fills out an evaluation form and under "Ability to Communicate" says "The teacher is hard to hear," then the problem can be addressed. Administrators could meet with the teacher and go over the evaluations. They could suggest to the teacher to speak up more clearly.

The objection that students might retaliate personally is really just a red herring. Students are already permitted to vote for the "Outstanding Teacher" award (or similar awards) given by most schools. Additionally, it would be obvious from the tone of the evaluations if teacher had been unfairly criticized. Statements like "A rotten teacher" or "Can't really help us" wouldn't carry much weight. Statements like "Speaks too softly" or "Doesn't answer questions about hard questions" are useful. Finally, a structured evaluation would make it less likely that students would comment on irrelevant factors like a teacher's personal habits.

If you listen to the debate about education, you can't help but notice that the issues are complicated. A quality education is not a simple matter. You need the right setting, the proper tools, motivated students, effective teachers, and good administration. It's like a complex recipe that calls for good ingredients mixed up in the right proportions and cooked at the right temperature for the correct length of time. Student evaluations of teachers is not going to solve all of the education world's problems. But student evaluations could be an important part of a successful recipe.

Position on issue:

The writer clearly states the position at the end of the second paragraph.

Topic Development and Essay Organization:

Although the structure of the essay isn't articulated in outline form (such as "Point 1; Point 2; etc.), the structure is evident. The writer uses transitional phrases such as "another advantage" and paragraphing to help the reader follow the train of thought. And the writer develops the points within each paragraph. In the next-to-the-last paragraph, for example, the writer offers three reasons for believing that the danger of personal retaliation is not very significant.

Language usage, sentence structure, and punctuation:

The essay might be subjected to two related criticism. One, the examples sometimes seem to be a little abstract. The example of "math scores" never really gets very specific, though it is a bit hard to say exactly how the writer could improve on what is written.

Additionally, the prose, while effective, seems a little dry. It lacks zip. Even the recipe analogy in the last paragraph seems a bit flat. Maybe the writer could have mentioned a specific dish, say Gumbo, in which a lot of ingredients have to be mixed together to get the desired result. Even that little flair would have lightened up the writing style.

Summary and conclusions:

This is a very strong response. It would surely get at least a "5" and more likely a "6" from most readers.

Answers and Explanations:
Step Three

ENGLISH

ENGLISH—CORE LESSON (p. 395)

1. A
2. B
3. B
4. C
5. D
6. B
7. C
8. C
9. B
10. A
11. A
12. E
13. E
14. A
15. D
16. B
17. D
18. C
19. C
20. D
21. C
22. A
23. E
24. C
25. E
26. D
27. A
28. B
29. A
30. D
31. B
32. D
33. A
34. D
35. B
36. D
37. D
38. D
39. B
40. B
41. C
42. D
43. B
44. A
45. B
46. B
47. A
48. E
49. D
50. C
51. C
52. C
53. D
54. C
55. A
56. A
57. D
58. A
59. A
60. B
61. A
62. C
63. B
64. C
65. C
66. B
67. E
68. B
69. C
70. B
71. B
72. D
73. C
74. A
75. C
76. C
77. E
78. B
79. C
80. B
81. E
82. E
83. E
84. A
85. E
86. B
87. C
88. A
89. C
90. B
91. C
92. E
93. E
94. B
95. C
96. D
97. E
98. A
99. A
100. B
101. D
102. C
103. B
104. B
105. D
106. B
107. E
108. E
109. -
110. D
111. D
112. D
113. B
114. B
115. A
116. C
117. B
118. E
119. D
120. B
121. D
122. B
123. A
124. B
125. F
126. D
127. H
128. A
129. F
130. B
131. J
132. D
133. H

ENGLISH—CHALLENGE ITEMS (p. 415)

1. A
2. J
3. B
4. H
5. A
6. F
7. A
8. F
9. D
10. H
11. A
12. F
13. A
14. J
15. A
16. G
17. B
18. G
19. D
20. G
21. D
22. G
23. B
24. J
25. A
26. H
27. A
28. F
29. B
30. H
31. B
32. H
33. A
34. G
35. D
36. G
37. C
38. G
39. A
40. F
41. A
42. H
43. C
44. H
45. A
46. F
47. B
48. H

ENGLISH—TIMED-PRACTICE QUIZZES (p. 424)

QUIZ I

1. B
2. F
3. B
4. F
5. C
6. F
7. D
8. J
9. A
10. J
11. C
12. J
13. B
14. H
15. A
16. J
17. B
18. H
19. C
20. J
21. C
22. F
23. A
24. G
25. B
26. H
27. D
28. G
29. C
30. G
31. B
32. H

QUIZ II

1. D
2. F
3. D
4. J
5. C
6. F
7. B
8. G
9. A
10. F
11. B
12. F
13. B
14. G
15. D
16. F
17. D
18. F
19. C
20. G
21. A
22. J
23. B
24. H
25. D
26. H
27. D
28. F
29. B

QUIZ III

1. B
2. H
3. B
4. F
5. C
6. F
7. C
8. H
9. D
10. J
11. C
12. G
13. A
14. F
15. C
16. J
17. C
18. J
19. C
20. F
21. A
22. G
23. A
24. G
25. A
26. H
27. C
28. J
29. A
30. G
31. B

MATHEMATICS

MATHEMATICS—CORE LESSON (p. 451)

1. C	32. F	63. C	94. K	125. E	156. H	187. C	218. J
2. H	33. C	64. K	95. D	126. G	157. D	188. F	219. C
3. D	34. G	65. B	96. J	127. A	158. J	189. B	220. J
4. J	35. C	66. K	97. B	128. J	159. B	190. H	221. A
5. C	36. J	67. C	98. K	129. B	160. H	191. C	222. K
6. F	37. A	68. H	99. C	130. H	161. C	192. F	223. A
7. E	38. K	69. A	100. H	131. B	162. H	193. C	224. J
8. G	39. A	70. F	101. D	132. J	163. E	194. K	225. E
9. C	40. J	71. C	102. H	133. E	164. G	195. D	226. F
10. J	41. D	72. K	103. A	134. H	165. D	196. K	227. B
11. B	42. H	73. B	104. F	135. E	166. G	197. C	228. H
12. J	43. D	74. J	105. E	136. H	167. C	198. K	229. C
13. D	44. G	75. B	106. J	137. E	168. K	199. E	230. K
14. J	45. D	76. G	107. A	138. G	169. E	200. F	231. B
15. E	46. K	77. D	108. H	139. B	170. G	201. E	232. K
16. J	47. E	78. F	109. A	140. G	171. E	202. H	233. D
17. C	48. J	79. C	110. F	141. A	172. F	203. C	234. G
18. K	49. C	80. J	111. E	142. G	173. A	204. J	235. B
19. C	50. J	81. D	112. F	143. E	174. F	205. C	236. F
20. G	51. B	82. J	113. A	144. F	175. C	206. J	237. B
21. D	52. K	83. E	114. G	145. E	176. J	207. C	238. G
22. H	53. D	84. J	115. D	146. J	177. C	208. J	239. B
23. B	54. H	85. C	116. H	147. C	178. J	209. D	240. J
24. H	55. C	86. H	117. D	148. H	179. E	210. G	241. D
25. D	56. F	87. D	118. J	149. B	180. H	211. B	
26. K	57. A	88. K	119. C	150. H	181. D	212. H	
27. E	58. J	89. B	120. G	151. B	182. K	213. C	
28. H	59. D	90. J	121. C	152. H	183. E	214. K	
29. D	60. H	91. D	122. G	153. A	184. H	215. D	
30. H	61. A	92. F	123. C	154. J	185. C	216. K	
31. C	62. K	93. D	124. F	155. E	186. H	217. A	

MATHEMATICS—CHALLENGE ITEMS (p. 502)

1. B	6. J	11. A	16. K	21. B	26. F	31. D
2. H	7. B	12. J	17. B	22. G	27. E	32. H
3. C	8. J	13. C	18. G	23. A	28. H	33. E
4. K	9. C	14. K	19. C	24. G	29. C	34. K
5. D	10. J	15. B	20. H	25. B	30. J	

MATHEMATICS—TIMED-PRACTICE QUIZZES (p. 510)

QUIZ I

1. A	3. D	5. D	7. E	9. B	11. D	13. D	15. A
2. K	4. H	6. J	8. J	10. H	12. H	14. F	16. J

QUIZ II

1. C	4. G	7. B	10. H	13. D	16. H	19. E
2. F	5. C	8. J	11. D	14. K	17. B	20. J
3. C	6. H	9. A	12. J	15. E	18. H	21. D

QUIZ III

1. C	2. H	3. E	4. G	5. D	6. G	7. B	8. F

9. D	12. F	15. C	18. G	21. C	24. G
10. J	13. A	16. G	19. E	22. G	25. E
11. D	14. F	17. C	20. G	23. D	26. H

READING

READING—CORE LESSON (p. 529)

1. C	6. J	11. A	16. G	21. B	26. F	31. A	36. J
2. F	7. C	12. J	17. D	22. G	27. A	32. G	37. C
3. A	8. H	13. A	18. F	23. A	28. H	33. D	38. J
4. J	9. D	14. H	19. D	24. G	29. C	34. G	39. A
5. B	10. J	15. C	20. H	25. A	30. F	35. D	

READING—EXTENDED LESSON (p. 540)

1. A	13. C	25. B	37. B	49. B	61. B	73. A	85. D
2. F	14. H	26. F	38. J	50. F	62. J	74. H	86. F
3. D	15. B	27. D	39. B	51. D	63. B	75. D	87. B
4. F	16. J	28. J	40. J	52. G	64. J	76. G	88. H
5. D	17. C	29. C	41. C	53. A	65. D	77. A	89. A
6. H	18. F	30. G	42. H	54. J	66. H	78. J	90. J
7. B	19. D	31. A	43. C	55. C	67. D	79. C	91. C
8. G	20. H	32. H	44. G	56. G	68. J	80. F	
9. B	21. B	33. C	45. D	57. D	69. A	81. D	
10. J	22. H	34. G	46. F	58. H	70. J	82. J	
11. B	23. D	35. B	47. B	59. C	71. C	83. C	
12. H	24. G	36. F	48. J	60. H	72. H	84. G	

READING—CHALLENGE ITEMS (p. 565)

1. D	9. B	17. C	25. C	33. D	41. B	49. A	57. D
2. G	10. J	18. G	26. J	34. F	42. H	50. H	58. F
3. C	11. B	19. D	27. A	35. D	43. D	51. D	59. D
4. J	12. F	20. F	28. J	36. H	44. H	52. G	60. H
5. A	13. C	21. D	29. C	37. D	45. D	53. A	61. C
6. F	14. F	22. J	30. J	38. G	46. F	54. H	62. G
7. C	15. B	23. C	31. A	39. B	47. B	55. A	
8. J	16. F	24. G	32. J	40. F	48. G	56. F	

READING—TIMED-PRACTICE QUIZZES (p. 584)

QUIZ I

1. A	2. H	3. A	4. G	5. A	6. H	7. D	8. J

QUIZ II

1. D	2. G	3. B	4. H	5. A	6. J	7. C

QUIZ III

1. C	2. G	3. D	4. F	5. B	6. G	7. C	8. F

QUIZ IV

1. B	3. B	5. D	7. A	9. C
2. G	4. F	6. H	8. F	10. G

QUIZ V

1. B	3. D	5. D	7. D	9. C
2. J	4. F	6. H	8. H	10. G

QUIZ VI

1. D	3. D	5. D	7. A	9. B
2. J	4. H	6. H	8. G	10. G

SCIENCE REASONING

SCIENCE REASONING—CORE LESSON (p. 603)

1. B
2. F
3. C
4. G
5. C
6. H
7. D
8. H
9. C
10. H
11. A
12. H
13. D
14. F
15. D
16. F
17. B
18. H
19. C
20. H
21. A
22. J
23. D
24. G
25. A
26. H
27. A
28. J
29. B
30. G
31. B
32. F
33. D
34. J
35. C
36. J
37. A
38. G
39. D
40. G
41. B
42. H
43. C
44. J
45. A
46. H
47. B
48. H
49. D
50. G
51. C
52. F
53. D
54. F

SCIENCE REASONING—CHALLENGE ITEMS (p. 617)

1. D
2. F
3. B
4. G
5. C
6. G
7. C
8. G
9. B
10. J
11. A
12. G
13. D
14. H
15. A
16. G
17. C
18. J
19. A
20. G
21. B
22. H
23. A
24. G
25. C
26. H
27. D
28. H
29. B
30. G
31. C
32. H
33. C
34. H
35. C
36. J
37. B
38. G
39. D
40. G
41. B
42. H
43. C
44. J
45. B
46. H
47. C
48. F
49. D
50. G
51. C
52. H
53. B
54. G
55. B
56. F
57. D
58. F
59. C
60. G
61. A
62. F
63. C
64. J
65. A
66. G
67. A
68. G
69. B
70. H
71. C
72. J
73. C
74. F
75. D
76. G
77. C
78. J

SCIENCE REASONING—TIMED-PRACTICE QUIZZES (p. 634)

QUIZ I

1. D
2. J
3. D
4. H
5. C
6. J
7. B
8. H
9. A
10. G

QUIZ II

1. A
2. F
3. A
4. J
5. C
6. H
7. D
8. F
9. C
10. G

QUIZ III

1. C
2. G
3. C
4. H
5. A
6. F
7. A
8. H
9. B
10. G
11. C

Answers and Explanations:
Step Four

PRACTICE TEST I

DIRECTIONS: For the *correct* answers in each ACT test subject, check the corresponding unshaded box. Then, total the number of checkmarks for each of the content areas, and add these totals in order to determine the raw score for that particular test.

TEST 1: ENGLISH (p. 672)

#	Answer	UM	RH
1.	B		✓
2.	J	✓	
3.	D		✓
4.	G	✓	
5.	A		✓
6.	H	✓	
7.	A	✓	
8.	G		✓
9.	A	✓	
10.	G	✓	
11.	C		✓
12.	J		✓
13.	B	✓	
14.	H		✓
15.	A	✓	
16.	H		✓
17.	D	✓	
18.	G	✓	
19.	A		✓
20.	F	✓	
21.	D	✓	
22.	H	✓	
23.	A	✓	
24.	G	✓	
25.	C	✓	
26.	J	✓	
27.	D		✓
28.	G	✓	
29.	C	✓	
30.	G	✓	
31.	B		✓
32.	H		✓
33.	A		✓
34.	J	✓	
35.	A		✓
36.	F	✓	
37.	B	✓	
38.	H	✓	
39.	B		✓
40.	H	✓	
41.	D	✓	
42.	H	✓	
43.	A		✓
44.	F	✓	
45.	C		✓
46.	F		✓
47.	D	✓	
48.	G	✓	
49.	C		✓
50.	F		✓
51.	B	✓	
52.	F		✓
53.	B	✓	
54.	J		✓
55.	D		✓
56.	G		✓
57.	D	✓	
58.	H	✓	
59.	A		✓
60.	J	✓	
61.	C	✓	
62.	H		✓
63.	D		✓
64.	G	✓	
65.	D	✓	
66.	F	✓	
67.	A		✓
68.	F		✓
69.	C	✓	
70.	J		✓
71.	A		✓
72.	G		✓
73.	B		✓
74.	J		✓
75.	B		✓

Usage/Mechanics (UM): ______/40 Rhetorical Skills (RH): ______/35 English Raw Score (UM + RH): ______/75

TEST 2: MATHEMATICS (p. 684)

#	Answer	EA	AG	GT
1.	A	✓		
2.	K	✓		
3.	C	✓		
4.	K	✓		
5.	E	✓		
6.	H	✓		
7.	D		✓	
8.	H		✓	
9.	D			✓
10.	G	✓		
11.	B		✓	
12.	H	✓		
13.	C	✓		
14.	G	✓		
15.	D			✓
16.	H	✓		
17.	B		✓	
18.	K			✓
19.	A	✓		
20.	H		✓	
21.	D		✓	
22.	G	✓		
23.	C		✓	
24.	F			✓
25.	E			✓
26.	G		✓	
27.	C	✓		
28.	J			✓
29.	E	✓		
30.	H	✓		
31.	C	✓		
32.	H			✓
33.	A		✓	
34.	K			✓
35.	D	✓		
36.	H	✓		
37.	C		✓	
38.	G	✓		
39.	C			✓
40.	G		✓	
41.	D	✓		
42.	H	✓		
43.	A	✓		
44.	G	✓		
45.	B			✓
46.	K			✓
47.	A			✓
48.	F			✓
49.	C		✓	
50.	K		✓	
51.	C		✓	
52.	J		✓	
53.	A		✓	
54.	F		✓	
55.	D		✓	
56.	H			✓
57.	B		✓	
58.	K			✓
59.	A			✓
60.	J			✓

Pre-Algebra/Elementary Algebra (EA): ______/24 Intermediate Algebra/Coordinate Geometry (AG): ______/19

Plane Geometry/Trigonometry (GT): ______/17 Mathematics Raw Score (EA + AG + GT): ______/60

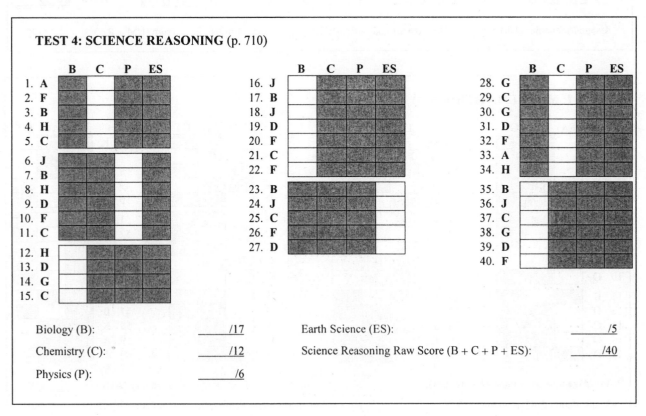

TEST 3: READING (p. 702)

		SS	NS	H	PF
1.	B				
2.	F				
3.	D				
4.	J				
5.	C				
6.	F				
7.	C				
8.	H				
9.	C				
10.	G				
11.	A				
12.	J				
13.	B				
14.	H				
15.	A				
16.	H				
17.	C				
18.	J				
19.	A				
20.	H				
21.	B				
22.	H				
23.	A				
24.	J				
25.	C				
26.	F				
27.	A				
28.	G				
29.	B				
30.	H				
31.	C				
32.	J				
33.	B				
34.	J				
35.	A				
36.	G				
37.	A				
38.	F				
39.	B				
40.	F				

Social Science (SS): ______/10

Natural Science (NS): ______/10

Humanities (H): ______/10

Prose Fiction (PF): ______/10

Reading Raw Score (SS + NS + H + PF): ______/40

TEST 4: SCIENCE REASONING (p. 710)

		B	C	P	ES
1.	A				
2.	F				
3.	B				
4.	H				
5.	C				
6.	J				
7.	B				
8.	H				
9.	D				
10.	F				
11.	C				
12.	H				
13.	D				
14.	G				
15.	C				
16.	J				
17.	B				
18.	J				
19.	D				
20.	F				
21.	C				
22.	F				
23.	B				
24.	J				
25.	C				
26.	F				
27.	D				
28.	G				
29.	C				
30.	G				
31.	D				
32.	F				
33.	A				
34.	H				
35.	B				
36.	J				
37.	C				
38.	G				
39.	D				
40.	F				

Biology (B): ______/17

Chemistry (C): ______/12

Physics (P): ______/6

Earth Science (ES): ______/5

Science Reasoning Raw Score (B + C + P + ES): ______/40

PRACTICE TEST II

DIRECTIONS: For the *correct* answers in each ACT test subject, check the corresponding unshaded box. Then, total the number of checkmarks for each of the content areas, and add these totals in order to determine the raw score for that particular test.

TEST 1: ENGLISH (p. 728)

#	Answer	UM	RH
1.	B	☐	■
2.	G	■	☐
3.	D	☐	■
4.	F	■	☐
5.	B	☐	■
6.	F	☐	■
7.	A	■	☐
8.	F	■	☐
9.	D	☐	■
10.	F	■	☐
11.	D	☐	■
12.	J	■	☐
13.	B	☐	■
14.	J	■	☐
15.	D	■	☐
16.	F	■	☐
17.	A	■	☐
18.	H	☐	■
19.	D	■	☐
20.	F	☐	■
21.	A	■	☐
22.	F	■	☐
23.	A	■	☐
24.	F	■	☐
25.	D	☐	■
26.	J	■	☐
27.	C	■	☐
28.	H	☐	■
29.	D	☐	■
30.	J	■	☐
31.	B	☐	■
32.	J	■	☐
33.	B	☐	■
34.	J	☐	■
35.	D	■	☐
36.	J	☐	■
37.	D	☐	■
38.	H	☐	■
39.	A	☐	■
40.	H	■	☐
41.	B	☐	■
42.	G	☐	■
43.	A	■	☐
44.	H	☐	■
45.	D	■	☐
46.	J	☐	■
47.	D	■	☐
48.	G	■	☐
49.	B	☐	■
50.	H	☐	■
51.	A	☐	■
52.	H	☐	■
53.	D	■	☐
54.	F	■	☐
55.	A	☐	■
56.	F	☐	■
57.	B	■	☐
58.	J	■	☐
59.	A	■	☐
60.	F	■	☐
61.	A	■	☐
62.	J	☐	■
63.	B	☐	■
64.	J	■	☐
65.	A	■	☐
66.	G	☐	■
67.	B	☐	■
68.	F	☐	■
69.	A	☐	■
70.	F	■	☐
71.	B	☐	■
72.	F	☐	■
73.	B	☐	■
74.	J	☐	■
75.	B	☐	■

Usage/Mechanics (UM): ______/40 Rhetorical Skills (RH): ______/35 English Raw Score (UM + RH): ______/75

TEST 2: MATHEMATICS (p. 740)

#	Answer	EA	AG	GT
1.	B	☐	■	■
2.	K	☐	■	■
3.	C	☐	■	■
4.	K	☐	■	■
5.	A	☐	■	■
6.	F	☐	■	■
7.	C	■	■	☐
8.	G	■	■	☐
9.	C	☐	■	■
10.	F	☐	■	■
11.	E	■	■	☐
12.	K	■	■	☐
13.	A	■	■	☐
14.	G	☐	■	■
15.	C	☐	■	■
16.	K	■	☐	■
17.	C	■	■	☐
18.	G	■	■	☐
19.	B	☐	■	■
20.	J	☐	■	■
21.	A	■	☐	■
22.	K	■	■	☐
23.	D	☐	■	■
24.	J	■	☐	■
25.	D	☐	■	■
26.	G	☐	■	■
27.	B	☐	■	■
28.	G	☐	■	■
29.	D	☐	■	■
30.	F	☐	■	■
31.	C	■	■	☐
32.	G	■	■	☐
33.	C	■	■	☐
34.	H	■	■	☐
35.	C	☐	■	■
36.	H	☐	■	■
37.	E	■	☐	■
38.	K	■	☐	■
39.	C	■	■	☐
40.	J	■	☐	■
41.	D	☐	■	■
42.	K	☐	■	■
43.	B	■	☐	■
44.	G	■	■	☐
45.	C	■	☐	■
46.	H	■	■	☐
47.	A	■	☐	■
48.	H	■	■	☐
49.	C	■	☐	■
50.	J	■	☐	■
51.	A	■	☐	■
52.	H	■	■	☐
53.	E	■	■	☐
54.	K	■	☐	■
55.	B	■	☐	■
56.	G	■	☐	■
57.	D	■	☐	■
58.	J	■	☐	■
59.	C	■	☐	■
60.	H	■	☐	■

Pre-Algebra/Elementary Algebra (EA): ______/23 Intermediate Algebra/Coordinate Geometry (AG): ______/19

Plane Geometry/Trigonometry (GT): ______/18 Mathematics Raw Score (EA + AG + GT): ______/60

TEST 3: READING (p. 756)

#	Answer	SS	NS	H	PF
1.	C	■	■	■	
2.	F	■	■	■	
3.	C	■	■	■	
4.	G	■	■	■	
5.	D	■	■	■	
6.	G	■	■	■	
7.	A	■	■	■	
8.	G	■	■	■	
9.	A	■	■	■	
10.	H	■	■	■	
11.	B	■	■		■
12.	J	■	■		■
13.	C	■	■		■
14.	J	■	■		■
15.	C	■	■		■
16.	J	■	■		■
17.	B	■	■		■
18.	F	■	■		■
19.	C	■	■		■
20.	J	■	■		■
21.	A		■	■	■
22.	F		■	■	■
23.	C		■	■	■
24.	F		■	■	■
25.	B		■	■	■
26.	J		■	■	■
27.	B		■	■	■
28.	H		■	■	■
29.	B		■	■	■
30.	H		■	■	■
31.	D	■		■	■
32.	H	■		■	■
33.	B	■		■	■
34.	H	■		■	■
35.	B	■		■	■
36.	H	■		■	■
37.	D	■		■	■
38.	G	■		■	■
39.	C	■		■	■
40.	H	■		■	■

Social Science (SS): ______/10

Natural Science (NS): ______/10

Humanities (H): ______/10

Prose Fiction (PF): ______/10

Reading Raw Score (SS + NS + H + PF): ______/40

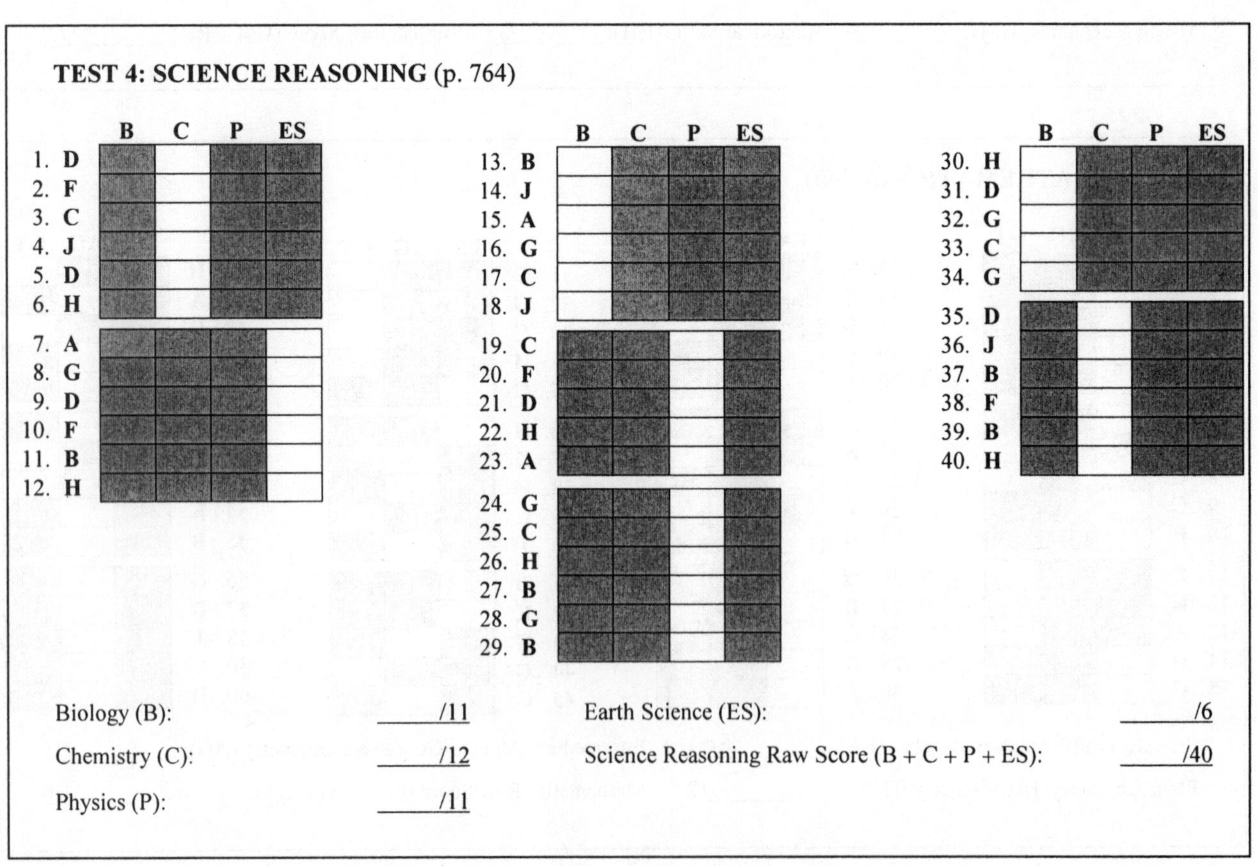

TEST 4: SCIENCE REASONING (p. 764)

#	Answer	B	C	P	ES
1.	D	■		■	■
2.	F	■		■	■
3.	C	■		■	■
4.	J	■		■	■
5.	D	■		■	■
6.	H	■		■	■
7.	A	■	■	■	
8.	G	■	■	■	
9.	D	■	■	■	
10.	F	■	■	■	
11.	B	■	■	■	
12.	H	■	■	■	
13.	B		■	■	■
14.	J		■	■	■
15.	A		■	■	■
16.	G		■	■	■
17.	C		■	■	■
18.	J		■	■	■
19.	C	■	■		■
20.	F	■	■		■
21.	D	■	■		■
22.	H	■	■		■
23.	A	■	■		■
24.	G	■	■		■
25.	C	■	■		■
26.	H	■	■		■
27.	B	■	■		■
28.	G	■	■		■
29.	B	■	■		■
30.	H		■	■	■
31.	D		■	■	■
32.	G		■	■	■
33.	C		■	■	■
34.	G		■	■	■
35.	D	■		■	■
36.	J	■		■	■
37.	B	■		■	■
38.	F	■		■	■
39.	B	■		■	■
40.	H	■		■	■

Biology (B): ______/11

Chemistry (C): ______/12

Physics (P): ______/11

Earth Science (ES): ______/6

Science Reasoning Raw Score (B + C + P + ES): ______/40

PRACTICE TEST III

DIRECTIONS: For the *correct* answers in each ACT test subject, check the corresponding unshaded box. Then, total the number of checkmarks for each of the content areas, and add these totals in order to determine the raw score for that particular test.

TEST 1: ENGLISH (p. 782)

Columns: UM RH

1.	C	16.	J	31.	B	46.	H	61.	D
2.	F	17.	A	32.	G	47.	D	62.	F
3.	C	18.	H	33.	A	48.	G	63.	B
4.	G	19.	D	34.	J	49.	B	64.	J
5.	B	20.	G	35.	B	50.	F	65.	C
6.	F	21.	A	36.	J	51.	A	66.	H
7.	B	22.	G	37.	D	52.	G	67.	A
8.	F	23.	D	38.	F	53.	D	68.	G
9.	B	24.	H	39.	A	54.	G	69.	D
10.	H	25.	D	40.	J	55.	B	70.	H
11.	A	26.	F	41.	B	56.	H	71.	C
12.	F	27.	B	42.	F	57.	A	72.	G
13.	D	28.	F	43.	A	58.	H	73.	D
14.	H	29.	D	44.	G	59.	A	74.	H
15.	B	30.	J	45.	A	60.	J	75.	D

Usage/Mechanics (UM): ______/40 Rhetorical Skills (RH): ______/35 English Raw Score (UM + RH): ______/75

TEST 2: MATHEMATICS (p. 794)

Columns: EA AG GT

1.	B	16.	G	31.	A	46.	K
2.	F	17.	D	32.	J	47.	D
3.	C	18.	F	33.	D	48.	H
4.	J	19.	B	34.	K	49.	D
5.	E	20.	K	35.	E	50.	G
6.	K	21.	E	36.	F	51.	C
7.	D	22.	F	37.	B	52.	G
8.	J	23.	C	38.	K	53.	D
9.	D	24.	G	39.	B	54.	K
10.	G	25.	A	40.	K	55.	D
11.	B	26.	H	41.	E	56.	G
12.	G	27.	A	42.	J	57.	A
13.	E	28.	G	43.	D	58.	F
14.	H	29.	C	44.	J	59.	D
15.	C	30.	K	45.	C	60.	G

Pre-Algebra/Elementary Algebra (EA): ______/24 Intermediate Algebra/Coordinate Geometry (AG): ______/18

Plane Geometry/Trigonometry (GT): ______/18 Mathematics Raw Score (EA + AG + GT): ______/60

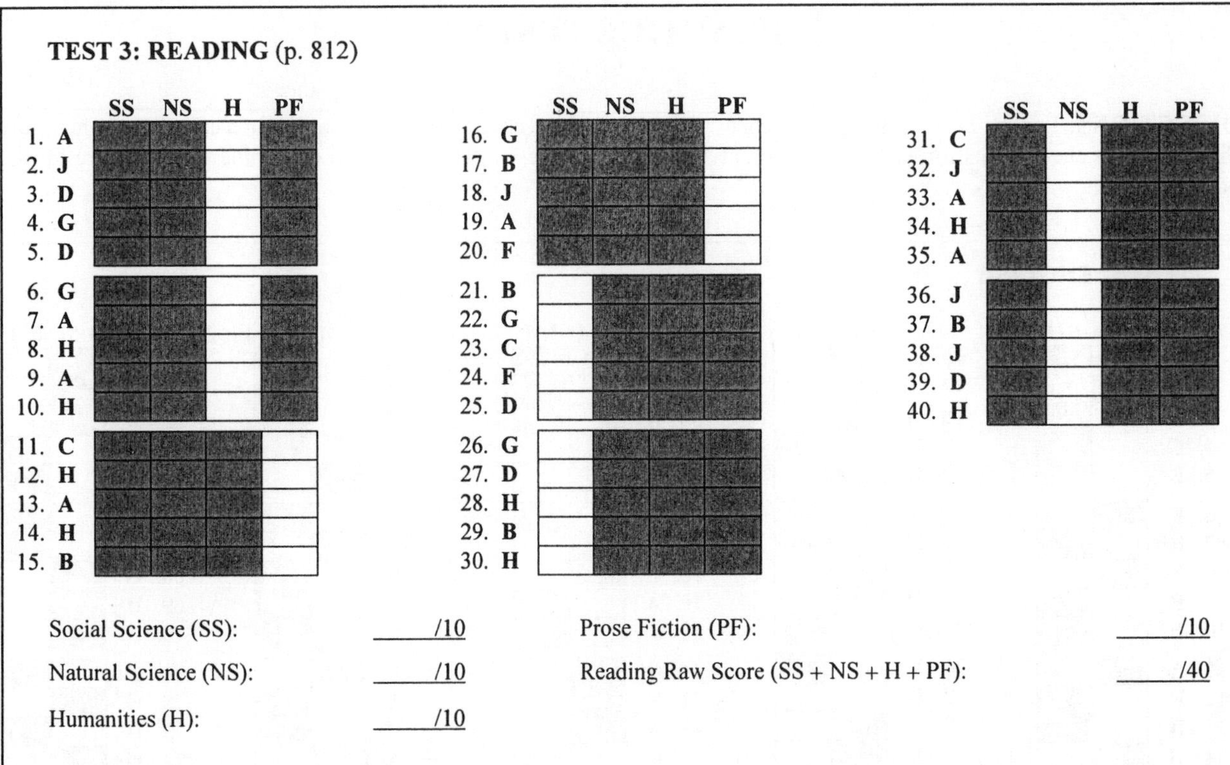

TEST 3: READING (p. 812)

Question	Answer	Category (open box)
1.	A	H
2.	J	H
3.	D	H
4.	G	H
5.	D	H
6.	G	H
7.	A	H
8.	H	H
9.	A	H
10.	H	H
11.	C	PF
12.	H	PF
13.	A	PF
14.	H	PF
15.	B	PF
16.	G	PF
17.	B	PF
18.	J	PF
19.	A	PF
20.	F	PF
21.	B	SS
22.	G	SS
23.	C	SS
24.	F	SS
25.	D	SS
26.	G	SS
27.	D	SS
28.	H	SS
29.	B	SS
30.	H	SS
31.	C	NS
32.	J	NS
33.	A	NS
34.	H	NS
35.	A	NS
36.	J	NS
37.	B	NS
38.	J	NS
39.	D	NS
40.	H	NS

Social Science (SS): ______/10

Natural Science (NS): ______/10

Humanities (H): ______/10

Prose Fiction (PF): ______/10

Reading Raw Score (SS + NS + H + PF): ______/40

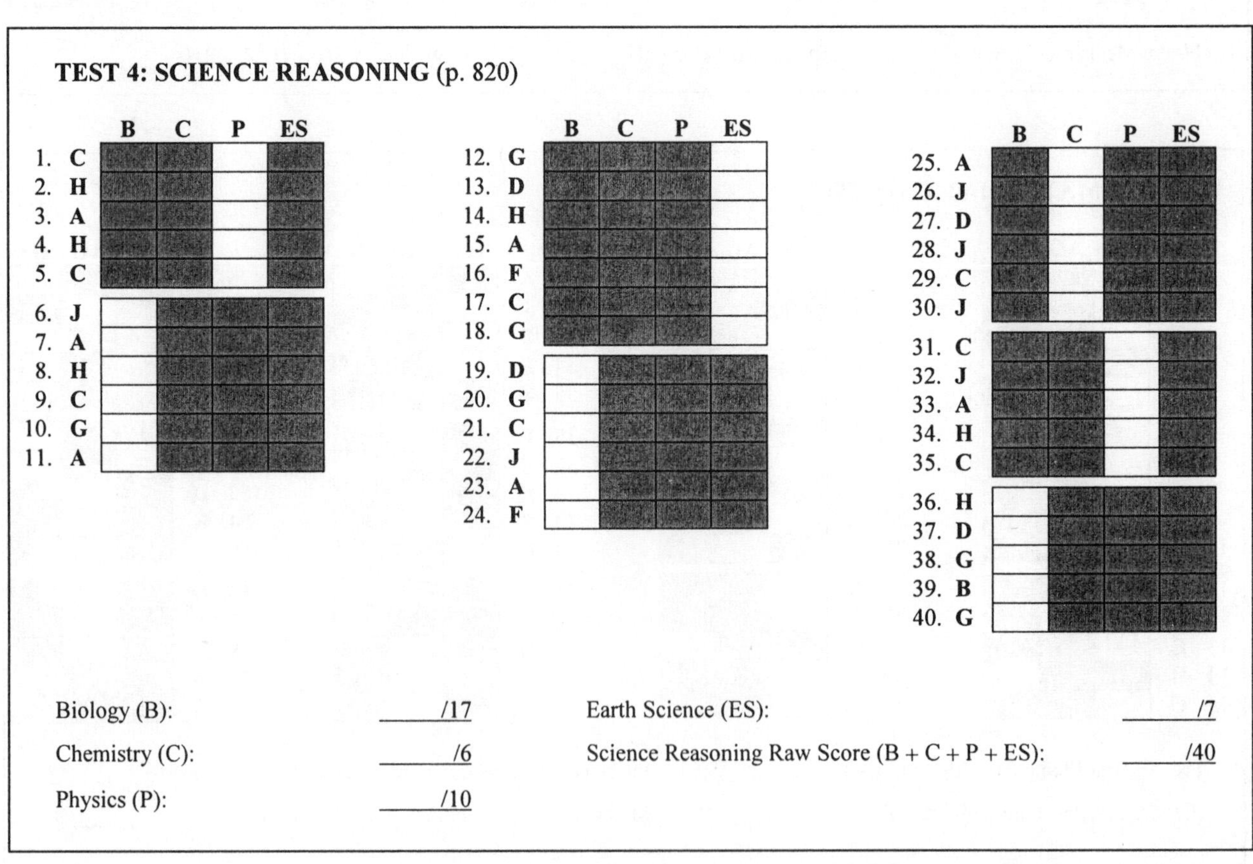

TEST 4: SCIENCE REASONING (p. 820)

Question	Answer	Category (open box)
1.	C	P
2.	H	P
3.	A	P
4.	H	P
5.	C	P
6.	J	B
7.	A	B
8.	H	B
9.	C	B
10.	G	B
11.	A	B
12.	G	ES
13.	D	ES
14.	H	ES
15.	A	ES
16.	F	ES
17.	C	ES
18.	G	ES
19.	D	B
20.	G	B
21.	C	B
22.	J	B
23.	A	B
24.	F	B
25.	A	C
26.	J	C
27.	D	C
28.	J	C
29.	C	C
30.	J	C
31.	C	P
32.	J	P
33.	A	P
34.	H	P
35.	C	P
36.	H	B
37.	D	B
38.	G	B
39.	B	B
40.	G	B

Biology (B): ______/17

Chemistry (C): ______/6

Physics (P): ______/10

Earth Science (ES): ______/7

Science Reasoning Raw Score (B + C + P + ES): ______/40

TEST 1: ENGLISH (p. 782)

1. **(C)** The original sentence has low-level usage. *On account of* should not be used as a substitute for *because of.* (C) makes the needed correction. (B) is wrong because *since* is a conjunction that introduces a dependent clause, but the material that follows is not a clause—it contains no verb. As for (D), although *for* can be a preposition, its meaning is not appropriate in this context.

2. **(F)** The original sentence is correct. *Nonetheless* means "in spite of this." (G) and (H) are wrong because the author means to say that smuggling grew in spite of government efforts, not because of government efforts. As for (J), although *on the contrary* does signal an opposition, it does not have the "in spite of" meaning needed here.

3. **(C)** The original sentence contains two errors. First, an adverb is needed to modify the adjective *timbered—heavy* should be *heavily.* Second, since *countless* is intended to modify *islands* and not *heavily timbered,* a comma must be placed after *countless.* (C) makes both of these corrections.

4. **(G)** The original sentence and (H) and (J) are not idiomatic. The correct idiom is *well founded.*

5. **(B)** The tense of the verb in the original sentence is not consistent with the other verbs in the paragraph. The author is describing past events, so the past tense *seized* should be used. Although (C) and (D) can be used to refer to past actions, they have meanings that are inappropriate in this context. First, *were seizing* (the progressive form of the past tense) implies an action that continued for some time in the past (*e.g.,* During this period, customs officials were seizing tons of wool each month). Second, *have seized* (the present perfect) implies an action that began in the past but continues into the present (*e.g.,* The British have repeatedly seized our ships).

6. **(F)** The original sentence is correct. By comparison, (G) and (J) are awkward and needlessly wordy. In (H), *technically* modifies *being*, whereas *technical* modifies the *violation.*

7. **(B)** The original sentence contains an error of diction. *Principle* means "rule"; *principal* means "main or important." (C) fails to correct this problem. (D) makes the needed correction, but the verb *was* will not agree with the subject of the sentence. The subject of the sentence is a compound subject—a series of elements joined by *and*—requires the use of a plural verb.

8. **(F)** *In fact* signals an idea that will provide an illustration of or give special emphasis to a point that came just before. This is exactly what the author does. As for (G) and (H), these words are used to alert the reader that what follows is a continuation of an idea and that the following idea has the same status as the first idea. Thus, (G) and (H) are not suited to this sentence. Finally, as for (J), *on the contrary* signals a contrast of ideas, but the author does not intend to present contrasting ideas.

9. **(B)** The only role for *selling* in the original sentence would be that of an adjective, but there is nothing for *selling* to modify. (B) corrects this problem by converting *selling* to a conjugated form. The sentence reads: *was smuggled... and sold.* (C) is wrong because *would be sold* is not parallel to *smuggled.* (D) is wrong for the same reason. There is no logical role for the infinitive *to sell.*

10. **(H)** The idiom *so much...that* is not completed in the original sentence. (H) completes the idiom: *so much was smuggled and sold... that one....* (G) and (J) fail to complete the expression.

11. **(A)** The original sentence is correct. The *although* sets up the contrast between the ideas *settlers welcomed national control* and *they did not like the restrictions.*

12. **(F)** The original sentence is correct. The simple past tense is consistent with the other verbs in the passage. (G) is wrong because it eliminates the only conjugated verb in the clause introduced by *although.* (H) is wrong because the tense is inconsistent with the other tenses in the paragraph. (J) destroys the logic of the sentence.

13. **(D)** The original sentence is not idiomatic—the correct idiom is *were fearful,* not *were fearing.* (D) avoids the problem by using *feared,* and the past tense is parallel to the other verb in the sentence, *wanted.* (B) fails to correct

the problem of the original sentence. (C) uses the correct idiom, but the verb *was* does not agree with the subject of the sentence, *they*.

14. (H) The original sentence contains two errors. First, the underlined verb is in the present tense and is therefore inconsistent with the use of the past tense in the rest of the paragraph. Second, *in the losing of* is not idiomatic; the phrase *in the loss of* is better used. (H) makes both the needed corrections. (G) makes one correction but not the other. (J) uses the indicative *results,* but it lacks the element of contingency: "they feared that this results." A verb is needed that suggests something might or might not occur: "they feared that this would result or might result."

15. (B) The passage should be arranged in chronological order. [1] should come first because it describes the first event (the opening of the customs office). [3] should be second because it describes the events that come next in time (Americans were leery of the new office). [2] should be last because it is the final development (the fears turned out to be true).

16. (J) The author describes events, so *narrative* is a part of the passage. The author also gives a specific example of a ship—the *Beaver*—that was seized. The author gives statistics about wool. However, the author does not quote from another source.

17. (A) The original sentence is the best choice. The other choices are awkward and needlessly wordy.

18. (H) The original sentence suffers from a lack of parallelism. All three verbs *can step outside, gaze,* and *become* are governed by the *can,* so the additional *can* in the original sentence creates a series in which the elements do not have the same form. (H) brings the third verb into line with the other two. (G) fails to provide the needed parallelism, and (J) is wrong because *becomes* does not agree in number with the subject, *anyone.*

19. (D) The original sentence is incorrectly punctuated. The comma creates a run-on sentence. (D) solves this problem by starting a new sentence, while (B) and (C) do not.

20. (G) The original sentence is ambiguous. *Ending* seems to be an adjective modifying *suns,* but the author intends for *ending* to modify *island universe.* (G) corrects this problem by creating a relative clause that modifies *island universe.* (H) also creates a new clause but *ends* does not agree with the antecedent of *that,* which is *universe.* Finally, (J) suffers from the same defect as the original because *ended* seems to modify *suns.*

21. (A) The original sentence is correct as written. (B) is not idiomatic. Correct English requires the use of the infinitive *to chart* in this situation, not the gerund *charting.* (C) is wrong because there is nothing for a participle like *having charted* to modify. (D) destroys the logic of the sentence.

22. (G) The verb tense of the original sentence is wrong. The past perfect *had been made* implies that the progress was made at a time in the past completely separated from our own time. However, the phrase *in the twentieth century* indicates that the author is describing an action that is still going on. The correct verb tense to show this is the present perfect. *Has been made* correctly implies that the progress began in the past and is still going on. (H) is wrong because the present tense *is made* lacks the implication of a past action. (J), which uses the future tense, indicates that the progress has not yet been made.

23. (D) In the original sentence, *as such* signals that the second idea is what it is by virtue of the first idea. However, the Milky Way is not called the Milky Way because our solar system is a part of it. (B) and (C) also disrupt the logical connection between the two ideas.

24. (H) The material in this sentence belongs with that of the next paragraph. Thus, a new paragraph should be started here, and no new paragraph should be started at the end of the sentence. (H) and (J) make the required change. However, (J) is wrong because *as* is used to introduce a dependent clause, resulting in a dependent clause with no supporting independent clause.

25. (D) The original sentence is incorrect because a comma and not a semicolon must be used to separate an appositive phrase from the main part of the sentence. The semicolon is too powerful and makes a fragment out of everything that follows it. (B) is wrong because it is necessary to place the phrase "crown jewels" in quotation marks. (C) is wrong because the verb *is* does not agree with *Clouds.*

26. (F) The original sentence is correct as written. The other choices simply are not idiomatic.

27. (B) *To* is superfluous and makes the phrasing stilted. Eliminate it. (B) and (C) both make the needed correction, but (C) is wrong because *provide* does not agree with the subject of the sentence, *galaxy.*

28. (F) The original sentence is the best rendering. Study the other choices—they are all stilted or needlessly wordy.

29. (D) The author poses the questions because they are questions about the stars that are still unanswered. He will not provide answers.

30. (J) At first, it appears that *graduated* is intended to be a verb in a phrase such as *graduated from test pilot schools.* Unfortunately, the structure of the sentence does not permit that reading. (J) clarifies the issue by making *graduated* a noun, and *graduates* can function as an appositive for *pilots.* (G) and (H) are wrong because the appositive must be set off by a comma and nothing else.

31. (B) The original sentence has two errors. First, *were* fails to agree in number with its subject, *each.* Second, the use of the gerund *having* is not idiomatic. (B) corrects both errors. (C) fails to correct the second error. (D) corrects both errors, but the past perfect *had been required* is inconsistent with the other verbs in the paragraph.

32. (G) The original sentence contains low-level usage. Do not use *got* to suggest the passive voice. Use some form of the verb *to be.* (G) makes the needed correction. (H) is a form of the passive voice, but the use of the past perfect is not consistent with the other verbs in the paragraph. (J) is wrong for two reasons. First, the present perfect *has been* is not consistent with the other verbs in the paragraph. Second, *has* is a singular verb, but the subject *seven* is plural.

33. (A) The information contained in the parentheses explains why only seven astronauts were chosen. However, it is not vital to the development of the passage. By placing the remark in parentheses, the author signals to the reader that the information is not vital.

34. (J) The original sentence contains a comma splice. (J) corrects the problem of the run-on sentence by starting a new sentence. Neither (G) nor (H) addresses the problem.

35. (B) The second paragraph introduces the topic of failures. (B) provides a good transition by signaling to the reader that this will be the topic of the paragraph.

36. (J) The original sentence uses the ubiquitous *they. They* has no referent. (H) and (J) correct the error; however, the usage of *fortunately* is not correct in (H).

37. (D) The original sentence is needlessly wordy as indicated by comparison with (D).

38. (F) By using the word *spectacular*, the author is suggesting that the incident was sensational, but it did not actually have particularly significant consequences. The irony is intended due to the incongruity between the anticipated and actual results of the incident.

39. (A) The original sentence is correct. An adverb, such as *relatively,* is needed to modify an adjective, such as *simple.*

40. (J) The underlined verb is not parallel to the other verb: *to ignite* and *shutting down.* (J) corrects the problem: *to ignite and then to shut down.* Neither (G) nor (H) solve the problem. (H) suffers from the further defect that *they* does not have a referent.

41. (B) This is another example of irony. The rocket was never really launched. The quotation marks signal that the author is using the word *flight* in a non-standard way.

42. (F) The original sentence is correct as written. A new paragraph should be started here because the author is taking up a new topic, switching from a discussion of failures in the problem to a discussion of animals in flight. Therefore, (G), (H), and (J) are wrong.

43. (A) The original sentence is the most concise. The other choices are stilted and wordy.

44. (G) The verb tense of the original sentence is wrong. *Delay* and *leak* belong to the same time frame, so both should be in the same tense.

45. (A) The original sentence is correct. None of the other suggested positions for *unharmed* are idiomatic.

46. (H) *Returning* is not a conjugated verb and thus it cannot be the main verb. All three choices supply conjugated verbs, but (H) is the only tense that is consistent with the other verbs in the paragraph.

47. (D) The question mentioned was, at the time, still unanswered. Thus, the choice of verb should reflect that: *could tolerate.*

48. (G) *Like* in the original sentence is both superfluous and not idiomatic. (G) corrects the error by eliminating the extra word. (H) and (J) are not idiomatic.

49. (B) The original sentence contains an error of grammar: *longer flights would require that astronauts to have.* The infinitive cannot be the verb for the subject *astronauts.* Instead, a conjugated verb is needed. Each of the alternatives supplies a conjugated verb form, but only (B) is consistent with the rest of the sentence. (C) is wrong because the past perfect *had had* suggests a sequence of events that is not supported by the meaning of the sentence. (D) is wrong because the sentence now reads: *would require that the astronauts are sure to have.*

50. (F) The author emphasizes the successes of the program and downplays its failures. (F) best summarizes this development.

51. (A) The original sentence is correct. (B) makes two mistakes. First, it leaves out an essential comma. The end of the aside beginning with *in* must be marked. Second, *of* introduces a prepositional phrase that has nothing to modify. (C) is wrong because it fails to mark the close of the aside. (D) is wrong because *of helping* is not idiomatic.

52. (G) The original sentence is needlessly wordy. *And* and *also* mean the same thing, so they should not both be used. (G) solves this problem by substituting *as well as,* a phrase which also means *and.* (H) is wrong because *with* does not have an appropriate meaning in this context. (J) is wrong because *as opposed to* signals a contrast between two ideas that is not suggested by the content of the sentence.

53. (D) The verb tense of the original sentence is inconsistent with that of the other verb in the sentence: *aided* and *had been emerging.* The simple past verb form should be used: *aided* and *emerged.* Only (D) makes the needed correction.

54. (G) The original sentence is incorrect because *was enjoying* does not agree with the subject of the sentence, *aspects.* (G) makes the needed correction. (H) and (J) are wrong because they are singular.

55. (B) The original sentence is not idiomatic. The correct idiom is *not only this but that.* (B) supplies the correct idiom. (C) is wrong because *not only this consequently that* is not idiomatic. As for (D), although it supplies the correct idiom, it also contains two errors. First, the comma following *but* illogically disrupts the idiom. Second, the verb *would have* is inconsistent with the other verb in the sentence.

56. (H) The original sentence does not contain any grievous errors. A comma should be inserted following *treatment* because the two clauses are long. Additionally, *also* is redundant of *and.* However, the main problem with the original sentence is its excessive wordiness. (H) expresses the thought more concisely. (G) is wrong because *but* illogically signals a contrast where none is intended. (J) destroys the parallelism of the sentence:*...the doctor could select...and can mitigate...*

57. (A) The original sentence is correct. (B) and (C) use inappropriate verb forms: *require that something was available* and *require that something is available.* The technical explanation for this is that it is one of the last vestiges in English of the subjunctive. (D) is wrong because *as* does not have the same meaning as *to.*

58. (H) In the original sentence, the present tense *presupposes* conflicts with the other past tense verbs in the paragraph. Although (G) also makes the correction, the passive voice is needlessly indirect. (H) makes the needed correction and is more concise.

59. (A) The original sentence is correct. A new paragraph is required here because the author is taking up a new topic (a discussion of a particular doctor). Therefore, (B) and (D) are wrong. As for (C), *since* is a subordinate conjunction and is used to introduce a dependent clause. The resulting construction would be a dependent clause with no supporting independent clause.

60. (J) The first three paragraphs are a general discussion of medical advances in the nineteenth century. The last two paragraphs are a discussion of a particular advance. The first sentence of the fourth paragraph sets the stage for this transition.

61. (D) The original sentence, (B), and (C) are all needlessly wordy. (D) clearly conveys the idea.

62. (F) The original sentence is correct. A new paragraph should not be started here because the following material continues the discussion about Dr. Beaumont. Thus, (G) and (J) are wrong. (H) is awkward. Compare the wording of (H) with the more direct wording of the original sentence.

63. (B) The original sentence is grammatically correct; however, *but* signals an inappropriate contrast. The second clause explains the outcome of the first clause. (B) solves this problem. (C) is wrong because the resulting construction would be a comma splice. (D) is grammatically correct; however, *but* is out of place.

64. (J) The original sentence suffers from faulty parallelism. The verb *describe* has the same function in the sentence as the verb *demonstrate,* so they need parallel forms. Only (J) makes the needed correction. The verb forms of (G) and (H) do not create the needed parallelism.

65. (C) The original sentence contains an error of pronoun usage. *Him* refers to *babies.* (C) makes the needed correction by using the plural *them.* (B) and (D) are wrong because, among other things, they use singular pronouns.

66. (H) The original sentence is not idiomatic. The correct idiom is *endowed with.* As for (J), although *endowed by* is idiomatic, it is not appropriate here. It would be used in a different way: *...endowed by their Creator with certain inalienable rights.*

67. (A) The original sentence is correct. The other choices, however, are not acceptable. (B) and (C) both create run-on sentences. (D) destroys the logical structure of the sentence. Two occurrences of *it* are required: one to be the object of *hears* and the other to function as the subject of the second clause.

68. (G) The sentence intends to state that an infant's cry causes two parallel reactions, one biological and the other emotional. As written, *including* illogically implies that an emotional reaction is a kind of biological reaction. Only a word like *and* will do the trick.

69. **(D)** The word *unfortunately* has a meaning that is not appropriate here. The author intends the last sentence of the paragraph to be a conclusion that is proved by the remainder of the paragraph: the infant does this and that, so he is in possession of certain attributes. The *in fact* conveys this idea and adds a special emphasis.

70. **(H)** The original sentence is needlessly indirect and wordy. (H) is more direct and concise. (G) also is concise, but it uses a verb tense that is inconsistent with the other verbs in the paragraph. (J) is too wordy. Furthermore, the verb *are* does not agree with the singular subject of the sentence.

71. **(C)** In English, sometimes the present progressive is used to give special emphasis to an idea: (*e.g.,* But Mom, I am doing my homework!). But nothing suggests that the author would want special emphasis here. (C) corrects the problem by using the simple present tense, which is the same tense used for the other verbs. (B) is wrong because the past tense is out of place. (D) is wrong because the subject of *guarantee* is *that,* which in turn refers to the singular *collection.*

72. **(G)** Although *whether or not* is a typical English idiom, its use here is not idiomatic. The first *whether* in the sentence has set up the comparison: *whether* this or *whether* that. (G) makes the needed correction. (H) and (J) are wrong because *whether if* is not idiomatic.

73. **(D)** *Although* introduces a long and complex dependent clause that ends with the period. The original sentence is wrong because the dependent clause is not attached to an independent clause. (D) makes the needed correction.

74. **(H)** The final sentence serves to summarize in an emphatic way the point the author has been laboring to prove: the newborn infant is not a passive creature.

75. **(D)** The passage is an argument. The author is trying to persuade the reader that the newborn infant is not a passive creature. The author uses examples of behavior to prove this point.

TEST 2: MATHEMATICS (p. 794)

1. **(B)** Perform the indicated operation: $5.75 - 4.5 = 1.25$.

2. **(F)** The product of 4 times x is written as $4x$. 3 less than that would be $4x - 3$.

3. **(C)** This question really just tests fractions. If $\frac{3}{4}$ of x equals 36, then: $\frac{3}{4}x = 36 \Rightarrow x = 36 \bullet \frac{4}{3} = 48$ and $\frac{1}{3}$ of 48 is 16.

4. **(J)** The measure of the unlabeled angle in the top triangle is 90°. The angle vertically opposite it in the bottom triangle is also equal to 90°. Therefore: $x + y + 90° = 180°$ and $x + y = 90°$.

5. **(E)** There are two ways to attack this question. One is to reason as follows:

A. $2 + n$ cannot be a multiple of 3. Since n is a multiple of 3, when $2 + n$ is divided by 3 there will be a remainder of 2.
B. $2 - n$ cannot be a multiple of 3 for the same reason that $2 + n$ cannot be a multiple of 3.
C. $2n - 1$ cannot be a multiple of 3. Since n is a multiple of 3, $2n$ will also be a multiple of 3, and $2n - 1$ cannot be a multiple of 3.
D. $2n + 1$ cannot be a multiple for the same reason that $2n - 1$ cannot be a multiple of 3.
E. $2n + 3$ is a multiple of 3. $2n$ is a multiple of 3; 3 is a multiple of 3; thus, $2n + 3$ is a multiple of 3.

Alternatively, substitute an assumed value into the choices. Let $n = 3$:

A. $2 + n = 2 + 3 = 5$ (Not a multiple of 3)
B. $2 - n = 2 - 3 = -1$ (Not a multiple of 3)
C. $2n - 1 = 2(3) - 1 = 6 - 1 = 5$ (Not a multiple of 3)
D. $2n + 1 = 2(3) + 1 = 6 + 1 = 7$ (Not a multiple of 3)
E. $2n + 3 = 2(3) + 3 = 6 + 3 = 9$ (A multiple of 3)

6. **(K)** A ratio is just another way of writing a fraction. Simply inspect each of the answers. As for (F), $(\frac{1}{5})^2$ is equal to $\frac{1}{25}$, and both 1 and 25 are whole numbers. As for (H), $\frac{1}{5}$ is the ratio of 1 to 5, so (H) is not the correct choice. As for (J), 0.25 is equal to $\frac{1}{4}$, the ratio of two whole numbers. Answer choice (G) is not the correct because 5 percent can be written as $\frac{5}{100}$, or $\frac{1}{20}$, which is the ratio of two whole numbers. Finally, $\sqrt{5}$ is not a whole number, so the expression in (K) is not the ratio of two whole numbers.

7. **(D)** If the area of a square is known, the perimeter can be found, and vice versa. Area = side • side = $16 \Rightarrow s^2 = 16 \Rightarrow s = \pm 4$. Distances are always positive. Therefore, the perimeter is equal to $4s$, or $4 \bullet 4 = 16$.

8. **(J)** This problem presents one equation with two variables. It is not possible to solve for x or y individually, but that is not necessary. Just rewrite the equation in the form of $x + y$: $12 + x = 36 - y \Rightarrow x + y = 36 - 12 = 24$.

9. **(D)** The coefficients are 3, 6, and 2, and 1 is the only common factor of those numbers. The smallest term containing the variable x is simply x. Thus, the greatest factor of those terms is just x. The same is true for the terms containing y and z and the greatest common factor is xyz.

10. **(G)** This item can be analyzed as follows: the sum of $3k$, $4k$, $5k$, $6k$, and $7k$ is $25k$, a number that will be divisible by 7. If, however, the coefficient of k were divisible by 7, then that number would be divisible by 7 regardless of the value of k. Dropping the term $4k$ from the group, the sum of the remaining terms is $21k$. Since 21 is divisible by 7, $21k$ will be divisible by 7 regardless of the value of k.

11. **(B)** Do not try to convert each of these fractions to decimals to find the value that lies between $\frac{1}{3}$ and $\frac{3}{8}$. Instead, find an escape route. Use a benchmark, approximate, or use whatever else is available.

First, eliminate (E): $\frac{1}{2}$ is more than $\frac{3}{8}$. Next, eliminate (A): $\frac{3}{15}$ is equal to $\frac{1}{3}$, so $\frac{3}{16}$ is smaller than $\frac{1}{3}$. (B) is close to and slightly less than $\frac{18}{48}$, which is $\frac{3}{8}$. Therefore, (B) is the correct choice. As for (C), $\frac{9}{24}$ is equal to $\frac{3}{8}$, not less than $\frac{3}{8}$. Finally, as for (D), $\frac{5}{12}$ is equal to $\frac{10}{24}$, and $\frac{3}{8}$ is equal to $\frac{9}{24}$.

12. **(G)** Simply factor the expression: $x^2 - y^2 = (x + y) \bullet (x - y)$. Since $(x - y) = 3$, then $(x + y)(3) = 3 \Rightarrow x + y = 1$.

13. **(E)** As for (A), whether $n + 1$ is odd or even will depend on whether n is odd or even. The same is true for (B) and (C) since whether $3n$ is odd or even will depend on whether n is odd or even. As for (D), n^2 will be odd or even depending on whether n is odd or even. However, (E) is even regardless of whether n is odd or even. $n^2 + n$ can be factored as $n(n + 1)$. Since either n or $n + 1$ is even, the product must me even.

14. **(H)** Since the square has an area of 16, it has a side of 4 and a diagonal of $4\sqrt{2}$. The diagonal of the square is also the diameter of the circle. Therefore, the circle has a diameter of $4\sqrt{2}$ and a radius of $2\sqrt{2}$. Finally, a circle with a radius of length $2\sqrt{2}$ has an area of $\pi r^2 = \pi(2\sqrt{2})^2 = 8\pi$.

15. **(C)** First, calculate the sale price: \$120 – (25% of \$120) = \$120 – (0.25 • \$120) = \$120 – \$30 = \$90. Next, calculate the sales tax: Tax = 8% of \$90 = 0.08 • \$90 = \$7.20. Therefore, the total price was \$90 + \$7.20 = \$97.20.

16. (G) Use the "is-over-of" equation. The "of," which is the denominator of the fraction, is the mixture. How much of the mixture is there? $2.5 + 12.5 = 15$. The "is," which is the numerator of the fraction, is the 2.5 kilograms of gravel. Thus: $\frac{\text{is}}{\text{of}} = \frac{\text{gravel}}{\text{mixture}} = \frac{2.5}{15} = \frac{1}{6}$. Remember that $\frac{1}{6} = .01666 = 16\frac{2}{3}\%$.

17. (D) The triangle has sides of 6, 8, and 10 (multiples of 3, 4, and 5). Therefore, the triangle is a right triangle. The sides of 6 and 8 form the right angle, so they can be used as altitude and base for finding the area: Area $= \frac{1}{2} \bullet$ altitude $\bullet$ base $= \frac{1}{2} \bullet 6 \bullet 8 = 24$.

18. (F) Proportions make this calculation easy. First, complete the calculation for Motorcycle A: $\frac{\text{Fuel Used } X}{\text{Fuel Used } Y} = \frac{\text{Miles Driven } X}{\text{Miles Driven } Y} \Rightarrow \frac{1}{x} = \frac{40}{300} \Rightarrow 300 = 40x \Rightarrow 40x = 300 \Rightarrow x = 7.5$. Thus, Motorcycle A uses 7.5 liters of fuel for the 300-mile trip. Now, do the same for Motorcycle B: $\frac{1}{x} = \frac{50}{300} \Rightarrow 300 = 50x \Rightarrow 50x = 300 \Rightarrow x = 6$. Therefore, Motorcycle B uses 6 liters of fuel for the trip. Since Motorcycle A uses $7.5 - 6 = 1.5$ liters more than Motorcycle B, the fuel for Motorcycle A costs $1.5 \bullet \$2 = \$3$ more.

19. (B) First, substitute 3 for x: $f(3) = 3^2 - 2(3) + 1 = 9 - 6 + 1 = 4$. Now, substitute 4 for x: $f(4) = 4^2 - 2(4) + 1 = 16 - 8 + 1 = 9$. Therefore, $f(f(3)) = 9$.

20. (K) Factor $6k + 3$: $6k + 3 = 3(2k + 1)$. Substituting 1 for k in the answer choices also works. The correct answer choice, (K), yields the value 9: $6k + 3 = 6(1) + 3 = 6 + 3 = 9$.

21. (E) Devise the formula as follows. The formula will be x, the cost for the first ounce, plus some expression to represent the additional postage for each additional ounce over the first ounce. The postage for the additional weight is y cents per ounce, and the additional weight is w minus the first ounce, or $w - 1$. Therefore, the additional postage is $y(w - 1)$, and the total postage is $x + y(w - 1)$.

Alternatively, assume some numbers. For ease of calculations, assume that the first ounce costs 1 cent and every additional ounce is free. If $x = 1$ and $y = 0$, then a letter, of say, 10 ounces ($w = 10$) will cost 1 cent. Substitute 1 for x, zero for y, and 10 for w into the choices. The correct formula will generate the value 1. (A), (B), and (C) are eliminated. One more set of assumptions will give the correct answer.

22. (F) $|-3| = 3$ and $|-\frac{1}{2}| = \frac{1}{2}$. Therefore: $|-3| \bullet |2| \bullet |-\frac{1}{2}| + (-4) = 3 \bullet 2 \bullet \frac{1}{2} - 4 = 3 - 4 = -1$.

23. (C) The side of the square is also the radius of the circle. Since the square has an area of 2, its side is: $s \bullet s = 2 \Rightarrow s^2 = 2 \Rightarrow s = \sqrt{2}$. $\sqrt{2}$ is the radius of the circle. Therefore, the area of the circle is $\pi r^2 = \pi(\sqrt{2})^2 = 2\pi$.

24. (G) Test each statement. As for statement (I), 2 is the first prime number, and the product of 2 and any other number must be even. Thus, (I) is not part of the correct answer. As for (II), the sum of two prime numbers might be odd, (*e.g.*, $2 + 3 = 5$), but the sum of two prime numbers might also be even, (*e.g.*, $3 + 5 = 8$). As for (III), however, the product of two odd numbers is necessarily odd.

25. (A) The coordinates establish that this figure is a rectangle. The width of the rectangle is a, and the length is $b - a$. Therefore, the area is $a(b - a)$.

Alternatively, "test-the-test." Assume that $a = 2$ and $b = 4$. The rectangle has a width of 2, a length of $4 - 2 = 2$, and an area of $2 \bullet 2 = 4$. Substitute 2 for a and 4 for b into the answer choices and the correct formula will yield 4.

26. (H) $\sqrt{(43 - 7)(29 + 7)} = \sqrt{(36)(36)} = 36$.

27. (A) Set up a direct proportion: $\frac{\text{Cement } X}{\text{Cement } Y} = \frac{\text{Grit } X}{\text{Grit } Y} \Rightarrow \frac{4}{50} = \frac{20}{x} \Rightarrow 4x = (20)(50) \Rightarrow x = \frac{(20)(50)}{4} = 250$.

28. (G) Label the other two angles in the triangle:

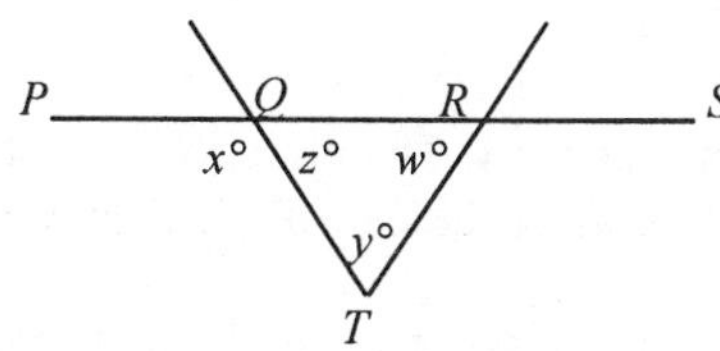

$x + z = 180 \Rightarrow 120 + z = 180 \Rightarrow z = 60$; $z + w + y = 180$. Since $\overline{QT} = \overline{QR}$, $y = w$. $60 + y + y = 180 \Rightarrow 2y = 120 \Rightarrow y = 60$.

29. (C) There is only one equation but two variables, so x and y cannot be solved for individually. Instead, look for a way to rewrite the first equation to give the information needed: $\frac{x}{y} = -1 \Rightarrow x = -y \Rightarrow x + y = 0$.

30. (K) Do not do lengthy calculations. Set up the cost of each fabric as a fraction and compare the fraction directly, using a benchmark:

F. $\frac{8}{3}$

G. $\frac{6}{2} = 3$

H. $\frac{9}{4}$

J. $\frac{7}{5}$

K. $\frac{4}{6}$

(K), $\frac{4}{6}$, is less than 1. The other fractions are greater than 1, so (K) is the smallest.

31. (A) Since $\overline{PQ} \parallel \overline{ST}$, the "big angle/little angle" theorem establishes that $x = y$. Solve for x since this equals y: $75 + 65 + x + x = 180 \Rightarrow 2x + 140 = 180 \Rightarrow 2x = 40 \Rightarrow x = 20$. Therefore, $y = 20$.

32. (J) $\frac{10^3(10^5 + 10^5)}{10^4} = \frac{10(10^4 + 10^4)}{10} = 2(10^4)$.

33. (D) Factor and solve for x: $x^2 - 5x + 4 = 0 \Rightarrow (x - 4)(x - 1) = 0$. So, either $x - 4 = 0$ and $x = 4$, or $x - 1 = 0$ and $x = 1$.

Alternatively, substitute the values in the choices back into the equation to find the set that works.

34. (K) Use the method for finding the missing elements of an average. The smallest possible sum for 6 different positive integers is $1 + 2 + 3 + 4 + 5 + 6 = 21$. The sum of all 7 integers is $7 \bullet 12 = 84$. Therefore, the largest that the seventh number could be (with the average of the seven numbers still 12) is $84 - 21 = 63$.

35. (E) To find b in terms of x and y, set b equal to x and equal to y:

$x = b + 4y = b - 3$
$x - 4 = by + 3 = b$

Combine the two equations by adding:

$$b = x - 4$$
$$+ b = y + 3$$
$$2b = x + y - 1 \Rightarrow b = \frac{x+y-1}{2}$$

Alternatively, substitute some numbers. Let $b = 1$. Therefore, $x = 1 + 4 = 5$, and $y = 1 - 3 = -2$. Substitute 5 for x and -2 for y into the answer choices. The correct choice will yield the value 1.

36. (F) Since $z = 5x = 3y$, and x, y, and z are integers, z is a multiple of both 3 and 5, so z is evenly divisible by 5, 3, and 15. z is divisible by both x and y individually, but z is not necessarily divisible by the product of x and y. Finally, since $5x = 3y$, and x and y are integers, x is a multiple of 3 (and evenly divisible by 3).

Alternatively, substitute some numbers. The most natural assumption is to let $z = 15$, so $x = 3$ and $y = 5$. However, on that assumption, every answer choice is an integer. Try the next multiple of 15. Let $z = 30$, so $x = 6$ and $y = 10$. (F) is no longer an integer: $30 \div (6 \bullet 10) = \frac{1}{2}$.

37. (B) Area of rectangle = width • length $\Rightarrow 48x^2 = w(24x) \Rightarrow w = \frac{48x^2}{24x} = 2x$.

Alternatively, substitute some numbers, such as $x = 2$. The area of the rectangle is $48(2^2) = 48(4) = 192$, and the length is 48. 48 times the width is equal to 192, so the width is $192 \div 48 = 4$. Therefore, if $x = 2$, the correct choice yields the value 4. Only (B) works.

38. (K) Rewrite the equation: $x = \frac{1}{y+1} \Rightarrow x(y+1) = 1 \Rightarrow y + 1 = \frac{1}{x} \Rightarrow y = \frac{1}{x} - 1 \Rightarrow y = \frac{1-x}{x}$.

39. (B) The length of the base of the triangle is $4x - x = 3x$, and the length of the altitude is $3x - 0 = 3x$ (the difference in the y coordinate). Use the formula for finding the area of a triangle to determine x: $\frac{1}{2}(3x)(3x) = 54 \Rightarrow (3x)(3x) = 108 \Rightarrow 9x^2 = 108 \Rightarrow x^2 = 12 \Rightarrow x = \sqrt{12} = 2\sqrt{3}$.

40. (K) This question is a little tricky, but it does not require advanced mathematics. If the room were completely dark and you were in a hurry to make sure you got at least one pair of each color, how many socks would you need to pull from the drawer? Well, what is the worst thing that might happen? You could pull 6 blue socks first. You might pull all 10 white socks on the next 10 tries. So far, you have only white socks and blue socks, and you have pulled 16 socks. Now, there is nothing left in the drawer but green socks. On the worst assumption, 18 picks will *guarantee* you a pair of each color.

41. (E) The question supplies the area of the shaded part of the figure, which is a portion of the circle. First, find what fraction of the circle is shaded. Then, use that value in order to determine the value of the unshaded angle at the center of the circle. The area of the entire circle is $\pi r^2 = \pi(4^2) = 16\pi$. $\frac{14\pi}{16} = \frac{7}{8}$ of the circle is shaded so $\frac{1}{8}$ is unshaded. Therefore, the unshaded angle at the center of the circle is $\frac{1}{8}$ of $360° = 45°$. Now, find x: $x + 45 + 90 = 180 \Rightarrow x + 135 = 180 \Rightarrow x = 45$.

42. (J) This is a composite figure. Redefine one figure in terms of another. The diameter of the smaller circle is equal to the side of the square. The diagonal of the square is the diameter of the larger circle.

Let r be the radius of the smaller circle, so the smaller circle has an area of πr^2. The diameter of the smaller circle is $2r$, which is also the side of the square:

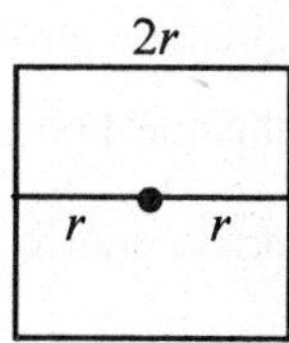

The diagonal of the square creates a 45°-45°-90° triangle with the sides. The hypotenuse of that triangle is equal to the side $s\sqrt{2}$. The diagonal of the square is equal to $2r \bullet \sqrt{2} = 2\sqrt{2}r$. This is also the diameter of the larger circle. Thus, the larger circle has a radius of $2\sqrt{2}r \div 2 = \sqrt{2}r$, and an area of $\pi(\sqrt{2}r)^2 = 2\pi r^2$. Therefore, the ratio is $2\pi r^2 : \pi r^2 = 2:1$.

43. (D) Just perform the indicated operations:

$$2^0 = 1$$
$$2^3 = 8$$
$$2^{-2} = \frac{1}{2^2} = \frac{1}{4}$$
$$1 + 8 - \frac{1}{4} = 8\frac{3}{4}$$

44. (J) Since the axis of symmetry of the parabola is given by the equation $x = 0$, the parabola is symmetric about the y-axis. The point symmetric to the point with coordinates (-1, -2) will have the same y-coordinate, and the x-coordinate of the point will be the same distance from the y-axis but in a positive direction: (1, -2). It might be easier to find the solution with a sketched graph of the equation:

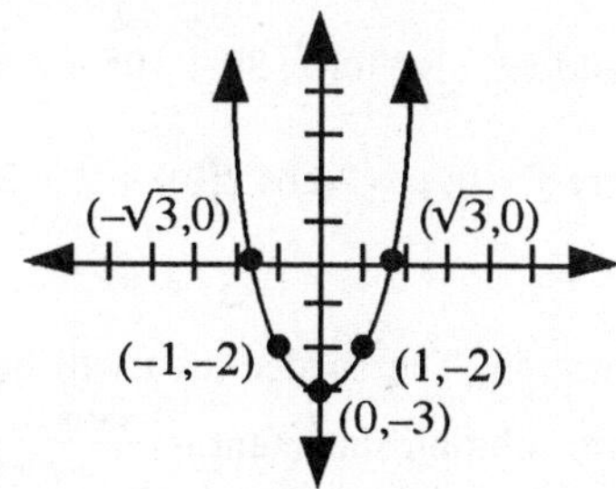

45. (C) If two lines in the coordinate plane are perpendicular to each other, then the product of their slopes is –1.

46. (K) Draw some additional lines to carve the figure up into some more familiar shapes, and use the Pythagorean theorem to determine the length of the shared third side of the two small triangles: $a^2 + 8^2 = 10^2 \Rightarrow a^2 + 64 = 100 \Rightarrow a^2 = 36 \Rightarrow a = 6$.

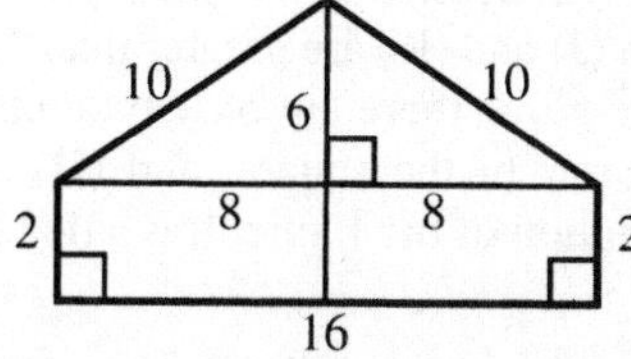

The area of the large rectangle is $16 \bullet 2 = 32$. Using 6 and 8 as the altitude and base of each triangle, respectively, determine the area of each triangle: $\frac{1}{2} \bullet 6 \bullet 8 = 24$. Therefore, the area of the composite figure is: $32 + 24(2) = 32 + 48 = 80$.

47. (D) Rationalize the denominator:

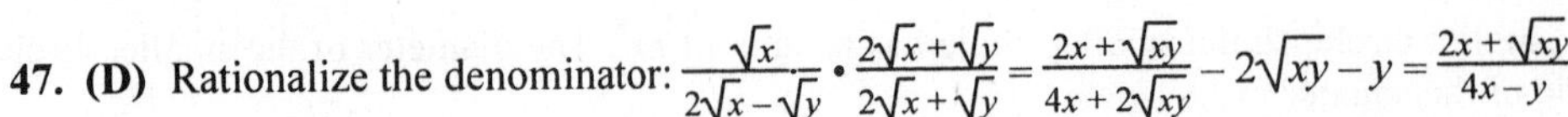

$\frac{\sqrt{x}}{2\sqrt{x}-\sqrt{y}} \bullet \frac{2\sqrt{x}+\sqrt{y}}{2\sqrt{x}+\sqrt{y}} = \frac{2x+\sqrt{xy}}{4x+2\sqrt{xy}-2\sqrt{xy}-y} = \frac{2x+\sqrt{xy}}{4x-y}$.

Alternatively, assume some values for x and y. Since the problem involves square roots, pick a couple of perfect squares, *e.g.*, $x = 9$ and $y = 4$. The expression in the question stem becomes: $\frac{\sqrt{9}}{2\sqrt{9}-\sqrt{4}} = \frac{3}{2(3)-2} = \frac{3}{4}$. Now, substitute 9 for x and 4 for y into the answer choices. The correct choice will generate the value $\frac{3}{4}$:

A.	$\frac{2\sqrt{x}-\sqrt{y}}{2} = \frac{2\sqrt{9}-\sqrt{4}}{2} = \frac{2(3)-2}{2} = 2$	✗
B.	$\frac{2\sqrt{x}+\sqrt{y}}{4xy} = \frac{2\sqrt{9}+\sqrt{4}}{4(9)(4)} = \frac{2(3)+2}{144} = \frac{8}{144}$	✗
C.	$\frac{2\sqrt{x}+\sqrt{xy}}{2x-y} = \frac{2\sqrt{9}+\sqrt{(9)(4)}}{2(9)-4} = \frac{6+6}{14} = \frac{12}{14}$	✗
D.	$\frac{2x+\sqrt{xy}}{4x-y} = \frac{2(9)+\sqrt{(9)(4)}}{4(9)-4} = \frac{18+6}{32} = \frac{24}{32} = \frac{3}{4}$	✓
E.	$\frac{4x+\sqrt{xy}}{4x-y} = \frac{4(9)+\sqrt{(9)(4)}}{4(9)-4} = \frac{36+6}{36-4} = \frac{42}{32}$	✗

48. (H) This question requires the deduction of further conclusions based on the given information. Since opposite angles are equal, the figure becomes:

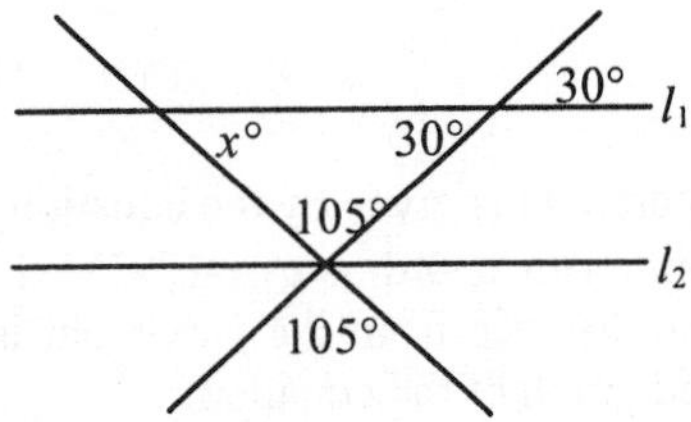

The center triangle has angles 30, 105, and x. Solve for x: $30 + 105 + x = 180 \Rightarrow x = 45$.

49. (D) The graph intersects the y-axis where $x = 0$: $y = 2(\cos 2[0]) + 2 = 2(\cos 0) + 2$. Since $\cos 0 = 1$: $y = 2(1) + 2 = 4$.

50. (G) This is a typical "shaded area" question. The shaded area will be the whole square minus the four circles: Shaded Area = □ – (4 • ○). The entire solution statement is: $\frac{\text{Shaded Area}}{\text{Square}}$. On the assumption that each circle has a radius of r, the side of the square must be $4r$, and the area of the square is $4r \bullet 4r = 16r^2$. This is the denominator of the solution statement, and it is also an element in the calculation of the shaded area. To complete the calculation of the shaded area, reason that each circle with radius r has an area of πr^2. Therefore, the shaded area is: $16r^2 - 4\pi r^2$. Fill in the solution statement: $\frac{16r^2 - 4\pi r^2}{16r^2} = \frac{4r^2(4-\pi)}{16r^2} = \frac{4-\pi}{4}$.

A little common sense goes a long way when applied to the answer choices. Since π is less than 4, (F) is a negative number and is therefore impossible. Both (J) and (K) are greater than 1, asserting that the shaded area is larger than the square, an equally absurd conclusion. Now, there are only two answer choices remaining: (G) asserts that the shaded area is a little less than one-quarter of the square, and (H) asserts that the shaded area is about three-quarters of the square. After careful inspection of the figure, it is safe to assume that (G) is correct.

51. (C) One of the Pythagorean identities is: $\sin^2 \theta + \cos^2 \theta = 1$. Therefore, the expression given in the question stem is equivalent to $\frac{1}{\sin \theta}$. The reciprocal identity for the sine function is the cosecant function.

52. (G) $\tan \theta = \frac{\text{side opposite } \theta}{\text{adjacent}}$. Therefore, $\tan 55° = \frac{6}{\overline{AC}}$: $1.4 \approx \frac{6}{\overline{AC}} \Rightarrow \overline{AC} \approx \frac{6}{1.4} \approx 4.28$.

53. (D) When $x = 1$, $x - 1 = 0$, so the entire expression is undefined. Similarly, when $x = -2$, $x + 2$ is 0, and the expression is undefined. When $x = -3$, then $x + 3$ is equal to 0, so the value of the expression is 0.

54. (K) Since the sum of x and y is less than or equal to 6, y will have its maximum value when x has its minimum value. The minimum value of x is 0; the maximum value of y is 6. $3(6) = 18$.

Alternatively, test the answer choices. Since the question asks for the maximum value of y, start with the largest choice: 18. If $3y = 18$, then $y = 6$. $x + y \leq 6 \Rightarrow x + 6 \leq 6 \Rightarrow x \leq 0$. Since x can be 0, $y = 6$ satisfies the system of inequalities. 18 is the largest answer choice, and therefore it must be the largest value possible for $3y$.

55. (D) Find the corresponding values for y:

$$y = |(-1)^2 - 3| = |1 - 3| = |-2| = 2$$
$$y = |(0)^2 - 3| = |-3| = 3$$
$$y = |(1)^2 - 3| = |1 - 3| = |-2| = 2$$

(D) is the correct plotting of the points $(-1, 2)$, $(0, 3)$, and $(1, 2)$.

56. (G) Calculate the slope: $m = \frac{(-2) + (-4)}{(2) - (-1)} = \frac{-6}{3} = -2$. Since the answer choices are equations of a line in slope-intercept form, each with a different slope, (G) is the correct answer.

57. (A) There are at least three different ways of attacking this problem, but one method is clearly superior. Use the roots to create the equation. If $x = a$ or $x = b$, then $x - a = 0$ or $x - b = 0$. The factors of the equation are $(x - a)$ and $(x - b)$, and the equation is: $(x - a)(x - b) = x^2 - ax - bx + ab = 0$. Given the roots of this equation, that will take a little time.

Similarly, substitute the solutions into each of the equations to find the equation that will accept both solutions. This, too, is a lot of work.

The best approach is to see that the roots are expressed in a form that is suggestive of the quadratic formula. Thus, $-b = -3$, so $b = 3$. Eliminate (B) and (D). Next, $2a = 2$, so $a = 1$; eliminate (E). Finally, $b^2 - 4ac = 5$. Since $b = 3$ and $a = 1$: $b^2 - 4ac = 5 \Rightarrow (3)^2 - 4(1)(c) = 5 \Rightarrow 9 - 4c = 5 \Rightarrow 4c = 4 \Rightarrow c = 1$. Thus, the equation is $x^2 + 3x + 1 = 0$.

58. (F) A function is a relationship such that each element of the domain is paired with one and only one element in the range. In the relationship given in the question stem, one element of the domain, *0*, is paired with two different elements in the range: 3 and 5. Therefore, the relationship given in the question stem is not a function. By dropping the first set of pairs, this duplication is eliminated and the set becomes a function.

59. (D) Consider the trapezoid as a composite figure. Draw a line from point B perpendicular to $\overline{CD}$. The trapezoid is a combination of a right triangle and a rectangle. Since the triangle has degree measures of 30, 60, and 90, the side opposite the 30° angle has a length half that of the hypotenuse, or a length of 4. Thus, the rectangle has sides of 4 and 9 and an area of 36. Then, the side of the triangle opposite the 60° angle has a length equal to $4\sqrt{3}$. The area of the triangle is: $\frac{1}{2}(a)(b) = \frac{1}{2}(4)(4\sqrt{3})$. The area of the triangle is $8\sqrt{3}$. So, the area of the trapezoid is $36 + 8\sqrt{3}$.

60. (G) There are several routes by which to reach the right conclusion. The shortest is to reason that the cotangent and tangent are reciprocal functions, so if $\cot\theta = \frac{4}{3}$, then $\tan\theta = \frac{3}{4}$.

TEST 3: READING (p. 812)

1. **(A)** The passage actually makes two points: Who Josquin is, and why we have never heard of him. (A) mentions both of these points.

2. **(J)** (F) is answered in the second paragraph ("Solace me"). (G) is answered in the final paragraph (sackbut). (H) is answered in the second paragraph (Ockeghem). (J) must be the correct answer since the author never makes reference to any students.

3. **(D)** In the fourth paragraph, the author lists certain difficulties in reading a Renaissance score: no tempo specified, missing flats and sharps, and no instrument/voice indication. Since these are regarded as deficiencies of Renaissance scoring, it is inferable that modern music notation contains all of these.

4. **(G)** In the third paragraph, the author discusses the distinction between concept and performance. The author states that music does not exist as printed notes. The notation is just a set of instructions for producing music. Therefore, the author would agree with (G).

5. **(D)** There is merit to each of the choices, but the best answer is the one that is most closely connected to the passage. The author discusses the lack of funding as one important reason for Josquin's obscurity, an obscurity that the author deplores. The argument might be used to support a proposal for funds to promote Josquin's music, (D).

6. **(G)** (H) and (J) are mentioned in the final paragraph. (F) is mentioned in the third paragraph. (G) is never mentioned. The author states that musicians who read modern notation have difficulty reading Renaissance notation—not that these musicians lack talent.

7. **(A)** The author compares Josquin to Galileo in order to praise Josquin. This suggests that the author has a very high opinion of Galileo.

8. **(H)** The first paragraph states that the dominant theme of liturgical music is reverence.

9. **(A)** In the third paragraph, the author says that in fine art such as painting and poetry, concept and performance are one. For example, the painting is what it is—a physical object. However, in music, the concept exists only during a performance. Ballet is like music in this respect.

10. **(H)** In the first paragraph, the author states that up to the time of Josquin des Prez, Western music was liturgical. In the second paragraph, the author says that Josquin des Prez wrote both religious and nonreligious music.

11. **(C)** At the beginning of the story, the child addresses the narrator as Miss Mix. At the end of the story, Mr. Rawjester calls her Mary Jane.

12. **(H)** As the narrator surmises, the highwayman is in reality Mr. Rawjester. He assumes the role of a robber in order to make sure that he is not suspected of setting the fire.

13. **(A)** The narrator is employed as a governess by Mr. Rawjester. Apparently, she is required to help Blanche make herself up. This is degrading since the narrator herself has feelings for the master of the house.

14. **(H)** This can be deduced from the conversation between the narrator and the child. It becomes clear when the narrator identifies herself to the highwayman as a governess.

15. **(B)** As he leaves the party, he calls his guests "idiots" under his breath.

16. **(G)** At the beginning of the story, the child tells the narrator that her father's sweetheart is about to become her mother.

17. **(B)** Since the narrator survives the encounter with the highwayman, she must have chosen to cooperate with him.

18. **(J)** As already noted, the highwayman is a trick designed to allow Mr. Rawjester to dispose of his three crazy wives while avoiding suspicion.

19. **(A)** Since the highwayman is Mr. Rawjester, he knows about the necklace.

20. **(F)** Notice that the conversation takes place in a low voice and a whisper.

21. **(B)** This is the only statement general enough to cover the specific information in the piece. (A) is contradicted by the text. (C) and (D) are specific details and, therefore, too narrow in scope to be the main idea of the passage.

22. **(G)** Since the policy approved by the board involves the payment of large bonuses to any management member who is fired after a takeover, the policy is, by definition, a golden parachute.

23. **(C)** According to the second paragraph, the defining characteristic of a hostile takeover is the existing management's opposition.

24. **(F)** This statement is supported by the beginning of the third paragraph, which tells of the methods used by raiders to raise the cash they need to buy a targeted company's stock.

25. **(D)** The fifth paragraph defines the three anti-takeover strategies. (A) defines the greenmail strategy. (B) defines the golden parachute theory. (C) is not supported by anything in the passage.

26. **(G)** This argument is made at the beginning of the last paragraph. The topics of statements (F), (H), and (J) are all mentioned in the passage, but the passage does not support any of these statements.

27. **(D)** The meaning of a proxy fight is presented in the second paragraph. The other choices are all true but do not involve a proxy battle.

28. **(H)** This point is explicitly made at the beginning of the last paragraph. All the other choices are properly defined in the second to last paragraph.

29. **(B)** The rule of the Securities and Exchange Commission is defined in the first sentence of the selection.

30. **(H)** In the fourth paragraph, the passage states that some people have been convicted of selling inside information about takeovers.

31. **(C)** In the first sentence of the passage, the author says a supernova occurs about twice every century, or about once every fifty years.

32. **(J)** (F) is stated in the second paragraph. (G) is stated in the first paragraph. (H) is stated in the second paragraph. Although the word "galaxy" is used in the selection, the author does not say that colliding galaxies cause supernovas. (J) is the one detail not mentioned in the selection.

33. **(A)** In the first paragraph, the author compares a star to a leaky balloon. That is an analogy.

34. **(H)** The key word for this question is *anomalous.* The author states that the unexpected makeup of the meteorites is evidence that a supernova helped form our solar system. However, this evidence supports the conclusion only if the strange content is foreign to our solar system. Only (H) explains the connection between the theory of the origin of our solar system and the strange makeup of the meteors.

35. **(A)** In the last two sentences of the second paragraph, the author states that supernovas emit most of their energy as x-rays and notes that x-ray observations provide the most useful insights into the nature of supernovas. He adds that remnants of supernovas have been found using x-ray studies. These remarks suggest that it is easier to find a supernova using equipment that detects x-rays than it is using equipment for viewing visible light.

36. **(J)** In the first paragraph, the author describes the start of the sequence of events that leads to a supernova. It begins when a star runs out of fuel and collapses.

37. **(B)** In the first paragraph, the author describes the collapse of an ordinary star. The result is a neutron star. In the second paragraph, the author describes what follows—a supernova. Thus, the neutron star is an intermediate stage between the ordinary star and its final phase, a supernova.

38. **(J)** (F), (G), and (H) are incorrect—each makes the mistake of elevating a part of the passage to the status of main idea. (J) is the best description of the passage. The author describes the sequence of events that leads to a supernova and then describes what events follow the supernova.

39. **(D)** The last paragraph dates the formation of our galaxy at over 4.5 billion years ago.

40. **(H)** The last paragraph notes that the cosmic radiation generated by supernovas is responsible for many of the genetic mutations that propel evolution.

TEST 4: SCIENCE REASONING (p. 820)

1. **(C)** Generally, the Wright data show lower lift at a given angle than the Lilienthal data.

2. **(H)** The highest point on the graph is at 16 degrees (approximately 5.5 pounds/sq. ft.).

3. **(A)** By extending both lines to the 50° mark, the difference between them is clearly observed to be less than 1 pound/sq. ft.

4. **(H)** Count the crossing points of the two curves.

5. **(C)** The widest region is between 18° and 43°.

6. **(J)** Since plastic beads are not alive, they cannot possibly carry out cellular respiration. This control is designed to detect any atmospheric changes (in the laboratory) that may cause a change in gas volume inside the tubes.

7. **(A)** Oxygen in the air of the tube is consumed by the peas during cellular respiration (see summary equation).

8. **(H)** Without KOH to remove the carbon dioxide produced during cellular respiration, the same number of gas molecules ($6CO_2$) would always be added to the tube as gas molecules were being consumed in the tube ($6O_2$).

9. **(C)** Experiment 2 was conducted at a higher temperature than Experiment 1. The greater decrease in gas in the same time period (15 minutes) demonstrates a faster consumption of oxygen.

10. **(G)** If results are identical in light and dark (Experiments 1 and 2), then light/dark conditions are irrelevant to cellular respiration rates in the experiment; only temperature conditions are important.

11. **(A)** Glucose must be consumed in order for cellular respiration to occur. Since cellular respiration did not occur at equal rates in Experiments 1 and 2, (A) is the only possible answer. Peas are seeds containing a supply of glucose.

12. **(G)** Scientist 1 believes that processes associated with sudden events in the past shaped the Earth, whereas Scientist 2 believes that the processes are continuing in the present.

13. **(D)** Mountains could not have formed only when land masses were raised at the beginnings of the Earth if recent fossils of sea creatures are found at mountain tops. This evidence suggests that the rocks were underwater relatively recently.

14. **(H)** Scientist 1 never refers to time or how old the Earth may be. Scientist 2 refers to "long" or "vast" periods of time.

15. **(A)** If the worldwide ocean precipitated granite first, it must be the lowest layer, with other precipitated materials covering it later.

16. **(F)** If the major rock types (three) formed when the worldwide ocean precipitated different materials on three occasions, no further types can be expected since this ocean no longer exists (possibly due to evaporation).

17. **(C)** Processes cannot be uniform from the beginning. Processes that formed the Earth at its origin must have differed from those that maintain and mold the Earth as an existing planet.

18. **(G)** Scientist 1 refers to three rock types forming during three separate precipitations. Regions of lava (with no present volcanoes), rivers presently continuing to cut their channels, and "related" fossils that could not have immigrated from other geographic areas are factors that support the views of Scientist 2.

19. **(D)** Ten individuals had their heart rates recorded every 10 minutes during a 30-minute experiment (three times). Therefore, 30 values were used to calculate the average heart rate for each of the experiments.

20. **(G)** Since Species B had an increase in heart rate when environmental temperature increased, it is the likely species to be poikilothermic (Species A's heart rate stayed about the same).

21. **(C)** Just by chance alone, any one individual might have an extremely high or extremely low heart rate. The larger the sample of individuals tested, the lower the chances of getting extreme average values.

22. **(J)** Since Species B (poikilothermic) had an increase in average heart rate when environmental temperature increased, a decrease in average heart rate is likely when temperatures drop. Species A should have approximately the same average heart rate at all three temperatures.

23. **(A)** At 22°C, Species A had an average heart rate of 150 beats/minute, while Species B averaged 100 beats/minute.

24. **(F)** The poikilothermic Species B should have an increase in body temperature in Experiment 2 (35°C conditions in the incubator compared to 22°C in Experiment 1). The homeothermic Species A should have no significant change in body temperature during the experiments.

25. **(A)** Each photon can promote an electron from level 1 to level 2 since the difference in energies is 0.60. (Note that the actual value of level 1 alone, which happens to be 0.60 also, does not determine the answer. Differences in energy are what matter.)

26. **(J)** There is no way to distinguish between the two emissions since each releases a photon of equal energy.

27. **(D)** Only the level 3 to level 1 emission has an energy difference of 0.92.

28. **(J)** Each electron can go from level 1 to any of 4 other levels, with each of the four transitions requiring a photon of a different energy.

29. **(C)** Since absorption of photons occurs first, then emission, electrons must be promoted (gaining the necessary energy from the absorbed photons), then emitted. Transitions between levels 3 and 4 have the necessary energies, namely 0.23.

30. **(J)** Although 2.07 is the absolute energy of level 5, there is no difference of energy levels anywhere on the diagram that equals 2.07; hence, the photons will not be absorbed.

31. **(C)** Note how θ_1 and θ_2 are defined on the original drawing, then imagine how the diagram will change as the angles become smaller. (B) would be correct if the angles were defined as those between the ray and the horizontal, not vertical, axis.

32. (J) Only the last choice fits both experiments.

33. (A) This question simply requires interpretation of the meaning of the diagram.

34. (H) The beam of light only passes into the air for observation in Experiment 2.

35. (C) This response covers all elements of the three diagrams.

36. (H) The number of butterflies captured for marking is found under the heading: "# marked". Reading across the table for each size group, the "dark brown" category always has the fewest butterflies marked.

37. (D) By comparing the number of butterflies recaptured to the number marked, students can derive a proportion that represents how easy it is to recapture each type of butterfly. The proportion for small, white butterflies (30/35) is much higher than that for any of the other choices.

38. (G) An examination of the table shows that for all colors, as size increases the number of butterflies marked gets larger.

39. (B) A poisonous chemical will have adverse effects on the butterfly after marking (perhaps by killing or by preventing flight). The group with the lowest number (and proportion) of individuals recaptured in flight (10/40 = 1/4 recaptured) is the group consisting of small, tan butterflies.

40. (G) For medium-sized butterflies, the proportion of individuals recaptured in each color is as follows: white (15/30 = 1/2), tan (20/40 = 1/2), and dark brown (10/20 = 1/2).

TEST 5: WRITING TEST (p. 830)

Sample Essay 1—Below Average Response

Some people will argue that a total ban on unhealthy food will interfere with the freedom of students to choose what they eat. Freedom to eat what one chooses is not like freedom of speech of freedom from policy brutality. In the big picture, being told that one cannot buy "Twinkle Cakes" from the machine in the cafeteria is not like being told that one can't criticize the government. Banning foods from school doesn't mean that these foods are banned altogether. One can still buy them and eat them before and after school and on weekends. All that the ban means is that you can't eat them in school when you are under the school's authority.

By banning unhealthy food from schools, students would be getting only healthy food. This means that for at least one meal (lunch), they wouldn't be eating junk. That would mean that they would be eating food that contains important nutrients and doesn't have all of the calories and additives that are usually found in regular junk food. This alone would probably have an important impact on the health of the country. Students would learn about good nutrition. Many students now may not understand that they need certain vitamins and minerals and these usually come from eating foods like broccoli and fresh fruit. You just don't find a lot of vitamins in "Twinkle Cakes." Junk food often contains additives and preservatives that are not good for us. Someone who eats too much junk food gets too much of these bad elements. This would be especially important for younger children because their nutritional needs are more significant than older children. They would begin to learn at an earlier age the important difference between healthy food and junk food. And these lessons would stay with them.

Having schools set a good example might help adults as well. When parents see that their children are eating right, they could also become interested in having better diets. If everyone were eating better, then there would be less incentive to eat things that are bad, and everyone would benefit.

Banning unhealthy foods in school is not the first step to a dictatorship. Schools prohibit a lot of behavior (think of obscene T-shirts) that is allowed outside of school. So a new policy really would hurt anyone. Plus, the new policy would have some definite benefits, so it should be accepted.

Position on issue:

The writer never clearly explains the position. The writer begins the essay with, "Some people will argue that a total ban on unhealthy food will interfere with the freedom of students to choose what they eat," which leaves the writer's actual position ambiguous.

Topic Development and Essay Organization:

This is obviously the same essay as the first but with some minor changes. Much of the organizational scheme has been removed. There is no "three benefits" and not other words to signal when the writer is passing from one point to another. The point is to see how very important the organizational scheme is in an essay. The two make essentially the same points, but the first is much more effective.

Language usage, sentence structure, and punctuation:

The essay should have a more formal tone.

Summary and conclusions:

This second essay would probably receive a "3" rather than a "4," although the elimination of the organization is artificial, so we can't say for certain. This much, however, does seem clear. The first would be more likely to receive the "4" than the second.

Sample Essay 2—Above Average Response

I think that it would be a good for schools to ban all food that is not healthy for students. Although some people will argue that a total ban on unhealthy food will interfere with the freedom of students to choose what they eat, there are two points to remember. One, freedom to eat what one chooses is not like freedom of speech of freedom from policy brutality. In the big picture, being told that one cannot buy "Twinkle Cakes" from the machine in the cafeteria is not like being told that one can't criticize the government. Two, banning foods from school doesn't mean that these foods are banned altogether. One can still buy them and eat them before and after school and on weekends. All that the ban means is that you can't eat them in school when you are under the school's authority.

Banning unhealthy food from schools would have three benefits. First, during the school day, students would be getting only healthy food. This means that for at least one meal (lunch), they wouldn't be eating junk. That would mean that they would be eating food that contains important nutrients and doesn't have all of the calories and additives that are usually found in regular junk food. This alone would probably have an important impact on the health of the country. Second, students would learn about good nutrition. Many students now may not understand that they need certain vitamins and minerals and these usually come from eating foods like broccoli and fresh fruit. You just don't find a lot of vitamins in "Twinkle Cakes." Also, junk food often contains additives and preservatives that are not good for us. Someone who eats too much junk food gets too much of these bad elements. This would be especially important for younger children because their nutritional needs are more significant than older children. They would begin to learn at an earlier age the important difference between healthy food and junk food. And these lessons would stay with them.

Third, having schools set a good example might help adults as well. When parents see that their children are eating right, they could also become interested in having better diets. If everyone were eating better, then there would be less incentive to eat things that are bad, and everyone would benefit.

Banning unhealthy foods in school is not the first step to a dictatorship. Schools prohibit a lot of behavior (think of obscene T-shirts) that is allowed outside of school. So a new policy really would not hurt anyone. Plus, the new policy would have some definite benefits, so it should be accepted.

Position on issue:

In this essay, the writer takes a clear position and begins by handling a possible objection to that position.

Topic Development and Essay Organization:

The writer develops three benefits that would flow from a school policy banning certain foods. The three benefits are each discussed in separate paragraphs, and the writer nicely signals for the reader what each paragraph is about. The one criticism that might be levied generally upon the essay is that it doesn't seem to develop the points in sufficient detail. Yes, the writer mentions examples such as "Twinkie Cakes" (presumably a humorous reference to "Twinkies" and a nice touch), broccoli, and fresh fruit; but the writer never connects these to the issue of obesity. To be sure, it would be legitimate to let the essay range over a lot of nutritional issues, but then the writer really should explain to the reader that these additional points are further thoughts about the issue, e.g., "In addition to having an impact on the obesity epidemic, a policy of "Healthy Foods Only" would improve nutrition in other ways."

Language usage, sentence structure, and punctuation:

In general, the writer uses correct grammar and ties ideas together logically.

Summary and conclusions:

As written, the essay makes some good points but they seem to be wide of the mark. A tighter focus would earn a higher mark. As it stands, this essay would probably get a "4." It's hard to imagine that anyone would think it a "3," and perhaps a handful of readers might think of it as a "5."

PRACTICE TEST IV

DIRECTIONS: For the *correct* answers in each ACT test subject, check the corresponding unshaded box. Then, total the number of checkmarks for each of the content areas, and add these totals in order to determine the raw score for that particular test.

TEST 1: ENGLISH (p. 838)

#	Answer	UM	RH
1.	C	☐	■
2.	J	■	☐
3.	D	■	☐
4.	G	☐	■
5.	A	☐	■
6.	H	☐	■
7.	C	■	☐
8.	F	☐	■
9.	B	☐	■
10.	G	■	☐
11.	D	☐	■
12.	H	☐	■
13.	C	■	☐
14.	H	■	☐
15.	D	☐	■
16.	F	☐	■
17.	B	☐	■
18.	J	■	☐
19.	D	☐	■
20.	H	☐	■
21.	A	☐	■
22.	J	☐	■
23.	A	■	☐
24.	H	■	☐
25.	C	☐	■
26.	J	■	☐
27.	A	☐	■
28.	J	■	☐
29.	C	☐	■
30.	F	■	☐
31.	A	☐	■
32.	J	☐	■
33.	B	■	☐
34.	G	☐	■
35.	D	■	☐
36.	G	☐	■
37.	A	■	☐
38.	H	■	☐
39.	B	☐	■
40.	J	■	☐
41.	A	☐	■
42.	H	☐	■
43.	D	■	☐
44.	H	☐	■
45.	B	■	☐
46.	J	■	☐
47.	B	■	☐
48.	F	☐	■
49.	D	■	☐
50.	H	■	☐
51.	B	☐	■
52.	F	☐	■
53.	D	☐	■
54.	G	☐	■
55.	D	■	☐
56.	J	■	☐
57.	C	☐	■
58.	H	☐	■
59.	A	■	☐
60.	G	■	☐
61.	A	☐	■
62.	H	■	☐
63.	B	■	☐
64.	J	☐	■
65.	D	■	☐
66.	H	☐	■
67.	C	☐	■
68.	G	■	☐
69.	B	■	☐
70.	F	☐	■
71.	D	☐	■
72.	J	☐	■
73.	C	■	☐
74.	F	■	☐
75.	A	■	☐

Usage/Mechanics (UM): _______ /40 Rhetorical Skills (RH): _______ /35 English Raw Score (UM + RH): _______ /75

TEST 2: MATHEMATICS (p. 852)

#	Answer	EA	AG	GT
1.	C	☐	■	■
2.	G	■	■	☐
3.	B	☐	■	■
4.	F	■	■	☐
5.	A	☐	■	■
6.	H	■	☐	■
7.	E	☐	■	■
8.	K	☐	■	■
9.	D	☐	■	■
10.	G	☐	■	■
11.	B	■	☐	■
12.	H	☐	■	■
13.	E	☐	■	■
14.	J	☐	■	■
15.	E	☐	■	■
16.	H	☐	■	■
17.	C	■	■	☐
18.	G	■	☐	■
19.	B	■	☐	■
20.	F	■	☐	■
21.	E	■	☐	■
22.	K	■	☐	■
23.	E	■	■	☐
24.	F	■	■	☐
25.	E	■	■	☐
26.	F	☐	■	■
27.	B	☐	■	■
28.	K	☐	■	■
29.	E	■	■	☐
30.	H	■	■	☐
31.	E	■	☐	■
32.	G	☐	■	■
33.	C	■	■	☐
34.	H	■	■	☐
35.	B	☐	■	■
36.	F	■	☐	■
37.	D	■	■	☐
38.	G	☐	■	■
39.	E	■	☐	■
40.	F	■	☐	■
41.	E	■	■	☐
42.	H	■	☐	■
43.	B	■	■	☐
44.	G	■	■	☐
45.	A	■	■	☐
46.	H	■	☐	■
47.	C	☐	■	■
48.	H	■	■	☐
49.	E	☐	■	■
50.	F	☐	■	■
51.	B	☐	■	■
52.	G	■	☐	■
53.	E	☐	■	■
54.	F	■	☐	■
55.	A	☐	■	■
56.	G	■	☐	■
57.	D	■	■	☐
58.	H	■	☐	■
59.	A	■	■	☐
60.	G	■	☐	■

Pre-Algebra/Elementary Algebra (EA): _______ /24 Intermediate Algebra/Coordinate Geometry (AG): _______ /18

Plane Geometry/Trigonometry (GT): _______ /18 Mathematics Raw Score (EA + AG + GT): _______ /60

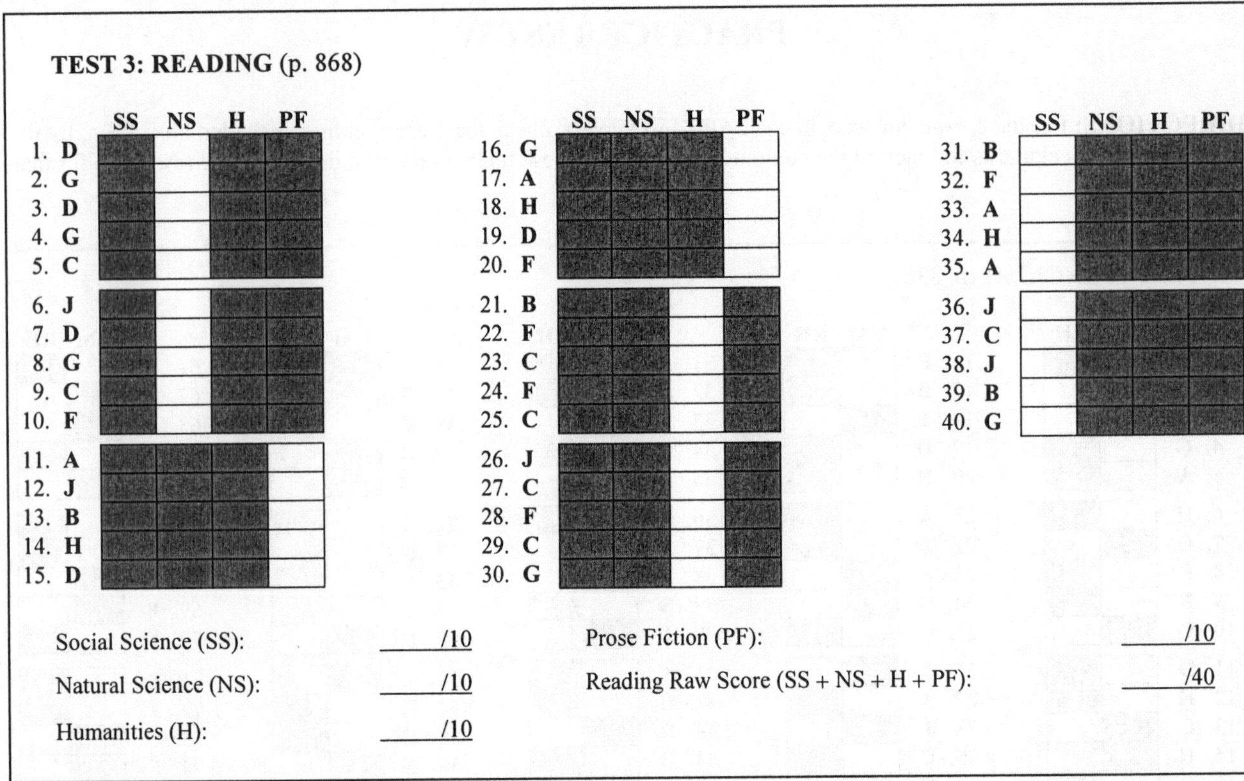

TEST 3: READING (p. 868)

#	Answer	SS	NS	H	PF
1.	D		☐		
2.	G		☐		
3.	D		☐		
4.	G		☐		
5.	C		☐		
6.	J		☐		
7.	D		☐		
8.	G		☐		
9.	C		☐		
10.	F		☐		
11.	A				☐
12.	J				☐
13.	B				☐
14.	H				☐
15.	D				☐
16.	G				☐
17.	A				☐
18.	H				☐
19.	D				☐
20.	F				☐
21.	B			☐	
22.	F			☐	
23.	C			☐	
24.	F			☐	
25.	C			☐	
26.	J			☐	
27.	C			☐	
28.	F			☐	
29.	C			☐	
30.	G			☐	
31.	B	☐			
32.	F	☐			
33.	A	☐			
34.	H	☐			
35.	A	☐			
36.	J	☐			
37.	C	☐			
38.	J	☐			
39.	B	☐			
40.	G	☐			

Social Science (SS): ______/10

Natural Science (NS): ______/10

Humanities (H): ______/10

Prose Fiction (PF): ______/10

Reading Raw Score (SS + NS + H + PF): ______/40

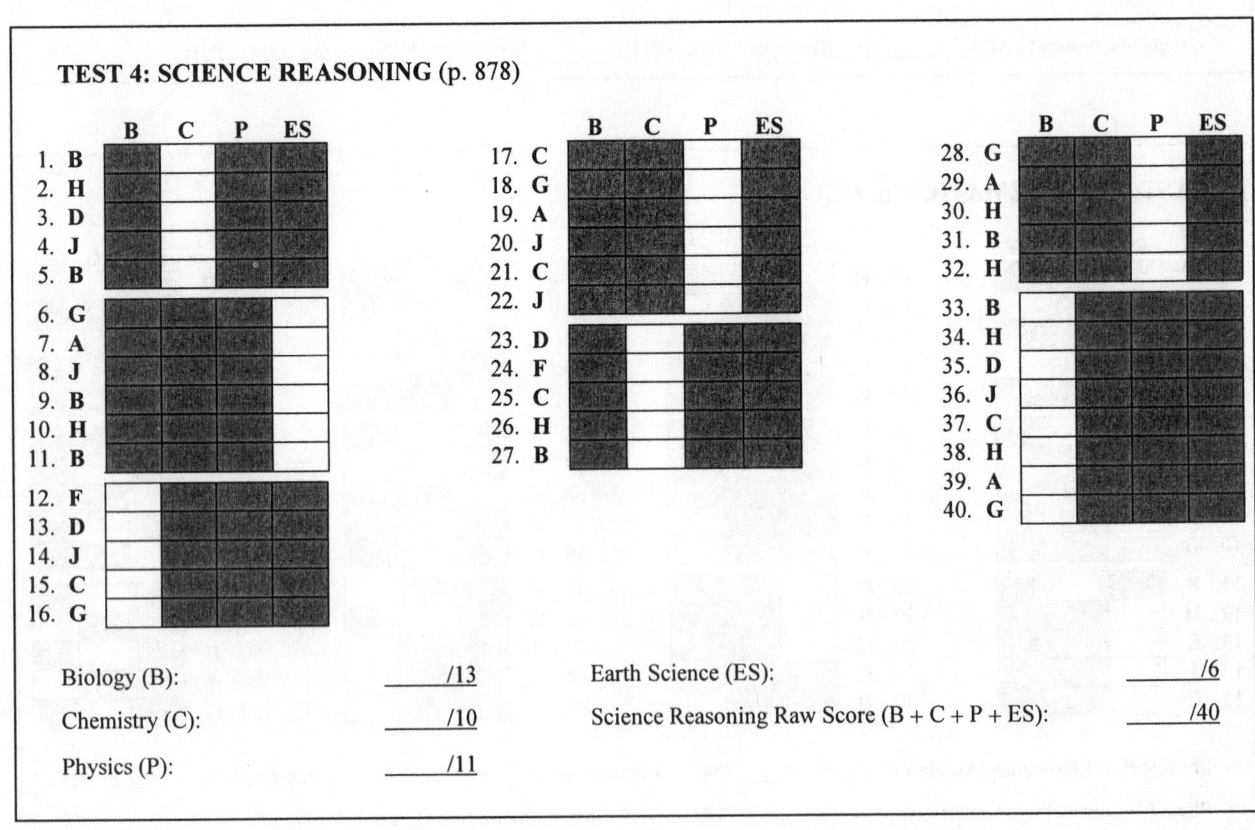

TEST 4: SCIENCE REASONING (p. 878)

#	Answer	B	C	P	ES
1.	B		☐		
2.	H		☐		
3.	D		☐		
4.	J		☐		
5.	B		☐		
6.	G				☐
7.	A				☐
8.	J				☐
9.	B				☐
10.	H				☐
11.	B				☐
12.	F	☐			
13.	D	☐			
14.	J	☐			
15.	C	☐			
16.	G	☐			
17.	C			☐	
18.	G			☐	
19.	A			☐	
20.	J			☐	
21.	C			☐	
22.	J			☐	
23.	D		☐		
24.	F		☐		
25.	C		☐		
26.	H		☐		
27.	B		☐		
28.	G			☐	
29.	A			☐	
30.	H			☐	
31.	B			☐	
32.	H			☐	
33.	B	☐			
34.	H	☐			
35.	D	☐			
36.	J	☐			
37.	C	☐			
38.	H	☐			
39.	A	☐			
40.	G	☐			

Biology (B): ______/13

Chemistry (C): ______/10

Physics (P): ______/11

Earth Science (ES): ______/6

Science Reasoning Raw Score (B + C + P + ES): ______/40

TEST 1: ENGLISH (p. 838)

1. **(C)** A semicolon is used between clauses joined by a coordinating conjunction when one or more of the clauses contain commas.

2. **(J)** This is redundant and not necessary to the sentence.

3. **(D)** The correct adjective is *characteristic*, which means distinctive.

4. **(G)** *When* is not used with *is*. Replace *when* with *is that*.

5. **(A)** The original sentence is correct. *Has become* is correct in both number and tense.

6. **(H)** Numbers are generally written out, especially at the beginning of a sentence.

7. **(C)** *As* is the standard usage for comparison.

8. **(F)** The dash is used for separation and emphasis.

9. **(B)** The apostrophe is used to show possession.

10. **(G)** The comma is needed for separation and clarity.

11. **(D)** *One's* is the correct possessive pronoun.

12. **(H)** Quotation marks indicate that *bowl* is used in an unusual way.

13. **(C)** The question gives the reader the main focus of the passage and piques his or her interest.

14. **(H)** The correct adjective is *distinguished*, which means separated from others by extraordinary qualities.

15. **(D)** The quoted material is the words of the imaginative Italian observer mentioned in the second sentence.

16. **(F)** *Easily* is the correct adverb modifying the verb *die*.

17. **(B)** *Likely* should be used to indicate probability. *Like* is incorrect as it is used in the original.

18. **(J)** This is redundant and not necessary since sociologists, by definition, study sociology.

19. **(D)** *Those kind of* is a nonstandard expression. *Those* is plural and *kind* is singular.

20. **(H)** The correct adverb is *around*.

21. **(A)** The original sentence is correct. The verb *compared* continues the past tense used throughout the sentence.

22. **(J)** Commas are used to separate items in a list.

23. **(A)** Criminology is a topic in the study of sociology, but the passage is not technical in nature; thus, (B) is wrong. (C) is too general, while (D) is too specific.

24. **(H)** [1] refers to the nineteenth century, [3] to the turn of the century, and [2] to the twentieth century.

25. **(C)** *Shows* is necessary for agreement with the singular subject *history*.

26. **(J)** *In depth* is the correct prepositional phrase.

27. **(A)** The original sentence is correct. *Effects* is the noun that means *results*.

28. **(J)** This information has no relevance to the paragraph, so it should be omitted.

29. **(C)** A comma is used to separate words, phrases, or clauses in a series.

30. **(F)** An example of the risks being discussed would make the discussion more concrete to the reader.

31. **(A)** The original sentence is correct. *An* is used before a word beginning with a vowel.

32. **(J)** *Neither* agrees with *nor* in the sentence.

33. **(B)** *And years to come* is redundant and not necessary to the sentence.

34. **(G)** *Persistence* is the correct noun.

35. **(D)** *Compared* is the correct verb and *to* is the correct preposition.

36. **(G)** No punctuation is necessary.

37. **(A)** The original order is correct. [1] introduces the topic of the entire essay: modern pollution problems—therefore, only (A) and (C) need to be considered. [2] begins with *These arguments*, which refers to arguments previously mentioned. Only (A) has [2] arranged before [3], so (A) is the correct choice.

38. **(H)** The passage discusses pollution problems, not a history of technology; thus, (F) is wrong. Because the information presented is general, not technical in nature, (G) is also wrong. (J) is too narrow; the passage covers radioactive substances and more.

39. **(B)** *Remaining* is the correct gerund. The addition of *around* or *up* is unnecessary.

40. **(J)** Use of *of had* in place of *have* is nonstandard. *Maybe* is an adverb, not a verb.

41. **(A)** The original sentence is correct. *Most* is used correctly to modify the adjective *able*.

42. **(H)** Commas are used to set off adverbs that compare or contrast some preceding idea.

43. **(D)** *Disrepute* is the correct noun. It means having a bad reputation.

44. **(H)** The singular pronoun *his or her* is needed for agreement with the singular noun *researcher*.

45. **(B)** The paragraph discusses a theory about the usefulness of the researcher after age 40. Thus, discussing contributions of older researchers would now be appropriate. (A) and (D) are irrelevant; (C) is too general. The correct answer is (B).

46. **(J)** *Of long ago* is redundant and not necessary to the sentence.

47. **(B)** *Be considered* is the correct verb phrase.

48. **(F)** *In* is the correct preposition.

49. **(D)** The most logical order is to contrast views of creativity in the past [3] with those of the present [2] and [1], and then of salary guideposts in the past [4] to those of today [5].

50. **(H)** The correct answer is (H). *However brilliant* should be emphasized.

51. **(B)** *Who* is correct as the subject of the verb phrase *have chosen*.

52. **(F)** Question marks are used after direct questions.

53. **(D)** *Greater* is the correct comparative adjective. *Greatest* is in the superlative and not required in this sentence.

54. **(G)** *Through,* meaning "by means of," is the correct preposition. *Threw* is the past tense of the verb *throw.*

55. **(D)** *In the past* is redundant.

56. **(J)** The conjunction *that* is the only word needed to introduce the clause that follows.

57. **(C)** *But* establishes the contrast between the two clauses and parallels the construction of the previous sentence.

58. **(H)** *Rising,* which means "moving upward," is correct. *Raising* means "causing to move upward."

59. **(A)** The original sentence is correct. *Quite the contrary* is the only phrase that makes sense in the sentence.

60. **(G)** The paragraph discusses the contributions that science and engineering have made. Therefore, specific examples are appropriate.

61. **(A)** The original sentence is correct. No punctuation is required here.

62. **(H)** The passage is concerned with solving problems in the fields of science and engineering. It begins by addressing those who have chosen these fields.

63. **(B)** [1] introduces the main concern of this section. [4], [2], and [3] begin with *First, Second,* and *Third,* respectively. [5] summarizes the author's point of view and is the conclusion.

64. **(J)** The singular subject *youth* requires the singular verb *is.*

65. **(D)** *This here* is nonstandard usage for the pronoun *this.*

66. **(H)** *Similarities* is not completed by *from.* It requires the preposition *to* (*similarities to* the American market).

67. **(C)** *Market's* is the correct possessive. The apostrophe followed by an "s" is used to show singular possession.

68. **(G)** The adverb *increasingly* correctly modifies the adjective *high.*

69. **(B)** The use of the comma creates a run-on sentence. The two sentences must be separated by a period, and then *generally* must be capitalized and also followed by a comma.

70. **(F)** *Transatlantic* is one word and an adjective, not a noun. No capitalization or hyphenation is necessary.

71. **(D)** *Adopted,* meaning "to have taken up and practice as one's own," is the correct verb. *Adapted* means "to have adjusted."

72. **(J)** *Between* is used for two persons or things and *among* and *amongst* are used for more than two persons or things.

73. **(C)** The correct answer is (C). Words in quotation marks have meanings that are specific to the context of this essay.

74. **(F)** The passage deals with the youth markets of Western Europe and America; therefore, its readers would probably be people who are interested in the consumer patterns of youth worldwide.

75. **(A)** The original sentence is correct. The dash sets off an illustration.

TEST 2: MATHEMATICS (p. 852)

1. **(C)** Two numbers that add up to zero are additive inverses. $(a) + (-a) = 0$. The additive inverse is the opposite of the original value. $\frac{2}{3}$ is the additive inverse of $-\frac{2}{3}$.

2. **(G)** $\angle AOC$ is a central angle and equals 70°. A central angle is equal to its intercepted arc. Arc AC = 70°. An inscribed angle is equal to one-half the measure of its intercepted arc. $m\angle ABC = \frac{1}{2}m \cdot (\text{Arc } AC) \Rightarrow \angle ABC = 35°$.

3. **(B)** $x^2 + 6x + 8 = 0 \Rightarrow (x + 4)(x + 2) = 0 \Rightarrow x + 4 = 0$ or $x + 2 = 0$. Therefore, $x = -4$ or -2.

4. **(F)**

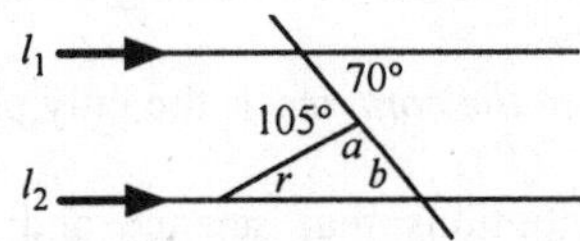

The measure of $\angle b$ is 70°, and because it is an alternate interior angle with $\angle x$. The measure of $\angle a$ is 75° because it is the supplement of $\angle y$. The three angles form a triangle: $m\angle r + m\angle a + m\angle b = 180°$. Thus, $m\angle r + 75° + 70° = 180° \Rightarrow m\angle r = 35°$.

5. **(A)** $A = \frac{2gr}{g+r} \Rightarrow 4 = \frac{2g(1)}{g+(1)} \Rightarrow 4 = \frac{2g}{g+1}$. Cross-multiply: $4(g + 1) = 2g \Rightarrow 4g + 4 = 2g \Rightarrow 2g = -4 \Rightarrow g = -2$.

6. **(H)** V-shaped graphs usually indicate absolute value functions. Substitute the given coordinates (2, 2), (0, 0), and (-3, 3) into the answer choices: Only $y = |x|$ satisfies all the ordered pairs.

7. **(E)** The distributive property indicates multiplication over addition ($a(b + c) = ab + ac$) and multiplication over subtraction ($a(b - c) = ab - ac$). Thus, $x(x + 2) = x^2 + 2x$.

8. **(K)** The sales tax is 7% of \$600: $\frac{7}{100} \cdot 600 = \frac{7(600)}{100}$ = \$42. Thus, the total cost = \$600 + \$42 = \$642.

9. **(D)** Substitute the value -1 for x: $-x^2 - 2x^3 \Rightarrow -(-1)^2 - 2(-1)^3 = -(1) - 2(-1) = -1 + 2 = 1$.

10. **(G)** The average is the sum of the numbers divided by the quantity of numbers: Average $= \frac{(n+3)+(2n-1)+(3n+4)}{3} = \frac{6n+6}{3} = 2n + 2$.

11. **(B)** Substitute 9 for x: $x^0 + x^{1/2} + x^{-2} = 9^0 + 9^{1/2} + 9^{-2} = 1 + \sqrt{9} + \frac{1}{9^2} = 1 + 3 + \frac{1}{81} = 4\frac{1}{81}$.

12. **(H)** In order to add radicals, the number in the square root must be the same: $4\sqrt{3} + 3\sqrt{27} = 4\sqrt{3} + 3(3\sqrt{3}) = 4\sqrt{3} + 9\sqrt{3} = 13\sqrt{3}$.

13. **(E)** The average is the sum of the test scores divided by the quantity of tests: Average $= 90 = \frac{87 + 93 + 86 + x}{4} \Rightarrow 4(90) = 87 + 93 + 86 + x \Rightarrow 360 = 266 + x \Rightarrow x = 94$.

14. **(J)** Each dime is 10 cents. Three dimes would be 3(10) = 30 cents. $4x$ dimes would be $4x(10) = 40x$ cents.

15. **(E)** ●indicates either $\geq$ or $\leq$. ○indicates either > or < without the equal. The arrow to the left, <, indicates less than. The arrow to the right, >, indicates greater than. The graph indicates $x \leq -5$ or $x > 3$. The answers are connected by an *or*. Therefore, the answer is $x \leq -5$ or $x > 3$.

16. **(H)** $2\frac{2}{5} - 1\frac{7}{8} = \frac{12}{5} - \frac{15}{8}$. The lowest common denominator is 40. Thus, $\frac{12}{5} - \frac{15}{8} = \frac{96}{40} - \frac{75}{40} = \frac{21}{40}$.

17. **(C)** Circumference $= 2\pi r = 2\pi(6) = 12\pi$. 2π is $\frac{2\pi}{12\pi} = \frac{1}{6}$ of the circumference. In turn, the central angle is $\frac{1}{6}(360°) = 60°$ or $\frac{\text{arc length}}{\text{circumference}} = \frac{x°}{360°} \Rightarrow \frac{2\pi}{12\pi} = \frac{x}{360} \Rightarrow \frac{1}{6} = \frac{x}{360} \Rightarrow 6x = 360 \Rightarrow x = 60$.

18. **(G)** $\frac{2x}{3\sqrt{2}} = \frac{3\sqrt{2}}{x} \Rightarrow 2x(x) = (3\sqrt{2})(3\sqrt{2}) \Rightarrow 2x^2 = 9(2) = 18 \Rightarrow x^2 = 9 \Rightarrow x = \pm 3$. The positive value of x is 3.

19. **(B)** $f(x) = 2x - x^2 \Rightarrow f(2) = 2(2) - (2)^2 = 4 - 4 = 0$. $g(x) = x - 4 \Rightarrow g(0) = 0 - 4 = -4$. Therefore, $g(f(2)) = g(0) = -4$.

20. **(F)** Since 7 is set equal to the absolute value of the equation involving x ($7 = |5 - 2x|$), then $5 - 2x = \pm 7$. Solve for the possible values of x: $5 - 2x = -7 \Rightarrow -2x = -12 \Rightarrow x = 6$ and $5 - 2x = 7 \Rightarrow -2x = 2 \Rightarrow x = -1$. Therefore, the possible solution set is {6, -1}, (F).

21. **(E)** Multiply the top and bottom of the fraction by the lowest common denominator, which is x:

$$\frac{x(3 - \frac{3}{x})}{x(x-1)} = \frac{x(3) - x(\frac{3}{x})}{x(x-1)} = \frac{3x-3}{x(x-1)} = \frac{3(x-1)}{x(x-1)} = \frac{3}{x}.$$

22. **(K)** slope $= m = \frac{y_2 - y_1}{x_2 - x_1} = \frac{7-5}{4-(-3)} = \frac{2}{7}$.

23. **(E)**

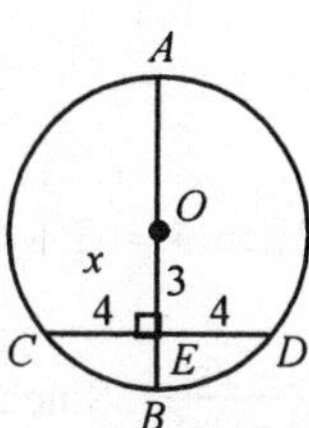

A diameter drawn perpendicular to the chord bisects the chord. Therefore, $\overline{AB}$ bisects $\overline{CD}$. A constructed radius $\overline{OC}$ forms right triangle OEC with $\overline{OC}$ as the hypotenuse. Since $\overline{OE}$ = 3 inches and $\overline{CE}$ = 4 inches, use the Pythagorean theorem: (Hypotenuse)^2 = (Leg 1)^2 + (Leg 2)^2 $\Rightarrow (\overline{OC})^2 = (\overline{OE})^2 + (\overline{CE})^2 \Rightarrow x^2 = 3^2 + 4^2 \Rightarrow x^2 = 25 \Rightarrow x = 5$.

24. **(F)**

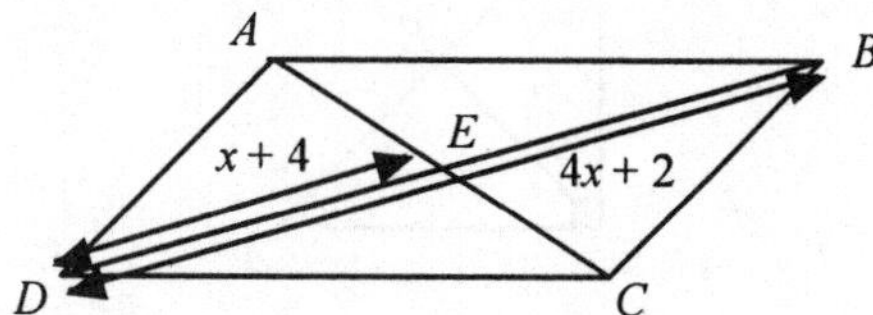

The diagonals of a parallelogram bisect each other. $\overline{DB} = 2(\overline{DE}) \Rightarrow 4x + 2 = 2(x + 4) \Rightarrow 4x + 2 = 2x + 8 \Rightarrow 2x = 6 \Rightarrow x = 3$.

25. (E)

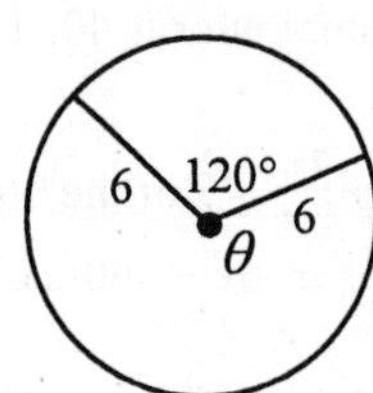

$\frac{\text{area of sector}}{\text{area of circle}} = \frac{\text{central angle}}{360°} \Rightarrow \frac{x}{\pi r^2} = \frac{120°}{360°} \Rightarrow \frac{x}{36\pi} = \frac{1}{3} \Rightarrow 3x = 36\pi \Rightarrow x = 12\pi.$

26. (F) If a statement is true, its contrapositive must be true. If the original statement is $p \Rightarrow q$, the contrapositive is "not $q \Rightarrow$ not p."

27. (B) Compare all the answer choices to the original using cross-multiplication. The original is: $\frac{a}{b} = \frac{r}{t} \Rightarrow at = br$.

A. $\frac{a}{r} = \frac{b}{t} \Rightarrow at = br$ ✓

B. $\frac{a}{t} = \frac{b}{r} \Rightarrow ar = bt$ ✗

C. $\frac{a+b}{b} = \frac{r+t}{t}$
$t(a+b) = b(r+t)$
$at + bt = br + bt$
$at = br$ ✓

D. $\frac{b}{a} = \frac{t}{r} \Rightarrow at = br$ ✓

E. $at = br$ ✓

28. (K) $-2x + 5 = 2 - (5 - 2x) = 2 - 5 + 2x = -3 + 2x \Rightarrow 5 = -3 + 4x \Rightarrow 8 = 4x \Rightarrow x = 2.$

29. (E) $\frac{(1+\sin x)(1-\sin x)}{(1+\cos x)(1-\cos x)} = \frac{1 - \sin x + \sin x - \sin^2 x}{1 - \cos x + \cos x - \cos^2 x} = \frac{1-\sin^2 x}{1-\cos^2 x}$. Since $\sin^2 x + \cos^2 x = 1$, $\sin^2 x = 1 - \cos^2 x$ and $\cos^2 x = 1 - \sin^2 x$. Therefore, by substitution: $\frac{1-\sin^2 x}{1-\cos^2 x} = \frac{\cos^2 x}{\sin^2 x} = \cot^2 x$.

30. (H) The median to the hypotenuse of a right triangle is equal in length to half the hypotenuse: $\overline{BE} = \overline{AE} = \overline{CE}$.

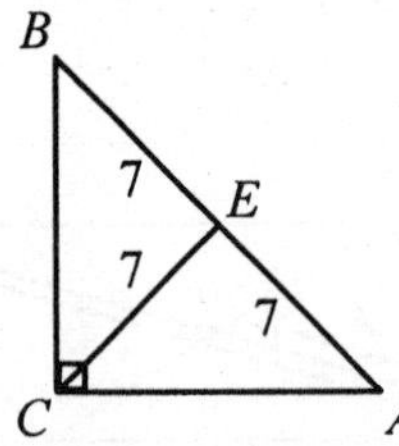

31. (E) y varies directly as x: $\frac{y_1}{x_1} = \frac{y_2}{x_2}$. Therefore, $\frac{10}{\frac{1}{5}} = \frac{y}{\frac{1}{2}} \Rightarrow 10(5) = y(2) \Rightarrow 50 = 2y \Rightarrow y = 25.$

32. (G) $\frac{(-1)(2)(-3)(4)(-5)}{(5)(-4)(3)(-2)(1)} = \frac{-120}{120} = -1.$

33. (C) The product of the segments of one chord is equal to the product of the segments of the other.

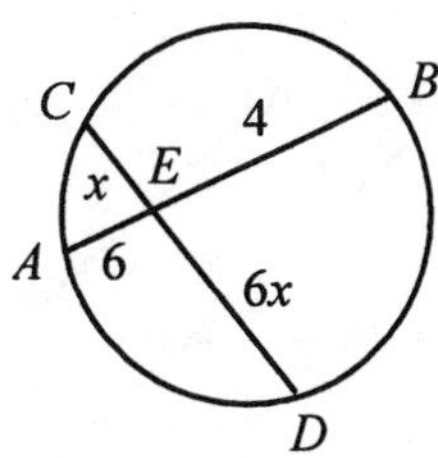

$\overline{CE} \cdot \overline{ED} = \overline{AE} \cdot \overline{EB} \Rightarrow x(6x) = 6(4) \Rightarrow 6x^2 = 24 \Rightarrow x^2 = 4 \Rightarrow x = \pm 2$. Lengths are positive, so $x = 2$.

34. (H) An isosceles triangle has two equal sides and two equal base angles: $50 + x + x = 180 \Rightarrow 50 + 2x = 180 \Rightarrow 2x = 130 \Rightarrow x = 65$.

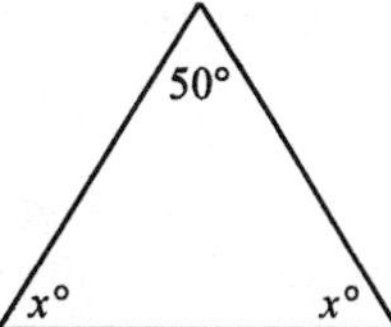

35. (B) The median is the "middle" data element when the data are arranged in numerical order: 20, 20, 20, 20, 30, 30, 30, 30, 50, 50, 50, 50, 50, 50, 50. The "middle" data element is 30.

36. (F) $x^2 - 2x - 3 > 0 \Rightarrow (x - 3)(x + 1) > 0$. This is true for two situations: (+) • (+) and (-) • (-). $x - 3$ is positive for $x > 3$ and negative for $x < 3$. $x + 1$ is positive for $x > -1$ and negative for $x < -1$. Therefore, the two situations for which $(x - 3) \cdot (x + 1) > 0$ are $(x > 3)(x > -1)$ and $(x < 3)(x < -1)$. To keep both parentheses true in each situation, x must be larger than 3 or less than -1. This is two intervals: numbers less than -1 and numbers greater than +3, (F).

37. (D) To evaluate $\frac{\sin x}{1}$, a common denominator is required in order to add the fractions. The lowest common denominator is $\sin x$: $\frac{\sin x}{1} \cdot \frac{\sin x}{\sin x} + \frac{\cos^2 x}{\sin x} = \frac{\sin^2 x}{\sin x} + \frac{\cos^2 x}{\sin x} = \frac{\sin^2 x + \cos^2 x}{\sin x}$. $\text{Sin}^2 x + \cos^2 x = 1$, so the expression reduces to $\frac{1}{\sin x}$.

38. (G) $(2.5 \cdot 10^5)^2 = (2.5 \cdot 10^5)(2.5 \cdot 10^5) = 6.25 \cdot 10^{10}$.

39. (E) $A * B = \frac{AB - B}{-B} \Rightarrow -2 * 2 = \frac{(-2)(2) - 2}{-2} = \frac{-4 - 2}{-2} = \frac{-6}{-2} = 3$.

40. (F) Substitute the root into the equation for the value of x: $0 = x^2 + kx - 12 = (4)^2 + k(4) - 12 = 16 + 4k - 12 = 4k + 4 \Rightarrow 4k = -4 \Rightarrow k = -1$.

41. **(E)** ΔABC and ΔDBE are similar; create a proportion between the sides of the two triangles. If $\overline{AB} = 10$ and $\overline{DB} = 4$, $\overline{DA} = 6$; if $\overline{BC} = 20$ and $\overline{EC} = x$, $\overline{BE} = 20 - x$.

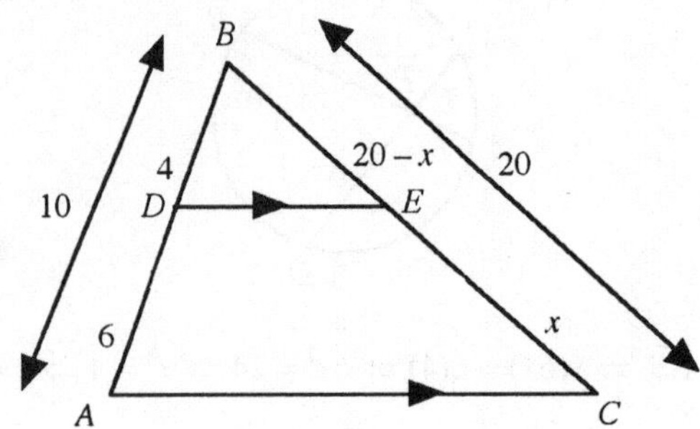

Therefore, $\frac{4}{10} = \frac{20-x}{20} \Rightarrow 80 = 200 - 10x \Rightarrow 10x = 120 \Rightarrow x = 12$.

42. **(H)** Evaluate the expression using the FOIL (First, Outer, Inner, Last) method: $(x + 2)(x - 4) - (x + 4)(x - 2) = x^2 - 4x + 2x - 8 - (x^2 - 2x + 4x - 8) = x^2 - 2x - 8 - x^2 + 2x - 4x + 8 = (x^2 - x^2) + (-2x + 2x - 4x) + (-8 + 8) = -4x$.

43. **(B)** The sum of the measures of the exterior angles of a polygon is 360° for all polygons. The sum of the measures of the interior angles of a polygon can be expressed as $180°(n - 2)$, where n is the number of sides. Therefore, $180(n - 2) = 360 \Rightarrow n - 2 = 2 \Rightarrow n = 4$.

44. **(G)** If the perimeter = 12, then each side is: $\frac{12}{3} = 4$. The area of a triangle $= \frac{1}{2}(bh)$, so draw a figure:

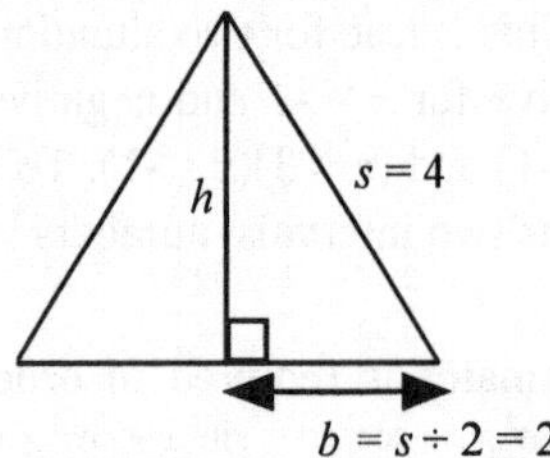

Use the Pythagorean theorem to solve for h: $2^2 + h^2 = 4^2 \Rightarrow h^2 = 16 - 4 = 12 \Rightarrow h = \sqrt{12} = 2\sqrt{3}$. $A = \frac{1}{2}(bh) = \frac{1}{2}(4)(2\sqrt{3}) = 4\sqrt{3}$.

45. **(A)** Let $8x$ equal one angle and x equal the other angle. Since complementary angles add to 90°, $8x + x = 90 \Rightarrow 9x = 90 \Rightarrow x = 10$.

46. **(H)** A square has four right angles; a rectangle has four right angles; a trapezoid does not have four right angles; a circle has no angles. Thus, the probability of four right angles is $\frac{\text{\# of successes}}{\text{\# of possibilities}} = \frac{2}{4} = \frac{1}{2}$.

47. **(C)** Distance = rate • time $\Rightarrow$ rate $= \frac{\text{distance}}{\text{time}} \Rightarrow \frac{\text{320 miles}}{\text{8 hrs}} = 40$ mph. Therefore, the total trip = 40 mph • 2 hrs = 80 miles.

48. **(H)** Use the common denominator ($\sin x \cdot \cos x$) to simplify the expression: $\frac{\sin x}{\cos x} \cdot \frac{\sin x}{\sin x} + \frac{\cos x}{\sin x} \cdot \frac{\cos x}{\cos x} = \frac{\sin^2 x}{\sin x \cos x} + \frac{\cos^2 x}{\sin x \cos x} = \frac{\sin^2 x + \cos^2 x}{\sin x \cos x} = \frac{1}{\sin x \cos x}$.

49. **(E)** The mode is the data element with the greatest frequency: 91°.

50. (F) $\frac{\text{part}}{\text{whole}} \cdot 100 = \frac{9}{30} \cdot 100 = 30\%$.

51. (B) Rearrange the expression and factor: $-7t + 6t^2 - 3 = 6t^2 - 7t - 3 = (3t + 1)(2t - 3)$.

52. (G) If $2^{x^2 + 2x} = 2^{-1}$, then $x^2 + 2x = -1$. Therefore, $x^2 + 2x + 1 = (x + 1)(x + 1) = 0$. This equation holds true only if $x = -1$.

53. (E) If Joshua is x years old now and Jessica is 3 years younger, then Jessica is now $x - 3$ years old. Four years ago she was $(x - 3) - 4 = x - 7$ years old.

54. (F) The amount collected = (# of students) • (amount each contributed). Therefore, $(x)(y) = 18$ and $(x + 3)(y - 1) = 18$.

55. (A) $\frac{1}{2}\sqrt{112} = \frac{1}{2}(\sqrt{16})(\sqrt{7}) = \frac{1}{2}(4)(\sqrt{7}) = 2\sqrt{7}$. $\sqrt{28} = \sqrt{4}\sqrt{7} = 2\sqrt{7}$. $2\sqrt{63} = 2(\sqrt{9})(\sqrt{7}) = 2(3)\sqrt{7} = 6\sqrt{7}$. Thus, $2\sqrt{7} - 2\sqrt{7} + 6\sqrt{7} = 6\sqrt{7}$.

56. (G) Add the two equations:

$$\begin{array}{r} \frac{1}{x} + \frac{1}{y} = \frac{1}{4} \\ + \quad \frac{1}{x} - \frac{1}{y} = \frac{3}{4} \\ \hline \frac{2}{x} = 1 \Rightarrow x = 2 \end{array}$$

57. (D) The sum of the lengths of any two sides of a triangle must exceed the length of the third side. Check each of the answer choices:

A.	$1 + 3 > 6$	✗
B.	$2 + 4 > 7$	✗
C.	$2 + 10 > 12$	✗
D.	$4 + 6 > 8$	
	$4 + 8 > 6$	
	$6 + 8 > 4$	✓
E.	$4 + 4 > 10$	✗

58. (H) To eliminate the variable y, multiply the first equation by -1 and add the equations:

$$\begin{array}{l} -1(ax + y = b) \\ + 2ax + y = 2b \\ \hline ax = b \Rightarrow x = \frac{b}{a} \end{array}$$

Substitute the value of x into the first equation and solve for y: $ax + y = b \Rightarrow a(\frac{b}{a}) + y = b \Rightarrow b + y = b \Rightarrow y = 0$. The solution set is $\{\frac{b}{a}, 0\}$.

59. (A) From the given information, draw a figure.

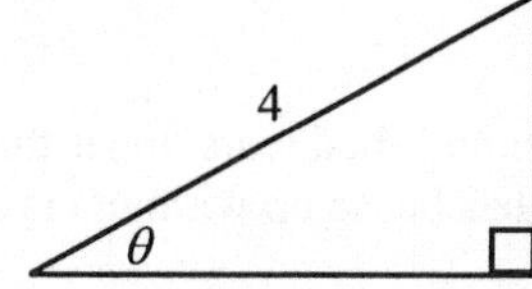

The third side of the triangle, x, is found using the Pythagorean theorem: $x^2 + r^2 = 4^2 = 16 \Rightarrow x^2 = 16 - r^2 \Rightarrow x = \sqrt{16 - r^2}$. Since $\cos\theta = \frac{\text{side adjacent to } \theta}{\text{hypotenuse}}$, $\cos\theta = \frac{\sqrt{16 - r^2}}{4}$.

60. **(G)** The number of sheets is directly proportional to the number of machines, as well as directly proportional to the amount of time. Thus, $(\frac{\text{sheets}}{\text{\# of machines} \cdot \text{time}})_1 = (\frac{\text{sheets}}{\text{\# of machines} \cdot \text{time}})_2 \Rightarrow \frac{300}{3(3)} = \frac{600}{6(t)} \Rightarrow \frac{300}{9} = \frac{600}{6t} \Rightarrow \frac{100}{3} = \frac{100}{t} \Rightarrow 100t = 300 \Rightarrow t = 3$.

TEST 3: READING (p. 868)

1. **(D)** In the fourth paragraph, lines 43-44 state that x-rays are found at wavelengths shorter than 100 Å, the lower end of ultraviolet radiation, (I). Lines 39-41 state that infrared radiation, (II), has wavelengths longer than 7,000 Å. Since (I), (II), and (III) are true, the answer is (D).

2. **(G)** As stated in lines 49-50, short wavelengths contain a high amount of energy, which makes them more dangerous than long wavelengths.

3. **(D)** This definition appears in lines 64-73.

4. **(G)** The first line of the paragraph states this main idea.

5. **(C)** The figure clearly shows that the visible spectrum ranges from 4,000 Å to 7,000 Å.

6. **(J)** Line 93 states that *T* refers to temperature: "…the temperature raised to the fourth power."

7. **(D)** Lines 74-84 refer to the temperature of stars. Line 81 states that "a hot star looks blue."

8. **(G)** Returning to lines 55-59 provides the answer to this question.

9. **(C)** (A) is never discussed. (B) is certainly not true, as the caption of the figure proves, and (D) is directly contradicted by the graph. Only (C) is true.

10. **(F)** As stated in lines 95-97: "doubling an object's temperature would radiate 16 times more energy."

11. **(A)** Only the first choice explains the subtitle. The other choices may be included under the idea "A Study in Temperament," but they are not the main idea.

12. **(J)** Paul is shown in a very unsympathetic light; one of the interesting things about this passage is the lack of sentiment in the description. Paul is plainly unpleasant, and even the narrator dislikes him.

13. **(B)** The first paragraph focuses on the faculty's feeling that Paul's dress and behavior are not properly contrite.

14. **(H)** Paul seems to be unable to control his odd mannerisms, but he is not actually frenzied, as (F), (G), or (J) would suggest.

15. **(D)** It is the inability to hide his contempt for others that has landed Paul in trouble, as evidenced in lines 40-51.

16. **(G)** The faculty "fell upon him without mercy, his English teacher leading the pack" (lines 54-55). The comparison is to a pack of wolves.

17. **(A)** "Older boys than Paul had broken down and shed tears under that baptism of fire" (lines 59-61). Paul has just undergone an inquisition by the faculty and has borne up without crying, unlike many other students.

18. **(H)** All of these choices could mean "smartness," but only *impudence* makes sense in context.

19. **(D)** There is evidence for every other choice in the descriptions of Paul's actions. The point is made in lines 25-27 that Paul often lies; he cannot be called "candid."

20. **(F)** Paul is physically revolted by the faculty, not vice versa, (J). The faculty's attack on Paul indicates their hatred for him.

21. **(B)** Jupiter is being asked to decide which of three goddesses is the fairest—it is a no-win decision since it is bound to anger two of the three.

22. **(F)** Ulysses has no inclination to embark on the adventure since he is happy at home with his family.

23. **(C)** Venus, one of the characters in the narrative, selected Helen as "the fairest of her sex." The other assertions are all opinions of the author.

24. **(F)** "Ulysses pretended to be mad" (lines 41-42), and one of the methods he chose was to hitch a mismatched team and sow something that could not grow.

25. **(C)** Palamedes does not buy Ulysses' mad act; he thinks up a way to test him. Since Ulysses is unwilling to run over his own son, he is obviously not as mad as he pretends to be.

26. **(J)** Rather than say that Thetis, being a sea-nymph, can read the future, the author merely mentions her immortal status and expects the reader to understand that this means that she knows "her son was fated to perish."

27. **(C)** The names in (A) are those of goddesses; Paris, (B), is a "beautiful shepherd." In (D), Eris is the goddess of Discord and Thetis is a sea-nymph.

28. **(F)** Readers are expected to understand Ulysses' clever ploy without its being spelled out. Achilles is disguised as a woman, but he is inappropriately interested in manly objects.

29. **(C)** Thetis' foreknowledge predicts Achilles' death, and the preparations for war on the part of the chieftains foreshadow the Trojan conflict.

30. **(G)** This is an accurate summary of the main themes in the passage.

31. **(B)** Lines 5-8 say that Hiram Revels was the first African American in Congress, but he was elected to the Senate, not the House of Representatives. Therefore, (A) is incorrect. However, lines 8-10 state that Rainey was the first African American elected to the House. (D) may be true but is not mentioned in the passage.

32. **(F)** The second paragraph says that the first African American representatives were from the South; the third paragraph describes the shift to northern cities.

33. **(A)** Compare lines 19-23 and 47-49.

34. **(H)** The context makes it clear that "turned to" means "concentrated on" or "devoted themselves to."

35. **(A)** Lines 37-40 indicate that many African Americans moved to northern cities during World War I and in the following decades.

36. **(J)** Voting rights are mentioned or implied in lines 29, 55, and 70; educational opportunities in lines 58 and 71; and employment in lines 62 and 71.

37. **(C)** Political organizations in southern states in the nineteenth century are mentioned in lines 15-19 and 30-33; political organizations in northern states in the twentieth century are cited in lines 37-40.

38. **(J)** This answer is a paraphrase of lines 66-69.

39. **(B)** The last paragraph specifically mentions "collected biographies of African Americans who served in the House and Senate" and "their stories."

40. **(G)** In an otherwise factual account, the author expresses admiration only in the last paragraph, where the representatives' "long struggle to extend the ideals of the founders to encompass all citizens of the United States" is cited.

TEST 4: SCIENCE REASONING (p. 878)

1. **(B)** The sharpest sloping curve is for potassium nitrate (KNO_3).

2. **(H)** The sodium salts, NaCl and $NaNO_3$, have different solubilities, indicating that solubility depends on more than the nature of sodium. Thus, (F) and (G) must be incorrect. (J) is incorrect because it is not known whether the solubility curves for all sodium compounds have been given. (H) is correct because it takes into account the differences in solubilities of different sodium salts.

3. **(D)** The table gives data only for aqueous solutions, not alcoholic.

4. **(J)** Since the solubility curves cross at 71° F, the temperature needs to be known.

5. **(B)** Soda goes flat as gas (carbon dioxide) leaves the liquid. The warmer the soda, the faster it goes flat. (A) shows the effect of pressure, not temperature, on solubility. (C) shows the solubility of a solid (sugar), which has nothing to do with the solubility characteristics of a gas. (D) deals with relative densities of gases and not with solubilities.

6. **(G)** Mercury's period of revolution equals 0.25 • period of Earth's revolution = 0.25 • 365.3 days ≈ 90 days. Mercury's period of rotation equals 60 • period of Earth's rotation = 60 • 1 day = 60 days. The ratio of revolution to rotation $= \frac{90}{60} = \frac{3}{2}$.

7. **(A)** Mercury's density equals that of the Earth. Density is mass divided by volume. Mercury's density = $\frac{\text{Mercury's mass}}{\text{Mercury's volume}} = \frac{0.58 \cdot \text{Earth's mass}}{0.58 \cdot \text{Earth's volume}} = \frac{\text{Earth's mass}}{\text{Earth's volume}} =$ Earth's density.

8. **(J)** Rate is distance divided by time. Divide the average distance to the sun by the period of revolution to get the relative rate. The smallest relative rate is the slowest. In this specific case, the planet with the greatest relative period of revolution orbits the sun at the slowest rate.

9. **(B)** Gravity depends on both the distance between the centers of objects (and thereby the volume—assuming the planets are roughly spherical in shape) and on the mass of the objects. Compare Mars and Mercury to see the effect of volume (by considering their diameters). Mars is more massive, but the smaller size of Mercury gives it an equivalent surface gravity. Density, a ratio of mass and volume, is not enough because gravity depends on the amount of mass and the amount of distance, not their ratio.

10. **(H)** $\frac{\text{Pluto's volume}}{\text{Earth's volume}} = 0.729 \Rightarrow \frac{\frac{4}{3}\pi r^3_{\text{Pluto}}}{\frac{4}{3}\pi r^3_{\text{Earth}}} = 0.729 \Rightarrow \frac{r^3_{\text{Pluto}}}{r^3_{\text{Earth}}} = 0.729 \Rightarrow \frac{r_{\text{Pluto}}}{r_{\text{Earth}}} = \sqrt[3]{0.729} = 0.9$. Pluto's diameter = 2 • (0.9 • Earth's radius) = 1.8 times the Earth's radius.

11. **(B)** The neighbors that are farthest from each other are Uranus and Neptune. Relative distances to the sun are as follows:

$$\frac{\text{Mercury}}{0.4} < \frac{\text{Venus}}{0.7} < \frac{\text{Earth}}{1} < \frac{\text{Mars}}{1.5} < \frac{\text{Jupiter}}{5.3} < \frac{\text{Saturn}}{10} < \frac{\text{Uranus}}{19} < \frac{\text{Neptune}}{30} < \frac{\text{Pluto}}{40}$$

The largest difference $(30 - 19) = 11$.

12. **(F)** The death rate for the 6-20 gram/day cholesterol eater from prostate cancer is 1.03, while that for a non-cholesterol eater is 2.02. Thus, (F) is correct. (G) contradicts the data for colon cancer; (H) ignores the direct relationship between coronary deaths and cholesterol intake; and cardiac arrest is a more common form of death than cerebral clots for the 20+ eaters.

13. **(D)** The death rate for all three groups of cholesterol-eaters from depression is 0.30. This number is lower than for non-cholesterol-eaters, so (A) and (B) are both wrong. According to the data, large amounts of cholesterol are just as effective in combating depression as small amounts, so (C) is incorrect.

14. **(J)** Although the 20+ diet increases coronary arrest to the highest absolute death rate, the percentage increase is less than 100% (from 6.00 to 11.00). The percentage increase for coronary thrombosis is greater than 100% (from 5.02 to 10.05).

15. **(C)** (C) is the only group in which low intake of cholesterol decreases the death rate from all three diseases. Intake of 0 to 5 grams raises the probability of death for lung and colon cancer only. This question is probably best answered by recognizing that fact and eliminating those choices that include either lung or colon cancer.

16. **(G)** Standardizing the death rate involves correcting for variables inherent in the subject groups but not involved in the experiment. Age, weight, genetic histories, and accidental deaths are just some of the variables that the scientist must consider. However, (F) does not correct for intrinsic variables; rather, it ignores results that might not conform to a "neat" result. This does not standardize the death rate so much as "fudge" it. (H) involves an arbitrary assumption that is in fact incorrect. Assuming a zero death rate in the male population distorts the result of this experiment and does not correct for variations within the subject groups. (J) is incorrect because this experiment does not consider women at all. It might be valid to compare results with a different experiment involving women, but the actual death rates for men and women for different diseases are not necessarily similar (*e.g.*, the gender-related differences for breast cancer).

17. **(C)** Since voltage is directly related to current, voltage increases by the same factor as current if other variables are held constant. The same applies for resistance; therefore, the only correct formula is (C).

18. **(G)** $V = IR$, so the circuit with the greater resistance would have the greater voltage. Since resistance is directly proportional to resistivity, the germanium circuit would have the greater resistance and voltage.

19. **(A)** The total resistance R_s of the series resistors is $R_1 + R_2 = 2 + 2 = 4$. This resistance is double that of the circuit where $R = 2$. If R doubles, then the voltage doubles as long as the current remains the same.

20. **(J)** According to the formula for resistors in parallel: $\frac{1}{R_p} = \frac{1}{4} + \frac{1}{4} = \frac{2}{4} = \frac{1}{2} \Rightarrow R_p = 2$.

21. **(C)** If R is constant, then P increases with I^2; this is the definition of exponential growth.

22. **(J)** $V = IR \Rightarrow I = \frac{V}{R}$. To keep I constant if V increases, R must be increased.

23. **(D)** Compare Trials 2 and 3 to see what changing the concentration of only one component has on rate. In this case, there is no change in rate with change in concentration of A, so rate is independent of concentration.

24. (F) Compare Trials 2 and 4 or Trials 1 and 3 to see what changing the concentration of only one component has on rate. In this case, rate increases with increasing A.

25. (C) Compare Trials 1 and 4 or Trials 2 and 3 to see what changing the concentration of only one component has on rate. In this case, rate increases by the square of the starting A concentration.

26. (H) Averaging or intermediate mechanisms do not work because one mechanism has no dependence on A with regard to rate. (G) is unlikely because a well-mixed solution should be homogeneous and have no pockets for mechanisms 1 and 2.

27. (B) This is a subtle question. (C) and (D) are incorrect because they over-generalize from a single case. It cannot be said that mechanisms can always be changed, (C), or that in every case the mechanism depends on solvent effects, (D). (A) is a special case of (D), where the claim is made that all reactions are solvent dependent. (B) alone allows for the possibility that solvents need not have an effect (note the word "may").

28. (G) acceleration $= \frac{D_v}{D_t} = \frac{\text{change in velocity}}{\text{change in time}}$.

Experiment 1 (steel ball): The acceleration is constant at 3.50 m/sec^2. This can be demonstrated by choosing a time interval and dividing the corresponding velocity change during the time interval by the length of the time interval. For example, between 1 and 2 seconds, the velocity changes from 3.5 m/sec to 7 m/sec; therefore, acceleration equals $\frac{\Delta v}{\Delta t} = \frac{7-3.5}{2-1} = \frac{3.5}{1} = 3.5$ m/sec^2.

For a time interval from 0.5 seconds to 1 second, the corresponding velocity would change from 1.75 m/sec to 3.5 m/sec; thus, the acceleration equals $\frac{\Delta v}{\Delta t} = \frac{3.5-1.75}{1-0.5} = \frac{1.75}{0.5} = 3.5$ m/sec^2.

Experiment 2 (sled): The acceleration is a constant 4.9 m/sec^2. For example, the change in velocity corresponding to the time interval from 0.5 seconds to 1 second is 4.90 m/sec – 2.45 m/sec = 2.45 m/sec. The acceleration $= \frac{\Delta v}{\Delta t} = \frac{4.90-2.45}{1-0.5} = \frac{2.45}{0.5} = 4.9$ m/sec^2.

Experiment 3 (box): The acceleration is constant at 0.66 m/sec^2.

29. (A) When friction is reduced in Experiment 4, the sled and the ball still travel at about the same accelerations as in the previous experiments. This can be demonstrated by using the equation $d = 0.5at^2$, which relates the distance that an object travels starting from rest to the time (traveling at constant acceleration) it takes to travel the indicated distance. Since the board is 10 meters in length, the distance that each travels is 10 meters.

For the sled:
$$d = \frac{1}{2}at^2$$
$$10 = \frac{1}{2}at(2.02)^2 \approx \frac{1}{2}(a)(4)$$
$$a = 5 \text{ m/sec}^2$$

For the ball:
$$d = \frac{1}{2}at^2$$
$$10 = \frac{1}{2}a(2.39)^2 \approx \frac{1}{2}a(5.7)$$
$$a = 3.50 \text{ m/sec}^2$$

The ball and sled travel at about the same accelerations before and after oiling, so the differences in their relative accelerations must be due to something other than friction. The difference is the rolling of the ball.

30. (H) Experiment 4 shows that friction affects the relative acceleration between the box and either the sled or ball. Calculate the acceleration for the box: $d = \frac{1}{2}at^2 \Rightarrow 10 = \frac{1}{2}a(4.08)^2 \approx \frac{1}{2}a(16) \Rightarrow a = 1.25$ m/sec^2.

Because the oiling in Experiment 4 caused a change in the box's acceleration, friction is a factor. Rolling must also be a factor as per the answer explanation to item #29.

31. **(B)** The acceleration of the ball is constant at 3.50 m/sec^2 (either Experiment 1 or 4). The acceleration of the sled is constant at 4.90 m/sec^2 (Experiment 2 or 4). Ratio $= \frac{3.50}{4.90} = \frac{5}{7}$.

32. **(H)** Although the acceleration of the ball is relatively insensitive to the amount of friction, the acceleration of the box is very sensitive to friction. Therefore, in a ratio, the effect of changing the amount of friction will change the numerator (ball acceleration) only slightly, whereas the denominator (box acceleration) will change significantly depending on friction. (J) is not correct because the acceleration remains constant within each experiment.

33. **(B)** Two genetically distant species cannot breed.

34. **(H)** For early modern humans to completely replace Neanderthals, there could not have been a region containing Neanderthals that did not also contain early modern humans.

35. **(D)** Neither hypothesis necessarily rules out isolated communities. Both are concerned about areas where contact occurred.

36. **(J)** This information suggests that early modern humans killed Neanderthals, which supports Scientist 2.

37. **(C)** This fact shows that even if two species can breed, they may not do so voluntarily. Scientist 2 can therefore use this case as an example of the fact that two genetically compatible but dissimilar-looking animals choose not to interbreed. (D) is not readily relevant because lions and tigers are brought together artificially. No one disputed the notion that animals can interbreed, so (A) does not enter the argument. (B) is incorrect because lions and tigers do not share the same niche (tigers are solitary forest hunters while lions are group-hunting plains dwellers), and their ranges rarely overlap.

38. **(H)** The mixing of traits is part of Scientist 2's objections to Scientist 1's hypothesis.

39. **(A)** Both hypotheses attribute the disappearance of Neanderthals to early modern humans.

40. **(G)** (F) is a perfectly logical argument but it does not strengthen the position of Scientist 1. (J) does not strengthen the position of Scientist 1 since there is no way to prove from the given information whether others also died violently (clubs may have been used, or spearpoints that were used may have been valuable and were taken by the victors). Even if (J) is acceptable, it does not strengthen the position of Scientist 1. It only casts doubt on the position of Scientist 2. (H) is true in general. The only possible answer that strengthens a scientist's argument is (G).

TEST 5: WRITING TEST (p. 890)

Sample Essay 1—Below Average Response

It is my opinion that they should let students ought of school to do some volunteering. In America, volunteering is a good idea, and everyone should be ready, willing, and able to help other people. But you can't always help someone else if you're too busy helping yourself. One way of avoiding this problem is to give students time to help other people. Once students learn that they will be allowed to volunteer instead of going to class, they will volunteer more. And more volunteers will help people more.

Position on issue:

The position is stated in the first sentence, however, the several grammar errors within the sentence, hinder it from being a strong opening sentence.

Topic Development and Essay Organization:

This essay lacks any form of development. The paragraph needs to be split into several organized paragraphs that discuss each point the writer will make. The writer fails to explain the reasoning behind the points that are listed in the paragraph. Although the writer presents an argument in a logical manner, it is not explained enough to present a strong essay.

Language usage, sentence structure, and punctuation:

This essay contains several grammar mistakes and does not flow well.

Summary and conclusions:

It's probably necessary after all of the examples to look at an essay that would likely receive a low score, a "1." There are many ways of talking about the deficiencies of this response: it lacks development, it doesn't engage the topic, the writer doesn't use examples, it has no organization. But ultimately these can all be traced back to a fundamental weakness: the writer really never gets started.

Sample Essay 2—Above Average Response

Volunteerism is an important American tradition, and schools should do more to encourage it. In today's world, most students are very busy. They attend classes for most of the day, and then may participate in one or two after school activities. Many students also manage to hold down part-time jobs such as working at a fast-food restaurant. Because they are so busy, most of them don't have time to volunteer to help others. Schools could encourage volunteering by giving students release time from school to participate in such activities.

In the first place, volunteerism is important. During emergencies, the Boy Scouts stuffing sandbags on the levee as the river rises are volunteers hoping to help their neighbors save their homes and businesses. The rescue workers the television shows walking through the woods all night with flashlights searching for a lost child are volunteers. The people who pass out cold drinks to marathon runners are volunteers. Without these volunteers, these efforts could not take place. While students may not be eligible to fight fires, they can do many other jobs, and the way to get involved is to join an organization that helps out.

Unfortunately, many students find it difficult to find time to join. To really be of service in an emergency, you need to have some sort of training, and that means going to meetings and learning what role to play in a rescue or disaster. Less dramatic, you can join a group that does things like visit sick people or clean up roads. You need to be an active member of the club or organization that is doing the public service. But if your day is booked solid with classes, there may just not be time left over to do meaningful volunteer work. If schools gave one or two hours a week off, say Friday after lunch, then many other students could volunteer.

Some people might say that release time is not really volunteering because you get something for your effort. But having free time that has to be used for volunteering isn't good for anything else. If you are working to clean up a public park, then you can't be making money at your job. So you really are giving up something by volunteering.

There are many other reasons why release time would work. But the most important one is that it gives students time to do some volunteer work.

Position on issue:

The position is nicely stated in the first paragraph.

Topic Development and Essay Organization:

The main weakness of the essay is that, in spite of the appropriate use of paragraphs and signals, it doesn't really engage the topic in an original and passionate way. To take just one point as an example, the writer, in a good authorly way, uses a paragraph to raise and dispose of a possible objection to the position. The writer argues that release time is not compensation because it cannot, under the terms of the program, be used except for volunteer work. The difficulty here is that this point doesn't come to grips with the objection raised in the prompt that being given the free time to do volunteer work doesn't require the sacrifice that one ordinarily expects with volunteerism. This idea is complex and needs to be explored in greater detail.

The same criticism could be applied to the other points made by the essay. The third paragraph, to be very critical, is really just a restatement of the problem posed by the prompt: students may not have a lot of time to volunteer. That point is probably not going to be disputed. No one has unlimited time. What the reader would probably expect to see is instead some discussion of the moral issue of giving up something for someone else's benefit, not just a statement that to volunteer requires sacrifice.

Language usage, sentence structure, and punctuation:

In general, the language is appropriate and the grammar adequate. There are, however, some errors throughout the essay.

Summary and conclusions:

This essay is a fairly consistent, if somewhat predictable, response to the prompt. It's not inspired; but it is not grossly deficient. For that reason, it is likely a "4."

This criticism should not be given too much weight because, after all, the essay is pretty good--a "4" is above average, and there are only two marks higher. But the criticism is intended to suggest a way in this essay, and essays of this sort, could be improved in general.